$150,00

The Oxford Handbook of
Language Production

OXFORD LIBRARY OF PSYCHOLOGY

Editor in Chief PETER E. NATHAN

The Oxford Handbook of Language Production

Edited by

Matthew Goldrick

Victor Ferreira

Michele Miozzo

OXFORD
UNIVERSITY PRESS

OXFORD
UNIVERSITY PRESS

Oxford University Press is a department of the University of Oxford.
It furthers the University's objective of excellence in research, scholarship,
and education by publishing worldwide.

Oxford   New York
Auckland   Cape Town   Dar es Salaam   Hong Kong   Karachi
Kuala Lumpur   Madrid   Melbourne   Mexico City   Nairobi
New Delhi   Shanghai   Taipei   Toronto

With offices in
Argentina   Austria   Brazil   Chile   Czech Republic   France   Greece
Guatemala   Hungary   Italy   Japan   Poland   Portugal   Singapore
South Korea   Switzerland   Thailand   Turkey   Ukraine   Vietnam

Oxford is a registered trademark of Oxford University Press
in the UK and certain other countries.

Published in the United States of America by
Oxford University Press
198 Madison Avenue, New York, NY 10016

Library of Congress Cataloging-in-Publication Data
The Oxford handbook of language production / edited by Matthew Goldrick, Victor Ferreira, Michele Miozzo.
     pages cm.—(Oxford library of psychology)
ISBN 978–0–19–973547–1
1. Language acquisition.   2. Cognition.   I. Goldrick, Matthew Andrew, editor of compilation.
II. Ferreira, Victor S., 1970– editor of compilation.   III. Miozzo, Michele, editor of compilation.
P118.O94 2014
401′.93—dc23
2013031616

9 7 8 6 5 4 3 2 1
Printed in the United States of America
on acid-free paper

ACKNOWLEDGMENTS

Thanks to Theodore Zeldin for providing the cover art illustration and Iva Ivanova for pointing us to his work.

SHORT CONTENTS

OXFORD LIBRARY OF PSYCHOLOGY

The *Oxford Library of Psychology*, a landmark series of handbooks, is published by Oxford University Press, one of the world's oldest and most highly respected publishers, with a tradition of publishing significant books in psychology. The ambitious goal of the *Oxford Library of Psychology* is nothing less than to span a vibrant, wide-ranging field and, in so doing, to fill a clear market need.

Encompassing a comprehensive set of handbooks, organized hierarchically, the *Library* incorporates volumes at different levels, each designed to meet a distinct need. At one level are a set of handbooks designed broadly to survey the major subfields of psychology; at another are numerous handbooks that cover important current focal research and scholarly areas of psychology in depth and detail. Planned as a reflection of the dynamism of psychology, the *Library* will grow and expand as psychology itself develops, thereby highlighting significant new research that will impact on the field. Adding to its accessibility and ease of use, the *Library* will be published in print and, later on, electronically.

The *Library* surveys psychology's principal subfields with a set of handbooks that capture the current status and future prospects of those major subdisciplines. This initial set includes handbooks of social and personality psychology, clinical psychology, counseling psychology, school psychology, educational psychology, industrial and organizational psychology, cognitive psychology, cognitive neuroscience, methods and measurements, history, neuropsychology, personality assessment, developmental psychology, and more. Each handbook undertakes to review one of psychology's major subdisciplines with breadth, comprehensiveness, and exemplary scholarship. In addition to these broadly-conceived volumes, the *Library* also includes a large number of handbooks designed to explore in depth more specialized areas of scholarship and research, such as stress, health and coping, anxiety and related disorders, cognitive development, or child and adolescent assessment. In contrast to the broad coverage of the subfield handbooks, each of these latter volumes focuses on an especially productive, more highly focused line of scholarship and research. Whether at the broadest or most specific level, however, all of the *Library* handbooks offer synthetic coverage that reviews and evaluates the relevant past and present research and anticipates research in the future. Each handbook in the *Library* includes introductory and concluding chapters written by its editor to provide a roadmap to the handbook's table of contents and to offer informed anticipations of significant future developments in that field.

An undertaking of this scope calls for handbook editors and chapter authors who are established scholars in the areas about which they write. Many of the nation's and world's most productive and best-respected psychologists have agreed to edit *Library* handbooks or write authoritative chapters in their areas of expertise.

For whom has the *Oxford Library of Psychology* been written? Because of its breadth, depth, and accessibility, the *Library* serves a diverse audience, including graduate students in psychology and their faculty mentors, scholars, researchers, and practitioners in psychology and related fields. Each will find in the *Library* the information they seek on the subfield or focal area of psychology in which they work or are interested.

Befitting its commitment to accessibility, each handbook includes a comprehensive index, as well as extensive references to help guide research. And because the *Library* was designed from its inception as an online as well as a print resource, its structure and contents will be readily and rationally searchable online. Further, once the *Library* is released online, the handbooks will be regularly and thoroughly updated.

In summary, the *Oxford Library of Psychology* will grow organically to provide a thoroughly informed perspective on the field of psychology, one that reflects both psychology's dynamism and its increasing interdisciplinarity. Once published electronically, the *Library* is also destined to become a uniquely valuable interactive tool, with extended search and browsing capabilities. As you begin to consult this handbook, we sincerely hope you will share our enthusiasm for the more than 500-year tradition of Oxford University Press for excellence, innovation, and quality, as exemplified by the *Oxford Library of Psychology*.

Peter E. Nathan
Editor-in-Chief
Oxford Library of Psychology

Matthew Goldrick

Matthew Goldrick is Associate Professor of Linguistics at Northwestern University, where he is affiliated with the Northwestern Cognitive Science Program and the Northwestern University Interdisciplinary Neuroscience Program. His research draws on behavioral experiments as well as computational and mathematical modeling to develop theories of the cognitive and neural mechanisms underlying the production, perception, and acquisition of sound structure.

Victor Ferreira

Victor Ferreira is Professor of Psychology and Associate Director of the Center for Research in Language at the University of California, San Diego. Dr. Ferreira's research focuses on language production and communication. Specific research questions center on how speakers form sentences, how speakers retrieve and produce individual words, and how the knowledge that speakers and listeners have of one another affects language production behavior.

Michele Miozzo

Michele Miozzo is Assistant Research Professor at Johns Hopkins and has held previous positions at Columbia University and the University of Cambridge. His research focuses on the organization of the brain mechanisms supporting word production in speaking, a topic he investigates with individuals with acquired language impairments and neuroimaging techniques.

CONTRIBUTORS

Hermann Ackermann
Department of General Neurology
Hertie Institute for Clinical Brain Research
University of Tübingen
Tuebingen, Germany

Mark Andrews
Cognitive, Perceptual, and Brain Sciences
University College London
Division of Psychology
Nottingham Trent University
Nottingham, UK

Molly Babel
Department of Linguistics
University of British Columbia
Vancouver, Canada

Eric Baković
Department of Linguistics
University of California San Diego
La Jolla, CA

James P. Blevins
Department of Theoretical and Applied
Linguistics
University of Cambridge
Cambridge, UK

Kathryn Bock
Department of Psychology
University of Illinois
Champaign, IL

Sarah Brown-Schmidt
Beckman Institute and Department of
Psychology
University of Illinois at Urbana-Champaign
Urbana, IL

Adam Buchwald
Steinhardt School of Culture, Education, and
Human Development
New York University
New York, NY

Alfonso Caramazza
Cognitive Neurology Laboratory
Harvard University
Cambridge, MA

Franklin Chang
School of Psychology
The University of Liverpool
Liverpool, UK

Herbert H. Clark
Department of Psychology
Stanford University
Stanford, CA

David P. Corina
Center for Mind and Brain
University of California Davis
Davis, CA

Albert Costa
Departament de Tecnologies de la Informació i
les Comunicacions
ICREA
Universitat Pompeu Fabra
Barcelona, Catalonia, Spain

Vanessa Costa
Center for Neurocognitive
Rehabilitation
Center for Mind/Brain Studies
University of Trento
Trento, Italy

Gary S. Dell
Department of Psychology
University of Illinois
Champaign, IL

Victor Ferreira
Language Production Laboratory
Department of Psychology
University of California, San Diego
La Jolla, CA

Simon Fischer-Baum
Department of Psychology
Rice University
Houston, TX

Hartmut Fitz
Max Planck Institute for
Psycholinguistics
Nijmegen, Netherlands

Matthew Goldrick
Department of Linguistics
Northwestern University
Evanston, IL

Louis Goldstein
Department of Linguistics
University of Southern California
Los Angeles, CA

Tamar H. Gollan
Department of Psychiatry
University of California, San Diego
La Jolla, CA

Michael Grosvald
Center for Mind and Brain
University of California Davis
Davis, CA

Frank H. Guenther
Departments of Speech, Language, and Hearing
    Sciences and Biomedical Engineering
Center for Cognitive Computation and Neural
    Technology
Boston University
Boston, MA

Eva Gutierrez
Center for Mind and Brain
University of California Davis
Davis, CA

Robert J. Hartsuiker
Department of Experimental Psychology
Ghent University
Ghent, Belgium

Argye E. Hillis
Departments of Neurology, Physical Medicine
    and Rehabilitation, and Cognitive Science
Johns Hopkins University
Baltimore, MD

Aneta Kielar
Aphasia and Neurolinguistics Research
    Laboratory
Department of Communication Sciences
    and Disorders
Northwestern University
Evanston, IL

Sotaro Kita
School of Psychology
University of Birmingham
Birmingham, UK

Agnieszka E. Konopka
Max Plank Institute for Psycholinguistics
Nijmegen, Netherlands

Judith F. Kroll
Department of Psychology
Program in Linguistics
Center for Language Science
The Pennsylvania State University
University Park, PA

Anna Leshinskaya
Cognitive Neuropsychology Lab
Department of Psychology
Harvard University
Cambridge, MA

Randi C. Martin
Department of Psychology
Rice University
Houston, TX

Gaurav Mathur
Department of Linguistics
Gallaudet University Washington, DC

Gabriele Miceli
Center for Neurocognitive Rehabilitation
Center for Mind/Brain Studies
University of Trento
Trento, Italy

Benjamin Munson
Department of Speech-Language-Hearing
    Sciences
University of Minnesota
Minneapolis, MN

Nazbanou Nozari
Department of Psychology
University of Illinois
Champaign, IL

David R. Olson
Ontario Institute for Studies and Education
University of Toronto
Toronto, Canada

Gary M. Oppenheim
Center for Research in Language
University of California San Diego
La Jolla, CA

Maya G. Peeva
Department of Speech, Language, and Hearing
    Sciences
Sargent College of Health and Rehabilitation
    Sciences
Center for Cognitive Computation and Neural
    Technology
Boston University
Boston, MA

Marianne Pouplier
Institut für Phonetik und Sprachverarbeitung
Ludwig-Maximilians-Universität
Munich, Germany

David S. Race
Departments of Neurology
Johns Hopkins University
Baltimore, MD

Brenda Rapp
Department of Cognitive Science
Johns Hopkins University
Baltimore, MD

Christian Rathmann
Institutfür Deutsche Gebärdensprache
Universität Hamburg
Hamburg, Germany

Elin Runnqvist
Laboratoire de Psychologie Cognitive
CNRS
Université Aix-Marseille
France

Stefanie Shattuck-Hufnagel
Speech Communication Group
Massachusetts Institute of Technology
Cambridge, MA

L. Robert Slevc
Language and Music Cognition Lab
University of Maryland
College Park, MD

Kristof Strijkers
Laboratoire de Psychologie Cognitive
CNRS
Université Aix-Marseille
France

Cynthia Thompson
Aphasia and Neurolinguistics Research
  Laboratory
Department of Communication Sciences and
  Disorders
Northwestern University
Evanston, IL
Department of Neurology and Cognitive
  Neurology
Alzheimer's Disease Center
Northwestern University Medical School
Chicago, IL

Jason A. Tourville
Department of Speech, Language, and Hearing
  Sciences
Sargent College of Health and Rehabilitation
  Sciences
Center for Cognitive Computation and Neural
  Technology
Boston University
Boston, MA

Gabriella Vigliocco
Cognitive, Perceptual, and Brain Sciences
University College London
London, UK

David Vinson
Cognitive, Perceptual, and Brain Sciences
University College London
London, UK

Wolfram Ziegler
Development Group Clinical Neuropsychology
Ludwig-Maximilians-University Munich
Munich, Germany

CONTENTS

PART 1

Speaking

Message Encoding

Agnieszka E. Konopka *and* Sarah Brown-Schmidt

Abstract

Speaking begins with the formulation of messages (i.e., with a thought and a desire to communicate). Depending on the complexity of the event, the conversational context, interlocutors' knowledge, success in establishing common ground, and a variety of other factors, messages can vary in content and breadth from speaker to speaker and from situation to situation. This article provides an overview of what is known from cognitive psychology about the process of planning the content of a message and the processes by which a message can be encoded linguistically. It begins by describing the relevant psycholinguistic research on message encoding, and then considers the content of messages including the question of the independence or interdependence of messages from language and the ways that contextual factors change the contents of messages.

Key Words: message encoding, message planning, language and thought, conversation

Speaking begins with the formulation of a message (i.e., with a thought and a desire to communicate. For example, a simple message might contain information about something that the speaker sees in the visual environment (*There's a wallet on the floor*); a description of a dynamic event (*The skier is losing his balance*); or a statement about a nonobservable mental state (*I have a headache*). Depending on the complexity of the event, the conversational context, interlocutors' knowledge, success in establishing common ground, and a variety of other factors, messages can vary in content and breadth from speaker to speaker and from situation to situation. This article provides an overview of what is known from a cognitive psychological point of view about the process of planning the content of a message and the processes by which a message can be encoded linguistically. It begins by describing the relevant psycholinguistic research on message encoding, and then considers the content of messages including the question of the independence

or interdependence of messages from language and the ways that contextual factors change the contents of messages. Finally, emerging areas of inquiry and future directions are noted.

Message Encoding: The Process

Message encoding, or message planning, is the first stage of language production (Levelt, 1989), but not much is known about this initial process. Only some of the information brought to mind on any given occasion is eventually expressed linguistically. Given this complexity, how does a speaker parse an event out of a sequence of actions and construct a message from this information? Understanding an event is sometimes assumed to be qualitatively different from the type of planning strictly necessary for production itself: the necessary mechanisms may range from perceptual encoding of a scene to conceptualization of event structure, and are sometimes assumed to fall within the realm of research on perception, concepts and categories, and abstract reasoning. The processing of this information specifically for the formulation of a message requires groundbreaking, or individuating something in the event that the speaker wants to communicate to someone else (Bock, Irwin, & Davidson, 2004; Tomlin, 1997).

Contemporary psycholinguists have been primarily concerned with the formulation of message content for linguistic encoding and the time course of this process. The heart of the debate on the characteristics of messages and their encoding in real time dates back to the beginnings of psychology as a science. In one of the first discussions of the language production architecture, Wundt (1900) proposed that speakers must complete planning of an entire message before speaking. A competing proposal was that the content of a message is planned in smaller units, interleaved with linguistic encoding (Paul, 1880). For example, on Wundt's view, a speaker describing the event in Figure 1.1 might need to encode the gist of the entire scene (i.e., the fact that one object is moving another object) and conceptualize the roles of all the protagonists (the truck as the agent, or the object acting on another object, and the car as the patient, or the undergoer of the action) before beginning linguistic encoding. In contrast, on Paul's view, this speaker might begin retrieving the words to describe one of the protagonists (i.e., either the truck or the car), which would then become the sentence subject, while at the same time still encoding the relational content of the event and identifying its other protagonists (the car or the truck).

Questions about the content and time course of message planning have traditionally been very difficult to address experimentally. Much like thoughts, messages are difficult to operationalize, and much like linguistic encoding, the formulation of a message proceeds very rapidly. Studies of message planning therefore require measures with high temporal resolution and a high degree of control over message content but enough flexibility to allow speakers to generate their own messages. The advent of the visual world eye-tracking technique in the last few decades (Tanenhaus, Spivey-Knowlton, Eberhard, & Sedivy, 1995; also Cooper, 1974) and its subsequent extension to production (Griffin & Bock, 2000; Griffin, 2004; Meyer, 2004; Meyer, Sleiderink, & Levelt, 1998; also see Pechmann, 1989) has provided the necessary means to link conceptual processing to the formulation of an utterance at a rapid time-scale. Insights from eye-tracking studies of message planning complement standard approaches that involve eliciting specific linguistic forms and analyzing speech onset times and various linguistic properties of the utterance.

In modern-day experimental studies of language production, messages are typically constrained to a pictured event of varying complexity that speakers describe while their gaze and speech are recorded. By necessity, the materials do not represent the full breadth of conceptual complexity in messages, nor do they exhaust the range of possible responses. Nevertheless, these paradigms allow for a systematic examination of the basic processes of message and sentence formulation, by monitoring shifts in eye fixation as the speaker plans a message and utterance. The link between cognitive processes and fixations is based on a reliable, albeit imperfect (Irwin, 2004) link between attention to task-relevant objects in a visual display and saccadic eye movements (Tanenhaus, Magnuson, Dahan, & Chambers, 2000). In this context, the first step in formulating a message is understanding something about the pictured event and selecting a starting point for the ensuing utterance. This has immediate consequences for the scope of conceptual planning, or the amount of information that can be prepared and passed on to grammatical encoding processes in one time step. The visual uptake of information from a scene, as indexed by the speaker's pattern of eye movements in the display, addresses both of

Figure 1.1 Example event eliciting active and passive sentences.

these questions by providing a wealth of data about the type of information that is relevant for early message formulation.

Starting Points

Messages need not map directly onto linguistic forms, so speakers must solve the so-called linearization problem in the production of any longer utterance: they must turn an alinguistic representation into a string of words produced sequentially[1]. To begin this sequence of words, they must select a starting point (Gernsbacher & Hargreaves, 1988; MacWhinney, 1977). To continue from this starting point, they must know something about the event they are going to describe. A highly consistent finding in eye-tracking studies of language production is that there is a tight relationship between gaze and speech: speakers overwhelmingly fixate the referents in a display in the order in which they are going to talk about them. For example, when describing the event in Figure 1.1, speakers who produce an active sentence (e.g., "*The truck is towing the car*"), typically look first at the truck (the agent) and then at the car (the patient). In contrast, when producing a passive sentence (e.g., "*The car is being towed by the truck*"), speakers show the reverse pattern of fixations. Under the assumption that shifts of visual attention say something about the development of a message plan, this result offers two testable theoretical alternatives about the selection of starting points (Bock et al., 2004).

One alternative is that visual properties of the display draw the speaker's eye to a particular element of the scene and thereby anchor this element as the starting point of the message and of the ensuing utterance. We refer to this hypothesis as perceptually driven or salience-driven message encoding. For example, Tomlin (1997) describes an experiment where speakers viewed displays in which two fish approached each other and in which one of the fish is ultimately eaten by the other. Before the end of the event, one of the fish was briefly cued by an arrow. Cuing influenced the assignment of the cued referent to subject position: speakers were more likely to produce an active sentence when the cued fish was the agent and a passive sentence when the cued fish was the undergoer of the action. Gleitman, January, Nappa, and Trueswell (2007) used a more subtle perceptual cue to test whether capturing visual attention biases the selection of a starting point for the message, and obtained similar results. This suggests that shifts of attention to specific message elements can influence the choice

of starting points before speakers have carried out more elaborate conceptual planning of the event as a whole. Combined with work showing that other visual and conceptual properties of referents, such as size and animacy, also make some objects more attractive starting points than others, this work indicates that individual properties of message elements are important variables in the early stages of message formulation (Bock, 1982; Bock, 1986; Bock & Warren, 1985; Flores d'Arcais, 1975; Kim, 1996; McDonald, Bock, & Kelly, 1993; Osgood & Bock, 1977).

Visual properties of a scene do not completely drive production. If they did, speaking would simply entail listing everything that is visible. Instead, the perceptually driven hypothesis proposes that the visual stimulus serves as an important scaffold in the formulation process for these types of messages. The salience of a message element could also arise from nonperceptual attributes, such as its role in the discourse (e.g., given-new status), linguistic codability (i.e., the number of acceptable lexical items referring to this entity), or lexical accessibility (i.e., the lexical frequency of the preferred referential term). This allows for a generalization of this hypothesis to messages about entities or events that are not visible or not easily picturable.

A second, alternative hypothesis is that gaze patterns closely match a conceptual plan because gaze reflects the formulation of a message plan, instead of preceding it. Under this view, speakers need a linguistic starting point to begin a sentence, but they also need to know how to proceed from that starting point; that is, they must know something of the propositional content of their utterance before committing to a starting point. Under this view, instead of being simply a perceptually salient element in a scene, a starting point is more likely to be an aspect of the scene that the speaker wants to say something about. This hypothesis predicts that naming an event like the one shown in Figure 1.1 begins with a short apprehension period during which neither character is preferentially fixated over the other one (Griffin & Bock, 2000): rather, what speakers do in the first 300–400 ms after stimulus onset is generate a rudimentary message plan to communicate the overall gist of the event. When speakers do begin preferentially fixating the person or object in the scene that they will name first, it is because this order of fixations is determined by a just formulated, provisional message plan.

These two views illustrate a dichotomy in factors that can influence the early formulation of simple messages. It is easy to think of real-life examples where speakers begin utterances with something that captured their attention at the moment of speaking, and examples where this information is not enough to support fluent production of an entire utterance. So, it becomes important to ask about the conditions under which speakers may and may not rely on perceptual cues. Another way of framing this question is that it is important to test when visual salience might influence the selection of starting points, and when other factors, such as compatibility with a larger message plan, determine the starting point instead.

Kuchinsky and Bock (2010) recently demonstrated that the contribution of perceptual salience to the selection of a starting point depends on the overall codability of the to-be-described event. In their experiments, speakers described transitive events that were either easy or difficult to encode linguistically: easy events were consistently described with a small set of verbs by most speakers (high-codability events), whereas difficult events elicited a wider range of verbs (low-codability events). One of the characters in each transitive event was cued as in Gleitman et al. (2007). The results showed that speakers were more likely to begin their sentences with the cued character when describing low-codability events, whereas the perceptual cue exerted a much smaller influence on descriptions of high-codability events. The ease of naming the characters themselves affected speakers' choice of starting points primarily in low-codability events: a cued referent in low-codability events was assigned to subject position more often when it was easy to name than when it was more difficult to name. This suggests that planning is facilitated by low-level attentional cues primarily when a higher-level, conceptual plan is not readily available. The implication for message planning is that there may be a hierarchy of factors influencing message formulation, with perceptual factors playing a role under limited circumstances.

Scope of Planning

Many theories concerning the scope of message planning follow from what is known about the selection of starting points. The scope of message-level planning refers to the amount of conceptual information that speakers can prepare in parallel, as a unit, or as an increment, before passing this information to linguistic encoding processes and beginning conceptual encoding of the next message unit. In many prominent models, overt production of a sentence can begin before the speaker has worked out the content of the entire utterance (Bock & Levelt, 1994; Kempen & Hoenkemp, 1987; Levelt, 1989; Pickering & Garrod, 2004), so central questions for an incremental production system concern the size of typical chunks of meaning, whether these chunks are uniform or whether they can vary, what factors influence chunk size, and finally what the lower limit might be on the size of these chunks.

Early evidence from speech errors suggested that the scope of message planning can span from one to two clauses. For example, an error like *I left the briefcase in my cigar* (Garrett, 1980) suggests that speakers may prepare multiple message elements before speaking: in this case, *briefcase* and *cigar* were both planned before speaking, and were then erroneously inserted into incorrect slot in the sentence frame. One limitation of offline data (such as properties of speech errors), however, is that they cannot indicate whether the underlying message elements were planned together in one increment or were planned sequentially and then passed on together to linguistic encoding processes. Some corroborating evidence for large planning units in extemporaneous speech comes from analyses of distributions of disfluencies within sentences, suggesting that speakers may plan sentences in conceptually coherent units that map easily onto syntactic units (Ford & Holmes, 1978).

Later work showed that speakers may indeed complete conceptual planning for one clause (Smith & Wheeldon, 1999) or, at the very least, a unit of meaning that cannot be broken down into simpler constituents (e.g., a "functional phrase" as in *the flower* or *above the house*; Allum & Wheeldon, 2007, 2009) before speaking. More specific predictions come from the two accounts described previously, positing reliance on perceptual cues and conceptual plans, respectively, when selecting starting points, because the types of processes implicated in the selection of starting points have straightforward implications for the breadth of conceptual planning. Although experimental evidence on this subject is rather scarce, both positions have recently received some attention.

Selecting a starting point based on the perceptual prominence of one message element implies little extensive, simultaneous conceptual planning beyond this point (Paul, 1880). If speakers can choose a starting point based on its visual or perceptual properties and if they need not have information about the role of this element in the event to begin their sentences, then planning windows might be as small as a single message element.

As illustrated in Figure 1.2, this sort of perceptually driven incremental message planning might begin with selection of the concept (truck) as the first message element, and thus production of *the truck* as the first words of the sentence. The rest of the message may then be built up with the uptake of new visual information, possibly in similarly sized chunks. In contrast, if a starting point is determined by the speaker's understanding of the event itself, the suitability of this starting point for expressing the gist of the event must already be supported by holistic planning of the sort advocated by Wundt (1900). Unlike the perceptually driven process, conceptually driven planning may result in initial processing of aspects of all the event participants. This initial message plan may be very rudimentary, in that it may involve little information about the identities of the protagonists (e.g., the event in Figure 1.2 involves two vehicles), but it is broad enough to specify the relationship between them: within a few hundred milliseconds of stimulus onset, the speaker already knows whether the display shows a transitive event (one object moving another) or a joint intransitive action (two objects independently moving in the same direction). The scope of planning, therefore, is wider in such cases than when starting points are driven solely by attention capture or other low-level perceptual factors.

In support of the first account, Gleitman et al. (2007) showed that speakers directed their gaze to the perceptually cued character in a transitive event within 200 ms of picture onset and reliably began their sentences with this character as subject. This very short time window between stimulus onset and the speaker preferentially fixating one of the characters (referred to as the eye-voice span) leaves little to no time for speakers to apprehend the event as a whole before speech onset. In support of the second account, Griffin and Bock (2000) observed longer eye-voice spans for the first character in descriptions of highly codable events. Corroborating evidence comes from production of well-learned time expressions from simple clock displays (Bock, Irwin, Davidson, & Levelt, 2003). Speakers normally look earlier at the hour hand when producing an absolute expression (*three twenty*) and earlier at the minute hand when producing a relative expression (*twenty past three*) from an analog clock, but more importantly, planning times for the sentence-initial element (e.g., *three...*) are longer than for the second element (*...twenty*). This is consistent with the idea that the first message increment includes more information than simply the identity of the sentence-initial element.

One implication of the debate about starting points is that the size of message increments is likely

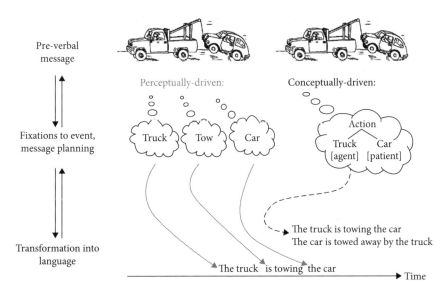

Figure 1.2 Message level concepts (e.g., truck) are transformed into lexical representations, either independently (perceptually driven planning), or along with a more complete event representation (conceptually driven planning). The concept (truck) is designated as an agent early in conceptually driven planning, whereas in perceptually driven planning concepts are incrementally selected on the basis of salience and thematic roles are not immediately assigned. Note that perceptual planning of individual concepts need not proceed in a left-to-right order isomorphic with syntactic structure, so "car" could be planned before "tow." For clarity, details concerning the timecourse of grammatical encoding are not included.

not uniform, but can range from encoding isolated pieces of information to conceptualizing the gist of an entire event. Another implication is that, as with questions regarding the selection of starting points, a productive approach to this problem may be to identify the conditions under which speakers plan either more or less message-level information in a single increment. As shown earlier, the codability of an event modulates the strength of perceptual cues attracting attention to a specific character (Kuchinsky & Bock, 2010). The availability of visual or conceptual information early in the formulation process may have similar effects, with speakers showing evidence of smaller planning windows when the message is too complex to plan holistically.

This last possibility provides a test of the lower limit of the size of conceptual planning windows and has been tested using a variant of the visual world paradigm (Tanenhaus et al., 1995). In these experiments, speakers are asked to describe one of many pictured objects to an addressee who views a similar display. This object can be referred to with a bare noun (*a butterfly*) on trials where there are no other butterflies in the display, but speakers need to add a modifier to uniquely identify the referent (*a small/large butterfly*) if the display includes a second, different-sized butterfly (Brown-Schmidt & Konopka, 2008; Brown-Schmidt & Tanenhaus, 2006). If speakers notice the contrast picture early, they have the time to incorporate this information into their message and produce a fluent modified expression (*the small butterfly*). Other times, speakers begin talking about one element in the display and then modify this initial message after noticing the contrast picture, resulting in disfluent utterances (*thee uh small butterfly, the small uh butterfly*). In both cases, the timing of fixations to the contrast object shows when new information is added to a message and this provides a way of gauging how much information speakers can encode in a single message unit.

In this type of message, a message chunk might minimally consist of information about a property of the pictured objects that can be expressed with a single word. Brown-Schmidt and Konopka (2008) tested this idea by examining the breadth of the time window during which speakers of English and Spanish plan adjectives like *big* or *small*. English syntax requires that speakers produce adjectives before nouns (*the small butterfly*), whereas Spanish syntax requires postnominal adjective placement (*la mariposa pequeña*). The prediction was that if speakers can plan such messages in two increments, one consisting of the object name and one consisting of

size information, then information about size can be added to the message at different times by speakers of the two languages. In fact, speakers of English who produced fluent modified expressions fixated the contrast picture showing a larger butterfly earlier than Spanish speakers who produced the same phrase in Spanish.

These studies are among the first to offer experimental evidence on the breadth of message-level planning scope. Using materials that require the preparation of very different types of messages, they have shown a wide range of possible planning windows. Although each study used highly controlled materials and sensitive methodologies, the most general conclusion is that no single approach may provide an accurate answer to questions regarding conceptual preparation before speaking. As one begins to explore these issues, such questions as "What is the basic unit of planning?" are likely to be set aside in favor of such questions as "What determines the limits of planning units?" (Konopka, 2009). Specific questions generated by this research as examples of subdomains where the field can make the most progress are discussed at the end of the article.

Message Encoding: Content

Testing the various hypotheses about the time-course of message planning requires a basic understanding of the composition of messages. Recall that a message is formed in response to an intention to communicate. This intention might be to declare a proposition (*There is a bear behind the tree*); to elicit some information from one's interlocutor (*What is under the rock?*); or to answer an interlocutor's question (*A spider*). The communicative intention might also be to simply manage the flow of information in dialog (e.g., *uh-huh, good bye*; Bangerter & Clark, 2003; Schegloff & Sacks, 1973), or express an emotion (e.g., *Yes!, Oh Sh!t*). Given that one can communicate this information in different ways, the question then becomes what determines what information makes it into the message.

So what is the stuff of messages? The general consensus is that messages are preverbal (i.e., not linguistic), nonlinear, and propositional in nature. For some, the message although preverbal may be of mixed composition of nonlinguistic and linguistic conceptualizations (Bierwisch & Schreuder, 1992). The structure of messages has been brushed on by many (e.g., Pickering & Garrod, 2004; Bock & Levelt, 1994; Bock, 1982; Kempen & Hoenkemp, 1987), but the focus here is on the somewhat more elaborated treatment offered by Levelt (1989),

Chang, Dell, and Bock (2006), and Brown and Dell (1987).

As an example in which messages are treated as nonlinguistic representations, consider Levelt (1989). He proposes that a message is a semantic representation of some event (including states, actions, and so forth), and is represented in a propositional form that indicates the relations among the event participants. These relations include a large number of potential thematic roles, and information about temporal structure (past, present, future) and mood (declarative, interrogative, and so forth). For Levelt, the message underlying sentence (1) can be described by (1a), in which the thematic roles are depicted through embedded parentheses.

(1) *Did Sarah throw the ball?*
(1a) ?(past(Sarah(throw(ball))))

The fact that the sentence has an interrogative mood is indicated by the initial "?", the tense is indicated by "past," and the embedding of *ball* within the verb, and of the verb within *Sarah*, indicates that the proposition under question is whether Sarah threw the ball (and not whether the ball threw Sarah).

In a different approach, Chang et al. (2006) describe a connectionist model of language production and language learning in which messages consist of bindings between concepts (e.g., girl, tuba, carry) and the roles that those concepts play in an event (e.g., girl = agent, tuba = patient, carry = action). These message-level representations are subsequently passed through the layers of the model to simulate production of the sentence. In their model, the conceptual (or lexical-semantic) information is represented in a "what" layer; information about roles is represented in a "where" layer; and information about the event semantics, such as the relative salience of the event participants, is represented separately (the analogy to the "what" and "where" processing streams in the visual system is intentional). In this model, sentence (2) is represented at a message level as (2a).

(2) *The orange is eaten by the girl.*
(2a)

Concepts:	Eat	Girl (definite)	Orange (definite)
Roles:	A = Action	X = transitive agent	Y = transitive patient
Event Semantics:	AA = .5	XX = .25	YY = .5

The conceptual representation indicates the nature of the primary event (eating); the participants in that event (girl, orange); and the fact that they are both definite referents (they are referred to with a definite determiner, *the*). The roles played by the two event participants are indicated by the X and Y role representations, allowing the girl to be the eater, and the orange the object that is eaten. Finally, in this model, the weights assigned to the event participants partially determine whether the sentence is active or passive. In this example, the event semantics facilitate the use of the passive voice in (2) by making the representation of the patient (YY = .5) more salient than that of the agent (XX = .25): as a result, the patient lexical item (*orange*) is accessed first and produced first (also see Bock & Levelt, 1994; Bock, Loebell, & Morey, 1992; McDonald et al., 1993).

Event semantics do not always dictate constituent ordering. In Chang et al.'s (2006) model, if the event semantics of the agent and patient are similar (e.g., XX = .451, YY = .475), the role sequencing system may produce a structure that inverts these roles when that structure is easier to assemble because of structural priming (in this case, an active sentence might be produced if a different active sentence had been produced recently, despite the relatively higher weighted patient-role for *orange*). The fact that the sequencing system interacts with message representations before production of the first word suggests that this model is a good candidate for explaining constituent ordering processes in cases where syntactic structure, rather than conceptual structure, leads to activation of subordinate lexical items first (Allum & Wheeldon, 2007, 2009).

In yet another account of the form of messages, Brown and Dell (1987) suggest that messages may be encoded in larger conceptual units referred to as macropropositions, followed by encoding of individual propositions. Speakers decide what level of conceptual detail to communicate during the formulation of a macroproposition (e.g., *the robber attacked the man; the robber stabbed the man; the robber stabbed the man with a knife; the robber stabbed the man with an icepick*). Information about the instrument of the action can be added to this message later in a separate clause if it is not part of the original macroproposition. In this example, the specificity of the verb or the proximity of the phrase describing the instrument to the main verb can indicate whether or not this information was encoded as a verb argument in the macroproposition or was added at a later point in time as independent information. This proposal also assumes that speakers monitor the degree to which the resulting utterance matches the content of the macroproposition before speaking and repair it when necessary.

With respect to the selection of referential terms for the event participants (e.g., girl, orange), a central issue in understanding the coordination of conceptual activation and lexical access is the degree to which the form of a message is isomorphic with linguistic form. Under one proposal, the decompositional view of lexical semantics, words can be decomposed into primitive semantic features (Bierwisch & Schreuder, 1992; McNamara & Miller, 1989). For example, the word *bachelor* might be represented as an "unmarried male." A competing proposal (the nondecompositional or antidefinitional view) posits that many, if not all, words are represented as nondecomposable wholes (see Fodor, Fodor, & Garrett, 1975, and Fodor, Garrett, Walker, & Parkes, 1980 for an excellent introduction to this issue). For the purposes of this discussion, whether the meaning underlying a lexical item can be decomposed or not has direct relevance to issues regarding the construction of prelinguistic messages, in particular to estimates of the lower limit on the size of message planning units. If words are decomposable, this opens the door to the possibility that individually planned message components could be features or parts of a word's meaning. For example, when preparing to say "*the ballerina*," the speaker could potentially plan the female component of the meaning separately from the dancer component of the meaning. In contrast, if word meanings are nondecomposable, this would support a one-to-one mapping between message elements and lexical items, creating a semantically imposed lower limit on planning units of the word.

In what follows, we set aside questions of the structure of messages, and focus on the factors that constrain their content. Specifically, three (of the undoubtedly many) constraints on message content are considered: (1) the language itself; (2) the discourse context (Salmon-Alt & Romary, 2000; Landragin, 2006); and (3) the intended addressee (Clark & Marshall, 1981; Fussell & Krauss, 1989).

The Language

As many learners of a second language know, languages differ widely in how they segment event structures and map this information onto linguistic forms (Talmy, 1985; Sapir, 1921). Language-wide constraints on what must be expressed in the language have clear impacts on message formulation.

For example, when producing a declarative sentence in Korean (or Turkish; Aksu-Koç, Ögel-Balaban, & Alp, 2009; Slobin & Aksu-Koç, 1982), speakers must use an evidential marker to express whether the evidence they have for the information is hearsay or whether they have direct evidence for it (Papafragou et al., 2007). In English, to express the same information, it is necessary to add extra words and phrases (*I heard that…*, vs. *I saw for myself that…*). Similarly, when describing the placement of one object into another object in Korean, it is necessary to indicate whether it is a tight or loose fit (Choi & Bowerman, 1991); again, English does not mark this distinction routinely. Other examples abound. Languages vary in whether they require their speakers to indicate the grammatical gender of each noun, as in French and Spanish, or whether the verbs typically encode information about manner (e.g., *skip, saunter*), as in English and Mandarin, or path (e.g., *enter, exit*), as in Greek and Turkish (Papafragou, Hulbert, & Trueswell, 2008). Languages also differ in whether nouns and verbs are routinely marked for number, as they are in many Indo-European languages, or whether they remain bare, as in Mandarin. In short, differences between languages are seen in a variety of subdomains (also see Evans and Levinson, 2009, for a comprehensive review of linguistic variability).

For both Slobin (1996) and Levelt (1989), this type of interlanguage difference in obligatorily expressed information leads to changes in how prelinguistic messages are designed (also see von Stutterheim & Nüse, 2003), whether or not such differences are of any communicative value (Levelt, 1989). Thus, when producing a declarative in Korean, information about the evidence the speaker has for the proposition being expressed is automatically included in the message at some point during message encoding; this process is absent in English. For others, however, the system that constructs messages (the "conceptualizer" in Levelt, 1989) has little to no contact with the part of the language production system that translates the message into language. For Bierwisch and Schreuder (1992), for example, the message that is passed on to linguistic encoding is more complex than what might be ultimately represented in the linguistic form, and a language-specific intermediary processing stage (the "Vbl," or verbalization-mapping) maps those aspects of the conceptual structure that are linguistically relevant onto the semantic structure. This includes the expression of evidentiality in Korean, and grammatical number in English, both of which would have been included in the prelinguistic messages in both languages. Thus, depending on assumptions about the message-conceptualization process (whether or not linguistic encoding processes have contact with message formulation) the message formulation system either is or is not equivalent across languages.

Finally, a separate question from whether and how between-language differences are encoded linguistically is the question of whether these between-language differences also influence perception of events, and "thinking" more generally, when an individual is *not* preparing to speak. A classic recurrent debate in philosophy and psycholinguistics is whether language is a necessary medium for abstract thinking or whether thinking and language rely at least partially on nonoverlapping cognitive processes. If the language of thought is somehow different from the language of linguistic encoding, similar thoughts may simply be expressed differently in linguistic form across languages. In this case, the question of between-language differences touches more closely on understanding the mechanisms that translate preverbal ideas into language-specific representations, such as the verbalization mapping (Bierwisch & Schreuder, 1992) or interfacing representations (Bock, 1982) that allow for fluent expression of a thought with different linguistic forms. The alternative possibility (i.e., the position that thought and language are interdependent) has implications for the content of messages themselves.

The debate dates back to Sapir (1921) and Whorf (1956) who proposed a causal relationship between linguistic knowledge and aspects of higher-level thinking, such as perception and categorization (see Gentner & Goldin-Meadow, 2003, for a review). Decades of work on Whorfian effects, beginning with the classic Rosch studies on color perception in Dani speakers, support either weaker claims about language-on-thought effects (Boroditsky, 2001; Hunt & Agnoli, 1991) or show no constraints of linguistic forms on thought in such domains as spatial cognition, reasoning about time, objects, and memory for events (see examples in Gennari, Sloman, Malt, & Fitch, 2002; Malt, Sloman, Gennari, Shi, & Wang, 1999; Papafragou, Massey, & Gleitman, 2006). The similarities in performance between speakers of different languages despite variability in their linguistic categories suggest that speakers are not bound by the grammatical defaults of their language.

Outside the domain of psycholinguistics, work with preverbal infants and special populations largely supports this hypothesis. For example, preverbal infants are capable of more sophisticated reasoning about the physics of simple objects (Baillargeon, 2008) and about other people's mental states (Onishi & Baillargeon, 2005) than was assumed on the basis of Piaget's work. Although these abilities are later honed with experience and linguistic interactions, they are demonstrated well before children have acquired the linguistic tools to understand or produce complex language (also see Pinker, 1994). On the other end of the spectrum, work with adults who have lost the ability to express themselves verbally for varying lengths of time (aphasics) also shows that some patients are capable of near-normal thinking in most everyday situations. Many patients report an unaffected intellectual "inner life" despite significant psychological difficulties and lack of normal linguistic interactions (Sacks, 2005).

A proposal explaining why speakers of different languages do show variability in the ways they talk but not think about similar concepts is Slobin's (1996, 2003) *thinking for speaking* hypothesis. The question goes back to the nature of the interfacing representations between thought and language. Under this view, speakers of different languages need not experience reality differently because language does not constrain the wide range of potential thought patterns to the more narrow range of language-specific grammatical tools. Rather, the properties of a language merely legislate what needs to be expressed overtly in a grammatical utterance. This results in, for example, some speakers explicitly encoding manner or aspect, but it need not imply a radically different conceptualization of the event itself or a different perspective on this event for speakers of different languages. Whether and how linguistic conventions might result in firmly ingrained, or learned, forms of reasoning after massive exposure to specific linguistic patterns remains an open question (Boroditsky, 2001; Hunt & Agnoli, 1991; Levinson, Kita, Haun, & Rasch, 2002; Li, Dunham, & Carey, 2009; Li & Gleitman, 2002; Lucy, 1992).

Discourse Context

Whatever the language used to communicate, speakers must decide how much and what type of information is important for the completeness of a message. In dialogue, an informative message is one that contains enough information for the addressee to decode the speaker's original communicative intention. For example, when producing a definite referring expression, this expression should uniquely identify the intended referent in a given context (Roberts, 2003). As a result, and perhaps in combination with the ease of eliciting referring expressions from experimental participants, much of the research on this topic focuses on the modification of referential expressions with adjectives (the *green* soup, the *tasty* tapenade) and postnominal clauses (the boy *playing soccer*, the girl *with the tattoo*). In our discussion of the influence of the discourse context on message form, we assume that the elements of a referential expression are planned at the message level (rather than being encoded at an intermediary processing stage). We can gain insights into what is included in a message by examining characteristics of the referential expression, such as noun choice and modifier use. In what follows, only two of the many aspects of the discourse context that shape the message plan are considered: the visual context and the linguistic context.

THE VISUAL CONTEXT

It has long been appreciated that the form of a referring expression must change depending on the context, so the same referent will be referred to quite differently in different contexts (Olson, 1970; Osgood, 1971). For example, to refer to the triangle on the left-hand side of quadrant 1 of Figure 1.3 (when not using a locative, such as *left-hand*), it is necessary to say *the striped triangle*. Describing the same image in quadrant 2 instead requires mentioning its size (*the big triangle*) given the change in the referential context. Similarly, to refer to the left-hand girl in quadrant 3, the speaker should indicate that she is *the girl wearing number 7*, whereas to refer to the same girl in quadrant 4, it is only necessary to mention her activity (*the girl playing soccer*). Empirical investigations of the role of visual context on the construction of referring expressions (and thus the construction of messages) have uncovered several noteworthy features of this process.

First, classes of adjectives vary in how likely they are to be used when not motivated by unique identifiability (Pechmann, 1989; Sedivy, 2005). Sedivy (2005) asked speakers to refer to objects in scalar contrast sets (e.g., a tall cup in the context of a short cup); color contrast sets (a green cup in the context of a blue cup); or material contrast sets (a wooden cup in the context of a metal cup). For all three types of modifiers, speakers were more likely to use an adjective in their object descriptions when a contrast object was present. For example, when referring to a wooden bowl, they were far more likely to produce a material adjective if the context contained a contrasting metal bowl than when the other object belonged to a different category (e.g., a teddy bear). Interestingly, there were large differences between the adjective categories in speakers' use of adjectives in the absence of contextual support: speakers infrequently used scalar or material adjectives (<10 percent of the time) in the absence of a contrast object, whereas they frequently used color adjectives in the absence of a contrast object (>90 percent of the time).

The fact that speakers reserve scalar adjectives for situations in which they are contextually required has since been replicated in both English and Spanish, and their use has been directly linked to the point in time when speakers notice the contrast object (Brown-Schmidt & Tanenhaus, 2006; Brown-Schmidt & Konopka, 2008). Further, the use of noncontextually motivated color and material adjectives may be modulated by their typicality with respect to the object class. For example, Sedivy (2003) reports that speakers are more likely to produce a color adjective in the absence of contextual support if the color of the referent is atypical (*the brown banana*) rather than typical

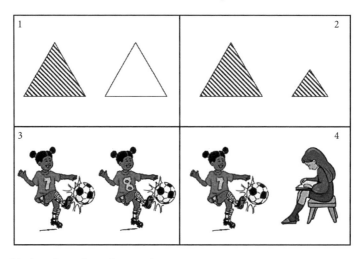

Figure 1.3 Examples of displays where referential context shapes naming patterns.

(*the yellow banana*). Taken together, these results suggest that speakers take into account information in the context that requires them to unambiguously frame a communicative intention.

An additional determinant of message content is the speaker's visual focus of attention. Specifically, the relevant referential context and thus the contents of the preverbal message are determined by what the speaker attends to, or what the speaker and addressee jointly attend to in face-to-face conversation. Similar attentional processes are likely at play when talking about non-copresent entities (e.g., a riveting conversation about politics may limit the attentional domain to foreign policy and away from the weather). Beun and Cremers (1998) argue that when referring to a specific entity, it is only necessary to specify that entity with respect to the other entities in the focus of attention, and that speakers can then refer to this entity with a reduced referential expression. In a task-based conversation, they characterized modification patterns by defining a spatial focus of attention determined in part by the referring history and use of pointing. Similarly, Brown-Schmidt and Tanenhaus (2006; Brown-Schmidt, Campana, & Tanenhaus, 2005) monitored the modification of definite referring expressions in a task-based conversation, and observed that two factors determined whether the speaker would distinguish the intended referent from other potential referents: the physical proximity of the intended referent to the just named referent and the relevance of the intended referent to the task at hand. When the intended referent was task-relevant and proximal to the last-mentioned referent, speakers tended to use reduced expressions (*the red one*), in a context including multiple red blocks. When the intended referent was further away or was less relevant, speakers produced richer descriptions to distinguish it from other competing referents (e.g., *the red horizontal block below the clown*). Interestingly, these same factors also predicted the degree to which addressees temporarily considered the competing referents when interpreting their partner's expression, suggesting that speakers and addressees may focus on similar factors when designing and interpreting language in dialog (Clark & Krych, 2004; Richardson & Dale, 2005; Richardson, Dale, & Kirkham, 2007).

THE LINGUISTIC CONTEXT

Related to the question of how a visual context shapes message formulation is the way in which the linguistic context shapes referring. Considered here are only two of the ways in which linguistic context shapes subsequent production: the use of elliptical speech and the use of overspecified speech. At the end of this section, the implications for message form are discussed. To illustrate the case of ellipsis, consider examples 3a-b below.

(3a)   *At what time do you wish to dine?*
(3b)   *At noon.*
(4a)   *What's the plan for today?*
(4b)   *I wish to dine at noon.*
(5)   *I threw the ball to Sally. Then, she threw it to the dog.*

When answering the question in (3a), a typical reply might be (3b). This response provides all the information necessary for the question-asker to understand the reply; however, the response in 3b is elliptical because all that the speaker says is the time (and the preposition *At*; see Levelt & Kelter, 1982). It is not necessary for the speaker to repeat information about the dining event because it is contained in the preceding question. If instead the question had been (4a), the second speaker would need to reply with (4b). Similar effects of the preceding linguistic context are observed in (5), where the first sentence introduces a new discourse referent (*Sally*), who can then be referred to with a pronoun (*she*) in the second sentence. The salience of the discourse referent established by the preceding linguistic context (Gundel, Hedberg, & Zacharski, 1993), in conjunction with form-specific characteristics of the referent (such as the fact that she is a solitary female: Kaiser & Trueswell, 2008; Brown-Schmidt, Byron, & Tanenhaus, 2005), afford the use of the personal pronoun *she*.

The force of linguistic context on messages is particularly evident in interactive dialog. Partners who discuss unusual objects typically establish joint referential terms for the objects over the course of the conversation, resulting in partner-specific abbreviated forms (e.g., *stair climber*, Wilkes-Gibbs & Clark, 1992; Clark & Wilkes-Gibbs, 1989). Interestingly, this form of linguistic context persists even when at odds with the visual context. For example, Brennan and Clark (1996) found that when the referential context changed so that there was now only one girl in the scene and it was no longer necessary to use a modifying phrase, such as *wearing number seven* (Figure 1.3, quadrant 4), speakers tended to stick to their conceptual pacts and overspecify their expressions (Van Der Wege, 2009).

These examples illustrate the fact that preceding linguistic exchanges shape what information is expressed linguistically. One important question for message encoding concerns the level of the production system at which speakers' choices to use ellipsis, a reduced referential form, or a contextually overmodified expression are encoded. Little experimental work has directly addressed how the message formulation process is guided by linguistic history, but there exist several proposals. In the case of ellipsis, Levelt (1989) suggests that when an utterance is elliptical, the underlying message is elliptical as well. However, it is unclear if the message underlying (3b), for example, completely lacks information about the dining event, and only includes temporal information, or whether the dining information is included too, and it is simply marked as needing to be elided. In the case of referential form, Levelt (1989) takes a different approach, suggesting that the information about the givenness of a referent is encoded at the message level, so the conceptual structure determines whether the speaker uses a pronoun or a definite referring expression. Similarly, for Chang et al., (2006), a single feature (DEFPRO) at the conceptual level determines whether each noun phrase is produced as a definite, indefinite, or a pronoun (e.g., the "definite" markings in example 2).

The Addressee

The final constraint on the content of messages considered here is the audience. The adjustments that speakers make for the needs of their addressees are known as *audience design* (Clark, 1996; Clark & Carlson, 1982). Based on assumptions about addressees, including what they do and do not know, speakers can tailor what they say and how they say it to increase understanding by the addressee.

Investigating whether and how speakers engage in audience design poses some challenges. The first is that, given the assumption that speaking begins with a desire to communicate, all language is in some sense designed for an addressee (i.e., it is designed to communicate a message to someone). Thus, to ask the question of *whether* speakers engage in audience design can be viewed as somewhat of a nonstarter. However, there are reasons to think that after the creation of an intention to communicate, some aspects of the production process may be driven more by speaker-internal processes and less by the needs of the addressee (Arnold, 2008; Dell & Brown, 1991). Understanding how speakers balance their own needs with those of the addressee and to what extent speakers accurately estimate the

needs of the addressee are central questions in this domain. A second challenge to examining audience design processes is that, in many cases, what is good for the speaker is also good for the addressee. Thus, although a high-frequency word may be selected by the speaker because it is easy to access and to produce, it may also be easy for the addressee to comprehend for the same reason (Dell & Brown, 1991). Discussed next are several ways in which speakers tailor their speech for the addressee. Again, much of this research focuses on the form of a linguistic expression, and the assumption is that any audience-driven changes in linguistic content are implemented at the message level.

Changes to the message in response to audience demands might reflect general adaptations to the category of the listener, as in the case of using one language over another, selecting child-appropriate topics when talking to an infant, or explaining difficult messages in more detail. For example, Fussell and Krauss (1992) examined the impact of the addressee's perceived familiarity with an image on the messages that speakers designed to describe these images. Speakers provided more detailed descriptions for their partners when the perceived identifiability of an image was low, suggesting that they were generally sensitive to the partner's need for more information. However, many of the expressions were simply bare names (e.g., *Clint Eastwood*), suggesting that speakers may sometimes opt to design potentially under-informative messages and wait for feedback from the addressee (e.g., Clark & Wilkes-Gibbs, 1986). Under-informative messages, such as messages where the speaker introduces new terms, may also be used in conjunction with elaborative descriptions, possibly as a teaching tool (Heller, Skovbroten, & Tanenhaus, 2009; also see Brown & Dell, 1987).

Speakers may also change their speech based on their understanding of the knowledge state of a particular addressee. Although some research has shown that speakers may produce syntactic constructions that are easier for the addressee to understand (Haywood, Pickering, & Branigan, 2005; Arnold, Wasow, Asudeh, & Alrenga, 2004; Ferreira & Dell, 2000; Kraljic & Brennan, 2005), much of the research in this area concerns whether speakers design referring expressions from their own perspective or from the perspective of the addressee. Several key findings have emerged in the literature. First, speakers produce longer, more elaborate expressions when the addressee is less knowledgeable about the topic (Heller et al., 2009; Horton & Gerrig, 2005;

Isaacs & Clark, 1989; Lockridge & Brennan, 2002; Schober & Clark, 1989; Brown & Dell, 1987). For example, in an interactive story-telling task, Lockridge and Brennan (2002) asked speakers to retell a story to an addressee that contained events with typical or atypical instruments (*stabbed with a knife/icepick*). When retelling the story, speakers were more likely to mention atypical than typical instruments; they also tended to introduce atypical instruments with indefinite articles (*an icepick*). These effects were eliminated when the addressee was looking at a picture of the event. Interestingly, this is true across a wide age range (Nadig & Sedivy, 2002; Brennan & Clark, 1996). For example, Nadig and Sedivy (2002) examined 5–6 year olds' descriptions of objects for a partner in a task in which the critical object was in a scalar contrast set (e.g., a large cup in the context of a smaller cup). The critical manipulation was whether the contrast object (small cup) was visible to the addressee; the target (large cup) was always visible to both speaker and addressee (Figure 1.4).

When both the speaker and addressee could see the large cup (left panel), children used scalar-modified expressions on 75 percent of trials. In contrast, when the large cup was visible to the child but not the addressee (right panel), the child used scalars only 50 percent of the time, demonstrating that even young children design their messages in ways that are sensitive to the perspective of the addressee.

The final, central finding that has emerged in this literature is that the process of designing messages with the addressee's needs in mind is modulated by a variety of speaker-internal factors. For example, when under time pressure, adult speakers are less sensitive to the addressee's knowledge state when designing such expressions as *the large cup* versus *the cup* in Figure 1.4 (Horton & Keysar,

1996). Memory for perspectives also plays a role; when designing messages for one of two addressees, speakers are better at tailoring the message for a given addressee when information associated with this person is more distinct, for example if the speaker always discusses *fish* with one addressee, and *birds* with the other addressee, rather than both species with both addressees (Horton & Gerrig, 2005; also see Horton, 2007, Heller et al., 2009). Additionally, speakers may also show more success at audience design after some practice with a task (Horton & Gerrig, 2002). Lastly, the relative salience of the speaker's and addressee's perspective is also relevant: for example, speakers are less able to suppress privately held information when this information is highly salient (Wardrow Lane, Groisman, & Ferreira, 2006; Wardlow Lane & Ferreira, 2008). Some of these effects can be counterintuitive. For example, Wardlow Lane et al. (2006) found that when a speaker was told to keep the object that only she could see a secret (e.g., the small cup in the right panel of Figure 1.4), speakers were actually more likely to refer to the target in a way that incidentally revealed the identity of that object (e.g., *the large cup*).

Loose Ends and New Directions

This section summarizes what has been learned about the formulation of messages and present current controversies in the field. It then concludes by highlighting empirical issues that remain unresolved and pointing out areas ripe for new research.

Recent Advances in the Field

Although at times the literature on message encoding seems a prickly nest of contradictions, there are several points of general agreement. Regarding the basic form of messages, it is generally agreed that messages are prelinguistic, nonlinear,

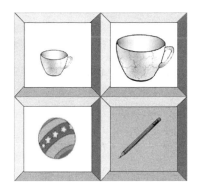 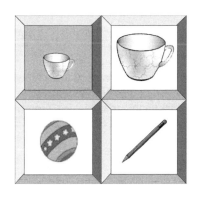

Figure 1.4 Example displays: items in gray are only visible to the speaker.

and propositional in nature. Recent research suggests that when planning messages, speakers must establish a starting point for the ensuing utterance; this starting point can be perceptually (Gleitman et al., 2007) or conceptually driven (Griffin & Bock, 2000), depending on event codability (Kuchinsky & Bock, 2010) and in all likelihood several to-be-documented factors. The scope of planning for messages seems to vary from the propositional content needed to express a single word (e.g., *small*, Brown-Schmidt & Konopka, 2008), up to an entire phrase or clause (Garrett, 1980; Allum & Wheeldon, 2009), although these points may or may not represent the ends of the continuum.

Although the details of the representations vary from account to account, it is generally assumed that complex messages contain all the information required to express the relationship between the concepts and their roles in the to-be-described event (Chang et al., 2006; Levelt, 1989), with the encoding of ellipsis and overspecification remaining an open question. Converging empirical and modeling evidence suggests considerable language-specific mediation on message content, and interaction between language-specific syntactic representations and message-level representations during formulation (Allum & Wheeldon, 2007, 2009; Bock, 1982; Chang et al., 2006). Finally, the content of messages is clearly shaped by the discourse context (Clark & Wilkes-Gibbs, 1989; Olson, 1970; Osgood, 1971; Sedivy, 2005) and characteristics of the addressee (Wilkes-Gibbs & Clark, 1992; Lockridge & Brennan, 2002). Importantly, messages are tailored by communicative intent and the real-time situation in which communication takes place.

Current Controversies

One of the theoretical questions for which there exists the clearest yet opposing theories concerns planning scope. Although the research on linguistic planning has described the process of grammatical encoding in rich detail, attempts to estimate planning scope in message generation have led to a number of diverging findings. Perhaps the most striking outcome of this research has been the observation of a wide range of planning windows, leading to the development of several promising and testable hypotheses about the time course of message encoding.

An important challenge for future research is to understand what determines the choice of planning strategies, whether it be highly incremental or holistic, or a combination of both. Such variables as message and sentence complexity may play an important role, with conceptually complex or conceptually coherent messages requiring more holistic planning. Planning may also take place in multiple stages, with initial encoding of basic relational information followed by more detailed planning of smaller message chunks containing some internal structure. Any number of these factors may interact with speaker-specific variables, such as individual differences in memory spans, linguistic abilities, background knowledge, or strategic choices made on the basis of immediate and changing communicative goals (Ferreira & Swets, 2002; Levelt & Meyer, 2000).

A second challenge is the development of mechanistic models of the message encoding process. Growing evidence for systematic variability in message planning suggests that model-building must consider questions about message complexity, communicative intent, and speaker-specific variables. Connectionist models, such as Chang et al.'s (2006; also Chang, 2009) model of language production, have been able to account for a range of findings in the literature in part because they use learning algorithms that reflect the model's history and experience with language, a strength that may be particularly pertinent in the domain of message planning where encoding outcomes are highly variable. As new findings shed light on these issues, the field will benefit from having a more specific operational definition of planning scope at the conceptual level and computationally feasible alternatives for mechanisms translating thought into language.

New Directions

In addition to these important issues, several new directions for research on message encoding deserve further attention. The answers to these questions are likely to have profound impact on the understanding of the content and encoding of messages.

One area that has been largely neglected is the fact that messages typically (if not always) carry nonlexical content. Consider the case of prosody. In English, given the right discourse context, whether an utterance has a rising or falling intonation (6a and b) makes the difference between understanding that utterance as a question and or a statement (Gunlogson, 2003).

(6a) *France is a monarchy.*
(6b) *France is a monarchy?*

Similarly, the prosodic form of individual words (including pitch accents, duration, and intensity) can convey changes in meaning (e.g., *he* vs. *HE*, Lakoff,

1971; also Dahan, Tanenhaus, & Chambers, 2002). Given that the choice between a rising and a falling prosodic contour, or an accented or unaccented pronoun, has clear implications for meaning, these prosodic choices reflect conceptual choices between emphasis and de-emphasis, and thus must originate in message-level planning (although other aspects of prosodic choices, such as syllabification of words, might be accomplished at other levels of the production system; see Levelt, 1989). As the domain of inquiry to nonlinguistic message-level content begins to open, other properties of spoken language that are relevant to message planning will become apparent, such as the use of disfluency (e.g., Fraundorf & Watson, 2008) and gesture, particularly when they convey information beyond what is in the speech stream (see McNeill, 2005; Cook & Tanenhaus, 2009).

A second area that deserves inquiry involves the complexities of the message encoding process in bilingual speakers, illustrated in the emerging research on conceptual representations in bilinguals (e.g., Ameel, Storms, Malt, & Sloman, 2005; Ameel, Malt, Storms, & Van Assche, 2009). Setting aside questions regarding mastery of lexical items, grammar, or phonology, bilingual speakers experience cross-talk between their languages at the level of individual words' semantic fields and larger categories. Semantic convergence and the processing requirements of *thinking for speaking* can have several consequences for online message preparation, including effects of processing load on the incrementality of message planning.

Conclusions

The field-defining theoretical positions were posed long ago by Wundt (1900) and Paul (1880), but the advent and increasing sophistication of experimental methods has recently made message planning a very active and attractive field of research. Although the intangibility of preverbal thoughts makes research on messages challenging, it also makes the topic all the more fascinating. Taken together, the state of the art of research in this domain suggests considerable flexibility in the process of message planning and considerable sensitivity and perspective-taking on the part of the speaker when designing messages in different conditions and for different listeners. The specific details of these operations remain a mystery, because the various research questions generate highly consistent findings in some subdomains and mixed results in others. Nevertheless, they provide the beginnings of a solid theoretical framework for future work on

this first, and most important, step in the transformation of thought to speech.

Acknowledgments

We are grateful to Kay Bock, Gary Dell, and Antje Meyer for helpful comments and discussions.

Note

1. For the purposes of this discussion, we make no distinction between conceptual structure and semantic structure. Questions regarding possible differences between an alinguistic representation of an event and its corresponding prelinguistic representation are taken up in the second part of the article.

References

Aksu-Koç, A., Ögel-Balaban, H., & Alp, I. E. (2009). Evidentials and source knowledge in Turkish. *New Directions for Child and Adolescent Development, 125*, 13–28.

Allum, P. H., & Wheeldon, L. R. (2007). Planning scope in spoken sentence production: The role of grammatical units. *Journal of Experimental Psychology: Learning, Memory, and Cognition, 33*, 791–810.

Allum, P. H., & Wheeldon, L. R. (2009). Scope of lexical access in spoken sentence production: Implications for the conceptual-syntactic interface. *Journal of Experimental Psychology: Learning, Memory, and Cognition, 35*, 1240–1255.

Ameel, E., Storms, G., Malt, B., & Sloman, S. (2005). How bilinguals solve the naming problem. *Journal of Memory and Language, 53*, 60–80.

Ameel, E., Storms, G., Malt, B., & Van Assche, F. (2009). Semantic convergence in the bilingual lexicon. *Journal of Memory and Language, 60*, 270–290.

Arnold, J. E. (2008). Reference production: Production-internal and addressee-oriented processes. *Language and Cognitive Processes, 23*, 495–527.

Arnold, J. E., Wasow, T., Asudeh, A., & Alrenga, P. (2004). Avoiding attachment ambiguities: The role of constituent ordering. *Journal of Memory and Language, 51*, 55–70.

Baillargeon, R. (2008). Innate ideas revisited: For a principle of persistence in infants' physical reasoning. *Perspectives on Psychological Science, 3*, 2–13.

Bangerter, A., & Clark, H. H. (2003). Navigating joint projects with dialogue. *Cognitive Science, 27*, 195–225.

Beun, R.J. & Cremers, A.H.M. (1998) Object Reference in a Shared Domain of Conversation. *Pragmatics and Cognition, 6*. 111–142.

Bierwisch, M., & Schreuder, R. (1992). From concepts to lexical items. *Cognition, 42*, 23–60.

Bock, K. (1982). Toward a cognitive psychology of syntax: information processing contributions to sentence formulation. *Psychological Review, 89*, 1–47.

Bock, J. K. (1986). Meaning, sound, and syntax: Lexical priming in sentence production. *Journal of Experimental Psychology: Learning, Memory, and Cognition, 12*, 575–586.

Bock, K., Irwin, D. E., & Davidson, D. J. (2004). Putting first things first. In F. Ferreira & J. Henderson (Eds.), *The integration of language, vision, and action: Eye movements and the visual world* (pp. 249–278). New York: Psychology Press.

Bock, K., Irwin, D. F., Davidson, D. J., Levelt, W. J. M. (2003). Minding the clock. *Journal of Memory and Language, 48*, 653–685.

Bock, J. K., & Levelt, W. J. M. (1994). Language production: Grammatical encoding. In M. A. Gernsbacher (Ed.), *Handbook of psycholinguistics* (pp. 945–984). San Diego: Academic Press.

Bock, K., Loebell, H., & Morey, R. (1992). From conceptual roles to structural relations: Bridging the syntactic cleft. *Psychological Review, 99*, 150–171.

Bock, K., & Warren, R. K. (1985). Conceptual accessibility and syntactic structure in sentence formulation. *Cognition, 21*, 47–67.

Boroditsky, L. (2001). Does language shape thought? Mandarin and English speakers' conceptions of time. *Cognitive Psychology, 43*, 1–22.

Brennan, S. E., & Clark, H. H. (1996). Conceptual pacts and lexical choice in conversation. *Journal of Experimental Psychology: Learning, Memory, and Cognition, 22*, 1482–1493.

Brown, P. M., & Dell, G. S. (1987). Adapting production to comprehension: The explicit mention of instruments. *Cognitive Psychology, 19*, 441–472.

Brown-Schmidt, S., Byron, D. K., & Tanenhaus, M. K. (2005). Beyond salience: Interpretation of personal and demonstrative pronouns. *Journal of Memory and Language, 53*, 292–313.

Brown-Schmidt, S., Campana, E., & Tanenhaus, M. K. (2005). Real-time reference resolution by naive participants during a task-based unscripted conversation. In J. C. Trueswell & M.K. Tanenhaus (Eds.), *Approaches to studying world-situated language use: Bridging the language as product and language as action traditions*. Cambridge, MA: MIT Press.

Brown-Schmidt, S., & Konopka, A. E. (2008). Little houses and casas pequeñas: Message formulation and syntactic form in unscripted speech with speakers of English and Spanish. *Cognition, 109*, 274–280.

Brown-Schmidt, S., & Tanenhaus, M. K. (2006). Watching the eyes when talking about size: An investigation of message formulation and utterance planning. *Journal of Memory and Language, 54*, 592–609.

Chang, F. (2009). Learning to order words: A connectionist model of heavy NP shift and accessibility effects in Japanese and English. *Journal of Memory and Language, 61*, 374–397.

Chang, F., Dell, G. S., & Bock, K. (2006). Becoming syntactic. *Psychological Review, 113*, 243–272.

Choi, S., & Bowerman, M. (1991). Learning to express motion events in English and Korean: The influence of language-specific lexicalization patterns. *Cognition, 41*, 83–121.

Clark, H. H. (1996). *Using language*. Cambridge: Cambridge University Press.

Clark, H. H., & Carlson, T. B. (1982). Hearers and speech acts. *Language, 58*, 332–373.

Clark, H. H., & Krych, M. A. (2004). Speaking while monitoring addressees for understanding. *Journal of Memory and Language, 50*, 62–81.

Clark, H. H., & Marshall, C. R. (1981). Definite reference and mutual knowledge. In A. K. Joshi, B. L. Webber, & I. A. Sag (Eds.), *Elements of discourse understanding* (pp. 10–63). Cambridge: Cambridge University Press.

Clark, H. H., & Wilkes-Gibbs, D. (1989). Referring as a collaborative process. *Cognition, 22*, 1–39.

Cook, S. W., & Tanenhaus, M. K. (2009). Embodied understanding: Speakers' gestures affect listeners' actions. *Cognition, 113*, 98–104.

Cooper, R. M. (1974). The control of eye fixation by the meaning of spoken language: A new methodology for the real-time investigation of speech perception, memory, and language processing. *Cognitive Psychology, 6*, 84–107.

Dahan, D., Tanenhaus, M.K. & Chambers, C.G. (2002). Accent and reference resolution in spoken language comprehension. *Journal of Memory and Language, 47*, 292–314.

Dell, G. S., & Brown, P. M. (1991). Mechanisms for listener-adaptation in language production: Limiting the role of the "model of the listener." In D. Napoli & J. Kegl (Eds.), *Bridges between psychology and linguistics* (pp. 105–129). New York: Academic Press.

Evans, N., & Levinson, S. C. (2009). The myth of language universals: Language diversity and its importance for cognitive science. *Behavioral and Brain Sciences, 32*, 429–492.

Ferreira, V. S., & Dell, G. S. (2000). Effect of ambiguity and lexical availability on syntactic and lexical production. *Cognitive Psychology, 40*, 296–340.

Ferreira, F., & Swets, B. (2002). How incremental is language production? Evidence from the production of utterances requiring the computation of arithmetic sums. *Journal of Memory & Language, 46*, 57–84.

Flores d'Arcais, G. B. (1975). *Some perceptual determinants of sentence construction*. In G. B. Flores d'Arcais (Ed.), *Studies in perception: Festschrift for Fabio Metelli* (pp. 344–373). Milan, Italy: Martello-Giunti.

Fodor, J. D., Fodor, J. A., & Garrett, M. F. (1975). The psychological unreality of semantic representations. *Linguistic Enquiry, 1*, 515–531.

Fodor, J. A., Garrett, M. F., Walker, E. C. T., & Parkes, C. H. (1980). Against definitions. *Cognition, 8*, 263–367.

Ford, M., & Holmes, V. M. (1978). Planning units and syntax in sentence production. *Cognition, 6*, 35–53.

Fraundorf, S., & Watson, D. G. (2008). Dimensions of variation in disfluency production in discourse. In J. Ginzburg, P. Healey, & Y. Sato (Eds.), *Proceedings of LONDIAL 2008, the 12th Workshop on the Semantics and Pragmatics of Dialogue* (pp. 131–138). London: King's College London.

Fussell, S. R., & Krauss, R. M. (1989). Understanding friends and strangers: The effects of audience design on message comprehension. *European Journal of Social Psychology, 19*, 509–525.

Fussell, S.R. & Krauss, R.M. (1992). Coordination of knowledge in communication: Effects of speakers' assumptions about others' knowledge. *Journal of Personality and Social Psychology, 62*, 378–391.

Garrett, M. F. (1980). Levels of processing in sentence production. In B. Butterworth (Ed.), *Language Production, Vol 1., Speech and talk* (pp. 177–220). London: Academic Press.

Gennari, S. P., Sloman, S. A., Malt, B. C., & Fitch, W. T. (2002). Motion events in language and cognition. *Cognition, 83*, 49–79.

Gentner, D., & Goldin-Meadow, S. (2003). *Language in mind*. Cambridge: MIT Press.

Gernsbacher, M. A., & Hargreaves, D. (1988). Accessing sentence participants: The advantage of first mention. *Journal of Memory and Language, 27*, 699–717.

Gleitman, L. R., January, D., Nappa, R., & Trueswell, J. C. (2007). On the give and take between event apprehension and utterance formulation. *Journal of Memory and Language, 57*, 544–569.

Griffin, Z. M. (2004). Why look? Reasons for eye movements related to language production. In F. Ferreira & J. Henderson (Eds.), *The integration of language, vision, and action: Eye movements and the visual world* (pp. 213–247). New York: Psychology Press.

Griffin, Z. M., & Bock, K. (2000). What the eyes say about speaking. *Psychological Science, 11*, 274–279.

Gundel, J. K., Hedberg, N., & Zacharski, R. (1993). Cognitive status and the form of referring expressions in discourse. *Language, 69*, 274–307.

Gunlogson, C. (2003). *True to form: Rising and falling declaratives as questions in English*. New York: Routledge.

Haywood, S. L., Pickering, M. J., & Branigan, H. P. (2005). Do speakers avoid ambiguities during dialogue? *Psychological Science, 16*, 362–366.

Heller, D., Skovbroten, K., & Tanenhaus M. K. (2009). Experimental evidence for speakers' sensitivity to common vs. privileged ground in the production of names. Paper presented at the PRE-CogSci Workshop on the Production of Referring Expressions, Amsterdam, The Netherlands.

Horton, W. S., & Gerrig, R. J. (2002). Speakers' experiences and audience design: Knowing *when* and knowing *how* to adjust utterances to addressees. *Journal of Memory and Language, 47*, 589–606.

Horton, W. S., & Keysar, B. (1996). When do speakers take into account common ground? *Cognition, 59*(1), 91–117.

Horton, W. S. (2007). The influence of partner-specific memory associations on language production: Evidence from picture naming. *Language and Cognitive Processes, 22*, 1114–1139.

Horton, W. S., & Gerrig, R. J. (2005). The impact of memory demands on audience design during language production. *Cognition, 96*, 127–142.

Hunt, E., & Agnoli, F. (1991). The Whorfian hypothesis: A cognitive psychology perspective. *Psychological Review, 98*, 377–389.

Irwin, D. E. (2004). Fixation location and fixation duration as indices of cognitive processing. In F. Ferreira & J. Henderson (Eds.), *The integration of language, vision, and action: Eye movements and the visual world* (pp. 213–247). New York: Psychology Press.

Isaacs, E. A., & Clark, H. H (1987) References in conversation between experts and novices. *Journal of Experimental Psychology: General, 116*, 26–37.

Kaiser, E., & Trueswell, J. C. (2008). Interpreting pronouns and demonstratives in Finnish: Evidence for a form-specific approach to reference resolution. *Language and Cognitive Processes, 23*, 709–748.

Kempen, G., & Hoenkemp, E. (1987). An incremental procedural grammar for sentence formulation. *Cognitive Science, 11*, 201–258.

Kim, M. (1996). Pragmatic determinants of syntactic subject in English. *Journal of Pragmatics, 24*, 839–854.

Konopka, A. E. (2009, March). *Variability in the scope of planning for simple and complex noun phrases: Effects of experience with messages, structures, and words*. Poster presented at the 22nd meeting of the CUNY Human Sentence Processing Conference, Davis, CA.

Kraljic, T., & Brennan, S. E. (2005). Prosodic disambiguation of syntactic structure: For the speaker or for the addressee? *Cognitive Psychology, 50*, 194–231.

Kuchinsky, S., & Bock, K. (2010). From Seeing to Saying: Perceiving, Planning, Producing. Paper presented at the 23rd meeting of CUNY Human Sentence Processing Conference, New York, NY.

Lakoff, G. (1971). Presupposition and relative well-formedness. In D. D. Steinberg & L. A. Jakobovits (Eds.), *Semantics: An interdisciplinary reader in philosophy, linguistics, and psychology* (pp. 329–340). Cambridge: Cambridge University Press.

Landragin, F. (2006). Visual perception, language and gesture: A model for their understanding in multimodal dialogue systems. *Signal Processing, 86*, 3578–3595.

Levelt, W. J. M. (1989). *Speaking*. Cambridge: MIT Press.

Levelt, W. J. M., & Kelter, S. (1982). Surface form and memory in question answering. *Cognitive Psychology, 14*, 78–106.

Levelt, W. J. M., & Meyer, A. S. (2000). Word for word: Multiple lexical access in speech production. *European Journal of Cognitive Psychology, 12*, 433–452.

Levinson, S. C., Kita, S., Haun, D. B. M., & Rasch, B. H. (2002). Returning the tables: Language affects spatial reasoning. *Cognition, 84*, 155–188.

Li, P., Dunham, Y., & Carey, S. (2009). Of substance: The nature of language effects on entity construal. *Cognitive Psychology, 58*, 487–524.

Li, P., & Gleitman, L. (2002). Turning the tables: Language and spatial reasoning. *Cognition, 83*, 265–294.

Lockridge, C. B., & Brennan, S. E. (2002). Addressees' needs influence speakers' early syntactic choices. *Psychonomic Bulletin & Review, 9*, 550–557.

Lucy, J. (1992). *Grammatical categories and cognition: A case study of the linguistic relativity hypothesis*. Cambridge: Cambridge University Press.

MacWhinney, B. (1977). Starting points. *Language, 53*, 152–168.

Malt, B. C., Sloman, S. A., Gennari, S., Shi, M., & Wang, Y. (1999). Knowing versus naming: Similarity and linguistic categorization of artifacts. *Journal of Memory and Language, 40*, 230–262.

McDonald, J. L., Bock, K., & Kelly, M. H. (1993). Word and world order: Semantic, phonological, and metrical determinants of serial position. *Cognitive Psychology, 25*, 188–230.

McNamara, T. P., & Miller, D. L. (1989). Attributes of theories of meaning. *Psychological Bulletin, 106*, 355–376.

McNeill, D. (2005). *Gesture and thought*. Chicago: University of Chicago Press.

Meyer, A. S. (2004). The use of eye tracking in studies of sentence generation. In F. Ferreira & J. Henderson (Eds.), *The integration of language, vision, and action: Eye movements and the visual world* (pp. 191–211). New York: Psychology Press.

Meyer, A. S., Sleiderink, A., & Levelt, W. J. M. (1998). Viewing and naming objects: Eye movements during noun phrase production. *Cognition, 66*, B25–B33.

Nadig, A. S., & Sedivy, J. C. (2002). Evidence of perspective-taking constraints in children's on-line reference resolution. *Psychological Science, 13*, 329–336.

Olson, D. R. (1970). Language and thought: Aspects of a cognitive theory of semantics. *Psychological Review, 77*, 257–273.

Onishi, K. H., & Baillargeon, R. (2005). Do 15-month-old infants understand false beliefs? *Science, 308*, 255–258.

Osgood, C. E. (1971). Where do sentences come from? In D. D. Steinberg & L. A. Jakobovits (Eds.), >*Semantics: An interdisciplinary reader in philosophy, linguistics and psychology* (pp. 497–529). Cambridge: Cambridge University Press.

Osgood, C. E., & Bock, K. (1977). *Salience and sentencing: Some production principles*. In S. Rosenberg (Ed.), Sentence production: Developments in research and theory (pp. 89–140). Hillsdale, NJ: Erlbaum.

Paul, H. (1880). *Prinzipien der Sprachgeschichte* (A. L. Blumenthal, Trans.). Halle: Niemeyer.

Papafragou, A., Hulbert, J., & Trueswell, J. (2008). Does language guide event perception? Evidence from eye movements. *Cognition 108*, 155–184.

Papafragou, A., Li, P., Choi, Y., & Han, C. (2007). Evidentiality in language and cognition. *Cognition* 103, 253–299.

Papafragou, A., Massey, C., & Gleitman, L. (2006). The cross-linguistic encoding of motion events. *Cognition, 98*, B75–B87.

Pechmann, T. (1989). Incremental speech production and referential overspecification. *Linguistics, 27*, 89–110.

Pickering, M. J., & Garrod, S. C. (2004). Towards a mechanistic theory of dialog. *Behavioral and Brain Sciences, 7*, 169–190.

Pinker, S. (1994). *The language instinct*. New York: Morrow.

Richardson, D. C., & Dale, R. (2005) Looking to understand: The coupling between speakers "and listeners" eye movements and its relationship to discourse comprehension. *Cognitive Science, 29*, 1045–1060.

Richardson, D. C., Dale, R., & Kirkham, N. Z. (2007). The art of conversation is coordination: Common ground and the coupling of eye movements during dialogue. *Psychological Science, 18*, 407–413.

Roberts, C. (2003). Uniqueness in definite noun phrases. *Linguistics and Philosophy*, 26, 287–350.

Sacks, O. (2005, October 31). A Neurologist's Notebook: "Recalled to Life." *The New Yorker* (p. 46).

Salmon-Alt, S., & Romary, L. (2000). Generating referring expressions in multi-modal contexts. *Proceedings of the INLG 2000 workshop on Coherence in Generated Multimedia,* Mitzpe Ramon, Israel.

Sapir, E. (1921/2006 ebook). *Language: An introduction to the study of speech [electronic version]*. Middlesex, UK: Echo Library.

Schegloff, E. A., & Sacks, H. (1973). Opening up closings. *Semiotica, VIII*, 4, 289–327.

Schober, M. F., & Clark, H. H. (1989). Understanding by addressees and overhearers. *Cognitive Psychology, 21*, 211–232.

Sedivy, J. C. (2003). Pragmatic versus form-based accounts of referential contrast: Evidence for effects of informativity expectations. *Journal of Psycholinguistic Research, 32*, 3–23.

Sedivy, J. C. (2005). Evaluating explanations for referential context effects: Evidence for Gricean mechanisms in online language interpretation. In J. C. Trueswell & M. K. Tanenhaus (Eds.), *Approaches to studying world-situated language use: Bridging the language as product and language as action traditions* (pp. 153–171). Cambridge, MA: MIT Press.

Slobin, D. I. (1996). From "thought to language" to "thinking for speaking." In Gumperz, J. J. and Levinson S. C. (Eds.), *Rethinking linguistic relativity* (pp. 70–96). Cambridge: Cambridge University Press.

Slobin, D. (2003). Language and thought online: Cognitive consequences of linguistic relativity. In D. Gentner and S. Goldwin-Meadow (Eds.), *Language in mind: Advances in the study of language and thought* (pp. 157–191). Cambridge: MIT Press.

Slobin, D. I., & Aksu-Koç, A. A. (1982). Tense, aspect, and modality in the use of the Turkish evidential. In: P. J. Hopper (Ed.), *Tense-aspect: Between semantics & pragmatics. Vol. 1 of typological studies in language* (pp. 185–200). Amsterdam/Philadelphia: John Benjamins.

Smith, M., & Wheeldon, L. (1999). High-level processing scope in spoken sentence production. *Cognition, 73*, 205–246.

Talmy, L. (1985). Lexicalization patterns: Semantic structure in lexical forms. In T. Shopen (Ed.), *Language typology and syntactic description* (pp. 57–149). New York: Cambridge University Press.

Tanenhaus, M. K., Magnuson, J. S., Dahan, D., & Chambers, C. (2000). Eye movements and lexical access in spoken-language comprehension: evaluating a linking hypothesis between fixations and linguistic processing. *Journal of Psycholinguistic Research, 29*, 557–580

Tanenhaus, M. K., Spivey-Knowlton, M. J., Eberhard, K. M., & Sedivy, J. C. (1995). Integration of visual and linguistic information in spoken language comprehension. *Science, 268*, 1632–1634.

Tomlin, R. (1997). Mapping conceptual representations into linguistic representations: the role of attention in grammar. In J. Noyts & E. Rederson (Eds.), *With Language in Mind* (pp. 162–189). Cambridge: CUP.

van der Wege, M. M. (2009). Lexical entrainment and lexical differentiation in reference phrase choice. *Journal of Memory and Language, 60*, 448–463.

von Stutterheim, C., & Nüse, R. (2003). Processes of conceptualization in language production: language-specific perspectives and event construal. *Language, 41*, 851–881.

Wardlow Lane, L., & Ferreira, V. S. (2008). Speaker-external versus speaker-internal forces on utterance form: Do cognitive demands override threats to referential success? *Journal of Experimental Psychology: Learning, Memory, and Cognition, 34*, 1466–1481.

Wardlow Lane, L., Groisman, M., & Ferreira, V. S. (2006). Don't talk about pink elephants! *Psychological Science, 17*, 273–277.

Whorf, B. L. (1956). *Language, thought, and reality: Selected writings of Benjamin Lee Whorf* (J. B. Carroll, Ed.). Cambridge: MIT Press.

Wilkes-Gibbs, D., & Clark, H. H. (1992). Coordinating beliefs in conversation. *Journal of Memory and Language, 31*, 183–194.

Wundt, W. (1900). *Völkerpsychologie: Eine Untersuchung der Entwicklungsgesetze von Sprache, Mythus und Sitte (Vol. 1). Die Sprache* [Language]. Leipzig: Kroner-Engelmann.

Syntactically Speaking

Kathryn Bock *and* Victor Ferreira

Abstract

Syntax is a construction project. It fills the conceptual holes and builds the conceptual bridges among words during ventures that speakers undertake in virtually every episode of talking. This chapter focuses on hypotheses and evidence about what speakers do and how they do it. The topics range over how construction proceeds from the draft of an idea through the creating of structural frames, the assembling of words, and the scheduling that brings words and frames together.

Key Words: syntax, sentence processing, structural frames

What you are reading is a product of language production. It contains sentences, clauses, phrases, and words that we are making up while we keep you, the reader, in mind. As you read, you might become aware of a faint echo of real speech in your head, a wraith of spoken language. You know the voice is only registering what you are reading (otherwise, please seek help). If everything is going as we intend, you also understand the ideas that we are trying to convey. To some unknown extent, we have made our thoughts into yours.

Suppose you exchange places with us. Imagine that you are the one with something to say, perhaps in reaction to the strange word *wraith*. Right here, right now, how do you turn your reaction to *wraith* into a comment that conveys your puzzlement, your sense of surprise, maybe the feeling that your reading stopped in its tracks? What arrangement of words would tell us what you experienced? That is, how could you use language to turn your thoughts into ours?

Questions like these are at the heart of research on syntax in language production. In more than 1,500 upcoming sentences, you will find more than 18,000 words that we put together with an aim to

explain what kinds of answers these questions call for. Some of the ideas behind the arrangements of words are our best guesses about what the answers are, drawn from what we have learned about language production during the hundreds of thousands of years that people have been talking.

Why Bother?

Most psycholinguistic research on language production focuses on producing single words (often object names) and the sounds of words. The production processes that support these abilities are fundamental to an explanation of talking, because words are building blocks of what people say. They are recurring, recognizable bits of language with sounds and meanings that are stable enough to be listed in dictionaries. They present interesting challenges: starting from nothing, they accumulate into the tens of thousands of words that adults can produce. Revealingly, they sometimes fall apart to disclose an intricate meshing of different kinds of information bound together in what looks like an individual word, inspiring important studies of single-word speech errors (see Dell & Reich, 1981, for a good example).

Yet almost all the words that people say occur in fluent strings with more than one word, unless the speaker is younger than about 3. Most of the connected strings of words that people utter will not be found in dictionaries, because there are too many of them, in fact an unlimited number. What speakers use to put the strings of words together is a set of abstract mechanisms collectively known as syntax. These syntactic mechanisms make sequences of words with structures that systematically convey sensible meanings. Because there are countless sequences with countless structures capable of conveying countless understandable meanings, speakers cannot memorize the strings and retrieve them from memory. Instead, they have to build syntax on the fly, virtually every time they talk. Single words are part of this process, but without the framework of syntax their communicative value is negligible.

The communicative limitations of single-word speech help to show why syntax is central to human language (and why the transition beyond one-word speech during the language development of toddlers is so significant). On its own, a word expresses too little or too much.

Sink.

Sink is a perfectly acceptable English word, and you know what it means, but if it comes out of the blue, as it did above, it is a mystery. You do not know if it is supposed to be the noun *sink* or the verb *sink*, which mean very different things. You might guess that there was a printing error. If the word comes from a speaker older than 3, you might wonder if you missed a question, since questions provide contexts in which single-word utterances *do* make sense. Questions, like the syntax of sentences, can supply the conceptual relationship between a single word and other things.

Conceptual relations are the heart of communication: communication is *about* things, *aboutness* being its very stuff. The linguistic vehicle of aboutness is syntax. Syntax identifies what a particular string of words is about (an "about-ee," roughly a topic that in English serves as a sentence's subject) and at the same time clarifies and enriches the aboutee with features from an "about-er" (a modifier of the aboutee that in English serves as a sentence's predicate). Without syntax, communication in language would be a shambles, heaps of words with baffling connections. So, to understand how people convey meaning when they talk, we have to explain how they make sentence structures with syntax. Let us look at what a speaker has to do to make this happen during a single fleeting episode of sentence production.

Building Structure with Syntax

Figure 2.1 illustrates a simple working hypothesis about the components of syntactic structure-building and their connections. From top to bottom, the components are arranged to broadly depict the flow of information from a speaker's *notion* (a hunk of thought, sometimes called a communicative intention) down to a rudimentary structure that corresponds to a syntactic *frame*. By *frame*, we mean a mental representation of relationships that can, as they fill in and fill out, guide the ordering of elements. In essence, a frame is a short-lived mental ensemble that transiently symbolizes how a sentence's separate parts are related and ordered with respect to each other. In more technical terms, a frame is a virtual cognitive instantiation of hierarchical structure.

If construction goes well, the ensuing frame will convey what went together in a speaker's notion, encoding aboutness links among disparate and sometimes distant pieces of an utterance. This is a definition of syntax that is known as Behaghel's First Law (Vennemann, 1973): syntax ties together linguistically what belongs together mentally, even when the things that belong together mentally lie far apart in a sentence.

Figure 2.1 breaks syntactic frame construction down into hypothesized processes that consist of *message formation, structural scaffolding, lexical identification, structural assembly*, and *morphological specification*. This chapter's focus is on structural scaffolding and structural assembly. Still, the

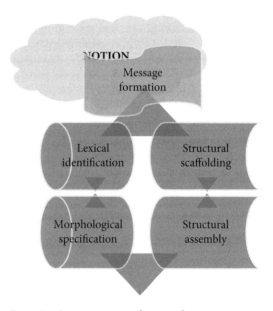

Figure 2.1 Basic components of sentence formation.

processes of message formation, lexical identification, and morphological specification are an integral and inescapable part of a sentence's history. They come up often in what follows, especially with respect to their links with structural scaffolding and structural assembly. In the discussions of these links we point to chapters in this volume that deal in more detail with messages (Konopka & Brown-Schmidt); words (Dell, Nozari, & Oppenheim; Race & Hillis; Leshinskaya & Caramazza; Vinson, Andrews, & Vigliocco); and morphology (Blevins).

We begin with the first link, the one between thought and the beginnings of linguistic structure, because it is the essential one that ideas must forge in order to become speech. This is the transition from message formation to sentence scaffolding.

Notions, Message Formation, and Structural Scaffolding

In a general account of cognitive processing, we place notions in the realm of *mentalese* (Fodor, 1975) or *mental models* (Johnson-Laird, 1983). Leaving conjectures about the layout of the information to braver souls, we define a notion simply as what a person has in mind when he or she is inclined to become a speaker. It is what a speaker intends to communicate.

A notion is embedded in ongoing mental activity from which it is set apart, because not everything that one has in mind when a notion arises is going to be worth saying. Someone who announces "It's time to feed the cat" is likely to be cognizant (even if not fully aware) of the listener, as well as an individual feline with a particular size, shape, color, and name, in a predictable state of agitation, in a particular place, at a particular time of day. Details about the cat food, the location of the cat food, and the feeding routine will also be on the threshold of awareness. In short, information is accessible at a level of unwieldy specificity, going far beyond what is situationally and communicatively viable or necessary. In this unfolding pageant of ideas, speakers have to spotlight what the situation requires to achieve a goal, calling on context, what they want the listener to do, and common ground, the knowledge that they believe they share with the addressee (Clark, 1996 and this volume).

As a focal point within an immediate perceptual, conceptual, emotional, social, and physical context, notions channel intended referents and relations in a nonlinguistic format. They are by definition non-linguistic, because they need not be converted into or conveyed in language. Sometimes gestures are better, or at least suffice for communication, given the setting. Other nonlinguistic devices work, too. But if language is the modality of choice, notions have to assume a form that is suitable for linguistic expression. For this to happen, a notion has to undergo on-the-fly categorization, the classification of notional elements (referents and relations among them) in terms of known concepts or ad hoc categories (Murphy, 2002). The product is a *message*.

Message Formation

Messages are analogous to locutionary forces in an analysis of speech acts (Searle, 1969), enveloped in illocutionary forces like questioning, asserting, commanding, and so on. The contents of messages are sometimes treated as *propositions*. Symbolically, propositions have a predicate (an abouter, often expressed with a verb and other modifiers that qualify aboutees) and arguments (one of which is the aboutee that the predicate modifies). In the sentences (a) *Dogs chase mailmen* and (b) *Mailmen are chased by dogs*, the predicate is *chase*. *Chase* puts two arguments (*dogs* and *mailmen*) that respectively perform and undergo chasing.

Unfortunately, a treatment of messages as propositions has drawbacks. Among other problems, propositional notation does not lend itself to representing the kinds of pragmatic information that sentences must convey. From a more practical standpoint, it leads to ambiguity in the treatment of syntax in language production. Propositional subjects sometimes are and sometimes are not sentence subjects: In *Dogs chase mailmen* and *Mailmen are chased by dogs*, the propositional subject argument is always *dogs*, while the grammatical subjects differ, corresponding to *dogs* and *mailmen*, respectively. To skirt this confusion, we avoid propositional terminology and instead talk about messages in terms of aboutness and the products of categorization, the *concepts* that play various aboutness roles. The message, then, is a prelinguistic representation of aboutness relations among concepts.

In the framework we adopt here, messages are the beginnings of syntax. Little is known about how transitions from messages to the formulation of syntax proceed, and even less about the timing and interaction of these processes. For now, this makes it risky to specify what is in a message before structural and lexical mechanisms come to the fore, despite the many empirical and theoretical efforts to pin answers down (e.g., Ford, 1982; Ford & Holmes, 1978; Osgood, 1971; see Levelt, 1989 for extended treatment).

A safe conjecture is that speakers do not always formulate complete messages before the mechanisms of language production get into gear (Brown-Schmidt & Tanenhaus, 2006; Brown-Schmidt & Konopka, 2008; Konopka, 2012; Lindsley, 1975). Even after speech begins, messages may undergo reformulation. This makes message formation and reformulation a culprit in the most pervasive disruptions of discourse, the disfluencies that punctuate almost all spontaneous speech (Barch & Berenbaum, 1997; Clark & Fox Tree, 2002; Deese, 1984; Goldman-Eisler, 1968; Maclay & Osgood, 1959). Disfluency is so common that as much as 50% of speaking time can be taken up by *umms* and *uhhhs* and silent pauses (estimate from Goldman-Eisler, 1968). Message formation is hard.

Because symptoms of message formation show up in disfluency, the distributions of pauses and hesitations should be valuable clues to how message creation works. The drawback of using hesitations for this purpose is that more than a half-century of research has failed to find unambiguous signals of alternative sources of hesitation. Message-rooted hesitations can be hard to distinguish from language-rooted hesitations. This could mean that there is no distinction to be made, that the thinking part of speaking actually flows seamlessly into the speaking part of speaking.

Fortunately, there is another kind of speech problem that is enlightening about both the etiology of hesitations (Garrett, 1982) and the transition from meaning to language. These are overt errors in saying sounds, words, and sentences. The properties of these errors hint that there is a buffer between message-making and structure-building. Because of this buffer, some of the problems of readying messages may have few direct consequences for the processes of readying language. We turn to this transition in the next section.

From Messages to Linguistic Structure

In the transition from a message to the structural domains of language processing, messages provide information relevant to assembling words and syntactic relations. This information is essential for conveying what the speaker has in mind, and at least some of it, at least briefly, has to be maintained in memory. In contemporary accounts of language production, the constraints from message contents must span cognitive chasms of sorts. The chasms have inspired terminology like *rift* (Levelt, 1993) in word retrieval and *syntactic cleft* (Bock, Loebell, & Morey, 1992) in structure-building. Figure 2.1

implies that the chasms differ, if only in the sense that what lies on the other side of the message is in one case a vocabulary or *mental lexicon*, and in the other the syntactic mechanisms for constructing sentences.

For the purposes of theoretically justifying a separation between the creation of notions and messages on the one side and the workings of syntax on the other, what is important is evidence for a qualitative dissociation. Separation presupposes a fundamental, natural discontinuity between thinking and speaking, and its tenability for language production is far from obvious or generally accepted (e.g., Boroditsky, 2001; Whorf, 1956), even among proponents of modularity (Fodor, 1983).

We think the assumption of discontinuity is not only tenable but unavoidable for explaining syntactic processes. In linguistics, the discontinuity is captured in the hard-to-dispute idea that language symbols (and here we include both the concrete lexical ones and the abstract structural ones) are to various degrees arbitrary with respect to human cognition. This holds even though the cognitive processes that motivate communication may be pretty much the same in format and content for speakers of different languages (e.g. Barner, Li, & Snedeker, 2010; Bock, Carreiras, & Meseguer, 2012; Iwasaki, Vinson, & Vigliocco, 2010).

The implication is that the products of a universal human ability to think are expressible with systems of symbols—languages—that bear no necessary relationship to underlying notions. The symbol systems vary in all the ways that languages around the world exhibit. At the same time, the lexical and structural constraints that languages impose on their human users have to be tightly organized. How tight we do not know, but tight enough to allow humans, within a couple of seconds or less, to retrieve suitable words and build suitable syntax for one of countless utterances to convey one of countless thoughts on any one of countless occasions throughout most of their lifetimes.

The consequences of a cognitive discontinuity between processes of thought and language are unveiled in research on the production of both words and structures. In word retrieval, clues come from sources that include research on familiar phenomena like tip-of-the-tongue states (Badecker, Miozzo, & Zanuttini, 1995; Vigliocco, Vinson, Martin, & Garrett, 1999), where the sense of discontinuity can be almost palpable (James, 1890), as well as the timing and accuracy of word production in controlled and natural settings (see chapters in the *Speaking* section of this volume). In the formulation of sentence structure, many of the clues come from analyses of speech errors.

Speech Error Analysis

With respect to structural processes, the discontinuities in language production were first disclosed in painstaking analyses of observed speech errors by Fromkin (1971), Garrett (1975, 1980, 1988), and others. By and large, these analyses encouraged the conclusion that when people make errors, the errors occur within well-formed structures. Even when words and their locations in utterances seem wrong, their syntax is right.

What makes them wrong? The fault lies in the havoc that errors can play with intended messages and the possibility of communicating them. A speaker who said that something was "costing the money more state" had a message in mind that is poorly communicated by the utterance. Nonetheless, the syntax of the error is impeccable. Likewise, "everyone expects high hopes of you," "I've got the whole thing wrapped around my arms," and "I enjoyed talking with these things about you" are perfectly fine examples of English syntax, but mishmashes of what the speakers intended (we leave it to you to figure out what those intentions were). Even "use the loose of her feet," which reverses an intended noun and verb, has a grammatical outcome (for reasons explained in Ferreira & Humphreys, 2001; Wardlow Lane & Ferreira, 2010).

Surprisingly, even the errors that analysts categorize as syntactic (excluding the rarefied minutiae of "school grammar") tend to be structurally well formed. These errors typically involve the abstract parts of whole-sentences frames, from phrases to whole sentences and syntactic relations. Among reported syntactic errors, one informal survey found 0.3% that contained clear structural violations (Bock, 2011). Note that this rate of ill-formedness is found *within* a type of speech error that is itself extremely rare: in large collections, syntactic errors constitute only about 2% of all the errors recorded (Fay, 1982; Stemberger, 1982). Disfluency aside, speech errors themselves are uncommon (Deese, 1984). This is not because of an irrevocable human ability to put words together in acceptable ways; attempts to speak languages that one knows poorly readily reveal how difficult it is to create consistent sentence structures. Speakers exhibit remarkably reliable production of syntax in their mother tongues.

These characteristics make it hard to resist the conclusion that the structural machinery of language continues to work when good messages go bad. This is the backbone of speech error analyses. It allows error properties to illuminate structural components of formulation like those in Figure 2.1, and strengthens the assumption of discontinuity between the activities of meaning and speaking.

The disparity between message preservation and syntax preservation also suggests that messages lose control of the formulation process, but the formulation process does not lose control of syntax. When speakers start thinking about what to say next, a current message can, and perhaps must, abandon its oversight of production. When structure-building takes control, it has its own priorities. Merrill Garrett summed up the operating principle with haiku-like austerity: "The production system must get the details of form "right" in every instance, whether those details are germane to sentence meaning or not" (1980, p. 216).

Putting a Sentence's Show on the Road

Even if there is some kind of qualitative transition between messages and sentence structure, something has to happen to bridge the gap. This "something" was the centerpiece of one of the longest, most heated debates about language production in the history of psycholinguistics (Blumenthal, 1970). The positions in the debate can be sketched like this: (a) Language production begins with an incremental concept-by-concept catapulting of message material into the lexicon, allowing concepts to identify corresponding words that arrange themselves one-by-one into phrase and sentence frames (Paul, 1886/1970); versus (b) Language production begins with a schematic, holistic configuration of message elements in aboutness relations. The relations serve as struts for a temporary bridge to linguistic-structural scaffolding and the lexicon. The bridge may give priority to salient or important elements, but only within the holistic framework (Wundt, 1912; see Levelt, 2012, chapter 6 for an unprecedented, lucid treatment of Wundt's views of language production). In line with the wellsprings of virtually all debates in cognitive psychology, one view (Paul's) emphasizes elements and the other (Wundt's) emphasizes the relationships among them.

Figures 2.2 and 2.3 (from Konopka and Bock, 2009; Kuchinsky & Bock, 2010) caricature the different accounts in terms of an experienced event that leads to structure-building. In both figures, the same experience gives rise to a message about one person shooting another. Figure 2.2 depicts a transition to language in which one part of the event and

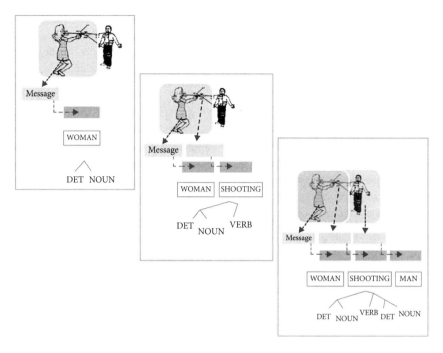

Figure 2.2 Word-driven development of utterance from attentional focus through structural assembly.

message and then another drive formulation successively, each one serving to identify relevant message concepts and appropriate words for expressing them. The words in turn arrange themselves into sentences. As shorthand, we call this *word-driven* sentence production (more precisely, production driven by the words that head initial phrases). Figure 2.3 depicts

structure-driven sentence production, in which relationships in the event (what is going on? what's it about?) dominate the transition to language, where the first order of business is building a structure that can eventually arrange words.

A fundamental property that word-driven and structure-driven production share is *incrementality*.

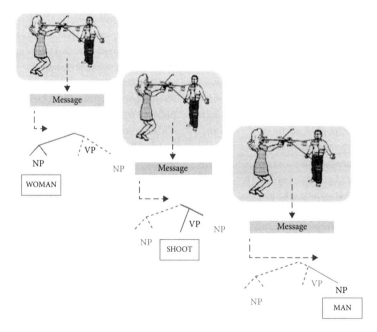

Figure 2.3 Structure-driven development of utterance from apprehension through structural assembly.

Sentences are not formulated as wholes or all at once, but as parts that are progressively linked to one another, and this incrementality is essential to an explanation of production. However, they are incremental in different ways. Word-driven production is *linearly incremental*: a sentence is built *up* from separate concepts in a message. Structure-driven production is *hierarchically incremental*: a sentence is built *out* from large structural joints that reflect relationships in a message.

Word- and structure-driven sentence formulation are far from mutually exclusive, and as we will see, they both play essential parts. Words and structures both have to be engaged, together or in succession, and integrated in the course of production. What is at issue here is the nature of the transition from messages to language. It could be that there is only one sort of steering that can lead off the structure-building process, with consequences for what happens later. Alternatively, it could be that either kind of steering can achieve the transition, as circumstances permit or demand. With that as background, let us look at the evidence for how language unfolds from messages.

Word-Driven Sentence Production

The word-driven view is in such good intuitive agreement with our sense of how we talk—one word at a time—that its rightness tends to be taken for granted. So, the typical question is not about whether the word-first approach is right, but about the factors that determine what the first word, the starting point, will be. A common answer to the starting-point question goes back at least to the ancient Greeks: speakers begin with the concept that is most important in the message.

Definitions of importance vary widely across the large literature dedicated to demonstrating word-driven ordering, and the results might best be taken as illustrating the many ways in which something can be important. Something can be important because it is perceptually salient, conceptually salient, personally significant, momentarily prominent in consciousness or attention, a topic of conversation, or a transient focus of shared interest (for reviews and discussion see Bock, 1982; Bock, Irwin, & Davidson, 2004; Levelt, 1989; MacWhinney, 1977). A different kind of importance, in terms of a speaker's priorities, is easiness: when possible, speakers begin with easy-to-use concepts, ones that are animate, concrete, familiar, frequent, simple, prototypical, at a basic level of categorization, and so on (e.g., Bock & Warren, 1985; Christianson

& Ferreira, 2005; Kelly, Bock, & Keil, 1986; McDonald, Bock, & Kelly, 1993; Onishi, Murphy, & Bock, 2008; Prat-Sala & Branigan, 2000). The easiness that matters most for speakers is not easiness for listeners, but easiness for themselves (Brown & Dell, 1987; Ferreira, 2008).

Oddly enough for something that seems so self-evident, research on word-driven language production has a long history of outcomes that would leave a skeptic unconvinced (see Bock, Irwin et al. 2004 for discussion). Fortunately, there is persuasive evidence from experiments by Gleitman, January, Nappa, and Trueswell (2007). The experiments manipulated the salience of alternative actors in pictured events using a subtle, almost imperceptible attentional cue (sidestepping a common problem in previous studies). The manipulation was accompanied by an assessment of eye fixations, to ensure that participants actually looked at the supposed salient object (remedying a source of circularity in earlier work). Gleitman et al. found a clear impact of attentional cuing on the choice of an initial phrase, often the subject phrase, of a sentence: cued referents were more likely to be mentioned first.

As an example, consider an event in which a woman is standing in front of a group of men, perhaps singing to them. Cueing the woman increased the probability of utterances along the lines of *The woman is performing for the men*, whereas cuing the men increased the probability of *The men are watching the woman*, mentioning the men first. This is credible support for a word-driven view of the transition between messages and utterances.

The structure-driven hypothesis that is depicted in Figure 2.3 is harder to assess for several reasons. First, the factors relevant to structural effects remain poorly understood. Second, there is no unambiguous link between the abstract components of sentence structure (whatever they might be) and potential manifestations of structural effects during production (e.g., prosody, latency, duration). Third, the suites of measures needed to converge on structural processes are far from obvious. Keeping these limitations in mind, there are several results that are consistent with initiation of formulation from a message-derived structural representation whose scope is broader than a word.

One of these results highlights what structure-driven sentence production looks like and at the same time provides illuminating counterpoint to Gleitman et al.'s (2007) work. The findings come from experiments that used the Gleitman et al. attention-cuing paradigm with eye-movement monitoring (Kuchinsky,

2009; Kuchinsky & Bock, 2010). As in Gleitman et al., speakers recounted pictured events in which alternative actors were covertly cued, and the impact of cuing on the choice of a sentence starting point was assessed. The major departure from the Gleitman et al. method was in the range of pictured events that speakers saw and described.

The events in Kuchinsky's experiments included those used by Gleitman et al. but went beyond them in an important way. The critical additions were events that varied in codability (Figure 2.4). Highly codable events are straightforwardly interpretable in terms of the relationship between two actors (e.g., the hitting that relates the ambulance to the car). In less codable events, the relationship between actors is ambiguous and hard to construe (e.g., a woman on an elevated surface being eyed by a group of men). Out of necessity, many of the Gleitman et al. materials had the latter kind of ambiguity, because their aim was to elicit verbs that offer different perspectives on the same event (e.g., *perform/watch; buy/sell, eat/feed*).

With less-codable pictures, Kuchinsky replicated the Gleitman et al. result that cued actors tended to be mentioned earlier than uncued actors. For the readily interpreted events, though, the results were different: attentional cuing had little effect on early mention. This was not due to failure to perceive or to use the cues, because the cues were highly effective in drawing the eyes: speakers consistently looked first at the actor that was cued, regardless of whether the event was more or less codable. But only for the less codable events was the cued actor likely to be used earlier in sentences than uncued actors. In other words, when events were hard to interpret, early attention to an object in the event elicited a word-driven production pattern, but in easy-to-interpret events, the cue had no consistent impact on the starting point.

What made codable events less susceptible to cuing? Putting together the results from several experiments, the account that stood up best in Kuchinsky's data was the fast emergence of structure, at least rudimentary structure, during the transition from a message to an utterance. This rudimentary structure (a *scaffold*) flags a suitable subject from referents represented in the message, projecting a tentative assignment on the basis of *accessible conceptual relations*. For this to happen, the relationship between actors in an event must be easily apprehended (categorized), for instance in terms of causality or intentionality, construed in terms of what the event is about. This construal allows subject selection.

When relational information is readily conceptualized, as it is in codable events, the relation can take precedence over momentary variations in attention to single referents. For example, a brief (500 milliseconds or less) glimpse of an event like the collision in Figure 2.4 can be enough for the general nature of the event to be apprehended and for an aboutee to come to the fore (Griffin & Bock, 2000; Schyns & Oliva, 1994).

Let us say that the aboutee is the car. With this construal in hand, there may be little inclination to construct an alternative interpretation provoked by a transient shift of attention to something else in the event. This is especially the case when a scene does not change during an eye movement. If the scene is the same, the event-world remains the same perceptually (unsurprisingly, because the stability of the visual world across eye movements is a classic phenomenon of vision; Irwin, 1991, 1996). In stable visual environments, efforts at recalibration are an extravagance; consider the effort required to discover alternative interpretations of newly encountered ambiguous figures. So, notwithstanding the movement of the eyes to the car, a speaker's initial construal of the car's centrality to the event is likely to remain in place and surface in an utterance like *The car is being hit by an ambulance*.

The findings of Kuchinsky and others (Brehm & Bock, 2011; Bock, Irwin, Davidson, & Levelt, 2003; Bock, Irwin et al. 2004; Griffin & Bock,

Figure 2.4 Events that are hard to interpret and easy to interpret.

2000; Konopka, 2012) imply that abstract structural relations *can* drive sentence production. What is harder to assess is how common structure-driven formulation occurs relative to word-driven formulation, or how common the circumstances are that promote one or the other.

The honest answer is that we do not know. Even so, it is worth keeping in mind that when people want to talk, they usually know what they want to talk *about*. (We all know people who blather on without discernible attention to aboutness, but they are rare enough to be distinctly annoying.) Speakers are often in possession of relational information before they start to talk, because what they are venturing to say starts out as a notion of their very own. Perhaps it is chiefly or only in situations like play-by-play announcing or pressured speech where speakers willingly start talking about something or someone that has an unknown role in an unknown event.

Structural Scaffolding and Structural Assembly

Regardless of whether a sentence is constructed in a word- or structure-driven way, structural relations arise at some point. So far, our only question has been whether a structure can emerge early, before lexical identification, as well as later. Now we have to get more explicit about what kind of structure we mean, what it contains, and how it gets there. We call it a *structural scaffold*.

Structural Scaffolding

A structural scaffold is the product of a mapping (the struts of the bridge in our earlier metaphor) between a message's conceptual instantiation of particular referents and a linguistic framing of particular words and syntactic relations. Syntactic relations are so far from receiving a satisfactory treatment, either linguistically or psycholinguistically, that Chang, Dell, and Bock (2006) resorted to the labels X, Y, and Z.

What we settle for here is a rough-and-ready characterization that combines the message terminology of *aboutness* with familiar, traditional grammatical-role labels. This yields an aboutee and an abouter, respectively the syntactic subject and its predicate. Predicates turn into verbs and other relations that can further specify (modify) an aboutee, including relations realized as the direct and indirect objects of verbs. Other relations may be expressed eventually in prepositional phrases, subordinate clauses, adverbs, and adjectives. These other relations (which we call *complements*, without

distinguishing among them) provide even greater precision for conveying aboutness.

A simple structural scaffold contains a subject-predicate relation. Subjects and predicates are really just one relationship looked at from opposite perspectives, predicates representing the abouters of subjects and subjects representing the aboutees of predicates. Accordingly, the terms *subject* and *predicate* each presuppose a subject-predicate relation, because they automatically implicate each other. In this way, a rudimentary or latent structure emerges as soon as a subject, the aboutee from the message, is flagged. If we had to depict a subject relation, we would sketch it something like this:

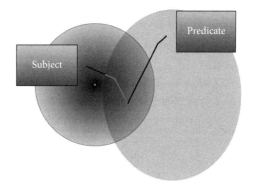

A direct object relation, if one emerges, intersects with the predicate, like this:

Other relations create other intersections, unions, and so on.

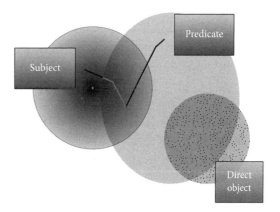

Each of the syntactic relations in a scaffold also has to have been rooted in the components of the message. The syntactic relations must likewise be bound to appropriate words, and going full circle, the words must be rooted in the same message components as their bound syntactic relations. For the subject relation shown below, the lexical binding is to a lexical entry and the message source is a referent-based concept:

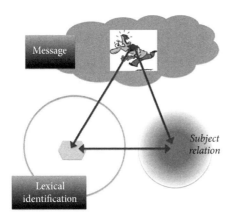

This is a sentence-production analogy of pulling off a triple play in baseball (ignoring the fact that baseball's triple plays are rare, while a syntactic relation's triple plays have to be the rule). Take Figure 4's collision event. In it, the message representation of the car (the initial tag for the triple play) can be linked to the subject relation (another tag in the play) and to the word identified to denote the car (completing the triple play). An essential feature in this configuration is that, given the message element and its link to the subject, the word identified for the scaffold had better be *car*, not *ambulance*. If it were *ambulance*, the resulting utterance could be *An ambulance is being hit by a car*, and that's not the right notion. Instead, it is a kind of error in which syntactic relations reverse.

Thus, for an accurate description of the collision in Figure 2.4, it is essential for the subject relation and an appropriate word to be rooted in the same component of the message. The creation of this small network in a referential-relational-lexical triple play is called *binding*, and it is a keystone of communication in language. Like a real triple play, the tagging of targets in the three-way binding may occur in any order, but some transitions will be more frequent and effective than others. Also like a real triple play, binding has to be fast-paced and short-lived, because successive messages have new elements that need binding to the same syntactic relations with different words. Unlike a real triple play, though, some or all of the bindings in a scaffold might arise simultaneously.

Triple-play binding means that in structure-driven formulation, where syntactic relations emerge before lexical identification, there is a strong lexical constraint: if the AMBULANCE concept

in a message is bound to a particular relation, the same relation must be bound to words that are capable of denoting the AMBULANCE concept. Conversely, in word-driven formulation, if the concept AMBULANCE is lexically identified as the noun *ambulance*, the noun must bind to a syntactic relation that is also linked to the AMBULANCE part of the message. Two possible options are to bind *ambulance* to the subject (*An ambulance is hitting a car*) or to an object in a passive sentence (*A car is being hit by an ambulance*). If message representations can be more or less ambiguous or neutral with respect to aboutness, either of these structures could convey the speaker's notion.

The constraint of triple-play binding, and the various ways in which it might be satisfied, lead directly to the topic of syntactic flexibility. Even if a triple-play constraint *can* be logically satisfied in one of several ways, it does not mean that language production mechanisms are configured in a way that allows options. The next section takes up the evidence for flexibility in production, which is a primary consideration in how words and structures work together.

Coordinating Words and Syntax

The prospect for flexibility in lexical and syntactic coordination raises questions with far-reaching implications for theories about the flow of information in language production (Bock, 1982; 1987b). The simplest and strongest claim about production comes from accounts in which formulation proceeds from a message through a defined sequence of encoding operations (Levelt et al., 1991). In such a framework, there is no natural accommodation for disruptions or failures in coordination. If trouble occurs or the circumstances that lead to trouble arise, failure at any point should instigate efforts at message recasting in order to resume speaking, perhaps with symptoms like disfluency. If adaptive mechanisms are present, however, they provide a recourse against brewing threats to utterances that avoids the revision of the original message.

A known source of trouble in sentence formulation comes from the need to identify suitable words. Links from messages to the lexicon may serve to automatically activate words, but sometimes too weakly for identification, sometimes too many at the same time (Cutting & Ferreira, 1999), and sometimes none at all (Burke, MacKay, Worthley, & Wade, 1991). Problems like these can stall production for an uncomfortably long time, or bring it to a complete halt. Like message formation, hitches in word retrieval are a culprit in disfluencies, particularly the disfluencies whose contexts of occurrence implicate upcoming content words (Clark & Wasow, 1998). Content words differ widely in ease of selection and retrieval that are attributable to variations in learning, experience, and circumstances of use (Griffin & Ferreira, 2006). They vary in the age at which they are learned, their objective frequency and subjective familiarity, their recency of occurrence, their contextual distinctiveness, their abstractness, their length, and so on. Variations like these can create roadblocks to ongoing but unfinished sentence formulation (Ferreira & Pashler, 2002), regardless of whether formulation is lexically or structurally driven.

To see how a roadblock could arise in the course of production, imagine that the AMBULANCE concept for Figure 4's collision event has been linked to the subject relation. Because the concept is a nonverbal conceptual categorization, it also has to activate and identify a specific word, optimally *ambulance*. However, *ambulance* is a complicated, infrequent word that could be hard to dredge up, interfering with launching the utterance. Had the other vehicle-concept in the message been designated as the subject and sought in the lexicon, the excellent and easy word could get things underway much faster. But with the ambulance-actor already occupying the subject relation, a different direction for the triple play has to be set up.

In a fully top-down formulation system, the only backup for lexical retrieval breakdowns is adjustment of the message. Perhaps, though, production processes are able to adapt to variability in retrieval without beginning a message anew (Bock, 1982). The feasibility of such adaptation in the internal mechanisms of structural and lexical processes gains considerable credence from the behavior of speech errors: when overt errors arise, they reliably come with any changes that are needed to make their structural contexts well formed, though with distortions to the message. It is a small step to the hypothesis that structural adaptation is possible without serious damage to a speaker's intended meaning.

This alternative gets support from another result of Kuchinsky (2009; Kuchinsky & Bock, 2010). Recall that speakers in Kuchinsky's experiments described events like those in Figure 2.4 after their attention was drawn to one or the other actor by an imperceptible cue. Although cuing had little impact on how speakers began utterances that recounted easy-to-interpret, codable events (suggesting fast

scaffolding that guided the identification of words), less codable events behaved differently.

In the less codable events, cuing was more effective in eliciting early mention of the cued actor. However, only a subset of the hard events showed this pattern. In these events, cued actors most often occurred early when they were *also* easy to name. This is an impact of lexical accessibility. It was measurable because the nameability of actors was manipulated in all of the events, both more and less codable, so that half of the events contained one hard-to-name actor (e.g., ambulance, audience) and one easy-to-name actor (car, woman). The other half was split into events in which both of the actors were easy or hard to name, providing controls for nameability effects.

When a cue targeted an easy-to-name actor in a less-codable event, the tendency to start with it was substantial. Since these events were less codable, though, speakers were unlikely to have a structure prepared. There was also no way to anticipate the cue, since the speakers were not even aware of it. But if words have the capacity to build their own scaffolds, instead of simply binding a directly message-controlled scaffold, another way to start off quickly is to use an accessible word to begin the scaffold. This is what the speakers in Kuchinsky's experiments seemed to be doing.

The difference between this apparent word-driven adaptation and message revision can be seen in what speakers did when the cue targeted a hard-to-name actor. In these cases, the cuing effect unexpectedly reversed: the tendency was to begin with the *uncued* object and to do so even when the uncued object was also hard to name. Apparently, the inaccessibility of words for referring to the cued object prompted speakers to shift attention to the other object and begin with it, as a sort of last-gasp effort. In contrast to what happened when cued actors were easily named, this looks like rethinking with message reformulation. In line with this conjecture, uncodable events in which the cues fell on hard-to-name actors also tended to be accompanied by eye-movements to the uncued actor.

The adjustments in sentence formulation that accommodate variations in event codability and lexical accessibility illustrate the intricate collaboration that is necessary between structural scaffolding and lexical identification. The triangular "bridge over the chasm" in Figure 2.1 represents this collaboration, allowing either lexical or structural initiation as circumstances require. For codable events, the commitment to a particular scaffold of syntactic relations may withstand variability in lexical identification (presumably within limits). With less codable events, pulling off the triple play against constraints from messages, syntactic relations, and words is less straightforward, requiring information to combine in ways that a strict sequence of production operations cannot easily accommodate. We turn to this with a discussion of word- and structure-driven coordination.

Word-Driven and Structure-Driven Coordination
Word-Driven Coordination

One way for sentence production to be resilient against lexical variability is to allow words to directly guide structural scaffolding. The results of Gleitman et al. (2007) taken together with those of Kuchinsky (2009; Kuchinsky & Bock, 2010) testify to the existence of a process of this kind and the circumstances that allow it to work. In fact, there is a substantial amount of converging evidence for word-driven formulation and the lexical opportunism that it signifies (Bock & Irwin, 1980; Bock, 1982; Bock, 1986a, 1987a; Ferreira & Dell, 2000; Ferreira & Firato, 2002; Kelly, 1986; Levelt & Maassen, 1981).

To work smoothly, word-driven formulation must proceed from messages through words into scaffolding, structural assembly, and morphological specification. This means that words have to take responsibility for constructing a set of grammatical relations. If they do not or cannot, effects of lexical accessibility could show up mostly as errors like word exchanges, errors along the lines of "costing the money more state" rather than *costing the state more money*. In fact, word exchanges and other word errors have a slight tendency to put more accessible words ahead of less accessible ones and to substitute more for less accessible words (Bock, 1987b; Dell & Reich, 1981; Stemberger, 1984). If speakers are to sidestep these errors, words have to know something about syntax.

Fortunately, it appears that they do. A lexically driven process can work because words come with built-in information about their structural privileges (Melinger & Dobel, 2005). In some languages, verbs are particularly rich in syntactic detail, but other words have it, too. The entries in the lexicon that make this kind of information available are often called *lemmas* (Kempen & Huijbers, 1983; for an explicit model of lemma access, see Levelt, Roelofs, & Meyer, 1999).

Lemmas work roughly like this. Suppose that the message for Figure 4's collision retrieves lemmas for the noun *car* and a verb like *hit*. *Car* can be a subject, but it requires a verb to build the subject-predicate scaffold. *Hit* serves this purpose. The verb hit also makes possible something more, additional "abouter" information that indicates more specifically what happened to the car. This generates another relation to add to the predicate in the scaffold. *Ambulance* supplies the necessary noun, filling out a scaffold that is suited to the transitive verb *hit* (subject[predicate(complement)]).

Lexical Accessibility with Structure-Driven Formulation

Sometimes, though, lexical accessibility may affect sentence structure when a structural scaffold is already underway. If some words are accessible for binding to a scaffold when others are not, the smart way to proceed is with an opportunistic grab-and-go process. With adjustments to the in-progress scaffold, structural assembly can proceed. Without adjustments, though, errors can appear in which words show up in the wrong structural relations. To avoid error, structure-driven opportunism requires scaffold adaptation.

Structure-driven opportunism, structural steering, comes about when a message creates the beginnings of a scaffold before adequate words are identified (analogous to how lexical steering begins with a message identifying words before a structural scaffold is built). This makes it the structural parallel of easy lexical retrieval. For it to happen, opportunism in a developing scaffold would sometimes lead to an adjustment of structural relations to accommodate accessible words. That is, if a structural relation cannot bind a word that suits it (i.e., the word spoils the triple play), the scaffold may reorganize its relation-to-message mapping in a manner that allows it to exploit a readily accessible, already identified word. To do this, it must be supple enough to adjust how its relations are linked to message referents so as to parallel the message referents that are linked to accessible words. Objects may have to become subjects and subjects may have to become objects. In short, for an existing scaffold to accommodate words, a revision of structural relations may be necessary.

The simplest way for an existing scaffold to accommodate lexical variability is in effect the inverse of how accessible words build scaffolds by calling on the structural options they possess. Ongoing construction of a scaffold should proceed more smoothly if it binds an accessible word that has the ability to adapt to the scaffold's developing relational configuration. This is in effect the reverse of Kuchinsky's finding, where an accessible word exploited its option to create a subject relation.

The benefits to structure-building from flexible words are illustrated in the outcomes of experiments by Ferreira (1996). Ferreira examined the effects of lexical flexibility with an anagram-style task in which speakers built sentences from sets of words. The sets of words differed only in that some contained a verb with more structural options than a corresponding set. The verbs had similar meanings, like the dative verbs *give* and *donate*, but one of them offers more structural flexibility. To illustrate, the options for *give* include *give some money to the church* as well as *give the church some money*, whereas *donate* offers only one, *donate some money to the church* (*donate the church some money* is unworkable for most English speakers).

With such verbs, there are two ways in which the coordination between a scaffold and lexical identification could proceed, one of them lexically driven and the other structurally driven. Suppose that just one of the possible dative scaffolds is under construction before the verb is selected, and the selected (in fact, provided) verb is *give*. Regardless of which dative scaffold is underway, it can continue to unfold regardless of its relational scheme given that there is a form of the verb that is consistent with either scheme. Now, imagine that the same scaffold is in progress, but the verb selected is *donate*. If the in-progress scaffold happens to be one with relations incompatible with *donate*'s only option, coordination could grind to a halt. In this scaffold-first, structure-driven scenario, the prediction is that *give* should be easier than *donate*.

The word-driven coordination account makes a different prediction. If the selected verb is what builds the scaffold, *give* demands that a choice in structure be made. This adds uncertainty to the process, along with the possibility of slowing formulation. With *donate* as the driver of formulation, however, there is no choice and no uncertainty. Now, the prediction is that *give* will be harder.

The result was that verbs with more options (like *give*) were easier, implying that the ability of the scaffold to bind a verb with different options was beneficial. Thus, a scaffold that was underway could proceed with the selected verb regardless of the relations under construction; a scaffold incompatible with an inflexible verb required time-taking adaptation. This result is consistent with the possibility of scaffolds selecting their words, capitalizing on lexical flexibility.

Another way to exploit lexical accessibility is when scaffolds contain relations that require multiple words. Common instances of this are conjoined structures (*car and ambulance; ambulance and car*). Here, the scaffold has the option of fairly free word ordering, naturally accommodating differences in the accessibility of words and the ease of binding them to relations. There is broad support for accessibility effects of this kind from research in the laboratory and in the wild (Cooper & Ross, 1975; Onishi et al., 2008; Kelly et al., 1986; Fenk-Oczlon, 1989).

Miscalculation in structure-driven coordination can create specific sorts of errors, just as miscalculations in word-driven coordination create word exchanges. Structure-driven errors show up on occasions when whole phrases seem to be linked to the wrong referents. Errors like these, apparent failures in the adjustment of structural scaffolds, show up in some intriguing mistakes that Garrett (1980) called functional errors. To keep our terminology consistent, we call them relational errors.

Table 2.1 lists some examples. The very first example, taken from Garrett (1980), illustrates why relational errors differ from single-word exchanges. The error looks like a mere reversal of pronouns. The flaw in that impression is that the speaker did not replace **He** *offends* **her** *sense of how the world should be* with **Her** *offends* **he** *sense of how the world should be,* but with "**She** offends **his** sense of how the world should be." The pronouns and syntactic relations are linked to opposite things in the message.

Let us look in more detail at the nature of this anomalous linkage. In traditional grammatical terminology, the intended and produced pronouns represent different cases (like nominative, accusative, genitive) that overtly signal syntactic relations. In the first error, the speaker's intention suggests that the male in the message was linked to the subject (nominative) relation and the female to a possessive (genitive). In the lexicon, the expected linkage would be to lemmas for masculine and feminine pronouns. If the subject binds the wrong lemma (the one for a feminine pronoun), the pronoun shows up in a form appropriate for a subject, the nominative *she*. This leaves the possessive relation to the male, yielding *his*.

Relational errors again illuminate the cornerstone of flexible interaction between lexical identification and structural scaffolding. For meaning to be preserved, it has to be possible to adjust existing mappings to message elements. In general, without remapping, scaffolds can exploit lexical accessibility only at the risk of creating meaning-changing errors (like the pronoun error), for the same reason that word-driven variations in lexical accessibility must revise the relations in scaffolds to prevent simple word exchanges like "costing the money more state."

Parallelism in Building Structural Scaffolds

The covert juggling that is needed to prevent message-changing errors, without changing the messages themselves, clearly requires deft coordination of lexical identification and structural scaffolding. Lexical and structural steering represent different ways of proceeding in the face of asynchronies in lexical and structural formulation. Together, they present at least one more option for coordination: Perhaps alternative scaffolds emerge simultaneously. Within a production system that is both word- and structure-driven, each route might yield a scaffold that then competes with the other. In effect, this is parallel word- and structure-driven formulation.

An argument for parallelism comes out of yet another kind of syntactic error that is shown in Table 2.1, *blends* (Butterworth, 1982; Coppock, 2010; Cutting & Bock, 1997). A unique feature of blends is that they combine two structurally and lexically different ways of expressing a notion, sometimes in ways that yield logical contradictions: "I miss being out of touch with academia" says exactly the opposite of what the speaker intended. Not all blends create contradictions, but many do, perhaps as many as half (45% in one estimate; Bock, 2011). Blends in general look suspiciously like a merger of separate scaffolds with different sources, one source biased to express the message in one way and the other in a different way. Oddly, even these convolutions look like all syntactic errors in having regular structural properties (Coppock, 2010). Odd or not, this is what we would expect from a system that is vastly better at creating well-formed than ill-formed utterances, semantic anomaly be damned.

Evaluating Word-Driven and Structure-Driven Coordination

There have been a few efforts to evaluate the consequences of word- and structure-driven formulation for lexical-structural coordination. One tactic for getting at their hypothesized differences compares the effects of lexical accessibility in structures where the accommodations to accessibility variations require smaller or larger changes in syntax with only subtle changes in message content. Examples of small changes include word order in conjunctions (e.g., *Herb and Eve/Eve and Herb*) and equative sentences (*Herb and Eve are the current and former Mitglieder/The current and former Mitglieder are Herb and Eve*). The role of accessibility in creating more substantial changes in syntactic relations has been examined with structures that include active and passive sentences (e.g., *Tania's intellect awed Herb and Eve/Herb and Eve were awed by Tania's intellect*) and dative sentences like the ones mentioned above.

There are provocative but somewhat mixed results from using this tactic to get at whether and how structural flexibility and lexical accessibility interact. The most suggestive findings point to a difference in the kinds of lexical and conceptual dimensions involved in word order changes (e.g., in conjunctions) compared with those that can change syntactic relations and the order in which they are expressed. Some of the conceptual factors that affect assignment and ordering of relations, such as animacy, concreteness, and givenness, have less consistent effects on word order (Bock & Warren, 1985; Kelly et al. 1986; McDonald et al. 1993; Onishi et al. 2008; Tanaka, Branigan, McLean, & Pickering, 2011). Conversely, factors that affect word order (including word length and prototypicality) less consistently affect the assignment and expression of syntactic relations.

An appealing account of these differences is in terms of a property called *predicability* (Keil, 1979; see Bock, Irwin et al. 2004 for a review of the relevant literature). Predicability (not to be confused with superficially similar but semantically different word *predictability*) refers to the relative ease of categorizing notional referents and their aboutness connections, as abouters and aboutees. It reflects differences in the aboutness possibilities of concepts in terms of the richness and simplicity of the relational possibilities they offer. Relations among animate referents are easier to categorize than those among inanimates; relations among concrete referents are easier to categorize than those among abstract referents; and relations to previously categorized referents (given information) are easier to categorize than relations to not-yet-categorized referents (new information). Predicability has additional consequences for scaffolding, in forging the three-way connection among concepts, lemmas, and structural relations. Thus, predicability affects the formation of aboutness in messages on the one hand (via the ease of conceptually categorizing relations among notional elements) and the translation into language on the other (via the ease of

Table 2.1. Production Errors Involving Abstract Syntactic Structures

Error type	What was intended	What was said
	Relational	
1.	He offends her sense of how the world should be	"She offends his sense of how the world should be"
2.	They're going to set their dog on you	"They're going to set your dog on them"
3.	You're staying with her	"She's staying with you"
4.	I enjoyed talking with you about these things	"I enjoyed talking with these things about you"
	Blends	
5.	I'm not going to solely blame all of climate change on man's activities/I'm not going to solely blame all changes in climate on man's activities	"I'm not going to solely blame all of man's activities on changes in climate"
6.	I think this is something that this movie might help/I think this is something that this movie might help him along with	"I think this is something that this movie might help him along"
7.	When a car seat is misused.../When a car seat is used improperly	"When a car seat is misused improperly"
8.	I miss academia/I'm out of touch with academia	"I miss being out of touch with academia"
	Attraction	
9.	How much correction of syntactic errors *is* there, anyway?	"How much correction of syntactic errors *are* there, anyway?"
10.	Dr. Bock's research on the processes of speech production ranks among the most important contributions to modern cognitive psychology	"Dr. Bock's research on the processes of speech production rank among the most important contributions to modern cognitive psychology"
11.	Processing of semantic selection errors was accompanied by a classical N400 effect	"Processing of semantic selection errors were accompanied by a classical N400 effect"
12.	The validity of some of the experimental paradigms was questioned	"The validity of some of the experimental paradigms were questioned"

converting aboutness relations into structural relations). These are the two sides of *conceptual accessibility* in the transition from notions to linguistic expression (Bock, 1987a; Christianson & Ferreira, 2005), and its effects may be observable in scaffolding, lexical identification, or both at once.

Predicability is fundamentally a property of conceptual relations. There can also be differences in the ease of putting particular message concepts into words, due to conceptual prototypicality, transient activation, familiarity, frequency, morphological complexity, and so on. Factors like these may create *lexical accessibility* in the absence of relational accessibility, affecting mainly the identification

of words, the speed of binding them to scaffolds, and their morphological specification. Differences in lexical accessibility should be more apparent in how speakers exploit the possibilities for ordering words or phrases where options exists, in structural incrementation, compared with how options in the creation of structural relations are exercised.

Regardless of the dynamics, what emerges from lexical-structural coordination is a representation of structural relations that includes bindings to lexical entries. It may be generally the case that the representation's lexical and structural components become incrementally available in the transition to structural assembly. The question we address in the next section is whether structural relations and lemmas are inextricably bound before they are assembled into a structural frame. The alternative is that they remain divisible parts of a transient lexical-relational binding, not yet fully integrated in the way that they must be for utterances to become speakable. What has to happen for this to be possible occurs during structural assembly. That is our remaining topic.

From Structural Scaffolding to Structural Assembly

As its label implies, a structural scaffold serves to support the construction of a frame (as in Figure 2.1) for grouping and ordering words. Frame construction has to be fluid and capable of proceeding incrementally, with some parts built earlier than others to enable speech to start before frame construction stops. Incrementation may be comparatively slow or comparatively fast and fluent, reflecting combinations of message difficulty, formulation events, and tactics for starting to talk (Ferreira & Swets, 2002). Because the details of frames need not be fully spelled out before speaking begins, there can be variability in frame construction due to the ease or speed of binding during lexical-structural coordination (Ferreira & Dell, 2000; Ferreira & Firato, 2002), and to the accessibility or viability of alternative procedures for assembling a frame.

One focus of current research on structural assembly can be thought of in terms of the question raised above about the triple-play binding among messages, words, and structural relations. By the time that frame construction begins, the links to a message are unlikely to remain. Empirically, this follows from the indifference of speech errors to message contents. Pragmatically, it follows from the improbability of a production process in which messages have to remain in place until they are expressed. Message formation is attention demanding (Ericsson & Simon, 1980), so when speakers turn their attention to the formation of new messages or other processes, the nuts-and-bolts of language production must proceed on their own.

This leaves the binding between words and structural relations as the major player in frame assembly. Against this background, a major debate about frame assembly centers on another division between word- and structure-driven mechanisms. Perhaps sentence frames issue from a tight binding between words and abstract structures in which lexical properties play the dominant role in frame assembly, making sentence frames the product of the specific words they contain. Alternatively, structural constraints on assembly might dominate, proceeding in part independently of the particular words destined to appear in the frame. A structural assembly process like this would give rise to the abstract constancies of speech errors, orderly structure with disorderly words (Bock, 1990).

In this further opposition between word- and structure-driven language production, the theoretical and empirical debates play out on a field shaped by research on structural priming and persistence. In the next section we look at what priming and persistence are, and then turn to the findings that dominate the debate.

Structural Priming and Structural Persistence

Speakers have a tendency to recreate and reuse surprisingly subtle relational features of utterances when they talk (Bock, 1986b). We call this *structural persistence*, the persistence of structural features from one sentence into another. On the assumption that the features represent basic properties of sentence frames, considerable effort has gone into exploring the factors that are responsible for the recreation and reuse of sentence structure. If the factors behind structural persistence themselves reflect properties of structural assembly, the findings from this research are important to how speakers group and order the words that they eventually produce.

To distinguish the phenomenon of structural persistence from the conditions that create it, we use the term *structural priming* for circumstances that evoke structural persistence. Accordingly, *structural priming* encompasses events that (adventitiously or intentionally) evoke later use of similar frames at greater-than-chance levels. The priming event is the structural prime, and a sentence in which the effect of priming can be observed is called the target. The increased tendency to use a frame is *structural persistence*.

Structural persistence can be observed over a wide range of conditions, over a wide range of ages, in a variety of languages, outside of awareness, within and between input and output processing modalities, using different kinds of exposure, tasks, structural forms, and measures. It persists across time, extraneous events, and changes in tasks, despite differences between primes and targets in content words, function words, bound morphology, and thematic roles. It is observable in the absence of discourse context, but also in the presence of discourse context, including conversation, ordinary speech, and writing. It has been found in different languages from different language families. It occurs *across* the languages of bilingual speakers (see Pickering & Ferreira, 2008, for review.) It occurs when primes lack linguistic meaning but have the requisite structural properties (Scheepers et al., 2011). Most important, it goes away when prime and target sentences are superficially similar in word order and metrical properties, but have different structural frames (Bock & Loebell, 1990, Experiment 3).

Many of the key properties of structural persistence have been observed in experiments using a structurally primed event-description paradigm. The features of the paradigm circumvent an array of objections to the hypothesis that structural persistence is indeed structural, and not a byproduct of speakers' intentions or nonstructural relationships between sentences. This makes it worth describing the method in some detail.

The procedure requires participants to do two things. One is a memory task, a standby of laboratory psychology, presented as the primary task in an experiment ostensibly directed at memory processes. The secondary task serves as a supposed aid to memory, requiring speakers to produce an utterance in response to an event on each trial. It is this secondary task that elicits the responses of interest.

The trials consist of a long, random-seeming sequence of unrelated sentences and pictures. The order of sentences and pictures looks haphazard, with only occasional cases in which sentences precede pictures. A few of these cases constitute structural priming trials that proceed no differently from other trials. For instance, on one trial a participant might hear and repeat the dative sentence

The governess poured a cup of tea for the princess.

On the next trial, a picture like that below appears. The participant says what is happening in his or her own words.

The covert relationship between the sentence and event is in the structure of the sentences produced. A sentence produced aloud as *The governess poured a cup of tea for the princess* may be followed by an event that can be described as either "The boy is giving an apple to the teacher" or "The boy is giving the teacher an apple." Other participants see the same event, but preceded by the sentence *The governess poured the princess a cup of tea.*

What happens as a result of this procedure is that the probability of the primed structure increases. *The governess poured a cup of tea for the princess* is a prepositional dative that raises the probability of the prepositional dative in the target description, "The boy is giving an apple to the teacher." Likewise, the participants who receive a double-object version of the prime *The governess poured the princess a cup of tea* exhibit an increased tendency to produce a double-object target, "The boy is giving the teacher an apple."

This task is simple for participants, despite its methodological complexity. It also has important advantages, especially in creating priming episodes that are incidental and noncoercive. The manipulation is covert, camouflaged by the pseudorandom arrangement of lexically and topically disjointed events, most of which are filler sentences and

pictures representing a variety of other structures and event types. Speakers virtually never notice the structural properties of what they hear and say, nor do they suspect that the point of the experiment is how they describe the pictured events. Even the artificiality of the procedure serves a purpose, minimizing the syntactically influential pragmatic pressures of conversations. As a result, what participants say is unforced. When a prime's structure persists in a target sentence, the structure arises in extemporaneous speech that is constrained only by the pictured event.

Despite its importance, the spontaneity of structural formulation in this task has a major disadvantage: Some responses have to be discounted because relevant structural features are absent. Fortunately, other methods have been developed to circumvent this limitation. Though they tend to reduce the covertness of the manipulation and the spontaneity of speaking, they have complementary strengths that help to establish the generality of the phenomenon. In fact, there is good evidence for structural persistence in corpora of spontaneous speech, confirming its presence in everyday language use.

The findings from all of this work illuminate the circumstances in which structural persistence arises. In fact, mere exposure to a structure can suffice, with no intention or even explicit capacity to remember the structure on the part of eventual speakers. Striking evidence comes from individuals with anterograde amnesia (Ferreira, Bock, Wilson, & Cohen, 2008). Amnesic patients and normal control subjects were tested for structural persistence at different intervals after priming occurred, from immediately after priming up to as many as 10 unrelated events later. Persistence was observed at all intervals for the normal and amnesic speakers, and to statistically similar degrees.

What makes this remarkable is the nature of anterograde amnesia. People with the disorder are typically unable to successfully probe the contents of their memories, even at short intervals after an experience. Consistent with this, the amnesic individuals in the priming experiment exhibited structural persistence even when their ability to recognize the priming sentences that they had just heard was profoundly impaired. Nonetheless, the levels of persistence were the same as in control speakers. This preservation of performance in the face of severe memory impairment is a well attested property of anterograde amnesia. In several domains, the ability to learn skills implicitly remains unimpaired, and even improves with practice, in the face of inability to recall performing the same task ever before (Cohen & Squire, 1980).

So, structural persistence is pervasive and durable. Though its effects tend to be subtle and small, they have been observed in so many circumstances that its contributions to first and second language learning, to structural acceptability, to language change, to social bonding, and more, have become topics of research, speculation, and discussion (Bock & Kroch, 1989; Loebell & Bock, 2003; Luka & Barsalou, 2005; Pickering & Garrod, 2004). Nonetheless, much remains uncertain about its mechanisms and limitations, and we come to that problem now.

Structure-Driven and Word-Driven Assembly of Frames

The persistence of structure in the absence of more salient kinds of similarity implies that ordinary sentences undergo an assembly process of the kind disclosed in speech errors. Here, though, the product of frame assembly successfully conveys what a speaker means, albeit without support in the speaker's message for all of the details of the sentence frame. The implication is that structural persistence can be exploited in finding out how frames are built. However, something more is needed to uncover the specific mechanisms of structural assembly, to shed light on the factors that support and inhibit frame construction.

One valuable approach to this problem puts a provocative spin on structural priming. The implicit strategy is to look at what happens when factors that *can* be decoupled from structural persistence (disclosing its abstract structural sources) are instead *recoupled* with it. Pickering and Branigan (1998) took this fruitful tack in experiments that combined structural priming with repeated-word priming in constrained sentence-completion tasks. This research sparked a line of investigation that reintroduced pragmatic variables (Branigan, Pickering, & Cleland, 2000), phonological variables (Cleland & Pickering, 2003; Santesteban, Pickering, & McLean, 2010), information-structure variables (Bernolet, Hartsuiker, & Pickering, 2009), and more.

The general outcome of increasing similarity and increasing pragmatic constraint is an increase, sometimes a massive increase, in the probability of the kinds and forms of sentences that are elicited, relative to the rate seen with structural priming in the absence of lexical and contextual support. The only major exception may be phonological relatedness, which is ineffective in increasing persistence in the absence of full phonological repetition between homophonic words (compare Cleland & Pickering, 2003, with Santesteban et al., 2010). What has emerged from this research is a theoretical debate that centers on the mechanisms behind the increased effectiveness of priming.

The bulk of the debate is about whether the impact of repeated words (often but not always verbs) occurs within a lexically or structurally driven framing process. Because the repetition of words across primes and target sentences raises the probability of structural persistence, the increase has come to be called the *lexical boost*. To distinguish lexically boosted performance from the persistence that arises in the absence of repeated words, we call the latter *abstract structural persistence*. In simple terms, the debate is about where the lexical boost comes from and whether its origin is in the same mechanisms that yield abstract structural persistence.

To tie the lexical boost to structural priming, Pickering and Branigan (1998) proposed a lexically based model for sentence production, with the further aim of explaining abstract structural persistence in the same framework. In the model, the lexicon consists of a network of lemmas through which activation spreads during the retrieval of words for production (Roelofs, 1992, 1993). Lemma activation makes schematic information available about the syntactic contexts or structural privileges of specific words. In the Pickering and Branigan account of structural persistence, the words in a prime activate their lemma representations, including the specific structural contexts in which the words appeared. So, when the verb *show* occurs in a sentence with a direct and an indirect object (*showed the painting to the gallery owner*), the representation of this structural context becomes more activated than an alternative that allows *show* to appear with two objects (*showed the gallery owner the painting*). If a subsequent sentence also contains the verb *show*, continued activation of *show*'s structural-context information predisposes the reuse of the verb in the same structure (e.g., *showed the hammer to the builder*).

The model's explanation for abstract structural persistence rests on the assumption that syntactic privileges of lemmas are themselves part of a network that captures similarities in the structural schemas for different lemmas. For instance, the verbs *show* and *give* share certain structural privileges that may be linked to each other. As a result, when prime and target sentences contain different verbs, structural persistence can still occur. The persistence is weaker than with word repetition, because the direct connection between a specific lemma and its structural privileges is missing. Nonetheless, because of the lingering activation in the structural information associated with a word from a priming sentence, a word with the same structural privileges can tap into and exhibit effects from residual structural activation. That is, verbs like *show* and *give* that share an activated representation of a particular structure may both become temporarily inclined toward the use of that structure. The result is a secondary form of structural persistence that is a reflection of lexical representation and retrieval, rather than structural formulation processes.

A structure-driven account treats the lexical boost as an incidental but influential byproduct of identifying and binding a suitable word to a structure (finding-and-binding). Ordinarily, when a primed structure finds and binds a word, structural assembly proceeds with an inclination to recreate the same structure, yielding persistence. However, when the word that a primed structure finds and binds repeats a word that occurred in the priming sentence, there is an additional facilitation in the binding process. The consequences of facilitation include support for structural operations that result from immediate repetition of the same binding within the same procedures. This arises over and above the facilitation from abstract structural priming.

The competing predictions about the lexical boost that follow from these broad accounts reflect the primary versus secondary roles of structural processes in structural and lexical steering. The major prediction from the lexical perspective is that lexical repetition and other kinds of lexical facilitation should increase structural priming. This prediction has been amply confirmed. The structural hypothesis instead focuses on the duration of structural persistence and the conundrum this poses for a model in which words are viewed as the portal to structural information. To account for the extended time-course of abstract structural persistence attested in several experiments (Bock & Griffin, 2000; Bock, Dell, Chang, & Onishi, 2007; Ferreira et al., 2008; Kaschak, Kutta, & Schatschneider, 2011) the lexical hypothesis has to predict that the lexical boost should have a similarly long time-course. That is, the amount of persistence should be magnified when a target sentence contains a repeated word, even if the target occurs well after the prime.

Tests of this prediction have yielded results that run counter to it: the lexical boost is brief, disappearing within one or two sentences after a prime (Hartsuiker, Bernolet, Schoonbaert, Speybroeck, & Vanderelst, 2008; Konopka & Bock, 2005). When the boost disappears, what remains is the amount of structural persistence that tends to be observed when words are not repeated.

The differences in time course suggest that distinct mechanisms are responsible for the abstract form of structural persistence and lexically enhanced persistence. In a structurally driven formulation process, the distinct mechanisms are binding and structure building. Because binding is transient, the lexical boost also is transient. The problem for the lexical account is the idea that a word's links to structural representations are the underpinnings of syntactic processing. The effects of these links cannot be transient if they are to account for the duration of structural persistence, but they cannot be long lasting without predicting a lexical boost that endures as much as does abstract persistence.

The syntax-driven alternative to the lexical account places the source of persistence in a procedural system that instantiates the abstract mechanisms of structural assembly (Chang et al., 2006). One of the noteworthy features of the model is that it accounts for the abstractness of structural priming and for its durability in a system that implicitly learns how to build sentence structures. Learning occurs throughout the lifespan, tuning the structural operations that formulate utterances every time they are used. The model accounts for the abstractness in the relationship between prime and target sentences, because the structural operations do not depend on the properties or repetition of specific words. It accounts for observed levels of priming in a wide range of experiments and for the duration of persistence in normal and amnesic speakers. Perhaps most intriguing is that the model's learning mechanisms are rooted in language comprehension rather than production, predicting the cross-modality and modality-general effects that have been observed. A strong prediction, recently confirmed, is that priming within comprehension and priming within production should exhibit similar changes in the probability of persistence (Tooley & Bock, 2012).

Structural Assembly and Morphological Specification

Morphological specification during sentence production has a lot to do with grammatical inflection (e.g., making words singular or plural). It comes together with structural assembly most saliently in the processes of grammatical agreement. There are several important kinds of agreement (e.g., subjects and verbs, pronouns and antecedents, and determiners and nouns) and features of agreement (e.g., number, person, natural and grammatical gender agreement). In English, agreement is familiar in the morphological variations that flag subject-verb number agreement: singular subjects occur with singular verbs (*The **girl sings**; The **mother was** proud*) and plural subjects appear with plural verbs (*The **girls sing**; The **mothers were** proud*). Subject-verb agreement is a fundamental part of morphological specification in sentence production, and a target of active research (see Bock & Middleton, 2011, for details).

Perhaps the most important thing to note about grammatical agreement, as a process of actual, everyday language production, is that its implementation calls on information from the notion on down: it depends on much more than morphology. Messages have to represent information about the construed one-or-more-than-oneness of things (*notional* number). This information has obvious consequences for lexical identification (whether a word will be singular or plural). Its consequences for scaffolding are less obvious but at least as important: the scaffold has to have information about whether the notional number of the subject's referent is one or more than one, separately from information about whether the subject noun is singular or plural.

Among the many reasons for why this must be, the most transparent is that the details of sentence formulation unfold in a way that varies with notional number, even when grammatical number stays the same. Take a subject like *her brother and best friend*. Appearances to the contrary, *her brother and best friend* can be either one person or more than one. When *brother and best friend* are separate individuals, a notional plural, speakers will produce a plural verb (*Her brother and best friend **are** coming to the wedding*) but if one and the same individual is both *brother and best friend* (a notional singular) the agreeing verb will be singular (*Her brother and best friend **is** coming to the wedding*).

Most people's awareness of subject-verb agreement is limited to a few forgettable lessons and occasional withering remarks about standards in contemporary grammar. Ironically, agreement is more appropriately cast as something that is unexciting (to most people) but complicated and important in its purpose, like a linguistic version of the pancreas. It is one of the most basic devices for doing what syntax does: tying together linguistically what belongs together mentally, even when the linguistic pieces are far apart. A sizeable majority of languages in the world have it. English-speaking children learn it and use it, mostly correctly, long before they start school. English speaking adults use it, mostly correctly, more than once every five seconds in running speech.

Once again, there are two components of agreement that have to be coordinated, a lexical part and a structural part. The grammatical number of a word can be different from the notional number of its referent: In English, the word *scissors* is plural (unlike other languages) even when the word refers to a single implement (i.e., the notional number is singular). However, when a single scissors-categorized referent in the message is about to become the sentence subject, it is not plural. This conflict has to be reconciled in order for agreement to occur, and the grammatical number of the word typically (though not always) wins. This is another lexical/structural coordination problem that has to be worked out in the scaffold. In turn, it has consequences for structural assembly and morphological specification, where agreement unfolds (for models of these processes, see Eberhard, Cutting, & Bock, 2005; Franck, Lassi, Frauenfelder, & Rizzi, 2006; Franck, Soare, Frauenfelder, & Rizzi, 2010; Franck, Vigliocco, Antón-Méndez, Collina, & Frauenfelder, 2008).

Fittingly, there are lexically and structurally driven accounts of agreement. Lexical accounts (Vigliocco, Butterworth, & Garrett, 1996; Vigliocco, Hartsuiker, Jarema, & Kolk, 1996) build on linguistic approaches that make the lexicon and morphology the center of grammar in general and agreement in particular (e.g., Pollard & Sag, 1994). In these frameworks, notional number variations drive variations in agreement morphology, not only noun number but also verb number. For example, on this view the abstract lexical representations behind the singular and plural forms of the verb *sing* (*sings* and *sing*) reflect a notional difference between individual and multiple instances of singing. A structural approach places the responsibility for verb number with the sentence subject, whose own number determines the number of the verb during structural assembly: verb inflection is not a consequence of lexical identification, but of structural relations.

Evidence for the structural view and against the lexical view comes from experimental comparisons of verb and pronoun number agreement. Pronoun number is in large part notionally determined, originating in a lexical identification process in which a singular or plural pronoun is selected from the lexicon. Because this is exactly the same kind of process hypothesized for verb agreement in lexical accounts, verb and pronoun number should have similar patterns of occurrence when pronoun antecedents and sentence subjects have the same referent. Contradicting this prediction, the distributions are strikingly different. While pronouns are extremely sensitive to notional number, verbs carry only weak vestiges (Bock et al., 2006; Bock, Nicol, & Cutting, 1999; Bock, Eberhard, & Cutting, 2004). These differences are well accounted for in the Eberhard et al. (2005) model of verb and pronoun agreement.

Likewise consistent with the structural account is a type of syntactic error called *attraction*. In a prototypical attraction error, verb number agrees not with the number of the subject, but with the grammatical number of another noun phrase in the sentence. So, in the first author's favorite attraction error ("Dr. Bock's research on the processes of speech production rank among the most important contributions to modern cognitive psychology"; #10 in Table 2.1), there is a singular subject noun (*research*) but a plural verb (*rank*), seemingly a reflection of a nearby plural noun (*processes*).

Attraction errors have two significant features that make their source more likely to be structural than lexical. The first is that the grammatical number of an attractor, not its notional number, is responsible for attraction. This indicates that the notional number of the referent of the attractor does not determine the number of the number of the affected verb (Bock & Eberhard, 1993; Bock, Eberhard, Cutting, Meyer, & Schriefers, 2001; Bock, Eberhard et al. 2004; Deutsch & Dank, 2009). Analogous effects are found in gender agreement, when the gender of an attractor creates a gender error: grammatical gender creates attraction, but notional (biological) gender does not (Deutsch & Dank, 2009; Vigliocco & Franck, 2001).

Where notional number does matter is in the formulation of sentence-subject number itself, throughout message formation, lexical identification, and structural scaffolding. Notional effects on agreement can then be explained as another facet of lexical and structural coordination that becomes observable in the interaction between morphological specification and structural assembly. When notional number gives a sentence subject an abstract plural feature, subjects take on a property that can show up in number agreement, even when it does not surface on a noun. They do. Beyond the variations in verb agreement with conjunctions that were mentioned earlier, there are well-attested cases of plural agreement with subject noun phrases that are grammatically but not notionally singular, in particular collective and distributive subjects.

Collective subjects for the most part take singular verbs in American English (e.g., *The jury is deadlocked*), though they refer to multiple people at the same time. They are nonetheless more prone to plural verb agreement than a subject noun like *judge* (Bock et al. 1999; Bock, Eberhard et al. 2004). Distributive subjects make a subtler but more convincing case. Like collectives, distributive phrases can be singular subjects that represent multiple referents in singular subjects: the phrase *the picture on the postcards* implicates multiple instances of a singular picture, one per postcard. Even though *picture* is singular, when phrases like these serve as sentence subjects, they show up with plural verbs more often than would be predicted by the rates of plural attraction alone. This has been observed in English (Eberhard, 1999) and other languages including Spanish, Dutch, French, and Italian (Vigliocco, Hartsuiker et al., 1996).

Significantly, harking back to the "chasm" between language and thought, effects like these can be the same in magnitude in different languages from different language families (Bock et al., 2012). If notional properties affect grammatical agreement in similar ways crosslinguistically, agreement falls squarely into the realm of devices that tie together linguistically what belongs together mentally. Like other structural devices in language, agreement plays an important part in what syntax does for human communication.

Conclusions

There are a few broadly important points about the production of syntax that deserve a reprise. A central one is a property that sets a psycholinguistic account of language apart from linguistic approaches. This property is the situatedness of sentence production in the circumstances of communication. Speakers have to do a whole lot more than create grammatically acceptable sentences. They have to create acceptable sentences that make sense. This means that they have to convey *particular* notions to *particular* people in *particular* circumstances in a *particular* language.

Getting the particulars right means that speakers cannot use any old words with any old structures at any old place and time, at least if they intend to communicate. They have to use words that fit their notions, selected from a vocabulary with upward of 40,000 items. They have to use structures that fit their notions, created from an incalculable number of possibilities. They have to fit the words and structures together. They have to do these things flexibly and opportunistically, in a fashion that can accommodate the vicissitudes of memory, perception, attention, and thinking, without neglecting muscles (i.e., the articulatory system, which has been said to encompass more working parts that any other human ability; Fink, 1986). Speakers have to accomplish all of this rapidly, at least fast enough to approximate a normal and socially tolerable speech rate, in the neighborhood of four words per second. Astonishingly, they *do* get the forms of utterances right, with surprisingly few exceptions, coping with disfluency as they go. Successful communication seems to be more the rule than the exception.

Out of this fundamental property of situatedness comes the problem that we see as the central one for explaining syntax in language production. The problem is explaining the nuts and bolts and gears of coordination, the mechanisms needed to turn notions into language (how speakers find pieces of language to start with, undertaking the heavy lifting needed to recruit words and syntax); explaining how words and syntax follow from linguistic starting points (in the opportunistic ways reflected in accessibility effects and structural persistence, as well as in lexical and syntactic errors); explaining how structural assembly and morphological specification forge linguistic links that flag what goes together mentally (as in the workings of grammatical agreement); and to achieve a grand union with sounds and speech.

Much of current research on language production goes after the components of coordination separately, with optimism that the pieces of the puzzle will eventually fit together. The puzzle in which all of the pieces fit will show how speakers create syntax from the interlocking components of coordination. It is not easy. But beguilingly, it feels easy enough that we will risk it one more time. The upcoming string of words was formulated from our here-and-now conscious contents, built with the intention to afford similar conscious contents to you, wherever you may be in time and space:

This is the end.

References

Badecker, W., Miozzo, M., & Zanuttini, R. (1995). The two-stage model of lexical retrieval: Evidence from a case of anomia with selective preservation of grammatical gender. *Cognition, 57*, 193–216.

Barch, D., & Berenbaum, D. M. (1997). Language generation in schizophrenia and mania: The relationships among verbosity, syntactic complexity, and pausing. *Journal of Psycholinguistic Research, 26*, 401–412.

Barner, D., Li, P., & Snedeker, J. (2010). Words as windows to thought: The case of object representation. *Current Directions in Psychological Science, 19*, 195–200.

Bernolet, S., Hartsuiker, R. J., & Pickering, M. J. (2009). Persistence of emphasis in language production: A cross-linguistic approach. *Cognition, 112*, 300–317.

Blumenthal, A. L. (1970). *Language and psychology: Historical aspects of psycholinguistics.* New York: Wiley.

Bock, J. K. (1982). Toward a cognitive psychology of syntax: Information processing contributions to sentence formulation. *Psychological Review, 89*, 1–47.

Bock, J. K. (1986a). Meaning, sound, and syntax: Lexical priming in sentence production. *Journal of Experimental Psychology: Learning, Memory, and Cognition, 12*, 575–586.

Bock, J. K. (1986b). Syntactic persistence in language production. *Cognitive Psychology, 18*, 355–387.

Bock, J. K. (1987a). An effect of the accessibility of word forms on sentence structures. *Journal of Memory and Language, 26*, 119–137.

Bock, J. K. (1987b). Coordinating words and syntax in speech plans. In A. Ellis (Ed.), *Progress in the psychology of language* (Vol. 3, pp. 337–390). London: Erlbaum.

Bock, J. K. (1989). Closed-class immanence in sentence production. *Cognition, 31*, 163–186.

Bock, J. K. (1990). Structure in language: Creating form in talk. *American Psychologist, 45*, 1221–1236.

Bock, J. K. (1996). Language production: Methods and methodologies. *Psychonomic Bulletin & Review, 3*, 395–421.

Bock, J. K. (2004). Psycholinguistically speaking: Some matters of meaning, marking, and morphing. In B. H. Ross (Ed.), *The psychology of learning and motivation* (Vol. 44, pp. 109–144). San Diego, CA: Elsevier.

Bock, J. K. (2011). "How much correction of syntactic errors *are* there, anyway?" *Language & Linguistics Compass, 5*, 322–335.

Bock, J. K., Butterfield, S., Cutler, A., Cutting, J. C., Eberhard, K. M., & Humphreys, K. R. (2006). Number agreement in British and American English: Disagreeing to agree collectively. *Language, 82*, 64–113.

Bock, J. K., Carreiras, M., & Meseguer, E. (2012). Number meaning and number grammar in English and Spanish. *Journal of Memory and Language, 66*, 17–37.

Bock, J. K., & Cutting, J. C. (1992). Regulating mental energy: Performance units in language production. *Journal of Memory and Language, 31*, 99–127.

Bock, J. K., Dell, G. S., Chang, F., & Onishi, K. H. (2007). Structural persistence from language comprehension to language production. *Cognition, 104*, 437–458.

Bock, J. K., & Eberhard, K. M. (1993). Meaning, sound, and syntax in English number agreement. *Language and Cognitive Processes, 8*, 57–99.

Bock, J. K., Eberhard, K. M., & Cutting, J. C. (2004). Producing number agreement: How pronouns equal verbs. *Journal of Memory and Language, 51*, 251–278.

Bock, J. K., Eberhard, K. M., Cutting, J. C., Meyer, A. S., & Schriefers, H. (2001). Some attractions of verb agreement. *Cognitive Psychology, 43*, 83–128.

Bock, J. K., & Griffin, Z. M. (2000). The persistence of structural priming: Transient activation or implicit learning? *Journal of Experimental Psychology: General, 129*, 177–192.

Bock, J. K., & Irwin, D. E. (1980). Syntactic effects of information availability in sentence production. *Journal of Verbal Learning and Verbal Behavior, 19*, 467–484.

Bock, J. K., Irwin, D. E., & Davidson, D. J. (2004). Putting first things first. In J. M. Henderson & F. Ferreira (Eds.), *The integration of language, vision, and action: Eye movements and the visual world* (pp. 249–278). New York: Psychology Press.

Bock, J. K., Irwin, D. E., Davidson, D. J., & Levelt, W. J. M. (2003). Minding the clock. *Journal of Memory and Language, 48*, 653–685.

Bock, J. K., & Kroch, A. S. (1989). The isolability of syntactic processing. In G. N. Carlson & M. K. Tanenhaus (Eds.), *Linguistic structure in language processing* (pp. 157–196). Dordrecht: Kluwer.

Bock, J. K., & Levelt, W. J. M. (1994). Language production: Grammatical encoding. In M. A. Gernsbacher (Ed.), *Handbook of psycholinguistics* (pp. 945–984). San Diego: Academic Press.

Bock, J. K., & Loebell, H. (1990). Framing sentences. *Cognition, 35*, 1–39.

Bock, J. K., Loebell, H., & Morey, R. (1992). From conceptual roles to structural relations: Bridging the syntactic cleft. *Psychological Review, 99*, 150–171.

Bock, J. K., & Middleton, E. L. (2011). Reaching agreement. *Natural Language & Linguistic Theory, 29*, 1033–1069.

Bock, J. K., & Miller, C. A. (1991). Broken agreement. *Cognitive Psychology, 23*, 45–93.

Bock, K., Nicol, J., & Cutting, J. C. (1999). The ties that bind: Creating number agreement in speech. *Journal of Memory and Language, 40*, 330–346.

Bock, J. K., & Warren, R. K. (1985). Conceptual accessibility and syntactic structure in sentence formulation. *Cognition, 21*, 47–67.

Boroditsky, L. (2001). Does language shape thought? Mandarin and English speakers' conceptions of time. *Cognitive Psychology, 43*, 1–22.

Branigan, H. P., Pickering, M. J., & Cleland, A. A. (2000). Syntactic co-ordination in dialogue. *Cognition, 75*, B13–B25.

Brehm, L., & Bock, K. (2013). What counts in grammatical number agreement?. *Cognition, 128*(2), 149–169.

Brown, P. M., & Dell, G. S. (1987). Adapting production to comprehension: The explicit mention of instruments. *Cognitive Psychology, 19*, 441–472.

Brown-Schmidt, S., & Konopka, A. E. (2008). Little houses and casas pequeñas: Message formulation and syntactic form in unscripted speech with speakers of English and Spanish. *Cognition, 109*, 274–280.

Brown-Schmidt, S., & Tanenhaus, M. K. (2006). Watching the eyes when talking about size: An investigation of message formulation and utterance planning. *Journal of Memory and Language, 54*, 592–609.

Burke, D. M., MacKay, D. G., Worthley, J. S., & Wade, E. (1991). On the tip of the tongue: What causes word finding failures in young and older adults? *Journal of Memory and Language, 30*, 542–579.

Butterworth, B. (1982). Speech errors: Old data in search of new theories. In A. Cutler (Ed.), *Slips of the tongue and language production* (pp. 73–108). Berlin: Mouton.

Chang, F., Bock, K., & Goldberg, A. E. (2003). Can thematic roles leave traces of their places? *Cognition, 90*, 29–49.

Chang, F., Dell, G. S., & Bock, J. K. (2006). Becoming syntactic. *Psychological Review, 113*, 234–272.

Christianson, K., & Ferreira, F. (2005). Conceptual accessibility and sentence production in a free word order language (Odawa). *Cognition, 98*, 105–135.

Clark, H. H. (1996). *Using language*. Cambridge, England: Cambridge University Press.

Clark, H. H., & Fox Tree, J. E. (2002). Using uh and um in spontaneous speaking. *Cognition, 84*(1), 73–111.

Clark, H. H., & Wasow, T. (1998). Repeating words in spontaneous speech. *Cognitive Psychology, 37*, 201–242.

Cleland, A. A., & Pickering, M. J. (2003). The use of lexical and syntactic information in language production: Evidence from the priming of noun-phrase structure. *Journal of Memory and Language, 49*, 214–230.

Cohen, N. J., & Squire, L. R. (1980). Preserved learning and retention of pattern analyzing skill in amnesia: Dissociation of knowing how and knowing that. *Science, 210*, 207–209.

Cooper, W. E., & Ross, J. R. (1975). World order. In R. E. Grossman, L. J. San, & T. J. Vance (Eds.), *Papers from the parasession on functionalism* (pp. 63–111). Chicago: Chicago Linguistic Society.

Coppock, E. (2010). Parallel grammatical encoding in sentence production: Evidence from syntactic blends. *Language and Cognitive Processes, 25*, 38–49.

Cutting, J. C., & Bock, J. K. (1997). That's the way the cookie bounces: Syntactic and semantic components of experimentally elicited idiom blends. *Memory & Cognition, 25*, 57–71.

Cutting, J. C., & Ferreira, V. S. (1999). Overlapping phonological and semantic activation in spoken word production. *Journal of Experimental Psychology: Learning, Memory, and Cognition, 25*, 318–344.

Deese, J. (1984). *Thought into speech: The psychology of a language*. Englewood Cliffs, NJ: Prentice-Hall.

Dell, G. S., & Reich, P. A. (1981). Stages in sentence production: An analysis of speech error data. *Journal of Verbal Learning and Verbal Behavior, 20*, 611–629.

Deutsch, A., & Dank, M. (2009). Conflicting cues and competition between notional and grammatical factors in producing number and gender agreement: Evidence from Hebrew. *Journal of Memory and Language, 60*(1), 112–143.

Eberhard, K. M. (1999). The accessibility of conceptual number to the processes of subject-verb agreement in English. *Journal of Memory and Language, 41*, 560–578.

Eberhard, K. M., Cutting, J. C., & Bock, J. K. (2005). Making syntax of sense: Number agreement in sentence production. *Psychological Review, 112*, 531–559.

Ericsson, K. A., & Simon, H. A. (1980). Verbal reports as data. *Psychological Review, 87*, 215–251.

Fay, D. (1982). Substitutions and splices: A study of sentence blends. In A. Cutler (Ed.), *Slips of the tongue and language production* (pp. 163–195). Amsterdam: Mouton.

Fenk-Oczlon, G. (1989). Word frequency and word order in freezes. *Linguistics, 27*, 517–556.

Ferreira, F., & Swets, B. (2002). How incremental is language production? Evidence from the production of utterances requiring the computation of arithmetic sums. *Journal of Memory and Language, 46*, 57–84.

Ferreira, V. S. (1996). Is it better to give than to donate? Syntactic flexibility in language production. *Journal of Memory and Language, 35*, 724–755.

Ferreira, V. S. (2003). The persistence of optional complementizer mention: Why saying "that" is not saying "that" at all. *Journal of Memory and Language, 48*, 379–398.

Ferreira, V. S. (2008). Ambiguity, accessibility, and a division of labor for communicative success. In B. H. Ross (Ed.), *Psychology of learning and motivation* (Vol. 49, pp. 209–246).

Ferreira, V. S., & Bock, J. K. (2006). The functions of structural priming. *Language and Cognitive Processes, 21*, 1011–1029.

Ferreira, V. S., Bock, J. K., Wilson, M. P., & Cohen, N. J. (2008). Memory for syntax despite amnesia. *Psychological Science, 19*, 940–946.

Ferreira, V.S., & Dell, G. (2000). Effect of ambiguity and lexical availability on syntactic and lexical production. *Cognitive Psychology, 40*, 296–340.

Ferreira, V. S., & Firato, C. E. (2002). Proactive interference effects on sentence production. *Psychonomic Bulletin & Review, 9*(4), 795–800.

Ferreira, V. S., & Humphreys, K. R. (2001). Syntactic influences on lexical and morphological processing in language production. *Journal of Memory and Language, 44*, 52–80.

Ferreira, V. S., & Pashler, H. (2002). Central bottleneck influences on the processing stages of word production. *Journal of Experimental Psychology: Learning, Memory, and Cognition, 28*, 1187–1199.

Fink, B. R. (1986). Complexity. *Science, 231*, 319.

Fodor, J. A. (1975). *The language of thought*. New York: Thomas Y. Crowell.

Fodor, J. A. (1983). *The modularity of mind*. Cambridge, MA: MIT Press.

Ford, M. (1982). Sentence planning units: Implications for the speaker's representation of meaningful relations underlying sentences. In J. Bresnan (Ed.), *The mental representation of grammatical relations* (pp. 797–827). Cambridge, MA: MIT Press.

Ford, M., & Holmes, V. M. (1978). Planning units and syntax in sentence production. *Cognition, 6*, 35–53.

Franck, J., Lassi, G., Frauenfelder, U. H., & Rizzi, L. (2006). Agreement and movement: A syntactic analysis of attraction. *Cognition, 101*, 173–216.

Franck, J., Soare, G., Frauenfelder, U. H., & Rizzi, L. (2010). Object interference in subject-verb agreement: The role of intermediate traces of movement. *Journal of Memory and Language, 62*, 166–182.

Franck, J., Vigliocco, G., Antón-Méndez, I., Collina, S., & Frauenfelder, U. H. (2008). The interplay of syntax and form in sentence production: A cross-linguistic study of form effects on agreement. *Language and Cognitive Processes, 23*, 329–374.

Fromkin, V. (1971). The non-anomalous nature of anomalous utterances. *Language, 47*, 27–52.

Garrett, M. F. (1975). The analysis of sentence production. In G. H. Bower (Ed.), *The psychology of learning and motivation* (Vol. 9, pp. 133–177). New York: Academic Press.

Garrett, M. F. (1980). Levels of processing in sentence production. In B. Butterworth (Ed.), *Language production* (Vol. 1, pp. 177–220). London: Academic Press.

Garrett, M. F. (1982). Production of speech: Observations from normal and pathological language use. In A. Ellis (Ed.), *Normality and pathology in cognitive functions* (pp. 19–76). London: Academic Press.

Garrett, M. F. (1988). Processes in language production. In F. J. Newmeyer (Ed.), *Linguistics: The Cambridge survey, III: Language: Psychological and biological aspects* (Vol. 3: Language: Psychological and biological aspects, pp. 69–96). Cambridge: Cambridge University Press.

Gleitman, L. R., January, D., Nappa, R., & Trueswell, J. C. (2007). On the *give* and *take* between event apprehension and utterance formulation. *Journal of Memory and Language*, *57*, 544–569.

Goldman Eisler, F. (1968). *Psycholinguistics: Experiments in spontaneous speech*. London: Academic Press.

Griffin, Z. M. (2001). Gaze durations during speech reflect word selection and phonological encoding. *Cognition*, *82*, B1–B14.

Griffin, Z. M., & Bock, J. K. (2000). What the eyes say about speaking. *Psychological Science*, *11*, 274–279.

Griffin, Z. M., & Ferreira, V. S. (2006). Properties of spoken language production. In M. J. Traxler & M. A. Gernsbacher (Eds.), *Handbook of psycholinguistics* (2nd ed., pp. 21–59). Amsterdam: Elsevier.

Griffin, Z. M., & Weinstein-Tull, J. (2003). Conceptual structure modulates structural priming in the production of complex sentences. *Journal of Memory and Language*, *49*, 537–555.

Hartsuiker, R. J., Bernolet, S., Schoonbaert, S., Speybroeck, S., & Vanderelst, D. (2008). Syntactic priming persists while the lexical boost decays: Evidence from written and spoken dialogue. *Journal of Memory and Language*, *58*, 214–238.

Hartsuiker, R., & Westenberg, C. (2000). Word order priming in written and spoken sentence production. *Cognition*, *75*, B27–B39.

Humphreys, K. R., & Bock, J. K. (2005). Notional number agreement in English. *Psychonomic Bulletin & Review*, *12*, 689–695.

Irwin, D. E. (1991). Information integration across saccadic eye movements. *Cognitive Psychology*, *23*, 420–456.

Irwin, D. E. (1996). Integrating information across saccadic eye movements. *Current Directions in Psychological Science*, *5*, 94–100.

Iwasaki, N., Vinson, D. P., & Vigliocco, G. (2010). Does the grammatical count/mass distinction affect semantic representations? Evidence from experiments in English and Japanese. *Language and Cognitive Processes*, *25*, 189–223.

James, W. (1890). *The principles of psychology* (Vol. 1). New York: Dover.

Johnson-Laird, P. N. (1983). *Mental models: Towards a cognitive science of language, inference, and consciousness*. Cambridge, England: Cambridge University Press.

Kaschak, M. P., Kutta, T. J., & Schatschneider, C. (2011). Long-term cumulative structural priming persists for (at least) one week. *Memory & Cognition*, *39*(3), 381–388.

Keil, F. C. (1979). *Semantic and conceptual development*. Cambridge, MA: Harvard University Press.

Kelly, M. H. (1986). *On the selection of linguistic options* (Unpublished doctoral dissertation). Cornell University, Ithaca, NY.

Kelly, M. H., Bock, J. K., & Keil, F. C. (1986). Prototypicality in a linguistic context: Effects on sentence structure. *Journal of Memory and Language*, *25*, 59–74.

Kempen, G., & Huijbers, P. (1983). The lexicalization process in sentence production and naming: Indirect election of words. *Cognition*, *14*, 185–209.

Konopka, A. (2012). Planning ahead: How recent experience with structures and words changes the scope of linguistic planning. *Journal of Memory and Language*, *66*, 143–162.

Konopka, A. E., & Bock, J. K. (2005, April). *Helping syntax out: What do words do?* Paper presented at the CUNY Sentence Processing Conference, Tucson, Arizona.

Konopka, A. E., & Bock, J. K. (2009). Lexical or syntactic control of sentence formulation? Structural generalizations from idiom production. *Cognitive Psychology*, *58*, 68–101.

Kuchinsky, S. E. (2009). *From seeing to saying: Perceiving, planning, producing* (Unpublished doctoral dissertation). University of Illinois, Urbana, IL.

Kuchinsky, S. E., & Bock, J. K. (2010, March). *From seeing to saying: Perceiving, planning, producing*. Paper presented at the CUNY Sentence Processing Conference, New York University, New York, NY.

Kuchinsky, S. E., Bock, J. K., & Irwin, D. E. (2011). Reversing the hands of time: Changing the mapping from seeing to saying. *Journal of Experimental Psychology: Learning, Memory, and Cognition*, *37*, 748–756.

Levelt, W. J. M. (1989). *Speaking: From intention to articulation*. Cambridge, MA: MIT Press.

Levelt, W. J. M. (1992). Accessing words in speech production: Stages, processes and representations. *Cognition*, *42*, 1–22.

Levelt, W. J. M. (1993). Lexical selection, or how to bridge the major rift in language processing. In F. Beckmann & G. Heyer (Eds.), *Theorie und Praxis des Lexikons* (pp. 164–172). Berlin: Walter de Gruyter.

Levelt, W. J. M. (2012). *A history of psycholinguistics: The pre-Chomskyan era*. Oxford, England: Oxford University Press.

Levelt, W. J. M., & Kelter, S. (1982). Surface form and memory in question answering. *Cognitive Psychology*, *14*, 78–106.

Levelt, W., & Maassen, B. (1981). Lexical search and order of mention in sentence production. In W. Klein & W. Levelt (Eds.), *Crossing the boundaries in linguistics* (pp. 221–252). Dordrecht: Reidel.

Levelt, W. J. M., Roelofs, A., & Meyer, A. S. (1999). A theory of lexical access in speech production. *Behavioral and Brain Sciences*, *22*, 1–38.

Levelt, W. J. M., Schriefers, H., Vorberg, D., Meyer, A. S., Pechmann, T., & Havinga, J. (1991). The time course of lexical access in speech production: A study of picture naming. *Psychological Review*, *98*, 122–142.

Lindsley, J. R. (1975). Producing simple utterances: How far ahead do we plan? *Cognitive Psychology*, *7*, 1–19.

Loebell, H., & Bock, J. K. (2003). Structural priming across languages. *Linguistics*, *41*, 791–824.

Luka, B., & Barsalou, L. (2005). Structural facilitation: Mere exposure effects for grammatical acceptability as evidence for syntactic priming in comprehension. *Journal of Memory and Language*, *52*, 436–459.

Maclay, H., & Osgood, C. E. (1959). Hesitation phenomena in spontaneous English speech. *Word*, *15*, 19–44.

MacWhinney, B. (1977). Starting points. *Language*, *53*, 152–168.

McDonald, J. L., Bock, J. K., & Kelly, M. H. (1993). Word and world order: Semantic, phonological, and metrical determinants of serial position. *Cognitive Psychology*, *25*, 188–230.

Melinger, A., & Dobel, C. (2005). Lexically-driven syntactic priming. *Cognition*, *98*, B11–B20.

Murphy, G. L. (2002). *The big book of concepts*. Cambridge, MA: MIT Press.

Onishi, K. H., Murphy, G. L., & Bock, J. K. (2008). Prototypicality in sentence production. *Cognitive Psychology*, *56*, 103–141.

Osgood, C. E. (1971). Where do sentences come from? In D. D. Steinberg & L. A. Jakobovits (Eds.), *Semantics: An interdisciplinary reader in philosophy, linguistics and psychology* (pp. 497–529). Cambridge: Cambridge University Press.

Paul, H. (1886/1970). The sentence as the expression of the combination of several ideas. In A. L. Blumenthal (Ed. & Trans.), *Language and psychology: Historical aspects of psycholinguistics* (pp. 34–37). New York: Wiley.

Pickering, M. J., & Branigan, H. P. (1998). The representation of verbs: Evidence from syntactic priming in language production. *Journal of Memory & Language, 39*(4), 633–651.

Pickering, M. J., & Ferreira, V. S. (2008). Structural priming: A critical review. *Psychological Bulletin, 13,* 427–459.

Pickering, M. J., & Garrod, S. (2004). Toward a mechanistic psychology of dialogue. *Behavioral and Brain Sciences, 27,* 169–226.

Pollard, C., & Sag, I. A. (1994). *Head-driven phrase structure grammar.* Chicago: University of Chicago Press.

Prat-Sala, M., & Branigan, H. P. (2000). Discourse constraints on syntactic processing in language production: A cross-linguistic study in English and Spanish. *Journal of Memory and Language, 42,* 168–182.

Roelofs, A. (1992). A spreading activation theory of lemma retrieval in speaking. *Cognition, 42,* 107–142.

Roelofs, A. (1993). Testing a non-decompositional theory of lemma retrieval in speaking: Retrieval of verbs. *Cognition, 47,* 59–87.

Santesteban, M., Pickering, M. J., & McLean, J. F. (2010). Lexical and phonological effects on syntactic processing: Evidence from syntactic priming. *Journal of Memory and Language, 63,* 347–366.

Scheepers, C., Sturt, P., Martin, C. J., Myachykov, A., Teevan, K., & Viskupova, I. (2011). Structural priming across cognitive domains: From simple arithmetic to relative-clause attachment. *Psychological Science, 22,* 1319–1326.

Schyns, P., & Oliva, A. (1994). From blobs to boundary edges: Evidence for time- and spatial-scale-dependent scene recognition. *Psychological Science, 5,* 195–200.

Searle, J. R. (1969). *Speech acts: An essay in the philosophy of language.* London, England: Cambridge University Press.

Stemberger, J. P. (1982). Syntactic errors in speech. *Journal of Psycholinguistic Research, 11,* 313–345.

Stemberger, J. P. (1984). Structural errors in normal and agrammatic speech. *Cognitive Neuropsychology, 1,* 281–313.

Tanaka, M. N., Branigan, H. P., McLean, J. F., & Pickering, M. J. (2011). Conceptual influences on word order and voice in sentence production: Evidence from Japanese. *Journal of Memory and Language, 65,* 318–330.

Tooley, K., & Bock, J. K. (2012). *On the parity of structural persistence in language production and comprehension.* Manuscript submitted for publication.

Vennemann, T. (1973). Explanation in syntax. In J. P. Kimballl (Ed.), *Syntax and semantics, Vol 2* (pp. 1–50). New York: Seminar Press.

Vigliocco, G., Butterworth, B., & Garrett, M. F. (1996). Subject-verb agreement in Spanish and English: Differences in the role of conceptual constraints. *Cognition, 61*(3), 261–298.

Vigliocco, G., & Franck, J. (2001). When sex affects syntax: Contextual influences in sentence production. *Journal of Memory and Language, 45*(3), 368–390.

Vigliocco, G., Hartsuiker, R. J., Jarema, G., & Kolk, H. H. J. (1996). One or more labels on the bottles? Notional concord in Dutch and French. *Language and Cognitive Processes, 11,* 407–442.

Vigliocco, G., Vinson, D. P., Martin, R. C., & Garrett, M. F. (1999). Is "count" and "mass" information available when the noun is not? An investigation of tip of the tongue states and anomia. *Journal of Memory and Language, 40,* 534–558.

Wardlow Lane, L., & Ferreira, V. S. (2010). Abstract syntax in sentence production: Evidence from stem-exchange errors. *Journal of Memory and Language, 62,* 151–165.

Whorf, B. L. (1956). *Language, thought, and reality.* Cambridge, MA: MIT Press.

Wundt, W. (1912). Die Sprache (A. L. Blumenthal, Trans.). In A. L. Blumenthal (Ed.), *Language and Psychology: Historical Aspects of Psycholinguistics* (First published 1900 ed., Vol. 1). New York: Wiley.

Neural Bases of Sentence Processing: Evidence from Neurolinguistic and Neuroimaging Studies

Cynthia Thompson *and* Aneta Kielar

Abstract

Sentence processing requires rapid integration of information over a short period of time. Models of language processing suggest that syntactic, semantic, and phonological detail must be accessed and coordinated within milliseconds to successfully produce or understand sentences. Exactly how this is accomplished and what neural mechanisms are engaged in real time to carry out these processes is not completely understood. Research examining the neural mechanisms associated with sentence processing elucidates a left hemisphere network involving both anterior and posterior brain regions, although studies show that the right hemisphere is also engaged to some extent. This chapter discusses what is known about the neural systems involved in sentence production and comprehension. Two bodies of research are discussed: neurolinguistic evidence derived from lesion-deficit studies with brain-damaged people, and neuroimaging research examining the neural correlates of sentence processing in healthy individuals.

Key Words: sentence processing, neuroimaging, syntax, neuroimaging, neurolinguistics

Introduction

Sentence processing requires rapid integration of information over a short period of time. Models of language processing suggest that syntactic, semantic, and phonological detail must be accessed and coordinated within milliseconds to successfully produce or understand sentences. Exactly how this is accomplished and what neural mechanisms are engaged in real time to carry out these processes, for either production or comprehension, is not completely understood. Research examining the neural mechanisms associated with sentence processing elucidates a (primarily) left hemisphere network involving both anterior and posterior brain regions, although studies show that the right hemisphere is engaged to some extent for some processes. This chapter discusses what is known about the neural systems involved in sentence production and comprehension. We do this by discussing two bodies of research: neurolinguistic evidence derived from lesion-deficit studies with brain-damaged people, and neuroimaging research examining the neural correlates of sentence processing in healthy individuals. Before proceeding with this discussion, we present a brief overview of models of sentence processing.

Models of Sentence Processing

How and when is syntactic structure assigned in sentence production or to an incoming sequence of words and how is word meaning integrated in sentence production or comprehension? A complete discussion of what is known about these processes is beyond the scope of this chapter. However, we point out here that both sentence production and comprehension engage at least three levels of processing, which for sentence production are engaged for mapping meaning or conceptual representations to phonological representations that guide articulatory processes (i.e., from meaning to form) and for comprehension are engaged for decoding phonological material and mapping it onto meaning representations (i.e., from linguistic form to meaning).

In the sentence production domain, models of language processing postulate conceptual (message level) encoding, grammatical encoding, and morphophonological encoding that build the surface structure of sentences (Bock, 1995, 1999; Bock & Levelt, 1994, 2002; Ferreira & Slevc, 2007; Garrett 1976, 1982, 1988; Levelt, 1989; Indefrey & Levelt, 2004; see Thompson & Shah, 2002, for review). Levelt and colleagues suggest that these levels are engaged in a serial fashion, whereas others argue that there is interaction among them such that all types of information interact in a constraint satisfaction manner (see Chang, Dell, & Bock, 2006; Dell, 1986; Dell & Sullivan, 2004; Marslen-Wilson & Tyler, 1980). First, the speaker encodes a nonlinguistic conceptual message and relevant lexical concepts. The output of this stage is a preverbal message, "for which there are words in the language" (Levelt, 1999, p. 87). Next, the message is transformed into a linguistic structure through the process of grammatical encoding, which on these models involves lexicalization and generation of functional structure. Lexical concepts activate corresponding lemmas containing semantic and syntactic information (e.g., word class [noun, verb]; grammatical markers, such as tense and gender; and verb argument structure). As lemmas are selected, syntactic structure building ensues, generating a hierarchically structured functional relation between lemmas. The syntactic properties specified within each lemma's entry enable the grammatical encoder to project phrasal nodes and concatenate them to generate the structure of the sentence. Via this syntactic unification process, each lemma is assigned a functional (semantic-to-grammatical) role, such as subject or object, and then assigned to their appropriate position in the sentence. At the morphophonological level, the morphological and phonological form (lexemes) of selected lemmas are specified and assembled into a linearly ordered structure (Figure 3.1). This output is then passed on for phonetic encoding and articulatory processing (Bock & Levelt, 1994).

For sentence comprehension, levels of processing similar to those engaged during sentence production are involved. Friederici (2002, 2006) proposed three stages as shown in Figure 3.2. After early acoustic analysis and phoneme identification, the first phase is purely syntactic. At this stage automatic first-pass parsing takes place, during which initial phrase structure is built based on lexical, word category information (e.g., verb, noun, determiner). Studies of sentence processing using event-related potentials (ERPs) show that the brain reacts immediately when the word category of incoming linguistic material does not match expectations based on the grammatical rules of a language. Early left anterior negativity (ELAN) with a latency between 100 and 300 ms has been reported in association with such violations (Friederici 1995; Hahne & Jescheniak, 2001; Kubota, Ferrari, & Roberts, 2003).

During the second stage, structural, semantic, and thematic relations are assigned. That is, lexicosemantic (i.e., meaning information relevant to content words [lemmas]) and morphosyntactic information (e.g., tense, syntactic gender) is retrieved. It is also during this stage that verb subcategorization and argument structure information is thought to be accessed and mapped onto the initial syntactic structure and the relation between words is established (Friederici & Kotz, 2003; Friederici, Hahne, & Mecklinger, 1996; Friederici & Meyer, 2004). Morphosyntactic violations, such as subject-verb agreement mismatches, have been found to evoke left dominant anterior negativity (LAN) between 300 and 500 ms across languages (Angrilli et al., 2002; Gunter, Stowe, & Mulder, 1997; Kutas & Hillyard, 1983; Penke et al., 1997; but see Osterhout & Nicol, 1999; Münte, Matzke, & Johannes, 1997), whereas subcategorization and verb argument structure violations may elicit a LAN or N400 (Coulson, King, & Kutas, 1998; Friederici & Frisch, 2000; Frisch, Hahne, & Friederici, 2004).

During the third and final phase of sentence processing, lexical and syntactic information is integrated and the final interpretation (meaning representation) is built. This model predicts interaction between semantic and syntactic information only at this latter stage of processing after the initial phrase structure has been built. When the parser encounters ungrammatical or ambiguous strings of words reanalysis and repair take place. Such conditions elicit late centroparietal positive deflection occurring at around 600 ms poststimulus onset, called the P600. This late positivity is assumed to reflect the third integration phase during which syntactic repair and reanalysis take place (Friederici, 2002; Friederici, Pfeifer, & Hahne, 1993). The P600 has been found to vary as a function of both syntactic and semantic information, indicating that both types of information interact during this later stage.

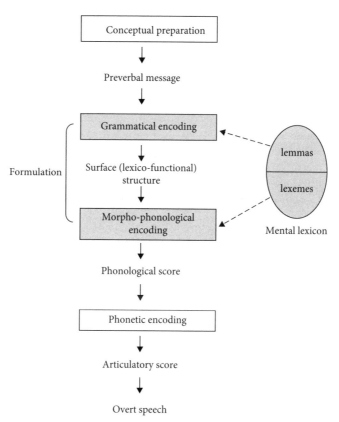

Figure 3.1 Stages of sentence production. Adapted from Levelt, W. (1999). Models of word production. *Trends in Cognitive Science, 3,* 223–232.

Stage/Phase	ERP Component	Temporal Window	Function/Process
Phase 0	N100	100 ms	Acoustic analysis Phonological identification /sequencing
Phase 1	ELAN	150-200 ms	Word form identification Word category identification Phrase structure building
Phase 2	LAN/N400	300-500 ms	Lemma access (morphosyntactic and argument structure) Thematic role assignment
Phase 3	P600	± 600 ms	Reanalysis/repair Integration

Figure 3.2 Event-related potential (ERP) signatures of sentence processing components. Adapted from Friederici, A. D. (1995). The time course of syntactic activation during language processing: A model based on neuro-psychological and neurophysiological data. *Brain and Language, 50,* 259–281; Friederici, A. D. (2002). Towards a neural basis of auditory sentence processing. *Trends in Cognitive Sciences, 6,* 78–84; and Friederici, A. D., & Kotz, S. A. (2003). The brain basis of syntactic processes: Functional imaging and lesion studies. *Neuroimage, 20,* S8–S17.

It is during this stage that semantic information is integrated into the syntactic frame, and in the case of incorrect or ambiguous sentences, reanalysis and repair take place.

VERB AND VERB ARGUMENT STRUCTURE PROCESSING

The processing mechanisms that map linguistic form onto meaning and vice versa and integrate this information into the syntactic frame are tied to verbs and the linguistic information that they encode. Hence, both sentence production and comprehension models emphasize the role of verb lemmas and associated syntactic information (i.e., subcategorization frames); verb argument structure or event structure (i.e., the participant roles entailed within the verb's representation); and thematic roles (e.g., agent, patient/theme). These participant roles or argument structure properties vary across verbs in terms of the number and type of arguments that they require. For instance, the intransitive verb *smile* requires only one external argument (i.e., an agent, as in: *John smiled*). The transitive verb *fix* requires two arguments (i.e. an agent [the one performing the action] and a theme [entity acted on] as in: *John fixed the car*). Other verbs take three arguments (e.g., *put*), requiring an agent, theme, and goal (e.g., *John put the book on the table*).

As a verb lemma is accessed so too is argument structure information, enabling humans to translate semantic representation into sentence forms for production, and to assign meaning to word strings encountered for sentence comprehension. On some theoretical linguistic accounts (e.g., "lexicalist" approaches; Caramazza, 1997; Chomsky 1995; Levelt et al., 1999), verb argument structure guides phrase structure building (but see Goldberg, 1995, 2003 for discussion of the "constructionist" approach, which argues that verb argument structure is dependent on semantics). According to the minimalist program (Chomsky 1995), verbs combine with other items selected from the lexicon and assign their thematic roles (e.g., agent, theme). Thus, during sentence production and comprehension verb argument structure information mediates sentence processing.

Several studies suggest that argument structure information is used for sentence production. Although experimental evidence supports word-by-word incrementality, that is as each lemma becomes available, morphophonological encoding begins (Griffin & Bock, 2000; Schriefers, Teruel, & Meinshausen, 1998; Spieler & Griffin, 2006,

and others), structural models of sentence production suggest that grammatical encoding proceeds in larger chunks of linguistic information (e.g., verb argument structure). On these latter models, building a hierarchical predicate structure requires prespeech planning at least up to the verb (Ferreira 2000; Kempen & Hujibers, 1983). Research also shows that verb argument structure is automatically accessed when people encounter verbs when listening to sentences (Arhens, 2003; Boland, 2005; Boland & Blodgett, 2006; Boland, Tanenhaus, & Garnsey, 1990; Boland, Tanenhaus, Garnsey, & Carlson, 1995; Ferretti, McRae, & Hatherell, 2001; Friedmann, Taranto, Shapiro, & Swinney, 2008; Shapiro, Brookins, Gordon, & Nagel, 1991; Trueswell & Kim, 1998; see also Trueswell, Tannenhaus, & Kello, 1993; MacDonald, Pearlmutter, & Seidenberg, 1994). In seminal research by Shapiro and colleagues, using a cross-modal lexical decision task, participants listened to sentences containing verbs with greater or lesser argument structure density (e.g., *fix* vs. *send*).[1] At the verb site, where visual lexical decision probes were inserted, healthy listeners showed longer reaction times for verbs with greater density, indicating automatic access to all argument structure entries for verbs when encountered in the sentence stream.

The question addressed in this chapter pertains to the neural mechanisms that support psycholinguistic processes associated with sentence production and comprehension. That is, can the aforementioned processes be mapped onto the brain and, if so, what structures are involved in sentence computation? The following sections directly address these issues.

Neurolinguistic Studies of Sentence Processing: Evidence from Aphasia

A starting point for discussing the neural mechanisms of sentence production and comprehension is to consider evidence from studies with brain-damaged patients with aphasia resulting from stroke and other neurological diseases. Indeed, before functional neuroimaging technology, lesion-deficit studies provided the primary source of information about how language is processed in the brain. This is because, according to classic aphasiology, aphasia syndromes were thought to arise from lesions in particular brain regions, with damage to anterior brain tissue (i.e., the left inferior frontal or Brodmann areas [BA] 44 and 45, and adjacent tissue) associated with a particular set of language deficits seen in Broca's aphasia and lesions in posterior regions of the brain (i.e., the posterior superior temporal gyrus and surrounding areas) associated with a different set of deficits seen in Wernicke's aphasia. Hence, examination of the abilities and disabilities of patients presenting with these two types of aphasia provided early notions about the neural mechanisms of language processing (Caramazza & Zurif, 1976; Damasio, 1992; Damasio & Damasio, 1989). Limitations to this approach are discussed later.

Broca's Aphasia and the Brain
SENTENCE PRODUCTION DEFICITS

The primary deficit seen in individuals with Broca's aphasia and concomitant agrammatism is difficulty producing grammatical sentences. These patients produce short, grammatically impoverished sentences or sentence fragments, consisting of primarily open class, content words with errors in grammatical morphology (e.g., omission or substitution of verb inflection; Faroqi-Shah & Thompson, 2003; Saffran, Schwartz, & Marin, 1980; Thompson, Kielar, & Fix, 2012). Consider the following narrative language sample from a 35-year-old man (LBS) with chronic agrammatic aphasia, telling the story of Cinderella:

> She's nice. Dusting (3 sec). Wash (3 sec). The old man (4 sec). Wicked uh sisters uh two three five uh. The horse (5 sec) dog uh bird (3 sec) mouse uh uh is (3 sec) cut (11 sec) dress (2 sec). Be (4 sec) alright. Pumpkin. Pull over uh uh. The uh prince (2 sec). The love uh. We dance (2 sec). Oh no uh noon. How uh get out uh uh? Shoe uh glass shoe (5 sec) found its uh uh. Pulling (3 sec) shoe uh. No ties. Yes. The end.

Linguistic analysis of LBS's speech using a method developed by Thompson and colleagues (see Thompson et al., 1995, 2012) revealed a greatly reduced speech rate (i.e., 14 words per minute; mean for healthy age-matched control subjects = 132.22 [SD = 5.22][2]) and utterance length (mean = 2.37 words; mean for healthy control subjects = 11.11 [SD = 0.56]). Only 10 percent of this patient's utterances were syntactically correct (normal control mean = 93 percent), with a complex to simple sentence ratio of 0.10. He also produced more open class compared with closed class words (open/closed class ratio = 2.41; healthy control mean = 0.95 [SD=0.03]) and evinced marked difficulty producing verb inflections (0 percent correct, with noun inflection 100 percent correct).

In constrained tasks these patients may show ability to produce simple active, canonical sentence structures; however, they show particular difficulty producing sentences with noncanonical word order. Using the Northwestern Assessment of Verbs and Sentences (Thompson 2012 also see Cho-Reyes & Thompson, 2012), which tests production of both canonical forms (i.e., actives, subject-wh questions, and subject-cleft structures) and noncanical forms (passives, object-wh questions, and object relative constructions) using a sentence production priming task, we documented this pattern in 35 patients with agrammatic aphasia with mild to moderately severe deficits. Mean production of canonical forms was 72 percent accuracy compared with a mean of 39 percent accuracy for noncanonical forms. Other work also has shown that finite verb inflection (e.g., third-person singular, past tense markers) is more impaired than nonfinite forms (e.g., infinitive forms, aspectual —ing; see Thompson et al., 2012; Lee, Mack, & Thompson, 2012).

VERB DEFICITS

People with agrammatic Broca's aphasia also often show difficulty producing verbs (compared with nouns; Kim & Thompson, 2000; Miceli, Silveri, Villa, & Caramazza, 1984; Zingeser & Berndt, 1990), and several studies have shown, cross-linguistically, that verb argument structure plays a role in verb production deficits (Dragoy & Bastiaanse, 2009; De Blesser & Kauschke, 2003; Jonkers & Bastiaanse, 1996, 1998; Kim & Thompson, 2004; Luzzatti et al., 2002; Thompson, 2003). These studies show that agrammatic individuals are able to produce one-argument verbs better than two- or three-argument verbs. In addition, agrammatic patients often delete obligatory verb arguments in sentences (Thompson, Lange, Schneider, & Shapiro, 1997) as did LBS, the speaker above who not only produced few verbs, but also produced correct arguments for only 25 percent of them (healthy control mean = 98 percent).

Recent online sentence production studies also show that argument structure complexity affects sentence production in agrammatic speakers (Lee, 2011; also see Lee & Thompson, 2011b; Thompson, Dickey, Cho, Lee, & Griffin, 2007). In an eye tracking study, healthy speakers and agrammatic aphasic speakers produced sentences with either nonalternating unaccusative or unergative verbs (e.g., *the black tube is floating* vs. *the black dog is barking*, respectively) while their eye movements were tracked. Results showed differential fixation patterns to the subject noun phrase in the unaccusative condition (in which the subject noun phrase is a theme) compared with the unergative condition (in which the subject noun phrase is an agent) for both healthy and aphasic participants. However, the aphasic speakers showed this effect before speech production, whereas the normal speakers showed the effect during production.

Collectively, these findings suggest that, based on models of sentence production, agrammatic speakers evince impaired grammatical encoding. Taking this a step further, given that some agrammatic aphasic speakers present with concomitant anterior perisylvian brain damage (e.g., the inferior frontal region), frontal lobe regions are thought to be engaged for this process.

Notably, in contrast, studies examining verb processing in individuals with Broca's aphasia show that they typically retain the ability to comprehend verbs, recognize verb argument structure violations, and automatically access verb argument (Grodzinsky & Finkel, 1998; Kim & Thompson, 2000, 2004; Shapiro, Gordon, Hack, & Killackey, 1993; Shapiro & Levine, 1990). In two studies, Kim and Thompson (2000, 2004) found that individuals with agrammatic Broca's aphasia performed at near normal levels in judging the grammaticality of sentences with argument structure violations, in which either an obligatory argument was omitted (e.g., *The woman is giving the sandwich; *The boy is carrying) or a noun phrase was added following an intransitive verb (e.g., *The dog is barking the girl). Grodzinsky and Finkel (1998) reported a similar result using a grammaticality judgment task. Shapiro and colleagues (Shapiro et al., 1993; Shapiro & Levine, 1990) also found in their online cross-modal priming work with patients with aphasia, that those with Broca's aphasia showed normal reaction time patterns when verbs with varying argument structure density were encountered during the temporal unfolding of sentences.

SENTENCE COMPREHENSION DEFICITS

Broca's aphasic deficits are not constrained to impairments in sentence production. These patients also show difficulty comprehending sentences. As in sentence production, they show particular difficulty with noncanonical forms with long-distance dependencies (e.g., filler-gap constructions; Caplan, Hildebrandt, & Makris, 1996; Caramazza & Zurif, 1976; Grodzinsky 2000). In these sentences, fillers (e.g., a wh-phrase [i.e., what in (1)]), are associated with a gap position (e.g., following the main verb see in [1]) and a coreferential relation exists between them, even though the two may be separated by linguistic material (Frazier & Clifton, 1989). Such

sentences, therefore, are difficult to process because the sentence parser must construct a filler-gap dependency to solve them.

(1) *What* did Zachary see __[gap]__that day in central park?

In a series of studies using a cross modal lexical priming paradigm in which participants listened to filler-gap sentences and at the same time performed a visual lexical decision task, with lexical probes strategically placed in sentences before the verb and at the gap site, Swinney, Zurif, and colleagues found that normal listeners "reactivate" the filler at the gap site (Swinney & Zurif, 1995; Swinney, Zurif, Prather, & Love, 1996; Zurif, Swinney, Prather, Solomon, & Bushell, 1993). For example, listening to sentences as in (2), semantic priming effects were found for normal participants at probe sites *1 and *2. That is, reaction times to lexical decision probes were faster for related probes (i.e., items related to the filler, such as wine) compared with unrelated probes. In addition, priming effects were stronger at probe site *2 (the gap site), compared with probe site *1, providing evidence of automatic gap-filling processes. However, listeners with Broca's aphasia did not show this pattern, although they showed a simple priming effect at both probe sites.

(2) The priest enjoyed the drink[i] that the caterer was *1 serving *2(t)[i] to the guests.

A strong interpretation of these findings is that Broca's area is specialized for computation of certain syntactic operations necessary to understand complex sentences, such as processing syntactic movement (i.e., as in filler-gap sentences; Grodzinsky, 2000, Grodzinsky & Friederici, 2006). However, more recent data indicate that the role of Broca's area in syntactic processing is not so clear-cut. Studies using an eyetracking-while-listening methodology indicate that individuals with Broca's aphasia show normal gap-filling ability. For example, in several studies we (Choy & Thompson, 2010; Dickey, Choy, & Thompson, 2007; Dickey & Thompson, 2009; Thompson & Choy, 2009) monitored the eye movements of aphasic and control participants while they listened to brief stories and looked at visual displays depicting objects mentioned in the stories (Figure 3.3). Results across studies showed that although agrammatic patients performed at chance level in understanding noncanonical sentences with filler-gap dependencies (e.g., object extracted wh-questions, object cleft structures), the eye movement data revealed that participants looked at pictures depicting displaced sentential elements

Subject: Boy; Object (target): Girl; Location: School; Distractor: Door.

Story:

This story is about a girl and a boy.
One day, they were playing at school.
The girl was pretty, so the boy kissed the girl.
They were both embarrassed after the kiss.

Target sentences:

A. Who did the boy kiss _____ that day at school?
B. It was the girl that the boy kissed _____ that day at school.

Figure 3.3 Sample visual panel used to examine gap filling during sentence processing. Participants listened to stories and their eye movements were monitored as they listened to target sentences following each.

at the gap site (e.g., looks to the theme, the *girl*, in Figure 3.3), and that their fixations were just as fast as control participants' fixations, even on incorrect off-line comprehension trials (see Blumstein et al., 1998, for similar findings using a unimodal lexical priming paradigm). On incorrect trials, however, the participants with aphasia showed eye fixations to competitor pictures downstream from the verb (e.g., looks to the *boy*).

These findings suggest that failure to comprehend complex sentences as seen in individuals with Broca's aphasia is associated with impaired lexical integration. That is, as sentences unfold in real time, these patients showed ability, albeit delayed, to access the lexical items in sentences, and they showed ability to fill gaps in a timely manner. However, they were unable to integrate the activated lexical items into the syntax and, hence, experience comprehension failure. Linking deficits in sentence comprehension to the disruption of lexical integration suggests that anterior brain regions (including Broca's area) are not the locus of syntactic processing per se. On Friederici's model, this suggests a breakdown in the final stage of sentence processing where semantic and syntactic information are integrated.

This interpretation is consistent with ERP studies with aphasic individuals. Hagoort, Wassenaar,

and Brown (2003a) and Wassenaar, Brown, and Hagoort (2004) found reduced or absent P600 responses to syntactic violations in patients with agrammatic, Broca's aphasia, in contrast to healthy control subjects. Instead, the patients displayed posterior negativity similar to the N400 effect. Further, the P600 component, thought to reflect the interaction of semantic and syntactic information, has been found to be attenuated in patients with lesions that include the left basal ganglia, which often is affected in Broca's aphasia (Frisch, Kotz, von Cramon, & Friederici, 2003). In addition, in a study examining the N400 effect, Swaab, Brown, and Hagoort (1997) found that, compared with unimpaired adults, aphasic listeners with comprehension deficits show reduced and delayed N400 effects when processing constructions with end-of-sentence semantic anomalies, once again reflecting lexical integration deficits (e.g., *The girl dropped the candy on the sky*).

Wernicke's Aphasia and the Brain

In contrast, patients with classic Wernicke's aphasia present with fluent speech output, with normal prosody and speech rate. In the most severe cases, speech is devoid of meaning as in the following narrative sample, taken from a 59-year-old woman (LH) with chronic Wernicke's aphasia (an excerpt from her telling of the Cinderella story).

She's working for these other three people that are not very nice. They're just grumpy all the time. And she's doing what she needs to do. But it's hard to always do what he wants her to do, what they want her to do.... Washing all the stuff or putting the cooking and everything on. That one in the other room helping. That's her friend. Dogs ha!... They're not people, people. They're [unintelligible], they're animals, ha.... But every time she's with this other group of people they're not nice. They're mean and hateful and just not nice. But then it turns out that she's supposed to find something to wear to the friend that she's going.. So she goes and these other not very friendly people are there [unintelligible].... And they're all coming, her and the children, or the animals, whatever. At any rate, she gets in line. And she goes to a friend. And on her way back home she lost one of her things.... She put it on. She thought it was really nice. And it's not going to raise the people that she got it from because they're not very nice people anyway.... Anyhow, they all try to come back together again and et cetera. And love whatever's before them. At any rate, or live what is before them…At any rate, they ended up loving each other again….and understanding that there's other people to face. Except that [unintelligible] un-fun ones over here…. It's all done and everybody's happy. I just like to see the happy people get happy.

Analysis of this patient's production indicated normal speech rate (i.e., 166 words per minute; healthy age-matched control subjects = 132.22 [SD=5.22]) and utterance length (mean = 9.13 morphemes; mean for healthy control subjects = 11.11 [SD = 0.56]). Seventy percent of her utterances were syntactically correct, with a complex/simple sentence ratio of 0.82. She also correctly inflected most nouns (96 percent) and verbs (95 percent), and 93 percent of verbs were produced with correct verb argument structure.

Research examining production in Wernicke's aphasia is consistent with LH's speech pattern. Von Stockert and Bader (1976) found that patients with Wernicke's aphasia form grammatically correct but semantically implausible sentences. Faroqi-Shah and Thompson (2003) also found that although patients with Wernicke's aphasia erroneously produce passivised sentences, close inspection of error patterns revealed semantic, rather than syntactic impairments. In addition, research shows that these patients typically show profound language comprehension deficits and often have difficulties understanding even single words and simple sentences in the face of putatively normal on-line processing of noncanonical sentence structures (Swinney & Zurif, 1995; Zurif et al., 1993). In contrast to patients with anterior lesions, Friederici, Hahne, and von Cramon (1998) reported an individual with a lesion involving the left posterior temporal and adjacent parietal areas who showed ELAN in response to phrase structure violations, but no P600 or N400.

Patients with Wernicke's aphasia also typically do not show word class production deficits as do individuals with agrammatic aphasic. However, several studies show that individuals with Wernicke's aphasia who have primary lesions in the posterior cortex present with a severe deficit in processing aspects of verb argument structure, with a lack of sensitivity to argument structure during on-line sentence processing (Shapiro & Levine, 1990). Similar findings were reported by McCann and Edwards (2002) who found that patients with Wernicke's aphasia with posterior perisylvian lesions did not detect argument structure violations (e.g., *John gives a card). Results from a study by Wu, Waller, and Chatterjee (2007) also support this pattern. They found that

brain-damaged individuals with lesions in the lateral temporal cortex showed deficits in argument structure knowledge. Consistent with these findings, in a lesion-deficit correlational study, Bonakdarpour et al. (2008) found a positive correlation between lesions in superior temporal and supramarginal gyri and argument structure processing ability.

In summary, the lesion-deficit literature suggests different roles for left anterior and posterior perisylvian brain regions. Data derived from individuals with Broca's aphasia suggest that frontal regions are associated with grammatical encoding, whereas posterior regions are required for semantic processing and integration. Recent studies show that, rather than syntactic processing per se, regions disrupted in Broca's aphasia are important for phrase structure building based on the subcategorization and argument structure properties of verbs. Difficulty producing verbs with complex argument structure results in impaired projection of syntactic frames for production. However, because posterior language regions are spared, processing of verb arguments proceeds normally. Patients with Wernicke's aphasia, with a sparing of frontal lobe tissue, but lesioned posterior brain regions show significant semantic deficits in the face of seemingly preserved syntactic processing. In addition, these patients do not typically show verb production deficits and appear to have little difficulty with phrase structure building in production. However, they fail to detect argument structure violations. These patterns suggest a primary role of posterior perisylvian regions for semantic and syntactic integration.

Limitations of Lesion-Deficit Studies

One problem with drawing conclusions about the neural mechanisms of sentence processing by observing the performance of brain-damaged individuals is that, even when disrupted language processes clearly result from disruption of particular brain regions, it cannot be concluded that these disrupted brain regions are responsible for carrying out the disrupted function. This is because the damaged regions are likely part of a large frontotemporal network. Thus, disruption of any part of the network could putatively disrupt function. In addition, stroke often affects neural tissue both adjacent to and distal to the lesion (e.g., tissue may be alive, but hypoperfused and, hence, nonfunctional). Furthermore and importantly, many lesion-deficit studies do not report the lesion characteristics of the patients under study, and the site and extent of lesions that patients with particular aphasic syndromes present vary considerably. Even for individuals who show clear behavioral patterns consistent with, for example, Broca's or Wernicke's aphasia, lesions are heterogeneous. In an early study examining computerized tomography (CT) scans derived from 20 individuals with Broca's aphasia, with concomitant agrammatism across languages, Vanier and Caplan (1990) found extensive variability in participant lesions, with some showing large left hemisphere lesions, some showing middle-sized lesions, and others showing small lesions. In another CT study, Caplan and colleagues (Caplan et al., 1996) further showed that lesions in different areas of the left perisylvian cortex resulted in syntactic processing deficits. Similarly, in a recent electroencephalogram (EEG) study of agrammatic patients with aphasia, inspection of magnetic resonance imaging (MRI) structural lesions revealed lesions ranging from large ones involving both anterior and posterior left perisylvian tissue to smaller ones constrained to the frontal region, but involving more than Broca's area (Figure 3.4). Notably, all participants showed the same patterns of sentence production and comprehension impairments, including verb and verb argument structure deficits, in both constrained tasks and in spontaneous speech. Further, Caplan et al. (2007) examined a large sample of brain-damaged individuals, localizing their lesions using both MRI and positron emission tomography (PET) and found that brain tissue associated with impaired sentence comprehension includes a wide range of perisylvian regions. In addition, areas outside the perisylvian regions, including the anterior temporal lobe and inferior and superior parietal regions, were involved in some patients.

Voxel-based lesion-symptom mapping studies have resulted in similar findings. Dronkers, Wilkins, Van Valin, Redfern, and Jaeger (2004) used this method to identify regions of lesioned tissue associated with sentence comprehension deficits, finding that regions adjacent to Broca's or Wernicke's areas contribute significantly to performance. Impaired performance on a sentence-picture matching task was associated with lesions in the left posterior middle temporal gyrus, anterior superior temporal, and superior temporal gyri. In addition, performance was affected by lesions in the left angular gyrus; middle frontal cortex (i.e., BA 46, BA 47); and the inferior frontal gyrus. However, lesions to Broca's and Wernicke's areas alone did not significantly affect language comprehension ability. In another study, Dronkers, Wilkins, Van Valin, Redfern, and Jaeger (1994) found that deficits in morphosyntactic processing correlated with lesions in the left

anterior temporal lobe (BA 22), but not Broca's area. Moreover, some patients with damage to the left inferior frontal gyrus did not show severe morphosyntactic impairment (Dronkers et al., 1994). In another study, Wilson and Saygin (2004) found an association between impaired performance on grammaticality judgment of noncanonical sentences (e.g., *Which woman did David think saw Pete?*) and lesions in the posterior superior and middle left temporal gyri. Although poor performance was observed in some patients with Broca's area lesions, more detailed lesion analysis indicated that damage to the inferior frontal cortex was not significantly associated with sentence comprehension ability.

These data indicate that both anterior and posterior regions of the brain play important roles in sentence production and comprehension. Furthermore, the results of lesion studies suggest that areas important for sentence processing are distributed throughout the left perisylvian region with support from areas outside this region.

Neuroimaging Studies of Sentence Processing in Healthy Individuals

The view that sentence processing involves a distributed neural network in anterior and posterior brain regions is supported by neuroimaging and ERP studies with healthy volunteers. Evidence from these studies suggests that semantic and syntactic aspects of sentence processing are supported by distinct, but highly interactive neural mechanisms involving primarily the left hemisphere (in left hemisphere–dominant speakers), but also regions in the right hemisphere.

Models of sentence production and comprehension describe several levels of processing required to transfer meaning to spoken production and phonological material to meaning. Research from brain-damaged individuals provides rudimentary information about how these processes are computed in the brain. However, for reasons pointed out previously, such data are insufficient for understanding the precise mechanisms involved in these complex computations. Neuroimaging studies are, therefore, useful and necessary to investigate how sentences are processed in healthy individuals. Functional neuroimaging, using functional MRI (fMRI) and PET, for example, provides information about spatial aspects of sentence processing (i.e., where in the brain neural activity occurs during sentence processing). Notably, however, these methods do not provide information about when, as sentences unfold in real time, particular regions

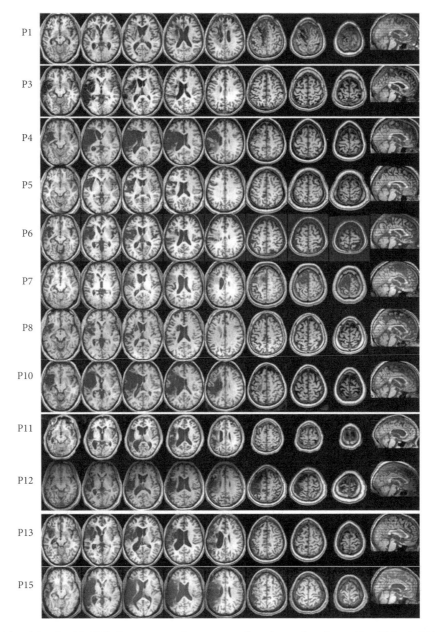

P1

P3

P4

P5

P6

P7

P8

P10

P11

P12

P13

P15

Figure 3.4 Selected slices from T1 MRIs of participants with agrammatic aphasia showing brain lesions. From Kielar, A., Meltzer-Aascher, A., & Thompson, C. K. (in press). Electrophysiological responses to argument structure violations in healthy adults and individuals with agrammatic aphasia. *Neuropsychologia.*

of the brain are recruited for processing. ERPs, however, provide temporal information, but the resulting data are quite imprecise with regard to the location of associated neural generators. This section discusses studies using fMRI and ERP to examine the neural mechanisms of sentence processing.

In one of the first neuroimaging studies of sentence processing, Bavelier et al. (1997) used PET to examine regional cerebral blood flow (rCBF) associated with processing visually presented English sentences versus consonant strings. Results showed activation in Broca's area, the posterior and middle temporal sulcus, the angular gyrus, and the anterior pole of the superior temporal sulcus. In another PET study, Mazoyer et al. (1993) found similar widespread activation in native speakers of French while they listened to French stories with and without semantically anomalous words; stories in a foreign language (Tamil); stories with pseudowords; and French word lists. Meaningful sentences activated a frontotemporal brain network, including the bilateral posterior superior temporally gyrus, the left middle temporal gyrus, and the left inferior frontal and superior frontal gyri. Humphries, Willard, Buchsbaum, and Hickok (2001) also found significant fMRI activation in the left posterior superior temporal cortex and in the anterior temporal region bilaterally, when participants listened to sentences describing an event (e.g., *There was a gunshot and then the man run away*) compared with environmental sounds of the same event (e.g., sound of a gunshot; see also Humphries, Binder, Medler, & Liebenthal, 2006). These findings are not surprising in that a distributed left hemisphere network has been found even for single word processing (i.e., left inferior frontal regions) and the middle temporal and angular gyri (posterior regions of the brain) are engaged for this purpose (Buckner, Koutstaal, Schacter, & Rosen, 2000; Demb et al., 1995; Devlin, Matthews, & Rushworth, 2003; Gabrieli, Poldrack, & Desmond, 1998; Thompson-Shrill, D'Esposito, Aguirre, & Farah, 1997; Thompson-Schill, D'Esposito, & Kan, 1999). Notably, however, these early studies were not designed to isolate semantic versus syntactic processing.

Breaking Down the Components of Sentence Processing: Evidence from Neuroimaging
PROCESSING SEMANTIC ASPECTS OF
SENTENCES

A crucial component of sentence processing involves attaching meaning to strings of words. Hence, in the aforementioned studies of general sentence processing, at least some of the activation noted is necessarily associated with semantic processing. PET and fMRI studies investigating semantic processing at the sentence level report a variety of activation loci in both frontal and temporal brain regions. Dapretto and Bookheimer (1999), using a task in which participants made similarity judgments about the meaning of sentence pairs (e.g., *The lawyer questioned the witness* vs. *The attorney questioned the witness*), found activation in the orbital portion of the inferior frontal gyrus (BA 47). Ni et al. (2000) also found small clusters of activation in the inferior and middle frontal gyri (BA10/46) in an fMRI study using a semantic anomaly judgment task (e.g., *Trees can grow* vs. **Trees can eat*).

Other studies using tasks requiring semantic judgment reported engagement of posterior temporal regions. In a PET study, using a visual plausibility judgment task, Caplan, Alpert, and Waters (1998)

observed bilateral activation in the middle and posterior temporal gyri for sentences with greater propositional content (e.g., *The magician performed the stunt that included the joke* vs. *The magician performed the stunt and the joke*). Similarly, in a German study using fMRI and an auditory anomaly judgment task, Friederici, Ruschemeyer, Hahne, and Fiebach (2003) found bilateral posterior and middle superior temporal activation when participants processed sentences containing semantic violations (versus those without violations). Bilateral posterior superior temporal activation (BA 22) also was found by Ni et al. (2000). These findings are in keeping with ERP studies, reporting an N400 effect associated with processing sentences with semantic violations (e.g., **They like their coffee with cream and the mustache*; Friederici, 2002; Friederici & Frisch, 2000; Frisch, Hahne, & Friederici, 2004; Friederici & Meyer, 2004; Hagoort, 2003; Kielar & Joanisse, 2010; Kutas & Federmeier, 2000; Kutas & Hillyard, 1980, 1984; Münte, Say, Clahsen, Schiltz, & Kutas, 1999). Although anatomically imprecise, the neural generators of the N400 have been associated with posterior brain regions. Available data from magnetoencephalography (MEG) also suggest involvement of the left anterior and superior temporal cortices (Friederici, Wang, Herrmann, Maess, & Oertel, 2000; Halgren et al., 2002; Helenius, Salmelin, Service, & Connolly, 1998; Service, Helenius, Maury, & Salmelin, 2007). Results of these studies indicate that semantic processing engages both hemispheres in frontal and temporal regions of the brain.

VERB ARGUMENT STRUCTURE PROCESSING

Another important aspect of sentence processing pertains to verb argument structure processing, considered an interface between semantics (e.g., who did what to whom) and syntax (e.g., word order). Several neuroimaging studies have found neural activation in posterior brain regions, including the left posterior superior temporal sulcus, supramarginal gyrus, and angular gyrus, associated with verb argument structure processing (Ben-Shachar, Hendler, Kahn, Ben-Bashat, & Grodzinsky, 2003; Bronkessel, Zysset, Friederici, von Cramon, & Schlesewsky, 2005; Hadar, Palti, & Hendler, 2002; Meltzer-Aascher, Shuchard, den Ouden, & Thompson, in press; Palti, Ben-Shachar, Hendler, & Hadar, 2007; Thompson, Bonakdarpour, & Fix, 2009; Thompson et al., 2007) (see Table 3.1 for a summary of studies). Using a lexical decision task with healthy young normal participants, Thompson et al. (2007) found graded

Table 3.1. fMRI Studies of Verb Argument Structure Processing

Study	Language	Task	Structures Tested	Main Findings
Ben-Shachar et al. (2003)	Hebrew	Auditory grammaticality judgment	Number of arguments; more > less	Left pSTS
den Ouden et al. (2009)	English	Naming action pictures/ videos	Transitive > intransitive	Left IFG (BA 44/45), SMG, AG
Newman et al. (2003)	English	Visual grammaticality judgment	Thematic role violation	Left IFG (BA 45), pSTS
Shetreet et al. (2007)	Hebrew	Auditory plausibility judgment	Number of arguments/subcategorization options; more > less	Left STG, BA 47
Shetreet et al. (2010)	Hebrew	Auditory plausibility judgment	Subcategorization options	Left STG, MFG, SFG
Thompson et al. (2007)	English	Visual lexical decision	Transitive > intransitive (transitive + ditransitive) > intransitive	Left SMG, AG Bilateral SMG, AG
Thompson et al. (2009)	English	Visual lexical decision	Transitive > intransitive (transitive + ditransitive) > intransitive	Bilateral AG Left AG
Meltzer-Aascher et al. (in press)	English	Visual lexical decision	Alternating transitive > unergative	Bilateral SMG, AG Bilateral MFG, SFG

Note. IFG = inferior frontal gyrus; pSTG = posterior superior temporal gyrus; AG = angular gyrus; SMG = supramarginal gyrus; pMTG = posterior middle temporal gyrus; aMTG = anterior middle temporal gyrus; STS = superior temporal sulcus; MFG = middle frontal gyrus.

activation in posterior perisylvian regions as a function of the number of arguments selected by the verb. Cortical tissue in the left supramarginal and angular gyri was active for processing of two- versus one-argument verbs (e.g., *follow* vs. *whistle*, respectively), whereas bilateral activation in these regions was found for processing three-argument verbs (e.g., *send*) versus one-argument verbs (Figure 3.5). This pattern was replicated by Thompson et al. (2009) in older healthy participants, who showed angular gyrus activation for verbs with greater argument structure density. Similar results were found by Meltzer-Aascher et al. (in press) in young normal listeners for alternating transitive verbs (e.g., *melt*) compared with unergative intransitive verbs (e.g., *sleep*). These findings indicate that the posterior perisylvian region is crucially engaged during processing of information related to verb argument structure. Some studies also find that anterior brain regions activate in response to increasing argument structure complexity. For example, Shetreet, Palti, Friedmann, and Hadar (2007) found left inferior frontal activation (BA 47), in addition to left posterior activation (BA 22), for verbs with denser subcategorization frames. These findings are in keeping with results reported by Friederici and colleagues (Bornkessel,

Zysset, Friederici, Cramon, & Schlesewsky, 2005; Friederici, Makuuchi, & Bahlman, 2009), that during sentence processing left inferior frontal gyrus activation was found when computation of a syntactic frame was required, whereas posterior superior temporal areas were engaged when interpretation of thematic roles and verb argument hierarchies ensued. Newman, Just, Keller, Roth, and Carpenter (2003) also observed greater activation in the pars opercularis for sentences containing syntactic violations, whereas the posterior left temporal area was engaged by both syntactic violations and thematic errors.

These results suggest that anterior and posterior language regions serve different functions, but need to work together to ensure efficient sentence comprehension and production. Anterior regions seem to support sequencing or building of hierarchical syntactic structure based on subcategorization and argument structure information, which in turn triggers posterior regions for syntactic and semantic integration. This is consistent with Humphries et al. (2006), who suggested that frontal regions may be crucial in extracting syntactic structure independent of sentential meaning, whereas temporal regions perform an integrative role.

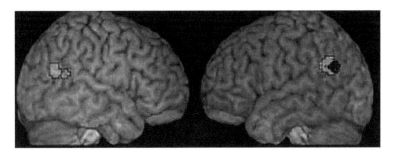

Figure 3.5 Posterior perisylvian regions (supramarginal gyrus and angular gyrus) activated as a function of argument structure complexity in healthy adults. From Thompson et al., 2007. Activation for two-argument minus one-argument verbs (blue); activation for two-argument and three-argument verbs compared with one-argument verbs (yellow).

ERP studies support this frontotemporal interaction. Friederici and colleagues found early anterior effects in response to violations of word-category constraints and violations of verb subcategorization requirements (e.g., *The cousin visited to the violinist*), reflecting interruptions in generation of syntactic structure. In contrast, violations of the correct number of arguments resulted in an N400 effect (Friederici & Frisch, 2000; Frisch et al., 2004; Frisch & Schlesewsky, 2001; Friederici & Meyer, 2004). Furthermore, several ERP studies of argument structure violations have found a biphasic N400-P600 response (Friederici, 2002; Friederici & Kotz, 2003; Friederici & Meyer, 2004; Friederici & Frisch, 2000; Kielar, Meltzer-Aascher, & Thompson, in press). The N400 seems to reflect attempts to integrate lexical-semantic information when arguments are missing (e.g., *John gives a car*), or when illicit arguments are present (e.g., *John sleeps a bed*; *John sneezed the doctor*) (Frisch & Schlesewsky, 2001; Kielar et al., in press). The P600 most likely reflects an attempt at reanalysis or repair after thematic integration failure. Wassenaar and Hagoort (2007) found a similar pattern when participants decided whether an auditorily presented sentence (e.g. *The cat licked the dog*) matched a visually displayed picture (e.g. of a dog licking a cat). That is, they showed on-line sensitivity to thematic role assignment, displaying an early negative effect followed by a later positive shift in response to thematic mismatches. This biphasic pattern also was found for sentences with two noun phrases marked as grammatical subjects (in German), arguably causing a similar failure of thematic integration. Again, although ERP effects do not provide precise anatomical information, early syntactic ERP components (i.e., ELAN and LAN) are thought to be generated in anterior perisylvian regions, whereas, the N400 and P600 are thought to be generated in posterior temporal regions. These findings are in agreement

with the proposal that generating phrase structure involves anterior brain regions, and that integration of meaning and syntax engages posterior perisylvian areas (see Grodzinsky & Friederici, 2006).

Syntactic Computation

PET and fMRI studies attempting to determine the neural correlates of syntactic processing have examined activation associated with computation of written or spoken grammatically incorrect versus correct sentences or grammatically complex versus simple sentences (see Table 3.2 for a summary of studies). Ni et al. (2000), comparing syntactically anomalous sentences (e.g., *Trees can grew*) with well-formed sentences (e.g., *Trees can grow*), found strong activation in the left frontal operculum (BA 44). Embick, Marantz, Miyashita, O'Neil, and Sakai (2000) also found significant activation in left Broca's area (BA 44/45) when comparing sentences with grammatical errors (e.g., *Mary asked question about theorem the in class*) with sentences with no grammatical errors (but incorrect spelling). In addition, clusters of activation were observed in the left posterior superior temporal cortex (BA 22) and angular gyrus (BA 39/40). Wartenburger et al. (2004) also found activation in the left inferior frontal gyrus (BA 44/45) and anterior superior temporal gyrus for grammatical versus ungrammatical sentences. Similarly, Meyer, Friederici, and von Cramon (2000) found a small area of activation in the left frontal operculum of the inferior frontal gyrus in addition to activation in anterior and posterior superior temporal gyri, and bilateral middle temporal gyri as a function of grammaticality (also see Friederici et al. [2003] for a similar pattern associated with syntactic phase structure violations). These results are in line with a MEG study that found that phrase structure violations based on word category errors (e.g., *The fish was in caught*) elicited activation in the left inferior

Table 3.2. Neuroimaging Studies of Syntactic Processing

Study	Language	Task	Structures Tested	Main Findings
PET Studies				
Caplan et al. (1998)	English	Visual plausibility judgment	Center embedded vs. right branching relative clauses Sentences with two vs. one propositions	Left IFG (BA 44), MFG, cingulate (BA 32) Bilateral ITG, pMTG
Caplan et al. (1999)	English	Speeded auditory plausibility judgment	Cleft-object vs. cleft-subject sentences	Left IFG (BA 45), MFG, SPL
Caplan et al. (2000)	English	Visual plausibility judgment	Center embedded subject-object vs. right branching object-subject	Left IFG (BA 45), MFG, cingulate (BA 31), MFG (BA 10)
Stowe et al. (1998)	Dutch	Reading sentences	Syntactically complex vs. simple sentences	Left aSTG, pSTG, pMTG
Stromswold et al. (1996)	English	Visual plausibility judgment	Center embedded vs. right branching relative clauses	Left IFG (BA 44)
Waters et al. (2003)	English	Visual speeded plausibility judgment	Subject-object vs. object-subject relative clauses	Bilateral IFG, STG, cingulate; left STS
fMRI Studies				
Ben-Shachar et al. (2003)	Hebrew	Auditory grammaticality judgment	Embedded complex and simple sentences	Left IFG, bilateral pSTS
Ben-Shachar et al. (2004)	Hebrew	Auditory sentence comprehension	Syntactic movement structures vs. topicalization	Left IFG, left ventral precentral sulcus, bilateral pSTS
Caplan et al. (2001)	English	Visual plausibility judgment (RSVP)	Subject-object vs. subject-subject relative clauses	Left AG, pSTG
Cooke et al. (2001)	English	Listening for speaker gender	Object/subject relatives; long and short antecedent-gaps	Long antecedent-gap: right pSTG; Long object relatives-subject relatives short: left IFG (BA 47)
Dapretto & Bookheimer (1999)	English	Auditory syntactic/ semantic sentence judgment	Sentence pairs	Syntactic judgment vs. rest: left BA 44/45, BA 22, 38, 40/39 Semantic processing vs. rest: bilateral BA 47, 45, left BA 22
Fiebach et al. (2005)	German	Visual comprehension	Object/subject wh-questions; Long and short antecedent-gaps	Left IFG (BA 44/45) Bilateral pSTS
Friederici et al. (2006)	German	Speeded visual acceptability judgment	Noncanonical vs. canonical Ungrammatical constructions	Complexity: left IFG (BA 44) Grammaticality: deep left frontal operculum
Friederici et al. (2009)	German	Visual comprehension judgment	Center embedded vs. simple sentences	pSTG, bilateral STS, BA 44
Friederici et al. (2000)	German	Auditory syntactic judgment	Syntactically/semantically normal sentences Syntactically correct sentences with pseudowords	Syntactic processing: deep left frontal operculum; bilateral aSTG

(continued)

Table 3.2. Continued

Study	Language	Task	Structures Tested	Main Findings
Friederici et al. (2003)	German	Auditory acceptability judgment	Syntactic violations Semantic violations	Syntactic violations: left aSTG, pSTG, posterior frontal operculum, basal ganglia Semantic violations: bilateral middle STG, insula
Friederici, Wang et al. (2000)	German	Auditory grammaticality judgment	Syntactically correct vs. incorrect sentences	Bilateral aSTG, left IFG
Just et al. (1996)	English	Sentence comprehension	Object relative vs. subject relative clauses	Left IFG (BA 44), pSTG
Makuuchi et al. (2009)	German	Visual sentence comprehension Semantic judgment	Center embedded sentences Long and short distance between subjects and verbs	Left IFG (BA 44) Left IFS
Meyer et al. (2000)	German	Auditory grammatical judgment	Grammatically correct vs. incorrect sentences	Left pSTG, aSTG, left frontal operculum, left anterior insula; bilateral MTG
Ni et al. (2000)	English	Auditory anomaly detection	Syntactically anomalous sentences Semantically anomalous sentences	Left IFG BA 44 Left pSTS, MTG, AG
Thompson et al. (2010)	English	Auditory sentence-picture verification	Object vs. subject cleft sentences	Left IFG (BA 44, 45), MFG, STG, AG
Wartenburger (2004)	German	Auditory grammaticality judgment	Noncanonical vs. canonical sentences	Bilateral STG, MTG Both sentence types: left BA 44 Grammaticality: left IFG (BA 44/45), insula, aSTG

Note. IFG = inferior frontal gyrus; IFS = inferior frontal sulcus; MFG = middle frontal gyrus; pSTG = posterior superior temporal gyrus; AG = angular gyrus; aSTG = anterior superior temporal gyrus; pMTG = posterior middle temporal gyrus; STS = superior temporal sulcus; SPL = superior parietal lobe; ITG = .

frontal cortex and bilateral anterior superior temporal gyrus (Friederici, Wang, Herrman, Maess, & Oertel, 2000).

ERP studies comparing ungrammatical with grammatical sentence processing also suggest a distributed network for syntactic processing. The neural signatures for syntactic processing include two main ERP components: the LAN and the P600. Anterior negativities (e.g., LAN) are usually larger over the left rather than right hemisphere, although bilateral distribution has been observed in some cases (Hagoort, Wassenaar, & Brown, 2003b). This component is most often elicited by outright syntactic violations, rather than nonpreferred structures or syntactic ambiguity (Kaan, Harris, Gibson, & Holcomb, 2000; Friederici et al., 1996). Left anterior negativities have been reported in response to violations of morphosyntax, such as number, tense,

and gender mismatches (Kutas & Hillyard, 1983; Münte, Heinze, & Mangun, 1993; Osterhout & Mobley, 1995) and phrase structure violations (Neville, Nicol, Barss, Forster, & Garrett, 1991). In other studies, the ELAN has been observed in correlation with word category errors (Friederici et al., 1996; Friederici et al., 1993). These early components are often followed by the P600 or syntactic positive shift, found in response to a broad range of syntactic violations (Ainsworth-Darnell, Shulman, & Boland, 1998; Friederici et al., 1996; Friederici et al., 1993; Hagoort & Brown, 2000; Kaan et al., 2000; Neville et al., 1991; Osterhout & Holcomb, 1992; Osterhout & Nicol, 1999; Rösler, Putz, Friederici, & Hahne, 1993; van den Brink & Hagoort, 2004).

Several studies using fMRI have compared brain activation associated with syntactically complex versus simple sentences. Several have found that processing complex syntax is accompanied by increased activation in the left inferior frontal region (BA 44/45). For example, using PET, Stromswold, Caplan, Alpert, and Rauch (1996) contrasted complex center-embedded subject-object sentences (e.g., *The limerick that the boy recited appalled the priest*) with simpler right branching constructions (e.g., *The bibliographer omitted the story that insulted the queen*) while participants performed a speeded plausibility judgment task. They found increased rCBF in the pars opercularis (BA 44) for the complex compared with simple sentences. Caplan et al. (1998) also found that processing of center-embedded subject-object clauses (e.g., *The juice that the child spilled stained the rug*) compared with simple object-subject relative sentences (e.g., *The child spilled the juice that stained the rug*) was associated with increased blood flow in the left pars opercularis (BA 44). Caplan and colleagues (Caplan, Alpert, & Waters, 1999; Caplan, Waters, & Alpert, 2003; Waters, Caplan, Alpert, & Stanczak, 2003) replicated these results, and further demonstrated that in comparison with subject relative sentences, structures with more complex subject-object relative clauses elicited greater activation in the left inferior frontal lobe areas (BA 45, BA 44/46).

Interestingly, in a study directly investigating the role of this region in sentence processing, Friederici, Fiebach, Schlesewsky, Bornkessel, and von Cramon (2006) compared neural responses associated with grammaticality with those varying in syntactic complexity. They found that ungrammatical sentences engaged the deep frontal operculum, whereas activation in BA 44 was modulated as a function of syntactic complexity. These data suggest that different parts of the inferior frontal gyrus may be engaged for distinct aspect of syntactic processing.

Inferior frontal activation during sentence processing also is often accompanied by substantial activity in the posterior temporal regions. For example, using fMRI, Just, Carpenter, Keller, Eddy, and Thulborn (1996) found increased activation in both Broca's area and parts of the left superior temporal gyrus when participants read and answered questions about the meaning of sentences in subject-object form (e.g., *The witness that the lawyer questioned impressed the judge*), compared with syntactically simpler subject-subject constructions (e.g., *The witness that questioned the lawyer impressed the judge*). Similarly, activation in the left inferior frontal and posterior superior temporal gyri was observed in a study comparing

processing of complex center embedded sentences to simple structures in German (Friederici et al., 2009). In another fMRI study, Friederici, Meyer, and von Cramon (2000) found that processing syntactic information was associated with activation in the deep left frontal operculum and the left posterior superior temporal gyrus and bilateral anterior superior temporal gyri. Similarly, in our own work (Thompson, den Ouden, Bonakdarpour, Garibaldi, & Parrish, 2010), we used fMRI to measure neural responses to object cleft (e.g., *It was the groom that the bride carried*), subject cleft (e.g., *It was the bride that carried the groom*), and simple active sentences while participants performed an auditory sentence-picture verification task. We found a left hemisphere network involving the inferior frontal gyrus, the premotor region, and the anterior and posterior superior temporal and middle temporal gyri associated with complex syntactic processing (Figure 3.6). ERP studies also show late positive shifts during complex sentence processing (Kaan et al., 2000; Kaan & Swaab, 2003; Osterhout, Holcomb, & Swinney, 1994), associated with later cognitive processes of syntactic reanalysis and repair (Münte et al., 1997) or syntactic integration (Kann et al., 2000).

Consistent with the role of a frontotemporal network for complex sentence processing, we also found evidence of functional connectivity between the left inferior frontal and posterior superior temporal cortices during processing of object-cleft sentences using dynamic causal modeling (den Ouden et al., 2012) (Figure 3.7). Results of this study indicated that complex sentence processing requires a flow of information between the inferior frontal cortex and both anterior and posterior temporal regions. Regional connectivity studies further indicate distinct fiber projections linking the two. The deep opercular part of the inferior frontal gyrus connects to the anterior temporal lobe through ventral white matter tracks, and BA 44/45 connects to the posterior temporal lobe through the arcuate fasciculus (Anwander, Tittgemeyer, von Cramon, Friederici, & Knosche, 2006; Friederici, Bahlmann, Heim, Schubotz, & Anwander, 2006).

THE ROLE OF WORKING MEMORY IN COMPLEX SENTENCE PROCESSING

One issue relevant to studies examining syntactically complex versus simple constructions is that complex structures differ from simple sentences not only in the syntactic operations required, but also in working memory demands. Successful

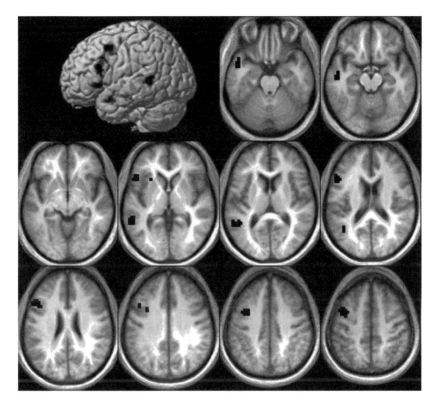

Figure 3.6 Left frontal (BAs 44, 45, 9, 8), temporal brain areas (BAs 21, 22), and angular gyrus (BA39) activated for the contrast object cleft > subject cleft for healthy adults. Adapted from Thompson, C. K., den Ouden, D. B., Bonakdarpour, B., Garibaldi, K., & Parrish, T. B. (2010). Neural plasticity and treatment-induced recovery of sentence processing in agrammatism. *Neuropsychologia*, 1–17.

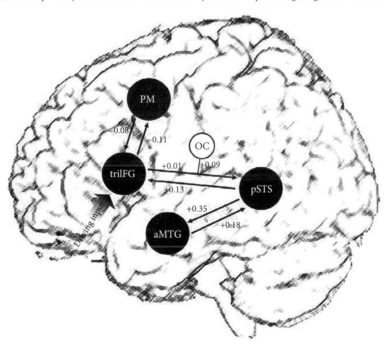

Figure 3.7 Model illustrating network of anterior and posterior brain regions involved in processing of complex syntax. Adapted from den Ouden, D. B., Saur, D., Schelter, B., Lukic, S., Wali, E., & Thompson, C. K. (2012). Network modulation during complex syntactic processing, *Neuroimage, 59*, 815–823. The driving input of the models is on the pars triangularis (triangular inferior frontal gyrus [triIFG]) and the connection between triIFG and pSTG is modulated by object-cleft processing. Mean parameter estimates are given alongside the connections and modulation. PM = ; OC = ; pSTS = ; aMTG = anterior middle temporal gyrus.

assignment of thematic roles in noncanonical sentences requires that the relationship between moved elements and their original position be established. For example, in sentences as in (2) above, the head noun of the relative clause (i.e., *the drink*) needs to be maintained in working memory from the time it is encountered until it can be integrated into the sentence at the gap site. This suggests the possibility that in addition to syntactic operations, activation in Broca's area during processing of complex syntactic structures may also reflect increased working memory demands. The main role of this area might be to maintain nonintegrated material active in a memory buffer when processing load increases. For example, Cooke et al. (2001) examined rCBF using fMRI while healthy participants read sentences differing in grammatical complexity (subject-relative vs. object-relative center embedded clauses) and short-term memory demands (short vs. long antecedent-gap linkages). Activation in the anterior inferior frontal gyrus was associated with reading object relative sentences that contained long-distance antecedent-gap linkages, indicating that this portion of the inferior frontal gyrus supports verbal working memory resources required to maintain long-distance syntactic dependencies. This activation was not observed when object relative long structures were compared with subject relative long structures, suggesting that the anterior inferior frontal gyrus is selectively sensitive to the additional memory cost associated with formation of long-distance dependencies. In another study, Fiebach, Schlesewsky, and Friederici (2001) found that direct comparison of object wh-questions with long versus short filler-gap distance revealed greater activity in the bilateral inferior frontal gyrus for the former constructions. Similarly, Fiebach, Schlesewsky, Lohmann, von Cramon, and Friederici (2005) reported increased activation in the anterior pars opercularis (BA 44) for long sentences with noncanonical word order, in which verbs were separated from their arguments over a long distance. However, no activation increase in this area was found in comparison of object-initial to subject-initial sentences that did not differ in length. These results indicate that the opercular part of Broca's area is involved in temporally maintaining unintegrated linguistic information in working memory during sentence comprehension.

In another study, Makuuchi, Bahlmann, Anwander, and Friederici (2009) found that activity in the left posterior pars opercularis (BA 44) increased as a function of structural complexity, whereas the distance between related elements modulated activation in the dorsal part of the pars triangularis (BA 45). In addition, diffusion tensor imaging showed that these two regions are connected through white matter fiber tracks and functional connectivity between these regions increases during processing of complex center embedded sentences. These results suggest that different parts of the inferior frontal cortex support distinct aspects of sentence processing; however, they are highly interconnected both functionally and anatomically and interact during language processing. The opercular region seems to subserve syntactic computations, whereas the pars triangularis (BA 45) supports increased working memory demands during processing of complex sentences.

Conclusion

The currently available neurolinguistic and neuroimaging data indicate that semantic and syntactic aspects of sentence processing are supported by separate but highly interactive frontal-temporal neuronal circuits, with a clear dominance in the left hemisphere. The results of lesion studies and neuroimaging experiments with healthy individuals indicate that anterior regions support computation of hierarchical syntactic structure based on subcategorization and argument structure information. In contrast, the posterior brain regions integrate semantic with syntactic information and activate when the interpretation of the verb and its argument structure are required. Thus, complex sentence processing requires an uninterrupted flow of information between the frontal and posterior temporal regions.

Regardless of the precise roles that these regions play, it is the interaction among these areas that makes sentence processing possible. Future studies with both patients and healthy individuals are needed to clarify these roles.

Notes

1. Fix is an obligatory two-argument verb (i.e., agent, theme) and, hence has only one theta-grid; *send* is an optional three-argument, alternating dative verb (i.e., agent, theme; agent, theme, goal; agent, goal, theme) and, therefore, has three theta-grids. Thus, *send* has a more dense argument structure representation than *fix*.
2. Data from Thompson et al., 2012.

References

Ainsworth-Darnell, K., Shulman, H. G., & Boland, J. E. (1998). Dissociating brain responses to syntactic and semantic anomalies: Evidence from event-related potentials. *Journal of Memory and Language, 38*, 112–130.

Angrilli, A., Penolazzi, B., Vespignani, F., De Vincenzi, M., Job, R., & Ciccarelli, L. (2002). Cortical brain responses to semantic incongruity and syntactic violation in Italian language: An Event-Related Potential study. *Neuroscience Letters, 322*, 5–8.

Anwander, A., Tittgemeyer, M., von Cramon D. Y., Friederici, A. D., & Knosche, T. R. (2006). Connectivity-based parcellation of Broca's area. *Cerebral Cortex, 17*, 816–825.

Arhens, K. (2003). Verbal integration: The interaction of participant roles and sentential argument structure. *Journal of Psycholinguistic Research, 32*, 497–516.

Bavelier, D., Corina, D., Jezzard, P., Padmanabhan, S., Clark, V. P., Karni, A., Prinster, A., ... Neville, H. (1997). Sentence reading: A functional MRI study at 4 Tesla. *Journal of Cognitive Neuroscience, 9*, 664–686.

Ben-Shachar, M., Hendler, T., Kahn, I., Ben-Bashat, D., & Grodzinsky, Y. (2003). The neural reality of syntactic transformations: Evidence from functional magnetic resonance imaging. *Psychological Science, 14*, 433–440.

Blumstein, S., Byma, G., Kurowski, K., Hourihan, J., Brown, T., & Hutchinson, A. (1998). Online processing of filler-gap constructions in aphasia. *Brain and Language, 61*, 149–168.

Bock, K. (1995). *Sentence production: From mind to mouth, speech, language and communication* (pp. 181–216). New York: Academic Press.

Bock, K. (1999). Language production. In R. A. Wilson & F. Keil (Eds.), *The MIT encyclopedia of cognitive sciences* (pp. 453–456). Cambridge, MA: MIT Press.

Bock, K., & Levelt, W. (1994). Language production: Grammatical encoding. In M. A. Gernsbacher (Ed.), *Handbook of psycholinguistics* (pp. 945–984). San Diego, CA; Academic Press.

Bock, K., & Levelt, W. J. M. (2002). Language production: Grammatical encoding. In G. T. M. Altmann (Ed.), *Psycholinguistics* (pp. 405–452). London: Routledge (Critical Concepts in Psychology, 5).

Boland, J. E. (2005). Visual arguments. *Cognition, 95*, 237–274.

Boland, J. E., & Blodgett, A. (2006). Argument status and PP-attachment. *Journal of Psycholinguistic Research, 35*, 385–403.

Boland, J. E., Tanenhaus, M. K., & Garnsey, S. M. (1990). Evidence for the immediate use of verb control information in sentence processing. *Journal of Memory and Language, 29*, 413–432.

Boland, J. E., Tanenhaus, M. K., Garnsey, S. M., & Carlson, G. N. (1995). Verb argument structure in parsing and interpretation: Evidence from wh-questions. *Journal of Memory and Language, 34*, 774–806.

Bonakdarpour, B., Lukic, S., Garibaldi, K., den Ouden, D. B., Fix, S., & Thompson, C. K. (2008). *Posterior perisylvian lesion volumes in agrammatism and associated sentence deficit patterns*. Presented at the Academy of Aphasia Conference, 19–21 October. Turku, Finland.

Bornkessel, I., Zysset, S., Friederici, A. D., von Cramon, Y., & Schlesewsky, M. (2005). Who did what to whom? The neural basis of argument structure hierarchies during language comprehension. *Neuroimage, 26*, 221–233.

Buckner, R. L., Koutstaal, W., Schacter, D. L., & Rosen, B. R. (2000). Functional MRI evidence for a role of frontal and inferior temporal cortex in amodal components of priming. *Brain, 123*, 620–640.

Caplan, D., Alpert, N., & Waters, G. (1998). Effects of syntactic structure and propositional number on patterns of regional cerebral blood flow. *Journal of Cognitive Neuroscience, 10*, 541–552.

Caplan, D., Alpert, N., & Waters, G. S. (1999). PET studies of syntactic processing with auditory sentence presentation. *NeuroImage, 9*, 343–351.

Caplan, D., Hildebrandt, N., & Makris, N. (1996). Location of lesions in stroke patients with deficits in syntactic processing in sentence comprehension. *Brain, 119*, 933–949.

Caplan, D., Waters, G., & Alpert, N. (2003). Effects of age and speed of processing on rCBF correlates of syntactic processing in sentence comprehension. *Human Brain Mapping, 19*, 112–131.

Caplan, D., Waters, G., Kennedy, D., Alpert, N., Makris, N., DeDe, G., ... Reddy, A. (2007). A study of syntactic processing in aphasia II. Neurological aspects. *Brain and Language, 101*, 151–177.

Caramazza, A. (1997). How many levels of processing are there in lexical access? *Cognitive Neuropsychology, 14*, 177–208.

Caramazza, A., & Zurif, E. (1976). Dissociations of algorithmic and heuristic processes in sentence comprehension: Evidence from aphasia. *Brain and Language, 3*, 572–582.

Chang, F., Dell, G. S., & Bock, J. K. (2006). Becoming syntactic. *Psychological Review, 113*, 234–272.

Cho-Reyes, S., & Thompson, C. K. (2012). Verb and sentence production and comprehension: Northwestern Assessment of Verbs and Sentences (NAVS). *Aphasiology, 26*, 1250–1277.

Chomsky, N. (1995). Bare phrase structure. In G. Webelhuth (Ed.), *Government and binding theory and the minimalist program* (pp. 385–439). Cambridge: Blackwell.

Choy, J. J., & Thompson, C. K. (2010). Binding in agrammatic aphasia: Processing to comprehension. *Aphasiology, 24*(5), 551–579.

Cooke, A., Zurif, E. B., DeVita, C., Alsop, D., Koening, P., Gee, J., Pinango, M., ... Grossman, M. (2001). Neural basis for sentence comprehension: grammatical and short term memory components. *Human Brain Mapping, 15*, 80–94.

Coulson, S., King, J. W., & Kutas, M. (1998). Expect the unexpected: Event-related brain potentials response to morphosyntactic violations. *Language and Cognitive Processes, 13*, 21–58.

Damasio, A. R. (1992). Aphasia. *New England Journal of Medicine, 326*, 531–539.

Damasio, H., & Damasio, A. R. (1989). *Lesion analysis in neuropsychology*. New York: Oxford University Press.

Dapretto, M., & Bookheimer, S. Y. (1999). Form and content: Dissociating syntax and semantics in sentence comprehension. *Neuron, 24*, 427–432.

De Blesser, R., & Kauschke, C. (2003). Acquisition and loss of nouns and verbs: Parallel and divergent patterns? *Journal of Neurolinguistics, 16*, 213–229.

Dell G. S. (1986). A spreading activation theory of retrieval in language production. *Psychological Review, 93*, 283–321.

Dell, G. S., & Sullivan, J. M. (2004). Speech errors and language production: Neuropsychological and connectionist perspectives. In B. H. Ross (Ed.), *The psychology of learning and motivation* (pp. 63–108). San Diego: Elsevier.

Demb, J. B., Desmond, J. E., Wagner, A. D., Vaidya, C. J., Glover, G. H., & Gabrieli, D. E. (1995). Semantic encoding and retrieval in the left inferior prefrontal cortex: A functional MRI study of task difficulty and process specificity. *The Journal of Neuroscience, 15*, 5870–5878.

den Ouden, D. B., Fix, S., Parrish, T. B., & Thompson, C. K. (2009) Argument structure effects in action verb naming in static and dynamic conditions. *Journal of Neurolinguistics, 22, 2,* 196–215.

den Ouden, D.B., Saur, D., Schelter, B., Lukic, S., Wali, E., & Thompson, C. K. (2012). Network modulation during complex syntactic processing, *Neuroimage, 59,* 815–823.

Devlin, J. T., Matthews, P. M., & Rushworth, M. F. S. (2003). Semantic processing in the left inferior prefrontal cortex: A combined functional magnetic resonance imaging and transcranial magnetic simulation study. *Journal of Cognitive Neuroscience, 15,* 71–84.

Dickey, M. W., Choy, J. J., & Thompson, C. K. (2007). Real-time comprehension of wh-movement in aphasia: evidence from eyetracking while listening. *Brain and Language, 100,* 1–22.

Dickey, M. W., & Thompson, C. K. (2009). Automatic processing of wh- and NP-movement in agrammatic aphasia: Evidence from eyetracking. *Brain and Language, 99,* 8–219.

Dragoy, O., & Bastiaanse, R. (2009). Verb production and word order in Russian agrammatic speakers. *Aphasiology, 24,* 28–55.

Dronkers, N. F., Wilkins, D. P., Van Valin, R. D., Redfern, B. B., & Jaeger, J. J. (1994). A reconsideration of the brain areas involved in the disruption of morphosyntactic comprehension. *Brain and Language, 47,* 461–463.

Dronkers, N. F., Wilkins, D. P., Van Valin, R. D., Redfern, B. B., & Jaeger, J. J. (2004). Lesion analysis of the brain areas involved in language comprehension. *Cognition, 92,* 145–177.

Embick, D., Marantz, A., Miyashita, Y., O'Neil, W., & Sakai, K. L. (2000). A syntactic specialization for Broca's area. *Proceedings of National Academy of Sciences, 97,* 6150–6154.

Faroqi-Shah, Y., & Thompson, C. K. (2003). Effect of lexical cues on the production of active and passive sentences in Broca's and Wernicke's aphasia. *Brain and Language, 85,* 409–426.

Ferreira, F. (2000). Syntax in language production: An approach using tree-adjoining grammars. In L. Wheeldon (Ed.), *Aspects of language production* (pp. 291–330). Cambridge, MA: MIT Press.

Ferreira, V. S., & Slevc, R. (2007). Grammatical encoding. In M. Gareth Gaskell (Ed.), *The Oxford handbook of psycholinguistics* (pp. 453–470) Oxford, UK: Oxford University Press.

Ferretti, T. R., McRae, K., & Hatherell, A. (2001). Integrating verbs, situation schemas, and thematic role concepts. *Journal of Memory and Language, 44,* 516–547.

Fiebach, C. J., Schlesewsky, M., & Friederici, A. D. (2001). Syntactic working memory and the establishment of filler-gap dependencies: Insight from ERPs and fMRI. *Journal of Psycholinguistic Research, 30,* 321–338.

Fiebach, C. J., Schlesewsky, M., Lohmann, G., von Cramon, D. Y., & Friederici, A. D. (2005). Revisiting the role of Broca's area in sentence processing: Syntactic integration versus syntactic working memory. *Human Brain Mapping, 24,* 79–91.

Frazier, L., & Clifton, C. (1989). Successive cyclicity in the grammar and the parser. *Language and Cognitive Processes, 4,* 93–126.

Friederici, A. D. (1995). The time course of syntactic activation during language processing: A model based on neuro-psychological and neurophysiological data. *Brain and Language, 50,* 259–281.

Friederici, A. D. (2002). Towards a neural basis of auditory sentence processing. *Trends in Cognitive Sciences, 6,* 78–84.

Friederici A. D. (2006). The neural basis of language development and its impairment. *Neuron, 52,* 941–952.

Friederici, A. D., Bahlmann, J., Heim, S., Schubotz, R. I., & Anwander, A. (2006). The brain differentiates human and non-human grammars: Functional localization and structural connectivity. *Proceedings of National Academy of Sciences, 103,* 2458–2463.

Friederici, A. D., Fiebach, C. J., Schlesewsky, M., Bornkessel, I. D., & von Cramon, D. Y. (2006). Processing linguistic complexity and grammaticality in the left frontal cortex. *Cerebral Cortex, 16,* 1709–1717.

Friederici, A. D., & Frisch, S. (2000). Verb argument structure processing: The role of verb-specific and argument-specific information. *Journal of Memory and Language, 43,* 476–507.

Friederici, A. D., Hahne, A., & Mecklinger, A. (1996). Temporal structure of syntactic parsing: Early and late event-related brain potential effects. *Journal of Experimental Psychology: Learning, Memory, and Cognition, 22,* 1219–1248.

Friederici, A. D., Hahne, A., & von Cramon, D. Y. (1998). First-pass versus second-pass parsing processes in a Wernicke's and a Broca's aphasics: Electrophysiological evidence for double dissociation. *Brain and Language, 62,* 311–341.

Friederici, A. D., & Kotz, S. A. (2003). The brain basis of syntactic processes: Functional imaging and lesion studies. *NeuroImage, 20,* S8–S17.

Friederici, A. D., Makuuchi, M., & Bahlmann, J. (2009). The role of the posterior superior temporal cortex in sentence comprehension. *NeuroReport, 20,* 563–568.

Friederici, A. D., & Meyer, M. (2004). The brain knows the difference: Two types of grammatical violations. *Brain Research, 1000,* 72–77.

Friederici, A. D., & Meyer, M., & von Cramon, D. Y. (2000). Auditory language comprehension: An event related fMRI study on the processing of syntactic and lexical information. *Brain and Language, 74,* 289–300.

Friederici, A. D., Pfeifer, E., & Hahne, A. (1993). Event-related brain potentials during natural speech processing: Effects of semantic, morphological and syntactic violations. *Cognitive Brain Research, 1,* 183–192.

Friederici, A. D., Ruschemeyer, S. A., Hahne, A., & Fiebach, C. J. (2003). The role of left temporal inferior frontal and superior temporal cortex in sentence comprehension: Localizing syntactic and semantic processes. *Cerebral Cortex, 13,* 170–177.

Friederici, A. D., Wang, Y., Herrmann, C. S., Maess, B., & Oertel, U. (2000). Localization of early syntactic processes in frontal and temporal cortical areas: A magnetoencephalographic study. *Human Brain Mapping, 11,* 1–11.

Friedmann, N., Taranto, G., Shapiro, L. P., & Swinney, D. (2008). The leaf fell (the leaf): The online processing of unaccusatives. *Linguistic Inquiry, 39,* 355–377.

Frisch, S., Hahne, A., & Friederici, A. D. (2004). Word category and verb-argument structure information in the dynamics of parsing. *Cognition, 91,* 191–219.

Frisch, S., Kotz, S. A., von Cramon, D. Y., & Friederici, A. D. (2003). Why the P600 is not just P300: The role of the basal ganglia. *Clinical Neurophysiology, 114,* 336–340.

Frisch, S., & Schlesewsky, M. (2001). The N400 reflects problems of thematic hierarchizing, *Neurophysiology, 12,* 3391–3394.

Gabrieli, J. D. E., Poldrack, R. A., & Desmond, J. E. (1998). The role of left prefrontal cortex in language and memory. *Proceedings of National Academy of Sciences, 95,* 906–913.

Garrett, M. F. 1976. Syntactic processes in sentence production. In R. J. Wales & E. C. T. Walker (Eds.), *New approaches to language mechanisms* (pp. 231–255). Amsterdam: North-Holland Publishing.

Garrett, M. F. (1982). Production of speech: Observations from normal and pathological language use. In A. W. Ellis (Ed.), *Normality and pathology in cognitive functions* (pp. 19–76). London, Academic Press.

Garrett, M. F. (1988). Processes in language production. In F. J. Newmeyer (Ed.), *The Cambridge survey of linguistics, language: Psychological and biological aspects* (vol. *3*, pp. 69–96). Cambridge: Harvard University Press.

Goldberg, A. E. (1995) *Constructions: A construction grammar approach to argument structure*. Chicago: ChicagoUniversity Press.

Goldberg, A. E. (2003). Constructions: A new theoretical approach to language. *Trends in Cognitive Sciences, 7*, 219–224.

Griffin, Z. M., & Bock, J. K. (2000). What they eyes say about speaking. *Psychological Science, 11*, 274–279.

Grodzinsky, Y. (2000). The neurology of syntax: Language use without Broca's area. *Behavioural Brain Science, 23*, 1–17.

Grodzinsky, Y., & Finkel, L. (1998). The neurology of empty categories aphasics' failure to detect ungrammaticality. *Journal of Cognitive Neuroscience, 10*, 281–292.

Grodzinsky, Y., & Friederici, A. D. (2006). Neuroimaging of syntax and syntactic processing. *Current Opinion in Neurobiology, 16*, 240–246.

Gunter, Th. C., Stowe. L. A., & Mulder, G. (1997). When syntax meets semantics. *Psychophysiology, 36*, 126–137.

Hadar, U., Palti, D., & Hendler, T. (2002). The cortical correlates of verb processing: Recent neuroimaging studies. *Brain and Language, 83*, 175–176.

Hagoort, P. (2003). How the brain solves the binding problem for language: A neurocomputational model of syntactic processing. *NeuroImage, 20*, S18–S29.

Hagoort, P., & Brown, C. M. (2000). ERP effects of listening to speech compared to reading: The P600/SPS to syntactic violations in spoken sentences and rapid serial visual presentation. *Neuropsychologia, 38*, 1531–1549.

Hagoort, P., Wassenaar, M., & Brown, C. M. (2003a). Syntax-related ERP effects in Dutch. *Cognitive Brain Research, 16*, 38–50.

Hagoort, P., Wassenaar, M., & Brown, C. M. (2003b). Real-time semantic compensation in patients with agrammatic comprehension: Electrophysiological evidence for multiple-route plasticity. *Proceedings of the National Academy of Sciences, 100*, 4340–4345.

Hahne, A., & Jescheniak, J. D. (2001). What's left if the Jabberwock gets the semantics? An ERP investigation into semantic and syntactic processes during auditory sentence comprehension. *Cognitive Brain Research, 11*, 199–212.

Halgren, E., Dhond, R. P., Christensen, N., Van Patten, C., Marinkovic, K., Lewine, J. D., & Dale, A. M. (2002). N400-like magnetoencephalography responses modulated by semantic context, word frequency, and lexical class in sentences. *NeuroImage, 17*, 1101–1116.

Helenius, P., Salmelin, R., Service, E., & Connolly, J. F. (1998). Distinct time courses of word and context comprehension in the let temporal cortex. *Brain, 121*, 1133–1142.

Humphries, C., Binder, J., Medler, D., & Liebenthal, E. (2006). Syntactic and semantic modulation of neural activity during auditory sentence comprehension. *Journal of Cognitive Neuroscience, 18*, 665–679.

Humphries, C., Willard, K., Buchsbaum, B., & Hickok, G. (2001). Role of anterior temporal cortex in auditory sentence comprehension: An fMRI study. *NeuroReport, 12*, 1749–1752.

Indefrey, P., & Levelt, W. J. M. (2004). The spatial and temporal signatures of word production components. *Cognition, 92*, 101–144.

Jonkers, R., & Bastiaanse, R. (1996). The influence of instrumentality and transitivity on action naming in Broca's and anomic aphasia. *Brain and Language, 55*, 50–53.

Jonkers, R., & Bastiaanse, R. (1998). How selective are selective word class deficits? Two cases of action and object naming. *Aphasiology, 12*, 245–256.

Just, M. A., Carpenter, P. A., Keller, T. A., Eddy, W. F., & Thulborn, K. R. (1996). Brain activation modulated by sentence comprehension. *Science, 274*, 114–116.

Kaan, E., Harris, A., Gibson, E., & Holcomb, P. (2000). The P600 as an index of syntactic integration difficulty. *Language and Cognitive Processes, 15*, 159–201.

Kaan, E., & Swaab, T. Y. (2002). The brain circuitry of syntactic comprehension. *Trends in Cognitive Sciences, 6*, 350–356.

Kaan, E., & Swaab, T. Y. (2003). Repair, revision, and complexity in syntactic analysis: An electrophysiological differentiation. *Journal of Cognitive Neuroscience, 15*, 98–110.

Kempen, G., & Huijbers, P. (1983). The lexicalization process in sentence production and naming: Indirect election of words. *Cognition, 14* (2), 185–209.

Kielar, A., & Joanisse, M. F. (2010). Graded effects of regularity in language revealed by N400 indices of morphological priming. *Journal of Cognitive Neuroscience, 22*, 1373–1398.

Kielar, A., Meltzer-Aascher, A., & Thompson, C. K. (2012). Electrophysiological responses to argument structure violations in healthy adults and individuals with agrammatic aphasia. *Neuropsychologia, 50*, 3320–3337

Kim, M., & Thompson, C. K. (2000). Patterns of comprehension and production of nouns and verbs in agrammatism: Implication for lexical organization. *Brain and Language, 74*, 1–25.

Kim, M., & Thompson, C. K. (2004). Verb deficits in Alzheimer's disease and agrammatism: Implications for lexical organization. *Brain and Language, 88*, 1–20.

Kubota, M., Ferrari, P., Roberts, T. P. L., (2003). Magnetoencephalography detection of early syntactic processes in humans: Comparison between L1 speakers and L2 learners. *Neuroscience Letters, 353*, 107–110.

Kutas, M., & Federmeier, K. D. (2000). Electrophysiology reveals semantic memory use in language comprehension. *Trends in Cognitive Sciences, 4*, 463–470.

Kutas, M., & Hillyard, S. A. (1980). Reading senseless sentences: Brain potentials reflect semantic incongruity. *Science, 207*, 203–205.

Kutas, M., & Hillyard, S. A. (1983). Event-related brain potentials to grammatical errors and semantic anomalies. *Memory and Cognition, 11*, 539–550.

Kutas, M., & Hillyard, S. A. (1984). Brain potentials during reading reflect word expectancy and semantic association. *Nature, 307*, 161–163.

Lee, J. (2011). Time course of grammatical encoding in agrammatism (Unpublished doctoral dissertation). Northwestern University, Chicago.

Lee, J., Mack, J., & Thompson, C. K. (2012). Verbal morphology in agrammatic and anomic aphasia: Comparison of structured vs. narrative elicitation tasks. Paper presented at the Clinical Aphasiology Conference, May 20–25.

Lee, J., & Thompson, C. K. (2011b). Real-time production of arguments and adjuncts in normal and agrammatic speakers. *Language and Cognitive Processes, 26* (8), 985–1021.

Levelt, W. (1989). *Speaking: From intention to articulation.* Cambridge, MA: MIT press.

Levelt, W. (1999). Models of word production. *Trends in Cognitive Science, 3,* 223–232.

Levelt, W. J. M., Roelofs, A., & Meyer, A. S. (1999). A theory of lexical access in speech production. *Behavioral & Brain Sciences, 22,* 1–75.

Luzzatti, C., Raggi, R., Zonca, G., Pistarini, C., Contardi, A., & Pinna, G. D. (2002). Verb-noun double dissociation in aphasic lexical impairments: The role of word frequency and imageability. *Brain and Language, 81,* 432–444.

MacDonald, M. C., Pearlmutter, N. J., & Seidenberg, M. S. (1994). Lexical nature of syntactic ambiguity resolution. *Psychological Review, 101,* 676–703.

Makuuchi, M., Bahlmann, J., Anwander, A., & Friederici, A. D. (2009). Segregating the core computational faculty of human language from working memory. *Proceedings of National Academy of Sciences, 106,* 8362–8367.

Marslen-Wilson, W. D., & Tyler, L. K. (1980). The temporal structure of spoken language understanding. *Cognition, 8,* 1–71.

Mazoyer, B. M., Tzourio, N., Frak, V., Syrota, A., Murayama, N., Levrier, O., Salamon, G.,…Mehler, J. (1993). The cortical representation of speech. *Journal of Cognitive Neuroscience, 5,* 467–479.

McCann, C., & Edwards, S. (2002). Verb problems in fluent aphasia. *Brain and Language, 83,* 42–44.

Meltzer-Asscher, A., Schuchard, J., den Ouden, D. D., & Thompson, C. K. (In press). The neural substrates of complex argument structure representations: Processing 'alternating transitivity' verbs. *Language and Cognitive Processes.*

Meyer, M., Friederici, A. D., & von Cramon, D. Y. (2000). Neurocognition of auditory sentence comprehension: Event related fMRI reveals sensitivity to syntactic violations and task demands. *Cognitive Brain Research, 9,* 19–33.

Miceli, G., Silveri, M. C., Villa, G., & Caramazza, A. (1984). On the basis of agrammatic's difficulty in producing main verbs. *Cortex, 20,* 207–220.

Münte, T. F., Heinze, H. J., & Mangun, G. R. (1993). Dissociation of brain activity related to syntactic and semantic aspects of language. *Journal of Cognitive Neuroscience, 5,* 335–344.

Münte, T. F., Matzke, M., & Johannes, S. (1997). Brain activity associated with syntactic incongruences in words and pseudo-words. *Journal of Cognitive Neuroscience, 9,* 318–329.

Münte, T. F., Say, T., Clahsen, H., Schiltz, K., & Kutas, M. (1999). Decomposition of morphologically complex words in English: Evidence from event related potentials. *Cognitive Brain Research, 7,* 241–253.

Neville, H., Nicol, J. L., Barss, A., Forster, K. I., & Garrett, M. F. (1991). Syntactically based sentence processing classes: Evidence from event-related brain potentials. *Journal of Cognitive Neuroscience, 3,* 151–165.

Newman, S. D., Just, M. D., Keller, T. A., Roth, J., & Carpenter, P. A. (2003). Differential effects of syntactic and semantic processing on the subregion of Broca's area. *Cognitive Brain Research, 16,* 297–307.

Ni, W., Constable, R. T., Mencl, W. E., Pugh, K. R., Fulbright, R. K., Shaywitz, S. E., Shaywitz, B. A.,…Shankweiler, D. (2000). An event related neuroimaging study distinguishing form and content in sentence processing. *Journal of Cognitive Neuroscience, 12,* 120–133.

Osterhout, L., & Holcomb, P. J. (1992). Event-related brain potentials elicited by syntactic anomaly. *Journal of Memory and Language, 31,* 785–806.

Osterhout, L., Holcomb, P. J., & Swinney, D. A. (1994). Brain potentials elicited by garden-path sentences: Evidence of the application of verb information during parsing. *Journal of Experimental Psychology: Learning, Memory, and Cognition, 20,* 786–803.

Osterhout, L., & Mobley, L. A. (1995). Event-related brain potentials elicited by failure to agree. *Journal of Memory and Language, 34,* 739–773.

Osterhout, L., & Nicol, J. (1999). On the distinctiveness, independence, and time course of the brain responses to syntactic and semantic anomalies. *Language and Cognitive Processes, 14,* 283–317.

Palti, D., Ben-Shachar, M., Hendler, T., & Hadar, U. (2007). The cortical correlates of grammatical category differences: An fMRI study of nouns and verbs. *Human Bain Mapping, 28,* 303–314.

Penke, M., Weyerts, H., Gross, M., Zander, E., M€unte, T. F., & Clahsen, H. (1997). How the brain processes complex words: An event-related potentials study of German verb inflection. *Cognitive Brain Research, 6,* 37–52.

Rösler, F., Putz, P., Friederici, A., & Hahne, A. (1993). Event-related brain potentials while encountering semantic and syntactic constraint violations. *Journal of Cognitive Neuroscience, 5,* 345–362.

Saffran, E. M., Schwartz, M. F., & Marin, O. S. M. (1980). The word order problem in agrammatization: II. Production. *Brain and Language, 10,* 263–280.

Schriefers, H., Teruel, E., & Meinshausen, M. (1998). Producing simple sentences: Results from picture-word interference experiments. *Journal of Memory and Language, 39,* 609–632.

Service, E., Helenius, P., Maury, S., & Salmelin, R. (2007). Localization of syntactic and semantic brain responses using magnetoencephalography, *Journal of Cognitive Neuroscience, 19,* 1193–11205.

Shapiro, L. P., Brookins, B., Gordon, B., & Nagel, N. (1991). Verb effects during sentence processing. *Journal of Experimental Psychology, 17,* 983–996.

Shapiro, L. P., Gordon, B., Hack, N., & Killackey, J. (1993). Verb-argument structure processing in complex sentences in Broca's and Wernicke's aphasia. *Brain and Language, 45,* 423–447.

Shapiro, L. P., & Levine, B. (1990). Verb processing during sentence comprehension in aphasia. *Brain and Language, 38,* 21–47.

Shetreet, E., Palti, D., Friedmann, N., & Hadar, U. (2007). Cortical representation of verbs processing in sentence comprehension: Number of complements, subcategorization, and thematic frames. *Cerebral Cortex, 17,* 1958–1969.

Spieler, D. H., & Griffin, Z. M. (2006). The influence of age on the time course of word preparation in multiword utterances. *Language and Cognitive Processes, 21,* 291–321.

Stowe, L. A., Broere, C. A. J., Paans, A. M. J., Wijers, A. A., Mulder, G., Vaalburg, W., & Zwarts, F. (1998). Localizing components of a complex task: Sentence processing and working memory. *NeuroReport, 9,* 2995–2999.

Stromswold, K., Caplan, D., Alpert, N., & Rauch, S. (1996). Localization of syntactic comprehension by positron emission tomography. *Brain and Language, 52,* 452–473.

Swaab, T., Brown, C., & Hagoort, P. (1997). Spoken sentence comprehension in aphasia: Event-related potential evidence for a lexical integration deficit. *Journal of Cognitive Neuroscience, 9,* 39–66.

Swinney, D., & Zurif, E. (1995). Syntactic processing in aphasia. *Brain and Language, 50,* 225–239.

Swinney, D., Zurif, E., Prather, P., & Love, T. (1996). Neurological distribution of processing resources underlying language comprehension. *Journal of Cognitive Neuroscience, 8,* 174–184.

Thompson, C. K. (2003). Unaccusative verb production in agrammatic aphasia: The argument structure complexity hypothesis. *Journal of Neurolinguistics, 16,* 151–167.

Thompson, C. K., Bonakdarpour, B., Fix, S. F., Blumenfeld, H. K., Parrish, T. B., & Gitelman, D. R. (2007). Neural correlates of verb argument structure processing. *Journal of Cognitive Neuroscience, 19,* 1753–1767.

Thompson C. K., & Choy, J. J. (2009). Pronominal resolution and gap-filling in agrammatic aphasia: Evidence from eye movement. *Journal of Psycholinguistic Research, 38,* 255–283.

Thompson C. K., den Ouden, D. B., Bonakdarpour, B., Garibaldi, K., & Parrish, T. B. (2010). Neural plasticity and treatment-induced recovery of sentence processing in agrammatism. *Neuropsychologia, 48,* 1–17.

Thompson, C. K., Dickey, W., Cho, S., Lee, J., & Griffin, Z. (2007). Verb argument structure encoding during sentence production in agrammatic aphasic speakers: An eye-tracking study. *Brian and Language, 103*(8), 24–26.

Thompson, C. K., Kielar, A., & Fix, S. (2012). Morphological aspects of agrammatic aphasia. In R. Bastiaanse & C. K. Thompson (Eds.), *Perspectives on agrammatism* (pp. 75–105). London: Psychology Press.

Thompson, C. K., Lange, K. L., Schneider, S. L., & Shapiro, L. P. (1997). Agrammatic and non-brain-damaged subjects' verb and verb argument structure production. *Aphasiology, 11,* 473–490.

Thompson, C. K., Meltzer-Asscher, A., Cho, S., Lee, J., Wieneke, C., Weintraub, S., & Mesulam, M. M. (2013). Syntactic and morphosyntactic processing in stroke-induced and primary progressive aphasia. *Behavioral Neurology, 26,* 35–54.

Thompson, C. K., & Shah, Y. (2002). Models of sentence production. In A. E. Hillis (Ed.), *Handbook of adult language disorders: Integrating cognitive neuropsychology, neurology and rehabilitation* (pp. 311–330). Philadelphia, PA: Psychology Press. Taylor & Francis Group.

Thompson, C. K., Shapiro, L. P., Tait, M. E., Jacobs, B., Schneider, S., & Ballard, K. (l995). A system for the linguistic analysis of agrammatic language production. *Brain and Language, 51,* 124–129.

Thompson-Shrill, S. L., D'Esposito, M., Aguirre, G. K., & Farah, M. J. (1997). Role of left inferior prefrontal cortex in retrieval of semantic knowledge: A reevaluation. *Proceedings of National Academy of Sciences, 94,* 14792–14797.

Thompson-Schill, S. L., D'Esposito, M., & Kan, I. P. (1999). Effects of repetition and competition on activity in left prefrontal cortex during word generation. *Neuron, 23,* 513–522.

Trueswell, J. C., & Kim, A. E. (1998). How to prune a garden-path by nipping it in the bud: Fast priming of verb argument structure. *Journal of Memory and Language, 39,* 102–123.

Trueswell, J. C., Tannenhaus, M. K., & Kello, C. (1993). Verb-specific constrains in sentence processing: Separating lexical preferences from garden-paths. *Journal of Experimental Psychology: Learning, Memory, and Cognition, 19,* 528–553.

van den Brink, D., & Hagoort, P. (2004). The influence of semantic and syntactic context constrains on lexical selection and integration in spoken-word comprehension as revealed by ERPs. *Journal of Cognitive Neuroscience, 16,* 1068–1084.

Vanier, M., & Caplan, D. (1990). CT correlates of agrammatism. In L. O. L. Menn & H. Goodglassa (Eds.), *A cross-language study of agrammatism* (pp. 97–114). New York: Benjamin.

von Stockert, T. R., & Bader, L. (1976). Some relations of grammar and lexicon in aphasia. *Cortex, 12,* 49–60.

Wartenburger, I., Heekeren, H. R., Burchert, F., Heinemann, S., De Bleser, R., & Villringer, A. (2004). Neural correlates of syntactic transformations. *Human Brain Mapping, 22,* 72–81.

Wassenaar, M., Brown, C. M., & Hagoort, P. (2004). ERP effects of subject-verb agreement violations in patients with Broca's aphasia. *Journal of Cognitive Neurosceince, 16,* 553–576.

Wassenaar, M., & Hagoort, P. (2007). Thematic role assignment in patients with Broca's aphasia: Sentence-picture matching electrified. *Neuropsychologia, 45,* 716–740.

Waters, G., Caplan, D., Alpert, N., & Stanczak, L. (2003). Individual differences in rCBF correlates of syntactic processing in sentence comprehension: Effects of working memory and speed of processing. *NeuroImage, 19,* 101–112.

Wilson, S. M., & Saygin, A. P. (2004). Grammatical judgment in aphasia: Deficits are not specific to specific syntactic structures, aphasic syndromes, or lesion sites. *Journal of Cognitive Neuroscience, 16,* 238–252.

Wu, D. H., Waller, S., & Chatterjee, A. (2007). The functional neuroanatomy of thematic role and locative relational knowledge. *Journal of Cognitive Neuroscience, 19,* 1542–1555.

Zingeser, L. B., & Berndt, R. S. (1990). Retrieval of nouns and verbs in agrammatism and anomia. *Brain and Language, 39,* 14 32.

Zurif, E., Swinney, D., Prather, P., Solomon, J., & Bushell, C. (1993). On-line analysis of syntactic processing in Broca's and Wernicke's aphasia. *Brain and Language, 45,* 448–464.

Computational Models of Sentence Production: A Dual-Path Approach

Franklin Chang *and* Hartmut Fitz

Abstract

Sentence production involves the complex interaction of meanings, words, and structures. These interactions are language-specific and to understand them, it is useful to build computational models of production that learn their internal representations. This chapter explores how a particular connectionist-learning model called the Dual-path model explains a range of sentence production behaviors, such as structural priming, heavy NP shift, and lexical-conceptual accessibility in structural choice. The model shows how learning can play an important role in explaining adult processing in different languages. This model is contrasted with other computational approaches to understand the strengths and weakness of each method.

Key Words: sentence processing, connectionism, incremental production, learning, structural priming

Talk is cheap. At least that is what we are told when action is required. But how do we do the action of talking? Is it as easy as the idiom suggests? Talking requires that we make decisions about words and structures. For example, if we find a big bag that belongs to Kris, we might say "Kris carries a big bag." Or, we could have also said, "she always has her bag" or "that bag is owned by Kris." To produce these sentences, we need to select language-specific words (e.g., "Kris" or "she") and structures (e.g., active, passive), and ensure that these elements are accessed in time and are appropriate for each other (we cannot say "that bag is owned by she"). The rules for ordering these elements are also language-specific. In Japanese, we could convey similar meanings as above with the utterances "kurisu wa kaban wo motte itta," "kaban wo kurisu ga motte itta," or "kaban wo motte itta." Are the same mechanisms used in English and Japanese? Or does learning a language change the way the sentence production system works? The goal of sentence production research is to explain how we make these language-specific word and structure choices, and how these separate decisions are integrated in time to create utterances.

To understand the complex interaction of factors in sentence production, researchers have developed computational models (Dell, 1986; Dell, Chang, & Griffin, 1999; Dijkstra & de Smedt, 1996). These models make explicit how different representations interact in the construction of sentences. As in other sciences, model building does not aim at replicating the complexity of the natural world, but focuses on simplifying a very complex mechanism into a system that can be understood. This simplification function of models can be seen in three broad approaches that have been taken in building models.

The first approach, which we call the *representational approach*, uses formal representations to embody the key features of the model. An influential exemplar of this group is the incremental procedural grammar developed by Kempen and Hoenkamp (1987). They developed a grammatical formalism that provided a way to build structures incrementally. In their account, meanings activated lexical entries called lemmas and these lemmas carried structural information. Combining the structural information from different lemmas allowed partial syntactic structures to be built. Thus, tightly linking lexical selection and structural choices provides a way to build trees incrementally and many representational theories have adopted similar structure-building mechanisms (e.g., tree-adjoining grammar; Ferreira, 2000).

The second group of models, which we call the *empiricist approach*, argues that behavior is strongly guided by statistical relationships in the linguistic environment (Bresnan, Cueni, Nikitina, & Baayen, 2004; Chang, Lieven, & Tomasello, 2008; Gries, 2005; Jaeger & Snider, 2007; Kempen & Harbusch, 2004). These modelers collect statistical data from labeled corpora and use those data to evaluate the fit of different models. Although formal representations are used in these models, representations are selected based on their ability to fit the data and hence these models have a weaker commitment to their representations compared with the representational approach. Those that take the empiricist approach are interested in demonstrating how probabilistic and distributional information in the input can help to explain production behavior and how abstract computational principles can provide deeper insight into the nature of the human language system.

The third approach, which we call the *brain systems approach*, assumes that the properties of the sentence production system are partially caused by the properties of the neural systems that implement them. One example of this approach is by Gordon and Dell (2003), who developed a model of how semantic and syntactic information interact in word selection in sentence production. Their model had separate pathways, one for linking conceptual semantics to words and another for linking syntactic categories to words, and this separation of pathways was inspired by evidence of double dissociations in the brain areas that support these types of knowledge in patients with aphasia. The brain systems approach looks for ways that brain organization and function can constrain models of language. This is in contrast to representational and empiricist models where neuropsychology does not strongly constrain modeling.

In this chapter we will examine the behavior of a particular model that takes the brain systems approach called the Dual-path model (Chang, 2002). This model provides an explicit account of a wide range of production phenomena, and hence it is a useful baseline for comparing different modeling approaches. By examining this account in detail and comparing it with other models, we can see how these three approaches differ in the models that they create. This chapter is organized into five sections. The first section on generalization motivates some of the basic choices made for the Dual-path model's architecture. The second section on structural priming provides evidence that adult priming behavior can be explained by the same learning mechanism that is used to explain language acquisition. The third section on word order in different languages provides evidence that the model can acquire different languages and explain differences in adult processing in those languages. The fourth section focuses on the production of complex sentences in development. In the conclusion, the strengths and weaknesses of the three different modeling approaches are compared.

Learning to Generalize in Production

As with the Gordon and Dell (2003) model, the Dual-path model assumes that the brain's neural processing mechanisms play an important role in language production. It represents its language knowledge within an artificial neural network and this knowledge is learned through a connectionist-learning algorithm, called back-propagation of error (Rumelhart, Hinton, & Williams, 1986). Activation spreads forward along links in the network with the strength of the activation modulated by weights associated with each link. This spreading activation generates an activation pattern on the output units that represents the model's expectations. Back-propagation assumes that the difference between these expectations and the actual input, which is called error, is used to change the weights in the network (similar to theories of classical conditioning; Rescorla & Wagner, 1972). By gradually adjusting its internal representations to encode the structure of the input, the model becomes better and better at reproducing the input. Although back-propagation has some features that are not neurally plausible, it is similar to neural systems in that it updates weights between neurons using only local information in adjacent neurons and learns by making small gradual changes that can approximate the biological growth processes that support plasticity in the brain (Klintsova & Greenough, 1999). In addition, back-propagation has been very successful at modeling a wide range of linguistic and nonlinguistic phenomena (e.g., Botvinick & Plaut, 2004; Cleeremans & McClelland, 1991; Oppenheim, Dell, & Schwartz, 2010; Plaut, McClelland, Seidenberg, & Patterson, 1996), which suggests that the algorithm can learn representations that resemble those in human brains.

Connectionist models of sequence learning often use an architecture called a simple recurrent network (SRN) in conjunction with back-propagation of error (Christiansen & Chater, 1999; Elman, 1990). SRNs predict the words in a sequence based on the previous word they receive as an input (Figure 4.1). In an SRN, the previous word input is linked to a hidden layer and then to the next word layer. In addition, the previous hidden layer activation is copied into a context layer (which functions as a memory buffer that enhances the ability to learn sequences) and this activation is fed back as input to the hidden layer at the next time step. The SRN learns how the previous word and the context representation could be used to predict the next word. The difference between the predicted next word and the actual next word is the error signal, and it is used to adjust the model's internal weights, so that in the future, the model is better able to predict the actual next word.

To allow this type of model to do production, Chang, Dell, Bock and Griffin (2000) augmented an SRN with a message (see also Dell et al., 1999). The message contained units that represented the combination of concepts and event roles, including a special role for the action (top part of Figure 4.1). For example, the sentence "The dog chased the cat" would have a message with three units: ACTION-CHASE, AGENT-DOG, PATIENT-CAT. When an SRN was augmented with this type of message, the resulting Prod-SRN could learn to generate sentences from meaning.

Analysis of the model revealed that it memorized the mapping between particular meanings and particular word sequences (Chang, 2002). This was because of the way that the model encoded the message. Because a single unit represented the binding of a role and concept (e.g., AGENT-DOG), the model could not use this unit to produce other agents or to produce the word "dog" in other event roles (e.g., PATIENT). Hence, a Prod-SRN that is trained with the message ACTION-CHASE, AGENT-DOG, PATIENT-CAT is able to produce the sentence "the dog chased the cat," but not the sentence "the cat chased the dog," from the message ACTION-CHASE, AGENT-CAT, PATIENT-DOG. This means that the model's syntactic knowledge did not have the property of systematicity, which is an important characteristic of human language syntax (Fodor & Pylyshyn, 1988; Hadley, 1994). The problem with the Prod-SRN was that the message did not have a separation between roles and concepts that would allow it to learn the right representations for mapping

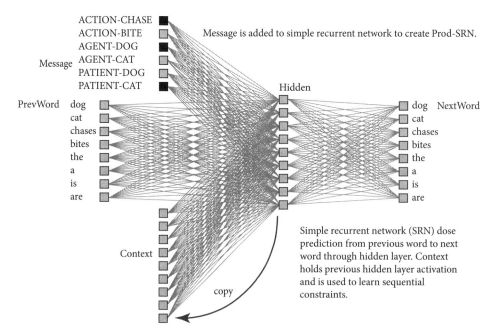

Figure 4.1 Architecture of Prod-SRN model.

novel role-concept pairings. This means that the Prod-SRN was unable to generalize in a human-like manner.

The Prod-SRN did not generalize because it used a binding-by-space representation where different neurons represented the same concept in different roles (AGENT-DOG vs. PATIENT-DOG). This is the standard approach for representing slot/filler relations in connectionist models (Miikkulainen, 1996; St. John & McClelland, 1990). Because these bindings were represented with individual units, these models had trouble learning separate regularities over slots and fillers (Chang, 2002; Fodor & Pylyshyn, 1988; Marcus, 1998). Computers, however, can distinguish variable slots and fillers, because filler identity is represented with a binary code and the code has the same meaning regardless of its memory location. If the binary code 1001 represents the concept DOG, then it still means DOG regardless if it is in a memory location for agents or patients. In neural systems, however, copying the neural activation for DOG from one location in the brain to any other location does not preserve the same DOG meaning. There are ways to achieve variable-binding in neural networks (Pollack, 1990; Shastri & Ajjanagadde, 1993), but it is not clear if these mechanisms can implement the extensive variable binding that is needed in most linguistic theories. In linguistic theories, a sentence could require the dynamic binding of multiple words, heads, nouns, verbs, clause elements, phrasal elements, gaps, traces, and event roles. If the mental states that support language require extensive variable binding and neural systems do not implement such variable binding mechanisms, then it is not clear how the syntactic mind can be implemented by the neural cells in the brain (a syntactic mind-body problem).

Chang (2002) asked whether it was possible to provide a connectionist account of the combinatorial nature of syntax by giving a model a limited variable-binding mechanism. In this model, which became the Dual-path model, the message was instantiated with temporary bindings between a layer for roles and a layer for concepts (in Figure 4.2, AGENT in the role layer has a link to DOG in the concept layer).

This binding mechanism for roles and concepts was assumed to be related to the brain's spatial processing mechanisms. It is known that the brain represents object and location/action information in different neural pathways and this information needs to be bound together for spatial processing (Goodale & Milner, 1992; Mishkin & Ungerleider, 1982). The model hypothesized that a fast variable-binding mechanism evolved for spatial processing and, when language arose in humans, this mechanism was adopted for linking roles to concepts in messages. The model provided a test of whether this limited set of message variables was sufficient to explain syntactic behavior, which is normally explained in representational theories with a much larger range of linguistic variables.

To take advantage of this fast binding message representation, the Dual-path architecture was developed. This architecture used an SRN with Compress layers between the Hidden layer and the

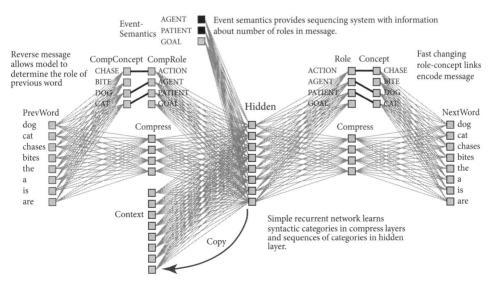

Figure 4.2 Architecture of Dual-path model.

PrevWord and NextWord layers (bottom half of Figure 4.2; Elman, 1993). The Compress layers had only a small number of units and therefore the hidden layer could only influence the production of words through a small number of categories (these come to act like syntactic categories, such as nouns or verbs). To allow the model to learn the mapping between concepts and words, the Concept layer was linked to the NextWord layer. The Hidden layer in the SRN was linked to the Role layer. Because the Role layer had temporary links to the concepts in the Concept layer, this Role-Concept-NextWord pathway could learn how to activate roles to ensure that message-appropriate words were produced (top right part of Figure 4.2).

This architecture allowed the model to generalize words to novel positions and even generalize a noun as a verb. For example, "friend" is a noun and might be learned from such sentences as "The mother called a friend" paired with a message like ACTION=CALL AGENT=MOTHER PATIENT=FRIEND (= represents a temporary variable binding). The Dual-path model would learn that the concept FRIEND maps to the word "friend" and this sentence would also strengthen its ability to sequence the roles in active transitive sentences (AGENT -> ACTION -> PATIENT). This knowledge is in a format that allows the model to generalize. For example, "friend" has recently become a verb that refers to the act of adding someone to your page in a social networking site (e.g., "reluctantly, he friended his mother"). If we assume that the concept FRIEND is bound to the ACTION variable, then when the ACTION role becomes activated in a transitive sequence, the model can produce the word "friend" as a novel verb.

Putting the message into role-concept variables that are inaccessible to the SRN sequencing system has the desirable outcome that the syntactic representations in the SRN are independent of lexical content. The SRN still needs to have some knowledge about the message to know which construction to select. This information is provided to the SRN through a layer called the event-semantics (top middle of Figure 4.2), which encodes the number and type of roles that are present in the message (e.g., one role for "the dog sleeps," two roles for "the girl chased the boy"). The activation of these units varied systematically with the structures in the input (e.g., AGENT might be less activated when a passive is to be produced) and the model could use this information to help select a structure when structural alternatives were available. Tense and aspect was also provided in the event-semantics, because this information was useful for planning the form of the verb.

With the role-concept message and the event-semantics, the model could learn different constructions with slots for each role. For example, in the active sentence "the dog chased the cat," the event-semantics would signal that there are two arguments (AGENT, PATIENT) and the model would learn that that event-semantics is associated with a sequence of role activations (AGENT -> ACTION -> PATIENT). However, two argument transitive utterances could also appear in the passive structure ("the cat is chased by the dog"). It has been found that the structural choice in this alternation is sensitive to the words that are in competition at the point where the structures diverge (the *choice point*). In the transitive alternation, the choice point is the subject noun phrase, where a speaker has to decide whether to say "dog" or "cat." If these words are made more available, then speakers are more likely to select structures that place these words earlier (Bock, 1986a; Bock & Irwin, 1980; McDonald, Bock, & Kelly, 1993).

To model this lexical sensitivity, a reverse message network was created by adding a CompConcept and CompRole layer (Figure 4.2, top left). The PrevWord layer was linked to the CompConcept layer and the CompRole layer was linked to the Hidden layer in the SRN. The CompConcept and CompRole links contained a reverse copy of the message. With this reverse network, the word that was produced at the choice point (e.g., "cat") could be mapped to its concept (e.g., CAT) and then to its role (e.g., PATIENT). This role information was then passed to the hidden layer where it combined with the event-semantics information (e.g., two arguments) and the information about the position in the sentence from the context (e.g., sentence-initial position). The model learned that activating the PATIENT role at this position with two arguments is associated with passive structures and therefore it would begin the production of this structure. Thus, even if the model was initially planning to produce an active sentence, lexical priming of "cat" could lead to the production of a passive.

An important feature of the model is the input language that the "child" model was trained on. The Dual-path model was trained on message-sentence pairs from an artificial language. The language had several types of verbs, such as intransitive, transitive, and dative verbs ("sleep," "hit," "give," respectively) and several structural alternations, such as active/

passive transitive, and double object/prepositional dative. Although connectionist models can be trained on real corpora, it is computationally intensive to train them with a large vocabulary, because each word requires its own input/output node (a localist representation) and this leads to a large number of weights that have to be adjusted in training. When an SRN learns syntactic categories, it learns to activate a set of word units that belong to that category, so the localist representation of words is critical for these models to exhibit syntactic knowledge (a distributed output representation would not allow the SRN to activate the multiple members of each category). In addition, because corpora do not always provide information about meaning, it is difficult to use real corpora with models that require meaning input. Empiricist approaches, in contrast, often use statistical regularities from real corpora, but they reduce the computational load by only modeling particular structural decisions rather than the whole process of mapping meaning into word sequences (Bresnan et al., 2004). Thus, the complexity of sentence production can be reduced either by simplifying the production model or the language used.

To determine if the architectural assumptions of the Dual-path model allowed it to capture human syntactic behavior better than the Prod-SRN model, Chang (2002) examined the generalization ability of both models in three experiments. The first experiment asked whether the models could generalize the word "dog" to goal positions in dative sentence (e.g., "the man gave **the dog** the bone"). This was done by restricting the model's input environment so that dog could occur in different roles, but not in the goal role. Then the models were given messages with "dog" in the goal role (ACTION=GIVE AGENT=MAN PATIENT=BONE **GOAL=DOG**) and the models were tested on whether they could correctly produce a sentence with "dog" in that position. An utterance was counted correct if it matched the target utterance word for word. The Dual-path model produced 82 percent correct *dog-goal* utterances, whereas the Prod-SRN only produced 6 percent (Figure 4.3). The Prod-SRN never trained the DOG-GOAL unit, so it was unable to generalize. But the Dual-path model separately learned to sequence the GOAL role and produce "dog" when the DOG concept was activated. Thus, when the GOAL role was linked to the DOG concept, the model was able to generalize appropriately.

Another test involved the identity construction (e.g., "a blicket was a blicket"; Marcus, 1998), where the model must generalize a novel word to two sentence positions. In training, only a subset of the possible nouns in the lexicon appeared in this construction and the remaining nouns were used for testing. The Dual-path model produced 88 percent of these novel utterances, whereas the Prod-SRN produced only 3 percent (Figure 4.3). A final generalization test used novel adjective-noun pairs. In training, one subset of adjectives was paired with animate nouns (e.g., "happy boy") and the other subset was unrestricted by animacy (e.g., "good cake"). Messages were created that bound animate adjectives with inanimate nouns (e.g., "happy cake"). When the two models were given these messages, the Dual-path model produced 73 percent of these novel adjective-noun phrases, whereas the Prod-SRN produced only 2 percent (Figure 4.3). For these three types of generalization, the Dual-path model performed better than the Prod-SRN and therefore it provides a closer match to human syntactic behavior.

The Dual-path model was able to generalize words to novel positions, and this ability was caused by the fact that syntactic knowledge in the SRN was independent of the lexical content in the message. This separation of lexicon and syntax was

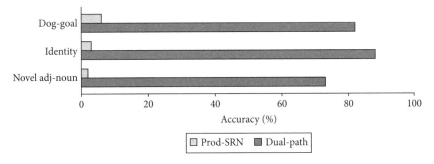

Figure 4.3 Generalization in Prod-SRN and Dual-path models. Adapted from Chang, F. (2002). Symbolically speaking: A connectionist model of sentence production. *Cognitive Science, 26*(5), 609–651.

needed to ensure that abstract syntax was learned in the model. However, representational models often have built-in abstract language-specific syntactic structures and they often advocate a tight linking of syntax and lexicon (Reitter, Keller, & Moore, 2011). It seems clear that there should be a link between the two (Ferreira, 1996), but this link needs to be weak enough to allow nouns to be used as verbs (e.g., "I friended my mother"; Clark & Clark, 1979) or verbs to be used in novel constructions (e.g., "I sneezed the napkin across the table"; Goldberg, 1995). The learning of how verbs pair with particular structures is an important challenge for all theories of syntactic development and use (e.g., Baker's paradox; Baker, 1979; Chang, 2002).

Structural Priming

Syntactic knowledge of language includes word order constraints across different structures. For example, both transitives and datives can appear in passive forms (e.g., "the dog was chased by the cat," "the books were given by the man to the girl"). In addition, in English, verbs agree in number with their subjects for intransitive, transitive, and dative structures. These examples suggest that syntactic representations are shared across constructions and work in structural priming has provided experimental evidence for these links.

Structural priming is a tendency to reuse previously heard syntactic structures (Bock, 1986b; Pickering & Ferreira, 2008). For example, if participants hear a prime sentence that uses the prepositional dative structure (e.g., "the man gave the car to the church"), they are more likely to use the same structure to describe a picture (e.g., "the children showed the picture to their teacher") than if they had heard a prime sentence in the double object dative structure ("the man gave the church the car"). Priming has been found between structures that have different roles and different function words, and this has been used to argue that priming involves an abstract structural representation that is shared across different constructions.

An important feature for understanding the mechanism behind structural priming is the duration of the effect. One mechanism that has been proposed to explain priming is residual activation on nodes that are used for planning structures (Pickering & Branigan, 1998). For example, hearing a prepositional dative prime could change the residual activation of an NP-PP structure node (say from an activation level of 0.2 to 0.3). If the node for the alternative double object NP-NP structure

was activated at 0.25, then the speaker would be more likely to choose the prepositional dative structure after this prime (0.3 > 0.25). Because activation is used for structural planning at various sentence positions, it is necessary for activation to dissipate quickly to allow the system to produce other words or structures. Therefore, an activation-based account predicts that priming dissipates quickly.

An alternative to this account of priming is the idea that priming is caused by learning. In this approach, learning strengthens the representations of the structure and these changes could persist in the system. To test this, Bock and Griffin (2000) separated the prime and target by 10 intervening filler sentences and they found that priming persisted over the processing of these fillers. The magnitude of priming was the same when there were 10 intervening sentences as when there were none; this finding supported a learning-based account.

The persistence of priming suggested that long-term adaptation processes were taking place in adult speakers. One possibility is that these long-term changes in adults were caused by the same learning processes that were used to learn the language initially (Chang, Dell, & Bock, 2006). Error-based learning in SRNs has been used to explain how adults learn and adapt to input sequences in various domains (Cleeremans & McClelland, 1991) and therefore these models might be able to explain structural priming in terms of adaptation.

Chang, Dell, and Bock (2006) examined whether error-based learning within the Dual-path architecture could model the persistence of priming. The model was first trained to map between meanings and English sentences. Once it had acquired the language, it was tested for priming by presenting the prime sentence with learning turned on. Thus, the prime sentence was treated the same way as the input sentences that the model had experienced to learn the language in the first place. For both dative and transitive prime-target pairs, the model processed a prime followed by 10 intransitive filler sentences with learning on, and then it was given a target message to produce. The model was more likely to describe the target message using the same structure as the prime and therefore it exhibited priming (see Bock & Griffin, 2000; Figure 4.4). Importantly, the magnitude of priming was the same regardless of the number of fillers, which suggests that immediate and long-term priming could be explained by a single mechanism.

The model assumes that error is generated during the prediction of the prime as it is comprehended.

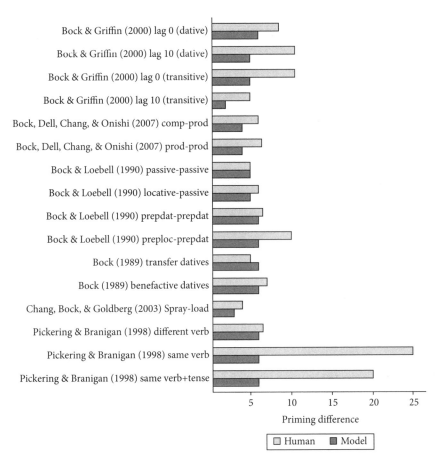

Figure 4.4 Structural priming in humans and Dual-path model. Adapted from Chang, F., Dell, G. S., & Bock, K. (2006). Becoming syntactic. *Psychological Review, 113*(2), 234–272.

Thus, priming should be similar when primes are only comprehended and when they are produced. Support for this hypothesis was found in Bock, Dell, Chang, and Onishi (2007), where priming persisted when primes were only comprehended and when they were comprehended and produced (Figure 4.4). Although it is clear that production representations must be learned from comprehended input, the model does not predict that comprehension-to-comprehension priming has the same properties. This is because comprehension of meaning requires a way to map from structures to meaning, and the next word prediction mechanism in the model does not naturally explain how this mapping is trained. Experimental work has found comprehension-to-comprehension priming in eye-tracking, but it seems to have different timing properties from priming in production (Arai, van Gompel, & Scheepers, 2007; Thothathiri & Snedeker, 2008a, 2008b).

Structural priming has provided evidence that the syntactic representations that support production are abstract, in that they do not seem to depend on overlap in event-roles or in function words. For example, Bock and Loebell (1990) examined whether the description of transitive pictures (e.g., "the postman was chased by the dog," "the dog chased the postman") would be primed by locative primes like "the 747 was landing by the control tower," passive primes like "the 747 was alerted by the control tower," and active control sentences like "the 747 radioed the control tower." If priming was caused by the order of agent and patient, then passives should prime differently from locatives, because only the passive has the same roles as the transitive. However, if priming was caused by the surface syntactic structure, then it is possible that passive and locatives would prime similarly, because both have a similar sequence of surface categories (something like DET NOUN AUX VERB PREP DET NOUN). In fact, they found that locatives and passives primed passives equally well relative to active primes. When the Dual-path model was tested with stimuli like those in this study, there was no difference in the magnitude of priming from locatives and passives (see Bock & Loebell, 1990; Locative/Passive-Passive in Figure 4.4). Similar results were found for prepositional dative structures like "the wealthy widow gave the Mercedes to the church" and prepositional locative structures like "the wealthy widow drove the Mercedes to the church") even though the "church" is a goal in the dative and a location in the locative. The model can reproduce these results (see Bock & Lobell, 1990, Preploc/Prepdat-Prepdat in Figure 4.4). Therefore as with humans, the model learned internal representations that encoded surface structural similarity between constructions with different meanings and structural priming in adults can be explained with error-based learning in an SRN.

Although locatives and passives shared similar surface orders, they also both used the word "by" and it is possible that priming was caused by the overlap in this function word. To examine whether function word overlap could influence priming, Bock (1989) tested whether the description of transfer dative pictures (e.g., "the girl gave the man the paintbrush," "the girl gave the paintbrush to the man") could be influenced by overlap in a function word in the prime. She compared benefactive dative primes that use the preposition "for" (e.g., "the cheerleader saved a seat for her boyfriend") with transfer dative primes that use the preposition "to" (e.g., "the cheerleader offered a seat to her friend"). She found that the amount of priming for prepositional dative primes relative to double object primes was the same for both transfer and benefactive datives, even though the benefactive dative uses a preposition that differs from the one in the transfer dative. This result suggested that priming was not simply caused by function word overlap, a finding that is difficult to explain in lexicalized accounts of priming (Reitter et al., 2011). When the Dual-path model was tested on such stimuli, there was no difference in the magnitude of priming from to-datives and for-datives (see Bock, 1989; Figure 4.4). Therefore, the model's syntactic representations are independent of function words and morphological overlap. Although priming is insensitive to function word overlap, it can be magnified by verb or noun overlap between prime and target (Cleland & Pickering, 2003; Pickering & Branigan, 1998). Because it also occurs without any lexical overlap, the minimal requirement for priming is structural similarity between prime and target.

In general, structural priming studies support the idea that syntactic representations are separable from the meaning representations that control them. Is this separation between meaning and structure universal or does it depend on the structure being tested? In a study that speaks to this issue, Chang, Bock, and Goldberg (2003) found that the choice of structure in the theme-location alternation (e.g., theme-location "the maid rubbed polish onto the table," location-theme "the maid rubbed the table with polish") could be primed by utterances that had the same order of event roles. Because the two orders in this alternation have similar sequences of syntactic categories (e.g., VERB NP PP), the fact that the order of theme and location influences priming shows that meaning is encoded in syntactic representations for this construction. The Dual-path model provides an error-based learning account of this result (see Chang et al., 2003; Spray-load in Figure 4.4). Initially, the SRN has a tendency to learn syntactic categories, because it does not have direct access to the message. Sequencing representations made of syntactic categories are sufficient to distinguish active and passive, but not the structures in the theme-location alternation because both are made up of the same sequence of syntactic categories. This generates error in learning and the model is forced to reorganize its representations to distinguish theme-location from location-theme structures by marking the order of roles in the syntax for this alternation. Thus, in contrast to representational theories that require syntactic knowledge to be of a consistent type across constructions (e.g., Ferreira, 2000), models that learn their syntactic representations can allow some constructions to be made up of abstract categories (e.g., passive), whereas others incorporate thematic roles (e.g., theme-location).

To understand how the model implements locative-passive priming, the hidden layer representations were analyzed. Connectionist models are often thought to make use of distributed representations, where knowledge is encoded by multiple units. Therefore, it is possible that the similarity between locatives and passives in structure would be distributed over multiple hidden units. In actuality, it was often the case that only one hidden unit was involved in locative-passive priming. One reason for this is that the model is trying to reduce error over all of the structures in the training corpus and hence it must organize the hidden units to best deal with the diverse structures in the input. This creates pressure to isolate each structural type to a small set of hidden units. Hence, the model suggests that abstractness of structural priming arises from the need to learn a large set of structures within a limited representational space.

The Dual-path model can account for a wide variety of priming effects, but does it make any predictions? One prediction arises from the model's error-based learning mechanism. If the prime is different from the utterance that the model expects, then error should be large and this should predict greater priming. Bernolet and Hartsuiker (2010) examined this prediction by looking at whether structural priming was influenced by verb bias. Verb bias is a tendency for particular verbs to be paired with particular structures, a bias that can influence sentence processing (Garnsey, Pearlmutter, Myers, & Lotocky, 1997; Wilson & Garnsey, 2009). Bernolet and Hartsuiker found that priming was greater when the verb's structural bias and the prime structure mismatched, supporting the idea that priming is caused by error-based learning. Jaeger and Snider (2007) offer an empiricist account of structural priming that can explain these effects. They argue that priming reflects the principles of surprisal and cumulativity. Surprisal measures how unexpected words or structures are given previous information. Cumulativity represents the idea that the effect of each prime structure accumulates within the language system. This model makes similar predictions to the Dual-path model, because surprisal can be implemented with error-driven learning and cumulativity can be implemented with gradual accumulation of knowledge in the weights in a neural network.

Another prediction of the Dual-path model arises from the assumption that learning is instantiated by physical changes in the connectivity of neurons and hence learning must take place slowly. This assumption is implemented by setting a parameter that controls the rate of learning in the model to a small value. A small learning rate is also behaviorally important for the encoding of frequency in the model. Each training episode makes a small change to the model's weights, so frequent episodes are better represented in the model's weights than infrequent ones. For example, if the verb "give" appears in a double object structure (e.g., "give him a book") more often than the prepositional dative structure (e.g., "give a book to him"), then the weights between "give" and animate noun phrases like "him" have been changed by a large number of training events and this can create verb-structure regularities (see Chang, 2002 for evidence that the Dual-path model learns verb-structure associations in acquisition).

A small learning rate means that the Dual-path model cannot explain large magnitude priming effects. One example of a large effect is the lexical boost, where priming is increased when prime and target share a verb or a noun (Pickering & Branigan, 1998). Sometimes this boost can create priming effects that are huge (73 percent priming; Hartsuiker, Bernolet, Schoonbaert, Speybroeck, & Vanderelst, 2008). If the lexical boost was caused by learning, then these large changes caused by priming would be making large changes to the speaker's language system and it would even be possible for structures to be primed out of existence (catastrophic interference; McCloskey & Cohen, 1989). These theoretical issues and the fact that the model did not exhibit a lexical boost (see Pickering & Branigan, 1998; Same Verb line in Figure 4.4) led Chang et al. (2006) to suggest that the lexical boost was caused by a different short-lived mechanism and the prediction of this Dual-mechanism account has been confirmed experimentally. Hartsuiker et al. (2008) found that the lexical boost dissipates quickly, whereas structure-based priming persists longer. Further evidence comes from acquisition, where Rowland, Chang, Ambridge, Pine, and Lieven (2011) found that abstract structural priming had a similar magnitude in 3- to 4-year-old children, 5- to 6-year-old children, and adults, but the lexical boost grew over development. Bringing these results together, Chang, Janciauskas, and Fitz (2012) argued that the slow and fast learning in complementary memory systems accounts of cortical and hippocampal learning provides a unified way of explaining both the large magnitude of the lexical boost and its variability over delay and development.

Word Order in Different Languages

The Dual-path model's account of syntactic generalization and priming suggests that it has the right properties for explaining English syntactic behavior. However, a language production system needs to be able to explain behavior in different languages, particularly those that are typologically different from English (Evans & Levinson, 2009; Jaeger & Norcliffe, 2009). Japanese differs from English in many ways. Japanese verbs occur at the ends of clauses, whereas English verbs tend to occur early in sentences. Japanese speakers can omit all arguments of a verb, where English speakers are required to use pronouns. For example, the English sentence "I gave it to them" could be expressed by the Japanese verb "ageta," because the arguments of the verb can often be inferred from the context. Also, whereas

English has structural alternations like active and passive, Japanese speakers typically convey similar changes with scrambling of case-marked arguments ("I gave the book to the man" can be conveyed by the canonical "otoko-ni hon-o ageta" or scrambled as "hon-o otoko-ni ageta"). Because the Dual-path model is an account of how syntax is acquired, it is necessary to test it on typologically different languages to see if it can acquire different languages to the same degree (Chang et al., 2008).

To test the model, English and Japanese versions of the Dual-path model were created (Chang, 2009). Both models were given the same messages, but the sentences paired with the messages differed in verb position, argument omission, and scrambling in accordance with the language being learned. When tested on a novel set of message-sentence pairs, both models were able to show similarly high levels of accuracy (grammatical output: English model 93%, Japanese model 95%). Grammaticality was measured by labeling the model's output with syntactic categories and seeing if the produced sequence was in the set of sequences derived by labeling the model's input with syntactic categories. Although the message-sentence mapping in these two languages was quite different, the model was able to learn both languages equally fast.

A cross-linguistic model of production should also be able to explain differences in production biases between these languages. One such cross-linguistic difference comes from a phenomenon called heavy NP shift (Arnold, Losongco, Wasow, & Ginstrom, 2000; Hawkins, 1994, 2004; Ross, 1967). English speakers have a tendency to prefer configurations where long phrases are placed later in sentences. For example, speakers might change the sentence "the man gave the woman that he met last week the book" into "the man gave the book to the woman that he met last week," where the long phrase "the woman that he met last week" is at the end of the sentence. Although English speakers have a short-before-long bias, Japanese speakers have a

long-before-short bias (Hawkins, 1994; Yamashita & Chang, 2001). A theory of sentence production needs to explain these cross-linguistic differences.

To examine the Dual-path model's heavy NP shift behavior, it was given dative messages where the patient or recipient phrase was made longer by modifying it with a relative clause (Chang, 2009). The model then produced the utterances and the order of short and long phrases was examined. The English version produced more recipient-before-patient orders when the patient was long than when the recipient was long (e.g., long patient "a man gave a girl a telephone that a dog touched" versus long recipient "a man gave a girl that a dog touched a telephone"). The Japanese model produced more recipient-before-patient orders when the recipient was long than when the patient was long. The model data are shown in Figure 4.5 (the Japanese human data come from the dative items in Yamashita & Chang, 2001, and the English human data were created by averaging the values in Figure 8 of Arnold, et al. 2000). The results show that the model can exhibit the English short-before-long and the Japanese long-before-short pattern.

Analysis of the model's internal representations suggested that heavy NP shift behavior was caused by a difference in the relative importance of meaning and surface structural information in the two languages at the choice point where the two word orders diverge. In English, the choice point was after the verb and at that point, the model tended to use structural cues, such as the fact that short-before-long utterances are more similar to simple main clause structures than long-before-short utterances. For example, the simple utterance "a man gave a girl a telephone" is more similar to the long patient utterance "a man gave a girl a telephone that a dog touched" than it is to the corresponding long recipient utterance "a man gave a girl that a dog touched a telephone" and therefore the high frequency of simple main clauses in the input could bias the model toward the short-before-long utterance.

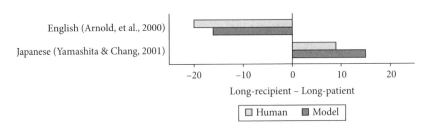

Figure 4.5 Heavy NP shift in English and Japanese in humans and Dual-path model (difference in use of recipient-before-patient order when recipient is long vs. when patient is long).

In Japanese, however, the choice point is at the beginning of the sentence, and at this position, it is difficult to use structural cues, because in Japanese the verb occurs late in the sentence and early structural configurations are highly variable because of argument omission and scrambling. Therefore, the Japanese model preferred to use meaning information at this position. Because the message signals that a relative clause should be produced and the model has learned that relative clauses go before their heads in Japanese, the model often prefers to start with a relative clause and that creates a long-before-short order.

Empiricist models have also addressed heavy NP shift by including phrase weight as a factor in predicting English word order (Arnold et al., 2000; Bresnan et al., 2004), but these models have not been extended to Japanese. One question with these models is the stability of the parameters across different corpora or languages. If a similar model was built from Japanese data, would it have similar parameters to the English models? It is crucial to determine which aspects of these models are universal and which are language- or corpus-dependent.

Another important phenomenon that differs between English and Japanese is lexical/conceptual accessibility. Accessible words are words that are easier to produce in naming studies. Many studies have found that English speakers tend to place accessible words early in sentences and this sometimes requires later changes in the structure to maintain the same meaning. For example, McDonald, Bock, and Kelly (1993) found that participants preferred to put animate elements early in transitive sentences and this sometimes required them to use a generally dispreferred structure like a passive (e.g., "the students were frightened by the sound"). However, when the same manipulation was done with conjunctions (e.g., "the manager and the key," "the key and the manager"), they found that animacy did not influence the word order. This difference seemed to align with the distinction between functional and positional levels in production theories (Garrett, 1988). Active and passive structures differ in the element that is assigned to the subject function and this assignment takes place at the functional level in the theory. The elements in conjunctions are assigned to the same syntactic function and the ordering of these two noun phrases takes place at the positional level. Therefore, the behavioral difference between transitives and conjunctions suggested that conceptual factors like animacy can have an influence on the functional but not on the positional level

(similar results for other factors have been found, such as imageability; Bock & Warren, 1985).

Although the functional/positional distinction has been useful for explaining results in English, it is a bit problematic for explaining behavior in Japanese. Syntactic functions in Japanese are signaled by case markers and the same case markers are used regardless of whether canonical or scrambled order is produced (e.g., "John eats rice" could be said in canonical order as "John-ga gohan-o taberu" or scrambled order as "gohan-o John-ga taberu"). Scrambling does not change syntactic functions and therefore it should be a positional-level effect. This would predict that conceptual factors do not influence scrambling in Japanese, but in fact it has been found that animacy and discourse status can influence Japanese scrambling (Ferreira & Yoshita, 2003; Tanaka, Branigan, McLean, & Pickering, 2011). To further complicate things, Tanaka et al. (2011) found that animacy does not influence the order of elements in Japanese conjunctions, which is similar to the behavior in English. Thus, production behavior for transitives and conjunctions differs in similar ways in English and Japanese, but in Japanese this distinction is difficult to explain in terms of functional and positional processing

Chang (2009) provided an alternative to the functional/positional account using the Dual-path model. One component of this account is to explain how lexical accessibility can influence structural choice or scrambling. The model has a reverse message system that maps from the previously produced word to its concept and then to its role in the particular message that is being expressed. For example, if a person started a sentence with "dog" and the dog was the patient in a transitive event, then the model could use the information in the PrevWord-CompConcept-CompRole system to produce a passive structure. Given this feature of the architecture, any factor that makes a word more likely to be produced early can influence the model's structural choices and this influence will be felt regardless of whether the language uses syntactic function assignment or scrambling to make these words prominent.

Because the Dual-path model learns its internal representations from input utterances, the prominence of words must be learned from the mapping of words to sentence positions. By giving the model input where animate words tended to occur earlier in sentences than inanimate elements, the model learned stronger weights from animate concepts to animate words and this made them more prominent. The learned prominence of words and the reverse word-role system can work together to create the accessibility-sensitive nature of structure selection in English and Japanese transitives.

If animacy can influence word order, why does it not influence the order of words in conjunctions? The data in McDonald et al. (1993) provide a clue as to why conjunctions were different from transitives. They gave participants utterances to recall and then examined how often they recalled the original order. What is interesting is that the participants rarely switched the order of words in conjunctions. To explain this, Chang (2009) argued that the model could use the activation of the units in the event-semantics to guide the word order that was produced. However, because the influence of the event-semantics was learned, effective use of this information required that both orders were trained equally often and this seems to be the case for conjunctions. Although the event-semantics also signaled word order for transitives, the low frequency

of structures like English passives or scrambled Japanese utterances made it hard for the model to use this information and therefore it was more likely to switch the structure in response to other factors, such as animacy. Thus in this account, learning plays an important role in explaining the difference between transitives and conjunctions in their sensitivity to animacy.

When given input with appropriate prominence and frequency information, the Dual-path model was able to reproduce the overall pattern of the human behavioral data (Figure 4.6). In the English model, passives were likely to switch to actives and these switches were sensitive to animacy. Meanwhile, the Japanese model was also likely to switch scrambled transitives back to the unscrambled version and the switch was also sensitive to animacy. Animacy had little effect on conjunctions, because in both languages the model rarely switched the order of nouns. Therefore, the Dual-path model's learning algorithm was

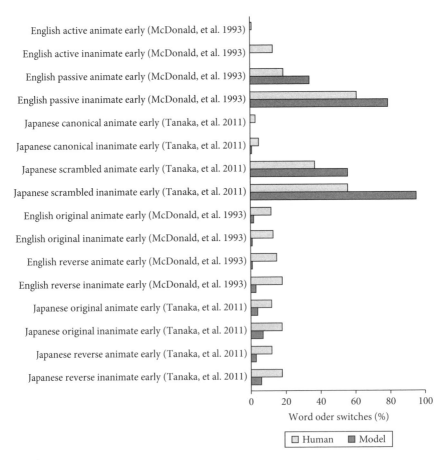

Figure 4.6 Accessibility in English and Japanese in humans and Dual-path model. Adapted from Chang, F. (2009). Learning to order words: A connectionist model of heavy NP shift and accessibility effects in Japanese and English. *Journal of Memory and Language,* *61*(3), 374–397.

| COMPUTATIONAL MODELS OF SENTENCE PRODUCTION

dependent on distributional regularities and meaning in a way that simulated the difference between transitives and conjunctions. Without an architectural functional/positional distinction, the model nonetheless could explain the behavioral data that support this distinction.

The brain systems approach, as implemented with the Dual-path model, allows us to separate out aspects of production that are universal (e.g., architecture, learning algorithm) from the parts that are learned. The Dual-path model was able to learn English-like and Japanese-like languages equally well and it provides an explicit account of word ordering differences in these two languages. It is possible to build representational models for typologically different languages, but this sometimes requires changes to the formalism (e.g., scrambling in tree-adjoining grammar; Rambow & Lee, 1994). Empiricist approaches can also be applied to different languages, as long as similar tagged corpora exist in each language. More work is needed to disentangle the parameters in the model that are just caused by fitting a corpus and those that reflect the underlying nature of production.

Production of Complex Syntax

In the previous section we saw that the Dual-path model could produce relative clauses. Relative clauses are theoretically important because they are a syntactic device that makes language structurally productive and they create long-distance dependencies between words. In the sentence "the dog that the cat chased loves the girl," the main clause verb "loves" has to agree in number with the subject "dog" and this dependency spans the relative clause (Bock & Cutting, 1992). Relative clause constructions, such as the one above, have also been characterized as an instance of recursion where a transitive structure is embedded within itself and it has been argued that recursion is universal, innate, and uniquely human (Hauser, Chomsky, & Fitch, 2002, but see Evans & Levinson, 2009, for an alternative view). Several studies have explored the learnability of recursive languages with SRN-type models (Cartling, 2008; Christiansen & Chater, 1999; Elman, 1993). An important aspect of recursion that has not been examined in great detail, however, is the role of meaning (or the message) in the generation of these utterances. For example, in the above sentence, "dog" is the subject and agent of the main clause verb "love," but also the fronted object and patient of the embedded clause verb "chased." If meaning helps to support recursion, then we can examine its influence within the Dual-path production model.

English relative clauses can be distinguished based on verb type and the grammatical function of the head noun in the relative clause. In S-relatives, for example, the relative clause has an intransitive verb and the head noun is the subject (e.g., "the boy that _ runs"; the underscore indicates the canonical position of the head noun "boy" in the relative clause). When the verb is transitive, the head noun can be the relative clause subject, as in "the boy that _ chased the dog" (A-relative), or the direct object, as in "the cat that the dog chased _" (P-relative). With dative verbs, three constituents can be relativized (e.g., the indirect object as in "the girl who the boy gave the apple to _"; IO-relative). The final type considered here is the case where the relative clause verb is intransitive and the head noun is an oblique argument as in "the boy who the girl played with _" (OBL-relative).

Diessel and Tomasello (2005) conducted an elicited production study with English and German children age 4;3 to 4;9, where subjects had to repeat sentences from an experimenter. They found that children were able to reproduce S-relatives the best, followed by A-relatives, then P-relatives, and finally OBL-relatives and IO-relatives (Figure 4.7). This order of acquisition also resembled results from adult production (Keenan & Hawkins, 1987), suggesting that the sources of difficulty might be similar for adults and children. A version of the Dual-path model was developed that could generate utterances with relative clauses (Fitz, 2009). The model had a message with multiple propositions and there were special units in the event-semantics that signaled the coreference of roles (similar to the message in Chang, 2009). During learning, the model was periodically tested on the structures used by Diessel and Tomasello (2005). In these structures, the five relative clause types defined previously were attached to a presentational main clause (e.g., "There is the boy that the dog was chasing"). The model eventually learned to produce all structures with more than 90 percent accuracy at the end of training.

It was found that early in development the model's behavior approximated the child data (Figure 4.7). S-relatives were easier than A- or P-relatives, because S-relatives are unambiguous about which element is relativized — there is only one participant in intransitive events. Transitive utterances, however, can relativize either the subordinate clause subject or object and this ambiguity increases the difficulty in producing the A- or P-relatives. Another

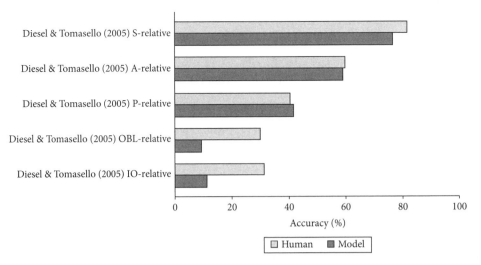

Figure 4.7 Elicited production of relative clauses in children and the Dual-path model. Adapted from Fitz, H., & Chang, F. (2008). The role of the input in a connectionist account of the accessibility hierarchy in development. In H. Chan, H. Jacob, & E. Kapia (Eds.), *Proceedings of the Boston University conference on language development* (Vol. 32, pp. 120–131). Somerville, MA: Cascadilla Press.

advantage of S-relatives over A- and P-relatives was that transitive relative clauses admitted passive alternations. Active and passive relative clauses had very similar messages in the event-semantics and the model had to learn both these structures over a single set of connection weights. This created competition between the syntactic alternations and complicated the meaning to form mapping for A- and P-relatives, but not for S-relatives. Transitive A-relatives were produced more accurately than the P-relatives, because A-relatives contained a sequence of surface syntactic categories that was shared with S-relatives (i.e., THAT VERB) and also occurred in subject-relativized obliques and datives (e.g., "that gave the toy to the dog"). For P-relatives this sequence was different (THAT ARTICLE NOUN VERB) and it was less frequent overall. Thus, although the Dual-path model was exposed to equal amounts of A- and P-relatives during learning, A-relatives had an advantage because of substructure overlap with other subject-relativized constructions in the input. The difference between P-relatives and OBL/IO-relatives was more complicated, but it was also caused in part by mapping and surface structure similarity. In summary, the Dual-path model was able to explain the performance ordering found in Diessel and Tomasello (2005) for English-speaking children, because the acquisition of each structure in the model depended on surface similarity, frequency, and the complexity of the mapping from meaning into utterances.

Representational and empiricist models have also been applied to explain differential processing of relative clause types. Hale (2006) was able to account for the Keenan and Hawkins (1987) adult data by using a word-prediction uncertainty mechanism based on a probabilistic grammar. This mechanism is similar to word-based error in SRNs, except that connectionist approaches suggest that uncertainty as error has value as a learning signal. The main difference between the Dual-path model and Hale's models is the fact that the Dual-path model learns syntactic representations that can be used in production. Hale's model depends on a particular set of English syntactic representations and those representations have not been integrated with theories of sentence production. Empiricist approaches have also correlated processing difficulty in adults and children with frequency of occurrence, especially for the subject/object relative clause asymmetry (Kidd, Brandt, Lieven, & Tomasello, 2007; Reali & Christiansen, 2007). Future work is needed to distinguish these different approaches to complex syntax.

Conclusion

This chapter focuses on the behavior of the Dual-path model, because it provides a unified account of several important phenomena in production: generalization, structural priming, heavy NP shift, accessibility, syntax acquisition, and recursion. Error-based learning explains both the model's ability to acquire internal syntactic representations and the persistence of structural priming. The Dual-path architecture helps to explain why structural priming can be abstract and why words can generalize to novel positions. When learning is combined with this incremental production architecture, the result is a model that can account for the behavioral differences in the production of word order in English and Japanese. The combination of meaning, incremental production, and learned substructure sequences allowed the model to explain the order of relative clause acquisition in children, providing foundations for a usage-based theory of recursion. Error-based learning and the Dual-path architecture provide an account of the aspects of production that are universal and make explicit the link between syntax acquisition and production.

There are many areas of language processing that need to be integrated with models of language production. One area of active research is the relationship between comprehension and production. Representational models of comprehension and production have argued for strong homologies between the two in representation and procedures (Kempen & Harbusch, 2002; Vosse & Kempen, 2000). Empiricist approaches have used similar mechanisms to explain data from both domains. For example, surprisal has been a useful construct for explaining comprehension parsing behavior (Frank, 2009; Hale, 2006; Levy, 2008) and for priming in production behavior (Jaeger & Snider, 2007). Surprisal is similar to error in the Dual-path model, and Chang et al. (2006) use prediction error to explain structural priming and to model preferential looking behavior in development, which suggests that aspects of comprehension can also be explained by this expectation-based mechanism. What needs to be clarified in the future is whether these surprisal/error effects reflect the parsing process itself or learning that takes place when we comprehend utterances.

It is clear from this chapter that there are deep similarities between representational, empiricist, and brain-system approaches. At the same time, these approaches have their own unique advantages and disadvantages. Representational theories can be formulated in a way that closely matches verbal theories. For example, Performance Grammar directly encodes the distinction between functional and positional levels (Kempen & Harbusch, 2002), and therefore it can explain English accessibility data. However, as seen previously, the same distinction does not provide a good explanation of accessibility effects in scrambling in Japanese and in these cases, the tight link between representations and theory can be a disadvantage. Empiricist approaches can be easily applied to different languages as long as

suitably labeled corpora are available. However, it can be difficult to determine which parameters in the model are fixed universal parts of the language processor and which can vary across corpora or languages. Therefore, one challenge for empiricist approaches is to create methods that allow them to make these distinctions.

One crucial feature of the brain systems approach is the importance of learning in explaining production behavior. Learning can help to explain variability between different structures in priming and variability across languages. However, the variability caused by learning can also lead to mismatches between verbal theories and the model (e.g., functional/positional distinction). It can be quite difficult to fit models with learned language representations to human data. For example, because the Dual-path model was not able to explain the lexical boost, Chang et al. (2006) were forced to posit that the lexical boost was caused by a separate mechanism and this prediction was confirmed experimentally. This suggests that the limitation of the neural mechanisms in the brain may provide important constraints on theorizing about human behavior and brain system modeling can expose these constraints. Regardless of the approach that is taken, researchers should try to develop coherent integrated models of sentence production. Unified models make stronger predictions that allow for comparison and falsification (Newell, 1994). More such models are needed. As they say, talk is cheap.

References

Arai, M., van Gompel, R. P. G., & Scheepers, C. (2007). Priming ditransitive structures in comprehension. *Cognitive Psychology, 54*(3), 218–250.

Arnold, J. E., Losongco, A., Wasow, T., & Ginstrom, R. (2000). Heaviness vs. newness: The effects of structural complexity and discourse status on constituent ordering. *Language, 76*(1), 28–55.

Baker, C. L. (1979). Syntactic theory and the projection problem. *Linguistic Inquiry, 10*(4), 533–581.

Bernolet, S., & Hartsuiker, R. J. (2010). Does verb bias modulate syntactic priming? *Cognition, 114*(3), 455–461.

Bock, K. (1986a). Meaning, sound, and syntax: Lexical priming in sentence production. *Journal of Experimental Psychology: Learning, Memory, and Cognition, 12*(4), 575–586.

Bock, K. (1986b). Syntactic persistence in language production. *Cognitive Psychology, 18*(3), 355–387.

Bock, K. (1989). Closed-class immanence in sentence production. *Cognition, 31*(2), 163–186.

Bock, K., & Cutting, J. C. (1992). Regulating mental energy: Performance units in language production. *Journal of Memory and Language, 31*(1), 99–127.

Bock, K., Dell, G. S., Chang, F., & Onishi, K. H. (2007). Persistent structural priming from language comprehension to language production. *Cognition, 104*(3), 437–458.

Bock, K., & Griffin, Z. M. (2000). The persistence of structural priming: Transient activation or implicit learning? *Journal of Experimental Psychology: General, 129*(2), 177–192.

Bock, K., & Irwin, D. E. (1980). Syntactic effects of information availability in sentence production. *Journal of Verbal Learning and Verbal Behavior, 19*(4), 467–484.

Bock, K., & Loebell, H. (1990). Framing sentences. *Cognition, 35*(1), 1–39.

Bock, K., & Warren, R. K. (1985). Conceptual accessibility and syntactic structure in sentence formulation. *Cognition, 21*(1), 47–67.

Botvinick, M., & Plaut, D. C. (2004). Doing without schema hierarchies: A recurrent connectionist approach to normal and impaired routine sequential action. *Psychological Review, 111*(2), 395–428.

Bresnan, J., Cueni, A., Nikitina, T., & Baayen, R. H. (2004). Predicting the dative alternation. In G. Bouma, I. Kraemer, & J. Zwarts (Eds.), *Cognitive foundations of interpretation* (pp. 69–94). Amsterdam: Royal Netherlands Academy of Science.

Cartling, B. (2008). On the implicit acquisition of a context-free grammar by a simple recurrent neural network. *Neurocomputing, 71*(7), 1527–1537.

Chang, F. (2002). Symbolically speaking: A connectionist model of sentence production. *Cognitive Science, 26*(5), 609–651.

Chang, F. (2009). Learning to order words: A connectionist model of heavy NP shift and accessibility effects in Japanese and English. *Journal of Memory and Language, 61*(3), 374–397.

Chang, F., Bock, K., & Goldberg, A. E. (2003). Can thematic roles leave traces of their places? *Cognition, 90*(1), 29–49.

Chang, F., Dell, G. S., & Bock, K. (2006). Becoming syntactic. *Psychological Review, 113*(2), 234–272.

Chang, F., Dell, G. S., Bock, J. K., & Griffin, Z. M. (2000). Structural priming as implicit learning: A comparison of models of sentence production. *Journal of Psycholinguistic Research, 29*(2), 217–230.

Chang, F., Janciauskas, M., & Fitz, H. (2012). Language adaptation and learning: Getting explicit about implicit learning. *Language and Linguistics Compass, 6*, 259–278.

Chang, F., Lieven, E., & Tomasello, M. (2008). Automatic evaluation of syntactic learners in typologically-different languages. *Cognitive Systems Research, 9*(3), 198–213.

Christiansen, M. H., & Chater, N. (1999). Toward a connectionist model of recursion in human linguistic performance. *Cognitive Science, 23*(2), 157–205.

Clark, E. V., & Clark, H. H. (1979). When nouns surface as verbs. *Language, 55*(4), 767–811.

Cleeremans, A., & McClelland, J. L. (1991). Learning the structure of event sequences. *Journal of Experimental Psychology: General, 120*(3), 235–253.

Cleland, A. A., & Pickering, M. J. (2003). The use of lexical and syntactic information in language production: Evidence from the priming of noun-phrase structure. *Journal of Memory and Language, 49*(2), 214–230.

Dell, G. S. (1986). A spreading-activation theory of retrieval in sentence production. *Psychological Review, 93*(3), 283–321.

Dell, G. S., Chang, F., & Griffin, Z. M. (1999). Connectionist models of language production: Lexical access and grammatical encoding. *Cognitive Science, 23*(4), 517–542.

Diessel, H., & Tomasello, M. (2005). A new look at the acquisition of relative clauses. *Language, 81*(4), 1–25.

Dijkstra, A., & de Smedt, K. (1996). *Computational psycholinguistics: AI and connectionist models of human language processing.* London: Taylor & Francis.

Elman, J. L. (1990). Finding structure in time. *Cognitive Science, 14*(2), 179–211.

Elman, J. L. (1993). Learning and development in neural networks: The importance of starting small. *Cognition, 48*(1), 71–99.

Evans, N., & Levinson, S. C. (2009). The myth of language universals: Language diversity and its importance for cognitive science. *Behavioral and Brain Sciences, 32*(5), 429–492.

Ferreira, V. S. (1996). Is it better to give than to donate? Syntactic flexibility in language production. *Journal of Memory and Language, 35*(5), 724–755.

Ferreira, F. (2000). Syntax in language production: An approach using tree-adjoining grammars. In L. Wheeldon (Ed.), *Aspects of language production* (pp. 291–330). Cambridge, MA: MIT Press.

Ferreira, V. S., & Yoshita, H. (2003). Given-new ordering effects on the production of scrambled sentences in Japanese. *Journal of Psycholinguistic Research, 32*(6), 669–692.

Fitz, H. (2009). *Neural syntax.* Amsterdam: University of Amsterdam. Institute for Logic, Language, and Computation dissertation series.

Fodor, J. A., & Pylyshyn, Z. W. (1988). Connectionism and cognitive architecture: A critical analysis. *Cognition, 28*(1–2), 3–71.

Frank, S. L. (2009). Surprisal-based comparison between a symbolic and a connectionist model of sentence processing. In N. A. Taatgen & H. van Rijn (Eds.), *Proceedings of the 31st annual conference of the cognitive science society* (pp. 1139– 1144). Austin, TX: Cognitive Science Society.

Garnsey, S. M., Pearlmutter, N. J., Myers, E., & Lotocky, M. A. (1997). The contributions of verb bias and plausibility to the comprehension of temporarily ambiguous sentences. *Journal of Memory and Language, 37*(1), 58–93.

Garrett, M. F. (1988). Processes in language production. In F. J. Newmeyer (Ed.), *Linguistics: The Cambridge survey, III. Language: Psychological and biological aspects* (pp. 69–96). Cambridge, UK: Cambridge University Press.

Goldberg, A. E. (1995). *Constructions: A construction grammar approach to argument structure.* Chicago: University of Chicago Press.

Goodale, M. A., & Milner, A. D. (1992). Separate visual pathways for perception and action. *Trends in Neurosciences, 15*(1), 20–25.

Gordon, J. K., & Dell, G. S. (2003). Learning to divide the labor: An account of deficits in light and heavy verb production. *Cognitive Science, 27*(1), 1–40.

Gries, S. T. (2005). Syntactic priming: A corpus-based approach. *Journal of Psycholinguistic Research, 34*(4), 365–399.

Hadley, R. F. (1994). Systematicity in connectionist language learning. *Mind & Language, 9*(3), 247–272.

Hale, J. (2006). Uncertainty about the rest of the sentence. *Cognitive Science, 30*(4), 643–672.

Hartsuiker, R. J., Bernolet, S., Schoonbaert, S., Speybroeck, S., & Vanderelst, D. (2008). Syntactic priming persists while the lexical boost decays: Evidence from written and spoken dialogue. *Journal of Memory and Language, 58*(2), 214–238.

Hauser, M. D., Chomsky, N., & Fitch, W. (2002). The faculty of language: What is it, who has it, and how did it evolve? *Science, 298*(5598), 1569–1579.

Hawkins, J. A. (1994). *A performance theory of order and constituency.* Cambridge, UK: Cambridge University Press.

Hawkins, J. A. (2004). *Efficiency and complexity in grammars.* New York: Oxford University Press.

Jaeger, T. F., & Norcliffe, E. J. (2009). The cross-linguistic study of sentence production. *Language and Linguistics Compass*, 3(4), 866–887.

Jaeger, T. F., & Snider, N. (2007). Implicit learning and syntactic persistence: Surprisal and cumulativity. *University of Rochester Working Papers in the Language Sciences*, 3(1), 26–44.

Keenan, E. L., & Hawkins, S. (1987). The psychological validity of the accessibility hierarchy. In E. L. Keenan (Ed.), *Universal grammar: 15 essays* (pp. 60–85). London: Croon Helm.

Kempen, G., & Harbusch, K. (2002). Performance Grammar: A declarative definition. *Language and Computers*, 45, 148–162.

Kempen, G., & Harbusch, K. (2004). Generating natural word orders in a semi–free word order language: Treebank-based linearization preferences for German. In A. Gelbukh (Ed.), *Computational linguistics and intelligent text processing* (pp. 350–354). Berlin: Springer.

Kempen, G., & Hoenkamp, E. (1987). An incremental procedural grammar for sentence formulation. *Cognitive Science*, 11(2), 201–258.

Kidd, E., Brandt, S., Lieven, E., & Tomasello, M. (2007). Object relatives made easy: A cross-linguistic comparison of the constraints influencing young children's processing of relative clauses. *Language and Cognitive Processes*, 22(6), 860–897.

Klintsova, A. Y., & Greenough, W. T. (1999). Synaptic plasticity in cortical systems. *Current Opinion in Neurobiology*, 9(2), 203–208.

Levy, R. (2008). Expectation-based syntactic comprehension. *Cognition*, 106(3), 1126–1177.

Marcus, G. F. (1998). Rethinking eliminative connectionism. *Cognitive Psychology*, 37(3), 243–282.

McCloskey, M., & Cohen, N. J. (1989). Catastrophic interference in connectionist networks: The sequential learning problem. In B. Ross (Ed.), *The psychology of learning and motivation: Advances in research and theory* (Vol. 24, pp. 109–165). San Diego, CA: Elsevier.

McDonald, J. L., Bock, J. K., & Kelly, M. H. (1993). Word and world order: Semantic, phonological, and metrical determinants of serial position. *Cognitive Psychology*, 25(2), 188–230.

Miikkulainen, R. (1996). Subsymbolic case-role analysis of sentences with embedded clauses. *Cognitive Science*, 20(1), 47–73.

Mishkin, M., & Ungerleider, L. G. (1982). Contribution of striate inputs to the visuospatial functions of parieto-preoccipital cortex in monkeys. *Behavioural Brain Research*, 6(1), 57–77.

Newell, A. (1994). *Unified theories of cognition*. Cambridge, MA: Harvard University Press.

Oppenheim, G. M., Dell, G. S., & Schwartz, M. F. (2010). The dark side of incremental learning: A model of cumulative semantic interference during lexical access in speech production. *Cognition*, 114(2), 227–252.

Pickering, M. J., & Branigan, H. P. (1998). The representation of verbs: Evidence from syntactic priming in language production. *Journal of Memory and Language*, 39(4), 633–651.

Pickering, M. J., & Ferreira, V. S. (2008). Structural priming: A critical review. *Psychological Bulletin*, 134(3), 427–459.

Plaut, D. C., McClelland, J. L., Seidenberg, M. S., & Patterson, K. (1996). Understanding normal and impaired word reading: Computational principles in quasi-regular domains. *Psychological Review*, 103(1), 56–115.

Pollack, J. B. (1990). Recursive distributed representations. *Artificial Intelligence*, 46(1), 77–105.

Rambow, O., & Lee, Y. S. (1994). Word order variation and tree adjoining grammar. *Computational Intelligence*, 10(4), 386–400.

Reali, F., & Christiansen, M. H. (2007). Processing of relative clauses is made easier by frequency of occurrence. *Journal of Memory and Language*, 57(1), 1–23.

Reitter, D., Keller, F., & Moore, J. D. (2011). A computational cognitive model of syntactic priming. *Cognitive Science*, 35(4), 587–637.

Rescorla, R. A., & Wagner, A. R. (1972). Variations in the effectiveness of reinforcement and nonreinforcement. In A. H. Black & W. F. Prokasy (Eds.), *Classical conditioning. II: Current research and theory*. New York: Appleton-Century-Crofts.

Ross, J. R. (1967). *Constraints on variables in syntax*. (Unpublished doctoral dissertation). MIT, Cambridge, MA.

Rowland, C., Chang, F., Ambridge, B., Pine, J. M., & Lieven, E. V. (2011). *The development of abstract syntax: Evidence from structural priming and the lexical boost*. Presented at the Conference on Architectures and Mechanisms for Language Processing, September 1–3, 2011, Paris.

Rumelhart, D. E., Hinton, G. E., & Williams, R. J. (1986). Learning representations by back-propagating errors. *Nature*, 323(6088), 533–536.

Shastri, L., & Ajjanagadde, V. (1993). From simple associations to systematic reasoning: A connectionist representation of rules, variables and dynamic bindings using temporal synchrony. *Behavioral and Brain Sciences*, 16(3), 417–451.

St. John, M. F., & McClelland, J. L. (1990). Learning and applying contextual constraints in sentence comprehension. *Artificial Intelligence*, 46(1–2), 217–257.

Tanaka, M. N., Branigan, H. P., McLean, J. F., & Pickering, M. J. (2011). Conceptual influences on word order and voice in sentence production: Evidence from Japanese. *Journal of Memory and Language*, 65(3), 318–330.

Thothathiri, M., & Snedeker, J. (2008a). Syntactic priming during language comprehension in three-and four-year-old children. *Journal of Memory and Language*, 58(2), 188–213.

Thothathiri, M., & Snedeker, J. (2008b). Give and take: Syntactic priming during spoken language comprehension. *Cognition*, 108(1), 51–68.

Vosse, T., & Kempen, G. (2000). Syntactic structure assembly in human parsing: A computational model based on competitive inhibition and a lexicalist grammar. *Cognition*, 75(2), 105–143.

Wilson, M. P., & Garnsey, S. M. (2009). Making simple sentences hard: Verb bias effects in simple direct object sentences. *Journal of Memory and Language*, 60(3), 368–392.

Yamashita, H., & Chang, F. (2001). "Long before short" preference in the production of a head-final language. *Cognition*, 81(2), B45–B55.

Word Production: Behavioral and Computational Considerations

Gary S. Dell, Nazbanou Nozari, *and* Gary M. Oppenheim

Abstract

Computational models of single-word production account fairly well for both errorful and errorfree production data. This chapter reviews influential models and argues that, through the models, the field has acquired a good understanding of the processing steps that occur when words are retrieved and spoken, and the role of cascading and interaction in those steps. Furthermore, the models clarify currently unresolved theoretical issues, such as the extent to which lexical selection is competitive, and the role of incremental learning in tuning the production system.

Key Words: computational models, lexical access, interactive activation, incremental learning, cascading, competitive selection, aphasia, speech errors

What happens when a person names a picture? To a first approximation, the answer to this question is uncontroversial. The speaker must identify the pictured object, determine that object's name, and say it. Putting it more formally, the production of a word in a task such as picture naming involves conceptualization, linguistic formulation, and articulation (Levelt, 1989). The controversy begins when we try to spell out these components in any detail. In this chapter, we discuss data that are informative about the linguistic formulation of single-word utterances, and focus on attempts to simulate its inner workings with computational models.

Behavioral Data for Word Production Models
Errors or Response Time?

For many production researchers, that is the question. Is word production best illuminated by the errors that the process generates, or by careful measurement of the time that it takes to correctly retrieve words while speaking? The field's Hamlet-like indecision on this issue reflects its

history. The first analyses of production from a psycholinguistic perspective were based on naturally occurring speech errors (e.g., MacKay, 1970; Nooteboom, 1969). Slips were viewed as a "window into linguistic processes [that] provides... the laboratory data needed in linguistics" (Fromkin, 1973, pp. 43–44). Natural errors can be divided into those in which whole meaningful units, such as words or morphemes, slip, and those in which the phonological parts of those units slip, thus echoing the fundamental duality of linguistic patterns: phonological units combine to make words and morphemes, and these then combine to make sentences. Slips can involve substitution ("knee" for "elbow," a word substitution); exchange ("lork yibrary" for "York library," a phonological exchange); shift; addition; or deletion of a linguistic unit or sequence of units. Moreover, errors are influenced by numerous linguistic, contextual, and psychological factors, even leaving aside potential "Freudian" influences on errors. The systematicity of the slip data provided the field with its first good look at the production process, and inspired its first true theory, that of

Garrett (1975). Moreover, error analyses led to the development of methods for generating slips in the laboratory (e.g., Baars, Motley, & MacKay, 1975), thus providing a degree of experimental control that was lacking in the natural error collections.

Speech errors show how the production process breaks down. But such data are limited by the tautological fact that a slip is the product of a system that, at that time, did *not* work correctly. Given this, perhaps normal production is better studied by measuring the properties of error-free, rather than erroneous, production. As Levelt, Roelofs, and Meyer (1999, p. 2) put it, "the ultimate test [of production models] cannot lie in how they account for infrequent derailments of the process but rather must lie in how they deal with the normal process itself." This perspective has led to many studies in which the response time to generate single-word utterances is measured. For example, picture naming times can be measured as a function of lexical variables, such as frequency (e.g., Oldfield & Wingfield, 1965). To fractionate the lexical-access process, though, researchers have enhanced naming tasks in several ways. An enhancement that is widely studied is the *picture-word interference paradigm* (Glaser & Düngelhoff, 1984; Schriefers, Meyer, & Levelt, 1990), in which a distractor word (either spoken or printed) is presented along with a target picture. The participant must name the picture as quickly as possible while ignoring the distractor. The distractor, which can be related in meaning or form to the picture's name, and can be presented at different times before or after the picture, affects the naming time. For example, a semantically related distractor presented closely before or at the same time as the picture will slow naming more than an unrelated distractor. There are several other response-time paradigms for studying single-word production, including *implicit priming* (e.g., Meyer, 1990); *blocked-cyclic naming* (e.g., Damian, Vigliocco, & Levelt, 2001); *symbol-cued naming* (e.g., Cholin, Levelt, & Schiller, 2006); *translation* (e.g., Jescheniak & Levelt, 1994); *repetitive recirculation* (e.g., O'Seaghdha, & Marin, 2000); and *multitask paradigms* in which the participant must do some other task in addition to naming a picture (e.g., Ferreira & Pashler, 2002). In all of these methods, the participant retrieves a target word from a cue that points to that word so effectively that error is unlikely, and the time to begin speaking is influenced by manipulation of the target's properties or the task context. The experimental procedures can get pretty complicated, but the payoff is that one can measure systematic differences in the time it takes to successfully produce the target.

Pathological Language Production

The error- versus reaction time (RT)-data debate becomes more pointed when language pathology is considered. Single-word production tasks, such as picture naming or auditory word repetition, are common clinical and research tools for aphasia. Moreover, some of the most important theories of single-word production rely on data from speakers with production deficits (e.g., Caramazza, 1997; Rapp & Goldrick, 2000). These theories, like the speech-error based theories of production, are based on the probability and the form of production errors; that is, they are based on episodes in which production failed in some way. On top of this, though, the production systems that generated these errors are themselves impaired. So, if the goal is to understand successful production, then the data from aphasic speakers suffer from a double whammy, at least from the perspective of researchers who focus on response times for correct productions.

The neuropsychological community has long been concerned by the fact that their data consist of erroneous responses generated by damaged brains. Consequently, theorists in this area have developed guidelines for inference from impairment patterns to conclusions about the unimpaired system, guidelines that they continue to debate and refine (e.g., Caramazza, 1984; Harley, 2004). Nonetheless, those who question the empirical value of slips made by unimpaired speakers have even more reason to be skeptical about aphasic data. One of our goals for this chapter is to show how computational models can allay this concern. Models can make error mechanisms concrete, thus showing how errors reflect the structure of the normal system. Furthermore, models can reveal the relationship between errors generated by a normal system and those that arise from a damaged one. If a model can simulate both the normal and the abnormal, that is, if it can explain the properties of erroneous and correct utterances *and* damaged and intact production systems, then error data can usefully add to the picture.

Theoretical Issues in Word Production Models
Representational Levels and Production Steps

We have introduced the conceptualization, linguistic formulation, and articulation components of production and said that our focus is on single-word lexical access within the formulation component. Can we further subdivide lexical access? All researchers agree that lexical access involves multiple levels of representation, including representations of word meaning or semantics, and representations of word form, or phonology. A stronger claim, which is accepted by most researchers, is that lexical access has steps, specifically two of them (Dell & Reich, 1981; Garrett, 1975; Levelt, 1989; Rapp & Goldrick, 2000). The first step (lemma access, word-access, L-access) consists of mapping a semantic representation onto an abstract lexical unit (*lemma* or *word node*), and the second of mapping that abstract unit onto a representation of the lexical unit's pronunciation (word-form access, phonological access).

Evidence for two steps comes from several sources. First, slips can profitably be divided into those that might have arisen during the first step (e.g., semantic errors such as "dog" for "cat") and those that could have happened in the second step (e.g., "cap" for "cat"). Later, we shall see how the two steps achieve this division using a model. Furthermore, the tip-of-the-tongue state that speakers experience when they cannot retrieve a word's phonology can be characterized as getting stuck between the steps. When speakers are stuck in this way, they can retrieve lexical properties that are associated with the first step—grammatical features such as gender for nouns—providing support for the view that the first step has been taken (Badecker, Miozzo, & Zanuttini, 1995; Miozzo & Caramazza, 1997; Vigliocco, Antonini, & Garrett, 1997). Response-time data can also be interpreted within the two-step framework. For example, in the picture-word interference paradigm, both semantically related and phonologically related distractors affect the time to name a target picture. But the strongest influences of these two distractor types occur at different stimulus-onset-asynchronies (SOAs) relative to the picture onset; the semantic effect is earlier than the phonological effect (e.g., Schriefers et al., 1990). Thus, the time course of the influence is consistent with an earlier semantic step and a later phonological step (Levelt et al., 1991; Peterson & Savoy, 1998).

Stages, Cascading, and Interaction

The two-step idea implies discreteness—step one, *then* step two—rather than a continuous evolution from semantics to phonology. There is, however, an even stricter form of discreteness, *modular stages*. If

the two steps are modular stages, the information that is accessed during each step is restricted to that which is appropriate for the step. Specifically, in the *WEAVER++ model* of Levelt, Roelofs, and Meyer (1999; Roelofs, 1997; 1992) described below, while lemma access is occurring, there is no activation of word-form information, and during word-form access, no semantic information is activated. We can relax this modularity by allowing for *cascading*. In a cascaded lexical access system, activation can flow to word-form information before lemma access finishes. To make this concrete, imagine that in an attempt to access the lemma CAT, there is also activation of the lemma DOG from either shared semantic features or other connections between their concepts. If lemma access is a modular stage, there would be no activation of word-form information until the stage is finished. But, if cascading happens, phonological properties of both CAT and DOG could become active before lemma-access completion. We can relax modularity even more by admitting a bottom-up flow of activation (feedback) from phonological information to words and from words to semantics. If bottom-up feedback and cascading are present, the system is said to be *interactive*: activation flows in both directions during both steps. The *interactive two-step model* described below (Dell, Schwartz, Martin, Saffran, & Gagnon, 1997) is interactive in this sense. During lemma access, phonological information becomes active (cascading) and can influence lemma selection (through feedback). During phonological access, activated phonological units can feed back to the lexical level, which in turn can affect which phonological units are chosen.

The question of the discreteness of lexical access thus boils down to whether the access steps are modular, cascading, or interactive. Support for cascading has largely come from response-time studies (but see Ferreira & Griffin, 2003). Peterson and Savoy (1998) asked participants to name pictures and, on some trials, interrupted the naming process by presenting printed probe words that the participant must read aloud as quickly as possible. They found that probes that were phonologically related to an alternate name of the picture, such as the probe "soda" related to the alternative name SOFA for a picture of a COUCH, were read faster than when the picture name was unrelated. Furthermore, when "count" (related to COUCH) was a probe, it was also associated with a comparable speed up. The facilitation for both "soda" and "count" occurred with a picture-probe SOA of 150 ms, but not with an SOA of 50 ms. These findings suggest that, during the first step of lexical access, the lemmas for both COUCH and SOFA were activated. Critically, the phonological properties of both words were also activated, even though for these participants, the pictured piece of furniture is nearly always referred to as a couch. If lexical access were modular, only the phonology of the selected item (couch) would be active. Consequently, the data indicate cascading from step one to step two. Step two information becomes active before step one has made its selection. Since the Peterson and Savoy study, several other response-time experiments have obtained findings consistent with cascading and it is now generally agreed that there is some degree of cascading during lexical access (e.g., Costa, Caramazza, & Sebastian-Galles, 2000; Cutting & Ferreira, 1999; Jescheniak & Schriefers, 1998) and in later phonetic processes (Goldrick & Blumstein, 2006).

What about interaction? Some speech-error findings have been interpreted as evidence for a bottom-up flow of activation during lexical access. The *mixed-error effect* is the tendency for semantic word substitutions to share phonological information. For example, US Vice President Joe Biden once referred to the pope as the "president." Both *pope* and *president* designate powerful offices and so clearly the slip is semantic. But it is tempting to conclude that both words beginning with /p/ helped the error happen. In fact, analyses of natural slips (e.g., Dell & Reich, 1981; Harley, 1984) and picture-naming errors from both control and aphasic speakers (e.g., Martin, Gagnon, Schwartz, Dell, Saffran, 1996; Rapp & Goldrick, 2000) show that semantic word substitutions exhibit phonological effects in excess of what would be expected by chance. The mixed-error effect is a natural consequence of interaction. During the first step of access, activation cascades to phonological units (e.g., to /p/ for the target POPE). This activation then feeds back to all /p/-initial word units including those that were already activated by virtue of their semantic relations to the target (e.g., PRESIDENT). This extra phonological activation gives these mixed semantic-phonological neighbors a boost over purely semantic neighbors, thus increasing the chance of the slip. Another speech-error phenomenon that can be explained by interaction is the *lexical-bias effect*—the tendency for phonological errors to create words, and particularly words related to the context, over nonwords (Baars et al., 1975; Motley & Baars, 1976). For example, saying "darn bore" instead of "barn door"

would be more likely because "darn" and "bore" are words. An interactive (two-way) flow of activation between word and phonological units can increase the activation of phonological units that correspond to words, thus creating lexical bias.

Although the mixed-error and the lexical-bias effects suggest some kind of interaction between processing levels, whether these effects are achieved by an automatic bottom-up spread of activation is controversial. Both the lexical bias and mixed-error effects can, instead, be explained by postulating that the lexical access system also includes a pre-articulatory editor—a system whose function is to detect and weed out errors before they are spoken (Baars et al., 1975). The lexical bias effect would require an editor that detects that the speaker is about to say a nonword and prevents articulation. Hence, errors that are nonwords become less likely. The mixed-error effect requires that the editor preferentially weed out semantic errors that are phonologically dissimilar to the target (Levelt et al., 1999). For example, when trying to say "cat," the editor can detect that "dog" is not "cat," better than it can tell that "rat" is not "cat." Hence, the mixed error, "rat," is more likely to be spoken. Although prearticulatory editing may require time and effort (e.g., Nozari & Dell, 2009) and existing theories of editing are poorly specified, there is little doubt that speakers monitor planned speech for purposes of error detection (Levelt, 1983; Hartsuiker & Kolk, 2001) and that at least some of the lexical bias effect can be attributed to this process (Hartsuiker, Corley, & Martensen, 2005; Nooteboom & Quene, 2008; Oppenheim & Dell, 2010). Note, however, that editorial explanations of these error effects do, in fact, involve bottom-up processing. Representations at a lower level (e.g., phonological level) are evaluated for their higher level (e.g., lexical) properties before articulation. In this way, the editorial explanations and the bottom-up feedback explanations are similar, with both asserting that production is not strictly top down (Dell & Reich, 1980; Rapp & Goldrick, 2004).

Competition in Lexical Selection

The first lexical-access step culminates in the selection of an abstract lexical item. In all of the models that we review below, the activation levels of the word or lemma units are the basis for selection. The interactive two-step model simply selects the most active word unit, which, as explained below, could be the wrong one thus creating a lexical error. Since this model is concerned with explaining errors rather than lexical selection time, the time at which the selection happens is a fixed parameter of the model. In contrast, the WEAVER++ model directly explains response times through its selection mechanism. The key property of this mechanism is that it is *competitive*. Not only does a more active target decrease selection time, but more active competitors have the opposite effect. So, if CAT is highly active and nothing else is, selection is rapid. But if DOG is activated, even if less so than CAT, CAT's selection time increases with DOG's activation level.

Competitive lexical selection is both intuitive and consistent with general cognitive theory (e.g., Miller & Cohen, 2001). Moreover, competition is a natural explanation for why a semantically related distractor word slows naming times in the picture-word interference paradigm (Schriefers et al., 1990). It nicely explains other phenomena, such as the fact that naming pictures from the same semantic category gets progressively slower (Damian et al., 2001; Howard, Nickels, Coltheart, & Cole-Virtue, 2006): the activation of the semantic competitor(s) increases the time taken to settle on the correct lexical item during the first access step, because it is harder to "see" the right answer when there are activated wrong answers in front of you. What could be simpler? In the last several years, though, some anomalous findings have surfaced. For example, Miozzo and Caramazza (2003) varied the frequency of an unrelated distractor word in the picture-word interference paradigm and found that low-frequency distractors retarded naming more than high-frequency ones. If selection were competitive, one would expect that the more active distractors, presumably the high-frequency ones, would be more potent. Instead, Miozzo and Caramazza suggested that the distractor's power to slow naming arises because it blocks the naming process at some point and that this block must be removed. Presumably, it is easier to latch onto a high-frequency distractor during this disposal process. Later on, other findings contrary to the competitive hypothesis emerged, such as instances in which related distractors actually speeded naming (e.g., Costa, Alario, & Caramazza, 2005). These findings have inspired alternative accounts of interference in the picture-word interference paradigm—accounts that deny that the first step of lexical access is competitive (e.g., Mahon, Costa, Peterson, Vargas, & Caramazza, 2007).

Whether lexical selection is competitive thus remains controversial. And resolving the issue is turning out to be more difficult than expected.

As a case in point, we will later present a model of semantic interference, a model that simulates response time effects in picture naming by using competitive selection. However, we will then show that the assumption of competitive selection is not necessary to explain the data.

Connectionism and Word Production

Before we turn to specific models, it is useful to review the principles that are common to those models. In general, the influential computational models of lexical selection in production are *connectionist* or at least have many connectionist properties. In fact, word production, like word recognition (e.g., McClelland & Rumelhart, 1981), was one of the first domains to be simulated through connectionist modeling.

A connectionist model contains a network of units. Like neurons, these units or "nodes" possess an *activation* value (often a real number between -1 or 0, and 1), and this value changes as activation passes from unit to unit through weighted links or *connections*. Processing in a connectionist model is carried out by *spreading activation*. The model is given an input by setting the activation levels of its *input units* to particular values. The input for a word production model might consist in setting the activations of units representing the word's concept to positive values. Then the activation spreads throughout the network via the connections. This spread is governed by the *activation rule*, which specifies how each unit's activation changes when it receives activation from its neighboring units. Finally, the output of the model is determined by examining the activation levels of a set of *output units*. In a model with two clear steps, there would first be a determination of the output for the first step, and the relevant output units would correspond to the selected lexical item. This selection would then affect the input to the next step, the output of which would be units representing that lexical item's phonological or phonetic form.

Many connectionist models, such as the model of cumulative semantic interference reviewed later, include a learning component that determines the weights of the connections. Such a model is trained by giving it many trials, each of which consists of an input activation pattern and (typically) a desired output activation pattern. After the activation has spread on a trial, each connection's weight may be changed by the model's *learning rule*, an equation that computes the weight change as a function of the activation and/or feedback associated with the units on the ends of the connection. For example, a model of word production might receive an input suitable for the CAT concept. But if the model has not yet been well trained, the activation might spread to the output units for RAT instead of CAT, resulting in an error. The learning rule might then change the connection weights so that the retrieval of /k/ is favored over the retrieval of /r/, when the CAT concept is input, thus decreasing the chance of this error in the future. If the model's learning rule is doing its job and the training regimen is a good one, then the network's weights will eventually become well adapted to its task, and its words will be accurately retrieved.

The next two sections summarize two models of lexical access in production: the interactive two-step model of Dell et al. (1997; Dell & O'Seaghdha, 1992), and the WEAVER++ model of Levelt et al. (1999). These models are more than 10 years old, but are still influential. Together, they embody the two empirical traditions of the field: the interactive two-step model simulates speech errors, while WEAVER++ accounts for unimpaired speakers' response times in experimental studies. Then, we present two newer computational models: an application of the interactive two-step model to aphasia, and a learning-based model of semantic interference during lexical access.

Interactive Two-Step Model

The interactive two-step model is succinctly described by its name. It has two clear steps, *word retrieval* and then *phonological retrieval*, but the interactive spread of activation allows for phonological information to influence the first step, and lexical-semantic information to affect the second one.

Both steps of lexical retrieval are carried out by the spread of activation through a network of semantic, word, and phonological units (Figure 5.1). Each network connection conveys activation between two units, according to a noisy linear activation rule. The activation sent to a unit is directly proportional to the sending unit's activation and the connection's weight, and the sent activation is just added to that of the receiving unit. Also, every unit's activation decays exponentially toward zero. In this model, all of the connection weights are positive and so decay is the only means by which activation levels are reduced. Importantly, every connection from one unit to another is associated with a connection that runs in the reverse direction. For example, there is a top-down connection from the word unit CAT to the phoneme /k/, and a bottom-up connection from /k/ to CAT. The influence of the bottom-up connections makes the model's retrieval process interactive.

During word retrieval, the semantic units of the target, say, CAT, are given a jolt of activation and this activation spreads through the network for a fixed period of time. This activates the word unit for CAT and potential error units as well. Semantically related word units, such as DOG or RAT, also get activation from semantic units shared with CAT, and phonologically related words, such as MAT or RAT, gain activation as well from the bottom-up spread of activation from shared phonemes (e.g., the /ae/ and /t/ units.). Word retrieval is

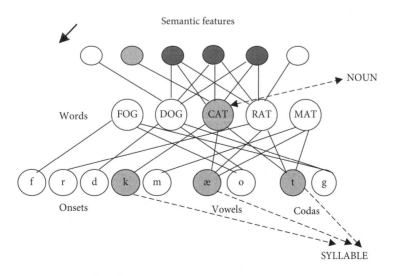

Figure 5.1 Interactive two-step model of lexical access.

concluded by the selection of the most activated word node of the proper grammatical category. Thus, the model assumes that the selection system "knows" that the system is looking, for example, for a noun. In this way, the selection process is affected by the anticipated syntactic structure of the sentence. For a task in which pictured objects are named, singular nouns are selected. Because of the noise in the activations, there is some chance that a semantic (DOG), mixed (RAT), formal (MAT), or in extreme cases, an unrelated word may be selected instead of the target. Thus, the model provides a simple mechanism for these lexical level errors.

Phonological retrieval begins by giving an activation jolt to the selected word (e.g., CAT), with all other nodes retaining their residual activation from the first step. The size of the jolt is large relative to the residual activation, thus providing a degree of discreteness to this interactive model. After the jolt is provided, activation spreads again through the network in both directions—up toward semantics and down toward the phonemes—for a fixed period of time. After that, the most activated phonemes are selected. Errors in this step would most likely create nonwords (CAG) or phonologically related words (MAT).

The interactive two-step model accounts for the kinds of errors that occur during lexical retrieval and particularly effects that suggest interaction between representational levels. For example, the model explains the mixed error effect, the tendency for semantic substitution slips to also exhibit phonological similarity. During the model's first step, word nodes for potential mixed errors, such as RAT (for CAT), gain activation from shared phonemes via bottom-up spreading activation as well as shared semantic features. Thus, mixed errors are especially likely in the model, as they are in the data. The tendency for phonological errors to create words, or lexical bias, is also due to activation feeding back from phonemes to words. During the second step, an activation pattern that corresponds to a word error (e.g., MAT for CAT) has an advantage over one that corresponds to a nonword (e.g., CAG for CAT). If the phonemes /m/, /ae/, and /t/ are highly activated, they will activate the word node for MAT, which will, in turn, further activate the phonemes, making the error even more likely. Patterns that correspond to nonwords do not have a corresponding word node and hence do not get this extra boost. Thus, slips tend to make words over nonwords. The model also explains other error phenomena through interaction including the repeated phoneme effect

(Dell, 1984), the error-proneness of words with few phonological neighbors (Vitevitch, 2002), and the tendency for phonological slips to be semantically related to their contexts (Motley & Baars, 1976). Furthermore, as we show below, the model can account for aphasic error patterns.

To summarize, the interactive two-step model has two clear steps. But its assumption of bi-directional spreading activation makes its retrieval processes both cascaded and interactive. Because the model assumes a fixed period of time for activation to spread, it does not simulate any response-time phenomena. Moreover, given its lack of sensitivity to time, the model does not take a stand on the question of whether lexical selection is competitive. In one sense, selection is competitive in that the most active word node is always chosen. But the time that passes before such selection is possible is not a factor in the currently implemented model.

WEAVER++

The WEAVER++ model of lexical access was based on Levelt's (1989) general theory of production and was formally developed in Roelofs (1992; 1997) and Levelt et al. (1999). It is similar to the interactive two-step model in that it, too, has a clear distinction between a lemma-access step and subsequent word-form encoding steps, and it retrieves lexical information through a linear spreading activation process that includes decay. In other respects, though, it differs, sometimes fundamentally.

The nodes in WEAVER++'s lexical network (Figure 5.2) represent lexical concepts (as single nodes, not collections of features), lemmas, morphemes, segments (analogous to phoneme nodes), and syllable programs. The connections between the nodes convey activation, but also represent information about the relation between the connected nodes. For example, the connection between the lexical concept **CAT** (lexical concepts are in bold) and the lemma for CAT indicates that the latter is the name of the former. So, it is not just a conduit for activation; it has a symbolic function as well.

During lemma access, the lexical concept (**CAT**) is flagged as the goal concept and activation spreads from this concept to related concepts (e.g., **DOG**) and lemma nodes (CAT and DOG). Because the lexical access steps in WEAVER++ are discrete, it does not allow cascading to word form levels during lemma access. Spreading continues until lemma selection is achieved, subject to two requirements. The first is that the lemma-to-be-selected realize the goal concept (e.g., that the selected lemma CAT is

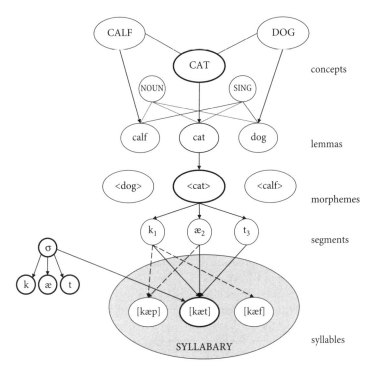

Figure 5.2 The WEAVER++ model of lexical access in production.

the *name* of **CAT** and that **CAT** is the *goal* concept). The second is that the lemma's activation be sufficiently greater than the activation of all the other lemma nodes. This latter requirement makes selection competitive because selection time will increase if other lemma nodes are active for whatever reason.

The semantic relations among the lexical concepts and the assumption of competitive selection enable WEAVER++ to give a good account of basic semantic interference effects in the picture-word interference effect. If a picture of a cat is to be named in the presence of an auditory or visual distractor, this distractor is a source of activation to the lemmas and concepts. In particular, a distractor such as "dog" will enhance the activation of the lemma DOG beyond what is gets from the lexical concept **CAT**, thus slowing the access of the CAT lemma. This semantic interference effect will only arise if the presentation of the distractor is timed so that it impacts lemma access, thus explaining the effects of distractor timing on naming RTs.

WEAVER++ is distinct from other production models in that it takes pains to have a fairly complete account of word-form retrieval, the processes that occur after lemma access, but before articulation. So, it is not just concerned with the retrieval and selection of phonological segments; it deals with how segments are organized into syllables,

and how the syllabified phonological representations are used to retrieve phonetic programs (e.g., Cholin et al., 2006). The model has been specifically applied to many studies using the implicit priming paradigm (Meyer, 1990; Roelofs & Meyer, 1998). In this paradigm, participants produce words from associative cues as quickly as they can (e.g., cue = INFANT, target response = "baby"). The critical trials are blocked based on phonological properties; for example, all the words in a block may begin with /b/. The RTs in these blocked trials are compared with those in control trials in which the targets in a block are not phonologically similar. The advance knowledge of the word form associated with the phonologically blocked trials can speed retrieval thus creating priming. It turns out that this only happens when the shared phonological material comprises an initial section of a word. For example, words sharing initial /b/ would benefit from blocking. Moreover, greater similarity leads to greater priming. Sharing initial /bey/ as in a block of "baby," "bacon," and "basin" would reduce RTs more than sharing just /b/ (Meyer, 1991). These findings were neatly explained in WEAVER++ by assuming that word-form encoding can be suspended at various points prior to articulation, and then resumed from that point (this suspend-resume mechanism is motivated by the incremental nature of production; Levelt et al., 1999). For example, in a block of words beginning with /b/, the production system can retrieve a /b/ and place it in a syllable-initial position, suspending planning at that point. This is all before the trial even begins. Then once the trial starts and the word to be spoken becomes known, the system resumes word-form encoding. The head start from the advance knowledge makes the response occur more quickly, thus explaining the priming.

In summary, the WEAVER++ model, in contrast to the interactive two-step model, treats lemma access and word-form encoding as discrete steps. Moreover, in both its treatment of lemma access and word-form encoding, it emphasizes accounting for performance in tasks in which production is accurate. In fact, the model's use of labeled relations to verify that what it selects correctly realizes its production goal makes it 100 percent accurate, unless assumptions about errors in the verification process are introduced. (WEAVER stands for Word Encoding by Activation and *VERification.*) Hence, WEAVER++ focuses on response-time studies, and it has achieved a high degree of success in explaining effects in the picture-word interference and implicit priming paradigms in particular. The model's ability to explain RT effects stems from its assumption that the selection times for both lemmas and word forms depend on the activation of competing representations as well as target ones. Thus, competitive selection is an important property of WEAVER++.

The final two models that we present are chosen because they represent recent developments in the study of single-word production, but more importantly, because they attempt to confront the challenges associated with studying production using error data, and particularly error data from brain-damaged speakers.

Modeling Aphasic Lexical Access

We mentioned earlier that studying speech errors to gain insight into production is not unanimously accepted. If the goal is to understand how the system functions, why look specifically at cases where it malfunctions? The objection only grows stronger when errors are generated by a damaged brain, for now an abnormal system is studied during a failed attempt at producing a correct utterance. In response, we claim that error data could in fact be quite informative, if the following two assumptions hold:

(1) *If the nature of speech errors is systematic rather than arbitrary.* This assumption clearly holds, as it is universally accepted that speech errors, even those

from aphasic speakers, follow systematic patterns. The errors respect grammatical and phonological constraints and are often quite similar to the target (Dell, 1986; Garrett, 1975). In short, slips are more right than wrong. Moreover, speech error probability is sensitive to the properties of the target word, such as frequency, age of acquisition, length, and neighborhood density (e.g., Kittredge, Dell, Verkuilen, & Schwartz, 2008), all of which have been shown in response-time studies to be indices of lexical retrieval. The error data thus clearly fit with other linguistic and psycholinguistic facts.

(2) *If speech errors produced by brain-damaged patients (aphasic errors) are qualitatively similar to those produced by normal speakers.* Freud (1891/1953) asserted that aphasic errors differ in degree rather than in kind from the blunders of normal speakers. If Freud is right, then a model of lexical access in unimpaired speakers must accommodate errors of aphasic speakers without a need for a change in the structure of the model, provided that one has an accurate characterization of dimension(s) that suffer damage in aphasia. Schwartz, Dell, Martin, Gahl, and Sobel (2006) employed the interactive two-step model of word production (Figure 5.1) to empirically test Freud's idea, which they called the "continuity thesis." The model simulates picture naming by generating responses in six categories: (1) correct response, (2) semantic error, (3) formal error, (4) mixed error, (5) unrelated word error, and (6) nonword error. When applied to aphasia, the model has two free parameters: the strength of the connections between the semantic and word nodes, called *s* (semantic); and the strength of the connections between the word and phoneme layers, called *p* (phonological). To illustrate how the model simulates picture naming, let us first consider a normal speaker. Since picture naming is a simple task, an unimpaired speaker would respond correctly on most trials (around 98 percent correct responses), with occasional errors, almost exclusively of semantic nature (2 percent semantic errors, 1 percent mixed errors). To get the model to generate a similar pattern, parameters *s* and *p* are varied until an acceptable fit is obtained. At $s = p = 0.04$-0.06, the model exactly mimics these proportions, thus successfully characterizing an unimpaired speaker.

Now, if the continuity thesis is correct, the model must be able to characterize a variety of aphasic patients under the same framework as an unimpaired speaker. Schwartz et al. (2006) tested this prediction by "lesioning" the model, or decreasing the values of the *s* and *p* parameters and therefore weakening the connectivity between the layers of the production system. They tested a sample of 94 aphasic patients on the 175-item Philadelphia Picture Naming Test and registered the proportion of their responses in each category. For each patient then, the model was lesioned to best simulate the response pattern of that patient by tweaking the s and p parameters. As an example, consider a patient from the Moss Aphasia Psycholinguistic Project Database (Mirman et al., 2010). This patient's naming profile comprised 58 percent correct responses, 2 percent semantic errors, 3 percent formal errors, 1 percent mixed errors, 1 percent unrelated errors, and 35 percent nonword errors. With $s = 0.034$ and $p = 0.011$ the model closely simulated this pattern (0.55, 0.02, 0.06, 0.02, 0.01, 0.34, for the six response categories, respectively). When comparing these values with those of an unimpaired speaker (s and p greater than 0.04) it becomes evident that the model characterizes this patient as having a more pronounced impairment in phonological retrieval rather than in word retrieval, as evidenced by the relatively larger discrepancy between the values of the normal and lesioned p weights.

This fitting procedure was completed for each of the 94 patients, with the fitted models accounting for 94.5 percent of the variance in the response-category proportions across the sample. The mean patient unadjusted root mean squared deviation was 0.024 (the root mean squared deviation for the patient above is 0.018, and so the mean fit for the study was slightly worse). Hence, the model can, for the most part, simulate the naming response patterns of a variety of aphasic patients, regardless of the depth of their impairment or clinical syndrome. The model shows a spectrum of graceful degradation from normal to profoundly impaired on the two dimensions of word retrieval and phonological retrieval, indexed by the decreasing values of the s and p parameters, respectively. The continuity thesis was thus supported.

In summary, speech errors show systematic and informative patterns even when they are generated by a damaged brain, making an error-based approach a reasonable and complementary companion to the response-time-based approach for studying normal production. This systematicity was made particularly apparent by the use of a computational model, one that could simulate both the normal and the abnormal using the same system. In the remainder of this section, we will briefly discuss two other capacities in which modeling aphasic errors has been used.

Making Predictions

Schwartz et al. (2006) showed that the interactive two-step model successfully simulates the picture-naming pattern of a variety of aphasic patients. But a model is most useful when it not only fits the data, but is capable of making predictions. Can the interactive two-step model do this? Dell, Martin, and Schwartz (2007) showed that once the model characterizes patients based on their naming performance, it can predict their scores on an auditory word repetition task, without any additional pieces of information. Based on the studies showing the influence of lexical properties, such as frequency on repetition, Dell et al. predicted that, at least in some cases, once the word to be repeated is recognized (i.e., selected at the word level), repetition could be accomplished simply by completing the phonological step of lexical access (the "lexical-route" model; see Figure 5.3). Therefore, by keeping the s and p parameters recovered from a patient's naming performance, the lexical-route repetition model can predict the patient's repetition score just by running the parameterized model on the phonological retrieval step alone. For example, for the patient with $s = 0.034$ and $p = 0.011$, the lexical-route model predicts 57 percent correct responses in word repetition. When compared with the actual performance of the patients in an auditory word repetition version of the 175 pictures used for naming, the lexical-route model was successful in predicting repetition accuracy of most patients. However, in some cases it underestimated the accuracy.

Investigation of the Alternative Models of Repetition

The fact that some aphasic patients outperformed the prediction of the lexical-route model in word repetition is hardly surprising. This model has no mechanism to accommodate repetition of a nonword, a task that normal speakers, at least, accomplish without much difficulty. When a "nonlexical route," or direct mapping from input to output phonology, is added to the lexical-route repetition model, a "dual-route" model of repetition is created (Hanley, Dell, Kay, & Baron, 2004; see Figure 5.3). As an example, recall the patient with $s = 0.034$ and $p = 0.011$, whose predicted accuracy in repetition, as estimated by the lexical-route model, was 57 percent. In reality, this patient repeated 74 percent of the words correctly. So, in this case, the lexical-route model underestimates accuracy. Let us now attempt to fit the patient to the dual-route model. To

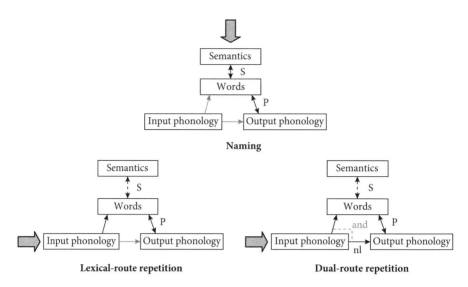

Naming

Lexical-route repetition   **Dual-route repetition**

Figure 5.3 Models of naming, lexical-route, and dual-route repetition with their relevant parameters. Dashed arrows represent involvement through feedback only. Gray arrows represent an inactive route. Patterned arrows represent the source of input to the model. Output phonology is always the output of the model. In the naming model, semantic (parameter s) and phonological (parameter p) connections operate bidirectionally. In the lexical-route repetition model, phonological connections are bidirectional, but semantic connections are used only through feedback. In the dual-route model the nonlexical route (parameter nl) is added to the lexical-route model.

characterize the patient's nonlexical route, the patient's ability to repeat nonwords, a task that must be carried out through the nonlexical route, is tested. This patient repeats only 15 percent of nonwords correctly. Then the strength of the patient's nonlexical route (*nl*) is estimated by determining what value of *nl* would lead to 15 percent correct repetition of nonwords in an implementation of the nonlexical route. A strength of 0.013 does this. Now, a dual-route model consisting of a lexical part (with parameters *s* and *p* determined through the naming simulation) and a nonlexical part (parameter *nl* = 0.013) is run with both lexical and nonlexical sources of activation adding together to yield the model's repetition output. This model predicts 75 percent accuracy on word repetition, quite close to the patient's actual performance.

Although the dual-route model solved the problem in cases where the lexical-route model failed, the nature of the model remained unspecified. Is labor divided equally between the two routes or is one route used by default? Which route is the default route? Nozari, Kittredge, Dell, and Schwartz (2010) addressed this question by comparing the effect of the frequency of the target word on repetition errors generated by different repetition models. It is well known that errors are more probable on low-frequency targets in both picture naming and word repetition. Furthermore, studies of naming have shown that frequency affects phonological retrieval more than word retrieval

(e.g., Kittredge et al., 2008). Recall that Dell et al.'s (2007) lexical-route model of repetition is simply the phonological step of naming, the step in which frequency exercises most of its influence. Now, if only the errors specific to that step are considered, then the structural overlap between naming and repetition through the lexical-route predicts a *similar-sized frequency effect* in the two tasks. To keep the focus on the phonological retrieval step instead of the word retrieval step, only errors that created nonwords were chosen. According to the model, nonword errors occur at the phonological step; errors in the previous step are necessarily words. Given this, the prediction from the lexical-route model of repetition is as follows: as the frequency of the target word increases, the probability of making a nonword error on that item should decrease by the same amount in naming and repetition. More formally, the slope of the logistic regression relating nonword error probability to the log of target-word frequency should be similar for the two tasks.

To examine this prediction more closely, Nozari et al. (2010) first simulated the interactive two-step model of naming, as well as three models of repetition: (1) the lexical-route, (2) dual-route, and (3) a pure-nonlexical route model. Specifically, they measured the effect of target-word frequency on the probability of making a nonword error (regression slopes) generated by each model. As expected, the lexical route model showed a strong frequency effect, similar to that produced by the naming model, and the pure nonlexical-route model, which directly maps input onto output phonology, showed very little frequency effect. Crucially, the frequency effect generated by the dual-route model was no different in magnitude from that of the lexical-route model and both were similar to that generated by the naming model. The simulated predictions for both the lexical-route and dual-route models were confirmed by real patient data. A comparison between the frequency effect in naming and repetition in a sample of 59 aphasic patients showed comparable and sizable effects in both tasks.

The fact that the frequency effects were equally strong in naming and repetition shows that word repetition is as heavily influenced by lexical information as is naming. This finding is consistent with the dual-route model as well as the lexical route model because the dual-route model's nonlexically generated activation is added on top of activations generated through the lexical route; any lexically sensitive differences in activation remain. So, which of these two repetition models is correct? Recall that, aside from frequency effects, the dual-route model predicts that there will be fewer nonword errors in repetition than there are in naming (because activation from the nonlexical route prevents these errors), and that this prediction is not made by the lexical-route model, which lacks the nonlexical route's contribution. In most patients, there were fewer nonword errors in repetition than in naming, even though the frequency effects on these errors were similar for the two tasks. Together, these findings support a dual-route model of word repetition. There is a default lexical route to which the nonlexical route is added by some patients to boost repetition's accuracy.

In summary, computational modeling of aphasic errors is useful for a variety of purposes, including understanding each patient's condition (e.g., fitting to naming data); making predictions about the patient's performance in other tasks (e.g., predicting repetition accuracy from naming); and even studying the architecture of the lexical access system (e.g., investigation of the alternative models of repetition).

Incremental Learning during Lexical Access: the Dark Side Model

According to Levelt (1989), unimpaired speakers successfully retrieve two to three words per second from an active vocabulary of 40,000. How is this feat of information processing possible? Much of

the research on lexical access that we have reviewed represents an attempt to answer this question. This research, however, neglects a key fact: the production system benefits from an extraordinary amount of practice; speakers retrieve an average of 16,000 words per day (Mehl, Vazire, Ramirez-Esparza, Slatcher, & Pennebaker, 2007). We claim that the production system learns from every one of these retrieval events, and generally that the system is continually tuned by an implicit-learning process.

The models that we have described until now have all approached speech production as a stable process. But mounting evidence suggests that production constantly adapts to new experience. This point has recently been emphasized for syntactic (e.g., Bock & Griffin, 2000; Chang, Dell, & Bock, 2006; Ferreira, Bock, Wilson, & Cohen, 2008) and phonotactic (e.g., Warker & Dell, 2006) information, but it has long been known that lexical access in production is sensitive to word frequency, repetition priming, and other effects of experience (e.g., Damian & Als, 2005; Howard et al., 2006). Word production models should be incorporating mechanisms for learning and adaptation. To illustrate, we next describe a recent model of lexical retrieval in speech production that learns through use.

Oppenheim, Dell, and Schwartz's (2010) Dark Side model of lexical access incorporates an incremental learning process to continually tune its semantic-to-lexical mappings. The model's name reflects a claim that incremental lexical learning has a light side and a dark side that work together in this tuning process. The light side learns a target mapping by strengthening connections from activated semantic features to a target word. The dark side unlearns competing mappings by weakening connections from the same semantic features to other activated words. Thus, lexical learning is sensitive to activated competitors, a point that we will return to later in this section.

The Dark Side model follows a tradition of division-of-labor models (including MacKay, 1982, the interactive two-step model, and more recently Gordon & Dell, 2003, and Chang, et al., 2006) in characterizing lexical retrieval as emerging from the interaction of semantic activation and syntactic selection. Although the model only deals with the first step of lexical retrieval (lemma or word retrieval), that step has two distinct phases, activation and selection, and a third process associated with learning. In the activation phase, words are activated through their associations with conceptual information, a process that we can tentatively

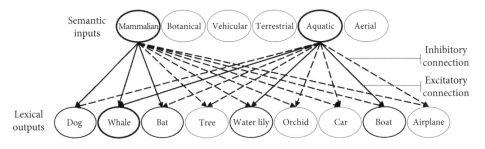

Figure 5.4 The lexical activation component of Oppenheim, Dell, and Schwartz's (2010) Dark Side model of lexical retrieval.

localize to the left anterior/middle temporal lobe (e.g., Schwartz et al., 2009). The mapping is implemented as a two-layer feedforward network, where an input of semantic features (e.g., MAMMAL, TERRESTRIAL) activates an output of localist word nodes (e.g., DOG; see Figure 5.4).[1] Noise in the lexical activations reflects a modicum of input from externalities and, as in the interactive two-step model, such noise provides a basis for lexical selection errors, particularly when the model is simulating brain damage.

The second phase entails selecting a single syntagmatically appropriate word for production, a process that we can associate with neural activity in the left inferior frontal gyrus (e.g., Schnur et al., 2009). As in the WEAVER++ model (and unlike the interactive two-step model), lexical selection in the Dark Side model unfolds over time, allowing it to account for response time data. Selection is implemented via a booster mechanism, which repeatedly floods the lexical layer with additional activation, combining nonlinearly with the existing lexical activations.[2] Boosting continues until the activation of one of the lexical nodes is sufficiently greater than that of other nodes, at which point that node is considered to be selected. Thus, selection latencies reflect target and competitor activations, as in WEAVER++. However, unlike WEAVER++, the Dark Side model is not bound to select the correct word. Omission errors occur when boosting continues for too long without producing a clear winner and, since the selection process is blind to the desired outcome, noisy activations can even lead to selecting an undesired word (e.g., BAT instead of DOG). Thus, the model predicts response time as well as errors.

Crucially, the model assumes that while people may rapidly acquire new vocabulary, they never truly stop learning the words that they already know. To understand how this works, we can imagine a trial in which the model attempts to retrieve the word DOG. As discussed earlier, two factors might make it difficult to quickly and accurately retrieve DOG: first, if DOG is too weakly activated; and second, if other words (e.g., BAT, WHALE) are too strongly activated. The Dark Side model addresses both of these problems by employing an error-based connectionist learning algorithm (specifically, the delta rule) to continually adjust each connection as a consequence of its use. The light side of incremental learning addresses the first problem by strengthening the connections that support retrieving the target word (e.g., MAMMAL→DOG), and dark side addresses the second problem by weakening the connections that would support retrieving its competitors (e.g., MAMMAL→BAT, MAMMAL→WHALE). With its stronger connections, retrieving DOG a second time will become faster and more accurate. But since its connection from the shared MAMMAL feature (i.e., MAMMAL→BAT) is now weaker, retrieving BAT will become slower and more error prone. Moreover, since the connections supporting DOG have just been strengthened, with a little noise in the lexical activations, DOG will be more likely to emerge as a semantic error on the BAT trial. Similarly, a subsequent attempt to retrieve WHALE will be even slower and more error prone because its connection from the shared MAMMAL feature will have been weakened twice. A further point to note is that, because learning is driven by relevant experience, any connection changes should persist indefinitely unless other learning overwrites them.

The Dark Side model offers an integrated account of effects in both speech errors and correct naming latencies that arise from persistent changes to semantic-to-lexical mappings, such as cumulative semantic interference. Cumulative semantic interference refers to the phenomenon that meaning-based lexical retrieval becomes increasingly difficult when speakers retrieve a series of semantically related words. For instance, when naming pictures from a single semantic category, like DOG, BAT, WHALE, the typical finding is that unimpaired speakers take slightly longer to name each picture (e.g., Howard et al., 2006; Navarrete, Mahon, & Caramazza, 2010), and speakers with aphasia make increasing numbers of semantic errors and omissions (e.g., Schnur, Schwartz, Brecher, & Hodgson, 2006). In the model, increasing response times chiefly reflect the dark side of incremental learning: previous competitors have weaker connections from shared semantic features, so they have weak activations that are more similar to those of their competitors, thus leading to slower retrieval. Retrieving multiple words from the same semantic category therefore elicits slower responses because each word from that category has previously acted as a competitor. Noise in the lexical activations (as one might expect to increase with brain damage) can turn these slow responses into omission errors. Semantic errors also require noisier activations in the model, but they further reflect the light side of incremental learning: competitors that have more recently served as targets retain stronger connections from shared semantic features and thus are more likely to emerge as errors. Semantic errors from aphasic patients particularly support this interpretation, because the words that speakers produce in error tend to match their most recent responses, irrespective of timing manipulations (Hsiao, Schwartz, Schnur, & Dell, 2009). In fact, all of the interference effects are robust to short timing manipulations (Howard et al., 2006; Schnur et al., 2006) and persist when same-category pictures are interspersed with unrelated ones (e.g., Damian & Als, 2005; Howard et al., 2006; Oppenheim, in preparation), suggesting that they reflect relatively persistent changes to the lexical access system. Indeed, there is some indication that the semantic interference that accumulates from naming a series of related pictures remains detectable even an hour later (Oppenheim, in preparation), strengthening the model's claim that cumulative semantic interference reflects the mechanisms by which people learn and maintain their vocabularies.

The Dark Side model can also inform the question noted earlier of whether lexical selection is competitive in the sense that having an activated competitor slows down target retrieval. Although cumulative semantic interference has been claimed as support for a competitive selection process (e.g., Howard, et al., 2006), Oppenheim et al. (2010) demonstrated that using a competitive algorithm for lexical selection did not contribute to the model's account of any aspect of the phenomenon. Instead, the model's performance indicated that the dark side of learning (i.e., weakening connections to activated competitors on previous trials) implemented sufficient "competition" to carry the effects. Thus, while there may be other reasons to hypothesize a competitive mechanism for lexical selection (as noted earlier), competitive selection may in practice be difficult to distinguish from competitive (error-based) learning.

Finally, we note that the Dark Side model is the only production model to simulate normal and aphasic speech errors, as well as response times, in the same task. By explaining all of these data, it addresses the quandary described at the beginning of this chapter. There is no longer any debate about whether one should explain errors or response times, if the same model can explain both. It should be recognized, however, that the model is purchasing its ability to explain a variety of data types by focusing on just a single step of the lexical access process and a specific set of phenomena that occur during this step, those associated with cumulative semantic interference.

Conclusion

Computational models of word production have achieved some success in explaining both the normal and the abnormal products of production. Also, through the models, we better understand theoretical notions, such as stages and steps, cascading and interaction, competitive selection, and implicit learning, and even have achieved a degree of consensus on some points, such as the role of cascading in a multistep production process. Much has been discovered since Garrett (1975) and Levelt et al. (1999) demonstrated the power of speech-error analysis and experimental methods, respectively, and although many issues are far from settled, lexical-access theory is in pretty good shape. Now that theory needs to transcend object-picture naming and other single-word methods and measures, and link up with the wider world of production, with theories of utterance generation in multispeaker interactions, acquisition, speech articulation, and with the cognitive neuroscience of language.

Acknowledgement

Preparation of this chapter was supported by the National Institutes of Health (HD-44458 and DC-00191).

Notes

1. While the implemented model only contains forward-spreading activation, this merely reflects the limited scope of the model, rather than a theoretical claim against cascading activation or feedback.

2. Although the constraint is not implemented in the model, it is assumed that the booster activation is limited to words that are syntagmatically appropriate for the current context. So, for example, selecting DOG would not entail boosting BARKED.

References

Baars, B. J., Motley, M. T., & MacKay, D. G. (1975). Output editing for lexical status in artificially elicited slips of the tongue. *Journal of Verbal Learning and Verbal Behavior, 14,* 382–391.

Badecker, W., Miozzo, M., & Zanuttini, R. (1995). The two-stage model of lexical retrieval: Evidence from a case of anomia with selective preservation of grammatical gender. *Cognition, 57,* 193–216.

Bock, K., & Griffin, Z. M. (2000). The persistence of structural priming: Transient activation or implicit learning? *Journal of Experimental Psychology: General, 129,* 177–192.

Caramazza, A. (1984). The logic of neuropsychological research and the problem of patient classification in aphasics. *Brain and Language, 21,* 9–20.

Caramazza, A. (1997). How many levels of processing are there in lexical access? *Cognitive Neuropsychology, 14,* 177–208.

Costa, A., Alario, F. X., & Caramazza, A. (2005). On the categorical nature of the semantic interference effect in the picture-word interference paradigm. *Psychonomic Bulletin & Review, 12,* 125–131.

Costa, A., Caramazza, A., & Sebastian-Galles, N. (2000). The cognate facilitation effect: Implications for models of lexical access. *Journal of Experimental Psychology: Learning, Memory, and Cognition, 26,* 1283–1296.

Chang, F., Dell, G. S., & Bock, K. (2006). Becoming syntactic. *Psychological Review, 113,* 234–272.

Cholin, J., Levelt, W. J. M., & Schiller, N. O. (2006). Effects of syllable frequency in speech production. *Cognition, 99,* 205–235.

Cutting, J. C., & Ferreira, V. S. (1999). Semantic and phonological information flow in the production lexicon. *Journal of Experimental Psychology: Learning, Memory, and Cognition, 25,* 318–344.

Damian, M. F., & Als, L. C. (2005). Long-lasting semantic context effects in the spoken production of object names. *Journal of Experimental Psychology: Learning, Memory and Cognition, 31,* 1372–1384.

Damian, M. F., Vigliocco, G., & Levelt, W. J. M. (2001). Effects of semantic context in the naming of pictures and words. *Cognition, 81,* B77–B86.

Dell, G. S. (1984). The representation of serial order in speech: Evidence from the repeated phoneme effect in speech errors. *Journal of Experimental Psychology: Learning, Memory, and Cognition, 10,* 222–233.

Dell, G. S. (1986). A spreading activation theory of retrieval in language production. *Psychological Review, 93,* 283–321.

Dell, G. S., Martin, N., & Schwartz, M. F. (2007). A case-series test of the interactive two-step model of lexical access: Predicting word repetition from picture naming. *Journal of Memory and Language, 56,* 490–520.

Dell, G. S., & O'Seaghdha, P. G. (1992). Stages of lexical access in language production. *Cognition, 42,* 287–314.

Dell, G. S., Reich, P. A. (1980). Toward a unified theory of slips of the tongue. In V. A. Fromkin (Ed.), *Errors in linguistic performance: Slips of the tongue, ear, pen, and hands* (pp. 273–286). New York: Academic Press.

Dell, G. S., & Reich, P. A. (1981). Stages in sentence production: An analysis of speech error data. *Journal of Verbal Learning and Verbal Behavior, 20,* 611–629.

Dell, G. S., Schwartz, M. F., Martin, N., Saffran, E. M., & Gagnon, D. A. (1997). Lexical access in aphasic and nonaphasic speakers. *Psychological Review, 104,* 801–838.

Ferreira, V. S., Bock, K., Wilson, M. P., & Cohen, N. (2008). Memory for syntax, despite amnesia. *Psychological Science, 19,* 940–946.

Ferreira, V. S., & Griffin, Z. M. (2003). Phonological influences on lexical (mis-) selection. *Psychological Science, 14,* 86–90.

Ferreira, V.S., & Pashler, H. (2002). Central bottleneck influences on the processing stages of word production. *Journal of Experimental Psychology: Human Learning and Memory, 28,* 1187–1199.

Freud, S. (1953). *On aphasia* (E. Stengel, Trans.). New York City: International University Press. (Original work published 1891).

Fromkin, V. A. (1973). Introduction. In V. A. Fromkin (Ed.), *Speech errors as linguistic evidence* (pp. 11–45). The Hague: Mouton.

Garrett, M. F. (1975). The analysis of sentence production. In G. H. Bower (Ed.), *The psychology of learning and motivation* (pp. 133–175). San Diego, CA: Academic Press.

Glaser, W. R., & Düngelhoff, F.-J. (1984). The time course of picture-word interference. *Journal of Experimental Psychology: Human Perception and Performance, 10,* 640–654.

Goldrick, M., & Blumstein, S. E. (2006). Cascading activation from phonological planning to articulatory processes: Evidence from tongue twisters. *Language and Cognitive Processes, 21,* 649–683.

Gordon, J. K., & Dell, G. S. (2003). Learning to divide the labor: An account of deficits in light and heavy verb production. *Cognitive Science, 27,* 1–40.

Hanley, J. R., Dell, G. S., Kay, J., & Baron, R. (2004). Evidence for the involvement of a nonlexical route in the repetition of familiar words: A comparison of single and dual route models of auditory repetition. *Cognitive Neuropsychology, 21,* 147–158.

Harley, T. A. (1984). A critique of top-down independent levels models of speech production: Evidence from non-plan-internal speech errors. *Cognitive Science, 8,* 191–219.

Harley, T. A. (2004). Does cognitive neuropsychology have a future? *Cognitive Neuropsychology, 21,* 3–16.

Hartsuiker, R. J., Corley, M., & Martensen, H. (2005). The lexical bias effect is modulated by context, but the standard monitoring account doesn't fly: Related reply to Baars, Motley, and MacKay (1975). *Journal of Memory and Language, 52,* 58–70.

Hartsuiker, R. J., & Kolk, H. H. J. (2001) A computational test of the perceptual loop theory. *Cognitive Psychology, 24,* 113–157.

Howard, D., Nickels, L., Coltheart, M., & Cole-Virtue, J. (2006). Cumulative semantic inhibition in picture naming: Experimental and computational studies. *Cognition, 100,* 464–482.

Hsiao, E., Schwartz, M. F., Schnur, T. T., & Dell, G. S. (2009). Temporal characteristics of semantic perseverations induced by blocked-cyclic picture naming. *Brain and Language, 108,* 133–144.

Jescheniak, J. D., & Levelt, W. J. M. (1994). Word frequency effects in speech production: Retrieval of syntactic information and of phonological form. *Journal of Experimental Psychology: Learning, Memory, and Cognition, 20,* 824–843.

Jescheniak, J. D., & Schriefers, H. J. (1998). Serial versus cascaded processing in lexical access in language production: Further evidence from the coactivation of near-synonyms. *Journal of Experimental Psychology: Learning, Memory and Cognition, 24,* 1256–1274.

Kittredge, A. K., Dell, G. S., Verkuilen, J., & Schwartz, M. F. (2008). Where is the effect of frequency in word production? Insights from aphasic picture-naming errors. *Cognitive Neuropsychology, 25,* 463–492.

Levelt, W. J. M. (1983). Monitoring and self-repair in speech. *Cognition, 14,* 41–104.

Levelt, W. J. M. (1989). *Speaking: From intention to articulation.* Cambridge, MA: MIT Press.

Levelt, W. J. M., Roelofs, A., & Meyer, A. S. (1999). A theory of lexical access in speech production. *Behavioral and Brain Science, 22,* 1–75.

Levelt, W. J. M., Schriefers, H., Vorberg, D., Meyer, A. S., Pechmann, T., & Havinga, J. (1991). The time course of lexical access in speech production: A study of picture naming. *Psychological Review, 98,* 122–142.

MacKay, D. G. (1970). Spoonerisms: The structure of errors in the serial order of speech. *Neuropsychologia, 8,* 323–350.

MacKay, D. G. (1982). The problems of flexibility, fluency, and speed-accuracy trade-off in skilled behavior. *Psychological Review, 89,* 483–506.

McClelland, J. L., & Rumelhart, D. E. (1981). An interactive activation model of context effects in letter perception: 1. An account of basic findings. *Psychological Review, 88,* 375–407.

Mahon, B. Z., Costa, A., Peterson, R., Vargas, K. A., & Caramazza, A. (2007). Lexical selection is not by competition: A reinterpretation of semantic interference and facilitation effects in the picture-word interference paradigm. *Journal of Experimental Psychology: Learning, Memory, and Cognition, 33,* 503–535.

Martin, N., Gagnon, D. A., Schwartz, M. F., Dell, G. S., & Saffran, E. M. (1996). Phonological facilitation of semantic errors in normal and aphasic speakers. *Language and Cognitive Processes, 11,* 257–282.

Mehl, M. R., Vazire, S., Ramirez-Esparza, N., Slatcher, R. B., & Pennebaker, J. W. (2007). Are women really more talkative than men? *Science, 317,*82.

Meyer, A. S. (1990). The time course of phonological encoding in language production: The encoding of successive syllables of a word. *Journal of Memory and Language, 29,* 524–545.

Meyer, A. S. (1991). The time course of phonological encoding in language production: Phonological encoding inside a syllable. *Journal of Memory and Language, 30,* 69–89.

Miller, E. K., & Cohen, J. D. (2001). An integrative theory of prefrontal cortex function. *Annual Review of Neuroscience, 24,* 167–202.

Miozzo, M., & Caramazza, A. (1997). Retrieval of lexical-syntactic features in tip-of-the-tongue states. *Journal of Experimental Psychology: Learning, Memory, and Cognition, 23,* 1410–1423.

Miozzo, M., & Caramazza, A. (2003). When more is less. A counterintuitive effect of distractor frequency in the picture-word interference paradigm. *Journal of Experimental Psychology: General, 132,* 228–252.

Mirman, D., Strauss, T. J., Brecher, A., Walker, G. M., Sobel, G. M., Dell, G. S., & Schwartz, M.F. (2010). A large searchable web-based database of aphasic performance on picture

naming and other tests of cognitive function. *Cognitive Neuropsychology, 27,* 495–504.

Motley, M. T., & Baars, B. J. (1976). Semantic bias effects on the outcomes of verbal slips. *Cognition, 4,* 177–187.

Navarrete, E., Mahon, B. Z., & Caramazza, A. (2010). The cumulative semantic cost does not reflect lexical selection by competition. *Acta Psychologica, 134,* 279–289.

Nooteboom, S. G. (1969). The tongue slips into patterns. In A. G. Sciarone, A. J. van Essen, & A. A. van Raad (Eds.), *Leyden studies in linguistics and phonetics* (pp. 114–132). The Hague: Mouton.

Nooteboom, S. G., & Quene, H. (2008). Self-monitoring and feedback: A new attempt to find the main cause of lexical bias in phonological speech errors. *Journal of Memory and Language, 58,* 837–861.

Nozari, N., Dell, G. S. (2009). More on lexical bias: How efficient can a "lexical editor" be? *Journal of Memory and Language, 60,* 291–307.

Nozari, N., Kittredge, A. K., Dell, G. S., Schwartz, M. F. (2010). Naming and repetition in aphasia: Steps, routes, and frequency effects. *Journal of Memory and Language, 63,* 541–559.

Oldfield, R. C., & Wingfield, A. (1965). Response latencies in naming objects. *Quarterly Journal of Experimental Psychology, 17,* 273–281.

Oppenheim, G.M. (in preparation). *Cumulative semantic interference persists over one hour.*

Oppenheim, G. M., & Dell, G. S. (2010). Motor movement matters: The flexible abstractness of inner speech. *Memory & Cognition, 38,* 1147–1160.

Oppenheim, G. M., Dell, G. S., & Schwartz, M. F. (2010). The dark side of incremental learning: A model of cumulative semantic interference during lexical access in speech production. *Cognition, 114,* 227–252.

O'Seaghdha, P. G., & Marin, J. W. (2000). Phonological competition and cooperation in form-related priming: Sequential and nonsequential processes in word production. *Journal of Experimental Psychology: Human Perception and Performance, 26,* 57–73.

Peterson, R. R., & Savoy, P. (1998). Lexical selection and phonological encoding during language production: Evidence for cascaded processing. *Journal of Experimental Psychology: Learning, Memory & Cognition, 24,* 539–557.

Rapp, B., & Goldrick, M. (2000). Discreteness and interactivity in spoken word production. *Psychological Review, 107,* 460–499.

Rapp, B., & Goldrick, M. (2004). Feedback by any other name is still interactivity: A reply to Roelofs' comment on Rapp & Goldrick (2000). *Psychological Review, 111,* 573–578.

Roelofs, A. (1992). A spreading-activation theory of lemma retrieval in speaking. *Cognition, 42,* 107–142.

Roelofs, A. (1997). The WEAVER model of word-form encoding in speech production. *Cognition, 64,* 249–284.

Roelofs, A., & Meyer, A. S. (1998). Metrical structure in planning the production of spoken words.*Journal of Experimental Psychology: Learning, Memory, and Cognition, 24,* 922–939.

Schnur, T. T., Schwartz, M. F., Brecher, A., & Hodgson, C. (2006). Semantic interference during blocked-cyclic naming: Evidence from aphasia. *Journal of Memory and Language, 54,* 199–227.

Schnur, T. T., Schwartz, M. F., Kimberg, D. Y., Hirshorn, E., Coslett, H. B., & Thompson-Schill, S. L. (2009). Localizing interference during naming: Convergent neuroimaging and neuropsychological evidence for the function of Broca's area. *Proceedings of the National Academy of Sciences, 106*, 322–327.

Schriefers, H., Meyer, A., & Levelt, W. (1990). Exploring the time course of lexical access in language production: Picture-word interference studies. *Journal of Memory and Language, 29*, 86–102.

Schwartz, M. F., Dell, G. S., Martin, N., Gahl, S., & Sobel, P. (2006). A case-series test of the interactive two-step model of lexical access: Evidence from picture naming. *Journal of Memory and Language, 54*, 228–264.

Schwartz, M. F., Kimberg, D. Y., Walker, G. M., Faseyitan, O., Brecher, A., Dell, G. S., Coslett, H. B. (2009). Anterior temporal involvement in semantic word retrieval: VLSM evidence from aphasia. *Brain, 132*, 3411–3427

Vigliocco, G., Antonini, T., & Garrett, M. F. (1997). Grammatical gender is on the tip of Italian tongues. *Psychological Science, 8*, 314–317.

Vitevitch, M. S. (2002). The influence of phonological similarity neighborhoods on speech production. *Journal of Experimental Psychology: Learning, Memory, & Cognition, 28*, 735–747.

Warker, J. A., & Dell, G. S. (2006). Speech errors reflect newly learned phonotactic constraints. *Journal of Experimental Psychology: Learning, Memory, and Cognition, 32*, 387–398.

Neural Bases of Word Representations for Naming

David S. Race *and* Argye E. Hillis

Abstract

Naming is a deceptively complex task that involves the interaction of multiple cognitive functions. This article provides an overview of the relationship between these functions and regions of the brain. It begins with an overview of the methods used to study the relationship between brain regions and naming. In particular, it focuses on lesions caused by stroke or degenerative disease, functional imaging, and transcranial magnetic stimulation. Next it discusses a generally accepted cognitive model of naming, which includes conceptual and word-form processing. Finally, it discusses the relationship that various brain regions have in relation to cognitive functions in the model. The literature indicates that naming, like much of language processing, is left lateralized, relying on an extended network of regions. Importantly it seems most of these regions participate in multiple cognitive functions in naming to varying degrees.

Key Words: naming, stroke, neurodegenerative disease, functional MRI, transcranial magnetic stimulation, cognitive model of naming

Introduction

Unless you are a language researcher, the representation of a word is not something you usually think about until you have some sort of difficulty homing in on it. The difficulty might range from an inability to produce the name of a famous actress or even an object that is sitting right in front of you, producing a name that is related but not quite the word you were looking for, to producing a nonword that is a blend of two separate words.

This review discusses the current state of knowledge regarding neural representations of words. The first section touches on three major methods of investigation: (1) lesion studies, (2) functional imaging, and (3) transcranial magnetic imaging (transcranial magnetic stimulation [TMS]). The main point to note is that there is no one best method. Rather, each method has its advantages and weaknesses, so

converging evidence is usually required to make definitive conclusions in any area of investigation.

The next section presents an overview of a general model of naming used as a framework for this article. For each stage of processing, there are corresponding debates as to the true nature of representation. Although discussing each debate in its entirety is beyond the scope of this review, we endeavor to touch on the major points of contention.

The final sections discuss the relationship between the stages of the model and the regions in the brain. Note here that there is not a strict one to one correspondence between a region and a particular function. Rather, it seems as though the brain is organized into networks of distributed regions that work together to perform particular tasks. Also, although naming in the model is described as a staged process, the current methodologies are not well suited to determine when or where one stage might end and another begins. Finally, as evidenced by imaging studies, language processing recruits areas in both hemispheres all over the brain. However, language seems to be lateralized such that only damage to regions of the left hemisphere results in major language deficits for naming, comprehension, and syntactic processing. For this reason, any mention of a region is in regard to the left hemisphere unless otherwise noted.

Methods of Investigation in Naming Studies

Determining how the brain processes words and language in general requires converging evidence from multiple types of methodologies. Three of the main methods for investigating the brain-language relationship are (1) lesion studies, (2) functional imaging and (3) TMS. The rest of this section provides a brief description of each method along with its advantages and weaknesses.

Lesions

Lesion studies involve investigating the correlation between damage to regions and performance on language tasks. Regions of the brain can become lesioned or damaged for numerous reasons including stroke, degenerative disease, tumor, encephalitis, and head trauma. Stroke occurs when one of the arteries in the brain becomes blocked, depriving regions supplied by that artery of oxygen and nutrients. The brain is supplied by three major arteries: (1) anterior cerebral artery, (2) middle cerebral artery, and (3) posterior cerebral artery. These arteries branch out and generally supply the frontal lobe, the temporal-parietal lobes, and the occipital lobe, respectively. Regions that lie at the ends of the arterial branches and therefore receive blood from multiple arteries are called watershed areas. Although these areas receive blood from multiple arteries, their location toward the end of the branches leaves them particularly vulnerable to ischemia (low blood supply) or infarction (tissue death).

Degenerative diseases tend to cause particular patterns of neural degeneration. A well-known example is Alzheimer's Disease, which usually affects memory regions, such as the hippocampus and parahippocampal gyrus, and leaves language processing intact until latter stages. An advantage to studying degenerative diseases is that they can occur in regions that are not usually affected by stroke, such as the anterior temporal lobes, allowing for a broader picture of the relation between brain and language.

An advantage to lesion studies is that they provide an indication of which regions are necessary for a particular function. The reasoning is straightforward. If the individuals were able to perform the function before damage to the region, and were unable to perform the function after damage to that area of the brain, then that particular area of the brain must be necessary for the function. However, lesions studies, especially stroke studies, suffer from the fact that damage is often not restricted to one focal region, which makes it difficult to pinpoint which particular area or areas are necessary to support the function. It is now thought that an entire network of brain regions may be necessary to support even a very simple task, such as reading a single word. Another disadvantage, again particularly so in stroke studies, is that patients are often studied long after the onset of their stroke. As time passes, the brain is likely to reorganize. This raises the question of whether normal performance on a task, when there is damage to a region, is because the area is not necessary for the task or it was initially necessary, but that there was recovery because of reorganization that followed the acute period. However, recent studies have tried to deal with this problem by testing patients in the acute stage before reorganization can take place. One problem with this approach is that imaging (computed tomography [CT] or structural magnetic resonance imaging [MRI]) often does not show the entire area of damage or dysfunction that may account for the deficits. Diffusion-weighted imaging is highly sensitive to dense ischemia or infarct, but does not reveal all areas that are dysfunctional because of hypoperfusion. This weakness can be addressed through more sensitive MRI scanning techniques using perfusion-weighted imaging with dynamic contrast (bolus-tracking) perfusion imaging, arterial spin-labeling MR perfusion imaging, or CT perfusion scans to show areas of hyperfusion or dysfunction imaging beyond the infarct that may account for some of the language deficits, particularly in acute stroke, but also in subacute or chronic stroke.

Functional Imaging

Functional imaging methods, such as positron emission tomography (PET) and functional magnetic resonance imaging (fMRI) studies, investigate hemodynamic responses in brain tissue that area correlated with language task performance or particular response types. As regions of neurons become more active, they require an increase in blood flow to deliver glucose and oxygen. Therefore, regions with increased blood flow in comparison with other regions are believed to be more involved in the task under investigation. An advantage of functional imaging studies is that they can be used to localize all the regions involved in a task. Furthermore, because this method is relatively noninvasive, this sort of imaging can be used to scan healthy participants, which allows for observation of activity in the normal brain. However, a disadvantage is that although functional imaging can indicate which regions are engaged in a task, they cannot be used to discern which regions are necessary for that task. In short, correlation does not equal causation.

Transcranial Magnetic Stimulation

TMS involves passing electricity through a coil of wires placed over a participant's head (see Pascual-Leone, Walsh, & Rothwell, 2000, for a review). Inducing a current creates a magnetic field that passes through the scalp and skull, and stimulates the neuronal tissue. A single pulse of stimulation is applied in TMS, whereas a series of pulses are applied in repetitive TMS. In many cases, stimulation is believed to be disruptive and is often used to, in effect, create a short-term lesion. An advantage to TMS studies is that, similar to lesion studies, it may be possible to determine if an area is necessary for a particular task by causing a temporary "lesion" in that area during performance of the task, and determining if performance is disrupted. In addition, performance cannot be due to reorganization as it is unlikely to occur in such a short timeframe. However, a disadvantage of TMS is that the stimulation can sometimes cause muscle movement in facial muscles, which can interfere with the task. Also, participants have reported varying amounts of pain, particularly in the temporal regions, limiting locations where it can be applied. There is also some controversy over how localized the "lesion" actually is; it is difficult to delineate the precise effects on the brain tissue.

Model of Naming

A model of naming is depicted in Figure 6.1. One of the fundamental findings in the literature is that naming is a process that occurs across two independent stages: conceptual and word-form processing. Semantic processing entails forming a unique semantic representation of an item, whereas word-form processing entails forming phonological and orthographic representations with the accompanying articulatory or written output. Evidence for this distinction comes from converging lines of evidence.

One line of evidence is that normal speakers can experience a tip-of-the tongue state in which they know what they want to say, but cannot find the word to say it. Conceptual knowledge is intact because they can often form an image of the item or person in their minds and can even give a verbal or gestural description. In trying to produce the name "horse" they might gesture a riding motion or describe it as an animal that eats hay and often races around a track. These abilities to describe the item suggest that the semantic representation is intact and that the problem stems from a latter, separate stage of processing.

Another line of evidence comes from patients with production anomia, which is characterized by production deficits in the face of intact comprehension. As an example, a patient might be unable to name the picture of a horse but would be able to match the word "horse" to a corresponding picture. Again, the fact that comprehension is intact indicates that the deficit does not originate with semantic processing and therefore likely occurs during word-form processing.

Semantics

The semantic stage consists of activating a semantic representation of an item and linking it to a word-form representation. It begins by constructing a conceptual representation that is tied to the modality of presentation. For example, a picture of a horse activates features in the visual cortex (e.g., hoofs, mane, tail) that helps to recognize the item as unique (horse) in relation to other visual representations (chair). Although modal representations are involved in activating a general semantic representation, they are not part of the core semantic representation of an item. When modal processing is interrupted, items can still be recognized through other modalities (Beauvois, 1982; Chanoine, Ferreira, Demonet, Nespoulous, & Poncet, 1998; Coslett & Saffran, 1992; Hillis & Caramazza, 1995; Iorio, Falanga, Fragassi, & Grossi, 1992; Lhermitte & Beauvois, 1973). For anyone who has had experience with horses, they would likely be able to recognize one from the sounds that it makes even if they are blindfolded. Furthermore, damage to modal processing does not seem it inhibit the ability to describe an item, which suggests that the semantic representation is intact.

At a certain point in the stream of processing, the semantic representation becomes amodal. The amodal representation of an item is constructed overtime by combining the features of that item across modalities

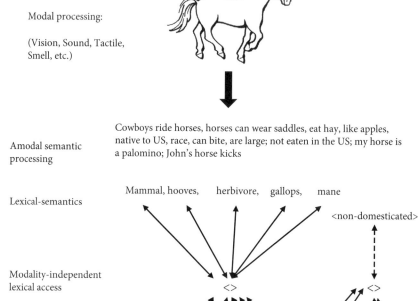

Conceptual stage

Modal processing:

(Vision, Sound, Tactile, Smell, etc.)

Amodal semantic processing

Cowboys ride horses, horses can wear saddles, eat hay, like apples, native to US, race, can bite, are large; not eaten in the US; my horse is a palomino; John's horse kicks

Lexical-semantics

Mammal, hooves,   herbivore,   gallops,   mane

<non-domesticated>

Modality-independent lexical access

<>   <>

Phonological processing (or orthographic processing)

/h/   /or/   /s/   /d/   /ir/   H o r s e   d e e r

Figure 6.1 Schematic representation of the cognitive processes underlying picture naming. The representations that receive the most activation, and are therefore selected for output, are shown in bold. Solid lines indicate processes involved in oral naming; dashed lines indicate processes involved in written naming. More peripheral mechanisms for output (e.g., output buffers, mechanisms for motor programming of output) are not shown.

to create a set of defining features or characteristics. These features can include modal information (mane, tail, whinney) as well as more complex information (eats hay, races around a track, ridden with a saddle). In comprehension tasks amodal representations are not disrupted by damage to modal processing regions and in production tasks they influence output across modalities. Another distinguishing feature of amodal semantics is that it encompasses nonlinguistic semantic processing, such that damage can result in difficulty in interacting with items. As an example, a person with damage to amodal semantics might try to ride a deer instead of a horse.

So, far we have used "conceptual" and "semantic" representation interchangeably. However, the

conceptual information might be considered to include everything a person knows about the item, whether or not it is import for "defining" that item or distinguishing it from other items. For example, the fact that many horses like carrots may be part of the conceptual representation of horses. However, it is not especially important for defining horses (nor does it distinguish them from deer or other hooved animals or even rabbits). We will now use "semantic" representation with a more restricted sense–i.e., the features that define the referent, that distinguish it from other related items.

Next, the semantic representation is linked to a word-form. The linking mechanism is not well understood, but likely consists of a representation that is intermediate between semantic and word-form representations. Furthermore, linking is likely a multi-step process over distributed regions of the brain. As such, the nature of the deficits should vary with damage to various stages of the linking process. This phenomenon is observed with damage to lexical-semantics, which is defined by deficits in comprehension as well as production, and with damage to lexical-access, which is restricted to deficits in production.

The system must be able to select the target concept in face of competition from other items. As the target is activated, competitor items, which share features with the target, are also activated. The degree to which a competitor is activated is related to the amount of overlap shared with the target. As such, competitors with high overlap (deer, zebra) tend to be more activated than competitors with low overlap (computer, chair). This effect is evidenced in cases of semantic priming in which the presentation of a word (doctor) tends to make it easier to recognize or generate semantically related words (nurse). Errors can occur when the target is not activated enough in relation to the competitors. A large proportion of these errors are semantic in nature such that a semantic competitor is produced instead of the target word (target = horse, semantic competitor = deer, saddle). Since most words share features with others in some semantic dimension, it is amazing that language is not filled with semantic errors.

Word-Form Stage, Phonology, and Articulation

The word-form stage encompasses activating a phonological representation of the word, followed by planning and executing the corresponding articulatory movements. In processing the phonological representation, the producer must be able to select the correct phonemes in the proper sequence, for each morpheme of the word. For example, for the word "horses" the producer needs to select the phonemes in the word "horse" and the plural marker "s." Next, the phonemic representation must be translated into a phonetic and motor plan for the articulators. Finally, the motor plan must be enacted for articulation to occur.

Syntax

In addition to semantic and phonological representations, words are also represented according to grammatical categories. We focus here on nouns and verbs because they are the most widely studied

in relation to naming. In linguistics, the determination of grammatical categories includes properties about their meaning, their inflections, and their distribution in the language. Nouns usually refer to physical entities (horse, saddle), whereas verbs tend to refer to actions (ride, gallop). Nouns are inflected for number (horse -> horses) and the possessive (Jim's horse). Verbs can be inflected for tense (race -> racing -> raced) or person (I think vs. He thinks). In English, nouns tend to appear after determiners, whereas verbs can occur after a noun but also appear after an auxiliary (e.g., will hit). Furthermore, verbs can vary in their argument structures. As an example, some verbs, such as "give," can appear in the double object structure ("Jim gave Dale the saddle") or the prepositional dative structure ("Jim gave the saddle to Dale"). Other verbs, which are similar in meaning, can appear in the prepositional dative structure ("Jim donated the saddle to Dale") or are ungrammatical in the double object dative structure ("Jim donated Dale the saddle").

At minimum, the major debates in this area concern two related questions. Are grammatical categories of words (specifically object and action names) differentially represented in the brain? Does syntax processing occur amodally before word-form processing (Levelt, Roelofs, & Meyer, 1999; Dell, 1986), or modality-specifically during word-form processing (Caramazza, 1997)? These debates are addressed elsewhere and are not discussed further here, except to recognize some evidence for independent neural substrates underlying some aspect of modality-independent (access to) representations of object and action names.

Timing and Interactivity

In the psycholinguistic literature, a major debate concerns the nature of information flow between stages of processing. In strictly feedforward models (Levelt et al., 1999), the conceptual representation of an item must be completed before activation begins at the word-form. Furthermore, activation during the word-form stage does not feedback to the conceptual stage. In contrast, interactive models allow activation during the conceptual stage to cascade into the next stage before the conceptual representation is completed and it allows for feedback from the word-form stage to the conceptual stage (Dell, 1986). Although there is some evidence that sheds light on the relation between timing of the stages of naming and corresponding activity in various brain regions (Levelt, Praamstra, Meyer,

Helenius, & Salmelin, 1998), the methodology has not moved to the point where definitive conclusion can be drawn.

Neural Representations of Naming
Conceptual Stage

Conceptual processing involves forming a unique concept of an item and linking it to a word-form. The evidence indicates that processing occurs in a network of distributed regions, mostly, but not exclusively, in the left hemisphere. These regions include portions of the temporal lobe, the angular gyrus, the fusiform gyrus, and perhaps the inferior frontal gyrus (IFG). There is no strict one to one correspondence between an aspect of semantic processing and a particular region. It seems that these regions participate to varying degrees in multiple functions that support conceptual processing (DeLeon et al., 2007). However, in general terms, modal representations correspond to regions specialized for that particular input modality (e.g., bilateral occipital lobe for vision, bilateral temporal lobe for audition); amodal representations correspond to the bilateral anterior temporal lobe; linking between semantics and word-form correspond to left posterior temporal regions; and selection mechanisms for output or task response correspond to portions of the left IFG.

MODAL PROCESSING

Modal processing is defined as forming a representation that allows for the recognition of that object in the modality of presentation and allowing for access to amodal semantics. Modal processing is related to regions that process input, such as the visual cortex, the somatosensory cortex, and the auditory cortex. Damage to these areas can result in agnosia, in which the object cannot be identified in a particular modality even though the basic sensory representations and semantic knowledge is intact. In such cases, the patient cannot name the object because they cannot recognize it.

The most common types of visual agnosia are apperceptive and associative agnosia. Apperceptive agnosia is characterized by the ability to process basic visual features, such as color, brightness, and motion, but an inability to combine these structural properties into a meaningful percept. As such, it is related to lesions in the visual cortex, often after a stroke or carbon monoxide poisoning, and is believed to occur because of damage to early visual processing. As an example, patients would be unable to copy the picture of a horse, or even tell which picture of a horse was different from other pictures of horses, unless its distinguishing feature was a basic visual characteristic, such as color or size.

Associative agnosia, also known as optic aphasia or visual object agnosia, is characterized by the ability to process the basic sensory information and form a percept of the item, but an inability to understand what that item is. For example, a person with optic aphasia can copy the picture of a horse, but cannot name the item. They might have trouble sorting pictures of horses and deer (Hillis & Caramazza, 1995). Naming often results in semantic errors suggesting that the locus of the problem may stem from difficulty with semantic access. Associative agnosia is more common than apperceptive agnosia and tends to result from lesions to the left occipital cortex and the splenium. This results in a disconnection from visual processing in the right hemisphere and language processing in the left hemisphere.

Auditory agnosia is generally characterized by the inability to process auditory material in a meaningful way. Deficits can range from the inability to hear words (verbal agnosia); the inability to hear music (amusia); or the inability to process environmental sounds, such as a car starting or a dog barking. Auditory agnosia results from damage to auditory cortex and surrounding areas.

Astereognosis, or tactile agnosia, is characterized by deficits in perceiving objects through tactile stimulation although basic tactile sensation is intact. There is a distinction between the inability to recognize basic features of an object, such as size, weight, and texture, and the inability to name or recognize the object. Patients who cannot recognize an object by touch may still be able to draw the object and recognize the object pictured in the drawing. Sometimes they can describe the physical features of the object but cannot recognize the object. Pure astereognosis is thought to be caused by lesions of the somatosensory cortex.

AMODAL SEMANTIC PROCESSING

Amodal semantics is described as a representation that sits at the core of nonlinguistic and linguistic semantics and therefore affects comprehension and production across modalities. Converging evidence suggests that amodal semantics is most closely associated with the bilateral anterior temporal lobe, especially Brodmann areas (BA) 38, 20, and 21.

Evidence for an amodal representation comes from patients with semantic dementia, which is a degenerative disease that results in bilateral damage to the anterior temporal poles (BA 38). Patients with semantic dementia have deficits in semantic tasks in contrast to relatively normal abilities in other aspects of cognition (e.g., executive functioning) and other aspects of language are normal (e.g., phonology). Comprehension and production deficits occur across all modalities. In comprehension tasks, patients have difficulty matching an object to: its spoken or written name; the sound that it makes; its smell (Bozeat, Lambon Ralph, Patterson, Garrard, & Hodges, 2000; Coccia, Bartolini, Luzzi, Provinciali, & Lambon Ralph, 2004); its tactile sensation; or a verbal definition (Lambon Ralph, Graham, Patterson, & Hodges, 1999). In production tasks, patients have difficulty with spoken or written production of an object presented in visual (Lambon Ralph, Graham, Ellis, Hodges, 1998; Lambon Ralph, McClelland, Patterson, Galton, Hodges, 2001), auditory, or tactile form. They even have trouble drawing a copy of an object, especially after delay (Bozeat et al., 2003). Naming is affected by frequency, familiarity, and complexity (Bozeat et al., 2000; Funnell, 1995; Jefferies & Lambon Ralph, 2006) and errors are consistent across tasks (Jefferies & Lambon Ralph, 2006).

A recent study of patients with unilateral chronic lesions of the anterior temporal pole (left or right) indicated that neither unilateral anterior temporal lesion caused substantial semantic impairment, and that bilateral damage was essential for the severe impairment of semantic memory seen in semantic dementia (Lambon Ralph, Cipolotti, Manes, & Patterson, 2010). A recent study of acute stroke patients with unilateral left anterior temporal lesions compared with acute stroke patients with lesions matched in volume in other regions of the left hemisphere also found no association between unilateral left anterior temporal pole (BA 38) damage and amodal semantic deficits (Tsapkini, Frangakis, & Hillis, 2011).

The functional imaging literature has been less clear on the matter, because several studies did not result in activation of the anterior temporal lobel (ATL) in semantic tasks. This has likely led to the exclusion of the ATL as a region of amodal processing in models of language processing that heavily rely on functional imaging data (Hickok & Poeppel, 2004; Indefrey & Levelt, 2004; Wise, 2003). To address this issue, Visser, Jefferies, and Lambon Ralph (2010) conducted a meta-analysis and found that when certain factors are taken into consideration, such as task type, ATL activation is more likely to be observed in semantic tasks.

Lexical-Semantics

The term *lexical-semantics* is defined as the processing required to link the semantic representation of an item to its word-form in both production and comprehension. Processing is associated with a relatively broad region that spans the posterior superior temporal gyrus (pSTG; BA 22), the angular gyrus (BA 39), and the posterior middle temporal gyrus (pMTG; BA 21). Lesions to pSTG often result in Wernicke aphasia, which is characterized by fluent, but meaningless speech and repetition as well as impaired sentence and word comprehension. Errors consist of a mixture of semantic errors (dog-bone) and phonological errors (dog-wog), which highlights the fact that this area sits at the interface between semantics and phonology. Similar deficits occur in reading and writing. In general, they are unaware of their errors.

Both chronic lesions and temporal lesions in BA 22 cause word comprehension deficits or impaired lexical semantics (Lesser et al., 1986; Hart & Gordon, 1990; Leff et al., 2009). Likewise, the severity of hypoperfusion in BA 22 correlates with severity of lexical-semantic deficits (Hillis et al., 2001b), and in the acute setting, restored blood flow to the area results in improved lexical semantic processing (Hillis et al., 2001a; Hillis and Heidler, 2002). Functional imaging data indicate that this region is highly involved in phonological processing (Buchsbaum, Hickok, & Humphries, 2001; Okada & Hickok, 2006; Price et al., 1996) and word comprehension (Leff et al., 2002; Fridriksson & Morrow, 2005).

Lesions to the areas adjacent to BA 22, most notably pMTG and the angular gyrus, often result in transcortical sensory aphasia, which is similar to Wernicke aphasia but differs in that repetition is relatively intact. The angular gyrus is an ideal site for lexical-semantic processing because it receives input from adjacent regions that process visual, auditory, and somatosensory information. Damage to the angular gyrus can result in naming deficits in naming tasks (e.g., of pictures) (Farias, Harrington, Broomand, & Seyal, 2005; Fridriksson & Morrow, 2005; Harrington, Buonocore, & Farias, 2006; Kemeny et al., 2006). Functional imaging studies have revealed activation for picture naming and semantic tasks (semantic relative to phonological judgments) (Mummery, Patterson, Hodges, & Price, 1998). However, this region may also play a role in translating between semantics, orthography, and phonology representations.

Modality-Independent Lexical Access

The occurrence of problems with lexical-access, also known as anomia, is defined as difficulty in naming with intact semantic processing as evidenced by relatively intact comprehension. The region most closely associated with lexical-access is the posterior inferior temporal gyrus BA 37. Lesions to BA 37 tend to result in naming errors that are semantic in nature (horse-zebra), and patients are usually aware of their mistakes. In the acute setting, reperfusion of BA 37 is associated with improvement in naming but not comprehension (Hillis et al., 2006).

The evidence suggests that left BA 37 is involved in amodal lexical access. Lesions result in naming deficits regardless of whether the task is to name an object in relation to a picture (DeLeon et al., 2007); the associated sound (e.g., naming "dog" to the sound of barking; Tranel, Grabowski, Lyon, & Damasio, 2005); or a tactile representation (Hillis & Caramazza, 1995). Furthermore, functional imaging studies indicate that BA 37 is activated during naming (Abrahams et al., 2003; Grabowski, Damasio, Eichhorn, & Tranel, 2003; Howard et al., 1992; Kemeny et al., 2006; Moore & Price, 1999; Price, Devlin, Moore, Morton, & Laird, 2005; Price et al., 2006; Saccuman et al., 2006); during spelling (Rapcsak & Beeson, 2004); and during reading (Cohen et al., 2000, 2002). Buchel, Price, and Friston (1998) found this region to be active during reading even in the congenitally blind reading Braille. All the evidence suggests that this region is a convergence zone between visual, semantic, and auditory information (Raymer et al., 1997; Foundas, Daniels, & Vasterling, 1998) and labels for these concepts.

Modality-Specific Lexical Selection

Lexical selection involves processing that activates the target in the face of competitors. Investigations into the nature of semantic processing suggest that the IFG, especially posterior anterior regions (BA 45, 47), is involved in working memory processing that guides lexical selection. In general, imaging studies have found greater relative activation of the posterior IFG during tasks that require semantic processing. These include categorization (e.g., living vs. nonliving), synonym judgments, and verb generation in which the participant must generate a verb after being presented with a noun (e.g., scissors -> cut) (Fiez, 1997; Poldrack, et al.,

1999). Furthermore, TMS studies have found that stimulating pIFG results in longer reaction times in tasks that require semantic processing (Devlin, Matthews, & Rushworth, 2003; Gough, Nobre, & Devlin, 2005). Devlin et al., (2003) concluded that although the IFG may not be necessary for semantic processing, it helped with efficiency. Semantic selection includes processing that helps to select the target word when there are multiple competitors (Thompson-Schill, D'Eposito, Aguirre, & Farrah, 1997), as well as activating stored representations of the target word when it is underspecified by context cues (Badre, Poldrack, Pare-Blagoev, Insler, & Wagner, 2005; Hindy, Hamilton, Houghtling, Coslett, & Thompson-Schill, 2009: Wagner, Pare-Blagoev, Clark, & Poldrack, 2001). Selection processing is claimed to take place in BA 45 postlexical selection processing, whereas BA 47 handles controlled retrieval.

However, this region appears to be activated during all selection tasks, not just semantic selection. The selection that takes place in the frontal lobes for the naming process seems to be post-semantic or even post-lexical (see Deleon et al., 2007 for evidence). That is, selection of phonological representations or even motor programs for articulatory planning may take place in posterior frontal cortex for production of the name of the object.

Phonological Processing

Word-form processing encompasses processing the phonological representation, and either the articulatory representation in naming or the orthographic/graphemic representation in writing. As with semantic processing, the literature indicates that word-form processing takes place in a network of regions distributed across the brain. In relation to aspects of word-form processing, these regions can broadly be grouped into left posterior superior temporal gyrus and supramarginal gyrus for phonology, and areas of the motor cortex and IFG (which includes Broca area) involved in the planning of articulatory movements. Together, these areas are believed to form the network for the phonological loop/working memory that consists of the storage, retrieval, and rehearsal of phonological material, with phonological material stored in the posterior areas of the network, rehearsal involving the IFG, and articulation involving the premotor and motor cortex. Certainly, these areas are crucial for monitoring one's own output and are activated by hearing one's own voice produce the name of an object in functional imaging studies.

Phonetics

Phonetic processing entails the planning of motor movements of the articulators. The areas most closely associated with phonetic processing are the IFG (notably Broca area); portions of the insular gyrus; and premotor and motor cortex. Damage to these areas is associated with deficits in fluency, which can include phonological errors, reduced phrase length, impaired melody, diminished words per minute, or agrammatic sentence production. Patients are aware of their errors and, in contrast to strictly phonological deficits, often struggle and show frustration during attempts to articulate the word correctly. Furthermore, fluency deficits are distinguished from problems with the muscles involved in articulation (dysarthria) because they are not associated with impairment in the rate, range, strength, or timing of movements of the jaw, palate, respiratory muscles, or vocal folds (Rohrer, Rossor, & Warren, 2010). Importantly, because the term *fluency* covers a broad range of deficits, the evidence indicates that it can manifest differently depending on the area of damage.

The IFG seems to be a multimodal region involved in the sequencing of phonological material across modalities. Broca aphasia, which is associated with damage to Broca area (roughly BA 44), is characterized by poor fluency and repetition, poor naming in oral and written modalities, poor spelling, and a decline in sentence comprehension as syntactic complexity increases (e.g. object relative clause: "The man that the woman is kicking is mean"). Additional supporting evidence comes from studies of nonfluent variants of primary progressive aphasia, which is associated with impairment of these language functions and atrophy in IFG (Ash et al., 2009), and also from the observation of similar deficits in the acute stage with hypoperfusion of left IFG and improvement in these language functions following reperfusion of left IFG (Davis et al., 2008).

Functional imaging evidence complements the lesion data in showing that the IFG, most notably anterior regions, is more closely associated with phonological tasks than with semantic tasks (Devlin et al., 2003; Gough et al., 2005). Furthermore, the data suggest that this region becomes more active as task difficulty increases, leading to claims of its involvement in phonological working memory tasks (Riecker, Brendel, Ziegler, Erb, & Ackermann, 2008; Poldrack et al., 1999; Price et al., 1996; Sekiyama, Kanno, Miura, & Sugita, 2003; Vigneau et al., 2006; Warburton et al., 1996). The IFG

(BA 44) and nearby insula have been implicated in articulatory planning in studies of chronic stroke (Dronkers, 1996) and progressive nonfluent aphasia (Ash et al., 2009; Gorno-Tempini et al., 2004), and acute infarct or hypoperfusion of the IFG (BA 44/45) is associated with impaired orchestration of speech articulation (Hillis et al., 2004b). The Supplementary cortex and the Premotor cortex are also involved in planning the articulatory movements of the word. Damage to these areas affects fluency in production, and functional imaging studies find that these areas tend to be more active during overt production (Indefrey & Levlet, 2004; Hickok & Poeppel, 2004); phonological judgments; and syllable judgments (Bookheimer, Zeffiro, Blaxton, Gaillard, & Theodore, 2000; Riecker et al., 2000).

Orthography

Tasks that involve reading or writing require some form of orthographic representation. Orthography seems to involve the superior temporal gyrus, the angular gyrus, and the supramrginal gyrus. These regions are involved in linking the phonological representations to the orthographic/graphemic representations (DeLeon et al., 2007; see Benson, 1979 or Hillis and Rapp, 2004, for review).

Grammatical/Syntactic Processing

The two main issues concerning the grammatical processing of word representations for naming have revolved around two questions. Are grammatical categories of words (specifically object and action names) differentially represented in the brain? Does grammatical processing of a word occur amodally before word-form processing, or modality-specifically during word-form processing?

In answer to the first question, there is ample evidence indicating that nouns and verbs are processed differently in the brain. Studies of grammatical categories usually involve such tasks as naming an item (noun) or action (verb), or inflecting the root of nouns and verbs. The general trend of evidence indicates that verb deficits occur with damage to the frontal lobe, especially portions of the IFG, and to regions of the parietal lobe. In contrast, noun deficits tend to occur with damage to the posterior middle and inferior temporal lobes (Damasio & Tranel, 1993; Zingeser & Berndt, 1990).

However, this evidence alone does not mean that the distinction is grammatical. There are several claims that the distinction could be due to differences in semantic features or complexity (Mätzig, Druks, Masterson, & Vigliocco, 2009). Numerous studies have shown that words from different semantic categories (living things vs. artifacts) are differentially represented in the brain (Damasio, Tranel, Grabowski, Adolphs, & Damasio, 2004). As such, it is not difficult to posit that the system would segregate processing along the semantic categories of items versus actions. In terms of complexity, verbs are generally thought to require a higher amount of processing (Mätzig, et al., 2009). As an example, nouns tend to rate higher on imageability scales (Bird, Howard, & Franklin, 2000, 2003), which are believed to reflect aspects of semantics and furthermore helps to explain why they are generally easier to process. Although frontal regions, such as the IFG, have been implicated in syntactic processing, as mentioned earlier it is also believed to be a region that is involved in word selection as it becomes more difficult to distinguish the semantic representation of the target from competitors. Therefore, processing in this area could be related to either syntactic features that involve distinctions of grammatical class or to processing difficulty, in which case higher levels of activation occur for verbs because they are generally more difficult.

In answer to the second question, there is evidence that grammatical category may be represented amodally and redundantly in the phonological and orthographic output modalities. Evidence for an amodal representation comes from studies in which grammatical deficits were found across class and across output modalities (Badecker, Miozzo, & Zanuttini, 1995; Gonon, Bruckert, & Michel, 1989; Miozzo & Caramazza, 1997; Shapiro & Caramazza, 2003; Vigliocco, Vinson, Martin, & Garrett, 1999). In these cases participants had knowledge of the grammatical properties of the word, such as gender or case, despite being unable to recover the phonological form.

The strongest evidence in favor of modality-specific representations of grammatical category comes from patients who have a deficit in naming tasks for a grammatical category (verb) in one output modality (spoken naming), in contrast to intact naming for the same grammatical category in another modality (written naming). Furthermore, naming is relatively intact for other grammatical categories, such as nouns, and comprehension is intact across categories. This general pattern of modality-specific deficits has been observed for both nouns and verbs (Hillis & Caramazza, 1991; Hillis, Rapp, & Caramazza, 1999; Hillis, Tuffiash, & Caramazza, 2002), which indicates that the differences seen between nouns and verbs

are not simply a reflection of processing difficulty. Finally, because these deficits are restricted to one modality, the evidence suggests that at least some aspects of grammatical processing are represented modality-specific. In sum, the evidence supports claims for both an amodal stage of grammatical processing and modality-specific grammatical processing. It will take future studies to determine the exact nature of processing at these two points of word representation.

Conclusions

This chapter discusses the relationship between the linguistic representation of words and their neural representation. The representation of a word encompasses semantic, phonological, orthographic, and syntactic representations and intermediate representations used to map between them. Converging evidence indicates that words are represented in networks of regions across mainly the left hemisphere of the brain. The regions work in parallel to perform tasks involving word comprehension and production. The general case of naming difficulty can have multiple underlying causes in terms of both cognitive impairments and sites and nature of lesions.

Acknowledgement

This work was supported in part by a grant from the National Institutes of Health (NIDCD RO1 DC 05375).

References

Abrahams, S., Goldstein, L. H., Simmons, A., Brammer, M. J., Williams, S. C. R., Giampietro, V. P.,...& Leigh, P. N. (2003). Functional magnetic resonance imaging of verbal fluency and confrontation naming using compressed image acquisition to permit overt responses. *Human Brain Mapping, 20*(1), 29–40.

Ash, S., Moore, P., Vesely, L., Gunawardena, D., McMillan, C., Anderson, C.,...& Grossman, M. (2009). Non-fluent speech in frontotemporal lobar degeneration. *Journal of Neurolinguistics, 22*(4), 370–383.

Badecker, W., Miozzo, M., & Zanuttini, R. (1995). The 2-stage model of lexical retrieval—evidence from a case of anomia with selective preservation of grammatical gender. *Cognition, 57*(2), 193–216.

Badre, D., Poldrack, R. A., Pare-Blagoev, E. J., Insler, R. Z., & Wagner, A. D. (2005). Dissociable controlled retrieval and generalized selection mechanisms in ventrolateral prefrontal cortex. *Neuron, 47*(6), 907–918.

Beauvois, M. F. (1982). Optic aphasia—A process of interaction between vision and language. *Philosophical Transactions of the Royal Society of London Series B-Biological Sciences, 298*(1089), 35–47.

Benson, D. F. (1979). *Aphasia, alexia and agraphia.* New York: Churchill.

Bird, H., Howard, D., & Franklin, S. (2000). Why is a verb like an inanimate object? Grammatical category and semantic category deficits. *Brain and Language, 72*, 246–309.

Bird, H., Howard, D., & Franklin, S. (2003). Verbs and nouns: The importance of being imageable. *Journal of Neurolinguistics, 16*, 113–149.

Bookheimer, S. Y., Zeffiro, T. A., Blaxton, T. A., Gaillard, W., & Theodore, W. H. (2000). Activation of language cortex with automatic speech tasks. *Neurology, 55*(8), 1151–1157.

Bozeat, S., Lambon Ralph, M. A., Graham, K. S., Patterson, K., Wilkin, H., Rowland, J.,…Hodges, J. R. (2003). A duck with four legs: Investigating the structure of conceptual knowledge using picture drawing in semantic dementia. *Cognitive Neuropsychology, 20*(1), 27–47.

Bozeat, S., Lambon Ralph, M. A., Patterson, K., Garrard, P., & Hodges, J. R. (2000). Non-verbal semantic impairment in semantic dementia. *Neuropsychologia, 38*(9), 1207–1215.

Buchel, C., Price, C., & Friston, K. (1998). A multimodal language region in the ventral visual pathway. *Nature, 394*(6690), 274–277.

Buchsbaum, B. R., Hickok, G., & Humphries, C. (2001). Role of left posterior superior temporal gyrus in phonological processing for speech perception and production. *Cognitive Science, 25*(5), 663–678.

Caramazza, A. (1997). How many levels of processing are there in lexical access? *Cognitive Neuropsychology, 14*, 177–208.

Chanoine, V., Ferreira, C. T., Demonet, J. F., Nespoulous, J. L., & Poncet, M. (1998). Optic aphasia with pure alexia: A mild form of visual associative agnosia? A case study. *Cortex, 34*(3), 437–448.

Coccia, M., Bartolini, M., Luzzi, S., Provinciali, L., & Lambon Ralph, M. A. (2004). Semantic memory is an amodal dynamic system: Evidence from the interaction of naming and object use in semantic dementia. *Cognitive Neuropsychology, 21*(5), 513–527.

Cohen, L., Dehaene, S., Naccache, L., Lehericy, S., Dehaene-Lambertz, G., Henaff, M. A., & Michel, F. (2000). The visual word form area—Spatial and temporal characterization of an initial stage of reading in normal subjects and posterior split-brain patients. *Brain, 123*, 291–307.

Cohen, L., Lehericy, S., Chochon, F., Lemer, C., Rivaud, S., & Dehaene, S. (2002). Language-specific tuning of visual cortex functional properties of the visual word form area. *Brain, 125*, 1054–1069.

Coslett, H. B., & Saffran, E. M. (1992). Optic aphasia and the right-hemisphere—A replication and extension. *Brain and Language, 43*(1), 148–161.

Damasio, A. R., & Tranel, D. (1993). Nouns and verbs are retrieved with differently distributed neural systems. *Proceedings of the National Academy of Sciences U S A, 90*, 4957–4960.

Damasio, H., Tranel, D., Grabowski, T., Adolphs, R., & Damasio, A. (2004). Neural systems behind word and concept retrieval. *Cognition, 92*, 179–229.

Davis, C., Kleinman, J. T., Newhart, M., Gingis, L., Pawlak, M., & Hillis, A. E. (2008). Speech and language functions that require a functioning Broca's area. *Brain and Language, 105*(1), 50–58.

Dell, G. S. (1986). A spreading-activation theory of retrieval in sentence production. *Psychological Review, 93*(3), 283–321.

DeLeon, J., Gottesman, R. F., Kleinman, J. T., Newhart, M., Davis, C., Heidler-Gary, J.,… & Hillis, A. E. (2007). Neural regions essential for distinct cognitive processes underlying picture naming. *Brain, 130*, 1408–1422.

Devlin, J. T., Matthews, P. M., & Rushworth, M. F. S. (2003). Semantic processing in the left inferior prefrontal cortex: A combined functional magnetic resonance imaging and transcranial magnetic stimulation study. *Journal of Cognitive Neuroscience, 15*(1), 71–84.

Dronkers, N. F. (1996). A new brain region for coordinating speech articulation. *Nature, 384*(6605), 159–161.

Farias, S. T., Harrington, G., Broomand, C., & Seyal, M. (2005). Differences in functional MR imaging activation patterns associated with confrontation naming and responsive naming. *American Journal of Neuroradiology, 26*(10), 2492–2499.

Fiez, J. A. (1997). Phonology, semantics, and the role of the left inferior prefrontal cortex. *Human Brain Mapping, 5*(2), 79–83.

Foundas, A. L., Daniels, S. K., & Vasterling, J. J. (1998). Anemia: Case studies with lesion localization. *Neurocase, 4*(1), 35–43.

Fridriksson, J., & Morrow, L. (2005). Cortical activation and language task difficulty in aphasia. *Aphasiology, 19*(3–5), 239–250.

Funnell, E. (1995). Objects and properties: a study of the breakdown of semantic memory. *Memory, 3*, 497–518.

Gonon, M. A. H., Bruckert, R., & Michel, F. (1989). Lexicalization in an anomic patient. *Neuropsychologia, 27*(4), 391–407.

Gorno-Tempini, M. L., Dronkers, N. F., Rankin, K. P., Ogar, J. M., Phengrasamy, L., Rosen, H. J.,… & Miller, B. L. (2004). Cognition and anatomy in three variants of primary progressive aphasia. *Annals of Neurology, 55*(3), 335–346.

Gough, P. M., Nobre, A. C., & Devlin, J. T. (2005). Dissociating linguistic processes in the left inferior frontal cortex with transcranial magnetic stimulation. *Journal of Neuroscience, 25*(35), 8010–8016.

Grabowski, T. J., Damasio, H., Eichhorn, G. R., & Tranel, D. (2003). Effects of gender on blood flow correlates of naming concrete entities. *Neuroimage, 20*(2), 940–954.

Harrington, G. S., Buonocore, M. H., & Farias, S. T. (2006). Intrasubject reproducibility of functional MR imaging activation in language tasks. *American Journal of Neuroradiology, 27*(4), 938–944.

Hart, J., & Gordon, B. (1990). Delineation of single-word semantic comprehension deficits in aphasia, with anatomical correlation. *Annals of Neurology, 27*(3), 226–231.

Hickok, G., & Poeppel, D. (2004). Dorsal and ventral streams: a framework for understanding aspects of the functional anatomy of language. *Cognition, 92*(1–2), 67–99.

Hillis, A. E., Barker, P. B., Beauchamp, N. J., Winters, B. D., Mirski, M., & Wityk, R. J. (2001a). Restoring blood pressure reperfused Wernicke's area and improved language. *Neurology, 56*(5), 670–672.

Hillis, A. E., & Caramazza, A. (1991). Lexical organization of nouns and verbs in the brain. *Nature, 349*(6312), 788–790.

Hillis, A. E., & Caramazza, A. (1995). Cognitive and neural mechanisms underlying visual and semantic processing—Implications from optic aphasia. *Journal of Cognitive Neuroscience, 7*(4), 457–478.

Hillis, A. E., & Heidler, J. (2002). Mechanisms of early aphasia recovery. *Aphasiology, 16*(9), 885–895.

Hillis, A. E., Kleinman, J. T., Newhart, M., Heidler-Gary, J., Gottesman, R., Barker, P. B.,… & Chaudhry, P. (2006). Restoring cerebral blood flow reveals neural regions critical for naming. *Journal of Neuroscience, 26*(31), 8069–8073.

Hillis, A. E., & Rapp, B. C. (2004). Cognitive and neural substrates of written language: Comprehension and production.

In M. S. Gazzaniga (Ed.), *The new cognitive neurosciences* (3rd ed., pp. 755–788). Cambridge, MA: MIT Press.

Hillis, A. E., Rapp, B. C., & Caramazza, A. (1999). When a rose is a rose in speech but a tulip in writing. *Cortex, 35*(3), 337–356.

Hillis, A. E., Tuffiash, E., & Caramazza, A. (2002). Modality-specific deterioration in naming verbs in non-fluent primary progressive aphasia. *Journal of Cognitive Neuroscience, 4*(7), 1099–1108.

Hillis, A. E., Wityk, R. J., Tuffiash, E., Beauchamp, N. J., Jacobs, M. A., Barker, P. B., & Selnes, O. A. (2001b). Hypoperfusion of Wernicke's area predicts severity of semantic deficit in acute stroke. *Annals of Neurology, 50*(5), 561–566.

Hillis, A. E., Work, M., Barker, P. B., Jacobs, M. A., Breese, E. L., & Maurer, K. (2004b). Re-examining the brain regions crucial for orchestrating speech articulation. *Brain, 127,* 1479–1487.

Hindy, N. C., Hamilton, R., Houghtling, A. S., Coslett, H. B., & Thompson-Schill, S. L. (2009). Computer-mouse tracking reveals TMS disruptions of prefrontal function during semantic retrieval. *Journal of Neurophysiology, 102*(6), 3405–3413.

Howard, D., Patterson, K., Wise, R., Brown, W. D., Friston, K., Weiller, C., & Frackowiak, R. (1992). The cortical localization of the lexicons—Positron emission tomography evidence. *Brain, 115,* 1769–1782.

Indefrey, P., & Levelt, W. J. M. (2004). The spatial and temporal signatures of word production components. *Cognition, 92*(1–2), 101–144.

Iorio, L., Falanga, A., Fragassi, N. A., & Grossi, D. (1992). Visual associative agnosia and optic aphasia—A single case-study and a review of the syndromes. *Cortex, 28*(1), 23–37.

Jefferies, E., & Lambon Ralph, M. A. (2006). Semantic impairment in stroke aphasia versus semantic dementia: a case-series comparison. *Brain, 129,* 2132–2147.

Kemeny, S., Xu, J., Park, G. H., Hosey, L. A., Wettig, C. M., & Braun, A. R. (2006). Temporal dissociation of early lexical access and articulation using a delayed naming task—An fMRI study. *Cerebral Cortex, 16*(4), 587–595.

Lambon Ralph, M., Cipolotti, L., Manes, F., & Patterson, K. (2010). Taking both sides: Do unilateral, anterior temporal-lobe lesions disrupt semantic memory? *Brain, 133,* 3243–3255.

Lambon Ralph, M. A., Graham, K. S., Ellis, A. W., & Hodges, J. R. (1998). Naming in semantic dementia—What matters? *Neuropsychologia, 36,* 775–784.

Lambon Ralph, M. A., Graham, K. S., Patterson, K., & Hodges, J. R. (1999). Is a picture worth a thousand words? Evidence from concept definitions by patients with semantic dementia. *Brain and Language, 70,* 309–335.

Lambon Ralph, M. A., McClelland, J. L., Patterson, K., Galton, C. J., Hodges, J. R. (2001). No right to speak? The relationship between object naming and semantic impairment: Neuropsychological abstract evidence and a computational model. *Journal of Cognitive Neuroscience, 13,* 341–356.

Leff, A., Crinion, J., Scott, S., Turkheimer, F., Howard, D., & Wise, R. A. (2002). Physiological change in the homotopic cortex following left posterior temporal lobe infarction. *Annals of Neurology, 51*(5), 553–558.

Leff, A. P., Schofield, T. M., Crinion, J. T., Seghier, M. L., Grogan, A., Green, D. W., Price, C. J. (2009). The left superior temporal gyrus is a shared substrate for auditory short-term memory and speech comprehension: evidence from 210 patients with stroke. *Brain, 132*(Pt 12):3401–3410.

Lesser, R. P., Luders, H., Morris, H. H., Dinner, D. S., Klem, G., Hahn, J., & Harrison, M. (1986). Electrical-stimulation of Wernicke's area interferes with comprehension. *Neurology, 36*(5), 658–663.

Levelt, W. J. M., Praamstra, P., Meyer, A. S., Helenius, P., & Salmelin, R. (1998). An MEG study of picture naming. *Journal of Cognitive Neuroscience, 10,* 553–567.

Levelt, W. J. M., Roelofs, A., & Meyer, A. S. (1999). A theory of lexical access in speech production. *Behavioral and Brain Sciences, 22*(1), 1–38.

Lhermitte, F., & Beauvois, M. F. (1973). Visual-speech disconnetion syndrome—Report of a case with optic aphasia, agnosic alexia and color agnosia. *Brain, 96,* 695–714.

Mätzig, S., Druks, J., Masterson, J., & Vigliocco, G. (2009). Noun and verb differences in picture naming: Past studies and new evidence. *Cortex, 45*(6), 738–758.

Miozzo, M., & Caramazza, A. (1997). On knowing the auxiliary of a verb that cannot be named: Evidence for the independence of grammatical and phonological aspects of lexical knowledge. *Journal of Cognitive Neuroscience, 9*(1), 160–166.

Moore, C. J., & Price, C. J. (1999). Three distinct ventral occipitotemporal regions for reading and object naming. *Neuroimage, 10*(2), 181–192.

Mummery, C. J., Patterson, K., Hodges, J. R., & Price, C. J. (1998). Functional neuroanatomy of the semantic system: Divisible by what? *Journal of Cognitive Neuroscience, 10*(6), 766–777.

Okada, K., & Hickok, G. (2006). Left posterior auditory-related cortices participate both in speech perception and speech production: Neural overlap revealed by fMRI. *Brain and Language, 98*(1), 112–117.

Pascual-Leone, A., Walsh, V., & Rothwell, J. (2000). Transcranial magnetic stimulation in cognitive neuroscience—virtual lesion, chronometry, and functional connectivity. *Current Opinion in Neurobiology, 10*(2), 232–237.

Poldrack, R. A., Wagner, A. D., Prull, M. W., Desmond, J. E., Glover, G. H., & Gabrieli, J. D. E. (1999). Functional specialization for semantic and phonological processing in the left inferior prefrontal cortex. *Neuroimage, 10*(1), 15–35.

Price, C. J., Devlin, J. T., Moore, C. J., Morton, C., & Laird, A. R. (2005). Meta-analyses of object naming: Effect of baseline. *Human Brain Mapping, 25*(1), 70–82.

Price, C. J., McCrory, E., Noppeney, U., Mechelli, A., Moore, C. J., Biggio, N., & Devlin, J. T. (2006). How reading differs from object naming at the neuronal level. *Neuroimage, 29*(2), 643–648.

Price, C. J., Wise, R. J. S., Warburton, E. A., Moore, C. J., Howard, D., Patterson, K.,…Friston, K. J. (1996). Hearing and saying. The functional neuroanatomy of auditory word processing. *Brain, 119,* 919–931.

Rapcsak, S. Z., & Beeson, P. M. (2004). The role of left posterior inferior temporal cortex in spelling. *Neurology, 62*(12), 2221–2229.

Raymer, A. M., Foundas, A. L., Maher, L. M., Greenwald, M. L., Morris, M., Rothi, L. J. G., & Heilman, K. M. (1997). Cognitive neuropsychological analysis and neuroanatomic correlates in a case of acute anomia. *Brain and Language, 58*(1), 137–156.

Riecker, A., Ackermann, H., Wildgruber, D., Meyer, J., Dogil, G., Haider, H., & Grodd, W. (2000). Articulatory/phonetic sequencing at the level of the anterior perisylvian cortex: A functional magnetic resonance imaging (fMRI) study. *Brain and Language, 75*(2), 259–276.

Riecker, A., Brendel, B., Ziegler, W., Erb, M., & Ackermann, H. (2008). The influence of syllable onset complexity and syllable frequency on speech motor control. *Brain and Language, 107*(2), 102–113.

Rohrer, J. D., Rossor, M. N., & Warren, J. D. (2010). Apraxia in progressive nonfluent aphasia. *Journal of Neurology, 257*(4), 569–574.

Saccuman, M. C., Cappa, S. F., Bates, E. A., Arevalo, A., Della Rosa, P., Danna, M., & Perani, D. (2006). The impact of semantic reference on word class: An fMRI study of action and object naming. *Neuroimage, 32*(4), 1865–1878.

Sekiyama, K., Kanno, I., Miura, S., & Sugita, Y. (2003). Auditory-visual speech perception examined by fMRI and. PET. *Neuroscience Research, 47*(3), 277–287.

Shapiro, K., & Caramazza, A. (2003). The representation of grammatical categories in the brain. *Trends in Cognitive Sciences, 7*(5), 201–206.

Thompson-Schill, S. L., D'Esposito, M., Aguirre, G. K., & Farah, M. J. (1997). Role of left inferior prefrontal cortex in retrieval of semantic knowledge: A reevaluation. *Proceedings of the National Academy of Sciences of the U S A, 94*(26), 14792–14797.

Tranel, D., Grabowski, T. J., Lyon, J., & Damasio, H. (2005). Naming the same entities from visual or from auditory stimulation engages similar regions of left inferotemporal cortices. *Journal of Cognitive Neuroscience, 17*(8), 1293–1305.

Tsapkini, K., Frangakis, C. E., & Hillis, A. E. (2011). The function of the left anterior temporal pole: evidence from acute stroke and infarct volume. *Brain, 134(10)*, 3094–3105.

Vigliocco, G., Vinson, D. P., Martin, R. C., & Garrett, M. F. (1999). Is "count" and "mass" information available when the noun is not? An investigation of tip of the tongue states and anomia. *Journal of Memory and Language, 40*(4), 534–558.

Vigneau, M., Beaucousin, V., Herve, P. Y., Duffau, H., Crivello, F., Houde, O.,…& Tzourio-Mazoyer, N. (2006). Meta-analyzing left hemisphere language areas: Phonology, semantics, and sentence processing. *Neuroimage, 30*(4), 1414–1432.

Visser, M., Jefferies, E., & Lambon Ralph, M. A. (2010). Semantic processing in the anterior temporal lobes: A meta-analysis of the functional neuroimaging literature. *Journal of Cognitive Neuroscience, 22*(6), 1083–1094.

Wagner, A. D., Pare-Blagoev, E. J., Clark, J., & Poldrack, R. A. (2001). Recovering meaning: Left prefrontal cortex guides controlled semantic retrieval. *Neuron, 31*(2), 329–338.

Warburton, E., Wise, R. J. S., Price, C. J., Weiller, C., Hadar, U., Ramsay, S., & Frackowiak, R. S. (1996). Noun and verb retrieval by normal subjects studies with PET. *Brain, 119*, 159–179.

Wise, R. J. S. (2003). Language systems in normal and aphasic human subjects: Functional imaging studies and inferences from animal studies. *British Medical Bulletin, 65*, 95–119.

Zingeser, L. B., & Berndt, R. S. (1990). Retrieval of nouns and verbs in agrammatism and anomia. *Brain and Language, 39*, 14–32.

Organization and Structure of Conceptual Representations

Anna Leshinskaya *and* Alfonso Caramazza

Abstract

This chapter addresses a question at the intersection of language production and semantic memory: what are representations of word meanings like? An important problem this raises is how the abstractions used in thought and language make contact with the world accessed through the senses. Proposals from embodied cognition deny the distinction between sensory representations and processes and conceptual ones. Evidence about the neural basis of conceptual knowledge is reviewed to critically assess the claims of the embodied view, and to support the opposing conclusion that conceptual representations are in part distinct from sensory-motor representations. Furthermore, any shared neural resources drawn on by perceptual and conceptual tasks are not interpretable until their representational properties are described. Instead, research that specifically characterizes supramodal representations in the brain may be the best route to understanding the neural basis of conceptual knowledge.

Key Words: cognitive neuroscience, conceptual knowledge, semantics, words, embodiment, perception, neuroimaging

Language production begins with the selection of meaning, before it can proceed to the selection and articulation of words. Thus, two important questions spanning both language production and semantic memory are: (1) What are representations of word meanings like? (2) How are these meanings attributed to words? Starting with the second question, which remains largely unanswered, this chapter proceeds to the first (what are meaning representations like), and considers in particular how neural evidence can inform the answer.

From Where do Words Obtain their Meaning?

One relatively simple solution to the question of how words map onto meanings is to assume that words obtain their meanings from associated lexical concepts (Levelt, Roelofs, & Meyer, 1999). This relationship is possible to the extent that there is a one-to-one mapping between lexical concepts and lexical nodes; unfortunately, there are several reasons this is not the case. First, there is a slippery relationship between words and their various related senses (i.e., polysemy; Caramazza & Grober, 1976; Ravin & Leacock, 2000; Murphy, 2002). A second reason is that the presumed borderline between world knowledge and the set of clearly defined lexical concepts is not only arbitrary, but also not psychologically real. Some encyclopedic knowledge must form part of the lexicon to allow us to understand even simple sentences, such as the distinction between "to bake a cake" and "to bake a potato," such that only in the former is there a sense of creation (Pustejovsky, 1995). If there are lexical concepts, one must explain how they are carved out of the rest of conceptual knowledge. Thus, the problem of word meanings is really a problem of semantic knowledge. It is with this topic that the rest of the chapter is concerned.

Models of Semantic Knowledge

There are two principal stances on the representation of meaning: either concepts[1] obtain their meaning from relations to other mental representations, or they obtain their meaning via a relationship to the world (Putnam, 1975; Margolis, 1998; Fodor, 1990). This distinction falls alongside the difference between views in which concepts are structured compositions of smaller units (componential view) and concepts that are holistic (atomic view). Under the atomic view, concepts have no structure or components; each concept's meaning is derived directly from its particular causal relationship with things in the world to which it refers[2] (Fodor, 1990; Laurence & Margolis, 1999). The holistic view has as its burden to explain how such a causal relationship is established and is maintained (see Margolis, 1998, for one possibility). Because an answer to this question must refer to mental representations and processes, the holistic view must face the same psychological problem as the componential view, of how something in the world is recognized and categorized.

The partial answer offered by componential theorists is that concepts break down into primitive components, by which we recognize instances of categories. This account must also explain the nature of this vocabulary of primitive elements, and how each of them links both to concepts and to the world.

Psychological investigation of concept knowledge typically assumes the componential stance (Muphy, 2002; Smith & Medin, 1981). Most of such research therefore begins with the question, what are the components? In which kinds of structures and processes do they participate? Two sorts of answers have classically been pitted against each other. In the *conceptual* componential view, the components are other concepts; in the empiricist version, the elements can be only sensory impressions. This distinction has been of recent concern in the literature on semantic memory, and therefore forms the focus of this chapter.

The Conceptual Componential Stance

In many models of semantic memory, the components comprising semantic knowledge are themselves categories (abstract properties, such as "wing" and "tail"; and taxonomic designations, such as "bird" and "animal"). For instance, semantic network models (e.g., Collins & Loftus, 1975) describe conceptual meanings as constituted by a set of links to other concepts. Distributed semantic network models (Rogers & McClelland, 2004) offer a related characterization, albeit without being implemented with localist units that explicitly stand in for components.[3] Yet other models propose that concepts are represented by the features of a prototypical member of a category rather than by a strict set of defining features (Rosch, 1978, 1999). The conceptual structure account (Tyler et al., 2000; Tyler & Moss, 2001) is another variant of the conceptual componential view, but further elaborates the importance of different conceptual components in composing concepts in different semantic domains (e.g., the importance of certain features is based on how well they can distinguish between members of a domain, such as living things). Despite the many differences among these briefly overviewed models, all of these characterizations depict semantic memory as made of conceptual units, and these units do not easily reduce to percepts or sensory impressions. For instance, the notion of a "wing" indicates a protrusion that helps with flying; it cannot be more specifically described without losing its function in these models, as a part shared by many birds.

Empiricist Models and Recent Incarnations

In the empiricist tradition, previously elaborated by Locke and Hume, the source of all knowledge is sensory experience. The elements out of which conceptual knowledge is built are therefore sensory primitives, and all concepts have their origin in, and are constituted reductively by, sensations.

Recent "embodied" theories are an instantiation of such views, but often go beyond these tenets. For instance, it has been suggested that concepts never need representations any more abstract than sensory impressions (Barsalou, 1999). Others suggest that conceptual mechanisms are really perceptual mechanisms, re-engaged in remembering just as they were engaged in perceiving (Allport, 1985; Martin, 2007; Barsalou, 2008). Embodiment is thus a claim against the presence of conceptual components in semantic memory and conceptual systems.

The Interface Problem

One of the main tensions in models of concepts is the dual role concepts must play in serving the demands of both generality and specificity. Smith and Medin (1981) pointed out that components, or "features," of concepts have to be formed out of the relevant units, units that are psychologically real (take part in categorization processes) and that can capture relations between concepts. For instance, the component "tail" is useful for establishing the similarity between dogs and cats; if it was more specific or more general, it may not properly serve this role. Thus, many components that seem to be useful for including in concepts are already recognized, whole objects and parts like "wing," "tail," and "red" (Smith & Medin, 1981; Fodor, 1975).

Such components may be useful for relating concepts to each other, but they do not describe objects in perceptual terms. As pointed out by critics and proponents (Laurence & Margolis, 1999; Jackendoff, 1987; Levelt et al., 1999), many models of semantic knowledge already assume a process that accomplishes the mapping from percepts to concepts, including the recognition of wings and tails. This mapping problem is not trivial; it is the core problem of object recognition.

The problem is difficult because conceptual units are not specified in perceptual terms. Tails are visibly highly different; and they may even differ more within a category than between categories. A golden retriever's tail is as different from a shih tzu's tail as it is from the tail of a cat. Thus, something makes tails similar across all these instances, but this "core" meaning of tail is not a good indicator of category membership from the point of view of object recognition.[4] In other words, concepts allow us to treat some things as similar and others as different, especially when category boundaries do not clearly correspond to surface similarity (Tversky, 1977; Shepard, 1980; Freedman et al., 2001). There is thus a tension between the role concepts have to play in being simultaneously specific and general.

This issue is a facet of the fundamental problem in cognition of how the abstractions we use in thought make contact with the world we access through the senses. Although this is a timeless problem that yet awaits a solution, one can consider whether some models of semantic memory offer better promise of an answer. To this end, the evidence for empiricist and conceptual compositional models is reviewed.

Evidence for and Against Embodiment
Tenets of Embodied Theories

Embodied theories have lately become increasingly influential. Various recent reviews of semantic knowledge have revealed empiricist commitments, and have suggested that the bulk of the evidence sides with embodied views (Thompson-Schill, 2003; Martin, 2007; Vigliocco & Vinson, 2007). This section reviews the tenets of embodied theory, and then considers the kinds of evidence used to

support it, and evaluate whether it might offer a viable solution to the interface problem.

As introduced above, the embodied proposal is that the representational format and mechanism of conceptual knowledge are identical to those involved in perception and action. Thus, in contrast to the conceptual componential view, here concepts are composed not of relations to other concepts, but entirely of various sensory-motor primitives, stored in modality-specific format, and implemented in perceptual systems. The solution offered to the interface problem is that, effectively, there is not such a problem: because conceptual representations are no different from percepts, there is no difficulty in mapping between percepts and concepts.

The embodied view of concepts can be summarized by two general claims:

1. *The Location Claim.* Semantic memory is housed in the same neural systems as those used to process sensory signals; remembering or knowing involves regenerating parts of the state of neural activity that occurred during the processing of those sensory signals (termed *simulation*).

2. *The Format Claim.* The representations within these systems are sensory-motor in nature; in other terminology, the format of representations in these perceptual systems is "modal." It is important to note that the claims are not about what is represented, but about format (e.g., Barsalou, 1999, 2008; Patterson et al., 2007; Stanfield & Zwaan, 2001; Paivio, 1991). The strongest version of the claims is that no amodal representations exist at all (Barsalou, 1999).

An influential formulation of the embodied view was postulated by Barsalou and colleagues (1999, 2008; Kan & Barsalou, 2003). The view that Barsalou *opposes* (the conceptual componential view) can be exemplified in the following quote: "The amodal symbols that represent the colors of objects in their absence reside in a different neural system from the representations of these colors during perception itself. In addition, these two systems use different representational schemes and operate according to different principles" (1999, p. 578). The rejection of this picture entails a commitment to both the Location claim and the Format claim. Although the idea of a "modal representational scheme" is still unspecified, the meaning and operationalization of this property are explored in the present chapter.

In a similar vein, Thompson-Schill (2003) offered the following overview of the evidence: "Semantic memory is not amodal: each attribute-specific system is tied to a sensorimotor modality (e.g., vision) and even to a specific property within that modality (e.g., color). Information about each feature of a concept is stored within the processing streams that were active during the acquisition of that feature. These findings are problematic for many current theories of semantic memory which represent concepts with amodal symbols…(p. 283)." In the following section, the evidence is reviewed to see whether and how what we know about semantic memory is in fact problematic for conceptual componential theories and supportive of embodied theory.

Examples of Evidence from Behavioral Paradigms

A series of experiments by Zwaan and colleagues (Zwaan et al., 2002; Stanfield & Zwaan, 2001) found that knowledge of what objects look like influences sentence processing, even when that particular information is not strictly relevant to the task. In one experiment, participants read sentences that denoted objects in particular configurations, such as an eagle in the sky (where wings are presumed to be outstretched) or an eagle in a nest (where wings are folded). They then saw a picture that contained an eagle with either outstretched wings or folded wings. Participants were slower to name the object in the picture if it mismatched the wing position denoted by the preceding sentence, than if it matched. Nothing in the lexical entry for eagle (or sky, or nest), as described by semantic network theories of word meaning, would directly specify the wing position of the eagle; yet, anyone with world experience easily infers the wing position. This information about wing position must have also been retrieved during sentence processing, because it primed the subsequent processing of the picture. Such information is typically called either "perceptual knowledge" or "world knowledge," and its activation during a linguistic task suggests that more than just core word meaning is engaged in reading sentences.

These findings are reminiscent of evidence used to illustrate the issue of compositionality in lexical semantics (e.g., Pustjevosky, 1999; Rips, 1995). Compositionality is the process of word combination to imply meanings that are not contained within the lexical entries for the component words (i.e., why *baking a cake* involves creating a new object, whereas *baking a potato* does not; or why a *smokey chimney* emits smoke, whereas a *smokey apple*

tastes like it). In all of these cases, additional meaning beyond the strict word meaning is automatically activated, much as in the case of the eagle sentences in the Zwaan et al. studies. In other words, the demonstration of how extralexical knowledge influences meaning comprehension is not novel, and has not given rise to embodiment claims in the past. It further does not help address the issue of what this additional knowledge is like.

In addition to world knowledge, other non-typically linguistic representations have also been shown to play a role in language tasks. Glenberg and Kaschak (2002) investigated an interaction between motor action and language processing, by having participants make actions that were either congruent or incongruent with a sentence meaning. Sentences implied either an "away" motion or a "toward" motion (i.e., by describing the opening or the closing of a drawer). Participants then judged the sensicality of the sentence by pressing a button either far or close in front of them, thus varying whether arm motion was toward or away from the body. When the response involved a "toward" motion but the sentence implied an "away" motion, responses were significantly slower than when the motion and sentence meaning were congruent. This suggested that sentence meaning interfaced with motion in a content-specific way, and that motion processes must be able to interact with semantic processes, rather than such systems being entirely encapsulated. There have been many other demonstrations of the influence of motor knowledge in semantic tasks, such as reading sentences that describe manual rotation actions (e.g., opening a water bottle) interfere with responses made by turning a knob, such that making a response in a congruent direction with the sentence facilitates the response (Zwaan & Taylor, 2006). Glover et al. (2004) showed that the affordances implied by the name of an object influence grasp aperture to a target block (i.e., reading "grape" leads participants to bias their grasp apertures to slightly smaller than the real block requires, if that block is larger than a grape). This result, much as the others above, suggests that information not typically considered linguistic has an influence on how participants reason about objects and their properties.

In yet another domain, Richardson, Spivey, Barsalou, and McRae (2003) demonstrated that language processing interfaces with spatial attention. In this study, participants read sentences containing verbs that had either a horizontal or a vertical denotation (e.g., *lift* and *respect*); then, participants had to identify a visual target (as either a circle or square). The target appeared away from fixation on either along a vertical axis (above or below) or horizontal axis (left or right). Participants were faster to identify the target if its position was *incongruent* with the axis of the verb, such that visual targets in vertical positions were identified faster when preceded by a horizontal verb than a vertical verb. Although the direction of the effect was opposite to that found in Glenberg and Kaschak (2002), the interaction was nonetheless content-specific. Such results reiterate that there must be an interface between word meaning and perceptual mechanisms. These results point to the importance of substantiating a mechanism for the interaction of linguistic and other semantic knowledge or perceptual mechanisms, and argue against a fully encapsulated language module.

At the same time, any number of findings supporting the above conclusions would not warrant the more extreme claims to which they have given rise. For instance, Glenberg and Kachak (2002) argued that their results (as described previously) could only be explained if language was processed via the same mechanisms that execute motor actions. Their reasoning was not that semantic networks simply lacked an interface to other systems, but that their format of representation was fundamentally of the wrong type. There is nothing, however, to suggest this latter option over the former. More importantly, it is also not clear from this evidence that the interactions between semantic reasoning and actions occurred at the level of actions, rather than at the level of semantics. Presumably, making an action involves semantic reasoning. Thus, the Glenberg and Kachak results could have occurred at the semantic level if actions were recoded into abstract terms, such as "away" and "toward" (Mahon & Caramazza, 2008). In other words, such effects could be caused by either the activation of motor sequences during the processing of the word "away," or the retrieval of the concept "away" while engaging in pushing. The question of how such interactions occur is largely open to investigation.

The findings of Richardson et al. (2003) regarding interface with spatial attention are less likely to be interpreted as an interface at a semantic level, because their spatial task was unlikely to engage a semantic coding of location. However, as the authors themselves concluded, the results likely show that spatial procedures (looking up or down) or representations of space might form part of the representation of a verb; and this may certainly be the case without supposing that meaning representations

literally *are* representations of space. After all, the vertical axis implied by "lift" cannot constitute the entire meaning of this verb, or else it could not be distinguished from the meaning of other verbs with similar motions, such as "rise." Overall, such findings might suggest that space-relevant representations can become tightly associated with the meanings of words, again illustrating the importance of an interface mechanism between conceptual knowledge and action.

The previously discussed results show the necessity of an interface between word meanings and world knowledge, perception, and action, but they do not elucidate what might be that interface mechanism (Mahon & Caramazza, 2008). The fundamental and empirical problem facing current research (and both embodied and nonembodied models) is how information is recoded and communicated between these systems; simply positing that no recoding takes place is a hypothesis, rather than a solution to this problem. Thus, other evidence needs to be considered to better understand the interface problem, and to lend support to either embodied or conceptual views.

Evidence from Semantic Deficits

Debates surrounding the nature of semantic knowledge, and its relation to perception, have long played out in the arena of neuropsychology. Evidence from this line of work has therefore been invoked in the context of current debates.

In neuropsychology, the strong version of sensory/motor theory of semantic memory might be a cousin of the empiricist/embodied view. One tenet of this view is multiple semantics, which is the notion that semantic memory is subdivided into modality-specific systems (vision, olfaction, motion), which together represent our knowledge of concepts (Allport, 1985; Shallice, 1988; Beauvois, 1982). According to this view, therefore, the semantic system closely parallels, if not entirely collapses onto, sensory/motor systems; and there is an important relationship between the semantic systems and their sensory/motor counterparts. In these ways, sensory/motor theory resembles embodiment theory. Support for sensory/motor theory may thus lend credence to the embodiment claim. However, such support hinges on the way the data allow one to interpret the notion of modality-specificity in the semantic system.

In one interpretation, a modality-specific semantic system is one that has a specific and privileged relationship to a sensory input channel for the acquisition and storage of semantic knowledge (Farah et al., 1989; Farah & McClelland, 1991; Humphreys & Forde, 2001; Warrington & Shallice, 1984; Warrington & McCarthy, 1987). Under this interpretation, evidence for modality-specificity in the semantic system is provided by reports of optic aphasia.

Patients with optic aphasia have a semantic deficit limited to a certain modality of access. For instance, patient JF (Beauvois, 1982) was unable to name objects presented as pictures, whereas he performed normally when touching the objects or hearing their sounds. The deficit could not be explained as a general difficulty with naming (aphasia) or as a problem with visual recognition: JF was able to use objects that he could not name, and to draw these objects from memory. Thus, the deficit was at a level in between visual categorization and naming; arguably, at the level of semantic memory. However, because this semantic deficit was limited to a certain input/output channel of access, it was suggested that semantic memory must be dissociable along the lines of modality.

However, as argued in Caramazza et al. (1990), the existence of modality-specific agnosias does not require that there are modality-specific modules in semantic memory with a special sensory format. Instead, it may be that semantic memory contains bona fide conceptual representations that, by virtue of their *content*, have privileged relationships to certain input channels. Thus, although there is a relationship between input/output channels and certain representations in semantic memory, these representations need not be composed of sensory features, and the relation to input channels is instead mediated by semantic relationships. This is therefore a very limited sense of modality-specificity, in the sense of having some (any) relationship to an input channel.[5] In conclusion, when interpreting modality-specific systems in terms of their relation to sensory input channels, not much can be concluded, and therefore, evidence from optic aphasia cannot adjudicate between the embodied view and the conceptual componential view.

The sensory/motor theory has also, alternatively, interpreted modality-specificity as a claim about representational format, rather than a strict relationship with a certain input channel for acquisition or access (Allport, 1985; Thompson-Schill, 2003; Farah & McClelland, 1991; Warrington & Shallice, 1984; Warrington & McCarthy, 1987). This interpretation of modality-specificity was developed as a way to account for patients with category-specific

semantic deficits, who show impairment in recognizing and reasoning about a particular class of objects, such as living things compared with nonliving things (Warrington, 1975). These deficits do not coincide with damage to the use of particular input/output channels, as in optic aphasia, but are rather present across multiple modes of presentation and multiple tasks. Initially, this type of deficit posed a problem for multiple semantics, because it suggested that the semantic system was not organized along the lines of modality, but along a semantic domain.

However, the theory was then adjusted to explain these patients (Farah & McClelland, 1991; Warrington & Shallice, 1984) by positing that each subsystem of semantic memory was characterized as a type of knowledge, rather than necessarily a strict reliance on a type of input channel (i.e., visual knowledge and functional knowledge; see Figure 7.1 for illustration). Furthermore, these different knowledge types (e.g., "sensory" features and "functional" features) were more or less important in processing each semantic category ("living," "nonliving"). Thus, because each semantic category has a privileged relationship with one of these feature types, a category-specific deficit could appear to be affecting a semantic domain ("living things") while really affecting a feature type ("visual"). With this proposal, one might still maintain that semantic memory is organized not along domains, such as "living" and "nonliving," but rather along feature type.

To evaluate this proposal, tests were made of patients' capabilities with these different feature types. For instance, Farah et al. (1989) used such questions as, "are the hind legs of a kangaroo larger than the front legs?" to test "visual" feature knowledge, and such questions as, "is peacock served in French

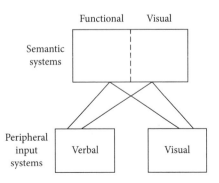

Figure 7.1 Schematic diagram of the parallel distributed processing model of semantic memory. Adapted from Farah and McClelland, 1991.

restaurants?" to test "functional" feature knowledge. Other assessments of a loss of visual or structural knowledge have included drawing named objects and making decisions about pictures of objects that are colored incorrectly or have untypical shapes or parts (Sartori & Job, 1988; Forde et al., 1997; Vandenbulcke et al., 2006). The aim of these studies was to demonstrate that patients with semantic impairments for living things also have greater difficulty with "visual" features than with functional features. Some studies indeed reported patients exhibiting such a pattern (Sartori & Job, 1988; Silveri & Gainotti, 1998; Farah et al., 1989; Hart & Gordon, 1992).

However, there are several obstacles to supporting the notion that living-domain deficits truly arise because of a deficit in a visual semantic store. First, it is not the case that all living-domain impairments are also impairments in "visual" feature knowledge. For instance, some patients with visual feature impairments have a deficit both for living things and for other categories of objects (Forde et al., 1997; Vandenbulcke et al., 2006; Laiacona et al., 1997; Caramazza & Shelton, 1998; Bright et al., 2007) or no deficit specific to living things (Lambon-Ralph et al., 1998). Yet others present with visual-knowledge impairments but no deficit for living things (Blundo et al., 2006). This patterning makes it difficult to conclude that living-things deficits arise because of visual-feature deficits, because these two dimensions (category and feature type) seem to operate independently, rather than consistently co-occuring. Thus, as concluded by Farah (1989), these two principles of organization are likely at work independently. This makes the notion that one type of deficit reduces to the other unlikely.

A second difficulty for the sensory/functional model, as reviewed in Caramazza and Shelton (1998), is its inability to explain the more specific category dissociations that have been reported, such as between animals and vegetables or between animals and musical instruments (e.g., Warrington & McCarthy, 1987; Hillis & Caramazza, 1991; Hart & Gordon, 1992). It is difficult to explain such dissociations on the basis of a differential reliance on visual versus functional properties among the dissociated categories. The distinctions are more fine-grained than sensory/functional theory originally postulated; although of course the theory can accommodate these findings post hoc by positing further distinctions between different sensory stores (Warrington & McCarthy, 1987).

Nonetheless, even if one accepts a sensory and functional feature typology, multiple semantics still lacks support. This is because of the questionable relationship between categories of features and sensory modalities. To maintain the multiple semantics tenet, one must also show that visual and functional feature types are also somehow *modality types* (i.e., that features of each kind were encoded in such a way that they could be said to have a modality-specific format). Thus, support for multiple semantics ultimately depends on the nature of these feature types.

However, in the patient cases reviewed previously, impairments in visual/physical knowledge do not relate specifically to certain input channels. Patients can be impaired in reasoning about visual properties without an impairment specific to the visual modality of presentation. In fact, their performance is very consistent between visual, verbal, tactile, or auditory presentations of objects (Forde et al., 1997; Silveri & Gainotti, 1988). Even more strikingly, Hart and Gordon (1992) reported a patient who was impaired in retrieving physical attributes of living things, while maintaining an ability to match pictures of animal bodies to their appropriate heads, and to decide if an animal picture was correctly colored. This illustrates the dissociation of two systems, both of which specifically enable the processing of physical attributes, but where one is more abstract and another more specific to a sensory processing channel. This further supports the conclusion that knowledge of the physical attributes of objects can be quite removed from modality-specific systems, including sensory processing, and thus retains few dependencies on any sensory modality. Thus, one's understanding of what are "visual" features has to depend on the nature of the information as it is stored, rather than its access through vision.

As discussed in Caramazza et al. (1990), there is a variety of possibilities for why certain features could end up in the "visual" feature store rather than some other store. One possibility is that certain kinds of information have certain kinds of format inherently; that is, information about *what things look like* has a particular kind of format when it is stored in the brain, and on this basis is located in the visual store. This seems to be what is implied by the multiple semantics hypothesis. Another option is that this information is placed in the visual store because it was originally acquired through the visual modality, but now can be accessed through any other input channel (Beauvois, 1982; Silveri & Gainotti, 1988). Here, the principle of organization is the history of acquisition. This becomes difficult to test; there are many cases in which one learns about "visual" attributes nonvisually (through a textbook or other means). One last option is that features end up in the visual store because they refer to a kind of content (i.e., are *about* what things look like). In this case, the distinction between semantic stores is *semantic* and no longer falls along the lines of sensory processing channels. If indeed the organizational principle is a type of content, then there is no reason to expect that each store is associated with a type of modality. Thus, the ambiguity of the basis of visual or functional stores is a persistent problem for the multiple semantics hypothesis, and it is still unclear what kind of evidence could explain why knowledge ends up in a "visual" store or otherwise.

In conclusion, evidence for multiple semantics from an input-channel interpretation of modality-specificity has not been borne out by the data. Under a feature-type interpretation of modality-specificity, it becomes unclear what provides semantic memory contents with a "modal" nature, and thus the distinction between modal and amodal views of semantic memory, remains without an empirical foothold.

Evidence from Neuroimaging

Neuroimaging has appeared to be a promising tool for settling the debate on the nature of semantic memory and its relationship to perception. In principle, all that is required to satisfy the embodied proposal (the Location claim and the Format claim) is to identify and delimit a perceptual/modal system in the brain, and then locate semantic representations within it. This endeavor relies on having a way to identify perceptual systems in the brain, and semantic representations, and comparing them directly. Neuroimaging has been invoked to do this task (i.e., by showing that a brain region has a privileged relation to some particular perceptual task or input channel and to a particular semantic task). Such evidence has been used to argue that perceptual systems and semantic systems are reducible to each other, and that semantic representations are modal, by virtue of residing in the same systems as perception.

It becomes clear, however, that relying on brain localization to identify either perceptual systems or semantic representations quickly becomes problematic. For one thing, a perceptual task (looking at a picture of an object) does not isolate perceptual processes from conceptual ones, as one unavoidably accesses semantic knowledge of that object. Likewise, any semantic task (e.g., retrieving properties of named objects) is unlikely to involve only semantic operations, but may conceivably also recruit representations with modality-specific properties (i.e., ones that allow the concept to interface with perception) making it difficult to isolate which process is which. Even under a conceptual componential view of concepts, sensory correlates of objects must be represented at some level or stage, and may become activated during a semantic task (Mahon & Caramazza, 2008). Thus, regardless of one's theoretical stance on semantic knowledge, concepts and percepts are expected to coincide, and are thus not easily extricable from one another using neuroimaging.

A further complication in the endeavor to characterize the semantic system with neuroimaging is that neuroimaging data offer only a description at the level of implementation, and do not immediately offer descriptions of representational format (Marr, 1972). Current state of knowledge does not permit making inferences from brain localization to the level of representational format (e.g., whether it is modal or amodal). Thus, evidence from brain systems can at best address the question of whether given processes share a brain system; however, to infer that this brain system also has a certain (modal or amodal) type of representation requires independent support. In other words, it is argued that support for the Format claim does not fall out of satisfying the Location claim.

Despite these hurdles, it is nonetheless possible to consider to what extent the Location claim is itself satisfied (namely, that perceptual and conceptual tasks rely on the same brain systems) and what implications might follow from such a state of affairs. To this end, several exemplary findings, organized by their implication, are described.

Is there Evidence for Overlap between Perceptual and Conceptual Systems?
SEMANTIC KNOWLEDGE MAY BE ORGANIZED BY ATTRIBUTES

Several studies have shown that retrieving different types of properties in response to object names differentially engages different brain regions (Martin et al., 1995; Mummery et al., 1998; Chao & Martin, 1999; Kellenbach, Brett, & Patterson, 2001; Noppeney & Price, 2002; Phillips, Noppeney, Humphreys, & Price, 2002).

For instance, using positron emission tomography imaging, Martin et al. (1995) found that asking participants to name a color or action associated with black and white pictures of objects recruited different brain areas: specifically, retrieving color properties activated the fusiform gyrus bilaterally, and action properties activated left middle and superior temporal gyri. The results were much the same when objects were presented as written names. Furthermore, the regions that were involved were nearby to regions previously reported during the perception of color and motion, respectively. However, the extent of proximity between these and the reported regions was not evaluated in most of these early studies (Martin et al., 1995; Mummery et al., 1998; Kellenbach et al., 2001).

Property type has been shown in several studies to affect the organization of semantic processing in the brain, although the specific regions engaged for a certain property are not always consistent among studies (Kellenbach et al., 2001; Kable, Kan, Wilson, Thompson-Schill, & Chatterjee, 2005; Phillips et al., 2002). For example, Mummery et al. (1998) reported an anteromedial left temporal region for color knowledge, relatively far from the region reported in Martin et al. (1995)

The observation that retrieving semantic knowledge activates different neural regions based on property rules out that a single neural locus is uniquely involved in retrieving object knowledge. This fact on its own has little relation to the present debate. Properties differ along a semantic dimension and in referring to different sensory attributes; thus, organization by property does not help determine whether semantic systems are organized by modality or sensory systems (Caramazza et al., 1990). Yet, this set of findings has, in fact, been taken to suggest exactly this (Thompson-Schill, 1999; Chao, Haxby, & Martin, 1999). These conclusions are not warranted because neural organization of semantic knowledge by attribute is not identical to organization by modality. For example, "action" is not itself a modality, particularly given that action properties have included such things as function (what an object is used for). Further studies have identified specific regions preferentially involved in abstract understanding of function as distinct from manipulation knowledge or knowledge of shape (Canessa et al., 2008; Creem-Regher, Dilda, Vicchrilli, Federer, & Lee, 2007). Furthermore, a study specifically looking for brain regions selective to words high in motion content (vs. low motion content) failed to find any region that cared about such a distinction (Bedny, Caramazza, Grossman, Pascual-Leone, & Saxe, 2008). Instead, a region in the left middle temporal gyrus (which has been implicated in action processing, as discussed previously), preferred verbs to nouns, independently of how much these words referred to motion. Thus,

the neural differences between property types cannot be reduced to differences in sensory modalities: it is difficult to imagine which sensory modality corresponds to either verb knowledge or function knowledge.

Thus, the fact that brain regions involved in property retrieval show organization by property does not support the idea that this organization reduces to, or overlaps with, a perceptual system organized by sensory modality, and rather suggests organization by semantic property.

CONCEPTUAL TASKS ACTIVATE BRAIN REGIONS PREVIOUSLY THOUGHT TO BE MODAL

Other neuroimaging evidence used in support of embodied claims has looked at neural regions that are traditionally sensory, and observed their involvement during conceptual tasks. Such evidence has been used to suggest that semantic properties really reside within modal brain areas. For example, Goldberg, Perfetti, and Schneider (2006) asked participants to perform a property verification task with attributes related to several sensory attributes (color, sound, touch, and taste). Functional magnetic resonance imaging (fMRI) evidence showed that the "predicted" sensory regions were activated according to attribute type (e.g., the somatosensory cortex was active during the processing of touch properties). Other research showed that sentences referring to mouth actions activate Broca area, which is loosely claimed to be important for articulation, and that hand-related sentences activate parts of the precentral gyrus thought to be involved in hand movement (Tettamanti et al., 2005).

These findings might be dismissed as being caused by mental imagery or motor preparation for action, processes that occur after actual language comprehension. However, research using event-related potential (ERP) and MEG has found that motor regions are activated automatically during language comprehension (Hauk & Pulvermuller, 2004; Pulvermuller, Hauk, Nikulin, & Ilmoniemi, 2005). In Hauk and Pulvermuller (2004), ERP signals were recorded during passive reading of arm-, leg-, or face-related words. The waveforms for each word type were differentiated in their topographic localization at 220 ms, suggesting that the localization differences occur early, and without explicit imagery. They appear to occur without much delay with respect to lexical access.

Although such results may be novel and intriguing, they do not directly support the Location claim. Neither the fMRI nor the ERP studies cited previously *directly* compared regions activated during language processing and those activated during motor action. Thus, although the language-related activations were roughly nearby to regions known to be involved in motor tasks, language comprehension and motor processing were not directly compared to see if they really involve entirely overlapping regions. It thus cannot be concluded that language comprehension and motor processing use identical mechanisms.

CONCEPTUAL TASKS ACTIVATE BRAIN REGIONS ACTIVE DURING PERCEPTION

Further studies have directly compared perceptual/motor and conceptual tasks to evaluate the extent of their overlap, and others have used transcranial magnetic stimulation (TMS) to evaluate the causal role of the implicated regions. Perceptual tasks typically involve the presentation of a stimulus, whereas conceptual tasks involve retrieval based on a cue. As will be discussed, it is unclear which processes or representations are isolated by contrasting such tasks; for now, the evidence is reviewed suspending this clarification.

Direct overlap between perceptual and conceptual tasks has not been very well supported. Chao and Martin (1999) compared regions activated during color perception with regions activated during color retrieval (naming the associated color of black and white objects, compared with viewing black and white abstract patterns). The regions activated were nearby, in the lingual gyrus, but were more lateral for color retrieval than for perception. The authors concluded that regions involved in color retrieval are distinct from those involved in perception.

On the other hand, Simmons et al. (2007) did find one locus of overlap between color perception and color naming tasks, but in a different region, a portion of the left fusiform gyrus. However, not all color-perception areas were active in color retrieval; in fact, the lingual gyrus was selectively active in color perception, indicating dissociation between perception and retrieval. Furthermore, the analysis was limited to regions active during color perception. No effects of color retrieval were visible with a whole-brain contrast. Thus, the study was underpowered in determining whether there are regions unique to color retrieval from memory that are *not* engaged while perceiving color. It was thus impossible to quantify the extent of overlap between perception and retrieval tasks. Nonetheless, it is clear from the results that were presented that overlap between the two tasks was quite limited.

Finally, as noted by Simmons et al. (2007), there is positive evidence illustrating the neural separability of color knowledge and color perception (Miceli et al., 2001; Luzzatti & Davidoff, 1994). Patient IOC (Miceli et al., 2001), for instance, selectively lost the ability to retrieve color properties of objects, but had normal color perception, and normal knowledge of other properties of objects. This illustrates even more clearly that the ability to perceive and recognize color has unique neural loci that are not essential for knowledge of typical object colors.

Another domain in which perceptual and semantic retrieval tasks have been compared is action concepts and the motor cortex. For example, Hauk, Johnsrude, and Pulvermüller (2004) used both a movement localizer and a language task to see whether words denoting actions also activate regions involved in moving one's own limbs. The findings revealed somatotopically organized activation of the motor-activated regions in response to arm, leg, and face words. Along similar lines, Buccino et al. (2005) found a content-specific decrease of motor evoked potentials in hand muscles and foot muscles when participants listened to hand- or foot-related sentences during concurrent TMS to hand or foot regions of their motor cortex, suggesting that effector-related signals had occurred in response to semantic processing of words. Finally, Pulvermuller et al. (2005) applied TMS to leg- and arm-related motor cortex, and showed that latency for reading leg- and arm-related words was modulated by these TMS pulses, respectively. Such results confirm that motor cortex activation is not simply epiphenomenal, but rather causally involved in language processing. Such evidence is reasonably convincing that there is involvement of motor regions in language comprehension.

The precision and specificity of motor region–action word overlaps has been questioned (Chatterjee, 2010; Postle et al., 2008), for instance on the basis of a failure to find somatotopically organized action word–related activation in cytoarchitectonically motor areas (Postle et al., 2008). Another concern is that, as in the case of color nouns, motor and nonmotor verb comprehension activates many regions besides the motor cortex, such as angular gyrus, precuneus, anterior temporal, and parahippocampal regions (Tomasino, Werner, Weiss, & Fink, 2007). It thus stands to reason that the overlap is not complete. Claims that action word comprehension literally consists of motor action simulation, and nothing else, are difficult to support.

Lastly, it is difficult to ignore evidence that often, areas involved in conceptual and perceptual processes do measurably diverge, as in the study by Martin et al. (1995), where language-activated regions were near to those activated during perceptual tasks. Another important case is action verb comprehension, which activates the left middle temporal gyrus and measurably diverges from regions involved in processing visually conveyed motion (Bedny et al., 2008). In fact, recent reviews note that nonoverlap appears to be more the rule than the exception (Chatterjee, 2010; Bedny & Caramazza, 2011). Thus, the fact that relatively blunt neuroimaging tools can reliably detect these distinctions is good evidence the overlap is not complete.

There is other positive evidence, from neuropsychology, that systems for action execution and conceptual processing of actions are in fact distinct. This includes reports of stroke patients exhibiting impaired ability to use objects but intact ability to reason about actions (e.g., Negri et al., 2007). Other evidence includes dissociations within apraxia. In "ideational" apraxia, the ability to execute an action dissociates from knowing the appropriate actions to undertake, whereas "ideomotor" apraxia can affect action execution without concomitant deficit in understanding what the appropriate action should be (De Renzi & Lucchelli, 1988; Heilman et al., 1997). For instance, patients with ideational apraxia can mimic meaningless actions, but are unable to use objects in the *appropriate* ways (e.g., given a key, such patients might perform a hammering motion rather a turning motion; De Renzi & Lucchelli, 1988).

In sum, there is evidence that although action understanding and motor execution share some neural geography, they are still dissociable subsystems, and do rely on distinct neural substrates.

Summary of Evidence from Brain Imaging

A wealth of brain imaging and neuropsychological evidence has been brought to bear on the first claim from the embodiment view: that sensory and semantic processes share neural substrates (the Location claim). Researchers have attempted to isolate these processes with tasks that involve the presentation of a stimulus and ones that require only retrieval from memory. The findings are mixed. Although certain portions of overlap have been identified between perceptual and semantic retrieval tasks, it appears that these tasks rely on regions that

remain to some extent distinct. Still, the partial overlaps that have been reported are important findings and deserve explanation.

What is the nature of the representations in these areas of overlap? There is much in common between perceiving an object's color and retrieving that color from memory, or from enacting an action and reading words denoting that action. The most obvious commonality is that they refer to similar content. Performing a perceptual task over meaningful objects inevitably engages conceptual knowledge; it is thus no surprise that overlaps should occur between perception and retrieval. Yet, the less intuitive explanation offered by embodiment theorists is by way of the Format claim: that the shared neural locus contains modality-specific representations encoded in a "perceptual" format. Which of these accounts is correct? Do we think with percepts, or do we perceive with concepts?

Evidence that Overlaps are Content-Based

A priori, it may appear unlikely that overlap between action understanding and action execution in primary motor cortex is a locus of abstract, conceptual knowledge rather than of motor commands specific to execution. However, there is evidence that makes the conceptual interpretation more likely than the other. This evidence comes from two principal sources: studies of mirror neurons in monkeys, and studies of cross-modal plasticity.

Mirror "neurons" are generally defined as a mapping system between observed actions (visible properties of actions performed by others) and execution of actions (the motor programs that are used to execute one's own actions; Di Pellegrino, Fadiga, Fogassi, Gallese, & Rizzolatti, 1992; Rizzolatti, Fadiga, Gallese, & Fogassi, 1996; Tettamanti et al., 2005; Rizzolatti & Sinigaglia, 2010). Such a system appears to exist in the premotor cortex of monkeys: certain neurons in nonhuman primates (located in area F5 of macaque cortex) respond to both execution and observation of corresponding actions; furthermore, they are engaged during meaningful or goal-related actions, such as grasping or tearing, by the hand and mouth (Rizzolatti et al., 1996). The responsiveness of these neurons to meaningful actions already suggests that they encode information more complex than motor programs. Further evidence of their abstract content is that such neurons respond to a variety of hand configurations during grasping, but only to actions that accomplish a grasp, and not motions that simply mimic grasping movements. Furthermore, Umiltà et al. (2008) reported neurons that responded to the use of two different pliers that are radically different in hand position and motion but which accomplish a similar goal. These findings and others (see review in Rizzolatti & Sinigaglia, 2010) suggest that these "motor" cortex neurons encode abstract relationship between hand, tool, and object (not specific motor patterns or motions) and are thus highly complex conceptual units. Thus, evidence from mirror neuron studies supports the view that regions thought to be modality-specific are in fact engaged in modality-general and abstract encoding, making it more likely that the role of premotor cortex in action word understanding reflects conceptual operations shared with action execution (rather than the activation of strictly motor representations as previously argued [e.g., Rizzolatti et al., 2001]).

Another line of work that has likewise expanded preconceived notions of "sensory" brain areas is the study of the neural organization of individuals who are blind from birth. Observations about multimodal plasticity (how brain functions change as a result of sensory deprivation) has led to the hypothesis of metamodality (Pascual-Leone & Hamilton, 2001), which proposes that the main principle of organization in the brain is not modality, but rather computation or function. This proposal emerges from observations that, whereas the sort of sensory channel that a brain region receives during development is not strictly fixed, its functional role persists despite early sensory loss. For instance, the occipital lobes of blind subjects are active during tactile discrimination (Sadato et al., 1998) and auditory localization tasks (Renier et al., 2010), rather than visual discrimination. It is well known that sensory deprivation leads to plasticity in modality-related areas; however, these findings additionally suggest that the novel role of the affected regions resembles its normal one computationally. In the previously mentioned cases, it could be said that the occipital lobe continues to be important for fine-grained spatial processing even in absence of vision.

One other strand of this research has explored the role of area MT, a superior portion of the middle temporal gyrus that is important in processing visually perceived motion (Zeki et al., 1991). Although considered a modality-specific visual region in sighted subjects, MT is activated in congenitally blind subjects in response to auditory motion (Bedny et al., 2010), indicating that this region adapts to sensory loss by continuing to process similar types of information from other input channels.

Another case is that of the lateral occipitotemporal cortex, which has been considered principally a visual area (Martin, 2007). Yet, this region appears to accomplish similar functions in subjects who have never had visual experience. Regions important in processing the shape of objects from visual input appear to be involved in processing shape properties of objects presented through the tactile modality in blind subjects (Pietrini et al., 2004). Furthermore, Mahon et al. (2009) demonstrated that in both sighted and congenitally blind participants, lateral temporo-occipital activation is spatially organized by object domain, such that responses to names of animals are located more laterally than responses to artifacts both in sighted and blind subjects. Thus, certain organizational principles and functions of the ventral stream are maintained even in the absence of visual input. This supports the idea that many regions maintain their functional role without input from a given sensory channel, and thus sensory channel is incidental to that functional role.

Despite the striking cross-modal plasticity of many parts of the brain, an embodied theorist might still object that in both sighted and blind, the brain regions involved in shape processing or motion processing are still modality-specific, but specific to a different modality in each case. To counter this objection, there is increasing evidence that even in sighted subjects multimodal functions can arise in putatively sensory areas with a relatively short amount of altered experience. For instance, Merabet et al. (2008) demonstrated that after just 5 days of blindfolding, sighted subjects displayed increased occipital responsivity to tactile stimulation, and enhanced tactile discrimination ability that is disrupted by rTMS to the occipital lobes. Equally dramatic are findings from Amedi et al. (2007) showing that subjects trained in interpreting auditory soundscapes (sound patterns that depict spatial topographies) show occipitotemporal activation when exposed to soundscapes depicting objects, whereas untrained control subjects do not. Because occipitotemporal cortex is involved in identifying object shape through vision, its expansion to the auditory domain is within the scope of its regular function. Thus, it appears likely that even in sighted subjects, occipitotemporal regions are not restricted to processing visual inputs, but rather can engage in functionally analogous tasks when the relevant information comes from a different sensory channel.

Overall, the evidence from monkey studies of premotor cortex and from cross-modal plasticity helps support the notion that classically unimodal brain areas are characterized not by a privileged relationship to a sensory channel, but by a type of computation or content (action goals, object shape, motion) that operates across inputs from a variety of sensory modalities.

Conclusion

Taking the weight of the research reviewed in this chapter, one might now consider whether the embodiment claims have been supported. Evidence from behavioral paradigms and from neuropsychology have contributed to our general understanding of conceptual knowledge, but have been unable to lend support to the embodiment view. Brain imaging evidence, with respect to the claim that semantic and perceptual tasks share neural mechanisms, has shown that there is a shared reliance on some brain areas, and unique reliance on others. This state of affairs makes it impossible to conclude that semantic and perceptual neural systems are entirely reducible, but does allow the observation that some overlaps exist.

The looming question is the significance of these overlaps, and whether their existence offers support for the second claim, that semantic knowledge is represented in a modality-specific format. The tasks that are contrasted (moving one's hand and listening to hand-related action words) do not pull apart what embodied theory needs; that is, representations with semantic content on the one hand, and those with purely modality-specific format on the other hand. Because of the difficulty of isolating such representational attributes, the nature of representations in many parts of the brain is still inadequately known. Furthermore, our understanding of "sensory" brain regions is rapidly shifting given findings from cross-modal plasticity and much other research. How then can one argue that the involvement of a certain brain area indicates the involvement of a certain representational format?[6]

Clearly, the engagement of certain brain regions is not appropriate evidence to specify the format (modality-specific or otherwise) of the representations involved. Aydede (1999) was the first to point out that much of such reasoning in fMRI research is circular: without an independent way to probe the format of information stored in a brain region, the difference between modality-specific and amodal format rests on the theory's own distinction, which cannot itself be based on brain area. It appears that the current state of brain-based evidence has not surpassed this circularity.

Returning to the question of whether one type of model (the conceptual componential model or

the strong empiricist model) is more promising, one might conclude that the reducibility of conceptual to sensory knowledge has not been supported by recent evidence. Rather, there seem to be conceptual operations that do more than recapitulate distinctions made by the senses. This makes a very strong empiricist view (the embodied view) seem unlikely. That said, little evidence has so far been able to address the interface problem, or how to answer questions about the format of representations, nor to really settle the debate between conceptual and empiricist views more generally.

Recent research has, however, made clear progress in characterizing the neural basis of word meaning. Neuroimaging has revealed systems for many types of semantic knowledge: goals, functions, verbs, shapes, and colors. These systems do not appear to reduce to neural systems that encode information from particular sensory channels. Novel approaches in imaging research have furthermore revealed the flexibility with which regions of the brain can take input from atypical sensory channels and robustly continue their functions. Overall, if one believes the picture emerging from these data, one would conclude that the brain's semantic system is organized by many fascinating dimensions, of which sensory modality is minimally prominent.

Notes

1. Concepts are defined very loosely as units of semantic knowledge; thus, "conceptual knowledge" and "semantic knowledge" are used interchangeably.

2. This is different from the idea that components may exist but are simply not retrieved during lexical access (e.g., Roelofs, 1992). Even in the nondecompositional model proposed by Roelofs (1992), DOG has its meaning by being connected to concept nodes, such as BARKS, and has a TAIL, but these are not obligatorily retrieved.

3. It is not clear, however, whether connectionist models would deny or support that concepts break down into conceptual elements at a level above their implementation in a distributed network.

4. An abstract set of features also fails to specify necessary and sufficient characteristics to define reference (Laurence & Margolis, 1999; Smith & Medin, 1981).

5. The nature of this privileged relationship was not explicated in the sensory/functional theory literature, nor are there data to be brought to bear on the question.

6. One difficulty might be that "format" is an improperly specified construct. In the more common view, format is distinct from content in that it describes the way that information is encoded and conveyed, rather than what is represented (Kosslyn, 1994). No embodied theorist has attempted a model of how manner of encoding distinguishes modalities. If one looks in primary motor cortex, is information encoded in some particular way that is different from V1, apart from the information they contain? Yet others have interpreted format as a way to make certain information explicit (Marr, 1978),

something in between format and content. Under this view, representations of different formats diverge in terms of which information is most available (Jackendoff, 1987; Kosslyn, 1994; Pylyshyn, 1979). One example is that "pictorial" representations are ones that have the most information about spatial extent and geometric form (Pylyshyn, 1979). There is some correlation between the most prominent information conveyed and sensory modality, but it is not equivalent because there are many more types of information than there are modalities. An emphasis on content as an organizing principle seems to be in line with evidence regarding the organization of the brain. It may also offer a better empirical foothold.

References

Allport, G. (1985). *Distributed memory, modular subsystems and dysphasia*. In S.K. Newman and R. Epstein (Eds.), *Current perspectives in dysphasia* (pp. 207–244). Edinburgh: Churchill Livingstone.

Amedi, A., Stern, W. M., Camprodon, J. A., Bermpohl, F., Merabet, L. B., Rotman, S.,... Pascual-Leone A (2007). Shape conveyed by visual-to-auditory sensory substitution activates the lateral occipital complex. *Nature Neuroscience, 10,* 687–689.

Aydede, M. (1999). What makes perceptual symbols perceptual? *Behavioral and Brain Sciences, 22,* 610–611.

Barsalou, L. W. (1999). Perceptual symbol systems. *Behavioral and Brain Sciences, 22,* 577–660.

Barsalou, L. W. (2008). Grounded cognition. *Annual Review of Psychology, 59,* 617–645.

Beauvois, M.-F. (1982). Optic aphasia: A process of interaction between vision and language. *Philosophical Transactions of the Royal Society B: Biological Sciences, 298,* 35–47.

Bedny, M., & Caramazza, A. (2011). Perception, action, and word meanings in the human brain: The case from action verbs. *Annals of the New York Academy of Sciences, 1224,* 81–95.

Bedny, M., Caramazza, A., Grossman, E., Pascual-Leone, A., & Saxe, R. (2008). Concepts are more than percepts: The case of action verbs. *The Journal of Neuroscience, 28,* 11347–11353.

Bedny, M., Konkle, T., Pelphrey, K., Saxe, R., & Pascual-Leone, A. (2010). Sensitive period for a multimodal response in human visual motion area MT/MST. *Current Biology, 20,* 1900–1906.

Bright, P., Moss, H. E., Longe, O., Stamatakis, E. A., & Tyler, L. K. (2007). Conceptual structure modulates anteromedial temporal involvement in processing verbally presented object properties. *Cerebral Cortex, 17,* 1066–1073.

Buccino, G., Riggio, L., Melli, G., Binkofski, F., Gallese, V., & Rizzolatti, G. (2005). Listening to action-related sentences modulates the activity of the motor system: A combined TMS and behavioral study. *Cognitive Brain Research, 24,* 355–363.

Canessa, N., Borgo, F., Cappa, S. F., Perani, D., Falini, A., Buccino, G.,... Shallice, T. (2008). The different neural correlates of action and functional knowledge in semantic memory: An FMRI study. *Cerebral Cortex, 18,* 740–751.

Caramazza, A., & Grober, E. (1976). Polysemy and the structure of the subjective lexicon. In C. Rameh (Ed.), *Georgetown University Round Table on Language and Linguistics* (pp. 181–206). Washington, D.C.: Georgetown University Press.

Caramazza, A., Hillis, A. E., Rapp, B. C., & Romani, C. (1990). The multiple semantics hypothesis: Multipleconfusions? *Cognitive Neuropsychology, 7,* 161–189.

Caramazza, A., & Shelton, J. R. (1998). Domain-specific knowledge systems in the brain the animate-inanimate distinction. *Journal of Cognitive Neuroscience, 10,* 1–34.

Chao, L. L., & Martin, A. (1999). Cortical regions associated with perceiving, naming, and knowing about colors. *Journal of Cognitive Neuroscience, 11,* 25–35.

Chao, L. L., Haxby, J. V., & Martin, A. (1999). Attribute-based neural substrates in temporal cortex for perceiving and knowing about objects. *Nature Neuroscience, 2,* 913–919.

Chatterjee, A. (2010). Disembodying cognition. *Language and Cognition, 2,* 79–116.

Collins, A. M., & Loftus, E. F. (1975). A spreading-activation theory of semantic processing. *Psychological Review, 82,* 407–428.

Creem-Regher, S. H., Dilda, V., Vicchrilli, A. E., Federer, F., & Lee, J. N. (2007). The influence of complex action knowledge on representations of novel graspable objects: Evidence from functional magnetic resonance imaging. *Journal of the International Neuropsychological Society, 13,* 1009–1020.

De Renzi, E., & Lucchelli, F. (1988). Ideational apraxia. *Brain, 111,* 1173–1185.

Di Pellegrino, G., Fadiga, L., Fogassi, L., Gallese, V., & Rizzolatti, G. (1992). Understanding motor events: A neurophysiological study. *Experimental Brain Research, 91,* 176–180.

Farah, M. J., Hammond, K. M., Mehta, Z., & Ratcliff, G. (1989). Category-specificity and modality-specificity in semantic memory. *Neuropsychologia, 27,* 193–200.

Farah, M. J., & McClelland, J. L. (1991). A computational model of semantic memory impairment: Modality specificity and emergent category specificity. *Journal of Experimental Psychology, General, 120,* 339–357.

Fodor, J. A. (1975) *The language of thought.* New York: Crowell.

Fodor, J.A. (1990). Information and representation. In S. Laurence & E. Margolis (Eds.), *Concepts: Core readings* (pp. 513–524). Cambridge, MA: MIT Press.

Forde, E., Francis, D., Riddoch, M. J., Rumiati, R. I., & Humphreys, G. W. (1997). On the links between visual knowledge and naming: A single case study of a patient with a category-specific impairment for living things. *Cognitive Neuropsychology, 14,* 403–458.

Freedman, D. J., Riesenhuber, M., Poggio, T., & Miller, E. (2001). Categorical representation of visual stimuli in the primate prefrontal cortex. *Science, 291,* 312–316.

Glenberg, A. M., & Kaschak, M. P. (2002). Grounding language in action. *Psychonomic Bulletin &Review, 9,* 558–565.

Glover, S., Rosenbaum, D. A., Graham, J., & Dixon, P. (2004). Grasping the meaning of words. *Experimental Brain Research, 154,* 103–108.

Goldberg, R. F., Perfetti, C. A., & Schneider, W. (2006). Perceptual knowledge retrieval activates sensory brain regions. *The Journal of Neuroscience, 26(18),* 4917–4921.

Hart, J., & Gordon, B. (1992). Neural subsystems for object knowledge. *Nature, 359,* 60–64.

Hauk, O., & Pulvermüller, F. (2004). Neurophysiological distinction of action words in the fronto-central cortex. *Human Brain Mapping, 21,* 191–201.

Hauk, O., Johnsrude, I., & Pulvermüller, F. (2004). Somatotopic representation of action words in human motor and premotor cortex. *Neuron, 41,* 301–307.

Heilman, K., Maher, L. M., & Greenwald, M. (1997). Conceptual apraxia from lateralized lesions. *Neurology, 49,* 457–464.

Hillis, A. E., & Caramazza, A. (1991). Category-specific naming and comprehension impairment: A double dissociation. *Brain, 114,* 2081–2094.

Humphreys, G. W., & Forde, E. (2001). Hierarchies, similarity, and interactivity in object recognition: Neuropsychological deficits. *Behavioral and Brain Sciences, 24,* 453–509.

Jackendoff, R. (1987). On beyond zebra: The relation of linguistic and visual information. *Cognition, 26*, 89–114.

Kable, J. W., Kan, I. P., Wilson, A., Thompson-Schill, S. L., & Chatterjee, A. (2005). Conceptual representations of action in the lateral temporal cortex. *Journal of Cognitive Neuroscience, 17*, 1855–1870.

Kan, I. P., Barsalou, L. W., Olseth Solomon, K., Minor, J. K., & Thompson-Schill, S. L. (2003). Role of mental imagery in a property verification task: fMRI evidence for perceptual representations of conceptual knowledge. *Cognitive Neuropsychology, 20*, 525–540.

Kellenbach, M. L., Brett, M., & Patterson, K. (2001). Large, colorful, or noisy? Attribute—and modality-specific activations during retrieval of perceptual attribute knowledge. *Cognitive, Affective & Behavioral Neuroscience, 1*, 207–221.

Laiacona, M., Capitani, E., Barbarotto, R., Foundation, S. M., & Hospital, S. P. (1997). Semantic category dissociations: A longitudinal study of two cases. *Riabilitazione, 3*, 441–461.

Laurence, S., & Margolis, E. (1999). Introduction. In S. Laurence & E. Margolis (Eds.), *Concepts: Core readings* (pp. 3–82). Cambridge, MA: MIT Press.

Levelt, W. J., Roelofs, A., & Meyer, S. (1999). A theory of lexical access in speech production. *The Behavioral and Brain Sciences, 22*, 1–38.

Luzzatti, C., & Davidoff, J. (1994). Impaired retrieval of object-colour knowledge with preserved colour naming. *Neuropsychologia, 32*, 933–950.

Mahon, B., & Caramazza, A. (2008). A critical look at the embodied cognition hypothesis and a new proposal for grounding conceptual content. *Journal of Physiology-Paris, 102*, 59–70.

Mahon, B. Z., Anzellotti, S., Schwartzbach, J., Zampini, M., & Caramazza, A. (2009). Category-specific organization in the human brain does not require visual experience. *Neuron, 63*, 297–405.

Margolis, E. (1998). How to acquire a concept. *Mind & Language, 13*(3), 347–369.

Marr, D. (1972). *Vision: A computational investigation into the human representation and processing of visual information.* New York: W. H. Freedman and Company.

Martin, A. (2007). The representation of object concepts in the brain. *Annual Review of Psychology, 58*, 25–45.

Martin, A., Haxby, J. V., Lalonde, F. M., Wiggs, C. L., & Ungerleider, L. G., (1995). Discrete cortical regions associated with knowledge of color and knowledge of action. *Science, 270*, 102–105.

Merabet, L. B., Hamilton, R., Schlaug, G., Swisher, J. D., Kiriakopoulos, E. T., Pitskel, N. B., . . . Pascual-Leone, A. (2008). Rapid and reversible recruitment of early visual cortex for touch. *PLoS ONE, 3*: e3046. doi:10.1371/journal.pone.0003046

Miceli, G., Fouch, E., Capasso, R., Shelton, J. R., Tomaiuolo, F., & Caramazza, A. (2001). The dissociation of color from form and function knowledge. *Nature Neuroscience, 4*, 662–667.

Mummery, C. J., Patterson, K., Hodges, J. R., & Price, C. J. (1998). Functional neuroanatomy of the semantic system: Divisible by what? *Journal of Cognitive Neuroscience, 10*, 766–777.

Murphy, G.L. (2002). *The big book of concepts.* Cambridge, MA: MIT Press

Noppeney, U., & Price, C. J. (2002). Retrieval of visual, auditory, and abstract semantics. *NeuroImage, 15*, 917–926.

Paivio, A. (1991). Dual coding theory: Retrospect and current status. *Canadian Journal of Psychology, 45*, 255–287.

Pascual-Leone, A., & Hamilton, R. (2001). The metamodal organization of the brain. *Progress in Brain Research, 134*, 427–445.

Patterson, K., Nestor, P. J., & Rogers, T. T. (2007). Where do you know what you know? The representation of semantic knowledge in the human brain. *Nature, 8*, 976–989.

Phillips, J. A., Noppeney, U., Humphreys, G. W., & Price, C. J. (2002). Can segregation within the semantic system account for category-specific deficits? *Brain, 125*, 2067–2080.

Pietrini, P., Furey, M. L., Ricciardi, E., Gobbini, M. I., Wu, W.-H. C., Cohen, L., . . . Haxby, J. V. (2004). Beyond sensory images: Object-based representation in the human ventral pathway. *Proceedings of the National Academy of Sciences of the United States of America, 101*, 5658–5663.

Postle, N., McMahon, K. L., Ashton, R., Meredith, M., & Zubicaray, G. I. de. (2008). Action word meaning representations in cytoarchitectonically defined primary and premotor cortices. *NeuroImage, 43*, 634–644.

Pulvermüller, F., Hauk, O., Nikulin, V. V., & Ilmoniemi, R. J. (2005). Functional links between motor and language systems. *The European Journal of Neuroscience, 21*, 793–797.

Pustejovsky, J. (1995). *The generative lexicon.* Cambridge, MA: MIT Press.

Putnam, H. (1975). The meaning of "meaning." In B. Beakley & P. Ludlow (Eds.), *The philosophy of mind* (pp. 539–555). Cambridge, MA: MIT Press.

Ravin, Y., & Leacock, C. (2002). Polysemy: An overview. In Y. Ravin and C. Leacock (Eds.), *Polysemy: Theoretical and computational approaches* (pp. 1–29). Oxford: Oxford University Press.

Renier, L. A., Anurova, I., De Volder, A. G., Carlson, S., Vanmeter, J., & Rauschecker, J. P. (2010). Preserved functional specialization for spatial processing in the middle occipital gyrus of the early blind. *Neuron, 68*, 138–148.

Richardson, D., Spivey, M., Barsalou, L. W., & McRae, K. (2003). Spatial representations activated during real-time comprehension of verbs. *Cognitive Science, 27*, 767–780.

Rips, L. J. (1995). The current status of research on concept combination. *Mind & Language, 10*, 73–104.

Rizzolatti, G., Fadiga, L., Gallese, V., & Fogassi, L. (1996). Premotor cortex and the recognition of motor actions. Brain research. *Cognitive Brain Research, 3*, 131–141.

Rizzolatti, G., Fogassi, L., & Gallese, V. (2001). Neurophysiological mechanisms underlying the understanding and imitation of action. *Nature Reviews Neuroscience, 2*, 661–672.

Rizzolatti, G., & Sinigaglia, C. (2010). The functional role of the parieto-frontal mirror circuit: Interpretations and misinterpretations. *Nature Reviews: Neuroscience, 11*, 264–274.

Rogers, T. T., & McClelland, J. L. (2004) *Semantic Cognition: A Parallel Distributed Processing Approach.* Cambridge, MA: MIT Press.

Rosch, E. (1978). Principles of categorization. In S. Laurence & E. Margolis (Eds.), *Concepts: Core readings* (pp. 189–206). Cambridge, MA: MIT Press.

Sadato, N., Pascual-Leone, A., Grafman, J., Ibanez, V., Deiber, M. P., Dold, G., & Hallet. M. (1996). Activation of the primary visual cortex by Braille reading in blind subjects. *Nature, 380*, 526–528.

Sartori, G., & Job, R. (1988). The oyster with four legs: A neuropsychological study on the interaction of visual and semantic information. *Cognitive Neuropsychology, 5*, 105–132.

Shallice, T. (1988). *From neuropsychology to mental structure*. Cambridge: Cambridge University Press.

Shepard, R. N. (1980). Multidimensional scaling, tree-fitting, and clustering. *Science, 210*, 390–398.

Silveri, M. C., & Gainotti, G. (1988). Interaction between vision and language in category-specific semantic impairment. *Cognitive Neuropsychology, 5*, 677–709.

Simmons, W. K., Ramjee, V., Beauchamp, M. S., McRae, K., Martin, A., & Barsalou, L. W. (2007). A common neural substrate for perceiving and knowing about color. *Neuropsychologia, 45*, 2802–2810.

Smith, E. E., & Medin, D. L. (1981). *Categories and concepts*. Cambridge, MA: Harvard University Press.

Stanfield, R. A., & Zwaan, R. A. (2001). The effect of implied orientation derived from verbal context on picture recognition. *Psychological Science, 12*, 153–156.

Tettamanti, M., Buccino, G., Saccuman, M. C., Gallese, V., Danna, M., Scifo, P.,…Perani, D. (2005). Listening to action-related sentences activates fronto-parietal motor circuits. *Journal of Cognitive Neuroscience, 17*, 273–281.

Thompson-Schill, S. L. (2003). Neuroimaging studies of semantic memory: Inferring "how" from "where." *Neuropsychologia, 41*, 280–292.

Tomasino, B., Werner, C. J., Weiss, P. H., & Fink, G. R. (2007). Stimulus properties matter more than perspective: An fMRI study of mental imagery and silent reading of action phrases. *NeuroImage, 36*, T128-T141.

Tversky, A. (1977). Features of similarity. *Psychological Review, 84*, 327-352.

Tyler, L. K., Moss, H. E., Durrant-Peatfield, M. R., & Levy, J. P. (2000). Conceptual structure and the structure of concepts: A distributed account of category-specific deficits. *Brain and Language, 75*, 195–231.

Tyler, L. K., & Moss, H. E. (2001). Towards a distributed account of conceptual knowledge. *Trends in Cognitive Sciences, 5*, 244–252.

Umiltà, M. A., Escola, L., Intskirveli, I., Grammont, F., Rochat, M., Caruana, F.,…Rizzolatti, G. (2008). When pliers become fingers in the monkey motor system. *Proceedings of the National Academy of Sciences of the United States of America, 105*, 2209–2213.

Vandenbulcke, M., Peeters, R., Fannes, K., & Vandenberghe, R. (2006). Knowledge of visual attributes in the right hemisphere. *Nature Neuroscience, 9*, 964–970.

Vigliocco, G., & Vinson, D. (2007). Semantic representation. In G. Gaskell (Ed.), *Oxford handbook of psycholinguistics* (pp. 195-215). New York: Oxford University Press.

Warrington, E. K. (1975). The selective impairment of semantic memory. *The Quarterly Journal of Experimental Psychology, 27*, 635–657.

Warrington, E. K., & Shallice, T. (1984). Category-specific semantic impairments. *Brain, 107*, 829–854.

Warrington, E. K., & McCarthy, R. A. (1987). Categories of knowledge: Further fractionations and an attempted integration. *Neurocase, 110*, 1273–1296.

Zeki, S., Watson, J. D., Lueck, C. J., Friston, K. J., Kennard, C., & Frackowiak, R. S. (1991). A direct demonstration of of functional specialization in human visual cortex. *Journal of Neuroscience, 11*, 641–649.

Zwaan, R., Stanfield, R. A., & Yaxley, R. H. (2002). Language comprehenders mentally represent the shapes of objects. *Psychological Science, 13*, 168–171.

Zwaan, R., & Taylor, L. J. (2006). Seeing, acting, understanding: Motor resonance in language comprehension. *Journal of Experimental Psychology: General, 135*, 1–11.

Giving Words Meaning: Why Better Models of Semantics Are Needed in Language Production Research

David Vinson, Mark Andrews, *and* Gabriella Vigliocco

Abstract

Meaning is the foundation of language production. The goal of communication is to express meaning to be understood by others. It is therefore no surprise that all accounts of lexical retrieval in production start with meaning representations of various types, implemented in various architectures, which drive retrieval of other types of lexical information. However, there is a vast gulf between the operationalization of semantic/conceptual representations in most models of lexical retrieval in production (using extremely simple assumptions about meaning similarity) and semantic/conceptual representations developed primarily by statistically or computationally oriented researchers. We argue that taking advantage of progress in computational modeling of semantics could help research in language production and, likewise, research on semantic modeling could also benefit from taking into account data arising from production research.

Key Words: semantics, concepts, distributional models, semantic features

Introduction

Meaning is the foundation of language production, with the goal of communication to express meaning to be understood by others. It is therefore no surprise that all accounts of lexical retrieval in production start with meaning representations of various types, implemented in various architectures, which drive retrieval of other types of lexical information. Throughout the existence of language production as a field of research, there have been debates and controversies concerning the relationship between meaning and other aspects of lexical retrieval, and vigorous discussions related to meaning continue in the literature. However, as we will discuss in more detail in this review, there is a vast gulf between the operationalization of semantic/conceptual representations in most models of lexical retrieval in production, and state-of-the-art accounts of semantic/conceptual representations developed primarily by statistically or computationally

oriented researchers. This separation is understandable, as extremely simple assumptions about meaning similarity seem sufficient to account for many findings in language production, whereas researchers in the statistical/computational tradition do not tend to be concerned with theories of language production (or language processing more generally). We will argue, however, that investigations of the mechanisms of lexical retrieval may be significantly limited due to these simplifying assumptions, and merging the two types of approaches could reveal aspects of lexical retrieval that are hidden behind the standard assumptions in the field.

We will start from a review of theoretical approaches to semantic representation and then move to present the assumptions about meaning representation and retrieval that have typically been applied in research on lexical retrieval over the years. We conclude with a brief discussion of how the current dissociation between these two domains may provide a significant impediment for addressing important issues at the junction of word meaning and word production. We argue that taking advantage of progress in computational modeling of semantics could help research in language production and, likewise, research on semantic modeling could also benefit from taking into account data arising from production research.

Theoretical Approaches to Semantic Representations

The current state of the art falls into two broad types of approaches, originating in theories of semantic representation developed in the 1970s (e.g. Rosch & Mervis, 1975; Smith, Shoben & Rips, 1974; Collins & Quillian, 1969; Minsky, 1975; Norman & Rumelhart, 1975; see Smith & Medin, 1981), and which can be described either as featural or holistic approaches (Vigliocco & Vinson, 2007). Until recently these two types of approaches have been pursued largely independently, with cognitive psychology/neuropsychology/cognitive neuroscience using more of a featural approach, versus the similarity-based (holistic) models used by computational linguistics/computer science. We discuss the development of semantic representations in these two domains, and then turn to some recent work aiming to bring these traditions together, and discuss how taking such approaches into account may provide a way forward for theories of lexical retrieval in production.

Meaning as Sets of Features

THE ORIGINS AND DEVELOPMENT OF FEATURAL THEORIES

The notion that word meaning can be decomposed into featural elements, whereby meanings are statements of the necessary and sufficient properties for membership in a set, has been pervasive for centuries (e.g., Aristotle's Categories, 350 BCE/1941). Although this classical view was influential for much of the 20th century (e.g., Cassirer, 1953; Bourne, 1970; Katz & Fodor, 1963), a variety of phenomena prove difficult to explain under such a view. In particular, some concepts, exemplified by Wittgenstein's (1953/1997) example of the word "game," are not clearly definable, and many other concepts appear to be fuzzy rather than sharply delimited (Rosch, 1973; Hampton, 1979). As a consequence, almost all contemporary feature-based accounts of semantic representation, following Rosch and Mervis (1975), Rosch, Mervis, Gray, Johnson, and Boyes-Braem (1976), view concepts as probabilistically rather than logically defined, and instances of concepts to be related by "family resemblance" rather than all-or-nothing category membership (see Smith & Medin, 1981, Murphy, 2002 for reviews).

A particularly useful application of this general approach is the use of features of meaning as a tool to provide insight into word meaning. One method is to assemble sets of words from a semantic domain of interest and decide a priori on their features but without claiming that these features constitute a complete set, and then use those features to build a computational model of representation that can then be tested against data. This method was taken by Hinton and Shallice (1991; also see Murphy, 2002 for reviews).

A particularly useful application of this general approach is the use of features of meaning as a tool to provide insight into word meaning. One method is to assemble sets of words from a semantic domain of interest and decide a priori on their features but without claiming that these features constitute a complete set, and then use those features to build a computational model of representation that can then be tested against data. This method was taken by Hinton and Shallice (1991, also see Plaut & Shallice, 1993), who created a set of semantic features that intuitively capture properties of common objects (e.g., <has-legs>, <hard>, <made-of-metal>, <part-of-limb>) and used these features to train an attractor network to learn the mapping between orthography and semantics. Lesioning this network produced semantic, visual, and visual/semantic errors consistent with patterns of performance in deep dyslexia. Plaut (1995) used the same approach to investigate dissociations between reading concrete and abstract words. A particular characteristic of the representations was that abstract words had fewer features than concrete words. This difference in featural properties between concrete and abstract words (possibly in conjunction with other differences) translated into different consequences when different aspects of the model were damaged: abstract words were more impaired when the feedforward connections were lesioned, whereas concrete words were more impaired when the recurrent connections were lesioned. Such findings suggest that even double dissociations can arise from a model with a (single) common level of semantic representation, depending on underlying characteristics of the featural input.

However, a potential problem with this computational modeling approach is that the semantic features used were chosen by the investigators, and may reflect the investigators' theoretical biases, or may not be true of the full range of meaning of the words in question. Other authors have addressed this concern by investigating those dimensions of meaning that are considered to be psychologically salient by others. Several models of semantic representations based on this kind of input have been implemented to date, differing mainly in the manner in which semantic representations are derived from the input. One class of models uses connectionist frameworks that develop representations from semantic input. These models are used to demonstrate how particular patterns of semantic impairment may be observed as a consequence of differential featural composition. This entails training a connectionist network with input that, although not directly obtained from speakers, is informed by characteristics of feature norms that are hypothesized to play a role. For example, Farah and McClelland (1991) constructed a model in which words referring to living or nonliving entities were associated with different proportions of visual-perceptual and functional features (the former predominant for living things, the latter predominant for nonliving entities). In this case, the proportions were derived from dictionary definitions, which were presented to naive participants who were asked to rate the individual elements of meaning in each definition in terms of sensory/perceptual or functional content. When the model was lesioned, different category-related effects were found, depending on whether the lesion targeted the visual-perceptual features (with living things more impaired) or functional features (with nonliving things more impaired). A similar approach was taken by Devlin, Gonnerman, Andersen, and Seidenberg (1998) who investigated the role of intercorrelated features (those features that frequently co-occur, such as <has wings> and <has a beak>) and distinguishing features (those that allow similar entities to be distinguished from each other) on impairment over time for living or nonliving things as a consequence of dementia. Because living things have many intercorrelated features but few distinguishing ones, and the situation is reversed for nonliving entities (McRae, de Sa, & Seidenberg, 1997), differences in their composition were able to explain the progression of relative impairment for living and nonliving things in dementia within a single representational system (see also Rogers et al., 2004)

In these examples, semantic representations are based on specific characteristics derived from independently generated information about meaning (e.g., more visual-perceptual features for living

things, as in Farah & McClelland, 1991; more intercorrelated but fewer distinguishing features, as in Devlin et al., 1998). Such approaches, however, require making a priori assumptions about the particular properties that are relevant to explain a particular pattern of data, and do not allow for the possibility that other properties not explicitly embedded in the semantic representations may also play important roles. Indeed, the theories of Farah and McClelland and Devlin et al. are not necessarily incompatible with each other, but their implementations do not permit direct comparison. This is because each model only embeds certain specific properties of featural input, and not others that are hypothesized to play a role under other theories, rather than simultaneously embedding multiple characteristics of featural input.

THE USE OF SPEAKER-GENERATED FEATURES

Another class of models based on independently obtained input avoids the need of deciding in advance which properties are relevant to explain a given pattern of data by using speaker-generated features: separable aspects of meaning that naive participants believe are important in defining and describing the meaning of a given word, which could be considered as a proxy for the types of primitive features that may actually underlie their meanings. These features are used to develop a model of representation, and then the properties of the resulting model are analyzed to identify those properties that affect the representations (Hampton, 1979, 1981; Hampton & Gardiner, 1983; Rosch & Mervis, 1975; Rosch et al., 1976; Smith et al., 1974; Tversky & Hemenway, 1984). The first work along these lines to be carried out on a larger scale was conducted by McRae et al. (1997), who collected speaker-generated features for a large number of nouns referring to concrete objects (animals, plants, fruits, vegetables, artifacts, vehicles, and so forth).

Subsequent work by McRae and colleagues has used these features to address several questions of semantic representation and impairment (e.g., Cree & McRae, 2003; Cree, McNorgan, & McRae 2006; Cree, McRae, & McNorgan, 1999; McRae & Cree, 2002; McRae, Cree, Seidenberg, & McNorgan, 2005; McRae, Cree, Westmacott, & de Sa, 1999), and on theoretical questions concerning the nature of multimodal sensory integration into word meaning (McNorgan, Reid, & McRae, 2011). Work based on speaker-generated features has also been conducted by other groups (Garrard, Lambon Ralph, Hodges, & Patterson, 2001; Randall, Moss,

Rodd, Greer, & Tyler, 2004; Rogers & McClelland, 2004; Vinson & Vigliocco, 2008), collectively providing comprehensive data sets which allow investigation of semantic representations from numerous directions.

However, one crucial characteristic of many of these models is that they still tend to discuss the featural input in terms of one particular dimension (or just a few) to explain particular patterns of data. To permit the evaluation of such models more generally as theories of semantic representation, it is necessary to consider classes of models that do not depend on selecting particular characteristics of the featural input, but that still permit features to be analyzed in such terms if desired. Such an approach was taken by Vigliocco, Vinson, Lewis, and Garrett (2004), using speaker-generated features to generate a similarity space of reduced dimensionality, and then establishing that distance in this representational space predicts a variety of fine-grained semantic effects in speech errors, priming in lexical decision, and picture-word interference (although see Mahon, Costa, Peterson, Vargas, & Caramazza, 2007 for alternative interpretation of the latter). Such findings can be seen, not necessarily as convincing evidence that the specific assumptions of Vigliocco et al's model are true, but as more of an existence proof that models of semantic similarity derived from speaker-generated features are capable of predicting behavioral effects at the item level. The featural approach is also appealing because it provides a natural link to the large body of neuroscientific evidence showing that sensory-motor characteristics of words' referents words are reflected in neural representation (e.g., Cappa, 2008; Martin, 2009 for recent reviews).

THE LIMITS OF FEATURAL APPROACHES

Although we have discussed several instances where the featural approach can provide insight into semantic representations, we quickly reach the limit of what such featural approaches can do for us. First of all, speaker-generated features are clearly only a proxy for those true properties that are assumed to underlie word meaning. Some of these are sensory-motor in nature and presumably derived from low-level sensory input, but it is unclear how others are represented, such as encyclopedic features (e.g., <from Africa>, <grows on trees>). Verbal features are also limited in expressing all but the most basic details of size, shape, or configuration (e.g., one of the participants from the data set published in Vinson & Vigliocco, 2008, attempted to describe

the shape of a hammer by describing it as having a cylindrical part, and a part with a more complicated shape—a correct description but one that clearly misses most of the nuances of a hammer's shape; a few others described a hammer as long or thin but most made no attempt to describe its shape). Participants also have much more trouble generating features for more abstract concepts, and when they do there tends to be much less in common from one participant to the next (Vinson & Vigliocco, unpublished data). Finally, it is enormously time-consuming to obtain such data on even a moderately large scale (i.e., hundreds of words, as in the studies cited previously) because substantial effort is required to combine responses across participants and items into an integrated whole. One way forward that has been explored by some groups is automated or semiautomated property extraction from very large corpora of text (e.g., Poesio & Almuhareb, 2008; Baroni, Murphy, Barbu, & Poesio, 2010; Davidov & Rappaport, 2008), but it is unclear how successful such approaches can be, given the inherent difficulties related to verbal features mentioned previously.

Meaning as Relations between Words

A very different approach to word meaning can be taken, by considering word meaning not in terms of the features an individual word may be decomposed into, but in terms of words' relations to other words. Beginning in the early 1990s, computational modeling of semantic representation has been increasingly influenced by what can be termed *distributional models*. In general, distributional models are based on the assumption that the meaning of a word can, at least in part, be inferred from its statistical distribution across spoken and written language. All distributional models aim to provide a statistical description, of some kind or other, of the different contexts in which any given word is used. To the extent that the contexts in which a word occurs provide information about what that word means, these statistical descriptions can thus provide a semantic representation for the word. As we will describe, many studies in cognitive science have now provided evidence for the general validity of these representations.

As such, distributional models are now widely accepted as plausible models of semantic representations. This trend is noteworthy for at least two independent reasons. First, distributional models are usually large-scale and based on large natural language corpora. This entails that they can usually provide detailed information on an extensive vocabulary range. Their vocabulary coverage is thus usually far greater than those based, out of necessity, on small and vocabulary-limited data-sets of features. Second, and from a more theoretical perspective, distributional models provide an alternative perspective on the nature and origin of semantic representation. In particular, distributional models show how intra-linguistic information is itself a valuable source of information about what words mean. How words are used within language itself, and not just how they are used to denote perceptible objects and events in the world, may be a rich source of information by which humans, whether as children or adults, learn and develop their semantic knowledge. In this section, our aim is to provide some brief history of the use distributional models and then to outline the current state-of-the-art of the use of distributional models in contemporary cognitive science.

THE ORIGINS OF THE DISTRIBUTIONAL HYPOTHESIS

Firth (1957) is often credited as one of the first to consider how the statistical distribution of word across spoken and written language may be related to its meaning. In this work, Firth proposed that we may learn the meaning of a word by examining the various contexts of its common usage. Firth suggested that "You shall know a word by the company it keeps" and that we may learn the meaning of a word from "its habitual collocation" with other words. Defining the "habitual collocation" of a word as "the mere word accompaniment, the other word material in which they are most commonly or most characteristically embedded," Firth suggested that words that are dissimilar in meaning should not be likely to be found in similar contexts, whereas words that are found in identical or similar environments can be taken to share some of their meanings.

Although Firth's principal concerns were primarily related to lexicography, he drew inspiration from the philosophy of Wittgenstein (1953/1997), which seemed to argue against a conception of meaning and language whereby words in a language refer to objects in the world, whereas the propositions of the language consist of these words arranged into a logical structure that mirror the structured interrelationships of their referents. Against this traditional view, Wittgenstein argued that the meaning of a word is based on how it is used within a language, or as he put it "for a large class of cases...in which we employ the term meaning, it can be defined thus: The meaning of a word is its use in the language" (Section 43; p. 21).

At the same time as Firth (1957), Harris (1954) proposed his distributional hypothesis whereby word meanings are derived in part from their distribution across different linguistic environments. Harris suggests, for example, that "If we consider oculist and eye-doctor, we find as our corpus of actually occurring utterances grows that these two occur in almost the same environments," whereas "there are many environments in which oculist occurs but lawyer does not." More formally, he proposed that "If A and B have almost identical environments...we say they are synonyms" whereas "If A and B have some environments in common and some not...we say that they have different meanings" with "the amount of meaning difference corresponding roughly to the amount of difference in their environments (p. 157)." Taken together, Firth (1957) and Harris (1954) introduce what can be termed the distributional hypothesis. At its most general, this is the hypothesis that the distribution of words across and written language is a rich source of information from which we learn word meanings. This hypothesis is a precursor and forms part of the theoretical background of many contemporary distributional models in cognitive science.

MOVING FROM THE DISTRIBUTIONAL HYPOTHESIS TO DISTRIBUTIONAL MODELS

The distributional hypothesis was destined to remain untested and perhaps obscure until computing resources grew to sufficient power. Moreover, the early computational models that can be said to have addressed this hypothesis (e.g., Schütze, 1992; Deerwester, Dumais, Furnas, Landauer, & Harshman, 1990) were primarily motivated by the practical concerns of information retrieval rather than philosophical, linguistic, or psychological matters. These models, however, were to influence models in cognitive science that aimed to specifically address questions concerning distributional structure in human semantic representations. Schütze (1992) strongly influenced the work of Lund and Burgess and their hyperspace analog of language model (e.g., Lund, Burgess, & Atchley, 1995; Lund & Burgess, 1996; Burgess & Lund, 1997), whereas Deerwester et al. (1990) was the foundation of the latent semantic analysis (LSA) work of Landauer and colleagues (e.g., Landauer & Dumais, 1997; Landauer, Laham, & Foltz, 1998; Landauer, Laham, Rehder, & Schreiner, 1997).

To date, LSA remains one of the mostly widely used methods in cognitive science to learn semantic representations from how words are distributed in language. LSA defines words as frequency distributions over a large set of documents. For example, if we have a corpus of J documents and a vocabulary of I words, we can create a $J \times I$ document by word frequency matrix M where element M_{ji} gives the frequency of occurrence of word i in document j. The ith column of M is the frequency distribution over all documents by word i. As such, any word can be seen as a point in a highly correlated J-dimensional space. LSA aims to find an uncorrelated low-dimensional representation of this space, where the axes of this space now correspond to the major latent dimensions in the original data. Every word can then be mapped to a point in this space. This provides a representation of the word in terms of the major types of contexts in which words occur. The cosine of the angle between points in this low dimensional space can be taken as a measure of the similarity between the corresponding words in terms of the contexts in which they occur.

In the original LSA work of Landauer and Dumais (1997), a 4.6-m word corpus comprising approximately 30,000 documents and 60,000 word types was used. The corpus was described as a word-document co-occurrence matrix, and a singular value decomposition (SVD) analysis of this matrix was carried out, resulting in a lower-dimensional latent-space representation of each word, as explained previously. The cosine of the angle between vectors in this space could be taken as a measure of interword similarity. Using this measure, Landauer and Dumais reported comparable performance between LSA and humans. For example, using items from a Test of English as a Foreign Language synonym-test, the authors reported a performance of 64.4 percent correct for LSA, compared to 64.5 percent by nonnative English speakers applying to US colleges. They also showed that in cases where LSA was incorrect, its choices were positively correlated ($r = .44$) with the choices made by the college applicants.

Although LSA has been shown to be successful in domains such as those discussed previously, it has some serious limitations. From a psychological point of view, as discussed next for distributional models in general, it lacks "grounding" (e.g., Glenberg & Robertson, 2000), namely, it does not provide an account for how words come to refer to objects and actions in the world. From a computational point of view, it lacks a well-defined probabilistic model of the distribution of words across spoken and written language. In practical terms, this entails that it is difficult to provide precise interpretations of the variables or measures of their relationship in

an LSA model. Likewise, without a well-defined probabilistic model, it is challenging to extend LSA beyond its original usage. In response to this, alternative probabilistic models have been introduced that can be viewed as the probabilistic counterparts of LSA. Chief among these is the Latent Dirichlet Allocation (LDA) model of Blei, Ng, and Jordan (2003). According to LDA, each text is a bag-of-words (i.e., a frequency distribution over a vocabulary) that is taken to be a sample from a mixture of component probability distributions over the vocabulary. Each component is a distribution over words that emphasize a specific discourse topic, such as sport, politics, finance, love, film, and so forth. For example, a component corresponding to the sport discourse topic may place most of its probability mass on such words as game, ball, play, team, competition, and so forth. Accordingly, each text is the product of a specific probabilistic weighting of these sets of discourse topics. For example, one text might be based 0.5 on sports, 0.35 on finance, and 0.15 on love. Another might be based 0.65 on love, 0.3 on film, and 0.5 on politics.

The aim of learning in LDA is to infer the model's component topic distributions, as well as the mixing proportions for each text. In other words, the topics are not predetermined but are inferred from the corpus of data and, as such, describe characteristic patterns in the data. On the basis of these learned distributions, it is then a straightforward application of Bayes rule to infer each word's latent semantic representation, which is interpreted as the typicality of a given word for each component topic. Words that are representative of similar topics have similar latent semantic representations. This is the direct LDA analog of the latent-semantic representation as a point in the latent-space of a LSA model.

In Griffiths, Steyvers, and Tenenbaum (2007), LDA is presented as a model of human semantic representation. In this model, latent distributions corresponding intuitively to discourse topics are discovered by the model. Each word in the model can be represented as a distribution over these latent-topics, and this can be taken to be its semantic representation. These distributions are inferred using Bayes rule and can be seen as measuring the typicality of each word for each latent topic, such that words that are typical of similar topics have similar representations. Using these representations, the relationships between words (i.e., interword similarities) can also be inferred. For the purposes of comparison between the similarity relationships inferred by the model and those of human judgments, the

Nelson word-association norms (Nelson, McEvoy, & Schreiber, 2004) were used as a standard. These norms provide lists of close associates (according to human judgments) of a set of approximately 5,000 common English words. Griffiths et al. (2007) reported that across this set, the rank assigned by the model to these highly associated words was high, and that in a large number of cases the most highly related word according to their model was exactly that of the most highly associated word according to the norms. They also reported superior performance of their model, according to this measure, compared with the original LSA model (Landauer & Dumais, 1997).

CRITICISMS OF DISTRIBUTIONAL MODELS

As a whole, the distributional models just described have shown that rich semantic information can be derived solely from the statistical distribution of words in spoken and written language. In other words, they have provided compelling support for the plausibility of the distributional hypothesis. However, by focusing exclusively on distributional data, these models deliberately neglect the obvious semantic role of the information that we acquire through our senses and through our interaction with the environment. As a consequence, distributional models, and the distributional hypothesis in general, have become open to criticism. The neglect of word-world relationships is taken by some as a definitive argument against the plausibility of distributional models as accounts of human semantic representation, especially those that are sympathetic to embodied cognition. For example, Glenberg and Robertson (2000) argue that because distributional approaches propose that "the meaning of an abstract symbol (a word) can arise from the conjunction of relations to other undefined abstract symbols," this is grounds for their rejection as psychologically valid models of semantic representation. Glenberg and Robertson use arguments including the famous Searle (2000) Chinese Room thought-experiment to argue that no purely symbolic interrelationships can describe a semantic system. For Glenberg and Robertson, to know "the meaning of an abstract symbol such as…an English word, the symbol has to be grounded in something other than more abstract symbols (p. 382)."

Even if Glenberg's specific argument is not found to be convincing, the disconnected nature of distributional data does present serious challenges for distributional models of semantic representation. For example, distributional models are also challenged by the considerable body of neuroscientific data (e.g., Aziz-Zadeh, Wilson, Rizzolatti, & Iacoboni, 2006; Beauchamp, Lee, Haxby, & Martin, 2002; Buccino et al., 2005; Chao, Haxby, & Martin, 1999; Chao, Weisberg, & Martin, 2002; Chao & Martin, 2000; Damasio et al., 2001; Gerlach, Law, & Paulson, 2002; Grabowski, Damasio, & Damasio, 1998; Ishai, Ungerleider, Martin, Schouten, & Haxby, 1999; Martin, Haxby, Lalonde, Wiggs, & Ungerleider, 1995; Martin, Wiggs, Ungerleider, & Haxby, 1996; Oliveri et al., 2004; Phillips, Noppeney, Humphreys, & Price, 2002; Pulvermüller, 1999, 2001; Pulvermüller, Hauk, Nikulin, & Ilmoniemi, 2005; Pulvermüller & Hauk, 2005; Tettamanti et al., 2005; Vigliocco et al., 2006; Vuilleumier, Henson, Driver, & Dolan, 2002) showing that words are represented in the brain according to the sensory-motor characteristics of their referents. These data have shown, for example, how the motor cortices are activated in the processing of tools or other manipulable objects, or how processing words whose referents have salient visual properties corresponds to activation in visual brain areas. The grounded and sensory-motor nature of these representations clearly indicates the role of experiential data in the representation of words.

Bringing Together Featural and Distributional Models

The criticism just raised, that of neglecting the role of perceived data from the world in the formation of semantic representation of words, may be dealt with by extending the scope of the distributional hypothesis. In its original form, the distributional hypothesis considers how a word is distributed across different linguistic contexts. We may extend this hypothesis by extending the definition of the context in which a word is used to include both the physical or real-world context as well as contexts within language itself. In other words, a word's usage can be seen in terms of its distribution across both spoken and written language and the various physical or real-world contexts in which it is used. The latter type of contexts will obviously also include the various referents of a word and their perceived properties.

This extended distributional hypothesis can be illustrated in the following scenario: On the basis of perceptual experience, a child learns that the term dog refers to a kind of domestic animal that makes barking noises, has four legs, a wagging tail, and so forth. In addition, through general experience with language, the child learns that the term dog co-occurs with terms like pet, animal, and so forth. In this scenario, it is as if there is a dual, or parallel, corpus of data. On the one hand, there is the stream of words that is the language itself, and on the other there is the set of perceived physical properties that are associated with these words. From this, knowledge that the word dog refers to those creatures with four legs and tails and that bark can be integrated with the knowledge that dog co-occurs with pet and animal. The two sources of information could then be combined to provide a richer understanding of the semantics of the word dog than could be possible otherwise.

In recent years, a growing number of studies have considered how perceptual and distributional information could be integrated to form semantic representations. For example, in Andrews, Vigliocco, and Vinson (2009), we present a Bayesian model of how semantic representations are learned by combining these two forms of information. Beginning with the premise that words are encountered simultaneously within two rich contexts (i.e., the physical world itself and the discourse of human language), we argued that the data from which we learn semantic representations is akin to a parallel corpus: a text is set of words, and each word is a set of perceptual features. Such a set up can easily be realized in a straightforward extension of the LDA model just described. Specifically, each word is sampled from a latent distribution over words while simultaneously the word's properties are sampled from a latent distribution over features. By modeling semantic representations in this way, we demonstrated that combining distributional and perceptual information leads to richer and more comprehensive semantic representation than those learned from either distributional or perceptual information alone.

In related work, Johns and Jones (2012) explored the integration of distributional and perceptual information, focusing particularly on how words for which no perceptual information is directly available may be perceptually grounded through chains of lexical associations. In this way, Johns and Jones address the criticism that distributional models are disembodied from the world, by treating the statistical information related to a word as a joint distribution over perceptual features and text occurrence frequencies. Using a single model for this joint distribution, they are able to make inferences from words to perceptual features and vice versa. In this way, even if a word is not observed to have any perceptual properties, it is possible to infer their possible features on the basis of their lexical associations with other words for which features are available. Thus, all words can eventually be grounded in perceptual experience, even if they do not have directly perceptible referents.

While Andrews et al. (2009) and Johns and Jones (2012) have used speaker-generated features as a rough proxy of perceptual data, Bruni, Tran, and Baroni (2011) have explored the issue of the integration of perceptual and distributional data using the actual visual information in images labeled by words. In particular, just as a text can be treated as a bag-of-words, Bruni et al. treat a visual image as a bag of visual-words. As such, statistical information for a given word is both in terms of word-to-word co-occurrences within texts and word-to-visual-word co-occurrences arising from words and their physical referents. Bruni et al. have shown that augmenting state-of-the-art distributional models with visual information related to the referents of words improves these models, particularly by allowing them to more easily learn the semantic similarities between concrete words.

These studies, along with Steyvers (2010) and Riordan and Jones (2011) among others, are beginning to address the persistent criticism of distributional models being disembodied from the world. The solution to this problem does not limit or compromise the scope of the distributional hypothesis, but extends it. Rather than the relevant context of a word being just its linguistic context, we can extend the definition of context to include the extralinguistic or real-world context in which the world occurs, "combined models" in other words. From this, the more general distributional hypothesis is that the meaning of a word is acquired from the contexts of its usage, regardless of whether these contexts are intralinguistic or extralinguistic.

Interim Conclusions

This section has presented the main computational approaches to semantic representation. Current models that attempt to bring together experiential and linguistic information are especially relevant here because they bear promise to be psychologically plausible, to cover a large amount of semantic domains, and to provide interesting novel hypotheses of how children learn vocabulary. These models seem to provide an ideal representation to be used as the starting point in computational models of language production. However, this is not the case. As we will see below, production models only make extremely simplified assumptions concerning meaning representation.

Semantics and Theories of Language Production

In this section we discuss in some detail two areas of theoretical disagreement where progress requires considering fine-grained models of semantic representation (in particular, combined models, which we believe offer the most promise). The first concerns the core assumptions of lexical retrieval in speech, an area in which alternative hypotheses have illustrated a clear need for greater attention to semantic representation; and the second concerns the representation and retrieval of grammatical properties during production, an area in which some progress has already been made by taking fine-grained models of semantics into account, and where such an approach bears clear promise for future developments.

Lexical Retrieval in Speech

Two highly influential models are WEAVER++ (e.g., Levelt, 1989; Levelt, Roelofs, & Meyer, 1999; Roelofs, 1992, 2011) and the Interactive Activation model advanced by Dell and colleagues (e.g., Dell, 1986, 1988; Dell, Burger, & Svec, 1997; Dell, Schwartz, Martin, Saffran, & Gagnon, 1997). Although there are many differences in the specific details of these models and the types of phenomena to which they have been applied, they have in common explicit computational implementations, extremely broad scope in making specific predictions of behavior across a wide variety of production domains (e.g., encompassing semantics, syntax, phonology, articulation, and so forth), and a wide variety of tasks. Most importantly for our purposes, both models include representation and processing of meaning (at a stage preceding the retrieval of wordform), the origins of which map clearly onto earlier theoretical accounts of meaning representation.

WEAVER++ is nondecompositional. Activation spreads among meaning-related concepts, within a conceptual network consisting of nodes with labeled links reflecting the nature of the link between concepts (see Roelofs 1992), very much in the spirit of network models of semantic memory, such as proposed by Collins and Loftus (1975). On the other hand, Interactive Activation is decompositional. Word meaning is represented in terms of some kind of separable features of meaning (see Dell, Schwartz et al., 1997), akin to semantic accounts put forward by Rosch and Mervis (1975) and Smith et al. (1974). Crucially, in both of these models, it is possible to operationalize semantic similarity at any level of granularity, from broad classes of words

(e.g., the distinction between actions and objects; or between living and nonliving entities) right down to individual lexical items (e.g., the distinction between apples and pears). With few exceptions, however, investigations related to the role of meaning relations in lexical retrieval have focused on one particular aspect of meaning similarity: the contrast between words related in meaning (more specifically, nouns belonging to the same semantic category), and those unrelated in meaning. This approach has frequently been used to investigate how meaning-based retrieval is coordinated in time with phonological retrieval, to distinguish between different accounts of information flow (see Vigliocco & Hartsuiker, 2002). For example, Levelt et al. (1991a) carried out an extensive series of picture naming + acoustic lexical decision studies, manipulating stimulus onset asynchrony (SOA) and the type of relation between the acoustically presented probe word and the picture name (identical, semantically related, phonologically related, unrelated) to address whether retrieval of semantic and phonological information could be best conceived of as discrete staged processes or not. Although the interpretation of their findings is disputed (see Dell & O'Seaghdha, 1991; Levelt et al., 1991b), it was essential to carry out these studies under conditions where semantic similarity is maximized to reliably observe semantic effects where they indeed obtain. One clear advantage of taking an approach like this is that any account of semantic representation would agree on classifying items as "related" and "unrelated," regardless of whether similarity is the result of shared features of meaning, proximity in conceptual networks, or other spatial models of similarity. Because this approach does not necessarily require taking any particular theoretical stance on conceptual/semantic similarity it has until now been a widely accepted approach in most production studies. The clear downside is that it does not allow one to assess any but the most basic hypotheses on how words related in meaning might be activated during lexical retrieval. As discussed next, this fact has led to an inability to adjudicate among theoretical alternatives.

In recent years, there have been a number of controversies in the field related to the representation of meaning and its consequences for lexical retrieval, for which explicit attention to the structure of meaning representations is necessary. Some of these controversies precisely concern the nature of semantic representations and how they are accessed in production. For example, the question on whether meaning representations underlying lexical retrieval can be considered to be decomposed or not (Roelofs, 1997) clearly cannot be answered without making explicit assumptions concerning semantic representation and attention to how meaning similarity among individual words arises (e.g., to what extent shared and correlated features, for example, can account for similarity effects; McRae et al., 1997), not just the coarsest of similarity relationships. Next we discuss two cases in which we believe that progress has been limited because of lack of detailed models of semantic representation.

COMPETITION VERSUS RESPONSE EXCLUSION

An area where lack of detailed accounts of semantic representation has generated controversies that, however, cannot be resolved unless semantic representations are further spelled out is the controversy concerning whether competition among lexical candidates for selection is a core property of lexical retrieval. Standard models held the assumption that lexical retrieval is a competitive process; namely, on the basis of speakers' intentions, a number of semantically related lexical entries would be activated and would compete among each other for retrieval. In successful production, the semantically appropriate entry would then be retrieved. However, the competitive nature of lexical retrieval process would also be responsible for semantically related slips of the tongue, cases in which speakers produce a word similar in meaning to their target (e.g., saying "mouth" when "nose" was intended; Butterworth, 1989; Dell, 1986; Garrett, 1984, 1992, 1993; Levelt, 1989; Levelt et al., 1999; Vigliocco et al., 2004). Semantic competition in lexical retrieval has also been argued to account for results of chronometric studies, especially those using picture-word interference or cyclic naming tasks. In picture-word interference studies (descendant of the original color-naming studies by Stroop, 1935), participants are presented with a picture and a word together, and are asked to name the picture aloud while ignoring the word. The standard finding in these studies is that semantically related words interfere with picture naming (in contrast to phonologically related words, which facilitate naming), consistent with the notion that words related in meaning compete for selection (e.g., Dalrymple-Alford, 1972; Damian & Bowers, 2003; Damian & Martin, 1998; Glaser & Düngelhoff, 1984; Rosinski, 1977; Rosinski, Golinkoff, & Kukish, 1975; Schriefers, Meyer, & Levelt, 1990, and countless others). Similar results also occur in cyclic naming, where participants repeatedly name pictures (or translate words from one language to another) that are presented either in semantically related or unrelated blocks. Naming latencies are slower in semantically related contexts, again consistent with the notion that lexical selection is competitive (e.g., Belke, Meyer, & Damian, 2005; Damian, Vigliocco, & Levelt, 2001; Kroll & Stewart, 1994; Vigliocco, Lauer, Damian, & Levelt, 2002; Vigliocco, Vinson, Damian, & Levelt, 2002; see also Howard, Nickels, Coltheart, & Cole-Virtue, 2006; Oppenheim, Dell, & Schwartz, 2010).

However, this standard assumption of semantic competition has been questioned by Mahon and colleagues (Mahon et al., 2007), who presented the "response exclusion hypothesis" as an alternative account for chronometric experimental findings. Under this account semantic interference effects in cyclic naming, as well as similar effects in such tasks as the picture-word interference paradigm, would occur substantially later in the production process, when potential responses to fully retrieved names of nontarget items are excluded from a production buffer (see also Janssen, Schirm, Mahon, & Caramazza, 2008; Mahon, Garcea, & Navarrete, 2012). Crucially, under this account response exclusion is argued to be broadly sensitive to the semantic characteristics of the target, rather than maintaining redundant representations of all aspects of semantic representations:

> ... the decision mechanism that clears the output buffer of nontarget words is sensitive to the provenance of the representations over which it operates. The claim is not that semantic information is duplicated ... rather, response level representations can index general properties of their corresponding concepts (e.g., semantic category) as well as their source (picture or word). Stated differently, task constraints determine certain parameters that are used to filter out production ready representations that do not correspond to the target. The efficacy with which the system can exclude such representations affects the time required to name the target pictures. (Mahon et al., 2007, p. 524)

Both the traditional selection-by-competition view and the response-exclusion view predict the same kind of difference between broadly defined semantically related and unrelated contexts (interference for related, whether caused by heightened competition or by response relevance), but differential predictions are made for finer-grained semantic relationships. Under selection-by-competition, degree of semantic similarity among related concepts should correlate to the magnitude of interference effects (at least up to a certain point at which items are no longer sufficiently similar; Vigliocco et al., 2004). On the other hand, response exclusion predicts instead that interference effects occur not because of semantic relatedness per se but instead because their response class (e.g., same semantic category, or other discrete criteria determined by the experimental context) is relevant to the target response and thus more difficult to exclude. Fine-grained semantic similarity effects, of a facilitatory nature, can be observed for nonresponse-relevant stimuli only after response relevance is taken into account.[1]

To test these predictions, one has to go beyond a simple distinction between related and unrelated making additional assumptions concerning how semantics is represented. Indeed, Mahon and colleagues did precisely that in a series of studies. In a first study, they found that semantically related nouns interfered with naming noun pictures (e.g., naming BED was slower with the distractor TABLE than with distractor RIFLE), whereas semantically related verbs facilitated naming the same picture (e.g., naming BED was faster with distractor SLEEP than with distractor SHOOT). In order to make the argument that similarity between BED-TABLE and BED-SLEEP is equated, they collected naive subjects' similarity ratings. The authors argue that these results are incompatible with selection-by-competition, because both TABLE and SLEEP should be viable competitors to BED, both being semantically related to the target word. However, a first implicit assumption here is that subjects will use the same scale in rating noun-noun pairs and noun-verb pairs. This is far from uncontroversial; there is a strong separation between a set of similarity measures derived from speaker-generated features for objects and actions, even for closely associated object-action pairs (see Vinson & Vigliocco, 2002; Vigliocco et al., 2004). If this measure of semantic similarity actually reflects underlying similarity structure (and this structure differs from those characteristics of meaning that affect speaker ratings of similarity between word pairs), the differential effects of same class versus different class distractors may simply be due to semantic similarity structure after all, while speaker ratings may be influenced by other types of similarity (e.g., lexical/situational association) that may not reflect semantic organization. In addition, differences in the observed effects for noun and verb distractors may also come about in terms of engagement of integration processes for verbs but not

for nouns (discussed next; see Vigliocco, Vinson, Druks, Barber, & Cappa, 2011 for discussions).

In another study, they manipulated category membership while holding a measure of semantic similarity constant (shared semantic features based on the norms from Cree & McRae, 2003). Under selection-by-competition, words at similar semantic distance should interfere regardless of category membership. However, interference effects differed; naming STRAWBERRY was slower in the context of LEMON (category coordinate) than in the context of LOBSTER (different category but similar according to the specific featural measure). However, again, explicit assumptions concerning the structure of semantic organization are necessary here to justify why differences in shared features (as measured from speaker-generated features) should represent the only critical dimension of similarity. One may argue, in fact, that the example of STRAWBERRY-LEMON and STRAWBERRY-LOBSTER clearly highlights a flaw with similarity measures derived from speaker-generated features, because sharing a single feature appears to be weighted overly highly in creating a similarity metric (at least according to our intuition) at least according to these measures.[2] However, it is unclear whether other models of semantic similarity would converge in classifying LOBSTER and LEMON as comparably similar to STRAWBERRY. As our discussion of state-of-the-art models of semantic representation should have made clear, the underlying organization of semantic memory takes advantage of many other dimensions in addition to shared features including linguistic distribution of words in the language. It is a task for future research to establish how these different hypotheses can be better operationalized taking into account state-of-the-art models of semantics, such as those described previously. Our goal in discussing these studies was simply to raise awareness among production researchers of the benefits of taking such models into account.

Lexical Syntactic Properties

In addition to the oversimplification of meaning representations in models of lexical retrieval, a similar situation is present when it comes to the representation of lexically specified syntactic information, such as grammatical class, grammatical gender, and other aspects of lexical representations that determine their functions in sentences. In the past decade, our group has begun to assess the extent to which such grammatical properties depend on semantic similarity, investigations that have gone some way toward detailed models of semantic representations (e.g., Vinson & Vigliocco, 2002; Vigliocco et al., 2011).

HOW GRAMMATICAL CLASS IS REPRESENTED IN MODELS

Theories greatly differ in how grammatical properties are represented and retrieved during language production. Vigliocco et al. (2011) distinguish between three broad classes of theoretical views concerning how syntactic properties, such as grammatical class, are represented and retrieved during production. In a first class of theories, grammatical properties are specified at the lexical level. These are also known as lexicalist theories of sentence production, based on the assumptions of Lexico-Functional Grammar developed in linguistics (Kaplan & Bresnan, 1982; see Dalrymple, 2001). Lexicalist theories assume that grammatical properties are retrieved along with semantic and phonological information of words. It is often assumed that lexically specified syntactic information (including grammatical class, but also other properties, such as subcategorization frames and grammatical gender) guides the process of syntactic encoding of sentences (see e.g., Levelt, 1989; Kempen and Hoenkamp, 1987). In production models that belong to this class, grammatical properties are represented as nodes in a lexical network (e.g., Caramazza, 1997; Levelt et al., 1999; Pickering & Branigan, 1998). In word production, the finding that grammatical class is preserved in nearly all lexical errors (e.g., saying "dog" when "cat" is intended; Garrett, 1980) is compatible with such views (Levelt, 1989). Lexicalist theories may be "strong," arguing that grammatical properties are automatically and necessarily retrieved whenever a word is produced (e.g., Levelt, 1989; Pickering & Branigan, 1998); or "weak," assuming instead that grammatical properties, although lexically represented, would only be activated when necessary, namely when sentences are produced and not when processing single words (e.g., Levelt et al., 1999).

In a second class of theoretical proposals, which Vigliocco et al, (2011) referred to as combinatorial views, morphosyntactic information is not considered to be lexically specified, but rather, to be part of combinatorial/integration processes that apply to words during the sentence production (e.g., Garrett, 1976, 1984). The manner in which these combinatorial operations have been described in the literature varies from strictly syntactic operations (based

on phrase structure grammar, X-bar theory, and so forth; e.g., Garrett, 1984) to a more general distinction between declarative (lexical) and procedural (integrative) knowledge (e.g., Ullman et al., 1997). Critically, all these views assume that grammatical properties would only be relevant to processes of integration, and that they would be processed by a system clearly distinguishable from the one used for lexical retrieval. As a more extreme position, Vigliocco et al. (2011) discuss emergentist views, in which grammatical properties are neither part of our lexical nor combinatorial knowledge, but rather a property emerging from a combination of constraints. Regarding grammatical class, for example, we would have semantic constraints (i.e., the fact that prototypical nouns refer to objects and prototypical verbs refer to events) playing a critical role. For example, Elman (2004) discusses how simple recurrent networks can learn to predict, in a probabilistic manner, grammatical properties of words, and can categorize words according to their grammatical class simply on the basis of semantic and contextual constraints.

SEMANTIC SIMILARITY AND GRAMMATICAL CLASS

A large number of studies have demonstrated selective impairments of nouns or verbs in different patient groups (e.g., Miceli, Silveri, Nocentini, & Caramazza, 1988; Miceli, Silveri, Villa, & Caramazza, 1984; see Mätzig, Druks, Masterson, & Vigliocco, 2009 for a review); noun-verb differences in processing have also been reported in a wide range of behavioral, electrophysiological, and neuroimaging studies (for a review see Vigliocco, et al., 2011). However, as Vigliocco et al. (2011) pointed out, issues related to meaning representation undermine the possibility of unambiguously attributing many of these findings to fundamental differences in the representation of grammatical class per se. Most crucially, in many studies addressing this issue the grammatical distinction between nouns and verbs has been conflated with the semantic difference between objects and actions. In this manner it is not possible to decide between lexicalist and other theories of syntactic representation. This issue was spelled out by Vinson & Vigliocco (2002), who argued that the best way to tease apart grammatical class effects from this broad semantic distinction between objects and actions was to investigate the processing of nouns and verbs referring to actions and events, such as *ascend*, *ascent*, *plea*, *plead* for which there are no obvious semantic differences corresponding to the noun-verb distinction. In their work, they propose for the first time a fine-grained manner to assess the semantic similarity of words referring to events so that grammatical class differences can then be assessed. Following McRae et al. (1997), Vinson and Vigliocco (2002) and Vigliocco et al, (2004) propose to use speaker-generated features to develop models of the semantic space for objects and actions. In these models, while nouns referring to objects and verbs referring to actions and events dissociated strongly both in representational space and in simulated impairments, no hint of grammatical class differences for nouns and verbs within the action/event domain was observed. Similar results were also found in behavioral studies contrasting nouns and verbs but controlling semantic distinctions by drawing materials only from the domain of actions and events. In comprehension, Vigliocco, Vinson, Arciuli, and Barber (2008) found that semantically related primes facilitated lexical decisions for verb targets regardless of the primes' grammatical class (nouns vs. verbs), with no difference in the magnitude of the priming effects for nouns and verbs (i.e., no interaction between semantic similarity and grammatical class). In production, semantically related distractor words, whether noun or verb, exhibited similar degrees of interference on naming of action pictures (using verbs) both in Italian (Vigliocco, Vinson, & Siri, 2005) and Japanese (Iwasaki, Vinson, Arciuli, Watanabe, & Vigliocco, 2008).

These results are problematic for strong lexicalist views of grammatical class, as we found that grammatical class does not affect single word production, whereas the situation is very different once words are comprehended or produced in contexts where grammatical class is relevant. In Vigliocco et al.'s (2008) lexical decision study, grammatical class effects were observed for the same items as soon as prime words were presented in phrasal contexts. The same was true in picture-word interference (Vigliocco et al., 2005): grammatical class effects were observed when participants named the same action pictures using inflected verb forms. These findings, taken together with the lack of strong evidence in favor of neural separability of integration processes that apply to nouns and those that apply to verbs, led Vigliocco et al. (2011) to argue for cognitive views in which words from different grammatical class do not use specialized neural or cognitive systems, thus, models in which both noun and verb processing are carried out by a shared combinatorial procedural system, or in which the noun-verb distinction emerges as a consequence of different constraints.

As in the previous section concerning competition in lexical retrieval, we have shown here how using finer-grained models of semantic representation can help us decide among alternative theoretical accounts concerning production. Regarding grammatical properties, our previous work has already shown the importance of such an approach, albeit based on speaker-generated features and therefore potentially subject to the criticisms we raised previously. The use of even better semantic representations, such as those that we can derive from the combined models presented previously, may permit us to draw stronger conclusions about the nature of grammatical properties, as well as further testing questions related to the "emergentist" nature of grammatical properties.

A Two-Way Road to Progress: Researchers Developing Computational Models of Semantics Should Pay Attention to Production Research

We are not simply faced with a situation in which production researchers need to silently receive guidance from researchers concerned only with semantic representations to bring semantic representations in production models up to date. After all, processes involved in production are ignored in the development of semantic representation theories, at least as a cognitive process by which words are retrieved and produced in real time (although some of the corpora used to train distributional models contain a small quantity of spoken, rather than written material). Moreover, the test cases on which the quality of semantic models is judged are extremely limited in scope at present, in our opinion leading to a situation in which model performance seems to have reached a plateau, and in which incremental improvements may be related to particular characteristics of the specific test cases rather than similarity more generally. The current gold standards in the field by which models are evaluated are, for example, similarity relations as reflected in the structure of Wordnet (wordnet.princeton.edu), large normative samples of word associates (e.g., Edinburgh Associative Thesaurus, Kiss, Armstrong, Milroy, & Piper, 1973; University of South Florida Association Norms, Nelson, McEvoy, & Schreiber, 2004), and comparatively very small samples of word pair ratings (WordSimilarity-353 Test Collection, Finkelstein et al., 2002). All of these may fail in reflecting the sort of similarity relations that affect online language processing, at least in the tasks typically used by production (and many comprehension) researchers interested in lexical representations. Perhaps most relevant to these issues is that all of these measures derive from offline judgments of similarity that may incorporate a mixed bag of relations (see McRae, Khalkhali, & Hare, 2012 for specific discussion of word association norms in this context, and our previous discussion of cases like BED-SLEEP). As a result, developments in computational semantics are by and large ignored by language processing researchers, but this need not be the case; we see a relationship between production and computational semantics as offering mutual benefit.

How can computational semantics benefit from production research? First, production data can provide additional data sets that may prove useful to distinguish between models of semantic representation (as in Andrews et al., 2009, which used data from lexical substitution errors and picture-word interference in addition to more standard types of data usually used to test such models). Specific production data may also provide other means to improve the quality of semantic models. The usual approach taken in this latter domain is to compare models in terms of their ability to fit a large set of data, usually without regard to the specific types of lexical items contained therein. Data from production studies may highlight classes of words for which current models of semantic representation perform poorly. To make this more concrete we can return to Mahon et al. (2007) who highlight the substantial differences that are observed in lexical tasks in which subordinate or superordinate terms are used, versus those involving only basic level terms. Because basic level terms are more frequent than terms at other levels (Rosch, 1978), any given model of semantic representation judged across a large set of words may, for example, appear extremely successful while utterly failing to produce adequate representations for superordinate terms. Paying closer attention to those domains of words that seem to exhibit different patterns of performance in studies of production may, in the long term, lead to more successful models of semantics in general.

Conclusions

In this review we have described the state of the art in semantic theory as bringing together two long-separate classes of theoretical approaches, either considering word meaning as componential in nature (featural theories) or in terms of relationships among word meanings (holistic theories, Vigliocco

& Vinson 2007). Combined models of semantics, bringing together words' linguistic contexts with extralinguistic contextual information, have a real advantage in addressing the shortcomings of purely featural or purely distributional models. As a result they are likely to provide suitable semantic representations that could actually provide leverage to theoretical questions (like the core assumptions of lexical retrieval, or the representation of lexically specified syntactic information) that are intractable when a gross caricature of semantics is the basis for models. Production theory and semantic theory have remained separate, however, because the related-unrelated distinction has been considered "good enough" to address many theoretical issues in the field; and because researchers working on semantic representations have not been concerned with the mechanics of language production, except (rarely) as providing a source of additional data for training and testing models of comprehension. We suggest it is time for this to change as production theory and semantic theory offer mutual benefit to resolving some of the vexing issues in both domains.

Notes

1. Semantic relatedness effects alone are not the only evidence relevant to the questions of selection-by-competition or response exclusion in language production. For example, the response exclusion hypothesis also predicts that effects can be observed in delayed naming tasks, when lexical competition effects should no longer be relevant (Janssen et al., 2008). Moreover, it also accounts for the distractor frequency effect in picture-word interference: picture naming is slower with low-frequency distractor words (Miozzo & Caramazza, 2003; Janssen et al., 2008) but only if they are visible (Dhooge & Hartsuiker, 2010), and this effect persists in delayed naming (Dhooghe & Hartsuiker, 2011), all apparently problematic for selection-by-competition accounts. However, the implications of these findings are still a matter of debate (e.g., Mädebach, Oppermann, Hantsch, Curda, & Jescheniak, 2011; Roelofs, Piai, & Schriefers, 2011, 2012; Piai, Roelofs, & Schriefers, 2012). Because our present focus is on how the typical assumptions about semantic representation and access can impede progress toward making theoretical conclusions, rather than on adjudicating between these theoretical approaches, we will not address them further.
2. A similar issue applies for the example of interference or facilitation in color naming as discussed by Mahon et al. (2012, p. 375). In the classic Stroop (1935) effect, naming the color of a color word (e.g., RED printed in green ink) is slowed when the printed word refers to an incongruent color. But, as Mahon et al. point out, this is not the case if instead the printed words are strongly color-associated (e.g., GRASS or FIRE; Dalrymple-Alford, 1972). In this case the associated color facilitates naming, and hence is problematic for competition-based selection. However, this hinges on the assumption that words like FIRE-RED are strongly semantically similar; whether this is the case depends on the assumptions about semantic representations (as in BED-SLEEP).

References

Andrews, M., Vigliocco, G., & Vinson, D. P. (2009). Integrating experiential and distributional data to learn semantic representations. *Psychological Review, 116,* 463–498.

Aristotle (350 BCE/1941). Categoriae [Categories] (E.M. Edghill, Trans.). In R. McKeon (Ed.), *The basic works of Aristotle* (pp. 7–37). New York: Random House.

Aziz-Zadeh, L., Wilson, S. M., Rizzolatti, G., & Iacoboni, M. (2006). Congruent embodied representations for visually presented actions and linguistic phrases describing actions. *Current Biology, 16,* 1818–1823.

Baroni, M., Murphy, B., Barbu, E., & Poesio, M. (2010). Strudel: A corpus-based semantic model based on properties and types. *Cognitive Science, 34,* 222–254.

Beauchamp, M. S., Lee, K. E., Haxby, J. V., & Martin, A. (2002). Parallel visual motion processing streams for manipulable objects and human movements. *Neuron, 34,* 149–159.

Belke, E., Meyer, A.S., & Damian, M.F. (2005). Refractory effects in picture naming as assessed in a semantic blocking paradigm. *Quarterly Journal of Experimental Psychology A, 58A,* 667–692.

Blei, D., Ng, A., & Jordan, M. (2003). Latent dirichlet allocation. *Journal of Machine Learning Research, 3,* 993–1022.

Bourne, L.E. (1970). Knowing and using concepts. *Psychological Review, 77,* 546–556.

Bruni, E., Tran, G.B., & Baroni, M. (2011). Distributional semantics from text and images. In Proceedings of the EMNLP 2011 Geometrical Models for Natural Language Semantics (GEMS) (pp. 22–32). Stroudsburg (PA): Association for Computational Linguistics.

Buccino, G., Riggio, L., Melli, G., Binkofski, F., Gallese, V., & Rizzolatti, G. (2005). Listening to action-related sentences modulates the activity of the motor system: A combined TMS and behavioural study. *Cognitive Brain Research, 24,* 355–363.

Burgess, C., & Lund, K. (1997). Modeling parsing constraints with high-dimensional context space. *Language and Cognitive Processes, 12,* 177–210.

Butterworth, B. (1989). Lexical access and representation in speech production. In W. Marslen-Wilson (Ed.), *Lexical representation and process* (pp. 108–135). Cambridge, MA: MIT Press.

Cappa, S.F. (2008). Imaging studies of semantic memory. *Current Opinion in Neurology, 21,* 669–675.

Caramazza, A. (1997). How many levels of processing are there in lexical access? *Cognitive Neuropsychology, 14,* 177–208.

Cassirer, E. (1953). *The philosophy of symbolic forms. Volume 1: Language* (R. Manheim, Trans.). New Haven: Yale University Press.

Chao, L. L., Haxby, J., & Martin, A. (1999, October). Attribute-based neural substrates in temporal cortex for perceiving and knowing about objects. *Nature Neuroscience, 2* (10), 913–919.

Chao, L. L., & Martin, A. (2000). Representation of manipulable man-made objects in the dorsal stream. *NeuroImage, 12,* 478–484.

Chao, L. L., Weisberg, J., & Martin, A. (2002). Experience-dependent modulation of category related cortical activity. *Cerebral Cortex, 12,* 545–551.

Collins, A. C., & Loftus, E.F. (1975). A spreading-activation theory of semantic processing. *Psychological Review, 82,* 407–428.

Collins, A. M., & Quillian, M.R. (1969). Retrieval time from semantic memory. *Journal of Verbal Learning and Verbal Behavior, 12,* 240–247.

Cree, G. S., McNorgan, C., & McRae, K. (2006). Distinctive features hold a privileged status in the computation of word meaning: Implications for theories of semantic memory. *Journal of Experimental Psychology: Learning, Memory, & Cognition, 32,* 643–658.

Cree, G. S., McRae, K., & McNorgan, C. (1999). An attractor model of lexical conceptual processing: Simulating semantic priming. *Cognitive Science, 23,* 371–414.

Cree, G.S., & McRae, K. (2003). Analyzing the factors underlying the structure and computation of the meaning of chipmunk, cherry, chisel, cheese and cello (and many other such concrete nouns). *Journal of Experimental Psychology: General, 132,* 163–201.

Dalrymple, M. (2001). *Lexical functional grammar.* San Diego: Academic Press.

Dalrymple-Alford, E. (1972). Associative facilitation and interference in the Stroop color-word tests. *Perception & Psychphysics, 11,* 274–276.

Damasio, H., Grabowski, T. J., Tranel, D., Ponto, L. L. B., Hichwa, R. D., & Damasio, A. R. (2001). Neural correlates of naming actions and of naming spatial relations. *NeuroImage, 13,* 1053–1064.

Damian, M. F., & Bowers, J. S. (2003). Locus of semantic interference in picture-word interference tasks. *Psychonomic Bulletin and Review, 10,* 111–117.

Damian, M. F., & Martin, R. C. (1998). Is visual lexical access based on phonological codes? Evidence from a picture-word interference task. *Psychonomic Bulletin and Review, 5,* 91–95.

Damian, M., Vigliocco, G., & Levelt, W.J.M. (2001). Effects of semantic context in the naming of pictures and words. *Cognition, 81,* B77–B86.

Davidov, D., & Rappaport, A. (2008). Classification of semantic relationships between nominals using pattern clusters. *Proceedings of ACL,* 227–235.

Deerwester, S., Dumais, S., Furnas, G., Landauer, T., & Harshman, R. (1990). Indexing by latent semantic analysis. *Journal of the American Society for Information Science, 41,* 391–407.

Dell, G. S. (1986). A spreading activation theory of retrieval in sentence production. *Psychological Review, 93,* 283–321.

Dell, G.S. (1988). The retrieval of phonological forms in production: Tests of predictions from a connectionist model. *Journal of Memory and Language, 27,* 124–142.

Dell, G. S., Burger, L. K., & Svec, W. R. (1997). Language production and serial order: A functional analysis and a model. *Psychological Review, 104,* 123–147.

Dell, G.S., & O'Seaghdha, P.G. (1991). Mediated and convergent lexical priming in language production: A comment on Levelt et al. (1991). *Psychological Review, 98,* 604–614.

Dell, G. S., Schwartz, M.F., Martin, N., Saffran, E.M., & Gagnon, D.A. (1997). Lexical access in aphasic and nonaphasic speakers. *Psychological Review, 104,* 801–838.

Devlin, J. T., Gonnerman, L. M., Andersen, E. S., & Seidenberg, M. S. (1998). Category-specific semantic deficits in focal and widespread brain damage: A computational account. *Journal of Cognitive Neuroscience, 10,* 77–94.

Dhooge, E., & Hartsuiker, R. J. (2010). The distractor frequency effect in picture–word interference: Evidence for response exclusion. *Journal of Experimental Psychology: Learning, Memory, and Cognition, 36:* 878–891.

Dhooge, E., & Hartsuiker, R. J. (2011). The distractor frequency effect in a delayed picture–word interference task: Further evidence for a late locus of distractor exclusion. *Psychonomic Bulletin & Review, 18:* 116–122

Elman, J.L. (2004). An alternative view of the mental lexicon. *Trends in Cognitive Sciences, 8,* 201–206.

Farah, M. J., & McClelland, J. L. (1991). A computational model of semantic memory impairment: Modality-specificity and emergent category-specificity. *Journal of Experimental Psychology: General, 120,* 339–357.

Finkelstein, L., Gabrilovich, E., Matias, Y., Rivlin, E., Solan, Z., Wolfman, G., & Ruppin, E. (2002), Placing search in context: The concept revisited. *ACM Transactions on Information Systems, 20,* 116–131

Firth, J. R. (1957). A synopsis of linguistic theory 1930–1955. In J. R. Firth et al. (Eds.), *Studies in Linguistic Analysis* (special volume of the Philological Society, Oxford) (pp. 1–32). Oxford: Blackwell.

Garrard, P., Lambon Ralph, M. A., Hodges, J. R., & Patterson, K. (2001). Prototypicality, distinctiveness, and intercorrelation: Analyses of the semantic attributes of living and nonliving concepts. *Cognitive Neuropsychology, 18,* 125–174.

Garrett, M. F. (1976). Syntactic processes in sentence production. In R. J. Wales & E. Walker (Eds.), *New approaches to language mechanisms* (pp. 231–255). Amsterdam: North Holland Publishing Company.

Garrett, M.F. (1980). Levels of processing in sentence production. In B. Butterworth (Ed.), *Language production, Volume 1: Speech and talk* (pp. 177–220). London: Academic Press.

Garrett, M. F. (1984). The organization of processing structure for language production: Applications to aphasic speech. In D. Caplan, A. R. Lecours, & A. Smith (Eds.), *Biological perspectives on language* (pp. 172–193). London:The MIT Press.

Garrett, M. F. (1992). Disorders of lexical selection. *Cognition, 42,* 143–180.

Garrett, M. F. (1993). Errors and their relevance for models of language production. In G. Blanken, J. Dittman, H. Grim, J. Marshall, & C. Wallesch (Eds.),*Linguistic disorders and pathologies* (pp. 72–92). Berlin:de Gruyter.

Gerlach, C., Law, I., & Paulson, O. B. (2002). When action turns to words. Activation of motor-based knowledge during categorisation of manipulable objects. *Journal of Cognitive Neuroscience, 14* (8), 1230–1239.

Glaser, W. R., & Düngelhoff, R.J. (1984). The time course of picture-word interference. *Journal of Experimental Psychology: Human, Perception and Performance, 10,* 640–654.

Glenberg, A. M., & Robertson, D. A. (2000). Symbol grounding and meaning: A comparison of high-dimensional and embodied theories of meaning. *Journal of Memory and Language, 43* (3), 379–401.

Grabowski, T. J., Damasio, H., & Damasio, A. R. (1998). Premotor and prefrontal correlate of category-related lexical retrieval. *NeuroImage, 7,* 232–243.

Griffiths, T. L., Steyvers, M., & Tenenbaum, J. B. (2007). Topics in semantic representation. *Psychological Review, 114* (2), 211–244.

Hampton, J.A. (1979). Polymorphous concepts in semantic memory. *Journal of Verbal Learning and Verbal Behavior, 18,* 441–461.

Hampton, J.A. (1981). An investigation of the nature of abstract concepts. *Memory & Cognition, 9,* 149–156.

Hampton, J.A., & Gardiner, M.M. (1983). Measures of internal category structure: A correlational analysis of normative data. *British Journal of Psychology, 74,* 491–516.

Harris, Z. (1954). Distributional structure. *Word, 10,* 146&162.

Hinton, G.E., & Shallice, T. (1991). Lesioning an attractor network: Investigations of acquired dyslexia. *Psychological Review, 98,* 74–95.

Howard, D., Nickels, L., Coltheart, M., & Cole-Virtue, J. (2006). Cumulative semantic inhibition in picture naming: Experimental and computational studies. *Cognition, 100,* 464–482.

Ishai, A., Ungerleider, L. G., Martin, A., Schouten, J. L., & Haxby, J. V. (1999). Distributed representation of objects in the human ventral visual pathway. *Proceedings of the National Academy of Science, 96,* 9379–9384.

Iwasaki, N., Vinson, D.P., Arciuli, J., Watanabe, M., & Vigliocco, G. (2008). Naming actions in Japanese: Effects of semantic similarity and grammatical class. *Language and Cognitive Processes, 23,* 889–930.

Janssen, N., Schirm, W., Mahon, B.Z., & Caramazza, A. (2008). Semantic interference in a delayed naming task: Evidence for the response exclusion hypothesis. *Journal of Experimental Psychology: Learning, Memory, and Cognition, 34* (1), 249–256.

Johns, B. T., & Jones, M. N. (2012). Perceptual inference through global lexical similarity. *Topics in Cognitive Science, 4,* 103–120.

Kaplan, R.M., & Bresnan, J. (1982). Lexical-functional grammar: A formal system for grammatical representation. In J. Bresnan (Ed.), *The mental representation of grammatical representations* (pp. 173–281). Cambridge MA: MIT Press.

Katz, J. J., & Fodor, J. A. (1963). The structure of a semantic theory. *Language, 39,* 170–210.

Kempen, G., Hoenkamp, E. (1987). An incremental procedural grammar for sentence formulation. *Cognitive Science, 11,* 201–258.

Kiss, G.R., Armstrong, C., Milroy, R., & Piper, J. (1973). An associative thesaurus of English and its computer analysis. In A. J. Aitken, R. W. Bailey, & N. Hamilton-Smith (Eds.), *The computer and literary studies* (pp. 153–165). Edinburgh: University Press.

Kroll, J.F., & Stewart, E. (1994). Category interference in translation and picture naming: Evidence for asymmetric connections between bilingual memory representations. *Journal of Memory and Language, 33,* 149–174.

Landauer, T., & Dumais, S. (1997). A solutions to Plato's problem: The Latent Semantic Analysis theory of acquisition, induction and representation of knowledge. *Psychological Review, 104,* 211–240.

Landauer, T., Laham, D., & Foltz, P. (1998). Learning human-like knowledge by singular-value decomposition. In M. I. Jordan, M. J. Kearns, & S. A. Solla, (Eds.), *Advances in Neural Information Processing Systems 10* (pp. 45–51). Cambridge, MA: MIT Press.

Landauer, T., Laham, D., Rehder, B., & Schreiner, M. (1997). How well can passage meaning be derived without using word order: A comparison of LSA and humans. In *Proceedings of the Nineteenth Annual Conference of the Cognitive Science Society.*

Levelt, W. J. L. (1989). *Speaking: From intention to articulation.* Cambridge, MA:MIT Press.

Levelt, W. J. M., Roelofs, A., & Meyer, A. S. (1999). A theory of lexical access in speech production. *Behavioral and Brain Sciences, 22,* 1–38.

Levelt, W. J. M., Schriefer, H., Vorberg, D., Meyer, A. S., Pechmann, T., & Havinga, J. (1991a). The time course of lexical access in speech production: A study of picture naming. *Psychological Review, 98* (1), 122–142.

Levelt, W. J. M., Schriefers, H., Vorberg, D., Meyer, A. S., Pechmann, T., & Havinga, J. (1991b). Normal and deviant lexical processing: Reply to Dell and O'Seaghdha. *Psychological Review, 98* (4), 615–618.

Lund, K., & Burgess, C. (1996). Producing high-dimensional semantic spaces from lexical co-occurrence. *Behavior Research Methods, Instrumentation, and Computers, 28*, 203–208.

Lund, K., Burgess, C., & Atchley, R. A. (1995). Semantic and associative priming in high dimensional semantic space. In J. D. Moore & J. F. Lehman (Eds.), *Proceedings of the seventeeth annual conference of the cognitive science society*. Mahweh, NJ: Lawrence Erlbaum Associates.

Mätzig, S., Druks, J., Masterson, J., & Vigliocco, G. (2009). Noun and verb differences in picture naming: Past studies and new evidence. *Cortex, 45*, 738–758.

Mahon, B.Z., Costa, A., Peterson, R., Vargas, K.A., & Caramazza, A.(2007). Lexical selection is not by competition: A reinterpretation of semantic interference and facilitation effects in the picture-word interference paradigm. *Journal of Experimental Psychology: Learning, Memory and Cognition, 33*, 503–535.

Mahon, B.Z., Garcea, F.E., & Navarrete, E. (2012). Picture-word interference and the Response-Exclusion Hypothesis: A response to Mulatti and Coltheart. *Cortex, 48*, 373–377.

Martin, A. (2009). Circuits in mind: The neural foundations for object concepts. In M. Gazzaniga (Ed.), *The cognitive neurosciences*, 4th edition (pp. 1031–1045). Cambridge (MA): MIT Press.

Martin, A., Haxby, J. V., Lalonde, F. M., Wiggs, C. L., & Ungerleider, L. G. (1995). Discrete cortical regions associated with knowledge of color and knowledge of action. *Science, 270* (5233), 194–201.

Martin, A., Wiggs, C., Ungerleider, L., & Haxby, J. (1996). Neural correlates of category specific knowledge. *Nature, 379*, 649–652.

McNorgan, C., Reid, J., & McRae, K. (2011). Integrating conceptual knowledge within and across representational modalities. *Cognition, 118*, 211–233.

McRae, K., & Cree, G. S. (2002). Factors underlying category-specific semantic deficits. In E. Forde & G. Humphreys (Eds.), *Category specificity in brain and mind* (pp. 211–249). Hove: Psychology Press.

McRae, K., Cree, G. S., Seidenberg, M. S., & McNorgan, C.(2005). Semantic feature production norms for a large set of living and nonliving things. *Behavioral Research Methods, Instruments, and Computers, 37*, 547–559.

McRae, K., Cree, G. S., Westmacott, R., & de Sa, V. R. (1999). Further evidence for feature correlations in semantic memory. *Canadian Journal of Experimental Psychology: Special Issue on Models of Word Recognition, 53*, 360–373.

McRae, K., de Sa, V., & Seidenberg, M.(1997). On the nature and scope of featural representations of word meaning. *Journal of Experimental Psychology: General, 126*, 99–130.

McRae, K., Khalkhali, S., & Hare, M. (2012). Semantic and associative relations: Examining an tenuous dichotomy. In V.F. Reyna, S.B. Chapman, M.R. Dougherty, & J. Confrey (Eds.), *The adolescent brain: Learning, reasoning and decision making* (pp. 39–66). Washington, DC: APA.

Miceli, G., Silveri, M.C., Nocentini, U., & Caramazza, A. (1988). Patterns of dissociation in comprehension and production of nouns and verbs. *Aphasiology, 1*, 351–358.

Miceli, G., Silveri, M. C., Villa, G., & Caramazza, A. (1984). On the basis for the agrammatic's difficulty in producing main verbs. *Cortex, 20*, 207–220.

Minsky, M. (1975). A framework for representing knowledge. In P. H. Winston (Ed.), *The psychology of computer vision* (pp. 211–277). New York:McGraw-Hill.

Miozzo, M., & Caramazza, A.(2003). When more is less: A counterintuitive effect of distractor frequency in the picture–word interference paradigm. *Journal of Experimental Psychology: General, 132*: 228–252.

Murphy, G.L. (2002). *The big book of concepts*. Cambridge, MA: MIT Press.

Nelson, D., McEvoy, C., & Schreiber, T. (2004). The University of South Florida word association, rhyme and word fragment norms. *Behavior Research Methods, Instruments, & Computers, 36*, 408–420.

Norman, D. A., & Rumelhart, D. E. (1975). *Explorations in cognition*. San Francisco:Freeman.

Oliveri, M., Finocchiaro, C., Shapiro, K., Gangitano, M., Caramazza, A., & Pascual-Leone, A.(2004). All talk and no action: A transcranial magnetic stimulation study of motor cortex activation during action word production. *Journal of Cognitive Neuroscience, 16* (3), 374–381.

Oppenheim, G. M., Dell, G. S., & Schwartz, M. F. (2010). The dark side of incremental learning: A model of cumulative semantic interference during lexical access in speech production. *Cognition, 114*, 227–252.

Phillips, J., Noppeney, U., Humphreys, G. W., & Price, C. J. (2002). Can segregation within the semantic system account for category-specific deficits? *Brain, 125*, 2067–2080.

Piai, V., Roelofs, A., & Schriefers, H. (2012). Distractor strength and selective attention in picture-naming performance. *Memory and Cognition, 40*, 614–627.

Pickering, M. J., Branigan, H. P. (1998). The representation of verbs: Evidence from syntactic priming in language production. *Journal of Memory and Language, 39*, 633–651.

Plaut, D. C. (1995). Double dissociation without modularity: Evidence from connectionist neuropsychology. *Journal of Clinical and Experimental Neuropsychology, 17*, 291–321.

Plaut, D. C., & Shallice, T. (1993). Deep dyslexia: A case study of connectionist neuropsychology. *Cognitive Neuropsychology, 10*, 377–500.

Poesio, M., & Almuhareb, A. (2008). Extracting concept descriptions from the Web: The importance of attributes and values. In P. Buitelaar & P. Cimiano (Eds.), *Bridging the gap between text and knowledge* (pp. 29–44). Amsterdam: IOS Press.

Pulvermüller, F. (1999). Words in the brain's language. *Behavioral and Brain Sciences, 22*, 253–336.

Pulvermüller, F. (2001, December). Brain reflections of words and their meanings. *Trends in Cognitive Sciences, 5* (12), 517–524.

Pulvermüller, F., & Hauk, O. (2005). Category-specific conceptual processing of color and form in left fronto-temporal cortex. *Cerebral Cortex, 16*, 1193–1201.

Pulvermüller, F., Hauk, O., Nikulin, V. V., & Ilmoniemi, R. J. (2005). Functional links between motor and language systems. *European Journal of Neuroscience, 21*, 793–797.

Randall, B., Moss, H.E., Rodd, J.M., Greer, M., & Tyler, L.K. (2004). Distinctiveness and correlation in conceptual structure: Behavioral and computational studies. *Journal of Experimental Psychology: Learning, Memory and Cognition, 30*, 393–406.

Riordan, B., & Jones, M. N. (2011). Redundancy in perceptual and linguistic experience: Comparing feature-based and distributional models of semantic representation. *Topics in Cognitive Science, 3*, 303–345.

Roelofs, A. (1992). A spreading-activation theory of lemma retrieval in speaking. *Cognition, 42*, 107–142.

Roelofs, A. (1997). A case for nondecomposition in conceptually driven word retrieval. *Journal of Psycholinguistic Research, 26*, 33–67.

Roelofs, A. (2011). Modeling the attentional control of vocal utterances: From Wernicke to WEAVER++. In J. Guendouzi, F. Loncke, & M. J. Williams (Eds.), *The Handbook of psycholinguistic and cognitive processes: Perspectives in communication disorders* (pp. 189–207). Hove, UK: Psychology Press.

Roelofs, A., Piai, V., and Schriefers, H. (2011). Selective attention and distractor frequency in naming performance: Comment on Dhooge and Hartsuiker (2010). *Journal of Experimental Psychology: Learning, Memory, and Cognition, 37*: 1032–1038.

Roelofs, A., Piai, V., & Schriefers, H. (2012). Context effects and selective attention in picture naming and word reading: Competition versus response exclusion. *Language and Cognitive Processes, 28*, 655–671.

Rogers, T. T., Lambon Ralph, M. A., Garrard, P., Bozeat, S., McClelland, J. L., Hodges, J. R., & Patterson, K. (2004). The structure and deterioration of semantic memory: A neuropsychological and computational investigation. *Psychological Review, 111*, 205–235.

Rogers, T. T., & McClelland, J. L. (2004). *Semantic cognition: A parallel distributed processing approach*. Cambridge, MA: MIT Press.

Rosch, E.H. (1973). Natural categories. *Cognitive Psychology, 4*, 328–350.

Rosch, E. H. (1978). Principles of categorization. In E. Rosch & B. B. Lloyd (Eds.), *Cognition and categorization* (pp. 27–48). Hillsdale, NJ: Erlbaum.

Rosch, E., & Mervis, C.B. (1975). Family resemblance: Studies in the internal structure of categories. *Cognitive Psychology, 7*, 573–605.

Rosch, E.H., Mervis, C.B., Gray, W.D., Johnson, D.M., & Boyes-Braem, P. (1976). Basic objects in natural categories. *Cognitive Psychology, 8*, 382–439.

Rosinski, R. R. (1977). Picture-word interference is semantically based. *Child Development, 48*, 643–647.

Rosinski, R. R., Golinkoff, R. M., & Kukish, K. S. (1975). Automatic semantic processing in a picture-word interference task. *Child Development, 46*, 247–253.

Schriefers, H., Meyer, A. S., & Levelt, W. J. M. (1990). Exploring the time course of lexical access in language production: Picture-word interference studies. *Journal of Memory and Language, 29*, 86–102.

Schütze, H. (1992). Dimensions of meaning. In *Proceedings of supercomputing '92* (pp. 787–796). Washington, DC: IEEE Computer Society Press.

Searle, J. R. (2000). Minds, brains, and programs. In R. Cummins & D. D. Cummins (Eds.), *Minds, brains and computers: The foundations of cognitive science* (pp. 140–152). Oxford, United Kingdom: Blackwell.

Smith, E. E., & Medin, D. L. (1981). *Categories and concepts*. Cambridge, MA: Harvard University Press.

Smith, E. E., Shoben, E.J., & Rips, L.J. (1974). Structure and process in semantic memory: Featural model for semantic decisions. *Psychological Review, 81*, 214–241.

Steyvers, M. (2010). Combining feature norms and text data with topic models. *Acta Psychologica, 133*, 234–243.

Stroop, J.R. (1935). Studies of interference in serial verbal reactions. *Journal of Experimental Psychology, 18*, 643–662.

Tettamanti, M., Buccino, G., Saccuman, M. C., Gallese, V., Danna, M., Scifo, P., Fazio, F.,... Perani, D. (2005). Listening to action-related sentences activates fronto-parietal motor circuits. *Journal of Cognitive Neuroscience, 17*, 273–281.

Tversky, B., & Hemenway, K. (1984). Objects, parts, and categories. *Journal of Experimental Psychology: General, 113*, 169–193.

Ullman, M.T., Corkin, S., Coppola, M., Hicock, G., Growdon, J.H., Koroshetz, W.J., Pinker, S. (1997). A neural dissociation within language: Evidence that the mental dictionary is part of declarative memory and that grammatical rules are processed by the procedural system. *Journal of Cognitive Neuroscience, 9*, 266–276.

Vigliocco, G., & Hartsuiker, R.J. (2002). The interplay of meaning, sound & syntax in language production. *Psychological Bulletin, 128*, 442–472.

Vigliocco, G., Lauer, M., Damian, M., & Levelt, W. (2002). Semantic and syntactic forces in noun phrase production. *Journal of Experimental Psychology: Learning, Memory and Cognition, 28*, 46–58.

Vigliocco, G., & Vinson, D.P. (2007). Semantics. In G. Gaskell (Ed.), *Oxford handbook of psycholinguistics* (pp. 195–215). New York: Oxford University Press.

Vigliocco, G., Vinson, D.P., Arciuli, J., Barber, H. (2008). The role of grammatical class on word recognition. *Brain and Language, 105*, 175–184.

Vigliocco, G., Vinson, D.P., Damian, M.F., & Levelt, W. (2002). Semantic distance effects on object and action naming. *Cognition, 85*: B61–B69.

Vigliocco, G., Vinson, D.P., Druks, J., Barber, H., & Cappa, S.F. (2011). Nouns and verbs in the brain: A review of behavioural, electrophysiological, neuropsychological and imaging studies. *Neuroscience and Biobehavioral Reviews, 35*, 407–426.

Vigliocco, G., Vinson, D.P., Lewis, W., & Garrett, M.F. (2004). Representing the meanings of object and action words: The featural and unitary semantic space hypothesis. *Cognitive Psychology, 48*, 422–488.

Vigliocco, G., Vinson, D.P., & Siri, S.(2005). Semantic and grammatical class effects in naming actions. *Cognition, 94*, B91–B100.

Vigliocco, G., Warren, J., Siri, S., Arciuli, J., Scott, S.K., & Wise, R. (2006). The role of semantics and grammatical class in the neural representation of words. *Cerebral Cortex, 16* (12), 1790–1796.

Vinson, D. P., & Vigliocco, G. (2002). A semantic analysis of noun-verb dissociations in aphasia. *Journal of Neurolinguistics, 15*, 317–351.

Vinson, D.P., & Vigliocco, G. (2008). Feature norms for a large set of object and event concepts. *Behavior Research Methods, 40*, 183–190.

Vuilleumier, P., Henson, R. N., Driver, J., & Dolan, R. J. (2002). Multiple levels of visual object constancy revealed by event-related fMRI of repetition priming. *Nature Neuroscience, 5* (5), 491–499.

Wittgenstein, L. (1953/1997). *Philosophical investigations* (G. E. M. Anscombe, Ed.). Oxford, UK: Blackwell.

The Morphology of Words

James P. Blevins

Abstract

Morphology is usually understood as the branch of linguistics that investigates word structure, a topic of central relevance to the systematic study of language and language processing. The Western grammatical tradition begins with the identification of words as the smallest meaningful elements of speech, a conception that survives largely intact in contemporary word-based models of morphology and grammar. Synchronic, historical, and behavioral evidence also suggests that words are not only organized into syntagmatic units but also into paradigmatic collections. On the syntagmatic dimension, words are composed of morphs and themselves form parts of larger syntactic constructions. Orthogonal to these structures, inflected and derivational forms exhibit an organization into inflectional paradigms and larger morphological families. This chapter outlines some of the linguistic issues that arise in describing words and their structure.

Key Words: morphology, morphological theory

Why words?

Morphology is usually understood as the branch of linguistics that investigates "word structure." One dimension of this investigation focusses on "the study of morphemes and their arrangement into words" (Nida, 1949, p. 1). A second, complementary, dimension examines "the forms of words in different uses and constructions" (Matthews, 1991, 3). Words are central to both of these investigations, reflecting the position they have occupied in models of language description and analysis since classical antiquity. The Western grammatical tradition begins with the identification of words as the smallest meaningful elements of speech, a conception that survives largely intact in contemporary word-based models of morphology and grammar. A similar perspective is represented in reference and pedagogical traditions that describe the lexical resources of a language primarily in terms of its word stock. Even Bloomfield (1933) freely conceded the

practical value of words for dictionaries and reference grammars.

> For the purposes of ordinary life, the word is the smallest unit of speech. Our dictionaries list the words of a language; for all purposes except the systematic study of language, this procedure is doubtless more useful than would be a list of morphemes. (p. 178)

The treatment of words as the smallest meaningful units of language is also implicit in procedures of phonemic analysis, which distinguish allophones from phonemes in terms of whether a given phone distinguishes the meaning of two words. The salience of words reinforces their role as the primary exponent of form variation in a language. Words are the smallest grammatical units that are demarcated with any consistency in the speech stream. They are also the smallest units that can function as utterances in isolation. Stages of first language acquisition are commonly defined in terms of the number of words per utterance. Behavioral correlates of word frequency, measured both in terms of "types" and "tokens," have been observed in psycholinguistic and neurolinguistic studies of language processing. Synchronic, historical, and behavioral evidence also suggests that words are not only organized into syntagmatic units but also into paradigmatic collections. On the syntagmatic dimension, words are composed of morphs and themselves form parts of larger syntactic constructions. Orthogonal to these structures, inflected and derivational forms exhibit organization into inflectional paradigms and larger morphological families.

Word structure is thus of central relevance to the "systematic study of language" and language processing. To set the context for the experimental and computational studies presented in subsequent sections, this chapter outlines some of the linguistic issues that arise in describing words and their structure.

Words

A treatment of words and word structure must begin by acknowledging that the definition of words is far from settled. Despite this lack of consensus, there are points of broad agreement. Most contemporary accounts recognize the usefulness of distinguishing three types of units, each corresponding to an established sense of the notion "word." Phonological words or WORDFORMS are simple sequences of phonemes (or graphemes). Grammatical words are phonological words with a morphosyntactic interpretation. Lexical words or LEXEMES correspond to the units that would be entered in a dictionary. Each of these units has a characteristic role in the morphology of a language, and each determines a corresponding notion of "word count." Yet the partial overlap between these notions also raises descriptive and analytic issues that need to be clarified.

Grammatical and Phonological Words

The notion of "word" proposed in Bloomfield (1926) provides the classic definition of the "grammatical" word. Bloomfield's notion of a "minimimum free form" also comes closest to capturing the sense of word as it is normally understood.

A minimum free form is a WORD.

A word is thus a form which may be uttered alone (with meaning) but cannot be analyzed into parts that may (all of them) be uttered alone (with meaning). (p. 156)

On this interpretation of "word," the three homophonous occurrences of *cut* in (1) are different words, realizing the preterite, past participle, and infinitive forms of the verb CUT. This is the notion of word that is most relevant to measures of token frequency, which treat each occurrence of a form as a separate "token."

(1)   a. He *cut* the flowers. (PRETERITE)
      b. He has *cut* the flowers. (PAST PARTICIPLE)
      c. He will *cut* the flowers. (INFINITIVE)

The Bloomfieldian notion of a "minimimum free form (with meaning)" also captures the sense of "word" that is mainly relevant for (extended) "word and paradigm" models (Robins, 1959; Anderson, 1992) and for other "word-based" approaches (Blevins, 2006). As Robins (1959, p. 120) puts it, the word in this sense is "a grammatical abstraction," but it is a maximally useful abstraction.

The word is a more stable and solid focus of grammatical relations than the component morpheme by itself. Put another way, grammatical statements are abstractions, but they are more profitably abstracted from words as wholes than from individual morphemes. (p. 128)

In most languages, the abstraction of words is facilitated by cues that enhance their perceptual salience. Open-class items are often subject to a minimum word constraint, whether measured in terms of moras, syllables, or metrical feet, and there is experimental evidence that speakers exploit these constraints in the segmentation of continuous speech (Norris, McQueen, Cutler, & Butterfield, 1997). Words often define the positions at which stress, pitch, or other suprasegmental features are realized, and word edges maybe marked by processes, such as boundary lengthening (Bybee, 2001). The perceptual salience of words is further enhanced by the fact that words (unlike subword units, such as phonemes or morphemes) may stand on their own as independent utterances. In addition, if there is any basis to notions like "the one-word stage" (Dromi, 1987), it would appear that the word is the canonical utterance during early stages of language acquisition. As one might expect, the functional load of individual cues varies across languages, reflecting general differences in phonological systems, so that no single cue identifies words cross-linguistically. This leads, as Robins (1959) acknowledges, to discrepancies between the notion of "word" relevant for the description of grammatical relations, and the sense of "word" that is marked phonetically.

WORDFORMS

The qualification "grammatical" reflects this contrast between the Bloomfieldian word and "phonological" (or, by extension, "orthographic") words. A more concise term for minimal free forms WITHOUT a fixed meaning or function is "wordform." In example (1) above, the phonological word *cut* realizes the preterite, past participle, and infinitive forms of the verb CUT. The same wordform realizes other forms of CUT, as well as the corresponding noun in *he has a cut*.

Wordforms are, by definition, the units that are most clearly demarcated in the speech stream by phonetic cues. As sequences of phonemes (or graphemes), they are also the most straightforward units to distinguish and count. Although wordforms are not traditionally of significant grammatical interest, they are central to many current frequency-based models. In accounts that treat phonetic reduction as a frequency effect, it is often wordform frequency that is taken to determine the rate or extent of reduction. Hence in the frequency-based model of Bybee (2010), the operative notion of "words" corresponds to "wordforms."

> A robust finding that has emerged recently in quantitative studies of phonetic reduction is that high-frequency words undergo more change or change at a faster rate than low-frequency words, (p. 20)

> [S]ubstantial evidence has recently been reported showing that phonetic reduction occurs earlier and to a greater extent in high-frequency words than in low-frequency ones…[I]f we postulate that reduction occurs online as words are used, then words that are used more often are exposed to reduction processes more often and thus undergo change at a faster rate. (p. 37)

Although grammatical words maybe realized by single wordforms, the correlation between these units is often disrupted by phonological or syntactic processes. Cliticization creates sequences in which multiple grammatical words correspond to a single phonological word. In example (2a), the contracted phonological word *he's* corresponds to the grammatical words *he* and *has*. Separable particles illustrate the converse case, in which a single grammatical word such as German *ablehnen* "reject" is realized by the wordforms *lehnen* and *ab* in (2b).

(2) a. *He's* cut the flowers.
    b. Sie lehnen den Vorschlag ab.
    they "lean" the proposal "away"
    "They reject the proposal."

CUES AND CORRELATIONS

The divergence between grammatical and phonological word has led some scholars to question the status and even the usefulness of the notion "word" in the analysis of a grammatical system.[1] Although this question has attracted renewed attention in the recent literature, it articulates a longstanding criticism of traditional word-based approaches. Thus the difficulty of demarcating words is taken by Bloomfield (1914) as evidence for the primacy of the sentence.

> it has long been recognized that the first and original datum of language is the sentence—that the individual word is the product of a theoretical reflection that ought not to be taken for granted. (p. 38)

One need not dispute the epistemological priority of utterances or downplay the discrepancies between phonological and grammatical words to realize that these discrepancies arise precisely because there *are* phonetic cues that, with varying degrees of reliability, mark word boundaries or otherwise guide the segmentation of utterances into words. The existence of mismatches should not obscure the fact that the two notions of "word" overlap, at least partially, in many languages, and that this overlap permits speakers to isolate grammatical words. Although grammatical words may be imperfectly demarcated, subword units—including, significantly, roots—are rarely if ever cued at all by phonetic properties. There is no discrepancy between the "grammatical morpheme" and the "phonological morpheme" for the simple reason that there is no such thing as a "phonological morpheme." Hence the objection that grammatical words are not reliably and invariantly cued in the speech stream provides no motivation for shifting the focus of morphological analysis onto units smaller than the word (such as morphemes), since these units require an even greater degree of abstraction from the speech signal. The observation that words are abstractions just falls under the broader generalization that *all* linguistic units smaller than utterances are abstracted from larger sequences of connected speech.

It is also possible that much of the debate about the alignment of grammatical and phonological words is fundamentally misconceived. Nearly all linguistic approaches to this issue frame the problem in terms of specifying reliable and cross-linguistically valid cues for demarcating grammatical words. Underlying these approaches is the assumption that there should be some set of necessary and sufficient conditions for defining words in a given language, or across languages. However, in parallel to theoretical and descriptive studies, there exists a large and diverse psycholinguistic and computational literature on word segmentation and recognition. This literature includes the work on identifying "uniqueness points" in Marslen-Wilson and Welsh (1978) and Marslen-Wilson and Tyler (1980), neural network-based predictive models (Elman 1990), and statistical models of word segmentation (Goldwater, Griffiths, & Johnson, 2009). The models of word segmentation developed in these studies are based on the observation that entropy (roughly, uncertainty about the segments that follow) declines as more of a word is processed, then peaks again at word boundaries. These sorts of prediction-based approaches suggest that the search for invariant cues may be futile and that the observable phonetic properties that have been assumed to be definitional are secondary cues for what is an essentially statistical notion.

> Observations about predictability at word boundaries are consistent with two different kinds of assumptions about what constitutes a word: either a word is a unit that is statistically independent of other units, or it is a unit that helps to predict other units (but to a lesser degree than the beginning of a word predicts its end). (Goldwater et al., 2009, p. 22)

From this perspective, the phonological word might correspond to phonetic sequences between entropy "peaks," with phonetic cues representing one source of entropy reduction. The correlation between phonological and grammatical words could be similarly probabilistic rather than defined by discrete criteria.

Grammatical and phonological words represent two kinds of word tokens. In examples (1) and (2), there are four occurrences of the wordform *cut*, corresponding to two occurrences of the past participle *cut*, and one occurrence each of the preterite and infinitive. Given that grammatical words are defined as wordforms with fixed meanings, their identification depends on assumptions about the parts of speech and morphosyntactic features in a language. For example, a classification that recognizes distinct perfect and passive participles in English will treat the two occurrences of *cut* in (3) as distinct grammatical words. On an account that recognizes a unitary past participle in perfect and passive constructions, there will be two occurrences of a past participle *cut*. More generally, the identification of grammatical words is always defined relative to a grammatical analysis (or, in the case of corpora, a set of grammatical "tags").

(3)   a. He has *cut* the flowers. (PERFECT/PAST PARTICIPLE)
      b. The flowers have been *cut*. (PASSIVE/PAST PARTICIPLE)

Lexemes and Lemmas

Insofar as occurrences of grammatical words are tokens of a common word "type," they imply another, more abstract notion of "word." This notion of "word type" usually goes under the name LEXEME. Matthews (1972, p. 160) characterizes the lexeme in this sense as "the lexical element...to which the forms in [a] paradigm as a whole...can be said to belong."[2] In a later discussion of the same point, Matthews (1991, p. 26) suggests that a lexeme is "a lexical unit and is entered in dictionaries as the fundamental element in the lexicon of language." Lexemes are thus reminiscent of the lexicographer's notion of a LEMMA, which is the citation form of an item or the headword under which it is listed in a dictionary.[3] The connection between these notions is reinforced by the fact that lexemes are conventionally represented by the citation form of an item in small caps (i.e., by the lemma of the item). However, whereas a lemma is a distinguished FORM, for example, the infinitive *cut*, a lexeme is a set of grammatical WORDS.

The contrast between wordforms, grammatical words, and lexemes resolves a systematic ambiguity in the use of the term "word" as applied to the pure form *cut*, the preterite *cut*, and the lexeme CUT. Not all items give rise to a full three-way split, since different notions of word may coincide in particular cases. There is usually at least a partial correlation between grammatical words and wordforms. For closed-class categories, the distinction between lexeme and grammatical word may not be especially relevant or useful, since a preposition or conjunction will usually be associated with a single grammatical word. Much the same will be true of open-class categories in an isolating language, such as Vietnamese, if nouns and verbs are represented by single grammatical WORDS.

PARADIGMS AND FAMILIES

Determining which grammatical words are part of a lexeme also introduces the kinds of issues that confront lexicographers when they attempt to distinguish primary "word entries" from "word senses" in a language. These issues bear in a direct way on the delineation of inflectional and derivational processes. From a traditional perspective, inflectional processes are said to define (or, more generally, relate) forms of a lexeme (i.e., grammatical words), whereas derivation derives (or relates) lexemes. It is typically assumed that the grammatical words that comprise a lexeme must belong to the same word class, preserve a core lexical semantics and argument structure, and even share a set of "intrinsic" features that are invariant for a given item. Inflectional processes are accordingly regarded as monotonic processes that add features to the invariant properties that can be associated with stems. In contrast, processes that alter class or argument structure are treated as derivational, since these changes create new lexemes.

Yet traditional descriptive practices are not entirely consistent with this split, as noted in a number of recent works, including Booij (1996), Haspelmath (1996), and Spencer (1999). In particular, conjugational paradigms often include categorial hybrids, such as participles, which exhibit adjectival properties, and gerunds or masdars, which exhibit nominal properties. The inclusion of passive participles also introduces argument structure variation into conjugational paradigms. This inconsistency undermines the coherence of the notion "lexeme," along with associated conceptions of the inflection/derivation divide, if, as these authors assume, the notions "lexeme" and "inflectional paradigm" are taken to coincide.

Alternatively, one can interpret traditional descriptions as inexplicit rather than inconsistent, and reconstruct lexemes as sets of forms that occupy an intermediate position between inflectional paradigms and morphological families. This interpretation has the additional benefit of resolving a systematic ambiguity in the use of the term "paradigm." Nouns and adjectives typically have a unified set of forms, inflected for case, number, definiteness, and so forth, which can be consolidated within a single declensional paradigm. In contrast, the inflected forms of verbs often exhibit a suborganization into sets of forms that share the same tense/aspect/mood features and vary in their agreement features. The term "paradigm" is applied to these smaller sets when one refers to the present indicative paradigm of French PARLER "to speak" and to the full set of inflected forms when one refers to the paradigm of PARLER toute court. To resolve this ambiguity, the term "paradigm" can be reserved for the first, smaller set of forms and the term "lexeme" applied to the complete set of inflected forms. Hence the present indicative paradigm of PARLER comprises a subset of the lexeme PARLER. The third member in

this concentric classification is the "morphological family," which contains a lexeme, such as PARLER, and any lexemes-related PARLER.

A coherent split between inflection and derivation can then be maintained by assigning related forms to the appropriate form class associated with an item. Consider first the challenges presented by categorial hybrids. If active participles are treated as neutralizing the categorial distinction between verbs and adjectives, they can be included in the lexeme of a verb provided that the lexeme is defined as a set of grammatical words with NONCONTRASTIVE (rather than identical) values for word class and other intrinsic features. A similar analysis extends to other elements that neutralize rather than alter word class distinctions. However, a derived deverbal nominal will, irrespective of how productively it is formed, comprise a separate lexeme in the morphological family of a verb.

The classification of passive forms likewise depends on the treatment of argument structure. Passive forms will be included in the lexeme of a verb if the forms in a lexeme need only share a common logical (or thematic) argument structure. If the words that make up a lexeme must also have common surface valence (subcategorization) demands, then active and passive words will belong to different lexemes but again to a common morphological family. Either choice restores coherence to a traditional perspective in which lexemes occupy a position between inflectional paradigms and morphological families.[4] A lexeme such as CUT will contain a set of grammatical words, including finite and nonfinite verb forms. However, CUT can itself be located within a morphological family that includes the predictable agentive nominal lexeme CUTTER, which contains the singular grammatical word *cutter* and its plural counterpart *cutters*.

ENDOCENTRIC AND EXOCENTRIC PROCESSES

Given a systematic contrast between lexemes and morphological families, the somewhat overloaded contrast between "inflection" and "derivation" can be construed in terms of a distinction between ENDOCENTRIC or "within-lexeme" processes, and EXOCENTRIC or "cross-lexeme" processes. Characteristics that correlate with the endocentric-exocentric split need not then enter into the DEFINITION of this contrast. The fact that inflection operates over a closed, relatively uniform space makes inflectional processes interpredictable and productive. From the class of an open-class item, it is usually possible to determine the features that are distinctive for the class and predict the number of forms of the item; apart from irregular items, paradigms and lexemes are comparable in size and structure within a word or inflection class.[5] The closed, uniform feature space of an inflectional system thus defines a "grid" populated by interpredictable forms.[6]

The uniform organization of inflectional paradigms contrasts starkly with the more variable structure exhibited by families of derivational forms. Exocentric processes that can change word class, valence, or other intrinsic properties clearly do not define a finite set of forms within a uniform feature space. From the class of an item, one cannot in general predict the number and type of derivational formations in which it occurs. Given a list of derivational processes active in a language, it is of course possible to assign a uniform family of "potential" forms to all of the members of a word class. Yet the uniformity achieved is deceptive, because it collapses a critical distinction between those forms that are ESTABLISHED in a language and those that are merely possible in principle. The status of derivational forms that are possible but unattested is similar to that of acceptable phoneme sequences that "merely" lack a conventionalized meaning. Moreover, defining expanded derivational paradigms does not make it any easier for a speaker to predict the derivational formations that are attested and in use within a language. The issue is perhaps clearer in connection with compounds. Of the infinitely many possible noun compounds in English only a comparatively small number are established, and a speaker cannot predict the set of established compounds containing an item from the item itself.

These contrasts between inflection and derivation are reflected in the ways that morphological systems are described and analyzed. It is rare for an individual inflected form to be described as established on its own. The availability of a form correlates instead with the productivity of a whole pattern. Conversely, notions like "morphological gap," "suppletion," and even, to a large degree, "syncretism" are mainly or exclusively applied to inflectional paradigms. Derivational families do not usually have "gaps" because they do not define implicational relations over a closed and uniform space that give rise to expectations about the existence of specific forms, even where the shape would be predictable. Suppletion can likewise only arise where there are definite assumptions about the shape of particular members of a form set. Whereas inflectional paradigms generate strong assumptions of this nature, derivational families do not.

Syncretism presupposes a similar structure, as syncretic patterns imply the existence of independent cells that can be associated with fully or partially identical forms. But the notion of a derivational cell is not clearly defined in the absence of features that specify a morphosyntactic grid within which to place the cells.

Although there is a strong correlation between endocentricity and predictability, it is neither possible (nor desirable) to define inflectional/endocentric processes in terms of predictability or productivity. It is possible for endocentric processes to be unpredictable and for exocentric processes to be predictable. Neither of these patterns raises practical or theoretical difficulties. An unpredictable inflected form is usually described as sporadic or lexically idiosyncratic and must, in the general case, be learned on an item-by-item basis. The "past subjunctive" forms of German fall into this category, as do comitative, abessive, or instructive case forms in Finnish. Exocentric processes can likewise be highly predictable while defining new lexemes, with their own inflectional paradigms.

For example, agentive nominals in -er can be formed for virtually any verb in English, so that the predictability of agentive nominals in -er approaches that of inflected verb forms. Nevertheless, there are two important differences between an agentive nominal, such as WALKER, and an inflected form, such as *walks*. The first is that WALKER is associated with its own nominal paradigm, containing singular *walker* and plural *walkers*. Treating the process that defines -er nominals as inflectional/endocentric would make the lexeme WALK a categorially incoherent collection of inflected verb and noun forms. The second difference is that inflected forms are associated with a specific paradigm within a lexeme, whereas derivational forms tend to be associated with the lexeme. This distinction can be illustrated even in the simple conjugational system of English. Whereas *walks* is associated with the present indicative paradigm, *walker* is not the agentive nominal of any particular paradigm but of the verb lexeme WALK.

Implications

The contrast between wordforms, grammatical words, and lexemes clarifies the principal senses of the notion "word." The distinction between paradigms, lexemes, and families in turn defines the paradigmatic organization relevant to the split between endocentric and exocentric morphological processes. The resulting classification reconstructs a traditional perspective in a form that is compatible with, and even to some degree supported by, recent psycholinguistic studies.

Traditional claims about the "psychological reality" of words and paradigmatic structure receive a measure of support from experimental studies of frequency effects on lexical processing. A number of studies have shown that the frequency of inflected forms and the size of derivational families have a robust effect on lexical processing. One line of research has investigated the correlation between response latencies for inflected forms and the token frequency of the elements of their inflectional paradigms (Taft, 1979; Baayen, Lieber, & Schreuder, 1997; Hay, 2001). A second line of research has demonstrated that the processing of an item is facilitated by the semantically transparent items in its morphological family and inhibited by the semantically opaque items (Schreuder & Baayen, 1997; de Jong, 2002; Moscoso del Prado Martín, 2003). A third line of research attempts to provide a single information-theoretic measure that subsumes the token-frequency effects relevant to inflectional paradigms and the type-frequency effects relevant to morphological families (Kostić, Marković, & Baucal, 2003; Moscoso del Prado Martín, Kostić, & Baayen, 2004). More recent studies (Milin, Filipović Đurdjević, & Moscoso del Prado Martín, 2009; Milin, Kuperman, Kostić, & Baayen, 2009) have also shown that speaker responses are conditioned in part by the relation between relative frequencies. In particular, speakers appear to be sensitive to the relation between the probability distribution of the inflected forms of a lexical item and the probability distribution of exponents within the inflection class to which the item belongs. The more that these distributions diverge, the longer are the response latencies and the higher are the error rates in lexical decision tasks.

The traditional contrast between inflection and derivation may likewise contribute to an explanation for the observation that the processing of inflectional forms is more sensitive to token frequencies, whereas the processing of derivational formations is more sensitive to the type frequencies (Baayen et al., 1997). The relevant assumption is just that members of a given paradigm or inflection class have a comparable number of forms, whereas the size of derivational families may vary by orders of magnitude. Hence, if the type frequencies for inflected forms are relatively constant, only token frequencies will be distinctive.

Experimental methods and results are described greater detail in later sections. However, two points are worth mentioning here. The first is that all available research suggests that speakers are sensitive to frequency and distributional relations, information that is almost completely absent from theoretical models. The second is that the processing of a form appears to be influenced (whether facilitated or inhibited) by related forms, an effect that conflicts with the theoretical idealization that individual forms are defined in isolation. Morphological family effects seem to indicate that related forms are not only present as elements of a speaker's mental lexicon but that they are in some sense "activated" in the processing of a given form. These effects appear particularly compatible with models that link families of wordforms into networks of elements with shared formal, grammatical, and/or semantic properties (Bybee, 1985, 2010).

Word Structure

The models of morphology that grew out the classical Greco-Roman tradition recognized no grammatical unit intervening between sounds and words, and did not even see the need to isolate roots (Law, 1998, p. 112). However, since at least the early Neogrammarian period (Schleicher, 1859) the study of morphology has been centrally concerned with the morphotactic organization of words. The recurrent structural patterns exhibited by words in turn defined the familiar models of morphological typology initially proposed in Sapir (1921). The following sections summarize this organization, from patterns through types.

Patterns

Morphotactic patterns fall broadly into affixal (concatenative) and nonaffixal (nonconcatenative) classes. Affixal patterns are characterized by the presence (or absence) of a formative. Nonaffixal patterns may be distinguished by a stress pattern, a tonal melody, a length contrast, an accentual pattern, or another change in the properties of a segment or sequence of segments.[7]

AFFIXATION

The most common type of affixation is suffixation. Thus the pattern represented by the suffixation of -s in English *books* is more common than the prefixation of *re-* in *reread*, and both are more prevalent than other types of affixation. INFIXATION tends to arise as a prosodically conditioned variant of prefixation or suffixation. Hence, few infixes do not have prefixal or suffixal variants. In English, additional emphasis can be placed on expletives, such as *bloody*, by interposing them between two prosodic feet of the noun that they are modifying: *bloody unlikely~un-bloody-likely* (McMillan, 1980; McCarthy, 1982). In Tagalog, the "actor focus" marker *um* is prefixed to vowel-initial verb root *alís* in (4a), but infixed after the initial consonant of the consonant-initial root *bása* in (4b).

(4) Infixation in Tagalog (Aspillera 1981, p. 45f.)

    a. *alís ~ **um**alís* "to leave"
    b. *bása ~ b**um**ása* "to read"

CIRCUMFIXATION (or parafixation) is the most sparsely attested type of affixation, and many cases invite a reanalysis in terms of successive affixation. In German, for example, the formation of the perfect participle is sometimes described in terms of circumfixation. A regular verb like SAGEN "say" has a basic stem *sag-* and a perfect participle *gesagt*. However, there is no clear motivation for a circumfix *ge-...-t*, given that the preterite series is based on a stem *sagt*, so that *gesagt* can be formed by prefixing *ge-* to this stem (Blevins, 2003). More plausible cases of circumfixation are illustrated by the Georgian superlative marker *u...esi* in (5a) and the Chuckchee negative marker *e...ke* in (5b).

(5) Circumfixation in Georgian and Chuckchee

    a. *q'ru* 'deaf ~ ***u**-q'ru-**esi***' "the most deaf" (Tschenkéli, 1958, p. 225)
    b. *tejkev-ǝk* "fight" ~ ***e**-tejkev-**ke**-it-ǝk* "not to fight" (Comrie, 1981, p. 247)

REDUPLICATION is sometimes regarded as a type of parasitic affixation that copies all or part of a base form. The future in Tagalog is formed by reduplicating the first syllable of a root, for example, *a* in *al.ís* in (6a), but *bá* in *bd.sa* in (6b).

(6) Reduplication in Tagalog (Aspillera, 1981)
    a. *alís ~ **a**alís* "leave.FUT"
    b. *bása ~ **ba**bása* "read.FUT"

NONAFFIXAL PATTERNS

Nonaffixal patterns are fairly heterogeneous, and correspond to any phonetic contrast that is stable and discriminable enough to be morphologized. SUBTRACTION (or truncation) involves the loss of a segment, usually under prosodic conditions. The formation of Hidatsa imperatives in (7a) illustrates a subtractive pattern cited by Harris (1942, p. 110). The Papago forms in (7b) provide another familiar case, in which perfectives lack the final *-m* of the imperfectives.

(7) Truncation in Hidatsa and Papago

    a. *cicic* "he jumped" ~ *cic* "jump!" *ika.c* "he looked" ~ *ika* "look!"
    b. *him ~ hi* "walking," *hihim ~ hihi* "walking.PL" (Zepeda, 1983)

In patterns of ABLAUT (or vowel modification), a morphological contrast is signaled by a change in vowel quality. In German, present, preterite, and participial forms of strong verbs exhibit the residual ablaut patterns in (8a) and (8b). In the Lezgian examples in (8c) and (8d), the inessive form of a noun "is marked by lowering the final vowel of the oblique stem" (Haspelmath, 1993).

(8) Ablaut in German and Lezgian
    a. *singe* "sing.1SG.PRES" ~ *sang* "1SG.PRET" ~ *gesungen* "PART."
    b. *nehme* "take. 1SG. PRES" ~ *nahm* "1SG. PRET" ~ *genommen* "PART."
    c. *čarxú* "rock" ~ *čarxá* "INES.SG"
    d. *arčí* "paper" ~ *čarčé* "INES.SG"

The phenomenon of morphological GRADATION is illustrated by Estonian, which exhibits a three-way quantity distinction between Q1 (short), Q2 (long), and Q3 (overlong) syllables. In the morphological system, the contrast between Q2 and Q3 distinguishes weak and strong (quantitative) grade. In the class of nouns represented in (9), the genitive and partitive singular forms differ solely in grade: a weak genitive singular contrasts with a strong partitive singular.[8]

(9) Grade in Estonian declensions (Mürk 1997; Blevins, 2008)

    a. *luku* "lock. GEN.SG" (Q2) ~ *'lukku* 'lock. PART.SG (Q3)
    b. *kooli* "school.GEN.SG" (Q2) ~ *'kooli* "school. PART.SG" (Q3)

Although the contrasts in these examples cannot be keyed to segmental formatives, the elements of each of the patterns can be associated with a particular morphological function or meaning. Even this constancy is missing in EXCHANGE patterns, in which a morphological contrast is encoded by a symmetrical or "reversable" opposition. In Spanish, the contrast between indicative and subjunctive mood is marked by a process of *a~e* "vowel reversal" (Matthews, 1991, p. 198) illustrated in (10a) and (10b). The contrast between the Estonian partitive

Alternation	Absolutive	Oblique	
$\grave{v} \sim \hat{v}$	àjît	àjît	'chicken'
$\hat{v} \sim \grave{v}$	àrêw	àrèw	'tortoise'

Figure 9.1 Contrastive modulation in Dinka. Adapted from Andersen (2002).

singulars and plurals in (10c) and (10d) is encoded by an *i ~ e* alternation.

(10) Exchange patterns in Spanish and Estonian
    a. *compra* "buy.3SG.IND" ~ *compre* "buy.3SG.SUB"
    b. *come* "eat.3SG.IND" ~ *coma* "eat. 3SG.SUB"
    c. *'kooli* "school.PART.SG" ~ *'koole* "school. PART.PL"
    d. *'lille* "flower. PART.SG" ~ *lilli* "flower.PART.PL."

Dinka exhibits a similar pattern of "variable interpredictability," in which suprasegmental tonal contrasts distinguish absolutive from oblique case.

> The oblique is distinguished from the absolutive in virtually all monosyllabic nouns that have a short vowel… and in most disyllabic nouns with the prefix *à-* and a short root vowel… The rule for such nouns is that if the absolutive has a low root tone… then the oblique gets a falling root tone, and if the absolutive has a high or falling root tone… then the oblique gets a low root tone. *(Andersen, 2002, p. 9)*

The near-minimal contrast between *àjît ~ àjît* and *àrêw ~ àrèw* in Figure 9.1 illustrates the alternation between low-falling and falling-low tonal melodies.

METHATHESIS represents an extreme version of a nonaffixal strategy in which a morphological contrast is expressed by a process that rearranges the relative order of segments or formatives. In Rotuman (Churchward, 1940; Blevins & Garrett 1999, p. 510) CV metathesis distinguishes the CV "complete phase" (corresponding roughly to a definite form) from the VC "incomplete phase."

(11)   a. *seséva ~ seséav* "erroneous"
     b. *tíko ~ tíok* "flesh"

Morphological types

Although different patterns and strategies often predominate in different parts of a language, it is common to classify languages by positioning them relative to a number of ideal morphological types. At one extreme are languages of the ISOLATING type, in which each morpheme functions as a grammatical word. Modern English approaches this ideal, at least insofar as inflectional morphology is concerned, although Southeast Asian languages, such as Vietnamese, are usually regarded as paradigm examples of the isolating type. At the other extreme are AGGLUTINATIVE languages, in which words consist of a sequence of discrete formatives, each of which realizes a single property. Many inflectionally complex languages contain structures that conform to this ideal. For example, a Finnish noun, such as *taloissansa* "in their houses," can be assigned the agglutinative analysis in (12a). However, in few languages is this transparency maintained through the entire morphology. In Finnish, agglutination breaks down already in the nominative plural *talot* "houses" in (12b), which lacks the distinct plural marker *-i-* and the discrete case marker found in other forms.

(12) Agglutination in Finnish (Karlsson, 1999)
    a. *talo-i-ssa-nsa* "house-PL-INES-3PL.POSS"
    b. *talo-t* "house-NOM.PL"

The "fusion" of nominative case and plural number in the single suffix *-t* in (12a) is—like the realization of third person and plural by the ending *-nsa* in (12a)—a salient characteristic of languages of the (IN)FLECTIONAL type. Fusional patterns are ubiquitous within Indo-European languages, and particularly well represented in Latin and Ancient Greek. As Matthews (1972, p. 132ff.) shows, the Latin verb *re:ksisti:* "you had ruled" (*rexisti* in the standard pedagogical orthography) exhibits the many-many relations between features and forms displayed in Figure 9.2. The ending *-ti:* exhibits a fusional pattern,

Figure 9.2 Morphological analysis of Latin *re:ksisti:*. Adapted from Matthews (1972).

e	le	lý	k	e	te
	PERF		PAST IND		2ND PLU
Past	ACTIVE				

Figure 9.3 Morphological analysis of Greek *elelýkete*. Adapted from Matthews (1991).

realizing perfective aspect, second person and singular number. The perfective feature exhibits a converse "fis-sional" pattern, as it is realized by each of the formatives *-s-*, *-is-*, and *-ti:*.

Nor is this an extreme or unrepresentative example. Classical Greek exhibits even more tangled feature-form associations, as illustrated by the verb *elelykete* "you had unfastened," in Figure 9.3 below. Just as *re:ksisti:* occupies the second person perfective active cell of REGO "rule," *elelykete* realizes the second person past perfective indicative active cell in the paradigm of LYO "unfasten." But as Matthews (1972, 1991) observes, the scattered realization of aspect and voice confounds any attempt to impose an agglutinative structure on these forms. Simpler cases of extended exponence are illustrated by the combination of a suppletive future stem *ir-* and a future ending *-ai* in French *irai* "go.1SG." More "exuberant" patterns are likewise attested in Batsbi, as shown by Harris (2009).[9]

Morphological analysis

It may be useful to bring this summary of the linguistic properties of words to a close with a brief discussion of some of the analytical issues that arise in assigning wordforms a morphotactic structure or associating them with sets of paradigmatic alternatives. Interestingly, the interaction between paradigmatic alternatives and morphotactic structure plays a significant role in morphological systems. The implicit "competition" between alternatives gives rise to a type of "paradigmatic deduction" that

allows forms to be interpreted based on the absence of a marker. Noun paradigms in English provide a simple example. Plural nouns in English are marked by the suffix /z/ (represented orthographically as -s). There is, however, no marking of singular number, and none is needed, given that a singular noun is unambiguously identified by the lack of a plural marker. A zero morph adds no information to what speakers can already deduce from the absence of any realized exponent. Similar patterns are even more typical of more intricate paradigms. As Anderson (1992, p. 87) notes, Georgian verbal paradigms provide a striking illustration of the fact that that "information may sometimes be conveyed not by constituents that are present in the structure of a given word, but precisely by the fact that certain other material is ABSENT."

Cases of what are sometimes termed "gestalt exponence" likewise highlight the grammatical and semantic contribution of the morphotactic arrangement of formatives. The patterns of cumulative and extended exponence illustrated in the section on morphological types, together with the paradigmatic deduction described in English and Georgian, suggest that the properties of words are not, at least in any straightforward or direct way, reducible to the properties of their parts. A range of patterns cannot be made to conform to an agglutinative ideal in which the grammatical meaning of a word consists of discrete units of meaning that correspond to subword formatives. Instead, morphological systems tend to reuse common parts in different contexts in such a way that the arrangement of these parts contributes a "constructional" meaning. Expanding on the discussion of gradation in (9) will clarify how combinations of elements can have distinctive meanings within a language. The first four columns in Table 9.1 contain the singular grammatical case forms of nouns that exhibit productive "weakening" gradation in Estonian. The

Table 9.1. Singular nouns in Estonian. Adapted from Erelt, Erelt, and Ross (2000) and Blevins (2008).

Nominative	Sukk	Kukk	Pukk	Lukk	Lugu
Genitive	Suka	Kuke	Puki	Luku	Loo
Partitive	Sukka	Kukke	Pukki	Lukku	Lugu
Illative 2	Sukka	Kukke	Pukki	Lukku	Lukku
	"Stocking"	"Rooster"	"Trestle"	"Lock"	"Tale"

nominative forms of these nouns consist of a strong (Q3) stem, identified by the double consonant *-kk*. The remaining forms consist of a strong stem, or a weak stem in *-k*, followed by one of the "theme vowels" *a, e, i,* and *u*.[10]

Let us consider the locus of the property "partitive singular." This property can only be associated with subword units if the forms in Table 9.1 are analyzable into smaller meaningful parts. The partitive singulars of this class contain two "recurrent partials": a strong stem and a theme vowel. Thus *sukka* can be analyzed as *sukk + a, kukke* as *kukk + e, pukki* as *pukk + i*, and *lukku* as *lukk + u*. But partitive case cannot be associated either with strong stems or with theme vowels in isolation. The strong stems *sukk, kukk, pukk,* and *lukk* cannot be analyzed as partitive, because these same stems realize the nominative singular when they occur without a theme vowel, and also underlie the second "short" illative singular forms. Partitive case also cannot be associated with the theme vowels, because the same vowels occur in the genitive and illative singular forms.

Hence partitive case is an irreducibly word-level feature that is realized by the combination of a strong stem and a theme vowel. This type of gestalt exponence or "constructional" exponence (Booij, 2005) is difficult to describe if stems and theme vowels are represented separately. Because the grammatical meanings associated with strong stems and theme vowels are context-dependent, these elements cannot be assigned discrete meanings that "add up" to partitive singular when they are combined. From a traditional perspective, this context-dependence underscores the difference between "analyzability" and morphemic "decomposition." An individual wordform is often analyzable into parts that recur elsewhere in its inflectional paradigm or in the morphological system at large. But these parts may function solely to differentiate larger forms, so that the minimal parts that distinguish a pair of wordforms cannot be associated with the difference in grammatical meaning between the wordforms. To return to the patterns in Table 9.1, the theme vowel *-u* distinguishes the partitive singular *lukku* "lock" from the nominative singular *lukk*. In isolation, however, the vowel *-u* neither realizes a specific case value nor expresses "the grammatical difference" between nominative and partitive. Exactly the same is true of the grade contrast between partitive singular *lukku* and genitive singular *luku*.

These examples illustrate some of the fundamental challenges that arise in decomposing wordforms into their component parts. Given a set of

wordforms, it is often possible to segment them into roots or stems and derivational and inflectional exponents. Yet disassembling a word into its parts raises chronic and even recalcitrant problems in many languages. Perhaps the most extreme analytical problem is associated with the patterns of stem syncretism that Matthews (1972) calls "Priscianic" or "parasitic" and Aronoff (1994) later terms "morphomic." A pair of Latin examples discussed in Matthews (1991) are summarized in the quotations below. The first case involves a correspondence between present active infinitives and imperfect subjunctives. The second example concerns the relation between past passive and future active participles.

> For any Verb, however irregular it may be in other respects, the Present Infinitive always predicts the Imperfect Subjunctive. For the Verb "to flower," *florere → florerem;* for the irregular Verb "to be," *esse → essem,* and so forth without exception. (p. 195)
>
> There are a few exceptions; but, in general, if the stem of the Past Participle is *x*, no matter how irregular it may be, that of the Future Participle is *x* with *-ūr-* added. (p. 200)

Table 9.2. Full paradigm of LUKK **"lock." Adapted from Erelt et al. (2000).**

	Sing	Plu
Nominative	Lukk	Lukud
Genitive	Luku	Lukkude
Partitive	Lukku	Lukkusid
Illa2/Rart2	Lukku	Lukke
Illative	Lukusse	Lukkudesse
Inessive	Lukus	Lukkudes
Elative	Lukust	Lukkudest
Allative	Lukule	Lukkudele
Adessive	Lukul	Lukkudel
Ablative	Lukult	Lukkudelt
Translative	Lukuks	Lukkudeks
Terminative	Lukuni	Lukkudeni
Essive	Lukuna	Lukkudena
Abessive	Lukuta	Lukkudeta
Comitative	Lukuga	Lukkudega

The challenge posed by these patterns is that stems such *as florere* and *esse* (and past participle stems like *amāt* "to love") are non–meaning-bearing units. Hence, once isolated, they cannot be assigned features and meanings that they contribute to determine the features and meanings of the larger units that they underlie. The difficulties that arise in attempting to assign these stems grammatical meanings merely highlights the fact that the value of these units of forms resides solely in the predictions that they sanction about other forms.

The descriptive value of form-based predictions is illustrated by the kind of implicational network that they define within the paradigm of LUKK "lock" in Table 9.2. The nominative singular *lukk* underlies the partitive singular *lukku*, which is in turn identical to the short illative singular *lukku* and underlies the partitive plural *lukkusid* and the genitive plural *lukkude*. The genitive singular *luku* underlies the nominative *lukud* and the illative through comitative singular, whereas the genitive plural *lukkude* underlies the illative through the comitative plural.

Summary

In sum, the word occupies a central position in the morphotactic, paradigmatic, and implicational organization of a language. The traditional assignment of words to paradigms, lexemes, and families complements the analysis of wordforms into smaller parts, ultimately reflecting interrelated "outward-looking" and "inward-looking" perspectives on the most basic grammatical unit of a language.

Notes

1. See the papers in Dixon and Aikhenvald (2002) for extended discussion of this issue.
2. An earlier use of "lexeme" is found in Hockett (1958, p. 169ff.), who uses the term to designate sequences that always occur as grammatical forms in a context where they are not part of any larger unit that also invariably occurs as a grammatical form. This usage is now largely obsolete.
3. There is an alternative interpretation of the term "lemma" still in circulation. In psycholinguistic models of speech production, lemmas are often construed as abstract conceptual entries that represent "the nonphonological part of an item's lexical information" (Levelt, 1989).
4. Moreover, on either alternative, "morphosemantic" alternations (Sadler & Spencer, 1998) like causativization will relate distinct lexemes within a larger morphological family.
5. This predictability underlies the descriptive success of the realization-based models of inflection set out in Matthews (1972, 1991), Anderson (1992), Aronoff (1994), and Stump (2001).
6. The patterns exhibited by this network provide the analogical base for exemplar-based models of both the traditional (Paul, 1920) and modern (Bybee, 2010) variety.
7. Some theories of morphology regard affixal and nonaffixal patterns as different in character (Carstairs-McCarthy, 1994, 2005). Other approaches argue that "there is no theoretically significant difference between concatenative and non-concatenative inflection" (Stump, 2005, p. 284).
8. Since the Q3 quantity of partitive singular *kooli* is not marked orthographically (as by the consonant doubling in *lukku*), Q3 is marked diacritically by a single quotation mark.
9. The POLYSYNTHETIC patterns found in many Amerindian languages represent an orthogonal dimension of morphological variation, as these patterns essentially exhibit a distinctive division of grammatical labor. In many of the familiar languages of Europe and Asia, lexical meaning is expressed by roots or stems, and grammatical meanings by affixes and other types of exponents.
10. The choice of theme vowel is a lexical property of an Estonian noun, and is not conditioned by phonological properties of the stem or by morphosyntactic features of the noun.

References

Andersen, T. (2002). Case inflection and nominal head marking in Dinka. *Journal of African Languages and Linguistics*, *23*, 1–30.

Anderson, S. R. (1992). *A-morphous morphology*. Cambridge: Cambridge University Press.

Aronoff, M. (1994). *Morphology by itself: Stems and inflectional classes*. Cambridge, MA: MIT Press.

Aspillera, P. S. (1981). *Basic Tagalog*. Manila: M & L Licudine Enterprises.

Baayen, R. H., Lieber, R., & Schreuder, R. (1997). The morphological complexity of simple nouns. *Linguistics*, *35*, 861–877.

Blevins, J., & Garrett, A. (1999). The origins of consonant-vowel metathesis. *Language*, *74*, 508–556.

Blevins, J. P. (2003). Stems and paradigms. *Language*, *79*, 737–767.

Blevins, J. P. (2006). Word-based morphology. *Journal of Linguistics*, *42*, 531–573.

Blevins, J. P. (2008). Declension classes in Estonian. *Linguistica Uralica*, *44*, 241–267.

Bloomfield, L. (1914). Sentence and word. *Transactions of the American Philological Society*, *45*, 65–75. Reprinted in Hockett (1970), 38–46.

Bloomfield, L. (1926). A set of postulates for the science of language. *Language*, *2*, 153–164. Reprinted in M. Joos (1957), *Readings in linguistics I*. Chicago: University of Chicago Press (26–37).

Bloomfield, L. (1933). *Language*. Chicago: University of Chicago Press.

Booij, G. (1996). Inherent verses contextual inflection and the split morphology hypothesis. In G. Booij & J. van Marie (Eds.), *Yearbook of morphology 1995* (pp. 1–16). Dordrecht: Kluwer.

Booij, G. (2005). Compounding and derivation: Evidence for constructional morphology. In W. U. Dressier, P. Kastovsky, & F. Rainer (Eds.), *Morphology and its demarcations* (pp. 109–132). Amsterdam: John Benjamins.

Bybee, J. L. (1985). *Morphology: A study of the relation between meaning and form*. Amsterdam: John Benjamins.

Bybee, J. L. (2001). *Phonology and language use*. Cambridge: Cambridge University Press.

Bybee, J. L. (2010). *Language, usage and complexity*. Cambridge: Cambridge University Press.

Carstairs-McCarthy, A. (1994). Inflection classes, gender, and the principle of contrast. *Language*, *70*, 737–788.

Carstairs-McCarthy, A. (2005). Affixes, stems and allomorphic conditioning in Paradigm Function Morphology. *Yearbook of Morphology, 2*, 253–281.

Churchward, C. M. (1940). *Rotuman grammar and dictionary.* Sydney, Australia: Methodist Church of Australasia.

Comrie, B. (1981). *The languages of the Soviet Union.* Cambridge: Cambridge University Press.

de Jong, N. H. (2002). *Morphological families in the mental lexicon* (Unpublished doctoral thesis). University of Nijmegen, Nijmegen, the Netherlands.

Dixon, R. M. W., & Aikhenvald, A. Y. (Eds.). (2002). *Word: A cross-linguistic typology.* Cambridge: Cambridge University Press.

Dromi, E. (1987). *Early lexical development.* Cambridge: Cambridge University Press.

Elman, J. L. (1990). Finding structure in time. *Cognitive Science, 14*, 179–211.

Erelt, M., Erelt, T., & Ross, K. (2000). *Eesti keele käsiraamat.* Tallinn: Eesti Keele Sihtasutus.

Goldwater, S., Griffiths, T. L., & Johnson, M. (2009). A Bayesian framework for word segmentation: Exploring the effects of context. *Cognition, 112*, 21–54.

Harris, A. C. (2009). Exuberant exponence in Batsbi. *Natural Language and Linguistic Theory, 27*, 267–303.

Harris, Z. S. (1942). Morpheme alternants in linguistic analysis. *Language, 18*, 169–180. Reprinted in M. Joos (1957), *Readings in linguistics I.* Chicago: University of Chicago Press (109–115).

Haspelmath, M. (1993). *A grammar of Lezgian.* Berlin: Mouton.

Haspelmath, M. (1996). Word-class-changing inflection and morphological theory. In G. Booij & J. van Marle (Eds.), *Yearbook of morphology 1995* (pp. 43–66). Kluwer, Dordrecht.

Hay, J. (2001). Lexical frequency in morphology: Is everything relative? *Linguistics, 39*, 1041–1070.

Hockett, C. F. (1958). *A course in modern linguistics.* New York: MacMillan.

Hockett, C. F. (Ed.). (1970). *A Leonard Bloomfield anthology.* Chicago: University of Chicago Press.

Karlsson, F. (1999). *Finnish: An essential grammar.* London: Routledge.

Kostić, A., Marković, T., & Baucal, A. (2003). Inflectional morphology and word meaning: Orthogonal or co-implicative domains? In R. H. Baayen & R. Schreuder (Eds.), *Morphological structure in language processing* (pp. 1–44). Berlin: Mouton de Gruyter.

Law, V. (1998). The Technē and grammar in the Roman world. In V. Law & I. Sluiter (Eds.), *Dionysius Thrax and the Technē Grammatikē* (pp. 111–120). Münster: Nodus Publikationen.

Levelt, W. J. M. (1989). *Speaking: From intention to articulation.* Cambridge, MA: MIT Press.

Marslen-Wilson, W., & Tyler, L. K. (1980). The temporal structure of spoken language understanding. *Cognition, 8*, 1–71.

Marslen-Wilson, W. D., & Welsh, A. (1978). Processing interactions and lexical access during word recognition in continuous speech. *Cognitive Psychology, 10*, 29–63.

Matthews, P. H. (1972). *Inflectional morphology: A theoretical study based on aspects of Latin verb conjugation.* Cambridge: Cambridge University Press.

Matthews, P. H. (1991). *Morphology.* Cambridge: Cambridge University Press.

McCarthy, J. J. (1982). Prosodic structure and expletive infixation. *Language, 58*, 574–590.

McMillan, J. (1980). Infixing and interposing in English. *American Speech, 55*, 168–177.

Milin, P., Filipović Đurdjević, D., & Moscoso del Prado Martín, F. (2009a). The simultaneous effects of inflectional paradigms and classes on lexical recognition: Evidence from Serbian. *Journal of Memory and Language, 60*, 50–64.

Milin, P., Kuperman, V., Kostić, A., & Baayen, R. H. (2009b). Words and paradigms bit by bit: An information-theoretic approach to the processing of inflection and derivation. In. J. P. Blevins & J. Blevins (Eds.), *Analogy in grammar: Form and acquisition* (pp. 214–253). Oxford: Oxford University Press.

Moscoso del Prado Martín, F. (2003). *Paradigmatic structures in morphological processing: computational and cross-linguistic studies* (Unpublished doctoral thesis). University of Nijmegen, Nijmegen, the Netherlands.

Moscoso del Prado Martín, F., Kostić, A., & Baayen, R. H. (2004). Putting the bits together: An information-theoretical perspective on morphological processing. *Cognition, 94*, 1–18.

Mürk, H. W. (1997). *A handbook of Estonian: Nouns, adjectives and verbs.* Indiana University Uralic and Altaic Series, v. 163. Bloomington, IN: Indiana University.

Nida, E. A. (1949). *Morphology: The descriptive analysis of words.* Ann Arbor, MI: University of Michigan Press.

Norris, D., McQueen, J. M., Cutler, A., & Butterfield, S. (1997). The possible-word constraint in the segmentation of continuous speech. *Cognitive Psychology, 34*, 191–243.

Paul, H. (1920). *Prinzipien der Sprachgeschichte.* Tübingen: Max Niemayer Verlag.

Robins, R. H. (1959). In defence of WP. *Transactions of the Philological Society, 58*, 116–144. Reprinted in *Transactions of the Philological Society, 99*, 116–144.

Sadler, L., & Spencer, A. (1998). Morphology and argument structure. In A. Spencer & A. M. Zwicky (Eds.), *Handbook of morphology* (pp. 206–236). Blackwell.

Sapir, E. (1921). *Language.* New York: Harcourt Brace.

Schleicher, A. (1859). *Zur Morphologie der Sprache. Volume 1, Memoires de L'Académie de St Pétersbourg.* Leipzig: Leopold Voss.

Schreuder, R., & Baayen, R. H. (1997). How complex simplex words can be. *Journal of Memory and Language, 37*, 118–139.

Spencer, A. (1999). Transpositions and argument structure. In G. Booij & J. van Marie (Eds.), *Yearbook of morphology 1998* (pp. 73–101). Dordrecht: Kluwer.

Stump, G. T. (2001). *Inflectional morphology: A theory of paradigm structure.* Cambridge: Cambridge University Press.

Stump, G. T. (2005). Some criticisms of Carstairs-McCarthy's conclusions. *Yearbook of Morphology, 2*, 283–303.

Taft, M. (1979). Recognition of affixed words and the word frequency effect. *Memory and Cognition, 7*, 263–272.

Tschenkéli, K. (1958). *Einführung in die georgische Sprache.* Zurich: Amirani Verlag.

Zepeda, O. (1983). *A Papago grammar.* Tucson, AZ: University of Arizona Press.

Speech Planning in Two Languages: What Bilinguals Tell Us about Language Production

Judith F. Kroll *and* Tamar H. Gollan

Abstract

This chapter considers the consequences of bilingualism for planning speech in each of the bilingual's two languages. Two accounts are contrasted of bilingual language production that make different assumptions about why bilinguals are slower to speak the L2 and sometimes also slower to speak the L1 compared with monolingual speakers. The frequency-lag hypothesis assumes that bilinguals have fewer opportunities to speak each of their languages relative to monolinguals. In contrast, the competition for production model assumes that the parallel activation of the bilingual's two languages creates competition that requires resolution to allow the intended language to be spoken. Evidence for each of these alternatives is reviewed and how the process of language selection in production may relate to the consequences of bilingualism that have been reported for domain-general cognitive processes is considered.

Key Words: bilingualism, lexical production, language selection, inhibitory control

Of all of the skills that bilinguals possess, perhaps the most remarkable is the ability to speak in two languages, keeping each language separate when necessary but easily switching from one language to the other when interacting with others who are similarly bilingual. From the perspective of speech planning in the native language, the focus of most of the chapters in this volume, it may seem that speaking in a second language (L2) is a special condition, one that complicates an already complex process. Bilingual speakers differ among themselves in how proficient they are in the L2, whether the L2 is typologically similar or different than the first language (L1), and whether the bilingual is immersed in the L1 or L2 context. However, the surprising observation in the research on bilingual production is not that speaking an L2 is more difficult and variable than speaking the native language, but that the native language itself changes in response to active L2 use. As a consequence, bilingual speech production differs from monolingual speech production,

even in the native language. The changes that occur also tell us something important about the architecture of speech planning because the presence of two languages provides a window into interactions that are otherwise not visible in speakers of one language alone.

This chapter reviews recent evidence on bilingual production, with a focus on the two features of bilingual speech noted previously: bilinguals are not identical to monolinguals, even in their native language; and the native language changes in response to active use of the L2. Each of these observations has been at the center of alternative accounts of bilingual speech planning. Related to these two observations are seemingly contrasted effects of bilingualism on different types of linguistic and nonlinguistic processing tasks. When compared with monolinguals, bilinguals seem relatively less proficient on verbal tasks that reflect vocabulary knowledge and rapid lexical access but more proficient on nonlinguistic tasks that require cognitive control.

The frequency-lag or weaker links hypothesis (Gollan, Montoya, Cera, & Sandoval, 2008; Gollan, Montoya, Fennema-Notestine, & Morris, 2005; Gollan et al., 2011) was proposed to explain why bilinguals, who on the one hand seem like language-acrobats flying seamlessly from one language system to the other, at other times seem disadvantaged relative to monolinguals. This view assumes that bilinguals may be disadvantaged simply because they speak each of the two languages less often than monolinguals. The result is functionally lower frequency or reduced accessibility of words in each language with the consequence that production is slower not only in L2 relative to L1 but also within L1 for bilinguals relative to monolinguals. On this view, whatever mechanism is used to explain why monolinguals require more time to access low-frequency than high-frequency words is also used to explain bilingual disadvantages on lexical processing tasks. The appeal to frequency of use was logical given several identified bilingual disadvantages in lexical processing tasks, that frequency effects have been found in virtually all lexical processing tasks (Murray & Forster, 2004), that frequency effects are sometimes considered the signature of lexical access (Almeida, Knobel, Finkbeiner, & Caramazza, 2007), and also simply that frequency may be the most studied variable in psycholinguistic research (Balota, Pilotti, & Cortese, 2001).

The competition for selection hypothesis (e.g., Green, 1998; Kroll, Bobb, & Wodniecka, 2006) assumes that candidates in each of the bilingual's two languages compete for selection even when utterances are planned in one language alone. Although there are several distinct models for how competition might ultimately be resolved (e.g., Finkbeiner, Gollan, & Caramazza, 2006; Kroll, Bobb, Misra, & Guo, 2008; La Heij, 2005), there is general agreement that alternatives in both languages are activated, at least briefly, when speech is planned in each language. Recent accounts that assume cross-language competition is resolved by inhibition of the more dominant language, typically the L1 (e.g., Guo, Liu, Misra, & Kroll, 2011; Kroll et al., 2008; Linck, Kroll, & Sunderman, 2009; Philipp, Gade, & Koch, 2007), also demonstrate that there is a cost to the native language, with inhibition of the L1 when speech is planned in the L2. An interesting issue for inhibitory accounts is to understand what the long-lasting consequences may be for repeated inhibition of the L1. Like frequency-lag, the competition account predicts a processing cost for bilinguals relative to monolinguals, but most of the research on cross-language competition in production has focused on a comparison across the bilingual's two languages rather than between bilinguals and monolinguals.

A challenge for all models of bilingual production is to consider whether the mechanisms that enable speech in each language are related causally to the domain-general executive function benefits that have been reported for bilinguals relative to monolinguals (e.g., Bialystok, Craik, Green, & Gollan, 2009). One hypothesis about the bilingual advantage in executive control is that over the lifespan, bilinguals develop specialized expertise in selecting the intended language for production. That expertise is then hypothesized to generalize from language experience to cognition more generally. A recent study by Emmorey, Luk, Pyers, and Bialystok (2008) reported that bimodal bilinguals who use one spoken language (English) and another signed language (American Sign Language) do not exhibit an advantage on an executive function task relative to monolingual speakers. Because bimodal bilinguals can speak and cogesture at the same time, Emmorey et al. claim that there is no need to select between the two languages the way that unimodal bilinguals must select to enable them to speak one language at a time. Although this is only a single study, the results suggest that the selection processes that guide bilingual speech may hold critical implications for the observed cognitive consequences of bilingualism.

In what follows, we review the evidence for the frequency-lag/weaker links hypothesis and also for the competition for selection hypothesis, with particular attention in the latter case to models that assume eventual inhibition of the bilingual's more dominant language. As noted above, these alternative accounts often focus on different types of evidence and comparisons between bilingual and monolinguals or between the L1 and L2 within bilinguals. A goal of this chapter is to examine the distinct and shared sources of evidence for each account and to then consider whether there are new predictions that might be generated to test them or a means to reconcile the differences between them. We review data from behavioral experiments and also from neuroimaging studies, from studies on young adults and elderly bilinguals, and from intact and impaired populations of bilingual speakers.

Evidence that Calls for the Frequency-lag Account (or Weaker Links)

Bilinguals are disadvantaged relative to monolinguals in several lexical processing tasks. Although it is tempting to simplify the theoretical approach by attributing all of the consequences of bilingualism (whether advantage or disadvantage) to competition between languages (Bialystok et al., 2009), several qualitative manifestations of differences between bilinguals and monolinguals are very difficult to explain by appealing to competition for selection. These results inspired the frequency-lag hypothesis as a theoretical alternative, which instead appeals to a more emergent property of bilingual language use: by virtue of using each language only some of the time, bilinguals have accessed words particular to each language relatively less frequently than monolinguals. In other words, bilingualism entails a frequency-lag (Gollan & Silverberg, 2001; Gollan, Montoya, & Werner, 2002; Gollan et al., 2005, 2008, 2011; Sandoval, Gollan, Ferreira, & Salmon, 2010; for similar ideas see Ivanova & Costa, 2008; Lehtonen, & Laine, 2003; Mägiste, 1979; Nicoladis, Palmer, & Marentette, 2007; Pearson et al., 1993; Ransdell & Fischler, 1987). Although the frequency-lag hypothesis was inspired as an alternative to the competition account, and to explain data that are not easily explained by competition between languages, the two explanations are in fact mutually compatible (Gollan et al., 2008; for recent review see Runnqvist, Strijkers, Sadat, & Costa, 2011). Before considering how these two explanations contrast and sometimes dovetail, it is necessary to summarize some key features of the extant findings.

The Size of the Frequency Effect

How the frequency-lag hypothesis explains bilingual disadvantages is inextricably tied to whatever mechanism explains frequency effects in general (Gollan et al., 2008). Multiple alternatives are possible (for review see Murray & Forster, 2004), but frequency effects are often explained within an activation framework in which higher-frequency representations have assumed higher levels of baseline activation than lower-frequency words. A similar approach considers frequency to be a product of learning (e.g., Plaut, McClelland, Seidenberg, & Patterson, 1996), and connection strength, rather than baseline activations of lexical units, is frequency sensitive. Such models use error-based learning: as they learn more about a specific item (e.g., as words become higher frequency) weight changes become smaller; this effectively imposes a "ceiling effect" on performance. The assumption of a hard ceiling on the extent to which frequency can influence lexical accessibility is critical for explaining bilingual disadvantages in such a framework; lexical

representations evolve toward ceiling-level, stable end states, and the monolingual lexicon is closer to these ceiling levels of lexical accessibility than the bilingual lexicon. As language use and proficiency increases, low-frequency words begin to catch-up with high-frequency words in levels of activation, and frequency effects should become smaller. Thus, monolinguals exhibit smaller frequency effects than bilinguals tested in their dominant language, and bilinguals exhibit smaller frequency effects when tested in their dominant language than in their nondominant language.

Direct evidence for the frequency-lag hypothesis is that the bilingual disadvantage is especially large for retrieval of low-frequency words, whereas little or no bilingual disadvantage is found for production of high-frequency words. Similarly, slowing related to language dominance is particularly large for retrieval of low-frequency words in both comprehension (Duyck, Vanderelst, Desmet, & Hartsuiker, 2008) and production (Gollan et al., 2008, 2011; but see Ivanova & Costa, 2008). Given that bilinguals often have difficulty accessing low-frequency names in their nondominant language, the finding of a greater bilingual disadvantage for those words seems rather inconsistent with the competition account (Gollan et al., 2005, 2008). However, there may be a way to reconcile this finding with the competition account if it is also assumed that retrieval of low-frequency words is more likely to be affected by interference. This may seem ad hoc, but there are hints that seem to support this notion outside the literature on bilingual language production. For example, monolingual speakers are slower to name pictures with more than one alternative name (e.g., *TV, television*) but only when the two names are also relatively low-frequency (e.g., *limousine, limo*; Spieler & Griffin, 2006; but see Griffin, 2001).

Vocabulary

One of the earliest reported (Pearson, Fernandez, & Oller, 1993) and perhaps most apparent bilingual disadvantages is the lag in language-specific vocabulary knowledge. Clearly bilinguals know many more words than monolinguals if words in each language are counted, but several studies have documented that monolinguals obtain higher scores than bilinguals on vocabulary tests. A recent study with a very large number of participants identified this disadvantage to be relatively small (about two-thirds of a standard deviation) but significant in children (Bialystok, Luk, Peets, & Yang, 2010), and persistent into adulthood (Bialystok, Craik, &

Luk, 2008; Portocarrero, Burright, & Donovick, 2007). This bilingual disadvantage is unlikely to reflect active competition between languages because there is no requirement to respond quickly, and often all that is needed is to select the correct response (a synonym or a picture) out of several alternative options provided, or to produce a definition using whatever words are accessible to express the key meaning. Vocabulary knowledge is highly sensitive to experience and exposure, and for this reason vocabulary size continues to grow throughout the lifespan and is one of few aging-related cognitive advantages (Verhaegen, 2003). Thus, it seems likely that bilinguals (who divide their exposure and use of two languages) between the two systems have lower vocabulary in each language relative to monolinguals, particularly low-frequency words, which continue to be acquired later in life (as opposed to high-frequency words, which must be learned early on to allow language use to begin).

Tip of the Tongue States

A common experience for bilingual speakers is to have difficulty retrieving a known word, sometimes accompanied by access to partial phonological information about the word (e.g., "it starts with /p/"), and a feeling that retrieval is imminent. Such retrieval failures are called *tip of the tongue states* (TOTs). Bilinguals are more likely to fall into a TOT when speaking in their nondominant language than in their dominant language (Ecke, 2004), and when speaking in their dominant language bilinguals have more TOTs than monolinguals speaking the one language they know (for an exception see Gollan & Brown, 2006). The increased rate of TOTs for bilinguals relative to monolinguals might seem quite obviously related to the increased potential for competition during bilingual language production.

Two central problems arise when trying to explain why bilinguals have more TOTs with the assumption of competition between languages. The first is that researchers of the TOT phenomenon have largely rejected the notion that TOTs arise because of competition for selection (Cross & Burke, 2004; James & Burke, 2000; Meyer & Bock, 1992), and have instead assumed that TOT failures arise during phonological encoding, and after competition for selection between semantically related lexical candidates has already been resolved (Levelt, 1989; Bock & Levelt, 1994). A second problem is that bilinguals often have TOTs for words that they know in just one language. When bilinguals do not know the target word in both languages, TOTs obviously

cannot be occurring because of direct competition for selection between translation-equivalent lexical representations. Even more problematic is that some aspects of TOT data imply that translation equivalents may prevent TOTs. The ability to retrieve translation equivalents seemed to significantly reduce TOTs one study (Gollan & Acenas, 2004), and in another study, a contingency analysis revealed that prior retrieval of a translation equivalent name significantly reduced TOTs in a task that required bilinguals to produce target names in both languages (switching languages on every trial; Gollan & Silverberg, 2001).

It might seem that bilinguals could nevertheless be having more TOTs because there is an increased generalized load on the lexical system given that the number of representations is roughly doubled compared with monolinguals. To test the generalized load hypothesis, Gollan, Bonanni, and Montoya (2005) asked if bilinguals would have more difficulty retrieving proper names than monolinguals. For monolinguals, most naturally occurring TOTs are for proper names, and proper-name production is notoriously difficult (Cohen & Burke, 1993; Valentine, Brennen, & Brédart, 1996). The aging-related increase in TOTs is considerably robust for proper name targets (Burke, MacKay, Worthley, & Wade, 1991; Evrard, 2002; Rastle & Burke, 1996), and if the effect of bilingualism on TOTs was driven by an increased generalized load, then bilinguals should also have had particular difficulty retrieving proper names. Alternatively, there may be no generalized load underlying bilinguals' increased TOT rate. If so, bilinguals might have a relatively easier time retrieving proper names, because they are effectively monolingual for proper names given that these are generally shared across languages (e.g., *Michele Miozzo* is called *Michele Miozzo* in Italian *and* in English). Replicating prior work, bilinguals had more TOTs than monolinguals for object names (e.g., *funnel*); however, both when asked to retrieve famous names (e.g., *Arnold Schwarzenegger*) and personal names (e.g., *who was your 7th grade math teacher?*), bilinguals were equally successful in their retrieval attempts as monolinguals (Gollan et al., 2005).

Bilinguals' ability to retrieve proper names provides evidence against the notion that bilingualism introduces an increased generalized load on the lexical retrieval system. This, along with their frequent rate of TOTs for object names that they know in just one language, further suggests that something other than competition between specific translation-equivalent lexical representations must be influencing TOT rates in bilinguals. However, several open questions remain. Frequency-lag and competition are mutually compatible alternatives. The data just reviewed suggest that competition cannot be the only reason why bilinguals have more TOTs, but it remains to be determined if competition might sometimes increase TOTs in bilingual speakers. To test this hypothesis, it is necessary to determine if bilinguals are more or less likely to have a TOT after they are primed with a translation equivalent name. This question is difficult to test because TOTs are more likely to occur with very difficult to retrieve (i.e., very low-frequency) target words, and these same types of targets are the ones bilinguals are less likely to know in both languages. Recent data strongly suggest that experimentally pre-exposing bilinguals to translation-equivalent primes leads them to have significantly more TOTs relative to unrelated control primes (Gollan, Ferreira, Cera, & Flett, in press). A second challenge with interpreting TOT evidence is that TOTs can sometimes reflect increased (not decreased) ability to access an intended target. That is, although TOTs are failed retrievals, after correct retrievals they represent the next-best possible outcome (of all retrieval failures they are the closest thing to a correct retrieval). Thus, bilinguals do not always have more TOTs than monolinguals; when the targets are very low frequency, the bilingual effect on TOTs reverses, and monolinguals have more TOTs than bilinguals, whereas bilinguals report not knowing the target words (Gollan & Brown, 2006). In future work it will be important to determine how translation primes increase TOT rates (is this an interference or a facilitation effect), and how spontaneous retrieval of translation equivalents (as opposed to experimentally provided presentation of translation equivalents) during a TOT influences likelihood of TOT resolution.

Bilingualism in Aging and Alzheimer Disease

Another challenge for the competition account is to explain why some aspects of bilingual language use seem to become easier in older age, and how bilinguals with clear deficits in executive control seem to nevertheless manage the supposedly difficult problem of controlling interference from the nontarget language. If we assume that bilinguals rely on general cognitive mechanisms to control competition between languages, an assumption that is needed to explain why bilinguals outperform monolinguals on some

nonlinguistic measures of cognitive control, then we should predict that bilinguals have more difficulty controlling competition between linguistic systems when such mechanisms decline in aging or with cognitive decline. From this perspective, research in this domain reveals some surprising findings.

A powerful way to examine the role of general control mechanisms for resolving competition between languages is to ask bilinguals to speak in their nondominant language. When bilinguals speak in the dominant language there may be differing degrees of interference depending on the task (e.g., competition from the nondominant language may not be possible for words that are known only in the dominant language). In contrast, bilinguals with one clearly dominant language should more consistently, and to a larger extent, need to rely on general control mechanisms to suppress the dominant language when speaking in the nondominant language. If so, bilinguals with impaired cognitive control mechanisms should have more difficulty speaking a nondominant language. In contrast, if cognitive control plays a relatively small role in allowing bilinguals to function fluently in two languages, and instead frequency is the major relevant factor, then older bilinguals should fare relatively better than young bilinguals, simply because older bilinguals have had relatively more time to accumulate frequency of use in both languages to the point of fluent and experienced retrieval in each language.

Gollan and colleagues addressed this question by asking young and older Spanish-English bilinguals who were matched for education level and ability to translate English into Spanish and vice versa to name pictures with high- and low-frequency names in each language (in counterbalanced order; Gollan et al., 2008). Inconsistent with the predictions of the interference account, in this study most bilinguals were English-dominant, and aging-related slowing was greater for English than it was for Spanish (i.e., the opposite of what the interference account would have predicted). In addition, consistent with the hypothesis that what is critical is frequency of use, older bilinguals named low-frequency pictures in Spanish slightly more *quickly* than young bilinguals. In all other conditions older bilinguals names pictures more slowly than young bilinguals. These results imply that frequency of use is a more important factor in gaining proficiency in two languages than cognitive control. Another way of stating this result is to say that age-related slowing was more robust in the dominant than in the nondominant language. This result could come about if increased age improves bilingual proficiency by increased frequency of use (over years in time) and this benefits the most difficult-to-learn words (lower-frequency words in the nondominant language) the most.

A more recent study reached similar conclusions this time comparing healthy aging bilinguals with proficiency-matched bilinguals with Alzheimer's disease (Gollan, Salmon, Montoya, & Da Pena, 2010). On the competition account, bilinguals should have increasing difficulty naming pictures in a nondominant language as the disease progresses given the deficits in executive control that often accompany the disease. Against the competition account, the difference between patients and controls was greater for *dominant* language production even though bilinguals in this study named significantly and substantially more pictures in their dominant than in their nondominant language. Because patients and controls were matched for age, in this case frequency of use cannot explain why the dominant language was more sensitive to group differences; instead, the effect here may be attributed to processes related to Alzheimer disease (i.e., degradation of semantic representations).

Another powerful way to ask about the role of executive control in bilingual language production is to ask whether bilinguals with executive control deficits have reduced control over which language they speak. If so, they might be expected to prefer avoiding language switching whenever possible, and they might mistakenly produce words in an unintended language more often than younger bilinguals. This approach is more powerful in some ways than comparing dominant with nondominant language production because deciding which language is dominant can be tricky, and alternative interpretations are possible (e.g., the dominant language may be more sensitive to between-group differences because performance in the dominant language is less variable than performance in the nondominant language). In this domain, the evidence for or against the competition account, and for the role of executive control in bilingual language production, is somewhat more mixed. Supporting the role of executive control, production of cross-language intrusion errors (i.e., failures of language control) increases as bilinguals get older (Gollan, Sandoval, & Salmon, 2011), and also in bilinguals with Alzheimer disease (Costa et al., 2012). However, the rate of language failures remains extremely low even in bilinguals with marked impairments in nonlinguistic executive control (1 percent on average, ranging from 0–3 percent of spoken responses; Gollan et al., 2011). The evidence in the domain

of intended language switches is similarly mixed. Although older bilinguals were less efficient than young bilinguals at cued and forced language switching (Hernandez & Kohnert, 1999; Weissberger, Wierenga, Bondi, & Gollan, 2012), when tested in a voluntary switching paradigm (Gollan & Ferreira, 2009), few or no aging deficits in switching efficiency were observed and older bilinguals chose to switch languages as often as younger bilinguals. Together these findings support a role for executive control in bilingual language production, but also imply the presence of language-specific control mechanisms that may remain largely intact in aging, and with some forms of cognitive impairment.

Section Summary

Although the frequency-lag account cannot explain advantages in nonlinguistic control tasks, the studies just reviewed imply that these advantages might arise despite the fact that bilingual lexical production is marked by reduced frequency. The studies reviewed in this section also demonstrate the use of the frequency-lag hypothesis as an alternative framework for explaining differences between bilinguals and monolinguals on speaking-related tasks in cases where competition between languages seems very unlikely. This broadened view of the consequences of bilingualism as arising from multiple possible sources also increases the potential relevance of research on bilingualism for understanding language processing in general. In recent work (Gollan, Slattery, et al., 2011) we have argued that bilingual disadvantages appear to be more robust in production than in comprehension, a result that on its face seems to support the competition account given that in speaking (but not in comprehension) bilinguals are faced with direct competition, ultimately needing to choose one or the other languages in which to speak. However, what the bilingual disadvantages in this study ultimately revealed was a larger role for frequency (perhaps influencing multiple processing stages) in production but not in comprehension and *for all speakers* (bilinguals and monolinguals alike), extending beyond the specific question about how bilinguals control which language they use when they speak, and illustrating how bilinguals provide an informative thread to follow in trying to uncover the fundamental properties of human language production.

Evidence Supporting Competition between Languages

Although the evidence reviewed above on the reduced-frequency model provides an account for a range of phenomena in bilingual production, there are other contexts in which the evidence is more easily understood by assuming that those alternatives across the bilingual's two languages compete for selection. The later discussion returns to the issue of whether these two accounts are genuine alternatives or, as already suggested, characterize different aspects of speech planning. A critical observation in recent work (e.g., Kroll et al., 2008; Linck et al., 2009) is that the requirement to modulate the potential competition that arises when alternatives are activated in both languages may have the consequence of selectively affecting the dominant or native language. If the dominant language must be ignored or suppressed to enable production in the nondominant language, there may be momentary or sustained inhibition that produces a pattern of performance consistent with the reduced-frequency account. The evidence that has been taken to support the idea that there is cross-language competition in production is reviewed next.

Cross-language Interactions in Bilingual Speech Planning

When bilinguals plan to speak words in one language alone, there is abundant evidence suggesting that alternatives in the other language are available and influence speech planning. That evidence has been reviewed in a number of papers and chapters (e.g., Costa, 2005; Hanulová, Davidson, & Indefrey, 2011; Kroll et al., 2006; and see Runnqvist, Strijkers, & Costa, this volume). A curious aspect of the work on bilingual speech planning is that it seems that it should be possible in principle to select the language of production in advance. Models that assume that this is possible (e.g., La Heij, 2005) have relied primarily on evidence from production in the L1, a context that may not provide the most sensitive test. As noted next, advance knowledge of the language to be spoken does not appear to eliminate the influence of the language not in use. Likewise, experience with languages that differ in their form or modality does also not prevent the activation of the unintended language (e.g., Emmorey, Borinstein, Thompson, & Gollan, 2008; Hoshino & Kroll, 2008).

Several different approaches have been taken to determine whether and to what level the language not in use is activated during speech planning. One approach is similar to the logic that has demonstrated language nonselectivity in word recognition (e.g., Dijkstra, 2005; Marian & Spivey, 2003). If the target production is language ambiguous, in

that speech planning in one language is likely to activate features shared with the other language, then bilinguals, but not monolinguals, should be sensitive to the presence of those features. For example, bilinguals are faster to name pictures whose names are cognates across their two languages (e.g., Colomé & Miozzo, 2010; Costa, Caramazza, & Sebastián-Gallés, 2000; Hoshino & Kroll, 2008), presumably because parallel activation of the phonology of the name and its translation converge to produce facilitation. Using event-related potentials (ERPs), Strijkers, Costa, and Thierry (2010) recently demonstrated that these cognate effects appear early in bilingual speech planning, suggesting that they may reflect an induced word frequency effect rather than genuine parallel activation of the two languages. However, the increased functional frequency for cognates has to originate in a process that itself requires the activation of both languages to the level of the phonology. Other studies that have examined the activation of cross-language phonology in speech planning have shown that bilinguals are sensitive to the phonology of the nontarget language even when the translations are not cognates (e.g., Colomé, 2001).

A second approach to demonstrating the presence of activation of the nontarget language during speech planning is to use Stroop-type picture-word interference tasks in which distractors are presented in the language not in use and the question is whether bilinguals can effectively filter those distractors to produce monolingual-like utterances. The results of initial behavioral studies taking this approach (e.g., Costa, Miozzo, & Caramazza, 1999; Hermans, Bongaerts, De Bot, & Schreuder, 1998) suggested that distractor words in the language not in use had effects that were largely similar to the effects of distractor words in the target language. More recent ERP studies have produced similar evidence for cross-language activation in production and for the presence of these effects relatively early in the time course of speech planning (e.g., Hoshino & Thierry, 2011). A counterintuitive finding in the cross-language picture-word Stroop studies is that the presence of a distractor word that itself is the translation of the picture's name produces facilitation rather than interference (e.g., Costa et al., 1999). Costa et al. took that result as evidence against competition for selection because the translation of the picture's name should be the strongest possible competitor and yet it produced facilitation. Although the competition account might not have predicted translation facilitation effects a priori, the finding of translation facilitation within the picture-word Stroop paradigm does not itself adjudicate between alternative theoretical claims (Hermans, 2004). Indeed, the presence of words as distractors in the picture-word Stroop paradigm makes it difficult to identify the direction of the observed effects. They could be driven by the bottom-up processing of the lexical distractors, by the top-down initiation of speech planning engaged by the picture, or by an interaction between the two.

A third type of logic that has been applied to the problem of cross-language activation is to manipulate the requirement to use both languages. If bilinguals activate both languages when they plan to speech in one language only, then requiring that both languages be active should have little impact on performance. Behavioral, ERP, and functional magnetic resonance imaging (fMRI) studies have taken this approach to compare mixed with blocked picture naming (e.g., Christoffels, Firk, & Schiller, 2007; Guo, Liu, Misra, & Kroll, 2011; Kroll, Dijkstra, Janssen, & Schriefers, 2000) and studies of lexical switching have investigated the trial-to-trial consequences of switches of language (e.g., Costa & Santesteban, 2004; Meuter & Allport, 1999). The main result is that there appears to be a differential cost to the L1 when the L2 is required to be active or just precedes the L1, but the L2 remains relatively unaffected or less affected by the mixed conditions. Although there is debate about the interpretation of the lexical switching data (e.g., Gollan & Ferreira, 2009; Verhoef, Roelofs, & Chwilla, 2009), there are three features of the resulting data that are notable. First, the lack of dramatic effects for the L2 under the mixed/switched conditions suggests that the L1 is active even without the requirement for it to be engaged. Second, the significant cost to the L1 in the mixed conditions relative to blocked L1 naming suggests that the skill associated with the normal blocked production in the native or dominant language may allow L1 speech to be planned without the influence of the L2, unless the L2 is deliberately activated. A focus in recent comparisons of bilingual speech in the L1 versus L2 has been to understand why the L2 is slower than the L1 (e.g., Hanulová et al., 2011; Runnqvist et al., 2011). Although there is some disagreement about the locus of the apparent L2 deficit and whether it reflects slower lexical retrieval, as the frequency-lag account might suggest, greater vulnerability to competition from both other L2 alternatives and the L1, or less skill in specifying the L2 phonology, or some combination of these mechanisms, it seems clear

that the slower time course associated with the L2 makes it less likely to affect the L1 under normal blocked conditions when the more dominant L1 is spoken. However, the final result, and the one that we now focus on in the remaining discussion within this section, is that there is dramatic interference in L1 production when the L2 is required to be active, by virtue of uncertainty about the language to be spoken (e.g., Kroll et al., 2000), when there is a trial-to-trial switch from the L2 into the L1 (e.g., Meuter & Allport, 1999), and when a block of L1 naming trials follows naming in the L2 (e.g., Guo et al., 2011; Misra, Guo, Bobb, & Kroll, 2012). That disruption to L1 production demonstrates that even speech planning in the dominant L1 is open to influence by the L2. At issue is how to interpret the function of that disruption.

Evidence for Inhibition of the L1

The inhibitory control model (Green, 1998) accounted for the initial observation of asymmetries in switch-cost following lexical switching into the L1 by assuming that the requirement to control L1 activation during L2 speech planning leads to inhibition of L1 candidates. When L1 is subsequently required to be spoken, there is a momentary suppression that must first be overcome. This sort of inhibition would be relatively local, affecting the target words and perhaps their semantic relatives. Following the initial demonstration of a switch-cost asymmetry in language switching by Meuter and Allport (1999), there were several challenges to the interpretation that inhibition is the mechanism responsible for the asymmetry (e.g., Finkbeiner, Almeida, Janssen, & Caramazza, 2006; Verhoef et al., 2009). Similar challenges were outlined against inhibition interpretations of switch-cost asymmetries outside the bilingual literature (e.g., Yeung & Monsell, 2003). The asymmetry itself could be shown to come and go depending on the nature of the mappings to responses (e.g., Finkbeiner et al., 2006), whether the decision to switch was forced or voluntary (e.g., Gollan & Ferreira, 2009), whether there was time to plan the switch (e.g., Verhoef et al., 2009), and whether or not the bilingual speaker was highly proficient (e.g., Costa & Santesteban, 2004). Because the assessment of switch-costs occurs in the context of a mixed language list, it is also perhaps not surprising that in many of these switching studies, regardless of whether an asymmetric pattern of costs is found, language dominance fully reverses such that the time to speak the L1 is slower than the time to speak the L2 (Christoffels et al., 2007;

Costa & Santesteban, 2004; Gollan & Ferreira, 2009; Verhoef et al., 2009). That pattern held even for Costa and Santesteban's highly balanced and proficient bilinguals who failed to produce an asymmetric pattern of switch-costs. One hypothesis is that the delay in naming under these mixed conditions is the genuine index of L1 inhibition. To the extent that the L1 is typically advantaged relative to the L2 (e.g., Hanulovà et al., 2011; Runnqvist et al., 2011), the observed cost to the L1 in the mixed conditions is likely to be an underestimate of the actual costs. That is, because L1 is normally faster than L2 under blocked naming conditions, the reversal in the mixed conditions that produces slower naming times for L1 than L2 is likely to underestimate the true costs.

Several studies have taken a different approach in examining the hypothesized inhibition of the L1 in mixed language contexts. Here we focus on recent evidence from blocked naming paradigms (see also Philipp, Gade, & Koch, 2007, and Philipp & Koch, 2009, for evidence from the N-2 repetition paradigm). Although the language of naming is forced in these blocked paradigms, unlike the lexical switching paradigms, there is an opportunity for bilinguals to speak each language over a longer period of time, making the switching from one language to the other more similar to the type of switching in which a bilingual might engage during the normal course of a day. Misra et al. (2012) performed an ERP experiment in which relatively proficient Chinese-English bilinguals named pictures in Chinese and in English in separate blocks of trials. Either two blocks of Chinese naming were followed by two blocks of English naming, or vice versa, thus L2 following L1 or L1 following L2. Critically, the pictures named in each language were identical. Misra et al. predicted that the identical pictures should produce repetition priming across languages (e.g., Francis & Sáenz, 2007; Hernandez & Reyes, 2002). For naming in L2, the data supported the predictions. The ERP record was less negative when L2 followed L1, a pattern consistent with facilitation, and the behavioral responses were faster. However, for naming in L1, the opposite pattern emerged, with greater negativity in the ERP record when the L1 was named in the second set of blocks following the L2, and no evidence of facilitation in the behavioral data. Because the pictures were identical in the two languages, it was impossible to determine the scope of the observed inhibition for L1. However, the inclusion of two blocks of naming in each language made it possible to identify,

within limits, the time course of inhibition. What was notable in the Misra et al. data was that there was no immediate recovery of the L1 after a few trials of L1 naming. When L1 followed L2, there was long-lasting inhibition into the subsequent block. Misra et al. speculated that the long-lasting consequences for L1 naming following L2 appeared to be more consistent with a global than a local mechanism of inhibition (van Assche, Duyck, & Gollan, in press, reached similar conclusions based on testing order effects using a verbal fluency task).

In a related study, Guo et al. (2011) examined blocked picture naming performance in the two orders of naming used by Misra et al. (2012) but using fMRI and comparing the blocked naming performance with mixed naming. They found distinct patterns of brain activity for the two languages for mixing versus blocking and for the two languages. The dorsal anterior cingulate cortex and the supplementary motor area appeared to play important roles in mixed language naming, whereas the dorsal left frontal gyrus and parietal cortex appeared to be engaged during blocking. Like the ERP results of Misra et al., there was more activation comparing the mixed and blocked conditions for the L1 than for the L2.

The results of these two studies suggest that the L1 may be inhibited when preparing speech in the L2 and that the resulting inhibition may extend over time. Contrary to the claim that only second language learners who are relatively unskilled in the L2 rely on inhibitory mechanisms (e.g., Costa & Santesteban, 2004), these data reflect the performance of relatively proficient bilinguals. However, the question of how learners negotiate these processes and how they come to be able to speak the weaker L2 at all in face of a dominant L1 has important implications for models of bilingual production and for developing fluent L2 speech. A recent study by Linck et al. (2009) examined the performance of a group of US college students who were studying abroad in Spain. The students were all native English speakers learning Spanish as the L2 and at an intermediate level of L2 proficiency. They performed a comprehension task, translation recognition, and a production task, semantic fluency. In each task, relative to a matched control group of classroom learners at home, the immersed learners were less sensitive to L1. In the semantic fluency task, they generated as many exemplars as they could speak in a 30-second interval in each language. Unsurprisingly, the immersed learners were able to generate more words in Spanish than the classroom learners. Although both groups of learners generated more words overall in English than in Spanish, consistent with their marked dominance in English, the immersed learners produced significantly fewer English words than the classroom learners. Together with their insensitivity to lexical foils in English in the comprehension task, the reduced level of English production in the semantic fluency task was interpreted as inhibition of the native language (see Levy, McVeigh, Marful, & Anderson, 2007 for a similar result in a retrieval induced forgetting experiment; but see Runnqvist et al., in press).

The studies reviewed included proficient bilinguals and second language learners and a range of measures from ERPs that reflect the earliest stages of speech planning, to behavioral measures of latency and accuracy that reflect the aggregated result of those early processes, and fMRI measures that distinguish the localization of function associated with different tasks in each language. In each case, there was evidence for inhibition of the more dominant L1. We make no claims at present for the scope of the observed inhibition because it requires experiments that are underway to determine precisely what is inhibited in the L1 and how long that inhibitory pattern lasts. It is quite possible that there are both local and global components of inhibition (see De Groot & Christoffels, 2006, for a discussion of these processes in translation) and that the modulation of these components differs for learners and for proficient bilinguals; for speakers of structurally similar or dissimilar languages (Van Assche et al., under review); and under conditions that may impose particular processing requirements, such as simultaneous interpretation (e.g., Ibáñez, Macizo, & Bajo, 2010). The finding of persistent L1 inhibition is not predicted by a reduced frequency account (nor does it provide evidence for or against it), but is generally consistent with recent imaging studies that demonstrate the activation of cognitive control areas during bilingual speech (e.g., Abutalebi et al., 2008; Abutalebi & Green, 2007; Festman, 2012; Garbin et al., 2010; Luo, Luk, & Bialystok, 2010). These issues are discussed later after we consider a final source of evidence for inhibitory processes in bilingual speech.

Acoustic Measures of Produced Speech Reflect L1 Inhibition

There is a long tradition of using measures of produced speech to assess aspects of L2 proficiency, such as the degree of accentedness of nonnative speech (e.g., Piske, MacKay, & Flege, 2001). In contrast, there is little research that examines the consequences of higher level language processes on the realization of speech itself. In part, this gap in the literature may reflect the traditional assumption of serial and discrete models of language production that speech planning is complete at the point where articulation begins (e.g., Levelt, 1989; Levelt, Roelofs, & Meyer, 1999). Models of production that assume cascaded processing and interaction between stages of speech planning (e.g., Dell, 1986; Rapp & Goldrick, 2000) can more easily accommodate the case in which articulation may be initiated on the basis of an underspecified plan. An initial study by Kello, Plaut, and MacWhinney (2000) examined the hypothesis that the variables that affect speech planning might influence articulation under conditions in which stress is imposed. Kello et al. compared the performance of speakers under conditions of time stress or normal speech in a Stroop paradigm. Under normal speech conditions, they found the typical Stroop effect in response latencies but no Stroop effects in measures of articulatory duration. When speech was stressed, there were Stroop effects in both measures of duration and in reaction times (RTs), suggesting that there was spillover into the realization of speech when it was impossible to complete planning in advance (see Damian, 2003, for a failure to replicate this pattern). Likewise, Goldrick and Blumstein (2006) reported a similar spillover effect into articulation using a different method of inducing stress on the speaker, in this case by having them produce tongue twisters.

When monolingual speakers produce speech in their native language, the skill associated with speech planning may typically allow them to complete planning before articulation. For L2 learners and bilinguals, there may be circumstances under which they are required to speak before planning is complete or in contexts in which the juggling of cross-language activity imposes functional stress of the sort observed in the monolingual studies. Only a few past studies have investigated the consequence of cross-language activation for articulation (e.g., Engstler & Goldrick, 2007). Here we review two recently completed studies related to those described previously in which we used digital recordings of speech in L1 and L2 to ask whether the evidence for inhibition of the L1 that was observed in the ERP and behavioral data would also be seen in the acoustic measures of produced speech.

Gerfen et al. (in preparation) recorded the performance of relatively proficient Chinese-English bilinguals during an ERP study similar to the one described previously by Misra et al. (2012). The design was improved by including an interpolated picture naming block so that bilinguals either named pictures in L1, L2, and then L1, or in L2, L1, and then L2. The third picture naming block included some tokens repeated from the initial naming block and some repeated from the second naming block, so it was possible to begin to assess the scope of any observed inhibition. When L2 was named before and after L1, there was no change in articulatory duration. When L1 was named after L2, durations were significantly longer relative to the first block of L1, again suggesting an inhibition of L1 following L2, but in this instance, lasting into the actual realization of speech. The inhibitory effect was observed for both identical and nonidentical tokens.

A possible alternative explanation for the observed pattern is that L2 speech is simply more difficult than L1 speech. If a more-skilled task follows a less-skilled task, even for relatively proficient bilinguals, then the more-skilled task may suffer the spillover from the less-skilled task. Yudes, Kroll, and Guo (in preparation) tested this alternative in a similar picture naming paradigm but in which monolinguals named pictures in their native language, English, in each of three blocks. In the interpolated block, instead of naming pictures in an L2, the pictures were presented in different orientations and the monolinguals had to name them in the same way that they had named the canonically presented pictures. The time to name the noncanonically presented pictures was indeed longer than the time to name pictures that were normally oriented, suggesting that the task imposed additional processing difficulty. However, unlike the bilingual results, there was no inhibition in the measures of articulatory duration. If anything, there was facilitation in the form of shorter durations for repeated pictures in the final block. Taken together with the bilingual data, these results suggest that the inhibitory effects observed in L1 following naming in the L2 were due to the manner in which cross-language competition was resolved and not to processing difficulty per se.

Linck et al. (2009) showed that immersed L2 learners studying abroad in Spain produced fewer words in a semantic fluency task in English, their native language, than their classroom counterparts in the United States. The reduced fluency in the L1 was interpreted as a reflection of the inhibition of the native language. The number of words alone, however, does not provide an optimally sensitive measure of what precisely is suppressed under these conditions. Gerfen, Tam, McClain, Linck, and Kroll (in preparation) performed a detailed acoustic analysis of these data to determine whether the apparent L1 inhibition was a momentary phenomenon, quickly overturned once speaking in L1 was engaged, or an enduring property of the L1 in the immersion context. Using the approach developed by Rohrer, Wixted, Salmon, and Butters (1995) that has recently been adopted to examine cognitive control processes in bilinguals (Luo et al., 2010; Sandoval et al., 2010), Gerfen et al. analyzed the time course of production within the 30-second response interval. The analysis revealed that immersed learners not only produced fewer words overall in L1 relative to the classroom controls, but were also slower to begin to speak English, produced fewer words in English at all points across the 30-second trial, and had longer pauses between spoken words in English than classroom-only learners. The immersed learners were also less likely than the classroom control participants to intrude English when they performed the task in Spanish. What is notable is that the participants in these studies were native and dominant English speakers who were only moderately proficient in Spanish. Critically, the verbal fluency task itself is under the control of the speaker. Unlike the picture naming results of Misra et al. (2012), the fluency study did not require production of the same words in both languages. The appearance suppression of the L1 early in the verbal fluency trial (i.e., in the first 5 seconds) and its persistence throughout production of the list and across different words and categories is consistent with an interpretation of global inhibition of the native language. If this sort of inhibitory process can be observed in the short term, during immersion experiences of 6 months or less, then the implication is that individuals who are immersed for longer periods of time or permanently may show significant changes in language dominance that may be related to the observation of language attrition (e.g., Schmid, 2010).

Section Summary

In this section we have reviewed the evidence for cross-language activation when bilinguals plan to speak even a single word in only one of their two languages. Taken together, the available data suggest that both languages are engaged during speech planning, even for highly proficient bilinguals. It might not be surprising to discover that the L1 is engaged when bilinguals begin to plan speech in the L2. The deficits associated with production of the L2 (e.g., Hanulovà et al., 2011; Runnqvist & Costa, 2012) make the process of planning speech in the L2 more open to the influence of the L1 and to the influences of other contextual factors. However, the profile of bilingual production that we have presented suggests that both languages are affected by a speaker's bilingualism. The evidence presented in the first section of the chapter demonstrated that there may be reduced frequency for bilinguals relative to monolinguals in each of their two languages. The evidence presented in the second section of the chapter showed that the L1 may be inhibited to enable production of the weaker L2. Although the available data allow only preliminary speculation about the scope and time course of the observed inhibitory effects, and there may very well be multiple contributions to these effects that differ in scope and time course, they suggest at the least that there may be inhibition of the L1 that is more global and enduring than previously understood. In the final discussion we consider whether these alternative accounts of bilingual production with respect to frequency and/or inhibitory processes are necessarily mutually exclusive and we ask how well each account relates to recent claims about the consequences of bilingualism for cognitive control.

Discussion and Conclusions

This chapter began with two observations: bilinguals are not identical to monolinguals, even in their native language; and the native language changes in response to the active use of the L2. The goal was to bring together two alternative accounts of bilingual production that have been considered to be at odds with one another. If the disadvantages associated with bilingual speech can be understood as a consequence of reduced functional frequency in each of the bilingual's two languages, then perhaps it is not necessary to posit a mechanism of cross-language competition. The results presented in the first section of the chapter provide a compelling account of why bilingual speech may be characterized in terms of a frequency-lag (or weaker links) relative to monolingual speech. That account not only explains the apparent deficits observed for young adult bilinguals but also for healthy elderly bilinguals and for elderly bilinguals affected by the onset of dementia (Bialystok, Craik, & Freedman, 2007).

The second section of the chapter reviewed the evidence that suggests that there is activation of information in both of the bilingual's two languages when words are spoken in one language alone.

That evidence has been hypothesized to create cross-language competition that requires resolution to produce fluent speech but that also holds consequences for language use for the native language and for the L2. A notable omission in our review is the class of models that have been referred to as "mental fire wall" models (e.g., Kroll, Bogulski, & McClain, 2012) in that they assume that although information about both languages may be activated in parallel, the resulting cross-language alternatives are not hypothesized to compete for selection (e.g., Costa et al., 1999; Finkbeiner et al., 2006). On this view, bilinguals are able to ignore the activation of candidates in the language not in use to select only from among target alternatives. Some have argued that this sort of firewall model requires bilinguals to establish a principled basis on which the language in use can be identified (e.g., Kroll et al., 2008; Kroll et al., 2012). The problem with the firewall account is that there is very little evidence to demonstrate that bilinguals are able to exploit language cues that might enable them to establish such a separation between their two languages (e.g., Emmorey et al., 2008; Hoshino & Kroll, 2008; Schwartz & Kroll, 2006). Bilinguals appear to activate both languages and to experience the consequences of that activation regardless of whether they have prior information or context that strongly biases them to one language, regardless of whether the two languages themselves have features that enable such a separation to be more readily available, and regardless of whether it is beneficial or costly to processing. Aside from the feasibility of a selection mechanism that is biased toward one class of activated candidates relative to another, any sort of mechanism that enables separation must be based on a demonstration that it is possible to attend selectively to establish those class divisions.

The comparison of the two lines of research we have reviewed suggests a new hypothesis that has not, to our knowledge, been considered in the previous literature. It is possible that the repeated inhibition of the L1 is related to the observed reduced frequency of the L1. The L2 may independently suffer from reduced frequency relative to the L1 and relative to monolingual speech for reasons related to the nature and context of L2 learning and as the recent discussion of L2 disadvantages makes clear, there may be multiple loci in processing that account for the L2 deficit (e.g., Hanulovà et al., 2011; Runnqvist et al., 2011). The studies reviewed previously that support the frequency-lag hypothesis demonstrate that it is the low-frequency rather than high-frequency portion of the lexicon that is differentially reduced in bilinguals. It might seem that inhibition of the L1 in bilingual speech planning would differentially affect high-frequency vocabulary because those are the competitors that are most dominant and likely to interference in L2 speech. However, the profile of inhibitory effects we have presented suggests, at least based on the evidence to date, that inhibition is more global than local. The suppression of the entire language, for whatever time course it follows, may be differentially damaging to low-frequency and vulnerable aspects of the lexicon.

In the context of this discussion, it may also be important to recognize that there is compelling evidence for language convergence when the bilingual's two languages differ in their lexical mappings and grammatical commitments (e.g., Ameel, Storms, Malt, & Sloman, 2005; Dussias, 2003). What the research on convergence shows is not simply that there is transfer from the stronger L1 to the weaker L2 (e.g., Kroll & Stewart, 1994; MacWhinney, 2005) but that there is an accommodation of the two languages that reflects mutual adjustments. Language convergence makes clear that bilinguals are truly not two monolinguals in one (e.g., Grosjean, 1989). It is important to understand the consequences of those adjustments for lexical frequency, particularly when bilingualism imposes a shift in the way that concepts are mapped to their respective names. By this account, reduced frequency in each of the bilingual's languages may be less a matter of having less time and fewer opportunities to use each of the languages relative to monolingual experience, but rather a reflection of the interactions across the two languages. Ironically, it may be the increased vulnerability of the L1 that enables proficient use of the two languages to develop, to allow for relatively fluent and error-free speech and also code switching under appropriate circumstances (e.g., Kroll, Dussias, Bogulski, & Valdes-Kroff, 2012).

The research we have reviewed on bilingual production might be viewed from some perspectives as the downside of the story. Aside from the many rather obvious and immediately compelling advantages associated with being able to speak more than one language (i.e., the ability to communicate with a broader audience), there is now an impressive body of literature on the upside of bilingualism, showing that a life of using two languages may confer positive consequences to domain-general executive function skills (see Bialystok et al., 2009, for a recent review). As we noted at the start, a challenge

for the research on bilingual production is to determine whether the mechanisms that allow proficient speech in each language and that modulate the language selection process are causally related to the development of enhanced cognitive control. Although there is debate on the scope of bilingual advantages, it seems clear from the emerging work that there are benefits for the youngest crib bilinguals to young adult bilinguals and to elderly bilinguals relative to the matched monolinguals. It also seems clear that the cognitive benefits of bilingualism will ultimately be explicitly related to precisely what bilinguals do when they manage coactivation of and shifting between languages (e.g., Prior & Gollan, 2011; Weissberger et al., 2012). What is not yet certain is how many different components of executive function may be affected by bilingualism and how the network of brain regions that are sensitive to the effects of bilingual experience represent the contributions of different types of language processing consequences.

It is beyond the scope of this chapter to review the recent imaging evidence in detail. However, it is useful in this context in which we have considered the mechanisms that may allow proficient speech in the bilingual's two languages to ask whether different accounts of speech planning might produce consequences that would result in the observed domain-general cognitive benefits. The mental firewall account that was effectively rejected in the previous discussion provides one such alternative. If bilinguals are able to learn to attend selectively to the target language and identify with high accuracy the language not in use, then negotiating that separation may produce consequences that might be beneficial to domain-general functions, such as task switching and ignoring irrelevant information. It is interesting to note that the research on young infants with bilingual exposure suggests that they are indeed sensitive to the subtle cues that differentiate the two languages that they hear (e.g., Kovács & Mehler, 2009; Werker & Byers-Heinlein, 2008). In contrast, as we noted in the earlier discussion, there is little evidence for similar sensitivity by adult bilinguals.

The frequency-lag hypothesis characterizes the accessibility of words in each of the bilingual's two languages but this mechanism by itself, without the assumption of an additional mechanism, simply cannot provide an account of the documented cognitive advantages, and it also cannot explain how bilinguals do what they do (i.e., speak and control production of two languages). As noted in the earlier discussion, we do not yet have an adequate understanding of the scope or time course over which words, meanings, or an entire language may be suppressed momentarily or for an extended time. However, the need to activate one alternative in the face of a more dominant option appears to engage active cognitive mechanisms that might produce exercise effects of the sort that have been reported. For a topic that has been mistakenly ignored in the past, research on bilingual speech planning holds great promise for illuminating the relations between language processing and its cognitive and neural consequences.

References

Abutalebi, J., Annoni, J. M., Zimine, I., Pegna, A. J., Seghier, M. L., Lee-Jahnke, H., Khateb, A. (2008). Language control and lexical competition in bilinguals: An event-related fMRI study. *Cerebral Cortex, 18*, 1496–1505.

Abutalebi, J., & Green, D. (2007). Bilingual language production: The neurocognition of language representation and control. *Journal of Neurolinguistics, 20*, 242–275.

Almeida, J., Knobel, M., Finkbeiner, M., & Caramazza, A. (2007). The locus of the frequency effect in picture naming: When recognizing is not enough. *Psychonomic Bulletin & Review, 14*, 1177–1182.

Ameel, E., Storms, G., Malt, B. C., & Sloman, S. A. (2005). How bilinguals solve the naming problem. *Journal of Memory and Language, 53*, 60–80.

Balota, D. A., Pilotti, M., & Cortese, M. J. (2001). Subjective frequency estimates for 2,938 monosyllabic words. *Memory & Cognition, 29*, 639–647.

Bialystok, E., Craik, F. I. M., & Freedman, M. (2007). Bilingualism as a protection against the onset of symptoms of dementia. *Neuropsychologia, 45*, 459–464.

Bialystok, E., Craik, F. I. M., Green, D. W., & Gollan, T. H. (2009). Bilingual minds. *Psychological Science in the Public Interest, 10*, 89–129.

Bialystok, E., Craik, F. I. M., & Luk, G. (2008). Cognitive control and lexical access in younger and older bilinguals. *Journal of Experimental Psychology: Learning, Memory, and Cognition, 34*, 859–873.

Bialystok, E., Luk, G., Peets, K. F., & Yang, S. (2010). Receptive vocabulary differences in monolingual and bilingual children. *Bilingualism: Language and Cognition, 13*, 525–531.

Bock, K., & Levelt, W. (1994). Language production: Grammatical encoding. In M. Traxler & M. A. Gernsbacher (Eds.), *Handbook of psycholinguistics* (pp. 945–984). San Diego, CA: Academic Press.

Burke, D. M., MacKay, D. G., Worthley, J. S., & Wade, E. (1991). On the tip of the tongue: What causes word finding failures in young and older adults. *Journal of Memory and Language, 30*, 542–579.

Christoffels, I. K., Firk, C., & Schiller, N. O. (2007). Bilingual language control: An event-related brain potential study. *Brain Research, 1147*, 192–208.

Cohen, G., & Burke, D. M. (1993). Memory for proper names: A review. *Memory, 1*, 249–263.

Colomé, A. (2001). Lexical activation in bilinguals' speech production: Language-specific or language-independent? *Journal of Memory and Language, 45*, 721–736.

Colomé, A., & Miozzo, M. (2010). Which words are activated during bilingual word production? *Journal of Experimental Psychology: Learning, Memory, and Cognition, 36*, 96–109.

Costa, A. (2005). Lexical access in bilingual production. In J. F. Kroll & A. M. B. De Groot (Eds.), *Handbook of bilingualism: Psycholinguistic approaches* (pp. 308–325). New York: Oxford University Press.

Costa, A., Calabria, M., Marne, P., Hernández, M., Juncadella, M., Gascón-Bayarri, J., Reñe, R. (2012). On the parallel deterioration of lexico-semantic processes in the bilinguals' two languages: Evidence from Alzheimer's disease, *Neuropsychologia, 50*, 740–753.

Costa, A., Caramazza, A., & Sebastián-Gallés, N. (2000). The cognate facilitation effect: Implications for models of lexical access. *Journal of Experimental Psychology: Learning, Memory, and Cognition, 26*, 1283–1296.

Costa, A., Miozzo, M., & Caramazza, A. (1999). Lexical selection in bilinguals: Do words in the bilingual's two lexicons compete for selection? *Journal of Memory and Language, 41*, 365–397.

Costa, A., & Santesteban, M. (2004). Lexical access in bilingual speech production: Evidence from language switching in highly proficient bilinguals and L2 learners. *Journal of Memory and Language, 50*, 491–511.

Cross, E. S., & Burke, D. M. (2004). Do alternative names block young and older adults retrieval of proper names? *Brain and Language, 89*, 174–181.

Damian, M. F. (2003). Articulatory duration in single word speech production. *Journal of Experimental Psychology: Learning, Memory, and Cognition, 29*, 416–431.

De Groot, A. M. B., & Christoffels, I. K. (2006). Language control in bilinguals: Monolingual tasks and simultaneous interpreting. *Bilingualism: Language and Cognition, 9*, 189–201.

Dell, G. S. (1986). A spreading activation theory of retrieval in sentence production. *Psychological Review, 93*, 283–321.

Dijkstra, T. (2005). Bilingual word recognition and lexical access. In J. F. Kroll & A. M. B. De Groot (Eds.), *Handbook of bilingualism: Psycholinguistic approaches* (pp. 179–201). New York: Oxford University Press.

Dussias, P. E. (2003). Syntactic ambiguity resolution in L2 learners: Some effects of bilinguality on LI and L2 processing strategies. *Studies in Second Language Acquisition, 25*, 529–557.

Duyck, W., Vanderelst, D., Desmet, T., & Hartsuiker, R. J. (2008). The frequency-effect in second-language visual word recognition. *Psychonomic Bulletin & Review, 15*, 850–855.

Ecke, P. (2004). Words on the tip of the tongue: A study of lexical retrieval failures in Spanish-English bilinguals. *Southwest Journal of Linguistics, 23*, 1–31.

Emmorey, K., Borinstein, H. B., Thompson, R. L., & Gollan, T. H. (2008). Bimodal bilingualism. *Bilingualism: Language and Cognition, 11*, 43–61.

Emmorey, K., Luk, G., Pyers, J. E., & Bialystok, E. (2008). The source of enhanced cognitive control in bilinguals. *Psychological Science, 19*, 1201–1206.

Engstler, C., & Goldrick, M. (2007, September). *Lexically conditioned variation across languages*. Poster presented at the 4th International Workshop on Language Production, Muenster, Germany.

Evrard, M. (2002). Ageing and lexical access to common and proper names in picture naming. *Brain and Language, 81*, 174–179.

Festman, J. (2012). Language control abilities of late bilinguals. *Bilingualism: Language and Cognition, 15*, 580–593.

Finkbeiner, M., Almeida, J., Janssen, N., & Caramazza, A. (2006). Lexical selection in bilingual speech production does not involve language suppression. *Journal of Experimental Psychology: Learning, Memory and Cognition, 32*, 1075–1089.

Finkbeiner, M., Gollan, T., & Caramazza, A. (2006). Bilingual lexical access: What's the (hard) problem? *Bilingualism: Language and Cognition, 9*, 153–166.

Francis, W. S., & Sáenz, S. P. (2007). Repetition priming endurance in picture naming and translation: Contributions of component processes. *Memory & Cognition, 35*, 481–493.

Garbin, G., Sanjuan, A., Forn, C. Bustamante, J. C., Rodriguez-Pujadas, A., Belloch V., Avila, C. (2010). Bridging language and attention: Brain basis of the impact of bilingualism on cognitive control. *NeuroImage, 53*, 1272–1278.

Gerfen, C., Kroll, J. F., Poepsel, T., Tam, J., Guo, T., & Misra, M. (in preparation). *Blocked naming yields evidence for global inhibition in both the planning and production of speech.*

Gerfen, C., Tam, J., McClain, R. R., Linck, J. A., & Kroll, J. F. (in preparation). *Evidence for inhibition in native language production during immersion in the second language.*

Goldrick, M., & Blumstein, S. E. (2006). Cascading activation from phonological planning to articulatory processes: Evidence from tongue twisters. *Language and Cognitive Processes, 21*, 649–683.

Gollan, T. H., & Acenas, L.-A. R. (2004). What is a TOT? Cognate and translation effects on tip-of-the-tongue states in Spanish-English and Tagalog-English bilinguals. *Journal of Experimental Psychology: Learning, Memory, and Cognition, 30*, 246–269.

Gollan, T. H., Bonanni, M. P., & Montoya, R. I. (2005). Proper names get stuck on bilingual and monolingual speakers' tip-of-the-tongue equally often. *Neuropsychology, 19*, 278–287.

Gollan, T. H., & Brown, A. S. (2006). From tip-of-the-tongue (TOT) data to theoretical implications in two steps: When more TOTs means better retrieval. *Journal of Experimental Psychology: General, 135*, 462–483.

Gollan, T. H., & Ferreira, V. S. (2009). Should I stay or should I switch? A cost-benefit analysis of voluntary language switching in young and aging bilinguals. *Journal of Experimental Psychology: Learning, Memory, and Cognition, 35*, 640–665.

Gollan, T. H., Ferreira, V. S., Cera, C., & Flett, S. (in press). Translation-priming effects on tip-of-the-tongue states. *Language and Cognitive Processes.*

Gollan, T. H., Montoya, R. I., Cera, C., & Sandoval, T. C. (2008). More use almost always means a smaller frequency effect: Aging, bilingualism, and the weaker links hypothesis. *Journal of Memory and Language, 58*, 787–814.

Gollan, T. H., Montoya, R. I., Fennema-Notestine, C., & Morris, S. K. (2005). Bilingualism affects picture naming but not picture classification. *Memory & Cognition, 33*, 1220–1234.

Gollan, T. H., Montoya, R. I., & Werner, G. (2002). Semantic and letter fluency in Spanish-English bilinguals. *Neuropsychology, 16*, 562–576.

Gollan, T. H., Salmon, D. P., Montoya, R. I., Da Pena, E. (2010). Accessibility of the nondominant language in picture naming: A counterintuitive effect of dementia on bilingual language production. *Neuropsychologia, 48*, 1356–1366.

Gollan, T. H., Sandoval, T., & Salmon, D. P. (2011). Cross-language intrusion errors in aging bilinguals reveal the link between executive control and language selection *Psychological Science, 22*, 1155–1164.

Gollan, T. H., & Silverberg, N. B. (2001). Tip-of-the-tongue states in Hebrew-English bilinguals. *Bilingualism: Language and Cognition, 4*, 63–83.

Gollan, T. H., Slattery, T. J., Goldenberg, D., van Assche, E., Duyck, W., & Rayner, K. (2011). Frequency drives lexical access in reading but not in speaking: The frequency-lag hypothesis. *Journal of Experimental Psychology: General, 140*, 186–209.

Green, D. (1998). Mental control of the bilingual lexico-semantic system. *Bilingualism: Language and Cognition, 1*, 67–81.

Griffin, Z. M. (2001). Gaze durations during speech reflect word selection and phonological encoding. *Cognition, 82*, B1–B14.

Grosjean, F. (1989). Neurolinguists, beware! The bilingual is not two monolinguals in one person. *Brain and Language, 36*, 3–15.

Guo, T., Liu, H., Misra, M., & Kroll, J. F. (2011). Local and global inhibition in bilingual word production: fMRI evidence from Chinese-English bilinguals. *NeuroImage, 56*, 2300–2309.

Hanulovà, J., Davidson, D. J., & Indefrey, P. (2011). Where does the delay in L2 picture naming come from? Psycholinguistic and neurocognitive evidence on second language word production. *Language and Cognitive Processes, 26*, 902–934.

Hermans, D. (2004). Between-language identity effects in picture-word interference tasks: A challenge for language-nonspecific or language-specific models of lexical access? *International Journal of Bilingualism, 8*, 115–125.

Hermans, D., Bongaerts, T., De Bot, K., & Schreuder, R. (1998). Producing words in a foreign language: Can speakers prevent interference from their first language? *Bilingualism: Language and Cognition, 1*, 213–229.

Hernandez, A. E., & Kohnert, K. J. (1999). Aging and language switching in bilinguals. *Aging, Neuropsychology, and Cognition, 6*, 69–83.

Hernandez, A. E., & Reyes, I. (2002). Within- and between-language priming differ: Evidence from repetition of pictures in Spanish-English bilinguals. *Journal of Experimental Psychology: Learning, Memory, and Cognition, 28*, 726–734.

Hoshino, N., & Kroll, J. F. (2008). Cognate effects in picture naming: Does cross-language activation survive a change of script? *Cognition, 106*, 501–511.

Hoshino, N., & Thierry, G. (2011). Language selection in bilingual word production: Electrophysiological evidence for cross-language competition, *Brain Research, 1371*, 100–109.

Ibáñez, A. J., Macizo, P., & Bajo, M. T. (2010). Language access and language selection in professional translators. *Acta Psychologica, 135*, 257–266.

Ivanova, I., & Costa, A. (2008). Does bilingualism hamper lexical access in speech production? *Acta Psychologica, 127*, 277–288.

James, L. E., & Burke, D. M. (2000). Phonological priming effects on word retrieval and tip-of-the-tongue experiences in young and older adults. *Journal of Experimental Psychology: Learning, Memory, and Cognition, 26*, 1378–1391.

Kello, C. T., Plaut, D. C., & MacWhinney, B. (2000). The task dependence of staged versus cascaded processing: An empirical and computational study of Stroop interference in speech production. *Journal of Experimental Psychology: General, 129*, 340–360.

Kovács, A. M., & Mehler, J. (2009). Cognitive gains in 7-month-old bilingual infants. *Proceedings of the National Academy of Sciences, 106*, 6556–6560.

Kroll, J. F., Bobb, S. C., Misra, M. M., & Guo, T. (2008). Language selection in bilingual speech: Evidence for inhibitory processes. *Acta Psychologica, 128*, 416–430.

Kroll, J. F., Bobb, S., & Wodniecka, Z. (2006). Language selectivity is the exception, not the rule: Arguments against a fixed locus of language selection in bilingual speech. *Bilingualism: Language and Cognition, 9*, 119–135.

Kroll, J. F., Bogulski, C. A., & McClain, R. (2012). Psycholinguistic perspectives on second language learning and bilingualism: The course and consequence of cross-language competition. *Linguistic Approaches to Bilingualism, 2*, 1–24.

Kroll, J. F., Dijkstra, A., Janssen, N., & Schriefers, H. (2000). *Selecting the language in which to speak: Experiments on lexical access in bilingual production.* Paper presented at the 41st Annual Meeting of the Psychonomic Society, New Orleans, LA.

Kroll, J. F., Dussias, P. E., Bogulski, C. A., & Valdes-Kroff, J. (2012). Juggling two languages in one mind: What bilinguals tell us about language processing and its consequences for cognition. In B. Ross (Ed.), *The psychology of learning and motivation, Volume 56* (pp. 229–262). San Diego: Academic Press.

Kroll, J. F., & Stewart, E. (1994). Category interference in translation and picture naming: Evidence for asymmetric connections between bilingual memory representations. *Journal of Memory and Language, 33*, 149–174.

La Heij, W. (2005). Selection processes in monolingual and bilingual lexical access. In J. F. Kroll & A. M. B. De Groot (Eds.), *Handbook of bilingualism: Psycholinguistic approaches* (pp. 289–307). New York: Oxford University Press.

Lehtonen, M., & Laine, M. (2003). How word frequency affects morphological processing in monolinguals and bilinguals. *Bilingualism: Language and Cognition, 6*, 213–225.

Levelt, W. J. M. (1989). *Speaking: From intention to articulation.* Cambridge, MA: MIT Press.

Levelt, W. J. M., Roelofs, A., & Meyer, A. S. (1999). A theory of lexical access in speech production. *Behavioral and Brain Sciences, 22*, 1–75.

Levy, B. J., McVeigh, N. D., Marful, A. & Anderson, M. C. (2007). Inhibiting your native language: The role of retrieval-induced forgetting during second language acquisition. *Psychological Science, 18*, 29–34.

Linck, J. A., Kroll, J. F. & Sunderman, G. (2009). Losing access to the native language while immersed in a second language: Evidence for the role of inhibition in second language learning. *Psychological Science, 20*, 1507–1515.

Luo, L., Luk, G., & Bialystok, E. (2010). Effect of language proficiency and executive control on verbal fluency performance in bilinguals. *Cognition, 114*, 29–41.

MacWhinney, B. (2005). A unified model of language acquisition. In J. F. Kroll & A. M. B. De Groot (Eds.), *Handbook of bilingualism: Psycholinguistic approaches* (pp. 49–67). New York: Oxford University Press.

Mägiste, E. (1979). The competing language systems of the multilingual: A developmental study of decoding and encoding processes. *Journal of Verbal Learning and Verbal Behavior, 18*, 79–89.

Marian, V., & Spivey, M. J. (2003). Competing activation in bilingual language processing: Within- and between-language competition. *Bilingualism: Language and Cognition, 6*, 97–115.

Meuter, R. F. I., & Allport, A. (1999). Bilingual language switching in naming: Asymmetrical costs of language selection. *Journal of Memory and Language, 40*, 25–40.

Meyer, A., & Bock, K. (1992). The tip of the tongue phenomenon: Blocking or partial activation. *Memory and Cognition, 20*, 715–726.

Misra, M., Guo, T., Bobb, S. C., & Kroll, J. F. (2012). When bilinguals choose a single word to speak: Electrophysiological evidence for global inhibition in bilingual word production. *Journal of Memory and Language, 67*, 224–237.

Murray, W. S., & Forster, K. I. (2004). Serial mechanisms in lexical access: The rank hypothesis. *Psychological Review, 111*, 721–756.

Nicoladis, E., Palmer, A., Marentette, P. (2007). The role of type and token frequency in using past tense morphemes correctly. *Developmental Science, 10*, 237–254.

Pearson, B. (1997). The relation of input factors to lexical learning by bilingual infants. *Applied Psycholinguistics, 18*, 41–58.

Pearson, B. Z., Fernandez, S. C., & Oller, D. K. (1993). Lexical development in bilingual infants and toddlers: Comparison to monolingual norms. *Language Learning, 43*, 93–120.

Philipp, A. M., Gade, M., & Koch, I. (2007). Inhibitory processes in language switching? Evidence from switching language-defined response sets. *European Journal of Cognitive Psychology, 19*, 395–416.

Philipp, A. M., & Koch, I. (2009). Inhibition in language switching: What is inhibited when switching among languages in naming tasks? *Journal of Experimental Psychology: Learning, Memory, & Cognition, 35*, 1187–1195.

Piske, T., MacKay, I. R. A., & Flege, J. E. (2001). Factors affecting the degree of foreign accent in an L2: A review. *Journal of Phonetics, 29*, 191–215.

Plaut, D. C., McClelland, J. L., Seidenberg, M. S., & Patterson, K. (1996). Understanding normal and impaired reading: Computational principles in quasi-regular domains. *Psychological Review, 103*, 56–115.

Portocarrero, J. S., Burright, R. G., & Donovick, P. J. (2007). Vocabulary and verbal fluency of bilingual and monolingual college students. *Archives of Clinical Neuropsychology, 22*, 415–422.

Prior, A., & Gollan, T. H. (2011). Good language switchers are good task switchers: Evidence from Spanish-English and Mandarin-English bilinguals. *Journal of the International Neuropsychological Society, 17*, 1–10.

Ransdell, S. E., & Fischler, I. (1987). Memory in a monolingual mode: When are bilinguals at a disadvantage? *Journal of Memory and Language, 26*, 392–405.

Rapp, B., & Goldrick, M. (2000). Discreteness and interactivity in spoken word production. *Psychological Review, 107*, 460–499.

Rastle, K. G., & Burke, D. M. (1996). Priming the tip of the tongue: Effects of prior processing on word retrieval in young and older adults. *Journal of Memory and Language, 35*, 586–605.

Rohrer, D., Wixted, J. T., Salmon, D. P., & Butters, N. (1995). Retrieval from semantic memory and its implications for Alzheimer's disease. *Journal of Experimental Psychology: Learning, Memory, and Cognition, 21*, 1127–1139.

Runnqvist, E., & Costa, A. (2012). Is retrieval-induced forgetting behind the bilingual disadvantage in speech production? *Bilingualism: Language and Cognition, 15*, 365–377.

Runnqvist, E., Strijkers, K., Sadat, J., & Costa, A. (2011). On the temporal and functional origin of L2 disadvantages in speech production: a critical review. *Frontiers in Psychology, 2: 379*.

Sandoval, T. C., Gollan, T. H., Ferreira, V. S., & Salmon, D. P. (2010). What causes the bilingual disadvantage in verbal fluency: The dual-task analogy. *Bilingualism: Language and Cognition, 13*, 231–252.

Schmid, M. S. (2010). Languages at play: The relevance of L1 attrition to the study of bilingualism. *Bilingualism: Language and Cognition, 13*, 1–7.

Schwartz, A. I., & Kroll, J. F. (2006). Bilingual lexical activation in sentence context. *Journal of Memory and Language, 55*, 197–212.

Spieler, D. H., & Griffin, Z. M. (2006). The influence of age on the time course of word preparation in multiword utterances. *Language and Cognitive Processes, 21*, 291–321.

Strijkers, K., Costa, A., & Thierry, G. (2010). Tracking lexical access in speech production: Electrophysiological correlated of word frequency and cognate effects. *Cerebral Cortex, 20*, 912–928.

Valentine, T., Brennen, T., & Brédart, S. (1996). *The cognitive psychology of proper names: On the importance of being Ernest*. London: Routledge.

Van Assche, E., Duyck, W., & Gollan, T. H. (2013). Whole-language and item-specific control in bilingual language production, *Journal of Experimental Psychology: Learning, Memory, & Cognition*.

Verhaegen, P. (2003). Aging and vocabulary scores: A meta-analysis. *Psychology and Aging, 18*, 332–339.

Verhoef, K. M. W., Roelofs, A., & Chwilla, D. J. (2009). Role of inhibition in language switching: Evidence from event-related brain potentials in overt picture naming. *Cognition, 110*, 84–99.

Weissberger, G. H., Wierenga, C. E., Bondi, M. W., & Gollan, T. H. (2012). Partially over-lapping mechanisms of language and task control in young and older bilinguals. *Psychology and Aging, 27*, 959–974.

Werker, J. F., & Byers-Heinlein, K. (2008). Bilingualism in infancy: First steps in perception and comprehension. *Trends in Cognitive Sciences, 12*, 144–151.

Yeung, N., & Monsell, S. (2003). Switching between tasks of unequal familiarity: The role of stimulus-attribute and response-set selection. *Journal of Experimental Psychology: Human Learning & Memory, 29*, 455–469.

Yudes, C., Kroll, J. F., & Guo, T. (in preparation). *On the consequences of naming rotated objects for inhibitory processes in speech planning*.

Bilingual Word Access

Elin Runnqvist, Kristof Strijkers, *and* Albert Costa

Abstract

A challenge for any model of bilingual word access is to explain how speakers are able to select words from the intended language without experiencing intrusions from the coactivated unintended language. The authors provide an overview of current models of bilingual speech production, and then critically examine the hypothesis that the unintended language has to be inhibited in order to select words from the intended language. The authors focus on (a) lexical retrieval difficulties associated with bilingualism and second language production; (b) cross-language semantic contextual effects; (c) advantages in domain-general cognitive control associated to bilingualism; (d) the relationship between domain-general cognitive control, language control, and bilingual advantages and disadvantages; and (e) the impact of becoming bilingual on lexical retrieval, language control, and domain general cognitive control. The authors conclude that despite the appeal of a unified inhibitory control account, a systematic evaluation of the literature highlights that a single mechanism is likely insufficient to capture all data.

Key Words: bilingual language control, bilingual speech production disadvantage, cross-language semantic contextual effects, bilingual advantages in cognitive control, immersion learning

Introduction

The mental lexicon has had a privileged position since the birth of the psycholinguistic study of bilingualism and still continues to be at the core of the debate in psycholinguistics. While earlier investigations focused on the organization of the bilingual lexicon (are representations shared or separate across languages?), more recently emphasis is on lexical access and how bilingual speakers manage to avoid interference from the language not in use during speech production. In this chapter we focus on the latter issue and the exposition is structured as follows. First, we provide an overview of current models of bilingual speech production, focusing on their ability to account for the critical process of lexical selection. Second, we review several predictions that follow from these models and examine how recent findings support such predictions. Finally, we briefly

discuss the impact that becoming bilingual has on language production and related collateral effects. The major conclusions we reach in this chapter can be summarized as follows:

• We argue that the prototypical tasks employed to study language control in bilingual speech production do not suffice to settle the issue and novel paradigms must be explored.

• The few attempts to explore bilingual language control with novel tasks seems to bring forward evidence that is not readily explained by the dominant accounts, possibly indicating the necessity for a conceptual shift concerning language control.

• Despite the appeal to explain bilingual processing disadvantages between monolinguals and bilinguals, and between L1 and L2 on the one hand, and the bilingual executive advantages on the other hand in terms of a single inhibitory control account, systematic comparisons highlight that such common ground is likely insufficient to capture all data.

Language control in bilingual word production

Perhaps the most explored question in bilingual language production has been how a person who masters two languages is able to speak in one language without suffering massive intrusion from the other. Most of the answers to this question assume a language control mechanism that allows bilinguals to keep production in each language separate. The functioning of such a mechanism is referred to as bilingual language control.

Three major proposals on bilingual language control have been put forward. According to what is referred to as the concept selection account, the language a speaker wants to use at a given point in time is specified at the conceptual level as part of the preverbal message, which permits the brain to essentially activate words only in the target language (e.g., Bloem & La Heij, 2003; Bloem, van den Boogaard, & La Heij, 2004; La Heij, 2005). A second critical assumption of this account is that word production unfolds in a fully serial fashion thereby only the word corresponding to the selected concept is accessed at the lexical level. Under this proposal there is no cross-language interference because words in the language not in use will not (or only redundantly) be accessed. Critical in this interpretation is La Heij's proposal that a language cue at the conceptual level ensures that activation propagating from concepts only reaches the corresponding lexical representations in the target language (La Heij, 2005). Although the concept selection account provides a straightforward explanation of how bilinguals select words in the proper language, there are several problems with such a view. First, a host of data make a strong case against fully serial processing in language production (e.g., Caramazza, 1997; Dell, 1986; Levelt, Roelofs, & Meyer, 1999; Meyer, Belke, Telling, & Humphreys, 2007; Meyer & Damian, 2007; Morsella & Miozzo, 2002; Navarrete & Costa, 2005; Roelofs, 1992, 2003, 2006, 2008) as well as in other related (e.g., Barsalou, 1999; Collins & Loftus, 1975; Fowler, Brown, Sabadini, & Weihing, 2003; Lakoff & Johnson, 1999; Liberman & Whalen, 2000; Pulvermuller, 1999, 2005; Pulvermuller & Fadiga, 2010) and unrelated areas of cognition (e.g., Engel, Fries, & Singer, 2001;

Gilbert & Sigman, 2007; Mesulam, 1998; Ullman, 1995). Second, the concept selection account contrasts with the predominant view that words in both of a bilingual's languages become activated even when only one language is in use (e.g., Colomé, 2001; Costa, Caramazza, & Sebastián-Gallés, 2000; Hermans, Bongaerts, de Bot, & Schreuder, 1998; Poulisse, 1999; Thierry & Wu, 2007). Altogether, these problems question whether the concept selection account could fully capture the extent and complexity of bilingual language control.

Turning now to the two other proposals, they both embrace spreading activation differing primarily on whether they allow lexical items from distinct languages to compete for selection. According to the language-specific selection proposal advanced by Costa and collaborators (e.g., Costa, 2005; Costa & Caramazza, 1999; Costa, Miozzo, & Caramazza, 1999), target and related concepts activate the corresponding words in both languages; however, words in the nontarget language would not interfere since lexical selection mechanisms only consider words in the target language and selection only depends on the activation levels of the words in the target language. The selection mechanism is here conceptualized as a lexicon-external monitoring device capable of restricting lexical search exclusively to the intended language while ignoring activated words in the nonintended language. Other researchers proposed a nonspecific lexical selection account according to which words from both languages compete for selection. A word is selected in the in-use (target) language if its activation level surpasses those of the other words in both languages (e.g., Green, 1986, 1998; De Bot, 1992; Poulisse, 1997). Green's inhibitory control model (ICM) (e.g., Green, 1986, 1998) is probably the most popular nonspecific lexical selection account. As hinted by its name, the model proposes that cross-language interference is resolved by reactively inhibiting words in the nontarget language. In this way, words would reach comparatively higher activation levels in the target language. Because the words with the highest activation level are eventually selected for production, words can typically be uttered in the intended language. Inhibition is supposedly controlled by a task module outside the lexicon that continuously specifies and updates a speaker's goals by decreasing the activation strength of the lexical representations bearing language tags of the nonintended language. Next, we review some of the evidence accrued in support of language-specific selection and inhibitory control mechanisms, respectively, topics on which research on bilingual production has concentrated extensively over the last decade primarily using the paradigms of picture-word interference (PWI) and language switching.

In the PWI task participants typically name a target picture while ignoring a superimposed written word. Semantic interference is a standard finding in PWI. A picture (e.g., *table*) is named more slowly when the word distractor is semantically related to the target picture (e.g., *chair*) compared with an unrelated word distractor (e.g., *shirt*). Semantic interference is viewed by many researchers as reflecting competition between semantically related words during lexical selection (e.g., Glaser & Glaser, 1989; Levelt et al., 1991; Lupker, 1979; Schriefers, Meyer, & Levelt, 1990; Roelofs, 1992, 2003, 2006, 2008). Semantic interference is also found in the bilingual version of PWI where the target picture is named in one language (e.g., English; *table*) and the word distracter is presented in a different language (e.g., Spanish; *silla [chair]*) (e.g., Mägiste, 1984, 1985; Smith & Kirsner, 1982). Cross-language semantic interference has generally been viewed as supporting language nonspecific selection accounts like the ICM (e.g., Green, 1986, 1998). Indeed, the most straightforward explanation of this result is that the word distractor in the nontarget language competes for selection with the picture name from the designated language. However, Costa et al. (1999) proposed an alternative explanation according to which the locus of cross-language semantic interference is the target lexicon. Given that the distractor word in the nontarget language (*silla*) also activates its translation in the target language (*chair*), a delay in the selection of the picture name (*table*) could be induced by the translation (*chair*) rather than by the distractor word itself (*silla [chair]*). To find positive evidence for their proposal, Costa et al. (1999) conducted a series of PWI experiments where the (Spanish) distracter word (*mesa [table]*) was the translation of the (English) target picture-name (*table*). Since translation words are arguably the strongest between-language competitors in models like the ICM, such words are expected to produce the strongest form of interference if cross-language competition is at play. On the other hand, if cross-language semantic interference stems from within-language competition, as argued by Costa et al. (1999), then facilitation should appear since, through automatic translation, the distractor word coactivates the same lexical entry as the picture. Indeed, facilitation was observed by Costa et al. (1999). Proponents of cross-language competition have objected that this

facilitation could be accounted for by conceptual overlap, masking and even overruling the inhibitory effects at the lexical level (e.g., Abutalebi & Green, 2007; Green, 2002; Hermans, 2004; Kroll, Bobb, Misra, & Guo, 2008). In the end, the discussion boils down on determining in which proportion facilitation involves conceptual versus lexical levels of processing, presently a difficult issue to resolve experimentally. More generally, a further factor complicates the interpretation of results obtained using PWI. In the last few years the debate on PWI has shifted from how word distractors interfere with lexical selection to whether the paradigm is actually relevant for studying lexical selection in monolingual and bilingual speech production. Results obtained in studies where variables, such as semantic relationship, semantic distance, or lexical frequency, were manipulated strongly challenge the view that the PWI paradigm is relevant for lexical retrieval processes (e.g., Miozzo & Caramazza, 2003; Costa, Alario, & Caramazza, 2005; Dhooge & Hartsuiker, 2010, 2011a, 2011b, 2012; Finkbeiner & Caramazza, 2006; Janssen, Schirm, Mahon, & Caramazza, 2008; Mahon, Costa, Peterson, Vargas, & Caramazza, 2007; Abdel Rahman & Melinger, 2007, 2009). Until we have a clear picture of the nature of the interference it is unlikely that the PWI task could be decisive in resolving the current debate on bilingual language control.

Language switching (LS) is another paradigm that has been widely used in the investigation of bilingual language control, arguably with stronger impact on models of word production than PWI. In a seminal experiment conducted by Meuter and Allport (1999), participants named Arabic numerals in their first language (L1) or in their second language (L2) as prompted by the color in which the numerals appeared. In consecutive trials, participants either used the same language (non-switch L1, non-switch L2) or changed from one language to the other (switch L1, switch L2), much like in the typical settings of task switching experiments (e.g., Meiran, 1996; Monsell, 1996). While switching was always associated with a naming cost, crucially, switching to L1 was more costly than switching to L2. This seemingly paradoxical result, referred to as the asymmetrical switch cost, receives a readily explanation within inhibitory models of bilingual language control (e.g., Green, 1986, 1998). Since the inhibition applied to a given language is proportional to the strength of the lexical activation of that language, L1 words are inhibited to a greater extent when speaking in L2 than vice versa. In fact, when naming in L1, the lexical representations in L2 hardly have to be suppressed, therefore switching to L2 proceeds fairly easily. In contrast, when naming in L2, the lexical representations in L1 have to be strongly suppressed to avoid cross-language intrusions. When in the next trial there is a switch to L1, not only do participants have to change stimulus-response rules, but they also need to overcome the strong inhibition applied to L1 words on previous trials. This results in the extra cost visible in the increased naming latencies in L2-L1 switching. Also in electrophysiological and neuroimaging investigations of LS, asymmetrical switch costs that mimicked those observed behaviorally appeared in ERPs (event-related potentials) components (N2) and brain areas (e.g., anterior cingulate cortex [ACC]) believed to reflect inhibitory processes (e.g., Jackson, Swainson, Cunnington, & Jackson, 2001; Wang, Xue, Chen, Xue, & Dong, 2007). Further evidence for the use of inhibition in LS tasks comes from two studies carried out by Philipp and colleagues (Philipp, Gade, & Koch, 2007; Philipp & Koch, 2009). Participants switched between German, English, and French. The critical comparison was between n-2 language repetition sequences (e.g., L1-L2-<u>L1</u>) and n-2 language nonrepetition sequences (e.g., L3-L2-<u>L1</u>). Words at the end of the sequences were named more slowly in n-2 language repetition sequences compared with n-2 language nonrepetition sequence. Although collectively these findings make a strong case for persisting inhibition of task-schemas in LS tasks, it is less clear whether such findings actually reveal that inhibition is applied to lexical items. This latter point echoes concerns as to whether LS is a valid paradigm for exploring bilingual lexical access (e.g., Finkbeiner, Almeida, Janssen, & Caramazza, 2006; Finkbeiner, Gollan, & Caramazza, 2006). Furthermore, as we review next, there are issues related to proficiency, response preparation time, response valence, the level at which inhibition applies, and the feasibility and nature of inhibition that significantly complicate explanations of asymmetrical switch costs within the framework of inhibitory accounts.

Participants in each of the LS studies we reviewed above were bilinguals with low or intermediate L2 proficiency. When Costa and Santesteban (2004) systematically explored the effects of proficiency on language switch costs, a more complex pattern emerged: switch costs were asymmetrical with low proficient bilinguals (thus replicating prior findings) but symmetrical with high proficient bilinguals,

even when switching between L1 and a much weaker L3. The latter result is especially important. A symmetrical switch cost for high proficient bilinguals is expected under inhibitory accounts since comparable levels of inhibition are required in both languages. However, the same argument cannot be extended to L1-L3 switching. Furthermore, a number of studies have reported symmetrical switch costs also for low proficient bilinguals (e.g., Christoffels, Firk, & Schiller, 2007; Verhoef et al., 2010; Gollan & Ferreira, 2009). Related to such variability of switch cost patterns, switch costs can vary not only as a function of proficiency but also as a function of predictability, response preparation time, and response valence (e.g., Gollan & Ferreira, 2010; Verhoef, Roelofs, & Chwilla, 2009; Finkbeiner et al., 2006). For example, Verhoef et al. (2009) conducted an ERP study of LS where language cue and target stimulus were uncoupled. The results revealed that the occurrence of asymmetrical or symmetrical switch costs does not depend on language proficiency but rather on preparation time; and a modulation of the N2 ERPs component, which is taken to index language inhibition in the LS task (e.g., Jackson et al., 2001), only appeared on long cue-target intervals. On the basis of these results, Verhoef et al. (2009) concluded that while bilinguals may resort to inhibition as a strategy in the LS paradigm, they do not need inhibition to control their language use.

Interestingly, symmetrical switch costs typically appear along with slower naming latencies in L1 compared with L2 (i.e., reversed language dominance), both on switch and nonswitch trials, a finding that some take as evidence of global inhibition of the dominant language throughout the whole LS experiment (e.g., Abutalebi & Green, 2008; Christoffels et al., 2007; Gollan & Ferreira, 2010; Kroll et al., 2008). However, it is not clear how to relate the variability in switch cost patterns to the idea of inhibitory language control without assuming different types of inhibition between low and high proficient bilinguals. That is, inhibition would be static, continuous, and global in high proficient bilinguals, whereas it would be applied on a trial-by-trial basis in low proficient bilinguals (e.g., Gollan & Ferreira, 2010). At present, such variability in switch cost patterns and reversed language dominance does not seem to follow any stable pattern, emphasizing the possibility that the results reflect at least in part strategic differences in approaching the experimental task. Thus, despite extensive research with the LS paradigm whether the suppression of a whole lexicon is the way in which bilinguals control their speech output in normal conversation remains a controversial issue. Indeed, most of the time, bilinguals participate in conversations in monolingual settings, even in demographic groups where both languages are used on regular bases. A constant inhibition of the entire lexicon does not seem a particularly efficient mechanism, since it would make speech an extremely effortful endeavor for bilinguals.

Possibly due to the difficulties associated with interpreting the results of the PWI and LS tasks, the research on bilingual language production and control has shifted in the last few years toward different questions that could be investigated adopting other tasks than PWI and LS. Research has concentrated on key features of current proposals on bilingual language control. A first feature concerns the comparison between bilinguals and monolinguals and the degree in which word production is more effortful for bilinguals, even in contexts in which only one language is used. In a model such as the ICM, the constant presence of cross-language interference and suppression would result in more effortful processing for bilinguals. A second feature regards the interactions of inhibitory language control with semantic contextual effects. Inhibiting a representation or a language should presumably render that representation or language less accessible at a later point in time. On the other hand, as we will specify later on, applying inhibitory language control should abolish semantic competitor effects under certain circumstances. Finally, although both inhibitory and noninhibitory models assume that bilingual word production involves some sort of extracognitive control resources, such resources are differently characterized within each model. This, in turn, allows formulating different predictions on whether the experience of language control would spill over to other cognitive abilities. In what follows we examine the empirical evidence that is relevant for testing the different predictions derived from the models.

Is lexical processing more costly for bilinguals than for monolinguals?

Cross-language interference and its suppression would slow down lexical processing. This should be especially true when speaking in a second or non-dominant language, since the interference should be greater from the strongest language than vice versa. Consistent with this expectation, picture naming was found to be slower in nondominant than dominant languages, even when the task was performed exclusively in one language (e.g., Gollan, Montoya, Cera, & Sandoval, 2008; Ivanova & Costa, 2008). Such a naming delay cannot be attributed exclusively to low L2 proficiency. In fact, it persists with high proficient bilinguals (e.g., Gollan et al., 2008; Ivanova & Costa, 2008) and over several repetitions (e.g., Ivanova & Costa, 2008).

What is the locus of the naming delay in L2? Is it at the lexical level? Results addressing this question come from studies that used neurophysiological measures. It appears that the few results demonstrating differences in the neuronal activity between speech in L1 and L2 revealed a late source of this effect: postlexical syllabification (e.g., Lucas, McKhann, & Ojemann, 2004; Indefrey, 2006). This led some researchers to propose a postlexical locus of the naming delay (for more details regarding this proposal see Indefrey, 2006; Hanulová, Davidson, & Indefrey, 2010). However, greater activation in areas associated with postlexical processing was found only in studies where participants were either low proficient or late bilinguals, while studies that examined early or high proficient bilinguals generally failed to find similar differences. Furthermore, it should be noted that the neurophysiological findings contrast with the behavioral results, which, as reviewed earlier, showed that even early and/or high proficient bilinguals are slower in L2 naming compared with L1 naming. Taken at face value, the conclusion of a postlexical origin of differences in L2 processing in low proficient or late bilinguals is surprising as it seems to imply that no extra resources are required for lexical access in the weaker language. However, using ERPs, a technique with fine temporal resolution, recent studies on picture naming revealed early differences (~200 ms post picture presentation) between first and second language production in early and high proficient bilinguals (e.g., Strijkers, Baus, Fitz Patrick, Runnqvist, & Costa, 2013; Strijkers, Costa, & Thierry, 2010). These differences appeared within the time window corresponding to lexical access (Costa, Strijkers, Martin, & Thierry, 2009; Indefrey & Levelt, 2004; Sahin, Pinker, Cash, Schomer, & Halgren, 2009; Strijkers et al., 2010). In addition to showing that with the proper technique, early and subtle differences between L1 and L2 can be detected when using sufficiently sensitive techniques, these ERPs findings might be consistent with those accounts of bilingual language production that assume cross-language competition at the lexical level.

In apparent contrast with inhibitory accounts of language control are various lines of evidence that reveal disadvantages in naming in the dominant and/or first language. For example, in studies in which participants were asked to name pictures with very low-frequency names, bilinguals were more likely to experience tip-of-the-tongues (TOTs) than monolinguals in addition to report of being familiar with fewer words (e.g., Gollan & Acenas, 2004; Gollan & Silverberg, 2001). Similarly, in comparison with monolinguals, bilinguals named fewer items in standardized naming tests such as the Boston Naming Test (e.g., Gollan, Fennema-Notestine, Montoya, & Jernigan, 2007; Kohnert, Hernandez, & Bates, 1998; Roberts, Garcia, Desrochers, & Hernandez, 2002) and typically showed longer naming-latencies in simple picture naming tasks (e.g., Gollan et al., 2008; Gollan, Montoya, Fennema-Notestine, & Morris, 2005; Ivanova & Costa, 2008; Gollan, Sandoval, & Salmon, 2011; Sadat, Martin, Alario, & Costa, 2012). Finally, bilinguals produced fewer items than their monolingual peers in timed verbal fluency tasks that required generating as many words as possible from a given category (animals, clothes) or with specific letter onsets (A, P, S) (e.g., Bialystok, Craik, & Luk, 2008; Gollan, Montoya, & Werner, 2002; Sandoval, Gollan, Ferreira, & Salmon, 2010). Importantly, several studies have shown that this disadvantage is circumscribed to lexical retrieval as opposed to affecting the language production system as a whole. For example, bilinguals do not experience more TOTs than monolinguals when targets are proper names (e.g., Gollan, Bonanni, & Montoya, 2005), even though retrieval is more demanding for proper names than common words (e.g., Cohen & Burke, 1993; Valentine, Brennen, & Brédart, 1996) and proper names are known to be adversely affected by cognitive decline (e.g., Burke, MacKay, Worthley, & Wade, 1991; Evrard, 2002; Rastle & Burke, 1996). Furthermore, bilinguals categorize pictures with the same speed as monolinguals, a finding indicating that whatever the causes of their naming disadvantages, these occur at a postsemantic level (e.g., Gollan et al., 2005). Finally, the finding that bimodal bilinguals (users of spoken and sign languages) experience more TOTs than monolinguals (e.g., Pyers, Gollan, & Emmorey, 2009) rules out an exclusive origin of the disadvantages at the phonological level of processing—there is no phonological overlap between signs and spoken words—pointing instead to a lexical origin (for a review see Runnqvist, Strijkers, Sadat, & Costa, 2011). Of course, this does not preclude that differences exist also at later stages. Indeed, phenomena such as the foreign accent (e.g., Alario, Goslin, Michel, & Laganaro, 2010; Flege & Eefting, 1987; Flege, Schirru, & MacKay, 2003) seem to indicate postlexical processing difficulties for L2 speakers. Furthermore, Gollan and Goldrick (2012) showed that even early and highly proficient bilinguals who do not have an accent in their L2 nevertheless experience processing difficulties for sublexical representations.

Inhibitory accounts of language control could explain L1 naming disadvantages in the same way as they explain L2 naming disadvantages (i.e., by assuming that the simultaneous activation of the nontarget language interferes with target-language production and that inhibition yields delays and inefficiencies in lexical retrieval). However, while inhibitory accounts anticipate L1 interference when speaking in L2, it is not so clear that they also predict L2 interference when speaking in L1. Furthermore, there are results that are difficult to reconcile with an interference-based account of bilingual disadvantage. For example, several studies reported reduced disadvantages for words that bilinguals could translate into their nondominant language compared with words that they only knew in their dominant language (e.g., Gollan & Acenas, 2004; Gollan et al., 2005). This finding is the opposite of what would be predicted by inhibitory accounts since words that are not known in the nontarget language obviously would not compete for selection and should thus be easily retrieved in the target language. Another piece of evidence seemingly hard to accommodate within inhibitory accounts emerged in studies that showed reduced disadvantage when bilinguals could use both of their languages (e.g., Gollan & Silverberg, 2001). As it is reasonable to assume that the use of both languages leads to strong activation of the nontarget language, inhibitory accounts would anticipate increase (not reduction) of interference in such conditions.

An alternative explanation of the bilingual disadvantages observed in production in L2 as well as in L1 is offered by the weaker-links or frequency lag account (e.g., Gollan & Silverberg, 2001; Gollan et al., 2005; Gollan et al., 2008; Gollan et al., 2011). The account builds on the observation that bilinguals divide their speech production between two languages. Thus, assuming that monolinguals and bilinguals produce comparable amounts of speech, bilinguals have relatively less experience with each of their languages. The reduced use is thought to have effects analogous to frequency; therefore, words that are commonly produced would strengthen their links between semantics and phonology whereas words that are produced less often would have relatively weaker links. In sum, under the weaker-links account, disadvantages associated with bilingualism stem from general mechanisms at play with monolingual and bilingual speakers alike.

Studies testing the weaker-links account and accounts that assume interference have mainly focused on the alleged contrasting predictions of these accounts concerning the effects of lexical frequency and ageing on bilinguals' disadvantage. The weaker links account specifically anticipates that, as a result of bilinguals' reduced language exposure, words have lower frequencies with bilinguals than monolinguals. This frequency lag might not be observable with very high-frequency words (e.g., *car*) being instead noticeable only with low-frequency words (e.g., *pestle*) whose low baseline activation levels render them almost inaccessible. Thus, the weaker-links account predicts that frequency effects should be larger for bilinguals than monolinguals (at least for low-frequency words) and for the nondominant language relative to the dominant language. In contrast, it has been argued that inhibitory accounts anticipate that the high-frequent words should be the most adversely affected since words that are used often supposedly reach relatively high activation levels and should thus be subjected to large interference. Diverging predictions similarly arise with ageing effects. On the one hand, the weaker-links account predicts that as bilinguals get older, their disadvantage with respect to monolinguals should reduce reflecting their long exposure to L2 words. For the same reason, older bilinguals should demonstrate smaller frequency effects as compared with younger bilinguals. On the other hand, interference-based accounts predict a larger disadvantage for older adults since their abilities to handle conflicting information should decrease in parallel with the age-related decline of their executive control. Several studies tested these predictions and provided us with an interesting but complex set of results.

Bilinguals' disadvantage in picture naming has typically been more pronounced with low-frequency words (e.g., Gollan et al., 2008; Ivanova & Costa, 2008), thus confirming predictions derived from the weaker-links account. However, predictions regarding the nondominant language have not been borne out in an equally consistent manner: while Gollan et al. (2008) found a larger frequency effect for picture naming in the nondominant language,

Ivanova and Costa (2008) failed to replicate this result. Results reported by Sandoval et al. (2010) in the verbal fluency task complicate the picture even further. Bilinguals tended to produce more low-frequency words than monolinguals, a finding apparently inconsistent with the increased disadvantage for low-frequency words observed in picture naming, but also one in line with inhibitory accounts. Finally, regarding the performance of older adults, it seems like the bilingual disadvantage remains stable with increased age. Gollan et al. (2008) found smaller language dominance effects in older than in younger adults, but only for pictures with low-frequency names. However, none of the extant accounts predict bilingual disadvantages impermeable to ageing.

Are there ways to reconcile these findings? As highlighted by several researchers, it is unlikely that accounts that attribute the bilingual disadvantage to single sources (frequency of use, interference, postlexical processing difficulties) would be able to explain such a complex set of data (e.g., Gollan & Goldrick, 2012; Gollan, Ferreira, Cera, & Flett, in press). Furthermore, an interference account of the bilingual disadvantage does not really make any predictions about how frequency should modulate bilingual speech production. In the same way as one could argue that high-frequency translations should be stronger competitors for selection, one could argue that low-frequency targets should be more vulnerable to lexical competition, and especially from competitors in a stronger language. Thus, manipulating lexical frequency might not be as useful as initially thought for the purpose of discriminating between the two accounts. To conclude the section, it should be noted that more evidence and different approaches seems to be required to make any conclusive statements about which mechanism is responsible for the differences in performance between monolinguals and bilinguals.

Interactions of language control and semantic contextual effects

The continuous inhibition of words in the language not in use would render such words less accessible at a later point in time, and this should be true especially for L1 words since these should be strongly inhibited when L2 is in use. Long-lasting inhibitory effects could account not only for transient difficulties in L1 word retrieval—as those observed in language switching—but also for naming delays in L1 and even for the phenomenon known as first language attrition (the deterioration of L1; e.g., Köpke & Schmid, 2004; Schmid, 2002; Seliger & Vago, 1991). This hypothesis was tested in a recent experiment conducted by Levy and collaborators (Levy, Mc Veigh, Marful, & Anderson, 2007). The experiment included three tasks performed in sequence: (a) participants studied some pictures along with their L2 names; (b) depending on a color cue, pictures were named in L1 or L2 a varying number of times (ten, five, one or zero); (c) participants were presented with prompt words and retrieved the L1 picture names rhyming with the prompt words. Levy et al. observed that the retrieval of L1 words was impaired as the naming in L2 increased. An account assuming inhibitory mechanisms with long-lasting detrimental effects on L1 production could explain the findings of Levy et al. However, this account seems unable to accommodate two other results reported by Levy et al. First, the negative effect of naming in L2 on subsequent L1 memory was found only after 10 repetitions—after one or five repetitions L1 memory was facilitated or unaffected. Second, even after 10 repetitions the negative effects of L2 naming on L1 memory only appeared with participants with the lowest L2 fluency. Given that the people who experience either L1 attrition or slowing in L1 picture naming usually have high levels of fluency in L2, it is hard to see how this latter finding could be in line with the hypothesis of long-lasting detrimental effects on L1 production due to L2 production. These seemingly inconsistent results motivated a replication of the experiment originally conducted by Levy et al. (Runnqvist & Costa, 2012). Not only were the negative effects of L2 naming on L1 recall not found in this second study, but L1 memory was facilitated in each of the repetition conditions. The result pattern of this second experiment suggests that whatever the nature of the mechanisms responsible for bilingual language control, such mechanisms might not have detrimental consequences on memory retrieval. Although the source of the discrepancy between the experiments is presently unclear, the inconsistencies in the data demand us to be extremely cautious in interpreting Levy et al.'s results as supporting the hypothesis of inhibitory language control.

Along the same line of reasoning that producing words in one language should hamper subsequent production in another language due to inhibitory language control, Misra, Guo, Bobb and Kroll (2012) examined L1 and L2 speech production in a blocked naming context. The authors measured the RT's and the ERP waveforms in a picture naming task in which one group of participants first named pictures in L1 (2 blocks) and then named the same pictures in L2 (2 blocks), and another group of participants started in L2 and continued with L1. When comparing the first presentation for one group of participants with the third presentation for the other group of participants (i.e., the same picture in the same language preceded or not by naming in a different language) the authors found shorter RTs and more positive ERPs for repeated items when naming in L2 followed naming in L1. In contrast, for L1 naming after L2 naming, there was little evidence of repetition priming in RTs and more negative ERPs. All together, these data were interpreted as reflecting a sustained inhibition of L1 in contexts of blocked L2 speech.

Similarly, Van Assche, Duyck, and Gollan (in press) reported report two experiments in which Dutch-English and Chinese-English bilinguals completed a letter fluency task (i.e., produce as many words as possible beginning with the letter A). Language testing order was counterbalanced across participants and the task included one different category condition (different letters were used for the task in English and the other language) and one same category condition (the same letter was used for the task in English and the other language). The main finding replicated across the two groups of participants was that speakers produced fewer words in the same category condition in their dominant language after completing the task in their nondominant language. Additionally, there was some evidence that the Chinese bilinguals produced fewer words in the dominant language also in the different category condition after completing the task in the nondominant language. Again, this evidence was interpreted as being consistent with inhibitory models of language control. More specifically, the authors emphasized the importance of item-specific as opposed to whole-language control in the basic bilingual speech production architecture.

In evaluating these studies, it is important to keep in mind that inhibitory effects on behavior might not result only from inhibitory mechanisms. Indeed, recently other dynamics stemming from principles defined in the monolingual literature have been proposed to explain interference effects without the need of bilingual-specific language control structures (e.g., Runnqvist, Strijkers, Alario, & Costa, 2012; see also Runnqvist, Fitzpatrick, Strijkers, & Costa, 2012). This novel account capitalizes on the notion of persistent target strengthening thought responsible for semantic interference in monolingual speech production (e.g., see Howard, Nickels, Coltheart, & Cole-Virtue, 2006; Oppenheim, Dell, & Schwartz, 2010). In short, according to this account semantic interference effects are not caused by inhibition, but rather through the enhancement of the lexical representations and/or lexico-semantic connections of a just produced target, which in turn renders a semantically related word less accessible in future production through an increase in lexical competition. For example, producing the L2 word "perro" [dog], will strengthen this representation in the system. If, afterward, one wishes to utter its translation "dog," the previously strengthened "perro" [dog] will be a stronger competitor making the retrieval of "dog" harder. Note that in this explanation there is no need to assume inhibition within the system even though it elicits an inhibitory effect on behavior (for a similar reasoning in the field of memory see Raajmakers & Jakab, 2013).

Interestingly, also the exploration of another specific prediction made by the ICM is in fact better captured by the above speaker-general strengthening account. According to the ICM inhibitory control should lead in well-defined circumstances to the abolishment of semantic effects (both within and between languages) (Green, 1998). That is, when producing a word that is semantically related to a previously produced word, naming latencies should only be slower if there is no intervening language switch (regardless of the target language). This is because, according to the ICM, inhibition is applied to the nontarget lexicon as a whole, reducing the level of activation of all words in the nonintended language. Consequently, semantic effects are only predicted when the same language is used continuously, or immediately following a language switch (i.e., before the residual activation of the nontarget language has been successfully suppressed). That is, saying *cat* is predicted to interfere with the production of *gato* or *perro* only if they appear on consecutive trials (by means of a head start for *cat*). After that, inhibition is applied to the whole lexicon and *cat* will no longer have a higher resting level of activation than any other word and will thus not be a strong competitor for *gato* or *perro*. Similarly, the language-specific selection account only predicts transient effects of semantic relatedness, which are explained as within-language effects. That is, the activation of *cat* will coactivate *gato* and *perro* which (either on the same trial or a subsequent trial) may facilitate or interfere with, respectively, the

production of *gato* through residual activation. Such a mechanism should, however, not be functional for semantic relationships between items spanning more than one trial since it is known that residual activation alone cannot cause persistent priming (e.g., Howard et al., 2006).

One study (Lee & Williams, 2001) had provided evidence for the prediction of the ICM that semantic effects (e.g., production of *dog* slowing down subsequent production of *gato*) can be abolished by an intervening language switch. However, an attempt to replicate this study by Li and MacWhinney (2011) was only partially successful. A recent study tested the occurrence of cumulative semantic interference across languages (Runnqvist, Strijkers, et al., 2012). Cumulative semantic interference refers to the fact that naming a picture that belongs to the same semantic category as a previously named picture becomes increasingly harder (i.e., increases naming latencies) every time a new category member is named. This effect is thought to reflect the ease with which lexical items are accessed (either as a consequence of lexical competition or not; e.g., Costa et al., 2009; Howard et al., 2006; Oppenheim et al., 2010; Navarrete, Mahon, & Caramazza, 2010). In the bilingual version of this paradigm, cumulative semantic interference was obtained between languages and with the same magnitude as within-language, a result that cannot be accommodated by either the ICM or the language-specific selection model in their current forms. In contrast, these results are the predicted finding according to the simple strengthening and competition account discussed above, given that a strengthened item (due to previous production of that item) will induce the same amount of interference on a semantically related item, regardless of whether it is from the same language or not (for details see Runnqvist, Fitzpatrick, et al., 2012). We believe that further direct tests of this hypothesis may be a fruitful approach for future research and could offer a promising and simpler alternative to the existing accounts.

How do the collateral effects of bilingualism on attention relate to language control?

As described in the first section of this chapter, there is widespread agreement on the idea that bilingual speakers resort to some sort of cognitive control whenever speaking in one of their languages in order to avoid cross-language intrusions. Their extended experience of language control has been found to exert positive effects on attention processing across the life-span. For example, it has been observed that bilingual children outperform monolingual children in a card-sorting task that demands attention control (e.g., Bialystok, 1999) and that bilingual older adults experience reduced age-related cognitive decline as compared to monolinguals (e.g., Bialystok, Craik, Klein, & Viswanathan, 2004). Importantly, an advantage has also been found for young adults who are at the peak of their attentional abilities (e.g., Costa, Hernández, Costa-Faidella, & Sebastián-Gallés, 2009; Costa, Hernández, & Sebastán-Gallés, 2008; Hernández, Costa, Fuentes, Vivas, & Sebastián-Gallés, 2010). Therefore the bilingual advantage is not restricted to developmental stages in which the attention system is not at its maximum level of performance. In addition to provide a more comprehensive characterization of the bilingual experience, analyses of the bilingual advantages could inform us about the nature of bilingual language control. A primary thrust for pursuing this line of research derives from the observation that bilingualism advantages are not across the board; rather, they seem to be limited to the executive control network of attention that is plausibly involved in language control. In this section we summarize findings demonstrating the effects of bilingual experience on attention.

Several studies have reported smaller difference between congruent and incongruent trials in bilinguals as compared with monolinguals, a finding that was taken as indexing reduced conflict effect and therefore an advantage in conflict resolution in bilinguals (Bialystok et al., 2004; Bialystok et al., 2008; Costa et al., 2008; Hernández et al., 2010). This advantage seems to originate from a better ability to ignore irrelevant information as shown by several studies in which bilinguals outperform monolinguals in interference suppression but not in response inhibition (e.g., Martin Rhee & Bialystok, 2008). This can reasonably be put in relation to the continuous need to prevent massive interference from the nontarget language during speech production, the key assumption in inhibitory models of language control.

However, far from all studies that compared the performance of bilinguals and monolinguals in tasks requiring conflict resolution found reduced conflict effects with bilinguals, casting doubts on the robustness of this phenomenon (e.g., Costa et al., 2008). Enhanced conflict monitoring—overall faster responses than monolinguals in tasks involving conflict resolution—was the type of advantage typically reported (e.g., Bialystok, 2006; Bialystok et al., 2004; Bialystok, Martin, & Viswanathan, 2005; Bialystok et al., 2006; Costa et al., 2008; Martin-Rhee & Bialystok, 2008). Specifically, bilinguals are faster than monolinguals on both congruent and incongruent trials, but only in tasks that include both of these types of trials thus entailing high monitoring demands. This pattern of findings is believed to reflect the more efficient functioning, in bilinguals, of the system monitoring conflict resolution on trial-by-trial basis. The bilingual advantage manifests itself also in smaller costs in switching between different tasks or rules (e.g., Costa et al., 2008; Prior & MacWhinney, 2010), above all in those conditions in which switching is especially difficult (e.g., Costa et al., 2008). This could reflect a better ability of shifting mindsets, a property of executive control that is related to conflict monitoring. This specific advantage could stem from the need to continuously monitor the appropriate language for each communicative interaction. Assuming that it is possible to establish a direct link between components of executive control and components that have been proposed to underlie bilingual language control (i.e., monitoring vs. interference suppression), a better understanding of the relationship between executive and language control might help us to refine models of bilingual language production.

Before concluding this section, we want to draw attention to findings in early language acquisition of potential interest for understanding the nature of bilingual language control. Cognitive gains in executive control have been observed as early as 7 months of age in infants growing up in a bilingual environment (e.g., Kovacs & Mehler, 2009). The appearance of gains in preverbal infants calls into question accounts that trace bilinguals' enhanced executive control to interference suppression in language production. Instead, such precocious advantages suggest a link with *monitoring* the two languages. It is possible that some forms of conflict monitoring are needed to separate the acoustic input according to language. Forms of monitoring that originate in perception are later extended to production. Still, it is possible that the cognitive gains observed in infants and adults have different origins and are related to comprehension and production, respectively. The extent to which language control overlaps in production and comprehension is an important issue on which future research will hopefully make substantial progress.

Is there a common source for language control and the collateral effects of bilingualism?

The results we have reviewed so far in relation to mechanisms associated with language control, naming delays in L2 and L1, and bilingual advantages in executive control could be conceived as arising from a single processing or as stemming from different sources. If the inhibition of the nontarget language is common over all of these mechanisms, it should be possible to find correlated behavior and brain measures corresponding to these mechanisms. Some steps have already been taken towards examining such correlations.

In a meta-analysis, Abutalebi and Green (2007) examined the neuronal substrates of language switching and task switching. Results from patient studies and hemodynamic studies converged in showing that subcortical regions (particularly the left caudate), and regions in the frontal cortex (particularly the ACC and Broca area), are involved in tasks requiring language control. Interestingly, these regions have also been demonstrated to support nonlinguistic tasks that require increased cognitive control and attentional demands (e.g., Botvinick, Nystrom, Fissell, Carter, & Cohen, 1999; Brass, Ullsperger, Knoesche, von Cramon, & Phillips, 2005). This overlap suggests that the same network ensuring successful control over competing behavior is also engaged in the successful control of language output (e.g., Abutalebi & Green, 2007).

Abutalebi et al. (2012) directly examined whether there are neural structures commonly engaged by language control and general cognitive control. To this end, they tested the same participants on a language switching task (targeting language control) and a flanker task (target general cognitive control) while recording their brain activity with functional magnetic resonance imaging. It was observed that both tasks involved activation of the ACC, consistent with the previously discussed meta-analysis. Furthermore, when comparing the bilingual participants with a group of monolinguals performing the same flanker task, the authors observed a correlation between gray matter volume in the ACC and behavioral performance only for the bilingual group, as well as evidence for a more efficient use of the ACC (i.e., less activity) in the bilingual group compared with the monolingual group. Thus, altogether these results suggest that bilingualism, and in particular language control, induces functional neuroplasticity in the ACC, which has a positive impact on general cognitive control through a more efficient use of the ACC in situations of conflict. More generally, these data provide support for the hypothesis that bilingual language control is subsidiary to domain general executive control.

Using a different approach, Gollan et al. (2011) investigated whether language control failures increase with aging-related declines in executive control. It was observed that cross-language intrusions (e.g., inadvertently saying an English word on a Spanish-language trial) were strongly associated with flanker-task errors in older but not younger bilinguals, implying that executive control plays a role in maintaining language selection. On the other hand, the fact that such cross-language intrusions occurred rarely, also suggest the presence of independent forces that prevent language-selection errors. That is, this study suggest some but not a complete overlap between domain-general executive control and bilingual language control.

Also suggesting a certain independence of bilingual language control is another study by Calabria et al. (2012) in which high proficient bilinguals were tested in a language switching paradigm and a task switching paradigm. As discussed previously, high proficient bilinguals usually show symmetrical switch costs in language switching tasks (e.g., Costa & Santesteban, 2004). Hence, Calabria et al. reasoned that if bilingual language control is completely subsidiary to domain-general executive control, high proficient bilinguals should exhibit a symmetrical pattern also in a nonlinguistic switching task. Contrary to this prediction it was observed that switch costs between L1 and L2 were symmetrical, while switch costs between color and shape categorization were asymmetrical. Similarly, Weissberger, Wierenga, Bondi, and Gollan (2012) showed that aging-related slowing and aging-related increases in errors were larger in a nonlinguistic (color-shape) switching task than in a linguistic switching task. Thus, while the data of Abutalebi et al., (2011) show that language control overlaps to some extent with domain general executive control, the studies of Calabria et al. (2011) and Weissberger et al. (2012) show that such overlap is not complete, consistent with the study of Gollan et al. (2012).

Finally, while all the above studies tested the relationship between language control and domain general executive control, a study of Bialystok et al. (2008) aimed at testing whether the same processes underlie the bilingual advantage in executive control and the bilingual disadvantage in lexical access. The study was motivated by the following considerations on bilingual lexical retrieval. The language choices constantly made by bilinguals slow down lexical retrieval rendering it quite effortful. But to the extent that language choice engages the central control system of attention, control mechanisms become particularly efficient in this population. It is this constant experience in using attention to resolve conflict in online processing that ultimately determines the bilinguals' advantage in executive control. After having assessed participants' levels of executive control and lexical fluency, Bialystok et al. (2008) found that participants who showed the greatest access difficulties were not necessarily those who also showed the greatest advantages in executive control, leaving open the possibility that control advantage and access disadvantage are attributable to different causes in bilinguals.

To summarize, the attempts undertaken to examine the relationship between language control, executive control and the effects of bilingualism on language processing and nonlingusitic executive control processing have been fruitful in at least two ways: there is some evidence suggesting a common source for language control and executive control, but also evidence suggesting that such overlap is not complete; and evidence for both the beneficial effects in executive control and the detrimental effects in lexical processing has been obtained within the same participants, although they did not seem to correlate. With respect to bilingual language control, it is an area where promising results have been obtained but also one that merits further explorations particularly to determine whether the mechanisms proposed for domain-general control also extend to bilingual language control.

The development of language control and the collateral effects of bilingualism

An interesting question that concerns both the scope of all the issues we have addressed so far as well as the more general topic of brain plasticity is whether even relatively low proficient bilinguals show noticeable changes in language control, lexical access, and executive control. Throughout this chapter we have reviewed differences between high and low proficient bilinguals regarding both behavioral measures and patterns of brain activation. In most of these studies, age of acquisition and exposure were confounded. An attempt to untangle these variables was undertaken in two recent studies that investigated L2 acquisition in controlled environments that allow systematic variations in L2 exposure (immersed vs. classroom learning settings). Of particular interest here are the findings

reported by Linck, Kroll, and Sunderman (2009) in speech production using a semantic verbal fluency task. Immersed learners produced more words in L2 and fewer words in L1 compared with classroom learners. Together, these results suggest that becoming bilingual is associated with an early attenuation in L1 access. Similarly, Baus, Costa, and Carreiras (2013) tested immersed learners at the beginning of a learning program (pretest) and at its completion (posttest) on a picture naming and a verbal fluency task in L1. These authors observed that pictures with noncognate and low-frequency names were named slower at the posttest. Second, less noncognate names were generated in the fluency task at posttest. Thus, similarly to the findings of Linck et al. (2009), the findings of Baus and colleagues (2013) demonstrate a rather fast onset of the detrimental effects of bilingualism on L1 access. However, it is important to keep in mind that immersion learning is normally correlated with an increased use of the new language and a decreased use of the first language. Thus, as discussed by Baus et al. (2013), the most parsimonious interpretation of the above discussed results is that lexical access is a process with a considerable degree of plasticity making it susceptible to the effects of frequency of use, even on a rather short term. In the end what the results suggest is that the monolingual brain might successively lose its position as the default situation.

Conclusions

To summarize, although our knowledge regarding bilingual word production and language control mechanisms has increased impressively, it is our opinion that none of the current models can successfully account for the multitude of results. However, considerable progress in the research on bilingual language control has opened new paths in the investigation of bilingual word production, many of which were reviewed in this chapter. With respect to future research on language control more specifically, we hope we have been convincing in arguing that as it is necessary to widen the scope of the investigation beyond PWI and LS, it is essential to generate novel approaches. In addition, bilingual theories may benefit by taking notice of the progress made in other areas of cognition, for example memory where patterns of facilitatory and inhibitory effects that resemble those in bilingualism have been reported and promising theories have been developed (e.g., Anderson & Spellman, 1995; Carr & Dagenbach, 1990; Raajmaakers & Jakab, 2013). Finally, we should mention that the investigation of top-down influences of attention and speech intention on language production is an understudied topic. Over the last decade there have been compelling demonstrations of the importance of proactive goal-directed top-down influences on the retrieval of task-relevant information both in language (e.g., Delong, Urbach, & Kutas, 2005; Kutas & Federmeier, 2000; Strijkers et al., 2011) and other cognitive domains (e.g., Bar, 2003; Desimone & Duncan, 1995; Engel et al., 2001; Gilbert & Sigman, 2007; Kastner, Pinsk, De Weerd, Desimone, & Ungerleider, 1999). Research on bilingual language production would most certainly profit from exploring this type of control, especially in consideration of the fact that most of the time bilinguals know perfectly well in which language the communicative act will take place. In conclusion, a fruitful path to pursue in future research on bilingual word production appears to be one that combines the investigation of the collateral effects of bilingualism with the development of novel approaches to the study of language control.

References

Abdel Rahman, R., & Melinger, A. (2007). When bees hamper the production of honey: Lexical interference from associates in speech production. *Journal of Experimental Psychology: Learning, Memory and Cognition*, 33, 604–614.

Abdel Rahman, R., & Melinger, A. (2009). Semantic context effects in language production: A swinging lexical network proposal and a review. *Language and Cognitive Processes*, 24, 713–734.

Abutalebi, J., Della Rosa, P. A., Green, D. W., Hernandez, M., Scifo, P., Keim, R., Cappa, S. F., & Costa, A. (2012). Bilingualism tunes the anterior cingulate cortex for conflict monitoring. *Cerebral Cortex*, 22, 2076–2086.

Abutalebi, J., & Green, D. (2007). Bilingual language production: the neurocognition of language representation and control. *Journal of Neurolinguistics*, 20, 242–275.

Abutalebi, J., & Green, D. (2008). Control mechanisms in bilingual language production: Neural evidence from language switching studies. *Language and Cognitive Processes*, 23, 557–582.

Alario, F.-X., Goslin, J., Michel, V., & Laganaro, M. (2010). The functional origin of the foreign accent: Evidence from the syllable-frequency effect in bilingual speakers. *Psychological Science*, 21, 15–20.

Anderson, M. C., & Spellman, B. A. (1995). On the status of inhibitory mechanisms in cognition: Memory retrieval as a model case. *Psychological Review*, 102, 68–100.

Bar, M. (2003). A cortical mechanism for triggering top-down facilitation in visual object recognition. *Journal of Cognitive Neuroscience*, 15, 600–609.

Barsalou, L. W. (1999). Perceptual symbol systems. *Behavioral and Brain Sciences*, 22, 577–609.

Baus, C., Costa, A., & Carreiras, M. (2013). On the effects of second language immersion on first language production, *Acta Psychologica*, 142, 402–409.

Bialystok, E. (1999). Cognitive complexity and attentional control in the bilingual mind. *Child Development*, 70, 636–644.

Bialystok, E. (2006). Effect of bilingualism and computer video game experience on the Simon task. *Canadian Journal of Experimental Psychology*, 60, 68–79.

Bialystok, E., Craik, F. I. M., Klein, R., & Viswanathan, M. (2004). Bilingualism, aging, and cognitive control: Evidence from the Simon task. *Psychology and Aging*, 19, 290–303.

Bialystok, E., Craik, F. I. M., & Luk, G. (2008). Cognitive control and lexical access in younger and older bilinguals. *Journal of Experimental Psychology: Learning, Memory, and Cognition*, 34, 859–873.

Bialystok, E., Craik, F. I. M., & Ryan, J. (2006). Executive control in a modified anti-saccade task: Effects of aging and bilingualism. *Journal of Experimental Psychology: Learning, Memory, and Cognition*, 32, 1341–1354.

Bialystok, E., Martin, M. M., & Viswanathan, M. (2005). Bilingualism across the lifespan: The rise and fall of inhibitory control. *International Journal of Bilingualism*, 9, 103–119.

Bloem, I., & La Heij, W. (2003). Semantic facilitation and semantic interference in word translation: Implications for models of lexical access in language production. *Journal of Memory and Language*, 48, 468–488.

Bloem, I., van den Boogaard, S., & La Heij, W. (2004). Semantic facilitation and semantic interference in language production: Further evidence for the conceptual selection model of lexical access. *Journal of Memory and Language*, 51, 307–323.

Botvinick, M., Nystrom, L. E., Fissell, K., Carter, C. S., & Cohen, J. D. (1999). Conflict monitoring versus selection-for-action in anterior cingulate cortex. *Nature*, 402, 179–181.

Brass, M., Ullsperger, M., Knoesche, T. R., von Cramon, D. Y., & Phillips, N. A. (2005). Who comes first? The role of the prefrontal and parietal cortex in cognitive control. *Journal of Cognitive Neuroscience*, 17, 1367–1375.

Burke, D. M., MacKay, D. G., Worthley, J. S., & Wade, E. (1991). On the tip of the tongue: What causes word finding failures in young and older adults. *Journal of Memory and Language*, 30, 542–579.

Calabria, M., Hernández, M., Branzi, F. M., & Costa, A. (2012). Qualitative differences between bilingual language control and executive control: Evidence from task-switching. *Frontiers in Psychology*. 103389/psyg.2011.00399.

Caramazza, A. (1997). How many levels of processing are there in lexical access? Cognitive *Neuropsychology*, 14, 177–208.

Carr, T. H., & Dagenbach, D. C. (1990). Semantic priming and repetition priming from masked words: Evidence for a center-surround attentional mechanism in perceptual recognition. *Journal of Experimental Psychology: Learning, Memory and Cognition*, 16, 341–350.

Christoffels, I. K., Firk, C., & Schiller, N. (2007). Bilingual language control: An event-related brain potential study. *Brain Research*, 1147, 192–208.

Cohen, G., & Burke, D. M. (1993). Memory for proper names: A review. *Memory*, 1, 249–263.

Collins, A. M., & Loftus, E. F. (1975). A spreading-activation theory of semantic priming. *Psychological Review*, 82, 407–428.

Colomé, A. (2001). Lexical activation in bilinguals' speech production: Language-specific or language-independent? *Journal of Memory and Language*, 45, 721–736.

Costa, A. (2005). Lexical access in bilingual production. In J. F. Kroll & A. M. B. De Groot (Eds.), *Handbook of bilingualism: Psycholinguistic approaches* (pp. 308–325). New York: Oxford University Press.

Costa, A., Alario, F.-X., & Caramazza, A. (2005). On the categorical nature of the semantic interference effect in the picture–word interference paradigm. *Psychonomic Bulletin and Review, 12*, 125–131.

Costa, A., & Caramazza, A. (1999). Is lexical selection in bilingual speech production language-specific? Further evidence from Spanish-English and English-Spanish bilinguals. *Bilingualism: Language and Cognition, 2*, 231–244.

Costa, A., Caramazza, A., & Sebastian-Galles, N. (2000). The cognate facilitation effect: Implications for models of lexical access. *Journal of Experimental Psychology: Learning, Memory and Cognition, 26*, 1283–1296.

Costa, A., Hernández, A., Costa-Faidella, J., & Sebastián-Gallés, N. (2009). On the bilingual advantage in conflict processing: Now you see it, now you don't. *Cognition, 113*, 135–149.

Costa, A., Hernandez, M., & Sebastian-Gallés, N. (2008). Bilingualism aids conflict resolution: Evidence from the ANT task. *Cognition, 106*, 59–86.

Costa, A., Kovacic, D., Federenko, E., & Caramazza, A. (2003). The gender congruency effect and the selection of free-standing and bound morphemes: Evidence from Croatian. *Journal of Experimental Psychology: Learning, Memory, and Cognition, 29*, 1270–1282.

Costa, A., Miozzo, M., & Caramazza, A. (1999). Lexical selection in bilinguals: Do words in the bilingual's two lexicons compete for selection? *Journal of Memory and Language, 41*, 365–397.

Costa, A., & Santesteban, M. (2004). Lexical access in bilingual speech production: Evidence from language switching in highly-proficient bilinguals and L2 learners. *Journal of Memory and Language, 50*, 491–511.

Costa, A., Santesteban, M., & Ivanova, I. (2006). How do high-proficient bilinguals control their lexicalization process? Inhibitory and language-specific selection mechanisms are both functional. *Journal of Experimental Psychology: Learning Memory and Cognition, 32*, 1057–1074.

Costa, A., Strijkers, K., Martin, C., & Thierry, G. (2009). The time-course of word retrieval revealed by event-related brain potentials during overt speech. *Proceedings of the National Academy of Sciences, 106*, 21442–21446.

De Bot, K. (1992). A bilingual production model: Levelt's speaking model adapted. *Applied Linguistics, 13*, 1–24.

Dell, G. S. (1986). A spreading-activation theory of retrieval in sentence production. *Psychological Review, 93*, 283–321.

DeLong, K. A., Urbach, T. P., & Kutas, M. (2005). Probabilistic word pre-activation during language comprehension inferred from electrical brain activity. *Nature Neuroscience, 8*, 1117–1121.

Desimone, R., Duncan, J. (1995). Neural mechanisms of selective visual attention. *Annual Review of Neuroscience, 18*, 193–222.

Dhooge, E., & Hartsuiker, R. J. (2010). The distractor frequency effect in picture–word interference: Evidence for response exclusion. *Journal of Experimental Psychology: Learning, Memory and Cognition, 36*, 878–891.

Dhooge, E., & Hartsuiker, R. J. (2011a). How do speakers resist distraction? Evidence from a taboo picture-word interference task. *Psychological Science, 22*, 855–859.

Dhooge, E., & Hartsuiker, R. J. (2011b). The distractor frequency effect in a delayed picture-word interference task: Further evidence for a late locus of distractor exclusion. *Psychonomic Bulletin & Review, 18*, 116–122.

Dhooge, E., & Hartsuiker, R. J. (2012). Lexical selection and verbal self-monitoring: Effects of lexicality, context, and time pressure in picture–word interference. *Journal of Memory and Language, 66*, 163–176.

Engel, A. K., Fries, P., & Singer, W. (2001). Dynamic predictions: Oscillations and synchrony in top-down processing. *Nature Reviews Neuroscience, 2*, 704–716.

Evrard, M. (2002). Ageing and lexical access to common and proper names in picture naming. *Brain and Language, 81*, 174–179.

Finkbeiner, M., Almeida, J., Janssen, N., & Caramazza, A. (2006). Lexical selection in bilingual speech production does not involve language suppression. *Journal of Experimental Psychology: Learning, Memory and Cognition, 32*, 1075–1089.

Finkbeiner, M., & Caramazza, A. (2006). Now you see it, now you don't: On turning semantic interference into facilitation in a Stroop-like task. *Cortex, 42*, 790–796.

Finkbeiner, M., Gollan, T. H., & Caramazza, A. (2006). Lexical access in bilingual speakers: What's the (hard) problem? *Bilingualism: Language and Cognition, 9*, 153–166.

Flege, J. E., & Eefting, W. (1987). Cross-language switching in stop consonant perception and production by Dutch speakers of English. *Speech Commun, 6*, 185–202.

Flege, J. E., Schirru, C., & MacKay, I. R. A. (2003). Interaction between the native and second language phonetic subsystems. *SpeechCommun, 40*, 467–491.

Fowler, C. A., Brown, J. M., Sabadini, L., & Weihing, J. (2003). Rapid access to speech gestures in perception: Evidence from choice and simple response time tasks. *Journal of Memory and Language, 49*, 396–413.

Gilbert, C. D., & Sigman, M. (2007). Brain states: Top-down influences in sensory processing. *Neuron, 54*, 677–696.

Glaser, W. R., & Glaser, M. O. (1989). Context effects on Stroop-like word and picture processing. *Journal of Experimental Psychology: General, 118*, 13–42.

Gollan, T. H., & Acenas, L. A. (2004). What is a TOT? Cognate and translation effects on tip-of-the-tongue states in Spanish–English and Tagalog–English bilinguals. *Journal of Experimental Psychology: Learning, Memory, and Cognition, 30*, 246–269.

Gollan, T. H., Bonanni, M. P., & Montoya, R. I. (2005). Proper names get stuck on bilingual and monolingual speakers' tip of the tongue equally often. *Neuropsychology, 19*, 278–287.

Gollan, T. H., Fennema-Notestine, C., Montoya, R. I., & Jernigan, T. L. (2007). The bilingual effect on Boston Naming Test performance. *Journal of the International Neuropsychological Society, 13*, 197–208.

Gollan, T. H., & Ferreira, V. S. (2009). Should I stay or should I switch? A cost-benefit analysis of voluntary language switching in young and aging bilinguals. *Journal of Experimental Psychology: Learning, Memory & Cognition, 35*, 640–665.

Gollan, T. H., Ferreira, V. S., Cera, C., & Flett, S. (in press). Translation-priming effects of tip-of-the-tongue states. *Language and Cognitive Processes*.

Gollan, T. H., & Goldrick, M. (2012). Does bilingualism twist your tongue? *Cognition, 125*(3), 491–497.

Gollan, T. H., Montoya, R. I., Cera, C., & Sandoval, T. C. (2008). More use almost always means a smaller frequency effect: Aging, bilingualism, and the weaker links hypothesis. *Journal of Memory and Language, 58*, 787–814.

Gollan, T. H., Montoya, R. I., Fennema-Notestine, C., & Morris, S. K. (2005). Bilingualism affects picture naming but not picture classification. *Memory & Cognition, 33*, 1220–1234.

Gollan, T. H., Montoya, R. I., & Werner, G. (2002). Semantic and letter fluency in Spanish–English bilinguals. *Neuropsychology, 16*, 562–576.

Gollan, T. H., Sandoval, T., & Salmon, D. P. (2011). Cross-language intrusion errors in aging bilinguals reveal the link between executive control and language selection. *Psychological Science*, 22, 1155–1164.

Gollan, T. H., & Silverberg, N. B. (2001). Tip-of-the-tongue states in Hebrew–English bilinguals. *Bilingualism: Language and Cognition*, 4, 63–83.

Gollan, T. H., Slattery, T. J., Goldenberg, D., van Assche, E., Duyck, W., & Rayner, K. (2011). Frequency drives lexical access in reading but not in speaking: The frequency-lag hypothesis. *Journal of Experimental Psychology: General*, 140, 186–209.

Green, D.W. (1986). Control, activation and resource. *Brain and Language*, 27, 210–223.

Green, D. W. (1998). Mental control of the bilingual lexico-semantic system. *Bilingualism: Language and Cognition*, 1, 67–81.

Green, D. W. (2002). The bilingual as an adaptive system. *Bilingualism: Language and Cognition*, 5, 206–208.

Hanulová, J., Davidson, D. J., & Indefrey, P. (2010). Where does the delay in L2 picture naming come from? Psycholinguistic and neurocognitive evidence on second language word production. *Language and Cognitive Processes*, 26, 902–934.

Hermans, D. (2004). Between-language identity effects in picture–word interference tasks: A challenge for language-nonspecific or language-specific models of lexical access? *International Journal of Bilingualism*, 8, 115–125.

Hermans, D., Bongaerts, T., de Bot, K., & Schreuder, R. (1998). Producing words in a foreign language: Can speakers prevent interference from their first language? *Bilingualism: Language and Cognition*, 1, 213–230.

Hernandez, A. E., Dapretto, M., Mazziotta, J., & Bookheimer, S. (2001). Language switching and language representation in Spanish–English bilinguals: An fMRI study. *NeuroImage*, 14, 510–520.

Hernández, M., Costa, A., Fuentes, L., Vivas, A., & Sebastian-Gallés, N. (2010). The impact of bilingualism on the executive control and orienting networks of attention. *Bilingualism: Language and Cognition*, 13, 315–325.

Hirschfeld, G. H. F., Jansma, B., Boelte, J., & Zwitserlood, P. (2008). Interference and facilitation in overt speech production investigated with ERPs. *NeuroReport*, 19, 1227–1230.

Howard, D., Nickels, L., Coltheart, M., & Cole-Virtue, J. (2006). Cumulative semantic inhibition in picture naming: Experimental and computational studies. *Cognition*, 100, 464–482.

Indefrey, P. (2006). A meta-analysis of hemodynamic studies on first and second language processing: which suggested differences can we trust and what do they mean? In M. Gullberg & P. Indefrey (Eds.), *The cognitive neuroscience of second language acquisition* (pp. 279–304). Malden, MA: Blackwell Publishing.

Indefrey, P., & Levelt, W. J. M. (2004). The spatial and temporal signatures of word production components. *Cognition*, 92, 101–144.

Ivanova, I., & Costa A. (2008). Does bilingualism hamper lexical access in speech production? *Acta Psychologica*, 127, 277–288.

Jackson, G. M., Swainson, R., Cunnington, R., & Jackson, S. R. (2001). ERP correlates of executive control during repeated language switching. *Bilingualism: Language and Cognition*, 4, 169–178.

Janssen, N., Schirm, W., Mahon, B. Z., & Caramazza, A. (2008). The semantic interference effect in the picture-word interference paradigm: Evidence for the response selection hypothesis. *Journal of Experimental Psychology: Learning, Memory, & Cognition*, 34, 249–256.

Kastner, S., Pinsk, M., De Weerd, P., Desimone, R., & Ungerleider, L. (1999). Increased activity in human visual cortex during directed attention in the absence of visual stimulation. *Neuron*, 22, 751–761.

Kohnert, K. J., Hernandez, A. E., & Bates, E. (1998). Bilingual performance on the Boston Naming Test: Preliminary norms in Spanish and English. *Brain and Language*, 65, 422–440.

Köpke, B., & Schmid, M. S. (2004). Language attrition: The next phase. In B. Schmid, M. S. Köpke, M. Keijzer, & L. Weilemar (Eds.), *First language attrition: Interdisciplinary perspective on methodological issues* (pp. 1–43). Amsterdam & Philadelphia: John Benjamins.

Kroll, J. F., Bobb, S. C., Misra, M., & Guo, T. (2008). Language selection in bilingual speech: Evidence for inhibitory processes. *Acta Psychologica*, 128, 416–430.

Kutas, M., & Federmeier, K. D. (2000). Electrophysiology reveals semantic memory use in language comprehension. *Trends in Cognitive Science*, 4, 463–470.

La Heij, W. (2005). Selection processes in monolingual and bilingual lexical access. In J. F. Kroll & A. M. B. de Groot (Eds.), *Handbook of bilingualism* (pp. 289–307). Oxford: Oxford University Press.

Lakoff, G., & Johnson, M. (1999). *Philosophy in the flesh*. Basic Books.

Lee, M. W., & Williams, J. N. (2001). Lexical access in spoken word production by bilinguals: Evidence from the semantic competitor priming paradigm. *Bilingualism: Language and Cognition*, 4, 233–248.

Levelt, W. J. M., Roelofs, A., & Meyer, A. S. (1999). A theory of lexical access in speech production. *Behavioural and Brain Sciences*, 22, 1–75.

Levelt, W. J. M., Schriefers, H., Vorberg, D., Meyer, A. S., Pechmann, T., & Havinga, J. (1991). Normal and deviant lexical processing: Reply to Dell and O'Seaghdha (1991). *Psychological Review*, 98, 615–618.

Levy, B. J., Mc Veigh, N., Marful, A., & Anderson, M. C. (2007). Inhibiting your native language. The role of retrieval-induced forgetting during second-language acquisition. *Psychological Science*, 18, 29–34.

Li, H., & MacWhinney, B. (2011). Semantic competitor priming within and across languages: The interplay of vocabulary knowledge, learning experience and working memory capacity. *Bilingualism: Language and Cognition*, 14, 433–443.

Liberman, A. M., & Whalen, D. H. (2000). On the relation of speech to language. *Trends in Cognitive Sciences*, 4, 187–196.

Linck, J. A., Kroll, J. F., & Sunderman, G. (2009). Losing access to the native language while immersed in a second language: Evidence for the role of inhibition in second-language learning. *Psychological Science*, 12, 1507–1515.

Lucas, T. H., McKhann, G. M., & Ojemann, G. A. (2004). Functional separation of languages in the bilingual brain: A comparison of electrical stimulation language mapping in 25 bilingual patients and 117 monolingual control patients. *Journal of Neurosurgery*, 101, 449–457.

Lupker, S. J. (1979). The semantic nature of response competition in the Picture–Word Interference Task. *Memory and Cognition*, 7, 485–495.

Mägiste, E. (1985). Development of intra- and inter-lingual interference in bilinguals. *Journal of Psycholinguistic Research*, 14, 137–154.

Mahon, B. Z., Costa, A., Peterson, R., Vargas, K. A., & Caramazza, A. (2007). Lexical selection is not by competition: A reinterpretation of semantic interference and facilitation effects in the picture-word interference paradigm. *Journal of Experimental Psychology: Learning Memory and Cognition, 33,* 503–535.

Martin-Rhee, M. M., & Bialystok, E. (2008). The development of two types of inhibitory control in monolingual and bilingual children. *Bilingualism: Language and Cognition, 11,* 81–93.

Meiran, N. (1996). Reconfiguration of processing mode prior to task performance. *Journal of Experimental Psychology: Learning, Memory and Cognition, 22,* 1423–1442.

Mesulam, M. M. (1998). From sensation to cognition (review). *Brain, 121,* 1013–1052.

Meuter, R. F. I., & Allport, A. (1999). Bilingual language switching in naming: Asymmetrical costs of language selection. *Journal of Memory and Language, 40,* 25–40.

Meyer, A. S., Belke, E., Telling, A. L., & Humphreys, G. W. (2007). Early activation of object names in visual search. *Psychonomic Bulletin & Review, 14,* 710–716.

Meyer, A. S., & Damian, M. F. (2007). Activation of distractor names in the picture-picture interference paradigm. *Memory & Cognition, 35,* 494–503.

Miozzo, M., & Caramazza, A. (2003). When more is less: A counterintuitive effect of distractor frequency in picture–word interference paradigm. *Journal of Experimental Psychology: General, 132,* 228–252.

Misra, M., Guo, T., Bobb, S., & Kroll, J. F. (2012). When bilinguals choose a single word to speak: Electrophysiological evidence for inhibition of the native language. *Journal of Memory and Language, 67,* 224–237.

Monsell, S. (1996). Control of mental processes. In V. Bruce (Ed.), *Unsolved mysteries of the mind: Tutorial essays in cognition* (pp. 93–148). Hove, UK: Erlbaum.

Morsella, E., & Miozzo, M. (2002). Evidence for a cascade model of lexical access in speech production. *Journal of Experimental Psychology: Learning, Memory, and Cognition, 3,* 555–563.

Navarrete, E., & Costa, A. (2005). Phonological activation of ignored pictures: Further evidence for a cascade model of lexical access. *Journal of Memory and Language, 53,* 359–377.

Navarrete, E., Mahon, B. Z., & Caramazza, A. (2010). The cumulative semantic cost does not reflect lexical selection by competition. *Acta Psychologica, 134,* 279–289.

Oppenheim, G. M., Dell, G. S., Schwartz, M. F. (2010). The dark side of incremental learning: A model of cumulative semantic interference during lexical access in speech production. *Cognition, 114,* 227–252.

Philipp, A. M., Gade, M., & Koch, I. (2007). Inhibitory processes in language switching: Evidence from switching language-defined response sets. *The European Journal of Cognitive Psychology, 19,* 395–416.

Philipp, A. M., & Koch, I. (2009). Inhibition in language switching: What is inhibited when switching among languages in naming tasks? *Journal of Experimental Psychology: Learning, Memory, & Cognition, 35,* 1187–1195.

Poulisse, N. (1997). Language production in bilinguals. In A.M.B. de Groot & J. F. Kroll (Eds.), *Tutorials in bilingualism: Psycholinguistic perspectives* (pp. 201–224). Mahwah, NJ: Lawrence Erlbaum Associates.

Poulisse, N. (1999). *Slips of the tongue: Speech errors in first and second language production.* Amsterdam & Philadelphia: John Benjamins.

Poulisse, N., & Bongaerts, T. (1994). First language use in second language production. *Applied Linguistics, 15,* 36–57.

Prior, A., MacWhinney, B. (2010). A bilingual advantage in task switching. *Bilingualism: Language and Cognition, 13,* 253–262.

Pyers, J. E., Gollan, T. H., & Emmorey, K. (2009). Bimodal bilinguals reveal the source of tip-of-the-tongue states. *Cognition, 112,* 323–329.

Raajmakers, J. G. W., & Jakab, E. (2013). Rethinking inhibition theory: On the problematic status of the inhibition theory for forgetting. *Journal of Memory and Language, 68,* 98–122.

Rastle, K. G., & Burke, D. M. (1996). Priming the tip of the tongue: Effects of prior processing on word retrieval in young and older adults. *Journal of Memory and Language, 35,* 586–605.

Roberts, P. M., Garcia, L. J., Desrochers, A., & Hernandez, D. (2002). English performance of proficient bilingual adults on the Boston Naming Test. *Aphasiology, 16,* 635–645.

Roelofs, A. (1992). A spreading-activation theory of lemma retrieval in speaking. *Cognition, 42,* 107–142.

Roelofs, A. (2003). Goal-referenced selection of verbal action: Modeling attentional control in the Stroop task. *Psychological Review, 110,* 88–125.

Roelofs, A. (2006). The influence of spelling on phonological encoding in word reading, object naming, and word generation. *Psychonomic Bulletin & Review, 13,* 33–37.

Roelofs, A. (2008). Attention to spoken word planning: Chronometric and neuroimaging evidence. *Language and Linguistics Compass, 2,* 389–405.

Runnqvist, E., & Costa, A. (2012). Is retrieval-induced forgetting behind the bilingual disadvantage in word production? *Bilingualism: Language and Cognition, 15,* 365–377.

Runnqvist, E., Fitzpatrick, I., Strijkers, K., & Costa, A. (2012). An appraisal of the bilingual language production system: Quantitatively or qualitatively different from monolinguals? In T. K. Bhatia & W. C. Ritchie (Eds.), *The handbook of bilingualism and multilingualism* (2nd ed.) (pp. 244–265). Chichester, UK: John Wiley & Sons, Ltd.

Runnqvist, E., Strijkers, K., Alario, F.-X., & Costa, A. (2012). Cumulative semantic interference is blind to language: Implications for models of bilingual speech production. *Journal of Memory and Language, 66,* 850–869.

Runnqvist, E., Strijkers, K., Sadat, J., & Costa, A. (2011). On the temporal and functional origin of L2 disadvantages in speech production: A critical review *Frontiers in Psychology, 2,* 379

Sadat, J., Martin, C. D., Alario, F. X., & Costa, A. (2012). Characterizing the bilingual disadvantage in noun phrase production. *Journal of Psycholinguistic Research, 41,* 159–179.

Sahin, N., Pinker, S., Cash, S., Schomer, D., & Halgren, E. (2009). Sequential processing of lexical, grammatical, and phonological information within Broca's area. *Science, 326,* 445–449.

Sandoval, T. C., Gollan, T. H., Ferreira, V. S., & Salmon, D. P. (2010). What causes the bilingual disadvantage in verbal fluency? The dual-task analogy. *Bilingualism: Language and Cognition, 13,* 231–252.,

Schmid, M. S. (2002). *First language attrition, use and maintenance: The case of German Jews in Anglophone countries.* Amsterdam: Benjamins.

Schriefers, H., Meyer, A. S., & Levelt, W. J. M. (1990). Exploring the time course of lexical access in language production: Picture-word interference studies. *Journal of Memory and Language, 29,* 86–102.

Seliger, H. W., & Vago, R. M. (1991). The study of first language attrition: An overview. In H. W. Seliger & R. M. Vago (Eds.), *First language attrition* (pp. 3–16). Cambridge, UK: Cambridge University Press.

Smith, M. C., & Kirsner, K. (1982). Language and orthography as irrelevant features in colour–word and picture–word Stroop interference. *Quarterly Journal of Experimental Psychology, 34A,* 153–170.

Strijkers, K., Costa, A., & Thierry, G. (2010). Tracking lexical access in speech production: Electrophysiological correlates of word frequency and cognate effects. *Cerebral Cortex, 20,* 912–928.

Strijkers, K., Baus, C., FitzPatrick, I., Runnqvist, E., & Costa, A. (2013). The temporal dynamics of first versus second language speech production. *Brain & Language, 127,* 6–11.

Strijkers, K., Holcomb, P. J., & Costa, A. (2011). Conscious intention to speak proactively facilitates lexical access during object naming. *Journal of Memory and Language, 65,* 345–362.

Thierry, G., & Wu, Y. J. (2007). Brain potentials reveal unconscious translation during foreign-language comprehension. *Proceedings of the National Academy of Sciences of the United States of America, 104,* 12530–12535.

Ullman, S. (1995). Sequence seeking and counter streams: A computational model for bidirectional information flow in the visual cortex. *Cerebral Cortex, 1,* 1–11.

Valentine, P., Brennen, T., & Brédart, S. (1996). *The cognitive psychology of proper names: On the importance of being Ernest.* London: Routledge.

Van Assche, E., Duyck, W., & Gollan, T. H. (in press). Whole-language and item-specific control in bilingual language production. *Journal of Experimental Psychology: Learning, Memory and Cognition.*

Verhoef, K. M. W., Roelofs, A., & Chwilla, D. J. (2009). Role of inhibition in language switching: Evidence from event-related brain potentials in overt picture naming. *Cognition, 110,* 84–99.

Verhoef, K. M. W., Roelofs, A., & Chwilla, D. J. (2010). Electrophysiological Evidence for Endogenous Control of Attention in Switching between Languages in Overt Picture Naming. *Journal of Cognitive Neuroscience, 22,* 1832–1843.

Wang, Y., Xue, G., Chen, C., Xue, F., & Dong, Q. (2007). Neural bases of asymmetric language switching in second-language learners: An ERfMRI study. *Neuroimage, 35,* 862–870.

Weissberger, G. H., Wierenga, C. E., Bondi, M. W., & Gollan, T. H. (2012). Partially overlapping mechanisms of language and task control in young and older bilinguals. *Psychology and Aging, 27,* 959–974.

Phonology and Phonological Theory

Eric Baković

Abstract

This chapter provides an overview of some of the basic assumptions and results of phonology and phonological theory. The focus is on two main goals of phonological description and analysis: the establishment of generalizations about which members of a set of posited phonological constituents are irreducibly basic and that are derived, and the establishment of generalizations about the contexts in which phonological constituents are and are not found. These implicate four main sets of theoretical assumptions: representational assumptions about what phonological constituents are and what they consist of, analytical assumptions about the kinds of evidence that are brought to bear on the question of the basic versus derived nature of a constituent, computational assumptions about the mechanisms that relate representations of phonological constituents to each other, and architectural assumptions about how the phonological component interfaces with other grammatical components.

Key Words: phonology, phonological theory, distinctive features, inventories, phonotactics, alternations

The purpose of this chapter provide an overview of some of the basic assumptions and results of phonology and phonological theory.[1] Phonology is the study of the sound patterns of natural human languages (henceforth just "languages"). The workings of a language's sound patterns are generally assumed to be within the purview of a *phonological component* of the grammar of that language. Theories of phonology aim to adequately describe and explain the structure of the phonological components of languages by the analysis of their sound patterns.

My focus here is on two main goals of phonological description and analysis. The first of these is the establishment of generalizations about which members of a set of posited phonological constituents are irreducibly basic and which are derived. The description and analysis of these generalizations implicates two main sets of theoretical assumptions: *representational assumptions* about what phonological constituents are and what they consist of,

and *analytical assumptions* about the kinds of evidence that are brought to bear on the question of the basic versus derived nature of a constituent.

The second main goal is the establishment of generalizations about the contexts in which phonological constituents are and are not found. In addition to the two main sets of theoretical assumptions noted previously, the description and analysis of these generalizations typically implicates two other main sets of theoretical assumptions: *computational assumptions* about the mechanisms that relate representations of phonological constituents to each other, and *architectural assumptions* about how the phonological component interfaces with other grammatical components.

This chapter is organized by the four main sets of assumptions just mentioned. The details of all of these sets of assumptions vary widely. I make no effort to be comprehensive in my coverage here choosing instead to aim for generality and to focus on those assumptions I take to be more widespread among phonologists. After some very general remarks about the goals of phonological research, I begin with discussion of some basic representational assumptions to which I will make liberal reference in the sections that follow. This is followed by discussion of some basic analytical assumptions. Then I discuss some of the consequences of different computational assumptions. A few alternative grammatical architectures that are generally assumed are examined. Finally, I conclude with some summary remarks.

Goals of Phonological Research

Phonological research, and as a consequence phonological theory, is driven by two explanatory goals, which I simply assume to be complementary here.[2] One goal is essentially cognitive: to describe and explain how the sound patterns of a language are represented and computed in the mind/brain of a speaker/hearer of that language. The other goal is essentially typological: to describe and explain how the sound patterns of all languages are fundamentally the same and how they are superficially different.

The results of the pursuit of the cognitive goal are, at least on the face of it, most in line with what is probably of most immediate interest to readers of this volume: how are the representations and computations that phonologists theorize to be in the mind/brain of a speaker/hearer involved in the processing and production of speech? Results of the pursuit of the typological goal have also formed a great deal of the foundation for cognitive theories. Phonologists have generally presupposed, at least implicitly, that observed fundamental similarities across languages directly or indirectly reflect similarities across speakers/hearers in terms of a shared genetic cognitive endowment, regardless of the specifics of what this endowment may consist of. This presupposition in turn supports two other related assumptions that phonologists generally make: that speakers/hearers of all languages share a common vocabulary of representational constituents and computational devices, and that different speakers/hearers of the same language internalize essentially the same representations and computations (see de Lacy, 2009 for a specific probing of these and related assumptions).

Although I am agnostic on the specifics, in what follows I generally adopt the assumptions just sketched: that typological considerations are indicative of a prior genetic endowment shared by all language users, which leads to their adoption of essentially the same kinds of representations and computations.

Representational Assumptions

Any theory of phonology must make (and ideally, defend) assumptions about the cognitive representations of speech sounds. I discuss here a relatively conservative set of assumptions that many phonologists make about these representations.

One important assumption must be stated up front concerning the obvious fact that there is a distinction between the cognitive representations of speech sounds and the physical properties and manifestations of the sounds themselves. I adopt here the general assumption of many phonologists that the interface between cognitive representations and physical manifestations is mediated to some significant extent by *naturalness*; that cognitive representations are composed of constituents that are relatively directly motivated by and categorized according to their physical properties.

These physical properties can be divided into articulatory properties (properties of speech production) and acoustic/auditory properties (properties of speech perception). I focus more here on the interface between cognitive representations and articulation, but a thorough investment in the naturalness assumption also requires attention to the interface between cognitive representations and acoustics/audition. Cognitive representations must not only be mapped to the articulatory output produced by a speaker but must also be recovered from the acoustic/auditory input perceived by a listener.

Sustained arguments for and against naturalness can be found in Hayes, Kirchner, and Steriade (2004) and Hale and Reiss (2008), respectively. Simplifying greatly here, the argument for naturalness is that the nature, frequency, and distribution of different types of phonological patterns are best explained if we assume them to be constrained by cognitive biases that directly reflect our physical limitations. The argument against naturalness, however, is essentially Occamian: that the burden of proof is on the defenders of naturalness to explain why our physical limitations are not already sufficient to explain the nature, frequency, and distribution of different types of phonological patterns.

Segmentation

Natural speech is continuous: there are typically no pauses corresponding to the spaces between written words, much less clean breaks between the speech sounds corresponding (however roughly) to written symbols. However, a fundamental assumption of linguistic theory in general is that the cognitive representation of an utterance is categorically *segmented* at several levels; most significantly for phonological theory, at the level of the individual speech sound. The segmentation of speech into at least these individual speech sounds is a prerequisite to phonemic analysis.

There is some potential for disagreement about the particular segmentation of at least certain types of speech sounds, such as whether affricates (Lombardi, 1990; Clements, 1999) or diphthongs (Hayes, 1990; Schane, 1995) are one segment or two, and if one, whether they are simple or complex. There is even some denial of speech sound segmentation *tout court* (Port & Leary, 2005; Port, 2007). I proceed here under the assumptions of most phonologists, whereby segmentation is real and the lines are for the most part clear.

Speech sounds are themselves assumed to be complex constituents, made up of features that cross-classify them. Speech sounds are also assumed to be grouped into higher-order constituents, such as syllables.

Distinctive Features and Natural Classes

The production of an individual speech sound typically involves the coordination of various articulatory events, each contributing in some way to the overall acoustic signature of the sound. Speech sounds can be cross-classified according to these physical properties; some subset of the labels resulting from these cross-classifications are generally assumed to be part of our cognitive representations of speech sounds, typically going by the name of *distinctive features* (or often simply "features"). A rarely defended but practically always implicit assumption among feature theorists is that these features are innately available to language learners, but some recent work suggests that they are instead best understood to be emergent properties of learned phonological patterns (Mielke, 2008; see also several of the contributions to Ridouane & Clements, 2011).

One important function of incorporating distinctive features into a theory of phonological representation is to provide a physically grounded vocabulary for distinguishing speech sounds from one another; in fact, the "distinctive" part of "distinctive features" is meant to highlight this function. For example, a [p] is distinct from a [b] in that the former is a *voiceless* bilabial stop, whereas the latter is a *voiced* bilabial stop. Both speech sounds are classified as having a bilabial place of articulation (meaning they are articulated with the lips) and as stops (meaning that they involve a complete constriction at the specified place of articulation), but [b] involves vibration of the vocal folds (= voiced), whereas [p] does not (= voiceless). Especially if this physical difference between [p] and [b] serves some contrastive function in a given language (that is, if there are words the meanings of which are distinguished solely or primarily by whether one of the speech sounds is a [p] or a [b]) then this is taken to be evidence that "voicing" is a distinctive feature of that language. The more contrasts in voicing, the greater the evidence: if [p] and [b] are distinct, then so might [t] and [d] or [k] and [g] be, since the members of these pairs also differ from each other solely in terms of voicing.

Another important function of distinctive features is to provide a vocabulary for describing *natural classes* of speech sounds; that is, sets of speech sounds that pattern together in the phonologies of some languages.[3] Making reference to the features that define natural classes makes it possible to state generalizations about patterns that would only be less adequately described by listing the members of the sets of speech sounds involved in those patterns. For example, a language may distinguish voiced stops [b,d,g] from voiceless stops [p,t,k] before vowels but not elsewhere; reference to the natural class of "stops" leads to a more adequate description of this distribution.

Theories of distinctive features may differ in terms of the precise set of natural classes that are able to be described. Some of these differences are ad hoc, but some are caused by more principled differences in the sets of physical properties to which features are allowed to make reference. For example, some feature theories give more (or even exclusive) weight to the articulatory events of which speech sounds are composed (Chomsky & Halle, 1968; Halle, 1983, 1995; Clements & Hume, 1995; Halle, Vaux, & Wolfe, 2000), whereas others give some more weight to the acoustic contributions that these (clusters of) articulatory events make (Jakobson, Fant, & Halle, 1952; Flemming, 1995; Stevens, 2002, 2003).

Still other differences of this type may be caused by a principled difference between the number of "values" that distinctive features may have, and how computations may make reference to those values. Features may be unary (or "privative"), having only one value (the presence of the feature) to which reference may be made; binary (or "equipollent"), having two values (typically "+" or "–"); ternary, having three values ("+" / "–" / absent); or multivalued in some further form. Phonologists typically assume some combination of these distinctive feature types, such that some features are unary (e.g., those denoting a consonant's place of articulation; Sagey, 1986; Clements & Hume, 1995); others (e.g., the feature denoting a speech sound's voicing) are binary (Wetzels & Mascaró, 2001) or ternary (Inkelas, 1994); and still others are multivalued (e.g., the feature denoting the relative height of the tongue body during the production of a vowel; Clements, 1991; Parkinson, 1996).

Theories of distinctive features may also differ in terms of the relative autonomy enjoyed by those features. Earlier, "segmental" theories (Jakobson et al., 1952; Chomsky & Halle, 1968) adopted an essentially classificatory approach, where each speech sound is composed of an unstructured list of its features. Later, "autosegmental" theories (Goldsmith, 1976; Clements, 1985; Sagey, 1986; McCarthy, 1988; Clements & Hume, 1995) granted speech sounds more structure and features more independence, for instance by allowing a single instance of a feature to span more than one speech sound.

This distinction affects the character of the computations involved in describing phonological patterns involving features. For example, a language may distinguish among several places of articulation in nasal consonants [m,n,ŋ] (= the class of consonantal speech sounds that involve a lowering of the soft palate so that air escapes through the nasal cavity) when these appear before vowels, but these place of articulation distinctions may be neutralized before other consonants such that a nasal must have the same place of articulation as the following consonant (e.g., bilabial [m] before [p,b]). This pattern would be characterized as a *copying* of the place of articulation feature of the consonant to the nasal in segmental theories and as *spreading* of the place of articulation feature from the consonant to the nasal in autosegmental theories.[4]

One argument for the general autosegmental approach is computational simplicity: possible types of computations are limited to insertion, deletion, and spreading of features. Another argument is representational naturalness: for example, a shared place of articulation feature between a nasal and a following consonant reflects the phonetic reality that a single articulatory gesture spans the nasal+consonant cluster. This latter argument extends to a similar representation of long vowels and long (= geminate) consonants: a single speech sound "melody" shared between two "timing units" (McCarthy, 1979; Clements & Keyser, 1983; Hayes, 1989; Perlmutter, 1995).

Groupings of Speech Sounds

As some of the previous examples have shown, the distributions of (features of) speech sounds are influenced by the position of those speech sounds relative to other, neighboring speech sounds. Sometimes this influence is relatively direct, for instance when the place of articulation of a nasal is directly determined by the place of articulation of a following consonant. But other times this influence appears to be less direct, and appears to require reference to something other than the neighboring context. In many such cases, crucial reference is made to higher-order constituents; these constituents serve as domains of or boundaries for phonological patterns. The level of general acceptance of each of these posited higher-order constituents has depended on the degree to which they have been motivated by independent strands of converging evidence, both within a single language and across multiple languages.

Returning to one of the previous examples, a distinction between voiced stops [b,d,g] and voiceless stops [p,t,k] that holds before vowels may be neutralized when the stops appear elsewhere, that is, before any other consonant (regardless of that consonant's voicing) or at the end of the word. Because the voicing of the following consonant has nothing to do with this neutralization, and because being at the end of the word also conditions it, how to characterize the neutralization in terms of the neighboring context is not obvious.[5] Many phonologists assume that the higher-order grouping of speech sounds into syllables is responsible: to be "before a consonant or at the end of the word" is to be at the end of a syllable (Kahn, 1976; Blevins, 1995).

The syllable is more than a notational convenience; a syllable-based description can capture a generalization that otherwise may be more difficult to capture. For example, it is reasonable to assume that possible word-initial consonant clusters are also possible syllable-initial clusters, meaning that word-internal clusters that are also found word-initially are grouped together in the same syllable, whereas those that are not also found word-initially are divided between syllables. This has an obvious impact on the "before a consonant → at the end of a syllable" entailment in languages with word-initial consonant clusters: some consonants before other consonants are syllable-final, whereas others are not. Indeed, languages with word-initial consonant clusters that neutralize voicing distinctions as described previously typically do so only syllable-finally; that is, voicing distinctions are neutralized only in clusters that are not found word-initially.

Higher-order constituents other than syllables are also generally assumed to exist. Some of these are subsyllabic constituents, such as onsets (syllable-initial consonants and clusters), nuclei (vowels and vowel-like elements), and codas (syllable-final consonants and clusters) (Clements & Keyser, 1983; Davis, 1985; Blevins, 1995), and the timing units that are held to be responsible for vowel and consonant length. Others are suprasyllabic; for example, pairs of syllables may be grouped into metrical feet (Liberman & Prince, 1977; Hayes, 1995), primarily motivated by (and held to be responsible for) the rhythmic properties of word stress. There are also even larger constituents, such as the phonological (or "prosodic") word (Selkirk, 1980); the phonological phrase (Nespor & Vogel, 1986); and the intonational phrase (Pierrehumbert & Beckman, 1988).

The following diagrams provide a sense of how all of these representational pieces fit together. In (1) is a high-level overview of an utterance consisting of two intonational phrases (delimited by curly brackets), the first consisting of three phonological phrases (delimited by angled quotation marks), and the first of these consisting of three prosodic words (delimited by square brackets). In (2) is a close-up view of the second phonological phrase, showing the constituents of speech sounds into subsyllabic constituents (o = onset, n = nucleus, c = coda), themselves grouped into syllables (= σ), which are themselves grouped into metrical feet (delimited by parentheses). Finally, in (3) is an even closer look at some of the features that make up of the coda cluster [mpt].

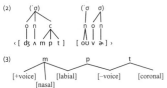

Analytical Assumptions

As noted in the introduction, I focus here on two main goals of phonological description and analysis: making generalizations about which members of a set of posited phonological constituents are basic and which are derived, and making generalizations about the contexts in which phonological constituents are and are not found. These goals are closely linked in ways that are made clear in this section.

The focus of the discussion in this section is on the most basic of the phonological constituents identified previously: speech sounds and distinctive features. Indeed, higher-order constituents are typically defined primarily in terms of their utility in describing and analyzing the distributions of speech sounds and features and only secondarily in terms of their own distributions and status as basic versus derived.

Inventories

Even a cursory description of the phonological patterns of a language typically includes a description of an *inventory* of the speech sounds used in the language. This inventory is typically defined at two levels: the set of speech sounds used *systematically*, and the proper subset of speech sounds used *distinctively* (there are a number of theoretical assumptions that can be tied up in the difference between the distinctive and systematic levels of phonological description and analysis; I side step many here).

For example, the inventory of speech sounds in English includes the bilabial stops [pʰ], [p], and [b], where [ʰ] indicates aspiration.[6] All three sounds are used systematically in English; compare [pʰæn] "pan," [spæn] "span," and [bæn] "ban." However, not all three are used distinctively: the meanings of two English words may be distinguished solely or primarily by the difference between [pʰ] and [b] (to wit, "pan" vs. "ban" above) or by the difference between [p] and [b] ([kʰæp] "cap" vs. [kʰæb] "cab") but not by the difference between [pʰ] and [p]. The difference between [pʰ] and [p] (the aspiration feature alone) is thus not distinctive in English; it is derived rather than basic.

Of course, every actual production of a speech sound differs in some way from any other production of a speech sound, even of one that is systematically "the same" speech sound. A systematic speech sound is thus an idealization; all else being ideally equal, the [pʰ] of [pʰæn] "pan" is systematically the same as the [pʰ] of [pʰɪt] "pit," both differ systematically from the systematically equal [p] of [spæn] "span" and [spɪt] "spit," and all of these differ systematically from the systematically equal [b] of [bæn] "ban" and [bɪt] "bit."

Languages differ in terms of one or both of these kinds of inventories. In Thai, for example, [pʰ], [p], and [b] are used systematically, but unlike English, the differences between all three of these stops are also distinctive: [pʰâː] "cloth" versus [pâː] "aunt" versus [bâː] "crazy." In both Spanish and Tamil, [p] and [b] are used systematically, but [pʰ] is not; the difference between [p] and [b] is also distinctive in Spanish ([peso] "weight" vs. [beso] "kiss"), but not in Tamil. In Quechua, [pʰ] and [p] are used systematically and distinctively ([wampʰu] "opening" vs. [wampu] "boat"), but [b] is not.

Distinctive speech sounds are known as *phonemes*, and the symbols representing them are typically enclosed in slashes as opposed to the square brackets reserved for systematic speech sounds (= *phones*). Thus, [b] is a phone associated with a phoneme of English that can be represented as /b/, whereas [p] and [pʰ] are phones associated with another phoneme that can be represented as either /p/ or /pʰ/ (or some voiceless bilabial stop representation unspecified for aspiration that can be unified with both).

Further analysis is typically required to determine whether two (or more) phones are associated with (= are *allophones* of) the same phoneme, and also to determine the representation of the phoneme with which those allophones are associated. The ultimate criterion is based on the assumption that the grouping of systematic phones into distinctive phonemes is psychologically real (Sapir, 1949); specifically, two phones are allophones of the same phoneme in some language given behavioral evidence that native speakers of that language treat the phones as "the same sound." The most compelling kind of evidence for phonologists comes from what are called *alternations* (discussed later).

Speech sound inventories are typically not random collections; rather, they appear to be largely organized in *series* that can be defined in terms of their features (Maddieson, 1984). For example, the systematic speech sound inventory of English includes a series of voiceless unaspirated stops [p,t,k], a series of voiceless aspirated stops [pʰ,tʰ,kʰ], a series of voiced stops [b,d,g], and a series of nasals [m,n,ŋ]. Each series contains a member from a given place of articulation: bilabial [p,pʰ,b,m]; alveolar [t,tʰ,d,n]; and velar [k,kʰ,g,ŋ]. Moreover, statements about the relationship between systematic and distinctive speech sound inventories typically apply in series: in English, the difference between all voiceless aspirated stops and their unaspirated counterparts is nondistinctive, whereas the difference between all

voiced and voiceless stops is distinctive. The same considerations apply to the other languages mentioned previously in the text: Thai distinguishes series of voiceless aspirated, voiceless unaspirated, and voiced stops; Spanish only distinguishes series of voiceless and voiced stops; Tamil uses a series of voiceless and voiced stops systematically but not distinctively; and Quechua only distinguishes series of voiceless aspirated and voiceless unaspirated stops.

The generality of such statements leads many phonologists to the conclusion that the features themselves are the foci of those statements. In other words, it is not that voiced stops are phonemes distinct from voiceless stop phonemes in English, but rather that the voicing feature *is phonemic* (= is basic) in English. Likewise, it is not that voiceless unaspirated stops are not distinct from voiceless aspirated stops in English, but rather that the aspiration feature is *not* phonemic (= is derived) in English.

Interactions

The systematic or distinctive deployment of a particular feature or speech sound can depend on a number of factors, including (but not limited to) interactions between features within the same speech sound; interactions between (features of) neighboring speech sounds; and interactions with higher-order constituents.

INTERACTIONS BETWEEN FEATURES WITHIN THE SAME SPEECH SOUND

The articulatory gesture associated with a given feature (or its acoustic/auditory consequence) may be incompatible with that of another feature to some degree. For example, complete closure of the vocal tract (as in the articulation of a stop) inhibits the maintenance of continuous vibration of the vocal folds, and this inhibition is greater for posterior places of articulation than for anterior ones (Ohala, 1983). Thus, it is not surprising to find languages with speech sound inventories lacking the velar (= posterior) voiced stop [g] (as in Thai) or voiced stops altogether (as in Quechua).

However, the articulatory gesture associated with a feature (or its acoustic/auditory consequence) may *enhance* that of another feature (Keyser & Stevens, 2006). For example, the acoustic difference between the English alveolar fricative [s] and postalveolar fricative [ʃ] (as in [sɪn] "sin" vs. [ʃɪn] "shin") is enhanced by lip rounding, which is not used to distinguish English consonants from each other on its own.

INTERACTIONS BETWEEN (FEATURES OF) NEIGHBORING SPEECH SOUNDS

The realization of a featural distinction often depends on neighboring speech sounds. This was noted previously with the example of a hypothetical (and in reality, quite common) language that distinguishes among several places of articulation in nasal consonants except before other consonants, where a nasal must have the same place of articulation as the following consonant. This is an example of *assimilation*, whereby one sound systematically takes on a feature of a neighboring sound; this particular type of example is known as *nasal place assimilation*. Other common types of assimilation are *voicing assimilation*, whereby the voicing of a consonant systematically matches the voicing of a neighboring consonant; *palatalization*, whereby the articulation of a consonant systematically matches the articulation of a neighboring palatal vowel (= a vowel with a raised or fronted tongue body); and *vowel harmony*, whereby one or more features of a vowel systematically match the same features of a neighboring vowel.[7]

Assimilations are often subject to restrictions on any or all of the following: the *target* of the assimilation (e.g., that it must be a nasal); the *trigger* of the assimilation (e.g., that it must be a stop); the *direction* of the assimilation (e.g., that the nasal must precede the stop); and the *domain* of the assimilation (e.g., within a prosodic word but not between words). Principled explanations of these restrictions (which ones are found, in what combinations, and so forth) are the focus of much research in phonological theory.

A speech sound may also systematically take on a *different* feature (or a different value of a feature) than a neighboring sound; this is called *dissimilation*. Two neighboring speech sounds may systematically trade places (*metathesis*); a consonant's articulation may be systematically weakened (= shortened, or its closure made less complete) when neighboring a vowel or other weakly articulated consonant (*lenition*); or the features of two neighboring speech sounds may merge into a single speech sound (*fusion*).

INTERACTIONS WITH HIGHER-ORDER CONSTITUENTS

Some of the interactions with neighboring speech sounds noted previously may also involve interactions with higher-order constituents; in some cases, for example, they appear to be motivated by resulting improvements in syllable structure. There are well-documented preferences for syllables with single onset (= syllable-initial) consonants and no coda (= syllable-final) consonants (Clements & Keyser, 1983), even in languages that (like English) tolerate clusters of consonants both within and across syllables; such clusters also tend to conform to similar apparent principles across languages (Selkirk, 1984; Clements, 1990; Morelli, 1999). These preferences and principles may be systematically furthered by metathesis or fusion; vowels may be given more consonant-like articulations or consonants more vowel-like articulations; entire speech sounds may be deleted or inserted outright (as in English [weɪʤd] "waged" vs. [weɪdəd] "waded").

Positions within the syllable also play a role in the featural realization of speech sounds; in particular, syllable codas tend to license a proper subset of the set of distinctions that are licensed in syllable onsets (Harris, 1983; Ito & Mester, 1993; Beckman, 1998). Such "edge effects," whereby one side or another of a higher-order constituent licenses more or fewer contrasts than other positions, are not uncommon. Other interactions with higher-order constituents include so-called "minimal word effects" (McCarthy & Prince, 1995), whereby the prosodic words of a language must be of some minimum size or length (usually a metrical foot), and domain boundedness, whereby an assimilation occurs only within a particular constituent (often a prosodic word).

Computational Assumptions

The various types of interactions discussed previously are generally assumed to be the results of computational mechanisms of the phonological component of the grammar, deriving the systematic patterns observed in *surface representations* of utterances (= the output of the phonological component) from arrays of distinctive constituents stored in *underlying representations* of lexical items (= the input to the phonological component). These representations are assumed to be the interfaces between the phonological component and other cognitive modules of linguistic knowledge; specifically, underlying representations are interfaces with the morphologic and syntactic components (which encode word and phrase formation patterns) and surface representations are interfaces with the phonetic component (which encodes the gradient detail of the production and perception of speech sounds).

For some phonologists, these mechanisms take the form of *rewrite rules* that both target and change features of underlying representations in a serial procedure leading to a particular surface representation (Chomsky & Halle, 1968). For others, the mechanisms take the form of resolutions of conflicts between constraints that define desirable surface configurations and constraints that penalize imperfect correspondences between underlying and surface representations; candidate surface representations are compared by the constraints in parallel, and conflicts are resolved by ranking (Prince & Smolensky, 1993) or numerical weighting (Smolensky & Legendre, 2006). Still others adopt other approaches, such as hybrid models with both constraints and rewrite rules (Calabrese, 2005) or ones with serial candidate comparison by ranked constraints (McCarthy, 2007, 2010).

Phonotactics

Evidence for these computational mechanisms is of two kinds. One kind is the straightforward distribution of (features of) speech sounds; the fact that they are found in some contexts and not in others. In these types of cases, generalized grammatical statements of these distributions (often called *phonotactic constraints*) are typically sufficient.

For example, the distributions of consonants in word-initial clusters in English are restricted in the following ways. Consider first the clusters of two consonants. If the second consonant is [r], then the first consonant may be any of the stops [p,t,k,b,d,g] or fricatives [f,ʃ]. If the second consonant is [l], however, then a preceding stop may only be one of [p,k,b,g] (i.e., not one of the alveolars [t,d]), and a preceding fricative may be one of [f,s] but not [ʃ]. If the second consonant is a nasal [m,n] or stop [p,t,k], then the first consonant must be [s]; in clusters of three consonants, the first must be [s], the second must be one of [p,t,k], and the third must be [r] or [l] (and the latter only if the second is not [t]). Restrictions like these are found in many different languages; they are structured, principled, and not arbitrary. Precise formal statements of phonotactic constraints expressing these restrictions differ, but phonologists generally agree that the phonological component of a language is made up in part by such statements.

Alternations

The second kind of evidence comes from *alternations*, a term that refers to examples of meaningful phonological units (= *morphemes*) the surface representations of which vary systematically according to their context within an utterance. The significance of this kind of evidence is predicated on the assumption that (the constituents of) the surface variants of a morpheme *correspond* with each other, via a single underlying representation that includes all idiosyncratic, unpredictable properties (and for some, only these).

For example, the English morpheme "atom" is systematically pronounced [ˈærəm] when unsuffixed but [əˈtʰɑːm] when suffixed with "-ic." Three of the four speech sounds of this morpheme have imperfect correspondences between these two pronunciations: stressed [æ] with unstressed [ə]; [r] in the onset of an unstressed syllable with [tʰ] in the onset of a stressed syllable; and unstressed [ə] with stressed [ɑː]. The root cause of all three is an idiosyncratic requirement of the suffix "-ic," that the syllable preceding it be stressed, trumping the conflicting requirement of the morpheme "atom" that its initial syllable be stressed. Unstressed syllables in English license fewer vowel contrasts than stressed syllables, reducing many of them to a mid-central vowel [ə]; voiceless stops are aspirated at the left edges of stressed syllables but not otherwise; alveolar stops are lenited to the tap [r] between vowels when the following vowel is unstressed. Reduction, aspiration, and lenition being predictable but other properties not, the underlying representation of this morpheme can be deduced to be /ˈætɑːm/. From this, the systematic surface variants are *derived* by computational mechanisms corresponding more or less to the statements of reduction, aspiration, and lenition given previously.

Some alternations provide solid evidence for the conclusion that two systematic phones are allophones of the same phoneme. For example, the fact that [r] in "atom" corresponds with [tʰ] in "atomic" demonstrates that these two phones are allophones of the same phoneme in English, /t/. In Spanish, the fact that the voiced bilabial stop [b] in [ˈbaso] "glass" corresponds with the voiced bilabial fricative [β] in [miˈβaso] "my glass" demonstrates that these two phones are allophones of the same phoneme, /b/ or /β/.[8]

Alternations can also provide evidence for the neutralization of particular phonemic distinctions. For example, the vowel alternations in "atom" and "atomic" demonstrate that the distinction between /æ/ and /ɑː/ ([ˈsæd] "sad" vs. [ˈsɑːd] "sod") is neutralized to [ə] in unstressed syllables, as indeed are many of the vowel distinctions in English. Likewise, the distinction between /t/ and /d/ ([ˈbæt] "bat" vs. [ˈbæd] "bad") is neutralized to [r] between vowels when the following vowel is unstressed: [ˈbærɚ] could be either "batter" or "badder," modulo systematic vowel length differences before the [r]. The "completeness" of these and other neutralizations has been challenged. See Flemming and Johnson (2007) on neutralization of unstressed vowels to [ə], Braver (2011) on neutralization of /t,d/ to [ɾ], and Port and Leary (2005) and van Oostendorp (2008) for examination of the relevant issues more generally.

Architectural Assumptions

The minimal architectural assumption, shared by all phonological theories making the kinds of representational, analytical, and computational assumptions outlined thus far in this chapter, is that there are two levels of representation for the computation of an utterance. One is an underlying representation, stored separately for every morpheme, which at the very least encodes basic distinctions among phonological constituents. The other is a systematic surface representation, the end result of the changes made by the rules or constraints that apply in the course of the computation.

Elaborations of these theories differ according to whether there are significant levels of representation other than these two; these additional levels of representation are typically motivated by observed interactions between the phonological component and other components of grammar, most significantly morphology and syntax. For example, many phonologists subscribe to some variant of the theory of lexical phonology and morphology (Kiparsky, 1982, in press), whereby phonological and morphological computations are interleaved such that the product of every morphological computation (e.g., the addition of an affix to a stem) is the input to a phonological computation. Research within this theory has identified significant differences between phonological computations applying to different morphological constituents, leading to models in which there are levels of representation corresponding to these differences.

The phonological component may also interact with the morphological and syntactic components by "interface constraints" regulating either the cross-component alignment of category edges (Selkirk, 1986; McCarthy & Prince, 1994) or the correspondence between morphophonological constituents (Burzio, 1994; McCarthy & Prince, 1995).

There is of course also the not-insignificant matter of the interface between the systematic surface representation level of the phonological component and the ultimate phonetic output. There is mounting evidence that much of what was once relegated to a universal, noncategorical "phonetic interpretation module" (and even some of what was once considered "low-level" systematic phonology) is both language-specific and gradient. This has led to the development of several detailed models of the interface between phonology and phonetics (e.g., Browman & Goldstein, 1992; Zsiga, 1997; Boersma, 1998; Flemming, 2001; Pierrehumbert, 2003; and Ladd, 2008).

Summary

Phonologists aim to adequately describe the structure of the phonological components of languages by the analysis of their sound patterns. The main goals of phonological description and analysis are the establishment of generalizations about the distribution and reducibility of phonological constituents in different languages. These goals have led to the development of four main sets of assumptions: (1) representational, (2) analytical, (3) computational, and (4) architectural. Phonologists generally share the assumptions laid out in this chapter, although of course the specifics differ from one theory to another.

Notes

1. It is of course not possible to delve as deeply as one would like into any of the areas covered here, and I attempt to counterbalance the resulting superficiality by citing some of the relevant literature. It is also not possible to reach out as broadly as one might like. I am afraid that I make far less of an effort to remedy this deficiency. My citation bias is in many cases at least modestly geared toward more recent work, in large part because previous work can be tracked down more easily that way than vice versa. I somewhat purposely do not cite the individual contributions to three recently published compendia of phonological research (de Lacy, 2007; van Oostendorp, Ewen, Hume, & Rice, 2011; and Goldsmith et al., 2011) and instead encourage the interested reader to consult any or all of these volumes for further detailed discussion. The second is especially comprehensive and accessible both by design and in fact.

2. These goals are sometimes assumed to be in conflict, but usually only when a particular set of theoretical assumptions made with one goal in mind is questioned or argued against with the other in mind.

3. But see Flemming (2005), where it is argued that natural classes derive not from the content of the set of available features but from the content of the set of constraints making reference to those features.

4. Sets of features (like individual places of articulation) that behave as a class in this way are assumed to be grouped together in some theories of autosegmental representation. See Padgett (2002) for a review and for arguments that these featural groupings are not best captured representationally.

5. Not obvious, but not impossible: Steriade (1999), for example, notes that a distinction between voiced and voiceless consonants before vowels is easier to perceive—and thus more likely to be maintained—than the same distinction before

consonants and utterance—finally. Failure to maintain a distinction utterance—finally is then carried over to word-final position by paradigmatic analogy (Steriade, 2000).

6. Standard feature theories typically categorize these three types of speech sound multidimensionally with [pʰ] and [p] together as voiceless and [p] and [b] together as unaspirated. It is also possible to categorize them on a unidimensional scale based on what is known as voice onset time (VOT; Lisker & Abramson, 1971), the time between the release of a stop and the onset of voicing on a following vowel (or other sonorant). The production of [b] involves a systematically shorter (typically negative) VOT than the production of [p], which involves a systematically shorter VOT than the production of [pʰ].

7. "Neighboring" is to be interpreted loosely here, because vowels typically harmonize across intervening consonants. This means either that these consonants must be ignored in some way (see Sagey, 1986; Archangeli & Pulleyblank, 1994; and Clements & Hume, 1995 for various proposals) or that they must participate in the harmony in some articulatorily measurable way (Gafos, 1996; see also Benus & Gafos, 2007).

8. This phoneme is traditionally assumed to be a basic stop (Harris 1969), but there are good reasons to think that it is instead a basic fricative or approximant (Lozano, 1979; Baković, 1994; Barlow, 2003).

References

Archangeli, D., & Pulleyblank, D. (1994). *Grounded phonology*. Cambridge, MA: MIT Press.

Baković, E. (1994). Strong onsets and Spanish fortition. *MIT Working Papers in Linguistics, 23*, 21–39.

Barlow, J. (2003). The stop-spirant alternation in Spanish: Converging evidence for a fortition account. *Southwest Journal of Linguistics, 22*, 51–86.

Beckman, J. (1998). *Positional faithfulness* (Unpublished doctoral dissertation). University of Massachusetts, Amherst, MA.

Blevins, J. (1995). The syllable in phonological theory. In J. A. Goldsmith (Ed.), *The Handbook of phonological theory* (1st ed., pp.206–244). Oxford: Blackwell.

Boersma, P. (1998). *Functional phonology: Formalizing the interactions between articulatory and perceptual drives* (Unpublished doctoral dissertation). University of Amsterdam, Amsterdam, the Netherlands.

Braver, A. (2011). Incomplete neutralization in American English flapping: A production study. *University of Pennsylvania Working Papers in Linguistics, 17.1*, 31–40.

Browman, C. P., & Goldstein, L. M. (1992). Articulatory phonology: An overview. *Phonetica, 49*, 155–180.

Burzio, L. (1994). *Principles of English stress*. Cambridge: Cambridge University Press.

Calabrese, A. (2005). *Markedness and economy in a derivational model of phonology*. The Hague: Mouton de Gruyter.

Chomsky, N., & Halle, M. (1968). *The sound pattern of English*. New York: Harper & Row.

Clements, G. N. (1985). The geometry of phonological features. *Phonology Yearbook, 2*, 225–252.

Clements, G. N. (1990). The role of the sonority cycle in core syllabification. In J. Kingston & M. E. Beckman (Eds.), *Papers in laboratory phonology I: Between the grammar and physics of speech* (pp. 282–333). Cambridge, UK: Cambridge University Press.

Clements, G. N. (1991). Vowel height assimilation in Bantu languages. In K. Hubbard (Ed.), *Proceedings of the 17th Annual Meeting of the Berkeley Linguistics Society, Feb. 15–18, 1991: Special Session on African Language Structures*, (pp. 25–64). Berkeley, CA: Berkeley Linguistics Society.

Clements, G. N. (1999). Affricates as noncontoured stops. In O. Fujimura, B. D. Joseph, & B. Palek (Eds.), *Proceedings of LP '98: Item order in language and speech*. (pp.271–299). Prague: The Karolinum Press.

Clements, G. N., & Hume, E. (1995). The internal organization of speech sounds. In J. A. Goldsmith (Ed.), *The handbook of phonological theory* (pp.245–306). Oxford: Blackwell.

Clements, G. N., & Keyser, S. J. (1983). *CV phonology: A generative theory of the syllable*. Cambridge, MA: MIT Press.

Davis, S. (1985). *Topics in syllable geometry* (Unpublished doctoral dissertation). University of Arizona, Tuscon, AZ.

de Lacy, P. (Ed.) (2007). *The Cambridge handbook of phonology*. Cambridge: Cambridge University Press.

de Lacy, P. (2009). Phonological evidence. In S. Parker (Ed.), *Phonological argumentation: Essays on evidence and motivation* (pp. 43–78). London: Equinox.

Flemming, E. (2002). *Auditory representations in phonology* (1995, doctoral dissertation, UCLA). New York: Routledge.

Flemming, E. (2001). Scalar and categorical phenomena in a unified model of phonetics and phonology. *Phonology, 18*, 7–44.

Flemming, E., & Johnson, S. (2007). Rosa's roses: Reduced vowels in American English. *Journal of the International Phonetic Association, 37*, 83–96.

Goldsmith, J. A. (1976). *Autosegmental phonology* (Unpublished doctoral dissertation). MIT, Cambridge, MA.

Goldsmith, J. A., Riggle, J., & Yu, A. C. L. (Eds.). (2011). *The handbook of phonological theory* (2nd ed.). Oxford: Blackwell.

Hale, M., & Reiss, C. (2008). *The phonological enterprise*. Oxford: Oxford University Press.

Halle, M. (1983). On distinctive features and their articulatory implementation. *Natural Language and Linguistic Theory, 1*, 91–105.

Halle, M. (1995). Feature geometry and feature spreading. *Linguistic Inquiry, 26*, 1–46.

Halle, M., Vaux, B., & Wolfe, A. (2000). On feature spreading and the representation of place of articulation. *Linguistic Inquiry, 31*, 387–444.

Harris, J. W. (1983). *Syllable structure and stress in Spanish: A nonlinear analysis*. Cambridge, MA: MIT Press.

Hayes, B. (1989). Compensatory lengthening in moraic phonology. *Linguistic Inquiry, 20*, 253–306.

Hayes, B. (1990). Diphthongisation and coindexing. *Phonology, 7*, 31–71.

Hayes, B. (1995). *Metrical stress theory: Principles and case studies*. Chicago: University of Chicago Press.

Hayes, B., Kirchner, R., & Steriade, D. (Eds.) (2004). *Phonetically-based phonology*. Cambridge: Cambridge University Press.

Inkelas, S. (1994). The consequences of optimization for underspecification. *Proceedings of the Northeast Linguistics Society, 25*, 287–302.

Ito, J., & Mester, R. A. (1993). Licensed segments and safe paths. *Canadian Journal of Linguistics, 38*, 197–213.

Jakobson, R., Fant, G., & Halle, M. (1952). Preliminaries to speech analysis. *MIT Acoustics Laboratory Technical Report* #13.

Kahn, D. (1976). *Syllable-based generalizations in English phonology* (Unpublished doctoral dissertation). MIT, Cambridge MA.

Keyser, S. J., & Stevens, K. N. (2006). Enhancement and overlap in the speech chain. *Language, 82*, 33–63.

Kiparsky, P. (1982). From cyclic phonology to lexical phonology. In H. van der Hulst and N. Smith (Eds.), *The structure of phonological representations* (Part 1, pp. 131–175). Dordrecht: Foris.

Kiparsky, P. (in press) *Paradigms and opacity.* Stanford: CSLI Publications.

Ladd, D. R. (2008). *Intonational phonology.* Cambridge: Cambridge University Press.

Liberman, M., & Prince, A. (1977). On stress and linguistic rhythm. *Linguistic Inquiry*, 8, 249–336.

Lombardi, L. (1990). The nonlinear organization of the affricate. *Natural Language and Linguistic Theory, 8*, 375–426.

Lozano, del Carmen, M. (1979). *Stop and spirant alternations: Fortition and spirantization processes in Spanish phonology* (Doctoral dissertation, The Ohio State University). Bloomington, IN: Indiana University Linguistics Club.

Maddieson, I. (1984). *Patterns of sounds.* Cambridge: Cambridge University Press.

McCarthy, J. J. (1979). On stress and syllabification. *Linguistic Inquiry, 10*, 443–465.

McCarthy, J. J. (1988). Feature geometry and dependency: A review. *Phonetica, 45*, 84–108.

McCarthy, J. J. (2007). *Hidden generalizations: Phonological opacity in optimality theory.* London: Equinox.

McCarthy, J. J. (2010). An introduction to Harmonic Serialism. *Language and Linguistics Compass, 4*, 1001–1018.

McCarthy, J. J., & Prince, A. S. (1994). Generalized alignment. In G. Booij & J. van Marle (Eds.), *Yearbook of morphology 1993* (pp. 79–153). Dordrecht: Kluwer.

McCarthy, J. J., & Prince, A. S. (1995). Prosodic morphology. In J. A. Goldsmith (Ed.), *The handbook of phonological theory* (pp. 318–366). Oxford: Blackwell.

Mielke, J. (2008). *The emergence of distinctive features.* Oxford: Oxford University Press.

Morelli, F. (1999). *The phonotactics and phonology of obstruent clusters in Optimality Theory* (Unpublished doctoral dissertation). University of Maryland, College Park, MA.

Nespor, M., & Vogel, I. (1986). *Prosodic phonology.* Dordrecht: Foris.

Ohala, J. J. (1983). The origin of sound patterns in vocal tract constraints. In P. F. MacNeilage (Ed.), *The production of speech* (pp. 189–216). New York: Springer-Verlag.

Parkinson, F. (1996). *The representation of vowel height in phonology* (Unpublished doctoral dissertation). The Ohio State University, Columbus, OH.

Perlmutter, D. (1995). Phonological quantity and multiple association. In J. A. Goldsmith (Ed.), *The handbook of phonological theory* (pp.307–313). Oxford: Blackwell.

Pierrehumbert, J. B. (2003). Probabilistic phonology: Discrimination and robustness. In R. Bod, J. Hay, & S. Jannedy (Eds.), *Probabilistic linguistics* (pp. 177–228). Cambridge, MA: MIT Press.

Pierrehumbert, J. B., & Beckman, M. E. (1988). *Japanese tone structure.* Cambridge, MA: MIT Press.

Port, R. F. (2007). How are words stored in memory? Beyond phones and phonemes. *New Ideas in Psychology, 25*, 143–170.

Port, R. F., & Leary, A. P. (2005). Against formal phonology. *Language, 85*, 927–964.

Prince, A., & Smolensky, P. (1993, 2004). *Optimality theory: Constraint interaction in generative grammar.* Medford, MA: Blackwell.

Ridouane, R., & Clements, G. N. (Eds.)(2011). *Where do phonological features come from? Cognitive, physical, and developmental bases of distinctive speech categories.* Amsterdam: John Benjamins.

Sagey, E. (1990). *The representation of features and relations in nonlinear phonology* (1986, doctoral dissertation, MIT). New York: Garland Press.

Sapir, E. (1949). The psychological reality of phonemes. In D. G. Mandelbaum (Ed.), *Selected writings of Edward Sapir in language, culture and personality* (pp.46–60). Berkeley and Los Angeles: University of California Press.

Schane, S. A.(1995). Diphthongization in particle phonology. In J. A. Goldsmith (Ed.), *The handbook of phonological theory* (pp. 586–608). Oxford: Blackwell.

Selkirk, E. O. (1980). The role of prosodic categories in English word stress. *Linguistic Inquiry, 11*, 563–605.

Selkirk, E. O. (1984). On the major class features and syllable theory. In M. Aronoff & R. Oehrle (Eds.), *Language sound structure* (pp. 107–136). Cambridge, MA: MIT Press.

Selkirk, E. O. (1986). On derived domains in sentence phonology. *Phonology Yearbook, 3*, 371–405.

Smolensky, P., & Legendre, G. (2006). *The harmonic mind: From neural computation to optimality-theoretic grammar.* Cambridge, MA: MIT Press.

Steriade, D. (2000). Paradigm uniformity and the phonetics-phonology boundary. In M. Broe & J. Pierrehumbert (Eds.), *Papers in laboratory phonology V: Acquisition and the lexicon* (pp. 313–334). Cambridge, UK: Cambridge University Press.

Stevens, K. N. (2002). Toward a model for lexical access based on acoustic landmarks and distinctive features. *Journal of the Acoustical Society of America, 111*, 1872–1891.

Stevens, K. N. (2003). Acoustic and perceptual evidence for universal phonological features. In *Proceedings of the XVth International Congress of Phonetic Sciences, Barcelona* (pp. 33–38).

van Oostendorp, M. (2008). Incomplete devoicing in formal phonology. *Lingua, 118*, 1362–1374.

van Oostendorp, M., Ewen, C. J., Hume, E., & Rice, K. (Eds.)(2011). *The Blackwell companion to phonology.* Oxford: Blackwell.

Wetzels, W. L., & Mascaró, J. (2001). The typology of voicing and devoicing. *Language, 77*, 207–244.

Zsiga, E. C. (1997). Features, gestures, and Igbo vowels: An approach to the phonology-phonetics interface. *Language, 73*, 227–274.

13

CHAPTER

The Temporal Organization of Speech

Louis Goldstein *and* Marianne Pouplier

Abstract

Research on speech production has historically been divided into two distinct areas: studies of the planning processes that control the sequencing of hierarchically organized discrete phonological units, and studies of the regularities observed in articulatory patterning in speech. How to relate these remains a largely unsolved problem. However, in recent years much progress has been made. Studies of articulatory patterning have revealed how the continuous speech signal can be understood as being structured of discrete (subsegmental) elements. A complete account of speech production must include a theory of these units, how they are planned, and how they are triggered over time. This article summarizes some of the general properties of this subsegmental structure in the context of Articulatory Phonology, which has provided a framework for systematizing observations of this structure and a model for how this structure could be planned and timed.

Key Words: phonetics, Articulatory Phonology, articulation, timing

Introduction

Research on speech production has historically been divided into two distinct areas: studies of the planning processes that control the sequencing of hierarchically organized, discrete phonological units (phrases, feet, words, syllables, segments, such as the models of Levelt, Roelofs, & Meyer, 1999, Dell, 1986, Goldrick & Blumstein, 2006); and studies of the regularities observed in articulatory patterning as speech is being executed (Perkell, 1997; Perrier, Loevenbruck, & Payan, 1996; Guenther, 1995). How to relate these two research areas of spoken language to each other remains a largely unsolved problem. However, in recent years much progress has been made and currently the speech and language disciplines in large part strongly embrace the view that there is a reciprocal relationship between abstract cognitive structures and the patterning of speech in the vocal tract. Studies of articulatory patterning, the focus of this article, have revealed how

the continuous speech signal can be understood as being structured of discrete (subsegmental) elements. This discovery opens the way for a commensurate description of speech that is able to capture the discrete abstract knowledge of grammar and the structuring principles underlying the continuous speech stream observed in articulatory and acoustic records of speech. Importantly, these structuring principles can be systematically related to the syllable and segment sequences that emerge from cognitive planning models, but they are not isomorphic with those sequences. Importantly, a complete account of speech production must also include a theory of how these subsegmental units are planned and triggered over time. There has been little attention to this, because it has fallen into the gap between the domains of research. This chapter summarizes some of the general properties of this subsegmental structure in the context of one approach (Articulatory Phonology) that has provided a framework for systematizing observations of this structure and a model for how this structure could be planned and timed. This is not intended to be an extended argument for the validity of this particular model; rather, it provides a useful framework synthesizing existing knowledge about the temporal structure of articulation.

Gestures

During speech, the vocal tract articulators are continuously in motion, and there are no discrete boundaries between individual segments analogous to the spaces between the letters of an alphabet, such as the International Phonetic Alphabet (IPA). This can be illustrated in the lower part of Figure 13.1, which shows the movements of the vocal tract

articulators as a speaker produced the sentence "Jane may earn more money by working hard." The panels show (from top to bottom) estimates of the degree of constriction (narrowing within the vocal tract) formed by the upper and lower lips; the tongue tip with the alveolar ridge; the tongue body with the soft palate; the tongue root with the rear pharyngeal wall; and the soft palate (velum) with the rear pharyngeal wall. These were obtained by analyzing real-time structural magnetic resonance imaging (MRI) of the vocal tract (Narayanan, Nayak, Lee, Sethy, & Byrd, 2004) for an utterance in the MRI-TIMIT database (Narayanan et al., 2011)[1]. Fundamental to Articulatory Phonology (e.g., Browman & Goldstein, 1992) and the related task dynamics model (Saltzman & Munhall, 1989)

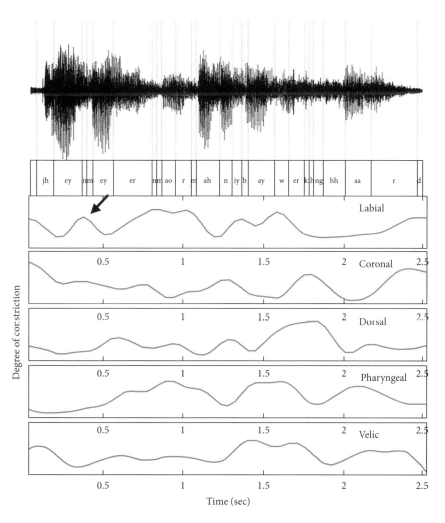

Figure 13.1 Upper panel: Audio waveform of the utterance "Jane may earn more money by working hard." Labels represent automatic segmentations using forced alignment. Lower panels: Degree of constriction formed by five vocal tract effectors over time, estimated from pixel intensities in real-time MRI images. The higher the value, the narrower the constriction. The arrow identifies the lip closure gesture associated with /m/ in "may."

is the idea that this continuous motion is the consequence of a set of articulatory events, or *gestures*, each of which is deployed within the vocal tract for a discrete interval of time. For example, the arrow in Figure 13.1 points to an interval in the lip function during which the lips close and then open again for the /m/ in "may." A gesture is modeled mathematically as an abstract dynamical system that accomplishes some task within the vocal tract. Most tasks are defined as the constrictions and releases of some vocal tract substructure (e.g., for the closing of the lips for /b/ or /m/), but others include changes in fundamental frequency of the voice (for tones or pitch accents) and the generation of turbulence (for fricatives like /s/). Because of the key properties illustrated in the following sections, task-dynamic modeling allows a small number of gestures to function as discrete, compositional units of the articulatory system. That is, the task dynamic model captures how the continuous motion arises in a principled way from abstract, macroscopic units without stripping the control units of their physical (spatiotemporal) properties, as symbolic representations do. Mathematically, the task dynamic model leverages properties of dynamical systems, which are defined by differential equations.

Differential Equations

Dynamical systems have the property that they define lawful change over time in the state of a system, even while the parameters of the system are fixed. For example, the simple equation below produces undamped spring-like oscillation in the state variable x, even though the system parameters (x_0, the equilibrium position of x; k, the stiffness of the elastic, or spring force; m, the mass) do not themselves change over time. In this way, the continuous change that seen in Figure 13.1 can be modeled by decomposing the time functions into local regions (epochs) during which the state of the articulatory system is lawfully regulated by a differential equation with a fixed set of parameter values. Those parameter values define the corresponding gestures and the epochs correspond to the *activation intervals* for each gesture.

$$\ddot{x} = \frac{k}{m}(x - x_0) \qquad (1)$$

Point Attractors and Equifinality

Point attractors are a class of differential equations that have the property that the state of the system always converges to the same value (the attractor) regardless of initial conditions under which the system is set into place. An example is to add a frictional force term to the equation in (1), which causes the state of the system to end up at its equilibrium position, x_0. This convergence property of point attractors is sometimes called *equifinality* when applied in the motor domain, the idea being that the same goal can be achieved from many different starting positions, such as reaching for a target from different initial postures. The equation governing the motion and the values of its parameters can be the same in every case, but the sequence of states that the system passes through differs as a function of initial condition, or context. For example, consider a differential equation whose state variable is the distance between the upper and lower lips (*lip aperture*). If we define point attractor dynamics for that system, with an equilibrium position x_0 near (or less than) 0, system state converges on lip closure from wherever the lips are at the time the system is put in place. A lip closure gesture, which is part of the production of /b/ or /p/ or /m/ can be defined by such a system. Given the properties of point attractor systems, the gesture's parameter settings can be invariant across the vowel contexts in which such a consonant can occur. For example, if the lips are wide open for a vowel like /a/ when the closure gesture is activated, the lips move a great deal in approaching closure. If the context is a vowel like /i/, the same system with the same parameter values exhibits much less movement on the way to the attractor. Generally, point attractors allow the modeling of context-conditioned variability (coarticulation) while maintaining an invariant control structure. The concept of point attractor is fundamental not only to the task dynamics model within articulatory phonology, but also to the equilibrium hypothesis model of Perrier and colleagues (Perrier, Ostry, & Laboissière, 1996) and the Directions into Velocities of Articulators (DIVA) model (Guenther, 1995).

Coordinative Structures and Functional Synergy

Skilled motor tasks can be described in two coordinate systems: the task coordinates and the independent articulatory degrees of freedom (DOF) that are relevant to performing the task goal. For example, when seated at the dinner table and reaching for an object on the table top, the task can be modeled using a point attractor dynamical system with a goal defined in the rectangular dimensions of the table top. The articulators included the shoulder joint, the elbow, and the wrist. As originally observed by Bernstein (1967), the number of DOFs is typically much larger than the dimensionality of the task coordinates, so there is redundancy in the system, and the same task can be produced in many different ways, exhibiting what has been called *motor equivalence*. The articulators relevant to performing a given task have been analyzed as constituting a coordinative structure, or functional synergy (Abbs, 1980; Turvey, 1977; Fowler, Rubin, Remez, & Turvey, 1980; Kelso, Tuller, Vatikiotis-Bateson, & Fowler, 1984). For example, in the case of the lip gesture described previously, the displacements of the jaw, the lower lip (with respect to the jaw), and the upper lip are the DOF relevant to the unidimensional lip closure task. In the task dynamics approach to redundancy (Saltzman & Kelso, 1987; Saltzman & Munhall, 1989), the invariant dynamical parameters in task coordinates (e.g., the equilibrium parameter value for the task coordinate of inter-lip distance, or lip aperture) are projected onto posturally dependent dynamical parameters for the individual DOFs (e.g., those of the jaw, upper and lower lips, depending on their current state), using articulatory weighting to resolve the redundancy, although other approaches can be used (see recent review in Guigon, Baraduc, & Desmurget, 2007).

Redundancy affords flexibility in the performance of tasks, which makes it possible to successfully perform multiple tasks concurrently. This can occur if two tasks are defined in such a way that their corresponding articulatory DOFs are at least partially nonoverlapping, for example, reaching for an object on a table while simultaneously standing up and sitting down. This is also commonly the situation in speech: redundancy allows multiple phonetic units to be produced in a temporally overlapping fashion, rather than in linear succession. Therefore multiple constriction tasks exert influence on articulators at the same time (examples are shown later). The differing constriction task dimensions along which speech gestures are defined within the task dynamics model and Articulatory Phonology satisfy this requirement for redundancy, and thus they can be produced concurrently (i.e., co-produced). The task dimensions (or vocal *tract variables*, as they have been dubbed) include lip aperture (distance between upper and lower lips), lip protrusion, tongue tip constriction degree location, tongue body constriction degree and location, glottal aperture, and velic aperture. Each of these six sets of task variables engage at least one articulator DOF that is not shared by other task dimensions. Because the task variables also do share some DOFs, the contribution of the individual articulatory DOFs to a gesture task differs as a function of other concurrently produced tasks. This context-dependence in the performance of a task underlies what is called *coarticulation*.

One ubiquitous instance of coproduction of gestures is that between the constriction gesture for a syllable-initial consonant and that for the following vowel (Öhman, 1967; Löfqvist & Gracco, 1999). These gestures are, in fact, produced concurrently, and this example of *parallel transmission* of consonantal (C) and vocalic (V) information is a hallmark property of human languages (Liberman, Cooper, Shankweiler, & Studdert-Kennedy, 1967). It is this coproduction that leads to the classical lack of acoustic invariance of an initial C across V contexts. However, while acoustic invariance is lacking, research has shown that the relationship between the acoustic properties of the C and that of the V are systematically (and linearly) related by "locus equations" that characterize a given C gesture's formants as a function of the vowel's formants. It has recently been shown that the parameters of these regression equations are empirically derived estimates of the DOF sharing (or synergy) between the C gesture and the V gesture (Iskarous, Fowler, & Whalen, 2010).

Articulatory Phonology hypothesizes that the task variables for gestures are constriction coordinates for the most part, although gestures controlling fundamental frequency have also been proposed (McGowan & Saltzman, 1995; Gao, 2008). It is certainly possible to hypothesize that speech tasks are defined in terms of their acoustical resonance properties (and their psychoacoustic consequences) and their somatosensory properties (Perkell et al., 2000) rather than their geometrical constriction properties, and this is the basis of the DIVA model (Guenther, 1995; Tourville, Peeva, & Guenther's "Perception-Production Interactions and Their Neural Bases"), which similarly relates a task-level description to articulatory DOF synergies that can perform the task. The differences between these choices of goal spaces can be quite subtle, particularly because it has been shown recently that constriction coordinates can be analytically recovered from resonance information, that is, formant frequencies and bandwidths (Iskarous, 2010). The relative merits of one or another goal space is bound up with the long history of debate about acoustic invariance of phonetic units, or the lack of it (e.g., Blumstein & Stevens, 1979; Liberman & Mattingly, 1985), and will not be debated here. The more relevant theoretical difference between the DIVA model and Articulatory Phonology is the latter's focus on formally characterizing temporal coordination of the subsegmental (gestural) elements into which speech can be analyzed, as is discussed in the rest of this article. The DIVA model, in contrast, assumes that the units of speech are isomorphic with phonetic segments, and produces acoustic tasks in sequence. Nonetheless, because of the way DIVA solves the redundancy problem, some important examples of coarticulation are modeled. The temporal regularities addressed in the next sections are, however, not explicitly addressed by that model.

Organization of Gestures in Time

It is possible to decompose speech into discrete, temporally overlapping units that correspond to intervals during which a particular gesture is active, controlling the formation or release of a contraction of a particular tract variable (or tract variable pair, such as tongue tip constriction location and constriction degree) with a fixed set of dynamical parameters. When articulatory movement data are available, this can be accomplished in simple examples by examining the time function of the articulatory components that directly shape the size and location of a constriction in the vocal tract, or by estimating the time functions of constriction task variables from the articulatory data. For example, Figure 13.2 shows movement data for a token extracted from the x-ray microbeam database (Westbury, 1994) for the utterance "two back."[2] The display includes the vertical position time functions of pellets attached to the upper lip, lower lip, tongue tip, and tongue dorsum, and also time functions of tract variables estimated from those pellet positions: lip aperture, tongue tip constriction degree, and tongue body constriction degree. Constriction degree is computed as the minimal Euclidean distance (from either tongue tip or tongue body) to the palate, and it approximates zero as closure is achieved. The boxes shown in Figure 13.2 locate the intervals of time associated with the lip closure gesture for /b/ and the tongue dorsum gestures for /ae/ and for /k/. The interval for a given gesture begins at the time at which the relevant constriction variable (e.g., lip aperture for /b/) begins to become more constricted, and ends when it starts to become less constricted again.

By determining the full set of controlled intervals for an utterance, a *gestural score* can be obtained. Figure 13.2 is thus a partial gestural score. The focus in this article is on the timing of these gestural activation intervals. There are timing regularities for a given syllable, but the actual durations of each gesture and their relative timing vary from token to token. In addition to stochastic variation, timing is significantly modulated by prosodic variables (e.g., Byrd & Choi, 2010; Hardcastle, 1985;

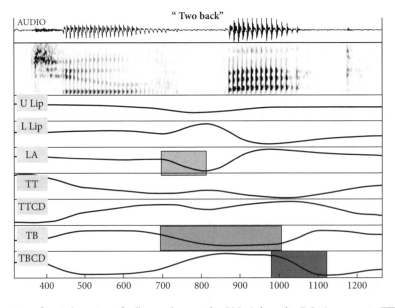

Figure 13.2 Time functions of vertical positions of pellets on the upper lip (U Lip), lower lip (L Lip), tongue tip (TT), and tongue body (TB) in one production of the phrase "two back." Also shown are time functions of tract variables lip aperture (LA), tongue tip constriction degree (TTCD), and tongue body constriction degree (TBCD); see main text for explanation. Boxes indicate activation intervals of gestures in the word "back."

Sproat & Fujimura, 1993). However, it is possible to find the same set of discrete gestural events across contexts.

In practice, determining the gestural score can be difficult to accomplish because of several factors. First, the technique of direct observation requires availability of articulatory data. Second, even in a database like the x-ray microbeam corpus, only data from the front part of the tongue, the lips, and the jaw are available. Using real-time MRI provides somewhat better coverage, adding the pharynx and the velum, but glottal data are still limited. Third, because of synergistic relations among gestures, it may not be possible to untangle the joint effects of a pair of overlapping gestures on the measured articulatory movements. For example, as discussed in following sections, tongue tip closure gestures (for /t/, /d/, or /n/) engage the tongue body to advance the tongue, which can make it difficult to parse the tongue body time function to determine when it is specifically being controlled by the vowel gesture in /dV/ utterances.

One solution to these problems is to take a model-based approach to finding the gestural score in a particular utterance. This is analogous to the use of forced alignment (Yuan & Liberman, 2008) of a phonetic transcription to a particular acoustic recording. This procedure takes a sequence of phones and an audio signal as input, and finds an optimal segmentation of the acoustics into phones, using a Hidden Markov Model trained on a large dataset. For example, the segmentation shown in the upper half of Figure 13.1 was obtained using such a procedure (Katsamanis, Black, Georgiou, Goldstein, & Narayanan, 2011).

A conceptually related procedure has recently been developed (Nam et al., 2012) to segment an acoustic signal into (temporally overlapping) gesture units (effectively a gestural transcription). The method leverages the TADA model (discussed later), which can generate a gestural score and resulting acoustics for arbitrary utterances. The procedure takes a phonetic transcription and audio signal as input (just like standard forced alignment); computes a model-based gestural score; and then uses an analysis-by-synthesis strategy to warp the timing of those gestures to find the optimal match to the input acoustics. Although the technique can be applied to any audio signal to derive a gestural score, by applying it to the x-ray microbeam corpus, Nam et al. were able to evaluate the model's articulatory output against the microbeam pellet time functions (for the gestures that can be directly observed in the pellets), and were able to show good correlations between model-generated constriction time functions and constriction time functions estimated from the acoustic data.

Gestures as Primitives of Phonological Encoding?

Because it is possible to decompose speech into discrete, context-invariant gestures, it is possible to hypothesize that those units of action are also informational primitives of phonology (Browman & Goldstein, 1989). Gestures and their abstract organization in time (as described later) could be part of the representation of words that is retrieved by lexical access. Indeed, there is substantial evidence that this subsegmental representation is relevant to grammatical representations and processes, such as allophony, assimilation, harmony, and template satisfaction, and to phonological encoding as revealed in speech errors. This evidence is reviewed in Gafos and Goldstein (2012). Nonetheless, this view remains somewhat controversial, and a discussion of these issues is outside the scope of this article. Yet, regardless of whether these discrete units of articulation are viewed as phonological primitives, their timing has to be explicitly controlled at some level of the speech production process. Which kinds of timing regularities can be observed and one possible model for their control constitute the topics for the remainder of this article.

Temporal Regularities

A comprehensive theory of speech production must account for how articulatory events are triggered in time. There is no generally accepted theory that accomplishes this completely. A simple, pretheoretical view is that gestures can be organized into segmental units, and that the gestures for a segment are triggered when each successive segment is triggered by a segment sequencing model (e.g., Bohland, Bullock, & Guenther, 2010). For example, a nasal consonant like /n/ can be analyzed as composed of an oral constriction gesture (tongue tip) and a velic gesture lowering the soft palate. However, the segment sequence bears only a complex relation to the triggering of gestures in time. The gestures that compose a single segment may be triggered sequentially, whereas the gestures that compose two successive segments may be triggered synchronously. There do seem to be principles that govern gestural timing, some language-specific, some apparently universal, that are also illustrated. Because they can be language-dependent, they must be explicitly planned at some level in the production system.

GESTURES OF SEQUENTIAL SEGMENTS CAN BE TRIGGERED SYNCHRONOUSLY

In simple consonant-vowel (CV) syllables with bilabial stops, kinematic data show that the lip movements for the bilabial closure and the tongue movements for the vowel constriction are initiated approximately synchronously (Löfqvist & Graco, 1999). The American English data show that the movements are initiated within 25 ms of one another, across speakers and vowel contexts. Similar data have been reported for Catalan, German, and Italian (Mücke, Nam, Hermes, & Goldstein, 2012; Niemann, Mücke, Nam, Goldstein, & Grice, 2011). Of course, as noted earlier, CV coproduction is a hallmark property of human language. Here, however, the point is not just that they can be coproduced, but rather that their activations begin synchronously. When an initial stop is coronal or dorsal, the articulatory synergies between the consonant and the vowel gesture make it difficult to determine exactly when the individual gestures are triggered, because both gestures engage the tongue body. Since a coronal consonant requires a fronted tongue body, systematic retraction of the tongue for a back vowel appears to be delayed by about 20 ms for coronal consonants (Mücke et al., 2012) compared with synchrony observed for labial consonants (Löfqvist & Graco, 1999). This departure from synchrony is not observed for coronals before front vowels (Niemann et al., 2011). Although CV gesture synchrony is the major example of this type, near synchronous triggering between a syllable-final stop consonant and the initial stop of the following syllable has been reported in Cantonese (Yanagawa, 2006), a language that exhibits variable place assimilation between those consonants.

GESTURES OF A SINGLE SEGMENT CAN BE TRIGGERED SEQUENTIALLY

Multi-gestural segments, such as nasal consonants, have been shown to exhibit distinct modes of temporal coordination in English depending on their syllable position (Byrd, Tobin, Bresch, & Narayanan, 2009; Krakow, 1993, 1999). In onset position (e.g., "see *more*"), the oral constriction (lips or tongue tip) and velic lowering are triggered synchronously, whereas in coda position ("see*m* ore"), they are triggered sequentially, the oral constriction beginning about when the velum gets to its maximally lowered position. Similar results have

been reported for English liquids, which can also be analyzed as bi-gestural segments. For example, the tongue tip closure and tongue dorsum retraction gestures into which English /l/ can be decomposed are triggered synchronously in onset, but in coda the gestures are sequential with the dorsum gesture preceding (Browman & Goldstein, 1995; Gick, 2003; Scobbie & Pouplier, 2010; Sproat & Fujimura, 1993). The parallelism of the nasal and lateral data are quite striking, given how different the gestures themselves are, which suggests a more general principle that relatively less constricted and more vocalic gestures are attracted to the syllable nucleus, particularly from coda position (Krakow, 1999; Gick, 2003; Scobbie & Pouplier, 2010; Sproat & Fujimura, 1993). The lack of synchronous triggering in coda, combined with the CV synchrony, demonstrates that the problem of gestural sequencing in speech production cannot be reduced to the problem of segmental sequencing. A more fine-grained plan at the gestural level has to be formulated at some point in the planning and execution process.

LANGUAGE DEPENDENCE

The need for an explicit plan at the gestural level is further underscored by the fact that the generalizations about gestural sequencing are language-dependent. Therefore, gestural sequencing cannot be the consequences of some basic neural or biomechanical aspect of the speech production system operating on a purely segmental sequence. For example, in the case of the nasals discussed previously, French (Cohn, 1993) and Arrernte (Butcher, 1999) are both languages in which the oral and velic constrictions are triggered synchronously in onset and coda. In the case of French, this could be explained by the need to maintain a difference between oral and nasal vowel *segments*, because these constitute phonologically contrastively units in French (as they are in Bengali, cf. related work of Lahiri & Marslen-Wilson, 1991). However, there is no oral-nasal vowel contrast in Arrernte; the plan is simply organized differently. Similarly, cross-linguistic variety in the coordination patterns for the multiple lingual gestures of liquid segments has been reported by Gick et al. (Gick, Campbell, Oh, & Tamburri-Watt, 2006). Synchronous or sequential organization could be observed in either onset or coda, as a function of language, although there is a trend toward synchrony in onsets and sequencing in coda. Language dependence is illustrated systematically in the case of consonant-consonant (CC) clusters later in this chapter.

ABSTRACTNESS OF TEMPORAL PLAN

Given the apparent complexity of intergestural timing relations, Levelt et al. (1999) propose the idea that gestural score-like representations for frequently produced syllables are stored in templates in a "syllabary" and serve as articulatory plans. Experiments showing the effect of syllable frequency on the time to initiate production of high- versus low-frequency syllables have supported this hypothesis (Levelt & Wheeldon, 1994; Cholin, Levelt, & Schiller, 2006). However, as these authors also acknowledge, the syllable template needs to be more abstract than the gestural scores shown (e.g., in Figure 13.2 in which one axis represents real time). The same syllable can be produced at different speaking rates, which changes the time scale. More problematical, however, is the fact that prosodic contexts cause *localized* changes in intergestural timing. For example, in the case of /l/ discussed previously, Sproat and Fujimura (1993) found that the timing between the tongue dorsum and tongue tip gestures is highly dependent on the strength of the prosodic boundary following the /l/. Specifically *nonlinear* time-warping techniques (e.g., Lee, Byrd, & Krivokapić, 2006) are needed to relate the kinematic time functions of a given syllable across contexts that differ in boundary strength. The results of such warping are consistent with prosodic gesture (π-gesture) theory of boundaries of (Byrd & Saltzman, 2003). In their model, the overall production clock is slowed in the presence of a prosodic boundary event (π-gesture). The effect is to make gestures near boundaries longer and slower, as a function of their proximity to the boundary, and to decrease the temporal overlap among them. However, this leaves the question of how to characterize the temporal relations among gestures in a particular unit (e.g., the syllable) in such a way as to generalize across the different contexts in which it can be produced. Also, if intergestural timing plans for frequent syllables are indeed stored in some form, it leaves open the question of how the plans for infrequent syllables are assembled. The model described in the next section attempts to address the issue of how to characterize timing relations in an abstract plan and also provides at least one possible way to go about assembly of the plan for a syllable.

The principles underlying these syllable plans also seem to be more general than just regulating the timing of consonant and vowel relations within a syllable. They also apply to the coordination of prosodic pitch accents with the consonant and vowel gestures. For example, it has been shown in Catalan (Mücke et al., 2012) and Italian (Niemann et al., 2011), that the onset of the F0 gesture associated with a nuclear pitch accent is synchronous with the onset of the C and V gestures. *Attraction to synchronous triggering* thus seems to be a general principle, and figures prominently in the model presented next. Syllable-onset based synchronization is also the basis for the model of syllable timing proposed in Xu & Liu (2006). Attraction to synchronous timing can be seen in experiments that involve qualitative changes in organization when syllables are repeated at fast rates (Stetson, 1951; Tuller & Kelso, 1991; de Jong, 2001), and recent work has also demonstrated that this attraction may underlie some examples of sound changes, both in progress (Parrell, 2012) and historical (Hsieh, 2010).

Coupled Oscillator Model of Planning Intergestural Timing within Syllables

The plan for the timing of gestures needs to be *stable* and *flexible*. Stability is necessary because the pattern of timing itself conveys phonological information (e.g., the same gestures compose words like "mad" and "ban," what differs is their timing). Second, if the timing departs from the pattern specified by the grammar of a language (see later for a discussion of how gestural coordination can be considered to be part of the phonological specification, or grammar of a language; a recent overview can also be found in Gafos & Goldstein, 2012), the speech may sound nonnative (Davidson, 2006; Yanagawa, 2006). Flexibility is needed, because the actual times of gestural triggering and activation are modulated by prosodic context.

One possible solution to the joint demands of stability and flexibility in timing lies in the domain of coupled oscillatory systems, and this direction has been pursued recently in a variety of approaches to timing regularities in speech at different levels (Cummins & Port, 1998; O'Dell & Nieminen, 1999; Goldstein, Byrd, & Saltzman, 2006; Nam, 2007; Saltzman, Nam, Krivokapić, & Goldstein, 2008; Tilsen, 2009). Stability in a system of oscillators (or clocks) is afforded by their potential to *entrain*. Coupled oscillators spontaneously synchronize with one another, in one of a small number of discrete modes, depending on how they are coupled (Pikovsky, Rosenblum, & Kurths, 2001). Applied at the level of gestures (Goldstein et al., 2006; Nam, 2007; Saltzman et al., 2008) this means that if each gesture is triggered by some phase of its internal clock, and the clocks for the gestures of syllable are coupled, then their triggering times tend to synchronize. This provides a way of beginning to account for the attraction to synchronous triggering discussed in the previous section. Synchronization has also been implicated in accounting for the speech errors that occur when sequences like "cop top" are repeated (Pouplier & Goldstein, 2005; Goldstein, Pouplier, Chen, Saltzman, & Byrd, 2007; Pouplier & Goldstein, 2010). In addition, systems of coupled oscillators also can provide the desired flexibility. Scaling the frequency of the oscillators alters the times at which gestures are triggered. Scaling the frequency also may lead to qualitative differences in the behavior of the system.

OSCILLATOR MODES

Systems of coupled oscillators have been used extensively to model the rhythmic behavior or systems of multiple limbs, as revealed in a variety of experiments (reviewed in Turvey, 1990). A key result is that when performers are asked to oscillate two limbs at the same frequency, they can successfully do so without any practice or learning in one of two modes, *in-phase* (limbs synchronized and moving in the same direction at the same time) and *anti-phase* (limbs synchronized but moving in opposite directions). Other eccentric modes of synchronization are possible but require learning (e.g., by skilled drummers). A further important result is that when oscillation rate is speeded up, spontaneous transitions are observed from anti-phase to in-phase modes (but not vice versa). This has been taken as evidence that in-phase mode is more stable. This transition in mode has been modeled by a particular coupling function among the oscillators (the HKB relative phase potential developed by Haken, Kelso, & Bunz, 1985) and the same coupling function has since been successfully applied to much data.

COUPLING GRAPH MODEL OF SYLLABLES

If the timing plan among gestures is modeled by coupling among planning clocks, or oscillators, the research just described suggests that there are just two modes for doing so that can be used without learning: in-phase (relative phase = 0°) and anti-phase (relative phase = 180°). The syllable coupling model (Goldstein et al., 2006; Nam, 2007; Saltzman et al, 2008), has hypothesized that these modes characterize (respectively) the phasing of an onset consonant to a vowel and the phasing of a coda consonant

to the vowel. If all gestures are triggered by a particular phase of their timing clocks (e.g., phase 0°), then an onset consonant and a vowel are triggered synchronously, because their clocks are in-phase. This produces the patterns of CV synchronization described previously. Whereas the triggering of a vowel and a coda C staggers in time by half a cycle, the coda C triggering can be specified as lagging the V. Modeling the difference between onset and coda consonants using these modes not only can account for their timing patterns, but also provides a possible account of the relative markedness/universality of CV versus VC syllables and their acquisition (Nam, Goldstein, & Saltzman, 2009). The HKB potential function predicts that in-phase mode should be more stable and more accessible (reachable from more initial conditions).

Differences in coupling mode for onset versus coda can also underlie differences in within-segment gesture timing. For example, for an initial nasal consonant, the oral and velic gestures are coupled in-phase, so that all the consonant gestures and the vowel gesture are synchronous in onset. In coda, the velic and oral gestures are coupled so as to be triggered sequentially (in an *eccentric* coupling mode).

In the TADA model developed from these hypotheses, the plan for a syllable can be represented in a *coupling graph*, in which the nodes correspond to the planning oscillators for the individual gestures and the edges define the coupling mode between pairs of oscillators. For example, the coupling graph for the word "back" is shown in Figure 13.3. The graph is the input to a task-dynamic oscillator simulation (Saltzman et al., 2008) in which the oscillators settle into stable relative phases as determined by the coupling parameters in the graph. Once settled, the oscillators trigger their corresponding gestures.

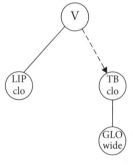

Figure 13.3 Coupling graph for "back." Nodes are oscillators that trigger the corresponding gestures: lip closure (LIP clo), vowel (V),velar closure (TB clo), and glottal abduction (GLO wide). Solid lines represent in-phase coupling, dashed line represents anti-phase coupling.

The activation duration of a gesture, once triggered, is specified for each gesture type. For example, V gestures have longer activation intervals than C gestures, so that in a CV, the vowel gesture is active after the C is deactivated. The resulting activation patterns constitute a gestural score that is input to the task-dynamic model of articulator coordination (Saltzman & Munhall, 1989) and from the resulting articulator and constriction time function, the output sound is produced. Although evaluating the model directly over a large corpus of data has not been possible because there is no corpus that provides tract variable constriction data, the model has been evaluated indirectly in the following way (Mitra, Nam, Espy-Wilson, Saltzman, & Goldstein, 2010, 2011). First, the model was used to generate a synthetic data corpus from which the inverse mapping from acoustics to tract variables and to gesture activations was learned using neural networks. This model-based mapping was then applied to noisy natural speech data, and when the automatically recovered tract variables and gesture activations were added as inputs to an automatic word recognition system, the performance was significantly enhanced over acoustic inputs alone. This suggests that the model is capturing important information about gestural structure.

As an abstract temporal plan for gestures constituting the syllable, the coupling graph appears to fill the role that the model of Levelt et al. (1999) assigns to the phonetically coded units in the syllabary. What needs to be considered in a model of planning is how the coupling graph for a given syllable is assembled, either during learning for cases in which the graph is stored or in real-time for the other cases. The limited set of coupling graphs considered here so far can, in fact, be derived by simple principles: in-phase coupling of onset consonant with the vowel, anti-phase coupling of coda consonant with the vowel; similarly, internal in-phase coupling of multigesture segments in onset, anti-phase in coda. However, it is important to consider more complex cases that show within- and across-language variability. For this, he coordination of sequences of consonant gestures must be considered.

Coordination of Consonant Gestures

There are three types of coordination relations among consonants to consider: (1) coordination of consonants in within-syllable clusters (either onset or coda); (2) coordination in syllables in which the nucleus is a consonant, rather than a vowel; and (3) coordination of consonant sequences across syllables.

Consonant Clusters in Onset and Coda

First consider an onset cluster like /sp/. The coupled oscillator theory hypothesizes that onset consonants are coupled in-phase to the vowel gesture. However, in the case of a cluster, it would appear that this is not possible, because if both the /s/ and the /p/ constrictions were to be in-phase with the vowel, they would also be in-phase with each other, and the resulting synchronized structure that would probably just sound like /p/. These narrow constrictions need to be at least partially sequential for both to be audible. One possible solution to this (first suggested in Browman & Goldstein, 2000) is to hypothesize that both consonants are in fact coupled in-phase to the vowel, but they are also coupled to one another with a relative phase other than 0°, which results in their being sequential. The result is a coupling graph with a loop like the one shown in Figure 13.4 (a) for the word "spa." The phase specifications around the loop are not compatible, so the oscillators in this case cannot settle into a pattern that satisfies all the target phase specifications. However, they do settle into a pattern that shows the influence of both of the competitive phasing specifications. This pattern was first reported empirically by Browman AND Goldstein (1988) and is called the *C-center*. As consonants are added to the onset, the center (defined as the temporal midpoint) of the consonant sequence as a whole maintains a fixed relation to the vowel, but the individual consonant gestures are no longer synchronous with the vowel gesture. For example, in a /pV/ sequence, the lip closure gesture is synchronous with the vowel gesture, as described previously. However, in /sp/, the lip gesture is triggered *after* the vowel onset, whereas the tongue tip fricative gesture is triggered *before* the vowel onset. The midpoint between the two gesture onsets is approximately synchronous with vowel gesture onset. The coupled oscillator simulation in TADA using coupling graphs like that in Figure 13.4 (a) produces the observed C-center pattern (Nam & Saltzman, 2003; Goldstein, Nam, Saltzman, & Chitoran, 2009).

The coupling between the consonant gestures in clusters was originally (Browman & Goldstein, 2000) hypothesized to be anti-phase (relative phase = 180°). However, recent modeling work suggests that coupling in some eccentric (i.e., not intrinsically accessible) relative phase pattern (e.g., 90°) fits the data better (Goldstein, 2011).

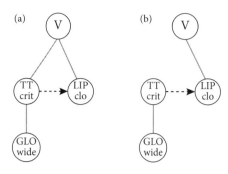

(a) V
TT crit → LIP clo
GLO wide

(b) V
TT crit → LIP clo
GLO wide

Figure 13.4 (a) Coupling graph for English word "spa." Nodes are oscillators that trigger the corresponding gestures: alveolar fricative (TT crit), lip closure (LIP clo), glottal abduction (GLO wide), and vowel (V). Solid lines represent in-phase coupling, dotted line represents eccentric coupling. (b) Possible coupling graph for syllable /spa/ in Italian.

This result is actually sensible, as it provides an account of why consonant clusters are acquired late: the phasing pattern has to be learned (Nam et al., 2009).

The C-center pattern has now been observed in word-initial consonant clusters in a variety of languages: English (Goldstein et al., 2009; Marin & Pouplier, 2010); French (Kühnert, Hoole, & Mooshammer, 2006); Georgian (Goldstein, Chitoran, & Selkirk, 2007); Italian (Hermes, Grice, Mücke, & Niemann, 2008); Mandarin (Gao, 2008); German (Pouplier, 2012); and Romanian (Marin, 2011). However, it does show some language dependence, which again argues that the information in the coupling graphs must be explicitly part of the temporal plan for production. For example, in Italian (Hermes et al., 2008), whereas stop-liquid onset clusters show the C-center effect, /s/-stop clusters fail to show it, unlike English, which exhibits the effect for both cluster types (Marin & Pouplier, 2010; Goldstein et al., 2009). As Hermes et al. note, this is consistent with existing phonological analyses of Italian in which the /s/-stop clusters are not truly complex syllable onsets; the /s/ is rather extrasyllabic. A possible coupling graph for this cluster is shown in Figure 13.4b. Similarly, data from languages in which word-onset clusters are never analyzed as complex syllable onsets also fail to exhibit the C-center pattern: Tashlihiyt Berber (Goldstein et al., 2007; Hermes, Ridouane, Mücke, & Grice, 2011) and Moroccan Arabic (Shaw, Gafos, Hoole, & Zeroual, 2009). This suggests a close isomorphism between the phonological syllable parse and the coupling graph, although the stochastic modeling and data analysis in Shaw et al. (2009)

illustrate that under specific conditions of variability, the C-center pattern may be observed even from the simplex onset type coupling graph (Figure 13.4 (b)). A more general exception to this isomorphism has been found in Slovak (Pouplier & Beňuš, 2011), a language in which word onset clusters are analyzed as true tautosyllabic onset clusters, yet they fail to exhibit the C-center pattern. This may be related to the fact that Slovak phonology allows complex onsets and syllabic consonants. Tashlhiyt Berber and Moroccan Arabic also have syllabic consonants, but they lack true complex onsets.

Although onset clusters in a variety of languages exhibit the C-center regularly, coda clusters have not been as systematically investigated, and the results are mixed. Data come almost exclusively from English, and studies reveal variability, both across cluster type and across talker, in whether the consonants shift to the left as more are added to a coda cluster (Browman & Goldstein, 1988; Byrd, 1995; Honorof & Browman, 1995; Marin & Pouplier, 2010). Pouplier (2012) notes for German, however, that coda clusters show less difference in their timing as a function of cluster composition compared with onsets. Browman & Goldstein (2000) propose that the coupling graph for coda clusters is a simple chain, rather than a loop, with the first coda C coupled anti-phase with the V, with each following C coupled only to the immediately preceding one and not to the V. They suggest that this is because anti-phase V-C coupling in coda is weaker than in-phase CV coupling in onset, and that the weaker forces do not reliably pull the more distant coda Cs into coupling with the V. This kind of topologic difference between onset and coda consonants could, they argue, provide a possible account of why coda consonants may in some languages contribute to syllable weight, whereas onset consonants very rarely do so (see also Nam, 2007). Coupled oscillator simulations (Saltzman et al., 2008) show that the distinction between loop representation of onset clusters and chain representation of codas not only accounts for the presence of the C-center effect in onsets and its absence in codas, but also the observed difference in stochastic variability: codas are much more variable in timing than onsets (e.g., Byrd [1996], but see Pouplier [2012] for different results for German). Still, the coda results are mixed, and this needs to be accounted for. A promising direction is the stochastic modeling approach of Shaw et al. (2009), which could make predictions about the relation between the variability of durations in particular conditions (speakers, contexts) and the expected stability pattern of the output.

Syllables without Vowels

Recent research on syllabic consonants has brought to light a lack of a simple, isomorphic relation between syllable organization and timing pattern. This further highlights the necessity for an explicit coupling graph to be part of the plan for speech production. Not many studies have been done on vowel-less syllables, and the results that have been obtained so far are briefly summarized here.

In the model as presented so far, the specific coordination patterns hypothesized to underlie gestural organization within the syllable's coupling graph assume that the vowel provides the organizational basis for syllabic organization. Languages can exploit in-phase coordination in onset-vowel coordination, because vowels have a different kinematic parameterization and activation duration compared with consonants. In a CV sequence, the movement into the constriction for both the consonant and the vowel may start synchronously, yet the vowel extends temporally beyond the consonant due to its "slower" movement (vowel gestures have a lower stiffness parameterization) and longer activation. This gives the impression of a strict serial ordering of consonant and vowel, even though in terms of speech planning and triggering there is no such strict linear order.

Importantly, the coupled oscillator theory of syllable structure has capitalized on a strong alignment between grammatical and coordination dynamic preferences: In-phase coordination, typical for onsets, is known to be behaviorally preferred in biologic systems generally. In the languages of the world, onsets are typologically preferred, providing strong evidence for the reciprocal relationship between grammatical structures and the physics of speech production (Nam et al., 2009; for a recent overview see Pouplier, 2012). Formal-linguistic theories of the syllable highlight the fundamental role of the vowel as the nucleus of prosodic organization (Blevins, 1995). Syllabic consonants such as they appear in Slovak or some dialects of Berber are from this perspective a particularly interesting phenomenon. There is no evidence that consonants are reparameterized kinematically if they are in the nucleus (i.e., they do not change their kinematics significantly to become more "vowel-like" (Fougeron & Ridouane, 2008; Pouplier & Beňuš, 2011). Therefore, an in-phase onset-nucleus coordination renders the perceptual recoverability of onset and nucleus problematic. Indeed, a study on Slovak (Pouplier & Beňuš 2011) shows that timing in syllables with consonantal nuclei differs significantly from timing in syllables with vocalic nuclei. Like several other Slavic languages, the Slovak lexicon features syllables with /l, r/ as syllable nuclei, giving rise to words containing long sequences of consonants, such as "štvrťvrstva" ([ʃtvrc.vrs.tva] "quarter layer"), with two syllabic /r/s. Since phonological processes targeting the syllable nucleus apply irrespectively of whether the nucleus is a consonant or vowel, the nucleus status of these consonants is uncontroversial in Slovak (Kenstowicz & Rubach, 1987). The results of the Slovak study showed that the degree of overlap between a sequence of the same consonants varies depending on the syllable position of these two consonants. If one of the consonants is in the nucleus (e.g., m-r or r-k in "mrk," with /r/ being in the nucleus), the consonant sequences shows less overlap compared to the same sequence in onset or coda (m-r in "mrak" or r-k in "park"). Importantly, also in vowel-less syllables, onset-nucleus timing differs significantly from nucleus-coda timing, which again underscores that syllabic organization is expressed in timing relations, even though the timing patterns may differ depending on whether the syllable nucleus is a consonant or a vowel. Interestingly, with regard to the gestural syllable model, vowel-less and canonical syllables behaved alike in that neither showed a C-center effect. For both syllable types, the timing of the release of the vowel-adjacent consonant remained the same across conditions, not the C-center. This means that as more consonants are added to the onset, in Slovak, these consonants are coordinated sequentially to the left of the nucleus. Overall, these results suggest that languages may stabilize a greater range of coordination patterns than has been thought possible (see also Kochetov, 2006). While it is not clear exactly what the coupling graph topology should be for syllables with consonant nuclei, it is clearly going to be different than that for syllables with vowel nuclei.

Much attention has paid to the syllabic consonants of Tashlhiyt Berber, one of the languages of Morocco (Dell & Elmedlaoui, 2002; Prince & Smolensky, 2004; Ridouane, 2003). In this language, any consonant can function as syllable nucleus, giving rise to words consisting solely of obstruents, such as "tkkststt" ("you took it off" fem.). Goldstein et al. (2006) include some examples of kinematic data comparing the Tashlhiyt words /tu.da/ and /tf.da/. The first syllable of both words includes a lip gesture as the nucleus, but in one it is a vowel gesture and in the other a consonant gesture. The kinematic data show that the lip gesture is triggered synchronously with the tongue tip /t/ gesture in /

tu.da/ but that the gestures are sequential in /tf.da/. This is consistent with the Slovak results, showing that the coupling graphs must be different depending on whether the nucleus is a C or V.

Overall, the work conducted on syllabic consonants thus far shows that in vowel-less syllables, syllabic organization is expressed in timing patterns, yet the specific patterns observed may differ as a function of the syllable nucleus. While there seems to be a strong cross-linguistic preference for in-phase onset-nucleus coordination, the Slovak and Berber data suggest that languages may grammaticalize other coordination patterns. The range of timing patterns utilized by the world's languages is not well understood at this point.

Coordination of Consonants Across Syllables

Strong arguments for incorporating spatio-temporal principles of gestural coordination into phonology, and hence grammar, comes from the existence systematic language-specific modes of articulatory timing. One source of evidence comes from the fact that these language-specific modes have been shown to crucially participate in phonological accounts of particular cases of allomorphy (e.g., template satisfaction in Moroccan Arabic, Gafos, 2002, and regular past-tense allomorphy in English, Goldstein, 2011). A second source of evidence is that there is typologic variation in gestural overlap similar to typologic variation in grammar. It has been pointed out that languages differ in their temporal (and hence coarticulatory) properties as early as the 1960s, for instance in a seminal paper by Öhman (1966). Yet it is only with the wider accessibility of techniques for recording of articulatory data since the mid-1990s that systematic cross-linguistic investigations comprising several subjects per language have become feasible. It has been shown that languages vary in their amount of vowel-to-vowel coarticulation (Beddor, Harnsberger, & Lindemann, 2002; Manuel, 1990; Mok, 2010) and in their amount of consonant-consonant coarticulation or overlap across syllable boundaries. It is the latter aspect that is discussed in the present section.

It is a well-known phenomenon of English (and many other languages) that adjacent consonants interact across word boundaries, giving rise to assimilation. For example, in fluent speech the phrase "miss you" ([mɪsju]) may come to be pronounced sounding similar to [mɪʃu]. It has been vigorously debated whether these changes are best accounted for as discrete symbolic changes of one sound into

another sound (/s/ being replaced by /ʃ/ in speech planning, independently of and before articulatory execution) or whether these changes are gradient and characterized by intermediate productions caused by /s/ and /j/ temporally sliding into each other, giving rise to a percept similar, but not identical to /ʃ/ (see Pouplier, Hoole, & Scobbie, 2011 for a recent overview). It is generally recognized that fluent speech assimilation overall arises from the spatio-temporal overlap of gestures. Depending on the degree of temporal overlap and the articulators involved, different consequences are observed. Overlapping /s+j/ sequences may come to sound similar to /ʃ/ even though the underlying articulatory pattern can clearly be distinguished from the production of an underlying /ʃ/ (Zsiga, 1995, 2000). In the case of a coronal-labial sequence, the labial may simply hide the coronal articulation altogether. For example, the phrase "perfect memory" may come to be perceived as perfe[km]emory because the coronal may still be fully produced, but be acoustically and perceptually hidden by the following labial gesture for /m/ (Browman & Goldstein, 1990; Surprenant & Goldstein, 1998).

Other languages do not allow their consonants to overlap to the same extent as English, whereas still other languages show even more overlap. One example of a less overlapping language is Russian. In Russian, final stops are obligatorily released, even when followed by a word-initial (nonhomorganic) stop (Zsiga, 2000, 2003). By contrast, in English, the relatively high degree of articulatory overlap auditorily obscures the release burst of C1 in any C1C2 sequence (Catford, 1977; Henderson & Repp, 1982). Kochetov, Pouplier, and Son (2007) further compared Russian with Korean and found that there are significant differences in C-C timing across syllable boundaries both within and across words, with Russian showing less overlap compared with Korean. Gibbon, Hardcastle, and Nicolaidis (1993) compared the timing of velar-liquid /VklV/ sequences for six languages (English, Catalan, Italian, French, German, and Swedish) and found Catalan to have the most and Swedish have the least overlap. In a further comparison of overlap patterns in English, German, Cantonese, and Japanese, Yanagawa (2006) found a considerably higher degree of overlap for Cantonese compared with German. It is therefore clear that languages exhibit systematic differences in timing, yet the ramifications of these observations are yet to be fully explored. For one, if consonant assimilation arises from gestural overlap, languages with generally little consonantal overlap should not show fluent speech assimilation in the same fashion as languages with a high degree of overlap. Indeed, Russian does not assimilate consonants at word boundaries as English or Korean do. For example in these latter languages, at word boundaries /tk/ may assimilate to /kk/, yet Russian shows no such assimilation. At the same time, even within languages like English and Korean, which are both "assimilating" languages, there are substantial differences in the detailed characteristics of gestural overlap. In English assimilation has been found to be characterized by gradiently overlapping gestures. The degree of overlap may vary with such factors as speaking rate and style. Depending on the degree of overlap and the particular consonants involved, in a C1C2 sequence, C1 and C2 may blend to different degrees rendering either intermediate productions or productions in which there is no measurable articulatory or auditory residue of C1 in the assimilated sequence, that is, C2 fully dominates. Studies on Korean place assimilation have revealed a different picture: assimilation is mainly characterized by a complete absence of C1. Intermediate or gradient productions may also be observed, but not as systematically as in English. At the same time, like in English, the occurrence of assimilation varies with speaking rate and style, characterizing it as a postlexical, fluent-speech phenomenon (Kochetov & Pouplier, 2008; Son, Kochetov, & Pouplier, 2007).

There are further factors that seem to constrain patterns of overlap cross-linguistically. At the same time, languages differ systematically in these noncontrastive properties of sound sequences, highlighting once more that these are not purely physical effects but have to be learned and have to be encoded as part of the abstract utterance plan when speaking. For instance, many studies have noted that in stop-stop C1C2 sequences, cases in which C1 has a more anterior place of articulation compared with C2 shows more overlap than cases in which C1 has a more posterior constriction. For example, a /pt/ (anterior-posterior) cluster shows less overlap than a /tp/ (posterior-anterior) cluster. This effect has come to be known as place order effect and has been observed for Georgian (a Kartvelian language), English, German, French, and Russian alike, even though these languages differ considerably in other aspects of their timing (Bombien, 2010; Byrd, 1996; Chitoran, Goldstein, & Byrd, 2002; Pouplier, 2012). The most popular hypothesis has been that this cross-linguistically shared pattern reflects constraints on perceptual

recoverability: a more anterior C2 consonant, such as /p/ in /tp/ would, under a high degree of overlap, obscure the coronal /t/ completely, while in a /pt/ sequence, an increasing amount of overlap has less effect on the recoverability of the labial closure. However, a complete overlap of a coronal by a following labial does occur on a regular basis in some languages, as the "perfect memory" case has shown for English; in running speech top-down effects may ensure the recoverability of the lexical item even if its final consonant may be acoustically hidden (Surprenant & Goldstein, 1998; Tiede, Perkell, Zandipour, & Matthies, 2001). Further, place order effects have been observed in cases in which perceptual recoverability is not at issue, that is, the place order effect is not limited to stop-stop clusters. The existence of the effect has been shown for instance in Georgian stop-liquid sequences (e.g., /kl/ being less overlapped than /pl/) (Chitoran & Goldstein, 2006), and also in French C/l/ and C/n/ clusters (Kühnert et al., 2006). This has led Kühnert et al. to hypothesize that the effect arises from low-level motor constraints rather than from (phonologically encoded) perceptual recoverability constraints. However, although the place order effect may have roots in the low-level constraints, the magnitude of the effect and the details of how it plays out may differ from language to language. Thus, these differences in overlap as a function of place also need to be part of a temporal plan.

Development of an explicit coupling graph analysis for language-specific regularities in planning cross-syllable consonant coordination presents a number of theoretical choices. One issue is whether the consonants are coupled to each other at all across boundaries; rather, their timing could result through coupling the vowels in successive syllables to one another or through coupling more abstract syllable clocks to one another (O'Dell & Nieminen, 1999; Saltzman et al., 2008). The answer to this itself could vary across languages, and this is one possible means of modeling some of the language differences in coordination data that has been explored (Yanagawa, 2006; Nava, Goldstein, Saltzman, Nam, & Proctor, 2008; Smith, 1995). For example, because of the variable number of consonants that can appear in onset or in coda in English, the timing of successive vowel gestures may be dependent on the number of consonants so that there is sufficient time for all the consonants. This suggests that consonants across syllables are directly coupled to each other. In contrast, in so-called syllable-timing languages with limited consonant clusters like Italian (Smith, 1995), the timing of successive vowels remains invariant across the number of intervening consonants, and thus cross-syllable coupling of the consonants is unnecessary, although the existing data at this point do not rule out such coupling. A second issue is whether the different cross-linguistic plans result from qualitative differences in graph topology (such as the one just discussed), or whether they require setting some quantitative parameters differently (e.g., relative coupling strength or target phase of eccentric coupling). The available data underdetermine model choice at present. Furthermore, to address these issues appropriately, dynamical models of rhythm and foot structure above the level of the syllable (Barbosa, 2001; O'Dell & Nieminen, 1999) need to be more tightly integrated with gesture-level coupling, as has been initiated by Saltzman et al. (2008) and Tilsen (2009).

From a broader planning perspective, the language differences in cross-syllable coordination are important, because the relevant timing plan (coupling graph or whatever alternative model) can obviously not be stored in a syllabary, nor can it be stored in a lexicon of the usual sort, because of the resyllabification phenomena that motivate the syllabary in the first place (Levelt et al., 1999). Experiments on planning in various languages, including kinematic data, are going to be crucial in understanding the planning and execution of speech, because of the nature of subsegmental structure of speech as outlined here.

Notes

1. Recent advances in MRI scanning have enabled the recording of structural MRI data in real time with frame rates above 20 Hz (Narayanan, et al., 2004; Uecker, Zhang, Voit, Karaus, Merboldt, & Frahm, 2010). See examples at http://sail.usc.edu/span/.
2. X-ray microbeam is, like articulography, a flesh-point tracking technique in which the movement of the articulators are tracked in time by the means of pellets or receiver coils attached to the articulators. For an overview of articulatory recording techniques see Stone (2010).

References

Abbs, H. J. (1980). Labial-mandibular motor equivalence in speech: A response to Sussman's evaluation. *Journal of Speech and Hearing Research*, 23, 702–704.

Barbosa, P. A. (2001). Generating duration from a cognitively plausible model of rhythm production. In *Proceedings of the Seventh European Conference on Speech Communication and Technology* (volume 2, pp. 967–970). Aalborg, Denmark: European Speech Communication Association.

Beddor, P. S., Harnsberger, J. D., & Lindemann, S. (2002). Language-specific patterns of vowel-to-vowel coarticulation: Acoustic structures and their perceptual correlates. *Journal of Phonetics*, 30, 591–627.

Bernstein, N. (1967). *The coordination and regulation of movements*. London: Pergamon.

Blevins, J. (1995). The syllable in phonological theory. In J. Goldsmith (Ed.), *Handbook of phonological theory* (pp. 206–244). Cambridge, MA: Blackwell.

Blumstein, S. E., & Stevens, K. N. (1979). Acoustic invariance in speech production: Evidence from measurements of the spectral characteristics of stop consonants. *The Journal of the Acoustical Society of America*, 66(4), 1001–1017.

Bohland, J. W., Bullock, D., & Guenther, F. H. (2010). Neural representations and mechanisms for the performance of simple speech sequences. *Journal of Cognitive Neuroscience*, 22(7), 1504–1529. doi:10.1162/jocn.2009.21306

Bombien, L. (2010). *Segmental and prosodic aspects in the production of consonant clusters* (Unpublished doctoral dissertation). Institute of Phonetics and Speech Processing, Ludwig-Maximilians Universität, München, Germany.

Browman, C. P., & Goldstein, L. (1988). Some notes on syllable structure in Articulatory Phonology. *Phonetica*, 45, 140–155.

Browman, C. P., & Goldstein, L. (1989). Articulatory gestures as phonological units. *Phonology*, 6(2), 201–251.

Browman, C. P., & Goldstein, L. (1990). Tiers in Articulatory Phonology, with some implications for casual speech. In J. Kingston & M. E. Beckman (Eds.), *Papers in laboratory phonology. I. Between the grammar and physics of speech* (pp. 340–376). Cambridge: Cambridge University Press.

Browman, C. P., & Goldstein, L. (1992). Articulatory Phonology: An overview. *Phonetica*, 49(3–4), 155–180.

Browman, C. P., & Goldstein, L. (1995). Gestural syllable position effects in American English. In F. Bell-Berti & L. J. Raphael (Eds.), *Studies in speech production: A festschrift for Katherine Safford Harris* (pp. 19–34). Woodbury, NY: American Institute of Physics.

Browman, C. P., & Goldstein, L. (2000). Competing constraints on intergestural coordination and self-organization of phonological structures. *Bulletin De La Communication Parlée*, 5, 25–34.

Butcher, A. (1999). What speakers of Australian aboriginal languages do with their velums and why: The phonetics of the nasal/oral contrast. In *Proceedings of the International Congress of Phonetic Sciences 1999* (pp. 479–482). San Francisco, CA.

Byrd, D. (1995). C-Centers revisited. *Phonetica*, 52(4), 285–306.

Byrd, D. (1996). Influences on articulatory timing in consonant sequences. *Journal of Phonetics*, 24, 209–244.

Byrd, D., & Choi, S. (2010). At the juncture of prosody, phonology, and phonetics—the interaction of phrasal and syllable structure in shaping the timing of consonant gestures. In Fougeron (Ed.), *Laboratory phonology 10*. Berlin: Mouton de Gruyter.

Byrd, D., & Saltzman, E. (2003). The elastic phrase: Modeling the dynamics of boundary-adjacent lengthening. *Journal of Phonetics*, 31, 149–180.

Byrd, D., Tobin, S., Bresch, E., & Narayanan, S. (2009). Timing effects of syllable structure and stress on nasals: A real-time MRI examination. *Journal of Phonetics*, 37(1), 97–110.

Catford, J. C. (1977). *Fundamental problems in phonetics*. Edinburgh: Edinburgh University Press.

Chitoran, I., & Goldstein, L. (2006). Testing the phonological status of perceptual recoverability: Articulatory evidence from Georgian. Poster presented at the 10th Conference on Laboratory Phonology, Paris.

Chitoran, I., Goldstein, L., & Byrd, D. (2002). Gestural overlap and recoverability: Articulatory evidence from Georgian. In C. Gussenhoven, T. Rietveld, & N. Warner (Eds.), *Papers in laboratory phonology 7* (pp. 419–447). Berlin: Mouton de Gruyter.

Cholin, J., Levelt, W., & Schiller, O. N. (2006). Effects of syllable frequency in speech production. *Cognition*, 99, 205–235.

Cohn, A. (1993). The status of nasalized continuants. In M. Huffman & R. Krakow (Eds.), *Phonetics and phonology V: Nasals, nasalization, and the velum*. Orlando: Academic Press.

Cummins, F., & Port, R. (1998). Rhythm constraints on stress timing in English. *Journal of Phonetics*, 26, 145–171.

Davidson, L. (2006). Phonology, phonetics, or frequency: Influence on the production of non-native sequences. *Journal of Phonetics*, 34, 104–137.

de Jong, K. J. (2001). Rate-induced resyllabification revisited. *Language and Speech*, 44(Pt. 2), 197–216.

Dell, F., & Elmedlaoui, M. (2002). *Syllables in Tashlhiyt Berber and in Moroccan Arabic*. Dordrecht: Kluwer.

Dell, G. S. (1986). A spreading activation theory of retrieval in sentence production. *Psychological Review*, 93, 124–142.

Fougeron, C., & Ridouane, R. (2008). On the phonetic implementation of syllabic consonants and vowel-less syllables in Tashlhiyt. *Estudios de Fonética Experimental*, 18, 139–175.

Fowler, C. A., Rubin, P. E., Remez, R., & Turvey, M. (1980). Implications for speech production of a general theory of action. In B. Butterworth (Ed.), *Language production* (pp. 373–420). New York: Academic Press.

Gafos, A., & Goldstein, L. (2012). Articulatory representation and organization. In A. Cohn, C. Fourgeron, & M. Huffman (Eds.), *Oxford handbook of laboratory phonology* (pp. 220– 231). Oxford: Oxford University Press.

Gafos, A. I. (2002). A grammar of gestural coordination. *Natural Language & Linguistic Theory*, 20(2), 269–337.

Gao, M. (2008). *Mandarin tones: An Articulatory Phonology account* (Unpublished doctoral dissertation). Yale University: New Haven, CT.

Gibbon, F., Hardcastle, W., & Nicolaidis, K. (1993). Temporal and spatial aspects of lingual coarticulation in /kl/ sequences: A cross-linguistic investigation. *Language and Speech*, 36, 261–277.

Gick, B. (2003). Articulatory correlates of ambisyllabicity in English glides and liquids. In J. Local, R. Ogden, & R. Temple (Eds.), *Papers in laboratory phonology VI: Constraints on phonetic interpretation* (pp. 222–236). Cambridge: Cambridge University Press.

Gick, B., Campbell, F., Oh, S., & Tamburri-Watt, L. (2006). Toward universals in the gestural organization of syllables: A cross-linguistic study of liquids. *Journal of Phonetics*, 34, 49–72.

Goldrick, M., & Blumstein, S. (2006). Cascading activation from phonological planning to articulatory processes: Evidence from tongue twisters. *Language and Cognitive Processes*, 21(6), 649–683.

Goldstein, L. (2011). Back to the past tense in English. In R. Bravo, L. Mikkelsen, & E. Potsdam (Eds.), *Representing language: Essays in honor of Judith Aissen* (pp. 69–88). Santa Cruz, CA: California Digital Library eScholarship Repository, Linguistic Research Center, University of California.

Goldstein, L., Byrd, D., & Saltzman, E. (2006). The role of vocal tract gestural action units in understanding the evolution of phonology. In M. A. Arbib (Ed.), *Action to language via the mirror neuron system* (pp. 215–248). Cambridge: Cambridge University Press.

Goldstein, L., Chitoran, I., & Selkirk, E. (2007). Syllable structure as coupled oscillator modes: Evidence from Georgian vs. Tashlhiyt Berber. In W. Trouvain & W. Barry (Eds.), *Proceedings of the XVIth International Congress of Phonetic Sciences* (pp. 241–244). Saabrücken, Germany.

Goldstein, L., Nam, H., Saltzman, E., & Chitoran, I. (2009). Coupled oscillator planning model of speech timing and syllable structure. In G. Fant, H. Fujisaki, & J. Shen (Eds.), *Frontiers in phonetics and speech science* (pp. 239–249). Beijing: The Commercial Press.

Goldstein, L., Pouplier, M., Chen, L., Saltzman, E., & Byrd, D. (2007). Dynamic action units slip in speech production errors. *Cognition*, 103(3), 386–412.

Guenther, F. (1995). Speech sound acquisition, coarticulation, and rate effects in a neural network model of speech production. *Psychological Review*, 102, 594–621.

Guigon, E., Baraduc, P., & Desmurget, M. (2007). Computational motor control: Redundancy and invariance. *Journal of Neurophysiology*, 97(1), 331–347.

Haken, H., Kelso, J. A., & Bunz, H. (1985). A theoretical model of phase transitions in human hand movements. *Biological Cybernetics*, 51, 347–356.

Hardcastle, J. W. (1985). Some phonetic and syntactic constraints on lingual co-articulation during /kl/ sequences. *Speech Communication*, 4, 247–263.

Henderson, J. B., & Repp, B. (1982). Is a stop consonant released when followed by another stop consonant? *Phonetica*, 39, 71–82.

Hermes, A., Grice, M., Mücke, D., & Niemann, H. (2008). Articulatory indicators of syllable affiliation in word initial consonant clusters in Italian. In *Proceedings of the 8th International Seminar on Speech Production*. Retrieved from http://issp2008.loria.fr/proceedings.html

Hermes, A., Ridouane, R., Mücke, D., & Grice, M. (2011). Kinematics of syllable structure in Tashlhiyt Berber: The case of vocalic and consonantal nuclei. In *9th International Seminar on Speech Production*. Retrieved from http://www.issp2011.uqam.ca/upload/files/proceedings.pdf

Honorof, D. N., & Browman, C. P. (1995). The center or edge: How are consonant clusters organized with respect to the vowel? In K. Elenius & P. Branderud (Eds.), *Proceedings of the XIIIth International Congress of Phonetic Sciences* (pp. 552– 555). Stockholm, Sweden: KTH and Stockholm University.

Hsieh, F.-Y. 2010. Gesture reorganization in Mandarin Tone 3 Sandhi [Abstract]. *Journal of the Acoustical Society of America*, 128, 2458.

Iskarous, K. (2010). Vowel constrictions are recoverable from formants. *Journal of Phonetics*, 38(3), 375–387.

Iskarous, K., Fowler, C. A., & Whalen, D. H. (2010). Locus equations are an acoustic expression of articulator synergy. *The Journal of the Acoustical Society of America*, 128(4), 2021–2032.

Katsamanis, A., Black, M. P., Georgiou, P. G., Goldstein, L., & Narayanan, S. (2011). Sailalign: Robust long speech-text alignment. In *Proceedings of the Workshop on New Tools and Methods for Very-Large Scale Phonetics Research*. doi:sailalign

Kelso, J. A., Tuller, B., Vatikiotis-Bateson, E., & Fowler, C. A. (1984). Functionally specific articulatory cooperation following jaw perturbations during speech: Evidence for coordinative structures. *Journal of Experimental Psychology: Human Perception and Performance*, 10(6), 812–832.

Kenstowicz, M., & Rubach, J. (1987). The phonology of syllabic nuclei in Slovak. *Language*, 63(3), 463–497.

Kochetov, A. (2006). Syllable position effects and gestural organization: Evidence from Russian. In L. Goldstein, D. Whalen, & C. Best (Eds.), *Papers in laboratory phonology VIII* (pp. 565–588). Berlin: Mouton de Gruyter.

Kochetov, A., & Pouplier, M. (2008). Phonetic variability and grammatical knowledge. An articulatory study of Korean place assimilation. *Phonology, 25,* 399–431.

Kochetov, A., Pouplier, M., & Son, M. (2007). Cross-language differences in overlap and assimilation patterns in Korean and Russian (1361–1364). In *Proceedings of the XVI International Congress of Phonetic Sciences.* Saarbrücken, Germany.

Krakow, R. (1993). Nonsegmental influences on velum movement patterns: Syllables, sentences, stress, and speaking rate. *Phonetics and Phonology, 5,* 87–116.

Krakow, R. (1999). Physiological organization of syllables: A review. *Journal of Phonetics, 27,* 23–54.

Kühnert, B., Hoole, P., & Mooshammer, C. (2006). Gestural overlap and C-center in selected French consonant clusters. In *Proceedings of ISSP '06—7th International Seminar on Speech Production* (pp. 327–334), Ubatuba, Brazil.

Lahiri, A., & Marslen-Wilson, W. (1991). The mental representation of lexical form: A phonological approach to the mental lexicon. *Cognition, 38,* 245–294.

Lee, S., Byrd, D., & Krivokapić, J. (2006). Functional data analysis of prosodic effects on articulatory timing. *Journal of the Acoustical Society of America, 119*(3), 1666–1671.

Levelt, W., Roelofs, A., & Meyer, A. (1999). A theory of lexical access in speech production. *Behavioral and Brain Sciences, 22,* 1–75.

Levelt, W., & Wheeldon, L. (1994). Do speakers have access to a mental syllabary? *Cognition, 50*(1–3), 239–269.

Liberman, A. M., Cooper, F. S., Shankweiler, D. P., & Studdert-Kennedy, M. (1967). Perception of the speech code. *Psychological Review, 74*(6), 431.

Liberman, A. M., & Mattingly, I. G. (1985). The motor theory of speech perception revised. *Cognition, 21,* 1–36.

Löfqvist, A., & Gracco, V. L. (1999). Interarticulator programming in VCV sequences: Lip and tongue movements. *Journal of the Acoustical Society of America, 105*(3), 1864–1876.

Manuel, S. (1990). The role of contrast in limiting vowel-to-vowel coarticulation in different languages. *Journal of the Acoustical Society of America, 88*(3), 1286–1298.

Marin, S. (2011, June). *Organization of complex onsets in Romanian.* Paper presented at the Proceedings of the 9th International Seminar on Speech Production, Montréal, Canada. Retrieved from http://www.issp2011.uqam.ca/upload/files/proceedings.pdf

Marin, S., & Pouplier, M. (2010). Temporal organization of complex onsets and codas in American English: Testing the predictions of a gestural coupling model. *Motor Control, 14*(3), 380–407.

McGowan, R., & Saltzman, E. (1995). Incorporating aerodynamic and laryngeal components into task dynamics. *Journal of Phonetics, 23,* 255–269.

Mitra, V., Nam, H., Espy-Wilson, C., Saltzman, E., & Goldstein, L. (2010). Robust word recognition using articulatory trajectories and gestures (pp. 2038–2041). In *Proceedings of Interspeech.* Makuhari, Japan.

Mitra, V., Nam, H., Espy-Wilson, C., Saltzman, E., & Goldstein, L. (2011). Articulatory information for noise robust speech recognition. *IEEE Transactions on Audio, Speech, and Language Processing, 19,* 1913–1924.

Mok, P. (2010). Language-specific realizations of syllable structure and vowel-to-vowel coarticulation. *Journal of the Acoustical Society of America, 128*(3), 1346–1356.

Mücke, D., Nam, H., Hermes, A., & Goldstein, L (2012). Coupling of tone and constriction gestures in pitch accents.

In P. Hoole, L. Bombien, M. Pouplier, C. Moohammer, & B. Kühnert, (Eds.), *Consonant clusters and structural complexity* (pp. 205–230). Berlin: Mouton de Gruyter.

Nam, H. (2007). Syllable-level intergestural timing model: Split-gesture dynamics focusing on positional asymmetry and moraic structure. In J. Cole & I. J. Hualde (Eds.), *Phonology and phonetics: Laboratory phonology 9* (pp. 483–506). New York: Mouton de Gruyter.

Nam, H., Goldstein, L., & Saltzman, E. (2009). Self-organization of syllable structure: A coupled oscillator model. In F. Pellegrino, E. Marisco, I. Chitoran, & C. Coupé (Eds.), *Approaches to phonological complexity* (pp. 299–328). Berlin: Mouton de Gruyter.

Nam, H., Mitra, V., Tiede, M., Hasegawa-Johnson, M., Espy-Wilson, C.Saltzman, E., & Goldstein, L. (2012). A procedure for estimating gestural scores from speech acoustics. *The Journal of the Acoustical Society of America, 132,* 3980–3989.

Nam, H., & Saltzman, E. (2003). A competitive, coupled oscillator model of syllable structure. *Proceedings of the International Conference on Phonetic Sciences* (vol. 1, pp. 2253–2256). Barcelona, Spain.

Narayanan, S., Bresch, E., Ghosh, P., Goldstein, L., Katasamains, A., Kim, Y., Zhu, Y., (2011) A multinodal real time MRI articulatory corpus for speech research. In *Proceeding of inter speech* (pp.837–840).Florence, Italy.

Narayanan, S., Nayak, K., Lee, S., Sethy, A., & Byrd, D. (2004). An approach to real-time magnetic resonance imaging for speech production. *The Journal of the Acoustical Society of America, 115*(4), 1771–1776.

Nava, E., Goldstein, L., Saltzman, E., Nam, H., & Proctor, M. (2008). Modeling prosodic rhythm: Evidence from L2 speech. *Journal of Acoustical Society of America, 124*(4), 2577–2577.

Niemann, H., Mücke, D., Nam, H., Goldstein, L., & Grice, M. (2011). Tones as gestures: The case of Italian and German. In *Proceedings of the XVIIth International Congress of Phonetic Sciences* (pp. 1486–1489). Hong Kong.

O'Dell, M., & Nieminen, T. (1999). Coupled oscillator model of speech rhythm. In *Proceedings of the XIVth International Congress of Phonetic Sciences* (vol. 2, pp. 1075–1078). San Francisco, CA.

Öhman, S. (1966). Coarticulation in VCV utterances: Spectrographic measurements. *Journal of the Acoustical Society of America, 39*(1), 151–168.

Öhman, S. (1967). Numerical model of coarticulation. *Journal of the Acoustical Society of America, 41,* 310–320.

Parrell, B. (2012). The role of gestural phasing in Western Andalusian Spanish aspiration. *Journal of Phonetics, 40,* 37–45.

Perkell, J. (1997). Articulatory processes. In J. W. Hardcastle & J. Laver (Eds.), *Handbook of phonetic sciences* (pp. 333–370). Oxford: Blackwell.

Perkell, J., Guenther, F. H., Lane, H., Matthies, M. L., Perrier, P., Vick, J., Zandipour, M. (2000). A theory of speech motor control and supporting data from speakers with normal hearing and with profound hearing loss. *Journal of Phonetics, 28*(3), 233–272. doi:10.1006/jpho.2000.0116

Perrier, P., Loevenbruck, H., & Payan, Y. (1996). Control of tongue movements in speech: The equilibrium point hypothesis perspective. *Journal of Phonetics, 24,* 53–75.

Perrier, P., Ostry, D., & Laboissière, R. (1996). The equilibrium point hypothesis and its application to speech motor control. *Journal of Speech and Hearing Research, 39,* 365–378.

Pikovsky, A., Rosenblum, M., & Kurths, J. (2001). *Synchronization: A universal concept in nonlinear sciences*. Cambridge: Cambridge University Press.

Pouplier, M., & Goldstein, L. (2005). Asymmetries in the perception of speech production errors. *Journal of Phonetics*, *33*, 47–75.

Pouplier, M., & Goldstein, L. (2010). Intention in articulation: Articulatory timing in alternating consonant sequences and its implications for models of speech production. *Language and Cognitive Processes, 25*, 616–649.

Pouplier, M. (2012). The gestural approach to syllable structure: Universal, language- and cluster-specific aspects. In S. Fuchs, M. Weirich, D. Pape, & P. Perrier (Eds.), *Speech planning and dynamics* (pp. 63–96). Berlin: Peter Lang.

Pouplier, M., & Beňuš, Š. (2011). On the phonetic status of syllabic consonants: Evidence from Slovak. *Journal of Laboratory Phonology*, *2*(2), 243–273.

Pouplier, M., Hoole, P., & Scobbie, J. (2011). Investigating the asymmetry of English sibilant assimilation: Acoustic and EPG data. *Journal of Laboratory Phonology*, *3*(1), 1–33.

Prince, A., & Smolensky, P. (2004). *Optimality theory: Constraint interaction in generative grammar*. Cambridge, MA: Blackwell.

Ridouane, R. (2003). *Suite de Consonnes en Berbère Chleuh: Phonétique et Phonologie* (Unpublished doctoral dissertation). Université de Paris III, Paris, France.

Saltzman, E., & Kelso, J. A. S. (1987). Skilled actions: A task dynamic approach. *Psychological Review, 94*, 84–106.

Saltzman, E., & Munhall, K. G. (1989). A dynamical approach to gestural patterning in speech production. *Ecologoical Psychology, 1*(4), 333–382.

Saltzman, E., Nam, H., Krivokapić, J., & Goldstein, L. (2008). A task-dynamic toolkit for modeling the effects of prosodic structure on articulation (pp. 175–184). In *Proceedings of the Speech Prosody 2008 Conference*. Campinas, Brazil.

Scobbie, J. M., & Pouplier, M. (2010). The role of syllable structure in external sandhi: An EPG study of vocalisation and retraction in word-final English/l. *Journal of Phonetics, 38*(2), 240–259.

Shaw, J., Gafos, I. A., Hoole, P., & Zeroual, C. (2009). Syllabification in Moroccan Arabic: Evidence from temporal stability in articulation. *Phonology, 26*, 187–215.

Smith, C. L. (1995). Prosodic patterns in the coordination of vowel and consonant gestures. In B. Connell & A. Arvaniti (Eds.), *Phonology and phonetic evidence: Papers in laboratory phonology IV* (pp. 205–222). Cambridge: Cambridge University Press.

Son, M., Kochetov, A., & Pouplier, M. (2007). The role of gestural overlap in perceptual place assimilation in Korean. In J. Cole & J. I. Hualde (Eds.), *Papers in laboratory phonology IX* (pp. 507–534). Berlin: Mouton de Gruyter.

Sproat, R., & Fujimura, O. (1993). Allophonic variation in English /l/ and its implications for phonetic implementation. *Journal of Phonetics, 21*(3), 291–311.

Stetson, R. (1951). *Motor phonetics. A study of speech movements in action* (2nd ed.). Amsterdam: North Holland Publishing Company.

Stone, M. (2010). Laboratory techniques for investigating speech articulation. In W. J. Hardcastle, J. Laver, & F. E. Gibbon (Eds.), *The handbook of phonetic sciences* (2nd ed., pp. 9–38). Malden, MA: Wiley-Blackwell.

Surprenant, A. M., & Goldstein, L. (1998). The perception of speech gestures. *Journal of the Acoustical Society of America*, *104*(1), 518–529.

Tiede, M., Perkell, J., Zandipour, M., & Matthies, M. (2001). Gestural timing effects in the "perfect memory" sequence observed under three rates by electromagnetometry [Abstract]. *Journal of the Acoustical Society of America, 110*, 2657.

Tilsen, S. (2009). Multitimescale dynamical interactions between speech rhythm and gesture. *Cognitive Science, 33*, 839–879. doi:10.1111/j.1551-6709.2009.01037.x

Tuller, B., & Kelso, J. (1991). The production and perception of syllable structure. *Journal of Speech and Hearing Research, 34*, 501–508.

Turvey, M. T. (1977). Preliminaries to a theory of action with reference to vision. In R. Shaw & J. Bransford (Eds.), *Perceiving, acting and knowing: Toward an ecological psychology* (pp. 211–265). Hillsdale, NJ: Lawrence Erlbaum Associates.

Turvey, M. T. (1990). Coordination. *American Psychologist, 45*(8), 938–953.

Uecker, M., Zhang, S., Voit, D., Karaus, A., Merboldt, K.-D., & Frahm, J. (2010). Real-time MRI at a resolution of 20 ms. *NMR in Biomedicine, 23*, 986–994.

Westbury, J. R. (1994). *X-ray microbeam speech production database user's handbook*. Madison, WI: University of Wisconsin Madison. Retrieved from Http://Www.Medsch.Wisc.Edu/Ubeam.

Xu, Y., & Liu, F. (2006). Tonal alignment, syllable structure and coarticulation: Toward an integrated model. *Italian Journal of Linguistics, 18*(1), 125.

Yanagawa, M. (2006). *Articulatory timing in first and second language: A cross-linguistic study* (Unpublished doctoral dissertation). Yale University, New Haven, CT.

Yuan, J., & Liberman, M. (2008). Speaker identification on the SCOTUS corpus. *Journal of the Acoustical Society of America, 123*, 3878.

Zsiga, E. (1995). An acoustic and electropalatographic study of lexical and postlexical palatalization in American English. In B. Connell & A. Arvaniti (Eds.), *Phonology and phonetic evidence. Papers in laboratory phonology IV* (pp. 282–302). Cambridge: Cambridge University Press.

Zsiga, E. (2000). Phonetic alignment constraints: Consonant overlap and palatalization in English and Russian. *Journal of Phonetics, 28*, 69–102.

Zsiga, E. (2003). Articulatory timing in a second language: Evidence from Russian and English. *Studies in Second Language Acquisition, 25*(3), 399–432.

Phonological Processing: The Retrieval and Encoding of Word Form Information in Speech Production

Matthew Goldrick

Abstract

Sound forms "give voice" to complex conceptual, syntactic, and morphological structures. This article examines the first steps in spoken production processing toward this goal. The first section argues for a stage of word form processing that is influenced by lexical factors (reflecting the input to phonological processes) but is not affected by phonetic factors (because these are represented in subsequent processes). The second section reviews behavioral and electrophysiological data suggesting that within phonological processes, multiple dimensions of phonological structure (segmental, syllabic, and metrical) are independently represented and retrieved; these are subsequently linked or coordinated with one another to provide input to phonetic processes. Finally, the influence of the input to phonological processing on the retrieval of phonological structure is examined (e.g., the influence of partially activated, semantically related words on the speed and accuracy of phonological processing).

Key Words: phonology, interaction, syllables, metrical structure

Sound forms are a linchpin of the link between speaker and hearer. They "give voice" to complex conceptual, syntactic, and morphological structures, providing the hearer with the information needed to recover the speaker's intentions. This article examines the level of processing that realizes the first steps towards the goal: phonological processes.

The first section of this article situates phonological processing within other processes in spoken production. As shown in Figure 14.1, phonological processes take as input information about the lexical representations that have been selected to express the speakers' intended message (see Word Production: Behavioral and Computational Considerations by Dell, Nozari, and Oppenheim for discussion). The word forms corresponding to these lexical representations are spelled out or specified by retrieving distinct dimensions of form information from long-term memory and linking them together, encoding a complex phonological representation

(these aspects of processing are sometimes discussed in the literature as separate processes, phonological retrieval, and phonological encoding.) As depicted at the bottom of Figure 14.1, these abstract phonological structures serve as input to phonetic and motor processes that produce articulatory gestures (for discussion, see "Phonetic Processing" by Buchwald; "The Temporal Organization of Speech" by Pouplier & Goldstein; and "Neural Bases of Phonological and Articulatory Processing" by Ziegler & Ackermann). The first section reviews evidence supporting this overall functional architecture. Data from a variety of methodologies and populations argue for a stage of word form processing that is influenced by lexical factors (reflecting the input to phonological processes) but is not affected by phonetic factors (as these are represented in subsequent processing stages).

The second section of the article examines the internal structure of phonological processing in greater detail. Behavioral and electrophysiologic

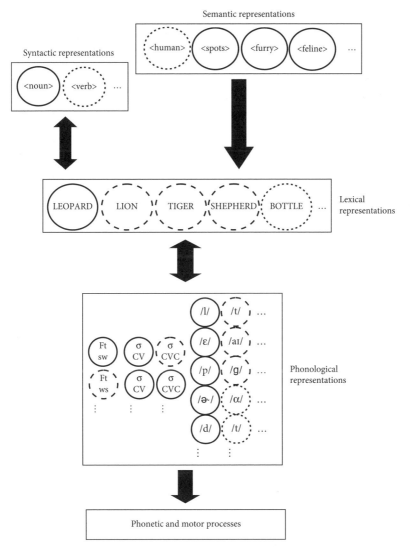

Figure 14.1 Representations and interrelationships among processes in speech production, illustrated for an English speaker producing "leopard" (see text for details). Dark circles denote highly activated representations; dashed lines, partially activated representations; dotted lines, inactive representations. Arrows denote activation flow between processes. Ellipses indicate the presence of additional (undepicted) representational units.

data suggest that within phonological processes, multiple dimensions of phonological structure (segmental, syllabic, and metrical; see "Phonology and Phonological Theory" by Baković for further discussion) are independently represented and retrieved; these are subsequently linked or coordinated with one another to provide input to phonetic processes. Figure 14.1 illustrates some of these dimensions of structure for the target word "leopard" segments (e.g., /l/); syllables (e.g., the first syllable is a stressed CV, /lɛ/); and metrical feet (e.g., "leopard" consists of a stressed followed by an unstressed syllable).

The following section examines in greater detail the influence of the input to phonological processing

on the retrieval of phonological structure. For example, as shown in Figure 14.1, interactions with semantic and phonological processes lead to the partial activation of lexical representations that are semantically (e.g., <tiger>) or phonologically (e.g., <shepherd>) related to the target. These in turn activate their corresponding phonological representations (e.g., <tiger> activates the segment /g/), influencing the speed and accuracy of phonological processing in production.

Finally, the article concludes with an overview of the advances in the understanding of phonological processing since the seminal work of Garrett (1975). Directions for future research that can build on these insights are discussed.

Linking Lexical and Phonetic Structure

The place of phonological processing within the production system is to bridge lexical/morphological representations and the processes that construct articulatory plans. This section argues for this functional architecture through a review of data from neuropsychological and neuroimaging studies and behavioral studies of unimpaired individuals.

Evidence from Acquired Neurological Deficits

If phonological processing is distinct from more peripheral phonetic processes, and the degree of interaction between these processes is sufficiently limited in strength, one should be able to observe cases of acquired neurologic impairments affecting word form processing that selectively target phonological vs. phonetic processing. Deficits to phonological processing should be marked by sensitivity to lexical factors and insensitivity to phonetic factors; deficits to subsequent phonetic processes should exhibit the contrasting pattern of performance.

Goldrick and Rapp (2007) argue that performance on picture naming versus repetition could be used to distinguish such impairments. Because picture naming requires access to lexical (word/morphological) representations, a selective impairment to phonological processing, in particular to the retrieval of phonological information, should impair naming. However, such a deficit should leave repetition performance intact; the task can be performed without accessing lexical representations (Hanley, Dell, Kay, & Baron, 2004). In contrast, a selective deficit to processes subsequent to phonological processing should equally impair all speech production tasks.

Goldrick and Rapp (2007) document two individuals that exhibit these contrasting patterns of performance. Both individuals produce a variety of sound-related errors (mitten→muffin, trumpet→chirpet) suggesting that their deficits affect processes subsequent to lexical access during the processing of word forms. Subsequent analyses reveal a nearly complementary set of factors influence these individuals' behavior. The performance of the individual with a phonological processing deficit is affected only by word-level variables (e.g., he is less accurate on low-frequency words) but not by phonetic complexity (e.g., he shows no difference in accuracy on high- vs. low-frequency sound structures). The individual with a deficit to processes subsequent to phonological processing exhibits the complementary pattern. These contrasting patterns

of performance are consistent with the view that phonological processing is sensitive to lexical properties and manipulates relatively abstract representations of sound structure.

Romani and colleagues (Romani & Galluzzi, 2005; Romani, Olson, Semenza, & Granà, 2002) also report patterns of acquired production impairments consistent with a distinction between more and less abstract word-form representations. They find that individuals with articulatory planning deficits (nonfluent speech in the absence of peripheral motor problems) are sensitive to phonetic complexity (e.g., complexity of syllable structures). In contrast, individuals with fluent speech show no such complexity effects but are sensitive to the word-level factor of lexical frequency. Note that in contrast to Goldrick and Rapp (2007), these fluent patients have deficits affecting all spoken output tasks. This may reflect disruptions to distinct aspects of phonological processing (e.g., retrieval of segmental structure vs. linking of segmental and syllabic structure).

Evidence from Functional Neuroimaging

If phonological processing serves to bridge lexical selection and phonetic processes, and the degree of interaction between phonological and phonetic process is sufficiently limited in strength, there should be brain regions involved in word form processing that are sensitive to word-level variables but not to phonetic complexity. Imaging studies of neurologic-intact individuals report results consistent with these predictions. Form-related processes in speech production engage a network involving posterior temporal and frontoparietal brain regions (Indefrey & Levelt, 2004; Indefrey, 2011; see "Neural Bases of Phonological and Articulatory Processing" by Ziegler & Ackermann for more detailed discussion). Activity in temporal regions (e.g., posterior superior temporal gyrus) is modulated by lexical frequency (Graves, Grabowski, Mehta, & Gordon, 2007; Graves, Grabowski, Mehta, & Gupta, 2008; Wilson, Isenberg, & Hickok, 2009) but not by phonetic complexity (i.e., frequency of sound structures; Graves et al., 2008; Papoutsi et al., 2009).[1]

In contrast, activity in frontal regions is reported to be modulated by these measures of phonetic complexity[2] (see Graves et al., 2008; Papoutsi et al., 2009, for discussion of specific regions). These contrasting patterns are consistent with a view that associates posterior temporal regions with an abstract level of phonological processing, sensitive to word-level properties (see Indefrey, 2011, for a detailed review of related spatial and temporal neuroimaging data concerning the contrast between phonological processing and phonetic encoding).

Evidence from Experimental Behavioral Studies: Speech Errors and Priming

Evidence from behavioral studies suggests that production processes operating at the granularity of segmental representations are sensitive to word-level factors but not sensitive to more fine-grained aspects of speech sounds, specifically, *features*. These are the most basic level of sound representation, specifying the distinctive acoustic/articulatory properties of sounds. For consonants, these include such aspects as the place of articulation (e.g., the placement of the tongue at the front of the hard palate for /t/ vs. the soft palate for /k/); the manner of articulation (e.g., the stopping of airflow for /t/ vs. the presence of frication noise in /s/); and voicing (roughly, whether the vocal folds are vibrating during the consonant constriction—contrast vibration during /z/ vs. its absence during /s/). Features are clearly represented within the speech production system. For example, featural similarity exerts a strong influence on the likelihood that two segments interact in a speech error. The highly similar segments /b/ and /p/, differing solely in voicing, frequently interact in errors. In contrast, /b/ is much less likely to interact with segments that differ not only in voicing but also in place and manner of articulation (e.g., /f/; Wilshire, 1999). *Segments* are a level of representation that links groups of features together and enforces their temporal coordination. For example, this level specifies that in "bat" the labial closure and voiced features of the /b/ are coordinated in time, whereas voiceless is coordinated with the alveolar closure in /t/. In contrast, the associations between voiced/voiceless and labial/alveolar are reversed for the word "pad."[3]

Oppenheim and Dell (2008, 2010) examine segmental errors produced in "inner speech," where participants monitor their silently produced speech. When conditions minimizing articulation are used (see Oppenheim & Dell, 2010, for discussion) segmental errors on tongue twisters produced during inner speech are less sensitive to featural similarity than overtly produced errors (Oppenheim & Dell, 2008, 2010).[4] This is consistent with a relatively abstract level of word-form processing, specified for segmental but not featural content. Furthermore, processing at this level is influenced by word-level information. Oppenheim and Dell find that inner speech errors exhibit a lexical bias; segmental errors are more likely to produce word outcomes than nonword outcomes (e.g., wreath → reef is more likely than wreath → leath). This is consistent with a level of word form processing that is sensitive to word-level factors but insensitive to fine-grained aspects of form (see Olson, Romani, & Halloran, 2007, for a report that errors arising due to a phonological processing deficit are sensitive to featural structure).

Chronometric paradigms provide additional support for a level of processing specified for segmental but not featural content. Roelofs (1999) uses a form-preparation paradigm (after Meyer, 1991) where Dutch participants name blocks of pictures. If all the names of pictures in a block shared the same initial segment (and only the initial segment; e.g., book, bear), participants named the pictures more quickly than when pictures in a block had highly dissimilar initial segments (e.g., file, kite). This form-overlap advantage is not found when the pictures in a block have initial segments that are highly similar (but not identical) in their featural content. For example, no priming is found for sets such as "book, pear," even those these initial segments are highly similar (sharing the same place and manner of articulation, differing solely in voicing). Roelofs (2003) finds similar results when the target segments are in the same language (e.g., book, bear) or different languages (e.g., book, *bloem*—"flower" in Dutch; note this study uses a paired-associates version of this paradigm, where speakers memorize prompt-response pairs instead of naming pictures). These findings suggest that segmental priming can occur at a level of processing that is not sensitive to featural structure.[5]

Two additional sets of findings from speech errors support a level of processing specified for segmental but not featural content. Stemberger (1990) examines a form of priming in spontaneous speech errors: the repeated phoneme effect. When a segment is repeated, there is an increased likelihood of errors on nearby phonological material (Dell, 1984). For example, initial consonant errors (e.g., "time life" → "lime tife") are more likely to occur in a sequences such as "time life," where the vowel /ai/ is repeated, compared with sequences such as "team laugh," where two distinct vowels (/i/ and /ae/) are used. Stemberger's (1990) analyses of English spontaneous speech errors shows that repetition of an identical sound increased error rates above chance, whereas repetition of highly similar sounds did not.

Stemberger (2009) examines another effect of repetition on speech errors. He reports analyses suggesting that repetition of identical sounds results in a higher-than-chance error rate on the second segment (e.g., the /b/ in *bill* will have more errors in a sequence like *bag bill* than *tag bill*). This segmental repetition effect occurs for repetitions of onset, nucleus, and coda segments. In contrast, across these positions there is no consistent, significant effect of repetition of features. The only exception to this is a weak effect of featural repetition (e.g., higher error rates on *peg bill*), limited to initial sounds. The overall pattern, showing highly attenuated featural similarity effects in the presence of strong segmental identity effects, supports a segmental level of processing that is relatively independent of featural structure.

Interim Summary: From Lexical to Phonetic Representations

In order to produce speech, it is clear that speakers must have representations of articulatory information. The data reviewed previously suggest a level of word-form processing that operates over more abstract representations (see Phonetic Processing by Buchwald for further discussion). Phonological processing is insensitive to phonetic complexity and does not specify featural structure. Furthermore, this level of processing is influenced by lexical properties, consistent with a cognitive process that receives input from lexical selection processes.

Form Representations in Phonological Processes
Phonological Representations Beyond the Segment

In addition to segmental representations, many phonological theories assume that segment-sized units are grouped into basic prosodic constituents, *syllables* (Selkirk, 1982). Syllables form the most basic level of a set of representations specifying the metrical structure of an utterance—roughly, the grouping of segments into structures that convey rhythm, stress, and intonation (see Goldsmith, 1990, for a review). Many of these are critical for understanding connected speech (see "Phrase-level Phonological and Phonetic Phenomena" by Shattuck-Hufnagel). In the case of single words it suffices to focus on the level of structure immediately superior to the syllable, the *foot*. These organize syllables and groups and express the relative prominence of different syllables (i.e., *stress*). Lexical stress refers to cases where the position of prominence is idiosyncratic to particular lexical items. For example, in Italian, stress tends to fall on the second to last syllable (e.g., *ancóra*, more/still) but sometimes (unpredictably) falls in other positions (e.g., *áncora*, anchor).

Distinct from segmental and syllabic structure is linguistic *tone* (Goldsmith, 1990). Roughly speaking, tonal distinctions are conveyed by variations in pitch. In languages such as English, tone patterns are used at the level of sentences to convey differences in meaning. For example, in American English, questions typically end with a rising pitch pattern, whereas statements typically end with a lower pitch (contrast "You saw Mary?" with "You saw Mary."). In other languages, tone patterns are associated with individual syllables and distinguish different lexical items. For example, in Mandarin, "ma" with a falling pitch pattern means "scold" while the same syllable with a rising pitch means "hemp." Because this latter type of tone pattern is associated with particular words, it is referred to as *lexical tone*.

The data reviewed next suggest that these distinct aspects of structure are represented within phonological processing. Given this, it is important to consider how they are integrated in representation and processing. As discussed in the following sections, much of the behavioral data suggest that these dimensions of structure are indeed linked together to encode a coherent phonological representation. However, there is also a considerable degree of independence between different dimensions. This accords with autosegmental phonological theories (see Goldsmith, 1990, for a review). These abandon the traditional focus on the segment as the central organizing structure of phonological representations. Instead, distinct aspects of phonological structure (e.g., segments, features, syllables) are viewed as independent representational "tiers" that are coordinated with one another. This "integrated-yet-independent" conception of representational structure provides a useful conceptual framework for understanding patterns in speech production (see Badecker, 1996, for further discussion).

SEGMENTAL AND SYLLABIC STRUCTURE

It is clear that segmental and syllabic structures are linked within phonological processes. In spontaneous speech, segmental speech errors tend to respect syllable position, suggesting an integration of syllabic and segmental structure (Vousden, Brown, & Harley, 2000). For example, for a target sequence like "bad cat," the error "bad *b*at" (where the misplaced segment occurs in the same syllable position in a different syllable) is more likely to occur than "bad ca*b*" (where the misplaced segment moves to a different position in a different syllable). These effects are at least partially attributable to phonological processes. Romani, Galluzzi, Bureca, and Olson (2011) report that the segmental errors of individuals with deficits to this process tend to preserve the syllabic structure of the target. Goldrick, Folk, and Rapp (2010) report that lexical substitutions arising subsequent to a deficit to phonological processes are sensitive to segmental and syllabic length. Finally, the implicit priming effects driven by overlap at the segmental, not featural, level (Roelofs, 1999; see above) are sensitive to whether or not words share the same number of syllables (Roelofs & Meyer, 1998). All of these results suggest that both aspects of phonological structure are integrated within phonological processing.

How can one account for the linking of segmental and syllable structure? Under one view, syllables serve as representational units controlling access to segmental information; alternatively, they are independent schemas or frames that organize and structure independently represented segments (see Sevald, Dell, & Cole, 1995, for a review). Under the former view, phonological processing involves the retrieval of an integrated representation of segmental and syllable structure (Romani et al., 2011). Under the latter, these two aspects of phonological structure are retrieved independently; subsequent processing integrates these two dimensions of structure into a single representation.

Independent Representation of Segment and Syllables

Consistent with the latter perspective, studies of languages such as English, German, Dutch, and Spanish suggest that syllabic and segmental information are represented independently during phonological processes. Although segmental speech errors tend to respect syllable position (suggesting an integration of syllabic and segmental structure), a significant number of errors violate such constraints. In English, this exceeds 20% in spontaneous errors (e.g., Vousden et al., 2000) with even higher rates of exceptions observed in experimental error-induction tasks (e.g., Dell, Reed, Adams, & Meyer, 2000). Damian and Dumay (2009) report priming results showing an effect of segments independent of syllable position. They find faster naming latencies when segments are repeated in English adjective-noun utterances, even when these segments occur in distinct syllable positions. These results suggest that the representation of segmental

identity is sufficiently independent from its syllable position to allow a separation during processing.

With respect to syllable structure, in some priming paradigms syllable structure can be primed independent of segmental content (see Schiller & Costa, 2006, for a full review of the mixed pattern of priming results across paradigms; see Hartsuiker, 2002, for a review of related evidence from speech errors). For example, using auditory and visually presented prime words, Costa and Sebastián-Gallés (1998) show that in Spanish shared syllable structure exerts a priming effect on picture naming independent of shared segmental structure. Sevald et al. (1995) found that English speakers can more quickly repeat pairs of words with overlapping syllable structure. For example, in the word pair *kil taf-ner* (where— indicates a syllable boundary), both words share an initial consonant-vowel-consonant (CVC) structure. This is repeated faster than *kil taft-ner* where the second word has an initial CVCC syllable (n.b. this effect is independent of length effects on naming). Sevald et al. find that there is no additional benefit for sharing the same segments, suggesting this effect derives purely from shared syllable structure (e.g., *kil kil-ner* is no faster than *kil taf-ner*). Spontaneous speech errors also provide support for the representation of the syllabic role (i.e., CV structure) independent of segmental identity. Hartsuiker (2002) finds that spontaneous speech errors in Dutch and Spanish are influenced by the CV structure of surrounding syllables (see also Stemberger, 1990). This set of findings supports a representational distinction between segments and syllable structure within the production system. However, the association of such effects with phonological processing is far from unambiguous. Because segmental and syllabic structure is also present in phonetic processes (see "Phonetic Processing" by Buchwald for discussion), in the absence of independent evidence it is possible to attribute these effects to other stages of word-form processing.

Assuming that effects such as these do arise within phonological processes, many authors have proposed the independent, parallel retrieval of segmental and syllabic structure during phonological processes, followed by a process that associates segments to specific syllable positions (see Shattuck-Hufnagel, 1979, for one of the first explicit proposals of such an account). Within this broad framework, a variety of contrasting proposals have been advanced for the representation and processing of these two aspects of structure (discussed in more detail in the following sections).

Structure of Syllabic and Segmental Representations

In addition to representing the identity of segments, phonological processes must represent their serial order; otherwise, one could not distinguish words like "cat" and "tack." Consistent with this observation, Goldrick et al. (2010) report that serial position influences the activation of form-related lexical representation during phonological processing. They examine word substitution errors (e.g., "beaver" → "weaver") produced by an individual with a deficit to phonological processes. The rate at which these errors shared segments with the target in specific linear positions exceeded that predicted by a theory in which the position of segments is not represented. However, these are also significantly more likely to share syllabic length with their targets than expected on the basis of shared segmental structure (Goldrick et al., 2010). Additionally, cross-position segmental transposition errors and priming effects (reviewed previously) suggest that the representation of segment identity is not intrinsically bound to particular serial positions. These observations raise the possibility that some aspects of the specification of segmental serial order are related to the linking of segmental and syllabic structure.

Theories disagree on the amount of syllabic information that is specified during retrieval. Levelt, Roelofs, and Meyer (1999) adopt a minimalist approach, assuming that only the number of syllables is retrieved. Under this account, the particular structure of each syllable is computed based on the retrieved segments. Others have proposed that more structure is specified. Shattuck-Hufnagel (1992) proposed that in addition to syllabic information (and other aspects of prosodic structure), segments are linked into a representation that specifies position within lexical items. Other studies suggest that the arrangement of consonants and vowels within each syllable is also stored and retrieved. This perspective is consistent with the effects of syllable structure independent of segmental content reviewed previously (assuming such effects arise within phonological processes).

Processing of Segmental and Syllabic Structure

A range of proposals have been advanced regarding how segmental and syllabic structure are retrieved and linked. Some theories assume that the retrieval of segments and their association to syllable positions are incremental (Levelt et al., 1999). Others have assumed that segments are retrieved in parallel but associated to the frame incrementally (O'Seaghdha & Marin, 2000). Additional debates concern the nature of mechanisms accomplishing the linking or binding of segments to syllable positions (for discussion of contrasting proposals, see Dell, Burger, & Svec, 1997; Levelt et al., 1999; Shattuck-Hufnagel, 1992; Vousden et al., 2000). Some authors (e.g., Jacquemot & Scott, 2006; Pate, Saffran, & Martin, 1987) have linked this linking/binding process to the phonological output buffer. This refers to a set of processes that maintain the activity of phonological representations while these linking processes (and perhaps subsequent phonetic and articulatory processes) are engaged (Caramazza, Miceli, & Villa, 1986; see Shallice, Rumiati, & Zadini, 2000, for a review).

Chronometric and electrophysiological studies provide support for some degree of incrementality in the retrieval or linking of segmental and syllabic structure. Meyer (1991) finds that implicit priming is contingent on prime words sharing initial structure; overlap in noninitial positions fails to produce priming. As discussed in preceding sections, this priming paradigm appears to tap into abstract segmental representations (Roelofs, 1999), suggesting this effect arises within phonological processes.

Further support for incrementality comes from studies of monitoring. Wheeldon and Levelt (1995; see also Wheeldon & Morgan, 2002) find that monitoring times for inner speech increase as segments appear at later positions in the word. Van Turennout, Hagoort, and Brown (1997) find a similar latency increase both behaviorally and in electrophysiological measures. Wheeldon and Levelt (1995) find that monitoring latencies for inner speech are sensitive to syllable boundaries. Participants are significantly faster at monitoring for a sequence of segments that falls within a single syllable (see also Morgan & Wheeldon, 2003). Furthermore, the increase in reaction times across linear positions in the word is influenced by syllable boundaries. Although reaction times increase for segments occurring at later positions in the word, there is a much greater increase in reaction times when syllables boundaries are crossed. For example, in the target word "lifter," the difference in monitoring times for /l/ and /f/ (within the same syllable) is much smaller than the difference between /t/ and /f/ (across syllables). Wheeldon and Levelt (1995) argue that these effects do not arise within phonetic processes because monitoring performance is not affected by performance of a concurrent articulatory task and there is no significant correlation between the acoustic durations of speakers' productions (indexing articulation time) and their monitoring latencies. The exclusion of phonetic processing supports phonological processes as the locus of these effects. However, performance in monitoring tasks may rely on processes outside of phonological processes in speech production proper (e.g., speech perception; Levelt et al., 1999). The incrementality effects observed here may therefore reflect the influence of these additional processes.

Segmental and Syllabic Representations across Languages

Research supporting the parallel, independent retrieval of segmental and syllabic structure has been almost exclusively drawn from a set of highly similar, historically related languages (e.g., Dutch, English, German, Italian, Spanish). A smaller body of data drawn from other languages suggests that the degree to which segments and syllabic structure are separated can vary as a function of linguistic experience.

Recent studies of Mandarin and Japanese suggest that for speakers of these languages segments are more tightly integrated with suprasegmental structure. Although speech errors in such languages as English frequently involve single segments (see above), Mandarin speech errors frequently involve movement of entire syllables (Chen, 2000). Priming studies in Mandarin also suggest a tighter coupling of syllables and segments. In English and Dutch, the implicit priming paradigm of Meyer (1991) requires only single segment overlap to induce priming; in contrast, implicit priming is observed in Mandarin speakers only when there is overlap of an entire syllable (Chen, Chen, & Dell, 2002; O'Seaghdha, Chen, & Chen, 2010). Japanese speakers also exhibit sensitivity to suprasegmental structure in this task. Syllables in Japanese have been argued to consist of two groupings of segments: the onset and vowel versus the coda (see Kubozono, 1985, for evidence from speech errors). Production priming in Japanese requires the overlap of the first of these units. In the implicit priming paradigm, effects are not found with onset overlap alone, but require overlap of the onset and vowel (Kureta, Fushimi, & Tatsumi, 2006). Similar results are found in masked onset priming (where word naming latency is reduced by presentation of a masked phonologically related word; Verdonschot et al., 2011).

On the other end of the scale from languages such as English and Dutch, phonological processes in Arabic speakers seem to have an even weaker coupling of segmental and syllabic representations. Berg and Abd-El-Jawad (1996) contrast spontaneous speech errors in English, German, and Arabic. Whereas in English and German most segmental speech errors tend to respect syllable position (in their study, >75% of errors), this constraint is respected by only a minority of within-word errors in Arabic (<40%). This is not to say that syllable position has no influence on production processes in Arabic; between-word errors respect syllable position at much higher rates (>80%).

These studies suggest that although speakers from a variety of language backgrounds make use of both segmental and syllabic structure, linguistic experience shapes the structure of processing mechanisms that integrate these dimensions of phonological representations. Future empirical and theoretical work is clearly needed to understand the factors that underlie these differences (see O'Seaghdha et al., 2010, for discussion).

Lexical Stress and Lexical Tone

Because they are associated with particular lexical items, it has often been assumed that lexical stress (Levelt et al., 1999) and lexical tone (Chen et al., 2002) are retrieved during phonological processes. Empirical evidence provides some support for these assumptions.

LEXICAL STRESS

Consistent with a distinct, independent functional role for the processing of lexical stress, Laganaro, Vacheresse, and Frauenfelder (2002) report a neurologically impaired Italian individual who misproduces lexical stress in all output tasks (reading, naming, repetition). Because this individual's stress production in nonwords matches that of neurologically intact individuals, his errors seem to reflect difficulty in retrieving the appropriate lexical stress position during phonological processes (see also Aichert & Ziegler, 2004, for a case of lexical stress impairment in German.) Segmental exchanges also support the independence of lexical stress. In most such exchanges, lexical stress does not shift with the vowel (e.g., marsúpial → musárpial; Garrett, 1980; Stemberger, 1983).

A defining property of lexical stress is its linear position within the word. For example, the Italian words áncora and ancóra do not have distinct kinds of stress; they are merely stressed in different locations. Behavioral and electrophysiological evidence suggests this linear order is reflected in incremental processing. In monitoring inner speech, speakers are faster at detecting lexical stress at earlier positions in the word (Schiller, Jansma, Peters, & Levelt, 2006). Schiller (2006) finds similar latency effects in electrophysiologic measures.

Although it is independently represented, lexical stress information is clearly integrated with syllabic and segmental structure. Typically, discussions of phonological processing use the cover term "metrical structure" to encompass syllable structure and lexical stress (e.g., Levelt et al., 1999). This reflects the assumption that both aspects of structure are stored and retrieved in an integrated format. Consistent with this, the implicit priming paradigm of Meyer (1991) is sensitive to overlap in syllabic length and stress position (Roelofs & Meyer, 1998). Stress also interacts with segmental structure. Interacting segments tend to occur in similar prosodic positions (Garrett, 1975). Such effects extend beyond lexical stress to include multi-word prosodic structures, such as intonational phrases (Croot, Au, & Harper, 2010).

LEXICAL TONE

Like lexical stress, lexical tone appears to have a functionally independent role within the production system. In languages with lexical tones, the segmental content of two syllables can be exchanged without disrupting the tonal pattern (Chen, 1999; Wan & Jaeger, 1998). Lexical tone information does not influence the implicit priming effects driven by syllabic and segmental overlap (Chen et al., 2002; O'Seaghdha et al., 2010). In monitoring inner speech, electrophysiologic data suggest speakers access segmental information earlier than tonal information (Zhang & Damian, 2009). Current empirical data do not clearly indicate how this independent dimension of structure is integrated with other information within phonological processes.

Interim Summary: Representational Structure in Phonological Processes

Phonological processes involve the retrieval of several distinct dimensions of phonological structure, specifying information regarding segmental and syllabic structure and the presence and location of lexical stress and tone. Although these dimensions are independently represented, properties along each dimension are coordinated with one another within phonological processing to form coherent phonological structures. The processes by which retrieval and coordination occur, and how the structure of such processes is influenced by linguistic experience, are less well understood.

Lexical Influences on Phonological Processes

During phonological processes, complex phonological representations are retrieved and encoded based on input from lexical selection processes. Evidence from a variety of methodologies suggests that word-level factors influence these retrieval and encoding processes. This section examines how specific lexical factors affect the processes of phonological processes.

Lexical Frequency and Age of Acquisition

Speakers learn to retrieve the phonological forms of certain words earlier than others (age of acquisition[6]); some words are retrieved more often than others (lexical frequency). Both of these aspects of target words influence phonological processing. Early acquired words are named faster (see Johnston & Barry, 2006, for a review) and more accurately (Kittredge, Dell, Verkuilen, & Schwartz, 2008). High-frequency targets are named faster (Jescheniak & Levelt, 1994) and more accurately (Kittredge et al., 2008). These reaction time effects are absent in delayed naming, suggesting the facilitation of high-frequency and early acquired words does not arise in postretrieval articulatory processes (Jescheniak & Levelt, 1994; Johnston & Barry, 2006). Data from patterns of acquired impairment provide further evidence that such effects arise specifically within phonological processes. With respect to errors, the facilitation of high-frequency targets and outcomes is found in the performance of individuals with deficits to phonological processes (in the context of intact semantic and phonetic processing; Goldrick et al., 2010; Kittredge et al., 2008); similarly, age of acquisition effects have been documented at this level of processing (Kittredge et al., 2008).

Theories have accounted for such effects by two different classes of mechanisms. Much of the available data fail to distinguish between these two possibilities (but see Knobel, Finkbeiner, & Caramazza, 2008, for simulation evidence in favor of the first account). One type of proposal assumes that variation in experience with different lexical items is encoded within the structure of phonological processes, affecting the strength or efficiency of processes by which phonological representations are retrieved (MacKay, 1987). If low-frequency/late-acquired words have weak connections to their associated phonological representations, phonological retrieval is slower and less accurate relative to high-frequency/early acquired words.

A second type of proposal assumes that variations in experience are reflected by properties of word-level representations themselves (e.g., resting activation levels, Stemberger, 1985; selection thresholds, Jescheniak & Levelt, 1994; time required for representations to accumulate activation, Miozzo & Caramazza, 2003; verification time for binding representations to previous representational levels, Roelofs, 1997). The varying strength of word-level representations could then influence the efficacy of retrieval of phonological representations. For example, if low-frequency words are less active than high-frequency words, they spread less activation to their associated phonological representations. The reduced activation of phonological representations leads to increased reaction times and higher error rates for low- versus high-frequency words (see Dell, 1990, for discussion).

Syntactic and Semantic Properties of Targets

Lexical selection processes are well known to be sensitive to syntactic and semantic properties of target words (Garrett, 1975, et seq.). There is some evidence that these also exert an influence on phonological processes. Studies of acquired deficits have shown selective modality-specific deficits to noun or verb processing, suggesting phonological processes distinguish among items from different grammatical categories. For example, Rapp and Caramazza (2002) present an individual with contrasting impairments across each modality. He has difficulty with speaking nouns (relative to verbs), whereas in writing he has difficulty with verbs (relative to nouns). These contrasting impairments suggest that his deficit does not arise at an amodal level of processing. Furthermore, because many of the errors produced by this individual were nonwords (e.g., "bird" → /prɛd/), it is likely that his deficit is not limited to lexical selection but extends to phonological retrieval. Other studies have documented complementary patterns (e.g., preserved spoken noun production), showing that such effects are not likely due to differences in form across these categories (see Rapp & Caramazza, 2002, for a detailed review). The finding of selective, modality-specific impairments within the set of open class words suggests that sentence production processes may exert a strong influence on the structure of phonological retrieval processes.

A somewhat smaller body of work has examined distinctions between lexical categories based around semantic dimensions. Selective impairments to lexical categories (or selective sparing of particular categories) have been used to argue that these distinctions are reflected within the structure of phonological processes. Particular dissociations that have been documented include proper versus common names (see Semenza, 2009, for a review), numerals versus non-number words, and abstract versus concrete words (see Rapp & Goldrick, 2006, for a review). For example, Rodriguez and Laganaro (2008) report the selective sparing of proper names (specifically, names of countries) in the context of a phonological processing deficit. Semenza et al. (2007) report an Italian-speaking individual with an acquired deficit affecting vowels more than consonants, suggesting an impairment to phonological processes (see also Caramazza et al., 2000). This individual made no phonological errors with number words (Bencini et al., 2011). Bachoud-Lévi and Dupoux (2003) also report spared number word production in a French speaking individual with an acquired deficit to phonological processes. This individual also shows less impairment on names of days and months and abstract nouns and verbs, even when words across categories are matched for variables that influence phonological retrieval (lexical frequency, phoneme length, and syllable structure).

Additional empirical work is required to clarify when—and why—such semantic distinctions are part of phonological processes. Bachoud-Lévi and Dupoux (2003) suggest that neural distinctions critical for other levels of processing (e.g., conceptual or syntactic) may be partially preserved when these levels project to phonological processes (see Watson, Armstrong, & Plaut, 2012, for a related connectionist account focusing on syntactic category distinctions).

Semantically Mediated Relationships between Words

A large number of studies from a variety of different methodologic approaches suggest that the phonological structures of words semantically related to the target (e.g., *dog* and *rat* for target *cat*) are activated during phonological processing (see Goldrick, 2006, for a review). The first source of evidence in support of this claim came from the mixed error effect, the observation that phonological errors are more likely to result in semantically related versus unrelated words (e.g., all else being equal, errors like cat→rat are more likely than cat→hat). This is found in errors in spontaneous speech (Dell & Reich, 1981), experimentally induced errors (Martin, Weisberg, & Saffran, 1989), and the errors of individuals with deficits to phonological processes (Rapp & Goldrick, 2000). More recent chronometric studies have provided additional support for this claim. For example, Peterson and Savoy (1998) demonstrate facilitation of the phonological structure of near-synonyms of the target. Finally, examination of hemodynamic responses during picture-word interference tasks suggests that semantically related distractor words influence phonological processes. Brain regions associated with form-based processing in production (e.g., posterior superior temporal gyrus) are modulated by visually (de Zubicaray, Wilson, McMahon, & Muthiah, 2001) and auditorily (de Zubicaray & McMahon, 2009; but see Abel et al., 2009) presented semantically related distractor words.

These effects are not limited to categorically related words within a single language. Translation equivalents (semantically related words in another language of bilinguals) also produce phonological facilitation effects. Costa, Caramazza, and Sebastián-Gallés (2000) find facilitation in picture naming of cognates, translation equivalents that overlap in form (e.g., gat—gato for a Catalan-Spanish bilingual). Colomé and Miozzo (2010) documented facilitation of phonologically related noncognate translation equivalents (e.g., Catalan *armilla* "vest"—Spanish *ardilla* "squirrel"). Within a single language, other meaning-based relationships result in the activation of phonological structure of nontarget words. These include semantic associates (e.g., *dance-ball*; Cutting & Ferreira, 1999); alternate target labels at different levels of categorization (e.g., subordinate-level *seagull* when basic-level *bird* is the typical label for a picture; Jescheniak, Hantsch, & Schriefers, 2005); and words predicted by a preceding sentence context (e.g., *nun*, primed by "The woman went to the convent to become a…"; Ferreira & Griffin, 2003). (n.b. Authors such as Ferreira & Griffin (2003) argue that some of these effects arise within lexical selection rather than phonological encoding processes.)

For these effects to emerge within phonological processing, theories must account for the coactivation of semantically related words and the influence of coactivated representations on phonological processing. Theories typically attribute coactivation to the structure of lexical selection processes. For example, spreading activation from overlapping semantic features (e.g., <furry, pet>) results in the coactivation of semantically related words (e.g., *dog*, *cat*; see "Word Production: Behavioral and Computational

Considerations" by Dell, Nozari, & Oppenheim for discussion). To allow these coactivated lexical representations to influence phonological retrieval, many theories have adopted a cascading activation mechanism (Peterson & Savoy, 1998). Instead of restricting phonological retrieval to a single selected representation, cascading activation allows all lexical representations to pass activation on to their associated phonological structures.

It is important to note that a wide variety of data suggest that there are critical limitations on the strength of this cascading activation (Rapp & Goldrick, 2000). In many situations, the activation level of the phonological structure of semantically related lexical representations is too weak to significantly influence processing (for a review, see Goldrick, 2006). These restrictions have led some authors to argue that cascading activation is typically restricted to a small number of exceptional situations (e.g., synonymy; Levelt, Roelofs, & Meyer, 1999) and is dependent on the varying attentional demands of production tasks (Roelofs, 2008). Although it is likely that these specific proposals are too restrictive (Goldrick, 2006; Humphreys, Boyd, & Warrier, 2010), the nature and magnitude of constraints on cascading activation remains an open area of investigation.

Rather than relying solely on active spreading activation processes, these effects could also be attributed, at least in part, to the structure of lexical representations. In parallel distributed processing accounts of language production (e.g., Plaut & Shallice, 1993), explicit lexical/morphological representations are replaced by acquired intermediate representations that mediate mappings between meaning and sound representations. The structure of intermediate representations is developed over the course of learning, typically resulting in distributed representations that reflect the structure of multiple representational domains (i.e., semantics and phonology). Thus, instead of relying solely on spreading activation processes to produce co-activation, the acquired "lexical" representations of *cat* and *dog* could encode their semantic similarity directly. When these distributed representations are provided as input to phonological retrieval, their overlapping structure automatically results in the coactivation of multiple phonological structures, producing the effects reviewed in the preceding section (see Plaut & Shallice, 1993, for discussion of related interactive effects in the context of reading impairments). One potential advantage of this perspective is linking the on-line co-activation of semantically related words and the patterns of selective impairment to semantic categories reviewed in the preceding section. Such impairments could reflect damage to the representational structure shared by these related words (see Watson, Armstrong, & Plaut, 2012, for discussion of similar effects related to grammatical categories). It is unclear how such category-specific impairments could be accounted for by a spreading activation mechanism. Of course, like pure spreading-activation based accounts, this perspective requires means to limit the influence of co-activated representations (see Rapp & Goldrick, 2000, for a critical assessment of the Plaut & Shallice, 1993, proposal). As little work has examined this, the contrast between these types of mechanisms remains an open area for research.

Phonological Relationships between Words: Lexical Neighbors

Complementing the work on semantically driven activation of nontarget lexical representations, research from a variety of different paradigms has shown that *phonologically* related lexical representations are activated during phonological processing (see Goldrick, 2006, for a review). The first source of evidence for such activation came from speech error research. The lexical bias effect refers to the observation that phonological errors are more likely to result in strings that correspond to words than nonwords (e.g., all else being equal, errors like cat→hat are more likely than cat→hap). This is found in errors in spontaneous speech (Dell & Reich, 1981), experimentally induced errors (Hartsuiker, Corley, & Martsensen, 2005), and the errors of individuals with deficits to phonological processes (Best, 1996). Costa, Roelstraete, and Hartsuiker (2006) found that experimentally induced errors are biased to result in words in the nontarget language of a bilingual. When performing a task in Spanish, participants are more likely to make phonological errors that result in strings that correspond to Catalan words versus nonwords in Catalan (even though both strings are nonwords in Spanish). To account for these effects, spreading-activation based theories have assumed that activation spreads bidirectionally between phonological and lexical representations.[7] This produces positive feedback loops that boost the activation of phonological representations corresponding to words versus nonwords, producing an advantage for the former representations (see Dell, 1986, for supporting simulation results).

Following research in visual word recognition (Landauer & Streeter, 1973), researchers have referred to these coactivated phonologically related lexical representations as *neighbors*. Dell and Gordon (2003; see also Chen & Mirman, 2012) used simulation results to argue that neighbors could facilitate phonological retrieval of target forms by enhancing the activation of the phonological structure they share with the target. Consistent with this, several studies show enhanced processing of words with more neighbors relative to those with few neighbors (see Goldrick et al., 2010, for a review). Picture-naming latencies are shorter for words with more versus fewer neighbors (Vitevitch, Armbrüster, & Chu, 2004)[8]. Words with more versus fewer neighbors are less susceptible to spontaneous (Vitevitch, 1997) and experimentally induced speech errors (Vitevitch, 2002). Individuals with deficits to phonological processes make fewer errors on words with more versus fewer neighbors (Middleton & Schwartz, 2011). Finally, neuroimaging results suggest enhanced processing of words with more versus fewer neighbors in regions associated with phonological processing (Peramunage, Blumstein, Myers, Goldrick, & Baese-Berk, 2011).

The first section of this article argued that during phonological processes, multiple dimensions of phonological structure are retrieved. However, the bulk of research on neighbors has focused exclusively on segmental structure (defining neighbors as those words differing from the target by the addition, deletion, or substitution of a single segment). Goldrick et al. (2010) find that speech errors arising in phonological processes shared length with their corresponding target forms at a rate greater than predicted by segmental overlap alone, suggesting that multiple aspects of phonological structure contribute to the activation of neighbors.

Nonphonological factors have also been argued to modulate the activation of neighbors (see Goldrick et al., 2010, for a review). Studies of errors arising spontaneously (del Viso, Igoa, & García-Albea, 1991) in experimental error-induction tasks (Goldrick, Baker, Murphy, & Baese-Berk, 2011; but see Dell, 1990) and subsequent to impairments to phonological processes (Goldrick et al., 2010) suggest that phonological errors are biased to result in words with high versus low lexical frequency. Baus, Costa, and Carreiras (2008) find that after controlling for the overall number of neighbors targets with more high-frequency neighbors exhibit greater facilitation than those with low-frequency neighbors. These effects are consistent with the mechanisms that result in effects of target frequency. If frequency influences the strength of connections between lexical and phonological representations, it modulates bottom-up as well as top-down activation flow. Similarly, if frequency modulates the strength of lexical representations, it affects the ability to influence error outcomes or target phonological processing.

Syntactic category also seems to influence the activation of neighbors. Phonological errors are biased to result in words that share syntactic category with the target (spontaneous errors, Harley & MacAndrew, 2001; subsequent to phonological processing impairments, Goldrick et al., 2010). This suggests that the syntactic representations and processes that influence lexical retrieval also exert an influence on phonological processes. This could be accounted for within a cascading activation framework. If syntactic representations boost the activation of nontarget words with the target-appropriate grammatical category (e.g., Dell et al., 1997), this enhanced activation could cascade and enhance the activation of associated phonological representations (see Goldrick & Rapp, 2002, for supporting simulation results).

Phonological Processes: Bridging Lexical and Phonetic Representations

Since the seminal work of Garrett (1975), drawing nearly exclusively on patterns of errors in the spontaneous speech of monolingual speakers of Germanic languages, research into phonological processes has noticeably diversified. Research in this area now draws on experimentally induced speech errors and chronometric and neurophysiological measures; it considers the performance of speakers from a (more) diverse array of languages, multilingual speakers, and individuals with acquired cognitive impairments.

These new techniques and populations have confirmed some of the original proposals based on speech error data. These findings support the claim that phonological processing involves the retrieval of relatively abstract phonological representations; these specify lexical stress, syllabic, and segmental structure, but lack featural information. Chronometric and electrophysiological data have extended and enriched the understanding of phonological processes by providing insight into the temporal structure of these processes, supporting incrementality in at least some aspects of retrieval and encoding. Consideration of data from a more diverse array of languages has revealed the role of lexical tone at this level of processing.

Other results have highlighted the limitations of early work on phonological processing.

Cross-linguistic research has revealed that apparently fixed features of the processing system are highly influenced by the linguistic environment. In particular, there is considerable variation in the degree to which syllabic and segmental representations are integrated during processing. Additional error-based, chronometric, and neurophysiologic research in monolinguals, bilinguals, and individuals with aphasia has documented substantial interactions between lexical and phonological processes in speech production. The strong constraints on such interactions are the likely source of disagreements between this research and earlier work. Because there are many situations under which significant lexical influences are not observed during phonological processes, the observation of such interactive effects requires consideration of a wide range of processing conditions.

A clear avenue for future investigations concerns the internal structure of phonological processes. Although many theories have distinguished retrieval of independent dimensions of structure (e.g., segmental, syllabic) from the encoding of an integrated phonological representation, the degree to which these two functions are subsumed by independent cognitive processes is unclear. Assuming they are independent, there is considerable disagreement regarding the nature of each aspect of processing (e.g., whether one or both of these processes are incremental). A challenge for future work is to more precisely delineate the empirical contrasts between these theoretical perspectives.

Although there are many issues that remain unresolved, recent research has clearly shown that phonological processes cannot be considered in isolation, either from other cognitive processes within the individual or from the linguistic environment in which the speaker is embedded. However, the substantial empirical base for such effects has not yet been matched by theoretical accounts that allow one to predict the nature and extent of such effects. The challenge for future work in this area is to understand the principles that allow these factors to shape representations and processes within phonological processing in speech production.

Author Note

Thanks to Simon Fischer-Baum and Jordana Heller for helpful comments on the manuscript. Preparation of this manuscript was supported by National Science Foundation Grant BCS0846147. Any opinions, findings, and conclusions or recommendations expressed in this material are those of the author and do not necessarily reflect the views of the National Science Foundation.

Notes

1. These posterior regions have been independently associated with phonologic retrieval by meta-analyses of functional imaging studies (Indefrey & Levelt, 2000, 2004).

2. In addition to being modulated by phonetic complexity, activity in these frontal regions has been argued to be modulated by lexical factors (lexical frequency: Wilson et al., 2009; lexical neighborhood density: Peramunage, Blumstein, Myers, Goldrick, & Baese-Berk, 2011). Such effects are consistent with feed-forward interactions (e.g., cascading activation) between phonologic and phonetic processes (see Phonetic Processing by Buchwald for further discussion).

3. Because the existing evidence does not provide clear evidence in favor of a particular representational type, the term "segment" is intended to encompass representational units as large as traditional phonologic segments (e.g., timing tier units, Goldsmith, 1990; root nodes, Archangeli & Pulleyblank, 1994) and smaller subgroups (e.g., nodes in feature geometry, Sagey, 1986; phasing relations between gestures, Browman & Goldstein, 1989).

4. Corley et al. (2011) report a significant phoneme similarity effect in inner speech errors; they argue this contradicts Oppenheim and Dell's (2008) claims. Oppenheim (2012) argues that Corley et al. do indeed find an attenuation of phoneme similarity effects in inner speech, consistent with the claims of Oppenheim and Dell (2010).

5. Damian and Bowers (2003) argued that this effect could arise due to orthographic influences in this paradigm (i.e., priming is disrupted because *b* and *p* are different letters). However, subsequent studies (Alario, Perre, Castel, & Ziegler, 2007; Roelofs, 2006) showed that such orthographic influences are unreliable and appear to be limited to tasks that have an explicit orthographic component.

6. Two concepts related to age of acquisition have also been argued to influence lexical access in production: frequency trajectory (reflecting shifts in the distribution of word occurrence over the lifespan) and cumulative frequency (total number of exposures to a lexical item over the lifespan). Although correlated, these measures are distinct from both age of acquisition and frequency; they have been argued to make independent contributions to production (for discussion, see Bonin, Barry, Méot & Chalard, 2004; Bonin, Méot, Mermillod, Ferrand, & Barry, 2009; Pérez, 2007).

7. Some authors (e.g., Levelt et al., 1999) have attributed such effects to monitoring processes (perhaps based in speech perception mechanisms; see Hartsuiker et al., 2005, for critical discussion of such proposals).

8. See Vitevitch and Stamer (2006) and Baus, Costa, and Carreiras (2008) for discussion of potential differential effects in Spanish.

References

Abel, S., Dressel, K., Bitzer, R., Kummerer, D., Mader, I., Weiller, C., & Huber, W. (2009). The separation of processing stages in a lexical interference fMRI-paradigm. *Neuroimage, 44*, 1113–1124.

Aichert, I., & Ziegler, W. (2004). Segmental and metrical encoding in aphasia: Two case reports. *Aphasiology, 18*, 1201–1211.

Alario, F.-X., Perre, L., Castel, C., & Ziegler, J. C. (2007). The role of orthography in speech production revisited. *Cognition, 102*, 464–475.

Archangeli, D., & Pulleyblank, D. (1994). *Grounded phonology.* Cambridge, MA: MIT Press.

Bachoud-Lévi, A.-C., & Dupoux, E. (2003). An influence of syntactic and semantic variables on word form retrieval. *Cognitive Neuropsychology, 20*, 163–188.

Badecker, W. (1996). Representational properties common to phonological and orthographic output systems. *Lingua, 99*, 55–83.

Baus, C., Costa, A. & Carreiras, M. (2008). Neighbourhood density and frequency effects in speech production: A case for interactivity. *Language and Cognitive Processes, 23*, 866–888.

Bencini, G. M. L., Pozzan, L., Bertella, L., Mori, I., Pignatti, R., Ceriani, F., & Semenza, C. (2011). When two and too don't go together: A selective phonological deficit sparing number words. *Cortex, 47*, 1052–1062.

Berg, T., & Abd-El-Jawad, H. (1996). The unfolding of suprasegmental representations: A crosslinguistic perspective. *Journal of Linguistics, 32*, 291–324.

Best, W. (1996). When racquets are baskets but baskets are biscuits, where do the words come from? A single case study of formal paraphasic errors in aphasia. *Cognitive Neuropsychology, 13*, 443–480.

Bonin, P., Barry, C., Méot, A., & Chalard, M. (2004). The influence of age of acquisition in word reading and other tasks: A never ending story? *Journal of Memory and Language, 50*, 456–476.

Bonin, P., Méot, A., Mermillod, M., Ferrand, L., & Barry, C. (2009). The effects of age of acquisition and frequency trajectory on object naming: Comments on Pérez (2007). *The Quarterly Journal of Experimental Psychology, 62*, 1132–1140.

Browman, C. P., & Goldstein, L. (1989). Articulatory gestures as phonological units. *Phonology, 6*, 201–251.

Caramazza, A., Chialant, D., Capasso, R., & Miceli, G. (2000). Separable processing of consonants and vowels. *Nature, 403*, 428–430.

Caramazza, A., Miceli, G., & Villa, G. (1986). The role of the (output) phonological buffer in reading, writing, and repetition. *Cognitive Neuropsychology, 3*, 37–76.

Chen, J.-Y. (1999). The representation and processing of tone in Mandarin Chinese: Evidence from slips of the tongue. *Applied Psycholinguistics, 20*, 289–301.

Chen, J.-Y. (2000). Syllable errors from naturalistic slips of the tongue in Mandarin Chinese. *Psychologia, 43*, 15–26.

Chen, J.-Y., Chen, T.-M., & Dell, G. S. (2002). Word-form encoding in Mandarin Chinese as assessed by the implicit priming task. *Journal of Memory and Language, 46*, 751–781.

Chen, Q., & Mirman, D. (2012). Competition and cooperation among similar representations: Toward a unified account of facilitative and inhibitory effects of lexical neighbors. *Psychological Review, 119*, 417–430.

Colomé, A., & Miozzo, M. (2010). Which words are activated during bilingual word production? *Journal of Experimental Psychology: Learning, Memory, and Cognition, 36*, 96–109.

Corley, M., Brocklehurst, P. H., & Moat, H. S. (2011). Error biases in inner and overt speech: Evidence from tongue twisters. *Journal of Experimental Psychology: Learning, Memory, and Cognition, 37*, 162–175.

Costa, A., Caramazza, A., & Sebastián-Gallés, N. (2000). The cognate facilitation effect: Implications for models of lexical access. *Journal of Experimental Psychology: Learning, Memory, and Cognition, 26*, 1283–1296.

Costa, A., Roelstraete, B., & Hartsuiker, R. J. (2006). The lexical bias effect in bilingual speech production: Evidence for feedback between lexical and sublexical levels across languages. *Psychonomic Bulletin & Review, 13*, 972–977.

Costa, A., & Sebastián-Gallés, N. (1998). Abstract syllabic structure in language production: Evidence from Spanish. *Journal of Experimental Psychology: Learning, Memory and Cognition, 24*, 886–903.

Croot, K., Au, C., & Harper, A. (2010). Prosodic structure and tongue twister errors C. Fougeron, B. Kuhnert, M. D'Imperio, & N. Vallee (Eds.), *Laboratory phonology 10: Variation, phonetic detail and phonological representation* (pp. 433–460). Berlin: Mouton de Gruyter.

Cutting, J. C., & Ferreira, V. S. (1999). Semantic and phonological information flow in the production lexicon. *Journal of Experimental Psychology: Learning, Memory, and Cognition, 25*, 318–344.

Damian, M. F., Bowers, J. S., (2003). Effects of orthography on speech production in a form-preparation paradigm. *Journal of Memory and Language, 49*, 119–132.

Damian, M. F., & Dumay, N. (2009). Exploring phonological encoding through repeated segments. *Language and Cognitive Processes, 24*, 685–712.

del Viso, S., Igoa, J. M., & García-Albea, J. E. (1991). On the autonomy of phonological encoding: Evidence from slips of the tongue in Spanish. *Journal of Psycholinguistic Research, 20*, 161–185.

Dell, G. S. (1984). Representation of serial order in speech: Evidence from the repeated phoneme effect in speech errors. *Journal of Experimental Psychology: Learning, Memory, and Cognition, 10*, 222–233.

Dell, G. S. (1986). A spreading activation theory of retrieval in sentence production. *Psychological Review, 93*, 283–321.

Dell, G. S. (1990). Effects of frequency and vocabulary type on phonological speech errors. *Language and Cognitive Processes, 4*, 313–349.

Dell, G. S., Burger, L. K., & Svec, W. (1997). Language production and serial order: A functional analysis and a model. *Psychological Review, 104*, 123–147.

Dell, G. S., & Gordon, J. K. (2003). Neighbors in the lexicon: Friends or foes? In N. O. Schiller & A. S. Meyer (Eds.), *Phonetics and phonology in language comprehension and production: Differences and similarities* (pp. 9–38). New York: Mouton de Gruyter.

Dell, G. S., Reed, K. D., Adams, D. R., & Meyer, A. S. (2000). Speech errors, phonotactic constraints, and implicit learning: A study of the role of experience in language production. *Journal of Experimental Psychology: Learning, Memory, and Cognition, 26*, 1355–1367.

Dell, G. S., & Reich, P. A. (1981). Stages in sentence production: An analysis of speech error data. *Journal of Verbal Learning and Verbal Behavior, 20*, 611–629.

de Zubicaray, G. I., & McMahon, K. L. (2009). Auditory context effects in picture naming investigated with event-related fMRI. *Cognitive, Affective, & Behavioral Neuroscience, 9*, 260–269.

de Zubicaray, G. I., Wilson, S. J., McMahon, K. L., & Muthiah, S. (2001). The semantic interference effect in the picture-word paradigm: An event-related fMRI study employing overt responses. *Human Brain Mapping, 14*, 218–227.

Ferreira, V. S., & Griffin, Z. M. (2003). Phonological influences on lexical (mis-) selection. *Psychological Science, 14*, 86–90.

Garrett, M. F. (1975). The analysis of sentence production. In G. H. Bower (Ed.), *The psychology of learning and motivation: Advances in research and theory* (Vol. 9, pp. 133–177). New York: Academic Press.

Garrett, M. F. (1980). Levels of processing in sentence production. In B. Butterworth (Ed.), *Language production* (Vol. 1, Speech and talk, pp. 177–220). New York: Academic Press.

Goldrick, M. (2006). Limited interaction in speech production: Chronometric, speech error, and neuropsychological evidence. *Language and Cognitive Processes, 21*, 817–855.

Goldrick, M., Baker, H. R., Murphy, A., & Baese-Berk, M. (2011). Interaction and representational integration: Evidence from speech errors. *Cognition, 121*, 58–72.

Goldrick, M., Folk, J., & Rapp, B. (2010). Mrs. Malaprop's neighborhood: Using word errors to reveal neighborhood structure. *Journal of Memory and Language, 62*, 113–134.

Goldrick, M., & Rapp, B. (2002). A restricted interaction account (RIA) of spoken word production: The best of both worlds. *Aphasiology, 16*, 20–55.

Goldrick, M., & Rapp, B. (2007). Lexical and post-lexical phonological representations in spoken production. *Cognition, 102*, 219–260.

Goldsmith, J. A. (1990). *Autosegmental and metrical phonology*. Oxford: Basil Blackwell.

Graves, W. W., Grabowski, T. J., Mehta, S., & Gordon, J. K. (2007). A neural signature of phonological access: Distinguishing the effects of word frequency from familiarity and length in overt picture naming. *Journal of Cognitive Neuroscience, 19*, 617–631.

Graves, W. W., Grabowski, T. J., Mehta, S., & Gupta, P. (2008). The left posterior superior temporal gyrus participates specifically in accessing lexical phonology. *Journal of Cognitive Neuroscience, 20*, 1698–1710.

Hanley, J. R., Dell, G. S., Kay, J., & Baron, R. (2004). Evidence for the involvement of a nonlexical route in the repetition of familiar words: A comparison of single and dual route models of auditory repetition. *Cognitive Neuropsychology, 21*, 147–158.

Harley, T. A., & MacAndrew, S. B. G. (2001). Constraints upon word substitution speech errors. *Journal of Psycholinguistic Research, 30*, 395–417.

Hartsuiker, R. J. (2002). The addition bias in Dutch and Spanish phonological speech errors: The role of structural context. *Language and Cognitive Processes, 17*, 61–96.

Hartsuiker, R. J., Corley, M., & Martensen, H. (2005). The lexical bias effect is modulated by context, but the standard monitoring account doesn't fly: Related reply to Baars et al. (1975). *Journal of Memory and Language, 52*, 58–70.

Humphreys, K. R., Boyd, C. H., & Watter, S. (2010). Phonological facilitation from pictures in a word association task: Evidence for routine cascaded processing in spoken word production. *The Quarterly Journal of Experimental Psychology, 63*, 2289–2296.

Indefrey, P. (2011). The spatial and temporal signatures of word production components: A critical update. *Frontiers in Psychology, 2*, article 255.

Indefrey, P., & Levelt, W. J. M. (2000). The neural correlates of language production. In M. Gazzaniga (Ed.), *The new cognitive neurosciences* (pp. 845–865). Cambridge, MA: MIT Press.

Indefrey, P., & Levelt, W. J. M. (2004). The spatial and temporal signatures of word production components. *Cognition, 92*, 101–144.

Jacquemot, C., & Scott, S. K. (2006). What is the relationship between phonological short-term memory and speech processing? *Trends in Cognitive Sciences, 10,* 480–486.

Jescheniak, J. D., Hantsch, A., & Schriefers, H. (2005). Context effects on lexical choice and lexical activation. *Journal of Experimental Psychology: Learning, Memory, and Cognition, 31,* 905–920.

Jescheniak, J. D., & Levelt, W. J. M. (1994). Word frequency effects in speech production: Retrieval of syntactic information and of phonological form. *Journal of Experimental Psychology: Learning, Memory, and Cognition, 20,* 824–843.

Johnston, R. A., & Barry, C. (2006). Age of acquisition and lexical processing. *Visual Cognition, 13,* 789–845.

Kittredge, A. K., Dell, G. S., Verkuilen, J., & Schwartz, M. F. (2008). Where is the effect of lexical frequency in word production? Insights from aphasic picture naming errors. *Cognitive Neuropsychology, 25,* 463–492.

Knobel, M., Finkbeiner, M., & Caramazza, A. (2008). The many places of frequency: Evidence for a novel locus of the lexical frequency effect in word production. *Cognitive Neuropsychology, 25,* 256–286.

Kubozono, H. (1985). Speech errors and syllable structure. *Linguistics and Philology, 6,* 220–243.

Kureta, Y., Fushimi, T., & Tatsumi, I. F. (2006). The functional unit of phonological encoding: Evidence for moraic representation in native Japanese speakers. *Journal of Experimental Psychology: Learning, Memory and Cognition, 32,* 1102–1119.

Laganaro, M., Vacheresse, F., & Frauenfelder, U. H. (2002). Selective impairment of lexical stress assignment in an Italian-speaking aphasic patient. *Brain and Language, 81,* 601–609.

Landauer, T. K., & Streeter, L. A. (1973). Structural differences between common and rare words: Failure or equivalence assumptions for theories of word recognition. *Journal of Verbal Learning & Verbal Behavior, 12,* 119–131.

Levelt, W. J. M., Roelofs, A., & Meyer, A. S. (1999). A theory of lexical access in speech production. *Behavioral and Brain Sciences, 22,* 1–75.

MacKay, D. G. (1987). *The organization of perception and action: A theory for language and other cognitive skills.* New York: Springer-Verlag.

Martin, N., Weisberg, R. W., & Saffran, E. M. (1989). Variables influencing the occurrence of naming errors: Implications for models of lexical retrieval. *Journal of Memory and Language, 28,* 462–485.

Meyer, A. S. (1991). The time course of phonological encoding in language production: Phonological encoding inside a syllable. *Journal of Memory and Language, 30,* 69–89.

Middleton, E. L., & Schwartz, M. F. (2011). Density pervades: An analysis of phonological neighbourhood density effects in aphasic speakers with different types of naming impairment. *Cognitive Neuropsychology, 27,* 401–427.

Miozzo, M., & Caramazza, A. (2003). When more is less: A counterintuitive effect of distractor frequency in the picture-word interference paradigm. *Journal of Experimental Psychology: General, 132,* 228–252.

Morgan, J. L., & Wheeldon, L. R. (2003). Syllable monitoring in internally and externally generated English words. *Journal of Psycholinguistic Research, 32,* 269–296.

Olson, A. C., Romani, C., & Halloran, L. (2007). Localizing the deficit in a case of jargonaphasia. *Cognitive Neuropsychology, 24,* 211–238.

Oppenheim, G. M. (2012). The case for sub-phonemic attenuation in inner speech: Comment on Corley, Brocklehurst, and Moat (2011). *Journal of Experimental Psychology: Learning, Memory and Cognition, 38,* 502–512.

Oppenheim, G. M., & Dell, G. S. (2008). Inner speech slips exhibit lexical bias, but not the phonemic similarity effect. *Cognition, 106,* 528–537.

Oppenheim, G. M., & Dell, G. S. (2010). Motor movement matters: The flexible abstractness of inner speech. *Memory & Cognition, 38,* 1147–1160.

O'Seaghdha, P. G., Chen, J.-Y., & Chen, T. M. (2010). Proximate units in word production: Phonological encoding begins with syllables in Mandarin Chinese but with segments in English. *Cognition, 115,* 282–302.

O'Seaghdha, P. G., & Marin, J. W. (2000). Phonological competition and cooperation in form-related priming: Sequential and nonsequential processes in word production. *Journal of Experimental Psychology: Human Perception and Performance, 26,* 57–73.

Papoutsi, M., de Zwart, J. A., Jansma, J. M., Pickering, M. J., Bednar, J. A., & Horwitz, B. (2009). From phonemes to articulatory codes: An fMRI study of the role of Broca's area in speech production. *Cerebral Cortex, 19,* 2156–2165.

Pate, D. S., Saffran, E. M., & Martin, N. (1987). Specifying the nature of the production impairment in a conduction aphasic: A case study. *Language and Cognitive Processes, 2,* 43–84.

Peramunage, D., Blumstein, S. E., Myers, E., Goldrick, M., & Baese-Berk, M. (2011). Phonological neighborhood effects in spoken word production: An fMRI study. *Journal of Cognitive Neuroscience, 23,* 593–603.

Pérez, M. (2007). Age of acquisition persists as the main factor in picture naming when cumulative word frequency and frequency trajectory are controlled. *Quarterly Journal of Experimental Psychology, 60,* 32–42.

Peterson, R. R., & Savoy, P. (1998). Lexical selection and phonological encoding during language production: Evidence for cascaded processing. *Journal of Experimental Psychology: Learning, Memory, and Cognition, 24,* 539–557.

Plaut, D. C., & Shallice, T. (1993). Deep dyslexia: A case study of connectionist neuropsychology. *Cognitive Neuropsychology, 10,* 377–500.

Rapp, B., & Caramazza, A. (2002). Selective difficulties with spoken nouns and written verbs: A single case study. *Journal of Neurolinguistics, 15,* 373–402.

Rapp, B., & Goldrick, M. (2000). Discreteness and interactivity in spoken word production. *Psychological Review, 107,* 460–499.

Rapp, B., & Goldrick, M. (2006). Speaking words: Contributions of cognitive neuropsychological research. *Cognitive Neuropsychology, 23,* 39–73.

Rodriguez, J., & Laganaro, M. (2008). Sparing of country names in the context of phonological impairment. *Neuropsychologia, 46,* 2079–2085.

Roelofs, A. (1997). The WEAVER model of word-form encoding in speech production. *Cognition, 64,* 249–284.

Roelofs, A. (1999). Phonological segments and features as planning units in speech production. *Language and Cognitive Processes, 14,* 173–200.

Roelofs, A. (2003). Shared phonological encoding processes and representations of languages in bilingual speakers. *Language and Cognitive Processes, 18,* 175–204.

Roelofs, A. (2006). The influence of spelling on phonological encoding in word reading, object naming, and word generation. *Psychonomic Bulletin & Review, 13*, 33–37.

Roelofs, A. (2008). Tracing attention and the activation flow in spoken word planning using eye movements. *Journal of Experimental Psychology: Learning, Memory, and Cognition, 34*, 353–368.

Roelofs, A., & Meyer, A. (1998). Metrical structure in planning the production of spoken words. *Journal of Experimental Psychology: Learning, Memory, and Cognition, 24*, 922–939.

Romani, C., & Galluzzi, C. (2005). Effects of syllabic complexity in predicting accuracy of repetition and direction of errors in patients with articulatory and phonological difficulties. *Cognitive Neuropsychology, 22*, 817–850.

Romani, C., Galluzzi, C., Bureca, I., & Olson, A. (2011). Effects of syllable structure in aphasic errors: Implications for a new model of speech production. *Cognitive Psychology, 62*, 151–192.

Romani, C., Olson, A., Semenza, C., & Granà, A. (2002). Patterns of phonological errors as a function of a phonological versus an articulatory locus of impairment. *Cortex, 38*, 541–567.

Sagey, E. (1986). *The representation of features and relations in nonlinear phonology* (Unpublished doctoral dissertation). Massachusetts Institute of Technology, Cambridge, MA.

Schiller, N. O. (2006). Lexical stress encoding in single word production estimated by event-related brain potentials. *Brain Research, 1112*, 201–212.

Schiller, N. O., & Costa, A. (2006). Activation of segments, not syllables, during phonological encoding in speech production. *The Mental Lexicon, 1*, 231–250.

Schiller, N. O., Jansma, B. M., Peters, J., & Levelt, W. J. M. (2006). Monitoring metrical stress in polysyllabic words. *Language and Cognitive Processes, 21*, 112–140.

Selkirk, E. O. (1982). The syllable. In H. Van der Hulst & N. Smith (Eds.), *The structure of phonological representations II* (pp. 337–383). Dordrecht: Foris Publications.

Semenza, C. (2009). The neuropsychology of proper names. *Mind & Language, 24*, 347–369.

Semenza, C., Bencini, G. M., Bertella, L., Mori, I., Pignatti, R., Ceriani, F.,…Caldognetto, E. M. (2007). A dedicated neural mechanism for vowel selection: A case of relative vowel deficit sparing the number lexicon. *Neuropsychologia, 45*, 425–430.

Sevald, C. E., Dell, G. S., & Cole, J. S. (1995). Syllable structure in speech production: Are syllables chunks or schemas? *Journal of Memory and Language, 34*, 807–820.

Shallice, T., Rumiati, R. I., & Zadini, A. (2000). The selective impairment of the phonological output buffer. *Cognitive Neuropsychology, 17*, 517–546.

Shattuck-Hufnagel, S. (1979). Speech errors as evidence for a serial-ordering mechanism in sentence production. In W. E. Cooper & E. C. T. Walker (Eds.), *Sentence processing: Psycholinguistic studies presented to Merrill Garrett* (pp. 295–341). Hillsdale, NJ: Lawrence Erlbaum Associates.

Shattuck-Hufnagel, S. (1992). The role of word structure in segmental serial ordering. *Cognition, 42*, 213–259.

Stemberger, J. P. (1983). *Speech errors and theoretical phonology: A review*. Bloomington: Indiana University Linguistics Club.

Stemberger, J. P. (1985). An interactive activation model of language production. In A. W. Ellis (Ed.), *Progress in the psychology of language* (Vol. 1, pp. 143–186). Hillsdale, NJ: Lawrence Erlbaum Associates.

Stemberger, J. P. (1990). Wordshape errors in language production. *Cognition, 35*, 123–157.

Stemberger, J. P. (2009). Preventing perseveration in language production. *Language and Cognitive Processes, 24*, 1431–1470.

Van Turennout, M., Hagoort, P., & Brown, C. M. (1997). Electrophysiological evidence on the time course of semantic and phonological processes in speech production. *Journal of Experimental Psychology: Learning, Memory, and Cognition, 23*, 787–806.

Verdonschot, R. G., Kiyama, S., Tamaoka, K., Kinoshita, S., La Heij, W., & Schiller, N. (2011). The functional unit of Japanese word naming: Evidence from masked priming. *Journal of Experimental Psychology: Learning, Memory, and Cognition, 37*, 1458–1473.

Vitevitch, M. S. (1997). The neighborhood characteristics of malapropisms. *Language and Speech, 40*, 211–228.

Vitevitch, M. S. (2002). The influence of phonological similarity neighborhoods on speech production. *Journal of Experimental Psychology: Learning, Memory and Cognition, 28*, 735–747.

Vitevitch, M. S., Ambrüster, J., & Chu, S. (2004). Sublexical and lexical representations in speech production: Effects of phonotactic probability and onset density. *Journal of Experimental Psychology: Learning, Memory, and Cognition, 30*, 514–529.

Vitevitch, M. S., & Stamer, M. K. (2006). The curious case of competition in Spanish speech production. *Language and Cognitive Processes, 21*, 760–770.

Vousden, J. I., Brown, G. D. A., & Harley, T. A. (2000). Serial control of phonology in speech production: A hierarchical model. *Cognitive Psychology, 41*, 101–175.

Wan, I-P., & Jaeger, J. (1998). Speech errors and the representation of tone in Mandarin Chinese. *Phonology, 15*, 417–461.

Wan, I. P., & Jaeger, J. (2003). The phonological representation of Taiwan Mandarin vowels: A psycholinguistic study. *Journal of East Asian Linguistics, 12*, 205–257.

Watson, C. E., Armstrong, B. C., & Plaut, D. C. (2012). Connectionist modeling of neuropsychological deficits in semantics, language and reading. In M. Faust (Ed.), *The handbook of the neuropsychology of language* (vol. 1, Language processing in the brain: Basic science, pp. 103–124). New York: Wiley-Blackwell.

Wheeldon, L. R., & Levelt, W. J. M. (1995). Monitoring the time course of phonological encoding. *Journal of Memory and Language, 34*, 311–334.

Wheeldon, L., & Morgan, J. L. (2002). Phoneme monitoring in internal and external speech. *Language and Cognitive Processes, 17*, 503–535.

Wilshire, C. E. (1999). The "tongue twister" paradigm as a technique for studying phonological encoding. *Language and Speech, 42*, 57–82.

Wilson, S. M., Isenberg, A. L., & Hickok, G. (2009). Neural correlates of word production stages delineated by parametric modulation of psycholinguistic variables. *Human Brain Mapping, 30*, 3596–3608.

Zhang, Q., & Damian, M. F. (2009). The time course of segment and tone encoding in Chinese spoken production: An event-related potential study. *Neuroscience, 163*, 252–265.

Phonetic Processing

Adam Buchwald

Abstract

Successful speech production requires a speaker to map from an encoded phonological representation of linguistic form to a more detailed representation of sound structure that may interface with the motor planning and implementation system. This chapter describes phonetic processing as this component of language production. Although the mapping from context-independent sound representations to context-specific sound representations may be largely predictable, there are a variety of factors that affect the outcome of these processes still being explored. This chapter reviews the recent literature addressing phonetic and articulatory processing, and considers the implications of an interactive language production system by exploring research that focuses on the interaction of phonetic processing with "earlier" and later processing systems. It also reviews data from normal and impaired speaker populations using both traditional psycholinguistic methods and articulatory and acoustic analysis.

Key Words: phonetic processing, articulation, acoustics, speech impairment

Introduction

As is evident from the variety of contributions to this volume, conveying messages through language production is a remarkably complex aspect of human cognition and behavior. This chapter focuses on a part of language production that links the more abstract representations of linguistic form with the more detailed aspects of speech production: phonetic processing. Here, phonetic processing is viewed as the process (or set of processes) involved in mapping from an encoded phonological representation (see the chapter by Goldrick in this volume) to a more detailed representation of sound structure that may interface with the motor planning and implementation system. Although this is a relatively predictable mapping (i.e., from context-independent representations to context-specific representations), a variety of factors that affect the outcome of these processes are still being explored. As has been widely noted (e.g., Goldstein, Pouplier, Chen, Saltzman, &

Byrd, 2007), this topic has typically been glossed over in psycholinguistics, because many of the seminal papers described models of the spoken production system that essentially collapsed the entire set of cognitive processes following phonological encoding (e.g., Shattuck-Hufnagel & Klatt, 1979; Garrett, 1980; Dell, 1986). Thus, this chapter largely focuses on the literature that has emerged over the past decade addressing these issues.

With respect to psycholinguistic accounts of speech production, the discussion of phonetic processing in this chapter is most closely related to the notions of postlexical phonological processing (as in Goldrick & Rapp, 2007) and phonetic encoding (Levelt, Roelofs, & Meyer, 1999). The goal of this chapter is to identify the type of information that is encoded at this level and to explore the nature of the processing mechanisms underlying phonetic processing. Given that these systems have been examined more directly in recent years, the focus here is on research from the past decade that has been particularly influential in moving this field forward.

The remainder of this introductory section presents a more detailed definition of the topic by exploring proposals that have been put forth, and relating this processing system to accounts in other domains. The chapter then reviews research that has directly explored articulatory processing and research that focuses on the interaction of articulatory processing with "earlier" processing systems (e.g., phonological encoding and lexical processing) and later processing systems (e.g., motor processing).

From Phonological Encoding to Articulatory Representations

Phonological encoding (see the chapter by Goldrick in this volume) is typically described as the process of retrieving a phonological representation from long-term memory into a code that can be used to generate more detailed forms for production (Butterworth, 1992; Stemberger, 1985, 1990; Levelt, 1989; Levelt et al., 1999). With respect to psycholinguistic accounts of language production, Goldrick and Rapp (2007) referred to this system as *lexical phonological processing*. As discussed in Goldrick (this volume), the factors that affect the likelihood of successful processing at this level are lexical-level factors (e.g., word frequency; neighborhood density). The output of these processes is then acted on by the postlexical phonological processes, resulting in a more detailed phonetic representation. This processing system is referred to here as phonetic processing (as in Levelt et al., 1999; also "post-lexical phonological processing" in Goldrick and Rapp, 2007).

Input to Phonetic Processing

Phonetic processing takes the output of phonological encoding and transforms it into a more detailed, context-specific representation that can interface with motor planning and execution processes. Traditional descriptions of the output of phonological encoding are as a sequence of phoneme-sized sound structure units (Levelt, 1989; Shattuck-Hufnagel, 1987; Fromkin, 1971; Stemberger, 1990), which may or may not be organized into syllables (see Goldrick, this volume). For example, the word *cat* is represented with its constituent phonemes /k/, /æ/, and /t/ represented as the sequence /kæt/. Accounts of spoken production differ in whether these representations are already specified for their subphonemic detail (i.e., their underlying feature structure, such that /k/ is [−voice], [+dorsal],[−continuant]; Wheeler & Touretzky, 1997) or not (Garrett, 1980; Stemberger, 1985; Dell, 1986, 1988; Shattuck-Hufnagel, 1987; Butterworth, 1992; Levelt et al., 1999; Goldrick & Rapp, 2007). Although debate remains regarding the content of these representations, most accounts hold that these representations are not yet context-specific; in other words, they are not yet specified for coarticulatory or allophonic detail. Thus, one critical function of phonetic processing is to specify the detail associated with these forms (e.g., that the /k/ in *cat* is aspirated, as in [kʰ]). In this way, phonetic processing is the system that generates the predictable details associated with a particular context, typically defined with respect to syllable position.

The most influential proposal offering an alternative to phonemic representations comes from the framework of articulatory phonology (Browman & Goldstein, 1986, 1988 et seq.; see the chapter by Goldstein & Pouplier in this volume). In this account, the primitive units of phonological representations are *articulatory gestures*, which are dynamic action units reflecting the structure of the vocal tract. A gesture consists of an active articulator having a particular degree of constriction and location of constriction. For example, the primary gesture associated with the voiceless velar stop /k/ is the tongue body having the constriction degree of "close" at the "velar" constriction location. These gestural representations are coordinated with one another in a *gestural score*, which specifies the target temporal coordination and spatial locations of adjacent gestures. Although this framework has not been directly integrated with a full processing account of spoken production, the processes involved in the generation of the gestural score from the component gestures (by the coupling graph; see the chapter by Goldstein & Pouplier in this volume and references within) are largely commensurate with the phonetic encoding processing system under discussion in this chapter. Thus, in this framework, the input to phonetic processing consists of articulatory gestures that are not yet specified for their context-specific temporal and spatial coordination patterns.

Generating Context-Specific Detail

The role of phonetic processing is to generate more detailed representations of these input representations that can be used to drive the motor planning, programming, and execution processes required for speech production. Linguists have long described the mapping from context-independent representations of sounds to context-sensitive representations as a language-specific mapping based on systematic principles (Chomsky & Halle, 1968; Prince & Smolensky, 1993/2004). Although there has been much debate about the nature of these mappings (e.g., inviolable rules vs. violable, ordered constraints), they are the core of phonological grammar (see the chapter by Baković in this volume).

In describing this mapping within the context of cognitive and neural processing, there are some issues that arise that have been and continue to be active areas of interest. First, what is the nature of the representations that are generated? There is a range of descriptions of the output of phonetic processing, including a string of phonetic representations incorporating (syllable-) position-specific allophonic detail (Dell, 1986, 1988), a string of syllables retrieved from the mental syllabary (Levelt et al., 1999; Cholin, 2008), and a gestural score specified for spatial targets and temporal coordination among elements (Browman & Goldstein, 1988, 1989).

A second critical issue in understanding phonetic processing is to determine the factors that affect the success of these processes. That is, given the mapping from one relatively abstract representation of sound structure (e.g., segments, gestures) to another relatively concrete level of sound structure (e.g., encoding context-specific spatiotemporal detail), one can ask whether the success of this process is determined by complexity at the former level, the latter level, or both. The third critical issue we will address is how these processes are affected by the interfaces with related processing systems, including both "higher" lexical processes and "lower" motor output processes.

This part of the language production system is critically affected by and defined by its interfaces with other parts of the production system. The remainder of this chapter focuses on the generation of context-specific detail and the factors that influence that detail. The next section reviews findings that directly examine phonetic processing by looking at normal and impaired speech production, and provides evidence supporting a variety of claims about the units in phonetic processing. Recent research indicating that information from higher-level processing (e.g., lexical and phonological processing) affects phonetic processing and articulatory detail is then explored. Finally, the relationship between phonetic processing and more peripheral motor speech systems is addressed.

Examining Phonetic Processing

As noted above, phonetic and articulatory processing has not typically been a focus of processing accounts of spoken language production. Although details of articulation and acoustics have been active areas of research both in phonetics (see Hardcastle & Laver, 1997 and papers within) and the motor speech literature (see McNeil, 2009 and papers within), this work has not typically been approached from an information processing view of spoken production. The next sections consider four sources of evidence regarding the structure of phonetic processes. These consider error patterns in impaired and unimpaired speakers, chronometric data, and phonetic data concerning context-specific variation.

A critical source of evidence in this domain has been instrumental analyses of speech. This contrasts with traditional analyses of sound structure processing within psycholinguistics that involved transcribing speech (both with and without errors) and analyzing the transcriptions, an approach that has been shown to be difficult to use in order to gain an accurate reflection of spoken production output. In particular, instrumental research has demonstrated that examining the articulation and acoustic output of speech allows us to obtain a more complete understanding of spoken production. This section explores some results from articulatory and acoustic analyses that have been influential in showing the need for this type of research.

Nature of Phonetic Representations: Evidence from Speech Errors

Given that most psycholinguistic research on the production of speech has focused on transcription, the use of acoustic and articulatory data to address issues related to spoken language processing has been relatively recent. One primary source of evidence has been speech errors, notably those that are elicited in the laboratory with a variety of tasks. Such errors from laboratory tasks (Dell, 1988, 1990) and naturally occurring speech errors (Fromkin, 1971; Nooteboom, 1969; Stemberger, 1983) have long been used to understand the nature of the spoken production system. Using transcription as the primary source of examining speech errors led to the widespread belief that naturally occurring or task-induced errors consist of well-formed canonical phonemic productions. The use of instrumental methods (both articulatory and acoustic) to address the nature of speech errors has been critical in debunking this notion. In contrast, a variety of evidence has indicated that speech errors often incorporate components of more than one production simultaneously. That is, these errors appear to reflect the competition among two competing sound structure targets (Mowrey & MacKay, 1990; Frisch & Wright, 2002; Pouplier, 2003; Pouplier & Hardcastle, 2005; Goldrick & Blumstein, 2006; Goldstein et al., 2007; McMillan, Corley, & Lickley, 2009; McMillan & Corley, 2010; Goldrick, Baker, Murphy, & Baese-Berk, 2011).

Goldrick and Blumstein (2006) reported on acoustic analyses of speech errors in a tongue twister task. Specifically, they analyzed errors in which a target voiceless sound (e.g., /k/) was erroneously produced as its voiceless cognate (e.g., [g]). The data indicated that the production of [g] when /k/ was the target had a longer voice onset times (VOT; i.e., was more [k]-like than correctly produced [g] targets. They used this pattern to argue that the spoken output reflects partial activation of both the target production and the error production. Thus, the combination of these elements active in phonological and phonetic processing leads to a production that incorporates components of both the target and the error.

Goldstein et al. (2007) reported on electromagnetic articulography studies of a tongue twister task in which participants were asked to quickly keep repeating the phrase *top cop*. They found a specific type of error in which participants produced the articulatory gestures associated with /t/ and /k/ simultaneously, clearly indicating that not all errors result in the production of well-formed phonemic productions. This result mirrored findings from electropalatography research in individuals with apraxia of speech (AOS; Hardcastle & Edwards, 1992; Wood & Hardcastle, 2000) who made similar errors in their stop productions (see later). Pouplier and Goldstein (2010) examined these "coproduction" errors from unimpaired participants and determined that the coproduced closures begin simultaneously, but that the target sound that was intended in any particular context is released later and has a longer duration, reflecting the relative differences of activation of the two gestures.

McMillan and Corley (2010) examined performance in a tongue twister task using both acoustic and articulatory methods and found that articulatory variability can be predicted by feature-based competition. Over two experiments, their participants read groups of four ABBA nonsense syllables where A and B differed by a single place feature (e.g., *kif tif tif kif*); a single voice feature (e.g., *kif gif gif kif*); both place and voice features (e.g., *kif dif dif kif*); or were identical (e.g., *kef kef kef kef*). The results indicated that, relative to the baseline (no change) condition, there was more variability in the VOT production (the main determinant of voicing in English) when A and B differed in voice only (e.g., *kif gif gif kif*), revealing competition at the level of the voice feature. Similarly, there was more variability in lingual contact with the palate (measured with electropalatography) when the competing syllables differed only in place of articulation (e.g., *kif tif tif kif*). In addition, variability of both VOT and of location of palate contact was significantly smaller when the onsets of the two syllables differed in both place and voice (e.g., *kif dif dif kif*), indicating that similarity among segments contributes to competition effects.

These findings from instrumental studies examining speech production clearly suggest that production processes can generate gradient errors that are described more accurately in terms of articulatory detail rather than phonemic representations. Given that the results discussed previously measure the result of the final motor speech output, it is not immediately clear that these results address the cognitive system that is the focus of this chapter. Thus, to verify that these findings inform us about phonetic processes, we must also establish that the output being measured reflects variation that arises during phonetic processing as opposed to during later motor processes or earlier lexical processes. One distinction that suggests many of these results do not arise in lexical processing is that many of the tongue twister tasks used focus either on nonwords or on CVC syllables that may be treated as nonwords in the context of the experiment. Furthermore, the gradient distortions of the type discussed here have been reported to be stronger for nonwords (Goldrick, 2006; McMillan et al., 2009). However, it remains somewhat less clear how we can distinguish effects arising in phonetic processing from those arising in motor planning.

Nature of Phonetic Processes: Evidence from Cognitive Neuropsychology

Goldrick and Rapp (2007) posited the distinction between lexical phonological processing and postlexical phonological processing (the system of interest here). They contended that we can use *task dissociation logic* to determine the level of the deficit of an individual with acquired impairment. Individuals with a lexical phonological processing impairment should be impaired at picture-naming tasks that require lexical items to be retrieved from long-term memory, but not necessarily at word and nonword repetition tasks in which the phonological representation of the word is provided to the individual. In contrast, impairment to postlexical phonological processing affects the ability to perform all tasks involving spoken output because this system is central in spoken production regardless of the task being produced.

Goldrick and Rapp (2007) used this task dissociation logic to explore the factors that influenced error rates in two individuals, CSS and BON. CSS fit the pattern of lexical phonological processing by exhibiting a more severe impairment in naming tasks than repetition tasks, and showed clear effects of lexical frequency and neighborhood density on his spoken production accuracy. In contrast, BON exhibited impairment in both naming and repetition, and displayed sensitivity to several sublexical linguistic factors, such as syllable position (onset > coda); place of articulation (coronal > velar); and phoneme frequency. The comparison between these two individuals showed a clear distinction between impairment affected by word-level properties (lexical phonological impairment) and impairment affected by factors involved in specifying the details of articulation (postlexical phonological impairment). It is worth noting, however, that each property that affected BON's production (phoneme frequency, place of articulation, and syllable position) have both phonological and articulatory correlates. For example, although onset consonants are described as unmarked relative to codas, they are also produced differently in that they are directly coupled with the following vowel that is produced. Thus, we are not able to determine whether BON's sensitivity to these sublexical properties followed from their phonological complexity or their articulatory complexity.

Romani, Olson, Semenza, and Granà (2002) compared the performance of two individuals (DB and MM) who made similar proportions of errors in speech production. DB's production was considered dysfluent and MM's speech was characterized as fluent. Although MM's production errors occurred at similar rates as DB's, the errors showed a different set of characteristics. In contrast to DB (Romani & Calabrese, 1998), MM's production errors did not improve the sonority profile of the target. Additionally, although DB's performance was affected by the sound structure complexity of the target word (he displayed a tendency to simplify consonant clusters, even at syllable boundaries),

MM's were not. Romani et al. argued that MM's performance was indicative of a deficit to phonological encoding, whereas DB's performance reflects an "articulatory planning" deficit. This contrast appears similar to that presented by Goldrick and Rapp (2007); however, it is unclear whether DB's deficit may actually impair the process of generating motor plans from the articulatory plan, rather than the generation of the articulatory plan itself.

Romani and Galluzzi (2005) performed a case-series study examining individuals with and without some articulatory deficit (defined through perceptions of speech) and reported that individuals with articulatory impairment were likely to be sensitive to effects of sound structure complexity (e.g., consonant clusters), whereas individuals who make phonological errors in the absence of articulatory errors were more likely to be sensitive to overall length of words regardless of the structural complexity (also see Nickels & Howard, 2004). If we assume that the individuals with articulatory impairment are impaired at the postlexical level, these findings may be relevant to the issue of what types of complexity affect error rate in individuals with impairment at this level. However, it is not possible to determine whether the individuals in Romani and Galluzzi's (2005) study have additional motor planning and implementation disorders leading to these patterns.

Distinguishing Impairment to Phonetic Processes from Impairment to Motor Processes

Although many psycholinguistic models of spoken production identify differences between lexical phonological processing and phonetic processing, these distinctions are not always clear in the literature on impaired speakers. AOS is a type of impairment associated with impairment to the speech motor planning system. Although the history of the description of this disorder includes defining it as a disorder affecting phonological processing (Wertz, Lapointe, & Rosenbek, 1984), it is now widely agreed that AOS is by definition a disorder affecting motor processing, leading to slowed, distorted, and prosodically abnormal speech (McNeil, Pratt, & Fossett, 2004; McNeil, Robin, & Schmidt, 2009). Given that this disorder affects a motoric level of processing, we may assume that the motor plans are generated based on the already existing context-specific detail. However, it has also been argued to be a deficit in phonetic processing (Aichert & Ziegler, 2004; Staiger & Ziegler,

2008; Ziegler, 2002). It remains possible that there is a terminological impasse here. In psycholinguistic models and in linguistics, phonetic processing typically refers to something that is still linguistic in nature, providing the interface between abstract representations of sound structure and the motor production of that structure by computing the language-specific context-specific detail associated with an utterance. We will return to a more detailed discussion of the relationship among these systems later in the chapter.

One type of error that has often been taken as an indication of speech motor planning impairment is intrusive schwa produced in legal consonant clusters of an individual with an acquired deficit (e.g., *clone* → [kəlon]). These errors are typically assumed to arise in this population as a function of mistiming the articulatory gestures, and similar mistimings have been observed for unimpaired English speakers producing consonant clusters that are not legal in English (e.g., /zgomu/; Davidson, 2006). Buchwald, Rapp, and Stone (2007) examined VBR, a native English speaker with both AOS and aphasia who regularly made these intrusive schwa errors on words with consonant clusters in all output tasks (i.e., the errors arose because of impairment after lexical phonological processing), and found that not all errors involving intrusive schwa are attributable to articulatory mistiming.

Using ultrasound imaging to track the movements of the tongue, Buchwald et al. (2007) compared VBR's articulation of words beginning with consonant clusters with words beginning with the same consonants with a lexical schwa between them (e.g., *clone* vs. *cologne*). If the error arose because of impairment in speech motor planning as opposed to phonetic processing, then there should have been a difference between the mistimed production and the production with a lexical schwa (as seen in Davidson's 2006 data), and this should have been reflected in the articulations associated with the two word types. However, this was not the case. VBR's productions of words with lexical schwa (e.g., *cologne*) and words with consonant clusters (e.g., *clone*) did not differ on a variety of articulatory and acoustic dimensions, and the schwa in the cluster words was produced with its own articulatory target, distinct from that of the neighboring consonants. Buchwald et al.'s data revealed that individuals with acquired deficits to phonetic processing may make true schwa insertion errors that are distinct from errors resulting from mistiming the planning and execution of the motor processes. This suggests the possibility of a distinction between errors arising during phonetic processing and errors arising during motor planning. It is worth noting that to observe this difference, it was critical to use instrumental measures (ultrasound and acoustics) to address the nature of the errors.

To further distinguish errors at these two levels, Buchwald and Miozzo (2011) directly examined the nature of the errors in two individuals with acquired impairment to phonetic processing who deleted /s/ from words that begin with /s/-stop clusters (e.g., *spill*). The question they addressed was whether the /s/ was deleted before (or while) generating the context-specific detail of the words or after the detail is generated. If /s/ is deleted before the completion of phonetic processes, then the errors should reflect a context without the /s/ (i.e., the /p/ should be produced with aspiration, as it is produced in *pill*). In contrast, if /s/ is deleted after the context-specific mapping takes place, then the resulting form should surface with an unaspirated /p/, as in *spill*. Buchwald and Miozzo (2011) examined two speakers and determined that one speaker (DLE) produced aspirated stops in the forms with /s/-deletion, and another (HFL) produced unaspirated stops in these contexts. This indicated that DLE's deletion occurred before specifying the output of phonetic processing, whereas HFL's deletion occurred as part of the motor planning or implementation processes. Taken together, these patterns indicate a distinction between individuals with phonetic processing impairment and motor impairment among those with deficits affecting postlexical processing.

The Role of Speaking Rate in Generating Phonetic Representations

An additional source of context-dependent variation comes from changes in speaking rate. Although speaking rate can be manipulated in experimental settings, these changes have also been reported to be extremely widespread in spontaneous speech (Miller, Grosjean, & Lomanto, 1984). In particular, changes in speaking rate have been reported to affect articulation of both vowel (Gay, 1968) and consonant (Miller, Green, & Reeves, 1986) segments, and consonant clusters (Byrd & Tan, 1996) and CV transitions (Agwuele, Sussman, & Lindblom, 2008). Additionally, the articulatory composition of sounds may alter rate effects (Byrd & Tan, 1996), and interspeaker variation has been reported in how speaking rate affects at least certain sounds (Theodore, Miller, & DeSteno, 2009).

Many of the effects of speaking rate that occur both within words and across words appear to result from changes in duration and temporal overlap of the gestures that compose the articulation. The articulatory phonology framework (Browman & Goldstein, 1986, 1988; Saltzman & Munhall, 1989) provides a clear and straightforward explanation of how and why speaking rate-induced context-dependent variation affects the production of particular sequences, and the variation that may exist can be explored with TADA, the task dynamic application developed at Haskins Laboratories (Saltzman & Munhall, 1989; Nam, Goldstein, Saltzman, & Byrd, 2004) that includes a rate parameter that can be changed to determine how the articulatory output of a particular sequence is altered by variation in speaking rate. The issue with respect to the gestural scores of individual words is addressed more in "The Temporal Organization of Speech" by Goldstein and Pouplier, and "Phrase-level Phonological and Phonetic Phenomena" by Shattuck-Hufnagel addresses this issue with respect to multiword utterances.

The Role of the Syllable in Phonetic Processing

Rather than simply focusing on context-specific variation of phonetic units, other research has looked at larger units of sound structure with respect to phonetic processing. In Levelt et al.'s (1999) influential account of spoken production, phonetic encoding consists of retrieving and encoding stored abstract syllable plans from the *mental syllabary* (also see Levelt, 1992). The mental syllabary contains context-dependent syllable-sized representations, and it is argued that retrieving syllables as holistic elements relieves the burden of generating syllables segment-by-segment during production (Schiller, Meyer, Baayen, & Levelt, 1996). In addition to the economy argument, there is ample evidence that syllable-sized units play an important role in word production. Most descriptions of the mental syllabary hold that syllable frequency influences ease of retrieval with high-frequency syllables, and that high-frequency syllables are retrieved faster than low-frequency syllables (the latter of which may not even be stored). Differences based on syllable frequency have been found in speech production tasks from a variety of languages in both unimpaired (Spanish, Carreiras & Perea, 2004; French, Laganaro & Alario, 2006; Dutch, Cholin, Levelt, & Schiller, 2006; Levelt & Wheeldon, 1994) and impaired speakers (German, Aichert & Ziegler, 2004; Staiger & Ziegler, 2008; French, Laganaro, 2005; Laganaro, 2008).

Although there is clear evidence that syllable frequency affects speech production, it remains less clear whether these effects arise during phonological encoding, phonetic processing, motor processing, or more than one of these levels. There is evidence that at least some syllable effects arise after lexical processing and phonological encoding. For example, Laganaro and Alario (2006) varied syllable frequency in a delayed naming task performed with and without articulatory suppression (i.e., participants repeating a syllable during the delay). Syllable frequency effects were obtained only with articulatory suppression, when the phonetic and motor processing systems were active during the delay. The authors concluded that this indicated that syllable frequency effects arise during those processes that were engaged during the delay that was filled by articulatory suppression—in other words, after phonological encoding (also see Cholin & Levelt, 2009). However, although some effects of syllable frequency have been reported to arise after phonological encoding, it remains difficult to pinpoint the level of these effects within phonetic and motor processing systems.

Interim Summary

This section explored a variety of findings regarding the nature of phonetic processing. It has been shown that a system incorporating only discrete, context-independent sound structure representations (e.g., segments) cannot account for the patterns seen in phonetic processing. These findings are seen in data from both unimpaired and impaired speakers. It is also likely that syllables are one type of unit of sound structure in phonetic processing, although it remains unclear whether they are the only units relevant at this level. Finally, the success of the processes at this level appear to relate to complexity at a variety of levels including sound structure sequences; frequency of sound structure sequences (e.g., syllable frequency); and the rate of speech production. These factors are all argued to be intrinsic to phonetic processing. The next section reviews research indicating that a variety of lexical variables that are extrinsic to phonetic processing can systematically affect the phonetic details of word production.

Interactions with Lexical Processing and Phonological Encoding

Many current descriptions of phonetic processing consider the interactions between articulatory detail and higher-level representations that are activated earlier in spoken production. In particular, the notion of lexical influences on articulatory detail has received a great deal of attention in recent years and several phenomena suggest that phonetic variation directly reflects differences in the activation dynamics of lexical entries. The details of how a word is articulated has been shown to be affected by a variety of properties (e.g., lexical frequency, neighborhood density, syntactic predictability) that are part of lexical processing, suggesting that lexical processing dynamics affect postlexical articulatory processing. This section explores results demonstrating this type of lexically conditioned phonetic variation, and reviews some of the prominent accounts of why this variation exists.

Lexical Frequency

It has long been reported that high-frequency words are more reduced than low-frequency words (Zipf, 1929), and a variety of studies have demonstrated effects of frequency on different aspects of speech production, ranging from durational differences to the degree to which a phonological process is applied (e.g., Bybee, 2001; Pierrehumbert, 2001; Munson, 2007; see Bell, Brenier, Gregory, Girand, & Jurafsky, 2009 for a recent review). To determine whether lexical frequency affects acoustic duration in word production, it is critical to ensure that the sound structure sequences being compared are matched on other properties relevant to sound structure processing (e.g., phonemic identity, word length). Several recent lines of research have shown clear effects of word frequency on articulatory detail when these other factors are controlled. Pluymaekers, Ernestus, and Baayen (2005) examined the production of the same affixes appearing in different words that varied in frequency, with the data coming from a spoken corpus of spontaneous speech in Dutch. They reported that frequency can affect the degree of reduction in the production the suffixes, with more reduction being obtained in higher-frequency words. These effects were seen over a variety of affixes, and interacted with other variables, such as speech rate.

Although the Pluymaekers et al. (2005) study used natural speech tokens that share sound structure sequences, one of the more compelling tests of the effect of lexical frequency on articulatory detail comes from Gahl (2008), who examined the production of English homophones that vary in frequency (e.g., *time ~ thyme*) from the Switchboard corpus of American English telephone conversations. Gahl reported that high-frequency homophones (e.g., *time*) were produced with shorter durations than their low-frequency counterparts (e.g., *thyme*), and a multiple regression analysis

indicated that frequency significantly predicted performance above the effects of several other relevant variables (e.g., measures of contextual predictability, likelihood of being phrase-final). Taken together, these findings indicate that lexical frequency affects the low-level articulation (e.g., duration) even when two words share the same phonemic content, indicating an effect of lexical frequency on articulatory detail (also see Goldrick et al., 2011).

Although these studies show that lexical frequency affects articulation even when other lexical effects are controlled, there is some evidence that frequency may alter production differently in different parts of the lexicon. In particular, Bell et al. (2009) reported that frequency effects on articulation affected content words (with more frequent words produced more quickly) but did not affect function words, where no frequency effect on production was observed. However, despite the lack of a frequency effect on the articulation of function words, Bell et al. reported that these words are produced with shorter durations than content words.

Neighborhood Structure

An additional type of lexical processing effect on phonetic detail comes from effects of phonological neighborhood structure. Phonological neighbors refer to the other words in the lexicon that are phonologically similar to a target word, and a large number of neighbors has been shown to inhibit word recognition in perception (through slower and less accurate word recognition; see Luce & Pisoni, 1998), but facilitate word production (Dell & Gordon, 2003; Vitevitch & Sommers, 2003). With respect to effects of phonological neighborhood structure on word production, one area that has been explored is that the production of the vowel space is expanded in the production of words from high-density neighborhoods compared with low-density neighborhoods (Munson, 2007; Munson & Solomon, 2004; Wright, 2004). Each of these studies shows that vowels in words from dense neighborhoods (i.e., words with several other words containing overlapping sound structure, see the chapter by Goldrick in this volume) are produced closer to the periphery of the vowel space (i.e., with more extreme articulation), whereas vowels in words from sparse neighborhoods are produced closer to the center of the vowel space. The effect of this difference is that there is an enhancement of distinctiveness in the vowels in words from high-density neighborhoods relative to vowels in words from low-density neighborhoods.

Vowel space expansion such as this is typical of what speakers do when they are producing "clear" speech (Bradlow, 2002), and has been associated with more intelligible speakers (Bradlow, Torretta, & Pisoni, 1996). Thus, when speakers are producing words from dense phonological neighborhoods, they adopt the strategies used in clear speech, referred to as "hyperarticulation" in Lindblom's *hyperspeech and hypospeech* theory (Lindblom, 1990). Additionally, Scarborough (2004) found that vowels in low-frequency words from high-density neighborhoods exhibit more coarticulation (e.g. V-to-V coarticulation) than vowels in high-frequency words from low-density neighborhoods. This pattern indicates that speakers produce more coarticulation among vowels for words that are harder for listeners to accurately recognize (low-frequency words in high-density neighborhoods; see Luce & Pisoni, 1998). Scarborough (2004) argued (contra Lindblom, 1990) it is helpful to the process of lexical access for the listener.

In recent work, Baese-Berk and Goldrick (2009) address a specific type of neighborhood effect: the presence or absence of a specific minimal pair lexical item. They examined the productions of words beginning with a voiceless consonant that have a voiced consonant-initial cognate (e.g. *cod ~ god*) and compared them with voiceless-initial words without a voiced cognate (e.g. *cop ~ *gop*). Their data revealed that participants produce more extreme VOT when producing words with the minimal pair neighbor than when producing words without a minimal pair neighbor. Because VOT is a key indicator of the voicing contrast (Lisker & Abramson, 1964), the enhanced VOT in the presence of a minimal pair neighbor can be viewed as another type of hyperarticulation due to a lexical item being from a lexical neighborhood with a particular neighborhood structure.

As can be inferred from this limited review of phonetic consequences of neighborhood density and structure, there have been relatively few attempts to understand how density can affect the acoustic details of speech production. Nevertheless, this remains a fruitful area of research and will likely lead to further insights regarding the relationship between lexical representations in the lexicon and the processing systems that allow those representations to be articulated in speech production.

Predictability Effects

In addition to effects from lexical properties of individual words, such as frequency and neighborhood density, an additional factor affecting articulatory detail is predictability within an utterance. Lieberman (1963) compared the production of words when they were predictable (as part of a formulaic expression) or unpredictable within an utterance. Acoustic measures indicated that unpredictable words are longer and exhibit clearer correlates of stress, such as increased amplitude. Additional investigations have shown that redundancy within a discourse (Aylett & Turk, 2004) and probability of producing a particular syntactic construction (Tily et al., 2009; Gahl & Garnsey, 2004, 2006) also affect articulatory detail, with less probable (and less redundant) forms produced with increased duration relative to more probable forms (also see Bell et al., 2009). Thus, the literature on articulatory detail shows that speakers are sensitive to a large number of factors (e.g., lexical, syntactic, discourse), which all affect the variation in how words are produced.

Relating Phonetic Processing to Speech Motor Planning

Throughout this chapter we have discussed phonetic processing as a part of spoken language production involved in mapping from a relatively abstract phonological representation (the output of phonological encoding) to a more detailed level of representation that may interface with the speech motor planning system. In this section we will discuss how the output of phonetic processing relates to speech motor planning, drawing on the literature from both unimpaired and impaired speech planning.

Speech Motor Planning: Targets of Production

One prominent debate in the literature on speech motor planning is whether the targets of speech sound production are articulatory targets (e.g., moving the tongue to a certain location; Saltzman & Munhall, 1989) or acoustic targets (e.g., achieving a particular formant structure; Guenther, Hampson, & Johnson, 1998). The main motor planning accounts focusing on articulatory targets are part of the articulatory phonology framework based on a coupled-oscillator model (Browman & Goldstein, 1986; Saltzman & Munhall, 1989). Given a description of phonetic planning that yields a representation akin to the coordinated gestural scores, the speech motor planning system can be viewed as a system that specifies these abstract gestural representations into specific vocal tract variables and yields a description of inter-articulator coordination that serve as plans to drive motor execution. The discussion of this speech planning mapping from gestural coordination to articulator coordination is couched in the dynamical systems framework (see Port & van Gelder, 1995 and papers within). A review of this literature is outside the scope of this chapter, and the reader is referred to Goldstein and Pouplier (this volume) for further discussion.

There exists some evidence that acoustic targets play a role in speech motor planning. This type of account is formalized in the DIVA model of speech production put forth by Frank Guenther and colleagues (Guenther, 1994; Guenther et al., 1998; Guenther & Perkell, 2004; Tourville & Guenther, 2011). Several lines of research have indicated that speakers make online adjustments to their productions to achieve an acoustic (not an articulatory) target when their production is disturbed with a bite block (Lane et al., 2005) or when the auditory feedback they receive from their own voice (over headphones) is modified to alter the acoustic details of their productions (see Guenther & Perkell, 2004). In addition, recent research suggests that even during covert syllable production, speakers generate an internal representation of the production of a word that generates activity in the auditory cortex that is consistent with hearing the syllable (Tian & Poeppel, 2010). The work of Guenther and others suggests the possibility that motor information is used to generate auditory representations and that those representations are assessed and then used to potentially modify motor production.

Relating Phonetic Processing to Motor Speech Impairment

Descriptions of impairment to speech motor control differentiate between the clinical categories of AOS (speech motor planning impairment) and dysarthria, typically viewed as impairment to speech motor production (McNeil et al., 2004; McNeil et al., 2009; Duffy, 2005). In relating acquired impairment to psycholinguistic models of speech production, there has been some debate as to whether AOS refers to phonetic encoding impairment (Ziegler, 2002; Varley & Whiteside, 2001) or whether a framework that accounts for the range of needs to distinguish phonetic encoding impairment (as a type of aphasia) from speech planning (AOS), programming, and execution (van der Merwe, 2009). Although most work relating AOS to psycholinguistic models holds the view that AOS is impairment to phonetic encoding (Ziegler,

Staiger, & Aichert, 2010), and this assumption has guided the interpretation of empirical findings, it has not been tested directly as a hypothesis other than to show that these individuals show a clear syllable frequency effect (e.g., Aichert & Ziegler, 2004). As mentioned earlier, the assumption may be based in part on the limited number of possible levels that could relate to AOS in the Levelt et al. (1999) framework, although some have proposed further refinement of the mechanisms involved in speech planning and production (van der Merwe, 2009; Maas, Robin, Wright, & Ballard, 2008).

Critically, psycholinguistic and linguistic accounts of phonetic processing typically hold that the phonetic processing level is linguistic in nature. In particular, phonetic processing acts as an interface between abstract representations of sound structure and the motor production of that structure by computing language-specific and context-specific detail associated with an utterance. To the extent that AOS is a disorder that is separate from linguistic processing (as argued by McNeil et al., 2009), it remains possible that the descriptions of these processing systems require additional elaboration. Although some have specifically argued for a distinction between phonetically driven impairment and motorically driven impairment among individuals with acquired sound production deficits (Buchwald et al., 2007; Buchwald & Miozzo, 2011), there is as yet no clear study that distinguishes between these two levels and verifies that AOS refers to a population distinct from individuals with phonetic impairment.

It is clear that determining whether there is a distinction to be made among individuals with AOS and individuals with phonetic processing impairment will help to further understand the unique roles of these cognitive systems. At present, it is important to note that much of the difficulty of clearly distinguishing these impairments arises from their frequent co-occurrence, with only a small number of influential papers helping to build a description of AOS based solely on individuals without comorbid aphasia or dysarthrias (McNeil, Odell, Miller, & Hunter, 1995; Odell, McNeil, Rosenbek, & Hunter, 1990; Odell, McNeil, Rosenbek, & Hunter, 1991). This type of work looking at additional psycholinguistic variables is necessary to integrate the research on AOS with psycholinguistic accounts of spoken language production.

Conclusion

This chapter has focused on a variety of issues with respect to phonetic processing, and has addressed a number of ongoing debates and challenges in research on this component of spoken language production. In particular, two critical issues that need to be addressed include the nature of the representations at this level and the degree of interaction between this processing system and related processing systems involved in language production. With respect to the nature of the representations, the gestural representations posited in Articulatory Phonology (Browman & Goldstein, 1986, 1988; 1989 et seq.) provide a clear means for discussing a variety of types of phonetic detail, including context-dependent effects of syllable position (Byrd, 1995), speaking rate (Byrd & Tan, 1996), and temporal overlap (Goldstein et al., 2007), although it is unclear how these representations may be integrated with the type of acoustic targets posited in the DIVA model (e.g., Tourville & Guenther, 2011).

One of the main obstacles to learning more about this system is to determine what data we can use to learn about phonetic processing. As we discussed, speech error data using instrumental measures of articulation and acoustics have been quite helpful in this regard, but there is still no means for forming a clear distinction between changes arising at the phonetic level and others arising at more peripheral stages of motor speech production. One attempt to understand processing systems that has been beneficial in cognitive science has been to examine individuals with selective impairment to that system. With respect to phonetic processing, these attempts have largely been based on the assumption that AOS reflects an impairment to phonetic processing and then to explore the nature of the errors in AOS (Varley & Whiteside, 2001; Ziegler, 2002). However, this strategy relies on the assumption that the clinical category of AOS reflects a selective deficit to phonetic processing; this assumption has not been verified, and the frequent co-occurrence of AOS with both aphasic impairments and dysarthria complicates these analyses unless these analyses are restricted to cases where there is a single level of impairment. Additional attempts to distinguish errors that occur in phonological processing from those arising in phonetic processing are necessary to make use of data from neurologically impaired populations in addressing these issues (see Buchwald et al., 2007; Buchwald & Miozzo, 2011 for examples).

References

Agwuele, A., Sussman, H., & Lindblom, B. (2008). The effect of speaking rate on consonant vowel coarticulation. *Phonetica*, *65*, 194–209.

Aichert, I., & Ziegler, W. (2004). Syllable frequency and syllable structure in apraxia of speech. *Brain and Language*, *88*, 148–159.

Aylett, M., & Turk, A. (2004). The smooth signal redundancy hypothesis: A functional explanation for relationships between redundancy, prosodic prominence, and duration in spontaneous speech. *Language and Speech*, *47*(1), 31–56.

Baese-Berk, M., & Goldrick, M. (2009). Mechanisms of interaction in speech production. *Language and Cognitive Processes*, *24*(4), 527–554.

Bell, A., Brenier, J. M., Gregory, M., Girand, C., & Jurafsky, D. (2009). Predictability effects on durations of content and function words in conversational English. *Journal of Memory and Language*, *60*, 92–111.

Bradlow, A. R. (2002). Confluent talker- and listener-related forces in clear speech production. In C. Gussenhoven & N. Warner (Eds.), *Papers in laboratory phonology* (Vol. 7, pp. 241–273). New York: Mouton de Gruyter.

Bradlow, A. R., Torretta, G., & Pisoni, D. B. (1996). Intelligibility of normal speech I: Global and fine-grained acoustic-phonetic talker characteristics. *Speech Communication*, *20*, 255–272.

Browman, C. P., & Goldstein, L. M. (1986). Towards an articulatory phonology. *Phonology*, *6*, 219–252.

Browman, C. P., & Goldstein, L. M. (1988). Some notes on syllable structure in articulatory phonology. *Phonetica*, *45*, 140–155.

Browman, C. P., & Goldstein, L. M. (1989). Articulatory gestures as phonological units. *Phonology*, *6*, 201–251.

Buchwald, A., & Miozzo, M. (2011). Finding levels of abstraction in speech production: Evidence from sound production impairment. *Psychological Science*, *22*, 1113–1119.

Buchwald, A., Rapp, B., & Stone, M. (2007). Insertion of discrete phonological units: An ultrasound investigation of aphasic speech. *Language and Cognitive Processes*, *22*(6), 910–948.

Butterworth, B. (1992). Disorders of phonological encoding. *Cognition*, *42*, 261–286.

Bybee, J. (2001). *Frequency and language use*. Cambridge: Cambridge University Press.

Byrd, D. (1995). C-centers revisited. *Phonetica*, *52*, 285–306.

Byrd, D., & Tan, C. C. (1996). Saying consonant clusters quickly. *Journal of Phonetics*, *24*, 263–282.

Carreiras, M., & Perea, M. (2004). Naming pseudowords in Spanish: Effects of syllable frequency. *Brain and Language*, *90*, 393–400.

Cholin, J. (2008). The mental syllabary in speech production: An integration of different approaches and domains. *Aphasiology*, *22*, 1–15.

Cholin, J., & Levelt, W. J. M. (2009). Effects of syllable preparation and syllable frequency in speech production: Further evidence for the retrieval of stored syllables at a post-lexical level. *Language and Cognitive Processes*, *24*, 662–684.

Cholin, J., Levelt, W. J. M., & Schiller, N. O. (2006). Effects of syllable frequency in speech production. *Cognition*, *99*, 205–235.

Chomsky, N., & Halle, M. (1968). *The sound pattern of English*. New York, NY: Harper and Row.

Davidson, L. (2006). Phonotactics and articulatory coordination interact in phonology: Evidence from non-native production. *Cognitive Science*, *30*(5), 837–862.

Dell, G. (1986). A spreading activation theory of retrieval in sentence processing. *Psychological Review*, *93*, 283–321.

Dell, G. (1988). The retrieval of phonological forms in production: Tests of predictions from a connectionist model. *Journal of Memory and Language*, *27*, 124–142.

Dell, G. (1990). Effects of frequency and vocabulary type on phonological speech errors. *Language and Cognitive Processes*, *4*, 313–349.

Dell, G., & Gordon, J. K. (2003). Neighbors in the lexicon: Friends or foes. In N. O. Schiller & A. S. Meyer (Eds.), *Phonetics and phonology in language comprehension and production: Differences and similarities* (pp. 9–38). New York: Mouton de Gruyter.

Duffy, J. R. (2005). *Motor speech disorders: Substrates, differential diagnosis, and management*. St. Louis: Elsevier Mosby.

Frisch, S., & Wright, R. (2002). The phonetics of phonological speech errors: An acoustic analysis of slips of the tongue. *Journal of Phonetics*, *30*, 139–162.

Fromkin, V. (1971). The non-anomalous nature of anomalous utterances. *Language*, *47*, 27–52.

Gahl, S. (2008). "Thyme" and "Time" are not homophones. Word durations in spontaneous speech. *Language*, *84*(3), 474–496.

Gahl, S., & Garnsey, S. M. (2004). Knowledge of grammar, knowledge of usage: Syntactic probabilities affect pronunciation variation. *Language*, *80*(4), 748–775.

Gahl, S., & Garnsey, S. M. (2006). Syntactic probabilities affect pronunciation variation. *Language*, *82*(2), 405–410.

Garrett, M. F. (1980). Levels of processing in sentence production. In B. Butterworth (Ed.), *Language production*. New York: Academic Press.

Gay, T. (1968). Effect of speaking rate on diphthong formant movements. *Journal of the Acoustical Society of America*, *44*(6), 1570–1573.

Goldrick, M. (2006). Limited interaction in speech production: Chronometric, speech error, and neuropsychological evidence. *Language and Cognitive Processes*, *21*, 817–855.

Goldrick, M., Baker, H. R., Murphy, A., & Baese-Berk, M. (2011). Interaction and representational integration: Evidence from speech errors. *Cognition*, *121*, 58–72.

Goldrick, M., & Blumstein, S. E. (2006). Cascading activation from phonological planning to articulatory processes: Evidence from tongue twisters. *Language and Cognitive Processes*, *21*, 649–683.

Goldrick, M., & Rapp, B. (2007). Lexical and post-lexical phonological representations in spoken production. *Cognition*, *102*(2), 219–260.

Goldstein, L., Pouplier, M., Chen, L., Saltzman, E., & Byrd, D. (2007). Dynamic action units slip in speech production errors. *Cognition*, *103*, 386–412.

Guenther, F. (1994). A neural network model of speech acquisition and motor equivalent speech production. *Biological Cybernetics*, *72*, 43–53.

Guenther, F. H., Hampson, M., & Johnson, D. (1998). A theoretical investigation of reference frames for the planning of speech movements. *Psychological Review*, *105*, 611–633.

Guenther, F. H., & Perkell, J. H. (2004). A neural model of speech production and its application to studies of the role of auditory feedback in speech. In B. Maassen, R. D. Kent, H. Peters, P. H. H. M. Van Lieshout, & W. Hulstijn (Eds.), *Speech motor control in normal and disordered speech* (pp. 29–49). Oxford: Oxford University Press.

Hardcastle, W. J., & Edwards, S. (1992). EPG-based description of apraxic speech errors. In R. D. Kent (Ed.), *Intelligibility in speech disorders* (pp. 287–328). Amsterdam: John Benjamins Publishing Company.

Hardcastle, W. J., & Laver, J. (Eds.). (1997). *The Handbook of phonetic sciences*. Oxford: Blackwell.

Laganaro, M. (2005). Syllable frequency effect in speech production: evidence from aphasia. *Journal of Neurolinguistics*, *18*, 221–235.

Laganaro, M. (2008). Is there a syllable frequency effect in aphasia or in apraxia of speech or both? *Aphasiology*, *22*(11), 1191–1200.

Laganaro, M., & Alario, F.-X. (2006). On the locus of the syllable frequency effect in speech production. *Journal of Memory and Language*, *55*, 178–196.

Lane, H., Denny, M., Guenther, F., Matthies, M. L., Menard, L., Perkell, J. S.,...& Zandipour, M. (2005). Effects of bite blocks and hearing status on vowel production. *Journal of the Acoustical Society of America*, *118*, 1636–1646.

Levelt, W. J. M. (1989). *Speaking: From intention to articulation*. Cambridge, MA: MIT Press.

Levelt, W. J. M. (1992). Accessing words in speech production: Stages, processes and representations. *Cognition*, *42*, 1–22.

Levelt, W. J. M., Roelofs, A., & Meyer, A. S. (1999). A theory of lexical access in speech production. *Behavioral and Brain Sciences*, *22*, 1–75.

Levelt, W. J. M., & Wheeldon, L. (1994). Do speakers have access to a mental syllabary? *Cognition*, *50*, 239–269.

Lieberman, P. (1963). Some effects of semantic and grammatical context on the production and perception of speech. *Language and Speech*, *6*, 172–187.

Lindblom, B. (1990). Explaining phonetic variation: A sketch of the H&H theory. In W. J. Hardcastle & A. Marchal (Eds.), *Speech production and speech modeling* (pp. 403–439). Dordrecht: Kluwer.

Lisker, L., & Abramson, A. S. (1964). A cross-language study of voicing in initial stops: Acoustical measurements. *Word*, *20*, 384–422.

Luce, P. A., & Pisoni, D. B. (1998). Recognizing spoken words: The neighborhood activation model. *Ear and Hearing*, *19*, 1–36.

Maas, E., Robin, D. A., Wright, D. L., & Ballard, K. J. (2008). Motor programming in apraxia of speech. *Brain and Language*, *106*(2), 107–118.

McMillan, C. T., & Corley, M. (2010). Cascading influences on the production of speech: Evidence from articulation. *Cognition*, *117*(3), 243–260.

McMillan, C. T., Corley, M., & Lickley, R. (2009). Articulation evidence for feedback and competition in speech production. *Language and Cognitive Processes*, *24*, 44–66.

McNeil, M. R. (Ed.). (2009). *Clinical management of sensorimotor speech disorders* (2nd. ed.). New York: Thieme.

McNeil, M. R., Odell, K., Miller, S. B., & Hunter, L. (1995). Consistency, variability, and target approximation for successive speech repetitions among apraxic, conduction aphasic, and ataxic dysarthria speakers. *Clinical Aphasiology*, *23*, 39–55.

McNeil, M. R.,Pratt, S. R., & Fossett, T. R. D. (2004). The differential diagnosis of apraxia of speech. In B. Maassen, R. D. Kent, H. Peters, P. H. H. M. Van Lieshout, & W. Hulstijn (Eds.), *Speech motor control in normal and disordered speech* (pp. 389–414). Oxford: Oxford University Press.

McNeil, M. R., Robin, D. A., & Schmidt, R. A. (2009). Apraxia of speech: Definition and differential diagnosis. In M.

R. McNeil (Ed.), *Clinical management of sensorimotor speech disorders* (pp. 249–268). New York: Thieme.

Miller, J. L., Green, K. P., & Reeves, A. (1986). Speaking rate and segments: A look at the relation between speech production and perception for the voicing contrast. *Phonetica, 43,* 106–115.

Miller, J. L., Grosjean, F., & Lomanto, C. (1984). Articulation rate and its variability in spontaneous speech: A reanalysis and some implications. *Phonetica, 41,* 215–255.

Mowrey, R. A., & MacKay, I. R. A. (1990). Phonological primitives: Electromyographic speech error evidence. *Journal of the Acoustical Society of America, 88,* 1299–1312.

Munson, B. (2007). Lexical access, lexical representation, and vowel articulation. In J. Cole & J. Hualde (Eds.), *Laboratory phonology* (Vol. 9, pp. 201–228). New York: Mouton de Gruyter.

Munson, B., & Solomon, N. P. (2004). The effect of phonological neighborhood density on vowel articulation. *Journal of Speech, Language, and Hearing Research, 47,* 1048–1058.

Nam, H., Goldstein, L., Saltzman, E., & Byrd, D. (2004). TADA: An enhanced, portable task dynamics model in MATLAB. *Journal of the Acoustical Society of America, 115*(5), 2430.

Nickels, L., & Howard, D. (2004). Dissociating effects of number of phonemes, number of syllables, and syllabic complexity on word production in aphasia: It's the number of phonemes that counts. *Cognitive Neuropsychology, 21,* 57–78.

Nooteboom, S. G. (1969). The tongue slips into patterns. In A. G. Sciarone, A. J. van Essen, & A. A. van Raad (Eds.), *Leyden studies in linguistics and phonetics* (pp. 114–132). The Hague: Mouton.

Odell, K., McNeil, M. R., Rosenbek, J. C., & Hunter, L. (1990). Perceptual characteristics of consonant production by apraxic speakers. *Journal of Speech and Hearing Disorders, 55,* 345–359.

Odell, K., McNeil, M. R., Rosenbek, J. C., & Hunter, L. (1991). Perceptual characteristics of vowel and prosody production in apraxic, aphasic and dysarthric speakers. *Journal of Speech and Hearing Research, 34,* 67–80.

Pierrehumbert, J. (2001). Exemplar dynamics: Word frequency, lenition, and contrast. In J. Bybee & P. Hopper (Eds.), *Frequency effects and the emergence of lexical structure* (pp. 137–157). Amsterdam: John Benjamins.

Pluymaekers, M., Ernestus, M., & Baayen, R. H. (2005). Lexical frequency and acoustic reduction in spoken Dutch. *Journal of the Acoustical Society of America, 118,* 2561–2569.

Port, R. F., & van Gelder, T. J. (Eds.). (1995). *Mind as motion: Explorations in the dynamics of cognition.* Cambridge, MA: MIT Press.

Pouplier, M. (2003). *Units of phonological encoding: Empirical evidence* (Unpublished doctoral dissertation). Yale University, New Haven, CT.

Pouplier, M., & Goldstein, L. (2010). Intention in articulation: Articulatory timing in alternating consonant sequences and its implications for models of speech production. *Language and Cognitive Processes, 25*(5), 616–649.

Pouplier, M., & Hardcastle, W. J. (2005). A re-evaluation of the nature of speech errors in normal and disordered speakers. *Phonetica, 62,* 227–243.

Prince, A., & Smolensky, P. (1993/2004). *Optimality theory: Constraint interaction in generative grammar* (Technical report). Rutgers University, New Brunswick and University of Colorado, Boulder.

Romani, C., & Calabrese, A. (1998). Syllabic constraints on the phonological errors of an aphasic patient. *Brain and Language, 64,* 83–121.

Romani, C., & Galluzzi, C. (2005). Effects of syllabic complexity in predicting accuracy of repetition and direction of errors in patients with articulatory and phonological difficulties. *Cognitive Neuropsychology, 22*(7), 817–850.

Romani, C., Olson, A., Semenza, C., & Granà, A. (2002). Patterns of phonological errors as a function of a phonological versus articulatory locus of impairment. *Cortex, 38,* 541–567.

Saltzman, E. L., & Munhall, K. G. (1989). A dynamical approach to gestural patterning in speech production. *Ecological Psychology, 1,* 333–382.

Scarborough, R. A. (2004). *Coarticulation and the structure of the lexicon* (Unpublished doctoral dissertation). UCLA, Los Angeles, CA.

Schiller, N. O., Meyer, A. S., Baayen, R. H., & Levelt, W. J. M. (1996). A comparison of lexeme and speech syllables in Dutch. *Journal of Quantitative Linguistics, 3,* 8–28.

Shattuck-Hufnagel, S. (1987). The role of word-onset consonants in speech production planning: New evidence from speech error patterns. In E. Keller & M. Gopnik (Eds.), *Motor and sensory processes of language* (pp. 17–51). Hillsdale, NJ: Lawrence Erlbaum Associates.

Shattuck-Hufnagel, S., & Klatt, D. H. (1979). The limited use of distinctive features and markedness in speech production: Evidence from speech error data. *Journal of Verbal Learning and Verbal Behavior, 18,* 41–55.

Staiger, A., & Ziegler, W. (2008). Syllable frequency and syllable structure in the spontaneous speech production of patients with apraxia of speech. *Aphasiology, 22*(11), 1201–1215.

Stemberger, J. P. (1983). *Speech errors and theoretical phonology: A review* (Unpublished manuscript). Distributed by the Indiana University Linguistics Club, Bloomington, IN.

Stemberger, J. P. (1985). An interactive activation model of language production. In A. W. Ellis (Ed.), *Progress in the psychology of language* (Vol. 1, pp. 143–186). Hillsdale, NJ: Lawrence Erlbaum Associates.

Stemberger, J. P. (1990). Wordshape errors in language production. *Cognition, 35,* 123–157.

Theodore, R. M., Miller, J. L., & DeSteno, D. (2009). Individual talker differences in voice-onset-time: Contextual influences. *Journal of the Acoustical Society of America, 125,* 3974–3982.

Tian, X., & Poeppel, D. (2010). Mental imagery of speech and movement implicates the dynamics of internal forward models. [Original Research]. *Frontiers in Psychology, 1,* 12.

Tily, H., Gahl, S., Arnon, I., Snider, N., Kothari, A., & Bresnan, J. (2009). Syntactic probabilities affect pronunciation variation in spontaneous speech. *Language and Cognition, 1–2,* 147–165.

Tourville, J. A., & Guenther, F. (2011). The DIVA model: A neural theory of speech acquisition and production. *Language and Cognitive Processes, 26,* 952–981.

van der Merwe, A. (2009). A theoretical framework for the characterization of pathological speech motor control. In M. R. McNeil (Ed.), *Clinical management of sensorimotor speech disorders* (2nd ed., pp. 3–18). New York: Thieme.

Varley, R. A., & Whiteside, S. P. (2001). What is the underlying impairment in acquired apraxia of speech? *Aphasiology, 15,* 39–49.

Vitevitch, M. S., & Sommers, M. S. (2003). The facilitative influence of phonological similarity and neighborhood frequency in speech production in younger and older adults. *Memory and Cognition, 31*, 491–504.

Wertz, R. T., Lapointe, L. L., & Rosenbek, J. C. (1984). *Apraxia of speech in adults: The disorder and its management.* Orlando, FL: Grune and Stratton.

Wheeler, D. W., & Touretzky, D. S. (1997). A parallel licensing model of normal slips and phonemic paraphasias. *Brain and Language, 59*, 147–201.

Wood, S., & Hardcastle, W. J. (2000). Instrumentation in the assessment and therapy of motor speech disorders: A survey of techniques and case studies with EPG. In I. Papathanasiou (Ed.), *Acquired neurogenic communication disorders: A clinical perspective* (pp. 203–248). London: Whurr.

Wright, R. A. (2004). Factors of lexical competition in vowel articulation. In J. J. Local, R. Ogden, & R. Temple (Eds.), *Laboratory phonology* (Vol. 6, pp. 26–50). Cambridge: Cambridge University Press.

Ziegler, W. (2002). Psycholinguistic and motor theories of apraxia of speech. *Seminars in Speech and Language, 23*, 231–243.

Ziegler, W., Staiger, A., & Aichert, I. (2010). Apraxia of speech: What the deconstruction of phonetic plans tells us about the construction of articulate language. In B. Maassen, & P. H. H. M. Van Lieshout (Eds.), *Speech motor control* (pp. 3–21). Oxford: Oxford University Press.

Zipf, G. K. (1929). Relative frequency as a determinant of phonetic change. *Harvard Studies in Classical Philology, 15*, 1–95.

Phrase-level Phonological and Phonetic Phenomena

Stefanie Shattuck-Hufnagel

Abstract

For many decades, investigators emphasized the search for invariant aspects of the speech signal that might explain the ability to extract a speaker's intended words despite wide variation in their acoustic shape. In contrast, over the past few decades, as the extraordinary range of phonetic variation has been revealed, the focus has shifted to documenting variation and determining the factors governing it. This review identifies two seemingly contradictory types of findings about connected speech: the extreme loss versus the concurrent preservation of word-form information. Based on these observations, a productive research strategy for understanding the planning and production of connected speech may be to focus on (1) the systematic nature of phonetic reduction patterns, making them a source of information rather than noise; (2) the ability of human listeners to interpret reduced and overlapped forms; and (3) the implications of these two ideas for speech production models.

Key Words: speech production planning, phrase-level phonetics, prosody, acoustic cues, phonological contrast, landmarks

For many decades after the development of technical tools enabled detailed analysis of the pronunciation of words in connected speech, investigators emphasized the search for invariant aspects of the speech signal that might explain the listener's striking ability to extract the speaker's intended words despite wide variation in their acoustic shape across different contexts. In contrast, over the past few decades, as the widespread availability of speech analysis freeware running on personal computers and of recorded utterances from corpora of typical communicative speech began to reveal the extraordinary range of this variation, the focus has shifted to documenting its nature and determining the factors that govern it, such as prosodic structure (constituent boundaries and prominences) and frequency of word use. This review identifies two seemingly contradictory types of findings about the surface forms of words in continuous speech (i.e., the extreme loss of word-form information vs.

the concurrent preservation of word-form information) and discusses the implications of these two observations for models of speech production planning at the sound level. Current knowledge about phrasally induced phonetic variation suggests that a productive research strategy for understanding how human speakers plan and produce connected speech may be to focus on (1) the systematic nature of phonetic reduction patterns, which makes them a source of information rather than noise; (2) the corresponding ability of human listeners to interpret reduced and overlapped forms in terms of the cues they nevertheless contain to the speaker's intended lexical items; and (3) the implications of these two ideas for speech production planning models.

Introduction: Phonetic Variation and Phonological Invariance

Human beings have a remarkable skill in the use of spoken language: speakers adapt word forms to different contexts, and listeners deal with these differences, recognizing the speaker's intended words without noticeable effort. Understanding the nature and extent of this contextual variation in word form has not been easy, because to a listener the intended words seem transparently available in the speech signal. It is only when the signal is particularly challenging (e.g., low in amplitude, produced by a non-native speaker, or conveyed over a poor channel) that the listener becomes aware of doing any cognitive work to understand what is said. Thus, when technical developments achieved by the mid-1900s, such as the sound recorder, the oscillograph, and the sound spectrograph, allowed speech scientists to study the fleeting acoustic events of spoken utterances in detail, the degree of variation revealed by these technologies was surprising. Instead of an orderly array of sequentially organized sound segments with their acoustic cues temporally aligned, these new tools revealed that information about successive speech sounds was spread more widely across time, with cues to adjacent parts of words overlapping each other (see, e.g., Lehiste, 1967). For example, the place of articulation cues for a stop consonant are not entirely contained within the temporal interval between the closure and release of the consonant; for voiceless stops this interval can be almost completely silent. Instead, cues are also found in the regions before and after these events, such as in the temporal course of changes in the resonant frequencies of the vocal tract (formant transitions) in the voiced regions associated with the adjacent vowels, and in the spectrum of the release noise. Similarly, in such words as *can* or *some*, the nasal quality of the coda consonant sometimes begins in the preceding vowel, well before the oral closure for the nasal. Another example is the migration of rhotic quality from the /r/ in utterances of *Africa* across the intervening /f/, to appear during the initial /ae/ (Espy-Wilson, 1987).

In addition to evidence for the temporal overlap of information about multiple speech sounds, these signal analysis tools also supported an idea that had long been promulgated by phoneticians attempting to capture the sound systems of dialects and undocumented languages: that the same contrastive sound category (e.g., the voiceless alveolar stop /t/ or the rounded high back vowel /u/) could be realized in quite different ways in different contexts. Such variants were called allophones, reflecting the idea that they were alternative implementations of the same phoneme. One of the first dimensions that investigators used to characterize the contexts

that evoked such distinctions in the phonetic realization of a sound category was position (e.g., structural location in a constituent, such as initial, medial, final in a word or syllable); or adjacent segments (e.g., singleton onset vs. consonant cluster); or adjacent stressed versus reduced vowel. A classic example is found in the positional allophones of /t/ in American English, which include at least the following:

- Word-initial or prestressed /t/ (*top, today, return*), where /t/ takes the form of an aspirated stop
- Following an /s/ in an onset cluster (*stop*), where the aspiration is reduced or missing
- Preceding an /r/ in an onset cluster (*try*), where the release is lengthened to resemble an affricate like /ch/
- Word-medially between a strong and a weak vowel (*city, lotto*), where the /t/ is usually shortened or even produced without a full closure to form a flap (ranging from a short closure with pressure buildup and release, through a dip in amplitude with continuous voicing and sometimes a small release burst riding on one pitch period, to no obvious amplitude reduction)
- In final position (*pot, repeat*), where the /t/ may be produced with closure but without release, may be strongly released, may be implemented acoustically as a sequence of irregular pitch periods at the end of the vowel with no obvious acoustic indication of oral closure, pressure buildup or release, or may be seemingly omitted altogether (e.g., in a cluster of alveolar coda consonants, such as the /st/ in *lost*)
- Between two nasals (as in some variants of *Clinton* or *mountain*), in which the following [-ən] is produced as a syllabic /n/ and the /t/ is implemented as a glottal closure and release

This is only one of many possible examples; a wide variety of English phonemes are realized in different ways depending on their segmental and structural contexts, and it was a natural assumption that these differences could be captured in terms of the same kinds of distinctive feature differences as those that relate the various forms of a morpheme that occur in different words. However, the weight of the evidence from increasingly detailed acoustic analysis of phrase-level phonetic phenomena suggests that a different vocabulary may be more appropriate for capturing these contextual variations.

Any discussion of phonetic variation and the factors that govern it must begin with the explicit recognition that words are made up of different combinations of a small number of elements. Early alphabetic systems reflected individual sound elements, sometimes morphemes, sometimes syllables, and at least once, for the Phoenicians, individual sound segments, and the development of orthographic symbols for these sound elements largely ignored the contextually governed phonetic differences. Early grammarians of sound (dubbed phonologists by Trubetzkoy, 1939) called these individual sound segments phonemes (Badouin de Courtenay, 1880s/1972), and later practitioners hypothesized that they were defined by distinctive features that differentiate the contrastive sound categories of a language and relate them to each other (Jakobson, 1941/1968). Several different frameworks for defining the distinctive features have been proposed, including both acoustic and articulatory characteristics (Jakobson, Fant, & Halle, 1952), or more purely acoustic (Stevens, 1998) or articulatory (Chomsky & Halle, 1968) characteristics. These distinctive features define natural classes of sounds (e.g., vowels and consonants; stops, fricatives and nasals, high and low vowels; labial and velar consonants) whose members undergo similar processes in similar contexts, and describe the kinds of systematic changes that occur when morphemes are combined into words. Chomsky and Halle's (1968) volume *The Sound Pattern of English* described feature-changing phonological processes, such as those reflected in the relationship between the final /k/ of *electric* or *domestic* and the corresponding /s/ in *electricity* or *domesticity*, as well as the relationship between their respective stress patterns.

The postulation of phonemes as bundles of distinctive features, some of which can change in within-word contexts, seemed to provide a natural way of describing the kinds of sound changes that occur in word combinations. For example, it seemed reasonable to draw a parallel between the change that occurs in the lexical form of the /n/ of the prefix *in-*, in such words as *important* (where it becomes the labial nasal /m/ under the influence of the following labial /p/), *indeed* (where it maintains its alveolar place feature under the influence of the following alveolar /d/), and *income* (where it becomes the velar nasal /ŋ/ under the influence of the following velar /k/), and the change that occurs in the /n/ of the preposition *in*, in phrase-level word combinations such as *in Boston*, *in Denver*, and *in Ghana*. Similarly, it was widely assumed that the ways in which positional allophones in a language, or differences in the implementation of a single contrastive category across languages, relate to each other is by changes in the value of individual distinctive features.

However, this picture of a single feature-changing mechanism as the only means of relating a word form to its variants in a language, or a sound category to its variants across languages, began to change as the understanding of phonetic variation in spoken word combinations grew deeper. This evolution resulted in part from the development of convenient tools for the display and analysis of speech signals. Following on the advent of acoustic recording devices in the late 1800s, important further tools were the sound spectrogram developed in the 1940s (which displayed changes in the distribution of energy across the frequency spectrum over time), and digital tools for further analysis and display of speech signals on mainframe computers and desktops, such as xWaves (Talkin, 1995) and the Klattools (Truslow, 2010), which enabled the convenient computation of an individual spectral slice at a particular time point, with quantitative estimates of the frequencies of peaks in the spectral distribution of energy. Finally, the advent of laptop computers and a powerful piece of analysis freeware called Praat (Boersma, 2001, Boersma & Weenik, 2012) brought convenient acoustic-phonetic analysis to just about anyone. These tools revealed even more clearly that speakers do not produce words as strings of discrete sounds, but as a sequence of overlapping and somewhat contextually distorted remnants of the original target sounds that defined the words. An extreme form of this view was described by Hockett (1955), who proposed the analogy of the individual sounds of a target word as being like a line of brightly patterned Easter eggs, and the speaking process as being like moving that line of distinct eggs down a conveyor belt toward a pair of rollers, which squeezes and smashes them into a flattened pattern of randomly arranged pieces. Although this metaphor captures the fact that spoken word forms do not preserve the temporal alignment of cues to each individual sound segment, it fails to do justice to the informative systematicity of phrase-level phonetic processes.

The Nature and Extent of Phonetic Variation Unveiled

The nondiscrete nature of sound segments in the speech signal inspired several proposals that moved away from the assumption that sound variation was best captured in terms of differences in categorical features. One particularly productive proposal was the importation, from task dynamics approaches to general motor control (Saltzman & Kelso, 1987), of the idea that variations in the phonetic implementation of word forms could be usefully described in terms of timing overlap and spatial reduction of the articulatory configurations that create the acoustic speech signal (Fowler, Rubin, Remez, & Turvey, 1980; Saltzman & Munhall, 1989; Browman & Goldstein, 1986, 1989, 1990, 1992). It seemed natural to press the matter further (i.e., to propose that lexical representations are stored in the form of such gestural scores). Joining the phonological representation in the lexicon and the phonetic adjustments in the speech signal into a common articulatory representation was felicitous in another way: more and more investigations began to reveal that phonetic variation is not always categorical (as feature-changing processing might predict), but instead is often continuous-valued.

For example, Zsiga (1997) described two different vowel-changing processes in the Igbo language: *vowel harmony* (in which the addition of a suffix to a root results in changes in the features of earlier vowels to harmonize with those of the suffix) and *interaction between two adjacent vowels*. Zsiga reported that although a harmonized vowel was indistinguishable from a nonharmonized vowel of the same category, a vowel influenced by an adjacent vowel showed a gradient distribution in measured formant values. Such continuous-valued changes are much more easily accounted for in a model that can adjust temporal and spatial specifications gradiently, than in a model that has only a single categorical feature-changing mechanism. Thus, Zsiga's result supports a model in which both mechanisms are available to a speaker: a feature-changing mechanism that results in categorical change; and a mechanism for computing articulatory overlap, which results in gradient change.

An additional advantage for mechanisms that could account for systematic multi-valued or continuous-valued variation lay in the ability to deal with the fact that speakers produce word forms with a range of phonetic values that vary with their location in hierarchical prosodic structures. In the 1970s and 1980s, several linguists had proposed the existence of a prosodic hierarchy of constituents, ranging from the utterance down through the intonational phrase, the prosodic word, and subword constituents, such as the foot, the syllable, and the mora (Hayes, 1984; Nespor & Vogel, 1986; Selkirk, 1984). Similarly, Beckman and Edwards (1994) proposed a hierarchy of prosodic prominences, ranging from the most prominent word or syllable in an intonational phrase (the nuclear accent; Halliday, 1967), down through prenuclear accents and unaccented full-vowel syllables bearing primary word stress, to full-vowel syllables without primary lexical stress and reduced syllables (Okobi, 2006). Various investigators tested the hypothesis that such hierarchical representations (derived in part from, but yet still independent of, the morphosyntactic structures of the sentence; Ferreira, 1993, 2007) play a role in speech production planning and implementation. These investigations uncovered systematic variation in the nature of phonetic implementation with level in the prosodic hierarchy.

For example, Pierrehumbert and Talkin (1992) and Dilley, Shattuck-Hufnagel, and Ostendorf (1996) reported more frequent occurrence of irregular pitch periods ("glottalization") for word-onset vowels that occur at the beginning of intonational phrases and of pitch accented words; Wightman, Shattuck-Hufnagel, Ostendorf, and Price (1992) and Ladd and Campbell (1991) reported monotonically increasing constituent-final lengthening with higher levels in the prosodic constituent hierarchy; and Jun (1993), studying Korean, reported longer voice onset times (the delay between release of a stop consonant and the onset of vocal fold vibration for the following vowel) at the onset of increasingly higher-level prosodic constituents. Keating and Fougeron (1997; see also Fougeron, 1998, 2001) reported a corresponding hierarchical articulatory correlate of prosodic structure in the form of articulatory strengthening at the onsets of prosodic constituents.

Variation of this kind is well-suited to signaling other kinds of information that are also highly relevant to acts of communication. For example, in a groundbreaking series of studies, Labov and colleagues (1966, 1972) demonstrated highly systematic variation in the subfeatural characteristics of vowels in different neighborhoods within a city. In addition to signaling the geographic origin and tribal affiliation of a speaker, several investigators have argued that such dimensions as noncontrastive variations in vowel quality, voice quality, and hyperarticulation can signal the attitudinal and emotional state of the speaker. Especially noteworthy in this regard is the work of Kohler (1990, 2011), Coleman (2002, 2003), and Hawkins (2003, 2011), discussed later.

Moreover, even noncategorical variation may nevertheless contribute to the listener's ability to identify the speaker's intended linguistic constituents and structure. For example, Klatt (1976) pointed out that the duration of a segment (in his case, /s/ in American English) can be influenced by many factors, including position in constituent structure, adjacent segments, and lexical stress. A well-known example of segmental cue ambiguity is found in some utterances of the sentence *The sky is blue*, which (with enough reduction in the first vowel) can be heard as *This guy is blue*, when lack of aspiration for the /k/ of *sky* (because of the preceding tautomorphemic /s/) and the ambiguous nature of the duration of /s/ (shortened because of its position in a word-initial /s/+stop cluster) make the cue pattern also consistent with a pronunciation of *This guy*. Like the visually ambiguous Nekker cube, a listener can find such an utterance flipping back and forth between the two possible interpretations on repeated listening. Phenomena like this are consistent with the view that perception involves the detection of individual cues rather than entire segments, with subsequent parsing and interpretation of those cues in ways that can be influenced by other aspects of the perceiver's knowledge (Cutler, 2010; Gow, 2002; Stevens, 2002).

A second example illustrates a parallel ambiguity for some prosodic contours: when the final syllables of an intonational phrase contain a sequence of two full vowels, as in words like *compact* or *digest*, realized with an F0 movement, such as a High→Low, it is sometimes difficult to determine whether or not the boundary-related intonation is also conveying a pitch accent. Thus, some pronunciations sound consistent with both interpretations: the noun *COMpact*, with a pitch accent on its initial and main-stressed syllable, or the verb *comPACT*, with a different type of pitch accent on its second and main-stressed syllable. Such ambiguities and ambiguity resolutions (Dilley & Shattuck-Hufnagel, 1998, 1999) provide a window into how listeners parse cues in context, and raise the possibility that speakers might plan the phonetics of their utterances in terms of such cue patterns (discussed later).

Another set of studies that illustrated continuous rather than categorical behavior examined the effects of word frequency/predictability on the phonetic implementation of phonological word forms. Fowler and Housum (1987) showed that the second mention of a word in a short discourse is more reduced than the first mention, and Bybee and colleagues (e.g., Bybee, 2001) took this concept further, documenting the effects of frequency on the phonetic implementation of words. For example, they examined the phonetics of homophonous words, such as the seldom-reduced numeral *four* and the often-reduced function word *for*, the various lexical items associated with *that* (e.g., the seldom-reduced pronoun, as in *That is the one*, vs. the often-reduced complementizer, as in *I knew that he was coming*), and found striking differences in the phonetic implementation of these separate words, despite their identical phonemic form. Johnson (2004) described a range of different types of phonetic variation in his landmark study. In a series of corpus studies, Jurafsky and colleagues (e.g., Jurafsky, Bell, Fosler-Lussier, Girand, & Raymond, 1998) described related phenomena and pointed out that it was difficult to disentangle the effects of word frequency from predictability in context, because high-frequency words are more predictable overall. Nonetheless, these studies revealed that the gradient nature of phonetic implementation of word forms was strongly influenced by patterns of use.

Interestingly, many blending and reduction phenomena occur over portions of utterances that are larger than a single word, and even over sequences of several words. Examples, described here in symbolic terms for convenience include such sequences as cuppa for *cup of*, doncha for *don't you*, [gɔɪnə] for *going to*, and such longer sequences as [amənə] for *I'm going to*, waintʃə for *why don't you*, and haudʒə for *how did you*. Like earlier examples cited to illustrate interactions within words and across word boundaries, these phenomena resist description in terms of sequences of segments or feature bundles, in part because the acoustic-phonetic cues are not segmentally aligned.

It should be noted that these empirical studies have not simply remained unconnected phonetic observation but have been incorporated into several theoretical perspectives. The theory of autosegmental phonology, proposed by Goldsmith (1976), explicitly suggested that distinctive features are not aligned into autonomous phonemic segments or feature bundles, but instead are represented on separate tiers, so that a given feature value could extend across material drawn from several traditional segments, including the segments of more than one word. At about the same time, Ogden and Local and their colleagues (e.g., Ogden & Local, 1994) were giving new emphasis to an idea proposed earlier by Firth (1948), termed "prosodies" (a term that should, for the present at least, be sharply distinguished from the hierarchy of prosodic structures described previously). A Firthian prosody is a region of an utterance over which a "phonetic exponent," such as nasalization or palatalization, is realized. Ogden and Local observed that such characteristics can extend over a relatively long region of an utterance, and that this region did not always correspond to a morphosyntactic constituent, just as Firth had proposed. Such a view, which has also been extensively explored in the work of Kohler and colleagues (German) and of Hawkins and colleagues (British English), is reminiscent of the multiword blending phenomena seen in the previous American English examples.

The foregoing brief and necessarily limited presentation highlights two contrasting trends in how speakers implement word forms in continuous speech. First, there is a high degree of apparent elimination of important information about the speaker's intended words, including blending, temporal overlap, apparently missing parts of words, and extreme reduction of articulatory gesture size and acoustic differentiation. Second, because this structure-governed variation is systematic, it is highly informative. Thus, the field was simultaneously moving deeper into phonetic detail (and documenting apparent loss of information), and higher into the structures that govern it (and finding gains in information). Additionally, as researchers attempted to delineate the range and nature of phonetic variation and how it arises, the field was also moving outside of traditional syntactic structures (to address prosodic structures) and traditional distinctive feature representations (to address continuous-valued variation). As Cho and Jun (2000) remark, this makes it necessary to control for position in prosodic structures when eliciting or selecting utterances for analysis, but it also indicates that speakers are providing information about those prosodic structures in the systematic nature of some aspects of that variation.

What has been learned about the patterns of phonetic variation in connected speech phenomena as a result of these developments? First, the kind of positional variation captured by the categories of the International Phonetic Alphabet (IPA; and other categorical, invariant-based theories) is just the tip of the iceberg. Many changes take place through interactions across word boundaries; others involve severe reduction (as when *and* in *black and white* becomes a single syllabic nasal, or *did you eat* in *did you eat yet* becomes *jeet* in something like *jeet jet*). Moreover, these changes do not always lend themselves to being captured by the traditional feature-changing rules of generative phonology. Instead, careful acoustic analysis has revealed that information about different target segments may overlap in the signal, as when the word *can't* is

produced with a partially nasalized vowel, no oral closure for the /n/, and a shortened nucleus combined with period of irregular phonation indicating the voiceless final /t/. Feature-changing rules and phonetic-category-selection mechanisms alike presumed a complete change in the category of a segment, whereas a growing body of evidence suggested that a more complex process involving more fine-grained specifications is at work. In fact, many types of variation that had been described in categorical terms were shown to leave traces of the original target segment in the signal, and further experiments showed that listeners could use this information to infer the original target string. Some of this evidence is described in the following section.

Information about Word Form Preserved Despite Reduction and Overlap

An example of information-preserving change in continuous speech is the production of the interdental voiced fricative /ð/ in American English. This sound, common at the onset of function words, such as *the*, *this*, and *that*, is often produced in a stop-like manner, and transcribed as /d/. However, Zhao (2010) showed in a careful analysis of the spectra of the release of stop-like /ð/ that such tokens are acoustically distinct from /d/; their spectra reflect an interdental constriction location. Another pervasive phenomenon that involves /ð/ in American English is commonly observed in /n+ð/ sequences, such as *in the*. When /ð/ is preceded by the nasal /n/, even across a word boundary, speakers often produce a single nasal segment, usually transcribed as /n/. This transcription suggests that the /ð/ has been deleted, leaving just an /n/ between the two vowels. However, Manuel et al. (1992) reported that, in a corpus of such tokens, the sequence *in the* was distinguished from the sequence *in a* by the longer duration of the intervocalic nasal region, indicating that there might be a perceptually useful duration cue to the presence of the /ð/, despite the absence of a region of voiced frication in the signal. Manuel (1995) took this question one step further, by asking whether, even in sequences like *win those* versus *win No's*, where both of the intervocalic sequences contain two consonants, there was an acoustic cue to the /ð/ in the form of a higher frequency for the second formant at the onset of the second vowel. The answer was yes; in cases where the /n+ð/ sequence was produced with no voiced fricative in the signal but only a nasal, the initial frequencies of following vowel formants differed significantly from /n+n/, consistent with the smaller front cavity for the interdental place of articulation versus the larger front cavity for an alveolar constriction. Thus, speakers seem to combine feature cues from two adjacent segments into a single interdental nasal articulation.

A particularly interesting aspect of Manuel's results was that the combination of cues to features of both /n/ and /ð/ was easily parsed by the listener into the underlying target sound sequence. When she tested listener's perceptions (using synthesized stimuli of *win those* and *win No's*, which differed only in the single cue of the frequency of F2 at release), they consistently distinguished the two sequences. Thus, the cue to the place of articulation feature of /ð/, which overlapped completely with the cues to the following vowel, allowed the listener to infer the underlying /n + ð/ sequence.

Related work by Gow (2002, 2003) similarly suggests that the speaker's tendency to overlap individual feature cues is complemented by the listener's ability to parse them to infer the intended segments. Gow elicited casual productions of sequences, such as *right berries* and *ripe berries*, and asked listeners to transcribe them orthographically. In this overt transcription task, many tokens of *right berries* were transcribed as *ripe berries*, presumably because the closure for the /b/ of *berries* began before or co-occurred with the closure for the preceding coda /t/. Such transcription results suggest that a substitution of /p/ for /t/ had occurred. However, using an online lexical decision task, Gow showed that for listeners, tokens of *right berries* that were transcribed as *ripe berries* nevertheless activated the word *right*, rather than *ripe*. This was shown by faster reaction times to decide that a word related to *right* was an existing lexical item of English, than for a word related to *ripe*. Like Manuel's finding for *win those*, this result supports the view that individual cues to a feature of an apparently missing segment can be preserved in production, overlapping with cues for a different segment; and listeners can disentangle these cues and infer the speaker's intended sequence of segments.

Other lines of work also support the view that speakers leave behind cues to apparently deleted segments, or to the original identity of apparently changed segments. For example, there is growing evidence that cases of "neutralization," such as for the voiced-voiceless distinction in final position in German (Port, Mitleb, & O'Dell, 1981) and in Dutch (Ernestus, Baayen, & Schreuder, 2002), may not be entirely neutralized. In a different domain

regarding sound-level speech errors, Goldrick and Blumstein (2006) found acoustic evidence for the "missing" target segment in apparent sound substitutions, and Pouplier and Goldstein (2010) found articulatory evidence for target and intrusion segments in errors elicited by repetitive regularly rhythmic tongue twisters. Kohler (1999), working on spontaneous speech in German, uses the term "articulatory residues" for such phenomena in continuous communicative speech:

> Nasalization may become a feature of a syllable or a whole syllable chain and not be tied to a delimitable nasal consonant. The same applies to labi(odent)alization. Both nasal and labi(odent)al consonants may be absent as separate units as long as the nasal and labial gestures are integrated in the total articulatory complex. This results in articulatory residues in the fusion of words. (p. 92)

Speakers not only provide cues to apparently missing or changed segments and their features; they also often signal the way those segments should be grouped into words. Lehiste (1960) documented a number of cues that signal the presence of a word boundary, disambiguating such sequences as *my seat* versus *mice eat*, and several investigators have reported an increased probability of irregular pitch periods for word-initial vowels (and sometimes sonorant consonants) at the beginnings of intonational phrases (Pierrehumbert & Talkin, 1992) and at accented syllables (Dilley et al., 1996), potentially signaling the constituent structure of word sequences; Surana and Slifka (2006) argued that this phenomenon could also aid in word segmentation. Phrase-final creak and phrase-final lengthening can presumably also reinforce the intonation cues to phrasing in languages like English. Thus, despite sometimes severe reduction or merging of sounds across constituent boundaries, the speaker nevertheless often produces enough cues to those boundaries to signal the intended structure.

Another such example is an early finding by Cooper (1991) showing that word-onset voiceless stops like /t/ are normally produced with an open glottis (and thus considerable aspiration noise) even before a schwa vowel, as in *today, tomorrow, tonight, Toledo, potato, polite, Canadian*, and *collection*. That is, the reduction to weaker versions of these stops that is usually seen before schwa vowels in word-medial position (e.g., *papa, mocha, beta*) or across a word boundary (*keep a, met a, block a*) is avoided in word-onset position, providing a cue to the word affiliation of the stop. Yet another example is found in a study by Manuel (1991) that compared the English word *sport* with reduced forms of the word *support*, which can sometimes be produced with no visible or audible first vowel. In such tokens of *s'port*, the /p/ was produced with aspiration after the release, rather than with the nonaspirated form seen after the tautosyllabic /s/ in *sport*. Thus, evidence for the original reduced vowel, and thus for the correct contrastive word form, is contained in the signal despite the lack of a "vocalic" region for the first syllable. Davidson (2006) reported a continuum of possible elision degrees for such vowels with increasing speaking rate, in such words as *potato*, arguing that this supports a gestural overlap rather than a schwa-deletion account.

Four additional lines of evidence are mentioned here. The first comes from analyses of possible "resyllabification" in American English by de Jong, Lim, and Nagao (2004). Although this term is often used, and deJong's work (and others) shows that some degree of reorganization does occur in repeated utterances of a VC syllable, so that they somewhat resemble CV syllables, the reorganization is not complete. That is, the characteristics of the C in such a transformed production are not exactly like those of the onset in an original CV. Shattuck-Hufnagel (2006) showed similar lack of full resyllabification for final /t/ in such phrases as *edit us*. Spinelli, McQueen, and Cutler (2003) studied the effects of elision in French, as when the final /t/ of *petit* restructures to become prevocalic in *petit agneau*, and found that this process had little if any effect on word recognition in French listeners, despite the seeming erosion of boundaries between the speaker's intended words. This result is expected if even after words were linked in elision, the signal nevertheless cued the original word affiliation of the features and segments. Additional support for the notion that it does comes from Scharenborg (2010): her laboratory's FastTracker algorithm detects boundary- and grouping-related phonetic markers in spoken Dutch, distinguishing syllables that make up monosyllabic words from those that are part of polysyllabic words, and word-initial from word-final /s/.

Taken together, the evidence for (a) widespread and sometimes extreme phonetic variation of word forms in continuous speech, (b) a role for both prosodic structure and frequency of word use (and lexical word structure) in governing that variation, (c) the gradient nature of at least some of that variation, and (d) the observation that the cues left in the signal often permit recognition of segments and their features, and the structural organization of these linguistic elements, inspired new approaches to modeling the cognitive process of speech production planning. Some highlights of these modeling developments are reviewed in the next section.

Models of Connected Speech Production

Up until the 1980s, speech production models were of three major types. The first type focused on broad characterizations of the planning process, largely based on evidence from studies of the systematic ways in which the system can go wrong, such as in speech errors (Fromkin, 1971, 1973; Garrett, 1975; Shattuck-Hufnagel, 1992) or in aphasia (Morton, 1969). These models provided constraints on what might constitute an adequate planning model, from the lexical retrieval process (Dell, 1986) through serial ordering of words and sounds. However, they did not extend to the phrase-level phonetic planning process, and there had been few efforts to model the entire process of speech planning and implementation from beginning to end. Most germane to the concerns here, there had been almost no modeling of how context-governed phonetic variation in connected speech might arise, other than the proposition that these processes were mechanical and universal (as suggested in Chomsky & Halle, 1968) or that they involved selection among allophonic categories (as suggested by IPA transcription conventions).

These gaps were filled by two modeling developments: Levelt's (1989) comprehensive model of the entire planning process that underlies speech production, from message conceptualization to motor movements of the articulatory system, and Browman and Goldstein's (1986, et seq.) proposal for articulatory phonology (discussed previously). Articulatory phonology modeled how at least some aspects of systematic phonetic variation might come about. It began with assumptions about the primacy of articulation in understanding the phonetics of speech, and worked its way back through the phonetic phenomena of word combinations to claims about word form representations in the lexicon and perhaps even earlier in the production process. The persuasive fit between this model and articulatory data made it unlikely that selection among symbolic categories would ever again be put forward as a serious model for all of phonetic variation.

In contrast, in his monograph *Speaking*, Levelt (1989) started at the other end of the production planning process, working his way down from message generation to articulation, and likewise changed the landscape of continuous speech planning models irrevocably. That volume integrated the available literature into a model of the entire speech production process, from generation of the message to movement of the articulators—marking a watershed in its degree of comprehensiveness and detail. This was followed a decade later by a paper with two of his colleagues, Antje Meyer and Ardi Roelofs (Levelt, Roelofs, & Meyer, 1999). This paper (henceforth LRM99; see also Levelt 2001 for a shorter summary statement) described Roelofs' computer implementation of the model, and a series of behavioral experiments that tested some of its predictions regarding reaction times to begin an utterance under various priming conditions. This implementation contained several important changes from the original 1989 description, including the explicit incorporation of articulatory phonology's mechanisms (Browman & Goldstein, 1986, inter alia) for storing and retrieving syllabic articulatory plans. Although it did not deal with adjusting these plans to fit their contexts, it represented a substantial advance over earlier "black box" models that simply fed phonological plans into a module labeled "articulation." Thus, even though Levelt et al. did not model the actual production of sound, they moved things substantially closer to that goal.

As discussed, prosodic grouping and prominence influence phrase-level phonetics, and in this domain, the LRM99 model made two important moves. First, it computed sound-level plans one prosodic word at a time, accounting for phonetic variation that involves constituents slightly larger than the lexical word, arguing principally from patterns of production of verb+pronoun sequences, such as *escort us* or *heat it*. Levelt et al. noted that in some varieties of British English, the final /t/ in such word combinations is produced with a noisy release, suggesting that it has been resyllabified to become an onset in the following vowel-initial word. The ability of a model to account for such cross-word-boundary interactions is critical, and the move to the prosodic word as the articulatory planning unit was an important step in this direction (although it is unlikely that this restructuring is complete).

A second important aspect of the LRM99 model was the inclusion of a later stage of phrase-level prosodic processing, as in the 1989 version. This component accounted for the planning of intonational contours as well as the structures (prosodic constituents and accents) that govern those contours. It could also, in theory, provide an account

of systematic boundary- and prominence-related adjustments to the proposed syllable-sized articulatory plans, such as the articulatory strengthening at constituent onsets and duration lengthening at boundaries described previously. However, no explicit mechanism was proposed for the adjustment of the selected syllable-sized articulatory plans to their prosodic contexts.

In addition to articulatory phonology and the LRM model of speech planning, a third development in the modeling of speech production has taken the form of exemplar-based models of production (Johnson, 1997; Pierrehumbert, 2001, 2002). These were inspired by several findings, starting with experimental results showing that listeners process auditorily presented words better (i.e., more accurately and more quickly) when they have previously heard them produced in the same voice (Goldinger, 1996). This suggested that listeners store tokens of earlier auditory experiences of each word in a multidimensional space that includes parameters of individual speaker productions, recognizing incoming words by accessing the best-fitting token from this cloud of stored memories (Goldinger, 1997; MacLennan, Luce, & Charles-Luce, 2003). This approach to modeling speech perception, which imported concepts from category learning (Nosofsky, 1986; Hintzman, 1986) into the cognition of language processing, opened the door to the possibility of formulating a production model that made use of a similar mechanism, such as selection of the most appropriate token from a set of memories of previously produced tokens stored in a multidimensional space that reflects the dimensions of variation that matter to the listener. Additional inspiration for this proposal came from findings of gradient and lexical-item-specific effects of frequency of word use and word predictability on the production of phonetic variation as described previously. Such word-specific differences are naturally accommodated in an exemplar-based framework, because each word in the lexicon has its own cloud of stored word forms. An exemplar-based approach is also consistent with results reported by Labov and colleagues (e.g., Labov, 1966, 1972) and others (e.g., Foulkes & Docherty, 2006), who used detailed acoustic analysis of vowel formants to establish the gradient nature of sociolinguistic variation and sound change. In exemplar models, such patterns can be captured by associating detailed phonetic forms to social/indexical labels.

The advantage of an exemplar-based model for production over a model based on feature-changing rewrite rules (i.e., selection from among phonemically distinct categories) is its ability to account for the nonbinary gradient nature of surface variation. It does this by storing so many remembered tokens of how a word has been produced in different contexts that there is always one available to fit the current context, at least for an adult who has had many decades of speaking experience. Pure exemplar-based theories, however, face several challenges in accounting for speaker behavior in the production of continuous speech. First, exactly how does the speaker decide which exemplar in the cloud of exemplars for a particular word to select as appropriate for a given context? Second, how is it that serial ordering errors involving word subconstituents can occur, if exemplars are retrieved as whole units? Thirdly, by precisely what mechanism does frequency of use lead to selection of exemplars with greater reduction? Fourth, how can such a model account for the speaker's ability to choose to produce any phrase, no matter how frequently it has been produced in the past, in a clear canonical (i.e., unreduced) or even hyperarticulated manner? Finally, when a speaker knows a word, he or she can do many things that an exemplar model might have trouble accounting for, such as manipulate the subparts of the word in language games and experimental tasks, judge the nature and location of similarities and differences among word forms, transform the word by inflection or derivation, and produce it in contexts that the speaker has not produced before, all abilities that can be accounted for in a unified manner by reference to a traditional phonological lexicon in which word forms are represented as sequences of discrete phonological segments (or feature bundles). Such considerations led to proposals for a hybrid model of production, in which each entry in a traditional phonological lexicon is also associated with a cloud of stored exemplars of that word as already produced (Pierrehumbert, 2002, 2003a, 2003b; Ernestus, in press). This set of exemplars stores previous experiences that include contextual variation and reduction patterns resulting from frequency of use, and that could be accessed during production, while still providing a mechanism to account for more traditional phonological abilities of the speaker. This approach is discussed further later.

In sum, the past few decades have seen the emergence of serious attempts to quantify the nature and extent of systematic surface variation in word forms, to identify the factors which govern it, and to model the mechanisms by which it occurs during speech production planning and articulation. There have been striking advances in the comprehensiveness of proposed models, and in their ability to make testable predictions about measurable aspects of the acoustics and the articulation of spoken utterances, and about the relationship between these two intertwined aspects of speech. However, one characteristic shared by many of these models is the rejection of traditional lexical representations of word form defined by sequences of phonemes, each of which is defined in turn by a bundle of distinctive features. The impetus to reject this traditional view has come from findings that feature cues are not aligned in the signal, that cue values are often distributed in a continuous-valued rather than a categorical way, and that entire chunks of words are sometimes apparently lost or changed unrecognizably in continuous speech. However, despite the indubitable occurrence of such phenomena, the remaining minimal cues to the distinctive features, phonemic segments, and grouping pattern of the speaker's intended words are often sufficient to allow the listener to infer those word forms with considerable accuracy. Thus, it might be time to ask in greater detail how the traditional model of lexical word form might be extended to account for the effects of experience on reduction patterns, particularly in light of how well it accounts for the wide variety of things that a speaker knows how to do with a word form.

Feature Cues as a Bridge between Abstract Invariant Lexical Representations and Surface Phonetic Variation

Insights gained from articulatory phonology show that many aspects of phonetic variation in continuous speech result from changes in the temporal overlap of adjacent articulatory movements and in their spatial and temporal extent. Relatedly, insights gained from work in exemplar theory, and a host of studies of phonetic variation in continuous speech, show that speakers produce systematic language-specific, dialect-specific, context-specific, and lexical-item-specific phonetic patterns when they implement a given word form or sound category. Moreover, countless analyses of the speech signal show that acoustic cues to the features of a given segment in a word are not reliably aligned together temporally in the signal. Do these collective observations render untenable the idea that speakers represent words as sequences of phonemes made up of feature bundles? The answer is no; not only are these observations compatible with this traditional view of the lexicon, but if one considers the full range of what a speaker knows about how to process words, then a phoneme-based lexicon (in the sense of phoneme as an abstract symbol for a bundle of distinctive features) may well provide the simplest account.

Several investigators working in various frameworks, such as Cutler (2010), Ernestus (in press), Munson, Beckman, and Edwards (in press), and Pierrehumbert (2001, 2002, 2006), have made a similar point: that the observed facts about phrase-level phonetic variation seem to require a hybrid model, with the advantages of both a phonemic lexicon and some way of storing more detailed phonetic knowledge. This section explores two aspects of a proposal for how this might work: that when speakers plan the surface phonetic form for a word in a particular utterance, they manipulate not segments or features, but individual acoustic cues to distinctive features; and that stored knowledge about frequency and its phonetic effects may be stored not for lexical items but for prosodic constituents that can correspond to more than one word.

The type of hybrid production model in mind here is, like those proposed previously, built around a lexicon whose word forms are represented in traditional phonological terms (i.e., as sequences of abstract symbols that correspond to bundles of distinctive features). Such a representation allows the speaker to generate a production plan for each word that specifies the effectors that will be used to articulate the acoustic cues for each feature bundle. This translation from abstract symbol to proto-motor plan produces a parameterizable representation (i.e., one for which temporal and spatial specifications can be developed for a particular utterance or speaking situation). Studies carried out in the Articulatory Phonology framework suggest that these paramterizable representations are gestural, specifying a sequence of articulatory configurations whose values for temporal overlap and reduction can be adjusted to fit the goals for a given utterance. Evidence from online acoustic perturbation studies (e.g., Cai, 2012; Houde & Jordan, 1998; Villacorta, Perkell, & Guenther, 2007), however, suggests that the goals are sensory, as assumed in Guenther's DIVA model (Guenther & Perkell, 2004; Guenther, this volume). In some way that is not yet entirely clear, there must be a mapping between the sensory (auditory and proprioceptive) goals and the motor movements that creates the articulatory configurations to accurately and appropriately produce those sensory goals.

Under some speaking conditions, such individual word plans are fitted together with appropriate phonetic adjustments for interactions across word boundaries and for the prosodic constituent structure and prominence structure of the particular utterance intended by the speaker. In other conditions, however, and perhaps typically in conversational speech, there is an additional route available, via retrieval from a set of stored but parameterizable representations of certain constituents that the speaker has produced before. The proposal here is that these stored representations of past production plans, with their parameterizable spatial and temporal targets, are the locus of frequency-based effects on production, specifying greater articulatory reduction and overlap for high-frequency constituents that can nevertheless be overcome, if the speaker prefers it, by the less-reduced instructions that emerge from the encoding process that starts with the traditional phonemic lexicon. However, these proposed stored plans differ from existing hybrid models in one significant dimension: they need not correspond to individual words, because they can correspond to prosodic constituents at any level of the prosodic hierarchy, from the highest to the lowest. Thus, they can in principle account for "reduction constituents" ranging from a pair of adjacent phonemes (as in the coda cluster /st/ in *lost* produced without a /t/ closure or release) to an entire utterance (as in *I don't know* produced as a low-high-low-high intonation contour on a single nasalized vowel sound [Hawkins, 2003]). Because the stored elements that support this second planning mechanism are not associated with single lexical items, their direct link to a single lexical meaning is severed. Instead, they form what might be called a prosodicon of constituents, separate from the form-meaning pairings in the lexicon. Activated by their corresponding lexical word sequences, these stored prosodic constituent plans facilitate specification of the phonetic shape of an utterance, because they are represented not in terms of abstract symbolic categories but in a vocabulary closer to what the motor system can use, such as abstract articulatory gestures.

Such a mechanism is consistent with the concept of optimization, as suggested in the DIVA model (Guenther & Perkell, 2004) and Keating's window model (Keating 1990), although it suggests that additional factors other than the balancing of efficient articulatory paths with meeting sensory goals may be involved. Note that this proposal provides a mechanism that frees the speaker from deterministic control by the mere arithmetic accumulation of exemplars of reduced forms. Past experience can be overridden by the speaker, because even high-frequency constituents can be produced in canonical or even hyperarticulated form when desired. The proposal that these stored elements are prosodic constituents is consistent with approaches like the Prosody First model of Keating and Shattuck-Hufnagel (2002), in which the planning frames for spoken utterances are made up of a hierarchy of prosodic constituents; elements of the prosodicon would fit neatly into such planning frames.

A second way in which this sketch of a hybrid model differs from existing models is in the elements that are manipulated in the setting of phonetic goals: it is proposed that these are the acoustic landmarks (i.e., the moments of abrupt spectral change associated with quantal changes in the acoustics at certain points during the continuous-valued changes in the articulatory configuration during the production of an utterance). Examples include the release burst of a stop consonant or the onset of frication noise for a fricative. In the perceptual domain, landmarks have been proposed as critical events that can be robustly detected by the perceptual system, so that their detection serves as the first step in the speech perception process. Stevens (2000, 2002) and Stevens and Keyser (1989; Keyser & Stevens, 2006) outline a model based on individual acoustic cues to the distinctive features that define, differentiate, and relate the word forms in the lexicon. In their model, a given feature contrast can be signaled by a number of different acoustic cues, and the speaker's cue selection can vary systematically with the other features in the feature bundle (e.g., labial is signaled differently for stops than for fricatives in English), with the nature of adjacent segments (different cues for a word-medial voiceless stop consonant before a stressed vowel vs. a reduced vowel), and with position in the larger context (word-initial /t/ has a different range of cues than word-final /t/). Although Stevens and Keyser do not propose a production model based on acoustic cue selection, one can envision extending their proposals for speech perception in this way. Individual feature-cue manipulation would be consistent with constraints on phonetic reduction that are not necessarily predicted by the physiology of the vocal tract; speakers may be constrained to preserve at least one cue to at least one feature of certain phonemes in a word in many reduction processes (although perhaps not in all of the most extreme cases), providing listeners with minimal cues to distinguish one contrastive word form from another. For example, informal observation suggests that when speakers produce a reduced form of the English phrase *why did you*, they can fully palatalize the cross-word-boundary sequence /-d+y-/ to produce something very close to the voiced palatal affricate /dʒ/, whereas when they produce a reduced form of *why do you*, there is much less overlap, resulting in less affrication and more of a glide-like production after the stop. This preserves cues to the difference between an interaction of the /y/ with a final /d/ in *why did you* but with the initial /d/ in *why do you*. These preserved cues are informative about the lexical items, whereas the pattern of cue loss and change may be informative about other aspects of the communicative act, such as the state of mind and social affiliations of the speaker. Moreover, intervals between acoustic landmark cues are good candidates for the computation of timing patterns for individual utterances, which are influenced by many phrase-level factors.

A critical aspect of this idea is that the speaker formulates a plan for phonetic implementation in terms of which cues to a distinctive feature will be realized, and what amplitude and timing with which they will be realized. On this view, one particularly informative class of feature cue (i.e., the abrupt changes associated with articulatory closures and releases called landmarks) are good candidates for the events that might be timed to implement duration shortening or lengthening. This move to the individual feature cue, rather than the feature or the segment, makes it possible to deal with many aspects of subfeatural variation.

Conclusion

The history of phonology and phonetics can be looked at as the evolution of attempts to find the appropriate set of elements to capture the invariance and the variability in word forms. From very early grammarians, such as Panini, who described sets of sounds with common characteristics in Sanskrit, through Badouin de Courtenay, Trubetzkoy, and de Saussure to Jakobson, and the development of the IPA as a system of for describing allophonic variation, there has been a search for the linguistic elements that define word forms and describe the relationships among them, and describe the range of systematic phonetic variation in their production. More recently, phonology and phonetics have focused on systematic subfeatural variation among word forms and their sounds, highlighting such phenomena as duration cues and articulatory strengthening at prosodic boundaries and prominences; differences in articulatory overlap with structural position; and language-specific, dialect-specific, and speaker-specific patterns of variation in phonetic implementation. For some investigators, these observations have cast doubt on the need for the phoneme (bundle of distinctive features) as a representational unit. Throughout this process, however, one bedrock fact has remained: one word form is distinct from other word forms in the language, and yet related to them and to the various surface forms it can take in speech, in highly systematic ways that a native speaker understands.

The best way to account for this set of facts is in terms of the speaker's knowledge of a lexicon of word forms made up of phonemes defined by contrasting features, and the set of acoustic-phonetic cues that are appropriate for signaling those contrasts in different contexts. Evidence consistent with this view is found in the observation that, even in reduced and overlapped tokens, speakers often provide cues to the features of segments that are apparently "missing" from the utterance, and to the higher-level structural affiliations of those features and segments. This suggests that speakers have the capacity to explicitly represent and manipulate individual cues during the production planning process, and that the goal of preserving cues to features and structures constrains phrase-level adjustments to word forms. In addition, speakers may store and retrieve precompiled motor programs for frequently produced prosodic components, permitting the further reduction of these elements.

The acid test of such a view will come from the development of a synthesis algorithm that combines lexical access, prosodic planning, and sound generation to produce natural-sounding speech. The resulting acoustic signals will allow evaluation of this approach by the most sensitive and appropriate instrument: the human speech perception system, which is exquisitely tuned to the appropriateness of phrase-level phonetic phenomena.

References

Badouin de Courtenay, J. (1800s/1972). *A Badouin de Courtenay anthology: The beginnings of structural linguistics* (Ed.//Trans. E. Stankiewicz). Bloomington: Indiana University Press.

Beckman, M. E., & Edwards, J. (1994). Articulatory evidence for differentiating stress categories. In P. A. Keating (Ed.), *Phonological structure and phonetic form: Papers in laboratory phonology III* (pp. 7–33). Cambridge: Cambridge University Press.

Boersma, P. (2001). Praat, a system for doing phonetics by computer. *Glot International, 5*(9/10), 341–345.

Boersma, P., & Weenink, D. (2012). Praat: doing phonetics by computer [Computer program]. Version 5.3.04. Retrieved from http://www.praat.org/

Browman, C. P., & Goldstein, L. (1986). Towards an articulatory phonology. *Phonology Yearbook, 3,* 219–252.

Browman, C. P., & Goldstein, L. (1989). Articulatory gestures as phonological units. *Phonology, 6,* 201–251.

Browman, C. P., & Goldstein, L. (1990). Tiers in articulatory phonology, with some implications for casual speech. In T. Kingston & M. E. Beckman (Eds.). *Papers in laboratory phonology I: Between the grammar and physics of speech* (pp. 341–376). Cambridge: Cambridge University Press.

Browman, C. P., & Goldstein, L. (1992). Articulatory phonology: An overview. *Phonetica, 49,* 155–180.

Bybee, J. (2001). *Phonology and language use.* Cambridge, England: Cambridge University Press.

Cai, S. (2012). *Online control of articulation based on auditory feedback in normal speech and stuttering: Behavioral and modeling studies* (Unpublished doctoral thesis). MIT, Cambridge, MA.

Cho, T., & Jun, S.-A. (2000). Domain-initial strengthening as enhancement of laryngeal features: Aerodynamic evidence from Korean. *CLS, 36,* 31–44.

Chomsky, N., & Halle, M. (1968). *The sound pattern of English.* New York: Harper & Row.

Coleman, J. (2002). Phonetic representations in the mental lexicon. In J. Durand, & B. Laks (Eds.), *Phonetics, phonology and cognition* (pp. 96–130). Oxford: Oxford University Press.

Coleman, J. (2003). Discovering the acoustic correlates of phonological contrasts. *Journal of Phonetics, 31,* 351–372.

Cooper, A. M. (1991). *An articulatory account of aspiration in English* (Unpublished doctoral thesis). Yale University, New Haven, CT.

Cutler, A. (2010). Abstraction-based efficiency in the lexicon. *Laboratory Phonology, 1*(2), 301–318. doi:10.1515/LABPHON.2010.016.

Davidson, L. (2006). Schwa elision in fast speech: segmental deletion or gestural overlap? *Phonetica, 63,* 79–112.

deJong, K. J., Lim, B. L., & Nagao, K. (2004). The perception of syllable affiliation of singleton stops in repetitive speech. *Language and Speech, 47,* 241–266.

Dell, G. (1986) A spreading activation theory of retrieval in sentence production, *Psychological Review, 93,* 283–321.

Dilley, L. C., & Shattuck-Hufnagel S. (1998). Ambiguity in prominence perception in spoken utterances of American English. In *Proceedings of the 16th International Congress on Acoustics and 135th Meeting of the Acoustical Society of America, Vol. 2* (pp. 1237–1238).

Dilley, L. C., & Shattuck-Hufnagel, S. (1999). Effects of repeated intonation patterns on perceived word-level organization. In *Proceedings of the ICPhS, San Francisco.*

Dilley, L., Shattuck-Hufnagel, S., & Ostendorf, M. (1996). Glottalization of vowel-initial syllables as a function of prosodic structure. *Journal of Phonetics, 24,* 423–444.

Ernestus, M. (in press). Acoustic reduction and the roles of abstractions and exemplars in speech processing. *Lingua.*

Ernestus, M., Baayen, H. R., & Schreuder, R. (2002). The recognition of reduced word forms. *Brain and Language, 81,* 162–173.

Espy-Wilson, C. (1987). *An acoustic-phonetic approach to speech recognition: application to the semivowels* (Unpublished doctoral thesis). Department of Electrical Engineering and Computer Science, MIT, Cambridge, MA.

Ferreira, F. (1993). The creation of prosody during sentence production. *Psychological Review, 100,* 233–253.

Ferreira, F. (2007). Prosody and performance in language production. *Language and Cognitive Processes, 22,* 1151–1177.

Firth, J. R. (1948). Sounds and prosodies. *Transactions of the Philological Society*. (Reprinted from *Prosodic analysis*, pp. 1–26, by F. R. Palmer, Ed., 1970, Oxford: Oxford University Press)

Fougeron, C. (1998) Variations articulatoires en début de constituants prosodiques de différents niveaux en français, Université Paris III.

Fougeron, C. (2001). Articulatory properties of initial consonants in several prosodic constituents in French. *J Phonetics*, *29*, 109–135.

Foulkes, P., & Docherty, G. (2006). The social life of phonetics and phonology. *Journal of Phonetics*, *34*, 409–438.

Fowler, C. A. (1988). Differential shortening of repeated content words produced in various communicative contexts. *Language and Speech*, *3*(4), 307–319.

Fowler, C. A., & Housum, J. (1987). Talkers' signalling of "new" and "old" words in speech and listeners' perception and use of the distinction. *Journal of Memory and Language*, *26*, 489–504.

Fowler, C. A., Rubin, P., Remez, R. E., & Turvey, M. T. (1980). Implications for speech production of a general theory of action. In B. Butterworth (Ed.), *Language production* (pp. 373–420). New York: Academic Press.

Fromkin, V. A. (1971). The nonanomalous nature of anomalous utterances. *Language*, *47*, 27–52.

Fromkin, V. A. (Ed., 1973). *Speech errors as linguistic evidence*. The Hague: Mouton.

Garrett, M. F. (1975). The analysis of sentence production. In: G. Bower (Ed.), *Psychology of learning and motivation* (Vol. 9, pp. 133–177). New York: Academic Press.

Goldinger, S. D. (1996). Words and voices: Episodic traces in spoken word identification and recognition memory. *Journal of Experimental Psychology: Learning, Memory, and Cognition*, *22*, 1166–1183.

Goldinger, S. (1997). Echoes of echoes: An episodic theory of lexical access. *Psychological Review*, *105*, 251–279.

Goldrick, M., & Blumstein, S. E. (2006). Cascading activation from phonological planning to articulatory processes: Evidence from tongue twisters. *Language and Cognitive Processes*, *21*(6), 649–683.

Goldsmith, J. A. (1976). An overview of autosegmental phonology. *Linguistic Analysis*. 2, 23–68.

Gow, D. W. (2002). Does English coronal place assimilation create lexical ambiguity? *Journal of Experimental Psychology: Human Perception and Performance*, *28*, 163–179.

Gow, D. W. (2003). Feature parsing: Feature cue mapping in spoken word recognition. *Perception & Psychophysics*, *65*, 575–590.

Guenther, F., & Perkell, J. (2004, June). *A neural model of speech production and supporting experiments*. In S. Manuel & J. Slifka (Eds.), *From sound to sense: 50 years of speech research*. Conference held at MIT, Cambridge, MA.

Halliday, M. (1967). *Intonation and grammar in British English* (Janua Linguarum, series practica, 48). The Hague: Mouton.

Hawkins, S. (2003). Roles and representations of systematic fine phonetic detail in speech understanding. *Journal of Phonetics*, *31*, 373–405.

Hawkins, S. (2011). On the robustness of speech perception. Plenary lecture presented at the International Congress of Phonetic Sciences 2011, Hong Kong.

Hayes, B. (1989). The prosodic hierarchy in meter. In P. Kiparsky & G. Youmans (Eds.), *Rhythm and meter* (pp. 201–260). Orlando, FL: Academic Press.

Hintzman, D. L. (1986). "Schema abstraction" in a multiple-trace memory model. *Psychological Review*, *93*, 411–428.

Hockett, C. (1955). *A manual of phonology*. Indiana University Publications in Anthropology and Linguistics 11. Baltimore, MD: Waverly Press.

Houde, J. F., & Jordan, M. I. (1998). Sensorimotor adaptation in speech production. *Science*, *279*, 1213–1216.

Jakobson, R. (1941/1968). *Child language, aphasia and phonological universals*. The Hague: Mouton

Jakobson, R., Fant, C. G. M., & Halle, M. (1952). *Preliminaries to speech analysis: The distinctive features and their correlates*. Cambridge, MA: MIT Press.

Johnson, K. (1997). Speech perception without speaker normalization: An exemplar model. In K. Johnson & J. Mullenix (Eds.), *Talker variability in speech processing* (pp. 145–166). San Diego, CA: Academic Press.

Johnson, K. (2004). Massive reduction in conversational American English. Spontaneous speech: data and analysis. *Proceedings of the 1st session of the 10th international symposium* (pp. 29–54). Tokyo: The National International Institute for Japanese Language.

Jun, S.-A. (1993). *The phonetics and phonology of Korean prosody* (Doctoral dissertation). Ohio State University, Columbus, OH. [Published in 1996 by Garland, New York].

Jurafsky, D., Bell, A., Fosler-Lussier, E., Girand, C., & Raymond, W. D. (1998). Reduction of English function words in Switchboard. In *ICSLP-98*, Sydney (Vol. 7, pp. 3111–3114). Canberra City, Australia: Australian Speech Science and Technology Association.

Jurafsky, D., Bell, A., & Girand, C. (2002). The role of the lemma in form variation. In C. Gussenhoven & N. Warner (Eds.), *Papers in laboratory phonology VII* (pp. 1–34). Berlin: Mouton de Gruyter.

Keating, P. A. (1990). The window model of coarticulation: Articulatory evidence. In J. Kingston & M. E. Beckman (Eds.), *Papers in laboratory phonology I* (pp. 451–470). Cambridge: Cambridge University Press.

Keating, P. A., & Fougeron, C. (1997). Articulatory strengthening at edges of prosodic domains. *Journal of the Acoustical Society of America*, *101*, 3728–3740.

Keating, P. A., & Shattuck-Hufnagel, S. (2002). A prosodic view of word form encoding for speech production. *UCLA Working Papers in Phonetics*, *101*, 112–156.

Keyser, S. J., & Stevens, K. N. (2006). Enhancement and overlap in the speech chain. *Language*, *82*(1), 33–63.

Klatt, D. H. (1976). Linguistic uses of segmental duration in English: Acoustic and perceptual evidence. *Journal of the Acoustical Society of America*, *59*, 1208–1221.

Kohler, K. (1990). Segmental reduction in connected speech in German: Phonological facts and phonetic explanations. In W. J. Hardcastle & A. Marchal (Eds.), *Speech production and speech modelling* (pp. 21–33). Dordrecht: Kluwer Academic Publishers.

Kohler, K. (1999). Articulatory prosodies in German reduced speech. *Proceedings of the XIVth International Congress of Phonetic Sciences*, San Francisco.

Kohler, K. (2011). Does phonetic detail guide situation-specific speech recognition. *Proceedings of the XVIIth International Congress of Phonetic Sciences*, Hong Kong.

Labov, W. (1966). *The social stratification of English in New York City*. Washington: Center for Applied Linguistics.

Labov, W. (1972). *Sociolinguistic patterns*. Philadelphia: University of Pennsylvania Press.

Ladd, D. R., & Campbell, N. (1991). Theories of prosodic structure: Evidence from syllable duration. *Proceedings of the XII ICPhS.* Aix-en- Provence, France.

Lehiste, I. (1960). An acoustic-phonetic study of internal open juncture. *Phonetica, 5*(Suppl.1), 5–54.

Lehiste, I. (Ed.). (1967). *Readings in acoustic phonetics.* Cambridge, MA: MIT Press.

Levelt, W. J. M. (1989). *Speaking: From intention to articulation.* Cambridge, MA: MIT Press.

Levelt, W. J. M. (2001). Spoken word production: A theory of lexical access. *Proceedings of the National Academy of Sciences, 98,* 13464–13471.

Levelt, W. J. M., Roelofs, A., & Meyer, A. (1999). A theory of lexical access in speech production. *Behavioral and Brain Sciences, 22,* 1–38.

Manuel, S. (1991). Recovery of "deleted" schwa. In O. Engstrand & C. Kylander (Eds.), *Current phonetic research paradigms: Implications for speech motor control (PERILUS XIV).* Stockholm: University of Stockholm.

Manuel, S. Y. (1995). Speakers nasalize /<eth>/ after /n/, but listeners still hear /<eth>/, *Journal of Phonetics, 23,* 453–476.

Manuel, S., Shattuck-Hufnagel, S., Huffman, M., Stevens, K., Carlsson, R., & Hunnicutt, S. (1992). Studies of vowel and consonant reduction. In *Proceedings of the 1992 International Congress on Spoken Language Processing,* 943–946.

MacLennan, C., Luce, P., & Charles-Luce, J. (2003). Representation of lexical form. *Journal of Experimental Psychology: Learning, Memory and Cognition, 29,* 539–553.

McQueen, J. M., Dahan, D., & Cutler, A. (2003). Continuity and gradedness in speech processing. In N. O. Schiller, & A. S. Meyer (Eds.), *Phonetics and phonology in language comprehension and production: Differences and similarities* (pp. 39–78). Berlin: Mouton de Gruyter.

Morton, J. (1969). Interaction of information in word recognition. *Psychological Review, 76*(2), 165–178.

Munson, B., Beckman, M., & Edwards, J. (2011). *Phonological representations in language acquisition: Climbing the ladder of abstraction.* In A. Cohn, C. Fougeron, & M. Huffman (Eds.), *Oxford handbook in laboratory phonology* (pp. 288–309). Oxford: Oxford University Press.

Nosofsky, R. (1986). Attention, similarity and the identification-categorization relationship. *Journal of Experimental Psychology: General, 115*(1), 39–57.

Nespor, M., & Vogel, I. (1986). *Prosodic phonology.* Dordrecht. Foris Publications.

Ogden, R., & Local, J. K. (1994). Disentangling autosegments from prosodies: A note on the misrepresentation of a research tradition in phonology. *Journal of Linguistics, 30,* 477–498.

Okobi, A. O. (2006). *Acoustic correlates of word stress in American English* (Unpublished doctoral thesis). MIT, Cambridge, MA.

Pierrehumbert, J. (2001). Exemplar dynamics: Word frequency, lenition, and contrast. In J. Bybee & P. Hopper (Eds.), *Frequency effects and the emergence of linguistic structure* (pp. 137–157). Amsterdam: John Benjamins.

Pierrehumbert, J. (2002). Word-specific phonetics. In C. Gussenhoven & N. Warner (Eds.), *Laboratory Phonology 7* (pp. 101–139). Berlin: Mouton de Gruyter.

Pierrehumbert, J. (2003a). Probabilistic phonology: Discrimination and robustness. In R. Bod, J. Hay, & S. Jannedy (Eds.), *Probability theory in linguistics* (pp. 177– 228). Cambridge, MA: The MIT Press.

Pierrehumbert, J. (2003b). Phonetic diversity, statistical learning, and acquisition of phonology. *Language and Speech, 46*(2–3), 115–154.

Pierrehumbert, J. (2006). *The statistical basis of an unnatural alternation.* In L. Goldstein, D. H. Whalen, & C. Best (Eds.), *Laboratory phonology VIII, varieties of phonological competence* (pp. 81–107). Berlin: Mouton de Gruyter.

Pierrehumbert, J. B., & Talkin, D. (1992). Lenition of /h/ and glottal stop. In G. Doherty & D. R. Ladd (Eds.), *Papers in laboratory phonology II: Gesture, segment, prosody* (pp. 90– 127). Cambridge: Cambridge University Press.

Port, R. F., Mitleb, F. M., & O'Dell, M. (1981). Neutralization of obstruent voicing is incomplete. *Journal of the Acoustical Society of America, 70,* S10.

Pouplier, M., & Goldstein, L. (2010). Intention in articulation: Articulatory timing of coproduced gestures and its implications for models of speech production. *Language and Cognitive Processes, 25*(5), 616–664.

Saltzman, E., & Kelso, J. A. S. (1987). Skilled actions: A task-dynamic approach. *Psychological Review, 94,* 84–106.

Saltzman, E., & Munhall, K. (1989). A dynamical approach to gestural patterning in speech production. *Ecological Psychology, 1,* 333–382.

Scharenborg, O. (2010). Modeling the use of durational information in human spoken-word recognition. *Journal of the Acoustical Society of America, 127*(6), 3758–3770.

Selkirk, E. O. (1984). *Phonology and syntax: The relation between sound and structure.* Cambridge, MA: MIT Press.

Shattuck-Hufnagel, S. (1992). The role of word structure in segmental serial ordering. *Cognition, 42*(1–3), 213–259.

Shattuck-Hufnagel, S. (2006). Prosody first or prosody last? Evidence from the phonetics of word-final /t/ in American English. In L. M. Goldstein, D. H. Whalen, & C. sT. Browman (Eds.), *Laboratory phonology 8: Varieties of phonological competence* (pp. 445–472). Berlin: de Gruyter.

Spinelli, E., McQueen, J., & Cutler, A. (2003). Processing resyllabified words in French. *Journal of Memory and Language, 48,* 233–254.

Stevens, K. N. (1998). *Acoustic phonetics.* Cambridge, MA: MIT Press.

Stevens, K. N. (2000). Diverse acoustic cues at consonantal landmarks. *Phonetica, 57*(2–4), 139–151.

Stevens, K. N. (2002). Toward a model for lexical access based on acoustic landmarks and distinctive features. *Journal of the Acoustical Society of America, 111,* 1872–1891.

Stevens, K. N., & Keyser, S. J. (1989). Primary features and their enhancement in consonants. *Language, 65,* 81–106.

Surana, K., & Slifka, J. (2006). Is irregular phonation a reliable cue towards the segmentation of continuous speech in American English? In *Proceedings of Speech Prosody 2006* (Paper 177). Dresden, Germany: ISCA Special Interest Group on Speech Prosody.

Talkin, D. (1995). A robust algorithm for pitch tracking (RAPT). In W. B. Kleijn & K. K. Paliwal (Eds.) *Speech coding and synthesis* (pp. 495–518). New York, NY: Elsevier. [xWaves is now embodied in Wavesurfer, www.speech.kth.se/wavesurfer/]

Trubetzkoy, N. S. (1939). *Grundzuge der phonologie.* Goettigen: Vandenhoeck and Ruprecht.

Truslow, E. (2010). *Xkl: A Tool for Speech Analysis* (Thesis, Union College). Retrieved from http://hdl.handle.net/10090/16913

[Xkl is the Unix implementation of the Klattools, which were developed by Dennis Klatt at MIT in the 1980s].

Villacorta, V. M., Perkell, J. S., & Guenther, F. H. (2007). Sensorimotor adaptation to feedback perturbations of vowel acoustics and its relation to perception. *Journal of the Acoustical Society of America, 122*(4), 2306–2319.

Wightman, C., Shattuck-Hufnagel, S., Ostendorf, M., & Price, P. (1992). Segmental durations in the vicinity of prosodic phrase boundaries. *Journal of the Acoustical Society of America, 91*(3), 1707–1717.

Zhao, S. (2010). Stop-like modification of the dental fricative / dh/: an acoustic analysis. *Journal of the Acoustical Society of America, 128*, 2009–2020.

Zsiga, E. (1997). Features, gestures and Igbo vowels: An approach to the phonetics/phonology interface. *Language, 73*(2), 227–274.

Neural Bases of Phonological and Articulatory Processing

Wolfram Ziegler *and* Hermann Ackermann

Abstract

This chapter supports the view of a coherent system interlacing the phonological network implicated in speaking with the central motor system controlling articulation. A pivotal role in this system is played by the left posterior-inferior frontal area, which is dedicated to the planning of speech motor patterns for syllables and words. This area constitutes the front end of an auditory-motor integration network and at the same time provides input to the speech motor execution system. Within this gross architecture, multiple interactions between subsystems take place. Moreover, the speech motor pathways are modulated by information from limbic structures by the basal ganglia and the supplementary motor area and receive sensory feedback from temporal and parietal cortex. Through these interconnections, speech movement control is influenced by the speaker's internal emotional and motivational state and by the sensory consequences of his or her speech motor activity.

Key Words: speech, phonology, motor, dorsal stream

Introduction

In many theories of speech production, phonology and articulation pertain to different worlds—phonology to the universe of abstract linguistic structures, articulation to the realm of vocal tract muscles and movements. Within the framework of the software-hardware metaphor, which has often been invoked to characterize the divide between these two domains, *phonology* comprises a system of rules and symbols subserving the generation of abstract linguistic data structures, whereas *articulation* describes the physical mechanisms launched by these representations. Aphasiologists have grown accustomed to this dualism for decades, drawing a strict demarcation line of their subject matter (i.e., aphasia) at the point where language is assumed to interface with speech motor control. In this vein, one of the most prevalent aphasic symptoms (i.e., phonemic paraphasia) is viewed as a *linguistic impairment*, whereas its close relative, the distorted

and laborious production of vowels and consonants in apraxia of speech, is considered to pertain to the *movement domain* on the opposite side of the language-motor rift. Against the background of this dichotomy, any interactions of the ostensibly disparate worlds of alleged symbols and motor actions remain elusive.

By contrast to this dualistic model, the theory proposed by Levelt and coworkers postulates a coherent chain of processing steps extending from phonological encoding to speech articulation. As soon as a word's phonological form has been retrieved from the lexicon, all further operations converge straightforward onto the unfolding of the movements bound to its pronunciation (Levelt, Roelofs, & Meyer, 1999). Several other theories likewise dispense with the assumption of a strict divide between phonology and articulation. *Articulatory Phonology*, for example, considers the abstract representations of words as bundles of gestural units that, unlike the phonemes of generative or structuralist phonology, are characterized by a transparent relationship with the unfolding speech movements (cf. Goldstein & Pouplier's "The Temporal Organization of Speech.") Modern phonetic theories try to elucidate the "dynamics of phonological cognition" by uncovering the link between discrete phonological representations and their continuous motor substrates (Gafos & Benus, 2006), and more recent phonological models seek to explain the structural regularities of phonological form as emergent patterns arising from the properties of the motor and sensory systems implied in speaking and of other external factors (Blevins, 2004). There is also growing psycholinguistic evidence of an interaction between lexical phonological units and the fine-grained phonetic properties of spoken words (Baese-Berk & Goldrick, 2009), suggesting that the boundary between phonological representations and their physical realization is permeable to a cascading flow of information (Goldrick & Blumstein, 2006; see also "Phonetic Processing" by Buchwald).

Given these disparate views of how phonology is linked to speech articulation, insights into the functional neuroanatomy of spoken language may provide important clues to a better understanding of the relationship between these two domains. This chapter provides a perspective on the functional-neuroanatomic correlates of the phonological and motor aspects of spoken language production, based on data derived from neuroimaging studies, clinical research, and animal experiments.

Outline of the Articulatory-Phonological Network

Figure 17.1 gives a gross outline of the anatomic architecture of the articulatory-phonological system. At the bottom of this network, the muscles implicated in vocal tract movements during speech production receive neural input from the motor nuclei of the cranial nerves in the brainstem and from spinal motor nuclei. This "final motor pathway" of spoken language is driven by two basically different systems. A first system originating in motor and premotor cortical areas is responsible for the volitional control of vocal tract muscles during willful motor activities. This *neocortical motor system* is at the core of speech motor control, but has only rudimentary functions in the vocal behavior of nonhuman primates. Knowledge about the architecture of this system derives predominantly from clinical studies in patients with motor speech disorders. Second, the cranial motor nuclei are also the target of a phylogenetically older motor system arising in limbic areas of the medial wall of the frontal lobe, which is associated with intrinsic and emotional vocal behaviors. This *limbic vocalization system* is also present in nonhuman primates and other mammals and has been studied most extensively by lesion experiments and electrical stimulation studies in squirrel monkeys and macaques. Only limited knowledge exists about the role of this system in human vocal behavior, especially speaking. Although numerous clinical observations of dissociations between impairments of volitional and emotional vocal tract movements indicate that the two pathways reach the motor nuclei along anatomically separate courses, speech motor activity can be modulated by the limbic vocalization system through interconnections at several levels.

Speaking as a highly overlearned motor skill must obviously be supported by an immense implicit knowledge of how a speaker's native sound patterns translate into movements. This knowledge base, conceptualized as *motor* or *phonetic plans*, is considered to reside in a premotor cortical network comprising anterior-perisylvian and subsylvian cortical areas of the dominant hemisphere (see Figure 17.1). Evidence relating to this neural system traces back to Broca's work in the 19th century and has since then been debated among clinicians studying patients with apraxia of speech. More recently, functional brain imaging in healthy subjects has accumulated further insights into the neural network supporting speech planning mechanisms.

Finally, the motor planning component is considered as the front-end of a so-called *dorsal stream* system, which reciprocally connects the anterior perisylvian speech motor areas to left superior-temporal and inferior-parietal cortex and thereby provides a neural basis for the supramodal processes and representations implicated in phonological planning. Knowledge about the dorsal stream has its roots in clinical studies of patients with phonological disorders and has received renewed attention in modern neuroimaging research, including more recent fiber-tracking methods.

The "Final Common Pathway": Motor Neuron Pools in the Brainstem

The cranial nerves steering the vocal tract muscles originate from motor neuron pools of the brainstem, including the trigeminal motor (Vmo), facial (VII), and hypoglossal (XII) nuclei and the nucleus ambiguus (X). These so-called lower motor neurons

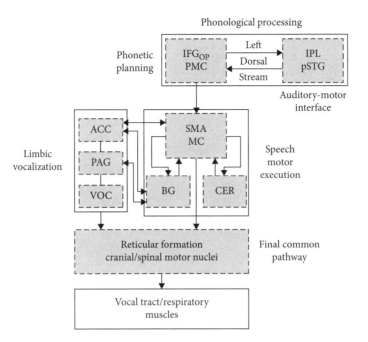

Figure 17.1 Gross architecture of the neural network subserving phonological and articulatory operations in speaking, delineating the phonological processing and phonetic planning components (top); the speech motor execution and the limbic vocalization system (middle); and the final common pathway (bottom). ACC = anterior cingulate cortex; BG = basal ganglia; CER = cerebellum; IFG$_{op}$ = (left) inferior frontal gyrus, pars opecularis; IPL = (left) inferior parietal lobe; MC = (primary) motor cortex; PAG = periaqueductal grey; PMC = (left) premotor cortex; pSTG = (left) posterior superior temporal gyrus; SMA = supplementary motor area; VOC = vocalization-related pontine neuron pool.

constitute a "final common pathway" for the control of mandibular, facial, lingual, and (intrinsic) laryngeal muscles during all types of motor activity, such as reflexive (coughing, swallowing); autonomous (breathing, yawning); affective (crying, laughing); or volitional (speaking, imitation of mouth movements). The extrinsic laryngeal and thoracic and abdominal muscles of the respiratory system are innervated by spinal nerves arising from the anterior horns of cervical, thoracic, and lumbar segments of the spinal cord (Jürgens, 2002).

The cranial nerve motor nuclei projecting to the laryngeal and supralaryngeal muscles are not mutually interconnected by direct pathways, but are embedded into a densely distributed network of neurons, the *reticular formation* of the brainstem, which coordinates conjoint vocal tract activities. In addition, the reticular formation encompasses nuclei mediating somatosensory information relevant for vocal tract motor functions, the *solitary tract nucleus* or the *spinal trigeminal nucleus* (Jürgens, 2002).

Disorders affecting the cranial nerve motor neurons give rise to a significant paresis of the respiratory, laryngeal, and supralaryngeal muscles, resulting in dysphagia and flaccid dysarthria. They impair the functioning of these muscles across all kinds of motor actions (reflexive, automatic, emotional, or voluntary).

Control of the Vocal Tract Muscles for Speaking: The Neocortical Motor System

During speaking, the cranial nerve motor nuclei receive direct and indirect input from the motor cortex, mainly from primary motor areas. These control signals are continuously updated and modulated by two parallel motor circuits: a basal ganglia and a cerebellar loop (Figure 17.2).

Motor Cortex and Corticobulbar Projections

The cortical region immediately rostral to the central (= Rolandic) sulcus, the Brodmann area (BA) 4, encompasses a somatotopic map of the musculature of the human body. The vocal tract muscles are represented within the lower third of the precentral motor strip, ventral to the hand area, occupying the anterior bank of the central sulcus and adjoining portions of premotor cortex. The functional topography of this system has originally been studied mainly by intraoperative electrical stimulation in patients suffering from drug-resistant epilepsy. Under these conditions, brief pulses of electrical current applied to the surface of the lower motor strip in awake patients were found to elicit speech arrest or vocalizations lacking a clear phonetic structure. More recently, noninvasive transcranial magnetic or electrical stimulation techniques, functional imaging methods, or the implantation of electrode grids were used to systematically delineate the representation of lips, tongue, larynx, and respiratory muscles along the precentral motor area (Brown, Ngan, & Liotti, 2008). Remarkably, a recent functional imaging study by Brown et al. (2009) revealed stronger speech-related hemodynamic responses within the larynx area compared with other vocal tract structures, which underscores the significant contribution of laryngeal motor skills in human communication.

More recent stimulation studies revealed a more elaborate picture of the somatotopic organization of primary motor cortex. It has been shown that the representations of functionally related body parts overlap with each other, and contractions of a specific group of muscles are usually associated with activation of multiple separate motor fields, often depending on the functional context of muscle recruitment, such as chewing or speaking (Sessle et al., 2007). Furthermore, it is also known that cortical motor maps can be modified through motor learning (Svensson, Romaniello, Wang, Arendt-Nielsen, & Sessle, 2006). Neurophysiologic studies of hand movements have demonstrated that long-term training of a specific sequential motor task "sculpts" the properties of motor cortex neurons, rendering them differentially sensitive for the trained motor function (Matsuzaka, Picard, & Strick, 2007). For these reasons it is plausible to assume that speaking—a motor skill established over a time-span of more than a decade—is based on highly specific motor cortical activation patterns in adult speakers.

The precentral motor fields of vocal tract structures send corticobulbar fibers to the cranial nerve motor nuclei of the brainstem. In humans, a large part of these fibers travels monosynaptically to the trigeminal, facial, and hypoglossal motor nuclei, and also to the laryngeal component of the nucleus ambiguus. Compared with humans, subhuman primates show a smaller proportion of monosynaptic projections and, even more importantly, lack any direct fiber connections to the nucleus ambiguus (Iwatsubo, Kuzuhara, Kanemitsu, Shimada, & Toyokura, 1990). These differences in corticobulbar connectivity represent one of the very few unambiguous anatomic specializations in our species directly related to the "faculty of linguistic

behavior." The direct corticoambigual projection must be considered a major prerequisite for the ability to engage laryngeal muscles into speech production (Passingham, 2008). The lack of direct cortical projections to the motor nuclei of the larynx in subhuman primates may explain why all the endeavors of training these species to produce spoken words have only resulted in voiceless, pant-like sounds (Wallman, 1992).

The descending corticobulbar projections also send collateral branches to the nuclei of the reticular formation, targeting the brainstem motor nuclei via interneurones (Jürgens, 2002). Such indirect corticobulbar connections are assumed to contribute to the regulation of muscle tone (see Figure 17.2).

The cranial motor nuclei of either side, with the possible exception of the lower facial nucleus, receive input from the motor cortices of both hemispheres. As a consequence, unilateral dysfunctions of the lower precentral cortex or its descending corticobulbar fibers usually cause only a mild and transient variant of paretic dysarthria, whereas damage to the corticobulbar system of both hemispheres (e.g., the Foix-Chavany-Marie syndrome), gives rise to severe speech motor deficits, in its extreme a complete paralysis of the vocal tract muscles (Ackermann

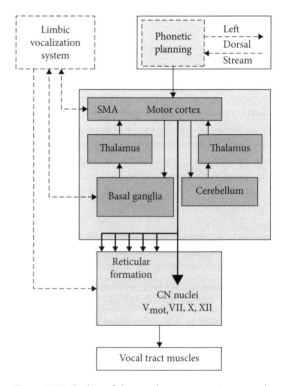

Figure 17.2 Outline of the speech motor execution network, including the direct and indirect corticobulbar projections and the striatal and cerebellar motor loops. For details see text.

& Ziegler, 2010). Despite this bilateral connectivity pattern, speech production appears to be characterized by a slight relative functional dominance of left-hemisphere motor cortex, as indicated both by imaging (e.g., Wildgruber, Ackermann, Klose, Kardatzki, & Grodd, 1996) and clinical data (e.g., the observation that dysarthria occurs more often after damage to the left than to the right corticobulbar system; Urban et al., 2006).

Basal Ganglia Circuit

The activity of primary motor cortex is continuously modulated by a motor loop traversing the basal ganglia. This circuit connects frontal motor areas with these subcortical nuclei and projects back via thalamic nuclei to its site of origin (see Figure 17.2). The striatum, especially the putamen, serves as the input zone of motor (and sensory) cortical efferent projections, whereas the internal segment of the globus pallidus and the substantia nigra, pars reticulata, constitute the output nuclei of the basal ganglia, projecting to the ventrolateral thalamus. As a remarkable feature of the architecture of this circuit, the putamen targets the output zone of the basal ganglia via two routes: a direct, monosynaptic connection; and an indirect pathway passing through the external segment of the globus pallidus and the subthalamic nucleus. Increased activity of the direct striatal loop reduces inhibitory internal segment of the globus pallidus output to the thalamus and, therefore, disinhibits thalamocortical drive, leading to a facilitation of movement execution. By contrast, stimulation of the indirect striatal pathway strengthens inhibitory basal ganglia output, giving rise to a decrease of thalamocortical motor drive. The balance of this system is regulated by the release of dopamine within the striatum. Obviously, the basal ganglia circuit contributes to the modulation of motor commands issued by motor cortex neurons (Desmurget, Grafton, Vindras, Grea, & Turner, 2004). In accordance with this model, basal ganglia disorders may give rise to reduced movement range and velocity (akinesia), as in Parkinson disease, or to overshooting and uncontrollable movements (hyperkinesia), as in choreatic conditions.

These two opposing pathomechanisms of striatal dysfunctions can also be encountered at the level of the vocal tract muscles. Speech production in individuals with Parkinson's disease is characterized by hypokinetic speech movements resulting in a decrease of loudness, a breathy and monotonous voice, and imprecise consonant production; whereas patients with Huntington disease may suffer from choreatic dysarthria, which is characterized by involuntary activity of the respiratory, laryngeal, and articulatory apparatus, resulting in uncontrolled pitch and loudness variations, vocal grunts, or other signs of a disinhibited vocal tract motor system (Duffy, 2005).

Besides the motor loop delineated so far, several further parallel circuits interconnect the basal ganglia with cortical structures, among them a pathway arising within anterior cingulate cortex (ACC) and projecting to the ventral striatum (Alexander, DeLong, & Strick, 1986). ACC pertains to the so-called limbic brain and is assumed to be implicated in motivational and affective aspects of behavior (see later). It is assumed that the motor and the limbic striato-thalamo-cortical circuit crosstalk at the level of the basal ganglia (Joel & Weiner, 1994), with the consequence that motivational or affective information may interact with motor control. In this view, the prosodic modulation of speech, especially its emotional and attitudinal components, might be considered as a remnant of the limbic vocalization pathway of the mammalian brain invading the speech motor network. From this perspective, the most salient symptoms of Parkinson dysarthria (i.e., a flattened prosody and a reduced voice volume) would be interpretable as signs of impaired limbic input. Likewise, vocal overflow symptoms occurring in some basal ganglia disorders, such as the prosodic mannerisms of patients with Huntington chorea or the palilalic syllable repetitions and compulsive verbal outbursts of patients with Tourette syndrome, might be viewed as a sign of a disinhibited limbic outflow.

The basal ganglia are also known to be implicated in the *acquisition* of motor (and cognitive) skills and the formation of habits and automatic routines (Ashby, Turner, & Horvitz, 2010). Yet, their role in speech motor learning is still elusive. Experimental studies in songbirds have suggested that the avian homologue of the basal ganglia contributes to vocal learning in those species (Ackermann & Ziegler, 2013), but direct evidence for a comparable role of the striatum in humans is still lacking, and the validity of the songbird model for a better understanding of speech motor learning is limited. More recently the striatal circuits have been identified as a major target of the evolutionary changes of the FOXP2-gene during mammalian evolution, with the interpretation that changes in FOXP2 in humans have contributed to the adaptations in corticobasal ganglia circuits that are deemed necessary for the emergence of vocal learning (Reimers-Kipping, Hevers, Pääbo, & Enard, 2011).

Human brain imaging studies of putaminal activity in L1- vs. L2-articulation in adult bilinguals yielded conflicting results regarding the implication of the putamen in the two conditions of early versus later speech acquisition (cf. Klein, Milner, Zatorre, Meyer, & Evans, 1995 vs. Frenck-Mestre, Anton, Roth, Vaid, & Viallet, 2005), and there is also limited clinical evidence of a striatal contribution to speech motor acquisition in infants. Hence, the role of the striatum in speech motor learning is a field of future research.

Cerebellar Circuit

Figure 17.2 also includes a second circuit operating in parallel to the descending corticobulbar pathway (i.e., a loop connecting motor cortex with the cerebellum). The cerebellum receives input from the frontal lobes (besides parietal and temporal input) via pontine nuclei, and projects back via the ventrolateral thalamus to, among other things, primary motor cortex (Schmahmann, 1997). A widely appreciated theory assumes that the cerebellum incorporates an "internal model" simulating cerebral cortical movement control mechanisms (Ramnani, 2006). More specifically, the motor cortex issues movement commands to the spinal and bulbar motor nuclei and, in addition, sends "efference copies" of these control signals to the cerebellar cortex. Ultimately, the cerebellum "learns" to predict the sensory consequences of these motor commands ("corollary discharge") and conveys copies of the predicted motor effects, via the deep cerebellar nuclei and the thalamus, back to the frontal lobe, thereby modulating the activity of primary motor cortex. Cerebellar output may also more directly impact motor commands at the spinal and bulbar level via efferent projections to the red nucleus. Within this theoretical scheme, the cerebellar loop appears to act as a feedforward-feedback control device that continuously updates and adapts cerebral cortical motor information and, consequently, supports distinct motor learning processes (Doyon & Benali, 2005). These concepts have also been absorbed in theories of speech motor control. According to a model proposed by Guenther, Ghosh, and Tourville (2006), for instance, cerebellar afferent input from auditory and somatosensory areas of the temporal and parietal lobes also contributes to the learning and maintenance of cerebellar feedforward commands to the motor cortex (cf. "Perception-Production Interactions and their Neural Bases" by Tourville, Peeva, and Guenther).

Auditory-perceptual evaluation of the dysarthric impairments in cerebellar disorders, concomitant with instrumental studies, provided a first approach to delineate the distinct contribution of the cerebellum to speech production. Patients with hereditary or acquired syndromes of cerebellar ataxia often display a slowed speech tempo; sometimes a scanning rhythm; irregular articulatory undershoot and overshoot; varying abnormalities of voice quality; and sometimes fluctuating pitch or loudness ("ataxic dysarthria.") Based on these observations it has been suggested that patients with ataxia have problems of regulating the interplay of their respiratory muscles during speech breathing, tuning the proper tension of their vocal folds for the orderly control of pitch and voice quality, precisely adjusting the direction and amplitude of vowel and consonant articulations, and molding their speech movements into a smooth sequence of syllables with a natural rhythm (Ackermann & Hertrich, 2000). Characteristically, these patients are disproportionately impaired in tasks requiring them to repeat a given syllable (e.g., /pa/, /ta/ or /ka/) as fast as possible (diadochokinesis), suggesting that they have a particular problem in adapting their vocal tract apparatus to the specific motor requirements of these quasi-speech tasks (Ziegler & Wessel, 1996). Another task that is sensitive to cerebellar involvement is *sustained vowel production*, which often reveals voice tremor and an inability to maintain a given laryngeal posture over a period of several seconds, possibly caused by impaired feedback control mechanisms (Ackermann & Ziegler, 1991).

Further evidence for a role of the cerebellum in speaking comes from imaging studies. The cerebellum "lights up" in practically all functional magnetic resonance imaging (fMRI) paradigms focusing on the motor aspects of spoken language production, and, most remarkably, its activation is sensitive to phonetic factors, such as utterance length (Shuster & Lemieux, 2005), segmental complexity (Bohland & Guenther, 2006; Riecker, Brendel, Ziegler, Erb, & Ackermann, 2008), or the interaction of syllable frequency and complexity (Riecker et al., 2008). Imaging studies point to a multifaceted role of the cerebellum in speech motor control, because hemodynamic activation is not restricted to overt speech, but emerges also during covert speaking. Furthermore, the cerebellum appears to engage both in "preparatory" activities preceding the onset of speaking and in the subsequent execution of movement sequences (Ackermann, 2008). Finally, some investigations point at functional lateralization effects toward the right cerebellar hemisphere (e.g., Brendel et al., 2011), an observation compatible with clinical findings of a slight preponderance of dysarthrias after right versus left cerebellar infarction (Urban et al., 2003). Given the crossed course of cortico-ponto-cerebellar projections, the assumed (relative) right-lateralization of cerebellar speech motor functions nicely corresponds with the reported slight overbalance of dysarthria in patients with infarctions of the left cerebral hemisphere (Urban et al., 2006).

The Neural Basis of Intrinsic Vocalizations: The Limbic Vocalization System

Similar to humans, nonhuman primates and other mammals use the vocal channel to communicate with their conspecifics. As one of their key properties, the vocalizations of monkeys and apes have a largely inborn acoustic structure and, furthermore, display a rather strict relationship to external or internal triggers, with very little experience-related plasticity and a low capacity of imitation learning (Fitch, 2010). Primate vocalizations have often been considered the behavioral analogues to the intrinsic vocalizations of humans, such as laughing, crying, or pain-related moaning, because these human vocal behaviors are also contingent on internal states or on external stimuli and are characterized by a relatively stereotypic pattern.

Primate Studies

Knowledge about the primate vocalization system is based predominantly on ablation and stimulation studies conducted in squirrel monkeys and macaques, or, more recently, from telemetric single-unit recording studies in freely moving animals (Jürgens, 2002; Hage & Jürgens, 2006). Because of its roots within rostral mesiofrontal cortex, the cerebral correlates of acoustic communication in subhuman primates have been termed the *limbic vocalization system* (see Figure 17.1). This network extends from ACC, a mesiofrontal cortical area surrounding the rostral pole of the corpus callosum, to the periaqueductal grey (PAG) and the adjacent tegmental area in the midbrain, and further to a pool of vocalization-related neurones (VOC) in the ventrolateral pons, from where it then projects onto the cranial motor nuclei to trigger vocalization-related muscular activity (see Figure 17.1).

Electrical stimulation of ACC in squirrel monkeys was found to elicit species-specific calls, whereas bilateral ablation of this region led to a decrease in spontaneous vocalizations, the acoustic

structure of calls being unaltered. Likewise, electrical stimulation of neurons in the PAG and adjacent tegmentum has also elicited natural, species-specific calls in squirrel monkeys, and lesions to this region are known to abolish spontaneous vocal behavior in monkeys and other mammals (for a review see Jürgens, 1994). More recently, Hage and Jürgens (2006) used a telemetric single-unit recording technique to measure vocalization-related neuronal activity in freely moving squirrel monkeys. They detected a pool of neurons in the ventrolateral pons whose activity was strongly correlated with the vocal calls of these animals. This network, termed VOC, is considered as a pattern generator that coordinates the firing of neurons in the trigeminal and facial nuclei and the nucleus ambiguus during specific calls (see Figure 17.1).

These findings suggest that anterior mesiofrontal cortex has a role in mediating internally generated primate vocalizations. ACC information is sent to midbrain PAG, which acts as an interface linking different vocalization-eliciting external and internal stimuli from sensory and limbic structures with the motor-coordinating mechanism in the brainstem. The motor coordination of the subsystems involved in vocalization is bound to a pontine pattern generator, VOC, which sends call-specific information to the brainstem motor nuclei.

The separation of this primate vocalization pathway from the neocortical speech motor network described previously explains the absence of vocal learning capacities in monkeys and apes and the restricted and strongly stimulus-contingent vocal repertoire of these animals (Fitch, 2000). Yet, there are a few single reports indicating that the functional segregation of the limbic vocalization pathway from neocortical volitional input is not entirely unbridgeable. Hihara, Yamada, Iriki, and Okanoya, (2003), for example, found that during the course of a tool-use training lasting for only a few days a Japanese macaque monkey started emitting different call types to demand either food or a tool. The authors interpreted their finding as an example of experience-induced vocal plasticity in macaques and developed a model of how in these animals motor cortex may gradually take over direct control of the mesencephalic vocal pattern generator.

Clinical Data

Only limited clinical data on the role of the limbic vocalization system of subhuman primates in acoustic communication of humans are available so far. ACC is assumed to engage in the initiation of laughter, because dysfunctions of this region may cause "gelastic epilepsy" (i.e., seizures associated with uncontrolled outbursts of laughter; Wild, Rodden, Grodd, & Ruch, 2003). Apart from its engagement in nonverbal vocal behavior, this mesiofrontal region appears to be related to motivational or activation aspects of spoken language production, which is in line with the more general view that it plays a role in self-generated action (Passingham, Bengtsson, & Lau, 2010). Bilateral lesions of the medial wall of the frontal lobes, including the ACC and the supplementary motor area (SMA), are known to result in a syndrome termed *akinetic mutism*, which is characterized by speechlessness or extreme poverty of speech, in the absence of significant paresis of the vocal tract muscles. Mesiofrontal lesions of the dominant hemisphere may cause sparsity of spontaneous utterances and halting or dysfluent speech, often associated with hypophonia and a monotonous intonation (Ackermann & Ziegler, 2010). Hypophonia and monotony also characterize the stage of recovery from complete akinetic mutism (Freedman, Alexander, & Naeser, 1984). This demonstrates that in humans rostral mesiofrontal cortex has a modulating influence on the speech motor system, which may be exerted via reciprocal ACC connections with the SMA or via mesiofrontal projections to the ventral striatum (Sutton & Jürgens, 1988; see Figure 17.1). The motor patterns of intrinsic vocalizations are not generated at the cortical level, because babies who are born without forebrain structures are still able to produce cries in response to pain. Instead, the structured neural activity associated with these innate vocalizations in humans, like in other mammals, is probably generated at the level of the mesencephalon. However, there is some clinical evidence that the mesencephalic structures pertaining to the primate limbic vocalization pathway (i.e., PAG and the adjacent tegmentum) are implicated in speaking, because damage to this midbrain region, similar to medial frontal cortical pathology, also cause a condition of akinetic mutism (Esposito, Demeurisse, Alberti, & Fabbro, 1999).

There is probably crosstalk between a limbic basal ganglia circuit with the striatal motor loop described previously, which may provide a gateway for limbic (i.e., activating, affective, and motivational) information to invade the neocortical speech motor system. The role of the basal ganglia as an interface between limbic and neocortical motor networks might explain why striatal dysfunction in Parkinson disease causes symptoms similar to those described in patients recovering from a mesiofrontal state of akinetic mutism (i.e., hypophonia, monotonous speech, and poverty of speech production).

Emotional Expressive Versus Voluntary Vocal Tract Movements

Clinical evidence for a largely separate course of emotional and volitional motor information in the human brain comes from observations of "voluntary-automatic movement dissociations" in patients with lesions to supranuclear structures. A striking dissociation occurs in patients with bilateral lesions to primary motor cortex or the descending pyramidal tract fibers of the facial-oral-laryngeal system (Foix-Chavany-Marie syndrome, pseudobulbar palsy), who present with almost complete paresis of the vocal tract muscles during voluntary motor activities and are therefore unable to produce voiced phonation or significant mouth movements during speaking. These patients often show normal or even exaggerated mimic movements during laughter or crying and are able to produce voiced phonation under these conditions (Ackermann & Ziegler, 2010).

Milder variants of this dissociation are known as volitional or emotional facial paresis, respectively. Unilateral lesions of face motor cortex or its projections to the facial nucleus in the brainstem regularly cause weakness of the contralateral lower face muscles, which is seen during speaking or in lip spreading on command ("show your teeth.") Remarkably, these patients may often show completely symmetrical mouth movements during spontaneous smiling or laughter ("volitional facial paresis.") Conversely, in a less frequent clinical condition patients are able to symmetrically abduct both corners of their mouth on command or during speaking, but show asymmetric lip movements during spontaneous smiling. This latter syndrome ("emotional facial paresis") has been observed after unilateral thalamic or putaminal lesions (Hopf, Müller-Forell, & Hopf, 1992). Taken together these clinical observations point to the existence of two separate pathways controlling vocal tract muscle activity: one in voluntary motor actions, such as speaking, the other one in emotionally expressive movements.

The Mesiofrontal "Go"-System

Mesial premotor cortex (BA 6), a region termed *supplementary motor area*, was mentioned previously as a structure participating in the transfer of motivational drive to the speech motor system. Unlike ACC, SMA regarding its cytoarchitectonic composition is part of the neocortex and resembles other motor cortical structures by its somatotopic organization (Roland & Zilles, 1996). Because it receives input from ACC and sends projections to primary motor cortex and to the motor components of the striatum, the SMA is in a position to mediate between limbic structures generating "internal drive" and the components of the motor execution system. Based on lesion and electrical stimulation studies in humans and monkeys SMA has been assumed to act as a neural "go-system" (cf. Ackermann & Ziegler, 2010). The metaphor of an SMA "starting mechanism" was inferred from clinical observations of patients with focal lesions to the SMA who, after bilateral damage, presented with akinetic mutism. Patients with this syndrome do not speak, although their vocal tract muscles are not paretic. After one-sided (left) SMA lesions, a pattern resembling "transcortical motor aphasia" may result, which is characterized by a reduced spontaneous verbal output, halting and hypophonic speech with little prosodic variation, sometimes stuttering-like symptoms, but otherwise a retained linguistic structure (Ziegler, Kilian, & Deger, 1997; Ackermann, Hertrich, Ziegler, Bitzer, & Bien, 1996). Interference of SMA lesions with the orderly timing of the syllabic-sequential aspects of speaking was interpreted as neurobiological evidence for the frame-content theory of speech production postulated by MacNeilage (1998). According to this theory, the SMA generates the basic "frame" of an utterance consisting of a chain of syllabic movement cycles, which is then filled by the segmental "content" generated by inferolateral premotor cortex (discussed next).

Hemodynamic SMA activation has also been found in almost all functional imaging studies of spoken language production. The SMA was classified as a part of a "preparatory loop" of speech motor control, because its activity was found to precede the activity of motor cortex and the basal ganglia (Riecker et al., 2005; Brendel et al., 2010). This finding is compatible with theories characterizing the SMA as a "supramotor" region that incorporates a starting mechanism for speaking.

Neural Basis of Speech Motor Planning

The neural signals generated by primary motor cortex in concert with striatal and cerebellar motor loops are assumed to originate in "higher" motor planning centers. As already mentioned, the speech motor execution apparatus probably undergoes significant structural and functional changes during the long-lasting process of speech acquisition (Smith,

2010) and, therefore, must be expected to accumulate implicit "knowledge" about the organization of vocal tract movements subserving speech production. On the top of this, the generation of proper motor commands for speaking is considered to depend on phonetically structured information specifying which movement sequences have to be instantiated for the production of a given string of phonemes or syllables. A "phonetic encoding component" providing such information is part of the speech production model proposed by Levelt et al. (1999).

Apraxia of Speech as a Clinical Model of Impaired Phonetic Planning

Clinical evidence for the idea of a hierarchical organization of the speech motor system, specifically the existence of a phonetic planning center, is based on the observation of severe and persisting motor speech impairments after lesions of the anterior perisylvian or intrasylvian cortex of the left hemisphere. The perceptual features of this syndrome, termed *apraxia of speech*, are not compatible with any of the "elementary" neuromotor pathomechanisms mentioned previously (i.e., paresis, akinesia or dyskinesia, or ataxia). Instead, some of the symptoms of apraxia of speech are rather reminiscent of the apraxic impairment seen in patients with limb apraxia, for instance the observation of an entirely undisturbed performance under certain conditions, the variability of aberrant motor behavior, or the occurrence of searching behavior and of self-corrections after off-target attempts (Ziegler, 2008). Moreover, apraxia of speech is definitely a syndrome of the dominant hemisphere. Hence, a clear-cut taxonomic distinction is usually drawn between the dysarthric syndromes bound to disorders of the *motor-executive* apparatus of speaking and apraxia of speech as a *motor planning* impairment (Ziegler, 2008). The finding that apraxic errors are influenced by syllable frequency (Aichert & Ziegler, 2004; Staiger & Ziegler, 2008) is compatible with expectations derived from the phonetic encoding model proposed by Levelt et al. (1999), because in this model a speaker's access to the speech motor plan for a syllable depends on the frequency of occurrence of this syllable in the speaker's language (cf. Cholin, 2008).

The intrahemispheric location of lesions causing apraxia of speech is still a matter of extensive debate. Originally, Broca (1861) assigned the seat of the "faculty of articulate language" to the posterior third of the inferior frontal gyrus (IFG), corresponding more or less to the opercular part of that convolution (BA 44). Still today, several researchers consider this region the structural correlate of acquired apraxia of speech (Hillis et al., 2004). However, several other lesion sites within rostral left-hemisphere perisylvian and subsylvian regions have been associated with this syndrome, among them the anterior portion of left insular cortex (Dronkers, 1996) or the lower left precentral and premotor cortex (BA4, BA6), including the respective underlying white matter (for reviews see Ziegler, 2008; Ackermann & Riecker, 2010). On a larger scale, it is plausible to assume that speech motor planning functions are distributed over a rather extended left-hemisphere cortical area rostral to and beneath the motor representation area of the vocal tract muscles (Figure 17.3).

Remarkably, a homologue of Broca area, engaged in the control of orofacial actions, has been detected in macaques (Petrides, Cadoret, & Mackey, 2005). Experimental ablation of this cortical area in monkeys does, however, not interfere with acoustic communication in these species (Ackermann & Ziegler, 2010), indicating that in humans Broca area pertains to an evolutionary novel circuitry specialized for spoken language production.

Functional Imaging Studies of the Speech Planning Network

More recently, various attempts have been made to identify speech motor planning areas by means of functional imaging techniques. As a significant problem common to these approaches, the activation paradigm must allow for a strict delineation of the planning aspects of speech production. For instance, several studies tried to delineate the regions of increased brain activation associated with the length (in numbers of syllables) or the complexity (presence of consonant clusters) of verbal stimuli (Shuster & Lemieux, 2005; Bohland & Guenther, 2006), but it is unclear if these stimulus variables are particularly sensitive to motor planning processes. Moreover, length and complexity may also influence activation of many other motor regions not specifically devoted to speech planning, and modulate the activity of structures involved in phonological encoding (Papoutsi et al., 2009). Hence, these studies revealed, not unexpectedly, an extended network of speech-related structures, comprising mesiofrontal cortex (SMA, ACC), inferior motor and sensory cortices of both hemispheres, left posterior IFG, left anterior insula, the basal ganglia, cerebellum, and thalamus (Shuster & Lemieux, 2005; Bohland & Guenther, 2006), but failed to specify those areas that are particularly engaged in phonetic planning.

To disentangle the contributions of these structures to speaking within the time domain of hemodynamic activation, Riecker et al. (2005) performed a combined functional connectivity and time series analysis of fMRI activation during syllable repetition. These authors identified a preparatory network consisting of left SMA, left anterior insula, left IFG, and superior parts of the cerebellum, whose responses preceded activation of a motor execution network comprising the motor cortex, basal ganglia, and cerebellum. Conceivably, the structures activated earlier are more engaged in planning and initiation than those activated later. Hence, the findings of Riecker et al. (2005) are compatible with the clinical evidence of a speech motor planning role of the left anterior insula and left posterior IFG (see Figure 17.3), although as a possible shortcoming this study was based on a syllable repetition task rather than on speaking.

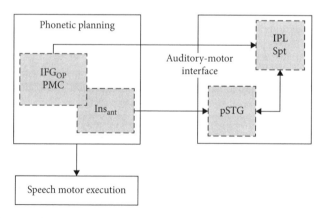

Figure 17.3 A simplified outline of the dorsal stream (left hemisphere). IFG$_{op}$ = inferior frontal gyrus, pars opecularis (BA 44); IPL = inferior parietal lobe; INS$_{ant}$ = anterior insular cortex; PMC = premotor cortex; pSTG = (left) posterior superior temporal gyrus; Spt = sylvian parietal-temporal region. For details see text.

Other approaches were motivated by model-based considerations regarding the factors that might influence speech motor planning more specifically. According to Levelt's theory, phonetic planning is sensitive to the frequency of occurrence of sublexical units, especially syllables (Cholin, 2008; Levelt et al., 1999). Therefore, the fMRI-studies of pseudoword reading by Brendel et al. (2011) and Riecker et al. (2008) independently varied syllable frequency and the complexity of syllable onsets in their test materials. No region was detected that showed a main effect of syllable frequency alone, but Riecker et al. (2008) found that functional connectivity between Broca area and the left anterior insula was significantly enhanced by a combination of low syllable frequency with high onset complexity. Papoutsi et al. (2009) later focused on the role of left IFG in phonetic encoding by systematically varying phoneme and biphoneme frequencies in their two- and four-syllabic pseudowords. They found enhanced hemodynamic activity in the ventral part of the pars opercularis of left inferior frontal cortex for stimuli with low phoneme and biphoneme frequencies and suggested that this region is specifically engaged in phonetic planning processes. Ackermann & Riecker (2010), who reviewed studies on the role of the insula in speech, identified a small area at the junction between anterior insular and opercular cortex to be sensitive to the phonetic structure of utterances in speaking and suggested a crucial role of this zone in speech motor planning.

More recently, Kellmeyer et al. (2010) sought a functional imaging approach based on a model derived from clinical data (Ziegler, 2005, 2009, 2010). Within this framework, the phonetic planning demands of words of differing lengths and complexities were simulated by a nonlinear regression model based on phonetic gestures and on a stepwise hierarchical integration of gestures into syllable constituents, syllables, and metrical feet. As a measure of the amount of phonetic planning required for the production of a word, articulatory accuracy of a set of words across a large number of speech samples from apraxic speakers was used. When this planning accuracy factor was included as a parametric modulator of BOLD signal changes in normal subjects who produced these words in a repetition setting, a network was found that comprised left posterior IFG, left anterior insular cortex, and the right cerebellum, in addition to superior temporal structures in the left and right hemisphere. This approach is unique in that it considers motor planning as a hierarchically nested process of combining gestural motor primitives to increasingly more complex motor patterns for words, up to the level of metrical properties. Our finding that left IFG activity is responsive to the tree-like nonlinear structure of the proposed model fits with the more general view that Broca area is engaged in hierarchical processing mechanisms (Friederici, 2009).

Neural Bases of Phonological Processing in Spoken Language Production

How can we identify the brain structures engaged in the *phonological* aspects of speaking? The answer to this question depends on how the encoding of the sound structure of language is conceptualized in operational terms. As a common denominator of most theories of speech production, phonological processes and representations are considered "more abstract" entities than the processes and representations of the motor planning and execution stages, but there is no generally accepted understanding of abstractness in this context. Usually, abstractness refers to the degree of detail of the motor (or sensory) information that is specified (e.g. Goldrick & Rapp, 2007), and to the property of phonological representations to be equally accessible to motor and perceptual processing (cf. "Phonological Processing: The Retrieval and Encoding of Word Form Information in Speech Production" by Goldrick).

The available neuroanatomic evidence points at a rather circumscribed network of the left hemisphere that can be considered to integrate the motor with the sensory domains involved in speaking. This system comprises anterior perisylvian regions, including the posterior part of left IFG and adjacent ventral premotor cortex, lateral temporal cortex, and inferior-parietal areas, encompassing the temporoparietal junction, and a complex network of bidirectional connections between these areas (see Figure 17.3). The functioning of this fronto-temporo-parietal circuitry has been a core issue of aphasiology since Wernicke's times and has attracted increased attention after the implementation of diffusion tensor imaging tractography (for a review see Catani & Mesulam, 2008). To date there is a gross discrepancy between the fine degree to which phonological processing mechanisms are dissected in cognitive-neurolinguistic models of aphasic phonological impairment and the lacking of appropriate neuroanatomic evidence supporting these models. Moreover, the results obtained from functional imaging studies of phonological processing in normal populations, which often use rather artificial metaphonological paradigms, offer still another perspective on the phonological component of speaking that cannot easily be conciliated with either the cognitive neurolinguistic models or the lesion analyses of aphasic phonological impairment.

Phonemic Paraphasia as a Clinical Model of Phonological Impairment

Current knowledge about the neural basis of the phonological mechanisms involved in speaking largely stems from lesion analyses of patients with aphasia who produce phonemic errors (i.e., substitute one phoneme of a word by another one, omit or add phonemes, or produce "abstruse" neologisms with no recognizable similarity to a target word). Typically, the paraphasic utterances of nonapraxic patients with aphasia are produced in a fluent manner, are well-articulated, and have a normal prosodic modulation. These characteristics distinguish them from the nonfluent, phonetically distorted output of apraxic speakers. Hence, phonemic paraphasias are assumed to result from linguistic pathomechanisms, representing some sort of misselection or misordering of phonemes or reflecting a compromised ability to maintain phonemic representations in a short-term buffer (Kohn, 1989; Schwartz, Saffran, Bloch, & Dell, 1994; Schwartz, Wilshire, Gagnon, & Polansky, 2004). Phonemic errors are among the most prevalent symptoms of aphasia and arise in almost all aphasia syndromes (Blumstein, 1973). In clinical lesion studies they are typically referred to as a unitary category reflecting a dysfunction at some weakly specified phonological processing level, whereas cognitive neurolinguistic theories are more differentiated regarding the mechanisms underlying these symptoms (Goldrick & Rapp, 2007).

CONDUCTION APHASIA

Historically, phonological impairment is considered the core deficit of *conduction aphasia*, a syndrome characterized by paraphasic word repetition in the presence of uncompromised word comprehension (Bernal & Ardila, 2009). Generally, two variants of this constellation are distinguished (the "repetition-type" mentioned previously and a "reproduction-type") giving rise to phonemic paraphasias in all modalities of spoken word production, concomitant with relatively fluent speaking and preserved speech comprehension (Shallice & Warrington, 1977).

From a neuroanatomic perspective, conduction aphasia has long been considered the prototype of a disconnection syndrome. Within the framework of the Wernicke-Lichtheim model, tracing back to the 1880s, impaired word repetition was assumed to arise from the interruption of the frontotemporal fiber tracts that connect Wernicke area, involved in the perception of spoken language, with Broca area, engaged in the generation of the corresponding motor output. The disconnection model, which was primarily based on case studies of repetition conduction aphasia, yielded a sustained interest in the fasciculus arcuatus, a fiber bundle that has its caudal roots in the posterior superior temporal gyrus (STG), courses around the posterior end of the sylvian fissure, and then targets inferior frontal cortical areas (Catani & Mesulam, 2008). It was hypothesized that damage to this tract impedes the transfer of auditory information from temporal regions to the motor areas of the frontal lobe of the language-dominant hemisphere. However, the role of the fasciculus arcuatus in conduction aphasia was questioned by reports of patients who presented with fluent phonemic paraphasia and preserved speech comprehension after lesions restricted to cortical (i.e., superior-temporal) inferior-parietal, and insular areas of the left hemisphere (Anderson et al., 1999). Geschwind (1965) had already assigned left inferior-parietal cortex, especially the supramarginal gyrus, a role in his disconnection account of conduction aphasia, considering this cortical area a relay station of the temporofrontal fiber tracts. He thus principally acknowledged that disconnection syndromes are not exclusively confined to white matter lesions, but may also result from damage to association areas of the cortex (Geschwind, 1965). Yet, other authors questioned this model and voted for a distinctive role of left posterior STG and inferior-parietal cortex in either phoneme assemblage or the conveyance of phonological information from the (temporal) perceptual to the (frontal) motor domain (Jacquemot, Dupoux, & Bachoud-Levi, 2007; Damasio & Damasio, 1980).

In cognitive-neurolinguistic terms, the phonological impairment discussed in the context of conduction aphasia has a postlexical locus. Patients with postlexical deficits of speech production typically show a length effect on word accuracy, and their verbal behavior indicates that they have successfully accessed a word representation, but must struggle for its realization (e.g., through self-corrections or the characteristic *conduite d'approche* behavior; Shallice, Rumiati, & Zadini, 2000).

IMPAIRED LEXICAL PHONOLOGY

A different variant of aphasic phonological impairment may occur at the level of lexical phonology, especially during retrieval of word form information from a conjectured lexicon or after corruption of stored lexical entries. Under these conditions patients may, despite a preserved semantic knowledge, be unable to retrieve the name of an object or misselect words during a naming task, typically with strong lexical effects (e.g., an impact of word frequency or age of acquisition; Howard & Gatehouse, 2006; Goldrick & Rapp, 2007).[1] Because impairments exclusively restricted to the (postsemantic) lexical component of spoken language production are rare, lesion data have provided only sparse insights into the anatomic correlates of stored word form information. Patients with lexical disorders usually suffer from lesions of the left temporal lobe (Lorenz & Ziegler, 2009). More specifically, damage to posterior parts of the inferior or middle temporal gyrus appears to be the critical correlate of impaired word retrieval in object naming tasks (Foundas, Daniels, & Vasterling, 1998). Because one of the debates in cognitive neurolinguistics deals with the question if lexical and postlexical processing stages need to be distinguished (see Goldrick & Rapp, 2007), it is important to evaluate the neuroanatomic basis of this distinction more systematically by lesion analyses with carefully controlled patient groups.

Frontotemporoparietal Connectivity and the Phonology of Speech Production: Functional Imaging

CONNECTIVITY OF PERISYLVIAN LANGUAGE REGIONS

The advent of diffusion-based methods for the in vivo imaging of effective fiber-tract connectivity (diffusion tensor imaging tractography) stimulated a series of studies addressing the architecture of the perisylvian language network, revealing a rather complex pattern of frontal-temporal-parietal pathways (Foundas et al., 1998). This network predominantly comprises segments of the superior longitudinal fascicle (SLF), a large intrahemispheric fiber tract connecting lateral frontal cortex with parietotemporal association areas (Makris et al., 2005). The arcuate fascicle mentioned in the preceding section represents one of the components of SLF. According to Catani, Jones, and Ffytche (2005) it comprises the "classical" direct pathway extending from posterior STG to Broca area and an indirect pathway connecting Broca territory with the inferior parietal lobe (anterior segment) and the inferior-parietal area with posterior STG (posterior segment; see Figure 17.3). The observation of an indirect pathway passing through the inferior-parietal lobe is consistent with Geschwind's idea of a temporofrontal relay station located within the supramarginal gyrus (see preceding section). Later studies by Frey, Campbell, Pike, and Petrides (2008) and Saur et al. (2008) modified this view and showed that the pars opercularis of Broca area (BA 44) is associated with the supramarginal gyrus (via the third segment of the SLF), whereas the more anterior (i.e., triangular) part of Broca area (BA 45) is connected with anterior parts of the STG via fibers running through the extreme capsule. According to these studies, the arcuate fascicle projects from posterior STG to dorsal premotor cortex (BA 6). A very similar connectivity was found in macaque monkeys, suggesting that this structure constitutes a precursor to the human perisylvian language system (Petrides & Pandya, 2009). However, the arcuate fascicle is much smaller or even absent in chimpanzees and macaques and, furthermore, the segments of the fasciculus arcuatus differ in their dominant temporal and parietal termination sites between monkeys and humans (Rilling et al., 2008). These observations point at a further differentiation and a specific contribution of this tract to language processing in humans. The linguistic role of the SFA is also underscored by the finding of a left-sided asymmetry of several SLF segments in humans (Nucifora, Verma, Melhem, Gur, & Gur, 2005).

FUNCTIONAL ROLE OF THE DORSAL STREAM

Hickok & Poeppel (2004) delineated a functional model of STG connectivity that distinguishes between a ventral stream, extending from auditory association cortex to posterior-inferior temporal areas, and a dorsal stream projecting from the same STG region to the temporoparietal junction adjacent to the caudal extension of the sylvian fissure (termed Spt [sylvian parietal-temporal]) and further to ventrolateral regions of the frontal lobe. The ventral stream is assumed to subserve the semantic interpretation of the incoming acoustic signal, whereas its dorsal cognate, which corresponds largely to the indirect temporofrontal pathway described by Catani et al. (2005), maps speech sounds onto corresponding motor representations. In particular, the temporoparietal area Spt is viewed as an auditory-motor interface engaged in the transformation of auditory data structures into a speech motor space, very similar to the idea of an auditory-based reference frame for speech movements proposed by Guenther, Hampson, and Johnson (1998). Warren, Wise, and Warren (2005) characterized the posterior-superior temporal plane as a region in which incoming speech sounds are mapped onto stored auditory templates, which can then be transformed, within the dorsal stream system, into an acoustically constrained sequence of motor representations.

Most of the functional imaging work addressing the perisylvian circuitry of the left hemisphere centers around speech comprehension paradigms and demonstrates that anterior motor areas contribute to the perceptual analysis of spoken language (Pulvermüller & Fadiga, 2010). These data fuelled discussions about the motor theory of speech perception and the existence of a mirror neuron system (Lotto, Hickok, & Holt, 2009). A further part of the published connectivity work was based on the word-repetition paradigm as a prototypical task that combines auditory input processing with motor output generation (e.g., Saur et al., 2008; Peschke, Ziegler, Kappes, & Baumgaertner, 2009). With these foci, the studies reviewed so far fail to resolve the question of how much the posterior components of the dorsal stream contribute to speech production under more natural conditions (i.e., in the absence of auditory input). An engagement of left parietal and temporal cortex in speaking is evidenced by lesion studies of patients who produce paraphasic speech, but are relatively unimpaired in auditory perception. More recently, however, the implication of posterior components of the dorsal stream in speaking has also been substantiated by several functional imaging studies. For instance, area Spt and the superior temporal sulcus of the left hemisphere have been shown to be activated during both the perception and the production of speech, suggesting that the auditory-motor integration processes bound to these regions indeed play a role in the generation of spoken words (Hickok, Okada, & Serences, 2009; Okada & Hickok, 2006; Hickok & Poeppel, 2007).

On the whole, the dorsal stream appears to mediate in a bidirectional manner between auditory and articulatory representations of speech and may therefore be conceived of as establishing the "parity" between auditory and articulatory representations and to constitute a neural substrate of abstract (i.e., supramodal) phonological processing. By virtue of its abstractness, the information evolving in the dorsal stream, particularly in its temporoparietal cortical relay station, is accessible to other cognitive and linguistic processes, such as verbal working memory or reading and writing, and more importantly to syntactic binding processes in inferior frontal cortex.

FUNCTIONAL ROLE OF THE VENTRAL STREAM

As concerns the interface between semantics and phonology in speaking, lesion studies have suggested a role of the ventral-most parts of the left posterior temporal lobe (discussed previously). This clinical model was corroborated by a recent functional imaging study in which left inferior temporal cortex concomitant with the left temporoparietal junction were activated during a naming task involving increased demands on lexical selection, suggesting that these two areas operate in conjunction during the retrieval and encoding of phonological information (Wilson, Isenberg, & Hickok, 2009). In accordance with these data and with the reported clinical evidence, the ventral stream component of the model proposed by Hickok & Poeppel (2004) was conceptualized as a system that maps auditory information, derived from superior temporal cortex, onto word meaning in the middle and inferior temporal lobe. This model was refined considerably by more recent tractography studies. For instance, the study by Saur et al. (2008), which was based on a listening paradigm (meaningful speech vs. meaningless pseudospeech), identified left middle and inferior temporal cortex as the posterior termination and left ventrolateral prefrontal cortex (BA 47 and BA 45) as the anterior endpoint of a fiber tract running through the extreme capsule. Conceptual and executive aspects of semantic processing and syntactic information may interact by way of this system with the lexical representations generated in the left temporal lobe.

Conclusions

The evidence reviewed in this chapter supports the view of a coherent system interlacing the phonological network implicated in speaking with the central motor system controlling articulation. A pivotal role in this system is played by the left inferior-frontal area, which is dedicated to the planning of speech movement sequences for syllables and words. This area constitutes the front end of an auditory-motor integration network (dorsal stream) and, at the same time, provides the input to the speech motor execution system (see Figure 17.3). Within this gross architecture, multiple interactions between subsystems take place. First, the phonetic planning center in the left posterior IFG and ventral-premotor area is in close proximity to and strongly interconnected with the vocal tract muscle representations in the left motor strip. Likewise, the cerebellum obviously houses speech planning and execution centers in close proximity. The functional interplay between these structures is still poorly understood.

Second, the speech motor pathways are modulated by information from limbic structures via SMA and the basal ganglia, and they also receive direct auditory and somatosensory feedback from temporal and parietal cortex to the cerebellum and the striatum. Through these interconnections, speech movement control is influenced by the speaker's internal emotional and motivational state and by the sensory consequences of his or her speech motor activity. Third, the higher speech motor centers in the left anterior perisylvian region interact with auditory regions in superior-temporal cortex and with inferior-parietal regions specialized for multimodal perceptuomotor integration processes, thereby incorporating the "common currency" of perception and action in speech. The information processed in the dorsal stream system appears sufficiently abstract to interact, along the course of the ventral stream, with semantic and morphosyntactic information during the production of spoken language.

Note

1. The "dual-origin" theory of phonemic paraphasia sketched here is not generally accepted. Connectionist models of spoken language production claim that the phoneme errors of patients with aphasia can be explained by a single lexical origin account (e.g., Schwartz et al., 2004).

References

Ackermann, H. (2008). Cerebellar contributions to speech production and speech perception: Psycholinguistic and neurobiological perspectives. *Trends in Neurosciences, 31*, 265–272.

Ackermann, H., & Hertrich, I. (2000). The contribution of the cerebellum to speech processing. *Journal of Neurolinguistics, 13*, 95–116.

Ackermann, H., Hertrich, I., Ziegler, W., Bitzer, M., & Bien, S. (1996). Acquired dysfluencies following infarction of the left mesiofrontal cortex. *Aphasiology, 10*, 409–417.

Ackermann, H., & Riecker, A. (2010). The contribution(s) of the insula to speech production: A review of the clinical and functional imaging literature. *Brain Structure & Function, 214*, 419–433.

Ackermann, H., & Ziegler, W. (1991). Cerebellar voice tremor: An acoustic analysis. *Journal of Neurology, Neurosurgery, and Psychiatry, 54*, 74–76.

Ackermann, H., & Ziegler, W. (2013). A birdsong perspective on human speech. In J. J. Bolhuis & M. Everaert (Eds.), *Birdsong, speech, and language. Converging views* (pp. 331–352). Boston, MA: MIT Press.

Ackermann, H., & Ziegler, W. (2010). Brain mechanisms underlying speech. In W. J. Hardcastle, J. Laver, & F. E. Gibbon (Eds.), *The handbook of phonetic sciences* (2nd ed., pp. 202–250). New York: Wiley-Blackwell.

Aichert, I., & Ziegler, W. (2004). Syllable frequency and syllable structure in apraxia of speech. *Brain and Language, 88*, 148–159

Alexander, G. E., DeLong, M. R., & Strick, P. L. (1986). Parallel organization of functionally segregated circuits linking basal ganglia and cortex. *Annual Review of Neuroscience, 9*, 357–381.

Anderson, J. M., Gilmore, R., Roper, S., Crosson, B., Bauer, R. M., Nadeau, S., ... Heilman, K. M. (1999). Conduction aphasia and the arcuate fasciculus: A reexamination of the Wernicke-Geschwind model. *Brain and Language, 70*, 1–12.

Ashby, F. G., Turner, B. O., & Horvitz, J. C. (2010). Cortical and basal ganglia contributions to habit learning and automaticity. *Trends in Cognitive Sciences, 14*, 208–215.

Baese-Berk, M., & Goldrick, M. (2009). Mechanisms of interaction in speech production. *Language and Cognitive Processes, 24*, 527–554.

Bernal, B., & Ardila, A. (2009). The role of the arcuate fasciculus in conduction aphasia. *Brain, 132*, 2309–2316.

Blevins, J. (2004). *Evolutionary phonology. The emergence of sound patterns.* Cambridge, MA: Cambridge University Press.

Blumstein, S. E. (1973). *A phonological investigation of aphasic speech.* The Hague: Mouton.

Bohland, J. W., & Guenther, F. H. (2006). An fMRI investigation of syllable sequence production. *Neuroimage, 32*, 821–841.

Brendel, B., Erb, M., Riecker, A., Grodd, W., Ackermann, H., & Ziegler, W. (2011). Do we have a mental syllabary in the brain? *Motor Control, 15*, 34–51.

Brendel, B., Hertrich, I., Erb, M., Lindner, A., Riecker, A., Grodd, W., & Ackermann, H. (2010). The contribution of mesiofrontal cortex to the preparation and execution of repetitive syllable productions: an fMRI study. *Neuroimage, 50*, 1219–1230.

Broca, P. (1861). Remarques sur le siège de la faculté du langage articulé; suives d'une observation d'aphémie. *Bulletin de la Société Anatomique, 6*, 330–357.

Brown, S., Laird, A. R., Pfordresher, P. Q., Thelen, S. M., Turkeltaub, P., & Liotti, M. (2009). The somatotopy of speech: Phonation and articulation in the human motor cortex. *Brain and Cognition, 70*, 31–41.

Brown, S., Ngan, E., & Liotti, M. (2008). A larynx area in the human motor cortex. *Cereb Cortex, 18*, 837–845.

Catani, M., Jones, D. K., & Ffytche, D. H. (2005). Perisylvian language networks of the human brain. *Annals of Neurology, 57*, 8–16.

Catani, M., & Mesulam, M.-M. (2008). The arcuate fasciculus and the disconnection theme in language and aphasia: History and current state. *Cortex, 44*, 953–961.

Cholin, J. (2008). The mental syllabary in speech production: An integration of different approaches and domains. *Aphasiology, 22*, 1127–1141.

Damasio, H., & Damasio, A. R. (1980). The anatomical basis of conduction aphasia. *Brain, 103*, 337–350.

Desmurget, M., Grafton, S. T., Vindras, P., Grea, H., & Turner, R. S. (2004). The basal ganglia network mediates the planning of movement amplitude. *European Journal of Neuroscience, 19*, 2871–2880.

Doyon, J., & Benali, H. (2005). Reorganization and plasticity in the adult brain during learning of motor skills. *Current Opinions in Neurobiology, 15*, 161–167.

Dronkers, N. F. (1996). A new brain region for coordinating speech articulation. *Nature, 384*, 159–161.

Duffy, J. R. (2005). *Motor speech disorders: Substrates, differential diagnosis, and management* (2nd ed.). St. Louis: Elsevier Mosby.

Esposito, A., Demeurisse, G., Alberti, B., & Fabbro, F. (1999). Complete mutism after midbrain periaqueductal gray lesion. *NeuroReport, 10*, 681–685.

Fitch, W. T. (2000). The evolution of speech: A comparative review. *Trends in Cognitive Sciences, 4,* 258–267.

Fitch, W. T. (2010). *The evolution of language.* New York: Cambridge University Press.

Foundas, A. L., Daniels, S. K., & Vasterling, J. J. (1998). Anomia: Case studies with lesion localization. *Neurocase, 4,* 35–43.

Freedman, M., Alexander, M. P., & Naeser, M. A. (1984). Anatomic basis of transcortical motor aphasia. *Neurology, 34,* 409–417.

Frenck-Mestre, C., Anton, J. L., Roth, M., Vaid, J., & Viallet, F. (2005). Articulation in early and late bilinguals' two languages: evidence from functional magnetic resonance imaging. *NeuroReport, 16,* 761–765.

Frey, S., Campbell, J. S., Pike, G. B., & Petrides, M. (2008). Dissociating the human language pathways with high angular resolution diffusion fiber tractography. *The Journal of Neuroscience, 28,* 11435–11444.

Friederici, A. (2009). Pathways to language: Fiber tracts in the human brain. *Trends in Cognitive Sciences, 13,* 175–181.

Gafos, A., & Benus, S. (2006). Dynamics of phonological cognition. *Cognitive Science, 30,* 905–943.

Geschwind, N. (1965). Disconnexion syndromes in animal and man. Part II. *Brain, 88,* 585–644.

Goldrick, M., & Blumstein, S. E. (2006). Cascading activation from phonological planning to articulatory processes: Evidence from tongue twisters. *Language and Cognitive Processes, 21,* 649–683.

Goldrick, M., & Rapp, B. (2007). Lexical and post-lexical phonological representations in spoken production. *Cognition, 102,* 219–260.

Guenther, F. H., Ghosh, S. S., & Tourville, J. A. (2006). Neural modeling and imaging of the cortical interactions underlying syllable production. *Brain and Language, 96,* 280–301.

Guenther, F. H., Hampson, M., & Johnson, D. (1998). A theoretical investigation of reference frames for the planning of speech movements. *Psychological Review, 105,* 611–633.

Hage, S. R., & Jürgens, U. (2006). Localization of a vocal pattern generator in the pontine brainstem of the squirrel monkey. *European Journal of Neuroscience, 23,* 840–844.

Hickok, G., Okada, K., & Serences, J. T. (2009). Area Spt in the human planum temporale supports sensory-motor integration for speech processing. *Journal of Neurophysiology, 101,* 2725–2732.

Hickok, G., & Poeppel, D. (2004). Dorsal and ventral streams: A framework for understanding aspects of the functional anatomy of language. *Cognition, 92,* 67–99.

Hickok, G., & Poeppel, D. (2007). The cortical organization of speech processing. *Nature Review Neuroscience, 8,* 393–402.

Hihara, S., Yamada, H., Iriki, A., & Okanoya, K. (2003). Spontaneous vocal differentiation of coo-calls for tools and food in Japanese monkeys. *Neuroscience Research, 45,* 383–389.

Hillis, A. E., Work, M., Barker, P. B., Jacobs, M. A., Breese, E. L., & Maurer, K. (2004). Re-examining the brain regions crucial for orchestrating speech articulation. *Brain, 127,* 1479–1487.

Hopf, H. C., Müller–Forell, W., & Hopf, N. J. (1992). Localization of emotional and volitional facial paresis. *Neurology, 42,* 1918–1923.

Howard, D., & Gatehouse, C. (2006). Distinguishing semantic and lexical word retrieval deficits in people with aphasia. *Aphasiology, 20,* 921–950.

Iwatsubo, T., Kuzuhara, S., Kanemitsu, A., Shimada, H., & Toyokura, Y. (1990). Corticofugal projections to the motor nuclei of the brainstem and spinal cord in humans. *Neurology, 40,* 309–312.

Jacquemot, C., Dupoux, E., & Bachoud-Levi, A. C. (2007). Breaking the mirror: Asymmetrical disconnection between the phonological input and output codes. *Cognitive Neuropsychology, 24,* 3–22.

Joel, D., & Weiner, I. (1994). The organization of the basal ganglia-thalamocortical circuits: Open interconnected rather than closed segregated. *Neuroscience, 63,* 363–379.

Jürgens, U. (1994). The role of the periaqueductal grey in vocal behaviour. *Behavioral Brain Research, 62,* 107–117.

Jürgens, U. (2002). Neural pathways underlying vocal control. *Neuroscience & Biobehavioral Reviews, 26,* 235–258.

Kellmeyer, P., Ewert, S., Kaller, C., Kümmerer, D., Weiller, C., Ziegler, W., & Saur, D. (2010). Neural networks for processing articulatory difficulty: A model for apraxia of speech. Human Brain Mapping Conference, Barcelona. Retrieved from https://www.aievolution.com/hbm1001/index.cfm?do=abs.viewAbs&abs=4406).

Klein, D., Milner, B., Zatorre, R. J., Meyer, E., & Evans, A. C. (1995). The neural substrates underlying word generation: A bilingual function-imaging study. *Proceedings of the National Academy of Sciences of the USA, 92,* 2899–2903.

Kohn, S. E. (1989). The nature of the phonemic string deficit in conduction aphasia. *Aphasiology, 3,* 209–239.

Levelt, W. J. M., Roelofs, A., & Meyer, A. S. (1999). A theory of lexical access in speech production. *Behavioral and Brain Sciences, 22,* 1–38.

Lorenz, A., & Ziegler, W. (2009). Semantic vs. word form specific techniques in anomia treatment: A multiple single case study. *Journal of Neurolinguist, 22,* 515–537.

Lotto, A. J., Hickok, G. S., & Holt, L. L. (2009). Reflections on mirror neurons and speech perception. *Trends in Cognitive Sciences, 13,* 110–114.

MacNeilage, P. F. (1998). The frame/content theory of evolution of speech production. *Behavioral and Brain Sciences, 21,* 499–511.

Makris, N., Kennedy, D. N., McInerney, S., Sorensen, A. G., Wang, R., Caviness, V. S., Jr.,& Pandya, D. N. (2005). Segmentation of subcomponents within the superior longitudinal fascicle in humans: A quantitative, in vivo, DT-MRI study. *Cerebral Cortex, 15,* 854–869.

Matsuzaka, Y., Picard, N., & Strick, P. L. (2007). Skill representation in the primary motor cortex after long-term practice. *Journal of Neurophysiology, 97,* 1819–1832.

Nucifora, P. G., Verma, R., Melhem, E. R., Gur, R. E., & Gur, R. C. (2005). Leftward asymmetry in relative fiber density of the arcuate fasciculus. *NeuroReport, 16,* 791–794.

Okada, K., & Hickok, G. (2006). Left posterior auditory-related cortices participate both in speech perception and speech production: Neural overlap revealed by fMRI. *Brain and Language, 98,* 112–117.

Papoutsi, M., de Zwart, J. A., Jansma, J. M., Pickering, M. J., Bednar, J. A., & Horwitz, B. (2009). From phonemes to articulatory codes: An fMRI study of the role of Broca's area in speech production. *Cerebral Cortex, 19,* 2156–2165.

Passingham, R. E. (2008). *What is special about the human brain?* Oxford: Oxford University Press.

Passingham, R. E., Bengtsson, S. L., & Lau, H. C. (2010). Medial frontal cortex: From self-generated action to reflection on one's own performance. *Trends in Cognitive Sciences, 14,* 16–21.

Peschke, C., Ziegler, W., Kappes, J., & Baumgaertner, A. (2009). Auditory-motor integration during fast repetition: The neuronal correlates of shadowing. *Neuroimage, 47*, 392–402.

Petrides, M., Cadoret, G., & Mackey, S. (2005). Orofacial somatomotor responses in the macaque monkey homologue of Broca's area. *Nature, 435*, 1235–1238.

Petrides, M., & Pandya, D. N. (2009). Distinct parietal and temporal pathways to the homologues of Broca's area in the monkey. *PLoS Biology, 7*, e1000170.

Pulvermüller, F., & Fadiga, L. (2010). Active perception: Sensorimotor circuits as a cortical basis for language. *Nature Review Neuroscience, 11*, 351–360.

Ramnani, N. (2006). The primate cortico-cerebellar system: anatomy and function. *Nature Review Neuroscience, 7*, 511–522.

Reimers-Kipping, S., Hevers, W., Pääbo, S., & Enard, W. (2011). Humanized Foxp2 specifically affects cortico-basal ganglia circuits. *Neuroscience, 175*, 75–84.

Riecker, A., Brendel, B., Ziegler, W., Erb, M., & Ackermann, H. (2008). The influence of syllable onset complexity and syllable frequency on speech motor control. *Brain and Language, 107*, 102–113.

Riecker, A., Mathiak, K., Wildgruber, D., Erb, M., Hertrich, I., Grodd, W., & Ackermann, H. (2005). fMRI reveals two distinct cerebral networks subserving speech motor control. *Neurology, 64*, 700–706.

Rilling, J. K., Glasser, M. F., Preuss, T. M., Ma, X., Zhao, T., Hu, X., & Behrens, T. E. J. (2008). The evolution of the arcuate fasciculus revealed with comparative DTI. *Nature Neuroscience, 11*, 426–428.

Roland, P. E., & Zilles, K. (1996). Functions and structures of the motor cortices in humans. *Current Opinion in Neurobiology, 6*, 773–781.

Saur, D., Kreher, B. W., Schnell, S., Kummerer, D., Kellmeyer, P., Vry, M. S.,…Weiller, C (2008). Ventral and dorsal pathways for language. *Proceedings of the National Academy of Sciences USA, 105*, 18035–18040.

Schmahmann, J. D. (1997). Rediscovery of an early concept. *International Review of Neurobiology, 41*, 3–27.

Schwartz, M. F., Saffran, E. M., Bloch, D. E., & Dell, G. S. (1994). Disordered speech production in aphasic and normal speakers. *Brain and Language, 47*, 52–88.

Schwartz, M. F., Wilshire, C. E., Gagnon, D. A., & Polansky, M. (2004). Origins of nonword phonological errors in aphasic picture naming. *Cognitive Neuropsychology, 21*, 159–186.

Sessle, B. J., Adachi, K., Avivi-Arber, L., Lee, J., Nishiura, H., Yao, D., & Yoshino, K. (2007). Neuroplasticity of face primary motor cortex control of orofacial movements. *Archives of Oral Biology, 52*, 334–337.

Shallice, T., Rumiati, R. I., & Zadini, A. (2000). The selective impairment of the phonological output buffer. *Cognitive Neuropsychology, 17*, 517–546.

Shallice, T., & Warrington, E. K. (1977). Auditory-verbal short-term memory impairment and conduction aphasia. *Brain and Language, 4*, 479–491.

Shuster, L. I., & Lemieux, S. K. (2005). An fMRI investigation of covertly and overtly produced mono—and multisyllabic words. *Brain and Language, 93*, 20–31.

Smith, A. (2010). Development of neural control of orofacial movements for speech. In W. J. Hardcastle, J. Laver, & F. E. Gibbon (Eds.), *The handbook of phonetic sciences* (2nd ed., pp. 251–296). New York: Wiley-Blackwell.

Staiger, A., & Ziegler, W. (2008). Syllable frequency and syllable structure in the spontaneous speech production of patients with apraxia of speech. *Aphasiology, 22*, 1201–1215

Sutton, D., & Jürgens, U. (1988). Neural control of vocalization. In H. D. Steklis & J. Erwin (Eds.), *Comparative primate biology. Vol. 4: Neurosciences* (4 ed., pp. 625–647). New York: Liss.

Svensson, P., Romaniello, A., Wang, K., Arendt-Nielsen, L., & Sessle, B. J. (2006). One hour of tongue-task training is associated with plasticity in corticomotor control of the human tongue musculature. *Experimental Brain Research, 173*, 165–173.

Urban, P. P., Marx, J., Hunsche, S., Gawehn, J., Vucurevic, G., Wicht, S.,…Hopf, H. C. (2003). Cerebellar speech representation. Lesion topography in dysarthria as derived from cerebellar ischemia and functional magnetic resonance imaging. *Archives of Neurology, 60*, 965–972.

Urban, P. P., Rolke, R., Wicht, S., Keilmann, A., Stoeter, P., Hopf, H. C., & Dietrich, M. (2006). Left-hemispheric dominance for articulation: A prospective study on acute ischaemic dysarthria at different localizations. *Brain, 129*, 767–777.

Wallman, J. (1992). *Aping language.* Cambridge, MA: Cambridge University Press.

Warren, J. E., Wise, R. J., & Warren, J. D. (2005). Sounds do-able: auditory-motor transformations and the posterior temporal plane. *Trends in Neurosciences, 28*, 636–643.

Wild, B., Rodden, F. A., Grodd, W., & Ruch, W. (2003). Neural correlates of laughter and humour. *Brain, 126*, 2121–2138.

Wildgruber, D., Ackermann, H., Klose, U., Kardatzki, B., & Grodd, W. (1996). Functional lateralization of speech production at primary motor cortex: A fMRI study. *NeuroReport, 7*, 2791–2795.

Wilson, S. M., Isenberg, A. L., & Hickok, G. (2009). Neural correlates of word production stages delineated by parametric modulation of psycholinguistic variables. *Human Brain Mapping, 30*, 3596–3608.

Ziegler, W. (2005). A nonlinear model of word length effects in apraxia of speech. *Cognitive Neuropsychology, 22*, 603–623.

Ziegler, W. (2008). Apraxia of speech. In G. Goldenberg & B. Miller (Eds.), *Handbook of clinical neurology* (pp. 269–285). London: Elsevier.

Ziegler, W. (2009). Modelling the architecture of phonetic plans: Evidence from apraxia of speech. *Language and Cognitive Processes, 24*, 631–661.

Ziegler, W. (2010). Apraxic failure and the hierarchical structure of speech motor plans: A non-linear probabilistic model. In A. Lowit & R. D. Kent (Eds.), *Assessment of motor speech disorders* (pp. 305–323). San Diego (CA): Plural Publishing.

Ziegler, W., Kilian, B., & Deger, K. (1997). The role of the left mesial frontal cortex in fluent speech: Evidence from a case of left supplementary motor area hemorrhage. *Neuropsychologia, 35*, 1197–1208.

Ziegler, W., & Wessel, K. (1996). Speech timing in ataxic disorders: Sentence production and rapid repetitive articulation. *Neurology, 47*, 208–214.

Spontaneous Discourse

Herbert H. Clark

Abstract

A discourse is an extended use of language, such as a conversation, novel, newspaper article, stage play, or comic strip. It may be long or short, fiction or nonfiction, printed or spoken, but the main divide is between spontaneous and manufactured varieties. A spontaneous discourse is one created on the fly, whereas a manufactured discourse is one that has been prepared, reworked, and turned into an artifact or performance. It is the spontaneous forms that are primeval. This chapter reviews how people work together to produce a spontaneous discourse. When people gossip, exchange information, make plans, or transact business, they must coordinate. Participants establish coordination by a succession of joint commitments. The discourse that emerges is a dialogue: part speech, part gesture; part spoken turns, part gestural actions; part simple turns, part longer narratives.

Key Words: discourse, gesture, dialogue, coordination

A discourse is an extended use of language, such as a conversation, novel, newspaper article, stage play, or comic strip. It may be long or short, fiction or nonfiction, printed or spoken, but the main divide is between *spontaneous* and *manufactured* varieties. A spontaneous discourse is one created on the fly, such as a conversation or personal story, whereas a manufactured discourse is one that has been prepared, reworked, and turned into an artifact or performance, such as a novel, newspaper article, stage play, or comic strip. It is the spontaneous forms that are primeval. In societies before the modern era (those without print, radio, or television) there were few manufactured forms, and yet everyone engaged in spontaneous forms. Spontaneous discourses are not only primeval, but the bases for most manufactured varieties.

Spontaneous discourses are distinguished by how they are produced. When Julia asks Ken, "What did you do last night?" Ken must decide broadly on the story he wants to tell and then, in a timely fashion,

formulate and produce his narrative one utterance at a time, correcting his own errors and Julia's misunderstandings as he goes along. If Julia had asked Ken by email, once again he would decide broadly on the story he wanted to tell. However, this time he would type out each sentence (at one-third speed), adding punctuation and correcting typos, and then rework his prose, all before sending it on to Julia. On the face of it, spontaneous and manufactured discourses are produced by different processes. This chapter is about the production of spontaneous discourses.

The basic form of spontaneous discourse is dialogue. Traditionally, dialogues have been treated as if they were speech alone—as if they were *bare dialogues*. However, when people are face-to-face, they use not only speech, but also gestures, eye gaze, and other signals. I will call these *full dialogues*. Research on full dialogues has led to significant changes in the accounts based on bare dialogues alone.

All dialogues are part of larger joint activities. The reason people talk is to solve problems, exchange addresses, buy and sell goods, assemble pieces of furniture, or play basketball—to carry out joint activities. Yet in most studies, dialogues are analyzed only after they have been surgically excised from the activities they are part of, obscuring why participants said what they said. Studies of *instrumental dialogues* — dialogues treated as parts of larger activities — have led to further changes in accounts of discourse.

Far more is known about bare dialogues than any other type of dialogue. The most extensive research was initiated in the 1970s by Harvey Sacks, Emanuel Schegloff, and Gail Jefferson in a tradition called *conversation analysis*. The first 35 years of this research is well summarized in a "primer in conversation analysis" by Schegloff (2007). The best way to understand spontaneous discourse is to start with bare dialogues and then move on to full and instrumental dialogues. This chapter discusses five features of dialogue: (1) turns, (2) paired actions, (3) joint projects, (4) grounding, and (5) narratives.

Turns in Speaking

In bare dialogues, people take turns speaking, moving from one turn to the next largely without gaps or overlap. How do they do this? According to Sacks, Schegloff, and Jefferson (1974), this is done by following rules.

Rules of Turn Taking

Turns, in the Sacks et al. (1974) analysis, consist of *turn-constructional units*, as illustrated in this excerpt from a telephone conversation between two secretaries in a British university. Jane has just called the Principal's office, and Kate has answered:

1	Jane	Is Miss Pink in-.
2	Kate	Well, she's in, but she's engaged at the moment, who is it?
3	Jane	Oh it's Professor Worth's secretary, from University College,
4	Kate	m,
5	Jane	Could you give her a message [for me,]
6	Kate	[certainly] (8.3d.230)[1]

[1] Examples from the London-Lund corpus (Svartvik & Quirk, 1980) are each marked with the text number (e.g., 8.3d) and beginning line (e.g., 230). Overlapping speech is marked in paired square brackets, as in "for me" and "certainly." Examples from the Switchboard corpus (Godfrey, Holliman, & McDaniel, 1992) are each marked with the conversation number.

Line 1 consists of one turn-constructional unit ("is Miss Pink in?"); line 2 of three units ("well, she's in" "but she's engaged at the moment" and "who is it?"); and line 3 of two units ("oh it's Professor Worth's secretary" and "from University College.") Turn-constructional units may be single words ("yes,"); phrases ("from University College,"); or full sentences ("is Miss Pink in?").

In the Sacks et al. (1974) analysis, transitions from one turn to the next are allowed only at the ends of turn-constructional units (at *transition-relevance places*) according to these pithy rules:

(1) For any turn, at the initial transition-relevance place of an initial turn constructional unit:

(a) If the turn-so-far is so constructed as to involve the use of a "current speaker selects next" technique, then the party so selected has the right and is obliged to take next turn to speak; no others have such rights or obligations, and transfer occurs at that place.

(b) If the turn-so-far is so constructed as not to involve the use of a "current speaker selects next" technique, then self-selection for next speakership may, but need not, be instituted; first starter acquires rights to a turn, and transfer occurs at that place.

(c) If the turn-so-far is so constructed as not to involve the use of a "current speaker selects next" technique, then current speaker may, but need not continue, unless another self-selects.

(2) If, at the initial transition-relevance place of an initial turn-constructional unit, neither la nor 1b has operated, and, following the provision of 1c, current speaker has continued, then the rule-set a-c reapplies at next transition relevance place, and recursively at each next transition-relevance place, until transfer is effected. (Sacks et al., 1974, p. 704)

These rules fit a great many features of bare conversations regardless of their length or number of participants.

Consider Jane and Kate. When Jane produces "Is Miss Pink in?" she uses a *current speaker selects next technique* (she is asking a question of Kate) so by rule (a), Kate "has the right and is obligated" to take the next turn at that point, and she does. Kate starts her own turn with the unit "well, she's in." This time rule (a) does not apply, so by rule (b) Jane could acquire the rights to the next turn by "self-selection," by speaking first, but she does not. So, by rule (c) Kate may continue, and she does. At the end of "but she's engaged at the moment," rule (a) does not apply, and Jane does not self-select by rule (b), so Kate continues by rule (c). At the end of "Who is it?" rule (a) does apply, so Jane "has the right and is obligated" to take the next turn at that moment, which she does, "Oh it's Professor Worth's secretary." And so it goes for the rest of the excerpt.

Projecting Turns

How do people know when to initiate the next turn? In a *reactive* view of the process, parties wait for the current turn-constructional unit to end and then initiate the transition to the next turn by rule (a) or (b). By waiting for the unit to end, a party can start speaking only after a gap of 200 ms, the minimum time it takes to react to any stimulus. In a *projective* view, in contrast, parties try to *project* the end of the current unit so that they can initiate the next turn *without* a gap. The projective view follows from rules (b) and (c). By rule (b), after Kate has completed "but she's engaged at the moment," Jane *could* start speaking, but to acquire the next turn, she would have to start before Kate. That is, by rules (b) and (c) Jane and Kate compete for the floor, and the one to speak first wins. This should motivate Kate to try to anticipate the end of Jane's turn and start without a gap.

There is good evidence for the projective view. In one study (de Ruiter, Mitterer, & Enfield, 2006), pairs of Dutch friends were recorded as they talked on the telephone; later, 1,500 of their turn transitions were measured for *turn offsets* (the time from the end of one turn to the onset of the next). A turn offset of –500 ms means the second turn overlapped the first by 500 ms; a turn offset of +500 ms means there was a 500 ms gap between the turns. A turn offset of 0 ms means there was neither a gap nor overlap. Remarkably, the average turn offset for these speakers was 0 ms. Individual offsets differed from 0 ms, of course, but 45 percent of them were between –250 and +250 ms, and 85 percent were between –750 and +750 ms. There was no evidence of systematic gaps between turns. Surprisingly, the average offset was the same whether the transition was triggered by rule (a) or by rule (b).

How can listeners project turn ends with such extraordinary accuracy? One proposal is that they base their projections on the *words and syntax* of the current turn-constructional unit, and another is that they base them mostly on *intonation*. In experiments by de Ruiter et al. (2006) on the same Dutch conversations, it was shown that listeners rely for this purpose on the words and syntax—on *what* speakers say—and make no use of intonation.

The Sacks et al. rules for taking turns were developed in 1974 for American speakers of English and yet claimed to be universal. The rules were soon disputed in reports of cultures that tolerate long overlaps or long gaps between turns. This dispute was examined by Stivers et al. (2009) in a study of 10 languages from five continents: Danish, Dutch, English, Italian, Japanese, Korean, Lao, and languages from Namibia, Mexico, and Papua New Guinea. For each language, the investigators video-recorded spontaneous conversations; identified 350 yes-no questions (questions to be answered yes or no); and then measured the turn offset for each transition from question to response. As before, a negative offset indicates overlap, and a positive offset indicates a gap. The shape of the curves for turn offsets looked much the same across the 10 languages. What varied was the median offset time: it ranged from 0 ms (for English, Japanese, and two other languages) to +300 ms (for Danish and two other languages). The median was +100 ms over the 10 languages. Languages vary a bit in the timing of the next turn, but most fit the projective view of turn transitions.

In the dialogues cited so far, people are chatting, gossiping, or discussing current events (joint *informational* activities). In the workplace, where people engage in joint *physical* activities, dialogues look very different. In the following excerpt, Ann and Burton were video-recorded in the middle of assembling a television stand from its parts:

Burton	Now let's do this one.
Ann	Okay
	(6.42 sec) ((**Ann & Burton place board**))
Ann	Should we screw the screws in? Or should we? I guess we don't have to.
	(23.10 sec) ((**Ann & Burton twist screws in**))
Burton	It's starting to look like a TV stand.
Ann	Heh-heh-heh-heh, it's starting to, yeah.
	(6.47 sec) ((**Ann & Burton screw screws, place board**))
Burton	Oh, wait. We've got this thing in backwards.

In the entire assembly, Ann and Burton spoke only 40 percent of the time. They clearly felt no pressure to minimize gaps between many of their turns. Instead, they timed what they said in relation to stages of the larger joint activity in which they were engaged (a point I return to later).

Paired Actions

Turns in bare conversations tend to come in pairs that Schegloff and Sacks (1973) called *adjacency pairs*. One such pair is the *question-answer pair*, as in this example from Jane and Kate's conversation:

Kate	Who is it?
Jane	Oh it's Professor Worth's secretary, from University College,

Adjacency pairs have these properties: (1) the two parts belong to different turns; (2) the two turns are from different speakers (here Kate and Jane); (3) the two parts belong to different utterance types (here question and answer); and (4) once one person has produced an utterance of the first type (a question), it is conditionally relevant for the second person to produce an utterance of the second type (an answer) as the next turn.

Adjacency pairs have a wide range of uses, from greetings to farewells, as illustrated with examples from Jane and Kate's conversation:

Pair parts	Example	
1. Greeting	Kate	hello,
2. Greeting	Jane	hello,
1. Question	Kate	who is it?
2. Answer	Jane	oh it's Professor Worth's secretary, from Pan-American College
1. Assertion	Jane	oh it's Professor Worth's secretary, from Pan-American College,
2. Acknowledgment	Kate	m,
1. Request	Jane	could you give her a message [for me,]
2. Promise	Kate	[certainly,]
1. Gratitude	Kate	thank you very much indeed,

Pair parts	Example	
2. Reply	Jane	right,
1. Farewell	Kate	bye bye,
2. Farewell	Jane	bye,

In Jane's and Kate's conversation, every turn contained either a first or a second part of an adjacency pair. First pair parts constitute a "current speaker selects next" technique, so Jane and Kate used them to give the other the right and obligation to speak next. Adjacency pairs were responsible for much of what the two of them did.

Timing

So far it may seem that people always try to produce the second parts of adjacency pairs with no gap and no overlap, but that would be misleading. When people need time to think of a response, they leave gaps, often long ones, without violating the rules of turn-taking. In one study (Smith & Clark, 1993), one student asked each of 25 student respondents a series of 40 questions, such as "In what sport is the Stanley Cup awarded?" The two students were in a conversational setting but separated by a visual barrier. The difficulty of the 40 questions had been calibrated on a separate set of students; the percentage of these students able to answer the questions correctly ranged from 0 percent to 97 percent. By this measure, the more difficult the question, the longer respondents delayed before giving an answer (e.g., "um [4 s] hockey.") In contrast, the more difficult the question, the less time they delayed before giving a nonanswer (e.g., "I can't remember.") Indeed, they took almost no time at all to respond "No idea!" Over all questions, the delays ranged up to 20 s. Still, the respondents realized that long delays might suggest they were uncooperative, ignorant, poor in judgment, or slow-witted, so they took pains to deal with those delays. The longer the delay, the more likely they were to add "uh" or "um"; talk to themselves audibly ("Stanley cup" in a low voice); and make excuses ("I should know that one"). They intended these moves to be taken not as parts of their answers, but as accounts for their delays.

People trying to answer questions also leave gaps for other reasons. Recall that the 10-language study (Stivers et al., 2009) measured turn offsets for yes-no questions (e.g., the time between "Is John going?" and "Yes" or "I don't know"). For all 10 languages, turn offsets were shortest for "yes" answers. In Japanese, indeed, the turn offsets for "yes" averaged −100 ms; that is, "yes" systematically overlapped the end of the question in violation of turn-taking rule (a).

Responses other than "yes" all took somewhat longer. Respondents took 250 ms longer on average to answer disconfirmatory answers (e.g., "no") Perhaps they needed more time to formulate "no" than "yes," or to signal disagreement than agreement. Turn offsets were also 300 ms longer for nonanswers (e.g., "I don't know") than for answers ("yes" or "no"). Respondents cannot say "I don't know" until, having searched memory, they discover they are unable to answer, and that usually takes time. Finally, turn offsets were 125 ms longer when respondents were not in the gaze of the questioner than when they were. Perhaps respondents felt pressed by the gaze to answer more quickly, or perhaps the gaze helped them project the end of the question more accurately. Remarkably, the delays added for nonconfirmatory answers, nonanswers, and absence of gaze were independent increments, and in all 10 languages. The goal of respondents is not to respond without a gap. It is to respond as soon as possible after they have decided on and formulated a response.

Projective Pairs

Adjacency pairs are really a type of *projective pair* (Clark, 2004). To be an adjacency pair, both parts must be spoken. To be a projective pair, the two parts may be any type of communicative act. Here are four different combinations with examples:

1.	Spoken	Server	I'll be right there. (in drugstore)
2.	Spoken	Clark	Okay.
1.	Spoken	Clark	Who needs a syllabus? (to classroom of students)
2.	Gestural	Student	((raises her hand)) (= "I do")
1.	Mechanical	Jane	(rings telephone) (= "I wish to speak to someone")
2.	Spoken	Kate	Miss Pink's office
1.	Gestural	Student	((holds up assignment in one hand, points at pile of papers with the other hand)) (= "Does my assignment go here?")
2.	Gestural	Clark	((nods)) (= "Yes")

All four pairs are projective pairs, but only the first is an adjacency pair.

Many of the properties that have been attributed to adjacency pairs are really properties of projective pairs. When Allan asks Barbara, "Is Susan around?" Barbara might respond "yes" or "no" or "I don't know," but she could equally well nod, shake her head, or shrug. A question projects an answer as the next communicative act, but the answer could be spoken, gestural, or both. In the 10-language study (Stivers et al., 2009), the responses to yes-no questions included not only "yes," "no," and "I don't know" (or their equivalents), but also head nods, head shakes, and shrugs (or their equivalents), either alone or in combination with words. In all 10 languages (with the right equivalents), one could answer "Are you hungry?" with "yes," a head nod, or both.

Joint Commitments

What then are projective pairs for? The basic answer is for establishing *joint commitments* (Clark, 1996, 2005). Suppose Allan wants to take Barbara shopping at noon. He cannot expect her to coordinate on her outing with him by accident. The two of them need to establish a joint commitment to going shopping at noon, and that takes commitments from both. The solution is for Allan to propose the joint action ("Would you like to go shopping at noon?") and for Barbara to take up his proposal and agree to it ("Yes, I'd love to"). Schematically:

Part 1	A proposes to B a joint position or action for A and B to commit to
Part 2	B takes up A's proposal

After Barbara agrees to his proposal, they establish a joint commitment to going shopping together at noon.

The uptake of a proposal can go in several directions. Suppose in part 1 that Allan asks Barbara, "Is Susan around?" proposing that she tell him whether or not Susan is around. In part 2, Barbara has at least five options. (1) She can accept the proposal outright by saying "Yes, she is." (2) She can accept an altered version of the proposal by saying something related but helpful, "Well, she was a minute ago." (3) She can decline the proposal because she is unable to tell Allan what he proposed, "I don't know." (4) She can dismiss the proposal because it is, for example, improper, "None of your business." (5) She can even disregard the proposal, "Well, I'm off now," refusing to address it at all. With alternatives like these, people can steer dialogues in many directions, even in unanticipated directions.

The proposals people negotiate with projective pairs are either for *joint positions* or for *joint actions*. A joint position is a proposition that people jointly accept for current purposes. When Burton asserts, "It's starting to look like a TV stand," and Ann responds "Heh-heh-heh-heh, it's starting to, yeah," the two of them establish the *joint* position, for current purposes, that their assembly is starting to look like a television stand. Joint positions can also be established with questions and answers. When Jane asks, "Is Miss Pink in," and Kate responds "Well, she's in, but she's engaged at the moment," the two of them establish the joint position, for current purposes, that Miss Pink is in but busy. Joint positions are generally introduced with assertions or questions.

A joint action is an action that two or more people perform jointly (Clark, 1996). When Jane makes a request, "Could you give her a message," and Kate says, "Certainly," the two of them establish a joint commitment to a future joint action: Kate giving Miss Pink a message at Jane's behest. Joint actions can also be established with promises. When a server in a drugstore told me, "I'll be right there," and I accepted her promise, "Okay," the two of us established a joint commitment to her serving me in a moment. Commitments to joint actions are generally initiated with directives or promises.

Joint Projects

People engage in dialogue to accomplish broader goals: to solve problems, exchange addresses, assemble furniture, play cards. How do they reach these broader goals when their only tool is projective pairs that link one action to the next? The answer is by using projective pairs to create larger joint projects, to create extended sequences.

Extended Sequences

One way to create extended sequences is to link projective pairs in chains. Here is an example:

1	Albert	How you do spell him?
2	Beth	P I E double L.
3	Albert	Thank you, (2.6.553)

Albert's question projects an answer, and Beth provides it in the next turn. Because Albert takes Beth's answer to be a favor, he responds to it in turn with "thank you." He links the favor-thanks pair (lines 2 and 3) to the question-answer pair (lines 1 and 2) to form a three-turn chain. Another common chain is a question-answer-acknowledgment:

1	Lou	Where have you been working?
2	Mary	I've been working as a research assistant for—Professor Leegate, on the collected notebooks of Etheridge.
3	Lou	Oh yes, (2.1.30)

Mary answers Lou's question with an assertion, but the assertion projects an acknowledgment, so Lou responds "oh yes." The assertion-acknowledgment pair (lines 2 and 3) is linked to the question-answer pair (lines 1 and 2) to form a chain of three turns. Chains may accumulate many links.

A more productive way to create extended sequences is to set them up with *presequences*. Here is an example of what Schegloff (1980) called a *prequestion*:

1	Ann	**Oh there's one thing I wanted to ask you,**
2	Betty	**mhm, -**
		((Ann and Betty take ten turns as Ann describes a type of belt))
13	Ann	Would you like one.
14	Betty	Oh I'd love one Ann ™ (7.1d.1320)

In line 1, Ann tells Betty that she has a question, an assertion that Betty acknowledges in line 2. Why did Ann not ask Betty the question then and there? The reason was that there were preliminaries she had to establish first, and they consumed the next 10 turns. Only then, in line 13, did Ann ask, "Would you like one?" The first two turns were used to establish the joint commitment to give Ann room for her preliminaries.

Prequestions are only one type of presequence (Schegloff, 2007). Here are four other common types:

| Prerequest | Customer | Do you have the pecan Danish today? |
| | Waitress | Yes we do. |

Preannouncement	Elizabeth	Well d'you know what they got,
	Duncan	What – (4.1.790)
Preinvitation	Rob	What are you doin'?
	Samuel	Nothin' what's up?
Prenarrative	Annabel	I acquired an absolutely magnificent sewing-machine, by foul means, did I tell you about that?
	Barbara	No, (1.3.215):

With the prerequest, the customer asks the waitress a question, expecting her to recognize it as preliminary to a request. Indeed, she preempts the customer's request by making him an offer, "Yes, we do. *Would you like one of those?*" The other three presequences prepare the way for an announcement, an invitation, and a narrative.

Extended Joint Activities

Presequences are especially useful in more extended joint activities. In 1974, a man called up Directory Enquiries at British Telecom in Cambridge, England and initiated the following conversation (from Clark & Schaefer, 1987):

1	Charles	((rings))
2	Operator	Directory Enquiries,
3		for which town, please?
4	Charles	In Cambridge
5	Operator	What's the name of the people?
6	Charles	It's the Shanghai Restaurant, it's not in my directory, but I know it exists
7	Operator	It's Cambridge 12345
8	Charles	12345
9	Operator	That's right
10	Charles	Thank you very much
11	Operator	Thank you,
12		good bye
13	Operator, Charles	((break contact))

The operator took it for granted that Charles had called Directory Enquiries for a telephone number, so she treated the "((ring))" in line 1 as a *preenquiry*. That way she could confirm his purpose with "Directory Enquiries" in line 2 and proceed directly to "For which town, please."

The structure that emerged was a *hierarchical joint project*, a hierarchy of joint positions:

1 C&O enter joint activity of exchanging telephone number (lines 1–2)
   1.1 C&O exchange number (lines 3–8)
   1.1.1 C&O exchange information needed by O (lines 3–6)
   1.1.1.1 C&O exchange name of town (lines 3–4)
   1.1.1.2 C&O exchange name of people (lines 5–6)
   1.1.2 C&O exchange number requested by C (lines 7–9)
   1.1.2.1 O tells C the number (line 7)
   1.1.2.2 C&O verify the number (lines 8–9)
   1.2 C&O exchange gratitude for O's assistance (lines 10–11)
2 C&O exit from joint activity (lines 12–13)

As a purely informational activity, Charles' and the operator's job was to establish a series of joint positions, and they did that with projective pairs alone. With "For which town please?" and "In Cambridge," they established the joint position that the town Charles wanted was Cambridge, and they used the remaining pairs to establish the other joint positions they needed to complete the enquiry.

When the joint activity is physical, participants need to agree less often on joint positions and more often on joint actions. In the middle of building the television stand, Ann and Burton carried out this hierarchy of joint actions:

1.4 A&B attach cross-piece to side-piece
   1.4.1 A&B stick pegs into side-piece
   1.4.1.1 A&B retrieve pegs
   1.4.1.2 A&B insert pegs into side-piece
   1.4.2 A&B affix cross-piece to side piece
   1.5 A&B attach top-piece to side-pieceEtc.

The two of them used projective pairs to commit to each of these joint actions. They agreed on 1.4 with these two turns:

Ann	Should we put this in, this, this little like kinda cross bar, like the T? Like the I bar?
Burton	Yeah we can do that

They agreed on 1.4.1.1 with a pair of gestures:

Burton	((extends hand with peg))
Ann	((grasps peg))

Participants in dialogues need to track hierarchies like these to know how to respond to each other. Recall that Kate and Jane produced this exchange:

Jane	Is Miss Pink in.
Kate	Well, she's in, but she's engaged at the moment,

If Kate had taken Jane's utterance to be a question and nothing more, she would have answered "Yes, she is" and stopped. Instead, she took it to be a prerequest, projecting a request to talk to Miss Pink. She answered Jane's question first ("well, she's in,") and then dealt with the projected request ("but she's engaged at the moment"). She was able to infer Jane's prerequest only from the emerging plan for the larger joint activity.

The role of emergent plans was demonstrated in several experiments in which a young woman named Susan made requests by telephone of local merchants (Clark, 1979). In one experiment, Susan telephoned 150 restaurants and asked the manager who answered one of three questions (50 restaurants per question):

1. Do you accept American Express cards?
2. Do you accept credit cards?
3. Do you accept any kinds of credit cards?

All three questions implied a larger plan in which Susan (a) would have dinner at the restaurant, perhaps that night, and (b) pay for it with a credit card. For question 1, Susan implied that she wanted to pay with an American Express card, so all she needed was a "yes" or "no." Indeed, all 50 managers responded with "yes" or "no" and nothing more. But for questions 2 and 3, Susan implied she was making a prerequest: she had one or more credit cards and, if the answer was "yes," she would ask which credit cards the restaurant accepted. For question 2, the managers who did accept credit cards went on to list the acceptable credit cards 54 percent of the time. For question 3, they did so 89 percent of the time. One manager went even further. After answering Susan's question, he dealt with her presumed plan of dining at the restaurant that night, "Uh, yes, we accept credit cards. But tonight we are closed." In brief, people engage in dialogues to do things together, and they produce what they do against the emerging plan of that activity.

Grounding

To communicate is, etymologically, to "make common," to establish information as common or shared. How do people in dialogues ensure themselves that they have made things common?

One answer focuses on failures in communication (e.g., Schegloff et al., 1977). The idea is that dialogues have "intrinsic troubles," such as when participants misspeak, mishear, misjudge each other, or change their minds. It is up to the participants to monitor for troubles like these and, when they find them, make repairs. Indeed, participants have a system for identifying troubles and repairing them.

Another answer focuses instead on success and failure together. The idea here is that participants look for evidence of success and failure. They try to establish, as they go along, the mutual belief that they have understood each other well enough for current purposes. Not only should they make repairs, but they should also display and acknowledge positive evidence of success. It takes both types of evidence to reach joint closure. The process of establishing these beliefs is called *grounding* (Clark, 1996; Clark & Brennan, 1991; Clark & Schaefer, 1989; Clark & Wilkes-Gibbs, 1986).

Evidence of Understanding

One source of positive evidence in dialogues is *acknowledgments*. In listening to extended descriptions, people regularly add "uh-huh," "m-hm," "yeah," "yes," and British "m" as positive claims of understanding-so-far (Jefferson, 1984, 2002; Schegloff, 1982). Here is a British description with four acknowledgments:

1	Beth	and I went to some second year seminars,
		where there are only about half a dozen people,
2	Ann	[**m,**]
3	Beth	[and] they discussed what a word was,
4	Ann	[**m,**]
5	Beth	[and -] what's a sentence,
		that's [ev] en more difficult,.
6	Ann	[**yeah,**]
7	Ann	**yeah**, -
8	Beth	And so on-.

With each "m" and "yeah," Ann claims to have understood the just previous clause well enough for them to go on, and she invites Beth to go on (Schegloff, 1982). Three of Ann's acknowledgments (lines 2, 4, and 7) come at clause boundaries, as did 77 percent of the acknowledgments in the corpus from which this example was drawn (Oreström, 1983). Acknowledgments are generally produced in the background, at a lower volume and often in overlap. Indeed, three of Ann's acknowledgements (lines 2, 4, and 6) are spoken in overlap, as were 45 percent in the full corpus (Oreström). If listeners want something stronger than "uh-huh" or "yeah," they can respond to the content of a clause with assessments such as "gosh," "really," "oh?" or "good God" (Goodwin, 1986).

Another source of positive evidence is second parts of adjacency pairs. Recall this question and answer:

1	Kate	Who is it?
2	Jane	Oh, it's Professor Worth's secretary, from University College,
3	Kate	m, (8.3d.230)

When Jane responds "oh, it's…" she passes up the chance to ask for clarification ("Do you mean me?") or a repeat ("What?"), and responds instead with what she believes is an appropriate answer. She is claiming, by implication, that she understands Kate's question well enough to answer it. But does she? She can only be sure once Kate acknowledges her answer in line 3 with "m." In this way, Jane and Kate each provide the other with positive evidence that Jane has understood Kate as intended. That, in turn, allows them to consider the question to be grounded (Clark & Schaefer, 1989).

Occasionally, of course the answer to a question yields negative evidence of understanding, and that normally leads to a repair. Here is an example:

1	Abe	Do do do you know, where you are, do the schools emphasize the metric system?
2	Bill	Yeah, in the engineering they all do pretty much.
3	Abe	**No, I I I meant I meant** down, like, in the elementary schools.
4	Bill	Oh, in the elementary schools. I don't know. (*continues*) (3476)

Although Bill thinks he understands Abe's question (in line 1), his answer (in 2) shows Abe that he does not, and so Abe makes the clarification (in 3) "No, I meant…" Bill, in turn, displays his

understanding of the clarification (in 4) "Oh, in the elementary schools…," which Abe does accept. Like Kate and Jane, Abe and Bill work to get joint closure. Both have positive evidence of Bill's understanding of Abe's question.

Repair Patterns

Repairing problems in dialogue, as illustrated in Abe and Bill's exchange, is an interactive process. As Schegloff et al. (1977) argued, participants have two preferences in the process. The first is for speakers to make their own repairs. Consider the following:

| 1 | Duncan | Or do they only know about the. **practical,**. excuse me **experimental** aspects, or reading,– |
| 2 | Ed | They they know (*continues*) (2.4a.735) |

Duncan's replacement of "practical" with "experimental" is a *self-repair*. Next consider:

1	Maggie	You fancy it yourself do you? -
2	Julia	**What, the men's doubles?**
3	Maggie	**Yeah,**
4	Julia	Well more than the singles, yes, - (7.3e.278)

When Julia did not understand Maggie's "it," she initiated a so-called *side sequence* in lines 2 and 3 to clear up the trouble. A side sequence (Jefferson, 1972) is a projective pair inserted within other units to deal with misunderstandings, mishearings, and other issues. In this pair, "the men's doubles" is Julia's repair, not Maggie's, making it an *other-repair*. In dialogue, so the evidence shows, participants prefer self-repairs to other-repairs.

The second preference is for speakers to *initiate* their own repairs. When Duncan repaired the word "practical," he made the repair without being prompted, a *self-initiated repair*. Compare his repair with the following:

1	Roger	Well there's no general agreement on it I should think,
2	Sam	**On what.**
3	Roger	**On uhm—on the uhm—the mixed up bits in the play,the [uhm]**
4	Sam	[yes] (3.5a.283)

In this case, Roger clarified the word "it" only after Sam asked him for clarification ("on what?"). Roger's repair was *other-initiated*. There is also much evidence for the preference of self- over other-initiation of repairs.

The basis for the two preferences seems clear (see Schegloff et al., 1977). Speakers know best what they want to say, making it prudent to give them the first chance to make the repair. That favors self-repairs. Speakers themselves have the opportunity to initiate self-repairs mid-utterance (as Duncan did), whereas others can initiate them only after the utterance is complete (as Julia and Sam did). That favors the self-initiation of repairs.

The two preferences also reflect the general goal of people in dialogue to minimize their joint effort (Clark & Wilkes-Gibbs, 1986). The repairs of Maggie's and Roger's problems, for example, were very costly in time and effort. Maggie's repair took two extra turns and five extra words, and Roger's took two extra turns and 14 extra words. These costs are characteristic of repairs either made or initiated by others. Duncan's self-initiated self-repair, in contrast, took no extra turns and only three extra words ("excuse me practical.") Minimizing joint effort favors both self-repair and the self-initiation of repairs.

To be efficient in making self-repairs, people need to monitor what they say and, the moment they detect a problem, try to repair it. There is good evidence that they do that (Levelt, 1983, 1989). Here are five types of self-repairs in spontaneous speech (the repaired elements are in boldface, and the point of suspension is a vertical line):

a.	we **must ha-** $\mid$ we're. big enough to stand on our own feet now, (1.2.33)
b.	he**'s done a** $\mid$ he's on a Ph.D., (1.2.787)
c.	if **she**'d been $\mid$ he'd been alive, (1.13.246)
d.	he **think** E- $\mid$ thinks Ella's worried about something, (2.13.1204)
e.	Everything is **mitch** $\mid$ much more complex, (2.8.304)

The problem that gets repaired may be an overall message (as in a); bad phrasing (as in b); or an incorrect word, inflection, or pronunciation (as in c, d, and e). In making a repair, speakers sometimes simply replace the item to be repaired (e.g., "much" for "mitch") and other times retrace earlier parts of the utterance first (as in a and b).

Speakers generally suspend speaking as soon as they detect a problem and initiate their repair as soon as they have formulated it (Levelt, 1983). For other strategies see Blackmer and Minton (1991); Fox Tree and Clark (1997); and Seyfeddinipur, Kita, and Indefrey (2008). Because speakers can monitor their "inner speech" before producing their actual speech, they are often able to suspend speaking even before completing the word to be corrected. In Levelt's study, speakers suspended their speech by the end of the to-be-corrected word 71 percent of the time, long before they could have heard and reacted to its audible version.

Grounding with Gestures

In full dialogues, grounding relies not only on speech, but also on head nods, gestures, smiles, and other actions, and that leads to quite a different process. In one study (Clark & Krych, 2004), one participant (the "director") was asked to guide a second participant (the "builder") in assembling a small model of Lego blocks. The two of them sat at opposite ends of a table. In the following excerpt, David and Ben could not see each other or each other's workspace:

David	And then you're gonna take a blue block of four.
Ben	M-hm.
David	And you're gonna put it on top of the four blocks— four yellow blocks farthest away from you.
Ben	Which are the ones closest to the green.
David	Yeah
Ben	Okay. But the green's still not attached.
David	Yeah. And then …

David makes a series of self-repairs, one initiated by himself and the rest by Ben. Everything they do is with speech, and they take 49 words in total. In the next excerpt, in contrast, Doris and Betty could see each other, and Doris could see Betty's workspace:

Doris	Take a short blue.
Betty	((*Retrieves a short blue block.*))
Doris	((*Looks at Betty's block.*)) Put it at the end of the yellow close to the green.
Betty	((*Places the blue block on the yellow block.*))
Doris	((*Looks at result.*)) Take a …

Although Doris and Betty are at precisely the same point in assembling the Lego model as David and Ben, they do most of their grounding by displaying blocks and looking at the result. Doris uses only 16 words, and Betty does not speak at all. This was typical. Assembling Lego models took half as much time, and fewer than half as many words, when the director could see the builder's workspace, as Doris could. The goals in grounding were the same for Doris and Betty as for David and Ben, but the results were radically different.

One way full and bare conversations differ is in acknowledgements. When people speak face-to-face, they often use nods instead of "uh-huh." In one study of spontaneous conversations (Dittmann & Llewellyn, 1968), 57 percent of the acknowledgments were words alone, 21 percent were head nods alone, and 26 percent were a combination of the two. People used head nods in almost half of their acknowledgements.

Head nods range from a single barely perceptible dip of the head to sustained vigorous nodding. As Morency, Sidner, Lee, and Darrell (2005) noted, spontaneous nods vary in: (1) length of the train of nods; (2) rate, or number of nods per second; and (3) size, the extent of up-down movement. Depending on people's choice of length, rate, and size, their nods mean different things. Playwrights, for example, specify nods in stage directions with a combination of form and meaning: "nods assent solemnly" (Dickens, Gilbert); "nods slowly," "smiling, with little nods" (Somerset Maugham); "nods her head slowly several times," "with a confidential nod," "nods thoughtfully" (Ibsen); and "answered by satisfied nods" (Twain). Nodding is a flexible method of signaling.

Where nods are placed is important. In one study (Matarazzo, Saslow, Wiens, Weitman, & Allen, 1964), an interviewer engaged 60 policemen and firemen in an employment interview, and for a third of each interview, the interviewer nodded slightly throughout each of their responses. The interviewer's nodding lengthened their responses by 50 percent. Apparently, the nodding signaled the interviewer's interest in what they were saying and encouraged them to say more (see also Kita & Ide, 2007).

In full dialogues, other methods of grounding rely on projective pairs that are partly gestural. In one example from the Lego study (Clark & Krych, 2004), Danny the director and Ed the builder can see each other, and Danny can see Ed's workspace:

1	Danny	and now get (.75) a-uh eight piece green, ((*waits 1.5 sec while Ed rummages through the blocks and retrieves an "eight piece green"*))
2	Ed	((**exhibits the block to Danny**)) (= "**I've got one**")
3	Danny	and join the two … (continues)

In line 1, Danny asks Ed to get a particular type of block, and when Ed gets one, he exhibits it to Danny, holding it out for Danny to see (line 2). In line 3, Danny accepts Ed's block as correct by continuing on. If Ed's workspace had not been visible to Danny, he would have responded "I've got one," completing an adjacency pair. Instead, he used a gesture, completing a different type of projective pair.

When people are face-to-face, they also use gestures in side sequences, as in the continuation of Danny and Ed's dialogue:

3	Danny	and join the two so it's all symmetric-
4	Ed	((**poises the block over a location in the model-so-far**)) (= "Does the block go here?")
5	Danny	**yeah, right in the center**
6	Ed	((*affixes the block to the model-so-far*))

In line 3, Danny tells Ed where to put the block he has just retrieved. Because Ed is not certain where to put it, he initiates the side-sequence in line 4 (an other-initiated repair) with a gesture, poising the block over the place he believes it should go. Danny takes him as asking, "Does the block go here?," so he answers in line 5, "Yeah, right in the center." After the location has been clarified, Ed affixes the block as instructed (line 6).

People try not to overlap each other when they are speaking, but there is no such prohibition when they are gesturing. In one example from the Lego study, Jane the director and Ken the builder can see each other, and Jane can see Ken's workspace:

1	Jane	And put it on the right half *of the-*
2	Ken	((**poises his block over a location in his model-so-far**)) (= "Does the block go here?")
3	Jane	**Yes**
4	Jane	of the green rectangle
5	Ken	((affixes block))

Jane initiates the request in line 1 to specify for Ken where to put the block he is now holding. Ken believes he knows where it should go by the middle of her utterance. If he had been speaking, he would have waited until the end of her utterance and asked "Does it go here?" Because he is gesturing, he does not wait. He poises the block over the assumed location as soon as he is able to, in the middle of her utterance. Jane, in response, interrupts herself to answer "yes" before finishing her utterance.

Examples like this raise questions about spoken turns in general. If Jane had not interrupted her utterance to deal with Ken's poise, he would have thought his guess was wrong and tried another location (as many builders did). Jane was forced to interrupt her utterance-so-far to say "yes" or she would have lost the opportunity to confirm his guess. Although she returned to her utterance and finished it, most directors did not. In similar circumstances, directors left their utterances incomplete 64 percent of the time. Interrupting and abandoning one's utterance like this is incompatible with the rules of turn taking. In full dialogues, participants systematically suspend speaking, when necessary, to deal with gestural acts of communication.

Instrumental Dialogues

In dialogues viewed as instrumental to a joint activity, grounding is often achieved with actions from the activity itself. Take this exchange in a hardware store (Merritt, 1976, p. 324):

1	Customer	Hi. Do you have uh size C flashlight batteries?
2	Server	Yes, sir.
3	Customer	I'll have four please.
4	Server	((*turns to get*))

In lines 1 and 2, the customer asks for information, and the server answers in words. In lines 3 and 4, the customer makes a request that the server takes up, instead, with "turning to get," the next action in their business transaction. The server does not intend the customer to take "turning to get" as disregarding his request, but as communicating "I'll get them for you." The server uses the move as the second part of the projective pair.

"Turning to get" is just one example of an action in a larger joint activity that is used as the first or second part of a projective pair. Here are other examples, some from dialogues already cited (others from Clark, 2005):

a	Poising a Lego block	Ed poises a Lego block over a location (= "Does it go here?")
b	Looking for a Lego block	When asked to get a Lego block, Ed manifestly begins to look for one, (= "I'm looking for one")
c	Holding up a screw	In building a TV stand, Connie holds out a screw for David (= "Do you want this screw?")
d	Placing hands on piano keyboard	In starting a duet, Jean places both hands on keyboard (= "I'm ready to start")
e	Lifting and dropping hands on piano keys	In starting a duet, Edward lifts and drops his hands to the piano keys in a rhythm (= "Begin *now*")
f	Stepping up to counter	In a coffee shop, a customer steps up to the counter (= "I am now the current customer")

The actions in (a) through (f) are inherent parts of assembling Lego models, playing duets, and transacting business, and yet they are simultaneously used as communicative acts for coordinating those activities (Clark, 2005). Using actions like this for two purposes is ubiquitous in playing basketball, ballroom dancing, and dining in restaurants, indeed, in all types of physical joint activities.

Narratives

Spontaneous narratives arise when people relate events, tell jokes, or narrate stories in dialogues. To narrate a story, a participant must be granted space enough in the dialogue to tell it, and that is something the participants must agree on (Sacks, 1974). Even after someone is granted space to tell a story, he or she collaborates with the others in telling it. Telling a story in a dialogue is as much a joint activity as the dialogue itself.

Narratives in Dialogue

The first problem for people in a dialogue is how to create the occasion for a story. One method is to request one, as in this example:

1	Barbara	How did you get on at your interview, do tell us.
2	Annabel	Oh—God, what an experience,—I don't know where to start, you know, it was just such a nightmare,—((*proceeds to give a ten minute narrative*)) (1.3.215)

In line 1 Barbara proposes a particular joint project: that Annabel tells Charles and her how she, Annabel, got on at her interview. In line 2 Annabel takes up the proposal and launches into her story. A second method is to use a prenarrative, as in this example from earlier in the same conversation:

1	Annabel	I acquired an absolutely magnificent sewing-machine, by foul means, did I tell you?
2	Barbara	No,
3	Annabel	Well when I was doing freelance advertising,—(*proceeds to give a brief narrative*) (1.3.96)

In lines 1 and 2, Annabel mentions a story and asks Barbara if she has told it to her, and Barbara answers "no." Annabel takes Barbara's "no" as offering her the space to tell her story, and she immediately launches in on it. For other methods, see Jefferson (1978).

Many accounts of narratives assume that people tell stories on their own. Once Annabel begins the sewing-machine story, in such a view, she holds forth by herself. But that is an illusion. In the course of Annabel's brief story, Barbara adds 12 acknowledgements (nine "m"s, one "m-hm," and two bouts of laughter) and a final "Marvelous!" In Annabel's interview-story, the two interlocutors Barbara and Charles alter its course several times with questions like "What sort of questions?" and "Who, who was doing the interviewing?" Full narratives are joint products of all the participants.

As Bavelas and her colleagues (2000) put it, listeners are really *conarrators*. In one of their experiments, one member of a dyad was asked to tell the other member a personal close-call story. In half of the dyads, listeners could pay full attention to the narrators, but in the other half, unbeknownst to the narrators, listeners had been asked to count all of the narrator's words that began with "t." Both the attentive and the distracted listeners used many *generic* acknowledgments, such as nodding, "uh-huh," and "yeah," although the distracted listeners used fewer. Only the attentive listeners made *specific* responses related to the story content, such as "motor mimicry [e.g., grimaces, winces], gesturing the content of the story, and supplying words or phrases that advance the content of the story." The specific responses helped narrators tell better stories. The stories that were told to attentive listeners were judged higher in quality than those that were told to distracted listeners.

Process of Narrating

In narratives, one must distinguish between the *story* one tells and the *discourse* by which one tells it. As Chatman (1978, p. 19) put it:

> [E]ach narrative has two parts: a story (*histoire*), the content or chain of events (actions, happenings), plus what may be called the existents (characters, items of setting); and a discourse (*discours*), that is, the expression, the means by which the content is communicated. In simple terms, the story is the *what* in a narrative that is depicted, discourse the *how*.

Creating the discourse is not easy. First you need a story to tell, a happening, or series of events, about which you can make a point. To tell the story, you need a rough plan, where to begin, what events and evaluations to include or emphasize, and where to end. Then, in producing the discourse, you must formulate utterances one by one, in a timely fashion, as you work out that plan.

An influential account of this process was proposed by Labov based on an analysis of narratives of personal experience (Labov, 1972; Labov & Waletzky, 1967). The narratives he elicited divided into six parts, as illustrated with Annabel's sewing-machine story:

1. *Abstract (a brief summary of the story)*. Annabel provided the abstract of her story by saying, "I acquired an absolutely magnificent sewing-machine, by foul means."

2. *Orientation (a stage setting about who, when, what, and where of the story)*. In some narratives, the orientation appears as a separate section, as in this teenager's story: "It was on Sunday and we didn't have nothin' to do after I—after we came from church. Then we ain't had nothing to do." In other narratives, the orientation is incorporated in the first lines of the complicating action that follows, as in the italicized pieces of Annabel's continuation:

> well when I was. doing freelance advertising,—the advertising agency,
> that I. sometimes did some work for,.
> rang me,

3. *Complicating action (what happened)*. Annabel continues with so-called *narrative clauses* (italicized) that raise the point to be resolved in her narrative:

> and said um—we've got a client,
> who wants um—a leaflet designed,.
> to go to s- uh instructions how to use a sewing-machine,

and I said I haven't used a sewing-machine for years,—
and uh he said well. go along and talk to them,
and I went along and tal-,
and I was quite honest about it,
I said you know I. I haven't used one for
years,(continues)

4. *Evaluation ("the point of the narrative, its raison d'être: why it was told, what the narrator is getting at")* (Labov, 1972, p. 266). The evaluation is usually expressed in background clauses set in among the narrative clauses. In Annabel's complicating action, evaluations are expressed in the clauses that are *not* highlighted—"who wants um—a leaflet designed,. to go to s- uh instructions how to use a sewing-machine" and "and I was quite honest about it."

5. *Result or resolution (how the complicating action got resolved)*. Annabel completes her story by returning to her original point, how she "acquired an absolutely magnificent machine, by foul means," adding a twist about her ignorance of sewing machines:

so I've got this fabulous machine,
which I—in fact and in order to use it,
I have to read my instruction booklet,
cos it's so complicated,

6. *Coda (a signal that the narrative is finished)*. In Annabel's narrative, the resolution itself signals the end of the narrative. In other narratives, the coda is explicit, such as "And that's what happened." Codas "bring the narrator and the listener back to the point at which they entered the narrative" (Labov, 1972, p. 365).

Imagining Stories

Labov's analysis suggests that narrators are really guides to *imagining* the stories—"the content or chain of events (actions, happenings)" plus "the existents (characters, items of setting)." Narrators start with us in the here-and-now of the current dialogue and then (with the abstract) point to a story-world in the distance. From there they guide us into the time-and-place of the story-world (with the orientation) and, once inside that world, guide us from one story event to the next (the complicating action) until we reach the event that resolves the story (the resolution). Then (with the coda) they guide us back to the world we started from—the here-and-now of the dialogue.

Narrators have many techniques for helping us imagine the story world vividly (Clark & Van Der Wege, 2001). One is to depict scenes in the story using gestures (Kendon, 2004; McNeill, 1992). In a story analyzed by Kendon (1980), Fran narrates a scene from the film *Some Like it Hot*. At one point she produces:

1	They wheel a big table in ((*sweeping her arm to depict the motion*)),
2	with a big with a big (1.08 sec) cake on it ((*tracing a horizontal circle to depict its shape*)),
3	and the girl ((*raises arm to depict jumping up*)), jumps up.

Fran uses gestures to trace the path of the table (line 1); outline the size and shape of the cake (line 2); and enact a girl jumping out of the cake (line 3). That is, she uses gestures not merely to clarify what she is saying (her audience now knows the cake's size) but to encourage them to imagine the scene in space with real characters. Other narrators use gestures to lay out scenes in the space in front of them and then point at places within the scenes to ground what they describe (Haviland, 1993, 2000).

Another technique is to depict the voices of characters in the story, as in this joke told by Sam to Reynard:

1	Let me tell you a story,—
2	a girl went into a chemist's shop, and asked for,. contraceptive tablets,—
3	so he said "well I've got. all kinds, and. all prices, what do you want,"
4	she said "well what have you got," (continues)

In lines 3 and 4, Sam does not describe what the chemist and girl said. He *enacts* what they said, perhaps raising and lowering his voice to match their male and female voices. In a narrative analyzed by Tannen (1989), the narrator enacted the speech of three different characters in what were described as an "innocent voice," "upset voice," "hysterically pleading voice," "bored voice," and "sobbing." Vocal enactments like these are particularly effective in helping the audience imagine what the characters mean by what they say (Wade & Clark, 1993).

Summary

Spontaneous discourses emerge as people gossip, exchange information, make plans, transact business, assemble television stands, and even play basketball. Engaging in these activities takes coordination, which the participants establish via a succession of joint commitments. Some commitments are to joint positions, such as "Miss Pink is engaged at the moment." Others are to joint actions, such as "Kate promises to give Miss Pink a message for Jane." The participants establish joint commitments via projective pairs in which one person proposes a joint position or joint action, and the other agrees to the proposal. For example, when Jane says, "Could you give her a message for me?" and Kate replies, "Certainly," the two of them establish a joint commitment to Jane's proposal. The discourse that emerges is a dialogue: part speech, part gesture; part spoken turns, part gestural actions; part simple turns, part longer narratives. Plainly, it takes people working together to produce a spontaneous discourse.

Bibliography

Bavelas, J. B., Coates, L., & Johnson, T. (2000). Listeners as co-narrators. *Journal of Personality and Social Psychology, 79*(6), 941–952.

Blackmer, E. R., & Mitton, J. L. (1991). Theories of monitoring and the timing of repairs in spontaneous speech. *Cognition, 39*, 173–194.

Chatman, S. (1978). *Story and discourse: Narrative structure in fiction and film.* Ithaca, NY: Cornell University Press.

Clark, H. H. (1979). Responding to indirect speech acts. *Cognitive Psychology, 11*, 430–477.

Clark, H. H. (1996). *Using language.* Cambridge: Cambridge University Press.

Clark, H. H. (2004). Pragmatics of language performance. In L. R. Horn & G. Ward (Eds.), *Handbook of pragmatics* (pp. 365–382). Oxford: Blackwell.

Clark, H. H. (2005). Coordinating with each other in a material world. *Discourse Studies, 7*(4–5), 507–525.

Clark, H. H., & Brennan, S. A. (1991). Grounding in communication. In L. B. Resnick, J. M. Levine, & S. D. Teasley (Eds.), *Perspectives on socially shared cognition* (pp. 222–233). Washington: APA Books.

Clark, H. H., & Krych, M. A. (2004). Speaking while monitoring addressees for understanding. *Journal of Memory and Language, 50*(1), 62–81.

Clark, H. H., & Schaefer, E. F. (1987). Collaborating on contributions to conversation. *Language and Cognitive Processes, 2*, 19–41.

Clark, H. H., & Schaefer, E. F. (1989). Contributing to discourse. *Cognitive Science, 13*, 259–294.

Clark, H. H., & Van Der Wege, M. (2001). Imagination in discourse. In D. Schiffrin, D. Tannen, & H. E. Hamilton (Eds.), *Handbook of discourse analysis* (pp. 772–786). Oxford: Basil Blackwell.

Clark, H. H., & Wilkes-Gibbs, D. (1986). Referring as a collaborative process. *Cognition, 22*, 1–39.

De Ruiter, J. P., Mitterer, H., & Enfield, N. J. (2006). Predicting the end of a speaker's turn; a cognitive cornerstone of conversation. *Language, 82*(3), 515–535.

Dittmann, A. T., & Llewellyn, L. G. (1968). Relationship between vocalizations and head nods as listener responses. *Journal of Personality and Social Psychology, 9*(1), 79–84.

FoxTree, J. E., & Clark, H. H. (1997). Pronouncing "the" as "thee" to signal problems in speaking. *Cognition, 62*, 151–167.

Godfrey, J. J., Holliman, E., & McDaniel, J. (1992). SWITCHBOARD: telephone speech corpus for research and development. In *Proceedings of the IEEE conference on acoustics, speech, and signal processing* (pp. 517–520). San Francisco, CA: IEEE.

Goodwin, C. (1986). Between and within: Alternative sequential treatments of continuers and assessments. *Human Studies, 9*, 205–217.

Haviland, J. B. (1993). Anchoring, iconicity and orientation in Guugu Yimithirr pointing gestures. *Journal of Linguistic Anthropology, 3*(l), 3–45.

Haviland, J. (2000). Pointing, gesture spaces, and mental maps. In D. McNeill (Ed.), *Language and gesture* (pp. 13–46). New York: Cambridge University Press.

Jefferson, G. (1972). Side sequences. In D. Sudnow (Ed.), *Studies in social interaction,* (pp. 294–338). New York, NY: Free Press.

Jefferson, G. (1978). Sequential aspects of storytelling in conversation. In J. Schenkein (Ed.), *Studies in the organization of conversational interaction,* (pp. 219–248). New York: Academic Press.

Jefferson, G. (1984). Notes on a systematic deployment of the acknowledgment tokens "Yeah" and "Mm hm." *Tilburg Papers in Language and Literature, 30*, 1–18.

Jefferson, G. (2002). Is "no" an acknowledgment token? Comparing American and British uses of (+)/(–) tokens. *Journal of Pragmatics, 34*, 1345–1383.

Kendon, A. (1980). Gesticulation and speech: Two aspects of the process of utterance. In M. R. Key (Ed.), *Relationship of verbal and nonverbal communication* (pp. 207–227). Amsterdam: Mouton de Gruyter.

Kendon, A. (2004). *Gesture. Visible action as utterance.* Cambridge: Cambridge University Press.

Kita, S., & Ide, S. (2007). Nodding, *aizuchi,* and final particles in Japanese conversation: How conversation reflects the ideology of communication and social relationships. *Journal of Pragmatics, 39*(7), 1242–1254.

Labov, W. (1972). The transformation of experience in narrative syntax. In W. Labov (Ed.), *Language in the inner city: Studies in the Black English vernacular* (pp. 354–396). Philadelphia, PA: University of Pennsylvania Press.

Labov, W., & Waletzky, J. (1967). Narrative analysis: Oral versions of personal experience. In J. Helm (Ed.), *Essays on the verbal and visual arts* (pp. 12–44). Seattle, WA: University of Washington Press.

Levelt, W. J. M. (1983). Monitoring and self-repair in speech. *Cognition, 14*, 41–104.

Levelt, W. J. M. (1989). *Speaking.* Cambridge, MA: MIT Press.

Matarazzo, J. D., Saslow, G., Wiens, A. N., Weitman, M., Allen, B. V. (1964). Interviewer head nodding and interviewee speech durations. *Psychotherapy: Theory, Research & Practice, 1*(2), 54–63.

McNeill, D. (1992). *Hand and mind.* Chicago: University of Chicago Press.

Merritt, M. (1976). On questions following questions (in service encounters). *Language in Society* 5, 315–357.

Morency, L. P., Sidner, C., Lee, C., & Darrell, T. (2005). Contextual recognition of head gestures. In *Proceedings of the 7th international conference on multimodal interfaces* (pp. 18–24). Toronto, Italy: ACM.

Oreström, B. (1983). *Turn-taking in English conversation* (Vol. 66). Lund, Sweden: Gleerup.

Sacks, H. (1974). An analysis of the course of a joke's telling in conversation. In R. Bauman & J. Sherzer (Eds.), *Explorations in the ethnography of speaking* (pp. 337–353). Cambridge: Cambridge University Press.

Sacks, H., Schegloff, E. A., & Jefferson, G. (1974). A simplest systematics for the organization of turn-taking in conversation. *Language, 50*, 696–735.

Schegloff, E. A. (1980). Preliminaries to preliminaries: "Can I ask you a question?" *Sociological Inquiry, 50*, 104–152.

Schegloff, E. A. (1982). Discourse as an interactional achievement: Some uses of "uh huh" and other things that come between sentences. In D. Tannen (Ed.), *Analyzing discourse: Text and talk. Georgetown University Roundtable on Languages and Linguistics 1981* (pp. 71–93). Washington, DC: Georgetown University Press.

Schegloff, E. A. (2007). *Sequence organization in interaction.* Cambridge, UK: Cambridge University Press.

Schegloff, E. A., Jefferson, G., & Sacks, H. (1977). The preference for self-correction in the organization of repair in conversation. *Language, 53*, 361–382.

Schegloff, E. A., & Sacks, H. (1973). Opening up closings. *Semiotica, 8*, 289–327.

Seyfeddinipur, M., Kita, S., Indefrey, P. (2008). How speakers interrupt themselves in managing problems in speaking: Evidence from self-repairs. *Cognition, 108*(3), 837–842.

Smith, V. L., & Clark, H. H. (1993). On the course of answering questions. *Journal of Memory and Language, 32*, 25–38.

Stivers, T., Enfield, N. J., Brown, P., Englert, C., Hayashi, M., Heinemann, T., Hoymann, G.,... Levinson, S. C. (2009). Universals and cultural variation in turn-taking in conversation. *Proceedings of the National Academy of Sciences, 106*(26), 10587–10592.

Svartvik, J., & Quirk, R. (Eds.). (1980). *A corpus of English conversation.* Lund, Sweden: Gleerup.

Tannen, D. (1989). *Talking voices: Repetition, dialogue and imagery in conversational discourse.* Cambridge: Cambridge University Press.

Wade, E., & Clark, H. H. (1993). Reproduction and demonstration in quotations. *Journal of Memory and Language, 32*, 805–819.

Producing Socially Meaningful Linguistic Variation

Molly Babel *and* Benjamin Munson

Abstract

Spoken language exhibits variability at multiple levels of linguistic structure. This chapter focuses on phonetic variation in speech, as governed by social categories and social functions. Before addressing socially meaningful variation in production, the way in which phonetic variation naturally makes its way into the speech chain through the mechanisms of speech production is described. A succinct history of sociolinguistic approaches to variation is provided, along with discussions of variation in production and perception from a laboratory phonology perspective. This provides a range of views on the topic, from macrosociologic perspectives to more microlevels in both naturalistic and experimentally controlled settings. This chapter argues that successful research on variation in speech production should build on current trends in the field by incorporating a range of methods and examining more fully the context under which speech is produced.

Key Words: speech production, speech perception, variation, sociophonetics, accommodation

Introduction

It is axiomatic that spoken language is highly variable, and that variability can be observed at nearly every level of linguistic structure, from the acoustic instantiation of speech sounds to the information structure of long stretches of spoken discourse. Many of the chapters in this volume discuss empirical and theoretical studies of the production of linguistic structures. A challenge to these has been to model the generation of variable linguistic forms. This chapter focuses on one type of variation, that which is related to social categories and social functions. We intentionally define "social" broadly in this chapter. Consequently, this chapter reviews numerous bodies of literature, including studies of linguistic differences between groups that differ in macrosociologic categories such as gender, age, social class, and regional origin; linguistic differences that reflect stances, attitudes, and ideologies; and linguistic differences that are elicited in

experimental tasks that manipulate different social variables.

This chapter considers empirical and theoretical studies of language variation, and suggests how they might be linked to the psycholinguistic models of production that are the focus of this volume. The specific focus of this chapter is on variability in speech sounds. The reason for this focus is partly practical and partly theoretical. Practically, this is because of the expertise of the authors: both of us are laboratory phonologists who study social variation in speech-sound production, processing, representation, and acquisition. Another practical reason relates to the content of the existing literature on variation: there is simply a larger body of research on speech-sound variation than on syntactic variation. The other motivation is theoretical, and relates to the imbalance in existing literature. Early variationist studies of language were based on linguistic models that posited a strong disconnect between competence and performance. Sociolinguistic variation was seen as variation in performance in a group of speakers whose competence was identical. In this view, phonological variation was seen as cases of variation in the performance of phonological categories whose abstract competence-level representations were equivalent across dialects. In contrast, syntactic variation was less amenable to this kind of modeling, because syntactic structures were seen as the product of a finite-state grammar that operated at the level of linguistic competence (e.g., Lavendara, 1978; Romain, 1984). The strict competence-performance distinction in phonology has been critiqued extensively in recent work (e.g., Munson, Edwards, & Beckman, 2012; Pierrehumbert, 2003). Although some work has extended this critique to syntax (e.g., Manning, 2003; Troutman, Clark, & Goldrick, 2008), research on socially meaningful syntactic variation remains very much in its infancy and is not discussed in this chapter.

By way of introduction, imagine the task of modeling the production of variants of /æ/ vowel, as in the word *cat*. Regional vernacular pronunciations of this vowel vary substantially. In the Inland North (using the geographic regions defined by Labov, Ash, & Boberg, 2006), the pronunciation is highly diphthongal, gliding from a high-front vowel to a mid-to low-front vowel, notated by Labov and colleagues as /iϒ/. In North California varieties, the vowel is typically lower and more central than in other dialects. In some Northeastern dialects, this vowel is pronounced differently in different phonetic contexts: before heterosyllabic nondorsal nasals, it is pronounced as in the Inland North, whereas in other phonetic contexts it is similar to its pronunciation in the pandialectal standard used in news media. Within dialects, pronunciation is also highly variable. In one small-scale study of the North dialect region, the use of different /æ/ variants was found to differ as a function of self and self-stated sexual orientation (Munson, McDonald, DeBoe, & White, 2006).

At first glance, two factors appear to govern this variation: regional dialect and social identity. If this were true, then modeling the production of dialectal variants would be easy to accomplish. Dialectal variants could be modeled by assuming that individuals were simply emulating the parametric phonetic detail that they were exposed to during acquisition. Modeling the effects of social identities on production would be similarly trivial if it were presumed that the acquisition of these variants was due to selective attention to selected speakers during childhood and consistent emulation of the phonetic characteristics of those speakers.

Unfortunately, this simple solution to modeling variation is likely to fail very quickly. A closer look at individuals' pronunciation patterns shows even more complex patterns of variation. Consider, for example, the pronunciation patterns of widely known US television host Oprah Winfrey. Hay, Jannedy, and Mendoza-Denton (1999) showed that the degree of monophthongization in /aɪ/ in Ms. Winfrey's speech varied as a function both of word frequency and of the identity of the person with whom she was speaking, with monophthongal variants being favored in high-frequency words and words spoken to African-American talk-show guests. Ms. Winfrey grew up in geographic regions where /aɪ/ monophthongization is common (i.e., rural Mississippi), and presumably in speaker communities where it is prevalent (i.e., African-American English-speaking communities, which we infer from the racial divisions in the Southern United States during the time Ms. Winfrey was growing up). As an adult, she lives in a community in which monophthongization is not prevalent (i.e., among speakers in Upper Class Chicago and in the media community). Hence, her variable pronunciation of /aɪ/ is consistent with the variable models that she has encountered in different speaking contexts across her lifespan. However, the *systematic* nature of this variation suggests that a much more complex process is at play than simply matching the probabilities of the different forms that have been encountered across a lifetime of language use. Specifically, it suggests that both cognitive and social processes work in concert to select different forms for production depending on the linguistic content, the meaning of the message to be conveyed, and the social context. A second telling example concerns the production of the word *Iraq*. Hall-Lew, Coppock, and Starr (2010) showed that differences in the production of the second vowel in the word *Iraq* were correlated with political attitudes, with /æ/ occurring more often in the speech of US Congressmen and women who support the Iraq war and /ɑ/ in those who opposed it. The relationship between the pronunciation of *Iraq* and political attitudes was most pronounced in speakers from dialect regions that do not have a global preference for /æ/ or /ɑ/ in the second syllable of similar words. Again, this variability suggests that pronunciation variability is the product of a complex set of interactions among a variety of forces.

The structure of the remainder of this chapter is as follows. The next section reviews studies of linguistic variation, chronicling a brief history of sociolinguistic and stylistic variation in studies that use quasi population-based samples, and in ethnographic studies of variation within individuals and communities. The third section reviews laboratory studies of variation, including both studies of the perception of variation and studies of its production. Suggestions for future research on this topic are provided in the fourth section. The chapter concludes with a brief summary.

Variation
Linguistic and Physiological Variation

A necessary prerequisite to building models of the production of variable forms is to understand some of the natural sources of variation in the signal. That is, even without variation based on social and cultural categories of class or race, given the nature of how speech is produced and how sounds are strung together into hierarchical sequences, significant variation in the signal is inevitable. In a classic article, Ladefoged and Broadbent (1957) presented a taxonomy that argued that variation can be roughly classified as originating in one of three sources: social, physiological, and linguistic. There is considerable overlap between these three sources of variation, such that one speech-sound variant cannot necessarily be classified as a member of just one of these categories. Because social variation is the theme of the chapter, most of the discussion in this section is on that type of variation. Before moving on, however, the physiological and linguistic sources of variation are briefly described.

The first in Ladefoged and Broadbent's taxonomy is called linguistic variation, for lack of a better term. This class of variation should be very familiar to readers of this handbook, and includes any variation that is secondary to linguistic organization. In the domain of speech sounds, this includes such phenomena as final strengthening and coarticulation. These processes are theoretically common to an entire speech community, regardless of who says them. Final strengthening, for example, is the process by which segments at word, phrase, or even syllable boundary become longer as a result of their prosodic position (Byrd et al., 2000, 2005; Cho & Keating, 2001; Fougeron & Keating, 1997; Keating, Cho, Fougeron, & Hsu, 2003; Klatt, 1976). Coarticulation is the way in which linguistic segments do not exist as actual individual segments, but inevitably involve the acoustic qualities

of surrounding segments. In other terms, each phonetic segment sounds different depending on the segmental context in which it is embedded. Some theories treat coarticulation as a mechanical consequence based on inertia of the articulators (Browman & Goldstein, 1990; Lindblom, 1990), but research has found that coarticulation is largely planned (Nolan, Holst, & Kühnert, 1996; Whalen, 1990) and its degree varies across languages (Hombert, Ohala, & Ewan, 1979; Manuel, 1990).

When one understands how speech is produced, it becomes apparent that physiological variation is inevitably reflected in sounds' spectral characteristics. The acoustics of the speech signal are determined by two main factors: the noise source and the filter through which that noise passes. In the production of voiced sounds with a relatively open vocal tract, the vibration of the vocal folds is the noise source and the supraglottal cavity is the filter. Differences in the size and shape of the vocal folds contribute to interspeaker differences in pitch and voice quality. A talker with bigger vocal folds has a voice that is lower in pitch than a talker with smaller vocal folds. Voice quality refers to whether a talker's voice is breathy or creaky, and it is determined largely by the closure duration of the vocal folds in the course of vibration, and by whether full vocal fold closure is achieved. The size and morphology of the supraglottal cavity determines the resonances of the filter. Again, the larger this oral cavity, the lower the resonant frequencies produced by the vocal tract; this property determines the position of a speaker's vowels within the acoustic-phonetic space of possible human vocalizations. Thus, individual anatomical and physiological differences contribute significantly to the variation within the signal, without necessarily acting as an ideologic or social identity marker.

On the surface, linguistic and anatomical variation appear to explain some of the speech-sound variation seen between different social groups. First, consider sex. Men's voices cluster together in having lower pitch and lower formant frequencies than women's voices. These differences are likely a consequence in part off the fact that men's vocal tracts and vocal folds are typically larger than women's. Next, consider age. Anatomical and physiological changes with age also naturally affect speech production. The extrinsic muscles that support the larynx become slack with age, and the mucosal tissue that covers the vocal folds loses its elasticity. This tends to change voice quality, and lower overall pitch and formant frequencies. Thus, at least some age and gender differences in the speech-sound production plausibly arise from sex- and age-based anatomical and physiological variation.

A closer look at a large set of data shows that variation in anatomy and physiology cannot account for all of the observed differences in groups that vary in gender or age. Classic studies describing the vowel patterns of males and females (Peterson & Barney, 1952) indeed find that women exhibit the predicted higher pitch and higher formant frequencies than men. However, a recent cross-linguistic study of male-female differences in vowel production found that the extent of these sex differences varies across languages, even when population height is controlled for statistically (Johnson, 2006). This suggests that some of the gender-based differences in speech production are the result of learned socially and culturally specific norms. This conjecture is supported by the findings of Van Bezooijen (1995), who examined the perception of vocal pitch in Japanese- and Dutch-speaking listeners. Van Bezooijen argued that Dutch and Japanese cultures place different weights on producing a canonically masculine or feminine voice. Given this, we might predict greater pitch differentiation between men and women in Japan than in the Netherlands, a finding partially supported by Yamazawa and Hollien (1992).

Moreover, children acquire some sex-specific speech characteristics before puberty, which is generally assumed to be the point at which the anatomical differences between males and females emerge (Perry, Ohde, & Ashmead, 2001; Sachs, Lieberman, & Erickson, 1973; though see Vorperian, Wang, & Chung, 2009 for recent evidence of sex differences in vocal-tract anatomy prior to puberty). Hence, despite the pre-existence of sex-related differences in speech production, the magnitude of the differences between men and women across cultures, and the age at which these differences are acquired, indicates that many of the speech patterns partly are learned socially and culturally specific behaviors.

The inadequacy of anatomical and physiological variation in explaining the full range of variation in speech is illustrated well by studies of sexual orientation and speech. Studies have found that self-identified members of the gay, lesbian, or bisexual (GLB) community use speech styles that are distinctive from those of the broader speech community (Crist, 1997; Gaudio, 1994; Linville, 1998; Moonwomon-Baird, 1997; Munson et al., 2006; Pierrehumbert, Bent, Munson, Bradlow, & Bailey, 2004; Smyth, Jacobs, & Rogers, 2003)

and that listeners are indeed sensitive to their variation. That is, GLB individuals can be identified as such at above chance levels from audio-only content-neutral speech samples (Carahaly, 2000; Gaudio, 1994; Linville, 1998; Munson et al., 2006; Smyth et al., 2003; see Munson and Babel, 2007, for a much broader and more in-depth treatment of sexual orientation and speech.) The specific speech differences that have been observed in these studies cannot be reduced to simple anatomical or physiological differences between GLB and heterosexual people, at least insomuch as can be inferred from acoustic analyses of their speech. Hence, they must reflect in part learned socially and culturally specific processes. We imagine that this situation is particularly complex when considering cultures in which sexualities are classified differently from how they are classified in English-speaking communities in North America (i.e., labels that go beyond the gender and sexuality labels used in Western cultures, like *man*, *woman*, *gay*, *straight*, and *bisexual*), such as the *hijras* of Indian society who have been shown to use distinctive linguistic forms (Hall, 2002; Hall & O'Donovan, 1996).

The Sociolinguistic Method

Having described what social variation is *not*, we now turn to what it *is*. The answer to this question is well illustrated through a brief summary of a seminal study on this topic, specifically Labov's pioneering (1963) work on of the distribution of speech-sound variants in Martha's Vineyard. This study arguably set the stage for the examination of how social structures motivate linguistic variation. In that study, sociolinguistic variation in a community was defined as differences in the incidence of linguistic forms across major sociological categories, such as gender, age, and race. Labov (1963) chronicled the centralization of the diphthongs /aɪ/ and /aʊ/(hallmarks of the local dialect) as a function three such variables: age, ethnic, and occupational groups. Labov's study occurred during a critical shift in the demographics in Martha's Vineyard, when the traditional fishing lifestyle was supplanted by a burgeoning tourism industry. Labov found that Vinelanders most threatened by tourism (men aged 31–45 years) had the highest rates of diphthong centralization. He interpreted this finding as evidence that centralization had a social meaning, which can be summarized broadly as "Vineyarder." That is, the fisherman's use of this variant was seen as marking their identity through their use of more-conservative pronunciation variants.

The general method in Labov (1963) fast became the norm in language variation research: identify a variable undergoing a sound change, examine the incidence of different variants of this linguistic variable in different major sociological categories in production tasks varying in complexity. The sociolinguistic stratification observed by Labov (1963) is regarded by many researchers as distinct from a second type of variation, stylistic variation. Stylistic variation is illustrated by Labov's (1966) in study of New York City English. In that study, spoken language was elicited from individuals in sociolinguistic interviews that had a variety of components intended to elicit categorically different productions: casual conversation, careful speech, the reading of a short passage, word lists, and minimal pair lists. The speakers in Labov's study came from a range of social classes and the linguistic variable of interest was the presence or absence of postvocalic /ɹ/. The principle finding of this study was that, while socioeconomic class groups differed *sociolinguistically* with respect to the use of postvocalic /ɹ/ (with /ɹ/ being more frequent in the middle class groups than the working and lower class groups) all social groups exhibited the same *stylistic* pattern. For all groups the lowest rates of postvocalic /ɹ/ were found in casual speech and the highest rates were found in readings of a minimal pair wordlist. This is taken as evidence that the minimal pair word-list elicits the most careful and formal speech style.

Giles (1973) argued that style shifting observed in sociolinguistic interviews like those in Labov's New York City study was an experimenter effect. That is, the subjects of the sociolinguistic interviews were accommodating their speech to the interviewer, who was modifying *his* speech style. Giles supports this argument with the results of a study he conducted in Bristol, where Bristol-accented speakers were either interviewed by a native speaker of Received Pronunciation (RP, the prescriptive standard for British English used by, among others, members of the British Broadcasting Corporation and by high-ranking public officials) or a native speaker of the regional variety spoken in Bristol. An independent group of listeners judged the voices of those who had interacted with the native Bristol interviewer as having stronger Bristol accents than those who had been interviewed by the native RP speaker. This result was based on running speech; hence, the accentedness judgments could have been based on the use of phonetic, syntactic, or lexical variables. Even without knowledge of what cued listeners' accentedness judgments, Giles demonstrated that shifts in speech style

may be prompted by the speech style of the interlocutor. Trudgill (1981) revealed a different and more intricate pattern in his sociolinguistic interviews. In interviews with speakers of Norwich English, the sociolinguist interviewer was found to move toward the level of /t/-glottalization of his interviewees, but not to their degree of /ɑ/-fronting, two linguistic features of Norwich English that vary as a function of speech style within speakers of that dialect. These two linguistic features, /t/-glottalization and /ɑ/-fronting, differ with respect to their social salience in the speech community, with /ɑ/-fronting being a linguistic variable that is ostensibly not consciously monitored by speakers or listeners. From his results, Trudgill concludes that accommodation, but not necessarily style shifting, occurs with only socially salient linguistic variables, and that the two processes are fundamentally different.

Variation in speech style is also illustrated in Coupland's (1980) case study of a single female travel agent in her workplace. Coupland tracked her use of five phonological variables while she interacted with clients, coworkers, family, and friends about a variety of topics, either in person or on the telephone. The frequency with which the travel agent used particular linguistic variables was correlated with the complex contextual dynamic (what she was speaking about, to whom, and through what communication medium).

The studies of Labov, Trudgill, and Giles lend themselves to a definition of speech style as variation in speech patterns in accordance with social context and demands. However, there is an active debate in the community of sociolinguistics on what is meant by style. Eckert (2001) defines style as any number of linguistics variables that indicate or mark a social identity on either an individual or group level, similar to the kind variation found in Coupland's study. Others view style as the sociolinguistic variation exhibited by a single speaker (Bell, 2001; Labov, 2001). Tied up in this latter meaning of style is the assumption that a variable will not be available for stylistic variation unless it is already in the speech community as a sociolinguistic variable. More recent analyses of speech style highlight how a single linguistic variable may be used in multiple contexts, and have a different social meaning in each of these contexts. For example, Podesva's (2007) study of a single gay man communicating in both professional and social contexts showed that the same variable, final stop-consonant release, can have the meaning "erudite" in one context and "prissy" in another.

Are speakers aware of the variation they are producing? In a great deal of sociolinguistic research, describing a process as social is often tantamount to describing the process as intentional. For example, Labov (2001, p. 85) described style shifting as a "controlled device" of language use. Similarly, Eckert (2001, p. 124) sees language use on the whole as a "fairly low-level process" but the social use of language is subject to "conscious manipulation." The earliest accounts of style, such as that of Labov (1966), argued that shifts to more standard speech styles would occur as a function of the amount of attention paid to speech. The key evidence for this claim was the higher proportion of nonstandard forms in spontaneous speech than in scripted speech or word list readings. Presumably, spontaneous speech has higher cognitive demands than does reading. Recent research has shown that this is clearly not always the case and that multiple factors may go into the selection of a speech style. Sharma (2005) illustrates that when speakers of Indian English in California pay more attention to their speech, they become *less* standard in their usage. Bell's (1984) investigation of four radio newsreaders in New Zealand also supports the argument that attention is not the sole determiner of style. In this study, Bell found that the four radio newsreaders used different stylistic variants when reading the news on a community radio station as opposed to a national radio station. In both contexts, the newscasters were reading the news and, therefore, using a style of speech demanding relatively high amounts of attention, but it was the audience to which the message was being delivered determining the speech style and not the act of reading.

These data, and others like it, provided the backbone for an alternative model of stylistic variation, Bell's theory of audience design. Within this model, a speaker is thought to consider not only the addressee, but also individuals who are in the roles of auditor, over-hearer, eavesdropper, and social group (Bell, 1984, 2001) in selecting his or her speech style. Bell (1984, p. 167) suggests three ways in which a speaker may select a stylistic variant: (1) a speaker evaluates an addressee's personal traits and a speech style is selected accordingly; (2) a speaker evaluates the general speech style of the addressee and a speech style is designed accordingly; or (3) a speaker listens for the use of particular linguistic variables and selects a speech style that reflects the speaker's uses. The underlying mechanisms or the level of automaticity with respect to how a stylistic variant is selected is not provided in Bell's model,

although it is acknowledged that a full understanding of a speaker's social and psychological networks, biases, and values is necessary to predict a speaker's behavior (Bell, 1984, p. 169). Bell's model is unique in sociolinguistic theory in that it attempts to predict when variation will arise in the signal, in lieu of simply describing its existence. In a similar vein, we reconnect the sociolinguistic concept of style with current speech production research next.

The Laboratory Method
Perception

Most studies of sociolinguistic variation have used the methods illustrated by Labov's (1963) study of Martha's Vineyard and his work on New York City English (Labov, 1966). This section reviews laboratory research on the perception of social categories through linguistic variation, as well as the influence of socially based expectations on linguistic processing. In the context of a volume on production processes, we see a section on perception as somewhat of a necessary evil. It is necessary because a model of production can only exist if there is first a model of the target message that talkers are attempting. Perception studies are one way of understanding the nature of this message. It is an evil (at least figuratively speaking) because the results of perception studies give at best an incomplete picture of production processes, and at worst a misleading one, a point elaborated on later. This section is a much briefer and slightly more current summary of perception studies given by Thomas (2002). We refer readers to that article for a fuller discussion of these studies and the issues they raise.

The first set of perception studies we review examines the attributes that listeners associate with different linguistic variants. Just as much of the research on sociolinguistics has focused on the influence of major sociological categories, such as age, gender, and social class on variation, so has much of the research examining the perception of these same categories. Some groups are perceived extremely robustly from phonetic variation. For example, listeners can identify a talker's sex from very brief signals that have had all linguistic content effectively removed (i.e., Bachorowski & Owren, 1999). Listeners can identify a talker's ethnicity, at least in tasks examining the perception of speech produced by African-American and Caucasian talkers. This is true when the categorical linguistic variation characteristic of African-American Vernacular English is removed (e.g., Purnell, Idsardi, & Baugh, 1999); however, this ability is much more strongly compromised when the signal is degraded than is the identification of sex (Lass, Almerino, Jordan, & Walsh, 1980). Listeners are able to identify regional dialects at greater-than-chance levels. In one study of American English (Clopper & Pisoni, 2004a), naive listeners in one Midwestern US town were found to be able to discriminate among three broad dialect regions. A subsequent study with the same stimuli found that individuals who had lived in multiple dialect regions were more accurate in classifying talkers than were those who had only lived in the Midwestern US (Clopper & Pisoni, 2004b). More recent research has examined social categories that were not examined in early sociolinguistic research in the variationist tradition. Munson et al. (2006) found that listeners could identify talkers' sexual orientation at greater-than-chance levels from productions of single words. Not all social variables are equally perceptible, even to familiar listeners. Drager (2010) reports on an ethnographic study of phonetic variation among different social groups in a single girl's high school in Christchurch, New Zealand. She found that the degree of glottalization in the vowel in the word *like* varied as a function of the word's function and of the social group of the speakers who produced it. A subsequent perception study found that listeners from the same population (i.e., students at the same school) could not identify either the function of *like* or the social group of the speaker who produced it from the degree of glottalization. A general tactic in all of these studies is to analyze which acoustic parameters are associated with which social judgments. For example, Clopper and Pisoni (2004a) found that a weak or absent postvocalic /ɹ/ was associated with listener judgments of a speaker being from the Northeast or New England. Munson et al. (2006) found that talkers who were identified as gay-sounding produced tokens of /s/ with a high peak frequency and a compact spectrum. This was also found to differ between self-identified gay and heterosexual men.

A second set of perception studies have shown that listeners calibrate their regular linguistic perception based on knowledge of or expectations about socially meaningful linguistic variation. One particularly striking example of this is given by Janson and Schulman (1983), who examined the perception of a synthetic /ɛ/-/æ/ continuum by speakers of Swedish. The /ɛ/-/æ/ contrast is preserved in some, but not all, dialects of Swedish. Jansen and Schulman found that listeners perceived this contrast when they thought they were listening to a speaker from a dialect that preserved the contrast,

but not when they thought they were listening to a speaker from one that did not. Similar results are presented by Drager (2011), Hay, Warren, and Drager (2006), Johnson, Strand, and D'Imperio (1999), Niedzielski (1999), Staum Casasanto (2008), and Strand and Johnson (1996). In each of those studies, listeners' identification of phonemes was affected by an experimental manipulation suggesting a particular attribute about a speaker.

Interestingly, this calibration does not extend to all perception tasks. Walker (2008) found that listeners did not judge nonstandard syntactic structures differently depending on whether they thought they were spoken by someone from a social group (here, New Zealanders with lower socioeconomic status) in which they are commonly used. Kraljic, Brennan, and Samuel (2008) and Kraljic, Samuel, and Brennan (2008) showed that listeners rapidly adapt to pronunciation characteristics of particular speakers and generalize them to new speakers who are presumed to share the same source of pronunciation variation (i.e., ones who they believe to speak the same dialect). Kraljic and colleagues also demonstrated that listeners are able to discern between sources of variation that are unique to speech communities (like dialects); to individuals (like those related to individual vocal-tract morphology); and to idiosyncratic conditions that led to a particular production (like having a pen in the mouth while speaking).

How do these studies inform models of the production of social variation? Consider the case of sexual orientation and speech. Given the findings by Munson et al. (2006), one might conclude that the particular high-frequency, compact-spectrum /s/ used by gay men and associated with judgments of gay-soundingness means *gay*, much in the way that the sequence of articulations and their acoustic consequences that are denoted by the phonetic symbols /kæt/ means "member of the class of animals *felis catus*." Producing this /s/ could be modeled by dictating that the articulatory spell-out of a lexical item would include a particular variant if that item was indexed to the social meaning "gay." One problem that this conjecture faces is that the same variant is potentially subject to many different interpretations. We can illustrate this with studies of two phenomena: the widely attested variation in the place of articulation of the nasal in the *-ing* morpheme by speakers US dialects of English and variation in the spectral detail of the vowel /æ/ by English speakers in the upper Midwestern United States. Campbell-Kibler (2007) showed that the use of an alveolar variant in the -*ing* morpheme can increase the tendency for a speaker to be labeled as Southern, and decrease the tendency to be rated as gay, although these specific perceptions seem to be strongly tied to other attributes about the same talker. That is, simply saying an [n] in -*ing* does not guarantee that someone will be labeled as heterosexual and Southern, but instead interacts with the perception of other attributes about the speaker. Smith, Hall, and Munson (2010) examined the perception of two variants of /æ/: one with a high-front on-glide, characteristic of a set of pronunciations known collectively as the Northern Cities Chain Shift (NCCS), and low, retracted variant, characteristic of a different set of pronunciations, the California Chain Shift (CCS). Previous work by Munson et al. (2006) showed that gay men produced vowels that were broadly similar to those produced by CCS speakers, and heterosexual men produced vowels more like those of the NCCS. In a perception experiment using single words, listeners identified NCCS vowels as more heterosexual sounding and CCS vowels as more gay sounding. Smith et al. examined the perception of tokens of /æ/ produced by trained speakers that had intentionally exaggerated NCCS and CCS characteristics. Although they failed to replicate Munson et al.'s original finding, they did show that different variants of /æ/ were associated with a variety of perceptions, including ones about the talker's age, height, and health habits (i.e., whether or not they smoked or drank alcohol). This finding was quite unexpected; indeed, these items were included only as fillers in an experiment whose primary goals were to examine the perception of sexual orientation! Nonetheless, the finding is further valuable evidence that a single linguistic variant can be perceived as indexing multiple social meanings.

As discussed in Munson (2010), there are two logical interpretations of the findings reviewed in the previous paragraph. The first is that variants like NCCS /æ/ are essentially homophones, much like the homophones that exist in other form-meaning relationships. The other is that the interpretations that people make reflect a hierarchy of meanings associated with forms like NCCS /æ/ versus CCS /æ/, or alveolar-in versus velar-finaling. This latter hypothesis has been discussed at length in recent works in sociolinguistics, including Campbell-Kibler (2009), Eckert (2008), and Silverstein (2003). Clearly, resolving the nature of the representation of socially meaningful variables is key to developing psycholinguistic models of its production.

Speech Production

The focus of this section is on studies of phonetic accommodation by psychologists, sociologists, and laboratory-oriented linguists. However, sociolinguists have long been interested in accommodation (e.g., Giles, 1973; Trudgill, 1981) and have recently displayed renewed interest in its role in dialect contact (Trudgill, 2004, 2008). Hence, before discussing recent laboratory studies, it is worthwhile revisiting the foundations of sociolinguistics, as it relates to current work on variation in speech production. In perhaps its earliest inception, sociolinguistics was a field interested in modeling sound change. The original list of primary interests included the *actuation* problem and the *transition* problem (Weinreich, Labov, & Herzog, 1968). The actuation problem involves understanding why a particular sound change is introduced into a particular speech community at a particular time. That issue is outside of the scope of this chapter. The transition problem, however, revolves around the path of the sound change, whether it behaves gradiently or categorically. In addition to this original goal of the field, we can consider another type of path: how does the sound change transition through the community? In this section on speech production we do not review the literature on macro-level sound changes, but rather we focus on laboratory- and corpus-based studies of phonetic convergence and imitation. This line of research has been fruitful in integrating methods and models of speech production that attempt to predict phonetic and phonological variation in the signal. This work is truly interdisciplinary, and represents an intersection of psychology, sociology, and several branches of linguistics. An understanding of an individual's social network also has bearing on the question of how a sound change spreads through a speech community (Milroy & Milroy, 1985), but from a different theoretical and methodologic perspective.

From the beginning, studies of phonetic convergence have been concerned with the social and contextual effects of speech production. Phonetic convergence (sometimes referred to as *phonetic imitation* or *accommodation*) is the process by which interacting talkers come to be more similar, both acoustically and perceptually. Some of the earliest studies considered the psychological and social factors that affect the direction of talkers' convergent or divergent behavior. For example, Natale (1975a) examined convergence of mean vocal intensity between conversational dyads. The intensity level of a confederate to the experiment was instrumentally manipulated three times through the course of the conversations; subjects generally converged toward the intensity level of the confederate. Natale's second task also used conversation dyads. Before participating, individuals completed the Marlowe-Crown Social Desirability test (Crown & Marlowe, 1964), which evaluates an individual's desire to be accepted by society. Through the course of three conversations, participants converged and individuals' contribution to their dyad's amount of convergence was positively correlated with their Marlowe-Crown score. In another study, Natale (1975b) examined same-sex dyads' convergence of temporal patterns across two conversations. Again, using the Marlowe-Crown test, Natale demonstrated that participants' degree of convergence was predictable by their desire to be accepted socially. This result was only significant, however, in the second conversation. This suggests that increased familiarity and more than a passing level of social engagement with a conversational partner prompts convergent speech behavior.

Gregory and colleagues (Gregory, Dagan, & Webster, 1997; Gregory, Green, Carrothers, & Dagan, 2001; Gregory & Webster, 1996; Gregory, Webster, & Huang, 1993) examined the role of vocal fundamental frequency (f0, changes in which are perceived as changes in vocal pitch) in phonetic convergence in conversations. Gregory et al. (1993) examined a corpus of 12 American English telephone conversations along with a corpus of 11 conversations from an Egyptian Arabic database. Spectral measures were averaged from a 62- to 192-Hz band-delimited region of the speech signal and with this long-term average spectra measure, Gregory and colleagues found convergence between the dyads. American English listeners evaluated the conversations from the English-speaking corpus in terms of how smoothly they went. This independent listener group rated the interviews more favorably when accommodation had occurred, suggesting the convergence between interlocutors affects the perceived quality of the conversation.

The role of social status in accommodation was explored by Gregory and Webster (1996). Drawing upon Communication Accommodation Theory (Giles & Coupland, 1991), a model that emphasizes the role of language as a tool for asserting identity and social relations, Gregory and colleagues interpreted the phenomenon of accommodation as a subconscious response to an interlocutor's higher status. They theorized that accommodation was an adaptation to another's communicative behavior

in the service of achieving a social goal or being accepted. Gregory and Webster (1996) measured accommodation in interview excerpts from the Larry King Live television program (a popular television program where a host, Larry King, interviews a range of guests, including both high-profile celebrities and politicians, and noncelebrities). The social status of the guest was used to predict King's behavior, specifically whether King would accommodate toward high status guests while lower status guests would accommodate toward him. Gregory and Webster's analysis indeed found that King accommodated more toward high status guests than lower status guests. The results from the f0 data illustrate that Larry King modulated his pitch less during interactions with talkers of a lower social status.

In another study, Gregory et al. (1997) filtered the audio signal of one member of a conversational dyad. Dyads in the control condition and those who were in a low-pass filtered condition exhibited convergence, whereas dyads in a high-pass filtered condition where the f0 frequency region had been removed did not. Groups of listeners also rated the conversations for quality. Generally, judgments were more negative for conversations that had been filtered, although the low-pass group did receive slightly more favorable ratings than the high-pass group. Gregory et al. (1997) argue their result indicates that low-frequency energy plays a significant role in convergence because of its role as a salient phonetic feature that transmits social information by conveying emotion and attitude. Using a similar design, Gregory et al. (2001) sought to determine how visual information influences accommodation. They replicated their finding that accommodation occurred in dyads in the control and low-pass filtered conditions. Additionally, Gregory and colleagues found that along with not accommodating phonetically, dyads in the high-pass filtered condition did not look up and interact visually as much as the dyads in the other conditions. This finding suggests that accommodating an interlocutor is part of the social structure of communication and when it does not go as intended, the level of engagement declines.

One recent and influential study on phonetic convergence is reported by Pardo (2006). Pardo examined phonetic convergence in same-gender dyads involved in jointly completing a map task, where one member of the dyad was the giver of map directions and one was the receiver whose task it was to navigate the dictated path. Pardo used an AXB task to examine the extent to which listeners modified their productions to match those of their conversational partner. In this AXB task, triplets of words were played to naive listeners. The middle "X" word was one person's production of a word elicited in a conversational dyad. The first and third "A" and "B" words were productions of the same word from the other conversational partner either in the conversation task itself (what Pardo called *task repetitions*); produced in a pretask reading list; or produced in a posttask reading list. Listeners judged which of the A or B words sounded most like the X word. Convergence was assumed to occur when the task repetitions were rated to sound more like the target than the pretask and posttasks readings. Using data from this AXB task, dyads were perceived to have converged on 62 percent of the experiment trials. Female dyads were found to converge toward the speaker who was receiving instructions, whereas male dyads patterned oppositely; they converged toward the speech of the male talkers giving instructions. Pardo concludes that particular social factors dependent on the situational context of a conversation determine the direction of phonetic accommodation. Subsequent research by Pardo, Jay, and Krauss (2010) found that when one member of a map-task dyad was given the instruction to imitate the other, social and interaction factors often overrode the instructions to imitate. Although they replicated Pardo's original finding that male dyads converged more than female dyads, pairs were judged to have converged when the map-directions receivers were instructed to imitate, but when the givers of directions were instructed to imitate, most dyads were judged to have diverged.

Pardo (2009) reports on the acoustic analyses of the speech of the same-gender dyads along with presenting results from the mixed-gender dyads whose data are not discussed in Pardo (2006). Like same-gender dyads, mixed-gender pairs converged, albeit to a lesser extent; listeners perceived mixed-gender pairs to have converged on 53 percent of the trials. Pardo (2010) also analyzed F0 and duration data to determine the cues on which listeners based their judgments; the acoustic measures were taken as the difference of F0 and duration between each pair for each AXB trial. These values accounted for 41 percent of the variance for the female talkers, but only 7 percent of the variance for the male data. Pardo also compared formant frequencies of vowels produced by participants in pretask and posttask sessions. Talkers were found to diverge or converge with their conversational partner, depending on the talkers' role (receiver or giver) and vowel identity; the high vowels converged and

low vowels diverged. Givers were found to centralize their vowel space more than receivers. These results are important because they indicate that convergent phonetic behavior does not stop simultaneously with the conversational partner with whom a talker is converging. Moreover, the vocalic changes found by Pardo (2010) suggest that the talker's entire phonological system was affected by exposure to the map task partner.

Researchers have also explored phonetic convergence using an auditory-naming paradigm. This paradigm elicits productions from research participants by having them repeat (i.e., name) words after hearing another talker say the words (i.e., the auditory object) over headphones or a loudspeaker. This paradigm uses single-word shadowing from a model talker as a way to elicit convergent or accommodating speech behavior. Although this method removes most, if not all, of the social aspects of actual language interaction, it is a useful tool because it demonstrates how even in the absence of social motivation, phonetic convergence (often termed *spontaneous imitation* when using this method) still occurs. Goldinger (1998), for example, found that the degree of phonetic imitation interacts with word frequency and amount of exposure. Lower-frequency words undergo more imitation than higher-frequency words and the more often a model talker's production of a word is heard, the more a participant spontaneously imitates its acoustic properties. This was later replicated in a study by Goldinger and Azuma (2004). Namy, Nygaard, and Sauerteig (2002) also replicated Goldinger's findings and expanded the result in revealing that female participants, in their study, imitated more than male participants. In using single-word production, researchers are able to probe in more detail what in the acoustic detail is imitated. With this in mind, Shockley, Sabadini, and Fowler (2004) revealed that participants readily imitate lengthened voice onset time in aspirated American English stops. Nielsen (2011) extended this finding in demonstrating that participants imitate lengthened voice onset time (VOT) and generalize lengthened VOT to all voiceless stops, not just those presented during an exposure phase. Following up on claims made by Gregory and colleagues, Babel and Bulatov (2011) used an auditory-naming paradigm to demonstrate that participants imitate less when presented with high-pass filtered single words, but that listener judgments of imitation and perceptual similarity do not simply correspond to the degree to which participants imitated f0.

We can gather from this research that imitation and convergent behavior appear to be, perhaps, an inevitable phenomenon. This idea is supported not only by the fact that it occurs across the language system (Pickering & Garrod, 2004), but by the fact that it is a pervasive behavior across human behavior in general (Bargh & Williams, 2006; Chartrand & Bargh, 1996; Dijksterhuis & Bargh, 2001;). Therefore, recent research has used the auditory-naming paradigm to examine the role of social factors with respect to low-level imitative tendencies.

Babel (2010) presents evidence demonstrating the relationship between social affinity and phonetic imitation. In this task, native speakers of New Zealand English shadowed single-word productions from an Australian model talker. Before auditory exposure to the model talker, half of the New Zealand participants were presented with a short statement regarding the Australian model talker's pejorative feelings toward New Zealand. The other half of the participants were presented with a statement which stated the Australian thought positively of New Zealand. Contrary to predictions based on previous work (Bourhis & Giles, 1977), the condition to which participants were assigned had no bearing on the degree of accommodation. Participants in both conditions accommodated to the speech of the Australian model talker. Participants' levels of implicit bias toward New Zealand and Australia as measured through an Implicit Association Task (Greenwald, McGhee, & Schwartz, 1998) did, however, predict the amount of imitation. Participants with pro-Australia bias were more likely to accommodate to the vowels of the Australian model talker. This suggests that simple liking can bolster the perception-production link (cf. Dijksterhuis & Bargh, 2001). In this study, imitation was not equally distributed across vowels; the DRESS vowel was the target of the most accommodation. This is worthy of mention because it is one of the vowels with the largest measurable psychoacoustic differences between New Zealand and Australian English, but is not perceptually one of the most salient differences to naive listeners (Bayard, 2000; Hay, Nolan, & Drager, 2006). This finding supports the claim that imitation and the social factors that mediate it are not the results of conscious choice, but are cognitive biases.

Using a participant population that was relatively homogenous with respect to dialect, Babel (2012) further explored the roles of cognitive and social bias in phonetic imitation. In this task, California-based participants were exposed with model talkers who were male native speakers of California English. Participants were presented with only one of the model talkers, one of whom was black and the other was white. Two groups of participants were assigned to an auditory-naming task that included still digital images of the model talkers. In these tasks, listeners were therefore aware of the physical make-up of the model talkers. After the speech production task, participants in the visual condition completed an Implicit Association Task that measured black and white racial bias. Both male and female participants were also asked to rate the model talkers' attractiveness on a scale of 1 (not at all attractive) to 10 (very attractive). All participants, male and female, succumbed to the same cognitive biases where the low vowels /a/ and /æ/ were imitated more than mid and high vowels /o i u/, but the genders differed with respect to the influence of the social measures on their degree of imitation. Female participants were more likely to imitate the white model talker when they were judged to be more attractive, whereas male participants were less likely to imitate when they judged the white talker as more attractive. The behavior of female participants with respect to the white talker can be interpreted as following directly from the predictions of Communication Accommodation Theory (e.g., Giles & Coupland, 1991) where accommodation or imitation takes place to decrease the social distance between interlocutors. One can imagine that female participants who view the model talkers positively would desire a decrease in social distance. These findings and these views coincide nicely with more recent work by Bargh and colleagues who suggest that liking is one of the simplest ways in which to intensify the perception-behavioral link (Bargh & Williams, 2006; Chartrand & Bargh, 1996; Dijksterhuis & Bargh, 2001).

Several key points fall out of the work on imitation. For one, the data suggest that participants default to imitating and converging, at least in laboratory settings. Indeed, recent modeling work demonstrates that convergence is inevitable unless there is in-group pressure to maintain linguistic features (Wedel & Van Volkinburg, in preparation). However, the fact that social factors mediate low-level behavior, such as imitation, suggests that speech production is never without social influence. The second major point also relates to the social factors, such as the desire to fit in, talkers' social status, and liking influence the degree to which talkers imitate. If we consider the dynamic ways in which talkers are modifying their speech in the corpus studies and experiments we have reviewed previously as a snapshot of style-shifting in real-world interactions, we can hypothesize that at least some of style-shifting is the result of behavioral imitation that is mediated by social factors.

Convergence, of course, does not always occur. In addition to there being clear instances of linguistic divergence (Bourhis & Giles, 1977), talkers are ineffective at accurately imitating themselves (Vallabha & Tuller, 2004). Although there is likely a host of reasons for the lack of convergence, part of the explanation lies in the role of auditory feedback in speech planning. In studies where what listeners hear as their own voices has been resynthesized and manipulated, for example, by lowering the first formant frequency, listeners partially compensate by raising the first formant frequency. This compensation finding has been reported for vowels (Houde & Jordan, 2002; Purcell & Munhall, 2006); fundamental frequency (Jones & Munhall, 2005); and fricative centroids (Shiller, Sato, Gracco, & Baum, 2009). The amount of compensation seems to vary considerably across individuals and is argued to be caused by individual differences in the weighting of auditory and somatosensory feedback (Katseff, Houde, & Johnson, 2012). Indeed, Larson, Altman, Lui, & Hain (2008) found that the amount of compensation in fundamental frequency manipulation increased when participants' vocal folds were anesthetized such that they were no longer privy to somatosensory feedback.

As an end to this section, let us visit a phenomenon that brings together social variation, accommodation, and self-monitoring of one's speech: new dialect acquisition in adults. When adults move to a new region, they generally accommodate their speech patterns to those of the new dialect, although they never sound completely native to the new dialect (Evans & Iverson, 2007; Munro et al., 1999). Without physical displacement, adults who are simply exposed to new social dialects also modify their speech patterns, a finding that has been illustrated in studies of changes in the pronunciation of HRM Queen Elizabeth II's pronunciation during her reign (Harrington, 2006, 2007; Harrington, Palethrope, & Watson, 2000a, 2000b). Moreover, pronunciation patterns can vacillate when speakers move back and forth between different language communities regularly, such as the adult that Sancier and Fowler (1997) studied, who lives part-year in Brazil and part-year in the Northeastern United States. We can hypothesize that acquisition of the new dialect features is not complete for adults for myriad reasons, but we would be remiss not to conclude that at least part of the issue revolves around the role of somatosensory and auditory feedback in self-monitoring. As a case in point, Howell, Barry, and Vinson (2006) show how adults who have acquired new dialects resort to their original native dialect when presented with shifted or delayed auditory feedback of their own voices. This finding was obtained with a dramatically different type of distorted feedback. Simply interfering with the normal self-listening process interfered with talkers' ability to monitor their speech style.

Areas of Future Research

This chapter considers different emerging areas of research that are crucial for developing psycholinguistics models of the production of socially meaningful linguistic variation. The cornerstone of many models of production (including the classic Leveltian models of production that inspired this volume) is the notion that communication starts out with a representation of the intended message in the mind of the speaker and ends when the listener has accessed that intended meaning. Hence a critical endeavor for researchers modeling the production of socially meaningful variation is to delimit precisely the nature of the meanings associated with the variation that we have reviewed thus far in this chapter. Although it is clear that much work needs to be done in this area, we can confidently make two generalizations from work that has been done previously. First, just because a listener *perceives* a linguistic variant as indexing a particular meaning does not mean that the talker *intended* it to index that meaning. Consider again the case of /æ/ variation, discussed previously. Presumably, speakers who use NCCS /æ/ do not do so because they intend to be perceived as overweight, heavy smokers, and older than 60 years old, although that is what the listeners in Smith et al. (2010) perceived talkers who use NCCS to be. Similarly, just because someone is perceived as sounding gay does not mean that gay was the intended meaning. This error of interpretation unfortunately pervades some work on the perception of socially meaningful variation, particularly work related to sexual orientation. For example, Rieger, Linsenmeier, Gygax, Garcia, and Bailey (2010) argue that gay-sounding speech is intentionally produced by gay people to signal sexual orientation to potential sexual partners. This ignores the fact that previous research predicts that the same voices would likely be identified as having many other attributes, such as being more-articulate and younger-sounding than heterosexual talkers, at least for men's voices.

The second conclusions that we can draw is that, if social categories are to be examined experimentally by psycholinguists, then the intended meanings that they index must be understood first. Understanding this requires rigorous investigations drawing on expertise from many different fields, including linguistic anthropology, psycholinguistics, sociolinguistics, and formal semantics, as argued by Smith et al. (2010) and Munson (2010), among others. The way to go about these investigations is by no means straightforward. There is at least one striking difference between the social meanings of linguistic variation and their regular semantic meanings, namely, they are not reinforced by prescriptive instruction in the same way that regular meanings are enforced by language arts instruction in schools. Consequently, many of the investigation tools that require explicit knowledge of a meaning (i.e., providing definitions, giving judgments of similarity in meaning) are likely to be of limited use in studying social meanings. In this sense, they parallel other types of meanings, such as the pragmatic meanings that guide the interpretation of utterances relative to the larger discourse. Here, a particularly useful model for this is work on the meaning of intonational contours (e.g., Pierrehumbert & Hirschberg, 1990). Work by Pierrehumbert and Hirschberg developed a formalism to account for speakers' use of different intonation contours to guide listeners' interpretation of speech. Such formalisms may prove fruitful for modeling the kind of meanings that are conveyed by social variation.

A second area of research that we regard as very important is to understand how socially meaningful variation interacts with and is affected by linguistic variation of the type discussed previously. There is a small body of research suggesting linguistic variation constrains socially meaningful variation. Consider first the general finding that words in highly semantically predictable contexts are spectrally and temporally reduced (e.g., Jurafsky, Bell, Gregory, & Raymond, 2001; Lieberman, 1963). Clopper and Pierrehumbert (2008) find that speakers of the Northern Cities dialect of American English produced vowels that were more advanced with respect to the Northern Cities vowel shift in highly semantically predictable positions relative to the same words in unpredictable contexts. What is unknown from this study is whether the

low semantically predictable production involves suppression of extreme vowel variants or whether the highly predictable position allows for more extreme-than-usual productions, perhaps because of lack of self-monitoring in such environments. Consider next the general finding that vowels in words that are in dense phonological neighborhoods (i.e., words that are only one-phoneme different from many other real words) are hyperarticulated relative to the same vowels in words in sparse neighborhoods (Munson & Solomon, 2004; Scarborough, 2010; Wright, 2004). This presumably reflects an attempt, either overt or tacit, to maintain the distinctiveness of words in dense neighborhoods: words from dense neighborhoods are generally harder to perceive than ones from sparse neighborhoods, and the hyperarticulated vowels partially counter this. Munson et al. (2006; see also Simpson, 2001 and Pierrehumbert et al., 2004) showed that larger-sized vowel spaces are associated with the speech of less-masculine sounding men and more-feminine sounding women. Munson (2007) showed an interaction between linguistic and social factors in vowel-space size: although more-masculine sounding men produced smaller-sized vowel spaces than did less-masculine sounding men, this difference was absent for high-density words.

Other research has shown that different patterns of socially meaningful variation can emerge in more-or-less difficult speaking tasks. Howell et al. (2006) showed that British English speakers who had relocated to other dialect regions in the United Kingdom and had reported losing their native accent were rated by listeners as sounding more like speakers of their original native dialects when producing speech in two challenging conditions (producing speech with acoustically altered feedback). This finding and those by Clopper and Pierrehumbert and by Munson may stem from a single source, if it were shown that production conditions that favored the production of socially marked variants in those latter two studies were found to be more difficult than the conditions that did not. Clearly, more work in this area is needed. This work should also examine whether the ability to perceive and produce socially meaningful linguistic variation has a reciprocal, positive effect on other aspects of language and cognition. Work by Bialystok and colleagues (e.g., Bialystok, 1999, Bialystok & Martin, 2004) has shown that bilingual children have superior executive function abilities, particularly those related to suppressing task-irrelevant information. It may be that there is a similar nonlinguistic cognitive advantage to perceiving and producing multiple, socially meaningful forms within a single language.

The third area of research we consider critical is to extend work on socially meaningful variation to various exceptional (i.e., clinical) populations. Speech production research has long examined production processes in exceptional populations as a means of testing different theories of production, as is reviewed in "Neural Bases of Sentence Processing: Evidence from Neurolinguistic and Neuroimaging Studies" by Thompson and Kielar; "Word Production: Behavioral and Computational Considerations" by Dell, et al; and "Phonetic Processing" by Buchwald. We consider two populations of great interest in understanding the cognitive bases of socially meaningful variation. The first of these is individuals with autism spectrum disorder (ASD). One influential view of ASD is that it arises in part from deficits in a theory of mind, the ability to correctly infer what others' know about a topic being discussed. Given this, we might predict that individuals with ASD would not make the proper inferences of when to use different linguistic forms socially. Indeed, we might expect that they would be unable to learn the systematic correspondences between speaker attributes and linguistic forms. There is some support for the latter hypothesis. Baron-Cohen and Staunton (1994) showed that children with ASD being raised by a non–native speaking parent were much more likely to emulate their mother's nonnative accent than were children without ASD. The possibility that individuals with ASD might process socially significant phonetic variability differently from other populations is made all the more likely by recent findings by Yu (2010) and Stewart and Ota (2008). These investigators showed that performance on a self-report measure of tendencies associated with ASD by individuals in the normal population predicts sensitivity to acoustic-phonetic detail in speech-perception tasks. Individuals with more behaviors characteristic of ASD showed reduced tendencies to use contextual information in speech perception. The second population of clinical interest is adults with acquired brain injury. In contrast to strokes, acquired brain injury typically results in diffuse brain lesions, often with significant damage to the part of the brain responsible for the executive functions related to cognitive control. Here we predict that individuals with acquired brain injury would be considerably poorer than typical individuals in switching among different socially meaningful linguistic variants.

Conclusions

This chapter reviews social variation from a very broad perspective, surveying classic work in traditional sociolinguistics and phonetics, in addition to more recent research on social variation in speech. The trends of the current research on social variation in speech attempt to predict when particular variation will arise based on the speech style of the interlocutor, the semantic predictability of the utterance, and the feelings of the talker toward the interlocutor. We would like to suggest that future work continue along this line, in tandem with traditional sociolinguistic work describing complex patterns of variation in speech and attempts to predict its presence. This often requires using methodologies considered nontraditional in speech research, but we hope the research reviewed in this chapter has convinced the reader that such a path is worthwhile.

References

Babel, M. (2012). Evidence for phonetic and social selectivity in spontaneous phonetic imitation. *Journal of Phonetics, 40,* 177–189.

Babel, M. (2010). Dialect divergence and convergence in New Zealand English. *Language in Society, 39,* 457–456.

Babel, M., & Bulatov, D. (2011). The role of fundamental frequency in phonetic accommodation. *Language and Speech, 55* 231–248..

Bachorowski, J., & Owren, M. (1999). Acoustic correlates of talker sex and individual talker identity are present in a short vowel segment produced in running speech. *Journal of the Acoustical Society of America, 106,* 1054–1063.

Bargh, J. A., & Williams, E. L. (2006). The automaticity of social life. *Current Directions in Psychological Science, 15,* 1–4.

Baron-Cohen, S., & Staunton, R. (1994). Do children with autism acquire the phonology of their peers? An examination of group identification through the window of bilingualism. *First Language, 42,* 317–352.

Bayard, D. (2000). The cultural cringe revisited: changes through time in Kiwi attitudes toward accents. In A. Bell & K. Kuiper (Eds.) *New Zealand English* (pp. 297–324). Amsterdam: John Benjamins.

Bell, A. (1984). Language style as audience design. *Language in Society, 13,* 145–204.

Bell, A. (2001). Back in style: Reworking audience design. In P. Eckert & J. R. Rickford (Eds.), *Style and sociolinguistic variation* (pp. 139–169). Cambridge: Cambridge University Press.

Bialystok, E. (1999). Cognitive complexity and attentional control in the bilingual mind. *Child Development, 70,* 636–644.

Bialystok, E., & Martin, M. (2004). Attention and inhibition in bilingual children: Evidence from the dimensional change card sort task. *Developmental Science, 7,* 325–339.

Bourhis, R. Y., & Giles, H. (1977). The language of intergroup distinctiveness. In H. Giles (Ed.), *Language, ethnicity, and intergroup relations* (pp. 119–136). London: Academic Press.

Browman, C. P., & Goldstein, L. (1990). Tiers in articulatory phonology, with some implications for casual speech. In J. Kingston & M. E. Beckman (Eds.) *Papers in laboratory phonology: Between the grammar and physics of speech* (341–376). Cambridge: Cambridge University Press.

Byrd, D., Kaun, A., Narayanan, S., & Saltzman, E. (2000). Phrasal signatures in articulation. In M. Broe & J. B. Pierrehumbert (Eds.), *Laboratory phonology V: Acquisition and the Lexicon* (pp. 70–89). Cambridge: Cambridge University Press.

Campbell-Kibler, K. (2007). Accent, (ING), and the social logic of listener perceptions. *American Speech, 82,* 32–64.

Campbell-Kibler, K. (2009). The nature of sociolinguistic perception. *Language Variation and Change, 21,* 135–156.

Carahaly, L. (2000). *Listener accuracy in identifying the sexual orientation of male and female speakers* (Unpublished master's thesis). Department of Speech and Hearing Science, Ohio State University, Columbus, OH..

Chartrand, T. L., & Bargh, J. A. (1996). Automatic activation of social information processing goals: Nonconscious priming reproduces effects of explicit conscious instructions. *Journal of Personality and Social Psychology, 71,* 464–478.

Cho, T., & Keating, P. A. (2001). Articulatory and acoustic studies on domain-initial strengthening in Korean. *Journal of Phonetics, 29,* 155–190.

Clopper, C., & Pierrehumbert, J. (2008). Effects of semantic predictability and regional dialect on vowel space reduction. *The Journal of the Acoustical Society of America, 124,* 1682–1688.

Clopper, C., & Pisoni, D. (2004a). Some acoustic cues for the perceptual categorization of American English regional dialects. *Journal of Phonetics, 32,* 111–140.

Clopper, C. G., & Pisoni, D. B. (2004b). Homebodies and army brats: Some effects of early linguistic experience and residential history on dialect categorization. *Language Variation and Change, 16,* 31–48.

Coupland, N. (1980). Style-shifting in a Cardiff work-setting. *Language in Society, 9,* 1–12.

Crist, S. (1997). Duration of onset consonants in gay male stereotyped speech. *University of Pennsylvania Working Papers in Linguistics, 4,* 53–70.

Crown, D. P., & Marlowe, D. (1964). *The approval motive: Studies in evaluative dependence.* New York: John Wiley & Sons, Inc.

Dijksterhuis, A., & Bargh, J. (2001). The perception-behavior expressway: Automatic effects of social perception on social behaviour. In M. Zanna (Ed.), *Advances in experimental social psychology* (Vol. 33, pp. 1–40). San Diego: Academic Press.

Drager, K. (2010). Sensitivity to grammatical and sociophonetic variability in perception. *Journal of Laboratory Phonology, 1,* 93–120.

Drager, K. (2011). Speaker age and vowel perception. *Language and Speech, 54*(1), 99–121.

Eckert, P. (2001). Style and social meaning. In P. Eckert, & J. R. Rickford (Eds.), *Style and sociolinguistic variation* (pp. 119–126). Cambridge: Cambridge University Press.

Eckert, P. (2008). Variation and the indexical field. *Journal of Sociolinguistics, 12,* 453–476.

Evans, B. G., & Iverson, P. (2007). Plasticity in vowel perception and production: A study of accent change in young adults. *Journal of the Acoustical Society of America, 121,* 3814–3826.

Fougeron, C., & Keating, P. (1997). Articulatory strengthening at the edges of prosodic domains. *Journal of the Acoustical Society of America, 101,* 3728–3740.

Gaudio, R. (1994). Sounding gay: Pitch properties in the speech of gay and straight men. *American Speech, 69,* 30–57.

Giles, H. (1973). Accent mobility: A model and some data. *Anthropological Linguistics, 15,* 87–105.

Giles, H., & Coupland, N. (1991). *Language: Contexts and consequences.* Milton Keynes, UK: Open University Press.

Goldinger, S. D. (1998). Echoes of echoes? An episodic theory of lexical access. *Psychological Review, 105,* 251–279.

Goldinger, S. D., & Azuma, T. (2004). Episodic memory in printed word naming. *Psychonomic Bulletin & Review, 11,* 716–722.

Greenwald, A. G., McGhee, D. E., & Schwartz, J. (1998). Measuring individual differences in implicit cognition: The implicit association test. *Journal of Personality and Social Psychology, 74,* 1464–1480.

Gregory, S. W., Dagan, K., & Webster, S. (1997). Evaluating the relation between vocal accommodation in conversational partners' fundamental frequencies to perceptions of communication quality. *Journal of Nonverbal Behavior, 21,* 23–43.

Gregory, S. W., Green, B. E., Carrothers, R. M., & Dagan, K. A. (2001). Verifying the primacy of voice fundamental frequency in social status accommodation. *Language Communication, 21,* 37–60.

Gregory, S. W., Webster, S., & Huang, G. (1993). Voice pitch and amplitude convergence as a metric of quality in dyadic interviews. *Language Communication, 13,* 195–217.

Gregory, S. W., & Webster, S. (1996). A nonverbal signal in voices of interview partners effectively predicts communication accommodation and social status perceptions. *Journal of Personality and Social Psychology, 70,* 1231–1240.

Hall, K. (2002). *"Unnatural" gender in Hindi.* In M. Hellinger & H. Bussman (Eds.), *Gender across languages: The linguistic representation of women and men* (pp. 133–162). Amsterdam, The Netherlands: John Benjamins.

Hall, K., & O'Donovan, V. (1996). *Shifting gender positions among Hindi-speaking hijras.* In V. Bergvall, J. Bingand, & A. Freed (Eds.), *Rethinking language and gender research: Theory and practice* (pp. 228–266). London: Longman.

Hall-Lew, L., Coppock, E., & Starr, R. (2010). Indexing political persuasion: Variation in the Iraq vowels. *American Speech, 85*(1), 91–102.

Harrington, J. (2006). An acoustic analysis of "happy-tensing" in the Queen's Christmas broadcasts. *Journal of Phonetics, 34,* 439–457.

Harrington, J. (2007). Evidence for a relationship between synchronic variability and diachronic change in the Queen's annual Christmas broadcasts. In J. Cole, & J. Hualde (Eds.), *Laboratory phonology 9: Phonetics and phonology* (pp. 125– 144). Berlin: Mouton de Gruyter.

Harrington, J., Palethrope, S., & Watson, C. I. (2000a). Does the Queen speak the Queen's English? *Nature, 408,* 927–928.

Harrington, J., Palethrope, S., & Watson, C. I. (2000b). Monophthongal vowel changes in Received Pronunciation: An acoustic analysis of the Queen's Christmas broadcasts. *Journal of the International Phonetic Association, 30,* 63–78.

Hay, J., Jannedy, S., & Mendoza-Denton, N. (1999). *Oprah and /ay/: Lexical frequency, referee design and style.* San Francisco, CA: Proceedings of the 14th International Congress of Phonetic Sciences.

Hay, J., Nolan, A., & Drager, K. (2006). From fush to feesh: Exemplar priming in speech perception. *The Linguistic Review, 23,* 351–379.

Hay, J., Warren, P., & Drager, K. (2006). Factors influencing speech perception in the context of a merger-in-progress. *Journal of Phonetics, 34,* 458–484.

Hombert, J.-M., Ohala, J. J., & Ewan, W. G. (1979). Phonetic explanations for the development of tones. *Language, 55,* 37–58.

Houde, J. F., & Jordan, M. I. (2002). Sensorimotor adaptation of speech I: Compensation and adaptation. *Journal of Speech, Language and Hearing Research, 45,* 295–310.

Howell, P., Barry, W., & Vinson, D. (2006). Strength of British English accents in altered listening conditions. *Attention, Perception, & Psychophysics, 68,* 139–153.

Janson, T., & Schulman, R. (1983). Nondistinctive features and their use. *Journal of Linguistics, 19,* 252–265.

Johnson, K. (2006). Resonance in an exemplar-based lexicon: The emergence of social identity and phonology. *Journal of Phonetics, 43,* 485–499.

Johnson, K., Strand, E. & D'Imperio, M. (1999). Auditory-visual integration of talker gender in vowel perception. *Journal of Phonetics, 27,* 359–384.

Jones, J. A., & Munhall, K. G. (2005). Remapping auditory-motor representations in voice production. *Current Biology, 15,* 1768–1772.

Jurafsky, D., Bell, A., Gregory, M., & Raymond, W. D. (2001). Probabilistic relations between words: Evidence from reduction in lexical production. In J. Bybee & P. Hopper (Eds.), *Frequency and the emergence of linguistic structure* (pp. 229–254). Amsterdam: John Benjamins.

Katseff, S., Houde, J., & Johnson, K. (2012). Partial compensation for altered auditory feedback: A tradeoff with somatosensory feedback? *Language and Speech 55,* 295–308..

Keating, P., Cho, T., Fougeron, C., & Hsu, C.-S. (2003). Domain-initial articulatory strengthening in four languages. In J. Local, R. Ogden, & R. Temple (Eds.) *Phonetic interpretation: Papers in laboratory phonology 6* (pp. 143–161). Cambridge: Cambridge University Press.

Klatt, D. (1976). Linguistic uses of segmental duration in English: Acoustic and perceptual evidence. *Journal of the Acoustical Society of America, 59,* 1208–1221.

Kraljic, T., Brennan, S. E., & Samuel, A. G. (2008). Accommodating variation: Dialects, idiolects, and speech processing. *Cognition, 107,* 54–81.

Kraljic, T., Samuel, A. G., & Brennan, S. E. (2008). First impressions and last resorts: How listeners adjust to speaker variability. *Psychological Science, 19,* 332–338.

Labov, W. (1963).The social motivation of a sound change. *Word,19,* 273–309.

Labov, W. (1966). *The social stratification of English in New York City.* Washington, DC: Center for Applied Linguistics.

Labov, W. (2001). The anatomy of style-shifting. In P. Eckert, & J. R. Rickford (Eds.), *Style and sociolinguistic variation,* (pp. 85–108). Cambridge: Cambridge University Press.

Labov, W., Ash, S., & Boberg, C. (2006). *Phonological atlas of North America.* New York: Mouton de Gruyter.

Ladefoged, P., & Broadbent, D. E. (1957). Information conveyed by vowels. *Journal of the Acoustical Society of America, 29*(1), 98–104.

Larson, C. R., Altman, K. W., Liu, H., & Hain, T. C. (2008). Interactions between auditory and somatosensory feedback for voice F 0 control. *Experimental Brain Research, 187,* 613–621.

Lass, N. J., Almerino, C. A., Jordan, L. F., & Walsh, J. M. (1980). The effect of filtered speech on speaker race and sex identifications. *Journal of Phonetics, 8,* 101–112.

Lavendara, B. (1978). Where does the sociolinguistic variable stop? *Language in Society, 7,* 171–182.

Lieberman, P. (1963). Some effects of the semantic and grammatical context on the production and perception of speech. *Language and Speech, 6,* 172–175.

Lindblom, B. (1990). Explaining variation: A sketch of the H and H theory. In W. Hardcastle & A. Marchal (Eds.), *Speech production and speech modeling.* Dordrecht, the Netherlands: Kluwer.

Linville, S. E. (1998). Acoustic correlates of perceived versus actual sexual orientation in men's speech. *Folia Phoniatrica et Logopaedica, 50,* 35–48.

Manning, C. (2003). Probabilistic syntax. In R. Bod, J. Hay, & S. Jannedy (Eds.), *Probablistic linguistics* (pp. 289–342). Cambridge, MA: MIT Press.

Manuel, S. (1990). The role of contrast in limiting vowel-to-vowel coarticulation in different languages. *Journal of the Acoustical Society of America 88,* 1286–1298.

Milroy, J., & Milroy, L. (1985). Linguistic change, social network, and speaker innovation. *Journal of Linguistics, 21,* 339–384.

Moonwomon-Baird, B. (1997). Toward a Study of Lesbian Speech. In A. Livia & K. Hall (Eds.) *Queerly phrased: Language, gender, and sexuality* (pp. 202–213). Oxford: Oxford University Press.

Munro, M. J., Derwing, T. M., & Flege, J. E. (1999). Canadians in Alabama: A perceptual study of dialect acquisition in adults. *Journal of Phonetics, 27,* 385–403.

Munson, B. (2010). Levels of phonological abstraction and knowledge of socially motivated speech-sound variation: A review, a proposal, and a commentary on the Papers by Clopper, Pierrehumbert, and Tamati; Drager; Foulkes; Mack; and Smith, Hall, and Munson. *Journal of Laboratory Phonology, 1,* 157–177.

Munson, B., & Babel, M. (2007). Loose lips and silver tongues, or, projecting sexual orientation through speech. *Language and Linguistics Compass, 1,* 416–449.

Munson, B., Edwards, J., & Beckman, M. E. (2012). Phonological representations in language acquisition: Climbing the ladder of abstraction. In A. C. Cohn, C. Fougeron, & M. K. Huffman (Eds.) *The Oxford handbook of laboratory phonology* (pp. 288–309). Oxford: Oxford University Press.

Munson, B., McDonald, E. C., DeBoe, N. L., & White, A. R. (2006). The acoustic and perceptual bases of judgments of women and men's sexual orientation from read speech. *Journal of Phonetics, 34,* 202–240.

Munson, B., & Solomon, N. P. (2004). The effect of phonological neighborhood density on vowel articulation. *Journal of Speech, Language, and Hearing Research, 47,* 1048–1058.

Namy, L. L., Nygaard, L. C., & Sauerteig, D. (2002). Gender differences in vocal accommodation: The role of perception. *Journal and Language and Social Psychology, 21,* 422–432.

Natale, M. (1975a). Convergence of mean vocal intensity in dyadic communication as a function of social desirability. *Journal of Personality and Social Psychology, 32,* 790–804.

Natale, M. (1975b). Social desirability as related to convergence of temporal speech patterns. *Perceptual Motor Skills, 40,* 827–830.

Niedzielski, N. (1999). The effect of social information on the perception of sociolinguistic variables. *Journal of Language and Social Psychology, 18,* 62–85.

Nielsen, K. (2011). Specificity and abstractness of VOT imitation. *Journal of Phonetics, 39*, 132–142.

Nolan, F., Holst, T., & Kühnert, B. (1996) Modelling [s] to [ʃ] accommodation in English. *Journal of Phonetics 24*, 113–137.

Pardo, J. S. (2006). On phonetic convergence during conversational interaction. *Journal of the Acoustical Society of America, 119*, 2382–2393.

Pardo, J. S. (2009). Expressing oneself in conversational interaction. In E. Morsella (Ed.), *Expressing oneself/expressing one's self: Communication, cognition, language, and identify* (pp. 183–196). Mahwah, NJ: Lawrence Erlbaum Associates.

Pardo, J. S., Jay, I. C., & Krauss, R. (2010). Conversational role influences speech imitation. *Attention, Perception, and Psychophysics, 72*(8), 2254–2264.

Perry, T. L., Ohde R., & Ashmead, D. (2001). The acoustic bases for gender identification from children's voices. *Journal of the Acoustical Society of America, 109*, 2988–2998.

Peterson, G., & Barney, H. (1952). Control methods used in a study of the vowels. *Journal of the Acoustical Society of America 24*, 175–184.

Pickering, M. J., & Garrod, S. (2004). Toward a mechanistic psychology of dialogue. *Behavioural & Brain Sciences, 27*, 169–226.

Pierrehumbert, J. (2003). Phonetic diversity, statistical learning, and acquisition of phonology. *Language and Speech, 46*, 115–154.

Pierrehumbert, J. B., Bent, T., Munson, B., Bradlow, A. R., & Bailey, J. M. (2004). The influence of sexual orientation on vowel production. *Journal of the Acoustical Society of America, 116*, 1905–1908.

Pierrehumbert, J., & Hirschberg, J. (1990). The meaning of intonation in the interpretation of discourse. In P. Cohen, J. Morgan, & M. Pollack, (Eds.) *Intentions in communication* (pp. 271–311). Cambridge, MA: MIT Press.

Podesva, R. J. (2007). Phonation type as a stylistic variable: The use of falsetto in constructing a persona. *Journal of Sociolinguistics, 11*, 478–504.

Purcell, D. W., & Munhall, K. G. (2006). Adaptive control of vowel formant frequency: Evidence from real-time formant manipulation. *The Journal of the Acoustical Society of America, 120*, 966–977.

Purnell, T., Idsardi, W., & Baugh, J. (1999). Perceptual and phonetic experimentation on American English dialect identification. *Journal of Language and Social Psychology, 18*, 10–30.

Rieger, G., Linsenmeier, J., Gygax, L., Garcia, S., & Bailey, J. M. (2010). Dissecting "gaydar": accuracy and the role of masculinity-femininity. *Archives of Sexual Behavior, 39*, 124–140.

Romain, S. (1984). On the problem of syntactic variation and pragmatic meaning in sociolinguistic theory. *Folia Linguistica, 18*, 409–439.

Sachs, J., Lieberman, P., & Erickson, D. (1973). Anatomical and cultural determinants in male and female speech. In R. W. Shuy, & R. W. Fasold (Eds.), *Language attitudes* (pp. 74–83). Washington, DC: Georgetown University Press.

Sancier, M., & Fowler, C. (1997). Gestural drift in a bilingual speaker of Brazilian Portuguese and English. *Journal of Phonetics, 25*, 421–436

Scarborough, R. A. (2010) *Lexical and contextual predictability: Confluent effects on the production of vowels*. In C. Fougeron, B. Kuhnert, M. D'Imperio and N. Vallee (Eds.) *Laboratory phonology 10* (pp. 557–586). Berlin: De Gruyter Mouton.

Sharma, D. (2005). Dialect stabilization and speaker awareness in non-native varieties of English. *Journal of Sociolinguistics, 9*, 194–224.

Shiller D., Sato, M., Gracco, V., & Baum, S. (2009). Perceptual recalibration of speech sounds following speech motor learning. *Journal of the Acoustical Society of America, 125*, 1103–1113.

Shockley, K., Sabadini, L., & Fowler, C. A. (2004). Imitation in shadowing words. *Perception & Psychophysics, 66*, 422–429.

Silverstein, M. (2003). Indexical order and the dialectics of sociolinguistic life. *Language & Communication, 23*, 193–229.

Simpson, A. P. (2001). Dynamic consequences of differences in male and female vocal-tract dimensions. *Journal of the Acoustical Society of America, 109*, 2153–2164.

Smith, E. A., Hall, K. C., & Munson, B. (2010). Bringing semantics to sociophonetics: Social variables and secondary entailments. *Journal of Laboratory Phonology, 1*, 121–155.

Smyth, R., Jacobs, G., & Rogers, H. (2003). Male voices and perceived sexual orientation: An experimental and theoretical approach. *Language in Society, 32*, 329–350.

Staum Casasanto, L. (2008). *Experimental investigations of sociolinguistic knowledge* (Unpublished doctoral dissertation). Palo Alto, CA: Stanford University Department of Linguistics.

Stewart, M., & Ota, M. (2008). Lexical effects on speech perception in individuals with "autistic" traits. *Cognition 109*, 157–162.

Strand, E., & Johnson, K. (1996). Gradient and visual speaker normalization in the perception of fricatives. In D. Gibbon (Ed.), *Natural language processing and speech technology: Results of the 3rd KONVENS Conference, Bielfelt, October 1996* (pp. 14–26). Berlin: Mouton de Gruyter.

Thomas, E. (2002). Sociophonetic applications of speech perception experiments. *American Speech, 77*, 115–147.

Troutman, C., Clark, B., & Goldrick, M. (2008). Social networks and intraspeaker variation during periods of language change. *Penn Working Papers in Linguistics, 14*.

Trudgill, P. (1981). Linguistic accommodation: Sociolinguistic observations on a sociopsychological theory. In R. Hendrick, C. Masek, & M. F. Miller (Eds.), *Papers from the Parasession on Language and Behavior* (pp. 218–237). Chicago: Chicago Linguistics Society.

Trudgill, P. (2004). *New dialect formation: The inevitability of colonial Englishes*. Edinburgh: Edinburgh University Press.

Trudgill, P. (2008). Colonial dialect contact in the history of European languages: On the irrelevance of identity in new-dialect formation. *Language in Society, 37*, 241–280.

Vallabha, G. K., & Tuller, B. (2004). Perceptuomotor bias in the imitation of steady-state vowels. *The Journal of the Acoustical Society of America, 116*, 1184–1197.

Van Bezooijen, R. (1995). Sociocultural aspects of pitch differences between Japanese and Dutch women. *Language and Speech 38*. 253–265.

Vorperian, H., Wang, S., & Chung, M. (2009). Anatomic development of the oral and pharyngeal portions of the vocal tract: An imaging study. *Journal of the Acoustical Society of America, 125*, 1666–1678.

Walker, A. (2008). *Phonetic detail and grammaticality judgements* (Unpublished master's thesis). Department of Linguistics, University of Canterbury, Christchurch, New Zealand.

Wedel, A., & Van Volkinburg, H. (in preparation). *Modeling simultaneous convergence and divergence of linguistic features between differently-identifying groups in contact.* http://dingo.sbs.arizona.edu/~wedel/publications/PDF/Wedel_VanVolkinburgSneetches.pdf

Weinreich, U., Labov, W., & Herzog, M. (1968) Empirical foundations for a theory of language change. In W. Lehmann & Y. Malkiel (Eds.), *Directions for historical linguistics.* Austin: University of Texas Press.

Whalen, D. H. (1990). Coarticulation is largely planned. *Journal of Phonetics, 18,* 3–35.

Wright, R. (2004). Factors of lexical competition in vowel articulation. In J. Local, J. R. Ogden, & R. Temple (Eds.), *Papers in laboratory phonology VI.* Cambridge: Cambridge University Press.

Yamazawa, H., & Hollien, H. (1992). Speaking fundamental frequency of Japanese women. *Phonetica, 49,* 128–140.

Yu, A. (2010). Perceptual compensation is correlated with individuals' "autistic" traits: Implications for models of sound change. *PLOS ONE, 5*(8): e11970.doi:10.1371/journal.pone.0011950.

PART 2

Beyond Speaking

Writing Systems, Language Production, and Modes of Rationality

David R. Olson

Abstract

Producing language in writing is importantly different from producing language in speaking. This chapter examines how the altered conditions of production and comprehension require an altered awareness of and attention to certain properties of language ranging from phonological form, to lexical and logical form that remain implicit in speaking. This awareness permits the development of a distinctive register of language and with it a distinctive mode of discourse and a distinctive mode of thought.

Key Words: writing, consciousness of language, prose, modes of thought, cognitive development, literacy

Speech and writing are sometimes seen as little more than alternative modes of language production. Consequently, the implications of writing for producing distinctive forms of discourse and distinctive modes of thought have been largely neglected. In this chapter it is argued that the differences between spoken and written language production result from the altered conditions or production and comprehension, which in turn require an altered awareness of and attention to certain properties of language ranging from phonological form, to lexical and logical form. This altered conception of language, rather than its contributions to memory, is what makes thinking for writing quite different from the knowledge required for speaking. The process of bringing implicit properties of language into awareness is one that has unfolded in historical time in a particular cultural context and is the same process that is reincarnated in the mental lives of children as they learn to competently participate in a modern written, textual tradition.

The chapter proceeds as follows. First I make the general case that language production in writing must be distinguished from language production in speech. After a brief review of the nature and historical development of writing systems, I go on to a more detailed analysis of how the written, literate tradition in the West gave rise to a new more formal register of language and with it an altered conception of meaning of both words and sentences. Next I consider how this altered conception of language brings with it a new conception of and new standards of rationality. The chapter concludes with some suggestions as to how writing gives rise to this new consciousness of linguistic forms and meanings.

Writing and Language Production

Modern industrial societies continue to advance a trend begun at the beginning of history, namely, to use writing as a major form or mode of language production. The trend took a dramatic turn in the 16th century with the invention of printing, an advance that put written language into the hands of the masses where it came to serve a diverse range of functions. The trend continues unabated with the rise of information technology and such "texting" resources as email and Twitter. Yet, the somewhat naive assumption prevails that writing and reading are just speaking and listening with different communication technologies with the consequence that, save the dramatic pronouncements of Marshall McLuhan (1962, 2003), the social and cognitive implications of writing have been largely ignored.

In fact, language production in oral conversational contexts has been shown to be dramatically different from at least some forms of written discourse, differences that are attributable to the conditions of production and reception. Chafe (1985) argued that the basic unit of speech was an "idea unit" consisting of a clause composed of a verb and one or more noun phrases with a single intonational contour, about seven words long and lasting some 2 seconds. The utterance corresponds roughly to the amount of information a speaker can focus on or hold in consciousness at a point in time. Written expression, however, subordinates these idea units to the grammatical structure of the sentence with one main clause to which one or more subordinate clauses are linked by means of conjunctions or relative pronouns. With education and training people may learn to produce orally utterances that hone more closely to the written norms, as indeed medieval scholars were taught to do (Carruthers, 1990).

Biber (1988, 2009) has conducted extensive empirical analyses of oral and written language in a variety of registers of language including conversation, fiction, newspaper language, and academic prose and showed that although there were clear differences between stereotypical spoken and written registers that derive from the different conditions of production, "there are few (if any) absolute linguistic differences between speech and writing" (2009, p. 75). A primary feature of the written mode is that it produces an artifact that, in contrast with person-to-person oral speech, is an object fixed in space that endures through time. This fixity allows for rereading and revising. Biber (2009) found that the linguistic constructions most associated with writing exhibited vastly greater lexical diversity and complex noun phrase constructions, expressions that "require extensive planning, revision, and editing—processes that are normally possible only in writing" (p. 90) some of which have been examined empirically (Hayes & Flower, 1986; Bereiter & Scardamalia, 1987). In modern societies these activities of rereading and rewriting have come to command their own disciplines, namely, hermeneutics and composition.

Hence, to understand the nature and uses of writing systems, it is necessary to both grant that writing exploits the properties of ordinary spoken language and at the same time acknowledge that some of these properties are made explicit and become subject to design (e.g., stipulating the meaning of terms) for particular social and intellectual purposes whether conveying information through personal letters, record keeping for public records, or summarizing arguments and advancing knowledge. As we shall see, writing tends to make explicit properties that remain implicit in speech (cf. Brandom, 1994).

This process of explication of implicit linguistic structures begins at the very beginning of attempts to read and write, namely, in the search for marks that may represent meaning. In learning to read an alphabet one must become aware of and think in a new way about the phonological properties of words that may be represented by a written letter, what has come to be called "phonological awareness." To produce written language by an alphabet requires that one both hear the requisite sounds and know their visual representation. Yet, those phonological properties are implicit in speech; literacy in a sense uncovers and brings into consciousness what was already there (Olson, 1994, pp. 259–260). However, there are different types of writing systems and each relates to spoken language in their distinctive ways.

Writing Systems

Within literate societies it has long been assumed that language production of any complexity or sophistication is a product of writing. Indeed, the evolution of writing systems was seen as the basis for the evolution of society, a tradition that was advanced by Vico (1744) and Rousseau (1754–1791). E. B. Tylor (1871) in his book *Primitive culture* (1881, Vol. 1, p. 142) forwarded the claim that the invention of writing was "the great movement by which mankind rose from barbarism to civilization." Modern theories of writing systems have abandoned general claims about civilization more generally and have focused on the classification of writing systems into types and advancing explanations of their origins and development. The most comprehensive of these accounts was that of I. J. Gelb (1963) who in his book *A study of writing* named the field "Grammatology" and offered an evolutionary theory of the advance of writing systems from the first communicative uses of visible marks to the unique invention of the Greek alphabet. Gelb saw a steady evolutionary progression of writing systems from images, to word signs, to syllable signs, to consonantal signs, culminating with the Greek invention of an alphabet with its explicit representations of both consonants and vowels and which could represent anything that could be said. All writing systems other than the alphabet were seen as steps toward or as failed attempts at representing the phonological properties of speech.

More recent writers have criticized this evolutionary approach, pointing out that writing systems evolved in response to the existing social demands and in relation to the linguistic properties of the existing spoken language. In regard to linguistic properties of the spoken language, Daniels (2009) has shown that all of the world's writing systems are representations of the spoken form of language, although the precise properties of speech captured by the visual signs differ from language to language and no writing system captures all of the properties of speech (e.g., tone of voice is largely unrepresented). The catalogue for the recent exhibit on the inventions of writing in the Ancient Middle East at the Oriental Institute Museum of Chicago shows the great diversity of attempts to use written marks for communicative and other purposes that preceded the development of full writing systems (Woods, 2010). However, some general principles relating spoken language to written signs have emerged.

The three independently invented ancient writing systems (the Sumerian, the Chinese, and the Mayan [some writers add Egyptian hieroglyphics to the list]) were based on languages that had a simple basic structure: most of their words contained a single morpheme and were expressed by a single syllable that in turn could be represented by a single visual sign. Writing systems representing languages that diverge from the one-syllable, one-morpheme pattern tend to be more complex, were invented later, and remain more difficult for children to master.

Writing systems first emerged in response to social demands. The origins of the earliest and best studied writing system, Babylonian cuneiform, has been traced to the use of tokens for recording economic transactions in Mesopotamia between 7500 and 3000 BC. Schmandt-Besserat (1996, 2007) found that the first written signs were inscribed copies of clay tokens each of which represented a particular traded commodity, such as sheep, corn, oil, or beer. The clay tokens had been modeled into many shapes, such as cones, spheres, cylinders, and disks used for inventorying those commodities: "Each token shape was a symbol for one particular unit of merchandise" (2007, p. 3). The tokens are representations of commodities rather than representations

of the names of those commodities and hence are best seen as prewriting. When the shapes of these tokens were later inscribed on a clay surface the meaning of these signs changed importantly from signs for objects into signs for the names of those objects. Whereas three identical tokens would be required to represent three sheep (thus, "sheep, sheep, sheep"), when inscribed the signs came to be treated as word signs, one sign representing the number "three" and the other representing the noun "sheep"; the signs, we may say, acquired a syntax thereby providing a basis for a comprehensive writing system. This cuneiform way of writing was widely adopted with modification to local language across the ancient Near East. This shift from signs for things to signs for words has been observed in children's attempts at writing; whereas their first signs represent things, later attempts represent the words and expressions for those things (Ferreiro & Teberosky, 1982; Olson, 1994). As mentioned, many Babylonian words were monosyllabic and thus readily represented by a single sign.

Schmandt-Besserat (1996) reports that around 3000 BC the state required that the names of recipients and donors of goods be entered on the tablets along with the inventoried goods. Unlike basic commodities, names were often multisyllabic. To represent such a name these single monosyllabic signs were redeployed, so to speak, for their phonological rather than semantic values. In this way multisyllabic words, including the names of kings, could be represented by a sequence of these original simple monosyllabic signs. For example, in one case the outlined shape of a man represented the monosyllabic word "lu" meaning "man" and the drawing of a man's mouth represented the monosyllabic word "ka" meaning "mouth," but the two signs could be borrowed and combined to represent the bisyllabic name "Luka." This use of signs for their phonological values is described as the "rebus principle." The Egyptians added some signs lacking phonological value, such the cartouche around a whole name to indicate royalty.

The invention of the Greek alphabet, distinctive for its invention for vowel signs, once seen as an indication of Greek genius (Havelock, 1982; Goody & Watt, 1968/1975) is now recognized as an important but more mundane invention. The neighboring Phoenicians had a writing system composed of 22 graphic signs with a memorized order beginning *aleph*, *bet*, *gemel* adequate for representing a full range of meanings. Such signs can be seen as representing not only syllables but also the consonantal sounds of the language because vocalic differences were not indicated. The Greek invention, around 750 BC and unique in the history of the world, occurred when the Phoenician script, suited to a Semitic language, was adopted for representing a non-Semitic language, Greek. Unlike a Semitic language, Greek like English, is an Indo-European language in which vowel differences make lexical contrasts: "big, bag, bog, beg, bug" differ only in their vowel sounds yet represent unrelated meanings. Furthermore, some words consist of a single vowel sound, some words begin with vowels, and words with pairs of vowels are not uncommon. To fill the gap, six Semitic characters that represented sounds unknown in Greek were borrowed to represent these isolated vowel sounds. Equipped with such signs, the Greeks were quick to see that those sounds also occurred within the syllables represented by the Semitic consonant signs. In this way syllables were dissolved into consonant-vowel pairs to form the alphabet (Olson, 1994, Chapter 4).

Chinese and Japanese writing systems, long thought to be primitive because of the somewhat pictorial nature of written signs (indeed, after World War II, western educators urged the Chinese and Japanese to abandon their writing system and adopt an alphabet; Gaur, 1984) are now acknowledged to be full writing systems with their distinctive advantages and disadvantages. They promote integration in that speakers of somewhat different language can read the same script and ancient documents can still be read. However, they also impose a large burden on learners in that some 400 characters must be memorized and indications of phonological values are somewhat indirect. Yet, in an extensive review of the history of Chinese literacy, Wang, Tsai, and Wang (2009) point out that "in every type of writing system, a reader always has access to the phonological information." Researchers comparing the reading processes involved in reading Asian and Western writing systems have stressed their similarities suggesting there is a "universal grammar of reading" (Perfetti, 2009; p. 219).

How Writing Relates to Speaking and Thinking

The invention of a system capable of representing everything that could be said is no doubt the most important fact about writing. Writing permits communication across space and time, it allows the formation of an archive and the accumulation of knowledge across generations, and it permits meetings of minds separated by oceans and generations.

However, writing is not just a way of preserving speech, nor is it simply an extension of memory. Writing allows the invention of new genres or ways of using language for far more specialized purposes than does speech. Writing takes diverse forms in different cultures and in different historical periods. Such differences are not simply cultural differences but cultural forms built around the particular properties of a writing system.

How writing is implicated in the development of particular linguistic and literary forms is indicated by the findings mentioned previously by Biber (1988, 2009). Biber used statistical methods to examine the linguistic variation in texts in English totaling some 20 million words drawn from a range of registers including conversation, fiction, newspapers, and academic prose. A second study examined typical linguistic characteristics of university spoken and written registers in both academic and nonacademic contexts. Although there were few absolute differences between speech and writing generally, there were large and significant differences in the typical linguistic characteristics of spoken and written language, writing allowing much more diversity in linguistic expression than did speech. Biber concludes

> there is a fundamental difference in linguistic expression associated with the production differences between speech and writing. Written production gives the addressor maximum freedom to manipulate the linguistic characteristics of a text in accordance with a number of situational parameters, including communicative purpose, interactiveness, and the degrees of personal involvement. As a result we find a wide range of linguistic styles within writing. In contrast, the real-time production circumstances of spoken registers restrict the types of linguistic complexity that are possible" (2009, p. 83).

Snow and Uccelli (2009), noting that the specializations devised for the written register can also be used in oral discourse, define the register of "academic language" in terms similar to those set out by Biber. Even if children become more acquainted with the forms of academic language through the school years, Berman and Ravid (2009) found that only late in their school careers were students able to express their ideas more effectively through writing than through speech. Olson (2010) adds to this story by arguing that writing confers this advantage by taking language "off-line" to make it more available for the writer to select or define words and design sentences that call for newer forms of reading and interpretation, indeed, to distinguish reading from interpretation. In this way the creation and interpretation of written expressions, he has argued, add new resources to the language that are distinctive from those available to a language and culture without writing.

Writing and Reasoning

The notion of a "primitive" people, bereft of the benefits of culture, and indicative of the first age or stage of mankind, dates from the age of discovery. Columbus in the 15th century and Cook in the 18th produced extensive accounts of the thought and actions of so-called primitive people. As we have seen, in the 18th century both Giambatista Vico and Jean-Jacques Rousseau not only speculated about the stages of civilization from primitive to modern, they related these stages to the ways of using visual marks for communicative purposes, claiming that the alphabet was the most advanced and uniquely associated with advanced rationality. Such claims were presumably used to justify the subjugation of less literate peoples to colonial rule.

The more careful empirical studies of the thinking processes of members of traditional (i.e., unlettered) societies was begun by Oxford University's first Chair in Anthropology, E. B. Tylor (Harris, 2009a) and was carried forward by Levy-Bruhl in his *Primitive mentality* (1923) and *How natives think* (1926). These works produced such a deluge of criticism because of their prejudicial implications that Levy-Bruhl abandoned the notion of "primitive" while continuing to maintain that such thought was indeed distinctive and he attributed this distinctiveness to a failure to "differentiate between sign and cause" or, as we would say, between a thing and a representation of a thing (1923, p. 43) a distinction that is now seen as central to literate Aristotelian cultures (see Olson, 1994, p. 29; Harris, 2009b). Thus, whereas the Huichol Indians of Mexico could, in a religious ceremony, claim that "Corn is deer," the literate tradition initiated in Classical Greece and carried into modern times would insist that the copula be replaced by "stands for" or "takes the place of" (see Olson, 1994, p. 29), "is" being reserved for statements with strict entailments. Similar disputes occurred during the Reformation over the Christian Eucharist, specifically the statement by Jesus, who taking a piece of bread, said "This is my body." As we shall see, arguments over rationality boil down to disputes over the meaning of such relational terms as "is," and including the meaning of so-called logical operators, such as "and," "not," and "or" and

overquantifiers, such as "all" and "every" when they occur in so-called "universalized" sentences, such as "All men are mortal." As Harris (2009a, p. 175) pointed out "What Aristotle did was to show how *so much* in argument can be made to depend on *so few* linguistic signs (particularly signs for 'all,' 'some' and 'not')." The meanings of those simple signs changed as they came to be used in the written sentences composing deductive arguments.

Writing and the Origins of Logic

Although language production generally reflects social and personal uses, some specialized forms or ways of using language, specifically those that call attention to the specific words and their meanings, depend on the availability of writing and the development of a textual tradition. How these have opened up in historical time in a particular cultural context has become an important issue in philosophy and science. In regard to philosophical logic, Harris (2009a, 2009b) has traced the origins of formal logic to Aristotle's focus on decontextualized sentences and the strict implications may be drawn from them. Harris points out that such sentences are abstract linguistic objects to be treated in terms of their explicit linguistic form quite independently of purpose or context. He writes, "With the arrival of 'the sentence,' a new forum is created for the discussion of human thinking" (p. 51) namely, the study of logic, of necessary implication. The sentence, Harris argues, is the basis of the Aristotelian syllogism. Aristotle rejected as a suitable basis for inference poetic utterances, such as *The salt sea is the sweat of the earth* (he would not have cared for "Corn is deer" either) and confined his analysis to sentences from which valid inferences could be drawn. In Harris's view this move imparted an unfortunate "scriptist" bias, the belief that rationality may be defined exclusively in terms of valid inference, thereby branding all non-Aristotlean cultures as primitive and irrational. Leezenberg (2001), too, has denied that literal meaning, the meaning determined by more or less decontextualized sentence meaning, is a neutral form of meaning. He argues that "literal meanings, then, are not the start of the life of the language, but rather the end product of a long social and historical process…Literal meanings depend on the stabilization and codification of linguistic norms; these are achieved with the aid of literacy, education, standardization of language and lexicography" (p. 302). Identifying the literal meaning of an expression is central to the logical reasoning but extracting such meaning is a specialized form of literate, academic competence quite different from that involved in ordinary uses of language (Snow & Uccelli, 2009). Indeed, the failure to recognize logical uses of language as a specialized form of literate academic discourse has given rise to claims about irrationality that harken back to 19th century claims about primitive thought.

The uncritical adoption of formal logic as a model of human reasoning generally, long a topic of experimental psychology, appears in the recent research by Kahneman and Tversky (1996) and Stanovich (2009), which shows that even educated adults are subject to "cognitive illusions" that lead them to make irrational judgments. Some of these claims are uncontroversial, such as that people are easily misled by advertising and especially that they have limited understanding of probability. However, these authors make more general claims about the irrationality of everyday reasoning. They base their claims on subjects "incorrect" understanding of the logical meanings of "and" and "or." Indeed, if these ordinary language terms are treated as synonymous with their logical counterparts "∧" and "∨," their claims have some merit. However, some philosophers and some psychologists deny the appropriateness of treating ordinary language terms as equivalent to their logical counterparts. In his William James lecture delivered in 1967 (published in 1989), Grice noted the differences between two philosophical stances "in regard to such words as *not, and, or, if,* and *all.*" Some saw these concepts as lacking in logical rigor and preferred the formal notations including "∧," roughly translated as "and," "∨" for "or," and "--" for "not." Others, like Grice himself, found ordinary language concepts as logically adequate but governed by rules of conversational discourse. He summarized these rules in terms of his "cooperative principle," which required that one be attuned to the purpose of the discourse and the needs of the listener. Thus, in parallel to the logican's formal implications, he offered the less formal, yet clearly rational, use of "implicatures" meanings that although not stated explicitly yet adequately and conventionally conveys a meaning. Thus we have two logics: one of the logician the other of ordinary discourse.

Olson (2010) like Harris (2009b) has argued that the formal uses of these logical terms, rather than being a basic human competence, is the product of literacy and education. These are the processes discussed by Leezenberg (2001), namely, "the stabilization and codification of linguistic norms" achieved through "literacy, education, standardization of language and lexicography." In ordinary discourse, "and" sometimes means "and then," sometimes "in order to," sometimes "only if," and the like. Only in formal, educated, literate, indeed logical discourse does "and" come to be treated as synonymous with "plus" such that "A and B" is synonymous with "B and A." In ordinary discourse the terms are not easily reordered: "Love and marriage" is not equivalent to "Marriage and love." Similarly, only in formal logical discourse can "or" violate the conventional function of contrasting mutually exclusive alternatives and allow "or" to contrast parts with wholes, as in Piaget's famous trick question: When shown a picture of three ducks and two rabbits children are asked "Are there more ducks or animals?" Most subjects, observing the Gricean cooperative principle, assume the speaker must have meant to say "Are there more ducks or *other* animals?" So do the subjects tested by Kahneman and Tversky (1996) and Stanovich (2009), who are presented with a narrative about a socially active person named Linda. They were then asked if it is more likely Linda becomes a bank teller or a bank teller active in the feminist movement. Subjects preferred the latter leading the researchers to attribute irrationality (How could the part [bankers who were feminists] be greater than the whole [all bankers]?). However, it is equally reasonable within ordinary discourse, and equally plausible, to infer that Linda may become a bank teller *only if* she could balance that choice with becoming active in the feminist movement; *and* here means *only if*. Similarly, "or," which conventionally divides mutually exclusive alternatives, here divides embedded alternatives that invite the inference that the speaker must have meant to ask whether it was more likely that Linda became a bank teller and feminist or a bank teller and not a feminist. Given Linda's history the former is more likely just as the subjects in the experiment claimed. It is the failure to recognize the two logics that led to such misleading conclusions about rationality. Children begin to distinguish these two logics in the early school years and so grant that if there are three cats and two dogs, there are, in fact, more animals than cats. As one sixth grade child to whom I posed this question replied "You have to count the cats twice." More serious is the failure to recognize that the formal, technical use of the language, including the precise stipulative definitions of these logical operators, is a product of not only literacy but of a particular use of formalized written language. That formal use is an aspect of linguistic competence that is developed through extensive literacy training.

A similar story may be told about the meaning of "is." As Bill Clinton famously retorted: "It depends on what the meaning of 'is' is." Christians debated the meaning of Jesus' statement "This is my body." Setting aside the fact the Aramaic, the oral language of Jesus, lacks the copula altogether, the "is" of this statement caused unresolved argument in part because, like "and" and "or" and "not" discussed previously, "is" came to acquire a somewhat technical meaning similar to the mathematical term "equals" or "is identical to" as in "Water is H_2O" or "The earth is round," the somewhat narrowed meaning that allows deduction. Debate over the precise meanings and usage of such terms is the product of a venerable Greek literary tradition (Johnson & Parker, 2009).

Writing and the Advance of Knowledge

Although it is misleading to identify a particular specialized literate use of language with rationality, there is no doubt that thinking and rationality have been advanced through the invention of specialized modes of discourse including logic and mathematics and the invention of an empirical scientific tradition. The dependence of these specialized modes of discourse on the availability of a written tradition requires some discussion.

The conventions of a writing system go beyond those dictating the relations between sound and visual sign to include the much more subtle set of conventions governing reading of what is written. These conventions are built on the oral genres of language use, such as conversation and storytelling, but they have evolved into the specialized written genre discussed by Biber, Snow and others. These distinctive written genres entail distinctive normative ways of reading and writing. Hence, the history of literacy is in part the history of ways of reading. Ways of reading, of course, dictate distinctive ways of writing. Historians have traced the development of the more specialized ways of reading and writing (according to the literal meaning of a text) that were instrumental in the rise of Protestantism and to the rise of early modern science (Bazerman, 1988; Olson, 1994, 2009). Protestantism established a new linguistic norm or standard according to which the text was to be read as meaning neither more nor less than what it said, the principle of *sola scriptura* (incidentally, this is the way of reading appropriate to the logical tasks studied by psychologists; its appropriateness to Scripture is open to question). Text, specifically Scripture, was taken to be fixed, its reading direct and transparent, devoid of "interpretation" and mystical meanings, and equally open to everyone. These norms conflicted with those of the established Church that had insisted on the authority of the Church in matters of interpretation, that Scripture was not fixed in writing but the expression of the living church, and that the power of scripture lay in its multiple levels of meaning. Whether or not the printing press facilitated the development of this new way of reading or only its widespread adoption remains contested (Eisenstein, 1979).

The equally interesting claim is that Protestant "way of reading" was readily applied to reading the book of nature, that is, to early modern science. Stock (1983) expressed the relation thus: "The growth of a more literate society did for naturalism what it had done for the Eucharist: it placed the whole matter on an intellectualist plane and dismissed as rustic, popular, and irrational all that did not accord with a *ratio* synonymous with the inner logic of texts" (p. 318). More recently, but in a similar vein, Forshaw and Killeen (2007) argued that "the transfer of methodologies between 'reading the Scripture' and 'reading the world'...is not a loose analogy but designates, rather, an almost technical procedure [such that] reading the Bible might be a model for reading the world" (pp. 16–17). Such reading established a new linguistic norm or standard; for writing, a "mathematical plainness of style"; for reading, "according to the very words" (Olson, 1994). This way of using language was based on a set of literate/literary conventions shared by a "textual community." These conventions included the assumption of the fixity of text, that a text had a given literal meaning, and that interpretation to be settled by appeal to the common reader or observer. This way of reading defined a new social group independent of political and religious authority of the day, whether in Protestant churches, in early modern scientific communities, or in the Dutch school of art (Alpers, 1983).

Writing and Consciousness of Language

Although writing systems share the universal properties of capturing the semantic and phonological properties of the languages they represent, they do so in importantly different ways with the result that they call into awareness only certain properties of the spoken language. Scribner and Cole (1981) studied the cognitive implications of learning to read and use three writing systems that co-occurred in a West African community: Vai, Arabic, and English. The uses of these systems differed dramatically, one for personal letters, another for religion, and the third for schooling and other bureaucratic functions. After learning to read Vai, a syllabic script, subjects were much more skilled in integrating separate syllables into phrases and decomposing phrases into such syllabic units than were nonreaders. Other researchers have shown that learning to read an alphabet, however, leads learners to a new awareness of the subsyllabic constituents of speech. Morais, Cary, Alegria, and Bertelson (1979), Petersson, Ingvar, and Reis (2009), and others have shown that this "phonological awareness" is a product not of normal development but of exposure to a writing system in which visual signs correspond to single phonemes, that is, an alphabet. However, once verbal expressions are written, other properties of language beyond those of phonemes and syllables have, in certain social contexts, become objects of awareness and subject to design and analysis. Among them, as we have seen, are the technical meanings of words, including the logical operators "and," "or," and "not"; universal quantifies "all" and "every"; the linking verb "is"; and the sentences in which they are embedded.

The invention of writing systems not only provided a novel way for producing language and communicating across time and space. More importantly, I have argued, writing set in train a set of procedures for reflecting on and analyzing the properties of language and shaping it to serve the new standards of rational discourse. Rather than taking consciousness of properties of language as a given, this consciousness must be seen as a by-product of literacy that offers a new way of producing language and distinctive mode of thought. A clearer understanding of the peculiar nature of the comprehension and production of language *in writing* promises to go far in advancing our understanding not only of language but of the mind.

References

Alpers, S. (1983). *The art of describing: Dutch art in the seventeenth century*. Chicago: University of Chicago Press.

Bazerman, C. (1988). *Shaping written knowledge: The genre and activity of the experimental article in science*. Madison: University of Wisconsin Press.

Bereiter, C., & Scardamalia, M. (1987). *The psychology of written composition*. Mahwah, NJ: Erlbaum.

Berman, R. A., & Ravid, D. (2009). Becoming a literate language user: Oral and written text construction across adolescence. In D. R. Olson & N. Torrance (Eds.), *Cambridge handbook of literacy* (pp. 92–111). Cambridge, UK: Cambridge University Press.

Biber, D. (1988). *Dimensions of register variation: A cross-linguistic comparison*. Cambridge, UK: Cambridge University Press.

Biber, D. (2009). Are there linguistic consequences of literacy? Comparing the potentials of language use in speech and writing. In D. R. Olson & N. Torrance (Eds.), *Cambridge handbook of literacy* (pp. 75–91). Cambridge, UK: Cambridge University Press.

Brandom, R. B. (1994). *Making it explicit*. Cambridge, MA: Harvard University Press.

Carruthers, M. (1990). *The book of memory: A study of memory in medieval culture*. Cambridge, UK: Cambridge University Press.

Chafe, W. (1985). Linguistic differences produced by differences between speaking and writing. In D. R. Olson, N. Torrance, & A. Hildyard (Eds.), *Literacy, language and learning: The nature and consequences of reading and writing* (pp. 105–123). Cambridge, UK: Cambridge University Press.

Daniels, P. (2009). Grammatology. In D. R. Olson & N. Torrance (Eds.) *Cambridge handbook of literacy* (pp. 25–45). Cambridge, UK: Cambridge University Press.

Eisenstein, E. (1979). *The printing press as an agent of change*. Cambridge, UK: Cambridge University Press.

Ferreiro, E., & Teberosky, A. (1982). *Literacy before schooling*. Exeter, NH: Heinemann.

Forshaw, P. J., & Killeen, K. (2007). Introduction. In K. Killeen & P. J. Forshaw (Eds.), *The word and the world: Biblical exegesis and early modern science* (pp. 1–20). New York: Palgrave Macmillan.

Gaur, A. (1984). *A history of writing*. London: The British Library.

Gelb, I. J. (1963). *A study of writing* (2nd ed.). Chicago: University of Chicago Press.

Goody, J., & Watt, I. (1968/1975). The consequences of literacy. In J. Goody (Ed.), *Literacy in traditional societies* (pp. 27–68). Cambridge, UK: Cambridge University Press.

Grice, H. P. (1989). *Studies in the ways with words*. Cambridge, MA: Harvard University Press.

Harris, R. (2009a). Speech and writing. In D. R. Olson & N. Torrance (Eds.), *Cambridge handbook of literacy* (pp. 46–58). Cambridge, UK: Cambridge University Press.

Harris, R. (2009b). *Rationality and the literate mind*. London: Routledge & Kegan Paul.

Havelock, E. (1982). *The literate revolution in Greece and its cultural consequence*. Princeton, NJ: Princeton University Press.

Hayes, R., & Flower, L. (1986). Writing research and the writer. *American Psychologist, 41*, 1106–1113.

Johnson, W., & Parker, H. (Eds.). (2009). *Ancient literacies: The culture of reading in Greece and Rome*. Oxford: Oxford University Press.

Kahneman, D., & Tversky, A. (1996). On the reality of cognitive illusions. *Psychological Review, 103*, 582–591.

Leezenberg, M. (2001). *Contexts of metaphor*. New York: Elsevier.

Levy-Bruhl, L. (1923). *How natives think*. New York: Washington Square Press.

Levy-Bruhl, L. (1923). *Primitive mentality*. London: George Allen & Unwin.

McLuhan, M. (1962). *The Gutenberg galaxy*. Toronto: University of Toronto Press.

McLuhan, M. (2003). *Understanding media: The extensions of man* (Critical edition). Corte Madera, CA: Gingko Press. (Original edition published in 1964)

Morais, J., Cary, L., Alegria, J., & Bertelson, P. (1979). Does awareness of speech as a sequence of phones arise spontaneously? *Cognition, 7*, 323–331.

Olson, D. R. (1994). *The world on paper: The conceptual and cognitive implications of writing and reading*. Cambridge: Cambridge University Press.

Olson, D. R. (2009). A theory of reading/writing: From literacy to literature. *Writing Systems Research, 1*, 51–64.

Olson, D. R. (2010). Narrative, cognition and rationality. In J. P. Gee & M. Handford (Eds.), *Routledge handbook of discourse analysis* (pp. 604–615). London: Routledge.

Perfetti, C. (2009). The universal grammar of reading. *Scientific Studies of Reading, 7*, 219–238.

Petersson, K. M., Ingvar, M., & Reis, A. (2009). Language and literacy from a cognitive neuroscience perspective. In D. R. Olson & N. Torrance (Eds.), *Cambridge handbook of literacy* (pp. 152–181). Cambridge, UK: Cambridge University Press.

Rousseau, J.-J. (1966). Essay on the origin of languages. In J. H. Moran & A. Gode (Eds.), *On the origin of language: Two essays by Jean-Jacques R'ousseau and Gohann Gottfried Herder* (pp. 5–85). New York: Frederick Unger. (Original work published in 1754–1791)

Schmandt-Besserat, D. (1996). *How writing came about*. Austin, TX: University of Texas Press.

Schmandt-Besserat, D. (2007). *When writing met art: From symbol to story*. Austin, TX: University of Texas Press.

Scribner, S., & Cole, M. (1981). *The psychology of literacy*. Cambridge, MA: Harvard University Press.

Snow, C., & Uccelli, P. (2009). The challenge of academic language. In D. R. Olson & N. Torrance (Eds.), *The Cambridge handbook of literacy* (pp. 112–133). New York: Cambridge University Press.

Stanovich, K. (2009). *What intelligence texts miss: The psychology of rational thought*. New Haven, CT: Yale University Press.

Stock, B. (1983). *The implications of literacy*. Princeton, NJ: Princeton University Press.

Tylor, E. B. (1871). *Primitive culture* (2 volumes). London: Murray.

Vico, G. B. (1744). *Scienza nuova* (3rd edition, Trans. by T. G. Bergin and M. H. Fish). Ithaca, NY: Cornell University Press.

Wang, F., Tsai, Y., & Wang, W. S.-Y. (2009). Chinese literacy. In D. R. Olson & N. Torrance (Eds.), *Cambridge handbook of literacy* (pp. 386–417). Cambridge, UK: Cambridge University Press.

Woods, C. (2013). *Visible language: Inventions of writing in the Ancient Middle East and beyond*. Chicago: Oriental Institute Museum of Chicago. Retrieved from (http://oi.uchicago.edu/pdf/oimp32.pdf)

Representation of Orthographic Knowledge

Brenda Rapp *and* Simon Fischer-Baum

Abstract

What is it that we know when we know the spellings of words? This chapter reviews current understanding of the answer to that question, focusing on evidence from written word production (spelling) and briefly reviewing convergent evidence from reading. We first establish that orthographic knowledge is independent from spoken word knowledge. With regard to the nature of orthographic representations, evidence indicates that orthographic knowledge is represented in a modality-independent code organized into units corresponding to morphemes, digraphs, and letters. Furthermore, a detailed examination of the representation of letter units reveals that they are multidimensional feature bundles specifying letter identity, consonant-vowel status, syllabic role, and letter position. This chapter shows that to know the spellings of words is to learn and process orthographic representations that are abstract, complex, and richly structured mental objects.

Key Words: spelling, orthographic representations, morphology, consonant-vowel status, syllables, letter position representation

Written language is an extraordinary human invention that has allowed for the communication and accumulation of knowledge across time and geography and, in so doing, has revolutionized human history. Furthermore, literacy, once limited to the elites and used only for specific functions, has become a priority across the globe and written communication is now pervasive in daily life. In fact, for some individuals, the time spent in written communication, through e-mailing, texting, chatting, instant messaging, tweeting, and so forth, may match or surpass the time spent speaking. What is the cognitive machinery that allows for this effective means of communication? What is it that we know when we know the spellings of words? The first question is the focus of Miceli and Costa "The Role of Lexical and Sublexical Orthography in Writing: Autonomy, Interactions, and Neurofunctional Correlates". The second forms the basis of this chapter, which is concerned with reviewing what is

known about the content of orthographic knowledge and the mental representations used in producing written language.

Before proceeding, we thought it useful to orient the reader regarding the focus and organization of the chapter. First, we should indicate that because of space limitations, the chapter is restricted to a discussion of the representation of orthographic knowledge in *alphabetic* or similar codes (rather than logographic or syllabic codes); in the *adult* system; and specifically as concerns *single-word* production. The chapter begins with several introductory sections in which some fundamental background issues are discussed. We then move on to the body of the chapter in which we discuss orthographic representation.

Here we also take the opportunity to explain why a great many of the findings we review come from cognitive neuropsychological studies of adults who, as a result of neural injury, have acquired dysgraphia. This is for two reasons. First, the bulk of research on orthographic representation in written language production has involved cognitive neuropsychological studies. Second, although neurologically intact individuals have been profitably studied to address issues of orthographic representation, it is often difficult to identify the processing locus of the empirical effects of interest. For example, as we will discuss below, doubling errors are often observed in "normal" typing and writing such that the wrong letter is doubled in a word that has a double letter (LETTER → LETEER). To understand what these errors reveal about orthographic representation, it is critical to determine whether the errors are produced at an abstract level of orthographic representation or in motor programming and execution. This determination is typically difficult in neurologically intact participants, but can often be accomplished with considerable ease in many cognitive neuropsychological case studies on the basis of independent characteristics of their performance.

The Relationship between Written and Spoken Language

This chapter is specifically interested in understanding how the orthographic content of words is mentally represented. We review evidence of the orthographic representation of morphologic and syllabic structure, consonants and vowels, segment quantity, the status of digraphs, and the reference system used for representing the position of letters in a string. Many of these concepts (e.g., syllable, consonant and vowel) are more typically used in describing phonological representations. It would not be surprising if readers were to wonder if these structures are appropriately described as orthographic or if they are not, instead, actually phonological. Such concerns are natural given that written language develops later than spoken language and clearly builds on it, both as it developed during human history and also as it is acquired in each individual. Furthermore, even in the adult expert reader and writer, spoken language knowledge and processes are often active when we are processing written language (e.g., Alario, de Cara, & Ziegler, 2007; Ashby, Sanders, & Kingston, 2009; Perfetti, Bell, & Delaney, 1988; see Rastle and Brysbaert, 2006 for review). One possibility, given written language's evolutionary "youth" compared with that of spoken language, is that written language is entirely parasitic both neurally and cognitively on spoken language substrates and processes. Although commonly held, the view that recently acquired skills are entirely dependent on evolutionarily older ones is not the only possible view. Another possibility is that written language processes and representations, although dependent on spoken ones during the course of learning, develop increasing cognitive and neural independence from spoken language until autonomy is achieved in the expert reader and speller.

This debate on the relationship between written and spoken language has been most clearly manifested in research on the question of whether or not phonological forms necessarily mediate between orthographic forms and meaning. In reading, the question has been whether the reader retrieves the spoken form of a written word to understand its meaning (obligatory phonological recoding). In spelling, the question has been whether if one has the meaning of a word in mind, must one first retrieve the spoken form of the word to recover the written form from long-term memory (LTM; obligatory phonological mediation).

With regard to spelling, the evidence indicates that phonological mediation is not obligatory, at least not for single word spelling (Ellis & Young, 1988). In fact, if we assume a functional architecture in which the spellings of words can be retrieved directly from their semantic representations without first retrieving their phonological forms (Figure 21.1), we would predict that the brain could be damaged such as to disrupt spoken naming while leaving written naming intact. This pattern has been described in several cases of individuals with acquired spoken language deficits who may, for example, orally misname pictures (e.g., naming an onion as a "banana") while correctly writing the name of the picture (O-N-I-O-N; Rapp, Benzing, & Caramazza, 1997; see also Miceli & Capasso, 1997; Tainturier, Moreaud, David, Leek, & Pellat, 2001). The architecture depicted in Figure 21.1 would also account for reports of disruptions to the production system

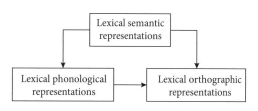

Figure 21.1 Cognitive architecture including orthographic autonomy. There is a direct link between lexical semantic representations and lexical orthographic representations, without obligatory phonological mediation.

that allow for different grammatical categories to be differentially disrupted in spoken and written output modalities (e.g., Rapp & Caramazza, 1997a). For example, in response to a picture of a horse jumping over a fence, an individual with difficulties producing nouns in spoken production but verbs in writing, might say the sentence "the /bedzoz/ jumps over the /θʌm/" but write THE HORSE *JERMING* OVER THE FENCE. If we consider neurologically intact individuals, the independence of written and spoken word production explains findings, such as those reported by Bonin, Fayol, and Peereman (1998), who found that conditions that facilitate the spoken production of word do not necessarily facilitate its written production. For example, the prior presentation of a written pseudohomophone prime (e.g., DANT, in French) facilitates the spoken naming of the picture "dent" (tooth), but the same pseudohomophone prime does not facilitate written naming of the picture D-E-N-T. This indicates that facilitating the retrieval of a spoken form does not necessarily affect the retrieval of the written form, a finding at odds with the hypothesis of obligatory phonological mediation of written production.

These examples illustrate how the findings from neuropsychological cases and neutrally intact individuals converge in revealing the autonomy of orthography from phonology that develops with increasing expertise.

The Basic Architecture of the Spelling System

To facilitate understanding of the findings we describe later that are specifically concerned with orthographic representation, we expand on the basic architecture represented in Figure 21.1 and briefly review the more complete set of processes involved in word spelling.

The basic architecture of spelling is represented in Figure 21.2 (along with related components of the spoken naming system). Individuals can retrieve lexical orthographic representations from orthographic LTM (Buchwald & Rapp, 2010) based on a variety of inputs: heard words (e.g., writing-to-dictation, taking notes in a lecture); pictures or objects in the world; or from internally generated word-meanings (e.g., writing letters, essays). The operations involved in processing these inputs and contacting meaning representations are not, however, specific to writing; rather they are engaged whenever heard words or pictures are processed. After lexical semantics is contacted, then retrieval from orthographic LTM (the orthographic lexicon) may occur. In addition to retrieval of orthographic lexical representations,

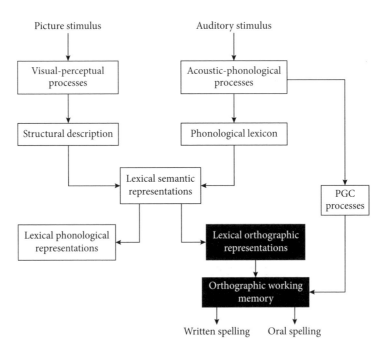

Figure 21.2 Cognitive architecture of the spelling system (expansion from Figure 21.1). Depiction of processes involved in word spelling based on a speech stimulus; visual object (or picture); or internally generated semantic representation. Highlighted are the lexical orthographic representations (orthographic long-term memory) and the orthographic working memory. PGC = phoneme-to-grapheme conversion. The nature of the orthographic representations at these levels constitutes the focus of this chapter.

heard words may be spelled through the application knowledge that has been acquired regarding the relationships between sounds and letters. On the basis of this information, the phoneme-grapheme conversion procedures generate plausible spellings for known words ("sugar" → SHUGER) or unfamiliar words ("flome" → FLOAM). Orthographic representations, whether retrieved from orthographic LTM or assembled through phoneme-grapheme conversion, are processed by an orthographic working memory (WM) system (often referred to as the graphemic buffer). Orthographic WM maintains orthographic information active and ensures the selection of letters in their correct order for production by subsequent processes involved in written or oral spelling. For written spelling, letter shapes are selected (specifying the desired case and font) and motor programs are executed to give form to the spellings (e.g., cat). For oral spelling, letter names are selected (from the phonological lexicon) and the necessary phonological, phonetic, and articulatory processes are deployed for spoken production of letter names (e.g., /si/ /ei/ /ti/). The different components of the spelling process have been shown to be sensitive to different variables (see Rapp, 2002, and Buchwald & Rapp, 2010 for reviews). Briefly, orthographic LTM is sensitive to lexical frequency but not the letter length of words. Orthographic WM shows the reverse sensitivity, where processes involved in letter shape production are generally sensitive to neither variable but instead are sensitive to letter shape. These differential sensitivities lead to different patterns of performance and different error types for different loci of disruption within the system, making it possible to identify the level of impairment in many neuropsychological cases. In the remainder of this chapter we specifically focus on the organization and content of the orthographic representations that are processed by orthographic LTM and WM.

The Internal Complexity of Orthographic Representations

Given the evidence that written and spoken language production machinery have developed considerable cognitive and neural independence, it is not surprising that phonological and orthographic representations themselves, although perhaps highly interdependent during written language learning (Treiman & Bourassa, 2000), have developed independent and modality-specific characteristics in the adult system.

The default hypothesis regarding the content of orthographic representations is that knowledge of

the spelling of a word consists simply of a string of letter identities and their positions, what has sometimes been referred to as "the linear string hypothesis" of orthographic representation (Caramazza, Miceli, & Villa, 1987). Although letter segment identity and position must certainly be represented, it is by no means obvious that this is the only information that is included in orthographic representations, or that representations necessarily have a one-dimensional "flat" structure. The alternative hypothesis is that orthographic representations, much like phonological ones, are internally rich, complex multidimensional structures (Badecker, 1996; Caramazza & Miceli, 1990).

We will review evidence revealing the internal complexity of orthographic representations, organizing our discussion into three sections. The first deals with the units of orthographic representation: abstract letters, digraphs, and morphemes. The second reviews evidence regarding the nature of the information that is associated with letters: consonant-vowel (CV) status, quantity, and syllabic role. In the third we discuss the manner in which letter position is represented.

Figure 21.3 depicts the internal structure of the orthographic representation of the word THICKNESS. Included are the various components of orthographic representation. Essentially, this figure serves as a graphic summary of this chapter, with the text dedicated to providing the empirical evidence supporting the components of orthographic representation depicted in this figure.

The Units of Orthographic Representation: Letters, Digraphs, and Morphemes

How can we identify the units of orthographic representation? Perhaps the clearest diagnostic is that the candidate units (e.g., morphemes, digraphs) can be affected independently of one another, that is, they exhibit "separate modifiability" (a term Sternberg, 2001, has used for the identification of independent processing modules). The separate modifiability of candidate representational units may be manifested in a variety of ways, such as differential effects of manipulating the levels of some experimental variable (e.g., frequency); differential susceptibility to disruption (or facilitation); or the possibility of independent "movement." In the review that follows we present examples of all of these types of evidence for orthographic units. In doing so, we will frequently use examples from cases of individuals with acquired dysgraphia who produce significant levels of perseveration errors in

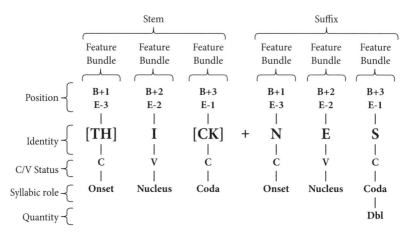

Figure 21.3 Proposed orthographic representation for the word THICKNESS. The bold elements represent the content and structure of the representation. Five features of orthographic unit representation are depicted: (1) letter position; (2) letter identity; (3) consonant vowel status (CV status); (4) syllabic role; and (5) letter quantity. For example, one orthographic unit has S in the identity dimension. Another feature associated with this unit identity position is represented as both three after the beginning of the morpheme (B+3) and one before the end of the morpheme (E-1). Also represented is the CV status of consonant (C), the syllabic role of Coda, and the quantity of double (Dbl). Note that the digraphs TH and CK are each represented within a single feature bundle. The brackets around [TH] and [CK] depict that these digraphs are single units in the letter identity dimension. Feature bundles are further organized into higher-level morphologic units. The first three feature bundles combine to form the stem morpheme THICK, and the final three feature bundles combine to form the suffix morpheme NESS. The plus symbol (+) between the two morphemes indicates processes that combine multiple morphemes into whole word representations. Not depicted here is the graded nature of position representations (see text).

their spelling. A perseveration error is the inappropriate intrusion of an element from a previous response into a subsequent response (Table 21.1). These errors are especially informative for identifying the units of orthographic representation under the simple logic that an element that can be shown to "travel" from one item to the next must have considerable independence from its neighboring elements.

Abstract Letter Units

It may seem obvious that letters are the basic units of orthographic representation. Nonetheless, critical questions remain concerning the *format* of these basic units of representation and the degree to which letter representations are indeed *independent* units. We consider each of these in turn.

The claim of abstract letter units is that there is a level of abstract letter representation that is used in representing our knowledge of the spellings of words. At this level of representation, letters are represented as abstract entities, lacking visual or motoric form, sounds, or names. This claim is perhaps less surprising if we consider that the same letter identities apply across a range of physical implementations and formats. For example, the quite different visual forms G, g, *g*, *G* and the name /gi/ all correspond to the same letter. The spoken names of letters do not resemble their visual shapes,[1] and even as concerns visual shapes, lower case forms do not

necessarily resemble their corresponding upper-case counterparts (e.g., A/a, G/g, E/e). In this way, letter identity transcends variation in visual form and even modality.

To be clear, it is certainly the case that there are modality- and form-specific representations of letters that allow us to express our orthographic knowledge in written and oral spelling; the question of interest is whether or not there are also abstract letter representations. The fact that letter identities can be expressed in a variety of formats does not, in and of itself, guarantee the existence of abstract letter representations. It could be that orthographic knowledge is stored in a specific format (e.g., spoken letter names) and then translated into another (visual/motor letter shapes). Thus, there are three candidate hypotheses: (1) orthographic information is represented in terms of abstract letter units that are converted into letter shapes or letter names as needed for oral or written spelling; (2) orthographic information is represented in terms of the spoken names of letters (e.g., CAT = /si/ /Ei/ /ti/) that are converted to letter shapes for written spelling; or (3) orthographic information is represented in terms of letter shapes that are converted into letter names for oral spelling.

There is a triplet of findings that distinguish among these three possibilities and strongly support the hypothesis of the abstract representation of letters. First, the hypothesis that the format of orthographic representations corresponds to spoken letter names (subsequently converted into letter shapes for written spelling) is challenged by the finding that, as a result of brain injury, an individual may have difficulties retrieving the spoken names of letters (e.g., oral spelling BED as /bi/ /ay/ /si/) and yet be able to spell words accurately in writing (e.g., Kinsbourne & Warrington, 1965). Second, the hypothesis that the format of orthographic representations corresponds to letter shapes (subsequently converted into letter names for oral spelling) is challenged by the complementary dissociation observed in individuals who have difficulties retrieving the correct shapes of letters (e.g., in written spelling producing TABLE as TAPLF) but who are accurate in oral spelling (Rapp & Caramazza, 1997b). Finally, the specific predictions of the hypothesis of abstract letter representation are upheld. Namely, as would be predicted for a deficit affecting central components of the spelling process (the orthographic lexicon or graphemic buffer), where orthographic information is hypothesized to be represented abstractly, there are individuals who have difficulties in both written and oral spelling that are virtually identical in their severity and in the distribution of errors, suggesting a common source (e.g., Caramazza & Miceli, 1990; Hillis & Caramazza, 1989; Jónsdóttir, Shallice, & Wise, 1996; Katz, 1991; McCloskey, Badecker, Goodman-Schulman, & Aliminosa, 1994). Additionally, when the letter substitution errors produced by these individuals are examined, the target and error letters (e.g., BEFORE → BEFOLE) are not any more similar visually or motorically than would be expected by chance (Rapp & Caramazza, 1997b). That is, as expected under the hypothesis that these errors arise at a level at which letters are abstractly represented, written and oral spelling are comparably affected and the errors do not reflect confusions of similar letter names, shapes, or sounds.

The evidence for abstract letter representations does not directly address the question of whether or not abstract letters can function as independent units. For example, one hypothesis is that letters are represented in multiletter units only (e.g., as open bigrams). The most obvious evidence for letters as units comes from the many observations of the spelling errors produced by both normal (Ellis, 1979; Hotopf, 1980; MacKay, 1969; Wing & Baddeley, 1980) and dysgraphic spellers indicating that *single* letters can be deleted (FUTURE → FUTUE); substituted (ABSENCE → ABSONCE);

added (COULD → COUNLD); and moved (RIOT → ROIT).

An analysis of single letter perseveration errors carried out by Fischer-Baum and Rapp (in preparation) underscores the independence of letter representations. Table 21.1 reports a sequence of spelling responses produced by an individual with an acquired dysgraphia originating from the central components of the spelling process (Fischer-Baum, McCloskey, & Rapp, 2010). Table 21.1 shows a sequence of trials leading up to the trial EDGE → ERGE in which the letter intrusion R is produced. Both the immediately preceding response (E-1: FRENCE) and two responses before the error (E-2: MORTCH) contained an R. One possibility is that the R was intruded into ERGE because it was perseverated from one of these prior responses.

The question that is relevant for the current context is whether or not the intruded letter was a *single* letter perseveration from previous responses. To address this question, we first identified 251 errors in which a single consonant intrusion was produced surrounded by correct vowels (EASILY → EASIBY). We found that for 69 percent of these errors, the response immediately preceding each intrusion contained the intruded letter. Further analyses (based on Monte Carlo methods first reported in McCloskey, Macaruso, & Rapp, 2006) indicated that this 69 percent rate was far greater than what would be expected by chance, with chance rates ranging from 14 to 29 percent. Thus, this example serves as a clear illustration of the "independent life" of individual letters, indicating that they can perseverate into subsequent responses as units independently of neighboring letters.

This section has reviewed evidence that there is a level of processing at which letters are represented as abstract units. Interestingly, the parallel claim from

Table 21.1. CM's error EDGE → ERGE and the five preceding trials (E = error trial)

Trial	Target	Response
E-5	CULT	CUNPH
E-4	HINT	HINT
E-3	WISH	WISH
E-2	MORTAL	MORTCH
E-1	FRENCH	FRENCE
E	EDGE	ERGE

spoken production about abstract phonemes and their role in spoken production is not uncontroversial, with many vigorous debates regarding the characterization of phonemes as abstract and distinct units of representation (e.g., Buchwald, Rapp, & Stone, 2007; Goldstein et al., 2007; Oppenheim & Dell, 2008; Pouplier & Goldstein, 2010; Roelofs, 1999). The issue is potentially more difficult to resolve in phonology given that, in contrast to orthography, what counts as a particular phoneme (e.g., /s/) is fully determined by the relevant set of form features. For example, there is a configuration of articulatory/acoustic features such that all tokens of /s/ will share some range of configurations of these features. This makes it difficult to distinguish abstract from more peripheral representations of language sounds. Furthermore, the complexities involved in characterizing the boundaries between phonemes contribute to questions regarding the status of phonemes as independent units of language sound (see Buchwald, "Phonetic Processing;" Goldrick "Phonological Processing: The Retrieval and Encoding of Word Form Information in Speech Production"). Many of these issues are avoided in the orthography because of the multiple modalities and formats in which written language can be expressed and the unitary character of letter representations.

Digraphs

Although there is clear evidence that single letters may be units of orthographic representation, there is also evidence that they are not the only orthographic units. In their computational work on the spelling process, Houghton and Zorzi (2003) proposed that the single or multiple letter sequences that correspond to single phonemes are represented as single orthographic units (note that these multiple letter sequences are referred to by some researchers as graphemes, by others as digraphs, and yet others as complex graphemes). Accordingly, the six letters of the three phoneme word "wreath" would be represented by three (digraph) units WR+EA+TH, whereas the six letters of the six-phoneme word "strict" would be represented by six units S+T+R+I+C+T. Houghton & Zorzi's arguments are computationally motivated because they found that this type of representation improved both the accuracy and the plausibility of errors produced by their connectionist simulation of single word spelling.

Consistent with the Houghton and Zorzi proposal are the findings of Kandel and Spinelli (2010), who found differences in the handwriting times of French words related to the presence or absence of digraphs. For example, they found that it took longer to produce the first letter of a digraph (e.g., the A in PRAIRIE) than a matched nondigraph letter (e.g., the A in CLAVIER) (see Kandel, Soler, Valdois, & Gros, 2006, for similar results with children). These systematic differences would not be predicted if the A in PRAIRIE was represented identically to the A in CLAVIER, as would be expected if digraphs did not have a special status. Further evidence of a very different type comes from Tainturier and Rapp (2004). They reported on two individuals with acquired dysgraphia who had documented deficits in orthographic WM (graphemic buffering), such that the probability of making an error on a letter increased with the length of the word. Tainturier and Rapp (2004) reasoned that if the graphemic buffer is sensitive to the number of orthographic units and if digraphs are indeed orthographic units, then digraphs should provide less of a burden than two-letter clusters to a damaged graphemic buffer. To test this hypothesis, they examined accuracy in writing matched two-letter clusters and digraphs (e.g., PO*CK*ET /BA*SK*ET). They found significantly more errors in the clusters than in the digraphs, consistent with the hypothesis that digraphs create less of a WM burden. Furthermore, in terms of types of errors, the constituents of digraphs were less likely to be separated than the constituents of clusters. That is, it was less likely in digraphs than in clusters that only one of the constituent letters was produced or that the two letters were produced in nonadjacent positions. A digraph error, such as PO*CK*ET → PO*CL*ER, was less likely than the cluster error BA*SK*ET → BA*SL*ET). This latter result is consistent with the notion that digraphs are unitized and that, therefore, constituent elements are more tightly coupled in a digraph than in a cluster.

In addition, Fischer-Baum and Rapp (in preparation) specifically presented evidence that the constituents of digraphs "travel" together. The dysgraphic individual (reported previously) who produced significant rates of perseveration errors in written production sometimes produced digraph "intrusions" ("soul" → SOU*CK*). The hypothesis of digraph unitization predicts that if digraphs are represented as single units, then digraph intrusion errors should occur at rates comparable with single letter intrusions. In contrast, the intrusion of adjacent consonants that do not form a digraph ("junk→ JU*LT*) are the result of the co-occurrence of two single unit intrusions and should occur less often than digraph intrusions. To examine this prediction, we compared the rate of digraph and consonant cluster perseverations to the rate of single consonant perseverations. We found significantly higher perseveration rates for both single consonants and digraphs than for consonant clusters, and digraph perseveration rates were not different from single consonant perseveration rates. Additionally, we considered the likelihood that individual constituent elements of a digraph (e.g., the S and the H in the digraph SH) would intrude into subsequent responses. Under the digraph unitization view, one would not expect separate movement for digraph constituents, but would expect to see this for cluster constituents. The results provided clear support for the digraph unitization hypothesis: single consonant intrusions ("cat" → CA*S*) were no more likely than chance to be preceded by responses that contained the intruded letter in a digraph ("fresh" → FRE*SH*), but were significantly more likely than chance to be preceded by responses that contained the intruded letter in a consonant cluster ("flask" → FLA*SK*).

The evidence for the status of digraphs as orthographic units raises a number of important questions: How is the internal structure of a digraph represented such that the ordering of its internal constituents can be correctly expressed in production? What is the relationship between the representations of digraph units, letter units, and digraph constituents? For some discussion of these and related questions see Tainturier and Rapp (2004), Jones, Folk, and Rapp (2009), and Kandel and Spinelli (2010).

Morpho-orthography

There have been hundreds of studies examining morphologic decomposition of written words in reading. In contrast, there has been only a handful examining this issue in spelling. Nonetheless, the evidence from spelling regarding the representation of orthographic morphemes is quite compelling.

Hillis and Caramazza (1989) and Badecker, Hillis, and Caramazza (1990) reported on the case of an individual whose spelling performance provided evidence that morphemes act as orthographic units in written language production. Specifically, this individual suffered from an orthographic WM deficit and Hillis and colleagues found that multimorphemic words yielded fewer errors than matched monomorphemic words. This suggested that the WM "load" was lessened by the possibility of separately processing the constituent morphemes. This hypothesis derived further support from the distribution of errors across letter positions within words. Within monomorphemic words, the probability of error was greater at the end of the word than at the beginning; however, with productively suffixed, prefixed, and compound words, accuracy decreased across each of the morphemes (Figure 21.4). For example, in a word such as WEIGHTLESS, accuracy decreased toward the end of the word stem WEIGHT, but then increased for the initial letters of the suffix LESS to the level of performance that was observed for the beginnings of words.

Further evidence of orthographic morpheme units was provided by Badecker, Rapp, and Caramazza (1996) who described a dysgraphic individual with selective disruption in the retrieval of stems but not affixes from the orthographic lexicon in written word production. Specifically, this individual made

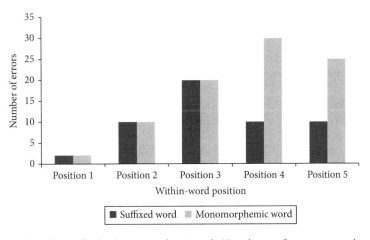

Figure 21.4 Patient errors in spelling suffixed and monomorphemic words. Note that very few errors are made on the fourth position in the suffixed word (the beginning of the affix) compared with the fourth position of the unaffixed word. Adapted from Badecker, W., Hillis, A., & Caramazza, A. (1990). Lexical morphology and its role in the writing process: Evidence from a case of acquired dysgraphia. *Cognition, 35*, 205–243.

phonologically plausible errors on irregularly spelled stems but not on irregularly spelled affixes. For example, in spelling to dictation, "surfed" was spelled as SOURPHED (not SOURPHT) and "cabooses" was spelled as CABUSES (not CABUSIZ). The fact that the errors were phonologically plausible indicates a deficit in lexical retrieval such that when lexical retrieval fails, the sublexical phoneme-to-grapheme conversion system is able to produce a plausible spelling (see Miceli and Costa "The Role of Lexical and Sublexical Orthography in Writing: Autonomy, Interactions, and Neurofunctional Correlates"). Importantly, the selective preservation of the spelling of the past tense suffix was not simply caused by a preference for spelling the unvoiced word stops in verbs with ED, because such words as "adjust," "erupt," and "draft" were never spelled as ADJUSED, ERUPED, or DRAFED. Instead, the fact that affixes were not regularized indicates that they were not subject to the same retrieval failure as stems. Thus, this selective retrieval difficulty with stems indicates that stems and affixes were available for retrieval as separate entities in the written production system.

The complementary pattern (selective difficulty with written affixes) was noted in the report by Berndt and Haendiges (2000), who described an aphasic individual with particular difficulty producing correct verb inflections in the written but not spoken modality. This was followed up by Rapp, Barriere, and Fischer-Baum (2006), who reported on four individuals who produced morphologic errors (affix deletions and substitutions) almost exclusively in written compared with spoken sentence production. For example, saying "Dave *is eating* an apple" but writing DAVE *IS EATS* AN APPLE. Further, Rapp et al. were able to rule out that these errors were simply difficulties with the ends of written words or were whole-word substitutions of orthographic neighbors. This set of findings provides critical evidence regarding the specifically orthographic nature of the morpheme representations because the difficulties these individuals exhibited exclusively or primarily affected the written modality, leaving spoken affix production largely intact. This brief summary reviews evidence that morphemes (both stems and affixes) are represented as separable entities in orthographic representations. This does not preclude that morphologically complex words may not also be represented as whole words.

Section Summary

This section presented evidence regarding the units of orthographic representations: abstract letters, digraphs, and morphemes, reviewing various types of evidence indicating the separate modifiability and movement of these orthographic units, and their specifically orthographic character. The next section reviews evidence regarding the content of abstract letter unit representations.

Letter Units as Multidimensional Feature Bundles: CV Status, Syllabic Role, and Quantity

We will argue that letter units can be conceived of as multidimensional feature bundles, each of which, in addition to specifying the identity of the letter, indicates specific values on additional dimensions. Specifically we will discuss evidence that information regarding CV status, syllabic role, and quantity (number of letters) form a part of each letter unit.

Orthographic Consonants and Vowels

The notion of consonants and vowels is a phonological one; however, it has been carried over into the orthography both explicitly and implicitly. Explicitly, letters are classified as consonants or vowels in the Roman alphabet, and in other alphabets, such as Hebrew or Amharic. Implicitly, the CV distinction may be critical to our representation of orthotactics, the knowledge that supports our ability to distinguish between unfamiliar yet "legal" letter sequences (e.g., STREBLE) and illegal ones (e.g., STREBL). Here we will specifically report on evidence that the orthographic (CV) identity of a letter is a component of the information bundle that constitutes each abstract letter unit.

In spelling, evidence of the representation of orthographic CV status includes the finding of selective deficits affecting either consonants or vowels in spelling. For example, Cubelli (1991) and Cotelli, Abutalebi, Zorzi, and Cappa (2003) described Italian-speaking, dysgraphic individuals who made significantly more errors on vowels than consonants (e.g., "uomo" [man] → IOMO) in spelling. The complementary dissociation was reported by Miceli, Capasso, Benvegnù, and Caramazza (2004) who described an individual for whom 99 percent of incorrectly spelled letters were consonants. These individuals did not suffer comparable deficits in their spoken production, underscoring the orthographic nature of the impairments. The conclusion is that the selectivity of the dissociations indicate that consonants and vowels are represented with sufficient neural independence that one category can be damaged while leaving the other relatively intact.

Additional evidence also comes from dysgraphic individuals (with graphemic buffer deficits) who, in their letter substitution errors, largely substitute consonants for consonants and vowels for vowels. For example, in 99 percent of the substitution errors produced by the individual reported by Caramazza and Miceli (1990), the CV status of each error matched that of the target letter (see also Buchwald & Rapp, 2006; Caramazza & Miceli, 1990; Cotelli et al., 2003; Jonsdottir et al., 1996; Kay and Hanley, 1994; McCloskey et al., 1994; Schonauer & Denes, 1994; Ward & Romani, 1998, 2000). Caramazza and Miceli (1990) proposed that this high CV matching rate in substitution errors is possible if one assumes that letter identity information may be disrupted while information regarding CV status may remain intact. For example, in such a word as THICKNESS (see Figure 21.3) if the letter identity "I" component is unavailable, the CV information would allow the system to produce a response that is consistent with the available information (e.g., THICKNESS → THACKNESS).

Buchwald and Rapp (2006) put this hypothesis to a test, examining if the matching of CV status in substitution errors could be attributed specifically to orthographic rather than phonological knowledge; and if the observed CV matching rates could be accounted for by the constraints of the local orthographic environment in which the substitution error occurred, rather than requiring the explicit representation of CV information.

In most cases, both the orthographic and phonological CV category of letters are the same (e.g., both C+A+T and /k ae t/ have a C+V+C structure). This quite naturally prompts the question of whether it is the phonological or orthographic CV information that constrains the substitution errors. However, in nontransparent languages, such as English, CV categories need not be the same orthographically and phonologically. For example, in the word "though" the phonological representation has a CV structure made up two phonemes (/ð ou/). The orthographic representation, however, is made of six letters with the following CV structure: CCVVCC. This allows one to ask whether if a substitution error is made on the final G or H in spelling "though," a consonant or vowel would be produced. If the phonological representation is guiding the substitution process, a vowel is expected because presumably the OUGH maps on to the V component of the phonological representation. Alternatively, if the error is constrained by orthographic CV status, then the G or H should be substituted by another consonant. To examine this, Buchwald and Rapp (2006) analyzed the performance of two individuals (with

deficits at the level of the graphemic buffer; see also Buchwald & Rapp, 2010). To distinguish between phonological and orthographic hypotheses, they examined substitution errors produced for letters for which the orthographic and phonological CV categories are mismatched, such as errors on the G or H in THOUGH or on the W in SHALLOW. Data analysis indicated that substitution errors on these critical letters matched the orthographic CV category of the target letters 91 percent and 70 percent of the time (for the two individuals, respectively). Examples include such things as writing "sleigh" → SLEIGT, an error in which orthographic consonant was substituted by another consonant. Further analyses revealed that these observed rates of orthographic CV matching on these critical segments occurred with significantly greater likelihood than would be expected by chance.

Having established that the results were genuinely orthographic, Buchwald and Rapp (2006) then examined the possibility that the system does not know the orthographic CV identity of the disrupted letter but rather that the constraints provided by the surrounding letters restrict the letter substitution to the appropriate CV category. To do so, they examined the performance of four individuals whose overall CV matching rates ranged from 70 to 97 percent. For each error produced by each participant they identified a complete list of words of the language that had the same orthographic environment as the error. These words were analyzed to determine the rate of CV matching that would be predicted by the orthographic characteristics of the language. In one analysis, for example, for the error GLOAT → GROAT, all five-letter words of English with G in the first position and O in the third were identified (ghost, gnome, goose, gross). These words were then examined to determine the rate of CV matching that would be predicted by the language for the letter in second position. In this case, in three out of the four words the critical second letter is a consonant, whereas in only one word is the critical letter a vowel, yielding a "language predicted" CV matching score of 0.75. That is, for this particular error, if CV information was not a part of the letter representation, the constraints of the language alone would predict a 0.75 CV matching rate. Based on this logic, each participant's error corpus was examined and several different ways of defining the relevant orthographic environment were evaluated (e.g., a three-letter window with the target letter in the center, two-letter windows with the target in the first or in the second position, and so forth). The results all clearly demonstrated that the orthographic regularities of the language (as characterized in the analyses that were performed) predict far *lower* rates of CV matching in letter substitutions than were observed in any of the four individuals examined. On this basis, Buchwald and Rapp (2006) concluded that additional information, such as the orthographic CV identity of target letters, is required to explain the high rates of CV matching that were observed in these individuals' spelling errors.

The Representation of Quantity: The Case of Letter Doubling

How are the double letters in the word MASS represented? There are two possibilities. One is that they are represented as adjacent elements in a string (M+A+S+S), no differently than any other adjacent pair of letters (M+A+S+T). The other is that letter quantity is one of the components of the multidimensional letter representation and that letter doubling is explicitly represented, perhaps as schematized by the representation of the SS in THICKNESS (see Figure 21.3).

Lashley (1951) suggested that the existence of typing errors in which there is a misplacing of the doubling of letter, such as LOOK → LOKK or ILL→ IIL, indicates an independence of order and identity information. Rumelhart and Norman (1982), in developing a typing simulation, discussed the critical implications of errors such as these for understanding the underlying representations. On the basis of these errors they rejected both representations in which double letters are represented just as any other pair of adjacent letters (B+O+O+T) and also those in which a double letter is represented as a single unit (B+[OO]+T). Instead, they argued that these errors indicate that doubling and identity schemata (representations) are independent (see Figure 21.3). In that way, the doubling information may occasionally be incorrectly bound to different identities. An important question that arises is whether this independent representation of identity and quantity occurs at the level of the motor plans, abstract letter representations, or both. This question is difficult to answer with nonimpaired writers or typists; in contrast, in dysgraphics with deficits at central levels of representations, before motor production, errors can be attributed to the level of abstract letter representation. In fact, several individuals have been described with graphemic buffer deficits who make a relatively large numbers of errors (compared with neurologically intact individuals) that involve the doubling of the wrong letter

in words with double letters (Caramazza & Miceli, 1990; Cipolotti, Bird, Glasspool, & Shallice, 2004; Jónsdóttir et al., 1996; McCloskey et al., 1994; Miceli, et al., 1995; Tainturier & Caramazza, 1996; Schiller, Greenhall, Shelton, & Caramazza, 2001).

Caramazza and Miceli (1990; see also Badecker, 1996) specifically proposed that letter identity and quantity are independently represented on different dimensions (or tiers) of the orthographic representation with quantity represented by an orthographic doubling feature[2] (as in Figure 21.3; see McCloskey et al., 1994 for an alternative representation). In support of their proposed representation of double letters, Caramazza and Miceli (1990) reported several important findings for an Italian-speaking individual with a deficit at the level of the graphemic buffer. First, a comparison of words with double consonants (e.g., FRUTTI) with those without (e.g., FLASCO) indicated that words with doubles were spelled with greater accuracy (75 percent correct) than those without doubles (57 percent). They argue that this is predicted under the hypothesis that double letters are represented by a single-letter identity unit (with a double feature), essentially making words with double letters "shorter" and less burdensome for the graphemic buffer. Second, the types of errors observed on words with double letters could be understood if there was a doubling feature that could be deleted, (SORELLA → SORELA); moved to a different letter (SORELLA→ SORRELA); or duplicated (SORELLA→ SORRELLA). Finally, they also failed to find errors that were predicted not to occur. Specifically, under the hypothesis that double letters consist of a single unit, the prediction is that there should be no errors in which the constituents of the double are separated (e.g., SORELLA→ SOLERAL, SOLELRA, SOLRELA, or SORLELA) and indeed they found no errors of this type. Furthermore, there should rarely be errors in which only one letter of a double is substituted (SORELLA→SORELTA). Consistent with this prediction, they found only five of these errors. The same basic patterns of results have been subsequently reported in cases in English (Jónsdóttir et al., 1996; McCloskey et al., 1994; Schiller et al., 2001; Tainturier & Caramazza, 1996) and other languages (German and Finnish: Blanken, Schäfer, Tucha, & Lange, 1999). In addition, Tainturier and Caramazza (1996) also specifically evaluated if double letters behaved like repeated letters (RA*BB*IT vs. *C*ACTUS) and found that they did not. They found, instead, that repeated letters were in fact no different than other (nonrepeated) letters in matched words with regard to their susceptibility to movement or the substitution of one of the two tokens of the letter.

Rapp, Fischer-Baum, and Pastor (2007) tested the prediction that in perseveration errors, the letter doubling feature can move from word to another without the letter identity perseverating along with it. In that case, one would expect spelling responses with erroneous doubling to be preceded by words with double letters even though the identities of the doubled letters do not match ("stay" → STOFF, preceded by FLOOR). In this example, the double feature from the previous response, FLOOR, may have perseverated into the subsequent response, STOFF. Rapp et al. (2007) identified 57 double letter intrusion errors, such as STOFF, and found that 54 percent of these were preceded by trials containing a different double letter. This is far greater than what would be expected by chance. These "quantity-but-not-identity" perseveration errors provide clear evidence of the independence of the representation of letter identity and quantity.

Orthographic Syllables

The notion of the syllable would seem to be quintessentially phonological. Phonologically, syllables are intimately related to consonants and vowels, with vowels almost always defining the syllabic units. However, by the same logic, orthographic vowels and consonants could similarly serve to define orthographic units. To distinguish the notions of orthographic and phonological syllables it is useful that, at least in some nontransparent languages, phonological and orthographic syllables need not be identical. For example, in English (and French) the final E, which is phonologically silent in many words, would be considered to be an orthographic syllable nucleus. That is, a word such as "France" would be monosyllabic phonologically, but bisyllabic orthographically (FRAN/CE).

There are various lines of experimental evidence that suggest a role for syllables in written language production. For example, there have been a number of studies indicating that, in motor programming, letters may be planned one syllable at a time in both children (Kandel et al., 2006; Kandel & Valdois, 2006) and adults (Kandel et al., 2006; Lambert et al., 2007). However, these studies did not distinguish between orthographic and phonological syllables. More recently, Kandel, Herault, Grosjacques, Lambert, and Fayol (2009), in an examination of stroke duration and fluency in third to fifth grade children, specifically compared writing of words that were phonologically monosyllabic ("barque") but orthographically bisyllabic (BAR/QUE) with words that were bisyllabic both phonologically ("bal/con") and orthographically (BAL/CON). They found increased duration and dysfluency at the syllable boundary for both types of words, indicating a role for orthographic syllables in written language production. The fact that the syllable boundary is prominent at the level of motor programming may indicate that the syllabic boundaries are represented at the earlier, abstract levels of orthographic representation that provide input into motor planning.

One of the earliest proposals of orthographic syllable structure in writing was put forward by Caramazza and Miceli (1990) in their detailed case study of an individual with acquired agraphia. Specifically, Caramazza and Miceli proposed that orthographic syllable structure is present at abstract levels of orthographic representation and serves to constrain the output of the spelling system. Their claim was based on several findings. First, they found that the syllable complexity of a word's spelling influenced accuracy, such that words with simple syllable structure, such as CVCVCV (e.g., GELATO), were produced more accurately than matched words with more complex syllable structure, such as VCCVCV (e.g., ALPINO). Further, syllabic structure also affected the types of errors that were produced, with 99 percent of errors in words with simple syllabic structure consisting of substitutions and exchanges, whereas words with more complex syllabic structures also yielded frequent deletions, insertions, and shifts. Finally, the syllable boundary and resulting subsyllabic structures influenced the probability of error. Most striking was the comparison of error rates on consonants in heterosyllabic positions (AL/PINO) versus tautosyllabic positions (A/BRIRE). There was a marked asymmetry between error likelihood across the two consonants in heterosyllabic clusters, with the coda of syllable 1 being more error-prone (18 percent) than the onset of syllable 2 (10 percent). In contrast, errors were equally likely (15 percent) across the two consonants in tautosyllabic clusters. Additional findings that are generally consistent with these have been reported by Ward and Romani (2000), Schonauer and Denes (1994), and in a study of the spelling of deaf individuals by Olson and Caramazza (2004; but see Jonsdottir, et al., 1996, and Kay and Hanley, 1994).

One may well wonder why this section on orthographic syllable was not included in the section on orthographic units. That is, one might have thought that syllables are units of orthographic representation. However, it is important to underscore that the evidence we have reviewed indicates that syllable boundaries may be represented and that the orthographic system may be sensitive to syllabic complexity. This would be consistent with the representation of the syllabic roles (whether they are onsets, nuclei, or codas). However, evidence of orthographic syllables as units that are separately modifiable, (e.g., that may move, exchange, and perseverate independently of one another) is scarce and typically subject to alternative interpretations. Interestingly, the failure to find clear evidence for orthographic syllables as units of representation parallels the situation in spoken production where, despite the pervasive effects of syllable structure and syllable position on a wide range of phenomena (speech errors, speech rate), there is relatively little evidence for syllables as units, at least an abstract level of representation (but see Cholin, Levelt, & Schiller, 2006). In sum, the precise representational implications of the syllabic influences on written word production have not been clearly resolved and, to our mind, syllabic structure currently represents the least well-understood component of orthographic representation.

Features and Feature Bundles

We have proposed that various orthographic features are bound together within letter units, including features that specify abstract letter identity, CV status, quantity, and syllabic role. We have described evidence indicating that these features may be selectively damaged, moved, and so forth. However, despite the evidence of their separability we would like to be clear that we are proposing that they are, nonetheless, bound together within multidimensional letter representations. In fact, although the various features can be separately modified, they are more likely to travel together than they are to "go their separate ways." For example, although it is clear that a doubling feature may travel from one word to the next independently of letter identity, it is, in fact, more common for the double feature and letter identity to travel together. That is, such errors as JACKET →JASSET preceded by DRESS are more common than such errors as STAY→STOFF preceded by FLOOR. In the former, the double feature and letter identity (S) are perseverated, whereas in the latter, only the double feature is perseverated.

In the next and final section we discuss another component of letter representation: letter position. Although it is also a part of the multidimensional letter-feature bundle, we have placed it in a separate section because the representation of position applies to and extends across all of the units of the orthographic representation of a word.

The Representation of Letter Position

The representation of letter position is obviously necessary to distinguish different words composed of the same letters (e.g., ACT vs. CAT). How is letter position represented? The question of the representation of the positions of elements in a sequence has been posed in many domains, such as WM, motor planning, and speech production. Many of the hypotheses we will review here in the context of spelling are the same or similar to those examined in other domains. Regardless of domain, what is common across theories of position representation (or the representation of serial order) is that the position of an item is defined with respect to some reference point external to the item itself. For example, the position of the E in the word NEST could be represented as the second letter from the beginning of the word, the letter between the N and the S, or the nucleus of the first orthographic syllable. In the first case, the position of the E is defined relative to a word-beginning reference point. In the second case, the position of the E is defined relative to the letters that precede and follow it. In the final case, the position of the E is defined by its syllabic position in the word. Each case is a viable alternative hypothesis (or *representational scheme*) for how letter position is represented in spelling.

Fischer-Baum et al. (2010) identified three different classes of representational schemes that apply in the orthographic context: (1) *content-independent* schemes, in which a letter's position is determined by distance (in number of letters) and direction from one or more reference points that do not themselves depend on the letters in the word (e.g., reference points include beginning, end, or center of the word); (2) *letter context* schemes in which a letter's position is defined relative to letters that precede or follow it (e.g., trigram, bigram, and open bigram schemes); and (3) *syllabic schemes* in which a letter's position is defined relative to the syllable in which it appears, and its role within that syllable (onset, nucleus, and coda).

Until recently, little work had been done on the question of letter position representation in written production. Caramazza and Hillis (1990) proposed a word-centered reference frame for letter position representation based on patterns of spelling (and reading) errors in an individual with unilateral spatial neglect. In computational work on spelling, Houghton, Glasspool, and Shallice (1994) adopted a "both edges" scheme according to which the position of every letter is encoded relative to the beginning and end of the word, whereas Brown and Loosemore (1994) proposed a trigram representation scheme. More recently, questions of letter position representation have gained considerable attention in the context of reading and we will refer to some of these findings next. However, a common limitation of much of this work has been that different representational schemes are rarely directly compared with one another in the same study; rather, a particular scheme is posited and data are presented that are consistent with the proposed scheme. Fischer-Baum et al. (2010) directly compared various letter position schemes in the context of spelling. We summarize that work here and then go on to briefly discuss related work.

Fischer-Baum et al. (2010) investigated the representational schemes for letter position through the analysis of the letter perseveration errors produced by two individuals with acquired dysgraphia. To evaluate representation schemes, Fischer-Baum et al. identified all potential perseveration errors. Then, for each error, they determined whether the position of the intruded letter in the *perseveration response* (e.g., E*R*GE) matched the position of that intruded letter in the earlier *source response* (e.g., F*R*ENCE). Table 21.2 shows how representational schemes differ with respect to the question: Does the position of the R in ERGE match the position of the R in FRENCE? According to a beginning-based scheme, the position of the R matches in the perseveration and source responses (two positions from the beginning in both responses). However, for the other schemes (center- and end-based, syllabic, trigram), the R is in different positions in ERGE and in FRENCE. For example, according to the syllabic scheme R is in Coda of the first syllable in ER/

GE, whereas it is in the onset of the first syllable in FRENCE.

From a series of analyses in which the observed rates of position matches were compared across all of the representational schemes, Fischer-Baum et al. found that the positions of the letter perseveration errors were significantly more likely to match the positions of the same letter in a source response when position was defined according to a "beginning- and end-based" representational scheme. That is, both dysgraphic individuals produced significant numbers of three types of perseveration errors: (1) errors in which the position of the intruded letter matched in the error and source words according to both beginning- and end-based schemes (SW*I*P preceded by DAM*P*); (2) errors in which error and source positions matched in terms of a beginning- but not an end-based scheme (E*R*GE preceded by F*R*ENCE); and (3) errors in which error and source positions matched according to an end- but not beginning-based scheme (KITCHE*M* preceded by SYSTE*M*). The observed values for letter perseveration errors that maintained either beginning- or end-based position or both were 78 and 87 percent for the two individuals. These values were greater than expected by chance, even when chance measures took into consideration the fact that three types of errors were predicted. Furthermore, these values were significantly greater than values obtained by any other single position representation scheme, or combinations of schemes.

Fischer-Baum et al. (2010) also considered whether letter position is represented in a discrete or graded fashion. Is the E in NEST represented as precisely the second from the beginning and the third from the end? Is the letter most strongly associated with these positions but also more weakly associated with adjacent positions, with strength of association diminishing in a graded manner with distance from the target position? To

Table 21.2. **Position match between R in perseveration response (ERGE) and source response (FRENCE) for five different representational schemes**

Scheme	R in ERGE	R in FRENCE	Same Position?
Beginning-based	Begin + 2	Begin + 2	Yes
Center-based	Center - 1	Center - 2	No
End-based	End - 3	End - 5	No
Syllabic	Coda Syl. 1	Onset Syl. 1	No
Trigram	Between E and G	Between F and E	No

evaluate these alternative accounts, positions adjacent to the precise beginning- or end-based positions were also counted as matches for a "graded" both-edges scheme. For example, the error "zebra" → ZEROBA was produced immediately after the response FLOWER. In this perseveration-source pair (ZEROBA—FLOWER) the perseverated O does not match exactly in terms of a position defined relative to both-edges but it does match on a graded both-edges scheme, because the O appears in a position in the source response adjacent to a position that would count as an exact match. When evaluated in this way, 94 and 97 percent of letter perseveration errors produced by the two individuals matched the position of the letter in the source response according to a "graded both-edges position scheme." These values were significantly greater than chance and greater than those found for the discrete, both-edges scheme when only exact matches were considered. Not only did the graded, both-edges scheme account for almost all of the letter perseveration errors, the remaining errors did not conform to any one of the other schemes. Fischer-Baum et al. examined several "multiple-scheme" combinations but none was as successful as the graded, both-edges account. There was no scheme that when added to the graded, both-edges scheme accounted for significantly more errors.

This work provides strong support for a graded, both-edges scheme for the representation of letter position in spelling. Consistent with these findings is the proposal of Houghton et al. (1994) and Glasspool and Houghton (2005) that this same representation scheme is required for their competitive queuing computational model of spelling to adequately simulate other aspects of the error patterns of individuals with graphemic buffer disorder.

Finally, it is important to note that representational schemes similar to the both-edges scheme have been proposed in other areas of cognition, such as verbal WM (Henson, 1998, 1999). Although the both-edges scheme is unlikely to be the only one used in representing the position of elements in different types of strings (e.g., Orlov, Amit, Yakovlev, Zohary, & Hochstein, 2006), the finding that it applies in multiple domains suggests that the representation of position relative to both-edges may reflect more general principles of position representation, a proposal recently put forward by Endress, Nespor, and Mehler (2009).

It seems likely that one of the components of each letter's representations is information regarding the letter's position in the word. On the basis of the findings reviewed here, this information is represented in a graded manner in terms of distance from both the beginning and end of the word (see Figure 21.4).

Orthographic Structure: Evidence from Reading

Although the focus of this chapter has been the production of written language, the issue of orthographic knowledge has been widely discussed in the literature on written language comprehension (reading). Both spelling and reading require various long-term and WM mechanisms that operate over letters and word spellings. These are responsible for the translation between letters/words and their corresponding sounds and, for words, there is the additional mapping between word spellings and word meanings. However, it is possible that written production and comprehension rely on entirely distinct orthographic representations. If so, then results from reading could be irrelevant to the study of the content of orthographic knowledge and mental representations used in producing written language.

Alternatively, reading and spelling may rely on shared representations and processes. If the same mental representations are used for both producing and comprehending written words, then results from both reading and spelling are relevant to the understanding of orthographic knowledge. Although there are relatively few studies specifically examining the relationship between written production and comprehension, existing behavioral, neuropsychological, and neuroimaging evidence most clearly supports the notion that at least some representations and processes are shared in reading and spelling, with the clearest evidence specifically indicating shared *lexical* processes and representations (but also see Tainturier and Rapp, 2003 for a review of evidence regarding shared orthographic buffering processes).

For example, behavioral studies with neurologically intact participants have found evidence of shared lexical orthographic representations in studies that have investigated word-specific performance similarities and differences in spelling and reading or have examined reading-spelling priming (e.g., Burt & Tate, 2002; Holmes & Carruthers, 1998; Monsell, 1987). In addition, the neuropsychological literature has provided several reports of well-studied individuals with lexical deficits in both reading and spelling (Philipose et al., 2007; Rapcsak & Beeson, 2004; Tsapkini & Rapp, 2010). Finally, with regard to neuroimaging, Rapp and Lipka

(2011) recently evaluated neural activation patterns in both reading and spelling in the same individuals, allowing a strong test of the hypothesis of shared components. They found two different neuroanatomic regions (left fusiform and inferior frontal junction) in which the locations of activation peaks for reading and spelling were statistically indistinguishable, providing some of the strongest evidence to date of components shared by reading and spelling. Given these results, it is likely that reading and spelling rely on some of the same orthographic representations, and that evidence from reading is likely to be relevant for understanding the nature of the orthographic representations used in spelling. Next we very briefly review converging evidence from the reading literature for some of the aspects of orthographic representation discussed in this chapter.

Research in reading supports the same units of orthographic representation as those identified in the spelling literature: abstract letters, digraphs, and morphemes. Evidence for abstract letter representation in reading primarily comes from cross-case priming. When briefly presented with a written prime word in one case (e.g., RADIO), participants are faster to respond to an identical written target presented in another case (e.g., radio), even when the upper and lower-case letters are visually dissimilar (Bowers, Vigliocco, & Haan, 1998) and in fact the effect size is comparable with that when the prime and target are in the same case (Arguin & Bub, 1995; for a more extensive review of research on this topic see Finkbeiner & Coltheart, 2009 and Whitney & Cornelissen, 2008). Rey, Ziegler, and Jacobs (2000) argued that digraphs (and other multiletter graphemes) function as perceptual units in reading. This claim was based on their finding that it is more difficult to identify a single letter in a written word when it occurs within a digraph (the letter O in BOAT) compared with when it does not (the letter O in HOPE). Along these lines, several studies have shown that visual "violations" of digraph structure (e.g., case alternation BREad vs. BReaD) affect reading times (Dickerson, 1999, Joubert & Lecours, 2000; Martensen, Maris, & Dijkstra, 2003; Pring, 1981). Finally, the reading literature also provides support for orthography-specific morpheme representation. For example, Longtin, Segui, and Hallé (2003; see also Diependaele, Sandra, & Grainger, 2005) showed significant cross-modal (auditory word prime–visual word target) and intramodal priming (visual word prime–visual word target) when the morphologic relationship

between the prime and target was transparent (e.g., teacher-TEACH), but only intramodal priming with pseudomorphologic items (e.g., brother-BROTH). Importantly, the intramodal result can be attributed to morphologic processes and not orthographic similarity because it was only observed when the words could be parsed into multiple possible morphemes (e.g., BROTHER primed BROTH but BROTHEL did not; Allen & Badecker, 1999; Fiorentino & Fund-Reznicek, 2009; McCormick et al., 2009; Rastle, Davis, & New, 2004). These results support a level of orthographic morphologic representation that identifies possible orthographic morphologic constituents regardless of whether the meaning of the (pseudo) multimorphemic form (BROTH/ER) corresponds to the sum of its parts.

Furthermore, there is support from the reading literature for the representation of CV status and syllabic role. Berent, Bouissa, and Tuller (2001) found faster nonword reading times when nonwords (e.g., DUS) were preceded by a prime with the same CV structure but different letters (e.g., fap) than a prime with different CV structure (e.g., ift). In addition, there are several studies indicating that orthographic consonants and vowels are processed differently from one another during reading (Carreiras, Vergara, & Perea, 2009; Lee, Rayner, & Pollatsek, 2001; Lupker, Perea, & Davis, 2008; Perea & Carreiras, 2006; Perea & Lupker, 2004). Prinzmetal and colleagues (Millis, 1986; Prinzmetal, 1990; Prinzmetal, Hoffman, & Vest, 1991; Prinzmetal & Keysar, 1989; Prinzmetal & Millis-Wright, 1984; Prinzmetal, Trieman, & Rho, 1986; see also Rapp, 1992) showed that readers are sensitive to orthographic syllabic boundaries in processing visually presented words. Specifically, they found that illusory conjunctions (confusing the colors of two letters in a briefly presented string of colored letters) occurred less often for two letters that straddled a syllable boundary (e.g., the NV and ANVIL) than for letters within the same syllable (the V and I in ANVIL). It is unlikely that these effects were phonological, not only because the errors themselves were visual, but also because the same effects have been observed in profoundly deaf participants (Olson & Nickerson, 2001), and because words that are bisyllabic orthographically, but either monosyllabic (WAIVE) and bisyllabic phonologically (NAIVE), produced similar effects (Doignon-Camus, Zagar, & Mathey, 2009; Seidenberg, 1987). One dimension of orthographic representation in which converging evidence from reading is not forthcoming is the representation of letter-quantity. In spelling there is clear evidence that quantity information is represented in association with letter-identity information. However, to our knowledge, this issue has not been investigated in the context of reading.

Finally, the question of letter position representation has been considered fairly extensively in the reading literature. One prominent theory of letter position representation in reading is the open bigram theory (Dehaene, Cohen, Sigman, & Vinckier, 2005; Grainger, Granier, Farioli, Van Assche, & van Heuven, 2006; Whitney, 2001). According to this proposal, the visual word processing system represents ordered letter pairs, such as the input word TUBE is represented by the units TU, TB, TE, UB, UE, and BE. Theories of reading that use open bigram position representations can explain a broad range of empirical findings. However, in spelling, there is clear evidence against open bigram representation of letter position (Fischer-Baum et al., 2010). Also worth noting is the fact that it is not clear if the available data in reading clearly support the open bigram scheme over alternative proposals. Reading theories that do not use open bigram representations can account for many of the same empirical results as those that use open bigram representations (e.g., Davis, 2010; Gomez, Ratcliff, & Perea, 2008). Moreover, Fischer-Baum, Charny, and McCloskey (2009) recently reported evidence consistent with both-edges position representation in reading. They found that substitution errors in reading briefly presented words (e.g., TUBE read as TUNE) were more likely given a simultaneously presented context word containing the substituted letter in the same beginning-based (TUBE → TUNE in the context of TANGLE) or end-based position (TUBE →TUNE in the context of THRONE) than when the context word contained the substituted letter in the same word-centered position (TUBE →TUNE in the context of TRANCE). In fact, a detailed analysis of the pattern of the substitution errors observed in this paradigm supported the both-edges scheme over the open bigram representation of position. Therefore, it seems possible that a both-edges representation of letter position is used in both reading and spelling. Further work is required to determine if the both-edges scheme can also account for other empirical findings in reading.

Summary and Conclusions

What is it that we know when we know the spellings of words? The goal of this chapter was to review our current understanding of the answer to that question. We focused on evidence obtained in the context of producing written words, while also briefly reviewing convergent evidence from reading. The evidence reveals that orthographic knowledge, although perhaps "inheriting" many representational principles of spoken word representation, is nonetheless independent from spoken word knowledge. Orthographic knowledge is represented in an abstract code that is independent of modality and format and is organized into units of various sizes: morphemes, digraphs, and letters. Their status as representational units is revealed by their separate modifiability and their ability to move independently of one another. When we turn our attention specifically to the representation of letter units, we find that they are internally complex, multidimensional feature bundles, each specifying information regarding letter identity, CV status, syllabic role, and letter position. The research literature reveals that the literate brain learns and manipulates orthographic representations that are abstract, complex, and richly structured mental objects.

Acknowledgements

The writing of this chapter was supported by NIH grant DC 006740 to the first author and the Dingwall Foundation Fellowship awarded to the second author.

Notes

1. Consider Korean as a possible exception (Kim, 1997).
2. Interestingly, this proposal is analogous not only to those that Rumelhart and Norman (1982) and others put forward in the context of typing and motor control but also to proposals in autosegmental phonology (e.g., Clements & Keyser, 1983) that refer to the representation of phoneme germination at abstract levels of phonological representation.

References

Alario, F.-X., De Cara, B., & Ziegler, J. C. (2007). Automatic activation of phonology in silent reading is parallel: Evidence from beginning and skilled readers. *Journal of Experimental Child Psychology*, 97, 205–219.

Allen, M., & Badecker, W. (1999). Stem homograph inhibition and stem allomorphy: Representing and processing inflected forms in a multi-level lexical system. *Journal of Memory and Language*, 41, 105–123.

Arguin, M., & Bub, D. N. (1995). Priming and response selection processes in letter classification and identification tasks. *Journal of Experimental Psychology: Human Perception and Performance*, 21, 1199–1219.

Ashby, J., Sanders, L. D., Kingston, J. (2009). Skilled readers begin processing phonological features by 80 ms: Evidence from ERPs. *Biological Psychology*, 80, 84–94.

Badecker, W. (1996). Representational properties common to phonological and orthographic output systems. *Lingua*, 99, 55–83.

Badecker, W., Hillis, A., & Caramazza, A. (1990). Lexical morphology and its role in the writing process: Evidence from a case of acquired dysgraphia. *Cognition, 35,* 205–243.

Badecker, W., Rapp, B., & Caramazza, A. (1996). Lexical morphology and the two orthographic routes. *Cognitive Neuropsychology, 13,* 161–175.

Berent, I., Bouissa, R., & Tuller, B. (2001). The effect of shared structure and content on reading nonwords: Evidence for a CV skeleton. *Journal of Experimental Psychology: Learning, Memory, and Cognition, 27,* 1042–1057.

Berndt, R. S., & Haendiges, A. N. (2000). Grammatical class in word and sentence production: Evidence from an aphasic patient. *Journal of Memory and Language, 43,* 249–273.

Blanken, G., Schäfer, C., Tucha, O., & Lange, K. W. (1999). Serial processing in graphemic encoding: Evidence from letter exchange errors in a multilingual patient. *Journal of Neurolinguistics, 12,* 13–39.

Bonin, P., Fayol, M., & Peereman, R. (1998). Masked form priming in writing words from pictures: Evidence for direct retrieval of orthographic codes. *Acta Psychologia, 99,* 311–328.

Bowers, J. S., Vigliocco, G., & Haan, R. (1998). Orthographic, phonological, and articulatory contributions to masked letter and word priming. *Journal of Experimental Psychology: Human Perception and Performance, 24,* 1705–1719.

Brown, G. D. A., & Loosemore, R. P. W. (1994). Computational approaches to normal and impaired spelling. In G. D. A. Brown & N. C. Ellis (Eds.), *Handbook of spelling: Theory, process and application* (pp. 319–335). Chichester: John Wiley & Sons.

Buchwald, A., & Rapp, B. (2006). Consonants and vowels in orthography. *Cognitive Neuropsychology, 23,* 308–337.

Buchwald, A., & Rapp, B. (2010). Distinctions between orthographic long-term memory and working memory. *Cognitive Neuropsychology, 26,* 724–751.

Buchwald, A., Rapp, B., & Stone, M. (2007). Insertion of discrete phonological units: An ultrasound investigation of aphasic speech. *Language and Cognitive Processes, 22,* 910–948.

Burt, J. S., & Tate, H. (2002). Does a reading lexicon provide orthographic representations for spelling? *Journal of Memory and Language, 46,* 518–543.

Caramazza, A., & Hillis, A. E. (1990). Levels of representation, co-ordinate frames, and unilateral neglect. *Cognitive Neuropsychology, 7,* 391–445.

Caramazza, A., & Miceli, G. (1990). The structure of graphemic representations. *Cognition, 37,* 243–297.

Caramazza, A., Miceli, G., & Villa, G. (1987). The role of the Graphemic Buffer in spelling: Evidence from a case of acquired dysgraphia. *Cognition, 26,* 59–85.

Carreiras, M., Vergara, M., & Perea, M. (2009). ERP correlates of transposed-letter priming effects: The role of vowels vs. consonants. *Psychophysiology, 46,* 34–42.

Cholin, J., Levelt, W. J. M., & Schiller, N. O. (2006). Effects of syllable frequency in speech production. *Cognition, 99,* 205–235.

Cipolotti, L., Bird, C. M., Glasspool, D. W., & Shallice, T. (2004). The impact of deep dysgraphia on graphemic buffer disorders. *Neurocase, 10,* 405–419.

Clements, G. N., & Keyser, S. J. (1983). *CV phonology: A generative theory of the syllable.* Cambridge (MA): The MIT Press.

Cotelli, M., Abutalebi, J., Zorzi, M., & Cappa, S. F. (2003). Vowels in the buffer: A case study of acquired dysgraphia with selective vowel substitutions. *Cognitive Neuropsychology, 20,* 99–114.

Cubelli, R. (1991). A selective deficit for writing vowels in acquired dysgraphia. *Nature, 353,* 258–260.

Davis, C. J. (2010). The spatial coding model of visual word identification. *Psychological Review, 117,* 713–758.

Dehaene, S., Cohen, L., Sigman, M., & Vinckier, F. (2005). The neural code for written words: A proposal. *Trends in Cognitive Science, 9,* 335–341.

Dickerson, J. (1999). Format distortion and word reading: The role of multiletter units. *Neurocase, 5,* 31–36.

Diependaele, K., Sandra, D., & Grainger, J. (2005). Masked cross-modal morphological priming: Unravelling morphoorthographic and morpho-semantic influences in early word recognition. *Language and Cognitive Processes, 20,* 75–114.

Doignon-Camus, N., Zagar, D., & Mathey, S. (2009). Can we see syllables in monosyllabic words? A study with illusory conjunctions. *European Journal of Cognitive Psychology, 21,* 599–614.

Ellis, A. W. (1979). Slips of the pen. *Visible language, 13,* 265–282.

Ellis, A. W., & Young, A. W. (1988). *Human cognitive neuropsychology.* Hove, UK: Erlbaum.

Endress, A. D., Nespor, M., & Mehler, J. (2009). Perceptual and memory constraints on language acquisition. *Trends in Cognitive Sciences, 13,* 348–335.

Finkbeiner, M., & Coltheart, M. (Eds.). (2009). *Letter representation: From perception to representation. Cognitive Neuropsychology, 26,* 1–127.

Fiorentino, R., & Fund-Reznicek, E. (2009). Masked morphological priming of compound constituents. *The Mental Lexicon, 4,* 159–193.

Fischer-Baum, S., Charny, J., & McCloskey, M. (2009). *The representation of letter position in reading.* Poster presented at the 50th Annual Meeting of the Psychonomics Society, Boston, MA.

Fischer-Baum, S., McCloskey, M., & Rapp, B. (2010). Representation of letter position in spelling: Evidence from acquired dysgraphia. *Cognition, 115,* 466–490.

Fischer-Baum, S., & Rapp, B. (in preparation). Units and bundles in orthographic representations.

Glasspool, D. W., & Houghton, G. (2005). Serial order and consonant-vowel structure in a graphemic output buffer model. *Brain and Language, 94,* 304–330.

Goldstein, L., Pouplier, M., Chen, L., Saltzman, E., & Byrd, D. (2007). Dynamic action units slip in speech production errors. *Cognition, 103,* 386–412.

Gomez, P., Ratcliff, R., & Perea, M. (2008). The overlap model: A model of letter position coding. *Psychological Review, 115,* 577–600.

Grainger, J., Granier, J. P., Farioli, F., Van Assche, E., & van Heuven, W. (2006). Letter position information and printed word perception: The relative-position priming constraint. *Journal of Experimental Psychology: Human Perception and Performance, 32,* 865–884.

Henson, R. N. (1998). Short-term memory for serial order: The Start-End Model. *Cognitive Psychology, 36,* 73–137.

Henson, R. N. (1999). Positional information in short-term memory: Relative or absolute? *Memory & Cognition, 27,* 915–927.

Hillis, A. E., & Caramazza, A. (1989). The graphemic buffer and attentional mechanisms. *Brain & Language, 36,* 208–235.

Holmes, V. M., & Carruthers, J. (1998). The relation between reading and spelling in skilled adult readers. *Journal of Memory and Language, 39,* 264–289.

Hotopf, W. H. N. (1980). Semantic similarity as a factor in whole-word slips of the tongue. In: V. A. Fromkin (Ed.), *Errors in linguistic performance: Slips of the tongue, ear, pen, and hand* (pp. 97–110). New York: Academic Press.

Houghton, G., Glasspool, D. W., & Shallice, T., (1994). Spelling and serial recall: Insights from a competitive queueing model. In G. D. A. Brown and N. C. Ellis (Eds.), *Handbook of spelling: Theory, process and intervention* (pp. 365–406). Chichester: Wiley.

Houghton, G., & Zorzi, M. (2003). Normal and impaired spelling in a connectionist dual-route architecture. *Cognitive Neuropsychology, 20,* 115–162.

Jones, A. C., Folk, J. R., & Rapp, B. (2009). All letters are not equal: Sub-graphemic texture in orthographic working memory. *Journal of Experimental Psychology: Learning, Memory, and Cognition, 35,* 1389–1402.

Jónsdóttir, M. K., Shallice, T., & Wise, R. (1996). Phonological mediation and the graphemic buffer disorder in spelling: cross-language differences? *Cognition, 49,* 169–197.

Joubert, S. A., & Lecours, A. R. (2000). The role of sublexical graphemic processing in reading. *Brain and Language, 72,* 1–13.

Kandel, S., Alvarez C., & Vallée, N. (2006). Syllables as processing units in handwriting production. *Journal of Experimental Psychology: Human Perception and Performance, 32,* 18–31.

Kandel, S., Herault, L., Grosjacques, G., Lambert, E., & Fayol, M. (2009). Orthographic vs. phonologic syllables in handwriting production. *Cognition, 110,* 440–444.

Kandel, S., Soler, O., Valdois, S., & Gros C. (2006). Graphemes as motor units in the acquisition of writing skills. *Reading & Writing: An Interdisciplinary Journal, 19,* 313–337.

Kandel, S., & Spinelli, E. (2010). Processing complex graphemes in handwriting production. *Memory & Cognition, 38,* 762–770.

Kandel, S., & Valdois, S. (2006). Syllables as functional units in a copyingtask. *Language and Cognitive Processes, 21,* 432–452.

Katz, R. B. (1991). Limited retention of information in the graphemic buffer. *Cortex, 27,* 111–119.

Kay, J., & Hanley, R. (1994). Peripheral disorders of spelling: The role of the graphemic buffer. In G. D. A. Brown and N. C. Ellis (Eds.), *Handbook of spelling: Theory, process and intervention* (pp. 295–318). Chichester: Wiley.

Kim, C. W. (1997). The structure of phonological units in Han'gul. In Y.-K. Kim-Reynaud (Ed.), *The Korean alphabet: Its history and structure* (pp. 145–160). Honolulu, HI: University of Hawaii Press.

Kinsbourne, M., & Warrington, E. K. (1965). A case showing selectively impaired oral spelling. *Journal of Neurology, Neurosurgery and Psychiatry, 28,* 563–566.

Lambert, E., Kandel, S., Fayol, M., & Esperet, E. (2007). The effect of the number of syllables when writing poly-syllabic words. *Reading & Writing: An Interdisciplinary Journal, 21,* 859–883.

Lashley, K. (1951). The problem of serial order in behavior. In L. A. Jeffress (Ed.), *Cerebral mechanisms in behavior* (pp. 478–503). Chichester: Wiley.

Lee, H.-W., Rayner, K., & Pollatsek, A. (2001). The relative contribution of consonants and vowels to word identification during reading. *Journal of Memory and Language, 44,* 189–205.

Longtin, C. M., Segui, J., & Hallé, P. A. (2003). Morphological priming without morphological relationship. *Language and Cognitive Processes, 18,* 313–334.

Lupker, S. J., Perea, M., & Davis, C. J. (2008). Transposed letter priming effects: Consonants, vowels and letter frequency. *Language and Cognitive Processes, 23,* 93–116.

MacKay, D. G. (1969). The repeated letter effect in the misspellings of dysgraphic and normals. *Perception and Psychophysics, 5,* 102–106.

Martensen, H., Maris, E., & Dijkstra, A. (2003). Phonological ambiguity and context sensitivity: On sublexical clustering in visual word recognition. *Journal of Memory and Language, 49,* 375–395.

McCloskey, M., Badecker, W., Goodman-Schulman, R. A., & Aliminosa, D. (1994). The structure of graphemic representations in spelling: Evidence from a case of acquired dysgraphia. *Cognitive Neuropsychology, 11,* 341–392.

McCloskey, M., Macaruso, P., & Rapp, B. (2006). Grapheme-to-lexeme feedback in the spelling system: Evidence from a dysgraphic patient. *Cognitive Neuropsychology, 23,* 278–307.

McCormick, S. F., Rastle, K., & Davis, M. H. (2009). Adore-able not adorable? Orthographic underspecification studied with masked repetition priming. *European Journal of Cognitive Psychology, 21,* 813–836.

Miceli, G., Benvegnù, B., Capasso, R., & Caramazza, A. (1995). Selective deficit in processing double letters. *Cortex, 31,* 161–171.

Miceli, G., & Capasso, R. (1997). Semantic errors as evidence for the autonomy and the interaction of phonological and orthographic forms. *Language and Cognitive Processes, 14,* 733–764.

Miceli, G., Capasso, R., Benvegnù, B., & Caramazza, A. (2004). The categorical distinction of vowel and consonant representations: Evidence from dysgraphia. *Neurocase, 10,* 109–121.

Millis, M. L. (1986). Syllables and spelling units affect feature integration in words. *Memory and Cognition, 14,* 409–419.

Monsell, S. (1987). On the relation between lexical input and output pathways for speech. In D. A. Allport, D. G. MacKay, W. Prinz, & E. Scheerer (Eds.), *Language perception and production: Relationships among listening, speaking, reading and writing* (pp. 273–311). London: Academic Press.

Olson, A. C., & Caramazza, A. (2004). Orthographic structure and deaf spelling errors: Syllables, letter frequency, and speech. *Quarterly Journal of Experimental Psychology: Human Experimental Psychology, 57A,* 385–417.

Olson, A. C., & Nickerson, J. F. (2001). Syllabic organization and deafness: Orthographic structure or letter frequency in reading. *Quarterly Journal of Experimental Psychology: Human Experimental Psychology, 54A,* 421–438.

Oppenheim, G. M., & Dell, G. S. (2008). Inner speech slips exhibit lexical bias, but not the phonemic similarity effect. *Cognition, 106,* 528–537.

Orlov, T., Amit, D. J., Yakovlev, V., Zohary, E., & Hochstein, S. (2006). Memory of ordinal number categories in macaque monkeys. *Journal of Cognitive Neuroscience, 18,* 399–417.

Perea, M., & Carreiras, M. (2006). Do transposed-letter similarity effects occur at a syllable level? *Experimental Psychology, 53,* 308–315.

Perea, M., & Lupker, S. J. (2004). Can CANISO activate CASINO? Transposed-letter similarity effects with nonadjacent letter positions. *Journal of Memory and Language, 51,* 231–246.

Perfetti, C. A., Bell, L. C., & Delaney, S. M. (1988). Automatic (prelexical) phonetic activation in silent word reading: Evidence from backward masking. *Journal of Memory and Language, 27,* 59–70.

Philipose, L. E., Gottesman, R. F., Newhart, M., Kleinman, J. T., Herskovits, E. H., Pawlak, M. A.,…Hillis A. E. (2007). Neural regions essential for reading and spelling of words and pseudowords. *Annals of Neurology*, 62, 481–492.

Pouplier, M., & Goldstein, L. (2010). Intention in articulation: Articulatory timing of coproduced gestures and its implications for models of speech production. *Language and Cognitive Processes, 25*, 616–649.

Pring, L. (1981). Phonological codes and functional spelling units: Reality and implications. *Perception & Psychophysics, 30*, 573–578.

Prinzmetal, W. (1990). Neon colors illuminate reading units. *Journal of Experimental Psychology: Human Perception and Performance*, 16, 584–597.

Prinzmetal, W., Hoffman, H., & Vest, K. (1991). Automatic processes in word perception: An analysis from illusory conjunctions. *Journal of Experimental Psychology: Human Perception and Performance*, 17, 902–923.

Prinzmetal, W., & Keysar, B. (1989). A functional theory of illusory conjunctions and neon colors. *Journal of Experimental Psychology: General, 118*, 165–190.

Prinzmetal, W., & Millis-Wright, M. (1984). Cognitive and linguistic factors affect visual feature integration. *Cognitve Psychology, 16*, 305–340.

Prinzmetal, W., Treiman, R., & Rho, S. H. (1986). How to see a reading unit. *Journal of Memory and Language*, 25, 461–475.

Rapcsak, S. Z., & Beeson, P. M. (2004). The role of left posterior inferior temporal cortex in spelling. *Neurology*, 62, 2221–2229.

Rapp, B. (1992). The nature of sublexical orthographic organization: The bigram trough hypothesis examined. *Journal of Memory and Language*, 31, 33–53.

Rapp, B. (2002). Uncovering the cognitive architecture of spelling. In A. Hillis (Ed.), *Handbook on adult language disorders: Integrating cognitive neuropsychology, neurology and rehabilitation* (pp. 47–69). Philadelphia: Psychology Press.

Rapp, B., Barriere, I., & Fischer-Baum, S. (2006). *Morpho-orthography: Evidence of modality specific morphological processes*. Talk given at the Fifth International Conference on the Mental Lexicon, Montreal, Canada.

Rapp, B., Benzing, L., & Caramazza, A. (1997). The autonomy of lexical orthography. *Cognitive Neuropsychology, 14*, 71–104.

Rapp, B., & Caramazza, A. (1997a). The modality specific organization of grammatical categories: Evidence from impaired spoken and written sentence production. *Brain and Language*, 56, 248–286.

Rapp, B., & Caramazza, A. (1997b). From graphemes to abstract letter shapes: Levels of representation in written spelling. *Journal of Experimental Psychology: Human Perception and Performance*, 23, 1130–1152.

Rapp, B., Fischer-Baum, S., & Pastor, T. (2007). Perseveration of letter doubling without perseveration of letter identity. *Brain and Language, 103*, 105–106.

Rapp, B., & Lipka, K. (2011). The literate brain: The relationship between spelling and reading. *Journal of Cognitive Neuroscience, 23*(5), 1180–1197.

Rastle, K., & Brysbaert M. (2006). Masked phonological priming effects in English: Are they real? Do they matter? *Cognitive Psychology, 53*, 97–145.

Rastle, K., Davis, M. H., New, B. (2004). The broth in my brother's brothel: Morpho-orthographic segmentation in visual word recognition. *Psychonomic Bulletin and Review, 11*, 1090–1098.

Rey, A., Ziegler, J. C., & Jacobs, A. M. (2000). Graphemes are perceptual reading units. *Cognition, 74*, 1–12.

Roelofs, A. P. A. (1999). Phonological segments and features as planning units in speech production. *Language and Cognitive Processes, 14*, 173–200.

Rumelhart, D. E., & Norman, D. A. (1982). Simulating a skilled typist: A study of skilled cognitive-motor performance. *Cognitive Science, 6*, 1–36.

Schiller, N. O., Greenhall, J. A., Shelton, J. R., & Caramazza, A. (2001). Serial order effects in spelling errors: Evidence from two dysgraphic patients. *Neurocase, 7*, 1–14.

Schonauer, K., & Denes, G. (1994). Graphemic jargon: A case report. *Brain and Language, 47*, 279–299.

Seidenberg, M. S. (1987). Sublexical structures in visual word recognition: Access units or orthographic redundancy? In M. Coltheart (Ed.), *Attention and performance XII: Reading* (pp. 245–263). Hillsdale, NJ: Erlbaum.

Sternberg, S. (2001). Separate modifiability, mental modules, and the use of pure and composite measures to reveal tem. *Acta Psychologica, 106*, 147–246,

Tainturier, M. J., & Caramazza, A. (1996). The status of double letters in graphemic representations. *Journal of Memory and Language, 35*, 53–73.

Tainturier, M. J., Moreaud, O., David, D., Leek, E. C., & Pellat, J. (2001). Superior written over spoken picture naming in a case of frontotemporal dementia. *Neurocase, 7*, 89–96.

Tainturier, M. J., & Rapp, B. (2003). Is a single graphemic buffer used in reading and spelling? *Aphasiology, 17*, 537–562.

Tainturier, M. J., & Rapp, B. (2004). Complex graphemes as functional spelling units: Evidence from acquired dysgraphia. *Neurocase, 10*, 122–131.

Treiman, R., & Bourassa, D. (2000). The development of spelling skill. *Topics in Language Disorders, 20*, 1–18.

Tsapkini, K., & Rapp, B. (2010). The orthography-specific functions of the left fusiform gyrus: Evidence from modality and category specificity. *Cortex, 46*, 185–205.

Ward, J., & Romani, C. (1998). Serial position effects and lexical activation in spelling: Evidence from a single case study. *Neurocase, 4*, 189–206.

Ward, J., & Romani, C. (2000). Consonant-vowel encoding and ortho-syllables in a case of acquired dysgraphia. *Cognitive Neuropsychology, 17*, 641–663.

Whitney, C. (2001). How the brain encodes the order of letters in a printed word: the SERIOL model and selective literature review. *Psychonomics Bulletin & Review, 8*, 221–243.

Whitney, C., & Cornelissen, P. (2008). SERIOL reading. *Language and Cognitive Processes, 23*, 143–164.

Wing, A. M., & Baddeley, A. D. (1980). Spelling errors in handwriting: A corpus and a distributional analysis. In U. Frith (Ed.), *Cognitive processes in spelling* (pp. 251–285). London: Academic Press.

The Role of Lexical and Sublexical Orthography in Writing: Autonomy, Interactions, and Neurofunctional Correlates

Gabriele Miceli *and* Vanessa Costa

Abstract

Writing words and nonwords involves distinct knowledge and processes in at least partly distinct neural substrates. In writing words, stored orthographic representations are retrieved from a semantic memory store. In writing nonwords, sublexical phoneme-grapheme correspondence procedures assemble the target string. Semantic-lexical and sublexical mechanisms interact, and target selection in the lexicon can be jointly constrained by semantic and sublexical input. Semantic-lexical processes involved in writing and speaking also interact—wordform selection for writing and speaking could result from an interaction of semantic-lexical and sublexical mechanisms. In addition to being functionally separable, lexical and sublexical knowledge and processes are also at least partially separable neurally. Left hemispheric regions are critical for the processing and representation of orthographic wordforms; several perisylvian structures are crucial for sublexical phoneme-grapheme correspondence procedures. The neural substrates involved in writing words and nonwords partially overlap with those involved in reading the same materials.

Key Words: autonomy of orthographic wordforms, lexical-sublexical interaction in writing, lexical/sublexical interactions in writing and speaking, neuroanatomical correlates of orthographic lexical and sublexical mechanisms

For a long time, studies on writing and dysgraphia raised relatively little interest in the scientific community. They focused on the classification of dysgraphia, based on its occurrence as an isolated sign or in combination with other cognitive deficits (aphasia, alexia, apraxia), rather than on the functional architecture of the writing process (e.g., Alajouanine & Lhermitte, 1960; Benson, 1979; Brown, 1972).

This state of affairs changed in the early 1980s, largely as a consequence of the development of cognitive models of reading (e.g., Coltheart, Patterson, & Marshall, 1980; Marshall & Newcombe, 1973; Morton, 1969). Initially, the main thrust behind studies of dysgraphia was the need to verify whether or not a similar functional architecture to that proposed for reading could be upheld also for writing. As soon as the question was answered in the affirmative,

however, experimental questions moved beyond the mere definition of the architecture of the system to include investigations on the knowledge and processes relevant for each stage of the writing process and on their interactions, both within the writing system and between writing and speaking. Remarkably, and in contrast to what happened in other areas of cognition, most investigations were conducted in neurological patients, to the point that studies on dysgraphia became a test case of the possibility to use data from brain damage in order to draw inferences on the functional architecture of cognitive systems.

This chapter reviews the evidence pertaining to the functional organization of the orthographic lexicon and of sublexical (phoneme-grapheme) conversion mechanisms. It presents data showing that the two sets of mechanisms work independently, as well as data attesting to their interaction. Studies that analyze the functional architecture of the orthographic lexicon and its relationships with the phonological lexicon (i.e., the relationships between writing and speaking) are also reviewed. Finally, the current evidence on the neural underpinnings of these mechanisms is briefly discussed.

Lexical-Semantic and Sublexical Mechanisms in Writing

The ability to write words is practiced in the context of various cognitive activities, such as writing a letter, writing the name of a picture/drawing, and writing to dictation. In addition to processing different types of input, writing tasks may require different types of output (handwriting, oral spelling, typing) (Figure 22.1). Consequently, writing a word involves both writing-specific and accessory processes. The latter are activated only as needed (i.e., as a function of the computational requirements of the task at hand), whereas the former are necessary for all writing tasks. It is generally acknowledged that word writing requires an orthographic lexicon (i.e., a complex set of knowledge and processes that allow retrieving stored graphemic sequences corresponding to meaning-related units).

When writing a word, a set of semantic features activates entries in the orthographic output lexicon (i.e., in the long-term memory store that represents the letter sequence corresponding to the target)[1].

Under normal conditions, the lexical entry that most closely corresponds to the stimulus receives the greatest activation, and semantically related words are also activated to some extent, in proportion to their conceptual similarity to the stimulus (Figure 22.2). For example, the picture of a tiger activates the semantic representation (animal, wild, feline, has claws, has fangs, has stripes, has yellow-black fur, lives in Asia, and so forth). Since the orthographic entry *tiger* fully matches this representation, it is selected for production. However, while the whole set of activated semantic features suffices to unambiguously specify *tiger*, subsets of features shared by other conceptual representations also activate to some extent other, semantically related orthographic wordforms. Thus, in our example, (animal, medium-sized, feline, has claws, has fangs) will activate *lion*, (animal, medium-sized, has stripes) will activate *zebra*, and so on. Since none of these representations fully match the semantic features activated by the stimulus, none are selected for output, even though they are partially activated. This mechanism ensures selection of the correct target when semantic and lexical mechanisms are intact, and accounts for the failures to respond (anomias) and for the production of semantically related, incorrect words (semantic paragraphias) when they are impaired, for example, as a consequence of brain damage (discussed later).

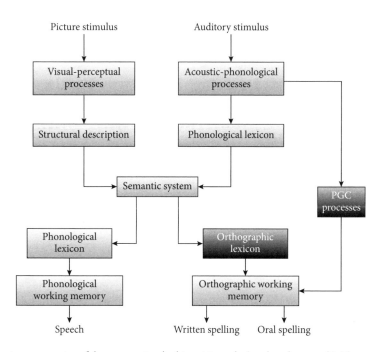

Figure 22.1 Schematic representation of the processes involved in writing tasks (words and nonwords). The components discussed in this chapter are shown with a dark background. PGC = phoneme-grapheme conversion.

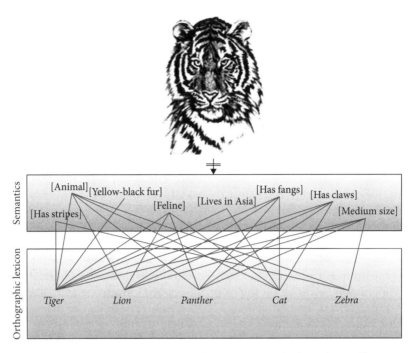

Figure 22.2 Schematic representation of the mechanisms involved in the activation of orthographic wordforms in picture naming.

Cognitively unimpaired individuals are able to write not only familiar words, but also unfamiliar words and nonwords (operationally defined here as pronounceable sequences that are not part of the vocabulary), typically in the context of writing-to-dictation tasks. In this case, a different set of mechanisms is recruited. Since the auditorily presented stimulus does not correspond to a meaning, or to a stored lexical representation, it serves as input to sublexical processing units. The input string is kept in phonological working memory, while phoneme-grapheme correspondence (PGC) procedures sequentially map it onto a plausible graphemic string (*feek, feak, pheek, pheak, pheeck, pheack*, etc. are all acceptable spellings for the nonword sequence /fik/). The latter is placed in an orthographic short-term memory component, while subsequent writing stages take place. PGC mechanisms can convert any pronounceable phonological string into a plausible sequence of letters. Although they are necessary in order to write unfamiliar strings, PGC procedures can also be used to spell familiar words, at least under some circumstances (see later).

The Autonomy of Lexical-Semantic and Sublexical PGC Mechanisms

Two contrasting patterns of impaired writing performance, repeatedly described in brain-damaged subjects, support the assumption of functionally independent lexical and sublexical mechanisms.

The first pattern of performance, often referred to as "phonological agraphia," is exemplified by P.R. (Shallice, 1981). This subject had normal comprehension. He wrote correctly to dictation 98% words, but only 18% nonwords. His performance on words was unaffected by frequency, length, and orthographic regularity. This already impressive discrepancy between words and nonwords is even more dramatic if one considers performance on length—and structure-matched subsets of items (Table 22.1). P.R. spelled flawlessly 10 words of six-letter and of eight-letter length, but only 0 of 10 and 1 of 10 matched nonwords. Writing errors on nonwords could not be attributed to memory problems, as P.R. often repeated correctly the target nonword after failing to write it (8 of 10 and 7 of 10 pseudowords from the six- and eight-grapheme subsets were repeated correctly). This pattern of performance is consistent with selective damage to PGC processes, in the face of spared lexical representations. Analogous performance profiles were reported in other subjects (e.g., Bub & Kertesz, 1982a; Langmore & Canter, 1983; Roeltgen, Sevush, & Heilman, 1983; Baxter & Warrington, 1985).

The second pattern of impairment, frequently labeled "surface dysgraphia" or "lexical agraphia,"

Table 22.1. Subject P.R. (Shallice, 1981): Percent incorrect responses in writing to dictation structure and length-matched words and nonwords, and in repeating nonwords after writing to dictation

	Word Writing	Nonword Writing	Nonword Repetition
Six letters	0%	100%	20%
Eight letters	0%	90%	30%

was documented for the first time in French-speaking subject R.G. (Beauvois & Dérouesné, 1981). This subject comprehended and repeated words normally, just like P.R., but his writing performance was substantially different. He wrote nonwords almost flawlessly (109 of 110 correct responses, or 99%), but produced many errors in response to words (174 of 238 correct responses, or 73.1%). Accuracy on words was constrained by orthographic regularity, defined as the number of mute letters and of ambiguous phonological segments, that admit to more than one graphemic mapping. R.G. wrote correctly to dictation 93% unambiguous words, 67% mildly ambiguous words, and 36% very ambiguous or exception words. Accuracy was unaffected by length, but was sensitive to frequency of usage (he spelled correctly approximately 70% high-frequency and 53% low-frequency words). Crucially, errors could be interpreted as an attempt to write words as they sound. For example, R.G. wrote "photo" as *fauto*; "rideau," ripple as *ridot*; "hangar" as *engare*; and "ascension" as *acention*. Analogous errors were reported in English-writing subjects, who produced errors like "subtle" → *suttel* and "duel" → *duwale* (Hatfield & Patterson, 1983; for additional cases, see Patterson, Marshall, & Coltheart, 1985). These so-called phonologically plausible errors (PPEs) occurred also in oral spelling ("pays," country → *paihi*; "septiéme," seventh → *saitiemme*; "calcium" → *calsiom*), and when spelling orally a word starting with a letter given by the examiner (e.g., "Spell a word starting with/i/" → *I-S-T-O-I-R-E* for *histoire*, history).

The pattern of performance documented for R.G. and similar cases (effects of frequency and regularity; PPEs in word writing in the face of accurate nonword writing) can be accounted for by assuming the selective unavailability of orthographic word-forms in the presence of spared PGC procedures. When asked to write to dictation a low-frequency word, R.G. sometimes fails to activate stored orthographic information on the target item, but can still produce a response via sublexical PGC mechanisms. However, these procedures operate on units that do not represent word-specific orthography, but rather encode plausible mappings between phonemic and graphemic subword units (that might correspond to phonemes, syllables, or short phonemic/orthographic sequences). In an orthographically opaque language like English or French, the spelling of a word cannot be predicted by its pronunciation (e.g., *night/knight; bed/bread*). Therefore, in these languages PGC processes allow correct responses to regular words, which typically contain unambiguous, high-probability mappings, but yield writing errors to words containing ambiguous or irregular segments. These errors take the form of PPEs. For example, since /o/ corresponds to *-au* in *rideau*, but to *-ot* in *gigot*, lamb, R.G. may spell *rideau* as *ridot*.

The behaviors reported in "phonological agraphia" are similar, as all these subjects show a disproportionate difficulty writing nonwords as compared with words. The same can be said of subjects with "surface dysgraphia," who present with a selective inability to write words, with incorrect responses resulting in PPEs. However, it cannot be stressed strongly enough that the patterns of performance documented for each set of subjects are heterogeneous and can result from disparate loci of impairments within each set of procedures. For example, a selective inability to write nonwords relative to words might result from damage to any component of PGC processes (auditory analysis, phonological working memory, parsing of the phonological input string, phoneme/grapheme mapping, and so forth). In these cases, an in-depth analysis of performance in all the relevant tasks allows localizing the functional damage. Thus, reduced phonological working memory will cause poor performance also in nonword repetition, as the damaged component is shared by writing and repetition (e.g., Caramazza, Miceli, & Villa, 1986), whereas damage to PGC rules themselves will not affect repetition (this was the case for P.R.). Similarly, in "surface dysgraphia" orthographic forms may be unavailable as a consequence of damage to semantic knowledge or of a lexical-level impairment. Also in this case, the pattern of performance observed in the relevant tasks allows identifying the functional locus of lesion. Selective damage to the orthographic lexicon will affect writing, but neither comprehension nor spoken production (e.g., Beauvois & Dérouesné, 1981); whereas, selective semantic damage will affect oral and written naming tasks, as well as auditory and visual word comprehension tasks to a similar extent (e.g., Hillis & Caramazza, 1991).

The Organization of the Orthographic Lexicon

Studies show the internal organization of the orthographic lexicon to be similar to that of the phonological lexicon. Since the latter is dealt with in detail elsewhere in this volume (Dell, Nozari, and Oppenheim Word Production: Behavioral and Computational Considerations; and Race and Hillis Neural Bases of Word Representations for Naming), here we only review very briefly the evidence specific to writing.

Grammatical class is obviously a critical dimension. For example, case G.O.S. (Baxter & Warrington, 1985) showed no effects of regularity and an insignificant effect of frequency when writing words, but fared worse on verbs than on nouns, even when stimuli were matched for abstractness/concreteness.

Compelling data on the role of grammatical class in the organization of orthographic lexical representations are provided by several studies in which subjects were asked to produce homonyms, which appeared as nouns or verbs in sentence context (e.g., "There is a crack in the mirror—Write crack" vs. "People crack under pressure—Write crack"; and for spoken production, *There is a crack in the mirror* vs. *People crack under pressure*—Read the underlined word). Subject S.J.D. (Caramazza & Hillis, 1991) fared poorly in writing verbs, while retaining the ability to write nouns and to read aloud both nouns and verbs. Subject M.M.L. (Hillis, Tuffiash, & Caramazza, 2002) showed a selective deterioration of verbs in spoken production, in the face of spared spoken output for nouns, and written output for nouns and verbs. Subject K.R.S. (Rapp & Caramazza, 2002) showed a double, grammatical class-by-modality dissociation; he fared significantly worse on verbs in writing, and on nouns in speech.

As a natural complement to the data supporting the role of grammatical category in the organization of the orthographic lexicon, other studies suggest that (consistent with the phonological lexicon) morphological structure is represented within the orthographic lexicon.

Subject B.H. (Badecker, Rapp, & Caramazza, 1996) suffered from severe damage to the orthographic lexicon (and perhaps from minor damage to semantics) in the face of spared PGC processes. As expected, he produced many PPEs in writing irregular words to dictation. On monomorphemic words, these errors occurred with comparable frequency in initial, middle, and final positions (e.g., "census" → *sensis*; "yacht" → *yaught*); whereas on inflected words they only occurred in root positions. If orthographic lexical forms correspond to whole words, errors in writing inflected words should occur in all within-word positions, just as in monomorphemic stimuli. For example, since the English past tense inflection -*ed* is phonologically ambiguous (it corresponds to /t/ in *passed*, to /d/ in *pulled*, and to /ɪd/ in *handed*), "surfed" and "kneeled" should yield PPEs like *sourphed* and *neiled*, as well as PPEs like *surft* and *kneeld*. In contrast with this prediction, B.H. produced PPEs on roots, but never on inflections (i.e., he wrote *sourphed* and *neiled*, but never *surft* nor *kneeld*). Furthermore, the opposite error never occurred: he never produced -*ed* as a PPE on a noninflectional word ending (e.g., he never wrote "adjust" as *adjused*).

Evidence for the representation of morphological structure in the orthographic lexicon is provided also by D.H. (Badecker, Hillis, & Caramazza, 1990). This subject suffered from damage to orthoare discussed more extensively in Rapp and Fischer-Baum "Representation of Orthographic Knowledge." Suffice it here to say that, since this component is activated after lexical selection, impaired performance is constrained by length, and errors result in substitutions, insertions, omissions, or transpositions of letters in the target string. D.H. produced many single-letter errors in writing to dictation morphologically simple and complex (prefixed, suffixed, compound) words. However, performance on monomorphemic words (*voyage*) and on pseudo-suffixed words (stimuli like *ballad* and *purchase*, in which the initial and final sequences, respectively, correspond to a word) clearly differed from that on affixed words (*smokes, dislike*)—i.e., as a function of morphological structure. First, monomorphemic words were spelled more accurately than polymorphemic words. Second, errors had a different distribution in the target string. On monomorphemic and pseudoaffixed words, they increased from initial to final word positions; on morphologically complex items, errors increased monotonically on the positions occupied by the root morpheme, and dropped on affixes (they were almost absent on prefixes, and rare on suffixes; see Badecker et al., 1990, Figures 6 and 7).

These patterns of performance are consistent with the view that roots and affixes are represented separately in the orthographic lexicon. In B.H., impaired retrieval of roots and spared retrieval of suffixes result in PPEs only on the roots of verbs that contain ambiguous or exceptional print-to-sound mappings. In D.H., the reduced error rate on morphologically complex words and different error distribution in monomorphemic as opposed to affixed words are compatible with the view that morphologically complex words are represented as root+affix (at least in the case of inflectional morphemes and of highly productive derivational affixes).

The Organization of PGC Mechanisms

Because they cannot activate orthographic lexical representations, dysgraphics with selective damage to orthographic wordforms respond to words by sequentially converting the phonological input into an orthographic output by means of PGC mechanisms. However, the graphemic information represented in these mechanisms does not correspond to stored, word-specific knowledge, but to smaller, submorphemic processing units. Therefore, in languages with opaque orthographies, in which the spelling of a word cannot be predicted from phonology, writing performance will be errorful. In English, orthographic regularity and consistency are the exception, rather than the rule. For some words, orthography is entirely predictable; each of the sounds that comprise the word admits to only one sound-to-print mapping. These regular words (e.g., *bit*) can be spelled correctly by either lexical or sublexical mechanisms. Much more frequently, however, English orthography is irregular. Some words (e.g., *yacht, colonel, choir, aisle,* and *sword*) have idiosyncratic spellings. In many others, irregularity takes less extreme forms, and results from the inconsistency of sound-to-print mappings. In these words, one or more phonological segments admit to more than one spelling (e.g., the sound / aɪt / corresponds to distinct spellings in *might/night/light*, and in *kite* and, to make an even more extreme example, / i / is spelled differently in *me, see, plea, people, women, chief, seize, ski,* and *fetus*). Furthermore, different mappings are associated more or less frequently to a given segment (in the first example, / aɪt / is associated much more frequently to -*ight* than to -*ite*). When orthographic wordforms are unavailable, written output is constrained by the consistency of print-to-sound mapping and by the frequency of occurrence of specific mapping rules. Words that contain irregular or inconsistent segments will be spelled by selecting graphemes among admissible sound-to-print mappings, regardless of whether or not the selected mappings are appropriate for the target. Analyses of the PPEs that result from this strategy provide a window into the functional organization of PGC mechanisms.

Subject J.G. (Goodman & Caramazza, 1986) resembles case R.G. under the critical respects. She wrote nonwords flawlessly, but her performance on words was inaccurate, and sensitive to frequency of usage (85% correct responses to high-frequency words and 46% to low-frequency words). Crucially, most errors to words (86%) resulted in PPEs ("coarse" → *korse*, "goals" → *goles*).

In writing words to dictation, J.G. responded correctly to low-frequency words when targets contained high-frequency PGC correspondences, but produced PPEs when they contained low-frequency mappings (PGC mapping frequency was based on Hanna, Hanna, Hodges, & Rudorf, 1966). Errors resulted from selecting a high-frequency PGC rule when a low-frequency rule would have been appropriate. In addition to frequency of usage, PGC mapping selection depended on within-string position, and closely paralleled the distribution of the same mapping in the language (Table 22.2). Consider as an example the different frequency of usage of *s* and *c* (the two most frequent options for / s /) in initial, middle, or final syllable position. In English, syllable-initial / s / corresponds to *s* in 78% of the cases (e.g., *sold*), and to *c* in 16%

Table 22.2. Percent incidence of /s/ → S and of /s/ → C mappings in various syllable positions, in J.G.'s responses and in the English language

| | Within-Syllable Position | | | | | |
| | Initial | | Medial | | Final | |
	J.G.	N	J.G.	N	J.G.	N
/s/> S	77.6	77.8	100.0	96.9	61.0	62.3
/s/> C	19.8	15.9	0.0	2.6	34.3	20.3
/s/> other	2.6	6.3	0.0	0.5	4.7	17.4

Note. N=norms.
Adapted from Hanna, R. R., Hannah, J. S., Hodges, R. E.,& Rudorf E. H. (1966). Phoneme-grapheme correspondences as cues to spelling improvement. US Department of Health, Education and Welfare. Office of Education. Washington, DC: US Government Printing Office.

(e.g., *cell*). In middle syllable position, /s/ is spelled as *s* in 96.9% of the cases (e.g., *cast*), and as *c* in 2.6% (e.g., *forced*). In syllable-final position, /s/ is mapped onto *s* in 61% of the times (e.g., *gas*), and onto *c* in 34.3% (e.g., *lace*). The frequency of occurrence of these mappings in the PPEs produced by J.G. closely parallels these figures. Finally, PGC selection is context-sensitive. To focus again on /s/, in syllable-initial position it occurs before consonants and before vowels. Before a consonant, it invariably corresponds to *s* (e.g., *spot*). Before a vowel, it corresponds to *s* when followed by *a, o,* or *u* (*salt, sold, super*) and to either *c* or *s* when the following vowel is *e, i,* or *y* (*cell, self, cider, side, cymbal, symbol*). J.G. invariably (34 of 34) spelled /s/+ *c* as *s*, and almost invariably (25 of 26) spelled /s/+ *a, o* or *u* as *s*. Overall, these observations suggest that units in the PGC system are associated with a threshold value that depends on their frequency of occurrence in the language, and that their selection is constrained, in addition to frequency, by within-syllable position and orthographic context.[2]

The Interaction between Lexical and Sublexical Mechanisms

The results reviewed so far show that lexical-semantic mechanisms and sublexical conversion procedures are functionally distinct. Observations on cognitively unimpaired subjects and on brain-damaged individuals also suggest that they interact.

This proposal was prompted by studies of acquired dyslexia (Caramazza & Hillis, 1991; Patterson & Hodges, 1992). Subject J.J. (Caramazza & Hillis, 1991) suffered from semantic damage in the presence of spared grapheme-phoneme conversion (GPC) procedures. When reading aloud irregular words, he produced the correct response to all the words he fully understood, and systematically produced PPEs to words (13 of 13) he totally failed to understand (in reading aloud, when semantic information is completely unavailable no phonological wordform is activated, and the response can only be produced via sublexical procedures that yield PPEs in opaque languages). Crucially, however, J.J. systematically (26 of 26) read aloud correctly words he comprehended partially.

As it applies to writing, the "interaction" hypothesis can be summarized as follows. Under normal conditions, even though the dictated stimulus is processed in parallel by lexical-semantic and sublexical PGC processes, intact lexical-semantic mechanisms suffice to ensure selection of the target word.

By contrast, when orthographic representations are activated less than optimally (due to semantic or lexical damage), the target form may not reach threshold, and entries related conceptually to the target may compete for production. For example, if only partial lexical-semantic information on "cake" is available, conceptually related entries like *pie, sweet, biscuit,* and *waffle* and *cake* itself compete for output. Under these circumstances, intact PGC procedures may convert "cake" into plausible graphemic strings (e.g., *caick, cake, kaick*). These sequences interact with lexical representations, and may coinstrain the selection of *cake*, by boosting its activation above threshold and/or blocking alternative responses. This hypothesis predicts that, in the event of lexical-semantic damage, the form taken by word writing errors should be critically constrained by the status of sublexical PGC procedures. Several pieces of evidence support this view.

J.J. is a first case in point. In addition to semantic damage, this subject suffers from additional, mild damage to PGC procedures and orthographic wordforms. He never produced PPEs to words he understood fully, and consistently produced PPEs when asked to write words he totally failed to understand. Crucially, however, he never produced PPEs to words he comprehended partially. Thus, for example, he showed no comprehension of "grew" and "riot," which he misspelled as *grue* and *wriett,* respectively, but spelled *book* correctly, after defining it vaguely as "a source of information." This pattern of performance, and especially the lack of PPEs to partially understood words, can be accounted for by assuming that in his case largely spared PGC procedures could still constrain the selection of the correct orthographic target from among semantically related alternatives.

When PGC mechanisms are severely damaged, the same lexical-semantic damage as in the previous case should yield a very different error pattern. In subjects of this type, dictating "cake" activates *pie, sweet, biscuit, cake,* and *waffle,* as in the previous example. However, since PGC rules are not functional, sublexical orthographic information cannot be used to constrain lexical selection. This should result in semantic paragraphias; subjects might respond to "cake" by writing *sweet, pie,* or *cake*. This is the pattern of performance referred to as "deep dysgraphia." Consistent with the interaction view, patients who produce semantic paragraphias invariably present with extremely severe disruption of PGC procedures, in addition to impaired lexical (e.g., Alario, Schiller, Domoto-Reilly, & Caramazza,

2003; Bub & Kertesz, 1982b; Caramazza & Hillis, 1991) or semantic knowledge (e.g., Alario et al., 2003; Miceli, Benvegnù, Capasso, & Caramazza, 1997; Miceli, Capasso, & Caramazza, 1999; Nolan & Caramazza, 1983).

Support for the interaction hypothesis comes also from the longitudinal study of case R.C.M. (Hillis, Rapp, & Caramazza, 1999). In this subject, semantic paragraphias amounted to 56% of overall writing errors at 1 week postonset, when PGC mechanisms were severely impaired (58% incorrect segments in writing nonwords), but dropped to 11% at 3 weeks postonset, when incorrect segments in nonwords fell to 33%. Analogous patterns were described in studies on the recovery of dyslexia (de Partz, 1986; Sherwood & Chatterjee, 2001).

Additional evidence consistent with an interaction between lexical-semantic and sublexical mechanisms is provided in a group case study of 13 Italian dysgraphics (Laiacona et al., 2009). The level of accuracy expected on the hypothesis that writing is mediated entirely by lexical processes, or entirely by sublexical processes, was calculated for each participant and compared with observed performance. In at least 4 of 13 cases, writing performance could only be accommodated by assuming the combined operation of lexical-semantic and PGC processes.

To sum up, it is reasonable to assume that lexical-semantic and sublexical mechanisms interact in writing (and reading and repetition), and that their interaction facilitates the activation of the target lexical string. It is worth stressing that PGC need not be totally spared to prevent PPEs in writing, nor completely abolished to allow semantic paragraphias. The extent of PGC damage needed to allow semantic paragraphias is still unclear (for quantitative data on GPC processes in reading, see Ciaghi, Pancheri, & Miceli, 2010). For the time being, a safe (albeit very weak) conclusion is that "functional" PGC rules will prevent semantic paragraphias, regardless of the extent and severity of semantic-lexical damage.

Possible Mechanisms Underlying the Interaction between Lexical and Sublexical Processes

The studies reviewed so far show that the wide spectrum of writing disorders observed in brain-damaged subjects is best accounted for by assuming an interaction between lexical-semantic and sublexical mechanisms. Evidence consistent with this possibility was obtained also in cognitively unimpaired spellers engaged in writing-to-dictation

tasks. In this case, the graphemic sequences selected to spell a nonword are influenced by the those produced for previously presented words. Thus, the nonword /preIn/ is more likely to be spelled as *prane* when preceded by *crane*, and as *prain* when preceded by *brain*; and /frit/ is more likely to be spelled as *freat* when preceded by *cheat*, and as *freet* when preceded by *greet* (Barry & De Bastiani, 1997; Barry & Seymour, 1988; Campbell, 1983).

Additional observations from cognitively unimpaired subjects suggest that the interaction might be mediated by both orthographic and phonological representations. In a study based on a priming task (Folk & Rapp, 2004), the examiner spoke a monosyllabic word prime, followed by a monosyllabic target that corresponded either to a word or to a nonword. When the target was a nonword, participants were asked to write it. Prime and target were related either phonologically + orthographically ("touch," /nʌtʃ/) or only orthographically[3] ("couch," /nʌtʃ/). Participants wrote the graphemic sequence corresponding to the vowel in the prime 22% of the times when prime and target were both phonologically and orthographically similar, and 7% of the times when they were related only orthographically. In other words, subjects wrote /nʌtʃ/ as *nouch* more often when the stimulus pair was "touch," /nʌtʃ/, than when it was "couch," /nʌtʃ/. These observations suggest that lexical information may constrain sublexical mechanisms in two ways. A first, more effective mechanism acts at the phonological level. The phonological vowel in the prime (/tʌtʃ/) activates the PGC mapping /ʌ/ → *ou*, thus increasing its activation level. Consequently, when the same phonological vowel occurs in the target pseudoword /nʌtʃ/, the just-activated graphemic mapping is more likely to be selected. A second, less effective mechanism is based on orthography; /au/ in /kautʃ/ activates the PGC correspondence /au/ → *ou*. This raises the activation level of *ou*, which is more likely to be used when spelling the target pseudoword (/nʌtʃ/) that follows. These observations add yet another dimension to the constraints under which PGC rules operate: the activation level of PGC mappings is affected by phonological and orthographic information retrieved during lexical processing.

The interaction between lexical-semantic and sublexical mechanisms was further investigated in a subject with Alzheimer disease (Rapp, Epstein, & Tainturier, 2002). All incorrect responses produced by L.A.T. were PPEs, but they contained many lexically correct, low-frequency PGC correspondences (for a similar behavior, see Baxter & Warrington, 1987; Sanders & Caramazza, 1990). For example, L.A.T. wrote "bouquet" as *bouket*, where *k* is an incorrect, high-probability mapping for /k/, and *et* is the correct, low-probability mapping for /eI/. Rapp et al. hypothesized that in this subject orthographic lexical information was impaired but not totally unavailable, and that enough of it was spared as to provide orthographic information on part of the target string. They interpreted PPEs in this subject as the combined result of lexical and sublexical information (in the example reported above, *bou* and *et* would be provided by the target orthographic entry, and /k/ → *k* by PGC mechanisms). Lexical information available on the target word allows producing the preserved segments, regardless of whether they correspond to high-frequency or low-frequency PGC rules; whereas PGC mechanisms provide the missing segments by activating sound-to-print mappings based on their frequency of occurrence. The temporal dynamics of the interaction are yet to be determined. One possibility is that the lexical entry is activated first and sublexical procedures are subsequently used to fill any remaining gaps. As an alternative, the two sets of mechanisms may be activated simultaneously, and each set may activate the candidate graphemes of the to-be-written response.

The writing-to-dictation performance of subject M.M.D. (Folk, Rapp, & Goldrick, 2002; see also Folk & Jones, 2004) provides further evidence for the hypothesis that the role of PGC mechanisms is to increase the activation level of the target word-form. This subject showed orthographic lexical damage (36% incorrect responses to words) and impaired PGC procedures (22% of the graphemes in dictated nonwords were written incorrectly). In a preliminary task, performance on words was sensitive to frequency and orthographic regularity. M.M.D. was asked to write to dictation 320 words, under baseline conditions and during articulatory suppression (i.e., while continuously producing a meaningless syllable), a condition that interferes heavily with PGC mechanisms (Table 22.3). Under baseline conditions, errors resulted in nonwords (62%); PPEs (31%); and form-related word substitutions, such as "loaf" → *leaf* (7%). During articulatory suppression, M.M.D. produced comparable numbers of nonword errors (66%), but more form-related errors (20%) and fewer PPEs (14%). This result is consistent with the view that under baseline conditions a substantial number of responses resulted from the interaction of

Table 22.3. Subject M.M.D. (Folk et al., 2002): Errors produced in writing words to dictation under baseline conditions and during articulatory suppression

	Dictation (Baseline)	Dictation (Articulatory Suppression)
Nonword errors	62%	66%
PPEs	31%	14%
Form-related word errors	7%	20%

semantic-lexical and sublexical processes (31% PPEs). Articulatory suppression disrupted PGC procedures, thereby reducing their influence on lexical selection, and licensing a greater number of form-related word errors, that raised from 7% to 20% of total incorrect responses. Additional evidence for this account comes from the observation that under baseline conditions M.M.D. produced incorrectly 8% high-probability PGC mappings and 23% low-probability mappings, whereas during articulatory suppression she produced comparable numbers of errors on PGC mappings of high (20%) and low (18%) probability.

Writing and Speaking

Individuals learn to speak before they learn to write. Therefore, it is fair to ask what relationship exists between the cognitive mechanisms involved in speech and those involved in writing. The assumption that writing necessitates phonological mediation is implied in the studies of classical authors (e.g., Lichtheim, 1885; Wernicke, 1886), and explicitly stated by Luria (1966; for a similar, more recent hypothesis, see van Orden, Johnston, & Hale, 1988). Stated differently, orthographic lexical representations cannot be activated directly from semantics, and must be activated from the corresponding phonological lexical representations, as sketched in Figure 22.3a. On this account, writing *table* in response to the picture of a table requires semantic knowledge to first activate the corresponding phonological lexical representation, which in turn activates its orthographic lexical counterpart. This could be accomplished either through direct links between a phonological representation and its corresponding orthographic representation (e.g., "table" → *table*), or by PGC procedures, that sequentially convert a phonological representation into the corresponding orthographic wordform.

In the face of it, obligatory phonological mediation is unlikely. While viable for a completely

(a) Obligatory phonological mediation hypothesis

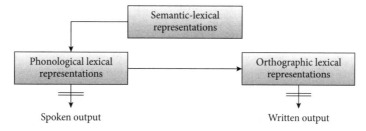

(b) Complete orthographic autonomy hypothesis

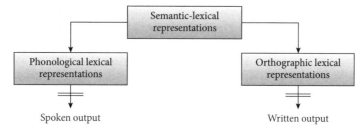

(c) Autonomy and interaction hypothesis

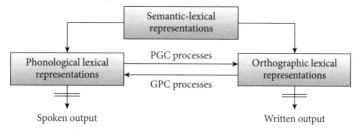

Figure 22.3 Schematic representation of the relationships between phonological and orthographic representations according to (a) the *obligatory phonological mediation* hypothesis, (b) the *complete orthographic autonomy* hypothesis, and (c) the *autonomy and interaction* hypothesis. GPC = grapheme-phoneme conversion; PGC = phoneme-grapheme conversion.

transparent language (i.e., for a language where the orthography of a word is unambiguously predicted from pronounciation), it is problematic in opaque languages like English, and even more problematic in ideographic systems (e.g., Japanese kana). Indirect evidence against obligatory phonological mediation is provided by subjects who present with superior performance in writing than in speaking (Assal & Buttet, 1981; Basso, Taborelli, & Vignolo, 1978; Ellis, Miller, & Sin, 1983; Hier & Mohr, 1977; Lhermitte & Dérouesné, 1974); if writing requires obligatory mediation, performance on spoken tasks should be similar to, or better than, performance on analogous written tasks. However, data from these subjects do not allow strong arguments against obligatory phonological mediation. For example, in several cases written naming is spared, in the presence of neologistic speech. Since neologisms can arise postlexically, in these subjects the correctly selected phonological wordform could still constrain the selection of the correct orthographic wordform, even though spoken output may be disrupted at later processing stages.

Clear evidence against obligatory phonological mediation comes from subjects whose errors in speaking and writing can be unambiguously attributed to lexical-semantic damage. Three sets of observations from these subjects suggest that orthographic lexical representations are autonomous from phonological representations and, just like the latter, are directly activated from semantics (Figure 22.3b).

First, there are subjects who produce semantic errors in only one output modality. For example, R.G.B. and H.W. (Caramazza & Hillis, 1990) produced many semantic errors in oral naming, but none in written naming, whereas J.C. (Bub & Kertesz, 1982) and S.J.D. (Hillis & Caramazza, 1991) produced many semantic paragraphias in the absence of semantic errors in reading.

Secondly, there are subjects who present with modality-specific grammatical class effects. There are reports of a selective difficulty producing verbs in oral tasks (Hillis & Caramazza, 1991; Hillis et al., 2002) or in written tasks (Hillis, Chang, Breese, & Heidler, 2004). Finally, subject K.R.S. (Rapp & Caramazza, 2002) demonstrated a double modality-by-grammatical class dissociation: he was selectively poor at producing verbs in writing and nouns in speech.

Finally, direct evidence against obligatory phonological mediation is provided by subjects who produce lexically inconsistent, consecutive responses in double (written and spoken) naming tasks. This pattern of responses was observed in W.M.A. (Miceli et al., 1997), P.W. (Rapp et al., 1997), M.G.K. (Beaton, Guest, & Ved, 1997), and W.B. (Alario et al., 2003; see Table 22.4 for examples). This incongruence cannot result from a memory deficit. Take for example W.M.A. This subject completed four naming tasks, all requiring two consecutive responses to 130 stimuli. In two tasks, he was asked to respond in different modalities (oral, then written; written, then oral). In two other tasks, he was asked to produce two responses in the same modality (two oral responses, or two written responses), but with a 5-second interval, spent performing a phonological interference task. Different-modality naming tasks yielded a substantial number of incongruent responses. A correct response was preceded or followed by a lexically incongruent incorrect response 21.5% times in the oral, then written task; and 19.2% times in the written, then oral task. By contrast, same-modality

Table 22.4. Subject W.M.A. (Miceli et al., 1997): Sequences resulting in lexically contrasting responses in the course of "repeated naming" tasks

	Stimulus	First Response	Second Response
Spoken, then written	TRUMPET	"orchestra"	*trumpet*
	MOUSTACHE	"moustache"	*beard*
	FORK	"spoon"	*knife*
Written, then spoken	SHOE	*socks*	"shoe"
	BUTTERFLY	*butterfly*	"dragonfly"
	ANKLE	*leg*	"arm"

tasks always resulted in the same correct or incorrect response being produced twice.

These observations support the hypothesis that orthographic and phonological wordforms are represented autonomously, and are both directly activated from semantics.

The Role of Sublexical Conversion Procedures in Writing and Speech

Data reviewed thus far allow one to rule out *obligatory* phonological mediation, and support orthographic autonomy. However, several observations show that orthographic and phonological wordforms interact. To begin with, case R.G. (Beauvois & Dérouesné, 1981) produced PPEs not only in writing to dictation and oral spelling, but also in spontaneous writing (e.g., fenêtre, window → *fenaitre*) and picture naming (e.g., bouilloire, boiler → *bouyoir*), which does not entail auditory presentation of the stimulus. These latter errors suggest an interaction between phonological and orthographic output mechanisms. In these examples, R.G. might have retrieved the correct phonological form, but not the corresponding orthographic form, and tried to write the target word as it sounds. The data reviewed so far suggest that sublexical conversion processes might be instrumental in this interaction (Figure 22.3c).

If orthographic and phonological lexical representations were *completely* independent, lexically inconsistent, consecutive responses to the same stimulus in "repeated naming" tasks (oral, then written; written, then oral) should be observed in all subjects with semantic damage (or, with damage to both phonological and orthographic lexical forms). Instead, error sequences like those reported for P.W., W.M.A., M.G.K., and W.B. are very rare, and subjects with semantic damage typically do not produce contrasting responses in these tasks (e.g., P.G.E. and G.M.A. in Miceli & Capasso, 1997; E.A. in Alario et al., 2003). The dimension that differentiates the subjects who produce lexically inconsistent responses in repeated naming tasks from those who do not is precisely the status of sublexical conversion procedures.

There are systematic contrasts in these subjects (Table 22.5). Subjects P.W., W.M.A., and W.B., who produce lexically inconsistent responses both in spoken, then written naming and in written, then spoken naming, show severe damage to both PGC and GPC rules. By contrast, PGC and GPC processes are spared in cases P.G.E., G.M.A., and E.A., who never produce similar response sequences. Sublexical conversion procedures show

Table 22.5. Performance profile of subjects with lexical or semantic damage who do/do not produce lexically inconsistent, consecutive responses in "repeated naming" tasks, and of subjects who produce semantic errors only in writing or only in reading

	Semantic Paralexias	Semantic Paragraphias	Severe GPC Damage	Severe PGC Damage	Inconsistent Sequences: Spoken, Then Written	Inconsistent Sequences: Written, Then Spoken
P.W.	+	+	+	+	+	+
M.G.K.	+	+	+	+	+	N/A
W.M.A.	+	+	+	+	+	+
P.G.E.	–	–	–	–	–	–
P.M.A.	–	–	–	–	–	–
E.A.	–	–	–	–	–	–
R.G.B.	+	–	+	–	N/A	N/A
H.W.	+	–	+	–	N/A	N/A
S.J.D.	–	+	–	+	N/A	N/A
J.C.	–	+	–	+	N/A	N/A
E.C.A.	–	+	–	+	–	+

Note: N/A = not administered.

interesting dissociations also in subjects who produce semantic errors in only one output modality. Cases R.G.B. and H.W. (Caramazza & Hillis, 1990), who produce semantic errors only in reading, present with severe damage to GPC (but not to PGC) processes; whereas subjects J.C. (Bub & Kertesz, 1982b) and S.J.D. (Caramazza & Hillis, 1991), who make semantic errors only in writing, suffer from severe damage to PGC (but not to GPC) mechanisms. Taken together, these observations suggest that sublexical conversion procedures, in addition to allowing sublexically assembled strings to constrain lexical selection for orthographic output in writing tasks and for phonological output in reading aloud (see previous sections), allow phonological and orthographic lexical representations to interact in all production tasks.

This hypothesis provides a straightforward account for all the performance profiles considered so far. Let us briefly consider how these mechanisms might allow or prevent contrasting responses in repeated naming tasks, when semantic damage co-occurs with varying impairment of sublexical mechanisms (Figure 22.4).

Since partial semantic information does not allow the correct word to reach threshold, related wordforms are activated, sometimes to a different extent in the phonological and in the orthographic lexicon, and compete for production. Thus, the picture of a cow might activate "horse," "chicken," "rabbit," and "donkey" in the phonological lexicon, to decreasing amounts of activation; and *rabbit, donkey, horse,* and *turkey* in the orthographic lexicon, also to decreasing amounts of activation. Once the first response is selected, it may or may not constrain selection of the second response, depending on the status of sublexical conversion procedures. "Functional" sublexical rules will ensure selection of the same word in both output modalities. In our example, once "horse" is selected, PGC procedures may assemble a graphemic string that constrains the selection of *horse,* even though *rabbit, donkey,* and *turkey* are also active. The same applies in the reverse task, when selecting *rabbit* for output allows GPC rules to constrain the selection of "rabbit" over "horse," "chicken," and "donkey." No such interaction is possible when both GPC and PGC mechanisms are functionally abolished. In this case, the most active entry in each lexical component is selected; the subject will produce "horse," then *rabbit* in the spoken, then written task, and *rabbit,* then "horse" in the written, then spoken task. Finally, when only one set of sublexical procedures is spared, the occurrence of lexically consistent or inconsistent response sequences in repeated-naming tasks should be constrained by the task at hand. Take for example

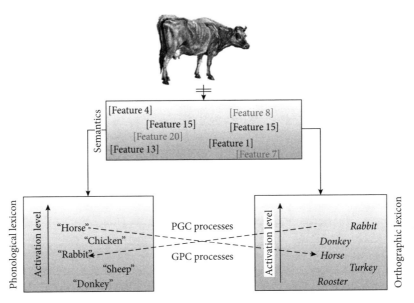

Figure 22.4 Schematic representation of the mechanisms that allow interactions between phonological and orthographic representations in a picture naming task. Semantic impairment is indicated by the lighter color of some semantic features corresponding to the stimulus.

subject E.C.A. (Miceli et al., 1994, 1999). This subject presented with semantic impairment and severe damage to PGC rules (only 9.6% correct responses to nonwords, with mostly unrelated errors), in the face of spared GPC mechanisms (97.4% correct segments in nonword reading). In this case, preserved GPC mechanisms allowed E.C.A. to read aloud 130 words almost flawlessly (0.8% errors). By contrast, impaired semantics and severely damaged PGC processes yielded many semantic paragraphias in writing the same words to dictation (12.3% of total responses). In the course of "repeated naming" tasks using the same words, the occurrence of lexically inconsistent sequences was constrained by the order in which responses had to be produced (Tables 22.5 and 22.6). In spoken, then written naming E.C.A. produced 15.4% lexically inconsistent sequences (e.g., crown → "king," then *throne*). In written, then spoken naming, he systematically produced the same word twice (e.g., hunter → *rifle*, then "rifle"). In this subject, inconsistent responses in spoken, then written naming were allowed by the inability of damaged PGC rules to constrain the selection of the orthographic form corresponding to the just-produced phonological form, whereas in the reverse task these sequences were blocked by functional GPC processes. Interestingly, this case also shows that lexical interaction is bidirectional; in output processes, there is not only (nonobligatory) phonological mediation but also, counterintuitively, (nonobligatory) orthographic mediation.

To conclude this section, observations from brain-damaged subjects suggest that the role of sublexical conversion procedures is not restricted to "transcoding" tasks, that is, to tasks that require converting a phonological input into an orthographic output (writing to dictation) or the reverse process (reading aloud). Available data suggest that they operate in all tasks requiring the retrieval of phonological or orthographic lexical forms. PGC and GPC processes output segmental (phonological or orthographic) information that interacts with information retrieved by lexical-semantic mechanisms, thereby facilitating the selection of target wordforms for production. This could be accomplished by "fixing" incomplete lexical knowledge, by boosting the activation level of less-than-optimally activated lexical entries, or by blocking incorrect responses. It is debatable whether these interactions are used under normal conditions, as intact lexical-semantic mechanisms suffice to ensure correct responses in writing and in speech. However, at least under conditions of damage, observations from neurological cases show that sublexical mechanisms play a critical role.

How Many Routes for Writing?

So far, we have assumed a dual-route model, that includes distinct lexical-semantic and sublexical PGC mechanisms. Two basic assumptions of this model are that word writing requires activating semantic knowledge, and that there are no direct,

Table 22.6. Subject E.C.A. (Miceli et al., 1994, 1999): Sequences that result in lexically contrasting responses in the spoken, then written naming task, but not in the reverse (written, then spoken) naming task

	Stimulus	First Response	Second Response
Spoken, then written	MOUSTACHE	+	*beard*
	JACKET	"suit"	+
	CROWN	"king"	*throne*
	HANGER	no response	*suit*
	VIOLIN	+	no response
Written, then spoken	MOUSTACHE	*sideburns*	+
	HUNTER	*rifle*	"rifle"
	CROWN	no response	no response
	HANGER	no response	no response

nonsemantic links between phonological input representations and orthographic output representations (see Figure 22.1).

Three-route models that include direct input-output lexical connections were originally proposed to account for the performance of dyslexic subjects with word comprehension disorders (e.g., Bub, Cancelliere, & Kertesz, 1985; Funnell, 1983; Sartori, Masterson, & Job, 1987; Schwartz, Saffran, & Marin, 1980) who produced correct responses instead of PPEs to irregular words (note that this direct, nonsemantic connection was not motivated independently). More recent cases also purportedly support this view (e.g., Blazely, Coltheart, & Casey, 2005; Cipolotti & Warrington, 1995; Lambon-Ralph, Sage, & Ellis, 1996; Wu, Martin, & Damian, 2002). The hypothesis is challenged by case reports (e.g., Hillis & Caramazza, 1991, 1995; Patterson & Hodges, 1992) showing that in subjects with lexical-semantic impairment and spared GPC procedures, and tested on the same words in all word processing tasks, reading performance was constrained by comprehension; PPEs occurred in response to words for which subjects showed no comprehension, but never in response to words they understood partially. This fact is accommodated more parsimoniously by a "dual route+interaction" model than by a "three-route" model. In fact, on the latter account, one would have to make the additional assumption that by chance, in these subjects direct input-output connections are damaged for just the items they fail to understand, and spared for just the items they understand partially.

"Dual-route+interaction" models also more parsimoniously accommodate other patterns of impairment. For example, they account for semantic paragraphias in writing to dictation by assuming the co-occurrence of damage to semantics or to orthographic lexical forms, with a severe disruption of PGC processes. In the direct-route framework, additional damage to the direct, nonsemantic route must be assumed, again just for the stimuli yielding semantic errors in writing to dictation.

To sum up, there are no compelling reasons to rule out direct, nonsemantic links between phonological and lexical orthographic forms. However, available results are accounted for more parsimoniously by models that do not include such direct links.

Cross-Linguistic Issues

The relative weight of lexical and sublexical mechanisms in various languages has been the object of discussion. In opaque languages like English, it is largely acknowledged that only stored lexical orthographic knowledge ensures accurate word writing. In very transparent languages, however, the possibility has been raised that errorless writing can be accomplished by relying solely on phonological lexical representations and phoneme-grapheme conversion procedures, with little or no role for orthographic lexical representations (see Ardila, 1991, for Spanish).

A strong version of this proposal can be rejected, as there is no evidence that orthographic opacity constrains the organization of the writing system in a major way. In fact, writing disorders consistent with selective damage to either lexical-semantic or to PGC procedures were reported in transparent languages, just as in English (e.g., Iribarren, Jarema, & Lecours, 2001; Luzzi et al., 2003; Miceli et al., 1997, 1999). However, it cannot be ruled out that orthographic transparency may constrain the neurofunctional organization of writing in subtler ways. For example, if word writing relies mostly on lexical mechanisms in opaque languages, but mostly on sublexical processes in transparent languages, the neural organization of writing might differ across languages as a function of their transparency. Even though there are no data on writing, this possibility is partially supported by recent neuroimaging studies suggesting that the very same tasks may involve different neural substrates in languages that differ along psycholinguistically critical dimensions (Jacquemot, Pallier, LeBihan, Dehaene, & Dupoux, 2003; Paulesu et al., 2000; Saur et al., 2009). To elucidate this issue, systematic cross-linguistic investigations are needed.

The Anatomoclinical Correlates of Writing

In the classical literature, the angular gyrus was thought to provide the critical neural substrate for writing (e.g., Déjérine, 1891). More recently, studies on both normal subjects and neurological cases have shown the involvement of a number of left hemisphere structures. In a large subject sample, magnetic resonance data (DWI-PWI) from acute vascular aphasia (<24 hrs from stroke onset) indicate that the ability to write words and nonwords is affected by damage to a large left hemisphere network including areas 37, 40, 22, and probably areas 39 and 44–45 (Philipose et al., 2007). Studies of subjects with selective damage to lexical-semantic mechanisms, or with disproportionate damage to sublexical conversion procedures, are providing increasingly detailed proposals on the anatomical correlates of specific components of the writing system.

The neural underpinnings of orthographic lexical mechanisms were investigated by lesion studies focusing on "surface" or "lexical" agraphia (i.e., on subjects who produce PPEs in response to words, in the face of good-to-normal nonword writing). These studies have drawn increasing attention to left inferior and inferomesial temporo-occipital regions, including Broca's area (BA) 37 (Philipose et al., 2007; Rapcsak & Beeson, 2004; Tsapkini & Rapp, 2010). Consistent evidence was obtained in

an functional magnetic resonance imaging study on normal spellers during a written word generation task (Beeson et al., 2003).

These data must be taken with caution, as they were obtained from subjects with cognitively and/or functionally heterogeneous deficits. As regards cognitive diversity, while D.P.T. (Tsapkini & Rapp, 2010) probably suffered from selective lexical damage (as shown by normal word comprehension), at least two of the eight (25%) subjects in Rapcsak and Beeson (2004), and a number of those studied by Philipose et al. (2007) suffered from semantic damage, which may or may not have been co-occurred with orthographic lexical damage. Thus, the area of greatest overlap in these studies is obtained from lesions observed in subjects with possibly heterogeneous cognitive impairments (selective lexical damage, selective semantic damage, combined semantic and lexical impairment). As for neural heterogeneity, cases were tested in the acute stage (Philipose et al., 2007) or in the chronic stage (Rapcsak & Beeson, 2004) of a vascular disease, or following surgery for the removal of slow-growing, low-grade gliomas (e.g., Gaillard et al., 2007; Tsapkini & Rapp, 2010). Clearly, very different compensatory mechanisms may be at work in these cases. Therefore, whereas data are consistent with an involvement of the fusiform gyrus in word writing, they do not allow clearly establishing its role (e.g., whether it represents orthographic forms, or allows access to orthographic forms stored elsewhere from meaning).

Even though in recent years the role of the angular gyrus has been downplayed, this structure appears to be critical for writing. Case R.G. (Beauvois & Dérouesné, 1979), who had a highly selective loss of orthographic lexical knowledge, presented with damage to the angular gyrus, extending to the inferior longitudinal fasciculus and the posterior part of the middle temporal gyrus. Four cases of "surface dysgraphia" suffered from lesions in the posterior portion of the angular gyrus (Roeltgen & Heilman, 1984). In a group study, angular gyrus damage was associated with disorders affecting both lexical and sublexical mechanisms (Henry, Beeson, Stark, & Rapcsak, 2007).

Prefrontal regions are also involved in word writing. In acute stroke cases with pure agraphia, the functional inactivation (DWI-PWI) of left BA 44, 45, and 6 was associated with orthographic lexical damage, as shown by lexicality and frequency effects in word writing (Hillis et al., 2004). In two cases, damage to the left inferior frontal gyrus and to the prefrontal gyrus resulted in a selective difficulty writing verbs (Hillis, Wytik, Barker, & Caramazza, 2003). The observation that in these cases the functional impairment is restricted to writing suggests that the posterior portion of the left inferior frontal gyrus and the anterior portion of the precentral gyrus may be involved in modality-specific (orthographic) lexical output processes.

To sum up, word writing is affected by damage to a network of left hemisphere structures that includes inferomesial temporo-occipital regions, the angular/supramarginal gyri, and the inferior frontal/premotor gyrus.

The neural underpinnings of PGC procedures were investigated in lesion studies focused on "phonological agraphia" (i.e., on subjects with a disproportionate difficulty writing nonwords as opposed to words). Results stress the role of left perisylvian regions (Alexander, Friedman, Loverso, & Fischer, 1992; Henry et al., 2007; Roeltgen & Heilman, 1984; Shallice, 1981). The putative neural substrate of PGC procedures is distributed over a large left hemisphere region that partially overlaps with the areas involved in word writing, and includes the posterior-inferior frontal gyrus (BA 44/45), the precentral gyrus (BA 4/6), the insula, the superior temporal gyrus/Wernicke's area (BA 22), and the supramarginal gyrus (BA 40) (Rapcsak et al., 2009; see also Roeltgen & Heilman, 1984). Interestingly, none of these studies showed an involvement of inferomesial temporo-occipital structures.

Also these data must be taken cautiously, for at least two reasons. In the first place, subjects with selective PGC damage are extremely rare (only 1 case in the 31-subject series by Rapcsak et al., 2009). Therefore, studies typically include subjects who fare significantly better on words than on nonwords, but who nonetheless make errors also on words. Consequently, these areas might be involved in the segmental assembly of graphemes (a stage common to word and pseudoword writing), rather than in PGC processes per se. In addition, the putative neural substrate for sublexical processes is identified by overimposing the lesions of subjects whose performance may result from damage to a variety of nonword processing stages (auditory/phonological input processing, phonological working memory, phonological/orthographic parsing mechanisms, damage to PGC procedures in the strict sense).

To sum up, studies on the anatomical correlates of lexical and of sublexical processes are beginning to shed light on the neural underpinnings of writing processes, emphasizing the role of left perisylvian regions in sublexical processes, and that of left perisylvian and extrasylvian (temporomesial) areas in word writing.

Using Neuroimaging Data to Understand the Cognitive Architecture of Reading/Writing Processes

Models of reading and writing maintain contrasting views on the representation of the lexical knowledge used in the two tasks (Figure 22.5). On one view (the *shared components* hypothesis), the same orthographic and phonological representations are shared by the two processes (e.g., Allport & Funnell, 1981; Behrmann & Bub, 1992;

(a) The *shared components* hypothesis. The same phonological and orthographic representations are used for writing to dictation and reading aloud. Solid lines represent the links used during the writing process; dotted lines represent the links used during the reading process.

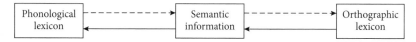

(b) The *independent components* hypothesis. Solid lines represent the representations and links used during the writing process; dotted lines represent the representations and links used during the reading process.

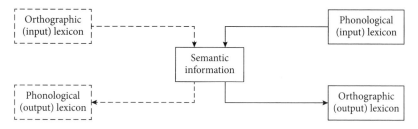

Figure 22.5 Schematic representation of the (a) *shared components* and (b) *independent components* hypothesis.

Coltheart & Funnell, 1987). On another view (the *independent components* hypothesis), independent input and output orthographic (as well as phonological) lexical components are needed to read and write (Ellis, 1982; Patterson & Shewell, 1986). Recent studies on reading and writing have revived the debate on this issue.

Neuroimaging studies suggest that a portion of the left mid-fusiform gyrus (the so-called visual wordform area) provides the critical substrate for input lexical processes in writing (Cohen et al, 2000; but for a contrasting interpretation of the data, see Price & Devlin, 2003). Consistent with this view, lesions in visual wordform area are associated with letter-by-letter reading (i.e., with a disorder characterized by slowed reading), in which response time increases linearly as a function of the number of letters in the to-be-read stimulus (e.g., Cohen et al., 2003, 2004; Damasio & Damasio, 1983; Gaillard et al., 2006). Data on the anatomical correlates of dysgraphia provide an interesting complement to this observation, as they suggest that the same regions may be critical for the stages of writing that require the availability of orthographic wordforms (e.g., Beeson et al., 2003; Philipose et al., 2007; Rapcsak & Beeson, 2004; Rapcsak et al., 2009; Tsapkini & Rapp, 2010).

Lesion studies focused on sublexical conversion impairments in reading and writing after brain damage yield similar results, as they typically document comparable disorders in nonword reading and writing. In a recent group study (Rapcsak et al., 2009) individual performance in the two tasks was compatible with damage to core phonological knowledge for 30 of 31 subjects; and in another study (Philipose et al., 2007) inactivation in BA 37 and 40 consistently resulted in co-occurring damage to words and nonwords, in reading and in writing. Data from neuroimaging studies in cognitively unimpaired participants are consistent with this possibility, as they show the same regions to be involved in phonological processing (Demonet et al., 1992; Paulesu, Frith & Frackowiak, 1993; Price, Moore, Humphreys, & Wise, 1997).

Support for a shared neural substrate for writing and reading comes from a neuroimaging study of normal spellers (Rapp & Lipka, 2011). In this study, a spelling task activated the mid-fusiform gyrus, the inferior frontal gyrus/junction, the superior frontal gyrus/sulcus, and the posterior superior temporal gyrus/sulcus in the left hemisphere, and the right anterior cingulate cortex. Of these areas, the left mid-fusiform, the left inferior frontal gyrus/sulcus, and the right anterior cingulate cortex were activated (more extensively than during spelling) also by a silent reading task.

Even though at face value these observations support the *shared components* hypothesis, observations of dissociated performance in reading as opposed to writing invite to exert caution in interpreting the previous results. A complete review of the contrasting evidence is beyond the scope of the present chapter. Some examples will suffice here. Case R.G. (Beauvois & Dérouesné, 1979, 1981) presented with phonological alexia and surface dysgraphia. He read aloud words correctly but made PPEs in word writing; and, he wrote nonwords to dictation without errors, but fared very poorly in reading aloud nonwords. One of the cases in Rapcsak et al. (2009) showed impaired PGC procedures and fully normal GPC procedures, whereas the reverse pattern was documented in A.M.P. (Iribarren et al., 2001). As regards the reading disorder associated with PPEs in writing, very different patterns were reported in the subjects described by Rapcsak & Beeson (2004), who mostly produced visually related incorrect responses (as opposed to PPEs), and the subject described by Tsapkini & Rapp (2010), who presented with letter-by-letter reading.

To sum up, observations are broadly consistent with both the *shared components* and the *independent components* hypothesis. The *shared components* hypothesis accounts smoothly for co-occurring impairments (e.g., for surface dyslexia and dysgraphia; for phonological alexia and agraphia). In the face of dissociated impairments, it assumes that representations themselves are spared, but that access/output mechanisms are selectively affected, and therefore are responsible for the observed dissociations (e.g., spared PGC in the presence of damaged GPC, or vice versa; spared word reading in the face of PPEs in word writing; modality-specific grammatical class effects; letter-by-letter reading in the presence of fully normal writing). The *independent components* hypothesis is more redundant, as it assumes distinct input and output lexical representations for both orthography and phonology. Therefore, it easily accounts for dissociated impairments, and accommodates parallel, co-occurring deficits by assuming that input and output lexical forms, albeit functionally distinct, are nonetheless represented in very close or even partially overlapping neural substrates.

Clearly, the debate is open, and a choice between the two alternative proposals cannot be made at this time. Answers to outstanding questions are unlikely to be provided merely by using increasingly refined technologies to localize and define anatomical damage in brain-lesioned subjects or activations in control subjects engaged in neuroimaging experiments. Progress in the understanding of the neural and functional underpinnings of writing and reading depends on the development of more detailed theories. The *shared components* view will have to provide more detailed hypotheses on the mechanisms involved in accessing orthographic representations. For example, it will have to account for how the same orthographic wordform can be accessed from visual input in reading but from semantic knowledge in writing; or, for how many access procedures must exist to allow impairments that can be specific for modality and for grammatical class. Conversely, the *independent components* hypothesis will have to spell out the properties that putatively distinguish the orthographic (and phonological) representations used for writing from those used for reading.

Conclusions

Writing words and nonwords involves distinct knowledge and processes, represented in at least partly distinct neural substrates. When writing familiar words, stored orthographic representations are retrieved from semantics in a long-term memory store. When a nonword must be spelled, sublexical PGC procedures sequentially assemble the target string. The two sets of mechanisms interact, and selection of the target lexical representation can be jointly constrained by combined semantic and sublexical input. Lexical-semantic processes involved in writing and speaking also interact, and also in this case wordform selection for written and spoken output could result from the interaction between semantic-lexical and sublexical mechanisms. In addition to being functionally separable, lexical and sublexical knowledge and processes are also represented in at least partially separable neural substrates. Left perisylvian and extrasylvian regions, including the inferior frontal/prefrontal, angular, and fusiform gyri, are critical for the processing/representation of orthographic wordforms; a variety of perisylvian structures are crucial for sublexical PGC procedures. The neural substrates involved in writing words and nonwords partially overlap with those involved in reading words and nonwords. Establishing if and to what extent the functional and neural underpinnings of the two processes are shared or autonomous is a central task for future studies.

Notes

1. For the time being, we will assume that semantics is the only source of information that activates word-specific orthographic knowledge stored in the lexicon. Alternative possibilities are discussed later in the chapter. The properties of the semantic component are discussed here only insofar as this component is involved in activating orthographic knowledge. For an extensive discussion, see Vinson, Andrews, and Vigliocco Giving Words Meaning: Why Better Models of Semantics Are Needed in Language Production Research; Leshinskaya and Caramazza Organization and Structure of Conceptual Representations.

2. Together with the fact that some phonemes correspond to >1 grapheme (e.g., /ʃ/, /θ/, /λ/), the observation that PGC rules are sensitive to context and to within-string position is one of the arguments for assuming that an orthographic short-term memory system is necessary for nonword writing.

3. In this latter case, a plausible spelling for the target pseudoword vowel (/ʌ/→ *ou*, as in /tʌtʃ/) corresponds to the orthographic sequence of the priming word.

References

Alajouanine, T., & Lhermitte, F. (1960). Les troubles des activités expressives du langage dans l'aphasie. Leurs relations avec les apraxies. *Revue Neurologique, 102*, 604–629.

Alario, F. X., Schiller, N. O., Domoto-Reilly, K., & Caramazza A. (2003). The role of phonological and orthographic information in lexical selection. *Brain and Language, 84*, 372–398.

Alexander, M. P., Friedman, R. B., Loverso, F., & Fischer, R. S. (1992). Lesion localization in phonological agraphia. *Brain and Language, 43*, 83–95.

Allport, D. A., & Funnell, E. (1981). Components of the mental lexicon. *Philosophical Transactions of the Royal Society of London, Series B, 295*, 397–410.

Ardila, A. (1991). Errors resembling semantic paraphasias in Spanish-speaking aphasics. *Brain and Language, 41*, 437–445.

Assal, G., & Buttet, J. (1981). Dissociations in aphasia: A case report. *Brain and Language, 13*, 223–240.

Badecker, W., Hillis, A. E., & Caramazza, A. (1990). Lexical morphology and its role in the writing process: Evidence from a case of acquired dysgraphia. *Cognition, 35*, 205–243.

Badecker, W., Rapp, B., & Caramazza, A. (1996). Lexical morphology and the two orthographic routes. *Cognitive Neuropsychology, 13*, 161–176.

Barry, C., & De Bastiani, P. (1997). Lexical priming of nonword spelling in the regular orthography of Italian. *Reading and Writing, 9*, 499–517.

Barry,C., & Seymour, P. (1988). Lexical priming and sound-to-spelling contingency effects in nonword spelling. *Quarterly Journal of Experimental Psychology, 40*, 5–40.

Basso, A., Taborelli, A., & Vignolo, L. A. (1978). Dissociated disorders of speaking and writing in aphasia. *Journal of Neurology, Neurosurgery and Psychiatry, 41*, 556–563.

Baxter, D., & Warrington, E. K. (1985). Category specific phonological dysgraphia. *Neuropsychologia, 23*, 653–666.

Baxter, D., & Warrington, E. K.(1987). Transcoding sound to spelling: A single or multiple sound unit correspondence? *Cortex 23*, 11–28.

Beaton, A., Guest, J., & Ved, R. (1997). Semantic errors of naming, reading, writing, and drawing following left-hemisphere infarction. *Cognitive Neuropsychology, 14*, 459–478.

Beauvois, M. F., & Dérouesné, J. (1979). Phonological alexia: Three dissociations. *Journal of Neurology, Neurosurgery, and Psychiatry, 42*, 1115–1124.

Beauvois, M., & Dérouesné, J. (1981). Lexical or orthographic agraphia. *Brain, 104*, 21–49.

Beeson, P. M., Rapcsak, S. Z., Plante, E., Chargualaf, J., Chung, A., Johnson, S., & Troiard, T. (2003). The neural substrates of writing: A functional magnetic resonance study. *Aphasiology, 17*, 647–665.

Behrmann, M., & Bub, D. (1992). Surface dyslexia and dysgraphia: Dual routes, single lexicon. *Cognitive Neuropsychology 8*, 209–251.

Benson, F. (1979). Agraphia. In K. M. Heilman & E. Valenstein (Eds.), *Clinical neuropsychology* (pp. 22–58). Oxford: Oxford University Press.

Blazely, A. M., Coltheart, M., & Casey, B. J. (2005). Semantic impairment with and without surface dyslexia: Implications for models of reading. *Cognitive Neuropsychology, 22*, 695–717.

Brown, J. V. (1972). *Aphasia, apraxia and agnosia*. Springfield, IL: Charles C. Thomas.

Bub, D., Cancelliere, A., & Kertesz, A. (1985). Whole-word and analytic translation of spelling-to-sound in a non-semantic reader. In K. E. Patterson, J. C. Marshall, & M. Coltheart (Eds.), *Surface dyslexia* (pp. 15–34). London: Lawrence Erlbaum Associates.

Bub, D., & Kertesz, A. (1982a). Evidence for lexicographic processing in a patient with preserved written over oral single word naming. *Brain, 105*, 697–717.

Bub, D., & Kertesz, A. (1982b). Deep agraphia. *Brain and Language, 17*, 146–165.

Campbell, R. (1983). Writing nonwords to dictation. *Brain and Language, 19*, 153–178.

Caramazza, A., & Hillis, A. E. (1990). Where do semantic errors come from? *Cortex, 26*, 95–122.

Caramazza, A., & Hillis, A. E. (1991). Lexical organization of nouns and verbs in the brain. *Nature, 349*, 788–790.

Caramazza, A., Miceli, G., & Villa, G. (1986). The role of the (output) phonological buffer in reading, writing, and repetition. *Cognitive Neuropsychology, 3*, 37–76.

Ciaghi, M., Pancheri, E., & Miceli, G. (2010). Semantic paralexias: A group study on the underlying functional mechanisms, incidence and clinical features in a consecutive series of 340 Italian aphasics. *Brain and Language, 115*, 121–132.

Cipolotti, L., & Warrington, E. K. (1995). Semantic memory and reading abilities: A case report. *Journal of the International Neuropsychological Society, 1*, 104–110.

Cohen, L., Dehaene, S., Naccache, L., Lehericy, S., Dehaene-Lambertz, G., Henaff, M. A., & Michel, F. (2000). The visual word form area: Spatial and temporal characterization of an initial stage of reading in normal subjects and posterior split-brain patients. *Brain, 123*, 291–307.

Cohen, L., Henry, C., Dehaene, S., Martinaud, O., Lehericy, S., Lemer, C., & Ferrieux, S. (2004). The pathophysiology of letter-by-letter reading. *Neuropsychologia, 42*, 1768–1780.

Cohen, L., Martinaud, O., Lemer, C., Léhéricy, S., Samson, Y., Obadia, M., Slachevsky, A., & Dehaene, S. (2003). Visual word recognition in the left and right hemispheres: Anatomical and functional correlates of peripheral alexias. *Cerebral Cortex, 13*, 1313–1333.

Coltheart, M., & Funnell, E. (1987). Reading and writing: One lexicon or two? In D. A. Allport, D. McKay, W. Prinz, & E. Scheerer (Eds.), *Language perception and production: Common processes in listening, speaking, reading, and writing* (pp. 313–339). London: Academic Press.

Coltheart, M., Patterson, K. E., & Marshall, J. C. (1980). *Deep dyslexia*. London: Routledge & Kegan Paul.

Damasio, A. R., & Damasio, H. (1983). The anatomic basis of pure alexia. *Neurology, 33*, 1573–1583.

de Partz, M. P. (1986). Re-education of a deep dyslexic patient: Rationale of the method and results. *Cognitive Neuropsychology, 3*, 149–178.

Déjérine, J. (1891). Sur un cas de cécité verbale avec agraphi.e., suivi d'autopsie. *Comptes Rendus Hebdomadaires del Séances et Mémoires del al Société de Biologie. Ninth series, 3*, 197–201.

Demonet, J. -F., Chollet, F., Ramsay, S., Cardebat, D., Nespoulous, J. L., Wise, R. J. S., Rascol, A., & Frackowiak, R. S. J. (1992). The anatomy of phonological and semantic processing in normal subjects. *Brain, 115*, 1753–1768.

Ellis, A. W. (1982). Spelling and writing (and reading and speaking). In A.W. Ellis (Ed.) *Normality and pathology in cognitive functions* (pp. 113–146). London: Academic Press.

Ellis, A., Miller, D., & Sin, G. (1983). Wernicke's aphasia and normal language processing: A case study in cognitive neuropsychology. *Cognition, 15*, 111–144.

Folk, J., & Jones, A. (2004). The purpose of lexical-sublexical interaction during spelling: Further evidence from dysgraphia and articulatory suppression. *Neurocase, 10*, 65–69.

Folk, J., & Rapp, B. (2004). Interaction of lexical and sublexical information in spelling: Further evidence from nonword priming. *Applied Psycholinguistics, 25*, 565–585.

Folk, J., Rapp, B., & Goldrick, M. (2002). The interaction of lexical and sublexical information in spelling: What's the point? *Cognitive Neurospsychology, 19*, 653–671.

Funnell, E. (1983). Phonological processes in reading: New evidence from acquired dyslexia. *British Journal of Psychology, 74*, 159–180.

Gaillard, R., Naccache, L., Pinel, P., Clémenceau, S.,Volle, E., Hasboun, D., Dupont, S., … Cohen, L. (2006). Direct intracranial, fMRI, and lesion evidence for the causal role of left inferotemporal cortex in reading. *Neuron, 50*, 191–204.

Goodman, R., & Caramazza, A. (1986). Aspects of the spelling process: Evidence from a case of acquired dysgraphia. *Language and Cognitive Processes 1*, 263–296.

Hanna, R. R., Hannah, J. S., Hodges, R. E., & Rudorf, E. H. (1966). *Phoneme-grapheme correspondences as cues to spelling improvement*. U.S. Department of Health, Education and Welfare. Office of Education, Washington, DC: US Government Printing Office.

Hatfield, F., & Patterson, K. E. (1983). Phonological spelling. *Quarterly Journal of Experimental Psychology, 35*, 451–458.

Henry, M. L., Beeson, P. M., Stark, A. J., & Rapcsak, S. Z. (2007). The role of left perisylvian cortical regions in spelling. *Brain and Language, 100*, 44–52.

Hier, D. B., & Mohr, J. P. (1977). Incongruous oral and written naming. *Brain and Language, 4*, 115–126.

Hillis, A. E., & Caramazza, A. (1991). Mechanisms for accessing lexical representations for output: Evidence from a category-specific semantic deficit. *Brain and Language, 40*, 106–144.

Hillis, A. E., & Caramazza, A. (1995). Converging evidence for the interaction of semantic and sublexical phonological information in accessing lexical representations for spoken output. *Cognitive Neuropsychology, 12*, 187–227.

Hillis, A. E., Chang, S., Breese, E., & Heidler, J. (2004). The crucial role of posterior frontal regions in modality specific components of the spelling process. *Neurocase, 10,* 175–187.

Hillis, A. E., Rapp, B., & Caramazza, A. (1999). When a rose is a rose in speech but a tulip in writing. *Cortex, 35,* 337–356.

Hillis, A. E., Tuffiash, E., & Caramazza, A. (2002). Modality-specific deterioration in naming verbs in non-fluent primary progressive aphasia. *Journal of Cognitive Neuroscience, 14,* 1099–1108.

Hillis, A. E., Wytik, R. J., Barker, P. B., & Caramazza, A. (2003). Neural regions essential for writing verbs. *Nature Neuroscience, 6,* 19–20.

Iribarren, I. C., Jarema, G., & Lecours, A. R. (2001). Two different dysgraphic syndromes in a regular orthography, Spanish. *Brain and Language, 77,* 166–175, 2001.

Jacquemot, C., Pallier, C., LeBihan, D., Dehaene, S., & Dupoux, E. (2003). Phonological grammar shapes the auditory cortex: A functional magnetic resonance imaging study. *The Journal of Neuroscience, 23,* 9541–9546.

Laiacona, M., Capitani, E., Zonca, G., Scola, I., Saletta, P., & Luzzatti, C. (2009). Integration of lexical and sublexical processing in the spelling of regular words: A multiple single-case study in Italian dysgraphic patients. *Cortex, 45,* 804–815.

Lambon-Ralph, M. A., Sage, K., & Ellis, A. W. (1996). Word meaning blindness: A new form of acquired dyslexia. *Cognitive Neuropsychology, 13,* 617–640.

Langmore, S. E., & Canter, G. J. (1983). Written spelling deficit of Broca's aphasics. *Brain and Language, 18,* 293–314.

Lhermitte, F., & Dérouesné, J. (1974). Paraphasies et jargonaphasie dans le langage oral avec conservation du langage écrit. *Revue Neurologique, 130,* 21–38.

Lichtheim, L. (1885). On aphasia. *Brain, 7,* 433–485.

Luria, A. (1966). *Higher cortical functions in man.* New York: Basic Books.

Luzzi, S., Bartolini, M., Coccia, M., Provinciali, L., Piccirilli, M., & Snowden, J. S. (2003). Surface dysgraphia in a regular orthography: Apostrophe use by an Italian writer. *Neurocase, 9,* 285–296.

Marshall, J. C., Newcombe, F. (1973). Patterns of paralexia. *Journal of Psycholinguistic Research, 2,* 175–199.

Miceli, G., Benvegnù, B., Capasso, R., & Caramazza, A. (1997). The independence of phonological and orthographic lexical forms: Evidence from aphasia. *Cognitive Neuropsychology, 14,* 35–69.

Miceli, G., & Capasso, R. (1997). Semantic errors as evidence for the independence and the interaction of orthographic and phonological forms. *Language and Cognitive Processes, 12,* 733–764.

Miceli, G., Capasso, R., & Caramazza, A. (1994). The interaction of lexical and sublexical processes in reading, writing and repetition. *Neuropsychologia, 32,* 317–333.

Miceli, G., Capasso, R., & Caramazza, A. (1999). Sublexical conversion procedures and the interaction of phonological and orthographic lexical forms. *Cognitive Neuropsychology, 16,* 557–572.

Morton, J. (1969). The interaction of information in word recognition. *Psychological Review, 76,* 165–178.

Nolan, K. A., & Caramazza, A. (1983). An analysis of writing in a case of deep dyslexia. *Brain and Language, 20,* 305–328.

Patterson, K. (1986). Lexical but nonsemantic spelling? *Cognitive Neuropsychology, 3,* 341–367.

Patterson, K., & Hodges, J. R. (1992). Deterioration of word meaning: Implications for reading. *Neuropsychologia, 30,* 1025–1040.

Patterson, K. E., Marshall, J. C., & Coltheart, M. (1985). *Surface dyslexia.* London: Lawrence Erlbaum Associates.

Patterson, K. E., & Shewell, C. (1986). Speak and spell: Dissociations and word-class effects. In M. Coltheart, G. Sartori, & R. Job (Eds.), *The cognitive neuropsychology of language* (pp. 273–294). London: Lawrence Erlbaum.

Paulesu, E., Frith, C. D., & Frackowiak, R. S. J. (1993). The neural correlates of the verbal component of working memory. *Nature, 362,* 342–345.

Paulesu, E., McCrory, E., Fazio, F., Menoncello, L., Brunswick, N., Cappa, S. F., Cotelli, M., ... Frith, U. (2000). A cultural effect on brain function. *Nature Neuroscience, 3,* 91–96.

Philipose, L. E., Gottesman, R. F., Newhart, M., Kleinman, J. T., Herskovits, E. H., Pawlak, M. A., Marsh, E. B., ... Hillis, A. E. (2007). Neural regions essential for reading and spelling of words and pseudowords. *Annals of Neurology, 62,* 481–492.

Price, C. J., & Devlin, J. T. (2003). The myth of the visual word form area. *Neuroimage, 19,* 473–481.

Price, C. J., Moore, C. J., Humphreys, G. W., & Wise, R. J. S. (1997). Segregating semantic from phonological processes during reading. *Journal of Cognitive Neuroscience, 9,* 727–733.

Rapcsak, S. Z., & Beeson, P. M. (2004) The role of left posterior inferior temporal cortex in spelling. *Neurology, 62,* 2221–2229.

Rapcsak, S. Z., Beeson, P. M., Henry, M. L., Leyden, A., Kim, E., Rising, K., Andersen, S., & Cho, H. (2009). Phonological dyslexia and dysgraphia: Cognitive mechanisms and neural substrates. *Cortex, 45,* 575–591.

Rapp, B., Benzing, L., & Caramazza, A. (1997). The autonomy of lexical ortography. *Cognitive Neurospsychology, 14,* 71–104

Rapp, B., & Caramazza, A. (1998). A case of selective difficulty in writing verbs. *Neurocase, 4,* 127–140.

Rapp, B., & Caramazza, A. (2002). Selective difficulties with spoken nouns and written verbs: A single case study. *Journal of Neurolinguistics, 15,* 373–402.

Rapp, B., Epstein, C., & Tainturier, M. J. (2002). The integration of information across lexical and sublexical processes in spelling. *Cognitive Neurospsychology, 19,* 1–29.

Rapp, B., & Lipka, K. (2011). The literate brain: The relationship between spelling and reading. *Journal of Cognitive Neuroscience, 23,* 1180–1197.

Roeltgen, D. P., & Heilman, K. M. (1984). Lexical agraphia: Further support for the two-system of linguistic agraphia. *Brain, 107,* 811–827.

Roeltgen, D. P., Rothi, L., & Heilman, K. M. (1986). Linguistic semantic agraphia: A dissociation of the lexical spelling system from semantics. *Brain and Language, 27,* 257–280.

Roeltgen, D. P., Sevush, R., & Heilman, K. M. (1983). Phonological agraphia: Writing by the lexical-semantic route. *Neurology, 33,* 755–765.

Sanders, R., & Caramazza, A. (1990). Operation of phoneme-to-grapheme conversion mechanism in a brain injured patient. *Reading and Writing, 2,* 61–82.

Sartori, G., Masterson, J., & Job, R. (1987). Direct route reading and the locus of lexical decision. In M. Coltheart, G. Sartori, & R. Job (Eds.), *Cognitive neuropsychology of language* (pp. 59–78). London: Lawrence Erlbaum Associates.

Saur, D., Baumagaertner, A., Moehring, A., Buchel, C., Bonnesen, M., Rose, M., Musso, M., & Meisel, J. M. (2009). Word order processing in the bilingual brain. *Neuropsychologia, 47,* 158–168.

Schwartz, M. F., Saffran, E., & Marin, O. S. M. (1980). Fractionating the reading process in dementia: Evidence for word-specific print-to-sound associations. In M. Coltheart, K. E. Patterson, & J. C. Marshall (Eds.), *Deep dyslexia* (pp. 259–269). London: Routledge & Kegan Paul.

Shallice, T. (1981). Phonological agraphia and lexical route in writing. *Brain, 104*, 413–429.

Southwood, M. H., & Chatterjee, A. (2001). The simultaneous activation hypothesis: Explaining recovery from deep to phonological dyslexia. *Brain and Language, 76*, 18–34.

Tsapkini, K., & Rapp, B. (2010). The orthography-specific functions of the left fusiform gyrus: Evidence of modality and category specificity. *Cortex, 46*, 185–205.

Van Orden, G. C., Johnston, J. C., & Hale, B. L. (1988). Word identification in reading proceeds from spelling to sound to meaning. *Journal of Experimental Psychology: Learning, Memory, and Cognition, 14*, 371–386.

Wernicke, C. (1886). Nervenheilkunde: Die neueren Arbeiten uber Aphasie. *Fortschritte der Medizin, 4*, 463–482.

Wu, D. H., Martin, R. C., & Damian, M. F. (2002). A third route for reading? Implications from a case of phonological dyslexia. *Neurocase, 8*, 274–293.

The Structure of Sign Languages

Gaurav Mathur *and* Christian Rathmann

Abstract

To understand the relationship between linguistic structure and modality, this chapter surveys the structure of sign languages at several levels of grammar, using the contrasting themes of sequentiality and simultaneity as a focus. Signs can be sequenced on the basis of phonological properties, such as handshape, orientation, and location, which are bundled simultaneously and co-occur with movement. Examples of both sequential and simultaneous morphology abound that have parallels in spoken languages. In addition, sign languages display a unique type of simultaneous morphology that requires interaction with gestural space. The use of gestural space to provide cohesion to the discourse and the simultaneous use of the two manual articulators to produce portions of syntax and discourse seem unique to sign languages. Such properties that are unique to the signed modality must be accounted for by models of language production that seek to cover both modalities.

Key Words: modality, sign language, sequentiality, simultaneity, phonology, morphology, syntax, discourse, gestural space

Introduction

This chapter examines the structure of sign languages, focusing on concepts that language scientists from different disciplines can use to understand the production of sign languages. Sign languages are of special interest, because they occur in a different modality than spoken languages. To date, the bulk of linguistic research has been on the structure of spoken languages and has uncovered many universal properties. The question is whether these universal properties can be attributed to linguistic structure alone, or whether they are due to the auditory-vocal modality of spoken languages. It is only by comparing spoken languages with sign languages that we can begin to distinguish the effects of structure from the effects of modality.

Although spoken and signed languages invoke different perceptual and articulatory systems, Meier (2002) notes two other important ways that spoken and signed languages are different. Sign languages have "greater potential...for iconic and/or indexic representation" by taking advantage of the gestural space in front of the signer (p. 6). For example, whereas a spoken language might use a pronoun to refer to an entity mentioned earlier in discourse, a sign language would achieve the same function by pointing directly to a location in the empty area in front of the signer's body, the same location that has been associated with the entity earlier in discourse.

The other difference Meier (2002) mentions is the relative youth of sign languages. Some sign languages, such as American Sign Language (ASL) and British Sign Language (BSL), are well-documented, but even their recorded history only goes as far back as two or three centuries, whereas most spoken languages have much longer histories. Moreover, there are unique demographic characteristics of the deaf community that affect the transmission of sign languages differently than spoken languages, as detailed by the collection of papers in Brentari (2010). Most speakers acquire spoken languages from infancy from people who are native speakers themselves, but that scenario occurs only for a small percentage of deaf signers. Just 5–10 percent of the deaf population is born to parents who are deaf (Mitchell & Karchmer, 2004) and acquires a sign language as a first language. The rest of the deaf signers acquire sign language later, usually when they enter a school for the deaf or meet deaf peers later in life. Mayberry (1993) has shown this late acquisition of a first language to be different from the acquisition of a second language, and it is possible that the late acquisition of sign language in each successive generation of deaf signers may affect the evolution of the sign language in a way that is not seen with spoken languages (Rathmann & Mathur, 2002).

The next question is how these cross-modal differences can impact linguistic structure. Meier (2002) entertains several possibilities. One possibility is that the impact is not much, because sign and spoken languages do share several properties in common, such as syntactic structure, productive morphology, and conventional vocabularies. In addition, they both display duality of patterning, that is the linguistic signal is divisible into discrete units (words), which can be arranged in multiple ways to produce different sentences and that themselves can be divided into smaller units (segments) that can be recombined to produce other units. Other related possibilities are that modality does not directly affect structure but could lead to statistical tendencies, major typological types, or limited variation. For example, the visual-gestural modality may lend itself naturally to a higher frequency of iconic lexical items in sign languages. The same modality may also lead to a typological bias for nonconcatenative morphology, whereas the auditory-vocal modality favors concatenative morphology. Alternatively, the visual-modality may just constrain the possibilities for structure, because the available research on various sign languages suggests that sign languages are more uniform than spoken languages with respect to certain properties, such as verb agreement (Newport & Supalla, 2000). The last possibility is that modality does affect structure and leads to specific rules and typological patterns, such as the systematic lack of the grammatical distinction between second and third person. This pattern seems unique to sign languages due to the fact that pronominal systems in sign languages interact with gestural space.

A common theme that runs through these possible modality effects is the tension between simultaneity and sequentiality. Stokoe (1960) notes that signs in ASL can be analyzed in terms of what he called "cheremes," namely, handshape, location, and movement, all of which co-occur simultaneously. He contrasts this situation with phonemes in spoken languages, which are arranged linearly. Liddell (1984) and Liddell and Johnson (1986) challenge this point and argue that segments exist in sign languages, and that they are ordered linearly, just as in spoken languages. Moreover, words and sentences are conveyed sequentially in both spoken and sign languages. Thus, the presence of sequentiality in linguistic structure is not unique to a particular modality.

However, it remains debatable whether each modality allows different possibilities for simultaneity. Klima and Bellugi (1979) highlight the simultaneous (nonconcatenative) nature of morphology in sign languages, whereas concatenative morphology seems more common in spoken languages. The volume by Vermeerbergen, Leeson, and Crasborn (2007) offers a more recent collection of papers examining other types of simultaneous constructions that appear unique to sign languages. Yet, spoken languages also display a wide range of simultaneous constructions. For example, the simultaneous combination of distinctive features into articulatory bundles and the coexistence of autosegmental tiers are comparable with Stokoe's (1960) "cheremes" for signs.

The rest of this chapter explores the tension between sequentiality and simultaneity at several levels of grammar: phonetics and phonology; lexicon and morphology; and finally, syntax and discourse. By examining the tension between sequential and simultaneous structure at different levels, we can begin to understand the relationship between modality and linguistic structure.

Phonetics and Phonology

The first levels of grammar to be considered are phonetics and phonology, which have to do with the sublexical structure, focusing on the smallest (meaningless) units that can be recombined to create words. The section first discusses examples of simultaneity in sign languages at these levels and then turns to instances of sequentiality.

Simultaneous Structure

Stokoe (1960), and later, Stokoe, Casterline, and Croneberg (1965), find, on the basis of minimal pairs, that signs can be broken down into the parameters of handshape, location, and movement. Battison (1978) argues for the addition of orientation as a fourth parameter, also based on minimal pairs, and some sign language researchers consider nonmanuals to be a fifth parameter (we come back to this particular parameter in the section on syntax and discourse). Evidence for the distinctness of these parameters comes from phonological processes and well-formedness conditions making reference only to one of the parameters and psycholinguistic (experimental) studies, which suggest the influence of a particular parameter on the task. A well-formed sign must have a complete specification for each of these parameters, all of which are produced simultaneously. We now discuss each parameter in turn, considering the possible values for the parameter. What follows is based on a composite of Liddell and Johnson (1989), Sandler (1989), van der Hulst (1993), and Brentari (1998), among other studies of sign language phonology, and unless otherwise specified, all the examples below come from ASL.

The handshape refers to the configuration of the hand and can be defined with respect to finger selection and finger configuration. Finger selection refers to the set of fingers that are prominent in a handshape. Some handshapes select one finger (THINK, DAY), whereas other handshapes select all the fingers (KNOW, SCHOOL) and yet other handshapes select other combinations of fingers. Finger selection usually does not change through a sign (Mandel, 1981), except in compounds (SHOCKED) and lexicalized fingerspelling loans from another language (J-O-B).[1] Finger configuration refers to whether the selected fingers are flexed or extended from the various knuckles. For example, in KNOW and THINK, the selected fingers are flat (i.e., extended with respect to all knuckles), whereas in COOKIE and DOUBT, the fingers are crooked (i.e., the fingers are partially flexed at the knuckles), and in SUPPORT and YES, the fingers are completely closed.

The next parameter, orientation, has been proposed to be another sublexical element of the sign, because there are minimal pairs with respect to orientation (e.g., STOP vs. AVERAGE and CHILDREN vs. THING). Orientation can be described in absolute terms (i.e., it can be defined as the direction in which the palm faces or in which the fingertip are pointing). For example, the palm is supine in THING, prone in CHILD, and facing to the side in TRUE. Orientation can also be defined relatively, in terms of the relationship between a part of the hand and a location on the body. In WARN, the fingerpads of the dominant hand contact the back of the nondominant hand; this relationship fixes the orientation of both hands in most cases.

Next on the list of parameters is location. A sign can be made at one of the following major locations: the head (THINK, FATHER); the neck (THIRSTY, PRIEST); the trunk (FEEL, HEART); the nondominant arm (IMPROVE, PUNISH); the nondominant hand (NICE, BOTHER); or neutral space, that is, the empty space in front of the signer (AWFUL, THROW). Moreover, each major location can be further specified with settings like "contralateral" (on the side opposite to the dominant hand) versus "ipsilateral" (on the same side as the dominant hand) (HEART vs. CANADA, which are made on the respective sides of the trunk) and "high" versus "low" (CONGRESS vs. NAVY, which are made at the top and the bottom of the trunk, respectively). Native signs are usually produced with one or two settings within a single major location.

Movement is possibly the most salient part of the sign and refers to the movement of the hands to or from locations. Movement can be described in articulatory terms (i.e., in terms of the joints of the arm/hand, such as the shoulder, the elbow, the wrist, and the knuckles). For example, MORNING involves the flexion of the arm at the elbow, whereas DRIVE involves extending the arm from the elbow. Movement can also be described in perceptual terms, which make reference to visual properties, such as the shape of the line traced by the hand (Brentari, 1998). The signs DAY and MORNING have arc-like movement, whereas YEAR and WORLD have circular movement and LIE and MAJOR have straight movement.

In addition to these parameters, signs are described in terms of whether they use one hand or both. The ability to use both hands in the production of a sign is a unique feature of the visual-manual modality. Battison (1978) observes that if a sign uses both hands, the two hands may be symmetrical with respect to all the parameters (as in ROW), or they may have an asymmetrical relationship (as in OWE), in which the two hands may have different handshapes, but the nondominant hand stays in place and is restricted to a small set of unmarked handshapes, whereas the dominant hand moves to, on, or from the nondominant hand.

Sequential Structure

The examples thus far show that signs can be formed from the simultaneous combination of handshape, orientation, location, and movement.

However, there are many examples where there is more than one specification for a parameter. For example, in SEND, the handshape changes from a closed fist to an open hand, and in FLOWER, the hand moves between the two nostrils. Then, there are signs with two movement patterns, such as CANCEL, which moves the extended index finger of the dominant hand diagonally across the palm of the nondominant hand in a crossing manner.

These examples have led Liddell (1984) and Liddell and Johnson (1989) to argue that signs have sequential structure in addition to simultaneous structure. Although there have been subsequent versions of their Hold-Move model for representing the structure of signs, this section considers the original version for the sake of simplicity. In this model, there are two types of segments, Holds and Movements. Hold (H) segments are defined as periods of time during which all aspects of the articulatory bundle are in a steady state ("posture"), whereas Movement (M) segments are characterized by a change in one or more of its articulatory features ("activity"). Each segment contains articulatory features that describe the current state of the hand: where the posture of the hand is, how it is oriented, and how its own moveable parts are configured. The change in articulatory specifications may occur in hand configuration (UNDERSTAND), orientation (DEAD), or location (CONGRESS). The H and M segments can be said to constitute the sequential structure of signs, whereas simultaneity is captured through the bundles of features associated with the segments. Liddell and Johnson (1989) is not the only model for representing the structure of signs sequentially; there have been other models, such as Sandler (1989), van der Hulst (1993), and Brentari (1998).

Sequentiality is seen not only between the segments of a sign (or sublexical units depending on the particular model assumed) but also between signs themselves. Brentari, Poizner, and Kegl (1995) present evidence that there is a distinction between intrasign movement and intersign movement with respect to their temporal properties. Signs may involve a sequence of handshapes as pointed out earlier; handshapes may also change between signs, because each sign has a different handshape. Brentari et al. (1995) measured the time it took to produce the sign-internal handshape change relative to the time for the whole sign and found that the ratio was roughly one-on-one. However, when they measured the ratio of the time for handshape change between signs to the time between signs, they found that the handshape change was made in the first 30–40 percent of the intersign interval. In other words, within signs, handshape changes unfold during the whole length of the sign, but between signs, handshape changes unfold much more rapidly and before the noticeable beginning of the second sign.

Moreover, several studies suggest that signers draw on phonological cues in segmenting the continuous input into a sequence of signs. In one experimental study in ASL (Brentari, 2006), signers depended on the locations and movement of the nonce signs to make word segmentation judgments; signers also used the handshapes of the signs, but to a lesser extent. These findings suggest that signers use a word-sized unit to parse the stream into discrete signs. Orfanidou, Adam, Morgan, and McQueen (2010) reach a similar conclusion for BSL in a sign-spotting study: the signers recognized real BSL signs more easily when they were embedded within phonologically possible nonce signs than within phonologically impossible nonce signs.

In sum, sign languages display both simultaneity and sequentiality at the levels of phonetics and phonology, just as in spoken languages, even when sign languages draw on a different articulatory system, and even when this articulatory system is unique in having two major articulators. The similarities between sign and spoken languages emerge most clearly when they are viewed from a sequential perspective, because words can be segmented into smaller sublexical units, which have different temporal properties than interword intervals, and these phonetic and phonological properties are exploited in segmenting the continuous stream into discrete words.

Lexicon and Morphology

We now turn to the levels of the lexicon and morphology, which deal with the mechanisms for building words. This section first considers examples of sequentiality in the lexicon and morphology of sign languages and then examines the more robust instances of simultaneity at these levels.

Sequential Structure

The combination of morphemes into signs can be sequential, in the sense that each morpheme has a complete set of phonological specifications. That is, each morpheme would have its own specification for handshape, orientation, location, and movement. Here, three representative examples of sequential morphology in sign languages are presented: (1) compounding, (2) affixation, and (3) reduplication.

Compounding forms a new sign by combining two or more existing signs sequentially. In contrast to synthetic compounds, which combines a lexeme with another lexeme and has the ability to keep on adding lexemes, root compounds usually combine two lexemes and are often entered into the dictionary as a new lexeme. Examples from ASL include EAT^MORNING ("breakfast"); LOOK^STRONG ("resemble"); SURE^WORK ("seriously"); and SLEEP+SUNRISE ("oversleep"). These compounds have morphological integrity such that they cannot be broken apart by other phrases. Thus, EAT^MORNING cannot be split by the expression "five o'clock," as in *EAT^FIVE^MORNING. The original morphemes of a compound can lose their original phonological form over time so that they fuse into a single lexeme and are no longer identifiable. For example, the ASL sign TOMATO looks like a simple sign, with a single specification for each parameter. However, when older versions of the sign are considered, the signs for RED and SLICE can be discerned. For further discussion of compounds, see Klima and Bellugi (1979) and Sandler (1989).

The other instances of sequential morphology, affixation and reduplication, are exemplified in (1a) and (1b) respectively.

(1) a. Prefixes (Aronoff, Meir, Padden, & Sandler, 2003)

Israeli Sign Language (ISL)	EYE+SHARP = DISCERN
	EYE+HOLE = SPITE
Suffixes:	
ASL:	SAME+ZERO "can't find one like yours"
	TELL+ZERO "not mention"
	TASTE+ZERO "not my type"

b. Reduplication in noun-verb pairs in ASL (Supalla & Newport, 1978)

Verb	*Noun*
SIT	CHAIR
OPEN-BOOK	BOOK
OPEN-DOOR	DOOR

All of the signs in (1a) consist of a root and an affix, and each root and affix has a complete set of phonological specifications. The affixes meet the usual criteria for a derivational affix. For example, EYE in ISL changes the meaning of SHARP to the meaning of "discern" and turns it from an adjective to a verb. The examples in (1b) show that sign languages display morphological reduplication, which can be considered sequential in the sense that the

root is repeated sequentially, albeit in a reduced form. In (1b), there is a systematic alternation between the verbs and the nouns. The verbs describe an activity and involve different kinds of movement, whereas all the nouns describe a thing related to the activity and have reduced and repeated movement. For example, the movement in SIT consists of moving the dominant hand (which has the index and middle fingers extended and touching) toward contact with the back of the nondominant fingers (also in the same handshape as the dominant hand), whereas the movement in CHAIR is the same but is repeated twice, and each instance of movement is shorter than that in SIT (i.e., the dominant hand starts closer to the nondominant hand in CHAIR). Sign languages exploit reduplication in various manifestations to convey not only the word formation process in (1b) but also other meanings, such as pluralization of certain nouns.

Simultaneous Structure

Although sign languages display sequential morphology to some extent, they reveal a much richer range of simultaneous morphology, in which the production of the morphemes overlap with one other. Five such morphological processes are described briefly here: (1) reduction, (2) numeral incorporation, (3) aspectual modulations, (4) verb agreement, and (5) classifier constructions.

In reduction, illustrated in (2), all the nouns have reduplicated movement, whereas all the adjectives describe some quality or property that is based on the meaning of the noun. The adjectives have a single movement that is reduced and tensed. For example, CHURCH involves moving the dominant hand (which curves the fingers and thumb in a C-like handshape) toward contact with the back of the nondominant fist, whereas the movement in PIOUS is similar but starts closer to the nondominant hand, so that the movement is reduced, and proceeds faster with greater effort from the forearm and results in a quick "bounce" off the nondominant hand, so that the movement appears tensed.

(2) *Noun*	*Adjective*
CHURCH	PIOUS
HISTORY	HISTORIC
NAME	HAVING-ESTABLISHED-A-REPUTATION

The noun is the root, and the derivational process converts the root into an adjective by manipulating the phonological units of the root. The root (noun) has two phonological units, each corresponding to a movement. The derivational process deletes one of these units; reduces the remaining unit; and inserts a tensed, sharp end to the unit.

Another example of simultaneous morphology is seen with numeral incorporation, a process that combines a numeral like "one" or "two" with a noun that quantifies elements like time, money, and order. In numeral incorporation, the handshape of numeral is substituted for the handshape of the noun root, while other phonological parameters (movement, orientation, and location) of the noun are held constant. Numeral incorporation is similar to compounding in that two lexemes are combined, except that they are combined simultaneously rather than sequentially. For this to work, each morpheme has an incomplete set of phonological specifications, but when they are combined, the result has a complete set. See Liddell (1996) for further discussion of numeral incorporation in ASL.

Aspectual modulations in sign language also constitute simultaneous morphology, because they change the movement of the verb root in some way. As suggested by Rathmann (2005), there are four morphological processes in ASL that encode situation aspect, which conveys a temporal view of the event or state: (1) continuative, (2) iterative, (3) habitual, and (4) conative. For example, consider the case where a certain person is involved in the activity of studying. The continuative form shows that the event of studying has gone on for a certain uninterrupted duration and is marked by the lengthening the movement of the root (verb). The iterative form indicates that the event of studying has occurred with some breaks in between and is expressed by reduplication of the root. The habitual form means that a certain person is accustomed to studying over time and is conveyed through quick and short reduplication of the root. Finally, the conative form expresses the meaning that studying is about to occur (the next sentence indicates whether or not studying happens successfully). The form is realized by holding the initial configuration of the sign (i.e., the hands take on the initial handshape of the sign and raise to the initial location of the sign but do not go through the usual movement). Again, all of these aspectual modulations are instances of simultaneous morphology, because they manipulate the phonological units of a root in some way (lengthening, reduplication, quick reduplication, and holding) to yield a new meaning.

A fourth example of simultaneous morphology in sign languages is verb agreement. There is a certain class of verbs that describe an action between two animate participants (e.g., ASK, INFORM, and INVITE). For example, to say the equivalent of "I asked her," an area in the gestural space in front of the signer, say on the right, is first associated with the referent of *her*. Then, while signing the verb (using the handshape of a crooked index finger in ASL), the palm of the hand faces to the right, and the hand moves from the signer's body to the right. In contrast, to say "she asked me," the palm of the hand faces the signer's body, and the hand moves toward oneself. The difference between the two sentences corresponds to differences in the person and number features of the subject and the object (first person singular and non–first person singular, respectively, in the first example, and vice versa in the second example). The difference in meaning is conveyed by a change in the orientation of the hands or the direction of movement. The realization of verb agreement is thus simultaneous, because the change to the verb is stem-internal and does not involve the addition of a segmental affix. Due to the nature of its interaction with gestural space, verb agreement has been one of the more heavily discussed topics in sign language linguistics. The preceding description reflects the featural perspective of Rathmann and Mathur (2008, 2011), but numerous studies, notably Meir (1998, 2002), Liddell (2003), and Lillo-Martin and Meier (2011), offer other perspectives on this phenomenon.

The last example of simultaneous morphology comes from classifier constructions, which are sometimes known as classifier predicates or polycomponential signs (Schembri, 2003). There are numerous types of classifier predicates, only one of which is briefly discussed here: whole entity classifiers. Whole entity classifier predicates depict the location or motion of an entity. The handshape in these predicates changes depending on the entity. If the entity is a vehicle, it is conveyed in German Sign Language (*Deutsche Gebärdensprache*—DGS) by a flat, palm-down handshape if the vehicle has four wheels and by a flat, mid-palm handshape if the vehicle has two wheels. In ASL, the same entity is conveyed by a different handshape, the "3" handshape (the thumb, index, and middle fingers are all extended), regardless of whether the vehicle has two or four wheels. In these examples, the handshape marking the entity combines simultaneously with the root specifying the location/motion, which depends on the conceptual representation of the location/motion and is conveyed through gestural space. This combination results in a sign with a complete set of phonological specifications. Along with verb agreement, classifier constructions have received much discussion in the sign language literature, again because of their interaction with gestural space; Supalla (1986) is one seminal study of the classifier system in ASL, whereas Emmorey (2003) contains a more recent sampling of the debate on the nature of classifier constructions in sign languages.

Other Lexical Processes

Thus far, we have seen several examples of sequential and simultaneous morphology in sign languages. However, these are not the only processes available for generating lexical items in sign languages. Sign languages also exploit other mechanisms for creating new words, which do not fit neatly into the sequential or simultaneous groups. For instance, sign languages borrow extensively from spoken languages by fingerspelling (Battison, 1978). The fingerspelled version of *job* becomes sign-like through the deletion of the middle letter, and reducing the movement to a single twist of the forearm that is cotemporaneous with a handshape change from J to B. Sign languages also borrow from other sign languages, especially the names of countries, such as RUSSIA, MEXICO, and CHINA in ASL. Then, sign languages may innovate new lexical items (neologisms) from iconic roots. The signs for the different generations of technology present a good example: the old ASL sign for TELEPHONE mimics holding the receiver to the ear with one hand and placing the speaker close to the mouth with the other hand; the current sign now places a phone-like handshape (thumb and pinky finger outstretched) at the ear. More recently, signs have emerged to describe texting; video telephone calls; and social networking media, such as Facebook and Twitter.

One last example of a lexical mechanism common to sign languages is the "lexical family," a group of signs that share the same specification for one or two phonological parameters, and that fall into the same semantic category (Fernald & Napoli, 2000). The closest equivalent in a spoken language is phonesthemes, which are "well-represented sound-meaning pairings, such as English *gl-*, which occurs in numerous words with meanings relating to light and vision" (Bergen, 2004, p. 290). In one lexical family in ASL, presented in (3), all the signs share the same movement and location: symmetrical semicircular movement of the two hands toward each other and in front of the chest. This form is consistently associated with the meaning "group"

but this correspondence does not necessarily have morphemic status, because the status of the remaining part is questionable. What sets the signs in this lexical family apart from each other is handshape; this handshape is not necessarily associated with a meaning but rather represents the initial letter of the corresponding English word. For example, CLASS uses a curved handshape with an open thumb and a midorientation, which represents the letter C (i.e., the initial letter of the English word *class*).

(3) Lexical family sharing "group" morpheme (expressed by movement)

CLASS	FAMILY
GROUP	TEAM
SOCIETY	ASSOCIATION

A Final Note on the Lexicon and Morphology of Sign Languages

Thus far, this section has illustrated both sequential and simultaneous morphology in sign languages. Sequential morphology abounds in spoken languages, but simultaneous morphology also exists in spoken languages to a great extent. Two examples from English suffice to support the latter point: stem-internal changes in the vowel quality of certain verbs to express past tense (*run ~ ran*, *see ~ saw*, and *take ~ took*), and stress placement to indicate a verb-noun distinction (*presént ~ présent*, *recórd ~ récord*, and *convért ~ cónvert*). That said, verb agreement and classifier constructions have been argued to represent a type of simultaneous morphology that is unique to sign languages and that does not have a counterpart in spoken languages (Mathur & Rathmann, 2010). These two morphological processes require interaction with gestural space for their realization. To our awareness, there are no analogous morphemes in spoken languages that must be realized through, say, a pointing in gestural space. Although speakers gesture while speaking, and some gestures may co-occur with specific words (Kendon, 2004; Liddell, 2000; McNeill, 2000, among others), it remains that the spoken words still have complete phonological specifications, and the addition of gesture is optional, whereas it is not for the unique type of morphology in sign languages.

Syntax and Discourse

The last levels of grammar to be examined are syntax and discourse, which are concerned with the structure of sentences and texts larger than a sentence. In keeping with the theme of the tension between sequentiality and simultaneity, this section first looks at examples of sequentiality in the syntax and discourse of sign languages and then turns to instances of simultaneity at these levels.

Sequential Structure

One obvious example of sequential structure lies in word order. On the basis of sentences with a reversible subject and object, Fischer (1975) argues that ASL has a basic word order of subject-verb-object, as shown in (4a). Elements like modals and negation occur in specific positions, including the preverbal position, as illustrated in (4b) and (4c), respectively. These examples illustrate the notational convention of the sign language linguistics field to show non-manual signals (facial expressions) with a line above the signs that co-occur with the nonmanual and with a symbol identifying the specific marker (e.g., "neg" = negation marker, which consists of shaking one's head).

(4) a. MAN NOTICE CHILD   Fischer (1975, p. 5)
"The man noticed the child."

     b. MAN MUST PAY B-I-L-L-S   Fischer (1975, p. 10)
"The man must pay his bills."

                            <u>   </u>*neg*
     c. J-O-H-N NOT BUY HOUSE   Neidle, Kegl, MacLaughlin, Bahan, and Lee (2000, p. 44)
"John is not buying a house."

In addition, sign languages like ASL display embedded structures, as in (5a), which Padden (1988) demonstrates through a number of linguistic tests to be distinct from conjoined structures like (5b). These examples illustrate another notational convention: the subscripts on the predicates refer to areas of gestural space that have been associated with the referents of noun phrases. The predicates are made in the direction of these areas, thus reflecting the arguments associated with the predicate. For example, the subscript *1* in (5b) refers to first person, which is associated with an area on the signer's body, so that the direction proceeds from this area and thus marks a (null) first person pronoun as the subject. Likewise, the subscript *i* in (5b) is associated with an area of gestural space that is used to refer to the referent of the mother, and when the predicate is directed toward this area, the direction marks the corresponding noun phrase (MOTHER) as a direct object.

(5) a. MOTHER SINCE _iPERSUADE_j SISTER _jCOME_i, _iINDEX
"My mother has been urging my sister to come and stay here, she has."

Padden (1988, p. 87)

b. _iPERSUADE_i BUT CHANGE MIND
"I persuaded her, but then I/he/she changed my mind."

Padden (1988, p. 95)

Although ASL has been to shown to have a basic word order, there are permissible changes to this order (Chen Pichler, 2002; Fischer, 1975; Liddell, 1980; and Sandler & Lillo-Martin, 2006, among others). For example, through topicalization, a constituent, such as a direct object, may be moved to the front of the clause as in (6a), resulting in an object-subject-verb order, provided that the direct object is marked with a specific nonmanual marker indicating topicalization (roughly, raised eyebrows). There are other instances where the direct object may be fronted without topicalization, as in (6b), where the "heaviness" of the aspectually marked verb places it at the end of the clause. The example in (6c) presents another case where interaction with signing space seems to license a subject-object-verb order: once the direct object has been signed in a particular area, the following verb is then directed to that area to mark its direct object. Even if word order in these examples diverges from the basic word order, there is sequentiality in that words still follow a particular order according to grammatical principles.

        <u>   </u>t
(6) a. MARY JOHN LIKE   Aarons (1994, p. 148)
"*Mary*, John likes."

           <u>   </u>q
     b. TOMATO GIRL EAT+durative aspect
"Did the girl eat tomatoes for a long time?"

Liddell (1980, p. 103)

     c. MAN _aMOVIE SEE_a
"The man saw the movie."   Liddell (1980, p. 90)

The property of having a set of permissible word orders has been attested in other sign languages, such as DGS (Rathmann, 2000), Brazilian Sign Language (Quadros, 1999), and Japanese Sign Language (Nihon Shuwa; Fischer, 1996). The collection of papers in Brennan and Turner (1994) examine word order in yet other sign languages. The overall picture suggested by these studies is that there is cross-linguistic variation with respect to word order and possible changes to word order. For example, subject-verb-object is argued to be the basic word order for some sign languages like ASL, BSL, and Brazilian Sign Language, whereas subject-object-verb is claimed to be the basic word order for other sign languages like DGS and Nihon Shuwa. The range of cross-linguistic variation is well within that for spoken languages, suggesting that modality effects are not necessarily seen at the level of sequential word order.

Sequential structure can likewise be discerned at the level of discourse, as seen through the use of turn-taking strategies, discourse markers, and narrative structure, for example. Baker (1977) finds that like spoken conversations, signed conversations are organized around "turn relevance places" where the interlocutors negotiate taking turns. There are strategies for initiating a turn, maintaining conversation, and shifting a turn, such as moving the hands out of a rest position, shifting one's posture, turning eye gaze to or away from the addressee, and getting one's attention by waving a hand (Baker, 1977). Just as discourse markers like *and* and *or* connect utterances in spoken languages, Roy (1989) and Metzger and Bahan (2001) find that certain ASL signs like FINE, NOW, and ON-TO-THE-NEXT-PART help to link discrete chunks of discourse. Locker McKee (1992) also describes a nonlexical discourse marker that seems unique to sign languages, in which a signer physically moves or leans to one side to convey an aside from a lecture. Another transparent example of sequential structure at the discourse level comes from Bahan and Supalla's (1995) study of one formal narrative in ASL. They find that the formal narrative can be broken down into the discourse units of chapters, sections, strophes, stanzas, and lines on the basis of specific cues. For example, each line can be marked by a pause, a head nod, eye blinking, or a change in eye gaze.

Simultaneous Structure

The syntax and discourse of sign languages also display multiple instances of simultaneity. At the level of discourse, simultaneity is manifested through several mechanisms, such as turn-taking, constructed dialogue/action, and cohesion. With regard to turn-taking, Metzger and Bahan (2001), drawing on other studies, note that simultaneous overlap between turns in signed conversations is relatively longer and more frequent compared with some spoken languages. One possible factor they discuss is that signers usually engage in high-style involvement, such as fingerspelling the name of a character fully the first time and then skipping the full fingerspelling the next time, because it is already familiar to both interlocutors.

Simultaneity is also seen through the use of constructed dialogue and action. The term refers to "'performatives' that use space to 'build' the elements of the narrative scene" (Metzger & Bahan, 2001, p. 133,

citing Winston, 1992), and they can be considered as subtypes of depiction in the sense of Liddell (2003). One example from Metzger (1995) illustrates the simultaneity of several components: "a signer is describing a card game in which one of the seated players looks up at someone who has just approached the table, signs LOOK-UP and at the same time moves his head up and to the right, as he constructs the actions of that character (looking up and holding a handful of cards) as well as his dialogue (his response to the newcomer's utterance)" (Metzger & Bahan, 2001, p. 134). There are several components occurring simultaneously in this snippet of discourse: the sign LOOK-UP; the constructed action (turning to the right, looking up, and holding a handful of cards, all at the same time); and the constructed dialogue of his response. Although constructed action and dialogue do appear with speech, as documented by McNeill (1992), what seems unique to the case of sign languages is the ability to sign something simultaneously with constructed action.

Another instance of simultaneity at the level of discourse can be seen through the technique of using gestural space to maintain cohesion across a text. Winston (1993, 1995) examined the mapping of comparative discourse frames in one lecture. The signer designated one side of gestural space to discuss poetry as art, and used the other side to refer to poetry as science. Once the signer had associated a particular area of gestural space with these frames, the signer produced signs in either area to refer back to a certain frame and to fill in each frame further. Gestural space thus makes it possible for the signer to convey the content about the frame simultaneously as the area associated with the frame. Using gestural space in this way is not only used to make comparisons but is also used for constructed action and constructed discourse. Moreover, gestural space is used for the mapping of temporal events (Winston, 1992; Emmorey, 2001; Rathmann, 2005). For example, a signer can associate one area of gestural space with the past (such as on the left side) and another area with the present (such as on the right), and then by signing content about an event in a certain area, it is already apparent which period of time the event has occurred in. The property of using gestural space to organize discourse seems unique to sign languages. Although gestural space is a principle available for spoken languages, in the sense that one can produce gestures in gestural space along with speech, the technique of organizing discourse through gestural space seems more conventionalized and pervasive in signed languages.

The volume by Vermeerbergen et al. (2007) offers a recent collection of papers examining other types of simultaneous constructions in sign languages at the level of syntax. One such example is manual-nonmanual simultaneity, in which the use of the hands is used simultaneously with other articulators, and each articulator contributes a different meaning. For example, Wilbur (2000) observes that articulators in the upper part of the face tend to be used to mark syntactic functions, whereas those in the lower part of the face, in particular the mouth, tend to be used to add adverbial functions. The sentences in (6a) and (6b) illustrate the simultaneous use of the hands with the use of the head and the eyebrows. In (6a), the head is tilted slightly back and the eyebrows are raised to mark the sign as topicalized; in (6b), the eyebrows are also raised, but the head is tilted slightly forward to mark the sentence as a yes/no question. The sentence in (4c) likewise shows the simultaneous use of the hands with the head; specifically, the head is shaken sideways to negate the sentence.

The hands can also be used simultaneously with articulators in the lower part of the face, such as the mouth. The sentence in (7) illustrates a mouth gesture notated as "mm," which indicates a pursing of the lips and carries the meaning of carrying out the event in a relaxed manner. Mouth gestures refer to idiomatic gestures of the mouth that are native to sign languages and that cannot be traced to a spoken language. Then, many of the signs (especially nouns) are sometimes accompanied by a mouthing, which refers to moving the mouth to convey a lexical item from a spoken language. For example, in (6b), the sign GIRL may be accompanied by a movement of the mouth that resembles the pronunciation of the English word *girl*. See Boyes-Braem and Sutton-Spence (2001) for a comprehensive perspective on both mouth gestures and mouthings.

$$\overline{\qquad} mm$$

(7) $_1$INDEX   DRIVE
    "I was driving along easily."   Padden (1988, p. 124)

There are additional facial expressions marking other constructions like wh-questions, rhetorical question and answer constructions, conditionals. The use of such nonmanual signals is almost always accompanied by the use of the hands. Neidle et al. (2000) note some cases in which the nonmanual may appear without the corresponding sign but even in these cases, the nonmanual co-occurs with other signs. For further discussion of the simultaneous use of nonmanuals with the hands at the syntactic and prosodic level, see Dudis (2004), Liddell (1980),

Neidle et al. (2000), Nespor and Sandler (1999), Sandler and Lillo-Martin (2006), and Wilbur (2000).

Comparable examples exist in spoken languages, in which the use of the vocal tract may be combined simultaneously with manual gesture, as in pointing to something when uttering "I would like to buy this." There is a growing body of literature examining the relationship between speech and gesture (e.g., Kendon, 2004; McNeill, 2000, which make it clear that some manual gestures contribute to the meaning of an utterance. This situation is plausibly analogous to signs being combined with formations of the mouth. Moreover, the use of suprasegmental features like duration, pitch, and stress to convey intonation or other aspects of prosody is comparable with the use of nonmanual signals (e.g., raising eyebrows, shifting eye gaze, leaning the body in a particular direction) to fulfill a range of semantic and pragmatic functions, as argued by Sandler and Lillo-Martin (2006).

The one type of simultaneous construction in sign languages that does not have an apparent counterpart in spoken languages is manual simultaneity (i.e., the use of both hands/arms to produce different content). This is one example where the modality of the language may affect the possibilities for linguistic structure and use. In the more common cases, one hand produces a sign and is then held in place, as the other hand produces another sign. In (8), H1 stands for one hand and H2 represents the other hand (usually the dominant hand and the nondominant hand, respectively, although they can switch dominance). Some signs require one hand like DRINK, which is notated only on the H1 tier, whereas other signs require two hands like READ, which is notated on the H1 and a series of xxx's below the gloss on the H2 tier. As the examples in (8) show, it is also possible for one part of the sign to continue through the articulation of the next sign. In (10a), both H1 and H2 work together to produce the sign READ. This is followed by one-handed signs, LOOK-AROUND and DRINK. At the same time, H2 remains in the flat upright handshape from the preceding sign of READ. This is indicated by a series of dashes in the example. Then, in the fourth sign, which repeats the first sign, H1 is returned to the original H1 of the first sign, namely, the extended index and middle fingers.

(8) a. H1: READ LOOK-AROUND DRINK READ
    H2: xxxxx ------------------------------------ xxxxxx
    "While I was reading, I took a look around and drank (coffee)."

b. H1: HOUSE CL:BLDG ----------------------------
   H2: xxxxxxxxxxxxxxxxx   BIKE CL:VEHICLE
   [note: CL:BLDG "located there" CL:VEHICLE "move"]
   "I biked past the house."

c. H1: BOOK RED   GREEN   BLUE
   H2: $_a$INDEX $_b$INDEX $_c$INDEX
   "The book here is red, the one there is green, and that one there is blue."

The sentence in (8a) also illustrates the point that the H2 part of the sign READ may continue through the articulation of more than two signs. This type of construction is especially common in classifier constructions, where each hand may be used as a classifier for an object, as in (8b), which starts with a two-handed lexical sign for "house." This is followed by a one-handed classifier form that establishes the location of the house in the signing space in front of the signer. This form then remains in place, as indicated by the dashed line, while the next two signs are articulated by H2. Note that BICYCLE is a two-handed sign, but in (8b), only H2 is used to articulate this sign, while H1 remains in the same handshape from the previous sign.

In the examples thus far, one hand first produces a sign and then is held in place as the other hand produces another sign. There are more extreme examples in which each hand simultaneously produces a different lexical item, as illustrated in (8c). In this example, the signer is identifying the colors of various books. After opening with the topic of BOOK, the signer points to one (imaginary) book and signs RED at the same time, and then moves on to another book and points out its color. In such examples, the lexical sign that can be produced simultaneously as another lexical sign is usually restricted and is often the pronoun INDEX, as shown in the above example. It is ungrammatical, for example, to produce the signs CAT and WHITE simultaneously (putatively meaning "The cat is white"), even though both signs are one-handed and could in theory be produced simultaneously.

Conclusion

This chapter surveys the tension between sequentiality and simultaneity at several levels of grammar in sign languages. At the levels of phonetics and phonology, we have seen that signs can be sequenced on the basis of phonological properties, such as handshape, orientation, and location, which are bundled simultaneously and co-occur with movement. Then, at the levels of the lexicon and morphology, we have seen

examples of sequential morphology, such as compounding and affixation, and examples of simultaneous morphology like stem-internal changes to mark aspect and numeral incorporation. Although both types of morphology are attested in spoken languages as well, sign languages also display a unique type of simultaneous morphology not seen in spoken languages: morphology that requires interaction with gestural space, as seen in verb agreement and classifier constructions. Finally, at the levels of syntax and discourse, there are instances of both sequential and simultaneous structure. All the instances of sequential structure in sign languages, such as basic word order, sentential embedding, word order changes, turn-taking strategies, the use of discourse markers, and narrative structure are found in spoken languages. Some instances of simultaneous structure like the simultaneous use of multiple articulators appear in both modalities; however, other instances like the use of gestural space to provide cohesion to the discourse and the simultaneous use of the two manual articulators to produce portions of syntax and discourse seem unique to sign languages.

The survey of sign language structure reveals properties unique to the visual-manual modality that must be accounted for by models of language production. For example, models of language production must account for interaction with gestural space, the root of many iconic constructions in sign languages, and the models must be able to handle the use of the two manual articulators, along with other nonmanual articulators, in simultaneous constructions.

To account for the unique properties of sign languages, language production models can be informed by studies of both adult and child language production of sign languages. For example, Klima and Bellugi (1979) and Hohenberger, Happ, and Leuninger (2002) have examined naturalistic and elicited slips of the hand, respectively; and Cheek, Cormier, Repp, and Meier (2001) and Mann, Marshall, Mason, and Morgan (2010) have analyzed naturalistic and elicited errors in child language production, respectively. Two issues with regard to the acquisition of sign languages are of particular interest to models of language production. First, as mentioned at the outset, most deaf signers are born to hearing parents and are usually not exposed to an accessible language (i.e., a sign language) until several years later, thus missing the critical period for language acquisition. Mayberry (1993), among numerous other studies, has found the delayed acquisition of L1 to have effects on grammatical processing that are not seen in adults who have undergone normal

L1 acquisition. It would be worthwhile to investigate whether delayed L1 acquisition also impacts language production, and if so, at which particular stages of language production.

The second issue is the confound between L2 and M2 acquisition. While L2 refers to "second language," M2 refers to "second modality." Thus, hearing people who have acquired English as a first language and then acquire ASL as a second language are also acquiring a language in a new modality, because the novice signers have to learn to apply their motor control system for the hands and arms to a new (linguistic) skill (Mirus, Rathmann, & Meier, 2001; Rosen, 2004). The challenge for adult learners in applying motor control systems to new skills is distinct from the challenge for child learners, which is the maturation of motor control skills (Cheek et al., 2001; Meier, 2006). Models of language production should take into account the different challenges posed by the acquisition of sign languages by L1, L2, and M2 signers.

There are now sophisticated motion capture systems, such as VICON and Optotrak, which are available for exploring sign language production in depth. These instruments have been successfully used in the study of ASL with respect to undershoot (Mauk, 2003), the coarticulation of handshape (Cheek, 2001), and verb agreement morphology (Cormier, 2002). Given the unique properties of sign languages and the unique issues raised by the acquisition of sign languages, and given the availability of sophisticated instruments to study sign language production, sign languages have the potential to make significant contributions to models of language production.

Note

1. Fingerspelling refers to the representation of written words by using handshapes that correspond to letters of the alphabet. The examples also illustrate notational conventions commonly used in the sign language linguistics field, such as indicating signs with English glosses in upper case and marking fingerspelling with dashes.

References

Aarons, D. (1994). *Aspects of the syntax of American Sign Language* (Unpublished doctoral dissertation). Boston University, Boston, MA.

Aronoff, M., Meir, I., Padden, C., & Sandler, W. (2003). Classifier complexes and morphology in two sign languages. In K. Emmorey (Ed.), *Perspectives on classifier constructions in signed languages* (pp.53–84). Mahwah, NJ: Lawrence Erlbaum Associates.

Bahan, B., & Supalla, S. (1995). Line segmentation and narrative structure: A study of eyegaze behavior and narrative structure in American Sign Language. In K. Emmorey & J. Reilly (Eds.), *Language, gesture and space* (pp.171–191). Hillsdale, NJ: Lawrence Erlbaum Associates.

Baker, C. (1977). Regulators and turn-taking in American Sign Language. In L. Friedman (Ed.), *On the other hand: New perspectives on American Sign Language* (pp. 215–236). New York: Academic Press.

Battison, R. (1978). *Lexical borrowing in American Sign Language*. Silver Spring, MD: Linstok Press.

Bergen, B. (2004). The psychological reality of phonaesthemes. *Language, 80*, 290–311.

Boyes-Braem, P., & Sutton-Spence, R. (Eds.)(2001). *The hands are the head of the mouth: The mouth as articulator in sign languages*. Hamburg: Signum Verlag.

Brennan, M., & Turner, G. (Eds.)(1994). *Word-order issues in sign language:Working papers*. Durham, UK: International Sign Linguistics Association.

Brentari, D. (1998). *A prosodic model of sign language phonology*. Cambridge, MA: MIT Press.

Brentari, D. (2006). Effects of language modality on word segmentation: An experimental study of phonological factors in a sign language. In L. Goldstein, C. Best, & D. Whalen (Eds.), *Papers from Laboratory Phonology VIII: Varieties of phonological competence* (pp.155–183). The Hague: Mouton.

Brentari, D. (Ed.) (2010). *Sign languages*. Cambridge: Cambridge University Press.

Brentari, D., Poizner, H., & Kegl, J. (1995). Aphasic and parkinsonian signing: Differences in phonological disruption. *Brain and Language, 48*, 69–105.

Cheek, A. (2001). *The phonetics and phonology of handshape in American Sign Language* (Unpublished doctoral dissertation). The University of Texas at Austin, Austin, TX.

Cheek, A., Cormier, K., Repp, A., & Meier, R. (2001). Prelinguistic gesture predicts mastery and error in the production of early signs. *Language, 77*, 292–323.

Chen Pichler, D. (2002). *Word order variability and acquisition in American Sign Language* (Unpublished doctoral dissertation). University of Connecticut, Storrs, CT.

Cormier, K. (2002). *Grammaticization of indexic signs: How American Sign Language expresses numerosity* (Unpublished doctoral dissertation). The University of Texas at Austin, Austin, TX.

Dudis, P. (2004). Body partitioning and real-space blends. *Cognitive Linguistics, 15*, 223–238.

Emmorey, K. (2001). *Language, cognition and the brain: Insights from sign language research*. Hillsdale, NJ: Lawrence Erlbaum Associates.

Emmorey, K. (Ed.) (2003). *Perspectives on classifier constructions in sign languages*. Mahwah, NJ: Lawrence Erlbaum Associates.

Fernald, T., & Napoli, D. (2000). Exploitation of morphological possibilities in signed languages. *Sign Language and Linguistics, 3*, 3–58.

Fischer, S. (1975). Influences on word order change in American Sign Language. In C. Li (Ed.), *Word order and word order change* (pp. 1–25). Austin, TX: University of Texas Press.

Fischer, S. (1996). The role of agreement and auxiliaries in sign languages. *Lingua, 98*, 103–120.

Hohenberger, A., Happ, D., & Leuninger, H. (2002). Modality-dependent aspects of sign language production: Evidence from slips of the hands and their repairs in German Sign Language. In R. Meier, K. Cormier, & D. Quinto-Pozos (Eds.), *Modality and structure in signed and spoken languages* (pp. 112–142). Cambridge: Cambridge University Press.

Kendon, A. (2004). *Gesture: Visible action as utterance*. Cambridge: Cambridge University Press.

Klima, E., & Bellugi, U. (1979). *The signs of language*. Cambridge, MA: Harvard University Press.

Liddell, S. (1980). *American Sign Language syntax*. The Hague: Mouton de Gruyter.

Liddell, S. (1984). THINK and BELIEVE: Sequentiality in American Sign Language. *Language, 60*, 372–399.

Liddell, S. (1996). Numeral incorporating roots and non-incorporating prefixes in American Sign Language. *Sign Language Studies, 92*, 201–226.

Liddell, S. (2000). Indicating verbs and pronouns: Pointing away from agreement. In H. Lane & K. Emmorey (Eds.), *The signs of language revisited: An anthology to honor Ursula Bellugi and Edward Klima* (pp. 303–320). Mahwah, NJ: Lawrence Erlbaum Associates.

Liddell, S. (2003). *Grammar, gesture and meaning in American Sign Language*. Cambridge: Cambridge University Press.

Liddell, S., & Johnson, R. (1986). American Sign Language compound formation processes, lexicalization and phonological remnants. *Natural Language and Linguistic Theory, 4*, 445–513.

Liddell, S., & Johnson, R. (1989). American Sign Language: The phonological base. *Sign Language Studies, 64*, 195–277.

Lillo-Martin, D., & Meier, R. (2011). On the linguistic status of "agreement" in sign languages. *Theoretical Linguistics, 37*, 95–141.

Locker McKee, R. (1992). *Footing shifts in American Sign Language lectures* (Unpublished doctoral dissertation). University of California, Los Angeles, CA.

Mandel, M. (1981). *Phonotactics and morphophonology in American Sign Language* (Unpublished doctoral dissertation). University of California at Berkeley, Berkeley, CA.

Mann, W., Marshall, C., Mason, K., & Morgan, G. (2010). The acquisition of sign language: The impact of phonetic complexity on phonology. *Language, Learning and Development, 6*, 60–86.

Mathur, G., & Rathmann, C. (2010). Two types of nonconcatenative morphology in signed languages. In D. Napoli & G. Mathur (Eds.), *Deaf Around the world: The impact of language* (pp. 54–82). Oxford: Oxford University Press..

Mauk, C. (2003). *Undershoot in two modalities: Evidence from fast speech and fast signing* (Unpublished doctoral dissertation). The University of Texas at Austin, Austin, TX.

Mayberry, R. (1993). First-language acquisition after childhood differs from second-language acquisition: The case of American Sign Language. *Journal of Speech and Hearing Research, 36*, 1258–1270.

McNeill, D. (1992). *Hand and mind: What gestures reveal about thought*. Chicago: University of Chicago Press.

McNeill, D. (Ed.) (2000). *Language and gesture: Window into thought and action*. Cambridge: Cambridge University Press.

Meier, R. (2002). Why different, why the same? Explaining effects and non-effects of modality in sign and speech. In R. Meier, K. Cormier, & D. Quinto-Pozos (Eds.), *Modality and structure in signed and spoken languages* (pp. 1–25). Cambridge: Cambridge University Press.

Meier, R. (2006). The form of early signs: Explaining signing children's articulatory development. In B. Schick, M. Marschark, & P. E. Spencer (Eds.), *Advances in the sign language development of deaf children* (pp. 202–230). New York: Oxford University Press.

Meir, I. (1998). *Thematic structure and verb agreement in Israeli Sign Language* (Unpublished doctoral dissertation). The Hebrew University of Jerusalem, Jerusalem, Israel.

Meir, I. (2002). A cross-modality perspective on verb agreement. *Natural Language and Linguistic Theory, 20*, 413–450.

Metzger, M. (1995). Constructed dialogue and constructed action in American Sign Language. In C. Lucas (Ed.), *Sociolinguistics in deaf communities* (pp. 255–271). Washington, DC: Gallaudet University Press.

Metzger, M., & Bahan, B. (2001). Discourse analysis. In C. Lucas (Ed.), *The sociolinguistics of sign languages* (pp. 112–144). Cambridge: Cambridge University Press.

Mirus, G., Rathmann, C., & Meier, R. (2001). Proximalization and distalization of sign movement in adult learners. In A. Baer, V. Dively, M. Metzger, & S. Taub (Eds.), *Signed languages: Discoveries from international research* (pp. 103–119). Washington, DC: Gallaudet University Press.

Mitchell, R., & Karchmer, M. (2004). When parents are deaf versus hard of hearing: Patterns of sign use and school placement of deaf and hard-of-hearing children. *Journal of Deaf Studies and Deaf Education, 9*, 133–152.

Neidle, C., Kegl, J., MacLaughlin, D., Bahan, B., & Lee, R. (2000). *The syntax of American Sign Language: Functional categories and hierarchical structure*. Cambridge, MA: MIT Press.

Nespor, M., & Sandler, W. (1999). Prosodic phonology in Israeli Sign Language. *Language and Speech, 42*, 143–176.

Newport, E., & Supalla, T. (2000). Sign language research at the millennium. In K. Emmorey & H. Lane (Eds.), *The signs of language revisited* (pp. 103–114). Mahwah, NJ: Lawrence Erlbaum Associates.

Orfanidou, E., Adam, R., Morgan, G., & McQueen, J. (2010). Recognition of signed and spoken language: Different sensory inputs, the same segmentation procedure. *Journal of Memory and Language, 62*, 272–283.

Padden, C. (1988). *Interaction of morphology and syntax in American Sign Language*. Outstanding Dissertations in Linguistics. New York: Garland Publishing.

Quadros, R. (1999). *Phrase structure of Brazilian Sign Language* (Unpublished doctoral dissertation). Pontificia Universidade Catolica do Rio Grande do Sul, Brazil.

Rathmann, C. (2000). *The optionality of agreement phrase: Evidence from signed languages* (Unpublished master's thesis). The University of Texas at Austin, Austin, TX.

Rathmann, C. (2005). *Event structure in American Sign Language* (Unpublished doctoral dissertation). The University of Texas at Austin, Austin, TX.

Rathmann, C., & Mathur, G. (2002). Is verb agreement different cross-modally? In R. Meier, K. Cormier, & D. Quinto-Pozos (Eds.), *Modality and structure in signed and spoken languages* (pp. 370–404). Cambridge: Cambridge University Press.

Rathmann, C., & Mathur, G. (2008). Verb agreement as a linguistic innovation in signed languages. In J. Quer (Ed.), *Signs of the time: Selected papers from TISLR 2004* (pp. 191–216). Hamburg: Signum Verlag.

Rathmann, C., & Mathur, G. (2011). A featural approach to verb agreement in signed languages. *Theoretical Linguistics, 37*, 197–208.

Rosen, R. (2004). Beginning L2 production errors in ASL lexical phonology: A cognitive phonology model. *Sign Language & Linguistics, 7*, 31–61.

Roy, C. (1989). Features of discourse in an American Sign Language lecture. In C. Lucas (Ed.), *The sociolinguistics of the deaf community* (pp. 231–251). San Diego: Academic Press.

Sandler, W. (1989). *Phonological representation of the sign*. Dordrecht: Foris.

Sandler, W., & Lillo-Martin, D. (2006). *Sign language and linguistic universals*. Cambridge: Cambridge University Press.

Schembri, A. (2003). Rethinking "classifiers" in signed languages. In K. Emmorey (Ed.), *Perspectives on classifier constructions in signed languages* (pp. 3–34). Mahwah, NJ: Erlbaum.

Stokoe, W. (1960) Sign language structure: An outline of the visual communication system of the American deaf. Studies in linguistics, occasional papers no. 8. (Revised and reprinted in 1978 as *Sign language structure*. Silver Spring, MD: Linstok Press.)

Stokoe, W. C., Casterline, D., & Cronenberg, C. (1965). *A dictionary of American sign language on linguistic principles*. Washington, DC: Gallaudet College Press.

Supalla, T. (1986). The classifier system in American Sign Language. In C. Craig (Ed.), *Noun classes and categorization* (pp. 181–214). Philadelphia: John Benjamins. 181–214.

Supalla, T., & Newport, E. (1978). How many seats in a chair? The derivation of nouns and verbs in American Sign Language. In P. Siple (Ed.), *Understanding language through sign language research* (pp. 91–132). New York, NY: Academic Press.

Van der Hulst, H. (1993). Units in the analysis of signs. *Phonology, 10*, 209–241.

Vermeerbergen, M., Leeson, L., & Crasborn, O. (Eds.) (2007). Simultaneity in signed languages: A string of sequentially organised issues. In M. Vermeerbergen, L. Leeson, & O. Crasborn (Eds.), *Simultaneity in signed languages* (pp. 1–25). Amsterdam: John Benjamins.

Wilbur R. (2000). Phonological and prosodic layering of nonmanuals in American Sign Language. In H. Lane & K. Emmorey (Eds.), *The signs of language revisited: Festschrift for Ursula Bellugi and Edward Klima* (pp. 213–241). Hillsdale, NJ: Lawrence Erlbaum.

Winston, E. (1992). Space and involvement in an American Sign Language lecture. In J. Plant-Moeller (Ed.), *Expanding horizons: Proceedings of the 12th National Convention of the Registry of Interpreters for the Deaf* (pp. 93–105). Silver Spring, MD: RID Publications.

Winston, E. (1993). *Spatial mapping in comparative discourse frames in an ASL lecture* (Unpublished doctoral dissertation). Georgetown University, Washington, DC.

Winston, E. (1995). Spatial mapping in comparative discourse frames. In K. Emmorey & J. Reilly (Eds.), *Language, gesture and space* (pp. 87–114). Hillsdale, NJ: Lawrence Erlbaum Associates.

Sign Language Production: An Overview

David P. Corina, Eva Gutierrez, *and* Michael Grosvald

Abstract

This chapter provides an overview of data from naturally occurring signed languages used by Deaf communities. This research has benefitted from linguistic, developmental, psycholinguistic, and, more recently, neurobiological investigations. Within each of these broad disciplines, researchers have examined different aspects of sign language production. Despite the obvious physical differences in the production of sign and speech, collectively these studies are beginning to illuminate some striking commonalities between signed and spoken languages. The similarities lead one to appreciate the seemingly indelible characteristics of human linguistic communication. At the same time, the comparison of signed and spoken languages reveals frank differences that arise from modality-specific characteristics of speech and sign articulation. The comparisons of signed and spoken languages continue to provide a powerful means to understand the human capacity for language.

Key Words: sign language, language acquisition, functional neuroimaging, aphasia

Introduction

Our understanding of naturally occurring signed languages used by Deaf communities has benefitted from linguistic, developmental, psycholinguistic, and, more recently, neurobiological investigations. Within each of these broad disciplines, researchers have examined different aspects of sign language production. Despite the obvious physical differences in the production of sign and speech, collectively these studies are beginning to illuminate some striking commonalities between signed and spoken languages. The similarities lead one to appreciate the seemingly indelible characteristics of human linguistic communication. At the same time, the comparison of signed and spoken languages reveals frank differences that arise from modality-specific characteristics of speech and sign articulation.

Linguists have posited formal representations to describe the properties of sign formation. Many of these devices, such as distinctive features and syllables, derive directly from linguistic traditions of spoken-language description. Other devices and constructions used, such as the need to represent multiple articulators (specifically the non-dominant hand as well as facial expressions), stem from the need to characterize modality-specific characteristics that are unique to signed languages.

Research on language acquisition, motivated by the question of whether sign language acquisition was similar to or different from the acquisition of spoken language, provided some of the earliest studies of sign production. These studies documented the form and progression of sign language production from its earliest prelinguistic stages.

Psycholinguistic studies of sign language production are relatively few in number. As with spoken language, the well-known bias toward studies of language comprehension over language production appears to hold for signed languages as well. However, the bias is not as egregious as the state of affairs seen in the spoken language literature, largely due to the fact that sign languages do not have well-accepted orthographic representations. This has permitted sign psycholinguists to sidestep the study of the processing of secondary codifications of languages (i.e., the reading of orthographic forms) that dominated so much of early spoken language psycholinguistics. Nevertheless, the technical demands of manipulating and measuring dynamic moving images (often video) required for psycholinguistic studies of signed languages presents its own set of challenges, which has hampered progress in this field.

Perhaps somewhat surprisingly, studies of the neurobiology of sign language production have received a good deal of attention. This follows in part from the long tradition in clinical aphasiology that tends to more objectively characterize aphasic impairments based upon descriptions of production over comprehension. For example, in the Boston Diagnostic Aphasic Examination (Goodglass & Kaplan, 1972), five out of seven characteristics of the Severity Rating Scale are putative measures of language production. The highly revealing studies of sign language aphasia follow in this tradition (see, e.g., Poizner, Klima, & Bellugi, 1987). Recent advances in brain imaging have provided new tools to examine the neural correlates of spoken and sign language production and provide a means to document the cortical signatures of languages expressed in different modalities and to disentangle neural systems supporting linguistic and motoric functions.

Sign Language Linguistics
Phonological Inventories and Representations

Early studies of the formal linguistic properties (see Mathur & Rathman "The Structure of Sign Languages") of American Sign Language (ASL) identified four major parameters associated with sign articulation: handshape, location, movement, and orientation (Battison, 1978; Stokoe, Casterline, & Croneberg, 1965). Sign linguists generally agree that these major parameters function distinctively in naturally occurring signed languages. In addition, specific facial expressions and body postures further serve to convey linguistic meaning (Baker, 1977; Baker-Schenk, 1983; Liddell, 1980).

Naturally occurring signed languages exist in communities of deaf users across the globe. Parameter inventories vary widely across signed languages largely as a function of historical relatedness, rendering less-related languages mutually unintelligible (e.g., McKee & Kennedy, 2000; Woodward, 2000).

For example, Figures 24.1a and 24.1b illustrate articulatory postures of handshapes in ASL that are shared in Cambodian Sign Language, while handshapes in Figures 24.1c and 24.1d illustrate handshapes observed in Cambodian Sign Language but not ASL. Typological studies of signed languages indicate that handshape postures are the most widely varying parameter, with many sign languages exhibiting inventories of the order of 45 distinct handshape postures. In contrast, distinctive body locations used in the articulation of signs (e.g., the forehead, the chest, the nondominant hand, the hip) number roughly on the order of 20–25 locations. Somewhat surprisingly to the nonsigner is the fact that distinct path movements show the fewest distinct forms and number only 5–10. This typology is interesting in part because the movement parameter in sign languages is often considered the most "sonorant" or "vowel-like," whereas handshape features may be described as more consonantal or aprosodic. Typological studies of the world's spoken languages have examined the ratio of consonants to vowel qualities and found a mean ratio of 4.25, with a median of 3.5, and a range of 1–29 (Maddieson, 2008). Assuming the higher-end approximations of distinct handshapes and movements stated above, sign languages yield a "consonant-vowel quality" ratio of 4.5 that is well within the range attested to in spoken languages.

Within models of ASL phonology, signs are considered to have two segment types. Sandler (1986), for example, proposes an M or movement segment and an L or location segment. These skeletal features serve as timing units to which "melodies" (i.e., specifications of handshape and place of articulation) are docked (Figure 24.2). Many have interpreted these segments to be similar to the consonants and vowels of spoken languages. This parallel in spoken and signed languages between consonants and vowels, and Location and Movement segments, is further exhibited in production errors arising from sign aphasia and naturally occurring slips of the hand.

Other linguists have adopted prosodic models to describe ASL phonology. In these models, the dynamic properties of sign languages, such as distinct path movement, or a handshape or orientation changes, are considered prosodic units, which in some analyses serve as a syllable nucleus (Brentari, 1990; Corina, 1990). Well-formedness constraints can be easily expressed with reference to sign syllabic domains, for example the constraint that essentially states that ASL can have only one handshape or orientation change per syllable (Brentari, 1998; Uyechi, 1996; Wilbur, 1993).

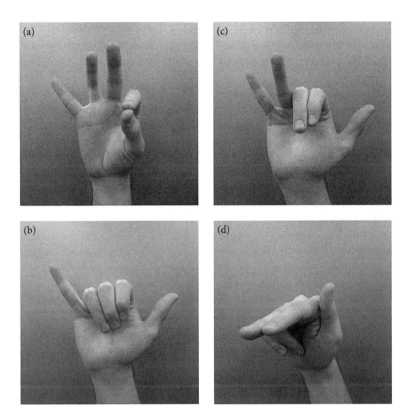

Figure 24.1 The F and Y handshapes are found in lexical signs in both ASL and Cambodian Sign Language (a and b). Handshapes found in lexical signs in Cambodian Sign Language but not ASL (c and d). (From Woodward, J., & The Cambodian Sign Language Production Team. (2010). Cambodian Sign Language-English and English-Cambodian Sign Language Dictionary. Hong Kong: The Centre for Sign Linguistics and Deaf Studies, The Chinese University of Hong Kong.

Cross-linguistic investigations of signed languages suggest that such a constraint on syllable form may be universal. Thus, the core lexicons ASL and many of the world's sign languages core lexicon would be considered largely monosyllabic, although reduplication is quite common.[1]

Phonetic studies of production in ASL suggest that syllable duration is influenced by the same pressures that can influence syllable production in spoken language, such as stress and phrase position. Phonetic studies of ASL syllables indicate their duration is comparable with that observed in spoken languages like English, roughly 250 ms (Corina, 1993; Wilbur & Nolan, 1986). While surface forms of sign and spoken words appear highly disparate, linguistic investigations have helped illuminate how structurally comparable signforms are to spoken words.

Rate of Sign Production

Some of the first studies of sign language production explored the question of the rate of articulation of sign language at the sentence and narrative level. These studies reported a rate of articulation for signs that was roughly half the rate for spoken-language words (Bellugi & Fischer, 1972; Grosjean, 1977; Klima & Bellugi, 1979). However, despite the slower overall articulation of signs in comparison with words, the propositional rate (that is the amount of information conveyed per unit time) is largely equivalent for spoken and signed language (Klima & Bellugi, 1979). This led Klima

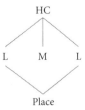

Figure 24.2 A canonical monomorphemic sign. L and M are skeletal features. HC (hand configuration) and Place (place of articulation) serve as autosegments attaching to the skeletal slots (Adapted from Sandler, W., & Lillo-Martin, D. C. (2006). Sign language and linguistic universals. Cambridge, UK: Cambridge University Press.)

and Bellugi to conclude, "there may be a common underlying temporal process governing the rate and production of propositions in language regardless of mode" (1979, p. 188).

The apparent "information compression" that occurs in sign sentences is related, in part, to the fact that in signed languages predicates are often multimorphemic and highly fusional (as opposed to sequentially concatenative), signaling such properties as person and number agreement, manner, and aspect. The fusional properties of sign language morphology have been likened to the morphological patterning observed in Semitic languages, whereby there is a invariant stem form (e.g., k_t_b_) from which nouns, adjectives, and verbs are formed in various ways by inserting vowels, doubling consonants, lengthening vowels, and/or adding affixes (e.g., kataba "he wrote"; katabtu "I wrote"; kutibat "it was written"; maktab "desk").

Adding to the multiple co-occurring layers of meaning within a sign, as noted earlier, facial expressions and head movements serve linguistic roles, for example, in signaling grammatical topics, conditionals, relative clause structure and WH and Y/N questions, as well as for marking adverbials and prominence. It has long been held that sign languages tend to favor the simultaneously packaging of information, while auditory language favors a more sequentially based kind of organization (Klima & Bellugi, 1979). These observations have led many to conclude that human languages capitalize upon the affordances of the modality of expression to create robust and efficient means for the transmission of information. Thus, signed language exploits the relative greater ability of the visual system to monitor and encode spatially disparate streams of information, while spoken languages are adapted to the temporal-sequential sensitivity of the auditory system.

Multiple Articulators

One aspect of sign language production that does not have a clear parallel in spoken language is the potential availability of two independent major articulators: the left and right hand. What is striking is that while one can in principle physically articulate two separate expressions, one using the left hand, the other the right hand, this type of "rub your stomach and while patting your head" phenomenon occurs only rarely in sign languages. Instead, just as there are well-formedness constraints on the internal composition of signs (e.g., the constraint that states that signed languages can

have only one handshape or orientation change per syllable), we also observe well-formedness constraints on the relationships between the two (logically) independent manual articulators. Battison (1978) discovered two major constraints on the nature of two-handed signs in ASL, which appear to be universal.

The first is symmetry condition. If both hands of a sign move independently during its articulation, then both hands must be specified for the same location, the same handshape, and the same movement (whether preformed simultaneously or in alternation), and the specifications for orientation must be either symmetrical or identical (Battison, 1978, p. 33). The second is dominance condition. If the hands of a two-handed sign do not share the same specification for handshape (i.e., they are different), then (a) one hand must be passive while the active hand articulates the movement and (b) the specification of the passive handshape is restricted to be one of a small set: A, S, B, 5, G, C, O (Battison 1978, p. 35).

As discussed in Emmorey (2002), such universals have been interpreted as suggesting that human languages may in fact have but one major articulator (either the tongue or the dominant hand; cf. Van der Hulst, 2000). Support for this contention comes from data on sign aphasia and neuroimaging, which confirms that neural correlates of linguistic programming for both the right and left hands emanate from primarily the left hemisphere (Corina, San Jose-Robertson, Guillemin, High, & Braun, 2003).

In summary, like wordforms, signforms are compositional structures whose makeup can be conceived as consisting of inventories of basic elements and constraints on the co-occurrence and patterns of those elements. Just as the production of spoken language adheres to language-specific and language-universal constraints on well-formedness, the emerging field of sign language linguistics has provided a scaffolding for the understanding of how universal and language-specific constraints govern the manifestation of signforms in the world's sign languages.

Coarticulation and Assimilation

The growing availability of low-cost motion capture systems has helped usher in a new era of phonetic studies of signed language (for an overview of relevant techniques, see Tyrone, 2001). These studies have begun to explore the phonetic properties of sign articulation and to examine whether lawful modification of signforms is observed in particular contexts. Much of this work concerns the phenomenon of coarticulation, the tendency of nearby elements in the flow of spoken or signed language to influence each other (or "overlap") during the articulatory process. For example, in measurements of speech production, one may find that a speaker begins rounding his or her lips during the production of putatively nonrounded consonants well in anticipation of a vocalic segment that is specified as rounded (e.g., the consonants in "two" and "strew"). Coarticulation may be anticipatory (later elements influencing earlier ones, as in the preceding example), or carryover (earlier elements influencing later ones). Both are of interest to researchers because of what they can reveal about language planning (particularly in the case of anticipatory effects) and articulator inertia (particularly for carryover effects).

Coarticulation in spoken language has been studied systematically for at least several decades (e.g., Öhman, 1966), but as is the case with many other aspects of language, coarticulation in signed language has been investigated by relatively few researchers. Such studies include Cheek's (2001) research on handshape coarticulation, Mauk's (2003) examination of location-related effects in the context of undershoot, and Grosvald and Corina's (2009) exploration of long-distance location effects.

Cheek (2001) used an infrared-based motion capture system (Vicon) to investigate handshape-to-handshape (HH) coarticulatory effects in a number of contexts, focusing on signs articulated with the "1" or "5" handshapes. Participants signed ASL sign pairs exemplifying various handshape sequences, such as "1"-"1" (e.g., TRUE SMART) and "1"-"5" (e.g., TRUE MOTHER), and the resulting motion-capture data were analyzed for evidence of HH effects. The metric that was used in determining whether such influence had been exerted was the distance between two markers (one on the tip of the pinky and the other on the base of the hand), which was assumed to be larger when the pinky was more extended (as in the articulation of a "5" handshape) and smaller when the pinky was more curled inward (as for a "1" handshape). Cheek found significant differences in this metric between the "1" and "5" handshape contexts, in both the anticipatory and carryover directions. In addition, faster signing conditions were often, although not always, associated with stronger HH effects.

Mauk (2003) investigated the phenomenon of undershoot in both spoken and signed language. Using a Vicon system, he examined location-to-location (LL) effects, making use of neutral-space signs, which are signs articulated in front of the signer and do not have a place specification for body contact. Subjects signed sequences of three signs, each of whose specified locations was either neutral space or the forehead. In each sequence, the first and third signs had the same location, whereas the middle sign's location varied. The sequences could therefore be classified as forehead-forehead-forehead (e.g., SMART FATHER SMART); forehead-neutral space-forehead (e.g., SMART CHILDREN SMART); neutral space-neutral space-neutral space (e.g., LATE CHILDREN LATE); or neutral space-forehead-neutral space (e.g., LATE FATHER LATE). It was expected that forehead location signs might influence the neutral-space signs, such that they would be articulated at a higher vertical position than they would be otherwise, and similarly, that coarticulatory influence of neutral-space signs on forehead-location signs would result in the latter being articulated at a lower vertical position.

Mauk (2003) found that forehead-location signs tended to exert significant coarticulatory influence on neutral-space signs, but that the reverse did not generally hold, indicating that signs specified for body contact may be less susceptible to coarticulatory influence than neutral-space signs. Like Cheek (2001), Mauk also found that faster signing conditions were generally associated with stronger coarticulatory effects.

Note that the coarticulatory effects found by Cheek and Mauk in their sign studies were influences of signs on immediately preceding or following signs. Grosvald and Corina (2012) examined the possibility that coarticulation may extend over greater distances in the flow of signed language, just as it has been found to do in spoken language (Magen, 1997; Öhman, 1966; Recasens, 1989). Grosvald and Corina used ultrasound-based motion-capture technology to investigate LL coarticulation in the signing of five ASL users. Each signer signed a number of ASL sentences that included multiple neutral-space signs followed by signs articulated at the periphery of signing space. For example, two sentences were "I WANT GO FIND HAT I" and "I WANT GO FIND PANTS I"; the signs HAT and PANTS are located on the top of the head and at waist level, respectively, whereas the preceding three signs are articulated in neutral signing space. It was expected that the neutral-space signs would be located higher in neutral space in the "HAT" context than in the "PANTS" context.

The study also investigated coarticulatory effects in nonlinguistic contexts involving a manual action.

The results were mixed. There was some evidence of significant LL coarticulatory influence of one sign on another across as many as three intervening signs. However, LL effects overall were much weaker and less frequent than the effects found in analogous spoken-language studies. In addition, the outcomes in the nonlinguistic and linguistic conditions did not substantially differ. The researchers argued that these results supported earlier research showing qualitative differences in motor behavior between oral and manual actions, for which the linguistic versus nonlinguistic distinction shows much less influence. For example, Ostry, Cooke, and Munhall (1987) found that movement patterns associated with the oral articulators were consistent whether or not linguistic in nature, but differed from those associated with the arms.

Research in spoken languages has found a great deal of variation among speakers in the strength of their coarticulatory tendencies (e.g., Grosvald, 2009; Magen, 1997). Given the heterogeneous nature of the signing community, it seems reasonably likely that such variation will also be seen among signers, and that many factors will be found to be involved. For example, in a study of sign assimilation, Lucas, Bayley, Rose, and Wulf (2002) investigated forehead-to-cheek location changes. They found that the location of the preceding sign was an important factor influencing whether such a location shift would occur in a target sign, but the grammatical category of the target sign was an even stronger predictor, and social factors including gender, geographic region, age, ethnicity, and social class were also influential to a significant degree (see also Bayley, Lucas, & Rose, 2002).

Tyrone and Mauk (2010) explored a number of factors relevant to the phenomenon of sign lowering, which they treated as an example of reduction in ASL. Sign lowering refers to the fact that in the flow of normal signing, signers sometimes articulate signs at a lower position than would be seen in a citation form. In this study, six native signers articulated the sign WONDER (whose citation form is located at the forehead) in two phonetic contexts and at three signing rates. All six of the signers exhibited sign lowering in at least some contexts. The data also showed that a number of factors known to be relevant in speech production also influenced these signers' sign productions: production rate, phonetic context, and position within an utterance.

Sign Language Acquisition

Studies of the acquisition of signed languages have provided a rich source of data regarding the development of sign production. Much of the early work aimed at understanding whether the developmental milestones observed in spoken languages also held for signed languages. These studies showed convincingly that similar milestones were achieved by deaf children who received sign language from primary caregivers in the home (Klima & Bellugi, 1979; McIntire, 1977; Newport & Meier, 1985).

In recent years, researchers have explored the details of language acquisition at a much more fine-grained level. These studies have pushed back the limits of our understanding of sign acquisition by examining the precursors to language development, specifically by exploring the phenomenon of manual babbling, as well as focusing more closely on the order of appearance and form of linguistic properties, such as handshape, movement, and place of articulation of children's first signs.

Sign Babble

A particularly interesting subdomain in this field of research has grown from work examining the phenomenon of sign babble. This work holds great promise as it provides a means to test hypotheses regarding the relationships between babbling and language development and to disentangle the effects of manual motoric development from language development in general. In a series of articles, researchers have documented stages of sign babbling in deaf and hearing infants exposed to sign languages. In an early study, Petitto and Marentette (1991) reported on two deaf signing infants at the ages of 10, 12, and 14 months comparing their development to that of three hearing non–sign-exposed children. They operationally defined manual babbling as those manual gestures that had no referential or manipulative purpose. While both hearing and deaf children produced actions that were coded as gestures and manual babbling, manual babbling accounted for 32 percent to 71 percent of manual activity in deaf infants and a mere 4 percent to 15 percent of the manual activity of hearing infants. These actions included single and reduplicated "syllabic" forms, exhibited a reduced inventory of handshapes, and were restricted to signing space (largely occurring in front of the body).

Work by Meier and colleagues (Cheek, Cormier, Rathmann, Repp, & Meier, 1998; Cormier, Mauk, & Repp, 1998; Meier & Willerman, 1995) also examined manual babbling in deaf and hearing infants. This work found far fewer differences in sign- and non–sign-exposed infants, both in terms of the frequency of occurrence of and the uniqueness of the manual forms observed. The researchers noted that in both groups, the most common forms included manual actions with relaxed handshapes with all fingers extended and with downward palm orientation. Movements displayed downward movements more often for babbles than for any other movement category; babies also demonstrated a preference for one-handed babbles over two-handed ones.

One developmental difference was noted between 7 and 13 months, at which time deaf babies decreased the frequency of two-handed babbles in favor of one-handed babbles. In contrast, hearing babies showed no such shift. The commonalities between sign-exposed and non–sign-exposed infants led the researchers to claim that deaf and hearing babies may be similarly constrained by their particular level of motor development. However, the increased production of one-handed babbles in deaf babies may indicate an effect of linguistic experience, as deaf babies see many one-handed signs in their linguistic environment.

Later work reported by Petitto, Holowka, Sergio, Levy, and Ostry (2004) used an Optotrack system to examine the rhythmic nature of manual actions in sign-exposed and non–sign-exposed infants at 6, 10, and 12 months. The data indicated differential distribution of the rhythmic components of gestures in these children, with sign-exposed children showing a bimodal distribution with peaks at 1 Hz and 2.5 Hz, and hearing non–sign-exposed children peaking at 3 Hz. Subsequent videotaped analysis guided by the Optotrack findings revealed that 80 percent of these 1-Hz gestures were consistent with criteria for sign babbling (e.g., showing evidence of being confined to a linguistically defined space). Petitto et al. (2004) suggested that this 1-Hz rate is characteristic of both babbling and speech output in adults. These figures, however, have been challenged with empirical data from infants suggesting a 3-Hz figure for rhythmic babbling (Dolata, Davis, & MacNeilage, 2008).

The work by Petitto and colleagues that highlights the observed differences between the form and frequency of occurrence of sign babbling in sign-exposed and non–sign-exposed infants leads to an interpretation that babbles reflect linguistic underpinning and are not simply by-products of motoric development. Moreover, the presumed uniformity of syllable production rates across vocal and manual babbling and sign and speech production has been taken as evidence for a uniform and invariant mechanism, attuned to specific frequencies, for human language production and recognition.

In contrast, the data offered by Meier and colleagues argue for a universal motoric account of these early gestures, with later differentiation into linguistic forms that persist for sign-exposed infants. In addition, comparing aspects of sign language movements with the syllabic cycle in speech, Meier (2000, p. 9) concludes that "analysts of syllable structure in sign may not be able to develop a simple articulatory model of syllable production comparable to the one which appears possible for speech." Dolata et al. (2008) state, "If articulatory components of basic syllable production are so different in the two modalities, it is unlikely that their rhythmic organization would be the same." Future work will no doubt strive to reconcile these differences; at the least, there appears to be a need for a careful evaluation of the forms being analyzed across laboratories, as operational definitions of sign babble, which appear derivative of descriptions of speech babble (e.g., Oller & Eilers, 1986), might not be readily borrowed and applied to sign languages.

First Signs

Meier and colleagues have also provided some of the most detailed accounts of the forms of first signs (Conlin, Mirus, Mauk, & Meier, 2000; Meier, Mauk, Mirus, & Conlin, 1998). They have noted that for the deaf infant there is continuity between the articulatory forms observed in babbling and signing "errors" observed in first signs. In one longitudinal study, they followed three deaf infants of deaf parents from the ages of 7 months to 19 months. They recorded handshape forms, places of articulation and movements, and evaluated the children's production relative to adult citation forms. Deviations from the adult forms were termed "errors" and catalogued. Analysis showed that children produced the fewest errors in place of articulation[2] (11.6 percent), with handshapes showing the greatest number of errors (75 percent) and movement intermediate (46 percent). The variability of each child's errors mirrored the observed errors' frequency count, with the least variability occurring in place of articulation and the most in handshape, with movement again intermediate. Consistent with previous studies, the handshapes produced were a restricted set and included 5(lax), G, baby-O, O, A, bent-5, C, and S. These handshapes, based partly on such developmental data, are often referred to as the unmarked handshapes in ASL. A significant trend in the data was noted for the movement parameter, with the insight that children tend to proximalize movement in their early signing—that is, to produce a movement from joints closest to the body such as the shoulder and elbow, rather than with the wrist or by using a change in handshape. This is consistent with literature on motor development showing that gross motor skills are acquired prior to fine motor skills.

Psycholinguistic Investigations

Psycholinguistic studies of sign production include naturally occurring "slips of the hand" and laboratory induced "tip-of-the-finger" (TOF) phenomena. Slips of the hand provide evidence for the psychological reality of sign parameters and the integrity of phonological segments, while the TOF phenomenon highlights the separability of lexical signform and meaning. Laboratory studies of sign naming have used sign-picture and implicit priming paradigms to further isolate the time course of semantic and lexical activation. Recent studies have sought to explore the relationship between production and perception of signing through studies of articulatory interference and visual self-monitoring.

Slips of the Hand

Seminal works by Fromkin (1971, 1973) and Garrett (1975) revealed how slips of the tongue could yield deep insights into the structure and organization of spoken languages. Early studies by Klima and Bellugi (1979) and Newkirk, Klima, Pedersen, and Bellugi (1980) reported similar phenomena in ASL. Analysis of videotaped conversation and self-reported errors revealed cases of exchanges of whole signs, as well as individual components of signs (i.e., handshapes, movements, or locations). The component errors included cases of metathesis, anticipation, and perseveration of components parts of ASL signs. Anticipation errors (where a component of one sign is replaced by a component of another sign occurring later in the signed sequence) were the most commonly reported error type, followed by preservative errors (in which a sign component is replaced by one appearing in a sign that occurs earlier in a sequence); least frequent were compete metathesis (where two components of sequentially ordered signs are exchanged). There

were frank differences in the frequency with which different sign parameters were subject to error, with the majority of form-based errors related to handshape. Importantly, in nearly all cases, errors were structure preserving, resulting in a possible sign rather than violation of sign structure.

Hohenberger, Happ, and Leuniger (2002) reported evidence of "slips of the hand" in German Sign Language (Deutsche Gebaerdensprache). In these data, semantic as well as phonological errors were found but dual errors (both semantic and form-based) were scarce: 38 out of 40 sign substitutions were semantically related but only one was both semantic and form-based. Sign language form-based errors were mostly perseverations and anticipations for whole signs ($n = 25$) or sublexical units ($n = 76$), consistent with previous research by Bellugi and colleagues.

It is interesting to note that both studies reported a lack of exchange errors, particularly those exchange errors in which there was an interaction with morphological elements (i.e., *turk*ing *talk*ish ⇓ *talk*ing *Turk*ish; Garrett, 1975). Such "stranding errors," which are prominent in spoken languages, appear largely absent in sign language. Hohenberger et al. (2002) entertain two possible explanations for this lack of error type, one based on the typological differences, and one based on a modality-specific account, which invokes the notion of an output editor. The typological account notes that although signed languages are extremely rich in inflectional and derivational morphology, the manifestation of the morphemes is highly fusional and is often coexpressed even within the domain of a single syllable in complex predicate forms, such as classifiers (Brentari, 1998; Shepard-Kegl, 1985; Supalla, 1986). Classifiers are morphological complex forms that are used to denote spatial relations and motion events and for characterizing the shapes and dimensions of objects (Sandler & Lillo-Martin, 2006). This degree of fusion may make these morphemes far more resistant to separation compared to concatenated morphemes (Hohenberger et al., 2002). The modality-specific account suggests that the longer duration of articulation of a sign may allow an output editor to capture mispronunciations earlier. In addition, the availability of the major articulators to visuokinesthetic monitoring may reduce the frequency with which errors escape detection prior to output (Hohenberger et al., 2002). These studies raise questions regarding the role of self-monitoring in sign language production, a topic to which we now turn.

Self-monitoring

Emmorey and colleagues (Emmorey, Bosworth, & Kraljic, 2009; Emmorey, Gertsberg, Korpics, & Wright, 2009) investigated the role of self-monitoring (see Hartsuiker, this volume) in ASL and concluded that a signer's somatosensory feedback plays a larger role than visual feedback during their own production of signing. In one experiment, they reported that signers were poor at recognizing ASL signs when viewed as they would appear during ones' own signing. In a second experiment, they showed that the absence or blurring of visual feedback did not affect production performance when deaf signers learned to reproduce novel signs from Russian Sign Language (Emmorey, Bosworth, et al., 2009). In a separate study, Emmorey, Gertsberg, et al. (2009) had signers produce signs in a carrier phrase under two conditions. In the first condition, signing was done in an unobstructed visual condition. In the second condition, signers wore a blindfold or tunnel vision goggles. Three-dimensional movement trajectories were obtained using a motion capture system. Tunnel vision caused signers to produce less movement within the vertical dimension of signing space, but blind and citation signing did not differ significantly on any measure, except duration. The researchers reported that signers do not "sign louder" when they cannot see themselves (as is common when hearing individuals cannot auditorily monitor their own speech), but do alter some aspects of signs production when vision is restricted. These studies suggest that signers may rely primarily on somatosensory feedback when monitoring language output.

Tip of the Finger

Thompson, Emmorey, and Gollan (2005) probed TOF (Newkirk et al., 1980) experiences for both lexical signs and fingerspelled names in ASL that were similar to speech users' "tip of the tongue" phenomenon. The tip of the tongue phenomenon is the failure to retrieve a word from memory, combined with partial recall and the feeling that retrieval is imminent (Brown, 1991). Participants were asked to fingerspell names of famous faces and to produce the lexical signs for lists of words. Results showed TOFs for fingerspelled names as well as for lexical signs. TOF states were more common for fingerspelled proper names; as often happens in spoken languages, participants mostly recalled the first letter of the first or last name or both. However, the contribution of the failure to retrieve the English spelling, rather than an ASL form, cannot be evaluated

in this paradigm. For the lexical signs, participants were typically able to recall some phonological information; specifically, handshape, location, and orientation were recalled more often than movement. The finding that partial phonological recall can dissociate from retrieval of the full lexical specification supports a two-stage model of lexical access that honors a distinction between activation of form (e.g., phonology) and meaning (e.g., semantics). In addition, the results indicate a similar role of location, handshape, and orientation as phonological onsets, suggesting that lexical retrieval may not be guided by a single phonological parameter.

Sign Naming: Semantic and Phonological Influences

Corina and Hildebrandt (2002) and Corina and Knapp (2006) investigated the time course of semantic and phonological form retrieval in a sign language production experiment. A sign-picture interference task, modeled after Schriefers, Meyer, and Levelt's (1990) word-picture paradigm was used. In the Schriefers et al. (1990) word-picture interference study, subjects were asked to name pictures of objects. Slightly before, simultaneously with, or slightly after picture onset, an auditory word (i.e., the interfering stimulus [IS]) was presented. The auditory IS was either phonologically or semantically related or unrelated to the to-be-named object (e.g., pictured target object: *cat*, phonological IS: *cab*; semantic IS: *pig*, unrelated IS: *beer*). The major findings of this research was that at the early time window (150 ms before picture onset), the semantic but not the phonological IS disrupted naming relative to the unrelated IS condition, whereas at the 0 and +150 ms stimulus onset asynchronies (SOAs) conditions the phonological IS facilitated picture naming, relative to the semantic or unrelated IS conditions. These data were taken as evidence for a two-stage model of word naming in which conceptual representation and activation of an associated lemma (a time that is most sensitive to the semantic IS) preceded the specification of a lexeme (a time sensitive to the effects of the phonological IS), which fed articulation.

In the ASL version, participants were asked to produce sign names of an object while ignoring a distracter sign transparently overlaid on top of the object at early (−130 ms) and late (0 and +130 ms) SOAs. Native signers of ASL exhibited longer naming latencies in the presence of semantically related sign distracters than in the presence of unrelated distracters at early, but not late, SOAs. On the other hand, phonologically related stimuli produced naming facilitation at both early and late SOAs. Thus, these effects mirrored those described in Schriefers et al. (1990). Furthermore, the direction and magnitude of the effects were influenced by the degree and type of phonological relatedness. Specifically, the degree of facilitation was larger when the target and distracter shared both movement and location. Similar to the accounts of spoken language described previously, these findings provide partial support for a serial account of naming in sign language production with a stage at which we posit activation of a lemma (susceptible to semantic interference) followed by specification of the lexeme (susceptible to phonological interference). Moreover, the differential effects of phonological overlap between IS and target signs provide evidence that structural components of signs may have different effects on phonological encoding.

Myers, Lee, and Tsay (2005) investigated the production of handshape changes in Taiwan Sign Language (TSL) using the implicit priming experimental paradigm modeled after Meyer (1990, 1991). In the original Meyer (1990, 1991) speech paradigms, subjects learned blocks of three to five paired associates consisting of a prompt word and a target under two conditions. In the homogenous condition, all the targets shared some feature of interest (first syllable, second syllable, onset, coda, and so forth), while in the heterogeneous condition all targets varied across the dimension of interest. For example, a researcher interested in testing the encoding of onsets in English might contrast a homogenous block (tent-pie; book-pot; stove-pen; cat-pill; truck-pat) with a heterogeneous list (tent-pie; book-head; stove-car; cat-town; truck-seed). Subjects are given a probe word and must recall and name the paired associate target. One observes that in some cases the naming times for the targets in the homogeneous conditions is faster than the heterogeneous condition (in our example, indicating that the initial onset could be primed across conditions). In the speech studies, Meyer reported that initial syllables in disyllabic forms could be primed, but not second syllables, and that word onsets could be primed, but not rhymes. These data were taken as evidence for structural limitations on the scope of activation in serial ordered sublexical constituents during speech production.

In the TSL experiment, participants were asked to memorize three nine-item sets of cue-target pairs. Sets were composed either of signs that shared a handshape change but varied in location, orientation movement path, and nonmanual features (homogeneous pairs), or of signs that had no phonological relationship (heterogeneous pairs). In addition, cue-pairs were semantically associated in order to facilitate memorization (although the nature of this association was not an experimental variable). After memorizing the pairs, participants were presented with the cue words, and latencies of targets' production were measured using the keyboard lift-off method. Participants produced fewer errors in the heterogeneous condition than in the homogeneous one, but there were no significant effects on reaction times. These results suggest an influence of form-based properties on the production of signs, although this influence was restricted to accuracy in this case. The authors suggested that these results mirrored effects found in spoken language implicit priming paradigms (Meyer, 1991) and suggested that the stages of phonological encoding seem to be essentially the same across modalities. This claim, however, may be premature, as the effects observed for TSL appear quite distinct from those reported by Meyer (1990, 1991) for speech. Specifically, the lack of facilitatory effects on reaction times for sign-naming in the homogenous condition, coupled with the presence of inference effects, may be more reflective of memory constraints than a reflection of the time course of language planning and production.

Baus, Gutiérrez-Sigut, Quer, and Carreiras (2008) also investigated semantic and phonological effects during sign production. Native and late learners of Catalan Sign Language (Llengua de Signes Catalana, LSC) were asked to perform a sign-picture interference task. Results suggested a difference between the retrieval processes associated with semantic and phonological properties of signs; differences in the roles played by the three phonological parameters under study were also apparent. Semantic overlap between the sign to be produced and the picture distracter produced interference, whereas phonological overlap led to facilitation for shared handshape or movement. However, when the target sign and the distracter (i.e., the sign that would name the picture) shared location, interference was found. This last finding suggests that there are differences between signed- and spoken-language production in the mechanisms underlying phonological encoding. Specifically, for signs, sublexical parameters appear to yield differential effects on language production, where handshape and movement lead to facilitation, whereas location produces interference. This difference suggests that there may not be a one-to-one correspondence between speech phonemes and the classes of articulatory features described in sign (i.e., handshape, location, and movements). Finally, no differences were found between groups; this might be due to the fact that all participants were highly competent users of LSC, although it also may also be case that that the task was not sensitive enough to capture differences between native and late-exposed signers.

Taken together, studies of naturally occurring TOF experiences and experimental studies of sign production provide compelling evidence for the commonalities between processes of sign- and spoken-language word production. The sign language studies suggest that, as predicted by most models of speech production (e.g., Caramazza, 1997; Dell & O'Seaghdha, 1992; Levelt, Roelofs, & Meyer, 1999), lexical selection of signs involves two different steps: semantic activation/selection and phonological encoding. A number of studies have shown interference effects from semantically related distracters. This interference can be explained in terms of activation levels of competitors. Provided that the target is selected from a cohort of semantically related representations, the higher the activation levels of the potential competitors the more demanding this selection process will be. The separation between semantics and phonology, as well as the inhibitory semantic effects, seem not to be modality-specific but rather part of a language-universal processing pattern.

However, the mechanisms underlying phonological encoding seem to show modality-specific effects. As noted in our discussion of TOF studies, deaf subjects in a TOF state show simultaneous accessibility of location, handshape, and orientation information. Moreover, the effects of these formed-based properties of signs on production show different degrees of interference (facilitation or inhibition) as a function of both the number of parameters that a distracter shares with the target (Corina & Knapp, 2006) and the specific parameters shared with the target (Baus et al., 2008). These effects on phonological encoding, specifically the simultaneous availability of multiple parameters, in many respects appears to mirror the status of the perception of signs. As noted earlier, sign structure has often been described as exhibiting far more structural simultaneity than has been attributed to spoken languages. That is, while a spoken word unfolds over time, exposing a great deal of phonological information about individual segments as they are sequentially produced, signs appear as

concurrent instantiations of values of each parameter (a simultaneously produced hand configuration, place of articulation, and movement). Thus, a great deal of phonological information is available quite early in a sign's production and is maintained throughout the duration of the sign (e.g., Corina & Sandler, 1993; Emmorey & Corina, 1990; Sandler, 1993). Thus, as in perception, the initial stages of phonological encoding during production seem in part to mirror this simultaneous structure, especially for nonmovement parameters.

Future psycholinguistic studies of sign production will be necessary to further explore the retrieval mechanisms for sublexical units of signs, not only to disentangle the specific role and temporal time-course of action related to the four major phonological parameters, but also to explore whether larger units of sign structure (such as syllables) are among the levels of phonological and phonetic encoding and can, therefore, be retrieved as whole entities. Another potentially revealing research question concerns the relationship between sign language production and age of sign language acquisition, as consistent differences are observed during the comprehension of signs by native versus nonnative signers (Carreiras, Gutierrez-Sigut, Baquero, & Corina, 2008; Emmorey, Bellugi, Friederici, & Horn, 1995; Emmorey & Corina, 1990; Mayberry & Eichen, 1991; Mayberry & Fischer, 1989; Mayberry & Witcher, 2006; Morford, Grieve-Smith, MacFarlane, Staley, & Waters, 2008). Moreover, these differences have often been attributed to the efficiency of phonological processing during on-line processing (for an attention-based account, see Morford et al., 2008). Whether such effects are present during the phonological encoding stages of sign production may shed light on the question of whether a single lexicon supports both comprehension and production. Aside from the one study of Baus et al. (2008) reported previously, this question has been largely unexplored.

Sign Perception and Production

Recent psycholinguistic work has reported that concurrent articulation of an ASL handshape may impact the ability to hold sign information in working memory (Wilson & Emmorey, 2000). This phenomenon mirrors well-known articulatory suppression effects observed in spoken language, suggesting an articulator or perhaps somatosensory component for working memory for users of signed languages. Recent attempts to closely examine perception-articulation effects for sign language have found that such effects are difficult to establish. In one study, subjects monitored for specific handshapes in signs and phonotactically possible nonsigns while rearticulating identical or contrasting handshapes. Only modest effects were observed in one study of 30 subjects (Grosvald, Lachaud, & Corina, 2009, 2012). While caution must be taken in interpreting negative effects, these data may indicate that sign-perception is relatively protected from the effect of overt differences in the state of the articulators. This would be consistent with physiological models of motor control which evoke the notion of forward-model or efference copy (Wolpert & Miall, 1996), which in part may serve to actively suppress mirror movements in the perceiver (Verstynen & Ivry, 2011).

Neurobioloigcal Studies
Sign Language Aphasia

In spoken language aphasia, chronic language production impairments are typically associated with left-hemisphere frontal anterior lesions that involve the lower posterior portion of the left frontal lobe (e.g., Broca's area). These lesions often extend in depth to the periventricular white matter (e.g., Goodglass, 1993; Mohr et al., 1978). The anterior insula has also been implicated in chronic speech production problems (Dronkers, Redfren, & Knight, 2000).

Profound sign language production problems have also been reported following left prefrontal damage. A well-described case is that of patient G.D., reported in Poizner, et al. (1987). G.D., a deaf signer with a large lesion in a left anterior frontal region encompassing BA 44/45, presented with nonfluent, aphasic signing with intact sign comprehension. Specifically, G.D.'s signing was effortful and dysfluent, with output often reduced to single-sign utterances. The signs she was able to produce were agrammatic, devoid of the movement modulations that signal morphosyntactic contrasts in fluent signing. A reduction in the use of linguistic facial expressions relative to affective expressions in this signer was also reported (Corina et al., 1999). As with hearing Broca's aphasics, this signer's comprehension of others' language productions appeared to be essentially undisturbed by her lesion. Both at the single sign and sentence level, her comprehension was on par with control subjects. That this deficit is not simply motoric in nature is indicated by the fact that the deficits were exhibited on both her motorically impacted and nonmotorically involved (i.e., ipsilesional) limb.

Neuropsychological case studies of deaf signers have provided evidence for dissociations between the production of sign language and human actions. Several reports have now documented cases in which, following damage to the left hemisphere, a deaf signer has completely or partially lost the ability to use sign language but has retained an ability to use pantomime and nonlinguistic gesture (Corina et al., 1992; Marshall, Atkinson, Smulovitch, Thacker, & Woll, 2004; Metz-Lutz et al., 1999; Poizner et al., 1987). A sampling of this literature cuts a broad swath across patient age and primary language. For example, Metz-Lutz et al. (1999) report a case of a child with acquired temporal-lobe epileptic aphasia who was unable to acquire French Sign Language, but was unimpaired on ideomotor and visuospatial tasks and produced unencumbered nonlinguistic pantomime. Corina et al. (1992) reported that adult patient W.L. demonstrated a marked ASL production (and comprehension) impairment following a lesion in left fronto-temporo-parietal regions, but retained intact pantomime production (and comprehension), using gestures to convey symbolic information that he ordinarily would have imparted with sign language. Marshall et al. (2004) report an interesting case study patient, Charles, whose communicative behavior following a left-hemisphere stroke makes clear that sign and gesture production in British Sign Language can be dissociated, even when the signs and gestures in question are physically quite similar. For example, when asked to produce the BSL sign for bicycle, he substituted a pantomimed bicycling motion. These cases emphasize that sign language impairments following left-hemisphere damage are not simply attributable to undifferentiated impairments in the motoric instantiation of symbolic representations, but in fact reflect disruptions to a manually expressed linguistic system that are not limited to any one language or stage of language development.

Sign Paraphasia

Sign language breakdown following left hemisphere damage is not haphazard, but clearly honors linguistic properties. The systematicity in sign and spoken language breakdown can be illustrated through consideration of paraphasic errors (Corina, 2000). In spoken language, the substitution of an unexpected word for an intended target is known as verbal paraphasia. Most verbal paraphasias have a clear semantic relationship to the desired word and represent the same part of speech; hence, they are referred to as "semantic paraphasias" (Goodglass, 1993). In contrast, phonemic or "literal" paraphasia refers to the production of unintended sounds or syllables in the utterance of a partially recognizable word (Blumstein, 1973; Goodglass, 1993). Alternatively, phonemic sound substitution may result in another real word, related in sound but not in meaning (e.g., *telephone* becomes *television*). Also attested are cases in which the erroneous word shares both sound characteristics and meaning with the target (e.g., *broom* becomes *brush*; Goodglass, 1993).

Several reports of signing paraphasia have been reported (Brentari, Poizner, & Kegl, 1995; Corina et al., 1992; Poizner et al., 1987). For example, a left posterior lesioned signer, subject P.D., (Poizner et al., 1987) produced clear lexical substitutions: BED for CHAIR, DAUGHTER for SON, QUIT for DEPART, etc.. In general, the semantic errors of P.D. overlap in meaning and lexical class with the intended targets; this pattern has been routinely observed in spoken language semantic paraphasia (Goodglass, 1993). These ASL semantic paraphasias provide additional evidence that the lexicon is structured according to semantic principles, whereby similar semantic items share representational proximity. In this view, coactivation of closely related representations and/or an absence of appropriate inhibition from competing entries may lead to substitutions and blends. As noted previously, such organization appears to hold across both signed and spoken languages.

Subject W.L. (Corina et al., 1992) evidenced interesting semantic blends in signing errors conditioned, in part, by perseverations from earlier cued items. For example, in the context of a picture-naming task, when shown a picture of a tree, W.L. signed TREE with the G handshape. Previously, W.L. had been asked to name the color green (which in ASL is made with a G handshape). The lexical signs GREEN and TREE also share a motion (repeated twisting of the wrist) and evidence similar articulatory postures. These errors appear to be similar to the blended errors described in spoken languages, which contain both semantic and formational properties of the intended target.

One of the most striking characteristics of aphasic signing is formational paraphasia or literal paraphasia. As with spoken languages, ASL formational errors encompass both phonological and phonetic levels of impairment (see Corina, 2000 for some discussion). A priori, we may expect to find phonological errors affecting the four major formational

parameters of ASL phonology: (1) handshape, (2) movement, (3) location, and (4) orientation. However, the distribution of paraphasic errors among the four parameters of sign formation appears to be unequal; handshape configuration errors are the most widely reported, while paraphasias affecting movement, location, and orientation, though attested, and are less frequent (see Poizner et al., 1987). The globally aphasic signer W.L. (Corina et al., 1992) produced numerous phonemic errors, nearly all of which were errors involving handshape specification. For example, W.L. produced the sign TOOTHBRUSH with the Y handshape rather than the required G handshape, and produced the sign SCREWDRIVER with an A handshape rather than the required H handshape.

The higher incidence of handshape errors is noteworthy, as we have seen handshape is the most frequently affected category in slips of the hand, in language acquisition, and here again in sign paraphasia. Moreover, as noted earlier, recent linguistic analyses of ASL have suggested that handshape specifications (and perhaps static articulatory locations) may be relatively consonantal in nature, whereas movement components of ASL may be analogous to vowels. In spoken language phonemic paraphasias, a homologous asymmetry exists; the vast majority of phonemic paraphasias involve consonant distortions (see also Caramazza, Chialant, Capasso, & Miceli, 2000). These errors demonstrate how functionally similar language categories (e.g., "consonants") may be selectively vulnerable to impairment. Although the surface manifestations differ, the underlying disruption may be related to a common abstract level of representation. Another similarity between spoken and sign paraphasic errors is that in both cases, errors do not compromise the syllabic integrity of a sign or word (Brentari et al., 1995; Corina, 2000).

An unusual case of sign paraphasia is reported by Hickok, Kritchevsky, Bellugi, & Klima (1996). This life-long signer, R.S., suffered an infarct to the left frontal operculum. Neurological examination revealed an initial expressive aphasia that largely resolved, although with lingering problems of word finding and frequent phonemic paraphasia. Particularly noteworthy is the nature of these errors, which in contrast to the handshape errors previously described, are errors that demonstrate the distinct way in which a language's modality may uniquely influence the form of the linguistic deficit, in this case an articulatory impairment with no clear parallels to spoken language disruption.

Sign languages, unlike spoken languages, require coordinated control of the two hands. The possibility of differential programming of two potentially independent articulators may place qualitatively different demands on the on the linguistic system. In the absence of limb apraxia, Patient R.S. exhibited paraphasia restricted to two-handed signs. For example, on signs that require two hands to assume different handshapes and/or move independently, R.S. would incorrectly fail to move one of her hands. In addition, during one-handed signing she mirrored movements and handshapes of the dominant hand on the nondominant hand, although with some reduction in degree of movement. Such mirroring was not seen during nonlinguistic movement and was qualitatively different from the mirror movements affecting distal movement that is sometimes seen in cases of hemiparesis (Hickok et al., 1996). The case of R.S. is important for our understanding of the neurobiology of language as it indicates that the modality and/or form of a human linguistic system may place unique demands on the neural mediation and implementation of language. The errors of R.S. can be taken as evidence for selective sign language–specific linguistic impairment.

Cortical Stimulation Mapping

Further clues to within-hemisphere specialization for sign language production come from rare clinical cases of cortical stimulation mapping performed in awake neurosurgical patients undergoing treatment for epilepsy. During the language mapping portion of the procedure, a subject is required to name pictures or read written words. Disruption of the ability to perform the task during stimulation is taken as evidence of which cortical regions are integral to the language task (Stemmer & Whitaker, 1998). Corina et al. (1999) reported the effects of cortical stimulation on sign language production in a deaf individual undergoing an awake cortical stimulation mapping procedure. The patient was to sign the names of items shown in line drawings. All elicited signs were one-handed, and the subject signed each with his left hand. As this subject was undergoing left hemisphere surgery, language disruption as a result of cortical stimulation cannot be attributed to primary motor deficits.

Stimulation to two anatomical sites led to consistent naming disruption. One of these sites, an isolated frontal opercular site, corresponds to the posterior aspect of Broca's area, BA 44. A second site, located in the parietal opercular region, also resulted in robust object-naming errors. This parietal area corresponds to the supramarginal gyrus (SMG, BA 40). Importantly, the nature of these errors was qualitatively different. Stimulation of Broca's area resulted in errors involving the motor execution of signs. These errors are characterized by a laxed articulation of the intended sign, with nonspecific movements (repeated tapping or rubbing) and a reduction in handshape configuration to a laxed-closed fist handshape. Interestingly, there was no effort on the part of S.T. to self-correct these imperfect forms. In addition, such errors were observed during trials of sign and nonsign repetition. These results are consistent with the characterization of the posterior portion of Broca's area as participating in the motoric execution of complex articulatory forms, especially those underlying the phonetic level of language structure.

The sign errors observed with stimulation of the SMG were qualitatively different. With stimulation to this site, S.T. produced both formational and semantic errors in this picture-naming task. Formational errors were characterized by repeated attempts to distinctly articulate the intended targets, and successive formational approximations of the correct sign were common. For example, the sign PEANUT is normally signed with a closed fist and outstretched thumb, and with a movement comprised of an outward wrist rotation (the thumb flicking off the front of the teeth). Under stimulation, this sign began as an incorrect, but clearly articulated, "X" handshape (closed fist with a protruding bent index finger) articulated at the correct location, but with an incorrect inward rotation movement. In two successive attempts to correct this error, the subject first corrected the handshape, and then went on to correct the movement as well. Notably, we did not find the laxed and reduced articulations characteristic of signing under conditions of stimulation to Broca's area. Instead, as these examples illustrate, under stimulation to the SMG, the subject's signing exhibited problems involving the selection of the individual components of signforms (i.e., handshape, movement, and, to a lesser extent, location). Adding to the specificity of these errors is the observation that in contrast to sign naming, sign and nonsign repetition were unaffected by stimulation to the SMG.

Semantic errors were also observed under stimulation of the SMG, and the form of these errors is particularly noteworthy. Specifically, all of these errors involved semantic substitutions that were formationally quite similar to the intended targets. For example, the stimulus picture "pig" elicited the sign FARM, the stimulus picture "bed" was signed as SLEEP, and the stimulus picture "horse" was signed as COW. In ASL, these semantic errors contain considerable formational overlap with their intended targets. For example, the signs PIG and FARM differ in movement, but share an identical articulatory location (the chin) and each are made with similar handshapes; the signs BED and SLEEP share handshapes and are both articulated about the face; finally, the signs COW and HORSE differ only in handshape.

In summary, these findings suggest that stimulation to Broca's area has a global effect on the motor output of signing, whereas stimulation to the parietal opercular site, the SMG, disrupts the correct selection of the linguistic components (including both phonological and semantic elements) required in the service of naming. The preponderance of formationally motivated semantic errors raises further questions regarding the coupling of semantic and phonological properties in sign languages, whereby some signforms may be historically influenced by iconic properties of their referents.

In a recent case (Knapp et al., 2005), stimulation mapping was performed in a right-hemisphere language-dominant (confirmed by Wada testing) deaf signer who grew up orally and learned ASL in early adolescence. As a fluent user of both speech and sign, this signer underwent thorough testing in both ASL and English. Stimulation of the right inferior ventral region (BA6) resulted in speech disruption with spared signing ability. A stimulation site dorsal to this region produced impaired sign naming, but spared speech abilities. This cortical organization thus mirrors primary motor cortex whereby hand representation is dorsal to mouth, lip, and tongue representation. Moving anteriorly, stimulation to superior pars triangularis disrupted both speech and sign; in the case of initiation of speech, naming was delayed and when produced, was executed with a low volume. Stimulation of this same site produced a laxed sign articulation of the left hand. Stimulation of the inferior portion of the pars triangularis affected the patient's ability to correctly produce movement components of signs and nonlinguistic gestures (i.e., repeated pincher movement of the index finger and thumb) and protruded tongue wagging. Finally, stimulation of a ventral region in the frontal orbitalis produced speech disruption but did not affect sign production. This pattern of disruption could be described by means of a mosaic of inferior frontal cortical regions that are differentially involved in unique and shared aspects of speech, oral movement, sign, and nonlinguistic gesture execution.

Parkinson Disease

Studies of deaf signers with Parkinson disease have provided evidence for the importance of extrapyramidal motor systems and basal ganglia in the production of signed languages (Brentari et al., 1995; Poizner & Kegl, 1992). Motor deficits observed in subjects with Parkinson disease are not specific to language but are evidenced across the general domain of motor behaviors. Signers with Parkinson disease have been described as signing in a monotonous fashion with a severely restricted range of temporal rates and tension in signing. Accompanying restrictions in limb movements are deficits in the motility facial musculature, which further reduce expressivity in signing.

Neuroimaging Studies
Lexical Naming

Neuroimaging studies of sign language production reveal further commonalities in the neural systems underlying core properties of language function in sign and speech. In an analysis of sign and word naming studies in deaf signers and hearing nonsigners, Emmorey, Mehta, and Grabowski (2007) reported common overlap in neural activation for single-sign and word production. In this positron emission tomography (PET) study, the naming of objects was placed in contrast to a low-level sensorimotor task in which participants were asked to indicate whether faces were presented upright or upside down. The naming responses covered several semantic categories, including animals, manipulable tools, and common objects. The comparison of blood flow from 29 deaf signers and 64 hearing nonsigners allowed the identification of regions supporting modality-independent lexical access. Common regions implicated included the left mesial temporal cortex and the left inferior frontal gyrus. Emmorey et al. (2007) suggest that left temporal regions are associated with conceptually driven lexical access (Indefrey & Levelt, 2004). For both speakers and signers, activation within the left inferior temporal gyrus may reflect prelexical conceptual processing of the pictures to be named, while activation within the more mesial temporal regions may reflect lemma selection, prior to phonological code retrieval. These results argue for a modality-independent frontotemporal network that subserves both sign and word production (Emmorey et al., 2004).

Differences in activated regions in speakers and signers were also observed. Within the left parietal lobe, two regions were more active for sign than for speech: the SMG and the superior parietal lobule. Emmorey et al. (2007) speculated that these regions might be linked to modality-specific output parameters of sign language. Specifically, activation within left SMG may reflect aspects of phonological processing in ASL (e.g., selection of hand configuration and place of articulation features), whereas activation within superior parietal lobule (SPL) may reflect proprioceptive monitoring of motoric output. This characterization of the role of the SMG based on imaging accords well with the stimulation data reported in Corina et al. (1999). Moreover, that sign languages may uniquely recruit superior-parietal cortical regions for proprioceptive/somatosensory monitoring to a greater degree than spoken language is consistent with the language-specific account of error types observed in data from slips of the hand—specifically the of lack of exchange errors in sign language compared to spoken language. It is also intriguing that errors produced with stimulation to SMG, a region proximal to SPL, resulted in a conscious effort to self-correct.

Verb Generation

In two studies of ASL verb generation, San José-Robertson, Corina, Ackerman, Guillemin, and Braun (2004) reported left-lateralized activation within perisylvian frontal and subcortical regions commonly implicated in spoken language generation tasks. In an extension of this work, Corina et al. (2005) reported that the observed left-lateralized patterns were not significantly different when the production of a repeat-generate task was conducted with a signer's dominant versus the signer's nondominant hand. This finding is consistent with studies of sign aphasic errors, which may be observed on the patient's nondominant hand following left hemisphere insult.

Discourse Production

A study of discourse production in ASL-English native bilinguals further underscores the similarities between speech and sign (Braun, Guillemin, Hosey, & Varga, 2001). In this study, spontaneous generation of autobiographical narratives in ASL and English revealed complementary progression from early stages of concept formation and lexical access to later stages of phonological encoding and articulation. This progression proceeds from bilateral to left lateralized representations, with posterior

regions (especially posterior cingulate, precuneus, and basal-ventral temporal regions) activated during encoding of semantic information (Braun et al., 2001). A separate study by Blank, Scott, Murphy, Warburton, and Wise (2002) investigating the contrast between self-generated propositional speech and nonpropositional speech provides strikingly similar patterns of activation. Taken together, these data offer evidence that higher-level processes involved in self-generated propositional language generation (beginning with the intention to speak or sign, formulation of linked concepts through activation and selection of relevant memories, followed by the selection of appropriate wordforms and signforms with elaboration of sentence frames appropriate for encoding this knowledge) are highly equivalent for sign and speech production.

Sign and Gesture Production

Data from aphasia shows convincingly that sign language can dissociate from pantomimic gestures. Neuroimaging studies by Emmorey and colleagues (Emmorey et al., 2004; Emmorey, McCullough, Mehta, Ponto, & Grabowski, 2010) provide further insight into the relationships between motoric encoding of sign nouns and verbs that resemble pantomimes compared with those whose forms are more arbitrary. In addition, these studies provide clear evidence for differences in the neural regions that underlie sign language and more general praxic functions.

Emmorey and colleagues (2004) used the PET technique to investigate sign-naming of tools and tool-based actions to determine whether motor-iconicity alters the neural systems that underlie lexical retrieval. Most ASL nouns denoting tools and ASL verbs referring to tool-based actions are produced with a handshape representing the human hand holding a tool and with an iconic movement depicting canonical tool use. So for example, the sign HAMMER appears similar to a pantomimic action of hammering and thus is said to have motor-iconicity. It was predicted that such forms would engage cortical systems involved in object manipulation, specifically left premotor and left inferior parietal cortex. These regions have been reported in hearing subjects naming or recognizing tools and tool-based actions (Chao & Martin, 2000; Grafton, Fadiga, Arbib, & Rizzolatti, 1997) and would differ from the naming of ASL actions whose signs do not exhibit motor-iconicity (e.g., YELL, READ).

As predicted, naming of tools and tool-based actions relative to a control task activated the left premotor and inferior parietal cortex. The control task here was an orientation judgment performed on the faces of unknown persons requiring the response YES if the face was in the canonical position (up) and NO if the face was inverted. Unique to tool naming was activation in left inferior temporal cortex; in contrast, tool-based action naming uniquely activated posterior middle temporal gyrus in the vicinity of MT. Naming of actions that do not exhibit motor-iconicity revealed activation in left posterior middle temporal gyrus but no activation in left premotor cortex or left inferior parietal lobule (IPL). The left premotor and left IPL activation may reflect retrieval of stored information about specific object features and attributes (Martin, Ungerleider, & Haxby, 2000), such as how to hold a tool, recognition of its visual characteristics, or the performance or perception of the action made with such a tool. However, given the low-level nature of the baseline in these studies, one cannot rule out that these activations also reflect the recognition of the stimuli themselves, rather than the activation of lexical features associated with naming.

Two additional points are noteworthy. In support of lexical contributions to these findings is the observation that all naming contrasts activated left hemisphere Broca's region, interpreted here as evidence for phonological encoding required for naming in ASL. Finally, when motor-iconic verbs were compared with noniconic verbs, no differences in neural activation were found. These results indicate that even when the form of a sign is indistinguishable from a pantomimic gesture, the neural systems underlying its production mirror those engaged when hearing speakers name tools or tool-based actions with speech.

In a recent study, Emmorey et al. (2011) compared the production of sign with the production of pantomimes. In this PET study, Emmorey and colleagues' deaf subjects generated action pantomimes or ASL verbs in response to pictures of tools and manipulable objects. Relative to baseline, where participants viewed pictures of manipulable objects and an occasional nonmanipulable object and decided whether the objects could be handled, gesturing "yes" (thumbs up) or "no" (hand wave), generation of ASL verbs engaged left inferior frontal cortex. In contrast, when nonsigners produced pantomimes for the same objects, no frontal activation was observed. Both groups recruited left parietal cortex during pantomime production. Thus, in the deaf group the production of pantomime versus ASL verbs (even those that resemble pantomime)

engages partially segregated neural systems that support praxic versus linguistic functions.

Conclusions

This chapter provides an overview of data from sign language production, including linguistic, developmental, psycholinguistic, and neurobiological investigations. Moreover, these studies include data from a diverse range of signed languages, attesting to the growth and interest in documentation of cross-linguistic properties of signed languages. These studies provide examples of how the properties and processes effecting sign language production appear highly similar to what is observed in spoken languages. These similarities illuminate the universal characteristics of human languages. In addition, we highlight several examples where we observed how properties and processes of signed language have come to reflect the manual-visual modality of expression. The comparisons of signed and spoken languages continue to provide a powerful means to understand the human capacity for language.

Acknowledgements.

This work was support by with grants from NIH-NIDCD 2ROI-DC03099 and NSF SBE-0541953 awarded to David Corina. We thank Mary Mendoza for her editorial support.

Notes

1. Arguments for the need for segmental and prosodic properties of signforms are motivated by data on the morphological processes of affixation, compounding, and verb agreement (see Sandler & Lillo-Martin, 2006 for a comprehensive overview of these issues).
2. This count excluded place of articulation errors that occurred outside of signing space; inclusion of these would raise the error rate for place of articulation to 18.6%.

References

Brown, A. S. (1991). A review of the tip-of-the-tongue experience. *Psychological Bulletin, 109*(2), 204–223.

Baker, C. (1977). Regulators and turn-taking in American Sign Language discourse. In L. Friedman (Ed.), *On the other hand: New perspectives on American Sign Language* (pp. 215– 236). New York: Academic Press.

Baker-Schenk, C. (1983). *A micro-analysis of the nonmanual components of questions in American Sign Language* (Unpublished doctoral dissertation). University of California, Berkeley, Berkeley, CA.

Battison, R. (1978). *Lexical borrowing in American Sign Language.* Silver Spring, MD: Linstok Press.

Baus, C., Gutiérrez-Sigut, E., Quer, J., & Carreiras, M. (2008). Lexical access in Catalan Signed Language (LSC) production. *Cognition, 108*(3), 856–865. doi: S0010-0277(08)00133-9 [pii] 10.1016/j.cognition.2008.05.012

Bayley, R., Lucas, C., & Rose, M. (2002). Phonological variation in American Sign Language: The case of 1 handshape. *Language Variation and Change, 14*, 19–53. doi: 10.1017.S0954394502141020

Bellugi, U., & Fischer, S. (1972). A comparison of sign language and spoken language. *Cognition, 1*(2-3), 173–200. doi: 10.1016/0010-0277(72)90018-2

Blank, S. C., Scott, S. K., Murphy, K., Warburton, E., & Wise, R. J. (2002). Speech production: Wernicke, Broca and beyond. *Brain, 125*(Pt 8), 1829–1838.

Blumstein, S. (1973). Some phonological implications of aphasic speech. In H. Goodglass & S. Blumstein (Eds.), *Psycholinguistics and aphasia* (pp. 123–137). Baltimore: The Johns Hopkins University Press.

Braun, A. R., Guillemin, A., Hosey, L., & Varga, M. (2001). The neural organization of discourse: an H2 15O-PET study of narrative production in English and American sign language. *Brain, 124*(Pt 10), 2028–2044.

Brentari, D. (1990). Licensing in ASL handshape change. In C. Lucas (Ed.), *Sign language research: Theoretical issues* (pp. 57–68). Washington, DC: Gallaudet University Press.

Brentari, D. (1998). *A prosodic model of sign language phonology.* Cambridge, MA: MIT Press.

Brentari, D., Poizner, H., & Kegl, J. (1995). Aphasic and parkinsonian signing: differences in phonological disruption. *Brain and Language, 48*(1), 69–105. doi: S0093-934X(85)71003-6 [pii] 10.1006/brln.1995.1003

Caramazza, A. (1997). How many levels of processing are there in lexical access? *Cognitive Neuropsychology, 14*(1), 177–208.

Caramazza, A., Chialant, D., Capasso, R., & Miceli, G. (2000). Separable processing of consonants and vowels. [10.1038/35000206]. *Nature, 403*(6768), 428–430.

Carreiras, M., Gutiérrez-Sigut, E., Baquero, S., & Corina, D. (2008). Lexical processing in Spanish Sign Language (LSE). *Journal of Memory and Language, 58*(1), 100–122. doi: 10.1016/j.jml.2007.05.004

Chao, L. L., & Martin, A. (2000). Representation of manipulable man-made objects in the dorsal stream. *Neuroimage, 12*(4), 478–484. doi: 10.1006/nimg.2000.0635 S1053-8119(00)90635-9 [pii]

Cheek, A., Cormier, K., Rathmann, C., Repp, A., & Meier, R. (1998). Motoric constraints link manual babbling and early signs. *Infant Behavior and Development, 21*(Supplement 1), 340–340. doi: 10.1016/s0163-6383(98)91553-3

Cheek, D. A. (2001). *The phonetics and phonology of handshape in American Sign Language.* (Doctoral dissertation, University of Texas at Austin, Austin). Retrieved from http://worldcat.org/oclc/49882712

Conlin, K. E., Mirus, G. R., Mauk, C., & Meier, R. P. (2000). The acquisition of first signs: Place, handshape, and movement. In C. Chamberlain, J. Patterson Morford, & R. I. Mayberry (Eds.), *Language acquisition by eye* (pp. 51–69). Mahwah, NJ: Lawrence Erlbaum Associates.

Corina, D. P. (1990). *Reassessing the role of sonority in syllable structure: Evidence from a Visual Gestural Language.* Paper presented at the Chicago Linguistic Society 26th Annual Regional Meeting/Parasession on the Syllable in Phonetics and Phonology, Chicago, IL.

Corina, D. P. (1993). To branch or not to branch: Underspecification in ASL handshape contours. In G. Coulter (Ed.), *Phonetics and phonology. Current issues in ASL phonology* (Vol. 3, pp. 63–94). San Diego, CA: Academic Press.

Corina, D. P. (2000). Some observations regarding paraphasia in American Sign Language. In K. Emmorey & H. Lane (Eds.), *The signs of language revisited: An anthology to honor Ursula Bellugi and Edward Klima* (pp. 493–507). Mahwah, NJ: Lawrence Erlbaum Associates.

Corina, D. P., Gibson, E. K., Martin, R., Poliakov, A., Brinkley, J., & Ojemann, G. A. (2005). Dissociation of action and object naming: Evidence from cortical stimulation mapping. *Human Brain Mapping, 24*(1), 1–10. doi: 10.1002/hbm.20063

Corina, D. P., & Hildebrandt, U. C. (2002). Psycholinguistic investigations of phonological structure in ASL. In R. P. Meier, K. Cormier, & D. Quinto-Pozos (Eds.), *Modality and structure in signed and spoken languages* (pp. 88–111). Cambridge, UK: Cambridge University Press.

Corina, D. P., & Knapp, H. P. (2006). Lexical retrieval in American Sign Language production. In L. M. Goldstein, D. H. Whalen, & C. T. Best (Eds.), *Papers in laboratory phonology 8: Varieties of phonological competence* (pp. 213–239). Berlin: Mouton de Gruyter.

Corina, D. P., McBurney, S. L., Dodrill, C., Hinshaw, K., Brinkley, J., & Ojemann, G. (1999). Functional roles of Broca's area and SMG: Evidence from cortical stimulation mapping in a deaf signer. *Neuroimage, 10*(5), 570–581. doi: 10.1006/nimg.1999.0499 S1053-8119(99)90499-8 [pii]

Corina, D. P., Poizner, H., Bellugi, U., Feinberg, T., Dowd, D., & O'Grady-Batch, L. (1992). Dissociation between linguistic and nonlinguistic gestural systems: A case for compositionality. *Brain and Language, 43*(3), 414–447. doi: 0093-934X(92)90110-Z [pii]

Corina, D. P., San Jose-Robertson, L., Guillemin, A., High, J., & Braun, A. R. (2003). Language lateralization in a bimanual language. *Journal of Cognitive Neuroscience, 15*(5), 718–730. doi: 10.1162/089892903322307438

Corina, D., & Sandler, W. (1993). On the nature of phonological structure in sign language. *Phonology, 10*(2), 165–207.

Cormier, K, Mauk, C., & Repp, A. (1998). *Manual babbling in deaf and hearing infants: A longitudinal study.* Paper presented at the Proceedings of the Twenty-Ninth Annual Child Language Research Forum, Stanford, CA.

Dell, G. S., & O'Seaghdha, P. G. (1992). Stages of lexical access in language production. *Cognition, 42*(1-3), 287–314. doi: 10.1016/0010-0277(92)90046-k

Dolata, J. K., Davis, B. L., & MacNeilage, P. F. (2008). Characteristics of the rhythmic organization of vocal babbling: Implications for an amodal linguistic rhythm. *Infant Behavior and Development, 31*(3), 422–431. doi: S0163-6383(08)00002-7 [pii] 10.1016/j.infbeh.2007.12.014

Dronkers, N. F., Redfern, B. B., & Knight, R. T. (2000). The neural architecture of language disorders. In M. S. Gazzaniga (Ed.), *The new cognitive neurosciences* (2nd ed., pp. 949–958). Cambridge, MA: MIT Press.

Emmorey, K. (2002). *Language, cognition, and the brain: Insights from sign language research.* Mahwah, NJ: Lawrence Erlbaum Associates.

Emmorey, K., Bellugi, U., Friederici, A., & Horn, P. (1995). Effects of age of acquisition on grammatical sensitivity: Evidence from on-line and off-line tasks. *Applied Psycholinguistics, 16*(01), 1–23. doi: 10.1017/S0142716400006391

Emmorey, K., Bosworth, R., & Kraljic, T. (2009). Visual feedback and self-monitoring of sign language. *Journal of Memory and Language, 61*(3), 398–411. doi: 10.1016/j.jml.2009.06.001

Emmorey, K., & Corina, D. (1990). Lexical recognition in sign language: Effects of phonetic structure and morphology. *Perceptual and Motor Skills, 71*(3 Pt 2), 1227–1252.

Emmorey, K., Gertsberg, N., Korpics, F., & Wright, C. E. (2009). The influence of visual feedback and register changes on sign language production: A kinematic study with deaf signers. *Applied Psycholinguistics, 30*(1), 187–203. doi: 10.1017/S0142716408090085

Emmorey, K., Grabowski, T., McCullough, S., Damasio, H., Ponto, L. L. B., Hichwa, R. D., & Bellugi, U. (2004). Motor-iconicity of sign language does not alter the neural systems underlying tool and action naming. *Brain and Language, 89*(1), 27–37. doi: 10.1016/S0093-934X(03)00309-2 S0093934X03003092 [pii]

Emmorey, K., McCullough, S., Mehta, S., Ponto, L. L. B., & Grabowski, T. J. (2011). Sign language and pantomime production differentially engage frontal and parietal cortices. *Language and Cognitive Processes, 26*(7), 878–901.

Emmorey, K., Mehta, S., & Grabowski, T. J. (2007). The neural correlates of sign versus word production. *NeuroImage, 36*(1), 202–208. doi: S1053-8119(07)00140-1 [pii] 10.1016/j.neuroimage.2007.02.040

Fromkin, V. A. (1971). The non-anomalous nature of anomalous utterances. *Language, 47*, 27–52.

Fromkin, V. A. (1973). Slips of the tongue. *Scientific American, 229*, 109–117.

Garrett, M. F. (1975). The analysis of speech production. *Psychology of Learning and Motivation, 9*, 133–177.

Goodglass, H. (1993). *Understanding aphasia*. San Diego: Academic Press.

Goodglass, H., & Kaplan, E. (1972). *The Boston diagnostic aphasia test*. Philadelphia: Lea and Febiger.

Grafton, S. T., Fadiga, L., Arbib, M. A., & Rizzolatti, G. (1997). Premotor cortex activation during observation and naming of familiar tools. *Neuroimage, 6*(4), 231–236. doi: S1053-8119(97)90293-7 [pii] 10.1006/nimg.1997.0293

Grosjean, F. (1977). The perception of rate in spoken and sign languages. *Perception and Psychophysics, 22*, 408–413.

Grosvald, M. (2009) Interspeaker variation in the extent and perception of longdistance vowel-to-vowel coarticulation. *Journal of Phonetics, 37*, 173–188.

Grosvald, M., & Corina, D. (2009, May 2008). *Location-to-location coarticulation: A phonetic investigation of American Sign Language*. Paper presented at the 24th Northwest Linguistics Conference, Seattle, WA.

Grosvald, M., & Corina, D. P. (2012) The perceptibility of long-distance coarticulation in speech and sign. *Sign Language and Linguistics, 15*(1), 73–103.

Grosvald M., Lachaud, C., & Corina D. (2009). Influences of linguistic and non-linguistic factors in the processing of American Sign Language: Evidence from handshape monitoring. Paper presented at the 35th Annual Meeting of the Berkeley Linguistics Society, Berkeley, CA.

Grosvald M, Lachaud C, Corina D. (2012). Handshape monitoring: Evaluation of linguistic and perceptual factors in the processing of American Sign Language. *Language and Cognitive Processes, 27*(1), 117–141.

Hickok, G., Kritchevsky, M., Bellugi, U., & Klima, E. S. (1996). The role of the left frontal operculum in sign language aphasia. *Neurocase: The Neural Basis of Cognition, 2*(5), 373–380.

Hohenberger, A., Happ, D., & Leuninger, H. (2002). Modality-dependent aspects of sign language production: Evidence from slips of the hands and their repairs in German Sign Language. In R. P. Meier, K. Cormier, & D. Quinto-Pozos (Eds.), *Modality and structure in signed and spoken languages* (pp. 112–142). Cambridge, UK: Cambridge University Press.

Indefrey, P., & Levelt, W. J. M. (2004). The spatial and temporal signatures of word production components. *Cognition, 92*(1-2), 101–144. doi: 10.1016/j.cognition.2002.06.001 S0010027703002294 [pii]

Klima, E. S., & Bellugi, U. (1979). *The signs of language*. Cambridge, MA: Harvard University Press.

Knapp, H. K., Corina, D. P., Panagiotides, H., Zanos, S., Brinkley, J., & Ojemann, G. (2005). *Frontal lobe representations of American Sign Language, reaching and speech: Data from cortical stimulation and local field potential*, Presentation at the San Francisco Neurological Society annual meeting, San Francisco, CA.

Levelt, W. J., Roelofs, A., & Meyer, A. S. (1999). A theory of lexical access in speech production. *Behavioral and Brain Sciences, 22*(1), 1–38; discussion 38-75.

Liddell, S. K. (1980). *American Sign Language syntax*. The Hague and New York: Mouton.

Lucas, C., Bayley, R., Rose, M., & Wulf, A. (2002). Location variation in American Sign Language. *Sign Language Studies, 2*(4), 407–440.

Maddieson, I. (2008). Consonant-vowel ratio. In M. Haspelmath, M. S. Dryer, D. Gil, & B. Comrie (Eds.), *The world atlas of language structures online*. Munich: Max Planck Digital Library. Retrieved from http://wals.info/feature/3.

Magen, H. S. (1997). The extent of vowel-to-vowel coarticulation in English. *Journal of Phonetics, 25*(2), 187–205. doi: 10.1006/jpho.1996.0041

Marshall, J., Atkinson, J., Smulovitch, E., Thacker, A., & Woll, B. (2004). Aphasia in a user of British Sign Language: Dissociation between sign and gesture. *Cognitive Neuropsychology, 21*(5), 537–554. doi: 713819159 [pii] 10.1080/02643290342000249

Martin, A., Ungerleider, L. G., & Haxby, J. V. (2000). Category specificity and the brain: The sensory-motor model of semantic representations of objects. In M. S. Gazzaniga (Ed.), *The cognitive neurosciences* (pp. 1023–1036). Cambridge, MA: MIT Press.

Mauk, C. (2003). *Undershoot in two modalities: Evidence from Fast speech and fast signing*. Austin, TX: University of Texas at Austin.

Mayberry, R. I., & Eichen, E. (1991). The long-lasting advantage of learning sign language in childhood: Another look at the critical period for language acquisition. *Journal of Memory and Language, 30*(486–512).

Mayberry, R. I., & Fischer, S. D. (1989). Looking through phonological shape to lexical meaning: The bottleneck of non-native sign language processing. *Memory and Cognit, 17*(6), 740–754.

Mayberry, R. I., & Witcher, P. (2006). What age of acquisition effects reveal about the nature of phonological processing. *Tech. Rept. No.17*(3). Retrieved from http://crl.ucsd.edu/newsletter/current/TechReports/articles.html

McIntire, M. (1977). The acquisition of American Sign Language hand configurations. *Sign Language Studies, 16*, 247–266.

McKee, D., & Kennedy, G. (2000). Lexical comparison of signs from American, Australian, British, and New Zealand Sign Languages. In K. Emmorey & H. Lane (Eds.), *The signs of language revisited: An anthology to honor Ursula Bellugi and Edward Klima*. Mahwah, NJ: Lawrence Erlbaum Associates.

Meier, R. P. (2000). Shared motoric factors in the acquisition of sign and speech. In K. Emmorey & H. Lane (Eds.), *The signs of language revisited: An anthology to honor Ursula Bellugi and Edward Klima* (pp. 333–356). Mahwah, NJ: Lawrence Erlbaum Associates.

Meier, R.P., Mauk, C., Mirus, G. R., & Conlin, K. E. (1998). *Motoric constraints on early sign acquisition.* Paper presented at the Proceedings of the Child Language Research Forum, Stanford, CA.

Meier, R. P., & Willerman, R. (1995). Prelinguistic gesture in deaf and hearing children. In K. Emmorey & J. Reily (Eds.), *Language, gesture, and space* (pp. 391–409). Mahwah, NJ: Lawrence Erlbaum Associates.

Metz-Lutz, M. N., de Saint Martin, A., Monpiou, S., Massa, R., Hirsch, E., & Marescaux, C. (1999). Early dissociation of verbal and nonverbal gestural ability in an epileptic deaf child. *Annals of Neurology, 46*(6), 929–932.

Meyer, A. S. (1990). The time course of phonological encoding in language production: The encoding of successive syllables of a word. *Journal of Memory and Language, 29,* 524–545.

Meyer, A. S. (1991). The time course of phonological encoding in language production: The phonological encoding inside a syllable. *Journal of Memory and Language, 30,* 69–89.

Mohr, J. P., Pessin, M. S., Finkelstein, S., Funkenstein, H. H., Duncan, G. W., & Davis, K. R. (1978). Broca aphasia: Pathologic and clinical. *Neurology, 28*(4), 311–324.

Morford, J. P., Grieve-Smith, A. B., MacFarlane, J., Staley, J., & Waters, G. (2008). Effects of language experience on the perception of American Sign Language. *Cognition, 109*(1), 41–53. doi: S0010-0277(08)00178-9 [pii] 10.1016/j.cognition.2008.07.016

Myers, J., Lee, H.-H., & Tsay, J, (2005). Phonological production in Taiwan sign language. *Language and linguistics, 6*(2), 319-359.

Newkirk, D, Klima, E. S., Pedersen, C. C., & Bellugi, U. (1980). Linguistic evidence from slips of the hand. In V. Fromkin (Ed.), *Errors in linguistic performance: Slips of the tongue, ear, pen, and hand* (pp. 165–198). San Diego, CA: Academic Press.

Newport, E. L., & Meier, R. P. (1985). The acquisition of American Sign Language. In D. I. Slobin (Ed.), *The cross-linguistic study of language acquisition.* Hillsdale, NJ: Lawrence Erlbaum Associates.

Öhman, S. E. (1966). Coarticulation in VCV utterances: spectrographic measurements. *The Journal of the Acoustical Society of America, 39*(1), 151–168.

Oller, D. K., & Eilers, R. E. (1986). Striking differences in the babbling of deaf and hearing infants. *The Journal of the Acoustical Society of America, 80*(S1), S79–S79. doi: 10.1121/1.2023976

Ostry, D. J., Cooke, J. D., & Munhall, K. G. (1987). Velocity curves of human arm and speech movements. *Experimental Brain Research, 68*(1), 37–46.

Petitto, L. A., Holowka, S., Sergio, L. E., Levy, B., & Ostry, D. J. (2004). Baby hands that move to the rhythm of language: Hearing babies acquiring sign languages babble silently on the hands. *Cognition, 93*(1), 43–73. doi: 10.1016/j.cognition.2003.10.007 S0010027703002245 [pii]

Petitto, L. A., & Marentette, P. F. (1991). Babbling in the manual mode: Evidence for the ontogeny of language. *Science, 251*(5000), 1493–1496.

Poizner, H., & Kegl, J. (1992). Neural basis of language and motor behavior: Perspectives from American Sign Language. *Aphasiology, 6,* 219–256.

Poizner, H., Klima, E. S., & Bellugi, U. (1987). *What hands reveal about the brain.* Cambridge, MA: MIT Press.

Recasens, D. (1989). Long range coarticulation effects for tongue dorsum contact in VCVCV sequences. *Speech Communication, 8*(4), 293–307. doi: 10.1016/0167- 6393(89)90012-5

San José-Robertson, L., Corina, D. P., Ackerman, D., Guillemin, A., & Braun, A. R. (2004). Neural systems for sign language production: mechanisms supporting lexical selection, phonological encoding, and articulation. *Human Brain Mapping, 23*(3), 156–167. doi: 10.1002/hbm.20054

Sandler, W. (1986). The spreading hand autosegment of American Sign Language. *Sign Language Studies, 50,* 1–28.

Sandler, W. (1993). Sonority cycle in American Sign Language. *Phonology, 10,* 243–279.

Sandler, W., & Lillo-Martin, D. C. (2006). *Sign language and linguistic universals.* Cambridge, UK: Cambridge University Press.

Schriefers, H., Meyer, A. S., & Levelt, W. J. M. (1990). Exploring the time course of lexical access in language production: Picture–word interference studies. *Journal of Memory and Language, 29,* 86–102.

Shepard-Kegl, J. A. (1985). *Locative relations in American Sign Language word formation, syntax and discourse.* Massachusetts Institute of Technology. Retrieved from http://dspace.mit.edu/handle/1721.1/15168

Stemmer, B., & Whitaker, H. A. (1998). *Handbook of neurolinguistics.* San Diego, CA: Academic Press.

Stokoe, W. C., Jr., Casterlime, D. C., & Croneberg, C. (1965). *A dictionary of American Sign Language on linguistic principles.* Washington, DC: Gallaudet press.

Supalla, T. (1986). The classifier system in American Sign Language. In C. Craig (Ed.), *Noun classes and categorization* (pp. 181–214). Philadelphia: John Benjamins.

Thompson, R., Emmorey, K., & Gollan, T. H. (2005). "Tip of the fingers" experiences by deaf signers. *Psychological Science, 16*(11), 856–860. doi: 10.1111/j.1467-9280.2005.01626.x

Tyrone, M. (2001). *Developing a methodology for studying sign language phonetics.* London: City University.

Tyrone, M. E., & Mauk, C. E. (2010). Sign lowering and phonetic reduction in American Sign Language. *J Phon, 38*(2), 317–328. doi: 10.1016/j.wocn.2010.02.003

Uyechi, L. (1996). *The geometry of visual phonology.* Stanford, CA: CSLI Publications.

van der Hulst, H. (2000). Modularity and modality in phonology. In N. Burton-Roberts, P. Carr, & G. J. Docherty (Eds.), *Phonological knowledge: Conceptual and empirical issues* (pp. 207–243). Oxford: Oxford University Press.

Verstynen, T., & Ivry, R.B. (2011). Network dynamics mediating ipsilateral motor cortex activity during unimanual actions. *Journal of Cognitive Neuroscience, 23,* 2468–2480.

Wilbur, R. B. (1993). Syllables and segments: Hold the Movements and move the Holds! In G. Coulter (Ed.), *Phonetics and phonology: Current issues in ASL phonology* (pp. 135–168). San Diego, CA: Academic Press.

Wilbur, R. B., & Nolen, S. B. (1986). The duration of syllables in American sign Language. *Language and Speech, 29* (Pt 3), 263–280.

Wilson, M., & Emmorey, K. (2000). When does modality matter? Evidence from ASL on the nature of working memory. In K. Emmorey & H. Lane (Eds.), *The signs of language revisited: An anthology to Honor Ursula Bellugi and Edward Klima* (pp. 135–142). Mahwah, NJ: Lawrence Erlbaum Associates.

Wolpert, D. M., & Miall, R. C. (1996). Forward models for physiological motor control. *Neural Networks,* 9(8), 1265–1279. doi: S0893608096000354 [pii]

Woodward, J. (2000). Sign languages and sign language families in Thailand and Viet Nam. In K. Emmorey & H. Lane (Eds.), *The signs of language revisited: An anthology to honor Ursula Bellugi and Edward Klima* (pp. 23-47). Mahwah, NJ: Lawrence Erlbaum Associates.

Woodward, J., & The Cambodian Sign Language Production Team (2010). *Cambodian Sign Language-English and English-Cambodian Sign Language Dictionary.* Hong Kong: The Centre for Sign Linguistics and Deaf Studies, The Chinese University of Hong Kong.

PART 3

The Interface of Production with Other Cognitive Systems

Monitoring and Control of the Production System

Robert J. Hartsuiker

Abstract

When speakers experience trouble in production, such as when they produce a speech error, they sometimes interrupt themselves and resume with a self-repair. There must therefore be a cognitive system that inspects language production processes and intervenes when necessary: a verbal self-monitoring system. This article reviews recent studies that have led to a better understanding of the processes of speech interruption and repair, their neural implementation, and their relationship to action monitoring in general. Importantly, it argues that self-monitoring has consequences for many of the speech parameters the field analyzes: the patterns of speech errors and disfluencies, and possibly also the patterns of reaction times. This means that any theory of language production is incomplete without a theory of self-monitoring.

Key Words: self-monitoring, speech interruption, speech repair, disfluency, speech errors

Introduction

When speakers experience trouble in production (e.g., when they produce a speech error) they sometimes interrupt themselves and resume with a self-repair. There must therefore be a cognitive system that inspects language production processes and intervenes when necessary: a verbal self-monitoring system (Levelt, 1989; Postma, 2000). Examples 1–4 below illustrate self-repairing; they are taken from a corpus of descriptions of networks like the one in Figure 25.1 (Hartsuiker & Notebaert, 2010).

(1) from there with a diagonal line straight line down to the right to the vest[1]

(2) from the vest with a short uh no small arch to the bomb

(3) from the radish left down uh diagonal arches a diagonal arch

(4) with a small arch to the left down to the buggy the pram

The troublesome item, such as *diagonal* in (1), is called the *reparandum*. The speech that replaces the troublesome material is called the *repair* (*straight line*). Sometimes, there are one or more editing terms between reparandum and repair, such as "uh," "no," "I mean," "or rather," and so on (2). Such terms can also occur in different contexts, such as the *uh* before the reparandum in (3). Speakers sometimes interrupt right after the reparandum (2), but they may also continue with one or more words (1). In about 20% of the repairs in Levelt's (1983) corpus (also with a network task), speakers even interrupted *within* the reparandum. Additionally, the repair does not always start with the word meant to replace the reparandum. In (4), the repair starts with an earlier correct word ("the"). Levelt (1989) calls these *anticipatory retracings*, and cases like (1–3) *instant repairs*.

The examples illustrate that the trouble to which the monitor responds can be of a diverse nature. In (1), the speaker started out with an adjective (*diagonal*) that directly provides information about the direction of the line; but then she changed her mind and chose a less informative adjective (*straight*) and encoded directionality with the help of the terms

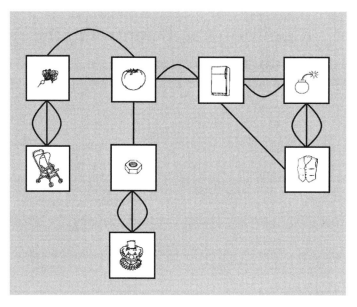

Figure 25.1 Example of the network description task.

down and *right*. In (2) and (4), the speaker instead replaced a lexical item with another one, in fact a synonym in (4). Instead in (3) the speaker produced a speech error, namely a plural instead of a singular noun phrase. Some authors (e.g., Levelt, 1989) distinguish between *error repairs* (3), where the speaker violates a linguistic norm or mistakenly produces a different word from intended, and appropriateness repairs (4), where the utterance is not strictly in error, but is not quite appropriate in its context. A speaker may decide that a term is not specific enough (saying *glass* instead of *tall glass*, or uses a different term from the one consistently used so far (saying *short* instead of *small* in 2). As discussed later, whether a repair is an error or appropriateness repair seems to have repercussions for how speakers interrupt, what editing terms they use, and how they repair.

A more contentious distinction is that between *overt* and *covert* repairs. In (5), the speaker begins to say *in a* but instead of continuing with *curve*, she repeats *in a*. One possibility is that the speaker experienced some sort of trouble right after the initial *in a*, interrupted before actually producing an overt error, and then started again. In other words, a repetition may be a side effect of a covert repair to covert trouble. Given that both the repair and the trouble remain covert, it is difficult to assess whether cases like (5) are really covert repairs (e.g., Postma & Kolk, 1993) or whether they have a different cause (see Clark & Wasow, 1998 for a different account).

(5) in a in a curve it goes to the right

Although the notion of covert repairing may be contentious, there can be no doubt that speakers can monitor their own speech before it is articulated. One reason is that interruptions sometimes follow errors with hardly any delay (Blackmer & Mitton, 1991; Oomen & Postma, 2001b). Such minimal delays are not compatible with monitoring of overt speech, because hearing the error and then interrupting takes much more time than these delays allow. Such incidents must therefore be based on a representation of speech before it is articulated. Furthermore, speakers can detect errors in speech without hearing themselves, for instance when they make speech movements without overt articulation ("mouthing") or when they speak covertly (Oppenheim & Dell, 2008; Postma & Noordanus, 1996). Additionally, speakers can detect errors in their speech when their speech is masked by loud noise (Lackner & Tuller, 1979; Oomen, Postma, & Kolk, 2001). Lackner and Tuller, for example, asked participants to press a button whenever they detected an error in their own speech. The speakers could do this in the noise-masked condition (although less accurately than in the unmasked condition), demonstrating that there is prearticulatory monitoring. Interestingly, response times were faster in the noise-masked condition. This makes sense, because in that condition all errors must have been detected by prearticulatory monitoring, which is quicker than normal monitoring, which combines slower postarticulatory monitoring and quicker prearticulatory monitoring.

What is the cognitive architecture of monitoring? One proposal (Figure 25.2) is the perceptual loop model (PLM; Hartsuiker & Kolk, 2001), which was based on Levelt's (1983, 1989) perceptual loop theory. The PLM assumes that the monitor uses the speech perception system for trouble detection. This system listens to overt speech (the external or postarticulatory channel) and to inner speech (the internal or prearticulatory channel). If the monitor detects the need to repair, it starts the processes of *interrupting* (note that interrupting actions is time-consuming in itself; Logan & Cowan, 1984) and *repairing*. These processes take place in parallel and this explains why repairs can sometimes follow the interruption with little or no delay (Blackmer & Mitton, 1991). Finally, the PLM assumes that overlap in meaning or form between reparandum and repair speeds up the repair process. The PLM is implemented as a computational model, and makes predictions about the time course of repairs (i.e., the time between error and interruption and between interruption and repair).

The PLM thus makes assumptions about three major components of monitoring: (1) a component of trouble *detection*, (2) a component that stops ongoing speech, and (3) a component that plans the repair. Most research on self-monitoring is concerned with the detection component (Postma's 2000 review paper focuses on this component only). Recently, however, interest in interruption and repair has increased (Hartsuiker, Pickering, & De Jong, 2005; Slevc & Ferreira, 2006; Xue, Aron, & Poldrack, 2008).

One may wonder how well the monitor generally detects trouble. Although estimates differ, and although the answer depends on the type of trouble in speech (not) detected, it is clear that the monitor is far from perfect. Nooteboom (1980) found that roughly 50% of lexical errors pass by unnoticed. However, this figure may be an underestimate if one acknowledges the possibility of prearticulatory editing. For instance, if the internal and external channels both have a detection rate of 50%, the combined detection rate looks much better: 75% (50% + 0.5 × 50%). Prearticulatory editing might prevent many more errors from happening.

This article argues that the study of the self-monitoring system is essential for understanding the language production system. First, the possibility of prearticulatory editing has important implications for two issues that are hotly debated in the literature: modularity versus interactivity, and the role of competition in lexical access. Second, understanding monitoring may have clinical implications given that monitoring may be implicated in various types of language pathologies, including Broca's aphasia, Wernicke's aphasia, Parkinson's disease, schizophrenia, and stuttering (Postma & Oomen, 2005). Third, self-monitoring is a prime example of metacognition: part of the speaker's mind is keeping an eye on what another part is doing. Investigating self-monitoring of speech might therefore contribute to the understanding of much wider issues having to do with how humans regulate their own behavior and their learning. It is interesting to note

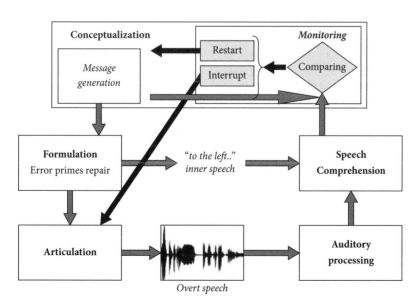

Figure 25.2 Sketch of Hartsuiker and Kolk's (2001) perceptual loop model. Detection of trouble takes place through the perception of inner speech and overt speech. If the monitor detects a problem it initiates the processes of interruption and repair in parallel.

that the notion of "inner speech" plays an important role in accounts of self-monitoring (Levelt, 1983, 1989), but also in accounts of self-awareness and self-regulation (Morin & Everett, 1990).

The remainder of this chapter is organized as follows. The second section discusses the three components of self-monitoring (detecting, stopping, and repairing), paying particular attention to theories in this domain. The third section discusses consequences of monitoring, in particular with respect to conversation, error patterns, reaction time patterns, and disfluencies. The fourth section discusses several challenges for future research.

Three Components of Self-Monitoring

This section discusses the trouble detecting, stopping, and repairing components, respectively. Although earlier findings are discussed, the emphasis is on recent studies.

Trouble Detection

MONITORING FOCI

What types of trouble can the monitor detect? Levelt (1983) argued that virtually every aspect of speech is a possible focus of monitoring. Repairs occur, for instance, at the level of the message. This is the case when the speaker changes his or her mind and so replaces a message with a different one, typically resulting in a so-called fresh start (6). Changes to messages are sometimes also necessary when the world changes in a critical aspect just at the moment someone is saying something about it (7). Finally, repairs to the message-level are necessary when people decide to say things in a different way, such as a change of a description scheme (1), or in a more informative way, by making an utterance more specific (8).

(6) Then we go to a take a small curve down to the right

(7) It is now three minutes past nine or rather four minutes past nine[2]

(8) With an arch small arch

Additionally, speakers can monitor at all linguistic levels; they repair lexical (9), phonological (10), prosodic (11), and morphosyntactic (4) errors. It is less clear how well people monitor aspects of their articulation. Repairs to speech rate or to the quality of articulation are usually triggered by interlocutors. There is some evidence that speakers monitor loudness; they automatically increase loudness when background noise levels increase, the so-called Lombard effect (e.g., Pick, Siegel, Fox, Garber, & Kearney, 1989).

(9) to the coat vest

(10) with a large curk curve[3]

(11) my PROsodic proSOdic colleagues[4]

Finally, speakers can also monitor the effects their speech has on the listener. Sometimes listeners explicitly indicate that they have not understood something a speaker said, but at other times the speaker can glean much information about the success of his or her contribution from the listener's facial expressions, nods, frowns, *uh-hm's*, and so on.

How does the monitor detect errors? One possibility is that the monitor always compares a representation of the actually produced word with the word that the speaker intended to say (Nozari & Dell, 2009). But it has also been suggested that the monitor uses more general criteria, similar to the case of monitoring for errors in another person's speech (when the intended word is unknown). Such general criteria might include lexicality (if I am about to say a nonword, it is presumably an error) and appropriateness (if I am about to say something inappropriate, I better not say it).

MONITORING CHANNELS

This multitude of monitoring foci raises the issue of which sources of information the speaker has available to inspect his or her speech. In his review of the monitoring literature, Postma (2000) distinguishes no fewer than 11 monitoring "channels" (Figure 25.3). It is important to note that this is not an 11-channel model (as is sometimes incorrectly assumed), but rather a list of all possible channels that different theorists have proposed over the years, within the framework of Levelt's (1989) blueprint of the speaker. In fact, every component of language production is associated with one or more monitoring channels. In particular, some theories (Levelt, 1983, 1989) assume a central monitoring system that is localized within the conceptualizer. According to this theory, one monitoring channel (the "conceptual loop") is internal to the conceptualizer and checks whether the preverbal message corresponds with the speaker's intentions. This channel has access to the earliest possible stage of the production process, but the repairs that it triggers (i.e., appropriateness repairs) tend to be produced more slowly than error repairs (Blackmer & Mitton, 1991). Postma suggests that the conceptual loop works this slowly because it may be difficult

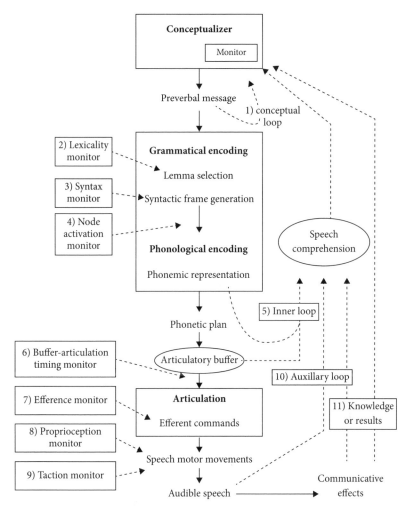

Figure 25.3 The 11 monitoring channels distinguished in Postma (2000).
Source: Postma, A. (2000). Detection of errors during speech production: a review of speech monitoring models. *Cognition, 77*, 97–131.

to determine the adequacy of an intention or to replace an intention with another one.

Two further proposed monitoring channels are internal to the grammatical encoder in Levelt's (1989) blueprint. These are specialized monitors that directly respond to trouble in each of the main functions of grammatical encoding: lemma selection and constituent structure building (Laver, 1980; Van Wijk & Kempen, 1987). A further type of monitor is also internal to the formulator, but can operate at every level of lexical access and phonological encoding. This type of monitor is sensitive to the activation levels of the units representing words, phonemes, and so on (MacKay, 1992; Mattson & Baars, 1992; Postma & Kolk, 1993). Specifically, this type of monitor could exploit the unusual pattern of feedback between levels (MacKay, 1992; Postma & Kolk, 1993) or the unusual amount of

competition within a level (Mattson & Baars, 1992) when an error is made.

The next level in Levelt's blueprint is the articulator. There are several candidate monitor channels related to this level, including a buffer-articulation timing monitor (Blackmer & Mitton, 1991) that responds to asynchronies between speech planning and execution; specifically, it executes the previous plan until a new plan has entered the articulatory buffer leading to multiple, fast repetitions. The articulator produces movements, which might provide information for monitors based on *proprioception* (i.e., short feedback loops between input and output neurons that provide information about the location and direction of movement of the articulators) and *taction* (i.e., somewhat later tactile feedback). It is not so clear, however, whether these monitors are restricted to detecting motoric errors, or whether they can also be used for detecting and correcting higher-level errors (Lackner & Tuller, 1979).

The same is true of feedforward monitoring (also known as "efferent copy" or "corrollary discharge"). The basic idea is that the (motor) planning system produces a copy of the commands to the motor system and sends this to a comparison center where it can be compared with some internal standard or with motor feedback from the actual movement. It is important to note there is considerable evidence for forward models in action monitoring more generally (Desmurget & Grafton, 2000) and the concept has even been used in robotics. Although Postma (2000) placed the forward monitor at the level of the articulator, it is a possibility that the formulator also makes forward models. Indeed, several authors have recently argued for forward models in the control of thought and higher cognition (Ito, 2008) and language (Pickering & Garrod, 2007).

People can of course hear themselves speak. Two further monitoring channels are related to speech perception. These are the channels of error detection in Levelt's (1983, 1989) perceptual loop theory of monitoring (i.e., in addition to the conceptual loop) and in the PLM (Hartsuiker & Kolk, 2001). First, people monitor their own overt speech for trouble. This *external* channel is relatively slow, given that speech perception, comparison, and stopping are all time-consuming processes. Second, Levelt also proposed a much quicker internal channel, which listens to "inner speech." In some versions of this account (Levelt, 1989) inner speech is the end-production of formulation processes, namely the phonetic plan that steers articulatory processing and that is stored in the articulatory buffer. In other versions of this account (Wheeldon & Levelt, 1995), inner speech consists of a phonological code. This is based on data obtained with a phoneme-monitoring task, in which bilingual participants are asked whether a given phoneme (e.g., /f/) occurs in the Dutch translation of an English target word (e.g., in *lifter*, which is the translation of hitchhiker). Response times were sensitive to position of the target phoneme (i.e., coda of first syllable in the example), but not to articulatory duration of the target word; performance hardly suffered when an articulatory suppression secondary task was added, contrary to what a phonetic account would lead one to predict.

The final monitoring channel is knowledge of results. Speakers can find out that they were unsuccessful in communication by perceiving the effect on others, which can range from a request for clarification, to a confused facial expression, to an unexpected behavior.

MONITORING THEORIES

As could be inferred from the previous section, several theories have been proposed that differ in which of the 11 channels they assume. There are several ways in which the theoretical landscape can be carved up. Levelt (1989) distinguished between *editor* theories and *connectionist* theories (Levelt, 1989). Editor theories assume that the output of production components is fed through an extrinsic device, such as the perception system. In connectionist theories, however, error detection results from an intrinsic property of the production system, such as feedback between adjacent layers of representation. One could also distinguish between theories based on *feedback* (i.e., direct feedback between layers or indirect feedback by comprehension) and *feedforward* (i.e., efferent copy). Perhaps the most frequently made distinction is that between *perception* monitoring and *production* monitoring (e.g., Postma, 2000).

Perception monitoring theories include the perceptual loop theory (Levelt, 1983, 1989) and the PLM based on it (Hartsuiker & Kolk, 2001). The key assumption is that detection uses the speech perception system. It considers monitoring a central function, which is therefore restricted by attentional focus and capacity. It is important to note that there is solid evidence that speakers monitor their overt speech: error detection gets worse when speakers cannot hear themselves (e.g., Lackner & Tuller, 1979; Oomen et al., 2001). However, the assumption that the prearticulatory channel is also based on speech perception is more controversial.

Production monitoring theories include Laver (1980) and Van Wijk and Kempen (1987), both of which postulate distributed monitoring devices within the production system. This class of theories also includes theories based on feedback or on forward models. The central assumption is that prearticulatory error detection is based on an information channel or channels that are located within the language production system. One theory that does not seem to fit the perception-production monitoring distinction very well is MacKay's (1992) node structure theory. This theory assumes that production and perception use the same network of representations, except for the most peripheral ones. It assumes that errors at level *n* in the system produce an unexpected (e.g., wrong word) or novel (e.g., nonword) pattern of activation at level n-1. Unexpected activation of a unit therefore leads to (almost immediate) perception of the error. Because most of the arguments that speak to production monitor theories (see later) also apply to the node structure theory, this discussion further treats the node structure theory as if it were a production monitoring theory. A potential problem for the node structure theory specifically, however, is the assumption that production and perception share the same network of representations, which some authors have argued is rather implausible (Levelt, 1989).

The remainder of this section focuses on the theoretical contrast between perception and production monitors. Based on principles of theory construction, such as parsimony and efficiency, there are some a priori reasons to prefer perception monitors to at least some versions of production monitoring. Levelt (1989) argued, for example, that a system that encodes both a representation to be spoken (e.g., that selects a word) and encodes an ideal representation (the word that should be selected) is highly inefficient; if some part of the system can determine the correct representation, why then was this correct representation not used in further processing? Additionally, some production monitor theories (Laver, 1980) assume that at each processing level, a completed unit needs to be checked and approved before it can undergo further processing at the next level ("hold-up monitors"). Such a system sounds highly unlikely, however, because this type of monitoring would severely jeopardize fluent delivery of speech. A further perhaps undesirable property of production monitors is that they allow one cognitive system to look into another cognitive system, in contrast to the notion of modular theories that subcomponents of production are autonomous specialists (Levelt, 1989). Finally, perception monitors can exploit cognitive machinery that is already in place. Speakers already have a speech perception system for listening to other people's speech. It is therefore parsimonious to assume that the same system can also be used for checking one's one overt and inner speech.

Although these considerations are rather compelling reasons to reject some versions of production monitoring, they do not speak against feedback monitors or theories based on forward models. Additionally, versions of the perceptual loop theory in which speakers have access to phonological codes before these are planned phonetically (Wheeldon & Levelt, 1995) allow the system to "look into" a specialized processing component. Such perception monitoring theories therefore also violate the principle of modularity, just like the production monitor theories.

Empirical evidence for perception versus production monitoring has yielded mixed results. *Perception monitoring* is mainly supported by evidence showing that the monitor is a central, flexible, and capacity-limited system. Thus, people can monitor for many aspects of speech but can also change their foci of monitoring as a function of task instructions (e.g., Vasic & Wijnen, 2005) or context (Baars, Motley, & MacKay, 1975; Hartsuiker, Corley, & Martensen, 2005). The monitor is also capacity-limited: the percentage of repaired errors decreases when speakers perform a secondary task during speech production (Oomen & Postma, 2002) and errors are more often repaired toward the end of phrases, when capacity for sentence planning is presumably freed up (Levelt, 1989). The PLM successfully simulated distributions of time-intervals from error to interruption (error to cut-off times) and from interruption to self-repair (cut-off to repair times) in Oomen and Postma's (2001b) data. The PLM also simulated effects of speech rate on these time intervals. Hartsuiker and Kolk (2001) therefore concluded that the observed temporal characteristics of monitoring are compatible with perception monitoring (but Postma & Oomen, 2005, have a different view).

More direct empirical support for perception-based monitoring comes from a study by Özdemir, Roelofs, and Levelt (2007). This study used the phoneme-monitoring task (Wheeldon & Levelt, 1995) but now presented line drawings instead of translations. Subjects had to indicate, for example, whether an /s/ occurs in the name of a picture of a glass. There is much evidence in the speech perception literature that listeners are sensitive to the *uniqueness* point, the phoneme in a word after which only one lexical candidate remains. Importantly, phoneme monitoring times in *perception* (push a button if you hear an /s/) vary with the uniqueness point. Özdemir et al. (2007) first demonstrated that this variable plays no role in production: there was no effect of the uniqueness point in a picture-naming task. Importantly, in the phoneme-monitoring task, conducted with the same materials as the picture-naming task, there was a clear effect of uniqueness point: the further the target phoneme was from the uniqueness point, the faster the response. The authors therefore argued that monitoring uses speech perception.

However, there are reasons to doubt that the phoneme monitoring task taps into processes that speakers also use to monitor their speech for errors and other kinds of trouble. A particularly important difference is that in phoneme monitoring, the participant is silent, whereas in normal situations he or she produces overt speech. It is likely that the presence of overt speech prevents speakers from perceiving inner speech; otherwise one would expect speakers to have awareness of inner speech and overt speech, experiencing echoes (Vigliocco & Hartsuiker, 2002).

There is also evidence that supports *production monitoring*. There are anecdotes (Postma, 2000) that speakers sometimes produce self-repairs without awareness of having done so. If speakers are instructed to push a button whenever they make an error, self-repairs sometimes occur that are unaccompanied by button presses (Postma & Noordanus, 1996). These findings are less in line with a perception monitor (in which error detection requires attention and so, presumably, awareness) than with a production monitor (which does not require awareness). However, as Postma (2000) acknowledges, it is also possible that Postma and Noordanus' subjects had a lapse in complying with task instructions.

Some further support for production monitoring comes from the examination of patients with brain damage. Patients with Wernicke's aphasia, for example, have severe problems in language comprehension and production, with little awareness of their production problems. Broca's aphasics, in contrast, have relatively good comprehension and seem to be highly aware of their production problems. Is it the case that monitoring success depends on the quality of comprehension skills? To investigate this, Schlenck, Huber, and Willmess (1987) examined 10 patients with Broca's aphasia, 10 with Wernicke's aphasia, and normal control subjects and brain-damaged control subjects. A sentence compehension[5] test revealed that patients with Wernicke's aphasia had much worse comprehension skills than those with Broca's aphasia, as is to be expected. Yet in a production task, both groups of patients produced far fewer overt speech repairs than the control subjects, with no difference between the aphasic groups. Additionally, both groups with aphasia produced considerable numbers of hesitations, repetitions, and so on, which the authors interpreted as evidence for covert repairing. These findings suggest that monitoring success does not depend on comprehension. It additionally suggests that those with aphasia may have impaired external-channel monitoring, but intact internal-channel monitoring (see also Oomen et al., 2001).

Nickels and Howard (1995) investigated 15 patients with aphasia with diverse syndromes and found that there were no correlations between measures of comprehension (assessed with three different auditory tasks) and monitoring, namely numbers of self-corrections and self-interruptions (where a word starts correctly but is then interrupted). In a reanalysis of these data, Roelofs (2005) found that a fourth comprehension task, judging which two out of three pictures have homophone names (e.g., with pictures of *hair, hare,* and *steak*), did correlate with the monitoring data, although the correlation was not significant in the case of self-corrections.

There is further evidence to suggest that monitoring and comprehension can be dissociated. Several case studies found monitoring impairments in patients with relatively intact comprehension (jargon aphasia: Marshall, Robson, Pring, & Chiat, 1998; Parkinson disease: McNamara, Obler, Au, Durso, & Albert, 1992; and dementia of the Alzheimer type: McNamara et al., 1992). Importantly, the reverse dissociation has also been reported: Marshall, Rappaport, and Garcia-Bunuel (1985) presented the case of a 62-year-old patient with both aphasia and auditory agnosia: the inability to comprehend sounds (words, sentences, familiar sounds from daily life) without audiological impairment. Surprisingly, this patient produced many self-corrections (often repeated repair attempts), demonstrating that spared comprehension is not a necessary condition for monitoring.

A production monitoring account might predict that monitoring impairments are related to production impairments. Oomen, Postma, and Kolk (2005) reported the case of G, a 71-year-old man with Broca's aphasia, whose data were consistent with this prediction. G performed the network task (Figure 25.1) in three conditions: (1) normal auditory feedback, (2) noise-masked speech, and (3) a listening condition in which he monitored for errors in someone else's description of the network. G produced many phonological errors but repaired very few of them, whereas he produced few semantic errors and repaired most of them. The deficit in phonological repair was not caused by an inability to perceive phonological errors: in monitoring other people's speech for phonological errors, he performed at the same level as normal control subjects. Thus, G's production deficit (but not comprehension deficit) mimicked his monitoring deficit, just as a production monitoring account would have it. However, G's monitoring deficit is not necessarily a problem of detecting phonological errors, but might be one of repairing them, so that many detected errors are left unrepaired.

Figure 25.4 Stimulus display used in Huettig and Hartsuiker's (2010) study. Eye movements were recorded while participants named the pictures.

More recently, Huettig and Hartsuiker (2010) used a visual-world eye-tracking study with normal participants to address this issue. Participants viewed displays containing a line drawing of one object and three written words (Figure 25.4). The instruction was always to name the line drawing and ignore the words. In the crucial conditions, one of the words (e.g., harp) was phonologically related to the name of the target object (e.g., heart). Visual-world studies in comprehension (e.g., Huettig & McQueen, 2007) have shown phonological competition effects, so that when people hear "heart" they tend to look at the written word "harp" more than at unrelated distractors. This effect begins approximately 300 ms after word onset. Huettig and Hartsuiker predicted that listening to one's own overt speech (i.e., external-channel monitoring) should have similar effects on eye-gaze behavior as does listening to another person, given that both involve speech perception. People should therefore look at the word "harp" roughly 300 ms after they begin to overtly say "heart." But perception monitoring further assumes that the internal channel also uses speech perception. Internal-channel monitoring should therefore have similar effects on visual attention but only much earlier (given that it bypasses time-consuming processes like articulation and low-level auditory processing). However, looks to the competitor started to increase only after 300 ms after the start of the speaker's articulation, just as in listening to another person's speech. This result is clearly not compatible with a perception monitoring theory.

Summarizing, the issue of whether the internal monitoring channel is perception- or production-based is far from resolved. Most of the evidence is rather indirect and the interpretation of studies often critically depends on assumptions about the task.

Interrupting

After speakers have detected trouble in their speech, how do they interrupt and where in the utterance do interruptions occur? According to the "main interruption rule" (Nooteboom, 1980) the answer is rather simple: speakers always try to interrupt themselves as soon as they can. It is important to note that "as soon as one can" still means that there is a delay between having the intention to stop and the actual moment speech is interrupted. In an early version of the stop-signal paradigm (Logan & Cowan, 1984; Verbruggen & Logan, 2008), Ladefoged, Silverstein, and Papçun (1973) found that people stopped about 200 ms after the presentation of a stopping cue, similar to the estimated time it takes to stop a manual response (Logan & Cowan, 1984). Indeed, recent work with this paradigm has demonstrated that stopping verbal and manual actions activate the same areas of the brain (Xue et al., 2008). Hartsuiker and Kolk's (2001) PLM also assumes that people begin stopping as soon as they have detected a need to do so; in their simulations they found the best fit between model and data when the interruption time was set at 150 ms ± 50 ms, which nicely corresponds to the 200-ms stopping time minus a short duration for detection of the signal.

The assumption of stopping as soon as one can seems to imply that interrupting has no respect for the linguistic integrity of the interrupted unit. Indeed, in Levelt's (1983) corpus analysis, there was no evidence that interruptions respected phrase boundaries. Additionally, 22% of interruptions fell within words, showing that lexical integrity is not always preserved (Levelt, 1989). Furthermore, within-syllable interruptions also occurred and this was independent of whether or not the part that was spoken was an existing syllable itself.

Levelt (1989) claimed, however, that there is one exception to the main interruption rule. Although word-internal interruptions did occur in the Levelt (1983) corpus, these were mostly restricted to words that were errors themselves. In contrast, words that were not errors themselves were completed. This was the case for appropriateness repairs and for words that follow an error. Brédart (1991) further showed that within-word interruptions for errors depended strongly on word length (the longer the word, the more likely that it can be interrupted word-internally), whereas a much weaker relation with word length was observed for within-word interruptions of inappropriate reparanda. Summarizing, Levelt's version of the main interruption rule holds that speakers interrupt as soon as they can unless this interrupts a correct word. Levelt further argued that speakers only interrupt errors so as to signal the nature of the trouble to the listener.

However, Tydgat, Stevens, Hartsuiker, and Pickering (2011) found data that do not confirm

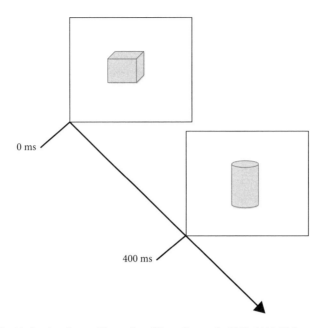

0 ms

400 ms

Figure 25.5 Example trial with the changing-world paradigm (Hartsuiker et al., 2005, 2008; Tydgat et al., 2012 a-b). The picture change (here after 400 ms) leads to responses, such as "yellow cu…yellow cylinder."

Levelt's version of the main interruption rule, using a "changing-world" paradigm (Hartsuiker, Pickering, & De Jong, 2005; Van Wijk & Kempen, 1987). In such paradigms, the world sometimes changes at the moment a speaker is saying something about it (9). Often, this results in the overt production of a reperandum followed by an interruption and repair (Figure 25.5). In contrast to analyses of speech corpora, this method of eliciting repairs allows for tight experimental control over the relation between reperandum and repair and particularly the moment of change (and so about the moment the speaker can detect a need to stop speech). Tydgat et al. presented pictures of colored geometric figures (e.g., of a yellow cube) that occasionally changed in either color (e.g., a brown cube) or shape (e.g., yellow cylinder). The stimulus onset asynchrony (SOA) between initial picture and changed picture varied from 400 ms to 850 ms. Participants were instructed to interrupt and self-repair whenever the picture changed. Consistent with the main interruption rule, the location of interruption depended on SOA, suggesting that people interrupted as soon as the trouble was detected. Importantly, participants as frequently interrupted the current correct word (*cube* in 12) as they interrupted erroneous words (or more precisely, words that were no longer correct).

(12)   yellow cu brown cube

At first glance, Tydgat et al.'s data seem to argue for Nooteboom's (1980) original version of the main interruption rule, that is, the version without Levelt's "strategic" exception. However, other findings argue for a more complicated model of interruption. Specifically, in a second experiment, Tydgat et al. instructed participants to stop *without repairing*. The data pattern differed in one important respect from the earlier data: speakers now much more often interrupted word-internally than in the previous experiment where they had to interrupt and repair. This is suggestive that the location of the interruption depends on the repair, that interruption and repair are coordinated.

Two further studies support the dependence of interruption on repair. In a corpus of spontaneous speech, Seyfeddinipur, Kita, and Indefrey (2008) investigated whether time intervals between interruption and repair depended on repair difficulty. They distinguished between minor repairs, such as phoneme or word substitutions, and major repairs, namely fresh starts. Time intervals between interruption and repair were longer for major than for minor repairs with interruptions after the word, but there was no effect of repair type with within-word interruptions. According to Seyfeddinipur et al., speakers postpone interruptions until they have the repair ready. As long as the repair is not ready, they continue to articulate all the material that is available in the articulatory buffer. This accounts for the observed data: if the repair is ready early, speakers can interrupt within a word and then resume right away with the repair. If the repair is not ready yet when the speaker has run out of buffered speech, the interval before resumption directly reflects the difficulty of planning the repair.

A changing-world study (Hartsuiker, Catchpole, De Jong, & Pickering, 2008) found experimental evidence for a dependence of the repair on the interruption. Participants named line drawings that were sometimes replaced with other drawings. There were two types of replacement drawings: visually intact drawings and visually degraded drawings. When presented as nonchanging initial pictures, the degraded pictures were named significantly more slowly than the intact pictures, confirming that they are more difficult to name. Importantly, in the change trials, participants interrupted themselves significantly later in the degraded than in the intact replacement picture condition, and this was true for both interruptions within-words and after the word. A control experiment, in which speakers interrupted without having to repair, found no effect of degradedness, ruling out that the effect observed in the first experiment resulted from a delay in change detection. This study offers further support for the hypothesis that interruption and repair are coordinated: more difficult repairs lead to later interruptions.

Summarizing, it seems that the main interruption rule does not do justice to the complexity of interruption. The moment speakers stop speech is related to the moment they detect trouble (as the main interruption rule predicts), but the interruption moment is also related to the difficulty of the following repair. Speakers might delay interruption until repair planning is complete (Seyfeddinipur et al., 2008); it is also possible that interrupting and repairing compete for a limited set of cognitive resources so that difficult repairs interfere more with interrupting than easy repairs do (Hartsuiker et al., 2008).

Repairing

How do speakers make the repair? Early work, summarized in Levelt (1989), focused on the surface characteristics of repair (i.e., their syntax and prosody). For instance, Levelt proposed a well-formedness rule that predicts that the repair in (13) is ill-formed but the one in (15) is well-formed. This rule states that an original utterance plus repair is well-formed if a version of the original utterance (completed with a hypothetical constituent if needed; e.g., with a noun phrase like *the surgeon*; see (14)) + the connective *or* + the repair (14 and 16, respectively) is well-formed.[6]

(13) Is the doctor seeing—er—the doctor interviewing patients?

(14) Is the doctor seeing the surgeon or the doctor interviewing patients?

(15) Is the nurse—er—the doctor interviewing patients?

(16) Is the nurse or the doctor interviewing patients?

Levelt found that most repairs in his corpus followed this rule. However, data with a changing-world study (Van Wijk & Kempen, 1987) showed many violations of this rule. The authors presented a scene with a bald man with spectacles pushing a clown; as the speaker began, the bald man's spectacles might disappear while a mustache appeared. This could lead to (17), which clearly violates the well-formedness rule (18)

(17) The bald man with the spectacles pushes—er—with the moustache pushes the sad clown

(18) The bald man with the spectacles pushes the skinny acrobat or with the moustache pushes the sad clown

Van Wijk and Kempen argued for two different ways of repairing: reformulation, which engages syntactic encoding and respects the well-formedness rule; and lexical substitution, which does not engage syntactic encoding and so does not respect the rule.

More recent changing-world studies asked whether representations of the original utterance are "wiped clean," or whether they remain active and affect the process of repairing. Boland, Hartsuiker, Pickering, and Postma (2005) presented participants with pairs of colored geometric objects, one of which had to be named (e.g., a blue square and a yellow square; a cue indicated which object had to be named). In the change trials, the context object changed. For instance, the yellow square could change into a blue square, although a darker blue than the target object. This made a response like "blue square" insufficiently specific; a specification like "light blue square" was now necessary. People were instructed to prepare a response on one trial and produce a response on the next one. Only a very small proportion of trials required a change. The most important finding was that repairs that added a word (blue square → light blue square) took much longer than repairs that deleted a word (light blue square → blue square); yet, in a simple naming task with the same materials, there was no effect of length on naming latencies. The authors argued that speakers can access a stored representation of planned speech and make changes to it; such changes take more time when they are more difficult to make.

Further evidence against a wiping-clean hypothesis comes from a study by Hartsuiker, Pickering, and De Jong (2005). This time the initial and replacement pictures were drawings of single objects and the names of replacement pictures were semantically or phonologically related or unrelated to the initial pictures. If representations of reparanda are discarded, then relatedness in meaning or form should have little effect on the ease of resuming with the name of the replacement picture. In contrast, there were semantic and phonological effects, although the pattern was complicated and depended on whether the name of the initial picture was interrupted or completed. A recent replication (Tydgat, Diependaele, Hartsuiker, & Pickering, 2012) confirmed that repair time is influenced by relatedness with the initial name, and found a clearer data pattern than Hartsuiker et al.: there was semantic facilitation and phonological interference independently of interruption type or SOA.

Summarizing, the process of repairing does not completely abandon representations of the reparanda. Corpus analysis suggests that repair and original utterance seem to be syntactically coordinated. Changing-world studies suggest the possibility that syntactic changes involve the editing of a stored representation and that relatedness between reparandum and repair affects repair time. Note that the PLM (Figure 25.1) is too simple in this respect, because it assumes facilitation, independent of type of relatedness.

Consequences of Monitoring

The presence of an error (or other type of problem) in speech may have as a consequence that the monitor will initiate an interruption and a self-repair, assuming that the monitoring system detects the error and is bothered enough about it to take action. However, interrupting and self-repairing have consequences themselves. Self-repairs and fresh starts are usually classified as disfluencies. So, by definition, self-repair of overt error creates a disfluency. Related to this, it can be expected that self-repairing creates a problem for the listener, because a stretch of speech is stopped and apparently needs to be fully or partly replaced by new speech. Thus, monitoring also has consequences for the flow of conversation. Finally, *covert* monitoring may also affect (and perhaps seriously bias) the data that the field gathers to understand speech production. It is therefore important to understand the ways in which monitoring and speech production processes can interact with each other. This section discusses these consequences.

Consequences for Conversation

Self-repairs might seriously hinder understanding in a conversational setting. When a speaker stops and repairs, the listener does not know which word was wrong, what was wrong about it, and which parts of the repair replaced which parts of the original utterance. According to Levelt (1989), the speaker attempts to minimize these negative consequences for conversation by "signalling" the type of problem to the listener. This signalling involves the location of interrupting, the choice of editing terms, the choice of where to begin the repair, and prosodic marking. Many of these signals would inform the listener about the type of trouble: is the speaker making an error repair or an appropriateness repair? First, word-internal interruptions would signal error repairs rather than appropriateness repairs (but see the study of Tydgat et al., 2011, discussed previously). Second, there are distinct editing terms preceding error repairs ("no!," "sorry," "I mean") and appropriateness repairs ("that is," "or rather"). Editing occurs more frequently with error repairs. Third, there are differences between the type of repairs: the most frequent type of appropriateness repairs are fresh starts, whereas error repairs tend to be instant repairs and anticipatory retracings. Fourth, Levelt and Cutler (1983) found that lexical repairs were sometimes clearly prosodically marked. This was the case much more often with error repairs, and more with terms from a small set (left RIGHT) than a larger set (blue YELLOW).

Levelt also proposed several "conventions" of restarting. For instance, if the restart begins with a word that is identical to one in the original utterance, the listener should interpret that word as the point of continuation. However, if it begins with a word of the same grammatical category as one in the original utterance, then it should be seen as a replacement for that word. Most of the repairs in Levelt's corpus followed these conventions.

One problem with Levelt's view on the consequences of repairs for conversation is that it is based on a rather small corpus, in only one language, and in a very restricted semantic domain (names of colors and of directions). Cross-linguistic studies and experimental investigations should test whether speakers really follow these conventions, whether they are similar in different languages, whether speakers follow such conventions deliberately to facilitate their interlocutor's comprehension, and whether listeners are sensitive to such signals.

Consequences for Disfluencies

Self-repairs are disfluencies by definition (just like pauses, *uhs* and *uhms*, and prolongations); thus, one might say that the price of self-repairing is that of being disfluent (rather than wrong). Levelt (1989) and Postma and Kolk (1993) further argued that internal-channel monitoring can sometimes proceed so fast that the process of interrupting and self-repairing can begin before articulation, while a previous stretch of speech is still being articulated. Hartsuiker and Kolk's (2001) model of the time-course of interruption and repairing is fully compatible with such early repairs. Covert repairing can have two consequences. The first possibility is that the error is filtered out without any obvious consequences for speech. The next two subsections address that possibility in detail. The second possibility is that the error is said partially, but is then interrupted. If the part that is said overtly is clearly incorrect, then the result is an overt repair (19); but if the spoken part is still correct (i.e., when a later phoneme of the internally planned word is wrong) the result may be a repetition (20).

(19) And then to the r left
(20) And then to the r right

Postma and Kolk's (1993; also Kolk & Postma, 1997) covert repair hypothesis makes the strong claim that *all* disfluencies are such covert repairs to hidden, phonological speech errors, both in people who do and do not stutter. However, there has been little empirical support for the covert repair hypothesis. Most attempts to test this hypothesis used a secondary task manipulation under the assumption that this would lead to reduced monitoring; reduced monitoring should lead to reduced rates of disfluencies. However, empirical findings run the gamut from reduced disfluency rates (Vasic & Wijnen, 2005), to no effect (Bosshardt, 2002), to increased disfluency rates (Oomen & Postma, 2001a) under divided attention.

Summarizing, it seems entirely possible that disfluencies (e.g., repetitions) sometimes result from covert repairs, just like other disfluencies (e.g., fresh starts) are overt repairs. However, there is no compelling support for the covert repair hypothesis' strong claim that all disfluencies are covert repairs (see Clark, 2002 and Clark & Wasow, 1998 for a different view on the causes of disfluency).

Consequences for Patterns of Speech Errors

If the monitor can sometimes intercept and replace errors before they become overt, then biases in monitoring (i.e., differences in likelihood of intercepting one type of error more often than another type) can affect patterns of speech errors (Hartsuiker, 2006). The possibility that error patterns are the joint product of encoding processes and monitoring processes has important implications for the field of language production. First, language production theories have traditionally been based on speech error patterns (e.g., Garrett, 1975) usually under the assumption that these patterns directly reflect production processes per se. Second, the field has been long divided between modular (e.g., Levelt et al., 1999) and interactive (e.g., Dell, 1986) views of production. Speech error patterns that seem to argue for interactivity have often been explained as resulting from biased monitoring (see Rapp & Goldrick, 2000; Vigliocco & Hartsuiker, 2002 for discussion). For example, the lexical bias effect (the tendency of phonological speech errors to result in existing words rather than nonwords at a higher rate than chance would predict) can be accounted for in terms of feedback between the phonological and lexical level (Dell, 1986), but also by prearticulatory monitoring, which uses a criterion of lexicality ("*is this a word?*") and so intercepts nonwords more than existing words (Baars, Motley, & MacKay, 1975; Levelt et al., 1999).

Recent evidence supports the notion that speech error patterns reflect an interaction between production and monitoring processes. One prerequisite for such a notion is that there is really prearticulatory editing (error detection and repair), so that the monitor can really discard and replace errors before they are made. Prearticulatory editing is supported by studies that elicited spoonerisms that varied in social appropriateness (Motley, Camden, & Baars, 1982; Severens, Kühn, Brass, & Hartsuiker, 2011; Severens, Kühn, Hartsuiker, & Brass, 2012). For instance, Motley et al. elicited the neutral spoonerism "cool tarts" for the target word pair "tool carts," and similarly, a taboo spoonerism for the pair "tool kits." There were fewer taboo than neutral spoonerisms, suggesting that the monitor used social appropriateness as a criterion. Importantly, correct production of potentially taboo-eliciting stimuli has physiological consequences: such measures as galvanic skin responses (Motley et al., 1982), evoked response potentials (ERPs; Severens et al., 2011), and functional magnetic resonance imaging (fMRI; Severens et al., 2012) showed indices of arousal, conflict, and inhibition in such trials, such as a focus of activation in the right inferior frontal gyrus, the same area involved in stopping speech and actions. These are most likely responses to internal taboo slips that were intercepted.

The issue of which error patterns are affected by prearticulatory editing is addressed at length in Hartsuiker (2006). Two often-cited candidates are the lexical bias effect (see above) and the mixed error bias—an overrepresentation of errors that are related in both form and meaning, such as *lemon-melon* or *cat-rat* (see Rapp & Goldrick, 2000; Roelofs, 2005 for discussion). Evidence that the lexical bias effect is (at least partially) caused by monitoring comes from a classical study of Baars et al. (1975). These authors elicited spoonerisms that could result in nonwords or real words, whereas the target stimuli were all nonwords. The crucial manipulation concerned the context. In the mixed context, some stimuli were words and some were nonwords. In the nonword context, all stimuli were nonwords. The authors observed the lexical bias effect in the mixed context, but not in the nonword context. They concluded that this modulation by context argues for a monitoring account; depending on whether words sometimes occur in the list, the monitor uses the criterion of lexicality. It is unclear how a feedback account, in contrast, could account for context effects.

Hartsuiker, Corley, and Martensen (2005) replicated Baars et al.'s (1975) experiment with several methodological improvements. Consistent with Baars et al., they observed a lexical bias effect in the mixed context, but not in the nonword context. However, there was a crucial difference in the form of the interaction (see Figure 25.6). Whereas Baars et al. found fewest errors in the nonword condition in the mixed context and comparable error rates in the other conditions, Hartsuiker et al. found most errors in word condition in the mixed context and comparable error rates in other conditions.

They accounted for this data pattern as follows. In the mixed context, lexical status is by definition uninformative about correctness, because correct responses are sometimes nonwords and sometimes words. Hence, the monitor does not care about lexicality, and the data pattern in this condition reflects the underlying bias of the production system, with more word errors than nonword errors. However, in the nonword context, all correct responses are nonwords. Hence, in this context, an upcoming real word response can be rejected as an error with complete certainty. Therefore, the monitor now uses the criterion of antilexicality and intercepts more word errors than nonword errors. Given that there are more word errors to begin with, the net result is that the lexical bias effect is wiped out.

Why then are there more word errors than nonword errors before monitoring? The simplest account has it that feedback between the phoneme and lexical levels creates an underlying lexical bias effect that interacts with the monitor. Normally, these two effects conspire to create the lexical bias, but in the highly unusual situation of having to produce nonwords only, they cancel each other out (see Nooteboom & Quené, 2008; Nozari & Dell, 2009 for further discussion).

Summarizing, a good case can be made for prearticulatory editing and for the idea that biases in prearticulatory editing can interact with underlying error biases in the production system per se. It is important to note that editing biases are usually invoked to explain certain observed error biases, especially ones that seem to argue for interactive processing. However, editing biases could just as well "wipe out" pre-existing biases, or interact with them in different ways (Hartsuiker, 2006). Indeed, that a particular error bias is influenced by monitoring in no way rules out that it is also affected by interactivity.

Consequences for the Speed of Production

If covert error detection and production processes can prevent errors, so that accuracy is preserved, this

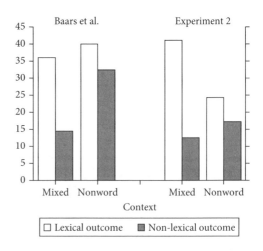

Figure 25.6 Interaction between context and lexical status in the studies of Baars et al. (1975) and Hartsuiker, Corley, and Martensen (2005).

Source: Hartsuiker, R. J., Corley, M., & Martensen, H. (2005). The lexical bias effect is modulated by context, but the standard monitoring account doesn't fly: Related reply to Baars, Motley, and MacKay (1975). *Journal of Memory and Language, 52*, 58–70.

might still lead to a delay. Indeed, the changing-world study of Boland et al. (2005) suggest that editing a prepared speech plan is time-consuming and that this cost depends on the difficulty of the repair: having to add a word took more time than having to delete one (also see Levelt & Maassen, 1981).

The possibility that the speed of production is affected by monitoring has repercussions for the field. Although the field has traditionally been informed by speech error data, the last three decades or so have clearly seen a shift toward the use of chronometric methods. The most popular method is undoubtedly the picture-word interference paradigm (e.g., Schriefers, Meyer, & Levelt, 1990) in which participants name a picture while ignoring a distractor word that is presented simultaneously, or somewhat earlier or later. Researchers using this task usually do not consider the possibility that the reaction times can be influenced by monitoring. It is absurd, however, to assume that the monitor is somehow "turned off" during this task. In fact, the monitor should be particularly vigilant during this task so as to prevent inadvertent naming of the distractor word. Starreveld and La Heij (1999) showed that if speakers are under enough time pressure, this is precisely what happens.

The possibility that monitoring affects picture-word data is relevant for a debate that currently divides the lexical access community, namely whether lexical access is by competition between lexical candidates, so that selection time depends on the activation level of competitor lexical items (e.g., Levelt et al., 1999) or not, so that selection only depends on the activation level of the target item (e.g., Dell, 1986). One noncompetition account is the response exclusion hypothesis (e.g., Janssen, Schirm, Mahon, & Caramazza, 2008; Mahon, Costa, Peterson, Vargas, & Caramazza, 2007), which assumes that distractor words have privileged access to the articulatory buffer. Hence, in a typical picture-word interference task, the distractor word enters the buffer and needs to be purged from it before the picture name can be articulated. The time it takes for this purging to end depends on the moment at which purging begins and how long purging takes. With these assumptions, the response exclusion hypothesis offers an account for several findings in the literature, including semantic interference and the distractor frequency effect, whereby low-frequency distractors interfere with picture naming more than high-frequency distractors do (Burt, 2002; Miozzo & Caramazza, 2003).

What is the mechanism of response exclusion? Dhooge and Hartsuiker (2010) suggested that this is the self-monitoring system. There is no reason to assume that self-monitoring is turned off during the task. Additionally, it is very unparsimonious to assume that speakers have a dedicated response-exclusion system, which evolved for good performance in the picture-word task, in addition to a monitoring system that has an identical function, namely exclusion of trouble that is detected prearticulatory.

Summarizing, it is possible that monitoring affects production latencies. A recent proposal is that the monitor is in fact the mechanism of response exclusion.

Self-Monitoring and the Brain

How is self-monitoring implemented in the brain? Ganushchak and Schiller (2006, 2008a, 2009) measured ERPs during the phoneme-monitoring task ("push the button if the target phoneme occurs in the picture name"). Incorrect go-responses were followed by an error-related negativity (ERN), a component that responds to action errors (e.g., Bernstein, Scheffers, & Coles, 1995) and which is generated in anterior cingulate cortex. This ERN was sensitive to manipulations such as time-pressure (Ganushchak & Schiller, 2006, 2009). However, it is possible that phoneme monitoring does not tap into normal speech monitoring processes (Vigliocco & Hartsuiker, 2002). Another issue is that this ERN does not reflect monitoring after trouble in speech: it is rather a response to errors in the monitoring task. More convincing evidence that self-monitoring elicits an ERN comes from another study of Ganushchak and Schiller (2008a) and one by Ries, Janssen, Dufau, Alario, and Burle (2011): both studies observed an ERN in an overt picture-naming paradigm.

Two further studies used the SLIP-task while the EEG was recorded. Möller, Jansma, Rodriguez-Fornells, & Münte (2007) observed a negativity, starting about 500 ms after stimulus onset, for trials that would subsequently result into spoonerisms compared to correct productions. They interpreted this component as reflecting conflict between the two alternative plans for production. Severens et al. (2012) observed a similar component, in a comparison involving correct productions only, namely correct productions where a Spoonerism would result in neutral words with correct productions where a Spoonerism would lead to a taboo word. The authors suggested that the component reflects a conflict-resolution process that is more pronounced in the potentially taboo-eliciting condition.

What about brain localization? From a meta-analysis of neuroimaging studies, Indefrey and Levelt (2004) concluded that *external*-channel monitoring is localized bilaterally in the superior temporal gyri. These areas are active in speech production and perception and more active in tasks involving overt than covert production. Additionally, these areas are activated in distorted speech feedback conditions (McGuire, Silbersweig, & Frith, 1996). Indefrey and Levelt did not have data to localize internal-channel monitoring, but suggested that this may involve similar areas as external-channel monitoring.

More recent studies suggest that self-monitoring involves a network of brain areas. An fMRI experiment of Christoffels, Formisano, and Schiller (2007) compared normal feedback with noise-masked and silent-speech conditions. It seemed that auditory feedback involved activation in areas including the anterior cingulate cortex, the supplementary motor areas, cerebellum, thalamus, and basal ganglia. Abel et al. (2009) found a very similar network of areas in a study that compared the brain response to speech errors with correct productions. Finally, Severens et al. (2012) argued that the right inferior frontal gyrus is involved in inhibiting the production of socially inappropriate speech errors. It is important to note that many of these areas "make sense": the anterior cingulate cortex is generally believed to be involved in monitoring actions. The cerebellum has been argued to be critically involved in forward models (Ito, 2008).

Future Challenges

The previous sections have already identified a number of important challenges for the future. The biggest challenge, no doubt, is to adjudicate between perception and production monitoring of prearticulatory speech, and to construct more precise production monitoring theories. Further challenges concern a more precise characterization of the interruption and repair processes and of the role monitoring plays in disfluencies, speech errors, and production latencies.

Three further issues are worthy of discussion. First, what is the place of speech monitoring in the broader domain of monitoring one's own thought and action? Second, how do monitoring processes differ in the context of conversation as opposed to monologue? Third, how is monitoring different in people with no full-fledged grammar of a particular language, such as second-language learners and children?

First, what is the place of self-monitoring of speech in the larger area of metacognition and self-regulation? Obviously, people can monitor much more than their speech production: they can monitor other thoughts and actions as well, including comprehension of words and sentences (Van Herten, Chwilla, & Kolk, 2006); text understanding (Dunlosky & Lipko, 2007); typing; and musical performance. People can even monitor their performance in a monitoring task (Ganushchak & Schiller, 2006). Signers can also monitor their signing; Emmorey, Bosworth, and Kraljic (2009) recently argued against a perception monitoring account of signing (i.e., an account using visual perception), because people cannot accurately see their own signs; they look at their hands from the wrong perspective and cannot see their own facial expressions, which are important grammatical markers. Traditionally, there has been little cross-talk between these different literatures, even though there are clear analogies between the type of monitor proposed by Mattson and Baars (1992) and the type of action monitor proposed by Botvinick, Braver, Barch, Carter, and Cohen (2001). More recently, several recent studies have argued for speech monitoring as an instance of more general action monitoring (Nozari, Dell, & Schwartz, 2011; Ries et al., 2011).

It is interesting to note that the field of action monitoring usually asks different questions than the field of speech monitoring (e.g., the question of whether actions following an error are performed more carefully); considers different kind of data (typically button presses in a two-alternative forced choice task; repair attempts are typically not analyzed); and has different kinds of theories (i.e., production monitor theories). Finally, speech production is typically for an audience. This is also true for other types of actions (e.g., performing arts and sports) but many daily activities are not. This difference may be fundamental, especially if it is true that the monitoring system takes the listener's needs into account, as suggested by Levelt.

A type of monitoring that is closer to home for psycholinguists is monitoring for comprehension (e.g., *did I hear this word correctly?*). According to Van Herten et al. (2006), such monitoring is particularly responsive when there is a conflict between two interpretations. For instance, in (21) there is nothing to suggest that the italicized item is correct and so this was presumably a spelling error. But in (22), there is a conflict between the interpretation derived from semantics and phonology (*book*) and the one derived from spelling, and so here the reader might doubt her own perception. Van Herten et al. claimed that comprehension monitoring is reflected in the P600 component of the ERP signal. Recently, Severens and Hartsuiker (2009) argued that comprehension and production monitoring both use lexicality as a criterion. They found a larger P600 for words than nonwords in a sentence context, in other words a lexical bias effect in comprehension.

(21) I went to the store and bought a *boul*

(22) I went to the book shop and bought a *bouk*

A second issue is how monitoring and self-repair are affected by the absence or presence of an interlocutor. Note that Levelt's (1983) evidence that speaker's interruptions, editing terms, and repairs are "signals" to the listener come from a study with recorded monologues. The situation of dialogue is more complex, because now the addressee also can make interruptions and repairs. This can happen when the addressee detects an outright error in the speaker's speech (perhaps a little bit earlier than the speaker does) but also when the two interlocutors have a different set of linguistic (or social) standards (when the speaker is a child, for instance, or a second-language learner). This is the case in the German example below (which I once overheard), where A is a second-language learner of German and B is a native German speaker. Interestingly, B's repair points out explicitly what was wrong with A's utterance. Future work should test whether other-repairs and self-repairs have different properties.

A: Es gibt Hummeln in das Vogelhaus
There are bumblebees in the[ACCUSATIVE] bird house
B: Es gibt Hummeln in DEM Vogelhaus. Datif.
There are bumblebees in THE[DATIVE] bird house. Dative.

Finally, how do people without full-fledged grammars of the language monitor themselves? An interesting suggestion is that children start to self-repair at an earlier time than they become aware of speech errors (Karmiloff-Smith, 1986). This has clear implications for the notion of perception-based theories that the monitor is a central, attentional process.

Multilingual people differ in whether they are speaking in a first or a second language and this varies from moment to moment. This raises a number of issues. For instance, language intrusions (in which a word from another language inadvertently appears) occur very rarely (Poulisse & Bongaerts,

1994). Is this because "target language" is a criterion for monitoring? Although this is possible, such a form of corrective control seems highly inefficient (Costa, Roelstraete, & Hartsuiker, 2006). Language selection might be much easier controlled directively, for instance by inhibiting the nontarget language (Kroll, Bobb, Misra, & Guo, 2008) or by language-specific selection rules (Costa, Miozzo, & Caramazza, 1999). Are monitoring in a first language and a second language quantitatively and qualitatively different? Van Hest (1996) argued for a quantitative difference, namely in the repair times. Kormos (1999) pointed out further differences including a lower repair rate in a second language and the existence of some types of repair that hardly ever occur in a first language.

A final issue for the future is what control mechanisms speakers have, in addition to self-monitoring. This issue is particularly important in bilingualism, where speakers need to control the language of production. Speakers in monolingual contexts also have many linguistic decisions to make, and so would benefit from control processes that keep them on the right track rather than by repairing the damage when one has already left the track.

Conclusion

This review on self-monitoring of speech makes clear that a key theoretical issue is whether the detection of errors before articulation should be seen as a function of speech perception, or of a component intrinsic to speech production. At the same time, recent work with a "changing world" paradigm has led to a better understanding of the processes of speech interruption and repair. Neuroimaging and ERP work has led to a better understanding of the way the brain implements self-monitoring and how this relates to action monitoring in general. Importantly, self-monitoring has consequences for many of the speech parameters the field analyzes: the patterns of speech errors and disfluencies, but quite possibly also the patterns of reaction times. This means that any theory of language production is incomplete without a theory of self-monitoring.

Notes

1. Unless otherwise noted, the examples in this chapter are based on real examples from the data collected by Hartsuiker and Notebaert (2010), but translated from Dutch into English.
2. I heard this example on the radio several months before writing it down; the actual wording may have been different
3. In the original Dutch: the nonword *boof* (/bo:f/) instead of the word *boog* (/bo:x/)

4. Example from Cutler (1983), cited in Levelt (1989).

5. But sentence compehension might not be the best measure of error detection skills in speech perception (Hartsuiker & Kolk, 2001).

6. Specifically, a completion of the last constituent of the original utterance. The completion can be empty if the original utterance already ends with a complete constituent, as in (15). Examples from Levelt (1989).

References

Abel, S., Dressel, K., Kummerer, D., Saur, D., Mader, I., Weiller, C., & Huber, W. (2009). Correct and erroneous picture naming responses in healthy subjects. *Neuroscience Letters*, *463*, 167–171.

Baars, B. J., Motley, J. T., & MacKay, D. (1975). Output editing for lexical status from artificially elicited slips of the tongue. *Journal of Verbal Learning and Verbal Behavior*, *14*, 382–391.

Bernstein, P. S., Scheffers, M. K., & Coles, M. G. H. (1995). "Where did I go wrong?" A psychophysiological analysis of error detection. *Journal of Experimental Psychology: Human Perception and Performance*, *21*, 1312–1322.

Blackmer, E. R., & Mitton, J. L. (1991). Theories of monitoring and the timing of repairs in spontaneous speech. *Cognition*, *39*, 173–194.

Boland, H. T., Hartsuiker, R. J., Pickering, M. J., & Postma, A. (2005). Repairing inappropriately specified utterances: Revision or restart? *Psychonomic Bulletin & Review*, *12*, 472–477.

Bosshardt, H. G. (2002). Effects of concurrent cognitive processing on the fluency of word repetition: comparison between persons who do and do not stutter. *Journal of Fluency Disorders*, *27*, 93–114.

Botvinick, M. M., Braver, T. S., Barch, D. M., Carter, C. S., & Cohen, J. D. (2001). Conflict monitoring and cognitive control. *Psychological Review*, *108*, 624–652.

Brédart, S. (1991). Word interrupting in self-repairing. *Journal of Psycholinguistic Research*, *20*, 123–138.

Burt, J. S. (2002). Why do non-color words interfere with color naming? *Journal of Experimental Psychology: Human Perception and Performance*, *28*, 1019–1038.

Christoffels, I. K., Formisano, E., & Schiller, N. O. (2007). Neural correlates of verbal feedback processing: An fMRI study employing overt speech. *Human Brain Mapping*, *28*, 868–879.

Clark, H. H. (2002). Speaking in time. *Speech Communication*, *36*, 5–13.

Clark, H. H., & Wasow, T. (1998). Repeating words in spontaneous speech. *Cognitive Psychology*, *37*, 201–242.

Costa, A., Miozzo, M., & Caramazza, A. (1999). Lexical selection in bilinguals: Do words in the bilingual's two lexicons compete for selection? *Journal of Memory and Language*, *41*, 365–397.

Costa, A., Roelstraete, B., & Hartsuiker, R. J. (2006). The lexical bias effect in bilingual speech production: Evidence for feedback between lexical and sublexical levels across languages. *Psychonomic Bulletin & Review*, *13*, 612–617.

Cutler, A. (1983). Speakers' conceptions of the function of prosody. In A. Cutler and D. R. Ladd (Eds.), *Prosody: Models and measurements* (pp. 79–91). Heidelberg: Springer.

Dell, G. S. (1986). A spreading-activation theory of retrieval in sentence production. *Psychological Review*, *93*, 283–321.

Desmurget, M., Grafton, S. (2000). Forward modeling allows feedback control for fast reaching movements. *Trends In Cognitive Sciences*, *4*, 423–431.

Dhooge, E., & Hartsuiker, R. J. (2010). The distractor frequency effect in picture-word interference: Evidence for response exclusion. *Journal of Experimental Psychology: Learning, Memory, and Cognition*, *36*, 878–891.

Dunlosky, J., & Lipko, A. R. (2007). Metacomprehension. A brief history and how to improve its accuracy. *Current Directions in Psychological Science*, *16*(4), 228–232.

Emmorey, K., Bosworth, R., & Kraljic, T. (2009). Visual feedback and self-monitoring of sign language. *Journal of Memory and Language*, *61*, 398–411.

Ganushchak, L. Y., & Schiller, N. O. (2006). Effects of time pressure on verbal self-monitoring: an ERP study. *Brain Research*, *1125*, 104–115.

Ganushchak, L. Y., & Schiller, N. O. (2008). Brain monitoring activity is affected by semantic relatedness: an event-related brain potentials study. *Journal of Cognitive Neuroscience*, *20*, 927–940.

Ganushchak, L. Y., & Schiller, N. O. (2009). Speaking one's second language under time pressure: An ERP study on verbal self-monitoring. *Psychophysiology*, *46*, 410–419.

Garrett, M. F. (1975). The analysis of sentence production. In G. H. Bower (Ed.), *The psychology of learning and motivation* (pp. 133–177). New York: Academic Press.

Hartsuiker, R. J. (2006). Are speech error patterns affected by a monitoring bias? *Language and Cognitive Processes*, *21*, 856–891.

Hartsuiker, R. J., Catchpole, C. M., de Jong, N. H., & Pickering, M. J. (2008). Concurrent processing of words and their replacements during speech. *Cognition*, *108*, 601–607.

Hartsuiker, R. J., Corley, M., & Martensen, H. (2005). The lexical bias effect is modulated by context, but the standard monitoring account doesn't fly: Related reply to Baars, Motley, and MacKay (1975). *Journal of Memory and Language*, *52*, 58–70.

Hartsuiker, R. J., & Kolk, H. H. J. (2001). Error monitoring in speech production: A computational test of the perceptual loop theory. *Cognitive Psychology*, *42*, 113–157.

Hartsuiker, R. J., & Notebaert, L. (2010). Lexical access problems lead to disfluencies in speech. *Experimental Psychology*, *57*, 169–177.

Hartsuiker, R. J., Pickering, M. J., & de Jong, N. H. (2005). Semantic and phonological context effects in speech error repair. *Journal of Experimental Psychology: Learning, Memory, and Cognition*, *31*, 921–932.

Huettig, F., & Hartsuiker, R. J. (2010). Listening to yourself is like listening to others: External, but not internal, verbal self-monitoring is based on speech perception, *Language and Cognitive Processes*, *25*, 347–374.

Huettig, F., & McQueen, J. M. (2007). The tug of war between phonological, semantic and shape information in language-mediated visual search. *Journal of Memory and Language*, *57*, 460–482.

Indefrey, P., & Levelt, W. J. M. (2004). The spatial and temporal signatures of word production components. *Cognition*, *92*, 101–144.

Ito, M. (2008). Control of mental activities by internal models in the cerebellum. *Nature Reviews Neuroscience*, *9*, 304–313.

Janssen, N., Schirm, W., Mahon, B. Z., & Caramazza, A. (2008). Semantic interference in a delayed naming task: Evidence for the response exclusion hypothesis. *Journal of Experimental Psychology: Learning, Memory, and Cognition*, *34*, 249–256.

Karmiloff-Smith, A. (1986). From meta-processes to conscious access: evidence from children's metalinguistic and repair data. *Cognition*, *23*, 95–147.

Kolk, H. H. J., & Postma, A. (1997). Stuttering as a covert-repair phenomenon. In: R. Corlee & G. Siegel (Eds.), *Nature and treatment of stuttering: New directions* (pp. 182–203). Boston: Allyn & Bacon.

Kormos, J. (1999). Monitoring and self-repair in L2. *Language Learning, 49*, 303–342.

Kroll, J. F., Bobb, S. C., Misra, M., & Guo, T. (2008). Language selection in bilingual speech: Evidence for inhibitory processes. *Acta Psychologica, 128*, 416–430.

Lackner, J. R., & Tuller, B. H. (1979). Role of efference monitoring in the detection of self-produced speech errors. In: W. E. Cooper & E. C. T. Walker (Eds.), *Sentence processing* (pp. 281–294). Hillsdale, N.J.: Erlbaum.

Ladefoged, P., Silverstein, R., & Papçun, G. (1973). Interruptibility of speech. *Journal of the Acoustical Society of America, 54*, 1105–1108.

Laver, J. (1980). Monitoring systems in the neurolinguistic control of speech production. In: V. A. Fromkin (Ed.), *Errors in linguistic performance: slips of the tongue, ear, pen, and hand* (pp. 287–305). New York: Academic Press.

Levelt, W. J. M. (1983). Monitoring and self-repair in speech. *Cognition, 14*, 41–104.

Levelt, W. J. M. (1989). *Speaking: From intention to articulation.* Cambridge, MA: MIT Press.

Levelt, W. J. M., & Cutler, A. (1983). Prosodic marking in self-repair. *Journal of Semantics, 2*, 205–217.

Levelt, W. J. M., & Maassen, R. (1981). Lexical search and order of mention in sentence production. In W. Klein & W. J. M. Levelt (Eds.), *Crossing the boundaries in linguistics* (pp. 221–252). Dordrecht, The Netherlands: Reidel.

Levelt, W. J. M., Roelofs, A., & Meyer, A. S. (1999). A theory of lexical access in speech production. *Behavioral and Brain Sciences, 22*, 1–75.

Logan, G. D., & Cowan, W. B. (1984). On the ability to inhibit thought and action: A theory of an act of control. *Psychological Review, 91*, 295–327.

MacKay, D. G. (1992). Awareness and error detection: New theories and research paradigms. *Consciousness and Cognition, 1*, 199–225.

Mahon, B. Z., Costa, A., Peterson, R., Vargas, K. A., & Caramazza, A. (2007). Lexical selection is not by competition. *Journal of Experimental Psychology: Learning, Memory, and Cognition, 33*, 503–533.

Marshall, J., Robson, J., Pring, T., & Chiat, S. (1998). Why does monitoring fail in jargon aphasia? Comprehension, judgment, and therapy evidence. *Brain and Language, 63*, 79–107.

Marshall, R. C., Rappaport, B. Z., & Garcia-Bunuel, L. (1985). Self-monitoring behavior in a case of severe auditory agnosia with aphasia. *Brain and Language, 24*, 297–313.

Mattson, M., & Baars, B. J. (1992). Error-minimizing mechanisms: Boosting or editing? In B. J. Baars (Ed.), *Experimental slips and human error: Exploring the architecture of volition* (pp. 263–287). New York: Plenum.

McGuire, P. K., Silbersweig, D. A., & Frith, C. D. (1996). Functional neuroanatomy of verbal self-monitoring. *Brain, 119*, 907–917.

McNamara, P., Obler, L. K., Au, R., Durso, R., & Albert, M. L. (1992). Speech monitoring skills in Alzheimer's disease, Parkinson's disease, and normal aging. *Brain and Language, 42*, 38–51.

Miozzo, M., & Caramazza, A. (2003). When more is less: A counterintuitive effect of distractor frequency in picture–word interference paradigm. *Journal of Experimental Psychology: General, 132*, 228–252.

Möller, J., Jansma, B. M., Rodriguez-Fornells, A., & Münte, T. F. (2007). What the brain does before the tongue slips. *Cerebral Cortex, 17*, 1173–1178.

Morin, A., & Everett, J. (1990). Inner speech as a mediator of self-awareness, self-consciousness, and self-knowledge—an hypothesis. *New Ideas in Psychology, 8*, 337–356.

Motley, M. T., Camden, C. T., Baars, B. J. (1982). Covert formulation and editing of anomalies in speech production—Evidence from experimentally elicited slips of the tongue. *Journal of Verbal Learning and Verbal Behavior, 21*, 578–594.

Nickels, L. A., & Howard, D. (1995). Phonological errors in aphasic naming: Comprehension, monitoring and lexicality. *Cortex, 31*, 209–237.

Nooteboom, S. G. (1980). Speaking and unspeaking: detection and correction of phonological and lexical errors in spontaneous speech. In V. A. Fromkin (Ed.), *Errors in linguistic performance* (pp. 87–95). New York: Academic Press.

Nooteboom, S. G., & Quené, H. (2008). Self-monitoring and feedback: A new attempt to find the main cause of lexical bias in phonological speech errors. *Journal of Memory and Language, 58*, 837–861.

Nozari, N., & Dell, G. S. (2009). More on lexical bias: How efficient can a "lexical editor" be? *Journal of Memory and Language, 60*, 291–307.

Nozari, N., Dell, G. S., & Schwartz, M. F. (2011). Is comprehension necessary for error detection? A conflict-based account of monitoring in speech production. *Cognitive Psychology, 63*, 1–33.

Oomen, C. C. E., & Postma, A. (2001a). Effects of divided attention on the production of filled pauses and repetitions. *Journal of Speech Language and Hearing Research, 44*, 997–1004.

Oomen, C. C. E., & Postma, A. (2001b). Effects on time pressure on mechanisms of speech production and self-monitoring. *Journal of Psycholinguistic Research, 30*, 163–184.

Oomen, C. C. E., & Postma, A. (2002). Limitations in processing resources and speech monitoring. *Language and Cognitive Processes, 17*, 163–184.

Oomen, C. C. E., Postma, A., & Kolk, H. H. J. (2001). Prearticulatory and postarticulatory self-monitoring in Broca's aphasia. *Cortex, 37*, 627–641.

Oomen, C. C. E., Postma, A., & Kolk, H. H. J. (2005). Speech monitoring in aphasia: Error detection and repair behaviour in a patient with Broca's aphasia. In R.J. Hartsuiker, R. Bastiaanse, A. Postma, & F. Wijnen (Eds.), *Phonological encoding and monitoring in normal and pathological speech* (pp. 209–225). Hove, England: Psychology Press.

Oppenheim, G. M., & Dell, G. S. (2008). Inner speech slips exhibit lexical bias, but not the phonemic similarity effect. *Cognition, 106*, 528–537.

Özdemir, R., Roelofs, A., & Levelt, W. J. M. (2007). Perceptual uniqueness point effects in monitoring internal speech. *Cognition, 105*, 457–465.

Pick, H. L., Siegel, G. M., Fox, P. W., Garber, S. R., & Kearney, J. K. (1989). Inhibiting the Lombard effect. *Journal of the Acoustical Society of America, 85*, 894–900.

Pickering, M. J., & Garrod, S. (2007). Do people use language production to make predictions during comprehension? *Trends in Cognitive Sciences, 11*, 105–110.

Postma, A. (2000). Detection of errors during speech production. A review of speech monitoring models. *Cognition, 77*, 97–131.

Postma, A., & Kolk, H. H. J. (1993). The covert repair hypothesis—prearticulatory repair processes in normal and stuttered disfluencies. *Journal of Speech and Hearing Research*, *36*, 472–487.

Postma, A., & Noordanus, C. (1996). Production and detection of speech errors in silent, mouthed, noise-masked, and normal auditory feedback speech. *Language and Speech*, *39*, 375–392.

Postma, A., & Oomen, C. C. E. (2005). Critical issues in speech monitoring. In R. J. Hartsuiker, R. Bastiaanse, A. Postma, & F. Wijnen (Eds.), *Phonological encoding and monitoring in normal and pathological speech* (pp. 157–166). Hove, England: Psychology Press.

Poulisse, N., & Bongaerts, T. (1994). 1st language use in 2nd-language production. *Applied Linguistics*, *15*, 36–57.

Rapp, B., & Goldrick, M. (2000). Discreteness and interactivity in spoken word production. *Psychological Review*, *107*, 460–499.

Ries, S., Janssen, N., Dufau, S., Alario, F. X., & Burle, B. (2011). General-purpose monitoring during speech production. *Journal of Cognitive Neuroscience*, *23*, 1419–1436.

Roelofs, A. (2005). Spoken word planning, comprehending, and self-monitoring: Evaluation of WEAVER++. In R. J. Hartsuiker, R. Bastiaanse, A. Postma, & F. Wijnen (Eds.), *Phonological encoding and monitoring in normal and pathological speech* (pp. 42–63). Hove, England: Psychology Press.

Schlenck, K. J., Huber, W., & Willmes, K. (1987). Prepairs and repairs: Different monitoring functions in aphasic language production. *Brain and Language*, *30*, 226–244.

Schriefers, H., Meyer, A. S., & Levelt, W. J. M. (1990). Exploring the time-course of lexical access in language production: Picture-word interference studies. *Journal of Memory and Language*, *29*, 86–102.

Severens, E., & Hartsuiker, R. J. (2009). Is there a lexical bias effect in comprehension monitoring? *Language and Cognitive Processes*, *24*, 910–927.

Severens, E., Kühn, S., Brass, M., & Hartsuiker, R. J. (2011). When the brain tames the tongue: Covert editing of inappropriate language. *Psychophysiology*, *48*, 1252-1257.

Severens, E., Kühn, S., Hartsuiker, R. J., & Brass, M. (2012). Functional mechanisms involved in the internal inhibition of taboo words. *Social, Cognitive and Affective Neuroscience*, *7*, 431–435.

Seyfeddinipur, M., Kita, S., & Indefrey, P. (2008). How speakers interrupt themselves in managing problems in speaking: Evidence from self-repairs. *Cognition*, *108*, 837–842.

Slevc, L. R., & Ferreira, V. S. (2006). Halting in single word production: A test of the perceptual loop theory of speech monitoring. *Journal of Memory and Language*, *54*, 515–540.

Starreveld, P. A., & La Heij, W. (1999). Word substitution errors in a speeded picture-word task. *American Journal of Psychology*, *112*, 521–553.

Tydgat, I., Diependaele, K., Hartsuiker, R. J., & Pickering, M. J. (2012). How lingering representations of abandoned context words affect speech production. *Acta Psychologica*, *140*, 218–229.

Tydgat, I., Stevens, M., Hartsuiker, R. J., & Pickering, M. J. (2011). Deciding where to stop speaking. *Journal of Memory and Language*, *64*, 359–380.

Van Herten, M., Chwilla, D. J., & Kolk, H. H. J. (2006). When heuristics clash with parsing routines: ERP evidence for conflict monitoring in sentence perception. *Journal of Cognitive Neuroscience*, *18*, 1181–1197.

Van Hest, E. (1996). *Self-repair in L1 and L2 production*. Tilburg: Tilburg University Press.

Van Wijk, C., & Kempen, G. (1987). A dual system for producing self-repairs in spontaneous speech: evidence from experimentally elicited corrections. *Cognitive Psychology*, *19*, 403–440.

Vasic, N., & Wijnen, F. (2005). Stuttering as a monitoring deficit. In R. J. Hartsuiker, R. Bastiaanse, A. Postma, & F. Wijnen (Eds.), *Phonological encoding and monitoring in normal and pathological speech* (pp. 226–247). Hove, England: Psychology Press.

Verbruggen, F., & Logan, G. D. (2008). Response inhibition in the stop-signal paradigm. *Trends in Cognitive Sciences*, *12*, 418–424.

Vigliocco, G., & Hartsuiker, R. J. (2002). The interplay of meaning, sound, and syntax in sentence production. *Psychological Bulletin*, *128*, 442–472.

Wheeldon, L. R., & Levelt, W. J. M. (1995). Monitoring the time course of phonological encoding. *Journal of Memory and Language*, *34*, 311–334.

Xue, G., Aron, A. R., & Poldrack, R. A. (2008). Common neural substrates for inhibition of spoken and manual responses. *Cerebral Cortex*, *18*, 1923–1932.

Language Production and Working Memory

Randi C. Martin *and* L. Robert Slevc

Abstract

The role of working memory in language production is considered at different levels of planning. At the message level, there is mixed evidence regarding a role for short-term memory or working memory in discourse fluency and coherence and stronger evidence for a role in the production of referring expressions. A somewhat larger body of evidence exists with respect to the level of grammatical encoding, with studies on accessibility and agreement implicating effects of retrieval interference in working memory. Regarding scope of planning, evidence drawn primarily from brain-damaged patients suggests a role for memory capacity at the lexical-semantic level rather than phonological level in phrasal planning. In contrast, some findings from neurally intact individuals implicate multiword planning at the phonological level, perhaps implicating a phonological output buffer. Future work is needed to integrate findings from production planning with different approaches to working memory.

Key Words: working memory, short-term memory, scope of planning, retrieval interference

In contrast to most research on the role of working memory (WM) in language comprehension (Caplan & Waters, 1999; Daneman & Hannon, 2007), relatively little research has been devoted to the role of WM in language production. Nonetheless, some important findings have been uncovered in the production domain from studies of normal and brain-damaged populations. This article provides an overview of these findings, organized primarily by the influence of WM at various stages in the production process. First discussed are some relevant theories in the WM literature before launching into the specifics of findings in production.

Working memory

The well-known standard model of WM originally proposed by Baddeley and Hitch (1974) consists of peripheral storage systems (specifically, the phonological loop and visuospatial sketchpad) and a central executive. The peripheral storage systems store information in a specific code (phonological or visuospatial) and rehearsal may be applied to these codes to keep them active, otherwise the representations decay over time. The central executive is an attentional control system involved in retrieving information from long-term memory and in allocating attention to the contents of the phonological loop and visuospatial sketchpad. More recently, Baddeley (2000) added a new component, termed the episodic buffer, which is involved in binding information from several sources to create a coherent episodic event. The information to be maintained in the episodic buffer may be retrieved from long-term memory, from one of the peripheral storage systems, or derived from external input.

In this model, one might assume that the phonological loop component would be centrally involved in language processing. However, contrary to this assumption, disruption of the phonological component, either through a secondary task, such as articulatory suppression, or through brain damage, has little effect on comprehension (Baddeley, Gathercole, & Papagno, 1998; Martin, 1993). During comprehension, the immediate construction of syntactic and semantic representations as each word is perceived obviates the need for phonological storage of an ordered representation of the input (Martin & Romani, 1994). For production, however, one must produce the phonological form of words in a specific order, and thus it is possible that the phonological loop (or some other temporary buffer for to-be-produced phonological information) is more involved. The central executive is another possible component involved in production. One might hypothesize, for instance, that an attention-allocation component plays a role in lexical selection, specifically in selecting a target word from competitors. Finally, the episodic buffer might play some role, such as in holding the intended message in mind during construction of the utterance.

There are many alternatives to the Baddeley (2000) approach, some of which may have more direct relevance to language production. Some of these proposals are specifically language-based (Martin & Saffran, 1997; Martin & Gupta, 2004; Martin, Lesch, & Bartha, 1999) and assume that representations at all levels during language processing are maintained either in specialized buffers for semantic and phonological information (Martin et al., 1999) or simply through the activation of the corresponding information in the lexicon (Martin & Saffran, 1997). In the model proposed by Martin et al. (1999), phonological retention is supported by two different buffers: one for maintaining input phonological representations and another for retaining output phonological representations. Another important approach in the language domain assumes that WM consists of a cognitive resource that is shared between processing and storage (Just & Carpenter, 1992). Complex tasks, such as language comprehension and production, are assumed to draw on the processing and storage components. Simple span measures (e.g., serial recall of a word list) are argued to tap primarily short-term memory (STM)—that is, the storage component of this WM resource—and as a consequence do not correlate highly with language comprehension (Daneman & Merikle, 1996). To measure individual differences in the processing-plus-storage resource, complex span tasks, such as reading span, are used (Daneman & Carpenter, 1980). In the reading span task, subjects must simultaneously retain words while reading sentences aloud. The speaking span measure

was developed specifically to tap into production processes (Daneman & Green, 1986). In this measure, individuals are given lists of words of varying length and must produce a sentence for each word in the list. Spans from these complex WM tasks correlate more highly with comprehension measures than do simple span measures. Complex measures have also been used to predict language production performance, with some success (as discussed later). According to the approach of Daneman and Green, the WM capacity tapped by complex span measures is a general capacity involved in language production, with the processing and storage capacity allocated to various types of representation. The approach thus differs from others that suppose a specific capacity allocated to syntactic parsing (Caplan & Waters, 1999) or specific capacities devoted to phonological versus lexical-semantic retention (Martin et al., 1999).

Another recent perspective on WM, the retrieval model, has been developed primarily to account for findings in basic memory tasks but also has been applied to language processing. This approach emphasizes attentional focus and cue-based retrieval from memory (e.g., Cowan, 2001; McElree, 2001; Unsworth & Engle, 2007). In the retrieval model, WM is assumed to be the activated portion of long-term memory. The items that are most highly activated are held in the focus of attention. The size of this focus varies across different instantiations of the theory, with some researchers arguing that the capacity is about four chunks of information (Cowan, 2001) and others suggesting that the capacity is only one chunk (McElree, 2001). Accessing information outside the focus of attention requires retrieval, which is assumed to involve parallel access to memory representations based on retrieval cues. These retrieval cues are likely to partially fit with multiple items in memory, resulting in interference in retrieval. Interference rather than decay is assumed to be the major source of forgetting (e.g., Berman, Jonides, & Lewis, 2009). Given the limited capacity of attentional focus, individual differences are often attributed to other factors, such as differences in the ability to switch the focus of attention (Verhaeghen & Basak, 2005) or in the ability to select appropriate search cues for retrieving information outside the focus of attention (Unsworth & Engle, 2007).

Because of the emphasis on retrieval, these interference-based models can readily be applied to sentence comprehension where it is often necessary to retrieve earlier information in a sentence to integrate with later information across several intervening words (e.g., for the sentence "The woman who was talking to the manager complained about the high prices," "woman" has to be retrieved as the subject of "complained," with "manager" potentially providing interference). Detailed investigations have been carried out assessing the ability of the interference-based model to account for patterns of sentence comprehension (e.g., Lewis, Vasishth, & Van Dyke, 2006; McElree, Foraker, & Dyer, 2003; Van Dyke, 2007) and the approach has met with considerable success. On the production side, the approach seems less clearly relevant because it is not as obvious how the retrieval of earlier parts of an utterance would be involved in production. There are situations, however, in which a case for retrieval can plausibly be made, such as in computing various types of agreement (e.g., retrieving the number or gender of the head noun in choosing inflectional markings on the verb or retrieving the number or gender of the anaphor when determining the pronoun to be produced; Badecker & Kuminiak, 2007; Lewis & Badecker, 2010).

In contrast to the previously mentioned proposals in which some relation between WM and language processing is assumed, McDonald and Christiansen (2002) have argued that individual differences in language comprehension can be attributed to variation in language experience and biological factors that influence the integrity of various types of language representations (e.g., the quality of phonological representations). Thus, in their view, neither specialized nor general storage capacity is involved in comprehension. This approach thus ascribes individual differences in comprehension to the quality of processing rather than to differences in storage capacity. Presumably, a similar argument could be made for production.

The following discussion considers how these different approaches have been applied to WM demands in language production.

Stages of Production and Demands on Working Memory

An analysis of the stages involved in production is important because WM requirements and the capacities involved could differ depending on the type of information represented at each stage, assuming that there are different capacities for different types of information. As shown in Figure 26.1, production begins with the nonverbal representation of the message to be expressed. The next stage, grammatical encoding, involves two parts: functional assembly, which involves the selection of lexical and grammatical units to represent the information in the message; and structural assembly, which involves linking lexical and structural forms into an ordered sequence. In the third stage, phonological forms are retrieved. Finally, the phonological forms are used to drive articulation. These stages should not be considered to be strictly serial. Processing of different parts of an utterance could be going on simultaneously at different stages. That is, phonological encoding could proceed for an early part of a sentence while structural assembly proceeds for a later part of the sentence. Also, even for what will become the same part of an utterance, processing at a later stage could feed back and affect processing at an earlier stage. For example, the unavailability of the phonological form of a word that was chosen at the grammatical encoding stage could lead to the selection of an alternative word at the structural assembly stage.

Much of the research on the role of WM in production has focused on the grammatical encoding stage, that is, on the capacity for maintaining representations during functional assembly and the influence of any capacity limitations on structural assembly. However, some consideration has also been given to WM effects at the message level and at the phonological level.

Working Memory in Message Encoding

At the message level, WM would seem to be required to maintain the central theme or topic of a conversation and keep track of what has occurred in the preceding discourse (e.g., questions typically require some type of contingent response). More generally, a successful conversation requires speakers to speak in a way that is relatively organized and fluent; to talk about things that are relevant to their audience; and to refer back to things that were previously brought up (by them or by others). Indeed, there is evidence that these processes of discourse fluency and coherence, audience design, and anaphora do rely on WM.

Early studies on the role of WM in language production found that WM span (as measured with the speaking span task; Daneman & Green, 1986) was positively correlated with discourse fluency (measured simply as the number of words produced in a picture description task) and negatively correlated with reading speed and errors in passage reading (Daneman, 1991). WM span (reading span) is also positively related to fluency (speech rate measures) and negatively related to production of hesitations (e.g., *ums* and repetitions) in first and second language narrative production (Fehringer & Fry, 2007b; Fortkamp, 2003). Although such findings could be taken to show a role of WM in production at the message level, fluency measures such as these seem unlikely to be the best measures of discourse quality. For one, a speaker could produce a great number of words with very few hesitations while nonetheless producing very little actual content, and this hardly seems to be high-quality discourse. Secondly, fluency measures depend on success at all levels of production, from message generation to articulation, so it is not clear that these findings implicate message level processing per se.

Fluency at the message level depends on efficient encoding of the semantic features of to-be-expressed entities, the relationships between these entities, and the roles of those entities in the larger context (Ferreira & Slevc, 2007). Thus, a more appropriate measure of fluency at the message level is probably *discourse coherence*, or how well utterances are linked with what has come before. Presumably this is often related to discourse fluency, but not always; for example, although older adults reduce their speech rate in a dual task situation (and thus have lower fluency scores), dual tasks have little effect on measures of their message content (Kemper, Herman, & Lian, 2003).

A small body of work has investigated the relationship between WM and discourse coherence (and other discourse measures) in patients with deficits in discourse production, on the idea that their discourse production problems might reflect underlying WM limitations. Caspari and Parkinson (2000) investigated various types of discourse and pragmatic production in an amnesic patient who additionally had a low WM span (as assessed with the Daneman and Carpenter [1980] reading span task) and in four control subjects: two with equivalently low WM spans and two with normal spans. Unsurprisingly, episodic long-term memory deficits predicted a number of problems in conversational discourse production; however, they found no relationship between WM measures and any aspect of discourse production.

In contrast, some studies with larger samples have reported relationships between STM and aspects of discourse production in patients with closed head injury, showing that discourse cohesion and production of words and content units are correlated (albeit modestly) with measures of STM (Brookshire, Chapman, Song, & Levin, 2000; Hartley & Jensen, 1991; Youse & Coelho, 2005). Importantly, these studies show a relationship between STM (not WM) and discourse cohesion, because memory ability was not measured with WM span tasks but with simple storage-based tasks (in particular, with simple span tasks and paired associate learning). Despite this, and despite the correlational nature of these studies, they do

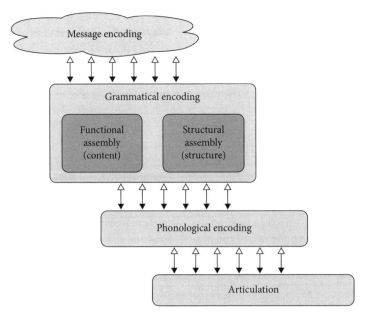

Figure 26.1 Stages of processing in language production (Adapted from Bock & Levelt, 1994; Ferreira & Slevc, 2007). Stages are staggered from left to right to indicate the flow of information over time. Solid arrows show feed-forward (primary) information flow and open arrows indicate possible feedback information flow.

provide some suggestion that discourse production deficits after brain injury may be related to STM or WM limitations.

Another aspect of discourse production that has been argued to rely on general memory processes is *audience design*, referring to the ways in which speakers tailor their utterances to their listeners. Effective audience design is generally thought to rely on speakers' understanding of what knowledge they share with their listener, that is, on their common ground (e.g., Clark, 1996). It is worth noting that the extent to which speakers actively engage in audience design is somewhat controversial (e.g., Brown & Dell, 1987; Ferreira & Dell, 2000; Lockridge & Brennan, 2002), but it is clear that at least some aspects of common ground are sensitive to speaker-internal cognitive pressures, which seem likely to include pressures on STM or WM (Nadig & Sedivy, 2002; Wardlow Lane & Ferreira, 2008; Wardlow Lane, Groisman, & Ferreira, 2006).

Indeed, an early conception of common ground was of an explicit, specialized memory system called a *reference diary* that maintained the co-occurrence of speakers, listeners, and referents (Clark & Marshall, 1981). More recently, it has been suggested that keeping track of common ground is a cognitively demanding task that occurs only as part of the monitoring function of production (Horton & Keysar, 1996; see also Clark & Krych, 2004; Hartsuiker's chapter in this volume titled Monitoring and Control of the Production System). Given proposals that this monitoring process relies on limited-resource WM (Oomen & Postma, 2002), this suggests that common ground also is WM dependent. Indeed, speakers are less successful at tailoring their utterances to their listeners' perspectives when under a greater memory load, be it a message-level load (i.e., increased message complexity) or a message-external digit load (Roßnagel, 2000, 2004).

However, another theory linking common ground to general memory processes does not implicate STM or WM, but rather suggests that common ground emerges by automatic associations between people and information in long-term episodic memory (Horton & Gerrig, 2005a, 2005b). Essentially, the idea is that specific listeners serve as cues that automatically activate information associated with them, and so speakers are likely to talk about information that is in common ground simply because that information is more accessible. This claim is supported by findings that speakers' degree of partner specificity (i.e., how much they

are using common ground) is affected by the complexity of the relevant partner-specific associations, but is not related to speakers' explicit memory for what information is shared with specific partners (Horton, 2007).

It is unclear to what extent speakers' use of common ground relies on WM versus long-term episodic memory. It is entirely possible (even likely) that both are correct: common ground is a fairly amorphous construct, and probably relies on a variety of underlying systems. A somewhat more specific domain of discourse production that seems to rely on WM processes is speakers' use of reference. Intuitively, choosing an appropriate referring expression to refer to an entity that has previously been mentioned (e.g., choosing whether to produce a full noun phrase, a demonstrative, a pronoun, and so forth) requires a memory of that previous mention.

Work on the comprehension of anaphors has implicated a form of WM that is susceptible to semantic interference (i.e., the retrieval model; Almor, 1999, 2004; Almor & Nair, 2007), although some recent work has not supported this account (Cowles, Garnham, & Simner, 2010). In production, choice of a referring expression (i.e., an anaphor) has been linked to *accessibility*, or how easy it is for a speaker to access the referred-to information. In several studies, Arnold and colleagues (see Arnold, 2010, for a review) show that accessibility is not just a function of discourse status, but is also influenced by pressures on WM. In particular, speakers tend to decrease pronoun production (i.e., to use of more specific forms of reference) when under a cognitive load (Arnold, Bennetto, & Diehl, 2009) and one relevant type of load is the existence of mental representations of other discourse entities (Arnold & Griffin, 2007).

In sum, work looking at the role of WM or STM in discourse production is somewhat mixed. There is evidence for a role of WM in discourse fluency (e.g., Daneman, 1991) and for a role of simple STM span in discourse coherence (Hartley & Jensen, 1991; Youse & Coelho, 2005), but the relative contributions of WM and STM have not been directly assessed. This work has largely been based on a framework of WM as a limited-capacity system (e.g., Baddeley, 2000); however, there also seems to be a relationship between executive functioning and discourse coherence (Brookshire et al., 2000) and these findings together might be well-explained by a retrieval model of WM (e.g., Cowan, 2001). The production of referring expressions (which is certainly part of discourse coherence) also seems to be better explained by interference effects than by capacity limits (Arnold, 2010). Work on common ground comes to somewhat mixed conclusions, with some work showing a role of WM (Roβnagel, 2000, 2004) and other work implicating episodic long-term memory (Horton, 2007; Horton & Gerrig, 2005a, 2005b). These findings are compatible with an interference-limited WM system, especially if the same types of cue-based retrieval mechanisms extend to the (automatic) retrieval of episodic associations. However, these findings may also fit with a capacity-limited system of WM if such automatic associations can be captured as operations of the episodic buffer (Baddeley, 2000). So far, however, there has been little attempt to distinguish between different models of WM in the discourse domain.

Working Memory in Grammatical Encoding

The role of STM and WM in sentence comprehension is controversial, with arguments that syntactic parsing relies on a language-specific WM store (e.g., Caplan & Waters, 1999); on a domain-general verbal WM store (e.g., Just & Carpenter, 1992); and on a cue-based (and interference-susceptible) retrieval mechanism (e.g., Lewis et al., 2006). The role of STM/WM in sentence production (i.e., in grammatical encoding) is less controversial, although perhaps only because there is relatively little research.

In studies of sentence production, syntactic complexity has been found to correlate with WM span in written production (Hoskyn & Swanson, 2003) and in second-language speech production (Fortkamp, 2003), although this does not hold for all ways of measuring complexity (Fehringer & Fry, 2007a). Moving beyond correlational evidence, speakers produce less syntactically complex speech when under a cognitive load (Kemper et al., 2003; Kemper, Schmalzried, Herman, Leedahl, & Mohankumar, 2009), and this effect is especially pronounced for people with lower WM spans (as assessed by the reading span task; Kemper et al., 2009). In parallel to a large body of work in sentence comprehension, syntactically complex sentences (in particular, object-extracted relative clauses) have been shown to be more cognitively demanding to produce than less syntactically complex (subject-extracted relative clause) sentences (Fedorenko, Badecker, & Gibson, 2007). This may reflect memory demands associated with syntactic

production processes themselves, or might instead reflect memory demands associated with constructing rarely produced lexical/structural pairings (Gennari & MacDonald, 2009).

Accessibility effects

One way that speakers might manage the memory demands of grammatical encoding is by taking advantage of syntactic flexibility afforded by the grammar (Bock, 1982; Ferreira, 1996). Indeed, speakers tend to choose structures that allow for later production of information that is relatively more complex (Arnold, Wasow, Losongco, & Ginstrom, 2000; Wasow, 1997) and allow for earlier production of information that is relatively more accessible, whether that be more animate, imageable, semantically primed, or previously mentioned (Bock, 1977; Bock, 1986; Bock & Irwin, 1980; Bock & Warren, 1985; Davidson, Zacks, & Ferreira, 2003; Ferreira & Yoshita, 2003; McDonald, Bock, & Kelly, 1993). These effects have often been framed as a way that speakers ease their processing load; the idea being that early production of easier-to-retrieve information reduces the need to temporarily maintain that information and allows more time and processing resources to be devoted to the more difficult to retrieve information while the accessible information is being articulated. Indeed, a concurrent verbal WM load (but not a spatial WM load) affects speakers' tendency to produce previously mentioned items early, suggesting that WM does underlie these accessibility effects (Slevc, 2011). In Slevc's study, however, a verbal WM load led to a reduction, rather than an increase, in accessibility effects. This pattern is unexpected under a workspace model of WM, where there should be a greater demand to produce items in active storage early (thereby freeing up "space" in WM). This pattern does, however, fit with a cue-based search model of WM because the memory cues used to retrieve a to-be-produced target are likely to overlap with the verbal WM load, thereby leading to interference. Put another way, under this account the accessibility of items is reduced when under a verbal load (see also Arnold & Griffin, 2007).

Computation of agreement

The accessibility effects described previously suggest that grammatical encoding processes can flexibly adapt to memory demands related to the availability of lexical items, but do not necessarily show that grammatical processing itself relies on WM. The bulk of the work relevant to this question has focused on processes of *agreement*. Most, if not all, work on agreement production has focused on agreement errors, relying on speakers' susceptibility to *attraction*. An attraction error occurs when a speaker produces a target item that agrees with an inappropriate controller (e.g., *The time for fun and games are over*; Bock & Miller, 1991). One reasonable account for such errors is that speakers must either maintain or retrieve the controller from WM during target production to determine the appropriate agreeing form to produce. Some work, however, has not found support for this account; finding weak or no correlations between WM span and agreement error rates in spoken English (Bock & Cutting, 1992) and no effect of a concurrent verbal WM load on agreement error rates (in the French imperfect tense) when writing to dictation (Chanquoy & Negro, 1996).

In contrast, written attraction errors (in the French present indicative) are more common when writing to dictation under a concurrent verbal WM load or when performing a secondary task (counting clicks; Fayol, Largy, & Lemaire, 1994). Spoken agreement error rates in Dutch are more likely when under a verbal WM load, but only for speakers with low WM spans (as assessed by a median split on speaking span scores; Hartsuiker & Barkhuysen, 2006). Some patients with asphasia also show an increased susceptibility to grammatical attraction in English, and this susceptibility is better predicted by the extent of the patients' STM deficit than by the extent of the patients' agrammatism (Slevc & Martin, 2011). Because patients' STM deficits seem to be related to deficits in verbal inhibition (Hamilton & Martin, 2005, 2007), these data fit well with Badecker and Kuminiak's (2007) proposal that agreement attraction errors reflect interference that occurs when retrieval cues for the appropriate controller overlap with other items in recent memory.

In sum, there is a small, but growing body of work showing that WM is involved in accessibility and agreement aspects of grammatical encoding. Some of this work is only suggestive at this point, such as demonstrations of syntactic complexity effects in production (Fedorenko et al., 2007) and correlations between speakers' WM span and the syntactic complexity in their speech or writing (Fortkamp, 2003; Hoskyn & Swanson, 2003). Other work manipulating memory load has found effects on syntactic complexity (Kemper et al., 2009) and syntactic choice (Slevc, 2011); these data seem most compatible with cue-based search

models of WM (e.g., Cowan, 2001; McElree, 2001) because a memory load seems to affect production by an increase in interference. Finally, work on agreement production suggests a role of an interference-susceptible form of WM in grammatical encoding itself (e.g., Badecker & Kuminiak, 2007; Slevc & Martin, in press). A relationship between WM and sentence production goes both ways: memory processes influence language production, but production processes also influence WM (Acheson & MacDonald, 2009; Martin, Shelton, & Yaffee, 1994). Recent work showing influences of morphosyntactic information on memory recall (Schweppe & Rummer, 2007) shows that this also holds at the level of grammatical encoding.

Working memory and scope of planning

The literature reviewed previously indicates that accessibility of lexical items influences the choice of syntactic structure and that accessibility effects are influenced by WM. Another issue regarding lexical retrieval and WM is the scope of planning (i.e., how far ahead speakers choose lexical representations before utterance onset). Early formulations based on speech error data suggested that planning at the functional assembly level occurred at a clausal level as word exchange errors occurred at some distance, with words often exchanging between different phrases (e.g., Garrett, 1975). Some recent theorizing has posited a much smaller scope, with some researchers arguing that planning at the grammatical stage proceeds word-by-word (Chang, Dell, & Bock, 2006; Griffin, 2003). Others take a middle ground, arguing that planning occurs at a phrasal level (Smith & Wheeldon, 1999; Martin, Crowther, Knight, Tamborello, & Yang, 2010). The hypothesized WM demands of grammatical encoding would vary depending on the assumed scope, with word-by-word planning making few demands on WM but clausal planning placing a large demand on WM capacity.

As discussed in Martin et al. (2010), the evidence for word-by-word planning has come principally from studies monitoring subjects' eye movements while they produced phrases or sentences to describe pictured scenes (e.g., Griffin & Bock, 2000; Meyer, Sleiderink, & Levelt, 1998). Studies using this methodology have shown a close correspondence between the timing of gazes to an object and the onset of the word corresponding to that object. If speakers plan several words in advance, one might expect that the time delay between fixation and name onset would be less for words occurring later in an utterance. Instead, this delay remains fixed irrespective of the word's position in the utterance. Also, Griffin (2001) showed that in producing a sentence like "The ball and the shirt are above the train" to describe stationary displays of objects, there was no effect of the frequency or name agreement for the second object (i.e., shirt) on onset latencies for the sentence, although there was an effect of frequency of the name of the first object. If the lexical representation for the second object had been accessed before utterance onset, one would have expected an effect of these lexical variables.

These findings with eye-tracking contrast with other findings showing that sentence onset latency increases with increasing number of lexical items in a sentence-initial phrase. For instance, Smith and Wheeldon (1999) contrasted onset latencies for sentences beginning with either a simple or conjoined noun phrase:

(1) The kite moves above the foot and the gate.
(2) The kite and the foot move above the gate.

They found longer onset latencies for sentences beginning with a conjoined noun phrase (i.e., speakers were slower to begin [2] than [1]) even though the two sentence types were matched in the initial noun, sentence length, lexical identities, and syntactic complexity. Recently, Allum and Wheeldon (2007) showed that for Japanese, which is a head-final language, the same pattern of an effect of number of lexical representations in the initial phrase was obtained even though the initial phrase consisted of a prepositional phrase rather than a head noun. In a related study, Allum and Wheeldon (2009) showed faster sentence-onset latencies after seeing a picture of a noninitial noun to be named in the first phrase but not from a picture of a noun to be named in a subsequent phrase, irrespective of whether the initial noun phrase was the head of the phrase. They concluded that planning occurred for what they termed a "functional phrase," defined as a grammatical unit with an irreducible semantic representation, such as agent or modifier.

Assuming that planning occurs across all of the elements in a functional phrase, one might expect WM demands to increase with the number of content words in the phrase. So far, there seem to be no studies of neurally healthy individuals taking a correlational or experimental approach to address this issue. Some relevant evidence has come from studies of patients with deficits in STM (Martin & Freedman, 2001; Martin, Miller, and Vu,

2004). Martin and Freedman showed that two patients with deficits in retaining lexical-semantic information in STM had difficulty producing adjective-noun phrases (e.g., "blonde hair"), even though they were able to produce the adjectives and nouns in isolation. Their performance improved if the noun and the adjective were in different phrases (e.g., "The hair is blonde"). Patients with a phonological STM deficit showed a normal level of accuracy for all conditions. Martin et al. (2004) reported that a patient with a lexical-semantic retention deficit showed a greatly exaggerated effect of initial phrase complexity with materials like those used by Smith and Wheeldon (1999; see sentences [1] and [2] above). A patient with a phonological STM deficit showed a complexity effect well within the normal range. The findings from both studies support the claim for a phrasal planning scope and suggest that this planning involves a capacity for maintaining lexical-semantic rather than phonological information. In terms of the model shown in Figure 26.1, this capacity may involve holding lexical items at the functional assembly stage, awaiting their insertion into syntactic frames in the structural assembly stage.

Although the data from Allum and Wheeldon (2007, 2009) and from Martin and colleagues (Martin & Freedman, 2001; Martin et al., 2004) are consistent with a phrasal scope of planning, the findings reported above are open to alternative explanations. Griffin (2003) has argued that speakers may plan ahead to avoid being disfluent rather than to fit with some syntactic constraint on planning. In the case of the sentence types with simple or conjoined noun phrases like those in examples (1) and (2), speakers may wait until they have access to some lexical or phonological information about the subsequent content word before beginning to utter the first content word. For the sentences beginning with a simple noun phrase in Smith and Wheeldon (1999) and Martin et al. (2004), the second content word was always the same ("moves"), which should be easier to retrieve than the second content word in the sentences beginning with a complex noun phrase, which was a noun that varied from trial to trial. Thus, assuming that speakers are awaiting some lexical information from the second content word, they would be able to begin the utterance more quickly in the simple noun phrase condition. Recently, however, Martin et al. (2010) showed that the phrasal complexity effect remained after equating the ease of retrievability of the second content word in both sentence types. In addition,

Martin et al. (2010) and Allum and Wheeldon (2007, 2009) presented other data that argued against this retrieval fluency hypothesis and other artifactual explanations based on differing features of the stimulus displays for sentences beginning with simple or conjoined noun phrases.

In summary, there is evidence that the scope of planning during grammatical encoding in sentence production is at the phrasal level, and thus several words may need to be maintained at the functional assembly stage during the planning of a phrase. Evidence from brain-damaged patients suggests that the critical capacity at this stage is the capacity to maintain lexical-semantic, rather than phonological representations. If so, then the findings are consistent with models hypothesizing specialized buffer capacities (Martin et al., 1999), rather than models assuming one general capacity (e.g., Just and Carpenter, 1992). A fruitful line of inquiry would be to test for converging evidence from neurally intact individuals that multiword phrases place demands on specifically a lexical-semantic capacity. It should be noted that an interference account might also be offered for these effects of phrasal complexity. That is, if planning proceeds at the phrasal level at the functional assembly stage, then several lexical representations would be activated simultaneously at this stage for multiword phrases. Selecting among these representations to fill slots at the structural assembly stage could lead to interference, particularly in selecting among words with the same word class (see Martin, 2007, for discussion).

Working Memory in Phonological Encoding

At the beginning of this article, we surmised that the phonological loop of Baddeley's (2000) WM model might be more relevant for production than for comprehension because of the need to produce an ordered sequence of phonological forms in production. In the studies discussed so far on message level and grammatical encoding, evidence for the involvement of a phonological storage capacity has been minimal. However, most studies on neurally healthy individuals have focused on the relation of complex span to production. The patient data from Martin and colleagues (Martin & Freedman, 2001; Martin et al., 2004) reviewed previously argued against a role for phonological storage in production. However, the patients in these studies had input phonological retention deficits—that is, they performed poorly on STM tasks even when production of the list was not required (e.g., in judging whether a probe word rhymed with any word in a preceding word list). To the extent that there are distinct buffers for maintaining input phonological representations involved in perception and output phonological representations involved in production (see Martin et al., 1999, for discussion), then the data from these patients would not bear on the role of (output) phonological retention involved in production.

On the input side, sentence comprehension has been investigated for patients with phonological STM deficits who have no difficulty comprehending single words (e.g., Martin et al., 1994). On the output side, there seem to be no studies of sentence production in patients with output buffer deficits who do not have difficulty producing single words. In the neuropsychological literature, the designation of "output phonological buffer deficit" has been given to patients making phonological errors in single word production (i.e., in naming, oral reading, and repetition) where these errors consist of substitutions, additions, deletions, and transpositions of phonemes (Caramazza, Miceli, & Villa, 1986; Shallice, Rumiati, & Zadini, 2000). The output buffer is assumed to be part of the word production system used to hold the phonological representations retrieved from the lexicon while the articulatory program is constructed. The patients' restricted buffer capacity or rapid decay of representations in the buffer is assumed to be the source of their segmental errors. Recently, however, Romani, Galluzzi, and Olson (2011) investigated the underlying cause of the word production errors in six patients showing the pattern typifying an output phonological buffer deficit. They provided convincing evidence that the patients' deficits could more easily be attributable to a disruption in access to phonological representations rather than restricted capacity for maintaining them. Thus, it seems that describing these patients, and similar patients reported in the literature as having a phonological output buffer deficit may be misleading.

Perhaps more consistent with the Romani et al. (2011) findings is the approach of Dell, Martin, and Schwartz (2007), who use the interactive word production model of Dell and colleagues (Dell, 1986; Foygel & Dell, 2000) to account for errors in patients' naming and word repetition by assuming that patients have reductions in the connection strength between semantic and lexical nodes and between lexical and phonological representations. Patients showing the "output buffer deficit" pattern would presumably be those who have a disruption of connections primarily between lexical and phonological nodes. Importantly, for this approach to be able to predict repetition from the parameters derived for naming, perfect perception has to be assumed in repetition (Dell et al., 2007). Such an assumption entails that there are different input and output connections from phonology to lexical representations.

In studies of neurally intact individuals, errors in repetition do not occur in single word repetition, but do occur in the typical serial list recall procedure that is used to obtain simple span measures (e.g., Conrad & Hull, 1964). Many proposals have been made that relate the activation of single word representations to list recall, with some researchers proposing that relative levels of activation in the lexicon could by themselves be sufficient to encode order information (e.g., Page & Norris, 1998; Ruchkin, Grafman, Cameron, & Berndt, 2003) and with others proposing that a multiword buffer (Martin & Gupta, 2004) or chaining process is needed to support serial recall (e.g., Burgess & Hitch, 2005). Whatever the mechanism underlying ordered recall of word lists, several researchers have claimed that the mechanisms used in list recall are those that underlie production of connected speech. As evidence, they cite the similarities in the phonological errors made in list recall and in spontaneous speech (e.g., Acheson & MacDonald, 2007; Ellis, 1980; Page, Madge, Cumming, & Norris, 2007).

Although such claims may have some plausibility, there is little evidence relating simple span measures and features of sentence production, although it seems that few studies have been carried out addressing the issue. The absence of such studies may have come about because of experimental evidence suggesting a small scope of planning at the phonological level—namely, one phonological word (i.e., a content word plus associated functions words; Wheeldon & Lahiri, 1997, 2002). Speech error data also suggest a small scope of phonological planning because anticipations, perseverations, and exchanges of phonological segments tend to occur within the same phrase and often involve adjacent syllables or words (Garrett, 1980; MacKay, 1970). One would assume that all neurally intact individuals have sufficient capacity for maintaining one phonological word. However, several findings on the production of noun phrases consisting of a determiner and/or adjective and noun have provided evidence of phonological encoding of all the content words in these short phrases before utterance onset, both when grammatical features of the noun specify the phonological form of determiners and adjectives (as in Dutch, Schriefers, 1992, and Spanish, Costa & Caramazza, 2002) and when they do not (as in English, Alario, Costa, & Caramazza, 2002, Damian & Dumay, 2007). For instance, Damian and Dumay (2007) showed that (English) distracter words phonologically related to the noun speeded onset latencies for noun phrases consisting of determiner + adjective + noun and that onset latencies for phrases consisting of an adjective and noun beginning with the same phoneme (e.g., blue bell) were faster than for those in which the two words began with different phonemes. These results imply that phonological access was at least initiated for the noun before voice onset. If so, then a phonological storage capacity of at least two phonological words would be needed to accommodate this advance phonological planning.

To investigate the role of a multiword buffer, one could identify patients showing normal STM span on input span tasks (e.g., involving recognition or matching) but impaired span for tasks requiring output (e.g., standard serial recall), but preserved single-word production. (A relevant patient was presented by Romani, 1992, but his sentence production was not investigated in detail.) One might hypothesize that such patients would show greater pausing between words in a phrase if the phonological planning of such a phrase was beyond their capacity, resulting in planning in smaller chunks. One might also hypothesize that for more severe cases, resyllabification at word boundaries would not take place normally if they could not maintain two words simultaneously in a phonological output buffer (Jacquemot & Scott, 2006). Studies of neurally healthy individuals might proceed by examining the relation between simple-span and phonological characteristics of the output. The effect of a simultaneous load could be examined by having subjects remember nonwords rather than words during a speech production task, to avoid the influence of lexical-semantic representations from the extraneous load interfering with production. To our knowledge, such investigations have not been carried out with patients or with healthy individuals. However, to the extent that the required phonological capacity for sentence production is quite small, it may be difficult to detect the effects of individual differences in output phonological buffer capacity on phrase or sentence production.

Summary and conclusions

Most of the research examining the role of WM in language production has focused on the grammatical encoding stage. In this research, it seems that a WM model that emphasizes retrieval interference provides the most parsimonious account of agreement phenomena. In terms of the scope of planning, WM research has highlighted the role of a buffer for maintaining lexical-semantic representations, which is presumably involved in mapping from the functional assembly to the structural assembly stages. However, an interference interpretation might also be offered for these findings.

At the message level, most research has examined the role of complex span or an external memory load, but has not contrasted the contribution from general WM capacity with that from more specialized memory representations. At the phonological level, one might most expect something akin to the phonological loop from Baddeley's (2000) WM model to be involved. Currently, however, there is little evidence on this proposal and it may be that the phonological capacity required for output is quite small, such that individual differences in this capacity would be minimal. It is possible, however, that other experimental approaches (e.g., an external load) could be taken to address this issue.

So far, the cognitive underpinnings of production have not been investigated with the intensity and thoroughness that has been devoted to comprehension. Clearly, there are several important theoretical questions for which only the beginnings of an answer have been obtained. As is evident in this and other reviews on production, however, experimental methodologies and theoretical approaches have been developed recently in the production realm that should lead to a rapid growth of knowledge about the role of WM and other cognitive processes in production in the near future.

Author Notes

Preparation of this manuscript was supported in part by National Institutes of Health grant F32 DC008723 to Rice University.

References

Acheson, D. J., & MacDonald, M. C. (2009). Verbal working memory and language production: Common approaches to the serial ordering of verbal information. *Psychological Bulletin, 135*, 50–68.

Alario, F., Costa, A., & Caramazza, A. (2002). Frequency effects in noun phrase production: Implications for models of lexical access. *Language and Cognitive Processes, 17*, 299–319.

Allum, P. H., & Wheeldon, L. R. (2007). Planning scope in spoken sentence production: The role of grammatical units. *Journal of Experimental Psychology: Learning, Memory, & Cognition, 33*, 791–810.

Allum, P. H., & Wheeldon, L. R. (2009). Scope of lexical access in spoken sentence production: Implications for the conceptual-syntactic interface. *Journal of Experimental Psychology: Learning, Memory, & Cognition, 35*, 1240–1255.

Almor, A. (1999). Noun-phrase anaphora and focus: The informational load hypothesis. *Psychological Review, 106*, 748–765.

Almor, A. (2004). A computational investigation of reference in production and comprehension. In J. C. Trueswell & M. K. Tanenhaus (Eds.), *Approaches to studying world-situated language use: Bridging the language-as-product and language-as-action traditions* (pp. 285–301). Cambridge, MA: MIT Press.

Almor, A., & Nair, V. (2007). The form of referential expressions in discourse. *Language and Linguistics Compass, 1*, 84–99.

Arnold, J. E. (2010). How speakers refer: The role of accessibility. *Language and Linguistics Compass, 4*, 187–203.

Arnold, J. E., Bennetto, L., & Diehl, J. J. (2009). Reference production in young speakers with and without autism: Effects of discourse status and processing constraints. *Cognition, 110*, 131–146.

Arnold, J. E., & Griffin, Z. M. (2007). The effect of additional characters on choice of referring expression: Everyone counts. *Journal of Memory and Language, 56*, 521–536.

Arnold, J. E., Wasow, T., Losongco, A., & Ginstrom, R. (2000). Heaviness vs. newness: The effects of structural complexity and discourse status on constituent ordering. *Language, 76*, 28–55.

Baddeley, A. (2000). The episodic buffer: A new component of working memory? *Trends in Cognitive Sciences, 4*, 417–423.

Baddeley, A., Gathercole, S., & Papagno, C. (1998). The phonological loop as a language acquisition device. *Psychological Review, 105*, 158–173.

Baddeley, A., & Hitch, G. (1974). Working memory. In G. H. Bower (Ed.), *The psychology of learning and motivation* (pp. 47–90). New York: Academic Press.

Badecker, W., & Kuminiak, F. (2007). Morphology, agreement and working memory retrieval in sentence production: Evidence from gender and case in Slovak. *Journal of Memory and Language, 56*, 65–85.

Berman, M. G., Jonides, J., & Lewis, R. L. (2009). In search of decay in verbal short-term memory. *Journal of Experimental Psychology: Learning, Memory, and Cognition, 35*, 317–333.

Bock, J. K. (1977). The effect of a pragmatic presupposition on syntactic structure in question answering. *Journal of Verbal Learning and Verbal Behavior, 16*, 723–734.

Bock, J. K. (1982). Toward a cognitive psychology of syntax: Information processing contributions to sentence formulation. *Psychological Review, 89*, 1–47.

Bock, J. K. (1986). Meaning, sound, and syntax: Lexical priming in sentence production. *Journal of Experimental Psychology: Learning, Memory, and Cognition, 12*, 575–586.

Bock, J. K., & Irwin, D. (1980). Syntactic effects of information availability in sentence production. *Journal of Verbal Learning and Verbal Behavior, 19*, 467–484.

Bock, J. K., & Levelt, W. J. M. (1994). Language production: Grammatical encoding. In M. A. Gernsbacher (Ed.), *Handbook of Psycholinguistics* (pp. 945–984). San Diego, CA: Academic Press.

Bock, J. K., & Warren, R. K. (1985). Conceptual accessibility and syntactic structure in sentence formulation. *Cognition, 21*, 47–67.

Bock, K., & Cutting, J. (1992). Regulating mental energy: Performance units in language production. *Journal of Memory and Language, 31*, 99–127.

Bock, K., & Miller, C. A. (1991). Broken agreement. *Cognitive Psychology, 23*, 45–93.

Brookshire, B. L., Chapman, S. B., Song, J., & Levin, H. S. (2000). Cognitive and linguistic correlates of children's discourse after closed head injury: A three-year follow-up. *Journal of the International Neuropsychological Society, 6*, 741–751.

Brown, P., & Dell, G. (1987). Adapting production to comprehension: The explicit mention of instruments. *Cognitive Psychology, 19*, 441–472.

Burgess, N., & Hitch, G. (2005). Computational models of working memory: Putting long-term memory into context. *Trends in Cognitive Science, 9*, 535–541.

Caplan, D., & Waters, G. S. (1999). Verbal working memory and sentence comprehension. *Behavioral and Brain Sciences, 22*, 77–126.

Caramazza, A., Miceli, G., & Villa, G. (1986). The role of the (output) phonological buffer in reading, writing, and repetition. *Cognitive Neuropsychology, 3*, 37–76.

Caspari, I., & Parkinson, S. R. (2000). Effects of memory impairment on discourse. *Journal of Neurolinguistics, 13*, 15–36.

Chang, F., Dell, G. S., & Bock, K. (2006). Becoming syntactic. *Psychological Review, 113*, 234–272.

Chanquoy, L., & Negro, I. (1996). Subject-verb agreement errors in written productions: A study of French children and adults. *Journal of Psycholinguistic Research, 25*, 553–570.

Clark, H. H. (1996). *Using language.* Cambridge, England: Cambridge University Press.

Clark, H. H., & Krych, M. A. (2004). Speaking while monitoring addressees for understanding. *Journal of Memory and Language, 50*, 62–81.

Clark, H. H., & Marshall, C. R. (1981). Definite reference and mutual knowledge. In A. K. Joshi, B. L. Webber, & I. A. Sag (Eds.), *Elements of discourse understanding* (pp. 10–63). Cambridge, UK: Cambridge University Press.

Conrad, R., & Hull, A. J. (1964). Information, acoustic confusion and memory span. *British Journal of Psychology, 55*, 429–432.

Costa, A., & Caramazza, A. (2002). The production of noun phrases in English and Spanish: Implications for the scope of phonological encoding in speech production. *Journal of Memory and Language, 46*, 178–198.

Cowan, N. (2001). The magical number 4 in short-term memory: A reconsideration of mental storage capacity. *Behavioral and Brain Sciences, 24*, 87–114.

Cowles, H. W., Garnham, A., & Simner, J. (2010). Conceptual similarity effects on working memory in sentence contexts: testing a theory of anaphora. *The Quarterly Journal of Experimental Psychology, 63*, 1218–1232.

Damian, M., & Dumay, N. (2007). Time pressure and phonological advance planning in spoken production. *Journal of Memory and Language, 57*, 195–209.

Daneman, M. (1991). Working memory as a predictor of verbal fluency. *Journal of Psycholinguistic Research, 20*, 445–464.

Daneman, M., & Carpenter, P. A. (1980). Individual differences in working memory and reading. *Journal of Verbal Learning and Verbal Behavior, 19*, 450–466.

Daneman, M., & Green, I. (1986). Individual differences in comprehending and producing words in context. *Journal of Memory and Language, 1*, 1–18.

Daneman, M., & Hannon, B. (2007). What do working memory span tasks like reading span really tell us? In N. Osaka, R. Logie, & M. D'Esposito (Eds.), *The cognitive neuroscience of working memory*. Oxford, UK: Oxford University Press.

Daneman, M., & Merikle, P. (1996). Working memory and language comprehension: A meta-analysis. *Psychonomic Bulletin and Review, 3*, 422–433.

Davidson, D. J., Zacks, R. T., & Ferreira, F. (2003). Age preservation of the syntactic processor in production. *Journal of Psycholinguistic Research, 32*, 541–566.

Dell, G. S. (1986). A spreading-activation theory of retrieval in sentence production. *Psychological Review, 93*, 283–321.

Dell, G. S., Martin, N., & Schwartz, M. F. (2007). A case-series test of the interactive two-step model of lexical access: Predicting word repetition from picture naming. *Journal of Memory and Language, 56*, 490–520.

Ellis, A. W. (1980). Errors in speech and short-term memory: The effects of phonemic similarity and syllable position. *Journal of Verbal Learning and Verbal Behavior, 5*, 624–634.

Fayol, M., Largy, P., & Lemaire, P. (1994). Cognitive overload and orthographic errors: When cognitive overload enhances subject–verb agreement errors. A study in French written language. *The Quarterly Journal of Experimental Psychology A, 47*, 437–464.

Fedorenko, E., Badecker, W., & Gibson, E. (2007). *Syntactic complexity effects in sentence production.* Poster presented at the 20th CUNY Conference on Human Sentence Processing, San Diego, CA.

Fehringer, C., & Fry, C. (2007a). Frills, furbelows and activated memory: Syntactically optional elements in the spontaneous language production of bilingual speakers. *Language Sciences, 29*, 497–511.

Fehringer, C., & Fry, C. (2007b). Hesitation phenomena in the language production of bilingual speakers: The role of working memory. *Folia Linguistica, 41*, 37–72.

Ferreira, V. S. (1996). Is it better to give than to donate? Syntactic flexibility in language production. *Journal of Memory and Language, 35*, 724–755.

Ferreira, V. S., & Dell, G. S. (2000). Effect of ambiguity and lexical availability on syntactic and lexical production. *Cognitive Psychology, 40*, 296–340.

Ferreira, V. S., & Slevc, L. R. (2007). Grammatical encoding. In M. G. Gaskell (Ed.), *The Oxford handbook of psycholinguistics* (pp. 453–469). Oxford, England: Oxford University Press.

Ferreira, V. S., & Yoshita, H. (2003). Given-new ordering effects on the production of scrambled sentences in Japanese. *Journal of Psycholinguistic Research, 32*, 669–692.

Fortkamp, M. B. (2003). Working memory capacity and fluency, accuracy, complexity, and lexical density in L2 speech production. *Fragmentos, 24*, 69–104.

Foygel, D., & Dell, G. S. (2000). Models of impaired lexical access in speech production. *Journal of Memory and Language, 43*, 182–216.

Garrett, M. F. (1975). The analysis of sentence production. In G. Bower (Ed.), *The psychology of learning and motivation, Vol. 9* (pp. 133–177). New York: Academic Press.

Garrett, M. F. (1980). Levels of processing in sentence production. In B. L. Butterworth (Ed.), *Language production Vol. 1: Speech and talk* (pp. 177–220). London: Academic Press.

Gennari, S. P., & Macdonald, M. C. (2009). Linking production and comprehension processes: The case of relative clauses. *Cognition, 111*, 1–23.

Griffin, Z. (2001). Gaze durations during speech reflect word selection and phonological encoding. *Cognition, 82*, B1–14.

Griffin, Z. (2003). A reversed word length effect in coordinating the preparation and articulation of words in speaking. *Psychonomic Bulletin & Review, 10*, 603–609.

Griffin, Z., & Bock, K. (2000). What the eyes say about speaking. *Psychological Science, 11*, 274–279.

Hamilton, A. C., & Martin, R. C. (2005). Dissociations among tasks involving inhibition: A single-case study. *Cognitive, Affective, & Behavioral Neuroscience, 5*, 1–13.

Hamilton, A. C., & Martin, R. C. (2007). Proactive interference in a semantic short-term memory deficit: Role of semantic and phonological relatedness. *Cortex, 43*, 112–123.

Hartley, L. L., & Jensen, P. J. (1991). Narrative and procedural discourse after closed head injury. *Brain Injury, 5*, 267–285.

Hartsuiker, R. J., & Barkhuysen, P. N. (2006). Language production and working memory: The case of subject-verb agreement. *Language and Cognitive Processes, 21*, 181–204.

Horton, W. S. (2007). The influence of partner-specific memory associations on language production: Evidence from picture naming. *Language and Cognitive Processes, 22*, 1114–1139.

Horton, W. S., & Gerrig, R. J. (2005a). Conversational common ground and memory processes in language production. *Discourse Processes, 40*, 1–35.

Horton, W. S., & Gerrig, R. J. (2005b). The impact of memory demands on audience design during language production. *Cognition, 96*, 127–142.

Horton, W. S., & Keysar, B. (1996). When do speakers take into account common ground? *Cognition, 59*, 91–117.

Hoskyn, M., & Swanson, H. L. (2003). The relationship between working memory and writing in younger and older adults. *Reading and Writing, 16*, 759–784.

Jacquemot, C., & Scott, S. K. (2006). What is the relationship between phonological short-term memory and speech processing? *Trends in Cognitive Sciences, 10*, 480–486.

Just, M. A., & Carpenter, P. A. (1992). A capacity theory of comprehension: Individual differences in working memory. *Psychological Review, 99*, 122–149.

Kemper, S., Herman, R. E., & Lian, C. H. (2003). The costs of doing two things at once for young and older adults: Talking while walking, finger tapping, and ignoring speech of noise. *Psychology and Aging, 18*, 181–192.

Kemper, S., Schmalzried, R., Herman, R. E., Leedahl, S., & Mohankumar, D. (2009). The effects of aging and dual task demands on language production. *Neuropsychology, Development, and Cognition. Section B, Aging, Neuropsychology and Cognition, 16*, 241–259.

Lewis, R., & Badecker, W. (April, 2010). *Short-term memory in sentence production and its adaptive control.* Paper presented at the CUNY Sentence Processing Conference 2010, New York, NY..

Lewis, R. L., Vasishth, S., & Van Dyke, J. A. (2006). Computational principles of working memory in sentence comprehension. *Trends in Cognitive Sciences, 10*, 447–454.

Lockridge, C. B., & Brennan, S. E. (2002). Addressees' needs influence speakers' early syntactic choices. *Psychonomic Bulletin & Review, 9*, 550–557.

MacDonald, M. C., & Christiansen, M. H. (2002). Reassessing working memory: Comment on Just and Carpenter (1992) and Waters and Caplan (1996). *Psychological Review, 109*, 35–54.

MacKay, D. G. (1970). Spoonerisms: the structure of errors in the serial order of speech. *Neuropsychologia, 8*, 323–350.

Martin, N., Gupta, P. (2004). Exploring the relationship between word processing and verbal short-term memory: Evidence from associations and dissociations. *Cognitive Neuropsychology, 21*, 213–228.

Martin, N., & Saffran, E. M. (1997). Language and auditory-verbal short-term memory impairments: Evidence for common underlying processes. *Cognitive Neuropsychology, 14*, 641–682.

Martin, R. C. (1993). Short-term memory and sentence processing: Evidence from neuropsychology. *Memory and Cognition, 21*, 176–183.

Martin, R. C. (2007). Semantic short-term memory, language processing, and inhibition. In A. S. Meyer, L. R. Wheeldon, & A. Knott (Eds.), *Automaticity and control in language processing* (pp. 161–191). Hove, England: Psychology Press.

Martin, R. C., Crowther, J. E., Knight, M., Tamborello, F. P., & Yang, C. (2010). Planning in sentence production: evidence for the phrase as a default planning scope. *Cognition, 116*, 177–192.

Martin, R. C., & Freedman, M. (2001). Short-term retention of lexical-semantic representations: Implications for speech production. *Memory, 9*, 261–280.

Martin, R. C., Lesch, M. F., & Bartha, M. C. (1999). Independence of input and output phonology in word processing and short-term memory. *Journal of Memory and Language, 41*, 3–29.

Martin, R. C., Miller, M., & Vu, H. (2004). Lexical-semantic retention and speech production: Further evidence from normal and brain-damaged participants for a phrasal scope of planning. *Cognitive Neuropsychology, 21*, 625–644.

Martin, R. C., & Romani, C. (1994). Verbal working memory and sentence comprehension: A multiple-components view. *Neuropsychology, 8*, 506–523.

Martin, R. C., Shelton, J., & Yaffee, L. (1994). Language processing and working memory: Neuropsychological evidence for separate phonological and semantic capacities. *Journal of Memory and Language, 33*, 83–111.

McDonald, J., Bock, K., & Kelly, M. (1993). Word and world order: Semantic, phonological, and metrical determinants of serial position. *Cognitive Psychology, 25*, 188–230.

McElree, B. (2001). Working memory and focal attention. *Journal of Experimental Psychology: Learning, Memory, and Cognition, 27*, 817–835.

McElree, B., Foraker, S., & Dyer, L. (2003). Memory structures that subserve sentence comprehension. *Journal of Memory and Language, 48*, 67–91.

Meyer, A. S., Sleiderink, A., & Levelt, W. (1998). Viewing and naming objects: Eye movements during noun phrase production. *Cognition, 66*, 25–33.

Nadig, A., & Sedivy, J. (2002). Evidence of perspective-taking constraints in children's on-line reference resolution. *Psychological Science, 13*, 329–336.

Oomen, C. C., & Postma, A. (2002). Limitations in processing resources and speech monitoring. *Language and Cognitive Processes, 17*, 163–184.

Page, M. P., Madge, A., Cumming, N., & Norris, D. G. (2007). Speech errors and the phonological similarity effect in short-term memory: Evidence suggesting a common locus. *Journal of Memory and Language, 56*, 49–64.

Page, M. P., & Norris, D. G. (1998). The primacy model: A new model of immediate serial recall. *Psychological Review, 105*, 761–781.

Roβnagel, C. (2000). Cognitive load and perspective-taking: Applying the automatic-controlled distinction to verbal communication. *European Journal of Social Psychology, 30*, 429–445.

Roßnagel, C. (2004). Lost in thought: Cognitive load and the processing of addressees' feedback in verbal communication. *Experimental Psychology, 51,* 191–200.

Romani C. (1992). Are there distinct input and output buffers? Evidence from an aphasic patient with an impaired output buffer. *Language and Cognitive Processes, 7,* 131–162.

Romani, C., Galluzzi, C., & Olson, A. (2011). Phonological-lexical activation: A lexical component or an output buffer? Evidence from aphasic errors. *Cortex, 47,* 217–235.

Ruchkin, D. S., Grafman, J., Cameron, K., & Berndt, R. S. (2003). Working memory retention systems: a state of activated long-term memory. *The Behavioral and Brain Sciences, 26,* 709–728.

Schriefers, H. (1992). Lexical access in the production of noun phrases. *Cognition, 45,* 33–54.

Schweppe, J., & Rummer, R. (2007). Shared representations in language processing and verbal short-term memory: The case of grammatical gender. *Journal of Memory and Language, 56,* 336–356.

Shallice T., Rumiati R. I., & Zadini A. (2000). The selective impairment of the phonological output buffer. *Cognitive Neuropsychology, 17,* 517–546.

Slevc, L. R. (2011). Saying what's on your mind: Working memory effects on sentence production. *Journal of Experimental Psychology: Learning, Memory, & Cognition, 37,* 1503–1514.

Slevc, L. R., & Martin, R. C. (2011). Short-term memory, agrammatism, and syntactic agreement. *Procedia Social and Behavioral Sciences, 23,* 102–103.

Smith, M., & Wheeldon, L. (1999). High level processing scope in spoken sentence production. *Cognition, 73,* 205–246.

Unsworth, N., & Engle, R. W. (2007). The nature of individual differences in working memory: Active maintenance in primary memory and controlled search from secondary memory. *Psychological Review, 114,* 104–132.

Van Dyke, J. A. (2007). Interference effects from grammatically unavailable constituents during sentence processing. *Journal of Experimental Psychology: Learning, Memory, and Cognition, 33,* 407–430.

Verhaeghen, P., & Basak, C. (2005). Ageing and switching the focus of attention in working memory: Results from a modified N-back task. *The Quarterly Journal of Experimental Psychology, 58,* 134–154.

Wardlow Lane, L., & Ferreira, V. S. (2008). Speaker-external versus speaker-internal forces on utterance form: Do cognitive demands override threats to referential success? *Journal of Experimental Psychology: Learning, Memory, and Cognition, 34,* 1466–1481.

Wardlow Lane, L., Groisman, M., & Ferreira, V. S. (2006). Don't talk about pink elephants! Speakers' control over leaking private information during language production. *Psychological Science, 17,* 273–277.

Wasow, T. (1997). End-weight from the speaker's perspective. *Journal of Psycholinguistic Research, 26,* 347–361.

Wheeldon, L. R., & Lahiri, A. (1997). Prosodic Units in Speech Production. *Journal of Memory and Language, 37,* 356–381.

Wheeldon, L. R., & Lahiri, A. (2002). The minimal unit of phonological encoding: Prosodic or lexical word. *Cognition, 85,* B31–41.

Youse, K. M., & Coelho, C. A. (2005). Working memory and discourse production abilities following closed-head injury. *Brain Injury, 19,* 1001–1009.

Production of Speech-Accompanying Gesture

Sotaro Kita

Abstract

When people speak, they often spontaneously produce hand gestures, which express information related to the information encoded in concurrent speech. This article discusses the relationship between speech production and gesture production, and presents a model based on Levelt's model of speech production. In the proposed model, speech and gesture production processes are closely linked at the conceptual planning stage. The following topics are covered: how physical and discursive contexts affect gesturing, how the addressee's knowledge status and perceptual capabilities affect gesturing, how grammatical and lexical choices in speech influences gestural expression of related contents, how the load on conceptualization for speech production influences gesture production, and how gesturing influences what information is expressed in speech and which grammatical structure is chosen in speech.

Key Words: gesture, discourse, grammatical planning, conceptual planning

Introduction

People spontaneously produce gestures when they speak. Gesture production and speech production are tightly linked processes. Speech-accompanying gesture is a cultural universal (Kita, 2009). Whenever there is speaking, there is gesture. Infants in the one-word stage already combine speech and gesture in a systematic way (Capirci, Iverson, Pizzuto, & Volterra, 1996; Iverson & Goldin-Meadow, 2005). Gesturing persists in situations where gestures are not communicatively useful, for example, when talking on the telephone (J. Bavelas, Gerwing, Sutton, & Prevost, 2008; Cohen, 1977). Congenitally blind children spontaneously produce gestures (Iverson & Goldin-Meadow, 2001), indicating gesture is resilient against poverty of input.

Speech-accompanying gestures come in different types. The most influential classification system by McNeill (1992) distinguishes iconic (metaphoric) gestures, deictic gesture, beat gesture, and emblem gestures. Iconic gestures can depict action, events, and shapes in an analogue and iconic way (e.g., a hand swinging as if to throw a ball can represent throwing, a flat hand moving downward can represent a flat object falling, or a hand can represent a shape by tracing the outline). Such gestural depiction can also represent abstract contents by spatializing them (e.g., the flow of time can be represented by a hand moving across). Iconic gestures with abstract contents are sometimes given a different label, metaphoric gesture (Cienki & Müller, 2008; McNeill, 1992). Deictic (pointing) gestures indicate the referent by means of spatiotemporal contiguity (Kita, 2003). Beat gestures are small bidirectional movements that are often performed in the lower periphery of gesture space (e.g., near the lap) as if to beat the rhythm. The form of beat gestures remains more or less the same, regardless of the content of the concurrent speech. One of the proposed functions is to mark shifts in discourse structure (McNeill, 1992). Emblem gestures have a conventionalized and often arbitrary form-meaning relationship (e.g., the OK sign with a ring created by the thumb and the index finger) (Kendon, 1992; Morris, Collett, Marsh, & O'Shaughnessy, 1979). In the remainder of the chapter, the focus will be on iconic and deictic gestures (i.e., "representational gestures") because the bulk of psycholinguistic work on production has been on these two types of gestures (but see Krahmer & Swerts, 2007 for work on beat gestures).

A Model of Speech and Gesture Production
General Architecture

Many of the empirical findings about speech-accompanying gestures can be explained by a model in which speech production and gesture production are regarded as separate but highly interactive processes, such as in Figure 27.1 (Kita & Özyürek, 2003). This model is based on Levelt's (1989) model of speech production. The goal of this chapter is to provide an overview of the literature on speech-accompanying gestures, using the model as a means to organise information.

In Figure 27.1, the rectangles represent information processing components and arrows represent how the output of one processing component is passed on to another component. The ovals represent information storage and dotted lines represent an access route to information storage.

As in Levelt (1989), two distinct planning levels for speech production are distinguished. The first concerns planning at the conceptual level ("Conceptualizer"), which determines what message should be verbally encoded. The content of the message is determined on the basis of what is communicatively needed and appropriate, based on information about the discourse context (Discourse Model) and on the relevant propositional information activated in working memory. The second concerns planning of linguistic formulation ("Formulator"), which linguistically encodes the message. That is, it specifies the words to be used, the syntactic relationship among the words, and the phonological contents of the words.

Levelt's Conceptualizer is divided into the Communication Planner and the Message Generator. The Communication Planner corresponds to "macroplanning" in Levelt's model. This process determines roughly what contents need to be expressed (i.e., communicative intention) in what order. In addition, the Communication Planner determines which modalities of expression (speech, gesture) should be used for communication (see de Ruiter, 2000 for a related idea that Conceptualizer determines which modalities of expression should be used), taking into account the extent to which the Environment is suitable for gestural communication (e.g., whether or not the addressee can see the speaker's gesture). Thus, the Communication Planner is not dedicated to speech production, but plans multimodal communication as a whole. The Message Generator corresponds to "microplanning" in Levelt's model. This process determines precisely what information needs to be verbally encoded (i.e., preverbal message).

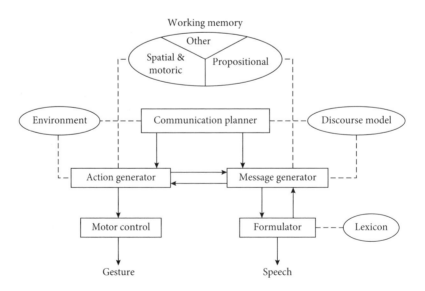

Figure 27.1 A model of speech and gesture production. (Adapted from Kita, S., & Özyürek, A. (2003). What does cross-linguistic variation in semantic coordination of speech and gesture reveal? Evidence for an interface representation of spatial thinking and speaking. *Journal of Memory and Language, 48,* 16–32.)

Gesture production follows similar steps to speech production. At the gross level, two distinct levels of planning are distinguished. The Communication Planner and the Action Generator carry out the conceptual planning for gesture production and the Motor Control module executes the conceptual-level plans. The Communication Planner determines roughly what contents need to be expressed in the gesture modality. The Action Generator determines precisely what information is gesturally encoded. The Action Generator is a general-purpose process that plans actions in real and imagined environments.

In the following sections, we will discuss interaction between the components in the model. We will start with the description of how the Communication Planner and the Action Generator work. Then, we will discuss how the Message Generator and the Formulator interact with gesture production.

The Communication Planner and the Discourse Model

The Communication Planner relies crucially on the Discourse Model in order to determine what information to encode, in what order, and in what modality. The Discourse Model has two subcomponents (Kita, 2010): the Interaction Record and the Addressee Model. The Interaction Record keeps track of what information has been communicated by the speaker and the communication partners. The Addressee Model specifies various properties of communication partners.

INTERACTION RECORD

Gesture production is sensitive to what has been communicated or not communicated in conversation. Based on qualitative analysis of when gestures appear in narrative, McNeill (1992) proposed that gestures tend to appear when the speech content makes a significant departure from what is taken to be given in the conversation (e.g., what has already been established in preceding discourse). Sometimes gestures explicitly encode the fact that certain information is in the Interaction Record. For example, during conversation, the speaker points to a conversational partner to indicate who has brought up a certain topic in an earlier part of the conversation (J. B. Bavelas, Chovil, Lawrie, & Wade, 1992). The Interaction Record includes not only what has been said but also what has been gestured and how gestures encoded the information. In a task in which participants describe a network of dots connected by lines, speakers sometimes produce a gesture that expresses the overall shape of the network at the beginning of a description. When such a preview gesture is produced, the verbal description of the network includes directional information less often, presumably because the initial overview gesture has already provided directional information (Melinger & Levelt, 2004). The Interaction Record also includes information about how certain information has been gesturally encoded. When the speaker gesturally expresses semantically related contents in different parts of a conversation, these gestures tend to share form features ("catchment" in McNeill, 2005). Similarly, when two speakers gesturally express the same referent in conversation, the handshapes of the two speakers' coreferential gestures tend to converge, but only when they can see each other (Kimbara, 2008). Thus, how the other speaker gesturally encoded a particular entity is stored in the Interaction Record and recycled in production. When the same entities are referred to repeatedly in a story, each tends to be expressed in a particular location in space (Gullberg, 2006; McNeill, 1992), not unlike anaphora in sign language (e.g., Engberg-Pedersen, 2003).

ADDRESSEE MODEL

Gesture production is modulated by what speakers know about the addressee. Relevant properties of the addressee include interactional potential, perceptual potential, cognitive potential, epistemic status, and attentiveness. The interaction potential refers to the degree to which the addressee can react to the speaker's utterances online, and it influences gesture frequency. When speakers have an interactive addressee (e.g., talking on the telephone), they produce gestures more frequently than when they do not have an interactive addressee (e.g., speaking to a tape recorder; J. Bavelas, et al., 2008; Cohen, 1977). The perceptual potential of the addressee also influences gesture frequency. Speakers produce gestures more often when the addressee can see the gestures (Alibali, Heath, & Myers, 2001; Cohen, 1977).[1] The cognitive potential of the addressee influences the gesture frequency as well as the way in which gestures are produced. When speakers use ambiguous words (homophones, drinking "glasses" vs. optical "glasses"), they are likely to produce iconic gestures that disambiguate speech (Holler & Beattie, 2003; Kidd & Holler, 2009). Similar sensitivity to the addressee's ability to identify the referent has been shown in a corpus analysis of naturalistic data (Enfield, Kita, & de Ruiter, 2007). In the corpus, speakers describe how their village and its surrounding area have changed to somebody who is not as knowledgeable about the area. Small pointing gestures often accompanied verbal expression of landmarks when it is likely but not certain that the referent can be identified by the addressee. The addressee's epistemic state, namely what the addressee knows, also influences the way gestures are produced. When the speaker talks about things for which the speaker and addressee have shared information, gestures tend to be less precise (Gerwing & Bavelas, 2004), although shared knowledge mostly does not make gestures less informative (Holler & Wilkin, 2009). Finally, the listener's attention state modulates the frequency of gestures. Speakers produce gestures more frequently when the addressee is attending to the speakers than when he or she is not (Jacobs & Garnham, 2007).

The Communication Planner and the Environment

One of the tasks of the Communication Planner is to decide roughly what information will be conveyed in what modality. This may depend on the properties of the Environment in which communication takes place. For example, imagine a referential communication task in which two participants, the director and the matcher, are seated side by side in front of an array of photographs of faces. The director describes one of the photographs, and the matcher has to identify which photograph is the referent. In this situation, participants use pointing gestures with deictic expressions, such as *this* and *here*, to identify a photograph more often when the participants are close to the array (arm's length or 25 cm) than when they are further away (50 cm—100 cm; Bangerter, 2004). Conversely, the participants use verbal expressions to identify a photograph less often when the array is close because gestures can fully identify the referent. That is, depending on the distance to the referent, speakers distribute information differently between the gesture and speech modalities in order to optimise communication (see also van der Sluis & Krahmer, 2007 for similar results).

The Action Generator and the Physical or Imagined Environment

The gesture production process needs access to the information about the Environment for various reasons. This is necessary when gestures need to take into account physical obstacles (e.g., so as not to hit the listener; de Ruiter, 2000) or when producing gestures that point at or trace a physically present target. Sometimes, gestural depiction relies on physical props. For example, a pointing gesture that indicates a horizontal direction and comes to contact with a vertical piece of timber in a door frame may depict a contraption with a horizontal bar supported by two vertical poles (Haviland, 2003). In this example, the vertical piece of timber represents the vertical poles. Production of such a gesture requires representation of the physical environment.

Gestures can be produced within an imagined environment that is generated on the basis of information activated in visuospatial and motoric working memory. Gestures are often produced as if there are imaginary objects (e.g., a gesture that depicts grasping of a cup). Gestures can take an active role in establishing and enriching the imagined environment (McNeill, 2003); that is, gestures can assign meaning to a specific location in the gesture space ("abstract deixis," McNeill, 1992; McNeill, Cassell, & Levy, 1993). The boundary between the physical and imagined environments is not clear-cut. For example, gestures can be produced near a physically present object in order to depict an imaginary transformation of the object. When describing how a geometric figure on a computer screen can be rotated, participants often produce gestures near the computer screen, as if the hand grasps the object and rotates it (Chu & Kita, 2008) (see also LeBaron & Streeck, 2000).

Interaction between the Message Generator and the Action Generator
SPEECH-TO-GESTURE INFLUENCE: SYNTACTIC PACKAGING

The speech production process can influence the gesture production process via the link between the Message Generator and the Action Generator. The Message Generator creates the propositional content for utterances. Given the evidence that a clause (a grammatical unit controlled by a verb) is an important planning unit for speech production (Bock & Cutting, 1992), it can be assumed that the Message Generator packages information that is readily verbalizable within a clause. The way speech packages information is reflected in the gestural packaging information, as demonstrated by studies summarized next.

The speech-gesture convergence in information packaging can be demonstrated in the domain of motion events. Languages vary as to syntactic packaging of information about manner (how something moves) and path (which direction something moves). Some languages (e.g., English) typically encode manner and path within a single clause (e.g., "he rolled down the hill"), whereas others (e.g., Japanese and Turkish) typically use two clauses (e.g., "he descended the hill, as he rolled"). When describing motion events with manner and path, English speakers are more likely to produce a single gesture that encoding both manner and path (e.g., a hand traces a circular movement as it moves across in front of the torso). In contrast, Japanese and Turkish speakers are more likely to produce two separate gestures for manner and path (Kita & Özyürek, 2003; Özyürek et al., 2008). The same effect can be shown within English speakers. One-clause and two-clause descriptions can be elicited from English speakers, using the following principle. When the strength of the causal link between manner and path (e.g., whether rolling causes descending) is weaker, English speakers tend to deviate from the typical one-clause description and increase the use of two-clause descriptions similar to Turkish and Japanese (Goldberg, 1997). English speakers tend to produce a single gesture encoding both manner and path when they encode manner and path in a single clause, but produce separate gestures for manner and path when they encode manner and path in two different clauses (Kita et al., 2007). Finally, the link between syntactic packaging in speech and gesture can also be seen in Turkish learners of English at different proficiency levels. Turkish speakers who speak English well enough to package manner and path in a single clause tend to produce a gesture that encodes both manner and path. In contrast, Turkish speakers whose proficiency level is such that they still produce two-clause descriptions in English (presumably transfer from Turkish) tend to produce separate gestures for manner and path (Özyürek, 2002).

SPEECH-GESTURE INFLUENCE: CONCEPTUALIZATION LOAD

In line with the idea that gesturing facilitates conceptualisation for speaking, gesture frequency increases when the conceptualization load is higher (Hostetter, Alibali, & Kita, 2007b; Kita & Davies, 2009; Melinger & Kita, 2007). For example (Figure 27.2), imagine the situation in which participants are instructed to describe the content of each of the six rectangles, while ignoring the difference between the dark versus light coloured lines. The dark lines disrupt how information should be packaged in the hard condition (e.g., in the left top rectangle in Figure 27.2b, it is difficult to conceptualize the entire diagonal line as a unit for verbalization), but not in the easy condition. Speakers produce more representational gestures in the hard condition than in the easy condition. When it is more difficult to package information into units for speech production, that is, when conceptualisation for speaking (in particular, microplanning in Levelt, 1989) is more difficult, gesture production is triggered.

GESTURE-TO-SPEECH INFLUENCE

The gesture production process can influence the speech production process via the link from the Action Generator to the Message Generator. The nature of this link has been investigated in studies that manipulated how and whether gesture is produced, as summarized next.

How information is grouped into gestures shapes how the same information is grammatically grouped in speech. When Dutch speakers describe motion events with manner and path components (e.g., rolling up), the type of gestures they are instructed to produce influence the type of grammatical structures (Mol & Kita, in press). When the speakers are instructed to produce a single gesture

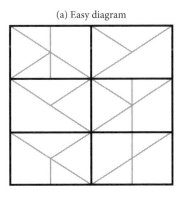
(a) Easy diagram

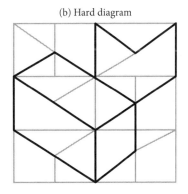
(b) Hard diagram

Figure 27.2 Example of a stimulus pair that manipulate conceptualization load during description. (Adapted from Kita, S., & Davies, T. S. (2009). Competing conceptual representations trigger co-speech representational gestures. *Language and Cognitive Processes, 24*(5), 761–775.)

encoding both manner and path, they are more likely to linguistically package manner and path in a single clause (e.g., "he rolls upwards"), but when they produced two separate gestures for manner and path, they are more likely to distribute manner and path expressions across two clauses (e.g., "he turns as he goes up"). In other words, what is encoded in a gesture is likely to be linguistically expressed within a clause, which is an important speech-planning unit (Bock & Cutting, 1992).

The information highlighted by gestures is fed into the Message Generator and is likely to be verbally expressed (Alibali & Kita, 2010; Alibali, Spencer, Knox, & Kita, 2011). When 5- to 7-year-old children are asked to explain answers to a Piagetian conservation task, the content of their explanation varied as a function of whether or not they were allowed to gesture (Alibali & Kita, 2010). In a Piagetian conservation task, the children are presented with two entities with the identical quantity (e.g., two identical glasses with water up to the same level). Then, the experimenter transforms the appearance of one entity in front of the child (e.g., pours water from one of the glasses into a wider and shallower dish) and asks which entity has more water. Five- to 7-year-old children find this task difficult (e.g., they tend to think that there is more water in the thinner and taller glass than in the wider and shallower dish). After children have answered the quantity question, the experimenter asks the reason for their answer. When children are allowed to gesture, they tend to gesture about various aspects of the task objects (e.g., width or height of a glass). Crucially, children's explanations include features of task objects in front of them (e.g., "because this one is tall and that one is short") more often when they are allowed to gesture than when they are not. That is, when gesture highlights certain information, that information is likely to be included in the message that speakers generate for their explanation (see also Alibali & Kita, 2010). That is, gesture influences "microplanning" (Levelt, 1989) in the conceptualization process, in which a message for each utterance is determined.

Manipulation of gestures influences fluency of speech production. When speakers describe spatial contents of an animated cartoon, the speech rate is higher and disfluencies are less frequent when the speakers are allowed to gesture than when they are prohibited from gesturing (Rauscher, Krauss, & Chen, 1996). This is compatible with the idea that gesture facilitates verbal encoding of spatial information.

The exact nature of the gestural influence on speech production is much debated in the literature.

There are three views, which are not mutually exclusive. The first view is that gesture facilitates conceptualisation for speaking (Kita, 2000), which is compatible with the model in Figure 27.1. There is substantial evidence for this view (Alibali & Kita, 2010; Alibali, Kita, Bigelow, Wolfman, & Klein, 2001; Alibali, Kita, & Young, 2000; Alibali, et al., 2011; Hostetter et al., 2007a, 2007b; Kita, 2000; Kita & Davies, 2009; Melinger & Kita, 2007; Mol & Kita, in press). The second view is that gesture facilitates lexical retrieval (Krauss, Chen, & Gottesman, 2000; Rauscher, et al., 1996). There is very limited evidence that uniquely supports this hypothesis (see Beattie & Coughlan, 1999 for further discussions; Kita, 2000; but see Rose, 2006). The third view is that gesture activates imagery whose content is to be verbally expressed (Bock & Cutting, 1992; de Ruiter, 1998; Wesp, Hesse, Keutmann, & Wheaton, 2001). The evidence for this view is that speakers produce more gestures when they have to describe stimuli from memory than when they can see the stimuli during description. In the memory condition, the image of the visual stimuli needs to be activated and, presumably, more gestures are produced in order to activate the necessary images. However, there is no study supporting this view that manipulated availability of gestures.

Other Models of Speech-Gesture Production

This article used Kita and Özyürek's (2003) model to summarize what is known about production of speech-accompanying gestures. However, it is important to acknowledge that there are other models. De Ruiter's (2000) model and Krauss and his colleagues' (2000) model are also based on Levelt's (1989) model of speech production. These models differ from the model in Figure 27.1 in the way gestural contents are determined. The content of gesture is determined by the conceptual planning process (the Conceptualizer in Levelt, 1989) in de Ruiter (2000) but in spatial working memory in Krauss et al. (2000). Unlike Figure 27.1, both models do not allow feedback from the formulation process to the conceptualization process. Consequently, they cannot account for the findings that syntactic packaging of information influences gestures.

It is also important to note theories of speech-gesture production that do not use the box-and-arrow architecture. Growth Point theory (McNeill, 1985, 1992, 2005; McNeill & Duncan, 2000) is very influential in its claim that speech and gesture production are an integrated process (see also Kendon, 1980). This theory brought gesture into psycholinguistics. According to the Growth Point theory, the information that stands out from the context forms a "Growth Point," which has both imagistic and verbal aspects. The imagistic aspect develops into a gesture and the verbal aspect develops into speech that is semantically associated with the gesture. Another more recent theory is the Gesture as a Simulated Action theory (Hostetter & Alibali, 2010). This theory assumes that underlying semantic representation for speech is motor or perceptual simulation (Barsalou, 1999) and gestures are generated from the same motor or perceptual simulation. When the strength of a simulation exceeds a certain threshold, a gesture is produced.

Other Important Issues

Due to space limitations, this article did not cover the following issues relevant to the relationship between speech and gesture production. The first issue is cultural variation in gesture production and reasons for the variation (Kita, 2009). The second issue is the model for how speech and gesture are synchronized. Most of the work on synchronization is on pointing gestures (de Ruiter, 1998; Levelt, Richardson, & La Heij, 1985). Representational gestures tend to precede coexpressive words (McNeill, 1992; Morrel-Samuels & Krauss, 1992); however, the mechanism for this synchronization has not been clarified. The third issue is how the relationship between speech and gesture production develops during childhood (Capirci, et al., 1996; Iverson & Goldin-Meadow, 2005; Nicoladis, 2002; Nicoladis, Mayberry, & Genesee, 1999; Özyürek, et al., 2008; Stefanini, Bello, Caselli, Iverson, & Volterra, 2009). The fourth issue concerns the neural substrates for the production of speech-accompanying gestures (Cocks, Dipper, Middleton, & Morgan, 2011; Hadar, Burstein, Krauss, & Soroker, 1998; Hadar & Krauss, 1999; Hadar, Wenkert-Olenik, Krauss, & Soroker, 1998; Hadar & Yadlin-Gedassy, 1994; Hogrefe, Ziegler, Tillmann, & Goldenberg, in press; Kimura, 1973a, 1973b; Kita, de Condappa, & Mohr, 2007; Kita & Lausberg, 2008; Lausberg, Davis, & Rothenhäuser, 2000; Rose, 2006). The fifth issue is how gesture production is affected in developmental disorders such as Specific Language Impairment, autism, Down syndrome, and Williams syndrome (Bello, Capirci, & Volterra, 2004; de marchena & Eigsti, 2010; Evans, Alibali, & McNeil, 2001; Stefanini, Caselli, & Volterra, 2007; Volterra, Capirci, & Caselli, 2001).

Conclusion

Speech-accompanying gestures are tightly coordinated with speech production. Gesture and speech are planned together as an integrated communicative move (Kendon, 2004). What is expressed in gesture and how it is expressed are shaped by information in the physical environment, discursive contexts, and how speech formulates information to be conveyed. Thus, it is not sufficient just to observe speech production to fully understand human communication.

Note

1. The Communication Planner has to also obtain information from the Environment to assess perceptual accessibility of gestures.

References

Alibali, M. W., Heath, D. C., & Myers, H. J. (2001). Effects of visibility between speaker and listener on gesture production: Some gestures are meant to be seen. *Journal of Memory and Language, 44*, 169–188.

Alibali, M. W., & Kita, S. (2010). Gesture highlights perceptually present information for speakers. *Gesture, 10*(1), 3–28.

Alibali, M. W., Kita, S., Bigelow, L. J., Wolfman, C. M., & Klein, S. M. (2001). Gesture plays a role in thinking for speaking. In C. Cavé, I. Guaïtella, & S. Santi (Eds.), *Oralité et gesturalité: Interactions et comportements multimodaux dans la communication* (pp. 407–410). Paris: L'Harmattan.

Alibali, M. W., Kita, S., & Young, A. J. (2000). Gesture and the process of speech production: We think, therefore we gesture. *Language and Cognitive Processes, 15*, 593–613.

Alibali, M. W., Spencer, R. C., Knox, L., & Kita, S. (2011). Spontaneous gestures influence strategy choices in problem solving. *Psychological Science, 22*(9), 1138–1144.

Bangerter, A. (2004). Using pointing and describing to achieve joint focus of attention in dialogue. *Psychological Science, 15*(6), 415–419.

Barsalou, L. W. (1999). Perceptual symbol systems. *Behavioral and Brain Sciences, 22*(4), 577–680.

Bavelas, J., Gerwing, J., Sutton, C., & Prevost, D. (2008). Gesturing on the telephone: Independent effects of dialogue and visibility. *Journal of Memory and Language, 58*(2), 495–520.

Bavelas, J. B., Chovil, N., Lawrie, D. A., & Wade, A. (1992). Interactive gestures. *Discourse Processes, 15*, 269–189.

Beattie, G., & Coughlan, J. (1999). An experimental investigation of the role of iconic gestures in lexical access using the tip-of-the-tongue phenomenon. *British Journal of Psychology, 90*, 35–56.

Bello, A., Capirci, O., & Volterra, V. (2004). Lexical production in children with Williams syndrome: spontaneous use of gesture in a naming task. *Neuropsychologia, 42*(2), 201–213.

Bock, K., & Cutting, J. C. (1992). Regulating mental energy: Performance units in language production. *Journal of Memory and Language, 31*, 99–127.

Capirci, O., Iverson, J. M., Pizzuto, E., & Volterra, V. (1996). Gestures and words during the transition to two-word speech. *Journal of Child Language, 23*(3), 645–673.

Chu, M., & Kita, S. (2008). Spontaneous gestures during mental rotation tasks: Insights into the microdevelopment of the motor strategy. *Journal of Experimental Psychology: General*, *137*, 706–723.

Cienki, A., & Müller, C. (Eds.). (2008). *Metaphor and gesture*. Amsterdam: John Benjamins.

Cocks, N., Dipper, L., Middleton, R., & Morgan, G. (2011). The impact of aphasia on gesture production: A case of condution aphasia. *International Journal of Language and Communication Disorders*, *46*(4), 423–436.

Cohen, A. A. (1977). The communicative functions of hand illustrators. *Journal of Communication*, *27*(4), 54–63.

de marchena, A., & Eigsti, I. M. (2010). Conversational gestures in autism spectrum disorders: Asycnrhony but not decreased frequency. *Autism Research*, *3*, 311–322.

de Ruiter, J. P. (1998). *Gesture and speech production* (Unpublished doctoral dissertation). University of Nijmegen, Nijmegen, the Netherlands.

de Ruiter, J. P. (2000). The production of gesture and speech. In D. McNeill (Ed.), *Language and gesture* (pp. 284–311). Chicago: University of Chicago Press.

Enfield, N. J., Kita, S., & de Ruiter, J. P. (2007). Primary and secondary pragmatic functions of pointing gestures. *Journal of Pragmatics*, *39*, 1722–1741.

Engberg-Pedersen, E. (2003). From pointing to reference and predication: Pointing signs, eyegaze, and head and body orientation in Danish Sign Language. In S. Kita (Ed.), *Pointing: Where language, cognition and culture meet* (pp. 269–292). Mahwah, NJ: Lawrence Erlbaum.

Evans, J. L., Alibali, M. W., & McNeil, N. M. (2001). Divergence of verbal expression and embodied knowledge: Evidence from speech and gesture in children with specific language impairment? *Language and Cognitive Processes*, *16*(2–3), 309–331.

Gerwing, J., & Bavelas, J. (2004). Linguistic influences on gesture's form. *Gesture*, *4*(2), 157–195.

Goldberg, A. E. (1997). The relationship between verbs and constructions. In M. Verspoor, K. D. Lee, & E. Seetser (Eds.), *Lexical and syntactical constructions and the construction of meaning* (pp. 383–398). Amsterdam: John Benjamins.

Gullberg, M. (2006). Handling discourse: Gestures, reference tracking, and communication strategies in early L2. *Language Learning*, *56*(1), 155–196.

Hadar, U., Burstein, A., Krauss, R., & Soroker, N. (1998). Ideational gestures and speech in brain-damaged subjects. *Language and Cognitive Processes*, *13*(1), 59–76.

Hadar, U., & Krauss, R. K. (1999). Iconic gestures: The grammatical categories of lexical affilates. *Journal of Neurolinguistics*, *12*, 1–12.

Hadar, U., Wenkert-Olenik, D. Krauss, R., & Soroker, N. (1998). Gesture and the processing of speech: Neuropsychological evidence. *Brain and Language*, *62*, 107–126.

Hadar, U., & Yadlin-Gedassy, S. (1994). Conceptual and lexical aspects of gesture: Evidence from aphasia. *Journal of Neurolinguistics*, *8*, 57–65.

Haviland, J. B. (2003). How to point in Zinacantán. In S. Kita (Ed.), *Pointing: Where language, cognition, and culture meet* (pp. 139–169). Mahwah, NJ: Lawrence Erlbaum.

Hogrefe, K., Ziegler, W., Tillmann, C., & Goldenberg, G. (2012). Non-verbal communication in severe aphasia: Influence of aphasia, apraxia, or semantic processing? *Cortex*, *48*, 952–962.

Holler, J., & Beattie, G. (2003). Pragmatic aspects of representational gestures: Do speakers use them to clarify verbal ambiguity with the listener? *Gesture*, *3*, 127–154.

Holler, J., & Wilkin, K. (2009). Communicating common ground: How mutually shared knowledge influences speech and gesture in a narrative task. *Language and Cognitive Processes*, *24*(2), 267–289.

Hostetter, A. B., & Alibali, M. W. (2010). Language, gesture, action! A test of the Gesture as Simulated Action framework. *Journal of Memory and Language*, *63*(2), 245–257.

Hostetter, A. B., Alibali, M. W., & Kita, S. (2007a). Does sitting on your hands make you bite your tongue? The effects of gesture prohibition on speech during motor description. In D. S. McNamara & J. G. Trafton (Eds.), *Proceedings of the twenty ninth annual conference of the Cognitive Science Society* (pp. 1097–1102). Mahwah, NJ: Lawrence Erlbaum.

Hostetter, A. B., Alibali, M. W., & Kita, S. (2007b). I see it in my hand's eye: Representational gestures are sensitive to conceptual demands. *Language and Cognitive Processes*, *22*(3), 313–336.

Iverson, J. M., & Goldin-Meadow, S. (2001). The resilience of gesture in talk: Gesture in blind speakers and listeners. *Developmental Science*, *4*(4), 416–422.

Iverson, J. M., & Goldin-Meadow, S. (2005). Gesture paves the way for language development. *Psychological Science*, *16*(5), 367–371.

Jacobs, N., & Garnham, A. (2007). The role of conversational hand gestures in a narrative task. *Journal of Memory and Language*, *56*(2), 291–303.

Kendon, A. (1980). Gesticulation and speech: Two aspects of the process of utterance. In M. R. Key (Ed.), *The relation between verbal and nonverbal communication* (pp. 207–227). The Hague: Mouton.

Kendon, A. (1992). Some recent work from Italy on quotable gestures (emblems). *Journal of Linguistic Anthropology*, *2*(1), 92–108.

Kendon, A. (2004). *Gesture: Visible action as utterance*. Cambridge: Cambridge University Press.

Kidd, E., & Holler, J. (2009). Children's use of gesture to resolve lexical ambiguity. *Developmental Science*, *12*(6), 903–913.

Kimbara, I. (2008). Gesture form convergence in joint description. *Journal of Nonverbal Behavior*, *32*(2), 123–131.

Kimura, D. (1973a). Manual activity during speaking. I. Right-handers. *Neuropsychologia*, *11*, 45–50.

Kimura, D. (1973b). Manual activity during speaking. II. Left-handers. *Neuropsychologia*, *11*, 51–55.

Kita, S. (2000). How representational gestures help speaking. In D. McNeill (Ed.), *Language and gesture* (pp. 162–185). Cambridge: Cambridge University Press.

Kita, S. (2003). *Pointing: Where language, culture, and cognition meet*. Mahwah, NJ: Lawrence Erlbaum.

Kita, S. (2009). Cross-cultural variation of speech-accompanying gesture: A review. *Language and Cognitive Processes*, *24*(2), 145–167.

Kita, S. (2010). A model of speech production. In E. Morsella (Ed.), *Expressing onself/expressing one's self: Communication, cognition, language, and identity* (pp. 9–22). New York: Psychology Press.

Kita, S., & Davies, T. S. (2009). Competing conceptual representations trigger co-speech representational gestures. *Language and Cognitive Processes*, *24*(5), 761–775.

Kita, S., de Condappa, O., & Mohr, C. (2007). Metaphor explanation attenuates the right-hand preference for depictive co-speech gestures that imitate actions. *Brain and Language*, *101*(3), 185.

Kita, S., & Lausberg, H. (2008). Generation of co-speech gestures based on spatial imagery from the right hemisphere: Evidence from split-brain patients. *Cortex*, *44*, 131–139.

Kita, S., & Özyürek, A. (2003). What does cross-linguistic variation in semantic coordination of speech and gesture reveal? Evidence for an interface representation of spatial thinking and speaking. *Journal of Memory and Language, 48*, 16–32.

Kita, S., Özyürek, A., Allen, S., Brown, A., Furman, R., & Ishizuka, T. (2007). How do our hands speak? Mechanisms underlying linguistic effects on representational gestures. *Language and Cognitive Processes, 22*(8), 1–25.

Krahmer, E., & Swerts, M. (2007). Effect of visual beats on prosodic prominence: Acoustic analyses, auditory perception, and visual perception. *Journal of Memory and Language, 57*, 396–414.

Krauss, R. M., Chen, Y., & Gottesman, R. F. (2000). Lexical gestures and lexical access: A process model. In D. McNeill (Ed.), *Language and gesture* (pp. 261–283). Cambridge: Cambridge University Press.

Lausberg, H., Davis, M., & Rothenhäuser, A. (2000). Hemispheric specialization in spontaneous gesticulation in a patient with callosal disconnection. *Neuropsychologia, 38*, 1654–1663.

LeBaron, C. D., & Streeck, J. (2000). Gesture, knowledge, and the world. In D. McNeill (Ed.), *Gesture and language* (pp. 118–138). Chicago: University of Chicago Press.

Levelt, W. J. M. (1989). *Speaking*. Cambridge, MA: The MIT Press.

Levelt, W. J. M., Richardson, G., & La Heij, W. (1985). Pointing and voicing in deictic expressions. *Journal of Memory and Language, 24*, 133–164.

McNeill, D. (1985). So you think gestures are nonverbal. *Psychological Review, 92*, 350–371.

McNeill, D. (1992). *Hand and mind*. Chicago: University of Chicago Press.

McNeill, D. (2003). Pointing and morality in Chicago. In S. Kita (Ed.), *Pointing: Where language, cognition, and culture meet.* (pp. 293–306). Mahwah, NJ: Lawrence Erlbaum.

McNeill, D. (2005). *Gesture and thought*. Chicago: University of Chicago Press.

McNeill, D., Cassell, J., & Levy, E. T. (1993). Abstract deixis. *Semiotica, 95*(1–2), 5–19.

McNeill, D., & Duncan, S. D. (2000). Growth points in thinking-for-speaking. In D. McNeill (Ed.), *Language and gesture* (pp. 141–161). Cambridge: Cambridge University Press.

Melinger, A., & Kita, S. (2007). Conceptualization load triggers gesture production. *Language and Cognitive Processes, 22*(4), 473–500.

Melinger, A., & Levelt, W. J. M. (2004). Gesture and the communicative intention of the speaker. *Gesture, 4*(2), 119–141.

Mol, L., & Kita, S. (2012). Gesture structure affects syntactic structure in speech. In *Proceedings of the thirty first annual conference of the Cognitive Science Society* (pp. 761–766). Austin, TX: Cognitive Science Society.

Morrel-Samuels, P., & Krauss, R. M. (1992). Word familiarity predicts temporal asynchrony of hand gestures and speech. *Journal of Experimental Psychology: Learning, Memory, and Cognition, 18*, 615–622.

Morris, D., Collett, P., Marsh, P., & O'Shaughnessy, M. (1979). *Gestures, their origins and distribution.* New York: Stein and Day.

Nicoladis, E. (2002). Some gestures develop in conjunction with spoken language development and others don't: Evidence from bilingual preschoolers. *Journal of Nonverbal Behavior, 26*(4), 241–266.

Nicoladis, E., Mayberry, R. I., & Genesee, F. (1999). Gesture and early bilingual development. *Developmental Psychology, 35*(2), 514–526.

Özyürek, A. (2002). Speech-gesture synchrony in typologically different languages and second language acquisition. In B. Skarabela, S. Fish, & A. H. J. Do (Eds.), *Proceedings from the 26th annual Boston University Conference in Language Development* (pp. 500–509). Somerville, MA: Cascadilla Press.

Özyürek, A., Kita, S., Allen, S., Brown, A., Furman, R., & Ishizuka, T. (2008). Development of cross-linguistic variation in speech and gesture: Motion events in English and Turkish. *Developmental Psychology, 44*(4), 1040–1054.

Rauscher, F. H., Krauss, R. M., & Chen, Y. (1996). Gesture, speech, and lexical access: The role of lexical movements in speech production. *Psychological Science, 7*, 226–230.

Rose, M. (2006). The utility of arm and hand gestures in the treatment of aphasia. *Advances in Speech-Language Pathology, 8*(2), 92.

Stefanini, S., Bello, A., Caselli, M. C., Iverson, J. M., & Volterra, V. (2009). Co-speech gestures in a naming task: Developmental data. *Language and Cognitive Processes, 24*(2), 168–189.

Stefanini, S., Caselli, M. C., & Volterra, V. (2007). Spoken and gestural production in a naming task by young children with Down syndrome. *Brain and Language, 101*(3), 208.

van der Sluis, I., & Krahmer, E. (2007). Generating multimodal references. *Discourse Processes, 44*, 145–174.

Volterra, V., Capirci, O., & Caselli, M. C. (2001). What atypical populations can reveal about language development: The contrast between deafness and Williams syndrome. *Language and Cognitive Processes, 16*(2–3), 219–239.

Wesp, R., Hesse, J., Keutmann, D., & Wheaton, K. (2001). Gestures maintain spatial imagery. *American Journal of Psychology, 114*, 591–600.

Perception-Production Interactions and their Neural Bases

Jason A. Tourville, Maya G. Peeva, *and* Frank H. Guenther

Abstract

Speech production is marked by rapid, coordinated movements of the vocal articulators. This is an impressive feat given the large number of muscles involved in producing even the simplest monosyllable. Yet, fluent speakers meet these demands with relative ease, producing as many as four to seven syllables per second. By 2 years of age, children learning American English have typically mastered the fine articulatory distinctions that differentiate the consonants /b/ and /d/ and the fine timing control that differentiates /b/ and /p/. By grade school they have mastered nearly the full inventory of phonemes, which they can combine in any syllable structure to produce long, complex, intelligible utterances. This article explores how the integration of auditory and somatosensory feedback with motor commands contributes to learning and maintaining these skills.

Key Words: articulation, somatosensory feedback, motor planning, motor learning

Overview: Perception-Production Interactions in Speech Production

Speech production is marked by rapid, coordinated movements of the vocal articulators. This is an impressive feat given the large number of muscles involved in producing even the simplest monosyllable (Zemlin, 1998). Yet, fluent speakers meet these demands with relative ease, producing as many as four to seven syllables per second (Tsao & Weismer, 1997). By 2 years of age, children learning American English have typically mastered the fine articulatory distinctions that differentiate the consonants /b/ and /d/ and the fine timing control that differentiate /b/ and /p/. By grade school they have mastered nearly the full inventory of phonemes, which they can combine in any syllable structure to produce long, complex, intelligible utterances (McLeod & Bleile, 2003). This article explores how the integration of auditory and somatosensory feedback with motor commands contributes to learning and maintaining these skills.

The brain orchestrates the finely tuned pattern of muscle activations needed for speech production using one or both of two broad classes of control. Under *feedback control*, sensory information guides motor execution. A well-known example of feedback control of speech is the increase in speech intensity in response to increasing environmental noise, the "Lombard Effect" (Lombard, 1911). Speakers also compensate for perceived errors in their auditory or somatosensory feedback (e.g., Abbs & Gracco, 1984; Jones & Munhall, 2002; Kelso, Tuller, Vatikiotis-Bateson, & Fowler, 1984; Purcell & Munhall, 2006b). Under *feedforward control*, task performance is executed from previously learned commands, or *speech motor programs*, without reliance on incoming task-related sensory information. The ease with which fluent speakers coordinate the rapid movements of multiple articulators is evidence of feedforward control (Neilson & Neilson, 1987). These movements are simply too fast to rely on sensory feedback for guidance.

Learning and maintaining the speech motor programs that support feedforward control, however, relies on sensory feedback. When we produce a speech sound, the motor commands that induce articulator movements are paired with the concomitant sensory feedback. The auditory and somatosensory signals that we expect to result from those motor commands are compared with this feedback. If a difference is encountered, the error is used to drive feedback-based corrective movements and to tune feedforward motor commands (e.g., Aasland, Baum, & McFarland, 2006; Houde & Jordan, 2002; Ito & Ostry, 2010; Jones & Munhall, 2002, 2005; Purcell & Munhall, 2006a; Villacorta, Perkell, & Guenther, 2007). This interplay between feedforward and feedback control systems subserves

a preschooler's initial speech motor learning and the updates necessitated by a growing vocal tract during puberty. At the same time, it supports rapid, online responses to a changing listening environment. This integration of motor and sensory information requires the recruitment and coordination of a diverse set of brain regions. Accordingly, a large portion of the brain is involved in even the simplest speech tasks, such as reading aloud a single word or syllable (e.g., (Fiez & Petersen, 1998; Ghosh, Tourville, & Guenther, 2008; Turkeltaub, Eden, Jones, & Zeffiro, 2002). This is demonstrated in Figure 28.1, which shows the cortical and subcortical brain regions involved in reading aloud one- or two-syllable words and pseudowords. When producing a speech sound, *motor commands* issued from

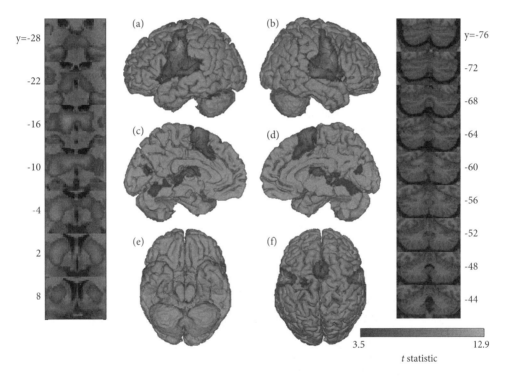

Figure 28.1 The brain regions involved in speech production. Activations (indicated by the red-yellow color gradient) were derived from pooled analysis of blood-oxygen level–dependent responses during three simple speech production tasks contrasted with a silent letter viewing baseline task (*speech—baseline*). The three speech tasks included in the analysis were production of monosyllable nonsense words (11 subjects), bisyllable nonsense words (13 subjects), and monosyllable American English words (10 subjects) for a total of 34 subjects. Thresholded statistical parametric maps (FDR <5 percent; $t > 3.48$) of the pooled *speech—baseline* contrast are shown superimposed on a representative brain to reveal the brain regions involved in speech production. *Far left*: A series of coronal slices through the central region of the brain reveals activation in the thalamus and basal ganglia. Numbers to the left of the images denote the anterior-posterior level (y coordinate) of the image in Montreal Neurological Institute (Mazziotta, et al., 2001) stereotactic space (higher y values are more anterior). *Center*: Activity is superimposed on renderings of the (a) left hemisphere lateral, (b) right lateral, (c) left medial, (d) right medial, (e) ventral, and (f) dorsal surfaces of the brain. The cortical regions associated with speech production include lateral sensorimotor cortex, medial and ventrolateral prefrontal cortex, perisylvian cortex, and superior temporal cortex. A more detailed illustration of the location of these regions on the cerebral surface is provided in Figure 28.2. *Far right*: A series of coronal slices through the cerebellum reveals widespread bilateral activation in superior cerebellar cortex and a small cluster of activation in right inferior cerebellar cortex.

motor and premotor cortex of the lateral frontal lobe induce articulator movements. These areas are highlighted and labeled in Figure 28.2. The articulator movements result in *auditory* and *somatosensory feedback*, which is processed in the superior temporal and lateral parietal cortex, respectively. These cortical regions interact with medial frontal cortex and subcortical structures including the cerebellum, basal ganglia, and brainstem (Figure 28.1). Together, these regions constitute the neural control system responsible for speech production.

The sections that follow describe how the motor and sensory components of this system interact during speech production and how their interplay enables a speaker to achieve his or her goals. In doing so, behavioral data characterizing the nature of auditory-motor and somatosensory-motor interactions during speech are discussed. Also reviewed is neurophysiological and neuroimaging research that has begun to reveal where and how these interactions are implemented in the brain. These neural mechanisms are described with reference to the Directions Into Velocities of Articulators (DIVA) model of speech acquisition and production (Guenther, Ghosh, & Tourville, 2006; Tourville & Guenther, 2010). DIVA provides a unified quantitative account of a wide range of speech production phenomena and neuroimaging data. The model consists of feedforward and feedback control

systems that are tuned by integrating motor output and sensory feedback and is therefore particularly useful for guiding a discussion of the sensorimotor interactions that underlie speech production.

Auditory-Motor Interactions in Speech

Many motor acts are aimed at achieving goals in three-dimensional space (e.g., reaching, grasping, walking, and handwriting). For such tasks, visual feedback of task performance plays an important role in monitoring performance and improving skill level (e.g., Held & Freedman, 1963; Helmholtz, 1925; Redding & Wallace, 2006). The primary goal of speech, however, is an acoustic signal that transmits a linguistic message by the listener's auditory system. Auditory feedback, like visual feedback during spatial task performance, plays an important role in monitoring vocal output and achieving fluency during speech production. We rely on instantaneous auditory feedback to modulate our voices in noisy environments (Lane & Tranel, 1971; Lombard, 1911), increasing the intensity and pitch of our voices and the duration of vowels (Summers, Pisoni, Bernacki, Pedlow, & Stokes, 1988; Tartter, Gomes, & Litwin, 1993) as ambient noise increases. This involuntary response improves the clarity of our speech, making it more easily comprehended by a listener (Pittman & Wiley, 2001). Disruption of normal auditory feedback can

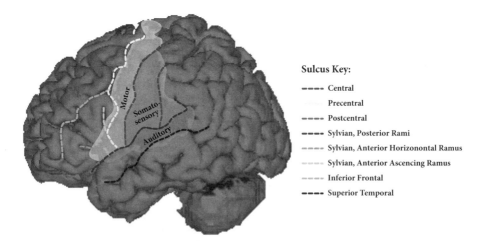

Sulcus Key:

‒‒‒‒ Central

⋯⋯ Precentral

‒ ‒ ‒ Postcentral

‒‒‒‒ Sylvian, Posterior Rami

‒ ‒ ‒ Sylvian, Anterior Horizonontal Ramus

⋯⋯ Sylvian, Anterior Ascencing Ramus

⋯⋯ Inferior Frontal

‒‒‒‒ Superior Temporal

Figure 28.2 Lateral cortical regions involved in speech production. Activity associated with motor, somatosensory, and auditory cortical processing during speech production is labeled on the lateral cortical surface. The activation overlays were generated from the pooled analysis of speech production tasks as described in the caption accompanying Figure 28.1. Sulci that mark relevant anatomic distinctions are marked by dotted lines (see key). The region labeled *motor* includes motor and premotor cortex on the ventral precentral gyrus and the posterior inferior frontal gyrus. The region labeled *somatosensory* includes primary and secondary somatosensory cortex on the ventral postcentral and anterior supramarginal gyri. The region labeled *auditory* includes primary and secondary auditory cortex along the superior temporal gyrus.

induce stuttering-like disfluencies in normally fluent speakers. This occurs when a short delay (approximately 200 ms) is introduced to a speaker's auditory feedback (Stuart, Kalinowski, Rastatter, & Lynch, 2002; Yates, 1963). A shorter delay, (approximately 50–75 ms), conversely, results in a transient *improvement* in the fluency of persons who stutter (e.g., Kalinowski, Stuart, Sark, & Armson, 1996; Ryan & Vankirk, 1974).

Auditory feedback does more than guide ongoing speech production by feedback-based control. In the absence of auditory feedback, development of verbal communication skills is profoundly disrupted. Infants born with severe hearing deficits experience delays in early speech development, including the onset of canonical babbling, which typically arises in the first year (Oller & Eilers, 1988). The intelligibility of speech later produced by such children covaries with residual hearing ability (Smith, 1975). Those born with profound hearing loss may never achieve intelligible verbal communication without interventions that provide some form of hearing ability. Speech development can be significantly improved by cochlear implants (Bouchard, Oullet, & Cohen, 2009), for instance, highlighting the critical role auditory feedback plays in the acquisition of *feedforward motor programs* that we rely on for fluent verbal communication.

The effects of hearing loss after language acquisition demonstrate another important contribution of auditory feedback to speech production. Although postlingually deaf individuals are able to communicate orally, difficulty controlling vocal pitch and intensity manifests shortly after hearing loss (Cowie & Douglas-Cowie, 1983; Lane & Webster, 1991). The precision of articulator movements and phonetic distinctions also deteriorate, reducing intelligibility (Lane & Webster, 1991; Waldstein, 1990). Auditory feedback is necessary to maintain speech motor skills long after they were first learned. Thus, speech production involves an ongoing, continuous interaction between the speech motor system and sensory systems that allows sensory feedback to modulate ongoing movements of the vocal articulators (feedback control) and to fine tune stored speech motor programs (feedforward control).

Since the Lombard effect was noted in the early 20th century, attempts to characterize auditory-motor interactions during speech have been made by unexpectedly and transiently modifying auditory feedback during speech production in near real-time. Speakers respond to these manipulations by altering their vocal output in the direction opposite the shift. For instance, when the amplitude of a speaker's auditory feedback is shifted down, the speaker responds by increasing his or her vocal intensity (Bauer, Mittal, Larson, & Hain, 2006; Heinks-Maldonado & Houde, 2005). Similarly, when fundamental frequency (F0), which is perceived as vocal pitch, is artificially shifted upward or downward, speakers respond by shifting the F0 in the opposite direction, below or above its normal level (e.g., Burnett & Larson, 2002; Elman, 1981; Jones & Munhall, 2002; Larson, Burnett, Kiran, & Hain, 2000). The speaker effectively corrects for the feedback manipulation, modifying vocal output so that the perceived feedback more closely matches the intended output

Manipulations of formant frequencies have demonstrated that control of the segmental content of speech is also influenced by online feedback-based control (e.g., Purcell & Munhall, 2006b; Tourville, Reilly, & Guenther, 2008). For instance, shifting the first formant (F1) of a speaker's acoustic output upward makes the word *bet* sound like *bat* (the vowel /ɛ/ shifts toward /ae/); a downward shift makes *bet* sound like *bit* (/ɛ/ shifts toward /I/). Such a shift alters the phonological and therefore lexical content of the auditory feedback. Speakers compensate for these segmental manipulations, again, by altering the F1 content of their vocal output in the direction opposite the shift, steering output closer to the intended auditory target. The compensatory response can occur within 108 ms of shift onset, fast enough to detect and correct the feedback within the typical duration syllable (Hillenbrand, Clark, & Nearey, 2001; Hillenbrand, Getty, Clark, & Wheeler, 1995) during conversational speech. Likewise, responses to F0 errors are fast enough to correct ongoing speech production. The compensatory response has been noted to persist well beyond the period during which the shift was applied (Donath, Natke, & Kalveram, 2002). Such aftereffects indicate that the change in vocal output is not simply a "reflexive" response to unexpected feedback. Rather, feedback errors and corrective responses are monitored and applied to future movements to pre-emptively avoid errors.

When a feedback error is repeatedly encountered, speakers adapt to the induced error (Houde, Nagarajan, Sekihara, & Merzenich, 2002; Jones & Munhall, 2000, 2005; Purcell & Munhall, 2006a; Villacorta, et al., 2007). For instance, repeated shifts of F1 in the same direction induce robust compensatory responses in the opposite direction (e.g., Purcell & Munhall, 2006a; Villacorta, et al., 2007). F1 in utterances made immediately after removal or masking of the persistent shift continues to differ from baseline formants in the direction opposite the shift. The "overshoots" or aftereffects that follow removal of the shift indicate a reorganization of the sensory–motor neural mappings that underlie feedforward control in speech. They are evidence of feedforward speech motor commands that have been updated in the presence of persistent auditory error to more accurately achieve auditory goals.

Neural Correlates

The interaction of auditory and motor systems during speech production is reflected in the findings of neuroimaging studies. As Figure 28.2 demonstrates, the motor-related activity of the frontal lobe is accompanied by activity in a large portion of the superior temporal gyrus, the seat of primary and secondary auditory cortices, during speech production. Responses in the more anterior and ventral portions of the superior temporal gyrus have been correlated with increasing intelligibility of speech sounds (Binder, et al., 2000; Giraud & Price, 2001; Scott, Blank, Rosen, & Wise, 2000). This region is thought to support auditory object recognition and speech perception (Rauschecker & Scott, 2009). Activation in the posterior superior temporal gyrus region extends to the inferior parietal cortex including the parietal operculum and anterior supramarginal gyrus, regions implicated in several processes related to speech production including verbal working memory (e.g., Becker, MacAndrew, & Fiez, 1999; Jonides, et al., 1998); phonetic discrimination (Caplan, Gow, & Makris, 1995); and an interface between orthographic, phonological, and lexical-semantic decision-making (Pugh, et al., 2001). Damage to this area results in several language production and perception deficits including Wernicke's aphasia and conduction aphasia (Damasio & Damasio, 1980; Goodglass, 1993).

It has become clear, however, that activity in the posterior portions of the superior temporal gyrus, including the planum temporale, the portion of the posterior superior temporal gyrus that lies within the Sylvian fissure and behind primary auditory cortex, does not solely reflect the afferent auditory input associated with speech production. Activity in this area changes even when subjects simply imagine speaking without moving the articulators (Hickok, et al., 2000; Numminen & Curio,

1999; Okada & Hickok, 2006; Okada, Smith, Humphries, & Hickok, 2003). Such "covert" speech results in no auditory feedback, yet induces a response in auditory cortex. Moreover, responses to one's own speech in this region are suppressed compared with responses when listening to recordings of others speaking (Wise, Greene, Buchel, & Scott, 1999) or even recordings of one's own speech (Curio, Neuloh, Numminen, Jousmaki, & Hari, 2000; Heinks-Maldonado, Mathalon, Gray, & Ford, 2005; Heinks-Maldonado, Nagarajan, & Houde, 2006; Numminen, Salmelin, & Hari, 1999). Single unit recordings from nonhuman primates have shown suppression of auditory cortical neurons immediately prior to self-initiated vocalizations (Eliades & Wang, 2003, 2005). These suppressed neurons become highly active, however, when auditory feedback is altered (Eliades & Wang, 2008). Attenuation of the auditory cortex suppression associated with speech production under altered auditory feedback conditions has also been noted in humans (e.g., Heinks-Maldonado, et al., 2006). The degree of suppression is modulated by how closely feedback matches expectations. Similar modulation of somatosensory responses to self-generated movements (e.g., Blakemore, Wolpert, & Frith, 1998; Wasaka, Hoshiyama, Nakata, Nishihira, & Kakigi, 2003) has been interpreted as evidence that an efference copy of outgoing motor commands sent from motor to sensory cortex encodes the expected sensory consequences of upcoming movements (Blakemore, Wolpert, & Frith, 2000; Wolpert & Flanagan, 2001). The efference copy attenuates the regions of sensory cortex responsive to the expected sensory feedback. In doing so, the efference copy "cancels" the sensory feedback response resulting from the movement (von Holst & Mittelstaedt, 1950).

Neuroimaging studies of perturbed auditory feedback during speech production have consistently noted increased response in posterior superior temporal gyrus bilaterally as a result of the feedback manipulation. This has been shown for delayed auditory feedback (Hashimoto & Sakai, 2003; Hirano, et al., 1997); noise masking (Christoffels, Formisano, & Schiller, 2007; Zheng, Munhall, & Johnsrude, 2010); F0/pitch shifts (Fu, et al., 2006; McGuire, Silbersweig, & Frith, 1996; Zarate & Zatorre, 2005; see Toyomura et al., 2007, for evidence of increased activity only in the right hemisphere); and formant shifts (Tourville, et al., 2008) during speech production. Greater attenuation of auditory cortical responses was noted when speakers

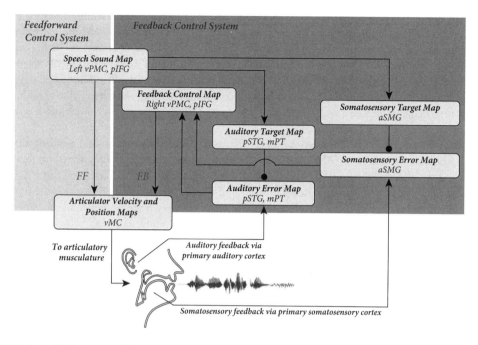

Figure 28.3 A simplified schematic of the DIVA model of the sensorimotor interactions underlying speech production. aSMG = anterior supramarginal gyrus; FF = feedforward motor command; FB = feedback motor command; mPT = medial planum temporale; pIFG = posterior inferior frontal gyrus; pSTG = posterior superior temporal gyrus; vMC = ventral motor cortex; vPMC = ventral premotor cortex.

heard normal rather than pitch-shifted auditory feedback. Collectively, these findings indicate that responses in posterior auditory cortex are modulated by input from the speech motor system during speech production. This input selectively suppresses the response to the expected auditory feedback. When feedback does not match this expectation, the response is elevated.

In addition to bilateral superior temporal activity, Tourville et al. (2008) noted increased inferior cerebellum activity in the left hemisphere and right lateralized increased activity in inferior frontal gyrus and lateral premotor cortex when formants were shifted during speech production. Structural equation modeling (McIntosh & Gonzalez-Lima, 1994) revealed greater effective connectivity between the bilateral superior temporal (auditory) areas that responded to the auditory perturbation and these inferior frontal/premotor regions of the right hemisphere. These findings suggest lateral premotor areas of the right hemisphere are selectively involved in the transformation of auditory errors into compensatory articulatory movements that forms the heart of the auditory feedback control network for speech (discussed later). Functional pathways between the lateral premotor areas

involved in speech production and posterior auditory cortex have been established in other studies (e.g., Matsumoto, et al., 2004), and more recently white matter tracts between these areas were identified using diffusion tensor imaging. These pathways provide a means for direct communication between the speech motor and auditory systems. Hickok and colleagues have described a region at the posterior end of this pathway, deep within the Sylvian fissure at the junction of the temporal and parietal lobes as a sensorimotor interface for speech (Hickok, Buchsbaum, Humphries, & Muftuler, 2003; Hickok & Poeppel, 2007). The DIVA model, detailed later, offers a mechanistic account of how this interface supports speech motor learning (Guenther, et al., 2006).

Somatomotor Interactions in Speech

Mechanoreceptors of the vocal tract provide the brain with information about the configuration of the speech articulators. Like auditory feedback, afferent somatosensory information is carefully monitored during speech production. When somatosensory feedback is unexpected, for instance when the shape of the vocal tract changes (Aasland, et al., 2006; Baum & McFarland, 1997, 2000; Jones

& Munhall, 2003; McFarland, Baum, & Chabot, 1996), the speech motor system adapts so that the intended speech target is reached. The influence of somatosensory feedback on speech motor control has been investigated extensively in experiments that have imparted an unexpected, transient perturbation of articulator movements. When speakers encounter disruptions of lip or jaw movements, they adjust movements of unimpeded articulators to compensate for the error (Abbs & Gracco, 1984; Folkins & Abbs, 1975; Gomi, Honda, Ito, & Murano, 2002; Gracco & Abbs, 1985; Kelso, et al., 1984; Shaiman, 1989). For instance, if the lower lip is displaced downward during production of /aba/, speakers adjust by moving their upper lips lower than normal (Abbs & Gracco, 1984). By doing so, they achieve the lip closure necessary for the /b/.

This compensatory response is fast (within 100 ms of the perturbation) and is functionally specific: compensatory movements are restricted to those that achieve the articulator or acoustic goal. For instance, a downward jaw displacement induces downward movement of the upper lip during the final bilabial closure in /baeb/ but not during the alveolar closure of /baez/ (Kelso, et al., 1984). A modification of the trajectory of the upper lip movement is unnecessary to produce the /z/. The compensatory movements are therefore not simply reflexive (i.e., the result of local stretch receptor dynamics). Rather, they are governed by the articulatory requirements of the intended sensory target, indicating that the compensatory responses are influenced by input from the cerebral cortex where the targets are likely stored. This has been confirmed by Ito and colleagues who demonstrated mediation of compensatory responses to a jaw perturbation by speech motor cortex (Ito, Kimura, & Gomi, 2005).

Although many of the somatosensory perturbations discussed so far were accompanied by a concomitant change in auditory feedback (making it possible that the responses were mediated by auditory feedback error that is transformed into compensatory articulator movements rather than somatosensory errors), other studies have shown correction for somatosensory perturbations in the absence of auditory errors. For example, Lindblom, Lubker, and Gay (1979) showed that subjects produced tongue movements that compensated for a bite block held between the teeth even before they produced acoustic output. More recent studies by Ostry and colleagues have shown that speakers compensate for small jaw perturbations that do not result in detectable changes of auditory feedback

(Nasir & Ostry, 2006; Tremblay, Shiller, & Ostry, 2003). Furthermore, when the perturbation is removed, speakers continue to make compensatory movements in anticipation of the perturbation for several trials. This aftereffect suggests that the somatosensory error resulted in modification of stored feedforward motor commands. Similar adaptation to the jaw perturbation was also observed from subjects with profound postlingual hearing loss (Nasir & Ostry, 2008). Together, these results indicate that somatosensory targets are indeed a goal of speech production, and that consistently applied somatosensory perturbations lead to changes in the feedforward motor commands for speech. This latter observation is consistent with the fact that children maintain fluent, intelligible speech in the face of dramatic growth in the vocal tract as they age; although the changes in vocal tract morphology occur relatively slowly, they are akin to the effects of bite blocks, false palates, or lip tubes that induce changes in vocal tract shape in experimental setups.

Neural Correlates

Few studies have investigated the brain regions associated with somatosensory feedback contributions to speech motor control. Compensatory responses to a jaw perturbation involve primary motor cortex. This was shown by targeting the left lateral motor cortex with transcranial magnetic stimulation; when the area was stimulated, compensatory responses to jaw perturbations were altered (Ito, et al., 2005). But what of the rest of the brain? Golfinopoulos et al. (2011) used functional magnetic resonance imaging (fMRI) to compare brain responses during speech under normal conditions and when jaw movements were unexpectedly restricted by the inflation of a small balloon. The perturbation resulted in increased activity throughout the brain regions involved in normal speech production (see Figure 28.1), peaking in the right anterior supramarginal gyrus, with additional activity in the right inferior frontal gyrus pars triangularis and anterior cingulate gyrus. Activity in several regions, including the supramarginal gyrus, lateral premotor cortex, and inferior frontal gyrus, was significantly greater in the right hemisphere. An earlier fMRI study of a static lip perturbation during speech (Baciu, Abry, & Segebarth, 2000) noted similar results, including a peak in right supramarginal gyrus and a shift to greater input from the right hemisphere during perturbed speech.

The anterior supramarginal gyrus lies immediately behind and is tightly connected with the lateral postcentral gyrus where the primary somato-sensory representation of the speech articulators lies (Boling, Reutens, & Olivier, 2002; Fesl, et al., 2003; Lotze, et al., 2000). It is therefore not surprising that this area is active when the speech articulators are perturbed. This area is strongly connected to the speech motor areas of the inferior frontal and lateral premotor cortex (Makris, et al., 2005; Matsumoto, et al., 2004; Rushworth, Behrens, & Johansen-Berg, 2006; Saur, et al., 2008, 2010). An analogous pathway in primates (Luppino, Murata, Govoni, & Matelli, 1999) is believed to contribute to the sensorimotor transformations required to guide movements, such as grasping (see Rizzolatti & Luppino, 2001). Relatedly, this area has been associated with corrective finger movements induced by unexpected load variations during lifting (Jenmalm, Schmitz, Forssberg, & Ehrsson, 2006; Schmitz, Jenmalm, Ehrsson, & Forssberg, 2005). In particular, it is associated with comparing expected sensory feedback and actual feedback from somatosensory afferents during movement. The imaging studies of articulator perturbations cited previously are consistent with this interpretation. It has been argued that speech motor commands and sensory feedback are integrated in the ventral parietal lobe (Guenther, et al., 2006; Hickok & Poeppel, 2004; Rauschecker & Scott, 2009), analogous to the integration of visual and motor signals demonstrated in the dorsal parietal lobe (Andersen, 1997; Rizzolatti, Fogassi, & Gallese, 1997). The next section describes a mechanistic account of this interaction and how it subserves speech motor learning and control.

Brain responses to jaw perturbation (Golfinopoulos, et al., 2011) offer interesting parallels to the auditory feedback perturbation findings discussed in the previous section (Tourville, et al., 2008). Both studies revealed increased bilateral activation of secondary sensory cortices in the modality of the perturbation and right lateralized increases of lateral premotor and inferior frontal activation when feedback was perturbed. Furthermore, both studies revealed increased effective connectivity between the posterior sensory regions and right lateral frontal regions in response to the perturbation, providing further evidence for increased recruitment of right inferior frontal and premotor regions during feedback-based control of speech.

Neural Computations Underlying Sensorimotor Interactions during Speech

Since 1992, our laboratory has developed an adaptive neural network model, the DIVA model, which provides a quantitatively explicit description of the sensorimotor interactions involved in speech motor control. The model represents a theory of how feedforward and feedback control systems interact during speech motor learning and production and is presented here to facilitate and guide a unified account of the findings discussed previously. A simplified schematic of the model is shown in Figure 28.3. DIVA consists of integrated feedforward and feedback control systems that learn to control a simulated vocal tract (a modified version of the synthesizer described by Maeda, 1990). Once trained, the model takes a discrete speech sound (typically a syllable) as input and generates a time varying sequence of articulator positions that command movements of the simulated vocal tract that produce the desired sound. The model provides a unified explanation of a number of speech production phenomena including motor equivalence, contextual variability, anticipatory and carryover coarticulation, velocity/distance relationships, speaking rate effects, and speaking skill acquisition and retention throughout development (e.g., Callan, Kent, Guenther, & Vorperian, 2000; Guenther, 1994; Guenther, 1995; Guenther, et al., 2006; Guenther, Hampson, & Johnson, 1998; Nieto-Castanon, Guenther, Perkell, & Curtin, 2005). Because it can account for such a wide array of data, the DIVA model has provided the theoretical framework for a number of investigations of normal and disordered speech production. Predictions from the model have guided studies of the role of auditory feedback in normally hearing persons, deaf persons, and persons who have recently regained some hearing through the use of cochlear implants (Lane, et al., 2007; Perkell, et al., 2007; Perkell, et al., 2000; Perkell, Guenther, et al., 2004; Perkell, Matthies, et al., 2004). The model has also aided investigations of the cause of stuttering (Max, Guenther, Gracco, Ghosh, & Wallace, 2004) and apraxia of speech (Robin, et al., 2008; Terband, Maassen, Guenther, & Brumberg, 2009).

The model is comprised of interconnected modules (blocks in Figure 28.3) that represent maps of neurons in specific regions of the human brain. The association of these modules to cortical, subcortical, and cerebellar regions of the brain is based on human clinical, neuroimaging, and microstimulation studies and nonhuman primate single cell recording and anterograde and retrograde tracing studies (Guenther, et al., 2006; Tourville & Guenther, 2010). Each module corresponds to a set of neurons, or map, which represents a particular type of information. The term *mapping* is used to refer to a transformation from one neural representation to another. These transformations are represented by arrows in Figure 28.3 and are analogous to axonal projections in the brain.

A hallmark of the DIVA model is the integration of input from feedforward and feedback control systems to generate the overall motor command that is sent to the articulatory musculature. The "motor programs" for speech sounds are stored in a *speech sound map* that is hypothesized to lie in lateral premotor cortex in the left hemisphere. Speech production in the model begins with the activation of one of these cells. Signals sent from the speech sound map directly to *articulator velocity and position maps* in motor cortex to represent *feedforward commands* (FF pathway in Figure 28.3). These projections encode a previously learned time series of articulatory movements for producing the desired speech sound; they can thus be thought of as a "gestural score" (e.g., Browman & Goldstein, 1989) for each learned speech sound.

In addition to activating the stored motor program (feedforward command) for the current speech sound, the speech sound map also sends signals to auditory and somatosensory cortex that represent the expected sensory feedback for the associated motor commands. Throughout speech production, sensory feedback is monitored; if a discrepancy between feedback and target is detected, error signals are generated in the *auditory and somatosensory error maps*, which project to the *feedback control map*, which in turn sends *feedback commands* (FB in Figure 28.3) to motor cortex, where they are added to the feedforward commands to produce the outgoing motor command to the articulatory musculature. When the model produces a highly practiced speech sound, the feedforward commands sent from the speech sound map to motor cortex are accurate and the resulting movements are driven primarily by feedforward control. Early in learning, however, speech production is guided primarily by feedback control because poorly tuned feedforward commands result in sensory errors that induce corrective feedback-based motor commands. Corrective feedback commands would similarly arise when the fully tuned system encounters an error caused by an artificial manipulation of sensory feedback (e.g., shifting a formant such that *head* sounds like *had*). The model responds to the error in the same way that speakers in auditory perturbation experiments do, producing speech that sounds more like the intended target. Like an adult speaker, the model

remains sensitive to errors while maintaining the ability to produce fluent speech.

DIVA's speech sound map can be likened to the "mental syllabary" described by Levelt and colleagues (Levelt, Roelofs, & Meyer, 1999; Levelt & Wheeldon, 1994). Each cell represents a phoneme or frequently encountered multiphonemic speech sound, with syllables being the most typical sound type represented. This representation is not entirely motor or sensory. Rather, cells of the speech sound map link the sensory goals of articulator movements to the motor commands that generate them. In doing so, these cells embody the core property of what Rizzolati and others have described as "mirror neurons" (Rizzolatti & Craighero, 2004; Rizzolatti, Fadiga, Gallese, & Fogassi, 1996). Mirror neurons are so termed because they respond during an action and while viewing (or hearing) that action performed by another animal or person. This describes the behavior of speech sound map cells: production of a speech sound requires activation of the appropriate speech sound map cells; the same cell becomes active when that speech sound is perceived by input from sensory cortex. In the DIVA model, this interaction between the production and perception systems supports speech motor learning. Others have suggested that mirror neurons may also contribute to speech perception (e.g., Gallese, Fadiga, Fogassi, & Rizzolatti, 1996; Rizzolatti & Arbib, 1998).

The Role of Sensory Feedback during Feedback Control and Motor Learning

Like an infant, the DIVA model must learn the association between sound and movement of the articulators before it can produce speech sounds. This is done during a training process analogous to infant babbling during which the model produces random movements of the articulators. The resulting auditory signal is then mapped back to that movement. For example, the model learns that the vowel sound /i/, as in *heed*, can be achieved by moving the tongue toward the hard palate. This sensory-to-motor mapping is a form of *inverse model* (e.g., Kawato, 1999; Wolpert & Kawato, 1998) because it implements the transformation between the desired sensory outcome and the appropriate motor actions, otherwise known as the *inverse kinematic* transformation. The auditory-to-motor inverse mapping is represented in Figure 28.3 by the pathway from the auditory error map to the feedback control map. Once learned, this mapping subserves both the feedback and feedforward controllers: it is the basis for the feedback-based corrective commands that, in turn, tune the feedforward motor programs of the speech sound map.

Following babbling, the DIVA model learns the auditory expectations, or targets, for frequently encountered speech sounds. The model "listens" to the speech sounds (e.g., phoneme, syllable, word) it is presented with, much like an infant listens to his or her mother, and learns the range of time-varying formants that are acceptable for each sound (see Guenther, 1995). As each new target is learned, it becomes associated with a cell in the speech sound map. When a speech sound map cell is activated during a production attempt, the corresponding auditory target becomes active in the *auditory target map*. Projections such as these, which predict the sensorimotor state resulting from a movement, represent a *forward model* of the movement (e.g. Davidson & Wolpert, 2005; Desmurget & Grafton, 2000; Kawato, 1999; Miall & Wolpert, 1996). The auditory target map inhibits the region in the *auditory error map* hypothesized to lie in the portion of the posterior superior temporal gyrus that has been described as a sensorimotor interface for speech (discussed previously). Direct connections between this region and lateral premotor cortex have recently been established (e.g., Bernal & Altman, 2010; Saur, et al., 2010). The auditory error map also receives excitatory input from primary auditory cortex that encodes afferent auditory feedback.

After a speech sound map cell is associated with an auditory target, the model begins to practice producing the speech sound. With each attempt, the resulting auditory feedback is compared with the target. Any difference between the two results in activation in the auditory error map that induces a feedback-based corrective command by the feedback control map. The feedback-based command improves the ongoing articulator output but also plays a key role in long-term speech motor development. This is because each feedback-based corrective command is added to the feedforward command that generated the articulator movement, thereby improving the feedforward command for the next attempt. With each subsequent attempt to produce the speech sound, the error is further reduced until the feedforward command is able to achieve the desired auditory target without input from the feedback system.

The model also includes a somatosensory feedback control subsystem that is analogous to the auditory feedback control system just described (see Figure 28.3). Projections from the speech sound map to the *somatosensory target map*, hypothesized to lie in ventral somatosensory cortex and anterior supramarginal gyrus, encode the expected proprioceptive and tactile feedback associated with each speech sound. According to the model, somatosensory targets are learned with each attempt to produce a speech sound (i.e., in parallel with feedforward learning). The target map inhibits a representation of the expected somatosensory feedback in the *somatosensory error map*, hypothesized to lie in the same cortical region (discussed previously). The error map also receives excitatory input from the primary somatosensory cortex along the ventral postcentral gyrus, immediately posterior to the motor articulator representations of the precentral gyrus. If somatosensory feedback falls outside the target, cells in the somatosensory error map become active resulting in the generation of a corrective motor command by the feedback control map.

Lateralized Control Subsystems

The view that the left hemisphere plays a dominant role in speech production has persisted for more than a century. Lesions to left inferior frontal and premotor cortex are far more likely to result in speech and language production deficits than those in the right hemisphere (see Duffy, 2005; Hillis, et al., 2004 for reviews). For a time, imaging data stood in conflict with this view; speech production was typically associated with bilateral frontal activity (e.g., Bohland & Guenther, 2006; Ozdemir, Norton, & Schlaug, 2006; Soros, et al., 2006; Wise, et al., 1999). There is growing evidence, however, that under normal speaking conditions, lateral premotor activity is indeed significantly greater in the left hemisphere (Ghosh, et al., 2008; Golfinopoulos, et al., 2011; Riecker, Ackermann, Wildgruber, Dogil, & Grodd, 2000; Sidtis, Gomez, Groshong, Strother, & Rottenberg, 2006; Tourville, et al., 2008). When an unanticipated auditory or somatosensory error is encountered, however, increases in premotor activity associated with compensatory responses are significantly greater in the right hemisphere (Golfinopoulos, et al., 2011; Tourville, et al., 2008).

In the DIVA model, these findings are expressed as lateralization of the feedforward and feedback inputs to motor cortex. Feedforward inputs derive from the speech sound map hypothesized to lie in left lateral premotor cortex. Feedback-based commands, however, are sent to motor cortex from a feedback motor control map in lateral premotor cortex of the right hemisphere. According to the model, under normal feedback conditions the articulators are primarily under the feedforward motor programs stored in left lateral premotor cortex.

When a sensory error is encountered, lateral premotor cortex of the right hemisphere is recruited to transform that error into corrective motor commands. The implication is that damage to the left lateral premotor region is more likely to disrupt stored feedforward speech motor commands, and is therefore more likely to result in disordered speech because the feedforward control system is more crucial for fluent speech than the sensory feedback control system (Neilson & Neilson, 1987).

There is additional clinical evidence to support lateralized feedforward and feedback control systems. Apraxia of speech, a disorder frequently associated with damage to left lateral premotor areas or posterior portions of the inferior frontal gyrus (Hillis, et al., 2004; Robin, Jacks, & Ramage, 2007) is typically characterized as involving impaired or missing motor programs for speech production. A speech disorder associated predominantly with right lateral premotor cortex and characterized by impaired feedback-based control has, thus far, not been identified. However, stuttering has been attributed to overreliance on feedback control (Max et al., 2004) and is associated with increased right lateral frontal activity (Brown, Ingham, Ingham, Laird, & Fox, 2005).

Future Directions
Other Regions Involved in Sensorimotor Interactions during Speech

The DIVA model does not account for all of the brain regions implicated in sensorimotor integration during speech production, especially areas where data are still rather uncertain and contradictory. For example, auditory and somatosensory feedback perturbations result in increased activity in the inferior intermediate cerebellar cortex (lobules VIIb and VIIIa; Golfinopoulos, et al., 2011; Tourville, et al., 2008). The intermediate cerebellum is structurally (Kelly & Strick, 2003; Schmahmann & Pandya, 1997) and functionally (O'Reilly, Beckmann, Tomassini, Ramnani, & Johansen-Berg, 2009) connected with motor, premotor, and sensory cortices and is known to play a crucial role in sensorimotor learning (Blakemore, Frith, & Wolpert, 2001; Criscimagna-Hemminger, Bastian, & Shadmehr, 2010; Diedrichsen, Hashambhoy, Rane, & Shadmehr, 2005; Smith & Shadmehr, 2005; Tseng, Diedrichsen, Krakauer, Shadmehr, & Bastian, 2007) and it contributes to movements of the vocal articulators (Grodd, Hulsmann, Lotze, Wildgruber, & Erb, 2001). The area found active when feedback was perturbed during speech has also been implicated in sensory error processing for reaching movements (Diedrichsen, et al., 2005). It is unknown, however, what specific role this area plays during feedback-based corrective movements during speech. It may contribute to the detection of sensory errors or to the calculation of the corrective motor command. There is evidence for both roles but a clear understanding of the contribution of the inferior cerebellum to sensorimotor integration awaits further study.

Studies have also found activity in the anterior cingulate gyrus and adjacent medial motor areas associated with auditory feedback monitoring during speech (Christoffels, et al., 2007; Fu, et al., 2006) and with somatosensory-based feedback control of speech (Golfinopoulos, et al., 2011). This region of the brain has been associated with a general role in conflict monitoring and error detection (Botvinick, Braver, Barch, Carter, & Cohen, 2001; Fiehler, Ullsperger, & von Cramon, 2004; van Veen, Cohen, Botvinick, Stenger, & Carter, 2001). A straightforward interpretation of its contribution to error correction in speech is hindered by the absence of activity in this area during auditory feedback perturbation (Tourville, et al., 2008; Toyomura, et al., 2007). Study design may explain the discrepancy (e.g., whether the error is expected or not, whether the error falls above or below conscious awareness) but, as with the cerebellum, further research is required before a detailed account of this region's contribution to sensorimotor interactions during speech is possible.

Effects of Motor Experience on Speech Perception

So far we have focused on how interactions between the sensory and motor systems influence speech production. Sensory feedback is used to correct ongoing movements and to tune speech motor programs. Recent work has suggested that motor experience can influence speech perception (see Houde, 2009 for review). For example, motor adaptation to a perturbation of auditory feedback during /s/ productions resulted in a concomitant shift in the perception of /s/ (Shiller, Sato, Gracco, & Baum, 2009). The perceptual shift acted to reduce the impact of the perturbation (i.e., the perturbed /s/ sounded more "/s/-like" to the subjects following motor adaptation). Perception was not shifted in a control group that passively listened to recordings of the perturbed utterances, indicating that the perceptual shift was not simply caused by exposure to the perturbed /s/ but was rather mediated by motor adaptation. Indeed, changes in auditory perceptual boundaries can be induced by motor adaptation to a somatosensory perturbation that does not alter auditory feedback (Nasir & Ostry, 2009). Subjects were asked to identify auditory tokens as *had* or *head* before and after speakers adapted to a jaw displacement (protrusion). Tokens were drawn from a continuum between *had* and *head* that varied only by the first and second formant values of the vowel. Those subjects that adapted to the perturbation were more likely to identify tokens in the middle of the continuum as *head* following motor learning. Subjects that did not adapt (5 of 23) and those in a control group that performed the experiment without the jaw perturbation did not demonstrate the perceptual shift.

These intriguing findings suggest that persistent errors encountered during adaptation experiments cause updates to the motor programs and the perceptual boundaries for a speech sound. The influence of motor experience on speech perception implies a tighter coupling than any of the previously discussed speech theories provide.

Integration of Somatosensory and Auditory Feedback

For simplicity, the DIVA model currently uses independent auditory and somatosensory channels. Feedback error is calculated within each channel and transformed into corrective commands in the feedback control map in right ventral premotor cortex. There is evidence, however, suggesting that the auditory and somatosensory systems interact during speech, influencing production and perception. A study showing a shift in auditory perception after motor adaptation to a somatosensory perturbation was described in the previous section (Nasir & Ostry, 2009). The influence of somatosensory feedback on auditory perception need not be through motor adaptation. Ito, Tiede, and Ostry (2009) found that perception of tokens on a continuum from *had* to *head* shifted when the facial skin of subjects was stretched while listening to the tokens. The direction of the perceptual shift depended on the pattern of the skin stretch: when the skin stretch resembled the pattern associated with production of *head*, perception was biased toward *head*; when it resembled *had* production, perception was biased toward *had*. Thus, it seems that somatosensory afferents modulate speech perception in normal-hearing individuals.

If somatosensory and auditory feedback systems are not independent, where are they integrated in the brain? A possible candidate is the medial portion of the planum temporale. This region, traditionally considered a unimodal auditory area, lies adjacent to the secondary somatosensory area of the opercular portion of the supramarginal gyrus, the parietal operculum. It was noted previously that the posterior portion of medial planum temporale is active during passive auditory speech perception and speech production, even if the articulation is silent (e.g., Buchsbaum, et al., 2005; Hickok, et al., 2003). Overlapping activity in this area has also been noted for overt speech and nonspeech movements of the jaw and tongue (Dhanjal, Handunnetthi, Patel, & Wise, 2008). According to the DIVA model, this area is the location of the auditory target and error maps (i.e., it receives inputs from low-level auditory cortex and from the motor system; Guenther, et al., 2006). Others have proposed a similar role for this region as an auditory-motor interface during speech (e.g., Hickok & Poeppel, 2007; Rauschecker, 2010; Wise, et al., 2001).

There is increasing evidence that somatosensory feedback is also sent to medial planum temporal by inputs from lateral parietal cortex. Projections from cortical and subcortical somatosensory areas to auditory cortex have been shown in rodents (Budinger & Scheich, 2009) and nonhuman primates (Cappe & Barone, 2005; Hackett, et al., 2007; Smiley, et al., 2007). Modulation of auditory cortical neurons in macaques by various forms of somatosensory stimulation has been demonstrated, providing functional evidence of these inputs (Brosch, Selezneva, & Scheich, 2005; Fu, et al., 2003; Lakatos, Chen, O'Connell, Mills, & Schroeder, 2007; Lemus, Hernandez, Luna, Zainos, & Romo, 2010; Schroeder, et al., 2001).

Several studies showing articulator movement-related activity in medial planum temporale have been discussed. As in the macaque, somatosensory stimulation alone, in the absence of movement, can also modulate activity in this region in humans (Beauchamp, Yasar, Frye, & Ro, 2008; Foxe, et al., 2002; Schurmann, Caetano, Hlushchuk, Jousmaki, & Hari, 2006). The anatomic substrates underlying somatosensory inputs to auditory cortex in humans have not been fully characterized. However, recent diffusion tensor imaging studies have shown white matter projections between supramarginal gyrus and posterior superior temporal gyrus (Oishi, et al., 2008) and further indicated that these regions (and lateral premotor cortex) may be connected by the superior longitudinal fasciculus (Saur, et al., 2008; Saur, et al., 2010). Anatomical and physiological studies in macaques (e.g., Cappe & Barone, 2005; Falchier, et al., 2010; Ghazanfar & Lemus, 2010; Kayser, Logothetis, & Panzeri, 2010; Kayser,

Petkov, Augath, & Logothetis, 2007; Smiley & Falchier, 2009) and functional imaging studies in humans (Lehmann, et al., 2006; Martuzzi, et al., 2007; Meyer, Baumann, Marchina, & Jancke, 2007; van Atteveldt, Formisano, Goebel, & Blomert, 2004) have also established modulatory visual input to auditory cortex. The "sensory" end of the sensory-motor interface identified in posterior medial planum temporale (Hickok, Okada, & Serences, 2009; Tourville & Guenther, 2010) may therefore be polysensory, an integration of relevant sensory information from the auditory, somatosensory, and visual systems (cf. Dhanjal, et al., 2008).

Acknowledgements

This work was supported by the National Institute on Deafness and other Communication Disorders (R01 DC02852 and R01 DC07683, Frank Guenther, PI).

References

Aasland, W. A., Baum, S. R., & McFarland, D. H. (2006). Electropalatographic, acoustic, and perceptual data on adaptation to a palatal perturbation. *Journal of the Acoustical Society of America, 119*(4), 2372–2381.

Abbs, J. H., & Gracco, V. L. (1984). Control of complex motor gestures: Orofacial muscle responses to load perturbations of lip during speech. *Journal of Neurophysiology, 51*(4), 705–723.

Andersen, R. A. (1997). Multimodal integration for the representation of space in the posterior parietal cortex. *Philosophical Transactions of the Royal Society of London Series B: Biological Sciences, 352*(1360), 1421–1428.

Baciu, M., Abry, C., & Segebarth, C. M. (June 19–23, 2000). *Equivalence motrice et dominance hémisphérique. Le cas de la voyelle [u]. Étude IRMf.* Paper presented at the XXIIIemes Journees d'Etude sur la Parole, Aussois, France.

Bauer, J. J., Mittal, J., Larson, C. R., & Hain, T. C. (2006). Vocal responses to unanticipated perturbations in voice loudness feedback: An automatic mechanism for stabilizing voice amplitude. *Journal of the Acoustical Society of America, 119*(4), 2363–2371.

Baum, S. R., & McFarland, D. H. (1997). The development of speech adaptation to an artificial palate. *Journal of the Acoustical Society of America, 102*(4), 2353–2359.

Baum, S. R., & McFarland, D. H. (2000). Individual differences in speech adaptation to an artificial palate. *Journal of the Acoustical Society of America, 107*(6), 3572–3575.

Beauchamp, M. S., Yasar, N. E., Frye, R. E., & Ro, T. (2008). Touch, sound and vision in human superior temporal sulcus. *Neuroimage, 41*(3), 1011–1020.

Becker, J. T., MacAndrew, D. K., & Fiez, J. A. (1999). A comment on the functional localization of the phonological storage subsystem of working memory. *Brain and Cognition, 41*(1), 27–38.

Bernal, B., & Altman, N. (2010). The connectivity of the superior longitudinal fasciculus: A tractography DTI study. *Magnetic Resonance Imaging, 28*(2), 217–225.

Binder, J. R., Frost, J. A., Hammeke, T. A., Bellgowan, P. S., Springer, J. A., Kaufman, J. N., & Possing, E. T. (2000). Human temporal lobe activation by speech and nonspeech sounds. *Cerebral Cortex, 10*(5), 512–528.

Blakemore, S. J., Frith, C. D., & Wolpert, D. M. (2001). The cerebellum is involved in predicting the sensory consequences of action. *Neuroreport, 12*(9), 1879–1884.

Blakemore, S. J., Wolpert, D. M., & Frith, C. D. (1998). Central cancellation of self-produced tickle sensation. *Nature Neuroscience, 1*(7), 635–640.

Blakemore, S. J., Wolpert, D., & Frith, C. (2000). Why can't you tickle yourself? *Neuroreport, 11*(11), R11–16.

Bohland, J. W., & Guenther, F. H. (2006). An fMRI investigation of syllable sequence production. *Neuroimage, 32*, 821–841.

Boling, W., Reutens, D. C., & Olivier, A. (2002). Functional topography of the low postcentral area. *Journal of Neurosurgery, 97*(2), 388–395.

Botvinick, M. M., Braver, T. S., Barch, D. M., Carter, C. S., & Cohen, J. D. (2001). Conflict monitoring and cognitive control. *Psychol Rev, 108*(3), 624–652.

Bouchard, M.-E., Oullet, C., & Cohen, H. (2009). Speech development in prelingually deaf children with cochlear implants. *Language and Linguistics Compass, 3*(1), 1–18.

Brosch, M., Selezneva, E., & Scheich, H. (2005). Nonauditory events of a behavioral procedure activate auditory cortex of highly trained monkeys. *Journal of Neuroscience, 25*(29), 6797–6806.

Browman, C. P., & Goldstein, L. (1989). Articulatory gestures as phonologiecal units. *Phonology, 6*, 201–251.

Brown, S., Ingham, R. J., Ingham, J. C., Laird, A. R., & Fox, P. T. (2005). Stuttered and fluent speech production: An ALE meta-analysis of functional neuroimaging studies. *Human Brain Mapping, 25*(1), 105–117.

Buchsbaum, B. R., Olsen, R. K., Koch, P. F., Kohn, P., Kippenhan, J. S., & Berman, K. F. (2005). Reading, hearing, and the planum temporale. *Neuroimage, 24*(2), 444–454.

Budinger, E., & Scheich, H. (2009). Anatomical connections suitable for the direct processing of neuronal information of different modalities via the rodent primary auditory cortex. *Hearing Research, 258*(1–2), 16–27.

Burnett, T. A., & Larson, C. R. (2002). Early pitch-shift response is active in both steady and dynamic voice pitch control. *Journal of the Acoustical Society of America, 112*(3 Pt 1), 1058–1063.

Callan, D. E., Kent, R. D., Guenther, F. H., & Vorperian, H. K. (2000). An auditory-feedback-based neural network model of speech production that is robust to developmental changes in the size and shape of the articulatory system. *Journal of Speech, Language, and Hearing Research, 43*(3), 721–736.

Caplan, D., Gow, D., & Makris, N. (1995). Analysis of lesions by MRI in stroke patients with acoustic-phonetic processing deficits. *Neurology, 45*(2), 293–298.

Cappe, C., & Barone, P. (2005). Heteromodal connections supporting multisensory integration at low levels of cortical processing in the monkey. *Eur J Neurosci, 22*(11), 2886–2902.

Christoffels, I. K., Formisano, E., & Schiller, N. O. (2007). Neural correlates of verbal feedback processing: An fMRI study employing overt speech. *Human Brain Mapping, 28*(9), 868–879.

Cowie, R. I., & Douglas-Cowie, E. (1983). Speech production in profound post-lingual deafness. In M. E. Lutman & M. P. Haggard (Eds.), *Hearing science and hearing disorders* (pp. 183–231). New York: Academic Press.

Criscimagna-Hemminger, S. E., Bastian, A. J., & Shadmehr, R. (2010). Size of error affects cerebellar contributions to motor learning. *Journal of Neurophysiology, 103*(4), 2275–2284.

Curio, G., Neuloh, G., Numminen, J., Jousmaki, V., & Hari, R. (2000). Speaking modifies voice-evoked activity in the human auditory cortex. *Human Brain Mapping, 9*(4), 183–191.

Damasio, H., & Damasio, A. R. (1980). The anatomical basis of conduction aphasia. *Brain, 103*(2), 337–350.

Davidson, P. R., & Wolpert, D. M. (2005). Widespread access to predictive models in the motor system: A short review. *Journal of Neural Engineering, 2*(3), S313–S319.

Desmurget, M., & Grafton, S. (2000). Forward modeling allows feedback control for fast reaching movements. *Trends in Cognitive Science, 4*(11), 423–431.

Dhanjal, N. S., Handunnetthi, L., Patel, M. C., & Wise, R. J. (2008). Perceptual systems controlling speech production. *Journal of Neuroscience, 28*(40), 9969–9975.

Diedrichsen, J., Hashambhoy, Y., Rane, T., & Shadmehr, R. (2005). Neural correlates of reach errors. *Journal of Neuroscience, 25*(43), 9919–9931.

Donath, T. M., Natke, U., & Kalveram, K. T. (2002). Effects of frequency-shifted auditory feedback on voice F0 contours in syllables. *Journal of the Acoustical Society of America, 111*(1 Pt 1), 357–366.

Duffy, J. R. (2005). *Motor speech disorders: Substrates, differential diagnosis, and management* (2nd ed.). St. Louis, MO: Elsevier Mosby.

Eliades, S. J., & Wang, X. (2003). Sensory-motor interaction in the primate auditory cortex during self-initiated vocalizations. *Journal of Neurophysiology, 89*(4), 2194–2207.

Eliades, S. J., & Wang, X. (2005). Dynamics of auditory-vocal interaction in monkey auditory cortex. *Cerebral Cortex, 15*(10), 1510–1523.

Eliades, S. J., & Wang, X. (2008). Neural substrates of vocalization feedback monitoring in primate auditory cortex. *Nature, 453*(7198), 1102–1106.

Elman, J. (1981). Effects of frequency-shifted feedback on the pitch of vocal productions. *Journal of the Acoustical Society of America, 70*(1), 45–50.

Falchier, A., Schroeder, C. E., Hackett, T. A., Lakatos, P., Nascimento-Silva, S., Ulbert, I.,.... & Smiley, J. F. (2010). Projection from visual areas V2 and prostriata to caudal auditory cortex in the monkey. *Cerebral Cortex, 20*(7), 1529–1538.

Fesl, G., Moriggl, B., Schmid, U. D., Naidich, T. P., Herholz, K., & Yousry, T. A. (2003). Inferior central sulcus: Variations of anatomy and function on the example of the motor tongue area. *Neuroimage, 20*(1), 601–610.

Fiehler, K., Ullsperger, M., & von Cramon, D. Y. (2004). Neural correlates of error detection and error correction: Is there a common neuroanatomical substrate? *European Journal of Neuroscience, 19*(11), 3081–3087.

Fiez, J. A., & Petersen, S. E. (1998). Neuroimaging studies of word reading. *Proceedings of the National Academy of Sciences of the United States of America, 95*(3), 914–921.

Folkins, J. W., & Abbs, J. H. (1975). Lip and jaw motor control during speech: Responses to resistive loading of the jaw. *Journal of Speech and Hearing Research, 18*(1), 207–219.

Foxe, J. J., Wylie, G. R., Martinez, A., Schroeder, C. E., Javitt, D. C., Guilfoyle, D., & Murray, M. M. (2002). Auditory-somatosensory multisensory processing in auditory association cortex: An fMRI study. *Journal of Neurophysiology, 88*(1), 540–543.

Fu, K. M., Johnston, T. A., Shah, A. S., Arnold, L., Smiley, J., Hackett, T. A.,... & Schroeder, C. E. (2003). Auditory cortical neurons respond to somatosensory stimulation. *Journal of Neuroscience, 23*(20), 7510–7515.

Fu, C. H., Vythelingum, G. N., Brammer, M. J., Williams, S. C., Amaro, E., Jr., Andrew, C. M.,...& McGuire, P. K. (2006). An fMRI study of verbal self-monitoring: Neural correlates of auditory verbal feedback. *Cerebral Cortex, 16*(7), 969–977.

Gallese, V., Fadiga, L., Fogassi, L., & Rizzolatti, G. (1996). Action recognition in the premotor cortex. *Brain, 119*(Pt. 2), 593–609.

Ghazanfar, A. A., & Lemus, L. (2010). Multisensory integration: Vision boosts information through suppression in auditory cortex. *Current Biology, 20*(1), R22–R23.

Ghosh, S. S., Tourville, J. A., & Guenther, F. H. (2008). An fMRI study of the overt production of simple speech sounds. *Journal of Speech, Language, and Hearing Research, 51*, 1183–1202.

Giraud, A. L., & Price, C. J. (2001). The constraints functional neuroimaging places on classical models of auditory word processing. *Journal of Cognitive Neuroscience, 13*(6), 754–765.

Golfinopoulos, E., Tourville, J. A., Bohland, J. W., Ghosh, S. S., & Guenther, F. H. (2011). fMRI investigation of unexpected somatosensory feedback perturbation during speech. *Neuroimage, 55*(3), 1324–1338.

Gomi, H., Honda, M., Ito, T., & Murano, E. Z. (2002). Compensatory articulation during bilabial fricative production by regulating muscle stiffness. *Journal of Phonetics, 30*(3), 261–279.

Goodglass, H. (1993). *Understanding aphasia.* New York: Academic Press.

Gracco, V. L., & Abbs, J. H. (1985). Dynamic control of the perioral system during speech: Kinematic analyses of autogenic and nonautogenic sensorimotor processes. *Journal of Neurophysiology, 54*(2), 418–432.

Grodd, W., Hulsmann, E., Lotze, M., Wildgruber, D., & Erb, M. (2001). Sensorimotor mapping of the human cerebellum: fMRI evidence of somatotopic organization. *Human Brain Mapping, 13*(2), 55–73.

Guenther, F. H. (1994). A neural network model of speech acquisition and motor equivalent speech production. *Biological Cybernetics, 72*(1), 43–53.

Guenther, F. H. (1995). Speech sound acquisition, coarticulation, and rate effects in a neural network model of speech production. *Psychological Review, 102*(3), 594–621.

Guenther, F. H., Ghosh, S. S., & Tourville, J. A. (2006). Neural modeling and imaging of the cortical interactions underlying syllable production. *Brain and Language, 96*(3), 280–301.

Guenther, F. H., Hampson, M., & Johnson, D. (1998). A theoretical investigation of reference frames for the planning of speech movements. *Psychological Review, 105*(4), 611–633.

Hackett, T. A., De La Mothe, L. A., Ulbert, I., Karmos, G., Smiley, J., & Schroeder, C. E. (2007). Multisensory convergence in auditory cortex, II. Thalamocortical connections of the caudal superior temporal plane. *Journal of Comparative Neurology, 502*(6), 924–952.

Hashimoto, Y., & Sakai, K. L. (2003). Brain activations during conscious self-monitoring of speech production with delayed auditory feedback: An fMRI study. *Human Brain Mapping, 20*(1), 22–28.

Heinks-Maldonado, T. H., & Houde, J. F. (2005). Compensatory responses to brief perturbations of speech amplitude. *Acoustics Research Letters Online, 6*(3), 131–137.

Heinks-Maldonado, T. H., Mathalon, D. H., Gray, M., & Ford, J. M. (2005). Fine-tuning of auditory cortex during speech production. *Psychophysiology, 42*(2), 180–190.

Heinks-Maldonado, T. H., Nagarajan, S. S., & Houde, J. F. (2006). Magnetoencephalographic evidence for a precise forward model in speech production. *Neuroreport, 17*(13), 1375–1379.

Held, R., & Freedman, S. J. (1963). Plasticity in human sensorimotor control. *Science, 142*, 455–462.

Helmholtz, H. (1925). *Treatise on physiological optics* (Electronic edition [2001]: University of Pennsylvania ed. Vol. 3). Rochester, NY: Optical Society of America.

Hickok, G., Buchsbaum, B., Humphries, C., & Muftuler, T. (2003). Auditory-motor interaction revealed by fMRI: Speech, music, and working memory in area Spt. *Journal of Cognitive Neuroscience, 15*(5), 673–682.

Hickok, G., Erhard, P., Kassubek, J., Helms-Tillery, A. K., Naeve-Velguth, S., Strupp, J. P.,...& Ugurbil, K. (2000). A functional magnetic resonance imaging study of the role of left posterior superior temporal gyrus in speech production: Implications for the explanation of conduction aphasia. *Neuroscience Letters, 287*(2), 156–160.

Hickok, G., Okada, K., & Serences, J. T. (2009). Area Spt in the human planum temporale supports sensory-motor integration for speech processing. *Journal of Neurophysiology, 101*(5), 2725–2732.

Hickok, G., & Poeppel, D. (2004). Dorsal and ventral streams: A framework for understanding aspects of the functional anatomy of language. *Cognition, 92*(1–2), 67–99.

Hickok, G., & Poeppel, D. (2007). The cortical organization of speech processing. *Nature Reviews Neuroscience, 8*(5), 393–402.

Hillenbrand, J., Clark, M. J., & Nearey, T. M. (2001). Effects of consonant environment on vowel formant patterns. *Journal of the Acoustical Society of America, 109*(2), 748–763.

Hillenbrand, J., Getty, L. A., Clark, M. J., & Wheeler, K. (1995). Acoustic characteristics of American English vowels. *Journal of the Acoustical Society of America, 97*(5 Pt 1), 3099–3111.

Hillis, A. E., Work, M., Barker, P. B., Jacobs, M. A., Breese, E. L., & Maurer, K. (2004). Re-examining the brain regions crucial for orchestrating speech articulation. *Brain, 127*(Pt 7), 1479–1487.

Hirano, S., Kojima, H., Naito, Y., Honjo, I., Kamoto, Y., Okazawa, H.,...& Konishi, J. (1997). Cortical processing mechanism for vocalization with auditory verbal feedback. *Neuroreport, 8*(9–10), 2379–2382.

Houde, J. F. (2009). There's more to speech perception than meets the ear. *Proceedings of the National Academy of Sciences USA, 106*(48), 20139–20140.

Houde, J. F., & Jordan, M. I. (2002). Sensorimotor adaptation of speech I: Compensation and adaptation. *Journal of Speech, Language, and Hearing Research, 45*(2), 295–310.

Houde, J. F., Nagarajan, S. S., Sekihara, K., & Merzenich, M. M. (2002). Modulation of the auditory cortex during speech: An MEG study. *Journal of Cognitive Neuroscience, 14*(8), 1125–1138.

Ito, T., Kimura, T., & Gomi, H. (2005). The motor cortex is involved in reflexive compensatory adjustment of speech articulation. *Neuroreport, 16*(16), 1791–1794.

Ito, T., & Ostry, D. J. (2010). Somatosensory contribution to motor learning due to facial skin deformation. *Journal of Neurophysiology, 104*(3), 1230–1238.

Ito, T., Tiede, M., & Ostry, D. J. (2009). Somatosensory function in speech perception. *Proceedings of the National Academy of Sciences of the United States of America, 106*(4), 1245–1248.

Jenmalm, P., Schmitz, C., Forssberg, H., & Ehrsson, H. H. (2006). Lighter or heavier than predicted: Neural correlates of corrective mechanisms during erroneously programmed lifts. *Journal of Neuroscience, 26*(35), 9015–9021.

Jones, J. A., & Munhall, K. G. (2000). Perceptual calibration of F0 production: Evidence from feedback perturbation. *Journal of the Acoustical Society of America, 108*(3 Pt 1), 1246–1251.

Jones, J. A., & Munhall, K. G. (2002). The role of auditory feedback during phonation: Studies of Mandarin tone production. *Journal of Phonetics, 30*, 303–320.

Jones, J. A., & Munhall, K. G. (2003). Learning to produce speech with an altered vocal tract: The role of auditory feedback. *J Acoust Soc Am, 113*(1), 532–543.

Jones, J. A., & Munhall, K. G. (2005). Remapping auditory-motor representations in voice production. *Current Biology, 15*(19), 1768–1772.

Jonides, J., Schumacher, E. H., Smith, E. E., Koeppe, R. A., Awh, E., Reuter-Lorenz, P. A.,...& Willis, C. R. (1998). The role of parietal cortex in verbal working memory. *Journal of Neuroscience, 18*(13), 5026–5034.

Kalinowski, J., Stuart, A., Sark, S., & Armson, J. (1996). Stuttering amelioration at various auditory feedback delays and speech rates. *European Journal of Disorders of Communication, 31*(3), 259–269.

Kawato, M. (1999). Internal models for motor control and trajectory planning. *Current Opinions in Neurobiology, 9*(6), 718–727.

Kayser, C., Logothetis, N. K., & Panzeri, S. (2010). Visual enhancement of the information representation in auditory cortex. *Current Biology, 20*(1), 19–24.

Kayser, C., Petkov, C. I., Augath, M., & Logothetis, N. K. (2007). Functional imaging reveals visual modulation of specific fields in auditory cortex. *Journal of Neuroscience, 27*(8), 1824–1835.

Kelly, R. M., & Strick, P. L. (2003). Cerebellar loops with motor cortex and prefrontal cortex of a nonhuman primate. *Journal of Neuroscience, 23*(23), 8432–8444.

Kelso, J. A., Tuller, B., Vatikiotis-Bateson, E., & Fowler, C. A. (1984). Functionally specific articulatory cooperation following jaw perturbations during speech: Evidence for coordinative structures. *Journal of Experimental Psychology: Human Perception and Performance, 10*(6), 812–832.

Lakatos, P., Chen, C. M., O'Connell, M. N., Mills, A., & Schroeder, C. E. (2007). Neuronal oscillations and multisensory interaction in primary auditory cortex. *Neuron, 53*(2), 279–292.

Lane, H., Matthies, M. L., Guenther, F. H., Denny, M., Perkell, J. S., Stockmann, E.,...& Zandipour, M. (2007). Effects of short- and long-term changes in auditory feedback on vowel and sibilant contrasts. *Journal of Speech, Language, and Hearing Research, 50*(4), 913–927.

Lane, H., & Tranel, B. (1971). The Lombard sign and the role of hearing in speech. *Journal of Speech Language and Hearing Research, 14*, 677–709.

Lane, H., & Webster, J. W. (1991). Speech deterioration in postlingually deafened adults. *Journal of the Acoustical Society of America, 89*(2), 859–866.

Larson, C. R., Burnett, T. A., Kiran, S., & Hain, T. C. (2000). Effects of pitch-shift velocity on voice F0 responses. *Journal of the Acoustical Society of America, 107*(1), 559–564.

Lehmann, C., Herdener, M., Esposito, F., Hubl, D., di Salle, F., Scheffler, K.,...& Seifritz, E. (2006). Differential patterns of multisensory interactions in core and belt areas of human auditory cortex. *Neuroimage, 31*(1), 294–300.

Lemus, L., Hernandez, A., Luna, R., Zainos, A., & Romo, R. (2010). Do sensory cortices process more than one sensory modality during perceptual judgments? *Neuron, 67*(2), 335–348.

Levelt, W. J., Roelofs, A., & Meyer, A. S. (1999). A theory of lexical access in speech production. *Behavioral and Brain Sciences, 22*(1), 1–38; discussion 38–75.

Levelt, W. J., & Wheeldon, L. (1994). Do speakers have access to a mental syllabary? *Cognition, 50*(1–3), 239–269.

Lindblom, B., Lubker, J., & Gay, T. (1979). Formant frequencies of some fixed-mandible vowels and a model of speech motor programming by predictive simulation. *Journal of Phonetics, 7*(2), 147–161.

Lombard, E. (1911). Le signe de l'elevation de la voix. *Annales des Maladies de l'Oreille du Larynx, 37*, 101–119.

Lotze, M., Erb, M., Flor, H., Huelsmann, E., Godde, B., & Grodd, W. (2000). fMRI evaluation of somatotopic representation in human primary motor cortex. *Neuroimage, 11*(5 Pt 1), 473–581.

Luppino, G., Murata, A., Govoni, P., & Matelli, M. (1999). Largely segregated parietofrontal connections linking rostral intraparietal cortex (areas AIP and VIP) and the ventral premotor cortex (areas F5 and F4). *Experimental Brain Research, 128*(1–2), 181–187.

Maeda, S. (1990). Compensatory articulation during speech: Evidence from the analysis and synthesis of vocal tract shapes using an articulatory model. In W. J. Hardcastle & A. Marchal (Eds.), *Speech production and speech modeling*. Boston: Kluwer Academic Publishers.

Makris, N., Kennedy, D. N., McInerney, S., Sorensen, A. G., Wang, R., Caviness, V. S., Jr., & Pandya, D. N.. (2005). Segmentation of subcomponents within the superior longitudinal fascicle in humans: A quantitative, in vivo, DT-MRI study. *Cereb Cortex, 15*(6), 854–869.

Martuzzi, R., Murray, M. M., Michel, C. M., Thiran, J. P., Maeder, P. P., Clarke, S., & Meuli, R. A. (2007). Multisensory interactions within human primary cortices revealed by BOLD dynamics. *Cerebral Cortex, 17*(7), 1672–1679.

Matsumoto, R., Nair, D. R., LaPresto, E., Najm, I., Bingaman, W., Shibasaki, H., & Lüders, H. O. (2004). Functional connectivity in the human language system: A cortico-cortical evoked potential study. *Brain, 127*(Pt 10), 2316–2330.

Max, L., Guenther, F. H., Gracco, V. L., Ghosh, S. S., & Wallace, M. E. (2004). Unstable or insufficiently activated internal models and feedback-biased motor control as sources of dysfluency: A theoretical model of stuttering. *Contemporary Issues in Communication Science and Disorders, 31*, 105–122.

Mazziotta, J., Toga, A., Evans, A., Fox, P., Lancaster, J., Zilles, K., . . . & Mazoyer B. (2001). A four-dimensional probabilistic atlas of the human brain. *Journal of the American Medical Informatics Association, 8*(5), 401–430.

McFarland, D. H., Baum, S. R., & Chabot, C. (1996). Speech compensation to structural modifications of the oral cavity. *Journal of the Acoustical Society of America, 100*(2 Pt 1), 1093–1104.

McGuire, P. K., Silbersweig, D. A., & Frith, C. D. (1996). Functional neuroanatomy of verbal self-monitoring. *Brain, 119*(Pt. 3), 907–917.

McIntosh, A. R., & Gonzalez-Lima, F. (1994). Structural equation modeling and its application to network analysis in functional imaging. *Human Brain Mapping, 2*, 2–22.

McLeod, S., & Bleile, K. (2003). *Neurological and developmental foundations of speech acquisition*. Paper presented at the American Speech-Language-Hearing Association, Chicago, IL.

Meyer, M., Baumann, S., Marchina, S., & Jancke, L. (2007). Hemodynamic responses in human multisensory and auditory association cortex to purely visual stimulation. *BMC Neuroscience, 8*, 14.

Miall, R. C., & Wolpert, D. M. (1996). Forward models for physiological motor control. *Neural Networks, 9*(8), 1265–1279.

Nasir, S. M., & Ostry, D. J. (2006). Somatosensory precision in speech production. *Current Biology, 16*(19), 1918–1923.

Nasir, S. M., & Ostry, D. J. (2008). Speech motor learning in profoundly deaf adults. *Nature Neuroscience, 11*(10), 1217–1222.

Nasir, S. M., & Ostry, D. J. (2009). Auditory plasticity and speech motor learning. *Proceedings of the National Academy of Sciences of the United States of America, 106*(48), 20470–20475.

Neilson, M., & Neilson, P. (1987). Speech motor control and stuttering: A computational model of adaptive sensory-motor processing. *Speech Communication, 6*, 325–333.

Nieto-Castanon, A., Guenther, F. H., Perkell, J. S., & Curtin, H. D. (2005). A modeling investigation of articulatory variability and acoustic stability during American English /r/ production. *Journal of the Acoustical Society of America, 117*(5), 3196–3212.

Numminen, J., & Curio, G. (1999). Differential effects of overt, covert and replayed speech on vowel-evoked responses of the human auditory cortex. *Neuroscience Letters, 272*(1), 29–32.

Numminen, J., Salmelin, R., & Hari, R. (1999). Subject's own speech reduces reactivity of the human auditory cortex. *Neuroscience Letters, 265*(2), 119–122.

O'Reilly, J. X., Beckmann, C. F., Tomassini, V., Ramnani, N., & Johansen-Berg, H. (2009). Distinct and overlapping functional zones in the cerebellum defined by resting state functional connectivity. *Cerebral Cortex, 20*(4), 953–965.

Oishi, K., Zilles, K., Amunts, K., Faria, A., Jiang, H., Li, X., . . . & Mori, S. (2008). Human brain white matter atlas: Identification and assignment of common anatomical structures in superficial white matter. *Neuroimage, 43*(3), 447–457.

Okada, K., & Hickok, G. (2006). Left posterior auditory-related cortices participate both in speech perception and speech production: Neural overlap revealed by fMRI. *Brain and Language, 98*(1), 112–117.

Okada, K., Smith, K. R., Humphries, C., & Hickok, G. (2003). Word length modulates neural activity in auditory cortex during covert object naming. *Neuroreport, 14*(18), 2323–2326.

Oller, D. K., & Eilers, R. E. (1988). The role of audition in infant babbling. *Child Development, 59*(2), 441–449.

Ozdemir, E., Norton, A., & Schlaug, G. (2006). Shared and distinct neural correlates of singing and speaking. *Neuroimage, 33*(2), 628–635.

Perkell, J. S., Denny, M., Lane, H., Guenther, F., Matthies, M. L., Tiede, M., . . . & Burton, E. (2007). Effects of masking noise on vowel and sibilant contrasts in normal-hearing speakers and postlingually deafened cochlear implant users. *Journal of the Acoustical Society of America, 121*(1), 505–518.

Perkell, J. S., Guenther, F. H., Lane, H., Matthies, M. L., Perrier, P., Vick, J., . . . & Zandipour, M. (2000). A theory of speech motor control and supporting data from speakers with normal hearing and profound hearing loss. *Journal of Phonetics, 28*, 232–272.

Perkell, J. S., Guenther, F. H., Lane, H., Matthies, M. L., Stockmann, E., Tiede, M., & Zandipour, M. (2004). The distinctness of speakers' productions of vowel contrasts is related to their discrimination of the contrasts. *Journal of the Acoustical Society of America, 116*(4 Pt 1), 2338–2344.

Perkell, J. S., Matthies, M. L., Tiede, M., Lane, H., Zandipour, M., Marrone, N., et al. (2004). The distinctness of speakers' /s/-/ʃ/ contrast is related to their auditory discrimination and use of an articulatory saturation effect. *Journal of Speech, Language, and Hearing Research, 47*(6), 1259–1269.

Pittman, A. L., & Wiley, T. L. (2001). Recognition of speech produced in noise. *Journal of Speech, Language, and Hearing Research, 44*(3), 487–496.

Pugh, K. R., Mencl, W. E., Jenner, A. R., Katz, L., Frost, S. J., Lee, J. R.,…& Shaywitz, B. A. (2001). Neurobiological studies of reading and reading disability. *Journal of Communication Disorders, 34*(6), 479–492.

Purcell, D. W., & Munhall, K. G. (2006a). Adaptive control of vowel formant frequency: Evidence from real-time formant manipulation. *Journal of the Acoustical Society of America, 120*(2), 966–977.

Purcell, D. W., & Munhall, K. G. (2006b). Compensation following real-time manipulation of formants in isolated vowels. *Journal of the Acoustical Society of America, 119*(4), 2288–2297.

Rauschecker, J. P. (2010). An expanded role for the dorsal auditory pathway in sensorimotor control and integration. *Hearing Research, 271*(1–2), 16–25.

Rauschecker, J. P., & Scott, S. K. (2009). Maps and streams in the auditory cortex: Nonhuman primates illuminate human speech processing. *Nature Neuroscience, 12*(6), 718–724.

Redding, G. M., & Wallace, B. (2006). Generalization of prism adaptation. *Journal of Experimental Psychology: Human Perception and Performance, 32*(4), 1006–1022.

Riecker, A., Ackermann, H., Wildgruber, D., Dogil, G., & Grodd, W. (2000). Opposite hemispheric lateralization effects during speaking and singing at motor cortex, insula and cerebellum. *Neuroreport, 11*(9), 1997–2000.

Rizzolatti, G., & Arbib, M. A. (1998). Language within our grasp. *Trends in Neurosciences, 21*(5), 188–194.

Rizzolatti, G., & Craighero, L. (2004). The mirror-neuron system. *Annual Review of Neuroscience, 27*, 169–192.

Rizzolatti, G., Fadiga, L., Gallese, V., & Fogassi, L. (1996). Premotor cortex and the recognition of motor actions. *Brain Research Cognitive Brain Research, 3*(2), 131–141.

Rizzolatti, G., Fogassi, L., & Gallese, V. (1997). Parietal cortex: from sight to action. *Current Opinions in Neurobiology, 7*(4), 562–567.

Rizzolatti, G., & Luppino, G. (2001). The cortical motor system. *Neuron, 31*(6), 889–901.

Robin, D. A., Guenther, F. H., Narayana, S., Jacks, A., Tourville, J. A., Ramage, A. E.,…& Fox, P. (2008). *A transcranial magnetic stimulation virtual lesion study of speech.* Paper presented at the Proceedings of the Conference on Motor Speech, Monterey, CA.

Robin, D. A., Jacks, A., & Ramage, A. E. (2007). The neural substrates of apraxia of speech as uncovered by brain imaging: A critical review. In R. J. Ingham (Ed.), *Neuroimaging in communication sciences and disorders.* San Diego: Plural Publishing.

Rushworth, M. F., Behrens, T. E., & Johansen-Berg, H. (2006). Connection patterns distinguish 3 regions of human parietal cortex. *Cereb Cortex, 16*(10), 1418–1430.

Ryan, B. P., & Vankirk, B. (1974). Establishment, transfer, and maintenance of fluent speech in 50 stutterers using delayed auditory feedback and operant procedures. *Journal of Speech and Hearing Disorders, 39*(1), 3–10.

Saur, D., Kreher, B. W., Schnell, S., Kummerer, D., Kellmeyer, P., Vry, M. S.,…& Weiller, C. (2008). Ventral and dorsal pathways for language. *Proceedings of the National Academy of Sciences of the United States of America, 105*(46), 18035–18040.

Saur, D., Schelter, B., Schnell, S., Kratochvil, D., Kupper, H., Kellmeyer, P.,…& Weiller, C. (2010). Combining functional and anatomical connectivity reveals brain networks for auditory language comprehension. *Neuroimage, 49*(4), 3187–3197.

Schmahmann, J. D., & Pandya, D. N. (1997). The cerebro-cerebellar system. *International Review of Neurobiology, 41*, 31–60.

Schmitz, C., Jenmalm, P., Ehrsson, H. H., & Forssberg, H. (2005). Brain activity during predictable and unpredictable weight changes when lifting objects. *Journal of Neurophysiology, 93*(3), 1498–1509.

Schroeder, C. E., Lindsley, R. W., Specht, C., Marcovici, A., Smiley, J. F., & Javitt, D. C. (2001). Somatosensory input to auditory association cortex in the macaque monkey. *Journal of Neurophysiology, 85*(3), 1322–1327.

Schurmann, M., Caetano, G., Hlushchuk, Y., Jousmaki, V., & Hari, R. (2006). Touch activates human auditory cortex. *Neuroimage, 30*(4), 1325–1331.

Scott, S. K., Blank, C. C., Rosen, S., & Wise, R. J. (2000). Identification of a pathway for intelligible speech in the left temporal lobe. *Brain, 123*(Pt. 12), 2400–2406.

Shaiman, S. (1989). Kinematic and electromyographic responses to perturbation of the jaw. *Journal of the Acoustical Society of America, 86*(1), 78–88.

Shiller, D. M., Sato, M., Gracco, V. L., & Baum, S. R. (2009). Perceptual recalibration of speech sounds following speech motor learning. *Journal of the Acoustical Society of America, 125*(2), 1103–1113.

Sidtis, J. J., Gomez, C., Groshong, A., Strother, S. C., & Rottenberg, D. A. (2006). Mapping cerebral blood flow during speech production in hereditary ataxia. *Neuroimage, 31*(1), 246–254.

Smiley, J. F., & Falchier, A. (2009). Multisensory connections of monkey auditory cerebral cortex. *Hearing Research, 258*(1–2), 37–46.

Smiley, J. F., Hackett, T. A., Ulbert, I., Karmas, G., Lakatos, P., Javitt, D. C., & Schroeder, C. E. (2007). Multisensory convergence in auditory cortex. I. Cortical connections of the caudal superior temporal plane in macaque monkeys. *Journal of Comparative Neurology, 502*(6), 894–923.

Smith, C. R. (1975). Residual hearing and speech production in deaf children. *Journal of Speech and Hearing Research, 18*(4), 795–811.

Smith, M. A., & Shadmehr, R. (2005). Intact ability to learn internal models of arm dynamics in Huntington's disease but not cerebellar degeneration. *Journal of Neurophysiology, 93*(5), 2809–2821.

Soros, P., Sokoloff, L. G., Bose, A., McIntosh, A. R., Graham, S. J., & Stuss, D. T. (2006). Clustered functional MRI of overt speech production. *Neuroimage, 32*(1), 376–387.

Stuart, A., Kalinowski, J., Rastatter, M. P., & Lynch, K. (2002). Effect of delayed auditory feedback on normal speakers at two speech rates. *Journal of the Acoustical Society of America, 111*(5 Pt 1), 2237–2241.

Summers, W. V., Pisoni, D. B., Bernacki, R. H., Pedlow, R. I., & Stokes, M. A. (1988). Effects of noise on speech production: acoustic and perceptual analyses. *Journal of the Acoustical Society of America, 84*(3), 917–928.

Tartter, V. C., Gomes, H., & Litwin, E. (1993). Some acoustic effects of listening to noise on speech production. *Journal of the Acoustical Society of America, 94*(4), 2437–2440.

Terband, H., Maassen, B., Guenther, F. H., & Brumberg, J. (2009). Computational neural modeling of speech motor control in childhood apraxia of speech (CAS). *Journal of Speech Language and Hearing Research, 52*(6), 1595–1609.

Tourville, J. A., & Guenther, F. (2010). The DIVA model: A neural theory of speech acquisition and production. *Language and Cognitive Processes.* Retrieved from doi:10.1080/01690960903498424

Tourville, J. A., Reilly, K. J., & Guenther, F. H. (2008). Neural mechanisms underlying auditory feedback control of speech. *Neuroimage, 39*(3), 1429–1443.

Toyomura, A., Koyama, S., Miyamoto, T., Terao, A., Omori, T., Murohashi, H., & Kuriki, S. (2007). Neural correlates of auditory feedback control in human. *Neuroscience, 146*(2), 499–503.

Tremblay, S., Shiller, D. M., & Ostry, D. J. (2003). Somatosensory basis of speech production. *Nature, 423*(6942), 866–869.

Tsao, Y. C., & Weismer, G. (1997). Interspeaker variation in habitual speaking rate: evidence for a neuromuscular component. *Journal of Speech, Language, and Hearing Research, 40*(4), 858–866.

Tseng, Y. W., Diedrichsen, J., Krakauer, J. W., Shadmehr, R., & Bastian, A. J. (2007). Sensory prediction errors drive cerebellum-dependent adaptation of reaching. *Journal of Neurophysiology,* 98, 54–62.

Turkeltaub, P. E., Eden, G. F., Jones, K. M., & Zeffiro, T. A. (2002). Meta-analysis of the functional neuroanatomy of single-word reading: Method and validation. *Neuroimage, 16*(3 Pt 1), 765–780.

van Atteveldt, N., Formisano, E., Goebel, R., & Blomert, L. (2004). Integration of letters and speech sounds in the human brain. *Neuron, 43*(2), 271–282.

van Veen, V., Cohen, J. D., Botvinick, M. M., Stenger, V. A., & Carter, C. S. (2001). Anterior cingulate cortex, conflict monitoring, and levels of processing. *Neuroimage, 14*(6), 1302–1308.

Villacorta, V. M., Perkell, J. S., & Guenther, F. H. (2007). Sensorimotor adaptation to feedback perturbations on vowel acoustics and its relation to perception. *Journal of the Acoustical Society of America, 122*(4), 2306–2319.

von Holst, E., & Mittelstaedt, H. (1950). Das reafferenzprinzip. *Naturewissenschaften, 37,* 464–476.

Waldstein, R. S. (1990). Effects of postlingual deafness on speech production: Implications for the role of auditory feedback. *Journal of the Acoustical Society of America, 88*(5), 2099–2114.

Wasaka, T., Hoshiyama, M., Nakata, H., Nishihira, Y., & Kakigi, R. (2003). Gating of somatosensory evoked magnetic fields during the preparatory period of self-initiated finger movement. *Neuroimage, 20*(3), 1830–1838.

Wise, R. J., Greene, J., Buchel, C., & Scott, S. K. (1999). Brain regions involved in articulation. *Lancet, 353*(9158), 1057–1061.

Wise, R. J., Scott, S. K., Blank, S. C., Mummery, C. J., Murphy, K., & Warburton, E. A. (2001). Separate neural subsystems within "Wernicke's area." *Brain, 124*(Pt. 1), 83–95.

Wolpert, D. M., & Flanagan, J. R. (2001). Motor prediction. *Current Biology, 11*(18), R729–R732.

Wolpert, D. M., & Kawato, M. (1998). Multiple paired forward and inverse models for motor control. *Neural Networks, 11*(7–8), 1317–1329.

Yates, A. J. (1963). Delayed auditory feedback. *Psychological Bulletin, 60,* 213–232.

Zarate, J. M., & Zatorre, R. J. (2005). Neural substrates governing audiovocal integration for vocal pitch regulation in singing. *Annals of the New York Academy of Science, 1060,* 404–408.

Zemlin, W. R. (1998). *Speech and hearing science anatomy and physiology* (4th ed). Needham Heights, MA: Allyn and Bacon.

Zheng, Z. Z., Munhall, K. G., & Johnsrude, I. S. (2010). Functional overlap between regions involved in speech perception and in monitoring one's own voice during speech production. *Journal of Cognitive Neuroscience, 22*(8), 1770–1781.

INDEX

Page numbers followed by *f* and *t* in italics refer to figures and page numbers respectively.

Folk, J., 233, 234, 239
Formisano, E., 432
Forshaw, P. J., 335
Fowler, C. A., 263, 317, 319
Freedman, M., 444
Frequency-lag hypothesis, 166–70, 172, 176–78, 187–88
Freud, S., 96
Frey, S., 287
Friederici, A. D., 54, 57, 58, 59, 60–61t, 62, 64
Friedmann, N., 58
Friston, K., 112
Fromkin, V. A., 400
Fujimura, O., 217
Fussell, S. R., 14

G
Gahl, S., 96, 252
Galluzzi, C., 233, 249, 445
Ganushchak, L. Y., 431
Garcia, S., 319
Garcia-Bunuel, L., 424
Garrett, M. F., 25, 33, 89, 101, 137, 145, 146, 240, 400
Gay, T., 466
Gelastic epilepsy, 282
Gelb, I. J., 331–32
Gerfen, C., 174–75
German Sign Language, 384, 387, 400
Gertsberg, N., 401
Geschwind, N., 286, 287
Gestural scores, 214–15, 214f, 219, 246, 468
Gesture as a Simulated Action theory, 457
Gestures. see also articulatory phonology; discourse
    abstraction, 451, 454
    Action Generator, 452f, 453, 454–56, 455f
    Addressee Model, 453–54, 457n1
    architecture, general, 452–53, 452f
    articulatory in phonetic processing, 246
    articulatory phonology, 211–14, 211f, 224n1
    beat, 451
    classification, 451–52
    Communications Planner, 452–54, 452f, 457n1
    conceptualization load, 455, 455f
    conceptualizer, 420–21, 421f, 452, 452f
    conceptual planning, 455–56, 455f
    coordination of consonant gestures, 219–24, 220f
    cultural variation, 457
    deictic (pointing), 451, 454, 457
    developmental disorders, 457
    discourse, 296, 301–3, 305
    Discourse Model, 452–53, 452f
    emblem, 451–52
    environment, 454
    Gesture as a Simulated Action theory, 457
    grammatical planning
    Growth Point theory, 456–57

iconic, 451
imagery activation, 456
Interaction Record, 453
lexical retrieval, 456
message encoding, 452–53, 452f, 455–56
Message Generator, 452–56, 452f, 455f
modality, 454
mouth, mouthings in sign language, 388
neural substrates, 457
organization of, 214–17, 214f, 224n2
perceptual loop model, 419, 419f, 422, 423, 425, 452–53, 452f
Piagetian conservation task, 456
syntax, 454–55, 455f
working memory, 456
Ghosh, S. S., 280
Giles, H., 312
Glasspool, D. W., 351, 352
Gleitman, L. R., 5, 6, 7, 27–28, 32
Glenberg, A. M., 121, 122, 140
Glover, S., 121
Goldberg, A. E., 78
Goldberg, R. F., 126
Goldinger, S. D., 317
Goldrick, M., 174, 187, 230, 233, 234, 239, 246, 248, 249, 253, 265
Goldsmith, J. A., 263
Goldstein, L., 219, 248, 265, 266
Golfinopoulos, E., 466
Gollan, T. H., 168, 169, 187, 188, 189, 192, 401
Gonnerman, L. M., 136
Gordon, B., 124
Gordon, J. K., 71, 239
GowD. W., 265
Grabowski, T. J., 407–8
Granà, A., 249
Gray, W. D., 135
Green, D. W., 183, 192
Green, I., 438
Gregory, S. W., 316
Grice, H. P., 334
Griffin, Z. M., 7, 72, 76, 238, 444
Griffiths, T. L., 139, 140
Grosjacques, G., 349
Grosvald, M., 397
Growth Point theory, 456–57
Guenther, F. H., 280, 287–88
Guillemin, A., 408
Guo, T., 173, 175, 189
Gutiérrez-Sigut, E., 402
Gygax, L., 319

H
Hadar, U., 58
Haendiges, A. N., 346
Hage, S. R., 281
Hagoort, P., 53, 59, 234
Hahne, A., 54, 57
Hain, T. C., 319
Hale, J., 84
Hall, K. C., 315
Halle, M., 261

Hallé, P. A., 353
Hall-Lew, L., 309
Hampson, M., 287–88
Happ, D., 400
Harris, A. C, 161
Harris, R., 333
Harris, Z., 138
Hart, J., 124
Hartsuiker, R. J., 79, 233, 239, 419, 419f, 423, 425–31, 425f, 426f, 430f, 433
Hauk, O., 126, 127
Hawkins, S., 84, 262, 264
Hay, J., 309
Herault, L., 349
Hermes, A., 220
Hickok, G., 57, 287, 288, 405, 465
Hihara, S., 281
Hildebrandt, U. C., 401
Hillis, A. E., 345, 350
Hinton, G.E., 135
Hirschberg, J., 320
Hitch, G., 437
Hockett, C. F., 163n2, 261
Hoenkamp, E., 70–71
Hohenberger, A., 400
Holowka, S., 399
Houghton, G., 344, 351, 352
Housum, J., 263
Howard, D., 424
Howell, P., 319, 320
Huber, W., 424
Huettig, F., 425, 425f
Humphries, C., 57
Huntington chorea, 279
Huntington disease, 279

I
Implicit priming, 89
Indefrey, P., 426, 432
Independent components hypothesis, 373, 374f, 375
Ingvar, M., 336
Interactive activation, 91–92, 142
Interactive two-step model, 90, 93–94, 93f, 96
Interactivity in naming, 109–10
International Phonetic Alphabet (IPA), 211, 264
Intrusive schwa errors, 250
Iriki, A., 281
Ito, T., 466, 471
Ivanova, I., 188

J
Jaeger, J. J., 55
Jaeger, T. F., 79
Janciauskas, M., 79
Jannedy, S., 309
Janson, T., 314
January, D., 5, 6, 7
Japanese Sign Language, 386–87
Jay, I. C., 317
Jefferies, E., 111

Shaw, J., 220
Shelton, J. R., 124
Shetreet, E., 58
Shetreet, E., 58t
Shockley, K., 317
Short-term memory. *see* working memory
Sign language
    acquisition, 379–80, 389–90, 393, 398
    affixation, 383
    American Sign Language (ASL), 379,
        381–87, 390, 394–95, 395f, 398–401,
        404, 408
    aphasia, 394, 404, 405, 408
    articulation rate, 395–96
    articulators, multiple, 381–82, 396, 406
    aspectual modulations, 384
    assimilation, 398
    babbling, 398–99
    bilingualism, 390
    borrowing, 385
    Boston Diagnostic Aphasic
        Examination, 394
    Brazilian Sign Language, 386–87
    British Sign Language (BSL), 379, 382,
        387, 404
    Broca's area errors, 406, 407, 409
    Cambodian Sign Language, 394, 395f
    Catalan Sign Language, 402–3
    classifier constructions, 384–85, 389, 400
    coarticulation, 396–98
    compounding, 383
    constructed dialogue and action, 387
    cortical stimulation mapping, 406–7
    discourse, 379, 386–89, 408
    dominance condition, 396
    embedded structures, 386
    finger configuration, 381
    finger selection, 381, 390n1
    fingerspelling, 381, 385, 390n1
    first signs, 399–400
    formal narrative, 387
    formational and semantic errors, 406–7
    frontal orbitalis stimulation, 407
    functional neuroimaging, 394
    German Sign Language, 384, 387, 400
    gestural space, 379, 387–88, 408–9
    hands, one *vs.* both, 381–82, 396, 406
    handshape, 381, 382, 384, 394, 395f,
        399–400
    handshape errors, 405
    Hold-Move model, 382
    inferior ventral region stimulation, 407
    information compression, 396
    interfering stimulus studies, 401–2
    Japanese Sign Language, 386–87
    lexical family, 385, 398
    lexicon, 382–85
    linguistic structure impacts, 380
    location, 381, 398
    manual-nonmanual simultaneity, 388
    manual simultaneity, 388–89
    memory, 403–4
    modality, 380, 390, 396, 400
    morphology, 382–85, 389, 395
    mouth gestures, mouthings, 388
    movement, 381, 382
    naming, 387, 400–403, 406–9
    negation, 386
    neuroimaging studies, 407–9
    new word creation, 385
    nonce signs, 382
    numeral incorporation, 384
    orientation, 381
    pantomimes, 409
    parameters, 381–82, 394
    paraphasia, 404–6
    Parkinson disease, 407
    phonesthemes, 385
    phonology, phonetics, 380–82, 389,
        394–95, 395f, 400–403
    priming studies, 402
    production errors, 394, 399–400
    prosody, 394–95
    reduction, 383–84, 398
    reduplication, 383
    research historically, 393–94
    Russian Sign Language, 401
    segments, 394
    self-monitoring, 401, 432
    sequentiality, 380–83, 386–87
    sign-picture interference task, 402–3
    simultaneity, 380–81, 383–85, 387–89,
        390n1, 396, 403
    "slips of the hand," 400
    spoken *vs.*, 379–80
    stimulus onset asynchronies, 401–2
    superior parietal lobule, 408
    superior pars triangularis stimulation, 407
    supramarginal gyrus errors, 406–8
    symmetry condition, 396
    syntax, 379, 386–89, 394–95, 403
    Taiwan Sign Language, 402
    "tip-of-the-finger," 400, 401, 403
    topicalization, 386
    turn relevance places, 387
    verb agreement, 384, 385
    verb generation, 408
    word order, 386–87
Silverstein, R., 425
Simmons, W. K., 127
Single-word production. *see* word
    production computational models
Slevc, L. R., 442
Slifka, J., 265
Slobin, D. I., 10
Smith, E. A., 315, 319, 320
Smith, E. E., 119, 142
Smith, M., 444
Snider, N., 79
Snow, C., 332
Sobel, P., 96
The Sound Pattern of English
    (Chomsky/Halle), 261
Speaking (Levelt), 266–67
Speech error studies
    analysis, syntax, 22f, 24, 25
articulation, 460, 465–66, 468–70
attraction errors, 41–42
back-propagation of error, 71–72
dysarthria, 278–80
emotional facial paresis, 282
error-based learning, 76–79
feedback errors, 463–66
intrusive schwa errors, 250
lexiccal phonology, impaired, 286–87,
    289n1
meaning, semantic models, 143
message encoding, 6
naming, 109, 111, 112
phonemic paraphasia, 286, 289n1
phonetic processing, 247–50
phonology, 231–40, 241nn3–5
word production computational
    models, 88–91, 94, 96–97
word substitution errors, 234
working memory, 443, 445–46
Speech error studies
    syntax, 22f, 24, 25, 33, 35t, 41–42
Speech motor pathways. *see*
    articulatory-phonological network
Spelling. *see* orthographic representations
Spinelli, E., 266, 344
Spivey, M., 121, 122
Spontaneous discourse. *see* discourse
Sproat, R., 217
Stanovich, K., 334
Starr, R., 309
Starreveld, P. A., 431
Staunton, R., 321
Stemberger, J. P., 231–32
Steriade, D., 207n5
Stevens, K. N., 270
Stevens, M., 425–26, 426f
Stewart, M., 321
Steyvers, M., 139, 140, 141
Stivers, T., 294
Stock, B., 335
Stokoe, W. C., 380–81
Stone, M., 250
Stowe, L. A., 60t
Strijkers, K., 171
Stroke, 106, 111, 128
Stromswold, K., 62
Stromswold, K., 60t
Stroop effect, 147n2
Structural priming, 36–37, 76–79, 77f
Sunderman, G., 193
Supalla, S., 387
Supalla, T., 385
Surana, K., 265
Surface dysgraphia/lexical agraphia,
    360–62, 361t, 373
Swaab, T., 53
Syllables
    coupling graph model of, 218–20, 218–20f
    cross-syllable coordination, 222–24
    intergestural timing within, 217–19, 218f
    orthographic representations, 341f,
        349–50, 353